# BUSINESS PLANNING: CLOSELY HELD ENTERPRISES

## Fourth Edition

■ ■ ■

By

## Dwight Drake

*University of Washington School of Law*

AMERICAN CASEBOOK SERIES®

**WEST**®

Mat #41508406

*American Casebook Series* is a trademark registered in the U.S. Patent and Trademark Office.

© West, a Thomson business, 2006, 2008
© 2011 Thomson Reuters
© 2013 LEG, Inc. d/b/a West Academic Publishing

    610 Opperman Drive
    St. Paul, MN 55123
    1-800-313-9378

West, West Academic Publishing, and West Academic are trademarks of West Publishing Corporation, used under license.

Printed in the United States of America

**ISBN:** 978–0–314–28960–5

*To Kath*

\*

# PREFACE

---

For decades, I have watched aspiring business lawyers enter the legal profession with no concept of the planning process. They have made it through law school and maybe a few years of practice without any real awareness of the strategic challenges that business owners, both large and small, face on a regular basis. They have a grasp of how their legal training helps in resolving disputes and executing transactions, but its role in the process of making strategic decisions that move a business forward often is completely undefined. Many lack any understanding or appreciation of the importance of forward planning and the need to identify and prioritize specific business objections. Others just figure that those challenges are for business people, not lawyers. Many times I have pondered the value of a book that would help law students and young lawyers understand what it takes to become a trusted advisor to business owners and executives. This book, now in its fourth edition, is my attempt at such an effort.

This fourth edition features many new, positive additions. Twelve new student case study problems have been added, bringing the total to 65 problems. New discussions have been added dealing with limited liability traps, undocumented partnership risks, the design and drafting of partnership and LLC operating agreements, capital structure basics, dividend challenges, going public realities, crowdfunding and the JOBS Act of 2012, oppression risks, healthcare reform, and judicial enforcement of buy-sell agreements. Perhaps the most significant addition is a recap (which includes three new student problems) of the statutory basics of limited liability companies and the four types of partnerships, designed for those students (there are many) who never gained a grasp of these core concepts. Of course, all tax discussions have been updated to include the significant changes of the American Taxpayer Relief Act of 2012 and thoughts on what might be coming in the future. Five case study examples have been added to the choice-of-entity "factor" discussion to better illustrate the impacts of various factors. And the discussions relating to securities law exemptions, deferred compensation, and business valuations have been revised, repositioned and substantially shortened. The net result for this fourth edition is only a three percent increase in word count and a reduction of 60 pages (due to a slight increase in page size).

Becoming a trusted advisor to business owners and executives requires training and the development of key skills. The core knowledge prerequisites are substantial. A solid grounding in tax and the ability to read financial statements, while both essential, are not enough. The advisor needs a broad grasp of legal issues that directly affect businesses. Many view this knowledge challenge as an unattractive burden and retreat to a specialty that narrows their focus and their relevance. Others perceive it as an excuse for ignorance and play over their heads every day. They regularly disappoint. Contrary to what many think, the successful business advisor is not a "generalist" who lacks specific knowledge. It is a person with a broad base of specific knowledge that positively impacts the decision-making process.

But core knowledge alone isn't enough. Many with deep reservoirs of legal knowledge are useless in the planning process. They lack one or more of three essential skills that a quality advisor must develop: the ability to identify and address business objectives, not just legal issues; the ability to evaluate and apply specific strategic options; and the ability to effectively communicate with non-lawyers. This book attempts to address the development of these three essential skills in the context of a number of common business challenges and the related core knowledge prerequisites.

As regards the first skill, any quality advisor knows that the identification and prioritization of specific business objectives is the threshold challenge in the planning process. Nearly all business owners, even the very brightest, need guidance and direction. From my experience, the best way to develop the ability to provide such guidance is to study examples that illustrate the varying scope of business objectives different types of business owners may have with respect to any planning challenge. For this reason, numerous case studies and examples are presented in text discussions and in the problems that accompany each chapter. The initial focus of each case study and problem is the identification of the client's business objectives. The names and the collateral facts of the case studies and problems are fictitious, but the underlying business objectives and planning challenges are based on real situations. To help the reader better understand and appreciate the difficulty of indentifying, prioritizing and accomplishing objectives as our nation and the world seeks to crawl out of a painful recession, this edition includes discussions on some of today's toughest challenges -- the drop in global demand and the associated deleveraging, the causes and affects of chronic unemployment, unprecedented government spending and deficits, the perpetual uncertainty of taxes, tax prospects for the future, and the business challenges of health care reform in the years ahead. There is also a section that provides a primer on basic business concepts and definitions.

The second skill—the ability to evaluate and apply specific strategies—requires knowledge of the strategic options and their business and legal limitations. I am continually amazed at how frequently a student studies a technical body of business or tax law without ever gaining any meaningful knowledge of the related options that impact businesses in their strategic planning. This effort attempts to address the issue by focusing on various strategic options for dealing with a number of specific business challenges. Of course, time and page constraints limit the scope of the challenges that can be discussed. The challenges selected were based on my experience, with "client appreciation" being the prime criterion. The key challenges examined include choice of entity, capital and business formation, entity conversion planning, co-owner planning, business valuations, exit and sellout strategies, key executive incentives, equity sharing, deferred compensation, life insurance planning, competitor collaborations, resource diversification planning, multi-entity estate and asset protection planning, select employee challenges, and business transition planning.

Perhaps the most vital skill is the third—the advisor's ability to effectively communicate with business owners. It also is the most difficult to develop. The lawyer who refines this skill wins in two big ways—clients respond very favorably, and the lawyer's understanding of the relevant subject matter is enriched. The best way to master a technical subject is to tackle the challenge of distilling and communicating the essence of the subject to a non-lawyer. It's not easy; it's something many don't even try. This, more than any other factor, explains why only a pitifully low 17 percent of the respondents in a survey of successful business owners (average annual company sales of $36.5 million) listed a lawyer as their most trusted outside advisor. The simple truth is that, when discussing technical issues, it is much easier to "talk Code" or use legalese that are designed to impress but communicate nearly nothing. Most business owners long for understanding but have little or no patience for legal dissertations that over-complicate and offend their intelligence. It is little wonder that so many turn to other advisors for guidance and, in the process, often become victims of sloppy planning or lost opportunities.

In this work, I attempt to address this all-important communication skill a couple of ways. The first is by example. The bulk of the following pages contain my words, most of which are designed to illustrate how I would discuss the relevant subject matter with an intelligent business owner who has no legal training. Lawyer talk and Code references are minimized. The focus is on planning solutions and potential traps, not abstract legal concepts and exceptions. Some bodies of technical law are distilled into a handful of pages to promote understanding of the relevant planning issues and impacts. Various educational formats are used, including question and answers, case studies, short examples, factor lists, and more. A few times I just tell a story. Beyond these examples, I included Chapter 17 to discuss specific practice techniques that I found helpful in building a practice to serve business owners and executives and to review common ethical challenges encountered in such a practice. The essence of many of the practice techniques discussed in that chapter is effective, value-added client communications.

I thank those lawyers who made direct contributes to this effort, each of whom is identified before his or her written words, the Seattle firm of Foster Pepper PLLC for use of the seven forms included in Chapter 18. Many others lawyers made indirect contributions by helping me with my personal development over the years. Two of these lawyers deserve special mention. Tim McDevitt and Kent Whiteley were superb planning lawyers who I had the privilege to work with for a long time. Beyond our joint efforts as law partners, the three of us for eight years struggled each month to produce a 50-minute audio planning program that was sent via audio cassette to planning professionals throughout the country. This project, known as "PlainTalk Planning," was a labor of love that made each of us (and hopefully many others) better advisors to business owners. Tim and Kent could not be part of this effort; their lives tragically were cut short years ago. But the impact of our collective PlainTalk experience will forever burn in me and is manifest throughout this book.

Finally, I want to acknowledge a vitally important group that made this effort possible. It is those business owners and executives who I had the privilege of serving for many years. These clients did much more than just give me a means to earn a living and practice my craft. They taught me; they inspired me. Jack Welch, the renowned former GE chief executive, once explained, "What we are trying relentlessly to do is get that small-company soul inside our big company." (As quoted in *USA Today*, February 2, 1993) Welch got it right. The happiest, most energetic, most interesting, most effective, most fun-to-be-with people I have ever known are those who build businesses. Many of them regularly experience the endless joy of self-discovery and improvement. They, plain and simple, enjoy life. That is why they are such an excellent career answer for the lawyer who develops the skills to play in their league.

DWIGHT DRAKE

Fall City, Washington
August, 2013

# SUMMARY OF CONTENTS

———

# TABLE OF CONTENTS

———

# Table of Cases

**References are to pages.**

# BUSINESS PLANNING: CLOSELY HELD ENTERPRISES

## Fourth Edition

\*

# CHAPTER 1

# AMERICA'S CLOSELY HELD BUSINESSES

---

## A.  THE BIG PICTURE

The big picture for America's closely held businesses has been rough since
2008.  The economy has been struggling to slowly crawl out of a protracted
recession that has delivered chronically high unemployment numbers, brought
our largest financial institutions to their knees, and forced many businesses to
close their doors. Million have given up their job-seeking efforts and are not even
included in the unemployment calculation.  The labor force participation rate hit
a 34-year low in 2013.[1] And millions who do have jobs consider themselves
grossly underemployed as they net only a fraction of what they used to earn.

All business advisers and owners should understand how we got to this
point. For more than two decades, the world markets have been fueled by
consumers in developed countries progressively spending at a faster pace. It was
done with leverage – debt backed by assets that were supposed to continually
grow in value and support perpetual borrowing and spending increases. The
leverage occurred at all levels: government debt escalated; financial institutions
leveraged derivative-based securities to the hilt; subprime mortgages and
government mandates pushed millions of families to buy homes they couldn't
afford; and households pumped up debt through home mortgage refinancing and
the use of easily available credit card leverage.  Then the momentum shifted.
Asset values turned and headed in the wrong direction, spiraling down as demand
shrank and fire sales escalated the descent. The largest financial institutions –
those "too big to fail" – saw their balance sheet values crumble. They were soon
on life support, begging the government for a lifeline.  The value of just about
every home in America plummeted, leaving millions of Americans underwater,
with more debt than assets.

The whole private sector was forced to deleverage by reducing debt and
cutting spending.  The resulting massive drop in demand forced employers to
slash payrolls, which further accelerated the drop in demand.  The government
and the Federal Reserve kept money flowing by cutting short-term interest rates
to nearly zero, driving annual federal deficits to unsustainable trillion-dollar
levels that no one could have imagined just a few years ago, and pumping

---

1. The labor participation rate, which reflects the percentage of Americans 16 years of age and older who
are in the labor force, dropped to 63.3 percent in March 2013, the lowest in 34 years.  United State Department
of Labor, Bureau of Labor Statistics Report for March 2013.

trillions into the economy through the Federal Reserve's "quantitative easing" plan. The big question now is whether these measures can offset the effects of the private deleveraging that drove buyers to the sidelines without doing untold damage in the long term.

Businesses, plain and simple, need more customers. Robust, sustained improvement for businesses and those seeking jobs will not occur until the deleveraging stops and the drop in demand bottoms out. Even then it may take time before companies have the confidence to start hiring in real numbers. Many will fear that positive signs are nothing more than short-term blips triggered by government manipulation.

The experiences of the recent past have once again confirmed that unrestrained, irresponsible asset-based leveraging is a double-edged sword; it has the capacity to either fuel wonderful growth or quickly put large financial institutions and millions of businesses and families on their backs. Debates will forever rage over the effectiveness of various government actions designed to help offset the massive private sector de-leveraging and the debilitating drop in global demand. But there is little doubt that when it comes to job creation, aggressive, creative government monetary policies are no substitute for new technologies and market opportunities that push American companies to build products and deliver services that the world wants and is capable of buying. And to that end there appears to be widespread agreement on one basic point: America's private business sector is the only hope for any real recovery.

In order to aggressively play to win, businesses need to know the rules of the game and have confidence that market forces are headed in the right direction. Today, the rules and forces are anything but certain. Far-reaching health care legislation has frightened nearly everyone who must meet a payroll. Unsustainable, unprecedented government deficits and recent tax increases triggered by the Fiscal Cliff legislation have discouraged many business owners and investors, who fear that more ongoing bad news is inevitable. Half our leaders are screaming for more regulation on all fronts and policies that foster social justice and wealth redistribution, while the other half proclaim that downsizing government and unleashing free market forces is our only hope. Meanwhile, the long-term business impact of massive federal spending, unprecedented deficits, and extreme monetary policies remains unknown, as we witness the economies of other nations implode and the entire global economy struggle to find its footing.

**U.S. House of Representatives Committee on Small Business**
**Small Business Fact Sheet**
*Updated May 21, 2013*

**Importance of Small Business to the Economy:**

- A small business is generally described as an independent company having fewer than 500 employees. (Small Business Administration). For the small business definition by industry used in government programs and contracting, see ww.sba.gov/content/small-business-size-standards. There are an estimated 27 million small businesses in the United States. (Census Bureau)

- America's small businesses are the engines of job creation. Small businesses employ about half of all private sector employees and create more than half of the nonfarm private gross domestic product. (Small Business Administration)

- Generally, 60 to 80 percent of all new jobs come from small businesses. This number fluctuates year-by-year when some small companies grow enough to become classified as large firms, and when new businesses are created. For example, from 1999 to 2000, small businesses accounted for 75 percent of all new jobs created. Small businesses have generated 65 percent of net new jobs over the past 17 years. (Small Business Administration)

- The so-called "gazelle" firms (ages three to five years) comprise less than one percent of all companies, yet generate roughly 10 percent of new jobs in any given year. The "average" firm in the top one percent of all companies contributes 88 jobs per year, and most end up with between 20 and 249 employees. (Kauffman Foundation)

- Small businesses are innovators. They produce 16.5 times more patents per employee than large firms. (Small Business Administration)

- From 1992 through 2010, small businesses outperformed large firms in net job creation 75% of the time, according to the latest the SBA Office of Advocacy's Small Business Economy 2011 report (released March 21, 2012).

- The U.S. ranks 13th in ease of starting a business in the world according to a World Bank report. In 2007, the U.S. ranked 3rd.

**Small Business Sentiment**

- The April 2013 Chamber of Commerce quarterly Small Business Outlook Survey found the vast majority of small businesses (79%) think our country is on the wrong track, and 27% lost employees in the past year, while 87% of small businesses are looking for more certainty, instead of more assistance from Washington. Also, 78% viewed the national debt and deficits as a threat to their success, and 79% favor comprehensive tax reform.

- The April 2013 BNA Economic Outlook Survey found that only 15% of small businesses intended to add full-time employees during the next six months, down from spring 2012 (28%), while 8% planned to reduce full-time staff.

- The 2013 surveys of small business owners by the National Federation of Independent Business have been a roller coast so far this year, up one month, down the next. The NFIB monthly optimism index improved to 92.1, still barely above the recovery average of 90.7. Only four percent of businesses think this is a good time to expand their businesses. NFIB's Chief Economist still calls the report lackluster and describes small business owners as pessimistic. As many small firms plan to cut inventory as plan to increase it.

- According to the April 2013 Gallup/Wells Fargo Small Business Index, the outlooks of small business owners are improving slightly. However, Gallup also reports flat consumer spending in April, and more workers still predict job losses than before the 2008 economic dip.

• In order to address America's high unemployment, Washington must provide more certainty and relief for small businesses that are continually burdened by threats of tax increases, the inconsistent flow of credit, unstable energy costs, unnecessarily burdensome federal regulations (including requirements from the health care law), and the dark cloud of an outrageous national debt over the economy.

### High Energy Prices Harm Small Business Job Creation

• Gas prices rose sharply by 11.19 cents on May 17, according to a Reuters-published Lundberg survey of 2,500 gas stations tracking increasing prices over a two-week span before the peak driving season begins Memorial Day weekend. In cities, gas rose 62 cents to $4.27 a gallon.

• A year ago, the Small Business & Entrepreneurship Council's survey showed that 72 percent of small businesses were concerned with the prices at that time – now reaching similar prices this season.

• The median commercial sector industry has a small business energy cost per sales ratio that is 2.7 times greater than that of larger businesses, which hinders their ability to compete during times of elevated energy prices. (SBA Office of Advocacy)

• Half of U.S. adults consider gas prices to be "too high" when it reaches $3.44 per gallon, according to a new consumer index developed by AAA. Forty-six percent of adults believe gas is too high when it reaches $3.00 per gallon; 61 percent believe it is too high when it reaches $3.50 per gallon; and 90 percent believe gas is too high when it reaches $4.00 per gallon.

### Regulatory Impediments Strangle Small Business Job Creation

• Small firms bear a regulatory cost of $10,585 per employee, which is 36% higher than the cost of regulatory compliance for large businesses. (2010 SBA study, The Impact of Regulatory Costs on Small Firms)

• Compliance with environmental regulations costs small businesses four times more than large firms. (2010 SBA study, The Impact of Regulatory Costs on Small Firms)

### Tax Increases Harm Small Business Job Growth

• The SBA reports that the average tax compliance cost per employee for small businesses is almost three times the per employee cost for the average large firm.

• Together, pass-throughs such as LLC's, partnerships, S Corporations and sole proprietorships, account for 54 percent of all business net income and they employ 54 percent of the private sector workforce. (Ernst & Young, April 2011)

• According to an NFIB's National Small Business Poll, about 75 percent of small businesses are structured as pass-through entities (S corporations, limited liability companies, sole proprietorships or partnerships) that must pay tax on their business income at the individual rate. Most small businesses do not pay the corporate tax.

### U.S. Senate Committee on Small Business and Entrepreneurship
### Democratic Page Excerpts

#### Business Development

Small firms employ half the American workforce and have created two-thirds of all new jobs. Yet, when the economy takes a downturn, small businesses are the first to get hit. In the 2008-2009 recession, 80 percent of the jobs lost came from small firms.

To help them survive, entrepreneurs can count on a muscular and valuable Small Business Administration (SBA). The SBA has a network of Small Business Development Centers, Women and Veteran Business Centers and other entrepreneurial development programs to help small businesses throughout the country. Whether small firms need help finding new financing options, ways to offer healthcare to their employees or have ideas they want to turn into reality, the centers provide the counseling and resources small businesses need in today's competitive global marketplace. The Committee on Small Business and Entrepreneurship helps small businesses find the centers near them and works with the SBA to strengthen these entrepreneurial programs by ensuring that they are receiving adequate financing and are operating with the sole purpose of aiding small firms.

#### Minority Entrepreneurs

The number of businesses in our minority communities continues to grow, adding to our competitive advantage. Over the last 10 years, minority business enterprises accounted for more than 50 percent of the two million new businesses started in the United States and created 4.7 million jobs. There are now more than four million minority-owned companies in the United States, with annual sales totaling close to $700 billion.

Yet, despite that growth, there is still a disparity when it comes to access to capital, contracting opportunities and other entrepreneurial development opportunities for minority-owned firms. Though minorities make up 32 percent of our population, minority business ownership represents only 18 percent of the population. Additionally, the Minority Business Development Agency (MBDA) noted in a recent report that even though the number of minority-owned firms has grown by 35 percent, the average gross receipts for those firms dropped by 16 percent.

Obviously, while the numbers of minority-owned businesses are a source of optimism and hold promise for the future, much more still needs to be done to encourage and strengthen the minority business community. That's why ensuring that all small businesses have access to federal contracts, access to capital and the technical assistance needed for success remains a top priority for the Committee on Small Business and Entrepreneurship. Diversity is one of the nation's greatest strengths, and diverse small-business ownership is essential to our nation's continued economic success and growth.

Women business owners employ more than 4 million workers and contribute about $1 trillion to the economy. But while women-owned enterprises now comprise the fastest-growing segment of the U.S. business community, they continue to struggle to obtain equal access to capital and contracts. Women entrepreneurs receive more loan denials - the share of dollars of loans to women was about 22 percent, according to a 2005 report - and only 3.5 percent of all federal contracts, far short of the 5 percent goal.

Senators Landrieu and Snowe are committed to reversing these trends and fostering women entrepreneurship in all sectors of our society. The Committee on Small Business and Entrepreneurship is focused on improving a network of women business centers to assure that women are on an equal playing field.

### Healthcare

One concern we hear over and over in the Senate Small Business and Entrepreneurship Committee from our nation's 27 million small businesses - the businesses that employ more than half America's workforce - is healthcare. Seventy-eight percent of small businesses recently reported that having access to stable, affordable, quality health insurance is their number one concern.

Skyrocketing premiums are crushing these businesses as they face yearly premium increases of as much as 20 percent for the past four years. These high costs have forced many small business owners to drop coverage altogether causing small business employers, employees and their families to make up nearly 23 million of American's 45 million uninsured. Most small business owners want to offer health insurance to their workers. But for small firms faced with the choice of cutting employees or cutting health insurance, the insurance is the first to go. And unfortunately, those who can afford to pay the least are today paying the most, and they're getting less bang for their buck. Small firms pay 18 percent more than large employers for health insurance.

As our nation's innovators and job creators, the cost of doing nothing to help small businesses is just too great. Without reform, we could lose 178,000 jobs and spend nearly $2.4 trillion on healthcare in the next ten years. With even a limited reform scenario, small businesses would save $546 billion and thousands of jobs in that same ten-year period.

### Access to Capital

For America's Main Street businesses, having access to capital means the difference between stocking shelves or hanging for sale signs, creating jobs or contributing to layoffs, exploring new technologies and new markets or stunting their own growth and potential.

The Committee on Small Business & Entrepreneurship oversees the U.S. Small Business Administration's (SBA) loan and venture capital programs. Because credit cards have become an increasing means of quick capital for small firms because of the credit crunch, the Committee also monitors the credit card industry. In fact, credit cards have overwhelmingly become the largest source of financing for small firms – with small business use of credit cards increasing from 16 to 44 percent from 1993 to 2008. As of April 2009, credit cards made up the largest source of small business financing at 59 percent, according to the National Small Business Association.

The use of credit cards has increased as entrepreneurs struggle to acquire bank loans, and specifically, SBA loans. More than 65 percent of banks have tightened lending on their 7(a) and 504 loans, which make up only 5 percent of financing for small businesses but represent 40 percent of their long-term capital. In 2007, more than 824,000 jobs were created or retained because of these programs. Additionally, the microloan program - which proportionally helps more women and minorities than other loan programs - provides loans of $35,000 or less to entrepreneurs. These mostly non-profit entities have seen their demand grow by as much as 75 percent as banks turn down borrowers.

The Committee also oversees the Small Business Investment Company (SBIC) and New Markets Venture Capital (NMVC) programs, which provide venture capital financing to small firms. SBICs and NMVCs differ from traditional venture capital firms in that they make smaller deals, between $250,000 and $5 million and spread their investments more broadly around the country and to a bigger variety of industries.

The American Recovery and Reinvestment Act took bold steps to increase access to capital for the nation's entrepreneurs by temporarily eliminating many fees on SBA-backed loans and increasing the guarantee on government-backed loans to 90 percent on SBA's largest loan program. The Act also included provisions to jumpstart the secondary market for SBA loans so banks could loan again. More than $50 million in microloans and management assistance also went to helping our smallest businesses adjust to the tough economy and to the unemployed to start their own companies. Additionally, SBA also implemented a temporary emergency loan program to help entrepreneurs in need of immediate help. Over time, these provisions will pump about $16 billion in loans and venture capital into small businesses in our communities, creating or saving thousands of jobs.

**Contracting**

Access to federal contracts often means the difference between surviving and thriving for our nation's small businesses. One of the principle oversight responsibilities of the Committee on Small Business and Entrepreneurship is to ensure that all small businesses have the opportunity to sell their goods and services to the federal government - this includes making sure women, minorities, veterans and other underserved groups have equal access to contracts.

The American government spent more than $378 billion on goods and services during Fiscal Year 2007, making the government the largest single purchaser in the world. But small businesses face significant challenges in competing for these contracts, including a maze of complicated regulations, contract bundling, size standards with loopholes for big businesses and a lack of protections for sub-contractors. Despite the fact that federal agencies' are mandated to spend 23 percent of their contract dollars on contracts to small firms

- 5 percent of which is required to go to women and disadvantaged firms and 3 percent to service-disabled veteran firms and HUBZones - the agencies often fall short of these requirements.

The American Recovery and Reinvestment Act helped bolster funding for the surety bond program to increase the number of small businesses competing for Federal contracts. But in the four months after the Act was passed, just over 10 percent of the $787 billion invested in contracts went to small businesses. As more of that $787 billion is spent over time, the Committee is working to ensure that the agencies remain true to their 23 percent goal.

Ensuring that small firms receive these contracts is important because putting government contracts into the hands of small businesses is not only good for entrepreneurs, but for all Americans. Small firms provide a strong, stable and diverse supplier base, allowing the government to get the best bang for its buck and assuring that taxpayer dollars are spent wisely.

### Congressional Budget Office
### The Budget and Economic Outlook: Fiscal Years 2013 To 2023
### (Excerpts Pages 1, 25 - 26)

Economic growth will remain slow this year, the Congressional Budget Office (CBO) anticipates, as gradual improvement in many of the forces that drive the economy is offset by the effects of budgetary changes that are scheduled to occur under current law. After this year, economic growth will speed up, CBO projects, causing the unemployment rate to decline and inflation and interest rates to eventually rise from their current low levels. Nevertheless, the unemployment rate is expected to remain above 7½ percent through next year; if that happens, 2014 will be the sixth consecutive year with unemployment exceeding 7½ percent of the labor force—the longest such period in the past 70 years.

If the current laws that govern federal taxes and spending do not change, the budget deficit will shrink this year to $845 billion, or 5.3 percent of gross domestic product (GDP), its smallest size since 2008. In CBO's baseline projections, deficits continue to shrink over the next few years, falling to 2.4 percent of GDP by 2015.

Deficits are projected to increase later in the coming decade, however, because of the pressures of an aging population, rising health care costs, an expansion of federal subsidies for health insurance, and growing interest payments on federal debt. As a result, federal debt held by the public is projected to remain historically high relative to the size of the economy for the next decade. By 2023, if current laws remain in place, debt will equal 77 percent of GDP and be on an upward path, CBO projects.

Debt held by the public consists mostly of securities that the Treasury issues to raise cash to fund the federal government's activities and to pay off its maturing liabilities. The amount the Treasury borrows by selling securities (net of the amount of maturing securities that it redeems) is influenced primarily by the annual budget deficit. However, several factors—collectively labeled other means of financing and not directly included in budget totals—also affect the government's need to borrow from the public. Among them are reductions (or increases) in the government's cash balance and in the cash flows associated with federal credit programs (such as those related to student loans and mortgage guarantees) because only the subsidy costs of those programs (calculated on a present-value basis) are reflected in the budget deficit.

CBO projects that Treasury borrowing will be $104 billion more than the projected budget deficit in fiscal year 2013, mainly to finance student loans. Each year from 2014 to 2023, borrowing by the Treasury is expected to exceed the amount of the deficit, mostly because of the need to provide financing for student loans and other credit programs. CBO projects that the government will need to borrow $76 billion more per year, on average, during that period than the budget deficits would suggest.

After accounting for all of the government's borrowing needs under current law, CBO projects that debt held by the public will increase from 73 percent of GDP at the end of fiscal year 2012 to 76 percent this year and 78 percent in 2014.

Under the assumptions that govern CBO's baseline, debt will fall to a low of 73 percent in 2018 and then rise for the remainder of the projection period, measuring 77 percent of GDP at the end of 2023.

Along such a path, federal debt held by the public will equal a greater percentage of GDP than in any year between 1951 and 2012 and will be far above the average of 39 percent over the 1973–2012 period. Moreover, it will be on an upward trend by the end of the decade.

Debt that is high by historical standards and heading higher will have significant consequences for the budget and the economy:

• The nation's net interest costs will be very high (after interest rates return to more normal levels) and rising. Higher costs for interest eventually will require the government to raise taxes, reduce benefits and services, or undertake some combination of those two actions.

• National saving will be held down, leading to more borrowing from abroad and less domestic investment, which in turn will decrease income in the United States relative to what it would be otherwise.

• Policymakers' ability to use tax and spending policies to respond to unexpected challenges, such as economic downturns, natural disasters, or financial crises will be constrained. As a result, unexpected events could have worse effects on the economy and people's well-being than they would otherwise.

• The likelihood of a fiscal crisis will be higher. During such a crisis, investors would lose so much confidence in the government's ability to manage its budget that the government would be unable to borrow funds at affordable interest rates.

### Excerpts from "The Moment of Truth"
### Report of the President's National Commission on
### Fiscal Responsibility and Reform (December 2010)

Throughout our nation's history, Americans have found the courage to do right by our children's future. Deep down, every American knows we face a moment of truth once again. We cannot play games or put off hard choices any longer. Without regard to party, we have a patriotic duty to keep the promise of America to give our children and grandchildren a better life.

Our challenge is clear and inescapable: America cannot be great if we go broke. Our businesses will not be able to grow and create jobs, and our workers will not be able to compete successfully for the jobs of the future without a plan to get this crushing debt burden off our backs.

Ever since the economic downturn, families across the country have huddled around kitchen tables, making tough choices about what they hold most dear and what they can learn to live without. They expect and deserve their leaders to do the same. The American people are counting on us to put politics aside, pull together not pull apart, and agree on a plan to live within our means and make America strong for the long haul.

As members of the National Commission on Fiscal Responsibility and Reform, we spent the past eight months studying the same cold, hard facts. Together, we have reached these unavoidable conclusions: The problem is real. The solution will be painful. There is no easy way out. Everything must be on the table. And Washington must lead.

We come from different backgrounds, represent different regions, and belong to different parties, but we share a common belief that America's long-term fiscal gap is unsustainable and, if left unchecked, will see our children and grandchildren living in a poorer, weaker nation. In the words of Senator Tom Coburn, "We keep kicking the can down the road, and splashing the soup all over our grandchildren." Every modest sacrifice we refuse to make today only forces far greater sacrifices of hope and opportunity upon the next generation.

Over the course of our deliberations, the urgency of our mission has become all the more apparent. The contagion of debt that began in Greece and continues to sweep through Europe shows us clearly that no economy will be immune. If the U.S. does not put its house in order, the reckoning will be sure and the devastation severe.

The President and the leaders of both parties in both chambers of Congress asked us to address the nation's fiscal challenges in this decade and beyond. We have worked to offer an aggressive, fair, balanced, and bipartisan proposal – a proposal as serious as the problems we face. None of us likes every element of our plan, and each of us had to tolerate provisions we previously or presently oppose in order to reach a principled compromise. We were willing to put our differences aside to forge a plan because our nation will certainly be lost without one.

We do not pretend to have all the answers. We offer our plan as the starting point for a serious national conversation in which every citizen has an interest and all should have a say. Our leaders have a responsibility to level with Americans about the choices we face, and to enlist the ingenuity and determination of the American people in rising to the challenge.

We believe neither party can fix this problem on its own, and both parties have a responsibility to do their part. The American people are a long way ahead of the political system in recognizing that now is the time to act. We believe that far from penalizing their leaders for making the tough choices, Americans will punish politicians for backing down – and well they should.

In the weeks and months to come, countless advocacy groups and special interests will try mightily through expensive, dramatic, and heart-wrenching media assaults to exempt themselves from shared sacrifice and common purpose. The national interest, not special interests, must prevail. We urge leaders and citizens with principled concerns about any of our recommendations to follow what we call the Becerra Rule: Don't shoot down an idea without offering a better idea in its place.

After all the talk about debt and deficits, it is long past time for America's leaders to put up or shut up. The era of debt denial is over, and there can be no turning back. We sign our names to this plan because we love our children, our grandchildren, and our country too much not to act while we still have the chance to secure a better future for all our fellow citizens.

**The Looming Fiscal Crisis**

Our nation is on an unsustainable fiscal path. Spending is rising and revenues are falling short, requiring the government to borrow huge sums each year to make up the difference. We face staggering deficits. In 2010, federal spending was nearly 24 percent of Gross Domestic Product (GDP), the value of all goods and services produced in the economy. Only during World War II was federal spending a larger part of the economy. Tax revenues stood at 15 percent of GDP this year, the lowest level since 1950. The gap between spending and revenue – the budget deficit – was just under nine percent of GDP.

Since the last time our budget was balanced in 2001, the federal debt has increased dramatically, rising from 33 percent of GDP to 62 percent of GDP in 2010. The escalation was driven in large part by two wars and a slew of fiscally irresponsible policies, along with a deep economic downturn. We have arrived at the moment of truth, and neither political party is without blame.

Economic recovery will improve the deficit situation in the short run because revenues will rise as people go back to work, and money spent on the social safety net will decline as fewer people are forced to rely on it. But even after the economy recovers, federal spending is projected to increase faster than revenues, so the government will have to continue borrowing money to spend. The Congressional Budget Office (CBO) projects if we continue on our current course, deficits will remain high throughout the rest of this decade and beyond, and debt will spiral ever higher, reaching 90 percent of GDP in 2020.

Over the long run, as the baby boomers retire and health care costs continue to grow, the situation will become far worse. By 2025 revenue will be able to finance only interest payments, Medicare, Medicaid, and Social Security. Every other federal government activity – from national defense and homeland security to transportation and energy – will have to be paid for with borrowed money. Debt held by the public will outstrip the entire American economy, growing to as much as 185 percent of GDP by 2035. Interest on the debt could rise to nearly $1 trillion by 2020. These mandatory payments – which buy absolutely no goods or services – will squeeze out funding for all other priorities.

Federal debt this high is unsustainable. It will drive up interest rates for all borrowers – businesses and individuals – and curtail economic growth by crowding out private investment. By making it more expensive for entrepreneurs and businesses to raise capital, innovate, and create jobs, rising debt could reduce per-capita GDP, each American's share of the nation's economy, by as much as 15 percent by 2035.

Rising debt will also hamstring the government, depriving it of the resources needed to respond to future crises and invest in other priorities. Deficit spending is often used to respond to short-term financial "emergency" needs such as wars or recessions. If our national debt grows higher, the federal government may even have difficulty borrowing funds at an affordable interest rate, preventing it from effectively responding.

Large debt will put America at risk by exposing it to foreign creditors. They currently own more than half our public debt, and the interest we pay them reduces our own standard of living. The single largest foreign holder of our debt is China, a nation that may not share our country's aspirations and strategic interests. In a worst-case scenario, investors could lose confidence that our nation is able or willing to repay its loans – possibly triggering a debt crisis that would force the government to implement the most stringent of austerity measures.

Predicting the precise level of public debt that would trigger such a crisis is difficult, but a key factor may be whether the debt has been stabilized as a share of the economy or if it continues to rise. Investors, reluctant to risk throwing good money after bad, are sure to be far more concerned about rising debt than stable debt. In a recent briefing on the risk of a fiscal crisis, CBO explained that while "there is no identifiable tipping point of debt relative to GDP indicating that a crisis is likely or imminent," the U.S. debt-to-GDP ratio is "climbing into unfamiliar territory" and "the higher the debt, the greater the risk of such a crisis."

If we do not act soon to reassure the markets, the risk of a crisis will increase, and the options available to avert or remedy the crisis will both narrow and become more stringent. If we wait ten years, CBO projects our economy could shrink by as much as 2 percent, and spending cuts and tax increases needed to plug the hole could nearly double what is needed today.

Continued inaction is not a viable option, and not an acceptable course for a responsible government...

The Government Accountability Office has said that we could have double-digit growth for a decade and still not grow out of the current fiscal situation. At the same time, we cannot get out of this fiscal hole without sustained economic growth. According to the Office of Management and Budget, a one-time 1 percent decrease in GDP would increase the deficit by more than $600 billion over the course of the decade; if annual growth were 1 percent lower every year, the deficit would be over $3 trillion larger. A plan to reduce the deficit must therefore promote economic growth and not undermine the economic recovery...

**Overview**

We propose a six-part plan to put our nation back on a path to fiscal health, promote economic growth, and protect the most vulnerable among us. Taken as a whole, the plan will:

- Achieve nearly $4 trillion in deficit reduction through 2020, more than any effort in the nation's history.

- Reduce the deficit to 2.3% of GDP by 2015 (2.4% excluding Social Security reform), exceeding President's goal of primary balance (about 3% of GDP).2

- Sharply reduce tax rates, abolish the AMT, and cut backdoor spending in the tax code.

- Cap revenue at 21% of GDP and get spending below 22% and eventually to 21%.

- Ensure lasting Social Security solvency, prevent the projected 22% cuts to come in 2037, reduce elderly poverty, and distribute the burden fairly.

- Stabilize debt by 2014 and reduce debt to 60% of GDP by 2023 and 40% by 2035.

The plan has six major components:

**1) Discretionary Spending Cuts:** Enact tough discretionary spending caps to force budget discipline in Congress. Include enforcement mechanisms to give the limits real teeth. Make significant cuts in both security and non-security spending by cutting low-priority programs and streamlining government operations. Offer over $50 billion in immediate cuts to lead by example, and provide $200 billion in illustrative 2015 savings.

**2) Comprehensive Tax Reform:** Sharply reduce rates, broaden the base, simplify the tax code, and reduce the deficit by reducing the many "tax expenditures"—another name for spending through the tax code. Reform corporate taxes to make America more competitive, and cap revenue to avoid excessive taxation.

**3) Health Care Cost Containment:** Replace the phantom savings from scheduled Medicare reimbursement cuts that will never materialize and from a new long-term care program that is unsustainable with real, common-sense reforms to physician payments, cost-sharing, malpractice law, prescription drug costs, government-subsidized medical education, and other sources. Institute additional long-term measures to bring down spending growth.

**4) Mandatory Savings:** Cut agriculture subsidies and modernize military and civil service retirement systems, while reforming student loan programs and putting the Pension Benefit Guarantee Corporation on a sustainable path.

**5) Social Security Reforms to Ensure Long-Term Solvency and Reduce Poverty:** Ensure sustainable solvency for the next 75 years while reducing poverty among seniors. Reform Social Security for its own sake, and not for deficit reduction.

**6) Process Changes:** Reform the budget process to ensure the debt remains on a stable path, spending stays under control, inflation is measured accurately, and taxpayer dollars go where they belong.

## B. FAMILY BUSINESS TRENDS
## AND CHALLENGES

Family dominated businesses comprise more than 80 percent of U.S. enterprises, employ more than 50 percent of the nation's workforce, and account for the bulk (some estimate as much as 64 percent) of America's gross domestic product.[2] In most situations, the business comprises the bulk of the family's wealth. In the recent survey, a startling 93 percent of the senior business owners acknowledged that the business is their primary source of income and security.[3] The following surveys highlight some of the key challenges faced by this all-important segment of the economy.

### PwC[4] Family Business Survey 2012/2013
### US findings

The economy and competition top the list of challenges that US family businesses say face them now and in the future. They know that business as usual won't suffice if they are to maintain — and grow — market share despite these challenges. To differentiate themselves, family firms will need to create new products and services, improve current offerings, and find new ways of engaging with customers — or even adopt an entirely new business model. Innovative leaders and a strong talent base will be essential to achieving these goals, which may be why innovation and talent also rank among the top challenges family businesses flagged in our survey.

US family businesses make their bid for the future. They're especially concerned about whether potential successors have a knack for innovation, flagging this as a top challenge their companies will face in five years' time

---

2. See generally R. Duman, "Family Firms Are Different," Entrepreneurship Theory and Practice, 1992, pp. 13–21; and M. F. R. Kets de Vries, "The Dynamics of Family Controlled Firms: The Good News and the Bad News," Organizational Dynamics, 1993, pp. 59–71; W. G. Dyer, Cultural Change in Family Firms, Jossey–Bass, San Francisco, 1986; and P. L. Rosenblatt, M. R. Anderson and P. Johnson, The Family in Business, Jossey–Bass, San Francisco, 1985; Arthur Anderson/Mass Mutual, American Family Business Survey, 2002.

3. Family to Family: Laird Norton Tyee Family Business Survey 2007, page 5 (Executive Summary).

4. PwC is a network of firms in 158 countries with more than 180,000 people who are committed to delivering quality in assurance, tax and advisory services.

(58%), surpassed only by economic challenges (66%) and price competition (61%). Economic challenges top the list of *near-term* concerns as well, with 68% of family businesses citing market conditions as a main issue for them over the next 12 months, though fewer companies registered concern this time around (88% flagged market conditions in 2010), suggesting that two years on, family businesses have adapted to the new normal of market volatility and economic uncertainty.

US family enterprises remain optimistic despite very real challenges ahead. They fully recognize that to thrive in a fast-evolving business landscape and still-uncertain economy, they'll need to out-innovate their peers and seek new avenues of growth.

Meeting these goals calls for entrepreneurship, which is a trait family businesses are known for — at least at their inception. Entrepreneurial instincts, however, aren't necessarily passed down the family line. Our survey participants appear to have no illusions about this. Many of them question whether the next generation has the ability and desire to steward the business into the future.

Competition is another challenge that's doing double duty as both a near- and long-term concern for family businesses. Increasingly, competition is coming in the form of aggressive, well-funded companies that are entering the US market from China and other rapidly growing economies. Business as usual won't suffice if family firms are to maintain — *and grow* — market share while dealing with this new breed of competitor. Differentiating themselves will require creating new products and services, improving current offerings, and finding new ways of engaging with customers. In some cases, it may even entail adopting an entirely new business model.

Competition from abroad is just one side of the international equation. Nearly half of US family businesses are venturing abroad themselves, selling goods and services outside their customary domestic markets. Fifty-four percent also expect they'll be selling internationally in the future. This is a striking increase from two years ago when just 30% of US respondents said they were planning to develop business in markets abroad.

Risk tends to be part of the bargain when a company seeks to increase its competitive edge, either at home or abroad. And yet risk-taking is often seen as somewhat contrary to the family-business ethos of protecting and preserving a legacy for future generations. This, coupled with a strong sense of commitment to their employees and the freedom to take a long-term approach to corporate strategy (rather than chase near-term results to meet quarterly earnings expectations), may give the impression that mature family businesses generally err on the conservative side when it comes to risk. What we're seeing among our family business clients in the United States, however, is that patience and preservation are not synonymous with risk-aversion.

**Steady growth**

Most US family businesses performed well over the past year, with nearly three-quarters of them experiencing sales growth. Roughly one-third said they had grown a lot. Looking ahead, almost all US family businesses are confident about growth for the next five years — 93% of US respondents, compared with 81% of their family-business peers globally. Aggressive growth, however, is not expected. Only 11% of US family businesses expect to grow quickly and aggressively over the next five years. Most (82%) are aiming for steady growth.

## Challenges

That companies are expecting to grow steadily rather than rapidly is not surprising. Various headwinds remain strong. Chief among them are tough competition and still-uncertain market conditions. There is also the ongoing challenge of finding workers with the right talents and skills. Meeting this third challenge is critical for companies looking to innovate their way past the competition and continue powering growth in a slow economy.

Family businesses worry about how to fill the skills gap now and in the future. Closing the skills gap has been a persistent challenge for family businesses, as well as for companies generally. Manufacturing businesses, in particular, are in need of workers with highly specialized skills — the kind requiring education beyond high school. To run the high precision machinery and technology that will keep US manufacturers competitive, more American workers will have to retool themselves with STEM (science, technology, engineering, mathematics) skills.

Across the country, states have begun to redress the problem by creating public-private partnerships (among other types of programs) that match workforce training with the vocational needs of local manufacturers. Community colleges are especially active in these partnerships. Here is where family businesses can play a decisive role, especially since many of them already have close ties to their communities and a strong sense of responsibility toward them. Indeed, almost all the US family businesses we surveyed say they believe their companies play a vital role in creating jobs and growing the economy.

### Weighing the role of government

The companies we surveyed have mixed feelings about the role government should play vis-à-vis family businesses. For instance, although a mere 9% of family businesses said taxes were among their top three "external issues/challenges" for the next year, they did voice a strong desire to see the inheritance tax go away and for the tax code overall to be simplified. As the leader of a fourth-generation family-owned producer of copper with more than $1 billion in annual revenue put it, "Government should reduce the tax burden on family businesses so that we can effectively pass on the business to the next generation. That means lowering the inheritance taxes or capital gains taxes so that family businesses do not find themselves in the position where they have to sell the company." His sentiments were echoed by many of our survey participants.

Government policy overall (regulation, legislation, and public spending) is of greater concern to family businesses than taxes per se. While a good many family businesses expressed displeasure over what they consider government interference (e.g., the Affordable Care Act, minimum wage), they also voiced a desire for government involvement in retraining the workforce, creating incentives for new product development (e.g., additional tax credits for investment and for research and development), and making it easier for businesses to access capital.

## Seeking new horizons

A key route that family businesses are taking to the future goes through international markets. Nearly half (47%) of US family businesses are currently selling goods and services outside the country, and even more (54%) expect they'll be selling internationally by 2017. This is a considerable leap from two years ago when just 30% of US respondents said they were intending to develop business in markets abroad, and an even bigger jump from our survey in 2007, when only 21% of family businesses planned to invest in business development outside the United States.

Top foreign destinations for US family businesses are the Americas (primarily Brazil, Canada, and Mexico) and the Asia Pacific region. China is the number one country on the itinerary — 14% of survey participants with global intentions plan to sell in that market five years from now, while more than one-quarter of internationally bound respondents are setting their sights on the Asia Pacific region overall. Thirty percent are aiming for the Americas, and 14% are eyeing Europe.

Despite family businesses' decisive uptick in international activity, they say that sales abroad account for just roughly 7% of their sales overall, and they don't foresee that changing much (they anticipate a 10% contribution in five years' time).

That picture may change if economic recovery in the United States remains slow and the demand for US goods in fast-growth markets abroad keeps rising. PwC's ongoing research shows that private companies selling abroad expect roughly 20% of total revenue to come from international sales over the next year. For the most part, those companies are also growing faster than their domestic-only peers, projecting a 12-month revenue growth rate of 9.7%, versus 6.9% for domestic-only businesses (private companies selling in key emerging markets project 11.3% growth). This has been a fairly consistent trend for several years now.

## Succession planning

Thirty-eight percent of the family businesses we surveyed say that succession planning will pose a substantial challenge for them in five years' time. This prompts an immediate question: Why in *five* years' time? The inferred answer: Because planning hasn't yet begun. Too often we find that family businesses either do not have a formal succession plan or, at best, have a loose one that is rarely revisited.

Lack of a formally documented and routinely updated succession plan signals uncertainty in a still-uncertain economy. That, in turn, can adversely affect not only the company's longevity, but also its near-term health. A clearly communicated plan, on the other hand, signals that the company is here to stay.

Just as importantly, the sooner a successor is identified, the sooner that individual can be groomed (or auditioned) for the leadership role, allowing ample time to cultivate innovative thinking and entrepreneurial skills — or, alternatively, time to select another candidate if the chosen successor's apprenticeship doesn't go well.

The earlier a business owner puts a well-considered plan in writing, the better he or she can prepare for an orderly transfer of the business, which should help the family maximize the business's value and reduce risk when the current leader steps down.

Early communication of a succession plan also gives the family time to resolve potential tensions between members who are actively involved in the business and those who are not. By informing these and other key stakeholders of the plan early on and soliciting their input, the business owner improves the likelihood of ultimately obtaining their support, even if at first they don't agree with certain aspects of the plan.

**Conclusion**

What most distinguishes family businesses from other types of companies? Although there are many distinguishing characteristics that family businesses can lay claim to, the majority would probably say that their closely knit structure and strong sense of personal responsibility for the business are the qualities that most set them apart.

On personal responsibility, Joe Sheetz of Sheetz, Inc., says, "I think that management pays a lot of attention to little details because in our case our name is on the building."

Regarding a closely knit structure, Cody Hughes of Hughes Rental remarks, "We can make decisions faster than other companies. That gives us a lot of flexibility." This last quality — flexibility — is a key reason so many of the family businesses we spoke with described themselves as nimble. And nimble they must be if they are to play their hand well at the right time and in the right way as new opportunities arise.

To make the most of new opportunities, family-business leaders may want to address the following questions when they meet with their management teams:

• Do we have the right mix of talent, technology, and innovation to stay ahead of our competitors?

• Will the strategies we're pursuing today help keep our company relevant five years from now?

• Are we making enough bold moves to grow our current market share, penetrate new markets, and possibly even *create* new markets (i.e., for novel products/services)?

• Have we done all we can to thrive in a global business environment?

• Is our company resilient enough for us to take the necessary risks to propel the business forward?

Using the answers to these questions as anchor points in setting future strategy should help family businesses hit their marks.

## American Family Business Survey
## Massachusetts Mutual Life Insurance Company – Kennesaw State University – Family Firm Institute
## (Excerpts - 2007)

### Methodology

As in previous years, we selected firms that were at least ten years old and had at least $1 million in sales. The median age of the companies was 22 years (the oldest four firms in the sample are from the 1800s).

### Company Characteristics

The opinions represented here are of the corporate decision makers as 71% of the respondents are the highest-ranked persons in their companies. The median age of the top executives was 50 years. Almost one fourth (24%) of the respondents were female. 67% of the respondents were family members, 25% were in-laws, and 8% were non-family executives. Family businesses are not limited to a particular industry. A broad range of industries are included in this survey...

The businesses represented are overwhelmingly controlled by families, with 83.1% of them being wholly family owned. More than three quarters (76.2%) of all firms own 100 percent of the voting shares, providing the owning families with total control of their firms. And the families decidedly want to keep their businesses in family hands, with 86.3 percent of the respondents believing that the business will still be controlled by the same family in five years. The vast majority of the firms are in their first (61.8 percent) or second (25.6 percent) generation of family ownership...

### 1. Optimism

Even amid a housing market crisis and generally depressed business conditions, family business owners express general optimism. Only 26.5 percent of the respondents expect no change or a decrease in revenues next year. The vast majority of respondents are optimistic about the future; 22.3 percent expect increases in revenue of more than 11 percent and 51.3 percent of respondents expect an increase in sales revenues of up to 10 percent. These figures confirm that family businesses are better able to weather economic hardship and stabilize the economy than their non-family counterparts.

### 2. Urgency

Family businesses face some significant challenges. Perhaps first among these is the issue of succession. Within 10 years, 40.3 percent of business owners expect to retire, creating a significant transition. Of these, fewer than half (45.5 percent) of those expecting to retire in five years and fewer than a third (29 percent) of those expecting to retire between six and 11 years have selected a successor, meaning there is much work to do and potential sources of instability for our economy. Of those who have selected a successor, the successor's median age is about 18 years younger than the current chief executive. Co-CEOs, as in previous years, are being considered at a similar rate (42.2 percent).

Many have less certainty about retirement, which is also a tremendous risk. Almost a third (30.5%) have no plans to retire, ever; and nearly another third (29.2%) report that retirement is more than 11 years away. Since the median age of the current leaders is 51, this means that many people plan to die in office, which is not beneficial to the family, the firm, its employees and its clients.

Further exacerbating the substantial succession risk is the fact that nearly a third (31.4 percent) have no estate plan beyond a will. This is worse than the 2002 survey, in which only 19 percent had no estate plan beyond a will. Likewise, in 2002, 68 percent had a good understanding of estate taxes that could be due, whereas in 2007 this number deteriorated to only 53.5 percent having a good understanding. This lack of financial preparedness jeopardizes the ability of the next generation to maintain the business, particularly because paying estate taxes can have a damaging effect on business prospects.

### 3. Gender

In a major advance from 2002, 24 percent of the businesses surveyed have a female CEO or President. In 2002 that number was only 10 percent (which was already double 1997 numbers). As a result, within the past decade there has been an almost five-fold increase in the number of women leaders in family businesses since 1997. This far outstrips the numbers in the world of non-family businesses where, for example, some 2.5 percent of Fortune 1,000 firms are led by women (Fortune Magazine, April 30, 2007.) The trend of female leadership of family businesses should continue as 31.3 percent of firms indicate they may have a female successor. And the prevalence of women in leadership positions carries through the organization even when moving down the org chart. Nearly 60 percent (57.2 percent) of all firms have women in top management team positions. On average, the family businesses in our sample each employ nearly five family members, of which 60 percent are men and fully 40 percent are women.

### 4. Ethical Behavior and Social Responsibility

If family businesses are family and relationship oriented, then it stands to reason that they operate more ethically.

Indeed, previous research shows they are less likely to lay off employees regardless of financial performance (Stavrou, Kassinis, & Filotheou, 2007). Our survey clearly shows family exerts a strong impact on the business; 83 percent state their families have a high influence on the business and 91 percent indicate that the owning family's values are emphasized in the business. Family orientation does indeed seem to translate into more ethical behavior. For example, 57 percent of the respondents answered that being a family business affected their firms' ethical behavior. While over one third (36.6 percent) of firms have a written code of ethical behavior, this does not mean that family businesses without written codes act irresponsibly or unethically, just that they have not made the investment in the kind of written code that is more common in larger firms. On the contrary, most of these family businesses (60 percent of respondents) believe that their ethical standards are more stringent than those of competing firms. The respondents also report ethical standards are discussed often or always at meetings with lower- and mid-level employees (54 percent), in discussions with customers (48 percent), in meetings with executives (45 percent) and suppliers (38 percent), and during board meetings (36.5 percent).

Furthermore, the firms in our sample are deeply embedded in their local communities, and proximity has been identified as an important factor that increases the likelihood of ethical decision-making and moral behavior. More than two-thirds (67.2 percent) of our respondents told us that their businesses contributed significantly to their family's identity in their communities. This finding is in line with research on larger family firms. In their study of S&P 500 firms, Dyer & Whetten (2006) find that family firms exhibit more social responsibility than non-family firms. The authors relate such behavior to the owning families' concern about image and community reputation.

### 5. Professionalism

There is a common misconception that due to the relational nature of family businesses they are less professional and rigorous in their behavior. In one way this may be true. Slightly more than one third of the firms (36.6 percent) have a written strategic plan. Similarly, a bit less than one third (31.1 percent) use a formal process to establish a strategic plan. Strategic planning though is only one higher level example of professional behavior. On the other hand, the fact that 20 percent had or do have a non-family CEO (a large increase from 14 percent in 2002) indicates a desire for high behavioral and professional standards.

Despite the apparent lack of formal strategic planning, the firms use other types of formal planning. For example:

• 37.4 percent have buy-sell agreements or other arrangements defining who can own stock and how it is transferred

• 64 percent have regular formal valuations of the worth of the business

• one third have an active board of directors and over half (50.9 percent) rate their contribution as outstanding, a major increase from 2002 which was only 22 percent

• over half (55.4 percent) have formal family meetings at least once a year

• and almost half of all firms (45.2 percent) have a full-time employee responsible for human resource management matters such as recruiting, performance appraisals, and benefits administration…

### 6. Family Unity

Family unity and cohesion are critical to family business success, especially when family have identified unity as an important goal. The families here are unified; 87 percent say family members share values. We interpret this agreement on values, attitudes, and beliefs among family members as indicative of family unity and cohesion. When it comes to the unity of the owning family in business matters such as strategy, ownership, and management, 82.9 percent of the respondents answered that they were completely or very unified as an ownership group. Research shows that the longest-lived family businesses can draw on various mechanisms stemming from family and business to bond their members closer together and increase family cohesion... In this research, unity of the ownership group is significantly associated with family commitment to the business in each generation, predictions of sales growth, and demonstrations of past growth; the more family unity, the more they grew in the last three years and the more they expect to grow in the future.

Family unity affects other stakeholders too. For example, unified families are more likely to share their values with employees; 85 percent report that the family shares values with employees to a large or even great extent. The overlap between individual and organizational values may result in increased levels of employee loyalty, commitment, and organizational citizenship behavior...

### 7. Most Trusted Advisor

Unlike all prior surveys, in 2007, the business owner's spouse is seen as the most trusted advisor, followed by accountant, business peer, parent, lawyer, and financial services advisor. This represents some large shifts, particularly for lawyers and spouses. Additionally, when considering their top three most-trusted advisors, business owners ranked their accountant first, just as they did in 2002; spouses second, up from fifth in 2002; and their lawyer third, down a spot from 2002.

# CHAPTER 2

# THE STARTING POINT: CLIENT OBJECTIVES

## A. INTRODUCTION

Business planning works only to the extent that it accomplishes the specific objectives of the client. Just about every business owner, when asked about his or her objectives, will respond with some combination of words that boils down to building a stable, respected business and making money. But such general bottom-line aspirations do nothing for the planning process. Quality planning requires knowledge of specific client objectives. A legal advisor's capacity to meaningfully assist in the identification and prioritization of a business owner's objectives is the key to effective planning – often the difference between good and bad.

Many business owners, even some of the very brightest, are incapable of identifying and articulating specific objectives with respect to a planning issue without the aid of a knowledgeable advisor. They need help in understanding the significance of the issue and eliciting the facts and considerations that will impact their objectives relative to the issue.

Take, for example, Joyce, the owner of a successful business, who is convinced that she must provide her star manager Jim an equity-based incentive in order to ensure his future loyalty and dedication – that is, as a hedge against the risk of Jim's jumping to a competitor. As we will see in Chapter 11, there are many factors and objectives that may affect the structure and design of such an incentive. After discussion of the relevant factors, Joyce concludes that she has four primary objectives: (1) she wants Jim to receive common stock in the business; (2) she doesn't want Jim to have to pay anything for the stock; (3) she doesn't want Jim to have any tax liability with respect to the stock except for the capital gains tax he will pay when he sells the stock to the company or Joyce (the only approved buyers); and (4) she wants Jim to forfeit all rights in the stock (including all value represented by the stock) if his employment with the company is terminated during the next eight years for any reason other than death or disability. Like most business owners, Joyce could not have formulated these objectives without input from a professional advisor.

Once identified, the objectives need to be prioritized. Prioritization is necessary because there are often many competing objectives. It's a balancing analysis that requires an understanding of the strategic options and trade-offs. In nearly every situation, this understanding is impossible without the knowledgeable input of a professional advisor. In Joyce's situation, there is no strategy that will accomplish all of her objectives, as we will see in Chapter 11. She will need to prioritize her objectives in order to evaluate the effectiveness of the available strategic options.

The ability to positively influence these all-important objective identification and prioritization processes with real knowledge and high quality dialogue is a fundamental prerequisite to being a good business advisor. The biggest mistake a legal advisor can make is to assume that all closely held business owners share the same basic objectives and require the same essential structural plans. Business planning is not a "one-size-fits-all" game.

The study of planning options and strategies is aided immensely by analysis of the objectives and priorities of different types of closely held business owners. This book focuses on many of the planning challenges that are routinely faced by such owners. The challenges are similar, but the objectives, controlling factors and optimum strategies vary significantly among the different types of owners. Although there are countless ways of classifying privately owned businesses, the following eight classifications, which are based on the type and mix of the owners of the businesses, are used in planning discussions throughout this book. These classifications are not perfect; overlaps, exceptions and omissions regularly surface in the real world. But they work for purposes of illustrating and analyzing the different and competing objectives that often must be addressed in evaluating the strategic options for resolving a specific challenge.

## B.  PRIVATE BUSINESS CLASSIFICATIONS

**1. THE SOLOIST.** The soloist has one owner – no partners, no co-shareholders. It may be a corporation, a limited liability company (LLC) or a sole proprietorship. Whatever the form, the planning focus is on a single owner. The soloist has no need for buy-sell agreements, control strategies, or the complexity of Subchapter K (the partnership provisions) of the Internal Revenue Code. But it still must be concerned with entity forms and structures, motivating and retaining key employees, funding and growing the enterprise, developing exit and transition strategies, controlling and managing risks, taxes, and other critical challenges. The planning usually is easier only because it is lonelier; there is no need to grapple with the competing objectives and perspectives of co-owners. The planner need only address the hopes and dreams of a single individual.

**2. THE TOILERS.** This business is owned by individuals who work full-time for the business. The owners toil in their business every day. To them, the business is much more than an investment; it is their jobs, their careers, and often their sole or primary means of support. They cherish the independence of working for themselves. They long for stability; above all, the business must continue to provide the owners their needed cash flows. The owners know that if the business folds, they likely will end up working for another or standing in an unemployment line. Among themselves, there often is a "democratic" spin on control issues, with minority rights being protected only on the most sensitive issues. The admission of a new owner is a carefully controlled event, because any new owner will become a true day-to-day colleague who will have the capacity to directly affect the success of the business. When one owner leaves the group, the survival and health of the ongoing entity always trumps the interests of the departing owner.

**3. THE GOLFERS.** This organization is owned by investors who do not work for the business. The owners often are heavily involved in the highest-level management decisions, but are free to play golf (or do whatever they want) while others sweat out the day-to-day challenges of the business. For most golfer owners, the business is not their primary or sole means of support; it's an investment. They are looking for a return on that investment – the sooner the better. Compared to toilers, golfers usually are less risk-averse and less concerned with the identity of their co-owners or ownership changes.

**4. THE HYBRID.** The hybrid organization has both toiler owners and golfer owners. Often it is the most difficult organization for planning purposes. The toilers who work for the business will usually put their careers, but not their checkbooks, on the line. They want to do everything in their capacity to protect their paychecks for the long run and to control the operations of the business. The golfer owners are concerned about the money they have at risk and the potential of having to put up more if things don't go as planned. They want equity growth and the flexibility to exit and cash out at the most opportune time.

**5. THE BIG FISH.** This organization has one majority owner and a few small minority owners. The dominant owner, the big fish, may be a toiler or a golfer. The minority owners are usually toilers. The planning dynamics are very different with this type of company. In almost every situation of this type, the big fish will want and expect special treatment. It's not about democratic votes or minority rights. From the big fish's perspective, real damage can be done by trying to create a level playing field on which all the owners are treated the same. The big fish usually will want exclusive control rights that can be passed on to chosen successors and special buy-out rights and liquidity protections to ensure that his or her position can always be preserved. Often the minority owners maintain their equity interests at the will of the big fish, who possesses broad rights to terminate and buy out their interests at any time.

**6. THE FAMILY AFFAIR.** The family affair is the organization that is owned and controlled by a single family. All planning issues are complicated by estate planning challenges and the dynamics among the family members. Usually the parents have family objectives that take priority over business issues, and often the children have special agendas. In many cases, the objectives of children who work in the business collide with the objectives of outside children. Liquidity issues often are magnified by estate tax realities. Control issues are usually affected by family considerations unrelated to the business.

**7. THE PERSONAL SERVICE ORGANIZATION.** This is an organization that generates income by its owners providing services in fields such as healthcare, law, engineering, accounting, actuarial science, the performing arts or consulting. It's actually a type of toiler organization, but it warrants its own classification for a few reasons. First, the owners are the instruments of production of the business; their talents generate the fees that drive everything. The owners are well educated, independent and have the flexibility to make a move at any time. Typically, their large incomes are exceeded only by their larger egos. As a result, these organizations tend to be fragile. Their existence is tied to professional talent that can die, become disabled, or just decide to walk if an ego is bruised. Transitions in and out are always a challenge. Often new blood must be recruited to replenish or expand the talent base. Second, professional service corporations have been a popular target of Congress. They have their own tax provisions, most of which are not friendly.[1] These include a unique tax avoidance and evasion provision that empowers the government to allocate income, deductions, credits and exclusions between a personal service corporation and its owner/employees.[2] There are severe limitations on a personal service corporation's ability to defer earnings by using a fiscal year.[3] But perhaps the harshest provision is the tax rate structure. Unlike all other C corporations, even other toiler organizations, a personal service corporation cannot benefit from the favorable graduated corporate rate structure that starts at 15 percent. All income accumulated in a personal service corporation is taxed at the maximum corporate rate from dollar one.[4]

**8. THE EMERGING PUBLIC COMPANY (EPC).** Only a tiny fraction of closely held businesses will ever consider "going public" – having their stock owned and regularly traded by a large number of public shareholders. All other closely held businesses (the masses) are just too small or not suited for public ownership and the associated regulatory hassles and horrendous expenses. But for those select few that are destined for the big time, going public is the ball game; it is their mission, their purpose, and a prerequisite to their success. Their closely held status is merely preparatory to their real life as a public company. Typically, these companies are developing and preparing to exploit proprietary intellectual property rights and are financed and controlled by professional investment funds. All planning is focused on the unique objectives of the deep pockets that are writing the checks and calling the shots in preparation for the big day when the public is invited to the party.

## PROBLEMS 2-A AND 2-B

**2-A.** Focus Industries, Inc. (Focus) is in the process of being organized. Initially, Focus will have three shareholders: Jason, Larry, and Jane. Their accountant has suggested that they consider entering into a shareholder agreement that would include a right of first refusal provision. The provision

---

1. The exception is the right afforded qualified personal service corporations to use the cash receipts and disbursements method of accounting under I.R.C. § 448(b). Any other corporation (unless in the farming business) may not use the cash method of accounting once its annual gross receipts hit $5 million.

2. I.R.C. § 269A. Allocations may be made when the services of the personal service corporation are performed for another corporation, partnership or entity, as is the situation where a professional uses a corporation to hold his or her interest in a broader organization of professionals.

3. I.R.C §§ 441(i). Use of an accounting period other than a calendar year is permitted only upon a showing of a business purpose for the different accounting period. The desire to defer income is not such a valid business purpose. A personal service corporation may adopt a fiscal year with a deferral period of no more than three months under I.R.C. § 444(b)(2), but in such event, the corporation is required to comply with the minimum distribution requirements of I.R.C. § 280H, which eliminate most deferral benefits.

4. I.R.C. § 11(b)(2).

would require that if a shareholder (Selling Shareholder) desires to sell all or any portion of his or her stock to another party (New Shareholder), the Selling Shareholder must first give Focus the right to purchase the stock on the same terms offered to the New Shareholder.  If Focus does not exercise the right within a designated time frame, the Selling Shareholder must then give the other shareholders a right to purchase the stock on the same terms offered to the New Shareholder.  If none of the other shareholders exercises the right to purchase the stock within a designated time frame, the Selling Shareholder may proceed to sell the stock to the New Shareholder on the same terms offered to Focus and the existing shareholders.  Your advice has been requested on the advisability of such a provision.  In each of the following scenarios, describe the likely objectives of the owners with respect to such a sale and whether the right of first refusal provision would further or frustrate those objectives.

**Scenario 1:**  Focus is a publishing business.  Jason, Larry and Jane are unrelated.  Jason will put up all the capital and own 80 percent of the stock of the company.  Larry and Jane will be the key employees of the company and will each receive 10 percent of the company's stock as incentive compensation.

**Scenario 2:**  Focus is a professional engineering firm.  Jason, Larry, and Jane are unrelated parties who will each work full-time for the firm and commit their careers to the firm.  The initial capital contributions of the three owners will be modest.  Start-up funding primarily will come from a bank line of credit that each owner will jointly and severally guarantee.

**Scenario 3:**  Focus is in the land development business.  Jason, Larry, and Jane are siblings who regularly invest together.  They each will contribute one-third of the substantial capital required by the business in return for one-third of the outstanding stock.  None of the shareholders will work for the business.  The president and CEO of the company will be an unrelated party who has a proven expertise in subdivision development.

**2-B.**  Brand Products Inc. is a four-year-old company that is in the business of providing branded promotional products to large companies through custom catalogs and custom websites.  Its four owners, Pete, Sue, Rick and James, recently developed a business plan for the next seven years that is based on an average annual growth rate of 12 percent.  It is likely that the company will soon develop the power to accelerate its growth to a rate faster than that reflected in the business plan.  Faster growth would create the potential for higher profits and a more visible industry position, but would also require more equity capital or more shareholder-guaranteed debt and accelerated hiring and training programs.  Plus, as more client programs are produced at a faster pace, the risk of program failures increases.  Any such failures would be very expensive, damage the company's reputation, and make it harder to attract profitable brands.

The planning issue now is: What type of owner approval will be required in the future to authorize a growth rate increase faster than that called for in the business plan?  You represent the corporation, not the owners, and your advice on this issue has been requested.  In each of the following scenarios, describe what additional facts should be elicited from the owners, the likely objectives of the different owners with respect to the issue, and the parameters of a potential solution.

**Scenario 1:** Pete, Sue, Rick and James are unrelated parties, each of whom works full-time for the business. They're toilers. They each own 25 percent of the outstanding stock and have each personally guaranteed the company's bank debt as joint and several obligors.

**Scenario 2:** Pete and Sue are unrelated golfers who each own 40 percent of the business but do not work in the business. They put up cash for their equity and arranged for the bank financing. Rick and James, also unrelated parties, manage the business full-time. Each was granted 10 percent of the outstanding stock of the company as part of his compensation package.

**Scenario 3:** Pete and Sue, both age 64, are husband and wife. They own 60 percent of the outstanding stock and provided all the capital for the business. Pete works full time for the business; Sue has no involvement. Rick and James, ages 36 and 28 respectively, are their only children. They were each gifted 20 percent of the outstanding stock when the company was formed. Rick is the vice president of operations and looks forward to taking over the reins from Pete in a few years. James is a writer who has no interest in business but very much appreciates the quarterly cash distributions that he receives from the business.

## C. BASIC BUSINESS CONCEPTS – A PRIMER

A legal advisor to business owners needs to understand basic business concepts. Without such an understanding, the advisor will struggle to comprehend core business objectives and to participate in intelligent business-focused conversations. Knowledge of sophisticated accounting principles is not necessary. What is required is a working knowledge of those basic concepts that drive all businesses: income, cash flow, leverage, opportunity costs, depreciation, return on equity, etc. The following simple description of a tiny company's first three years of operation is designed to illustrate 10 basic business concepts. It is for those students who need some elementary business tutoring. The veteran business or accounting student is encouraged to skip this primer and move on to the next section.

**Party Time Inc.** Jane knows food and is a party animal. After much thought and analysis, she quit her job at the end of 2008 to start her own catering business in early 2009. She formed a corporation named Party Time, Inc., contributed $60,000 for the stock, and started business on January 1. Initially, Party Time's targeted clients were high-income couples who wanted the very best when they threw a party. During the first year of operation, Jane was Party Time's sole employee and handled every detail of every event. When she needed assistance, Party Time hired temporary help for a flat hourly rate of $13. Party Time rented a small commercial kitchen and used $50,000 of its capital to buy a van and essential equipment items. In 2009, Party Time's gross client billings totaled $100,000, of which $80,000 was collected during the year. The uncollected $20,000 represented billings from the busy year-end holiday season that were collected during the first two months of 2010. Party Time's expenses in

2009 totaled $81,700, of which $11,000 remained unpaid at year-end. Key expenses included rent, food, advertising, temporary help, and gas. Jane took no compensation from the company during 2009.

   **1. INCOME.** What was Party Time's income in 2009? Income is an essential concept of business, but it has different meanings based on what it is measuring. The starting point for most business owners is operating income, which is the earnings from the business before any reductions for interest, income taxes, depreciation, and amortization. It is commonly referred to as "EBITDA." EBITDA measures the profitability of the company's operations. Party Time's EBITDA in 2009 was $18,300, the excess of its total billings of $100,000 over its operating expenses of $81,700.

### Exhibit 1
### Party Time Inc. Income Statements

|  | 2009 | 2010 | 2011 No-Debt | 2011 Debt |
|---|---|---|---|---|
| Revenues | $ 100,000 | $ 180,000 | $ 640,000 | $ 640,000 |
| Expenses |  |  |  |  |
| Rent | $ 18,000 | $ 18,000 | $ 18,000 | $ 18,000 |
| Food | 25,000 | 39,600 | 137,300 | 137,300 |
| Advertising | 22,000 | 22,000 | 22,000 | 22,000 |
| Salaries | - | 50,000 | 275,000 | 275,000 |
| Payroll Taxes | - | 4,500 | 24,750 | 24,750 |
| Gas | 1,100 | 1,900 | 7,500 | 7,500 |
| Help | 14,000 | 22,000 | 4,800 | 4,800 |
| Misc. Expenses | 1,600 | 2,900 | 3,400 | 3,400 |
| Total | $ 81,700 | $ 160,900 | $ 492,750 | $ 492,750 |
| Operating Income | $ 18,300 | $ 19,100 | $ 147,250 | $ 147,250 |
| Depreciation | 10,000 | 10,000 | 42,000 | 42,000 |
| Interest Expense | - | - | - | 13,500 |
| Income Before Taxes | $ 8,300 | $ 9,100 | $ 105,250 | $ 91,750 |
| Income Taxes | 1,245 | 1,365 | 24,297 | 19,445 |
| Net Income | $ 7,055 | $ 7,735 | $ 80,953 | $ 72,305 |

   The next income definition is net income before taxes. This definition factors in all expenses except the income taxes that the company must pay on its earnings. It is calculated by reducing the EBITDA by expenses for interest, depreciation, and amortization. Party Time had no interest expense in 2009 because it had no debt, nor did it have any amortizable assets. But it did own a van and equipment that will wear out over time and will need to be replaced. This wearing out cost is referred to as depreciation. It is not an expense that is based on a cash outlay; it reflects the diminution in value of assets owned by the business. Since the equipment purchased by Party Time for $50,000 at the beginning of 2009 was expected to wear out over a useful life of five years, Party Time's annual depreciation expense for that equipment was $10,000. Thus, Party Time's net income before taxes in 2009 was $8,300, its EBITDA of $18,300 less its depreciation expense of $10,000.

The third income component is net income after taxes. This component factors in the income taxes that need to be paid on the company's income. At a federal corporate tax rate of 15 percent on the first $50,000 of earnings, Party Time's income tax liability on its $8,300 of earnings in 2009 was $1,245. Thus, its net income after taxes equaled $7,055. All three of the income concepts described above are reflected in Party Time's income statement for 2009 (Exhibit 1, 2009 column).

**2. CASH FLOW.** Cash flow is a concept different than income, although it is heavily influenced by the income of the business. Cash flow is just what its name implies; it measures the cash that goes in and out of the business. The starting point for the cash flow analysis is the net income after taxes of the business, which was $7,055 in 2009.

**Exhibit 2**
**Party Time Inc. Cash Flow Summary**

| | |
|---|---:|
| Beginning Cash | $  60,000 |
| Plus: | |
| Net Income | $   7,055 |
| Accounts Payable Increase | 11,000 |
| Income Tax Payable Increase | 1,245 |
| Depreciation | 10,000 |
| Total Additions | $  29,300 |
| Less: | |
| Equipment Purchases | $  50,000 |
| Accounts Receivable Increase | 20,000 |
| Total Reductions | $  70,000 |
| Net Change | (40,700) |
| Ending Cash | $  19,300 |

To arrive at the cash flow, this income number must be increased for expenses that did not require any cash outlay during 2009, which for Party Time included the depreciation expense of $10,000, the $11,000 of operating expenses that remained unpaid at the end of the year (typically referred to as accounts payable increase), and the income tax liability of $1,245 that was not paid until the following year. For cash flow purposes, the net income must be decreased by the $20,000 of gross billings that were not actually collected during the year (the accounts receivable increase) and the $50,000 that was used to purchase the van and equipment. Exhibit 2 is Party Time's Cash Flow Summary for 2009.

As Exhibit 2 indicates, even though Party Time showed a net after-tax income of $7,055 in 2009, its cash resources plummeted from $60,000 at the beginning of the year to $19,300 at year-end. This is why many say "cash is king" in start-up operations and why undercapitalization is the reason so many promising businesses fail. The income statement and cash flow summary show the activity of the company over a given period of time, here calendar year 2009. This activity is reflected in the balance sheets of Party Time at the beginning and end of the year (Exhibit 3), each of which provides a snapshot of the assets and liabilities of the company at a specific point in time.

**Exhibit 3**
**Party Time Inc. Balance Sheet**

|  | As of 1/1/2009 | As of 12/31/2009 |
|---|---|---|
| **Assets** | | |
| Cash | $ 60,000 | $ 19,300 |
| Accounts Receivable | | 20,000 |
| Total Current Assets | | $ 39,300 |
| Equipment | | 50,000 |
| Less: Accum. Depreciation | | (10,000) |
| **Total Assets** | $ 60,000 | $ 79,300 |
| **Liabilities** | | |
| Accounts Payable | | $ 11,000 |
| Taxes Payable | | 1,245 |
| Total Current Liabilities | | $ 12,245 |
| **Owner Equity** | | |
| Contributed Capital | $ 60,000 | $ 60,000 |
| Retained Earnings | | 7,055 |
| **Total Owner Equity** | | $ 67,055 |
| **Total Liabilities and Equity** | $ 60,000 | $ 79,300 |

**3. CURRENT ASSETS AND CURRENT LIABILITIES.** A business needs to be able to meet its obligations as they become due. A popular technique for measuring a business' capacity to timely fund its obligations is to compare the company's current assets with its current liabilities. Current assets are those assets that will be converted to cash within one year, and current liabilities are those debts that must be paid within a year. The number obtained by dividing the current assets by the current liabilities is known as the "current ratio." Party Time's current ratio at the end of 2009 was 3.2, strong by any standard. Another ratio that is often used is known as a "quick ratio" or "acid test" ratio. It is the same as the current ratio, except that inventories are excluded from current assets in making the calculation. Since Party Time had no inventories, its quick ratio would be the same as its current ratio.

**4. OPPORTUNITY COSTS.** Beyond the costs actually incurred in operating the business, business owners must always consider the opportunity costs of any decision they make. Opportunity costs are the benefits that are lost because a particular course is pursued. In this case, Jane chose to form a new business that generated a bottom line profit of $7,055 in 2009 and consumed a large portion of the $60,000 that she contributed to the business. She worked hard in 2009, but drew no salary or income from the business. This course of action triggered at least three opportunity costs. First, if she had left the $60,000 that she invested in the company in a bank certificate of deposit that earns five percent annually, she would have earned $3,000 of interest in 2009, and she would have had all of her cash at year end. Second, if she had stayed at her old job, she would have earned a salary and other benefits valued at $75,000 in 2009. Third, if she had remained at her old job, she would have racked up another year of experience and seniority. These are big opportunity costs that she incurred in starting the business.

Smart business decisions are made by factoring in all costs, both real and opportunity. Standard financial statements do not reflect or account for opportunity costs. And often it isn't advisable to approach an opportunity cost analysis based solely on specific numbers. For example, when Jane decided to make her move in 2009, she knew that she would risk $60,000 of hard-earned capital, would work hard in 2009 for no pay, and would give up her secure job and all the benefits that it promised. Any short-term quantitative analysis of those opportunity costs likely would have encouraged Jane to sit tight and count her blessings. Many business plans never come to fruition because the short-term pain of making the move and taking the risks (the opportunity costs) is perceived as being too great. But in this case, Jane weighed these known opportunity costs against the opportunity benefits of doing something she loved and potentially building a valuable going concern that she would own. Although her numbers in 2009 were nothing to write home about, she knew momentum was building and the numbers would improve going forward. And they did.

**5. FIXED VS. VARIABLE EXPENSES.** Through word of mouth, the demand for Party Time's custom catering services grew rapidly in 2010. By mid-year, Jane was regularly turning away more business than she accepted. As her revenue (her top line) number grew, she noticed that her bottom line income number grew at a faster rate. This was due to the fact that certain key expenses – rent and advertising – were fixed in amount and did not increase with the growth in revenues. Other expenses, such as food and temporary labor, were variable with the revenues. The ability to leverage fixed expenses is very important in the growth cycle of any business. In 2010, Jane grew Party Time's total revenues to $180,000, but profitability grew fast enough to allow Jane to draw personal compensation benefits of $50,000 from the business and still drop $7,735 to the bottom line as income. Party Time's income statement for 2010 is in Exhibit 1, 2010 column.

**6. ECONOMIES OF SCALE.** Although Jane was pleased with the activity in 2010, she was frustrated with the work she was being forced to turn away. Many of her clients owned or ran businesses or professional practices, and she was constantly being offered lucrative opportunities to cater business events. She was forced to turn down all but the smallest of these jobs because of her limited personnel and her one-truck operation. She soon discovered that the economy of scale of her business was not large enough to accommodate the kind of growth she wanted.

Every business must be geared to operate at a given level of activity. Its resources and planning are based on a defined level of activity, commonly referred to as its economy of scale. Some businesses are very "scalable," which means they can easily adjust their economy of scale to accommodate more volume. On the other end of the scalability spectrum are those businesses that must make huge additional investments and take on much greater risks to build an expanded economy of scale. Jane quickly determined that she needed to build a new economy of scale to meet the expanded demand for her services. After careful analysis, she decided to purchase and outfit three large trucks and to hire three full-time "event lieutenants," each of whom would be paid compensation and benefits equal to $50,000 a year. Jane easily identified the best candidates from a talented pool of temporary assistants. She knew that each of the three candidates loved the business, would work hard, and would jump at the opportunity to have a full-time job that paid well. Jane's new economy of scale required an additional investment of $180,000 to cover the costs of the trucks and equipment and the necessary working capital to fund the expansion. Jane dipped deeper into her savings and made the additional investment.

Jane's expanded economy of scale was in full swing by the start of 2011. It all worked. Jane was able to effectively use her lieutenants to leverage her personal touch across all major events. As Party Time began catering larger corporate events, its reputation ballooned in all markets. Its gross revenues grew to $640,000 in 2011.

**7. LEVERAGE AND RETURN ON EQUITY.** Jane's expansion plan required an additional investment of $180,000, bringing her total investment in Party Time to $240,000. And it all paid off. In 2011, she was able to pay herself $75,000 from the business and still generate a bottom line net profit of $80,953, as indicated by Party Time's 2011 income statement (See Exhibit 1, 2011 No-Debt column). This net profit represented a 33.73 percent annual return on her total equity investment of $240,000.

Suppose that Jane did not fund her expansion plan with more private investment capital. Assume instead that she went to her local bank, presented her operating history and future plans, and secured a bank line of credit for $180,000 at an annual interest cost of seven and one-half percent. Jane would be spared the burden of having to come up with more personal capital, but Party Time would have a new annual interest expense of $13,500. This interest expense, net of income tax impacts, would reduce Party Time's net income in 2011 to $72,305, as illustrated in Party Time's revised income statement for 2011 (see Exhibit 1, 2011 Debt column). Although the net income would be reduced by the net after-tax cost of the interest expense, the yield on Jane's equity investment would skyrocket. Her original equity investment of $60,000 would generate an annual yield in 2011 of $72,305, more than 120 percent. This is known as positive leverage. The business operations created the opportunity to leverage the existing equity by generating a yield off borrowed funds that far exceeded the cost of the funds. This leverage is the key to maximizing business equity. It is business 101.

**8. DEBT-TO-EQUITY RATIO.** The potential of debt leverage encourages some to overdo it. The ratio of the debt to the equity of the business must be reasonable for business and tax purposes.[5] The reasonableness is measured by a debt-to-equity ratio, which is determined by dividing the company's debt by the equity of the business. Sometimes the ratio is based on all the debt of the business; other times it includes only the long-term debt. There is no mandated acceptable ratio. Debt-to-equity ratios vary widely among industries and particular businesses. Generally (and I really mean generally), a ratio of less than 5-to-1 is considered reasonable, and any ratio in excess of 10-to-1 is usually suspect. If Jane had used the bank line to finance her expansion plan, the book value of the owner's equity on the company's balance sheet at the end of 2011 would equal $147,095. This is calculated by increasing the owner's equity balance at the end of 2009 (Exhibit 3) by the net retained income in 2010 and 2011 (Exhibit 1, Debt Column). Thus, even with a bank line of $180,000, her debt-to-equity ratio would have been less than 2-to-1, reasonable by any standard.

**9. GROSS MULTIPLIERS AND CAPITALIZATION RATES.** By the end of 2011, many were aware of Jane's success. Party Time had a superb reputation, and Jane was known as the inspiration behind its success. A profitable high-end regional restaurant chain (Chain) had been planning a move into the corporate catering business. Chain was faced with a choice. It could endure the start-up expense and hassle of trying to compete with Party Time's reputation and Jane's golden touch, or it could try to buy Party Time and make Jane part of its team. Chain's management decided that a purchase would make sense if the purchased operation would generate a pre-tax operating yield of 13 percent on the price paid for the business. This is known as the capitalization rate, the rate used to determine the purchase price based on a known EBITDA. Party Time's EBITDA in 2011 was $147,250 (Exhibit 1, 2011 Debt column). Dividing this amount by the desired capitalization rate of 13 percent produced a purchase price of $1,132,692. If Jane accepted Chain's offer of this amount for the business, she would pay off the $180,000 bank line, pay her tax hit (see Chapter 8), put the rest in her pocket, and negotiate a lucrative employment contract (see Chapter 10), perhaps with deferred compensation and equity sharing benefits (see Chapters 11 and 12). Sometimes the capitalization rate is expressed as an equivalent income multiple. They are two sides of the same coin. In this case, an EBITDA income of $147,250 was the basis of a purchase price of $1,132,692 based on a 13 percent capitalization rate. This represents an income multiple of 7.69 (147,250/1,132,692). Thus, specifying an EBITDA income multiple of 7.69 is the equivalent of specifying a capitalization rate of 13 percent.

**10. GOODWILL AND GOING CONCERN VALUE.** Under the forgoing analysis, the corporate equity owned by Jane at the time of sale had a value of

---

5. For a related discussion, see section B.4. of Chapter 4.

approximately $953,000, after the purchase price of $1,132,692 was reduced by the $180,000 bank line of credit balance. But, as indicated above, the book value of Jane's equity on the company's balance sheet at the end of 2011 was only $147,095. Valuing the business' equity on the basis of the earnings power of the operation produced a value that was many times greater than the equity book value derived from the assets and liabilities of the company. This excess value, which is huge for many companies, is known as goodwill and going concern value. It recognizes that Jane has built an ongoing, profitable operation that has valued customers and employees and a coveted market reputation. A large, ever-growing goodwill and going concern value is the ultimate goal of all operating businesses.

## PROBLEM 2-C

Following are the Balance Sheet of ABC Inc. (ABC) as of December 31, 2013 and its income statement for the twelve-month period then ended.

**a.** Based on the following statements, what was ABC's:

- Current ratio at year-end?
- Quick ratio year end?
- Long-term debt-to-equity ratio at year-end?
- EBITDA for 2013?
- Net after-tax return on equity for 2013?
- Opportunity costs for 2013?

**b.** Assume that the management of ABC has determined that an expansion of its East Coast operation would enable the company to significantly increase revenues while maintaining its existing profitability margins. The expansion would require $5 million of additional capital.

There are two options for securing the needed capital: A 10-year loan from the company's bank or the sale of common stock to a group that is anxious to invest in the company.

What factors would ABC's management likely consider important in evaluating these two options?

If ABC's management would consider issuing more stock only on a basis that values the company's existing outstanding common stock at a capitalization rate of 12.5 percent on its current EBITDA, what percentage of the total outstanding stock of ABC would be issued for the $5 million of new equity capital?

## ABC Inc. Balance Sheet
### December 31, 2013

**Assets**

| | | |
|---|---|---:|
| Cash | $ | 451,871 |
| Marketable Securities | | 621,045 |
| Accounts Receivable | | 6,211,372 |
| Inventories | | 3,128,897 |
| Total Current Assets | $ | 10,413,185 |
| Property and Equipment | | 8,652,355 |
| Less: Accumulated Depreciation | | (2,768,754) |
| Other Tangible Assets | | 145,781 |
| Intangible Assets | | 24,521 |
| **Total Assets** | $ | 16,467,088 |

**Liabilities**

| | | |
|---|---|---:|
| Accounts Payable | $ | 2,276,541 |
| Accrued Payroll | | 115,432 |
| Current Portion Long Term Debt | | 556,321 |
| Taxes Payable | | 1,462,113 |
| Total Current Liabilities | $ | 4,410,407 |
| Notes Payable | | 6,398,776 |
| **Total Liabilities** | $ | 10,809,183 |

**Owner Equity**

| | | |
|---|---|---:|
| Common Stock | $ | 101,000 |
| Capital Surplus | | 234,698 |
| Retained Earnings | | 5,322,207 |
| **Total Owner Equity** | $ | 5,657,905 |
| **Total Liabilities and Equity** | $ | 16,467,088 |

## ABC Inc. Income Statement
### Twelve Months Ended December 31, 2013

| | | | |
|---|---|---:|---:|
| **Revenues** | $ | 31,542,111 | 100.0% |
| Cost of Goods Sold | | 14,603,997 | 46.3% |
| **Gross Profit** | $ | 16,938,114 | 53.7% |
| Expenses | | | |
| Selling | $ | 2,908,183 | 9.2% |
| Marketing | | 1,955,611 | 6.2% |

| | | |
|---|---:|---:|
| Warehouse and Distribution | 2,113,321 | 6.7% |
| General and Administrative | 4,258,185 | 13.5% |
| Outside Services | 252,337 | 0.8% |
| Other Operating Expenses | 1,327,923 | 4.2% |
| Total | $ 12,815,560 | 40.6% |
| **Operating Income** | $ 4,122,554 | 13.1% |
| Depreciation | 618,383 | 2.0% |
| Net Interest Expense | 461,200 | 1.5% |
| **Pre-Tax Income** | $ 3,042,971 | 9.6% |
| Income Taxes | 1,034,610 | 3.3% |
| **Net Income** | $ 2,008,361 | 6.4% |

## D. BUSINESS VALUATION BASICS

### 1. THE LAWYER'S NON-ROLE

A core objective of nearly all business owners is to continually increase the value of the business. Experts are often used on a regular basis to express an opinion on the value of the business as a going concern.

Foolish is the lawyer who attempts to value a client's business or even express an opinion on its value. It's not the job of the lawyer. It is beyond the lawyer's expertise or training. Other professionals are trained to tackle the tough job of pinning a value on an ever-evolving bundle of assets and income-generating operations. Let them take the heat. Avoid any temptation to start sounding like a valuation expert with clients.

This does not mean that a lawyer should not understand the vocabulary and basic techniques of business valuations. Such an understanding is essential to being a good legal advisor to business owners. At the most basic level, it makes intelligent conversation possible with those business owners who regularly analyze and ponder the importance of events, both internal and external, that may impact the value of the business they have devoted their working lives to building. They regularly talk of intangible asset indicators, capitalization and discount rates, EBITDA multipliers, and the like.

But the need to know goes beyond client relationships. The issue of value goes right to the heart of the planning effort in countless situations. It, for example, is center stage in buy-sell planning among co-owners, new owner admission challenges, executive-based equity incentives, insurance planning, all estate planning and related family planning challenges, and all exit strategy planning. Valuation challenges are always present in major transaction, including acquisitions, mergers, leveraged buy-outs, and initial public offerings. Business valuation issues often arise in a litigation context in connection with marital dissolution, bankruptcy, breach of contract, dissenting shareholder and minority oppression cases, economic damages computations, and other cases.

While the lawyer is not the valuation expert in these situations, the lawyer's working knowledge of the relevant factors and techniques can strengthen the quality of the entire planning effort. It facilities dialogue with the experts that may help identify or eliminate sloppy valuations. It enables the lawyer to spot unreasonable client valuation expectations. Often it makes it possible for the lawyer to assist the client in understanding the factors that impact the valuation determination and to explain the valuation to other parties who are impacted by the determination. And in most situations, it helps the lawyer lead the planning process.

Knowledge of valuation factors and techniques also can make a lawyer a much better negotiator. Most business negotiations are about value. A primary challenge in the negotiation process is to convince the other side that it is being offered a fair deal based on the values. The lawyer who is equipped to use valuation lingo and measurement techniques to make the case is often very effective. This is one situation where the lawyer can become a valuation advocate by applying favorable factors, drawing comparisons, and expressing "heat-of-battle" opinions. The difference here (and it is huge) is that the lawyer is not seeking to advise a client, but rather is seeking to prevail in a negotiation with one who is not a client. Often the lawyer who gets on a valuation soapbox in a tough negotiation is well advised to privately remind any client who witnessed the show that negotiation dialogue is no substitute for quality advice from a valuation expert.

## 2. THE CHALLENGE

Revenue Ruling 59-60[6] is a useful starting point in assessing the nature of the business valuation challenge. Although ancient, this ruling continues to provide relevant guidance. In the context of business valuations, it states the classic definition of "fair market value" as "the price at which the property would change hands between a willing buyer and a willing seller when the former is not under any compulsion to buy and the latter is not under any compulsion to sell, both parties having reasonable knowledge of the relevant facts." In lieu of prescribing a specific mathematical valuation formula, the ruling discusses the following factors that should be considered in arriving at a fair market value determination:

1. The nature of the business and the history of the enterprise from its inception.

2. The economic outlook in general and the condition and outlook of the specific industry in particular.

3. The book value of the stock and financial condition of the business.

4. The earning capacity of the company.

---

6. 1959-1 C.B. 237. Years later in Revenue Ruling 68-609, 1968-2 C.B. 327, the Service stated that the valuation principles of 59-60 also would apply to partnership interests.

5. The dividend-paying capacity.

6. Whether or not the enterprise has goodwill or other intangible value.

7. Sales of the stock and the size of the block of stock to be valued.

8. The market price of stocks of corporations engaged in the same or a similar line of business having their stocks actively traded in a free and open market, either on an exchange or over-the-counter.

Although the fair market value standard has been around forever and nearly a half century ago the Internal Revenue Service provided guidance on how it should be applied in valuing business interests, serious valuation disputes routinely erupt. These disputes teach two important lessons. First, secure the services of a professional appraiser. Valuing a business interest requires judgment calls that must be made by a professional. Second, get the best appraiser available. If a dispute breaks out, the quality, reputation, and competence of the appraiser may be the ultimate deciding factor. The Tax Court, for example, has consistently refused to accept an appraisal on its face; it has followed a practice of carefully examining the underlying details and assumptions and the quality of the appraiser's analysis.[7]

Revenue Ruling 59-60 also recognized that the size of the block of stock is a relevant valuation factor in valuing an interest in a business enterprise, specifically noting that a minority interest would be more difficult to sell. In many situations, valuation discounts become the name of the game and play an essential role in the planning process. The two most significant discounts associated with an interest in a closely held business enterprise are the minority interest (lack of control) discount and the lack of marketability discount. The minority interest discount recognizes that a willing buyer will not pay as much for a minority interest; there is no control. The lack of marketability discount reflects the reality that a willing buyer will pay less for an interest in a closely held business if there is no ready market of future buyers for the interest. Usually both discounts are applied in valuing the transferred interest.[8] Often the two discounts total as much as 35 to 40 percent when a minority interest is being valued.[9]

Of course, publicly traded companies and closely held enterprises present different valuation challenges. A public company's value is impacted by the demand for its stock, which can be heavily influenced by general market conditions and factors that are unrelated to the company's performance. A closely held enterprise's value tends to be more closely tied to specify industry factors and the company's track record. Stockholders of public companies generally have no significant influence on how the company is managed; owners of closely held enterprises usually run the whole show. And whereas profit maximization is premier objective in publicly traded companies, income

---

7. See, for example, Rabenhorst v. Commissioner, 71 TCM(CCH) 2271 (1996) and Estate of Kaufman v. Commissioner, 77 TCM (CCH) 1779 (1999).

8. See, for example, Dailey v. Commissioner, 82 TCM 710 (2001); Janda v. Commissioner, 81 TCM 1100 (2001); Barnes v. Commissioner, 76 TCM 881 (1998); Litchfield v. Commissioner, T.C. Memo 2009-21.

9. Id.

maximization often takes a back seat to tax planning for the owners of closely held businesses.

When it comes to business valuations, nothing is easy and uncertainty abounds. William Yegge, an experienced business valuation expert and author summed it as follows:

> For nearly 30 years I have wrestled with the question: What is business value? And to this day, assignment of intangible value in business remains the more perplexing task. There simply is no "pat" answer or formula. My way is neither right nor wrong, and the task is not really made easier with experience. If I have learned one common essential, it is to exercise caution in assigning intangible value and throughout the whole process. There will always be reams of theory and flames of discussion, because scientific formulas developed for intangible value can do no more than "attempt" to measure the art form of human enterprise.[10]

### 3. ALTERNATIVE VALUATION METHODS

It helps to have a basic understanding of the various methods that are used to value a business. The most appropriate method in any given situation depends on the nature and history of the business, market conditions, and a host of other factors. Often a combination of methods is used. In Section B above, the capitalized earnings method was illustrated. The business' value was determined by applying a capitalization rate to EBITDA or some other designated measure of income. Following is a brief description of select other methods.

**Book Value Method.** The book value method bases the value on the company's balance sheet. It is total assets less as total liabilities, using the balance sheet's historical dollar cost numbers. No attempt is made to account for the fair market value of the assets or the going concern value of the enterprise. For that reason, it is usually a poor measure of a company's real value. Its only virtue is its simplicity.

**Adjusted Book Value Method.** This is the same as the Book Value Method, with one important twist. Under this method, the assets are adjusted to reflect their current fair market values. The balance sheet is still the driving force, but asset values are restated. It works best in those situations where asset values are the key to the company's value. But it is a poor measure for an operating business whose value is predicated on its earning capacity and going concern value.

**Hybrid Method.** The hybrid method, in most situations, is a combination of the Adjusted Book Value Method and the capitalized earnings method illustrated in section B above (Item 9). A value is determined under each method and then the two values are weighted to arrive at a value for the business. For example, if a determination was made to base 20 percent of the value on the Adjusted Book Value Method and 80 percent on the capitalized earnings value, an amount equal to 20 percent of the Adjusted Book Value method would be

---

10. Yegge, A Basic Guide to Valuing a Company (John Wiley & Sons Inc. 2002).

added to an amount equal to 80 percent of the capitalized earnings value. The Hybrid Method works best in those situations where the business' value is attributable to a combination of asset values and its earning capacity.

**Excess Earnings Method.** This method incorporates the features of the Hybrid Method, but factors in the cost of carrying the assets of the business and financing impacts. The starting point is to multiply the "Net Tangible Assets" (aggregate fair market value of the tangible assets less liabilities) by a relevant applied lending interest rate to arrive at the annual cost of carrying the assets ("Cost of Money"). The designated income measure (EBITDA, for example) is reduced by the Cost of Money, and the result is divided by the designated capitalization rate to arrive at the business' "Intangible Value." The Intangible Value is then added to the Net Tangible Assets to arrive at the total value.

**Discounted Cash Flow of Future Earnings.** This method calculates the company's value by looking to the future. The applicable earnings measure (EBITDA, for example) is projected to increase at a given rate for a designated period of time, such as ten years. The present value of the projected EBITDA in each of such years is then calculated by applying a discount rate that reflects the level of risk and uncertainty associated with the business and the time value of money. The present value determinations for each of the years are then added together to arrive at the business' value. When this method it used, often it is done to confirm the conclusions of another method.

## PROBLEM 2-D

Based on the following are the balance sheet of XYZ Inc. at December 31, 2013 and its income statement for the twelve-month period then ended, calculate XYZ Inc.'s value under the following methods:

A. Book Value Method

B. Adjusted Book Value Method

C. Capitalized earnings method based on current years EBITDA and a capitalization rate of 16.67 percent (equivalent to a multiplier of 6).

D. Hybrid of B and C, with 30 percent allocated to B and 70 percent allocated to C.

E. Excess earnings method based on pre-tax income for 2010, a 7 percent applied lending rate, and a 12.5 percent yield rate (equivalent of multiplier of 8). Assume the Net Tangible Assets total $5.6 million.

F. Discounted cash flow of future earnings based on ten year projections of EBITDA earnings, assuming EBITDA earnings increase at 9 percent each year and the risk level return requirement is 18 percent.

**XYZ Inc. Financial Statements**

**December 31, 2013**

| | Book Value | Fair Market Value |
|---|---|---|
| **Assets** | | |
| Cash | $ 200,000 | 200,000 |
| Accounts Receivable | 2,400,000 | 2,400,000 |
| Inventories | 2,800,000 | 3,500,000 |
| Equipment | 1,400,000 | 2,600,000 |
| Total | $ 6,800,000 | $ 8,700,000 |
| **Liabilities** | | |
| Accounts Payable | $ 900,000 | $ 900,000 |
| Bank Line of Credit | 2,200,000 | 2,200,000 |
| Total | $ 3,100,000 | $ 3,100,000 |
| **Shareholder Equity** | | |
| Capital Stock | $ 200,000 | $ 200,000 |
| Retained Earnings | 3,500,000 | 3,500,000 |
| Asset Appreciation | | 1,900,000 |
| Total Equity | $ 3,700,000 | $ 5,600,000 |
| **Total Debt and Equity** | $ 6,800,000 | $ 8,700,000 |

**Income Statement Current Year**

| | |
|---|---|
| Gross Revenues | $ 18,500,000 |
| Cost of Sales | 11,100,000 |
| Gross Profit | $ 7,400,000 |
| Expenses (no depreciation) | 5,100,000 |
| Earnings Before Interest, Taxes Depreciation & Amoritization (EBITDA) | $ 2,300,000 |
| Depreciation | 260,000 |
| Interest | 140,000 |
| Pre-Tax Income | $ 1,900,000 |
| Income Taxes | 646,000 |
| Income After Taxes | $ 1,254,000 |

## E.  TAXES – THE FUTURE?

A core objective of most business planning strategies is tax reduction. Business owners need to be smart with taxes.  The objective is to minimize the government's bite, consistent with other objectives, and to avoid look-back planning blunders – those situations where an owner, faced with an ugly tax bill that could have been avoided with some advance planning, exclaims in disgust, "I sure wish someone had told me that five years ago."

Smart tax planning requires more than just strategizing against a static set of rules.  Changes in the rules must be anticipated and factored into the mix.  Tax planning has always favored those who can wisely anticipate a moving target. And there is little question that today, perhaps more than ever, the target is moving faster and is harder to predict.

All who witnessed Congress and the White House struggle during the last few days of 2010 and 2012 with vital, last-ditch tax changes were vividly reminded of four lessons regarding tax law changes.  First, timing is not a function of what makes sense for the economy, businesses, or the American people.  The timing of change is governed by what a few powerful individuals deem best for their political fortunes and those of their fellow party members. Given the stakes of the 2010 and 2012 election showdowns, there was no way future tax landscapes were going to be addressed until the critical election results in those years were in the rear view mirror.  It made no difference that the crucial drop-dead dates were set years ago, or that the prolonged uncertainty and delay hurt everyone, even as the economy struggled with chronic unemployment and a pitifully low growth rate. Timing predictions need to be based on the anticipated political motives of the White House and those few key players who control the agendas of the House and Senate.

Second, talk about fiscal responsibility and unsustainable deficits is just talk. In early December 2010, just a few weeks before the political theatrics of the 2010 Tax Bill, the President's National Commission on Fiscal Responsibility and Reform ("Commission") published its long-anticipated report entitled "The Moment of Truth."  Although the Commission's  recommendations were controversial, everyone professed agreement with the bottom line conclusions that mirrored exactly what Congress has repeatedly been told in years past: "America cannot be great if we go broke,"[11] "[I]f the U.S. does not put its house in order, the reckoning will be sure and the devastation severe,"[12] and our federal debt is "unsustainable."[13]  Yet just days later, fiscal responsibility was once again thrown out the window as the "compromise" of the 2010 Tax Bill granted unfunded unemployment benefit extensions and across-the-board tax breaks for everyone, triggering a new stimulus bill that promises to add nearly another trillion dollars to the national debt.  As each side rushed to proclaim victory for the bill, alleging that it had out-negotiated the other side, only a handful of elected representatives expressed any concern with the associated costs and

---

11.  "The Moment of Truth," Report of the National Commission on Fiscal Responsibility and Reform (December 2010) (the "Commission Report"), p. 6.
12.  Id.
13.  Commission Report p. 10.

deficits. And given the vote tallies in both the House and Senate,[14] the fiscal irresponsibility of the bill cannot be blamed on the lame-duckers. Once again each side has proven that, in the heat of battle to get what it wants, it will always sacrifice fiscal discipline in the spirit of compromise and the need to generate media sound bites for its base. That simple reality is why we face the mammoth financial crisis that the Commission's report once again laid out for Congress. The lesson in anticipating change is to not overreact to dialogue about the nation's unsustainable fiscal position. Elected representatives will pay lip service to the crisis, but most lack the capacity to understand the gravity of the situation or the political will to take any position based on difficult facts. It's always easier and more popular to be fiscally irresponsible.

Third, tax law changes are usually a product of negotiation, not reasoned tax policy or economic theory. For example, the elaborate theories and arguments advanced over the years regarding federal estate and gift taxes meant nothing when Congress had to take action by the close of 2010 and 2012. As usual, the end result was a function of down-and-dirty horse trading.

Finally, although many businesses thrive on stability and certainty, most tax changes provide neither. The plan of late is to pass a measure that will expire on a given date and revert to something that promises serious pain for everyone unless Congress timely extends the measure or adopts something different. This new normal practice of short-term tax rules facilitates Congressional procrastination and last minute horse-trading, eliminates the need for reasoned analysis and meaningful debate, and provides a measure of political cover for those who approve short-term compromises.

So with all this, what changes can America's businesses expect in the years ahead? No crystal ball is powerful enough to answer that question, but following are six factors to consider.

1. A consensus will continue to build that the moment of truth for Medicare and Social Security really has arrived and that reform of these mammoth, unsustainable programs can no longer be ignored. Medicare reform will be wrapped up in legislative fights to dismantle, frustrate, or defund the healthcare reform bill passed in 2010. The new 3.8 percent Medicare tax on investment income for couples earning over $250,000 ($200,000 for single individuals) will continue to be a key revenue factor. Although many claims will be made regarding the value of improving efficiencies, reducing waste, fraud and abuse, and considering other cost savings measures (i.e. tort reform), there likely will be an emerging consensus that the easiest and only effective means to reduce out-of-control Medicare costs is to replace expensive late-life procedures with inexpensive end-of-life counseling. As for Social Security, the "fix" will likely come by changing the rules for young Americans – increasing the age of retirement, reducing the benefit formula, skewing benefits even more in favor of those who make less, and increasing Social Security taxes by accelerating the annual increase in the wage base cap.[15] In short, Social Security will be actuarially "saved" by having young Americans pay more and get much less.

---

14. The Senate vote was 81-19; the House Vote 277-148.
15. See Commission Report pp. 48-55.

Unlike the large senior and baby boomer voting blocks that fixate on anything related to Social Security, most of America's young will have no clue what's been done to (or for) them.  No serious consideration will be given to other reform proposals that would promise much more for young America.[16]  The political fight over who should get the most credit for the "save" will likely be more intense than any dispute over the merits of the available options.

2.  Of course, the long-term tax picture will depend on which party has the longest-lasting upper hand.  No matter who is in control, the realities and pressures of unprecedented deficits will mandate increases in government revenues.  Many will advocate keeping tax rates down on the theory that lower taxes translate to stronger businesses and reduced unemployment, in turn leading to more income and payroll taxes for the government.  They will forever point to the Reagan years and the annual acceleration of revenues generated in the years following the Bush tax cuts.  Many others will dispute the link between lower rates and higher revenues, rejecting all trickle-down benefit theories, arguing that lower rates only benefit the rich, and pushing hard for the 30-percent minimum "Buffett" tax on those with adjusted gross incomes over $1 million (phased in between $1 million and $2 million) and a 28 percent cap on all deductions for those families earning more than $250,000.

3.  It is reasonable to expect that supporters of the "Moment of Truth" report issued by the Commission will push to raise revenues by fundamentally restructuring the Internal Revenue Code along the lines recommended by the Commission.[17]  Rates at all levels would be reduced (maximum rates in the 28 percent range) while the overall tax base would be broadened.  Capital gains and dividends would be taxed the same as ordinary income; itemized deductions would be eliminated (all taxpayers would get the standard deduction); interest on newly-issued state and municipal bonds would no longer be tax exempt; the home mortgage interest deduction would be eliminated, replaced with a watered-down 12 percent credit that would be capped for mortgages up to $500,000 and not be available for second homes or home equity loans; the charitable contribution deduction would be replaced with a watered-down 12 percent credit; the AMT would be gone; and numerous other "tax expenditure" loopholes would be closed.  All C corporations would be subject to a single lower rate (i.e. 28 percent), but all general business credits would be gone, along with the domestic credit deduction, the last-in, first-out (LIFO) method of valuing inventories, the deferral method of taxing active foreign source income, and various other tax incentives.  Although proponents would trumpet the perceived simplicity and fairness of the new structure, its biggest impact would be immediate increases in government revenues[18] and the potential to generate much more for the government down the road.  The fear of many would be that, shortly after the ink had dried on such a bill, some would start pushing to hike rates back to "more normal" levels, knowing that any rate bumps, when applied to a much broader

---

16.  See, e.g., The Interim and Final Reports of the President's Commission to Strengthen Social Security (August 2001 and December 2001).

17.  See Commission Report pp. 28-34.

18.  The Report indicates that the changes would increase government revenues to 21 percent of Gross Domestic Product (GDP) by 2022, up from 15 percent in 2010.  Commission Report pp. 10, 28.

tax base, would enable the government to take its share of the nation's gross domestic product to new highs even faster. Many would fight any such restructuring proposal, arguing that it would destroy key markets, reduce investment capital, hurt business development, assure chronic high unemployment, and ultimately lead to the government just having a bigger piece of a much smaller pie. As the impacts of any such proposal became clearer, more would join the fight, and the dissenters' volume would increase. Obviously, any such major change would force all investors and business owners to reanalyze and revise their strategies and business structures. And it is exactly that capacity to restructure that will guarantee, as always, that the projections used to support the changes will miss by a mile.

4. The recently created, significant tax rate differential between individual taxpayers and C corporations may continue to grow. For many years, this was not a factor, as both rate structures topped out at a maximum rate of 35 percent. But the 2012 Fiscal Cliff legislation and the Healthcare 3.8 percent tax have pushed high-end individual rates to 43.4 percent starting in 2013, creating a huge gap between top individual and corporate rates. There is an ongoing push to kick individual rates higher, and no one is advocating an increase in America's corporate rates (now the highest in the industrial world). Indeed, many on both sides of the aisle favor a reduction in corporate rates. Some predict that, when all potential components are factored in, high-end individual rates could ultimately rise to as high as 45 to 48 percent, with corporate rates still at the 34 percent level (and potentially lower) for all companies that make less than $10 million and 35 percent for those over the $10 million mark. For an enterprise looking to grow with reinvested earnings, the magnitude of such a rate differential may mandate the use of a C corporation. The difference between reinvesting 66 cents on every earned dollar and reinvesting 55 cents (a 20 percent spread), when compounded over five or 10 years and adjusted for leveraging differences, can dramatically affect a business' capacity to finance growth. And if corporate rates drop (as suggested below), the rate gap and related planning impacts will become more significant.

5. As regards federal estate and gift taxes, the 2012 Fiscal Cliff legislation likely resolved these issues for the foreseeable future. That legislation set the unified gift and estate tax exemption at $5.25 million starting in 2013 and the tax rate at 40 percent. It also provided for an annual inflation adjustment in the exemption amount and an automatic unused exemption rollover provision to a surviving spouse. Of course, opponents of these taxes (who reside on both sides of the political aisle) will continue to push for complete repeal, and there is always the possibility that they may succeed one day if proponents of these rich-focused taxes choose to use them as low-cost trading bait to secure far more substantial tax concessions from the other side. My suspicion is that political realities would never tolerate such a blatant tax break for the rich.

6. Business entity taxation will remain a centerpiece of all tax reform discussions, with rhetoric on both sides of the aisle focused on job creation and the need to bolster the ability of American companies to compete in a global economy that has embraced the value of lower business tax rates. The White

House and many Congressional members now openly favor a maximum federal corporate tax rate in the 25 to 28 percent range. The only question is how to fund the required revenue offsets. Substantial discussions of Subchapter S and partnership tax reforms are underway, with some proposing key substantive changes (e.g. elimination of the section 1375 tax for excessive passive income in an S corporation and reduction of the 10-year section 1374 built-in gains holding period) and others taking a more radical approach and proposing a new set of uniform tax rules for non-public companies that would eliminate the need for Subchapter S and complicated partnership tax provisions. It's reasonable to assume that any major tax reform may include significant changes for C corporations and all pass-through entities.

6. As the economy struggles to recover, it's likely that valuable tax perks will be available from time to time. Some will come and go; others will be extended time and again. Advisors need to help their clients take advantage of these perks when it makes business sense to do so. Potential examples could include enhanced bonus depreciation provisions, a variety of special credits (e.g. research and development, empowerment zone, renewal communities, and work opportunity), expanded section 1202 benefits (offering the potential of a 100 percent capital gain exclusion and freedom from AMT burdens) available to investors in small business stock, and the potential to avoid the section 1374 built-in gains tax by a corporation that converts from C status to S status. The planning challenge requires a timely awareness of the perks and an effective client communication program.

# CHAPTER 3

---

# THE CHOICE-OF-ENTITY CHALLENGE

---

## A. INTRODUCTION

A primary planning challenge for all businesses is to select the best form of business organization. Too many planning lawyers mistakenly assume that this challenge is limited to new ventures. Many mature businesses have a need, albeit often unrecognized, to re-evaluate their business structure from time to time to maximize the benefits of the enterprise for its owners.

Some perceive the "choice of entity" analysis solely as a tax-driven exercise. Although taxes are vitally important, there are many important non-tax factors that can impact the ultimate decision. The rules of the game have changed in recent years. Some factors, once deemed vitally important, no longer impact the final outcome, and there are new issues that now must be factored into the mix. In most situations, the analytical process requires the client and the planner to predict and handicap what's likely to happen down the road. There usually is a need to consider and project earnings, losses, capital expansion needs, debt levels, the possibility of adding new owners, potential exit strategies, the likelihood of a sale, the estate planning needs of the owners, and a variety of other factors. For this reason, the decision-making process is not an exact science that punches out a single, perfect answer for every client. There is a need to weigh and consider a number of factors, while being sensitive to the consequences of the alternative options.

The complexity of the challenge often is enhanced by the need to use multiple entities to accomplish the objectives of the client. Multi-entity planning is discussed in Chapter 16. Multi-entity planning can be used to protect assets from liability exposure, limit or control value growth, scatter wealth among family members, segregate asset-based yields from operation-based risks and yields, shift or defer income, enhance tax benefits from recognized losses, facilitate exit strategy planning, satisfy liquidity needs, and promote a structured discipline that helps ensure that all financial bases are covered. It complicates the process, but the benefits usually far outweigh any burdens of added complexity. From the client's perspective, often the use of multiple entities actually promotes an understanding of the different planning challenges and objectives because each entity is being used for specific purposes. The entity options are not limited to the business entity forms reviewed in this chapter; they also include a broad menu of different trusts that can be used to promote targeted objectives. More on this topic in Chapter 16.

## B. THE CHECK-THE-BOX GAME

A mammoth choice-of-entity burden was eliminated in 1997 when the Internal Revenue Service decided to abandon the difficult corporate resemblance tests used for classifying unincorporated businesses and instead adopted an infinitely easier and more certain "check-the-box" regime. The analytical challenge of selecting the best entity form was not made any easier, but the planner could now know for certain that the choice, once made, would stick. Prior to 1997, often there was a nerve-wracking uncertainty that some detail might trigger a retroactive tax reclassification of the entity by the Service – a disastrous result in nearly every situation. Great care was required to protect against this uncertainty. Often it required that less favorable substantive provisions be included in the governing documents in order to protect the entity's tax classification.

A corporation subject to the provisions of Subchapter C of the Internal Revenue Code is defined as including "associations."[1] There is no "associations" definition. Before 1997, the tough challenge was determining when an unincorporated business, such as a partnership or a limited liability company, was to be deemed an "association" taxable as a corporation under Subchapter C. In rare instances, the taxpayer desired corporate tax treatment, and the Service sought to deny "association" status. The most common example of this was the professional service organization that desired certain corporate tax benefits (such as lower rates, fringe benefits, and enhanced retirement plan options), but was not allowed to incorporate under state law.[2] The conflict ultimately prompted all states to render the issue moot by authorizing the formation of professional service corporations. But the far more common situation was the partnership or limited liability company that planned on the pass-through and other benefits of Subchapter K of the Code (the partnership provisions), only to find the Service arguing for "association" status.[3]

Although the pre-1997 classification regulations lacked an "association" definition, they provided that "an organization will be treated as an association if the corporate characteristics are such that the organization more nearly resembles a corporation than a partnership or trust."[4] The regulation listed six corporate characteristics: (1) Two or more associates; (2) an objective to carry on business and share profits; (3) continuity of life; (4) centralization of management; (5)

---

1. I.R.C. § 7701(a)(3).
2. See, e.g., United States v. Kintner, 216 F.2d 418 (9th Cir. 1954) and Morrissey v. Commissioner, 296 U.S. 344 (1935).
3. See Rev. Proc. 89-12, 1989-1 C.B. 798, Rev. Proc. 91-13, 1991-1 C.B. 477, and Larson v. Commissioner, 66 T.C. 159 (1976).
4. Reg. § 301.7701-2(a)(1), before amended in 1997.

limited liability; and (6) free transferability of interests.[5] For analytical purposes, the first two characteristics – associates and business purpose – were ignored because they were always common to both corporations and partnerships. The focus was on the last four, which were weighted equally. The entity was classified as a corporation if it possessed three of the last four characteristics. For planning purposes, this required a careful structuring of the organization to ensure that at least two of the last four characteristics were flunked. Since limited liability was an overriding objective in many cases, the focus often was on the need to destroy continuity of life, centralized management and free transferability of interests. This is why so many pre-1997 organizational documents contain tough provisions on these issues that never reflected the business objectives of the clients. It's a classic example of the tax tail wagging the dog.

This all changed in 1997. The Service threw in the towel on the difficult corporate characteristics test and opted for a simple "check-the-box" system. The new system provides certainty and, unlike the prior system, contains default provisions that greatly reduce the likelihood of the uninformed being punished. The regulations apply to any business entity that is separate from its owner and that is not a trust.[6] Following is a brief description of the key provisions of the "check-the-box" system:

**1. CORPORATIONS.** Any entity organized under a federal or state statute that uses the words "incorporated," "corporation," "body corporate," or "body politic" is taxed as a corporation.[7] Thus, all corporations formed under state law are taxed as corporations, either under Subchapter C or Subchapter S of the Internal Revenue Code.

**2. UNINCORPORATED ENTITY.** An unincorporated entity with two or more owners (i.e., a partnership, limited partnership, or limited liability company) is taxed as a partnership under the provisions of subchapter K unless the entity elects to be treated as a corporation for tax purposes.[8] Any such election may be effective up to 75 days before and 12 months after the election is filed.[9] The election must be signed by all members (including any former members impacted by a retroactive election) or by an officer or member specifically authorized to make the election.[10]

**3. SINGLE-OWNER ENTITY.** An unincorporated single-owner entity, such as a single-member limited liability company, is treated as a disregarded entity unless a corporate status election is made. Thus, the default is taxation as a sole proprietorship. A single-owner entity will never be subject to the partnership provisions of Subchapter K.[11]

**4. PRE-1997 ENTITIES.** With one exception, pre-1997 entities retain the

---

5. Id.
6. Reg. §§ 301.7701-1(a), 301.7701-2(a).
7. Reg. § 301.7701-2(b)(1).
8. Reg. §§ 301.7701-2(c)(1), 301.7701-3(a), 301.7701-3(b)(1).
9. Reg. § 301.7701-3(c)(1)(iii).
10. Reg. § 301.7701-3(c)(2).
11. Reg. §§ 301.7701-2(a), 301.7701–2(c)(2), 301.7701–3(a), 301.7701–3(b)(1).

same tax status they had under prior regulations unless a contrary election is made.  The exception is for single-owner entities that were taxed as partnerships; they are now taxed as sole proprietorships unless a corporate election is made.[12]

**5.  CHANGES.**  A classification election, once made, cannot be changed for 60 months unless the Service authorizes a new election or more than 50 percent of the ownership interests are acquired by persons who did not own any interest in the company at the time of the first election.[13]  A change in the number of owners does not affect a classification unless the change results in a single-owner unincorporated entity (in which case it will be taxed as a sole proprietorship) or changes a single-owner unincorporated business into a multi-owner entity (in which case the entity will go from being taxed as a sole proprietorship to being taxed as a partnership).[14]

**6.  ELECTION TAX CONSEQUENCES.**   If an entity that is taxed as a partnership elects to be taxed as a corporation, it will be deemed to have contributed all its assets and liabilities to the corporation in return for stock and then to have distributed the stock to the partners in liquidation of their partnership interests.[15]  If an unincorporated entity that is taxed as a corporation elects to be taxed as a partnership, it will be deemed to have distributed its assets and liabilities to the shareholders, who, in turn, will be deemed to have contributed the assets and liabilities to a newly formed partnership.[16]  Similar rules apply to a single-owner entity that elects corporate status or that elects sole proprietorship status after having elected and maintained corporate status for at least 60 months.[17]

## C.  THE ENTITY CANDIDATES

### 1.  SOLE PROPRIETORSHIP

Sole proprietorships are for soloists who operate simple businesses and do not want the hassles of dealing with a separate entity.  Everything is reflected through the individual owner's tax return.  Its greatest virtue is its simplicity, but it offers few other benefits.  For this reason, it generally is confined to small one-owner businesses that create no significant liability concerns for their owners.

### 2.  C CORPORATION

The C corporation is a regular corporation that pays its own taxes.  It is a creature of state law and is recognized as a separate taxable entity.  Its earnings and losses are not passed through to its shareholders. It may have different classes of stock and any number of shareholders.  It offers its shareholders personal liability protection from the liabilities of the business and a host of tax benefits.   It is a popular choice for many toiler organizations, big fish organizations, emerging public companies, and operating companies that need to

---

12. Reg. § 301.7701-3(b)(3).
13. Reg. § 301.7701-3(c)(1).
14. Reg. § 301.7701-3(f).
15. Reg. § 301.7701-3(g)(1)(i).
16. Reg. § 301.7701-3(g)(1)(ii).
17. Reg. § 301.7701-3(g)(1)(iii) & (iv).

retain modest earnings each year. Any corporation that does not qualify and elect to be taxed as an S corporation will be taxed as a C corporation.

### 3.  S CORPORATION

The S corporation is the preferred choice for many.  It is organized as a corporation under state law and offers all corporate limited liability protections. But it is taxed as a pass-through entity under the provisions of Subchapter S of the Internal Revenue Code.  These provisions are similar, but not identical, to the partnership provisions of Subchapter K.  The popularity of S status is attributable primarily to three factors: (1) accumulated earnings increase the outside stock basis of the shareholders' stock; (2) an S corporation is free of any threat of a double tax on shareholder distributions or sale and liquidation proceeds; and (3) S status can facilitate income shifting and passive income generation.  As described below, when compared to a C corporation or partnership, there are a variety of other tax perks and traps as well.  The S corporation is particularly attractive to golfers who own part of a corporate entity that makes regular earnings distributions and to a C corporation that wants to convert to a structure that offers pass-through tax benefits.

There are certain limitations and restrictions with an S corporation that can pose serious problems in the planning process.  Not every corporation is eligible to elect S status.  If a corporation has a shareholder that is a corporation, a partnership, a non-resident alien or an ineligible trust, S status is not available.[18] Banks and insurance companies cannot elect S status.[19]  Also, the election cannot be made if the corporation has more than 100 shareholders or has more than one class of stock.[20]  For purposes of the 100-shareholder limitation, a husband and wife are counted as one shareholder and all the members of a family (six generations deep) may elect to be treated as one shareholder.[21]  The one class of stock requirement is not violated if the corporation has both voting and nonvoting common stock and the only difference is voting rights.[22]  Also, there is an important straight debt safe harbor provision that easily can be satisfied to protect against the threat of an S election being jeopardized by a debt obligation being characterized as a second class of stock.[23]

In defining S status eligibility, trusts have received serious Congressional attention in recent years.  There has been a constant expansion of the trust eligibility rules.  Trusts that are now eligible to qualify as S corporation shareholders include: (1) voting trusts; (2) grantor trusts; (3) testamentary trusts that receive S corporation stock via a will (but only for a two year period following the transfer); (4) testamentary trusts that receive S corporation stock via a former grantor trust (but only for a two year period following the transfer);

---

18.  I.R.C. § 1361(b).
19.  I.R.C. § 1361(b)(2).
20.  I.R.C. § 1361(b)(1)(A) & (D).
21.  I.R.C. § 1361(c)(1).
22.  I.R.C. § 1361(c)(4).
23.  I.R.C. § 1361(c)(5).  To fit within the safe harbor, there must be a written unconditional promise to pay on demand or on a specified date a sum certain and (1) the interest rate and payment dates cannot be contingent on profits, the borrower's discretion, or similar factors; (2) there can be no stock convertibility feature; and (3) the creditor must be an individual, an estate, a trust eligible to be a shareholder, or a person regularly and actively engaged in the business of lending money.  For planning purposes, it is an easy fit in most situations.

(5) "qualified subchapter S" trusts (QSSTs), which generally are trusts with only one current income beneficiary who is a U.S. resident or citizen to whom all income is distributed annually and that elect to be treated as the owner of the S corporation stock for tax purposes; and (6) "electing small business" trusts (ESBTs), which are trusts whose beneficiaries are qualifying S corporation shareholders who acquired their interests in the trust by gift or inheritance, not purchase.[24] An ESBT must elect to be treated as an S corporation shareholder, in which case each current beneficiary of the trust is counted as one shareholder for purposes of the maximum 100 shareholder limitation and the S corporation income is taxed to the trust at the highest individual marginal rate under the provisions of the Internal Revenue Code [25]

Electing in and out of S status can present some planning challenges. An election to S status requires the consent of all shareholders.[26] A single dissenter can hold up the show. For this reason, often it is advisable to include in an organizational agreement among all the owners (typically a shareholder agreement) a provision that requires all owners to consent to an S election if a designated number of the owners at any time approve the making of the election. The election, once made, is effective for the current tax year if made during the preceding year or within the first two and one-half months of the current year.[27] If made during the first two and one-half months of the year, all shareholders who have owned stock at any time during the year, even those who no longer own stock at the time of the election, must consent in order for the election to be valid for the current year.[28] Exiting out of S status is easier than electing into it; a revocation is valid if approved by shareholders holding more than half of the outstanding voting and nonvoting shares.[29] For the organization that wants to require something more than a simple majority to trigger such a revocation, the answer is a separate agreement among the shareholders that provides that no shareholder will consent to a revocation absent the approval of a designated supermajority. The revocation may designate a future effective date. Absent such a designation, the election is effective on the first day of the following year, unless it is made on or before the fifteenth day of the third month of the current year, in which case it is retroactively effective for the current year.[30]

## 4. PARTNERSHIP OPTIONS

Partnership structures often are used for ventures that hold appreciating assets, such as real estate and oil and gas interests. Historically, they have been used as effective family planning tools to shift income to family members, freeze estate values, and facilitate gifting of minority interests at heavily discounted values. Often they are used in conjunction with one or more other business entities. Their use with operating businesses has diminished in recent years as the limited liability company has taken center stage.

---

24. I.R.C. §§ 1361(c)(2), 1361(d), 1361(e).
25. I.R.C. §§ 1361 (e)(1)(A), 1361(c)(2)(b)(v).
26. I.R.C. § 1362(a). See generally Reg. § 1.1362-6.
27. I.R.C. § 1362(b)(1).
28. I.R.C. § 1362(b)(2). For potential relief on a late election where there is reasonable cause for the tardiness, see I.R.C. § 1362(b)(5) and Rev. Proc. 2004-48, 2004-2 C.B. 172.
29. I.R.C. § 1362(d)(1).
30. I.R.C. § 1362(d)(1)(C) & (D).

Generally, there are four types of partnerships: general partnerships, limited liability partnerships, limited partnerships, and limited liability limited partnerships. In a general partnership, each partner is personally liable for the debts of the entity and has a say in the management of the business.

A limited liability partnership ("LLP") is a partnership that, pursuant to applicable state law, has filed a statement of qualification (sometimes called an "application") with the state's secretary of state to eliminate the personal liability exposure of the partners. The name of an LLP must end with the words "Registered Limited Liability Partnership," "limited liability partnership," or the abbreviation "R.L.L.P," "RLLP," "L.L.P.," or LLP."

A limited partnership is an entity that has one or more general partners ("GP") and one or more limited partners ("LP") and is formed under a state's limited partnership act. GPs have the authority to manage and conduct the business of the partnership and are personally liable for the debts and obligations of the partnership. LPs typically are investors who have limited or minimal control over daily business decisions and operations of the partnership and have no personal liability for the obligations of the partnership beyond their capital contributions to the partnership.

The limited liability limited partnership ("LLLP") is to a limited partnership what an LLP is to a general partnership. Its role is to eliminate the personal liability exposure that general partners have for the obligations of a limited partnership. It's a relatively new entity form that has been adopted in roughly half the states. An LLLP must elect LLLP status in the limited partnership's filed certificate and use a name that includes the phrase "limited liability limited partnership," "LLLP," or "L.L.L.P." With LLLP status, a general partner is not personally liable for an obligation of the limited partnership incurred while the partnership is an LLLP, whether arising in contract, tort, or otherwise. This limited liability exists even if the partnership agreement contained inconsistent provisions before making the election to become an LLLP.

Substantive details regarding the different types of partnerships and the related planning challenge are discussed in Chapter 5.

Although partnerships file separate returns, they are not taxpaying entities. The profits and losses of the partnership are passed through and taxed to the partners under the provisions of Subchapter K of the Internal Revenue Code.

## 5. THE LIMITED LIABILITY COMPANY

The limited liability company ("LLC") is a relatively new candidate. All states now have statutes authorizing LLCs, most of which were adopted during the 1980s. Many claim that the LLC is the ultimate entity, arguing that it offers the best advantages of both corporations and partnerships and few of the disadvantages. It's an overstatement, but not by much in some situations. There is no question that the arrival of the LLC has made the choice of entity challenge easier in many cases. Like a corporation, the LLC is an entity organized under state law. And as with a corporation, it offers liability protection to all owners, making it possible for its owners to fully participate in the management of the business without subjecting themselves to personal exposure for the liabilities of the business. LLCs are classified as either "member-managed" (managed by all members) or "manager-managed" (managed by designated managers).

Although similar to a corporation for state law purposes, a limited liability company is taxed as a partnership for federal income tax purposes unless it elects otherwise. As such, it offers better pass-through benefits than an S corporation and completely avoids all the S corporation eligibility and election hassles. It can have more than 100 owners, and partnerships, corporations, nonresident aliens, and any kind of trust can be included as owners. For these reasons, many wrongfully conclude that the LLC eliminates the need to consider S corporations and partnerships as viable pass-through entity candidates. As we will see, there are still many situations where an S corporation or a partnership will be the entity of choice.

The professional limited liability company ("PLLC") is a state-chartered entity that allows licensed professionals (i.e., doctors and lawyers) to enjoy the benefits of a limited liability company. A PLLC does nothing to reduce a professional's personal liability for his or her own mistakes, but does eliminate a professional's liability for the errors, omissions, negligence, incompetence or malfeasance of other professionals who are not under his or her supervision and control. It also eliminates personal exposure for contract liabilities that the professional has not personally guaranteed. States often require that a PLLC register with the applicable state licensing board before filing its organizational documents with the state.

## D. TAX PERKS AND TRAPS

The choice of entity analysis requires a careful assessment of all relevant income tax considerations. Each entity option offers certain tax benefits – perks – and traps that may pose problems down the road. The smart planner will review the perks and traps by carefully pondering their potential relevance under various scenarios that may be applicable to the client's situation. In most cases, it is advisable to review the tax consequences with the client, even those consequences that at first blush are not likely to impact the ultimate choice of entity decision. Such a review usually triggers a detailed dialogue that significantly improves the quality of the analysis and enhances the client's appreciation of the issues. Plus, it can go a long way in protecting against the potential for a "no one told me" complaint when a tax trap, deemed unimportant upfront, kicks in because circumstances change. The planner who quickly jumps to an ultimate conclusion and then becomes a dogmatic advocate for that conclusion usually shortchanges the analytical process and forfeits a valuable opportunity to educate the business owner about the relevant factors and trade-offs and the value of sound judgment and wisdom. It is a mistake to assume that business owners, like so many other clients, want to be spared the details. While a few may wave off discussion of the fine points, most business owners yearn for understanding that promotes confidence in major decisions.

Also, clients should be reminded that taxes are a moving target. The rules often change.  What works today may make no sense tomorrow.  Those who watched the eleventh-hour theatrics of the Congress and the White House during the closing days of 2010 and 2012 to prevent threatened tax chaos saw that it is all about politics and inherent uncertainty.  We can make predictions and try hard to access the political winds, but uncertainty is a given that makes choice of entity planning more challenging and exciting.

Our starting point is a brief review of some of the primary tax perks and traps of an entity being taxed as a C corporation, a partnership, or an S corporation.  This foundational review is followed by a discussion of the 16 factors that should be considered in the choice of entity analysis.

## 1.  C CORPORATION PERKS

**a.  Favorable Low-End Rates.**  The first $50,000 of a C corporation's taxable income each year is subject to a favorable 15 percent tax rate.  The rate jumps to 25 percent on the next $25,000 of taxable income.  Thus, the overall rate on the first $75,000 of taxable income is an attractive 18.33 percent, far less than the personal marginal rate applicable to most successful business owners.  Beyond $75,000, the rate advantage disappears as the marginal rate jumps to 34 percent.  Plus, if the corporation's income exceeds $100,000, the rate "bubbles" an additional five percent on taxable income over $100,000 until any rate savings on the first $75,000 is lost. The impact of this five percent "bubble" is that any C corporation with a taxable income of $335,000 or more will pay a rate of at least 34 percent from dollar one.  Earnings of a C corporation in excess of $10 million are taxed at 35 percent, and a three percent "bubble" applies to C corporation earnings in excess of $15 million until the 35 percent rate has been applicable to all income.[31]  And remember, there are no rate breaks for a professional service organization that is taxed as a C corporation; it is subject to a flat 35 percent rate from dollar one.[32]

**b.  Shareholder Employee Benefits.**  A shareholder of a C corporation who is also an employee can participate in all employee benefit plans and receive the associated tax benefits.  Such plans typically include group term life insurance,[33] medical and dental reimbursement plans,[34] section 125 cafeteria plans, dependent care assistance programs,[35] and qualified transportation reimbursement plans.[36]  Partners and most S corporation shareholder/employees (those who own more than 2 percent of the outstanding stock) are not eligible for the tax benefits associated with such plans.[37]  This factor alone makes the C corporation an attractive option for many toiler and professional service organizations.

**c.  Tax-Free Reorganization Potential.**  A C corporation may participate

---

31.  I.R.C. § 11(b)(1).

32.  I.R.C. § 11(b)(2).

33.  I.R.C. § 79.

34.  I.R.C. § 106.

35.  I.R.C. § 129.

36.  I.R.C. § 132(a)(5).

37.  The benefits are available only to "employees," a status that partners can never obtain.  Although S corporation shareholders may clearly qualify as "employees," Section 1372 provides that, for fringe benefit purposes, the S corporation will be treated as a partnership and any shareholder owning more than 2 percent of the stock will be treated as a partner.

in tax-free reorganizations with other corporate entities. It's possible for corporations to combine through mergers, stock-for-stock transactions, and assets-for-stock transactions on terms that eliminate all corporate and shareholder-level taxes.[38] This perk often is the key to the ultimate payday for those private business owners who cash in by "selling" their business to a public corporation. Cast as a reorganization, the transaction allows the acquiring entity to fund the acquisition with its own stock (little or no cash required) and enables the selling owners to walk with highly liquid, publicly traded securities and no tax bills until the securities are sold.

**d. Reduced Dividend Rates.** The economic stimulus package of 2003 resulted in a compromise that reduced the maximum tax rate on "qualifying corporate dividends" paid to non-corporate shareholders to 15 percent (5 percent for low-income shareholders otherwise subject to maximum marginal rates of 15 percent or less).[1] These reduced rates applied to all dividends received from January 1, 2003 to December 31, 2012. The American Taxpayer Relief Act of 2012 (the "Fiscal Cliff" legislation signed into law during the final days of 2012)[2] increased this low dividend rate to 20 percent starting in 2013 for couples with taxable incomes in excess of $450,000 and individuals with taxable incomes in excess of $400,000. Plus, in 2013, the 3.8 percent Medicare tax kicked in on interest, dividends, capital gains, and other "net investment income" to the extent that this income, when added to the taxpayer's other modified adjusted gross income, exceeds $200,000 in the case of unmarried individuals, $250,000 in the case of married individuals filing jointly, and $125,000 in the case of married individuals filing separately. The net result is that a couple with an adjusted income of less than $250,000 or a single person with an adjusted gross income of less than $200,000 will continue to pay the pre-2013 dividend rates (a maximum of 15 percent).[3] Couples or individuals with higher incomes will pay a combined income and Medicare dividend rate of either 18.8 percent or 23.8 percent, depending on whether the new $450,000 or $400,000 thresholds are exceeded.

**e. Tax Year Flexibility.** Unlike a partnership and an S corporation, a C corporation may adopt any fiscal year to ease its accounting and administrative burdens and to maximize tax deferral planning.[42] No special showing is required, and there are no special deferral limitations. The only exception is for personal service organizations that are taxed as C corporations.[43]

**f. Rollover Deferral.** Section 1045 permits non-corporate shareholders to defer the recognition of gain on the disposition of qualified small business stock held for more than six months by investing the proceeds into the stock of another qualified small business within 60 days of the sale.[44] This perk can excite the

---

38. I.R.C. §§ 368, 354, 361. See Chapter 7.
39. I.R.C. § 1(h)11(b).
40. Section 102 of the American Taxpayer Relief Act of 2012.
41. I.R.C. § 1411.
42. See generally I.R.C. § 441.
43. I.R.C. § 441(i).
44. Section 1045 incorporates the Section 1202(c) definition of "small business stock," which generally requires that the stock have been issued to the original issuee after the effective date of the Revenue Reconciliation Act of 1993 by a C corporation that actively conducts a trade or business and that has gross assets of $50 million or less at the time the stock is issued. I.R.C. § 1202(c), (d) & (e).

entrepreneur who is in the business of moving money from one deal to the next or the shareholder who has a falling out with his or her co-shareholders and wants to exit for another opportunity.

**g. Section 1202 Gain Exclusion.** Section 1202 allows a non-corporate shareholder to exclude 50 percent of the gain recognized on the sale or exchange of qualifying small business stock held for more than five years.[45] To qualify, the stock must have been issued after August 10, 1993, the shareholder must be the original issuee of the stock, and the company must be a C corporation whose aggregate gross assets did not exceed $50 million at the time the stock was issued.  The maximum amount of eligible section 1202 gain with respect to the stock of a single corporation is the greater of $10 million or 10 times the taxpayer's basis in the stock of the issuing corporation.  The perk has always sounded better than it really is because the taxable portion of the gain is subject to a high 28 percent capital gains rate and the tax break can trigger or enhance an alternative minimum tax.  So often section 1202 has been ignored in the planning process. The Small Business Jobs Act of 2010 gave this perk a huge shot in the arm by increasing the exclusion to 100 percent and eliminating the alternative minimum tax risk for stock bought between September 27, 2010 and January 1, 2011. Congress then extended these benefits for stock bought during 2011 under section 760 of the Tax Relief, Unemployment Insurance Reauthorization, and Jobs Creation Act passed during the final days of 2010 and then further extended the benefits through 2013 under section 324 of The American Taxpayer Relief Act of 2012.  For many companies formed during 2013, this mammoth change in section 1202 may be a big factor in any choice of entity analysis; it eliminates all the negatives of old section 1202 and provides a potential tax free exit for those shareholders who hold their stock for five years.  This factor, coupled with the different pressures on C corporation rates and individual rates (discussed below), could make the C corporation the darling choice for many in 2013.  And if by chance Congress down the road chooses to make this temporary 1202 perk a permanent fix, section 1202 will become an important threshold consideration in all choice of entity planning.

**h. Ordinary Loss Treatment.**   Section 1244 grants individuals and partnerships ordinary loss treatment (as opposed to the less favorable capital loss treatment) on losses recognized on the sale or exchange of common or preferred stock of a "small business corporation" (generally defined as a corporation whose aggregate contributions to capital and paid-in surplus do not exceed $1 million). In order to qualify, the shareholder must be the original issuee of the stock and the stock must have been issued for money or property (services do not count).[46] There is no longer a requirement that the corporation adopt a formal 1244 plan, although many legal advisors routinely include a directors' resolution in the organizational documents that makes specific reference to 1244 in authorizing the issuance of stock.  Again, this perk often sounds better than it is.  The problem is that the ordinary loss in any single year (usually the year of sale) is limited to $50,000 ($100,000 for married couples).[47]  This serious dollar

---

45. See I.R.C. §§ 1202, 57(a)(7), 1(h)(3), 1(h)(7).
46. I.R.C. § 1244.
47. I.R.C. § 1244(b).

limitation, together with the fact that bailout loss treatment is not an exciting topic during the start-up planning of any business, usually results in this perk having no impact on the choice of entity analysis.

**i.  Consolidated Return Option.**  Often it is advantageous to use multiple corporations to conduct the operations of an expanding business.  Multiple entities can reduce liability exposures, regulatory hassles, and employee challenges as the operations diversify and expand into multiple states and foreign countries.  While there may be compelling business reasons for the use of multiple entities, business owners often prefer that all the entities be treated as a single entity for tax purposes in order to simplify tax compliance, eliminate tax issues on transactions between the entities, and facilitate the netting of profits and losses for tax purposes.  All this is possible with multiple C corporations under the consolidated return provisions of the Code.[48]  The key, of course, is that the entities constitute an "affiliated group," which generally means that their common ownership must extend to 80 percent of the total voting power and 80 percent of the total stock value of each entity included in the group.[49]

**j.  Long-Term Capital Gain on Stock Sale.**  The stock of a C corporation is a capital asset that qualifies for long-term capital gain treatment if sold after being held for more than a year.[50]  Unlike an interest in a partnership-taxed entity, the disposition of which will generally trigger ordinary income treatment to the extent that the entity would recognize ordinary income on the disposition of its assets, the character of the gain on the disposition of C corporation stock is not impacted by the asset mix of the entity.  Today, this perk shines because the maximum capital gains rate (15 percent to 23.8 percent, depending on income level)[451] is substantially less than the maximum 43.4 percent rate on ordinary income. The difference is significant in some cases and can provide a compelling incentive.  The problem for planning purposes is that it is usually difficult, if not impossible, to accurately predict when the stock may be sold and even more difficult to predict what the state of the long-term capital gains break will be at that time.  Too often, planners and clients mistakenly assume that the status quo will remain the status quo.  History, even very recent history, confirms the fallacy of this assumption with respect to the capital gains tax.  Just over the past two decades, we have seen the gap between ordinary and capital gains rates completely eliminated, narrowed to levels that were not compelling for planning purposes, and (as now) widened to levels that get everyone excited.  The report

---

48.  See generally I.R.C. §§ 1501-1504.

49.  I.R.C. § 1504(a).

50.  I.R.C. §§ 1221(a), 1222(3).

51.  I.R.C. § 1(h).  The American Taxpayer Relief Act of 2012 (the "fiscal cliff" legislation signed into law during the final days of 2012)4 increased the capital gains rate to 20 percent starting in 2013 for couples with taxable incomes in excess of $450,000 and individuals with taxable incomes in excess of $400,000. Plus, in 2013, the 3.8 percent Medicare tax kicked in on interest, dividends, capital gains, and other "net investment income" to the extent that this income, when added to the taxpayer's other modified adjusted gross income, exceeds $200,000 in the case of unmarried individuals, $250,000 in the case of married individuals filing jointly, and $125,000 in the case of married individuals filing separately.  The net result is that a couple with an adjusted income of less than $250,000 or a single person with an adjusted gross income of less than $200,000 will continue to pay the pre-2013 capital gains rates (a maximum of 15 percent).4  Couples or individuals with higher incomes will pay a combined income and Medicare dividend rate of either 18.8 percent or 23.8 percent, depending on whether the new $450,000 or $400,000 thresholds are exceeded.

entitled "The Moment of Truth" issued by The National Commission on Fiscal Responsibility and Reform in December 2010 once again proposed a revised tax structure that would tax capital gains the same as ordinary income. The capital gains tax has always been a political football, and we have no reason to believe that this reality will ever change. Many powerful forces view it as nothing more than a sop to big business and the rich, while others passionately label it an essential element of a strong and vibrant economy.

**k. Corporate Dividend Exclusion.** Section 243 provides an attractive income deduction for dividends paid by one C corporation to another C corporation. The purpose of the deduction is to eliminate the potential of a triple tax on corporate earnings – one at the operating C corporation level, a second at the corporate shareholder level, and a third at the individual shareholder level. The deduction is at least 70 percent, and increases to 80 percent for corporate shareholders who own 20 percent of the operating entity's stock and 100 percent for members of an affiliated group.[52] There are special anti-abuse provisions designed to eliminate or water down the benefit of the deduction if the corporate-owned stock has been held for a very short period[53] or has been debt-financed,[54] or if extraordinary dividends are paid on stock held for less than two years.[55] Plus, use of the deduction to reduce the overall tax hit in a bootstrap corporate acquisition structured to include a corporate dividend bailout that has no bona fide business purpose is likely to trigger an attack from the Service.[56] This perk affects the choice of entity analysis only in those situations where all or a significant portion of the business enterprise is going to be funded and owned by one or more C corporations.

**l. True Separateness.** Often one of the most compelling benefits of a C corporation is that for tax purposes it truly is separate from its shareholders. Absent the payment of a dividend or the sale of stock (both uncommon events for closely held corporations), nothing the corporation does will affect the personal income tax returns of its shareholders. The absence of any pass-through impacts to the shareholders' personal returns is attractive to many. Some are fearful of anything that complicates their personal return or increases the risk that their personal return may be affected by a tax audit of an entity in which they have invested. This perk is often a compelling factor for many emerging public companies and those golfers who are looking for big capital gains on a relatively quick exit.

## 2. C CORP TRAPS

**a. Double Tax Structure.** The biggest negative of the C corporation is the double tax structure: a corporate level tax and a shareholder level tax. It surfaces

---

52. I.R.C. § 243(a) & (c).

53. I.R.C. § 246(c).

54. I.R.C. § 246A.

55. I.R.C. § 1059. Section 1059 requires that a corporate shareholder receiving an "extraordinary dividend" (generally defined as a dividend exceeding 5 percent of the basis of preferred stock and 10 percent of the basis of other stock) reduce its basis in the underlying stock by the deductible portion of the dividend if the corporation held the stock for two years or less before the dividend announcement date.

56. See, e.g., TSN Liquidating Corp. v. United States, 624 F.2d 1328 (5th Cir. 1980) and Waterman Steamship Corp. v. Commissioner, 430 F.2d 1185 (5th Cir. 1970).

whenever a dividend is paid or is deemed to have been paid, although the lower rates on dividends reduce the pain. Still, even with the lower dividend rates, 43.9 percent to 49.7 percent [57] of every dollar earned and distributed by a C corporation subject to a marginal 34 percent rate will be consumed in corporate and shareholder federal income taxes. Added to these numbers are the state income tax hits, which also are pumped up by the double tax structure. But the grief of the double tax structure is not limited to dividends; it kicks in whenever the assets of the business are sold and the proceeds distributed. The bottom line impact is that when it comes time to bail out of a C corporation, the selling shareholders often face an ugly dilemma: sell assets and pay corporate and personal income taxes that collectively may equal 43 to 50 percent of the gain recognized (depending on the capital gains rate at the time of sale), or sell stock and take a hit on the price because the buyer gets no basis step-up on the assets of the business. It's all a result of the inherent double tax structure of a C corporation.

**b. Trapped Losses.** Losses sustained by a C corporation are trapped inside the corporation. They may be carried backward or forward, but they will never be passed through to the shareholders.

**c. Locked-In Basis.** The basis of a shareholder's stock in a C corporation is not affected by the entity's income or losses. This can have a profound impact in a situation where a profitable C corporation has accumulated substantial earnings. Assume, for example, that XYZ Inc. has always had a single shareholder, Linda, who purchased her stock for $100,000, and that the company has accumulated $2 million of earnings over the last ten years. Linda's stock basis at the end of year ten is still $100,000. In contrast, if XYZ Inc. had been taxed as an S corporation or a partnership from day one, Linda's basis at the end of year ten would have grown to $2.1 million. [58] On a sale, the difference would be a capital gains hit on $2 million. This basis step-up potential may not be viewed as a big deal for the shareholder who plans on holding his or her stock until death and is confident that Section 1014 (the basis step-up rule at death) will still be around. But for all other business owners who anticipate substantial earnings accumulations, it can be a compelling factor in the choice of entity analysis.

**d. No Entity Capital Gains Break.** There is no rate break for any capital gain recognized by a C corporation. All income is subject to normal corporate rates. [59]

**e. Redemption Traps.** In contrast to the partnership provisions of the Code, Subchapter C is structured to maximize the recognition of income at the entity and owner levels whenever cash or property passes from the entity to the owners. A good example is a C corporation's redemption of a shareholder's stock. The double tax structure surfaces in a couple of ways. First, unless the

---

57. This number is obtained by first reducing the dollar by the 34 percent corporate tax rate and then applying the 15 percent dividend rate to the remaining 66 percent. The sum of the two taxes is 43.9 percent. The result increases to 49.7 percent if the 23.8 percent dividend rate is applicable.

58. I.R.C. § 1367(a). Partners experience the same basis adjustment for accumulated earnings under I.R.C. § 705(a).

59. I.R.C. § 1201(a).

transaction is structured to fit within one of the exceptions of Section 302(b), the full amount distributed in redemption of the stock is taxed as a dividend to the shareholder to the extent of the corporation's earnings and profits. [60]  So long as the maximum dividend and capital gains rates remain the same, this 302 issue is affected only by the stock basis.  If a 302 exception applies, the stock basis is recovered before any income is recognized.  If no exception fits, the full amount distributed is taxable.  Second, if the corporation distributes property in redemption of the stock, any built-in gain on the distributed property also is taxed to the corporation.  Built-in losses are not recognized. [61]  So if appreciated property is distributed to a shareholder in redemption of stock and a Section 302 exception does not apply, the corporation will pay taxes on the built-in gain at ordinary corporate rates and the full fair market value of the distributed property will be taxed to the shareholder as a dividend.

   **f. Disguised Dividend Trap.**  Any payment from a C corporation to a shareholder may be scrutinized by the Service to see if the payment constitutes a disguised dividend.  What's at stake is a deduction at the corporate level. Common examples of disguised dividends include excessive compensation payments to shareholder/employees or family members,[62] personal shareholder expenses that are paid and deducted as business expenses by the corporation, [63] interest payments on excessive shareholder debt that is reclassified as equity, [64] excess rental payments on shareholder property rented or leased to the corporation, [65] personal use of corporate assets, and bargain sales of corporate property to a shareholder.[66] The lower rates on corporate dividends soften the shareholder tax hit on any such payments being reclassified as a dividend, but the combined impact of the loss of the corporate deduction usually produces a significant net tax cost.

   **g. The Accumulated Earnings Trap.**  The C corporation double-tax structure produces more revenue for the government when larger dividends are paid and less income is accumulated in the corporation.  For this reason, Section 531 imposes a penalty tax on excess income accumulations in a C corporation. Some mistakenly assume that the 531 penalty only applied in years past when individual marginal rates exceeded corporate rates.  Not so.  Although the penalty may be applied whenever there are excessive income accumulations, there is some good news.  First, the current penalty rate, which is applied at the corporate level to the corporation's "accumulated taxable income" (taxable income for the current year, adjusted for certain items including dividends paid and deemed

---

60. The four exceptions of Section 302(b) that will qualify for exchange treatment are (1) redemptions that are not essentially equivalent to a dividend; (2) substantially disproportionate redemptions; (3) complete redemptions of a shareholder's stock; and (4) partial liquidations.  The attribution rules of Section 318 are applicable, although in select situations the family attribution rules do not apply to complete redemptions of a shareholder's stock.

61. I.R.C. § 311(b).

62. See, e.g., Exacto Spring Corp. v. Commissioner, 196 F.3d 833 (7th Cir. 1999); Elliotts Inc. v. Commissioner, 716 F.2d 1241 (9th Cir. 1983); and Charles McCandless Tire Service v. United States, 422 F.2d 1336 (Ct. Cl. 1970).

63. See, e.g., Hood v. Commissioner, 115 T.C. 172 (2000).

64. See the discussion accompany footnotes 99-111 in Chapter 4.  Also, see generally Hariton, "Essay: Distinguishing Between Equity and Debt in the New Financial Environment," 49 Tax L. Rev. 449 (1994).

65. See, e.g., International Artists, Ltd. v. Commissioner, 55 T.C. 94 (1970).

66. See, e.g., Honigman v. Commissioner, 466 F.2d 69 (6th Cir. 1972).

paid) is 20 percent.[67] Second, the tax doesn't kick in until the aggregate accumulated earnings exceed $250,000 ($150,000 in the case of certain professional service organizations). [68] And finally, the penalty tax can be avoided completely if the corporation can demonstrate that it accumulated the earnings in order to meet the reasonable business needs of the corporation.[69] Most companies need to retain earnings to finance operations and growth, and the best evidence is on the asset side of the balance sheet – there is little or no excess cash. If earnings above the statutory thresholds ($250,000 or $150,000, as the case may be) are being accumulated, what is required is an annual resolution of the corporate directors, ideally supported by a numbers analysis, that spells out why the income accumulations are necessary to meet the reasonable business needs of the company. There is a great deal of latitude in defining the reasonable business needs. For this reason, the accumulated earnings penalty usually is a trap for the uninformed who never saw it coming. Apart from being another nuisance that has to be watched as good things start to happen with a C corporation, it seldom is a factor in the choice of entity analysis.

**h. Personal Holding Company Trap.** The personal holding company trap is a close cousin to the accumulated earnings trap. Its purpose is to prohibit C corporations from accumulating excess amounts of investment income, compensation payments (the incorporated movie star or other talent), and shareholder rental income (the corporate yacht scenario). Unlike the accumulated earnings tax, the personal holding company penalty cannot be avoided by documenting reasonable business needs. Generally, the penalty is applicable if the company is closely held (defined as five or fewer individuals owning more than 50 percent of the outstanding stock value, with broad attribution rules[70]) and at least 60 percent of the corporation's "adjusted ordinary gross income" is "personal holding company income." [71] Personal holding company income is defined to include dividends, interest, annuities, most royalties, most rents, and personal service income. [72] The penalty rate of 20 percent is applied at the corporate level to the undistributed personal holding company income.[73] If the penalty becomes a threat, remedial actions include increasing compensation payments to shareholder/employees and paying dividends. Like the accumulated earnings penalty, it's just a nuisance that has to be monitored in select situations.

**i. The AMT Trap.** Large C corporations are subject to an alternative minimum tax. There are blanket exceptions for a company's first year of operation, for any company with average annual gross receipts of not more than $5 million during its first three years, and for any company with average annual

---

67. I.R.C. § 531.

68. I.R.C. § 535(c).

69. I.R.C. § 532 provides that the tax is applicable to any corporation that is "formed or availed of for the purpose of avoiding the income tax with respect to its shareholders..." Section 533(a) then provides that, unless the corporation can prove by a preponderance of evidence to the contrary, any accumulation of earnings and profits "beyond the reasonable needs of the business shall be determinative of the purpose to avoid the income tax..."

70. I.R.C. § 542(a)(2).

71. I.R.C. § 542(a)(1).

72. I.R.C. § 543.

73. I.R.C. § 541.

gross receipts of not more than $7.5 million during any three-year period thereafter.[74] The tax applies only to the extent it exceeds the corporation's regular income tax liability. The tax is calculated by applying a 20 percent rate to the excess of the corporation's alternative minimum taxable income (AMTI) over a $40,000 exemption.[75] AMTI is defined to include the corporation's taxable income, increased by a host of tax preference items and adjustments designed to reduce certain timing benefits (i.e., accelerated cost recovery deductions) of the regular corporate tax. [76] The greatest impact in recent years has been the expansion of AMTI to include an amount which, roughly speaking, is designed to equal 75 percent of the excess of the corporation's true book earnings over its taxable income.[77] This expansion was Congress' answer to those public companies that, through the maintenance of separate books, would report big earnings to their investors and miniscule tax liabilities. But as we will see in later chapters, the sweep of the expansion is broad enough to trigger problems for closely held C corporations in dealing with corporate-owned life insurance policies and other select planning issues.

**j. The Controlled Group Trap.** This trap is the flip side of the consolidated group perk described above. It is aimed primarily at the business owner who would like to use multiple C corporations to maximize low C corporation tax rates, the $250,000 accumulated earnings trap threshold, or the $40,000 alternative minimum tax exemption. For example, absent this trap, $500,000 of annual corporate earnings could be spread among ten C corporations ($50,000 each) at a 15 percent tax rate. If multiple corporations are deemed to be part of a controlled group, they are treated as a single entity for purposes of these tax perks, and the multiple-entity benefits are gone.[78]

There are three types of controlled groups. The first, known as a parent-subsidiary controlled group, exists when a chain of corporations is connected by common stock ownership such that at least 80 percent of the total voting power or total stock value of each corporation (other than the parent corporation) is owned by other corporations in the group, and a parent corporation owns at least 80 percent of the total voting power or total stock value of at least one of the other corporations.[79] For example, if corporation A (the parent) owns 80 percent of the stock of B and C, and B and C collectively own 80 percent of the stock of D, then A, B, C and D would constitute a parent-subsidiary controlled group.

The second type of controlled group is the brother-sister controlled group. Its reach was significantly expanded by the American Jobs Creation Act of 2004.[80] It exists when five or fewer individuals, estates or trusts own (i) more than 50 percent of the total combined voting power of all voting stock of two or more corporations, *or* (ii) more than 50 percent of the value of all classes of stock

74.[74] I.R.C. § 55(e).
75. I.R.C. §§ 55(b)(1)(B), 55(d)(2).
76. See generally I.R.C. § 56.
77. I.R.C. § 56(g).
78. I.R.C. § 1561.
79. I.R.C. § 1563(a)(1); Reg. § 1.1563-1(a)(2).
80. Prior to the American Jobs Creation Act of 2004, two or more corporations had to satisfy both an 80 percent test and a 50 percent minimum common ownership test to be treated as a brother-sister controlled group.

of each corporation, taking into account only each shareholder's identical stock ownership in each corporation.[81]   For example, assume that A corporation and B corporation each have 1,000 shares of voting common stock outstanding. Assume further that Jim owns 80 percent of the voting common stock of A corporation and 20 percent of the voting stock of B corporation, and that Linda owns 20 percent of the voting stock of A corporation and 80 percent of the voting stock of B corporation.   Under such facts, A and B would not be considered a brother-sister controlled group because the value of each of Jim and Linda's identical common ownership in the two corporations is only 20 percent.   Thus, their combined identical stock ownership is only 40 percent.   Under these facts, A and B would not satisfy the requisite 50 percent test.

The third type of controlled group, known as the combined controlled group, exists when three or more corporations are each part of a parent-subsidiary controlled group or a brother-sister controlled group, and at least one of the corporations is both a common parent of the parent-subsidiary controlled group and a member of the brother-sister controlled group.[82]   For example, assume that Jim and Linda each own 50 percent of the stock of A and B corporation, that A owns 80 percent of the stock of C corporation, and that B owns 80 percent of the stock of D corporation.   Under these facts, A, B, C and D would be considered a controlled group.   Special attribution and other rules apply in unique situations.[83] The existence of this trap requires, as part of the choice of entity analysis, a disclosure of other C corporation interests owned by those who are going to own an interest in the new entity that is considering C corporation status.

**k. The 482 Trap.**   Section 482 is that ominous provision that gives the Internal Revenue Service authority to "distribute, apportion, or allocate gross income, deductions, credits or allowances between and among" commonly controlled business interests "whenever necessary to prevent evasion of taxes or clearly to reflect the income" of any such businesses.   Although 482, by its terms, applies to any type of business organization, its application to related C corporations who do business with each other can trigger brutal double tax consequences.   The following short Revenue Ruling says it all.

## Rev. Rul. 69-630, 1969-2 C.B. 112

Advice has been requested as to the treatment of a 'bargain sale' between two corporate entities controlled by the same shareholder(s).

A, an individual, owns all of the stock of X corporation and all of the stock of Y corporation.   In 1967, A caused X to sell certain of its property to Y for less than an arm's length price.   It has been determined that such sale had as one of its principal purposes the avoidance of Federal income tax and resulted in a significant understatement of X's taxable income.

Section 482 of the Internal Revenue Code of 1954 provides authority to distribute, apportion, or allocate gross income, deductions, and credits among

---

81. I.R.C. § 1563(a)(2).
82. I.R.C. § 1563(a)(3).
83. I.R.C. § 1563(d) & (e).

related organizations, trades, or businesses if it is necessary in order to clearly reflect the income of such entities or to prevent the evasion of taxes.  Section 482 of the Code applies to bargain sale transactions between brother-sister corporations that result in significant shifting of income.  Where an allocation is made under section 482 of the Code as a result of a bargain sale between brother-sister corporations, the amount of the allocation will be treated as a distribution to the controlling shareholder(s) with respect to the stock of the entity whose income is increased and as a capital contribution by the controlling shareholder(s) to the other entity involved in the transaction giving rise to the section 482 allocation.

Accordingly, in the instant case, the income of X for 1967 will be increased under section 482 of the Code to reflect the arm's length price of the property sold to Y.  The basis of the property in the hands of Y will also be increased to reflect the arm's length price.  See section 1.482-1(d) of the Income Tax Regulations.  Furthermore, the amount of such increase will be treated as a distribution to A, the controlling shareholder, with respect to his stock of X and as a capital contribution by A to Y.

### 3. PARTNERSHIP PERKS

**a. Income Pass Through.**  The income of a partnership is passed through and taxed to its partners.  The entity itself reports the income, but pays no taxes.  The advantage, of course, is that there is no threat of a double tax.  There is only one tax at the owner level.  Unlike a C corporation, a distribution of cash or other assets generally does not trigger a tax at either the partnership or owner level.  Since there is no double-tax structure, all the C corporation traps tied to that menacing structure, including the redemption trap, the disguised dividend trap, the accumulated earnings tax trap, the personal holding company trap, and the consolidated group trap have no application to entities taxed as partnerships.  Even the 482 trap is less threatening because there is no threat of a double tax flowing from any allocation the IRS might make.

**b. Loss Pass Through.**  The losses of a partnership also pass through to its owners.  Unlike a C corporation, the losses are not trapped inside the entity.  Does this mean the partners can use the losses to reduce the tax bite on their other income?  Maybe.  There are three hurdles that first must be overcome, and they can be very difficult in many situations.  The first and easiest hurdle is the basis hurdle – the losses passed through to a partner cannot exceed that partner's basis in his or her partnership interest.[84]  This hurdle seldom presents a problem in a partnership, because each partner's share of the partnership's liabilities, even its nonrecourse liabilities, is treated as a contribution of money by the partner for basis purposes.[85]  The second hurdle, known as the at-risk hurdle, generally limits a partner's losses to only the amount that the partner actually has at risk.[86]  A partner's at-risk amount typically includes property contributed to the partnership by the partner and the partner's share of the partnership's recourse liabilities

---

84. I.R.C. § 704(d).
85. I.R.C. § 752(a).
86. I.R.C. § 465(a).

(those liabilities that create personal exposure for the partners).[87] Nonrecourse liabilities (those liabilities for which no partner has any personal exposure) generally do not count for purposes of the at-risk hurdle, but there is an important exception for qualified nonrecourse financing that makes it easy for many real estate transactions to satisfy the at-risk limitations.[88] The third hurdle (and usually the toughest) is the passive loss rule,[89] a 1980s creation that is designed to prevent a taxpayer from using losses from a passive business venture to offset active business income or portfolio income (i.e., interest, dividends, gains from stocks and bonds, etc.). It was created to stop doctors and others from using losses from real estate and other tax shelters to reduce or eliminate the tax on their professional and business incomes. Losses passed through from a passive venture can only be offset against passive income from another source. If there is not sufficient passive income to cover the passive losses, the excess passive losses are carried forward until sufficient passive income is generated or the partner disposes of his or her interest in the passive activity that produced the unused losses.[90] Whether a particular business activity is deemed passive or active with respect to a particular partner is based on the partner's level of participation in the activity – that is, whether the partner is a "material participant" in the activity. A limited partner is presumed not to be a material participant and, therefore, all losses allocated to a limited partner generally are deemed passive.[91] To meet the "material participation" standard and avoid the hurdle, a partner must show "regular, continuous, and substantial" involvement in the activity.[92] Given these three hurdles, in a choice of entity planning analysis, it is never safe to assume that use of a partnership-taxed entity will convert start-up losses into slam-dunk tax benefits for the owners.

    **c. Passive Income Potential.** Generally, taxable income is classified as portfolio income (dividends, interest, royalties, gains from stocks and bonds, and assets that produce such income), active income (income from activities in which the taxpayer materially participates), or passive income (income from passive business ventures). Passive income is the only type of income that can be sheltered by either an active loss or a passive loss. So the passive loss rule, by limiting the use of passive losses, exalts the value of passive income. An activity that generates passive income can breathe tax life into passive losses from other

---

87. I.R.C. § 465(b).

88. I.R.C. § 465(b)(6). To qualify as "qualified nonrecourse financing," the debt must be incurred in connection with the activity of holding real estate, must not impose any personal liability on any person, must not be convertible debt, and must have been obtained from a "qualified person" (generally defined to include a person who is in the business of lending money, who is not related to the borrower, and who is not the seller or related to the seller).

89. See generally I.R.C. § 469.

90. I.R.C. §§ 469(a), 469(b), 469(d)(1).

91. I.R.C. § 469(h)(2).

92. I.R.C. § 469(h)(1). Under the temporary regulations, a taxpayer meets the material participation standard for a year by (1) participating in the activity for more than 500 hours in the year; (2) being the sole participant in the activity; (3) participating more than 100 hours in the activity and not less than any other person; (4) participating more than 100 hours in the activity and participating in the aggregate more than 500 hours in significant participation activities; (5) having been a material participant in the activity for any five of the last ten years; (6) having materially participated in the activity in any three previous years if the activity is a personal service activity; or (7) proving regular, continuous and substantial participation based on all facts and circumstances. Temp. Reg. § 1.469-5T(a)(1)-(7).

activities. A C corporation has no capacity to produce passive income; it pays dividends or interest (both classified as portfolio income) or compensation income (active income). In contrast, a profitable entity taxed as a partnership can pass through valued passive income to those partners who are not material participants.

**d. Outside Basis Adjustment.** A partner's basis in his or her partnership interest is adjusted upward by capital contributions and income allocations and downward by distributions and loss allocations.[93] Unlike stock in a C corporation, there is no locked-in basis. This can be a valuable perk to the owner of a thriving business that is retaining income to finance growth and expansion. In the case of Linda above (C Corporation Trap c.), the $2 million of retained earnings in an entity taxed as a partnership would have increased the outside basis in her partnership interest from $100,000 to $2.1 million.

**e. Special Allocations Perk.** An entity taxed as a partnership has the flexibility to structure special allocations of income and loss items among its various partners. For example, one partner may be allocated 60 percent of all income and 30 percent of all losses. Although a C corporation has some limited capacity to create allocation differences among owners through the use of different classes of stock and debt instruments, that capacity pales in comparison to the flexibility available to a partnership. A partnership allocation will be respected for tax purposes only if it has "substantial economic effect," three words that make section 704(b) and its regulations one of the most complex subjects in the world of tax.[94] Generally speaking (and I do mean generally), an allocation that does not produce a deficit capital account for a partner will have "economic effect" if capital accounts are maintained for all partners and, upon liquidation of the partnership, liquidating distributions are made in accordance with positive capital account balances.[95] In order for an allocation that produces a deficit capital account balance to have "economic effect," the partner also must be unconditionally obligated to restore the deficit (i.e., pay cash to cover the shortfall) upon liquidation of the partnership,[96] or the partnership must have sufficient nonrecourse debt to assure that the partner's share of any minimum gain recognized on the discharge of the debt will eliminate the deficit.[97] An "economic effect," if present, will not be deemed "substantial" if it produces an after-tax benefit for one or more partners with no diminished after-tax consequences to other partners.[98] The most common examples of economic effects that are not deemed "substantial" are shifting allocations (allocations of different types of income and deductions among partners within a given year to reduce individual taxes without changing the partners' relative economic interests in the partnership) and transitory allocations (allocations in one year that are offset by allocations in later years).[99]

---

93. I.R.C. § 705(a).
94. I.R.C. § 704(b).
95. Reg. §§ 1.704-1(b)(2)(ii) (b)(1), 1.704-(b)(2)(ii) (B)(2).
96. Reg. § 1.704-1(b)(2)(ii) (b)(3).
97. Reg. §§ 1.704-(2)(c), 1.704-(2)(f)(1), 1.704-(g)(1), 1.704-2(b)(1) & (e).
98. Reg. § 1.704-1(b)(2)(iii).
99. Reg. § 1.704-1(b)(2)(iii) (b) & (c).

**f. Easy Bailouts.** It's easy to get money or property out of an entity that is taxed as a partnership. Both in the case of ordinary and liquidating distributions, the Code is structured to eliminate all taxes at the partnership and owner level. Built-in gains generally are deferred through basis adjustments.[100] There are a few exceptions. One is where a distribution of money to a partner exceeds the partner's basis in his or her partnership interest; the excess is taxable.[101] Another is where the partnership has unrealized accounts receivable or substantially appreciated inventory items; in these cases, ordinary income may need to be recognized to reflect any change in a partner's interest in such assets.[102] These easy bail-out provisions are a far cry from the harsh dividend, redemption, and liquidation provisions of C corporations, all of which are designed to maximize the tax bite at both the entity and owner levels on any money or property flowing from the corporation to its owners.

**g. Inside Basis Adjustments.** A partnership's basis in its assets may be adjusted whenever an interest in the partnership changes hands as a result of a sale or exchange of a partnership interest or the death of a partner.[103] The basis of that portion of the partnership assets attributable to the transferred interest is adjusted to reflect the current value of the assets. The result can be higher depreciation deductions and less taxable gain down the road. The adjustment requires that an election be made under Section 754. Nothing comparable exists for C or S corporations.

**h. Tax-Free Profits Interests.** Often a business entity desires to transfer an equity interest in future profits to one who works for the business. An entity taxed as a partnership can do this without triggering any current tax hit for the recipient.[104] A corporation generally cannot transfer an equity interest in return for services without creating a taxable event. Note: this perk only applies to an equity interest in future profits, not an interest in existing capital.

**i. Transfer for Value Exception.** Transfers of interests in life insurance policies among partners are exempt from the reaches of the transfer-for-value rule, that harsh provision that converts tax-free life insurance proceeds into taxable income.[105] No such similar exemption exists for transfers among co-shareholders of a corporation. As we will see in later chapters, this exemption makes insurance planning easier in a partnership-taxed entity.

## 4. PARTNERSHIP TRAPS

**a. Ordinary Income Asset Traps.** Section 751 is a complex provision designed to require a partner to recognize ordinary income whenever a change occurs in the partner's interest in ordinary income assets owned by the partnership. The change may be a result of a distribution, the partnership's purchase of the partner's interest, or a sale of a partnership interest to a third party. The result is that any gain represented by these assets is taxed to the

---

100. See generally I.R.C. §§ 731.
101. I.R.C. § 731(a).
102. I.R.C. § 751; Reg. §§ 1.751-1(b)(2)(ii), 1.751-1(b)(3)(ii), 1.751-1(g).
103. See generally I.R.C. §§ 743, 754.
104. See Rev. Proc. 93-27, 1993-2 C.B. 343 and Rev. Proc. 2001-43, 2001-2 C.B. 191.
105. I.R.C. § 101(2)(b).

partner as ordinary income, not capital gain. In contrast, the capital gain realized on the sale of corporate stock is not affected by the corporation's asset mix.

**b. Family Partnership Trap.** Family partnerships are subject to a special trap that is designed to prevent the use of a partnership to aggressively shift income among family members. If any person gifts a partnership interest to another, the donor must be adequately compensated for any services rendered to the partnership, and the income allocated to the donee, calculated as a yield on capital, cannot be proportionately greater than the yield to the donor.[106] In effect, special allocations to favor donees are out, as are attempts to shift service income. Any purchase among family members is considered a "gift" for purposes of this trap.[107]

**c. Conversion Trap.** As discussed in Chapter 6, usually it is prohibitive from a tax standpoint to convert from a C corporation to an entity taxed as a partnership. Such a change will produce a double tax triggered by a liquidation of the C corporation. The far better option in most cases is to convert to S corporation status if pass-through tax benefits are desired.

## 5. S CORPORATION PERKS

**a. Comparable C Corporation Perks.** Although taxed as a pass-through entity, an S corporation offers a few of the same tax perks as a C corporation that are not available to a partnership. An S corporation may enjoy all the benefits of the tax-free reorganization provisions of the Code, and, except for collectibles, the capital gains benefit realized from the sale or exchange of S corporation stock is not watered down by ordinary income assets owned by the S corporation. An S corporation may even have a multi-entity structure that offers benefits comparable to the C corporation consolidated return perk. An S corporation may own 100 percent of the stock of multiple domestic corporations, each referred to as a "qualified subchapter S subsidiary" (QSSS). Each QSSS is disregarded for tax purposes, and the parent S corporation is deemed the owner of its assets, liabilities, income, deductions and tax credits.[108]

**b. Pass-Through Income.** The income of an S corporation is passed through and taxed to its owners, much the same as a partnership. The entity itself pays no tax on the income, and the shareholders' recognition of the income is not affected by the corporation's retention or distribution of the income. This eliminates the double tax threat and the need for the C corporation traps that are designed to maximize the double tax impact. Also, like a partnership, the income passing through an S corporation may qualify as passive income for those shareholders who are not deemed "material participants." There are a few situations, all arising from an S corporation's prior history as a C corporation, where the pass-through benefits are lost and the S corporation itself is required to pay a tax or a distribution to a shareholder is taxed as a dividend. These are discussed in Chapter 6.

**c. Pass-Through Losses.** An S corporation's losses also are passed through

---

106. I.R.C. § 704(e).
107. I.R.C. § 704(e)(3).
108. I.R.C. § 1361(b)(3).

to its owners, subject to the same three loss hurdles applicable to partnerships. The big difference is that the first hurdle – the basis hurdle – is much tougher in the context of an S corporation. The reason is that the basis calculation considers only amounts that an S corporation shareholder actually pays out-of-pocket (for stock purchases and loans to the entity).[109] There is nothing comparable to the generous liability basis allocation provisions applicable to partnerships.

    **d. Stock Basis Perk.** An S corporation shareholder's stock basis is adjusted up and down for allocable income and losses and cash distributions, much as with a partnership.[110] There is no locked-in basis, as there is with a C corporation. However, as regards the entity's basis in its assets, there is nothing comparable to the 754 election available to an entity taxed as a partnership.

    **e. Bail-Out Potential.** The tax consequences of distributing money or property from an S corporation generally are much less severe than for a C corporation, but not nearly as painless as for a partnership. Distributions of allocated S corporation income are tax-free to the shareholders. Distributions of prior C corporation earnings are taxable,[111] as are liquidating distributions and redemptions that qualify for sale or exchange treatment. Also, unlike a partnership, an S corporation that distributes appreciated property gets no break; the appreciation is taxable income to the S corporation that is passed through to the shareholders.[112]

## 6. S CORPORATION TRAPS

    **a. Eligibility Limitations.** The eligibility requirements for an S corporation (qualifying shareholders, number of shareholders, one class of stock, etc.) are traps that can limit flexibility for an S corporation or result in the loss of S corporation treatment.

    **b. Tax Year Trap.** An S corporation generally is subject to the same limitations as a partnership in selecting a tax year.[113] As compared to a C corporation, there is much less flexibility.

    **c. No Special Allocations.** Unlike a partnership, an S corporation has no capacity to structure special allocations among its owners. Income and losses are allocated according to stock ownership percentages. As discussed in later chapters, employment agreements and shareholder loan arrangements may provide some planning flexibility in select situations.

    **d. Conversion Traps.** A C corporation's conversion to an S corporation is far easier from a tax perspective than a conversion to a partnership-tax entity, which often triggers prohibitive taxes. But there are traps even in an S

---

    109. I.R.C. § 1366(d). A shareholder's guarantee of an S corporation's loan will not result in a basis increase. See, e.g., Harris v. United States, 902 F.2d 439 (5th Cir. 1990); Brown v. Commissioner, 706 F.2d 755 (6th Cir. 1983); Uri v. Commissioner, 949 F.2d 371 (10th Cir. 1991); and Sleiman v. Commissioner, 187 F.3d 1352 (11th Cir. 1999). Contrary is Selfe v. United States, 778 F.2d 769 (11th Cir. 1985).

    110. I.R.C. § 1367(a).

    111. I.R.C. § 1368(c).

    112. I.R.C. § 1371(a) provides that the provisions of Subchapter C will be applicable to S corporations except as otherwise provided in Subchapter S or inconsistent with Subchapter S. As a result, the C corporation provisions dealing with redemptions, liquidations, appreciated property distributions, reorganizations and similar issues are directly applicable to S corporations.

    113. I.R.C. § 1378(b).

conversion (all discussed in Chapter 7) for built-in asset gains, accumulated earnings, LIFO inventory reserves, and excessive S corporation passive income. These traps can usually be managed or completely avoided with some basic planning.

## E.  THOSE OTHER TAXES

The choice of entity analysis may be impacted by self-employment, payroll, and new healthcare taxes in many situations. The self-employment/payroll tax is a regressive tax that's easy to ignore, but the consequences of neglect can be painful.  The tax is levied at a flat rate of 15.3 percent on a base level of self-employment earnings ($113,700 for 2013) and 2.9 percent above the base. Starting in 2013, the rate jumps to 3.8 percent on a  married couple's earnings in excess of $250,000 and an unmarried individual's earnings in excess of $200,000, and the new 3.8 percent healthcare tax applies to any interest, dividends, capital gains, and "net investment income" received by such taxpayers.[114] A self-employed person is entitled to an income tax deduction of one-half of self-employment taxes paid at the 15.3 percent and 2.9 percent rates.[115]

How does the payroll tax impact employees? An employee has one-half of the tax (7.65 percent) come directly from his or her paycheck in the form of payroll taxes.  The other half is paid by the employer who, in order to stay in business, must consider this tax burden in setting the employee's pay level.

For high-income taxpayers, including many business owners, the personal impact of the self-employment tax often is not significant because they are able to structure their affairs to reduce or eliminate its impact, or the base amount subject to the tax is considered small in relation to their overall earnings.  The tax, by design, is structured to punish middle- and low-income workers.  For 80 percent of American workers, the self-employment and payroll taxes paid on their earnings exceed the income tax bite, often by many times.[116]

Are these an important factor to consider in choosing the best form of business entity?  The answer is "yes" in many, but not all, situations. The form of business entity that is selected can affect the self-employment tax burden for the owners of the business.

Compensation payments from a C corporation to owner/employees are subject to payroll taxes.  Corporate dividends are now subject to the 3.8 percent tax to the extent a married couple's income exceeds $250,000 and an unmarried individual's income exceeds $200,000.[117]  For other taxpayers, dividends are not subject to the tax. In a C corporation context, the negative trade-off is that the dividends are subject to the double income tax structure.

The C corporation double-tax trade-off disappears for an S corporation

---

114.  I.R.C. § 1411.
115.  I.R.C. § 164(f).
116.  Report of the Congressional Budget Office, Economic Stimulus: Evaluating Proposed Changes in Tax Policy – Approaches to Cutting Personal Taxes (January 2002), footnote 7.
117.  I.R.C. §§ 1402(a)(2), 1411.

whose earnings are taxed directly through to its shareholders. Compensation payments to an S corporation shareholder are subject to payroll taxes. But a shareholder who works for an S corporation avoids all self-employment taxes on dividends, including the 3.8 percent Medicare tax.[118] An S corporation investor who does not materially participate in the venture will also avoid any self-employment tax on dividends unless the applicable $250,000/$200,000 threshold is exceeded, in which case the 3.8 percent tax will kick in.

Can a shareholder who works for an S corporation eliminate all self-employment and payroll taxes by paying only dividends? If a shareholder renders significant services to the S corporation and receives no compensation payments, the Service likely will claim that a portion of the dividends are compensation payments subject to payroll taxes.[119] The key is to be reasonable in taking advantage of the tax loophole for S corporation dividends paid to a shareholder/employee. Set a defensible compensation level and pay payroll taxes at that level. Then distribute the balance as dividends that are not subject to any self-employment or payroll tax burden.

As for a partnership, section 1402(a) of the Code specifically provides that a partner's distributive share of income from a partnership constitutes earnings from self-employment tax purposes.[120] There is a limited statutory exception for retired partners[121] and a broader exception for limited partners, but the new 3.8 percent Medicare tax will still be applicable to the extent the triggering income thresholds ($250,000 or $200,000) are exceeded.[122] Thus, the key to minimizing the tax in a partnership structure is to fit within this limited partnership exception.

What are the self-employment tax impacts with a limited liability company? It may be more difficult to avoid the tax for a member of a limited liability company that has no limited partners. The Service's first attempt to provide some guidance on the issue came in 1994 when it published its first Proposed Regulations. After public comment, new Proposed Regulations were issued in 1997, defining the scope of the limited partnership exception for all entities taxed as a partnership, without regard to state law characterizations.[123] Under the 1997 Proposed Regulations, an individual would be treated as a limited partner for purposes of the self-employment tax unless the individual was personally liable for the debts of the entity by being a partner, had authority to contract on behalf of the entity under applicable law, or participated for more than 500 hours in the business during the taxable year. The 1997 Proposed Regulations also drew criticism because LLC members who had authority to contract on behalf of the entity could never fit within the limited partner exception. The result was a statutory moratorium in 1997 on the issuance of any temporary or proposed

---

118. If an S corporation shareholder materially participates in the venture, dividends paid to that shareholder do not fall within the definition of "net investment income" in IRC § 1411. See IRS Guidance in Reg.130507-11 (November 30, 2012).

119. See, for example, Joseph Radtke, S.C. v. United States, 712 F.Supp. 143 (E.D. Wis. 1989), affirmed 895 F.2d 1196 (7th Cir. 1990); Spicer Accounting, Inc. v. United States, 918 F.2d 90 (9th Cir. 1990); and Dunn & Clark, P.A. v. Commissioner, 57 F.3d 1076 (9th Cir. 1995).

120. I.R.C. § 1402(a).

121. I.R.C. § 1402(a)(10).

122. I.R.C. §§ 1402(a)(13), 1411.

123. Proposed Reg. § 1.1402 (a)-2.

regulations dealing with the limited partnership exception.[124]

For planning purposes, where does this history leave us now with respect to entities taxed as partnerships? Any general partner under state law is exposed to the tax. Any limited partner under applicable state law is probably safe. As for LLC members, any member who can fit within the 1997 Proposed Regulations' definition is justified in relying on the statutory limited partner exception. Beyond that definition, it becomes more difficult and uncertain to evaluate the facts and circumstances of each situation. The risk escalates in direct proportion to the individual's authority to act on behalf of the entity and the scope of any services rendered. Note, however, that any member will now be subject to the new 3.8 percent Medicare tax to the extent the applicable triggering income thresholds ($250,000 or $200,000) is exceeded.

Is it smart to design a plan that reduces or eliminates self-employment tax burdens for the owners of a business? Most think it is. Of course, the payment of self-employment taxes may result in higher Social Security benefits down the road. The Social Security program, as presently structured, will become unsustainable in the future. Current benefit levels can be maintained long term only if tax rates or government borrowing levels are increased to unprecedented levels. There is a strong likelihood that, at some point in the not-too-distant future, forced structural reform of the program will reduce future government-funded benefits for all except those who are close to retirement or at the lowest income levels.[125]

## PROBLEM 3-A

Marsha is ready to start a business that will generate about $150,000 of earnings each year. Marsha will work full time for the business. Her plan is to withdraw $100,000 of earnings from the business each year. She will leave the remaining earnings in the business to retire debt and fund future needs of the business. Marsha wants to minimize the overall tax bite on these earnings.

What will be the total entity and personal tax cost under each of the following scenarios, assuming Marsha's ordinary income tax rate is 25 percent, her dividend rate is 15 percent, and the applicable self-employment/payroll tax rate is 15.3 percent? Ignore all potential state income tax consequences.

1. Marsha's business is a C corporation that distributes Marsha a $100,000 dividend each year.

2. Marsha's business is a C corporation that pays Marsha a salary of $100,000 each year for services she renders to the corporation?

3. Marsha's business is an S corporation that pays Marsha a $40,000 salary each year and distributes a $60,000 dividend to her each year.

4. Marsha's business is a limited liability company that is taxed as a partnership. Marsha owns 90 percent of the business, and Joe, an investor who

---

124. Tax Relief Act of 1997 § 935.
125. See generally The Interim and Final Reports of the President's Commission to Strengthen Social Security (August 2001 & December 2001).

does not work in the business, owns the remaining 10 percent. The LLC distributes $90,000 to Marsha each year and $10,000 to Joe. Assume Joe's marginal tax rate is also 25 percent.

## F. KEY FACTORS – FIVE CASE STUDIES

The choice of entity analysis requires a careful assessment of all relevant factors. This sections reviews 16 of the key factors, illustrated through five case studies. Each entity option offers certain benefits and traps that may pose problems down the road. The analysis should review the benefits and traps by carefully pondering their potential relevance under various scenarios that may be applicable to the specific situation.

Although each factor may be important, they never have equal weight in any given situation. It is not a game of adding up the factors to see which entity scores the most points. In many cases, one or two factors may be so compelling for the particular situation that they alone dictate the ultimate solution. But even in that situation, the other factors cannot be ignored because they help identify the collateral consequences of the decision that is about to be made.

The issue of limited liability protection for the owners of the business, once considered to be the most critical factor in the choice of entity analysis, is no longer included in the list of key factors. It's not that insulating the owners of a business from personal liability for the business' liabilities is no longer important; it's as important today as ever. Its absence from the critical factor list is due to the fact that, if desired, it can be accomplished in any given situation. Thus, it is a neutral consideration that no longer needs to affect the decision-making process. With the new check-the-box regime, there is no longer a fear that providing limited liability protection may result in an unincorporated business being inadvertently taxed as a corporation. Even a general partner can be protected by parking the ownership interest in a limited liability company or an S corporation.

### EXAMPLE CASE ONE: JASON

Jason, a seasoned entrepreneur, plans to start a new business that will offer specialized heavy equipment moving services in the western United States. Jason will own 60 percent of the new enterprise, and the remaining 40 percent will be owned equally by two investors, buddies of Jason. Jason will oversee the business, as he does with the other businesses that he has organized. He will not be a fulltime employee of the business.

The business will initially have about 30 employees. Jason anticipates that the business will be profitable by year two, and he has advised the investors that regular distributions will be made starting in year two. Plus, if things play out as planned, there might be a potential to sell to a larger strategic player down the road. Jason wants an entity that will minimize all tax bites, always leave him in complete control, and avoid, to the fullest extent possible, any potential hassles with the minority owners.

The best option for Jason's new company would be an S corporation. This case illustrates six key factors.

### Factor 1:  Earnings Bailout

In Jason's situation, an important factor in the choice of entity decision analysis is the tax cost of getting earnings out of the enterprise and into the hands of Jason and the other owners.  Bailing out earnings in S corporations, LLCs, partnerships and sole proprietorships usually is no big deal.  Profits generated by the business are passed through and taxed directly to the owners, so the distribution of those profits in the form of dividends or partnership distributions carries no tax consequences.  In contrast, bailing out the fruits of a C corporation may trigger substantial income tax consequences, because a C corporation is not a pass-through entity.

When a C corporation bails out its earnings by distributing them to its shareholders in the form of dividends, the dividend distribution is not deductible to the corporation.  The corporation pays a tax on the earnings, and the distribution of those earnings to the shareholders in the form of dividends is taxed a second time at the shareholder level.  This double tax is one of the negatives of a C corporation.

For some businesses, this double tax risk is more academic than real.  There are often ways to avoid it.  The most common is for the shareholders to be employed by the corporation and to receive earnings in the form of taxable compensation.  The payment of the compensation to the shareholders is deductible by the corporation, so that income is only taxed once, at the shareholder level.  But the compensation must be reasonable for the services actually rendered.  If it isn't, it may be re-characterized as a dividend.  In service corporations where the services are rendered by the shareholders, stripping out all of the earnings of the business through the use of compensation payments usually can be easily justified.  Since Jason does not plan on working for his new business, the compensation bailout structure isn't an option.

If earnings are piled up in a C corporation, keep an eye on the accumulated earnings tax.  As previously described, this penalty tax is imposed on accumulated earnings exceeding the greater of the reasonable needs of the business or $250,000 ($150,000 for personal service corporations).  The key is to have the board of directors document through resolutions the reasonable business needs that justify the retention of substantial earnings in the business.

### Factor 2:  Self-Employment Taxes

Self-employment taxes can be an important choice of entity factor in some situations.  In Jason's situation, use of an S corporation may create the opportunity to save self-employment taxes by just paying dividends that escape double income tax treatment by virtue of the S election.

If the plan is to bail out earnings as compensation payments to owners of a C corporation, the compensation payments will be subject to payroll taxes. Of course, except to the extent the new 3.8 percent Medicare tax is applicable to those with incomes above the triggering thresholds ($250,000 or $200,000), there is no self-employment tax imposed on dividends from a C corporation, but such dividends are subject to a double income tax structure.

In Jason's situation, the goal is for the owners to avoid the double income tax structure and self-employment taxes. S corporation dividends will do the job (subject to the 3.8 percent Medicare tax, where applicable), but distributions by a partnership-taxed entity, including a limited liability company, will not escape self-employment taxes unless the owners are limited partners. If the owners are limited partners of a limited partnership, there is a statutory exception that will protect them from self-employment taxes. The same exception should work in the context of a limited liability company where the owners have no management rights in the enterprise and are not personally responsible for the liabilities of the entity. The tough situation comes when a key owner, such a Jason, wants to exercise management rights. In Jason's case, reliance on the limited partnership exception in the LLC context may create an intolerable risk, given the uncertainty of current law. For self-employment tax purposes, a much smarter option would be an S corporation. Given the size of the self-employment tax, this factor may be the deciding issue in some cases.

### Factor 3: Tax-Free Reorganization Potential

If the business succeeds and a sellout opportunity surfaces, a corporate entity will be able to participate in a tax-free reorganization with a corporate buyer. Corporations may combine through mergers, stock-for-stock transactions, and assets-for-stock transactions on terms that eliminate all corporate and shareholder-level taxes. This benefit often is the key to the ultimate payday for those business owners who cash in by "selling" to a public corporation. Cast as a reorganization, the transaction allows the acquiring entity to fund the acquisition with its own stock (little or no cash required) and enables the selling owners to walk with highly liquid, publicly traded securities and no tax bills until the securities are sold.

A partnership-taxed entity, such as a limited liability company, can't enjoy the tax-free benefits of a corporate reorganization.

### Factor 4: Control Rights

Jason wants complete control over all business decisions with as little discussion and fanfare as possible. A corporation, either C or S, or a limited partnership automatically offers this type of ultimate control in favor of the majority, absent a special agreement to the contrary. Minority corporate shareholders often have no control rights; the majority elects the board of directors, and the board has the authority to manage the affairs of the corporation. Limited partner status and the benefits associated with that status (i.e., liability protection and freedom from self-employment taxes) mandate little or no control. For the majority player who wants control of all the reins, the idea of easily getting it all "the normal way" can be appealing.

Limited liability companies and general partnerships are different only in that the control rights need to be spelled out in an operating agreement among the owners. In some cases, the fear is that the need for a single operating agreement may result in more dialogue, more negotiation, and more compromise. Minority owners may see that there is no "standard" or "normal" way of locking in voting requirements and that the agreement can be crafted to address the control concerns of all parties.  Once minority expectations are elevated, the majority players' options become more difficult.  One option, of course, is to throw down the gauntlet and demand ultimate majority control.  Beyond the personal discomfort of having to overtly make such demands, the demands themselves may fuel suspicions, undermine loyalties, or, worst case, trigger the departure of a valuable minority player.  The alternative option is to build into the operating agreement "mutually acceptable" minority rights.

The lawyer's role in this scenario depends entirely on which side of the fence the lawyer sits on.  The lawyer who solely represents the interest of the big fish or the dominant golfer group may push for, even mandate, a corporate structure that automatically grants all control rights to the majority.  The lawyer who represents solely the interests of the minority players may appropriately push for key minority control rights in all situations, even in the corporate format.  As discussed in Chapter 4, state laws permit the use of shareholder agreements in closely held corporate situations to provide for voting restrictions and control limitations that are binding on all shareholders and the board of directors.  The dangerous scenario is where the lawyer sits on the fence by representing the entity and allows complete majority control to be automatically and quietly put in place through a corporate entity.  More on this in Chapter 4.  For choice of entity planning purposes, suffice it to say that specific control interests of the client and the dynamics between the parties (or lack thereof) may favor the use of a corporate entity or limited partnership in some cases.

### Factor 5:  Sellout Tax Hit

Many who start a new business are not focused on selling out down the road.  But this factor can be extremely important in selecting the right form of business organization.  If this factor is neglected, a business owner may find that, when it comes time to cash in, there is an added tax burden that could have been avoided. If Jason's business flourishes and its assets are ultimately sold within a pass-through entity, such as an S corporation, partnership or LLC, the gains realized on the sale of the assets are taxed to the owners in proportion to their interests in the business.  After those taxes are paid, the owners are free to pocket the net proceeds. Bailing out of a C corporation may carry a significant additional tax cost.  A simple example illustrates the impact.

Assume Jason started a C corporation with a $250,000 investment, that the assets in the company have a present basis of $750,000, and that the company is worth $3 million.  It's now time to cash in.  The buyer does not want to buy the stock, but is willing to pay $3 million for the assets in the business.

The C corporation would sell the assets for $3 million to the buyer, and the corporation would recognize a $2.25 million gain – the difference between the $3 million purchase price and the corporation's $750,000 tax basis in the assets.  After the corporation pays a corporate income tax on the gain, the balance of the proceeds would be distributed to the shareholders, who would pay a capital gains tax on the difference between the amount received and their low basis in the stock. The threat of this double tax at the time of sale is a major disadvantage for many C corporations.

Beyond this double tax impact, other important elements of this sellout factor should be considered. First, if a C corporation accumulates earnings within the corporation over an extended period of time, those accumulations do nothing to increase the shareholders' tax basis in their stock. If the shareholder sells stock down the road, the shareholder recognizes capital gains based upon the shareholder's original cost basis in the stock. In contrast, if the business organization is operated in a pass-through entity, such as an LLC, an S corporation, or a partnership, the earnings accumulated in the business will boost, dollar for dollar, the owner's tax basis in his or her stock or partnership interest. So if the owner down the road sells the stock or partnership interest, the earnings accumulated within the enterprise reduce the tax bite to the owner. This is a significant consequence, and it should not be ignored if the business plans to accumulate earnings in anticipation of a sale at a future date.

A second consideration is that, if a C corporation already has substantial value, it is not easy to convert to a pass-through entity and eliminate the threat of double tax. The business cannot make the conversion just before the sale and expect to get off tax free. Usually, it takes a significant period of time to wind out of the double-tax threat.

When all these factors are thrown into the mix, the S corporation looks attractive to Jason with respect to this sellout factor. As a pass-through entity, it eliminates the double tax hit and provides the basis booster. Plus, as a corporate entity, it offers the potential of tax-free reorganization benefits and eliminates the potential ordinary income asset mix complications of an entity taxed as a partnership.

### Factor 6: Passive Income Potential

If Jason uses a pass-through entity, such as an S corporation or an LLC, the income allocated to the owners who are not material participants in the business (a given in this situation) will be passive income that can be offset by tax losses, including passive losses. Even if the income is not distributed to the owners and is retained in the business to finance growth, the owners' losses from other activities can be used to reduce the tax bite on the business income. This capacity to use real estate and other passive losses of the owners to reduce current taxes on income from profitable activities often enhances the reinvestment of earnings in a profitable business to finance growth.

By comparison, if the business is operated as a C corporation, there is no way that the income of the business, whether retained in the business or distributed to the owners, can be sheltered by passive losses that the owners generate from other activities. The bottom line is that, for many income-producing enterprises, those owners who are not employed by the business (and perhaps the business itself) will be much better off with a pass-through entity.

### EXAMPLE CASE TWO: SUE AND JOYCE

Sue and Joyce are planning to form a new business that will offer specialized catering services. They will be the sole owners (in equal shares), and they will both work full time for the business. They will start out with eight other employees, but anticipate that the employee base could grow to 50 or more as they expand into neighboring markets.

They project that the business will need to reinvest $50,000 to $100,000 of earnings each year to finance growth and expansion. They will bailout the rest of the earnings as compensation income for the long hours they both will put into the business. They can't imagine ever selling the business and doubt anyone would be willing to pay much for it. The business is a means for them to each pursue a passion and earn a nice living along the way. It will be their careers. They want to maximize any fringe benefits for themselves.

The best option for the new company that is being organized by Sue and Joyce is a C corporation. This case illustrates three additional key choice-of-entity factors.

### Factor 7:  Owner Fringe Benefits

Sue and Joyce's desire for employee fringe benefits may be a compelling factor in selecting a business form. There are a number of fringe benefits that are available to shareholder/employees of a C corporation that generally are not available to owner/employees of pass-through entities, such as a partnerships, LLCs, or S corporations. The significance of these fringe benefits depends on their importance to the particular owners. Investor owners could care less; employee owners, like Sue and Joyce, often view them as big deals. Each owner needs to assess whether the tax advantages of the fringe benefits are attractive enough to impact the choice-of-entity decision. The most significant fringe benefits available to shareholder-employees of C corporations include group-term life insurance plans under Section 79, medical-dental reimbursement plans under Section 106, Section 125 cafeteria plans,[126] and dependent care assistance programs under Section 129. Note that health insurance premiums are usually a neutral factor because they can be deducted in full by a self-employed person, a partner or an S corporation shareholder.

### Factor 8:  The Bracket Racket

Only the C corporation offers the potential that the tax rate applied to the net income of the business may differ from the income tax rate applied to the owners of the business. All other entities (S corporations, LLCs, partnerships and sole proprietorships) are not separate taxpaying entities. Income earned by these entities is simply passed through and reported by the owners in proportion to their interests in the business. The C corporation may create an income splitting opportunity – to

---

126. A section 125 cafeteria plan may be adopted by a partnership, LLC, or S corporation, but S corporation shareholders holding two percent or more of the corporation's stock, partners of the partnership, and members of the LLC cannot participate in the plan. C corporation shareholders may participate so long as no more than 25 percent of the nontaxable benefits selected within the cafeteria plan go to key employees. Subject to the 25 percent limitation, C corporation shareholders can take full advantage of the tax benefits of the plan.

have the income retained in the business taxed at a rate lower than the rates paid by the owners.  In Sue and Joyce's situation, the different rate structure can be used to their advantage.  It's the bracket racquet.

C corporations have a tiered graduated rate structure.  This structure imposes a low 15 percent tax on taxable income up to $50,000 and 25 percent on taxable income between $50,000 and $75,000.  So if Sue and Linda can keep the corporation's taxable income to less than $100,000 each year, these low corporate rates will produce a significant bottom line tax savings.  If this reinvested income were passed through to them, it is likely that the income tax rate would be at least 28 percent and perhaps more, and payroll taxes would be on top of the income tax hit.  This bracket differential can be a big deal when the numbers are in these ranges.

Note that the potential negative consequences of a C corporation are no big deal in Sue and Linda's situation.  They will avoid all double tax fears by bailing out all available earnings as deductible compensation.  The C corporation accumulated earnings tax, personal holding company tax, and alternative minimum tax pose no threats.  The locked-in stock basis and other sellout costs are not a factor because Sue and Joyce have no plans to sell.

Note that this potential bracket rate advantage does not apply to personal service C corporations because they are subject to a single-tiered tax bracket of 35 percent.  For this reason, clients who are personal service C corporations will be better off stripping the income out as compensation on a tax-deductible basis.  A personal service corporation is defined as any corporation that meets two tests: a function test and an ownership test.  The function test requires that the corporation perform substantially all of its services in the fields of health, law, engineering, architecture, accounting, actuarial science, the performing arts or consulting.  The ownership test requires that substantially all of the stock be held directly or indirectly by employees who perform services in one of those fields.  For example, the typical medical professional corporation will be a personal service corporation.  Clients who fall within the personal service corporation definition should be advised to keep the taxable income of the corporation at or close to zero.  This can be accomplished by stripping out the earnings in the form of salaries, bonuses, rent, or other forms of deductible payments to the owners.  Generally, there are no advantages to accumulating earnings in the corporation.

In view of this tax bracket discrimination against personal service corporations, should a personal service C corporation convert to a partnership, an LLC, an S corporation, or a sole proprietorship? The answer is "no" for most clients.  First, the conversion itself might trigger an immediate tax cost.  Second, the owners can enjoy the single-tax benefits of a pass-through entity by stripping all the corporate earnings through compensation and other deductible payments.  And third, as discussed above, the owners may participate in tax-favored employee benefit programs by sticking with the C corporation.

### Factor 9:  Tax Year Flexibility

Most C corporations may select any fiscal year for tax reporting purposes.  Thus, use of a C corporation will give Sue and Joyce an opportunity to select a tax years that simplifies and accommodates their accounting and that may provide a tax deferral potential. Partnerships, LLCs, S corporations and sole proprietorships generally are required to use a calendar year unless they can prove a business purpose for using a fiscal year (a tough burden in most cases) or make a tax deposit under Section 7519 that is designed to eliminate any deferral advantage. C corporations that are personal service corporations may adopt a fiscal year with a deferral period of no more than three months, but the minimum distribution rules applicable to such personal service corporations under Section 280H substantially reduce any tax deferral potential.[127]

The income tax deferral potential of a C corporation that is not a personal service corporation is a fairly simple concept. Consider a toiler-owned manufacturing corporation that uses a calendar year for tax reporting. Its projected taxable income for 2013, its first year of operation, will be $240,000, and it will earn that income proportionately in each month during the year. For 2013, the choice for the owners of the corporation is to either report the income in the corporation or pay all or a portion of it to themselves as deductible compensation payments. With either approach, all of the $240,000 of taxable income will be reported in the 2013 tax returns of the owners or the corporation.

If the same corporation elects to use a fiscal year ending March 31, a one-year deferral can be achieved on $180,000 of the $240,000 of taxable income. This is accomplished by having the corporation file a short-year return ending March 31, 2013, reporting $60,000 of taxable income. The remaining $180,000 earned during the last nine months of 2013 is reportable in the fiscal year ending March 31, 2014. But during the first three months of 2014, the owners pay themselves bonuses totaling $180,000 plus any income earned by the corporation during those three months, thus zeroing out the corporation's tax liability for the fiscal year ending March 31, 2014. These bonuses are deducted from the corporation's income for the fiscal year ending March 31, 2014, but are not reported by the calendar year shareholders until they file their 2014 returns on April 15, 2015. The ability to use this technique is limited by the normal compensation reasonableness standards. Plus, the deferral impact is often watered down by withholding and estimated tax payment requirements. But the technique is fairly common and is a legitimate means of deferring taxes.

### EXAMPLE CASE THREE: CHARLES

Charles plans on buying and operating a large apartment complex. Charles will put up 10 percent of the equity capital, and the other 90 percent of the equity will come from four outside investors. The business will obtain debt financing equal to nearly four times the total equity capital, and is expected to generate substantial taxable losses during the first five years of operation, fueled in large part by big depreciation deductions.

Charles wants an entity that will allocate 99 percent of the losses to the investors, award him with 50 percent of the profits after the investors have recouped their investment, and, to the maximum extent possible, free him from minority owner hassles and contractual negotiations and dealings with minority

---

127. I.R.C. §§ 444(b)(2), 280(H).

owners. He wants total control. Plus, he would like to protect the investors from any self employment taxes.

Charles is going to need a partnership-taxed entity, either a limited liability company where he is the sole manager or a limited partnership where his investors are limited partners and his wholly-owned LLC or S corporation is the general partner. Of these two, the limited partnership option may make it easier for Charles to nail down his absolute control rights and reduce any self-employment tax risks for the investors. But either approach will work with some quality planning.

This case illustrates three additional choice-of-entity factors.

## Factor 10:  Different Ownership Interests

As Charles' deal illustrates, often owners want to structure different types of ownership interests in the entity.  Income rights, loss rights, cash flow rights, or liquidation rights may need to be structured differently for select owners to reflect varying contributions to the enterprise.  With a C corporation, different types of common and preferred stock may be issued to reflect the varying preferences.

An S corporation is extremely limited in its ability to create different types of equity ownership interests.  It is limited to voting and non-voting common stock, all of which must have the same income, loss, cash flow and liquidation rights.

Partnerships and limited liability companies offer the most flexibility in structuring different equity ownership interests.  These partnership-taxed pass-through entities can customize and define the different interests in the entity's operating agreement.  Although the design possibilities are almost unlimited, all allocations of profits, losses and credits will be respected for tax purposes only if the allocations are structured to have "substantial economic effect" within the meaning of section 704(b).

In Charles' situation, there's a clear need to use one of these flexible pass-through entities to create different types of ownership interests.   This is particularly true in situations where one group of owners is providing capital and another group of owners is providing management, services and expertise. Often, an LLC is the answer; it offers the centralized management and limited liability benefits of a corporation, and the structuring and tax flexibility of a partnership.

## Factor 11:  Loss Utilization

Like many organizers of businesses that are projected to generate losses in the early years, Charles wants to insure that such losses are funneled to the tax returns that will trigger the highest tax savings.  The threshold issue is whether the losses should be retained in the entity or passed through to the owners.

Losses generated by a C corporation are retained in the C corporation and are carried backward or forward to be deducted against income earned in previous or future years.  Losses sustained by S corporations, LLCs, partnerships and sole proprietorships are passed through to the business owners.  When losses are anticipated in the initial years of a business, using a pass-through entity may generate a tax advantage if the owners have other taxable income against which those losses can be offset, within certain limitations. The advantage is that the losses may produce immediate tax benefits.

In planning to pass through losses to the owners, never lose sight of the fact that the losses, even if passed through, may produce no benefit if one or more of the three loss hurdles mentioned get in the way. The at-risk and passive loss hurdles usually are not affected by the type of pass-through entity selected. The basis hurdle is different in this regard. The general rule is that losses generated by a pass-through entity are not available to an owner of the entity to the extent that the cumulative net losses exceed the owner's basis in the entity. For example, if an investor puts $50,000 into an S corporation, that owner's basis in the S corporation stock is $50,000. If the S corporation generates a loss of $150,000 in the first year and finances the loss through corporate indebtedness, the S corporation shareholder may only use $50,000 of the loss against his or her other income. The other $100,000 is suspended because it exceeds the owner's stock basis. It is carried forward to be used in future years if and when the basis is increased. In contrast, if the indebtedness is incurred in an entity taxed as a partnership, such as a limited liability company or a limited partnership, the indebtedness will increase the partners' basis in their partnership interests under the provisions of Section 752, and the basis limitation will no longer be a factor in assessing the current tax value of the losses.

This loss pass-through factor, perhaps more than any other factor, underscores the value of quality projections of the business operations for the first few years and an evaluation of the individual tax positions of the business owners.

### Factor 12:  Real Estate

The choice of entity analysis is always affected by the presence of real estate. The fact that most real estate tends to appreciate over time has some powerful consequences for planning purposes. First, it permits the owners to take advantage of the biggest fiction in the Internal Revenue Code – depreciation cost recovery deductions that are based on the premise that real estate improvements lose their value over time. Second, it facilitates the use of nonrecourse debt because lenders are willing to make loans that are secured only by the value of the real estate. The nonrecourse debt eliminates the loss basis hurdle for any entity taxed as a partnership and escapes the at-risk hurdle by virtue of the "qualified nonrecourse debt financing" exception that is applicable only to real estate.[128] And third, it is never prudent to subject the appreciation of the real estate to the double tax structure of a C corporation. As a general proposition, appreciating real estate should be kept out of C corporations. Plus, income from real estate activities that is passed through to the owners generally is not subject to the self-employment tax.[129]

---

128. I.R.C. §§ 752(a), 465(b)(6).

129. I.R.C. § 1402(a)(1).  The tax will apply to anyone who receives rental income in the course of a trade or business as a real estate dealer.

Given these consequences, real estate usually warrants its own entity, and in nearly all situations that entity should be a partnership-taxed entity.

### EXAMPLE CASE FOUR: JURDEN INC.

Jurden Inc. is a successful C corporation that is poised to explode.  It has five shareholders, all successful business investors.  The plan for the next five to10 years is to aggressively reinvest earnings to create a global presence and then sell out to a strategic buyer at the right time.  The shareholders want to shed the C status now.  They want the future tax benefits of a pass-though entity, including the stock basis booster for all reinvested earnings and the elimination or serious reduction of double tax bites at time of sale.

Jurden Inc's only option, as a practical matter, is to covert to an S corporation. This case illustrates a controlling choice-of-entity factor for many.

### Factor 13:  C Corporation Conversion Flexibility

As a C corporation, Jurden Inc. has only one option that makes any sense. If it converted to a partnership structure or an LLC, a gain on the liquidation of the corporation would be triggered at both the corporate and shareholder level at time of conversion – a disastrous scenario.  The corporation would recognize a gain on all its assets, and the shareholders would recognize a gain on the liquidation of their stock.  The tax costs of getting into a partnership or LLC pass-through entity usually are too great to even think about.

The only practical answer for Jurden Inc. is an S corporation.  At the present time, a C corporation may convert to an S corporation without automatically triggering the type of gain that would be triggered on a deemed liquidation of a C corporation.

The S corporate conversion, while clearly the preferred choice in most situations, is not a perfect solution and may trigger some additional tax costs at the time of the conversion and later down the road.   If, for example, the corporation values its inventories under the LIFO method, the corporation must recognize as income the LIFO reserve as a result of the S election conversion. Also, the conversion will not eliminate all threats of double taxation.  If a C corporation converts to an S corporation and liquidates or sells out within 10 years after the election, the portion of the resulting gain that is attributable to the period prior to the election will be taxed at the corporate level as if the corporation had remained a C corporation. If the C corporation had accumulated earnings and profits before the conversion, the shareholders may end up with taxable dividends after the conversion.  A completely clean break from C status often is not possible.   But in most situations, these tax consequences of conversion can be managed and do not provide a basis for rejecting the conversion to S status.

### EXAMPLE CASE FIVE: PETER

 Peter has developed a business plan for creating and exploiting a series of new Internet games that promise the potential of a huge success. He has attracted the attention of various investors, none of whom want their personal tax returns exposed to any venture and all of whom would love to see Peter's unique talents showcased and exploited through a public company at the right time. The plan is to reinvest all business earnings so that Peter can build the business as fast as possible.

Peter is going to want a C corporation. This case illustrates three additional choice-of-entity factors, two of which usually are controlling when they are applicable to the situation.

### Factor 14: Going Public Prospects

When a company is funded with outside capital and the plan is to go public at the first solid opportunity, the C corporation often is the mandated choice. The interests of the outside investors and the potential of going public trump all other considerations. Usually the audited track record of the company leading up to the offering is best reflected in the same form of entity that will ultimately go public, which is a C corporation in nearly all cases.

### Factor 15: The "Not My Return" Factor

This factor is one of those considerations that sometimes preempts everything else when it is present. It is the owner who has no interest in anything that will implicate or complicate his or her personal tax return. Some just cannot buy into the concept of having to personally recognize and pay taxes on income from a pass-through entity that has never been (and may never be) received in the form of hard cash. Others are spooked by the accounting and audit risks. The thought that their personal tax return and their personal tax liability could be affected by the audit of a company managed by others is too much to bear. Still others are just adamant about keeping all personal matters as simple and as understandable as possible. A stack of K–1 forms flapping on the back of their return is not their concept of simple. When this factor is present and cannot be eliminated, the only option is a C corporation that offers the benefit of complete "separateness."

### Factor 16: Reinvestment Growth

Like many companies, Peter hopes to grow his company by reinvesting all earnings. In recent years, the tax rate differential between individual taxpayers and a C corporation has not been a big deal. Both have topped out at a maximum rate of 35 percent. So the choice-of-entity analysis has not turned on the potential to reinvest after tax earnings and grow the business.

But that has changed in 2013. The American Taxpayer Relief Act of 2012 (the "Fiscal Cliff" legislation signed into law during the final days of 2012)[130] increased individual ordinary income tax rates to 39.6 percent starting in 2013 for couples with taxable incomes in excess of $450,000 and individuals with taxable incomes in excess of $400,000. Plus, in 2013, the 3.8 percent Medicare tax kicks in for couples with a modified adjusted gross income in excess of $250,000 ($200,000 for individuals). The net result is that a successful business owner who is allocated profits through a pass-through S corporation or LLC could end up

---

130. Section 101 of the American Taxpayer Relief Act of 2012.

paying federal taxes at a combined income and Medicare rate of 43.4 percent. In contrast, political leaders on both sides of the aisle and the Obama administration have agreed that top corporate tax rates should be reduced to the 25 to 28 percent range to remain competitive with other countries. The result is that we could end up with a condition that we haven't had for decades – a mammoth gap between top individual rates and top corporate rates.

For a company looking to grow with reinvested earnings, such a huge rate differential between individual and corporate rates may compel use of a C corporation. The difference between reinvesting 56 cents on every earned dollar and reinvesting 75 cents, when compounded over five or 10 years and adjusted for leveraging differences, may impact a business' capacity to finance growth by as much as 50 percent or more. As the push for such rate differentials intensifies, this may emerge as the newest and most dominant choice-of-entity factor for businesses that need to grow. The old C Corporation could emerge as the ultimate comeback kid.

### Factor Summary and Conclusion

A review of these 16 factors in a given situation will help the lawyer assist a client in choosing the best form of business entity and understanding the primary and collateral consequences. One conclusion is fairly obvious: The C corporation is a very different creature from the other forms, all of which are pass-through entities. Therefore, the starting point for many clients will be to take a hard look at the C corporation as an alternative. If it fails to pass muster (and it will in many situations), the alternative pass-through entity forms will need to be evaluated.

Having reviewed the tax perks and traps of each entity form and the 16 key choice-of-entity factors, you should be teed up to analyze the following 11 fact situations.

### PROBLEMS 3-B THRU 3-L

**3-B.** Lucy owns and manages two businesses. She now intends to start a third. Her new business will offer high-end catering services. Lucy will be the sole owner, but will spend very little time in the business. The inspiration and driving force behind the business will be Jane. In addition to Jane, the business will have ten employees and regularly have three trucks on the road. Lucy anticipates that the business will be profitable from the get-go. She anticipates withdrawing profits on a regular basis. She wants to have a separate entity for business purposes. What form of entity do you recommend? What additional facts would you like to have?

**3-C.** Sam, Larry and Joe are going into the business of offering management consulting and computer training services. The business will generate fees for professional services. Sam, Larry and Joe anticipate that they will always be the sole owners (in equal shares), and they will all work full-time for the business. They will start out with two staff employees, but will add other professional and staff employees as the business grows. The three owners intend to bail out the earnings of the business as compensation income, and they want to maximize their fringe benefits. What form of business entity do you recommend?

**3-D.** Roger plans on opening a specialized machine shop. He will put up 55 percent of the capital, receive 55 percent of the equity interests in the business, work full-time as CEO of the business, and draw a salary and a bonus based on his performance. Three other individuals have committed to fund the balance of the needed capital in equal shares, and they will each receive 15 percent of the equity of the business. The business will have minimal debt and is expected to be profitable by year two. Roger wants a structure that ensures, to the maximum extent possible, freedom from minority owner hassles and contractual negotiations and dealings with minority owners. He wants total control. He wants to ensure that his investors do not have to pay self-employment taxes on any income they receive from the business. You represent Roger. What form of business entity do you recommend?

**3-E.** Same as 3–C, except (1) Roger puts up only 10 percent of the equity capital; (2) the other owners put up 90 percent of the equity capital; (3) the business will incur debt financing equal to nearly four times the total equity capital; (4) the business will generate substantial start-up losses during the first three years; and (5) a primary incentive for the investors is big tax write-offs in the early years. What form of business entity do you recommend?

**3-F.** Ronda has developed a business plan for creating and exploiting a new flash-type Internet application that, if successful, will make streaming media obsolete. She has already attracted the attention of one venture fund. She anticipates the company will need up to three levels of venture financing before it is in a position to go public. When asked about the opportunity, she lights up and says, "It will either be out of the park or a complete bust." What form of business entity do you recommend?

**3-G.** The outstanding common stock of corporations X, Y and Z, all C corporations, are owned by Jim, Linda and Sam, unrelated parties, in the following percentages:

|       | X Corp | Y Corp | Z Corp |
|-------|--------|--------|--------|
| Jim   | 10%    | 40%    | 30%    |
| Linda | 80%    | 5%     | 25%    |
| Sam   | 10%    | 55%    | 45%    |

Jim, Linda and Sam plan to accumulate and reinvest $75,000 of income in each of the three corporations at the lowest corporate tax rates each year, and they assume that each of the corporations has an accumulated earnings tax threshold of $250,000. Will their plan work?

**3-H.** ABC Inc. and Smith Enterprises Inc. are friendly competitors in the medical supply industry. They are both C corporations owned and operated as successful family businesses. They now desire to form a joint venture to market their respective products in Europe. The venture will be a separate U.S. entity owned by ABC Inc. and Smith Enterprises and will have its own employees and facilities. Both parties want flexibility in transferring funds into and out of the new entity and a clear written understanding of how decisions will be made and control exercised. What form of business entity would you recommend?

**3-I.** Jones Industries ("JI") is a successful C corporation that provides brand promotion products to multi-national companies. It buys many of its products and components offshore. To strengthen its offshore operations, it wants to create a new entity that will only develop and source products in other countries and then import and sell the products to JI. The new company will be owned by JI's three shareholders and will have its own employees. The pricing between the new company and JI will be structured to enable the new company to cover its costs and expenses and make a nominal profit. What form of business entity would you recommend for the new company?

**3-J.** Jerry has plans to form a new company that will build large trawler yachts (measuring 55 to 65 feet) in China. At his own expense, he has completed the initial plans for the first four yachts, all of which will be built from the same mold. He has secured equity financing from five wealthy yacht enthusiasts, who collectively have agreed to put up $6 million for the first four yachts. The "deal" is that (1) Jerry will get a salary of $90,000 a year; (2) the investors will get their investment money back first; (3) Jerry will then be paid the $150,000 he has invested in the initial plans; and (4) profits then will be distributed 30 percent to Jerry and 70 percent to the investors. Any losses will be allocated 99 percent to the investors and one percent to Jerry. Jerry wants to ensure that he always is in complete control of all business decisions. You represent Jerry. What business form would you recommend?

**3-K.** Five individuals are going to form a new manufacturing company that should quickly become profitable (starting at $150,000 and growing to $800,000 a year within five years). None of the shareholders will work for the company. Their shareholders' plan is to reinvest the profits to quickly grow the company and then to sell to a strategic buyer as soon as possible. Ideally, the sale of the business might be structured as a tax-free reorganization that would provide the shareholders with stock in a publicly-traded company. The shareholders want a structure that will minimize taxes, limit liability exposure, and ensure that they all have equal control in future decisions. What business form would you recommend?

**3-L.** Wharton Enterprises Inc. ("WI") is a successful S corporation owned by three individuals, all of whom work full-time for the business. WI has now decided to expand into many other states. In order to limit its liability exposure and simplify regulatory requirements, WI believes it must form a separate business entity for each state. WI will own all the state business entities. The shareholders want to ensure that profits and losses from the various entities can be consolidated for tax purposes. What business form would you recommend for WI and the state entities?

# CHAPTER 4

# CORPORATE ORGANIZATIONAL PLANNING CHALLENGES

## A. DOCUMENTING THE DEAL

### 1. THE PROCESS AND THE DOCUMENTS

Every corporation needs organizational documents to get it going. The number, scope and complexity of the documents depend on the composition of the owners, the number and type of entities used, and the quality of the planning effort on the front end. Usually customization of the organizational documents increases as the planning effort improves. More customization results in more complexity and, most importantly, a better mutual understanding of the key deal points between the organizers and owners of the business.

Too often the temptation is to short-circuit the planning process up front. The business organizers want to focus on start-up business challenges, not legal documents. Plus, the lawyers' job is much easier if the document customization effort is minimized or avoided altogether. Why trigger potentially contentious dialogue on tough hypothetical scenarios that may never develop? Why not just perpetuate the common (but false) perception that there is a "normal" or "accepted" way of documenting issues between co-owners? The result is that, in far too many cases, everyone opts for the "standard stuff." The documentation effort is limited to filling in blanks on stock forms, and the dialogue is limited to descriptive pronouncements from the lawyers. The documents look and read complete and official, but they do nothing to reflect thoughtful, negotiated "deal points" that the owners have resolved with the assistance of skilled planning advisors.

In nearly all situations, the lawyer must take the lead in defining the scope of the front-end planning effort. This is done by identifying key operational issues, explaining the significance of the issues, and then helping the client carefully evaluate his or her objectives or priority concerns with respect to each issue. The following section briefly reviews 20 of the most common operational issues that need to be discussed and analyzed. In addition to the operational issues, there is the paramount challenge of structuring the buy-sell provisions between the co-owners of a closely held business. For most closely held businesses, the buy-sell provisions between the co-owners define how and when individual owners ultimately will realize a return on their investment in the venture. Although many business owners initially are confused by the need to give significant attention to provisions dealing with exit scenarios during the early planning stages of the business, the confusion usually disappears very quickly as the owners begin to realize that these provisions define what they will ultimately get in return for all of their invested capital and effort. This buy-sell agreement planning challenge is discussed in Chapter 8.

### a. Corporate Organizational Documents

A corporate entity requires more organizational documents than a partnership or an LLC. The advisor must have an understanding of the state corporate law that is going to be applicable to the entity in order to properly draft corporate organizational documents that will meet the client's objectives. This is essential because state corporate statutes specify important default rules that will apply unless the corporate organizational documents provide otherwise. These default rules vary from state to state. In many situations, a particular default rule will be perfectly consistent with a client's objectives, and there will be no need to call attention to the rule in the organizational documents and trigger the possibility of other owners raising an objection. In such a situation, saying nothing in the documents and letting the default rule automatically kick in may be the best course of action. In many other situations, a particular default rule will be inconsistent with the client's core objectives, and the organizational documents will need to be drawn to negate the default rule.

The starting point is to identify the applicable state corporate law. The traditional internal affairs doctrine is alive and well in nearly all states, including Delaware.[1] Simply stated, the doctrine provides that the law of the state of incorporation will govern any matter related to the internal affairs of the corporation.[2] Internal affairs generally include matters involving the relationship between the corporation and its officers, directors, and shareholders. Common examples of internal affairs subject to the doctrine include voting rights, the rights and liabilities of directors and officers, shareholder rights, distributions, indemnifications, mergers, and derivative litigation. The internal affairs doctrine does not apply to matters unrelated to internal corporate relationships or procedures, such as taxes, antitrust, employment matters, environmental issues, securities laws, intellectual property matters, consumer protection, and most tort and contract claims. Two big states – California and New York – have statutes that apply their corporate law to resolve specific internal affairs of a corporation organized in another state (a "pseudo-foreign" corporation) that conducts most of its activities in California or New York, as the case may be, and has most of its outstanding stock owned by residents of the state.[3] These pseudo-foreign corporation statutes will likely govern the outcome of any litigation in California or New York courts,[4] but it is highly unlikely that they will have a controlling impact in a dispute that breaks out in another state. In a significant 2005

---

1. See, e.g., Rogers McDermott Inc. v. Lewis, 531 A.2d 206 (Del. 1987), and Kozyris, Corporate Wars and Choice of Law, 1985 Duke L.J. 1, 98.

2. For a succinct statement and adoption of the doctrine by the United States Supreme Court, see Rogers v. Guaranty Trust Co. of New York, 288 U.S. 123, 130 (1933).

3. See Section 2115 of the California Corporation Code and N.Y. Bus. Corp. Law §§ 1317-20 (McKinney 1963 & Supp. 1981).

4. See, e.g., Wilson v. Louisiana-Pacific Resources, Inc., 187 Cal. Rptr. 852 (1982).

decision, the Delaware Supreme Court refused to apply California's pseudo-foreign corporate statute to a corporation that was organized in Delaware but had its closest ties to California.[5]  The court ruled that Delaware's "well-established choice of law rules" and the commerce clause of the federal constitution "mandated" the application of Delaware law to resolve the dispute.  For planning purposes, the legal advisor needs to understand the scope and impact of the internal affairs doctrine and potential wrinkles that may be triggered in New York or California under specific conditions.  And, of course, the legal advisor usually plays a key role in helping the client select the state of incorporation for the business.

**(1)  The State of Incorporation?**  Hands down, Delaware is the darling of the corporate world.  In the corporate charter game, Delaware is the reigning king, and it is highly unlikely that any other state will ever threaten its crown.  For the organizers of most closely held corporations, the question is: Should we incorporate in our home state or Delaware?  A number of factors may influence the answer to this basic question.

The starting point is to focus on the reasons that Delaware is the king, and whether those reasons have any relevance to the specific situation.  Delaware's dominance in large part is attributable to its judiciary's demonstrated competence to resolve corporate matters in an efficient and fair manner.  Many of its judges are accomplished corporate lawyers who have a massive body of corporate case law to work with and a deep appreciation of the importance of Delaware's corporate supremacy to the state.  Corporate managers and lawyers generally love the predictability offered by Delaware's established case law and its favorable statutory provisions relating to compensation, self-dealing contracts, and indemnification.[6]  Decades of doing deals in Delaware have caused money players and investment bankers to grow comfortable with Delaware's corporate mindset.  Everyone understands and appreciates the importance of corporate franchise fees in Delaware and Delaware's strong incentive to remain corporate-friendly on cutting edge issues.  Plus, unpopular statutory changes are unlikely given a state constitutional provision that requires a two-thirds vote of both legislative houses to change Delaware's corporation code.[7]

The importance of these factors in a given situation will depend in large part on the nature of the company's projected operations and ownership structure.  If the company is going to do business in many states, it will be required to register as a foreign corporation in all such states and likely will deal with important third parties in multiple states.  In such a case, the company may prefer to organize in Delaware to bolster its national or regional image and to remove any "local" taint.  Similarly, a company that has any hope of going public or that is, or may become, dependent on capital from established brokerage or venture firms generally would be well advised to incorporate in Delaware from the get-go.  The managers who run such firms and their lawyers will be saved the task of asking "Why not Delaware?" and taking necessary corrective actions.  In contrast, a

---

5.  Vantage Point Venture Partners 1996 v. Examen, Inc., 871 A.2d 1108 (Del. 2005).
6.  See 8 Del. C. §§ 143, 144, 145.
7.  Del. Const. art. IX, § 1.

closely held corporation that is going to be owned and controlled by a select group of local shareholders often has no need to look beyond its local corporate law.[8] The potential benefits of Delaware's deep body of case law and the trappings of being a Delaware player may not be worth the added hassle and expense of incorporating in Delaware and registering as a foreign corporation in the company's home state. In this very common situation, franchise fees and any specific oddities of the home state's corporate statutes may need to be factored into the mix. Often, the ultimate conclusion is to "stay local."

(2) **Articles of Incorporation.** The Articles of Incorporation is the charter document mandated by state statute. When this document is filed with the appropriate state authority, the corporation comes into existence. This is a public document that can be easily accessed by anyone. For this reason, often it is drawn to include only the minimum provisions, which typically include the identity and address of the incorporators, the corporate name, the registered agent and office of the corporation, the number of shares of stock that the corporation is authorized to issue, and usually (but not always) the number and identity of the initial directors of the corporation. Here, it is critically important that the state's default rules regarding certain matters be carefully evaluated. If a default rule is ill advised or unacceptable, it must be negated in the articles of incorporation. If the state's default rules favor cumulative voting or preemptive rights, specific provisions denying these rights are often needed in the articles of incorporation. Similarly, the articles of incorporation often must contain specific provisions dealing with the limited liability of directors, the indemnification of directors and related expense advances, shareholder consent voting procedures, the authorization of "blank check" stock, and supermajority shareholder voting requirements. See Chapter 18 for a sample form for Articles of Incorporation.

(3) **Bylaws.** The bylaws serve as the owners' manual for the corporation. This document describes the roles of the shareholders, directors and officers as well as the mechanics for calling and holding meetings, approving consent resolutions, and handling other administrative and procedural matters. Key provisions often include the number of directors; the authorized use of electronic transmissions for shareholder notices; special meeting notice requirements; annual meeting time and place; authorized participation via communication equipment; authorized board actions without a meeting; board of director compensation authorization; officer duties and titles; stock certificates and legends; stock transfer restrictions; indemnification provisions; fiscal year designation; bylaw amendment procedures; and special tax elections.

(4) **Employment Agreements.** These documents govern the employment relationship between the corporation and its key employees, including shareholders who are employed by the corporation. Often employment agreements are used to document important deal points between the owners. See Chapter 11 for details relating to such agreements.

---

8. Delaware does have a set of provisions in its corporation code that are directly applicable to close corporations, generally defined as corporations with no more than 30 shareholders that meet certain defined criteria. See 8 Del. C. §§ 341-356. These provisions, among other things, make it easier for shareholders to manage the affairs of the corporation and facilitate the appointment of a provisional director to help resolve disputes.

**(5) Directors' Resolutions.** These resolutions are approved by the board of directors and are essential for the organization and start-up of the business. The resolutions usually include provisions approving the articles of incorporation, adopting the bylaws, electing the officers, authorizing the issuance of stock and the receipt of consideration (money, property or services) for the stock, authorizing the establishment of corporate bank accounts, ratifying and approving any pre-incorporation business transactions, approving credit lines and other financing arrangements, authorizing the commencement of business operations, authorizing the execution of documents necessary for the acquisition of assets, leases, licenses and intellectual property rights, and approving any other significant matters related to the start-up of the business. The organizational directors' resolutions are documented either as written consent resolutions signed by all the directors or as minutes of an organizational meeting where the directors approved the resolutions. See Chapter 18 for a sample form for Organization Directors' Resolutions.

**(6) Stock Register and Stock Certificates.** Stock certificates are issued to the shareholders. Usually they include legends referencing the provisions of the Shareholder Agreement and transfer restrictions under applicable securities laws. The stock register is a record of when specific shares were issued and to whom they were issued.

**(7) Asset Transfer Documents.** Often documents are needed to transfer specific assets to the corporation. Examples include bills of sale, lease assignments, license agreements and, in rare instances, real estate deeds. Often the documents include provisions requiring the corporation to assume liabilities related to the transferred assets.

**(8) Pre-Incorporation Agreement.** In limited situations, the parties desire to document their mutual understandings regarding the formation of the corporation and their approval of the terms and conditions of all the organizational documents before steps are taken to officially form the corporation. This is accomplished with a pre-incorporation agreement, a comprehensive document that usually includes the other organizational documents as attachments. It is not a required document and is not used in many situations.

**(9) Required Government Filing.** Each state requires that certain documents be filed and fees paid in order to form the corporation. Typically these documents include the Articles of Incorporation, the written consent of the registered agent for the corporation in the particular state, and an application to obtain a state tax identification number. Also, a Form SS-4 needs to be filed with the Internal Revenue Service to obtain a federal tax identification number, and a Form 2553 is required if an S election is desired.

**(10) Shareholder Agreement.** An agreement between the shareholders of the corporation is critically important in nearly all situations involving closely held corporations. For planning purposes, this agreement is the most important document – by a long shot. It lays out the terms of the buy-sell agreements among shareholders and the details of those operational deal points that the shareholders have chosen to document. This is not a required document, and it is shamefully ignored in far too many situations. It takes more work, more dialogue and more customization than any other organizational document.

Although the authority to manage a corporation is vested in its board of directors, state corporate statutes generally authorize the use of shareholder agreements to establish rights among the shareholders of closely held corporations (those corporations whose stock is not publicly traded) that preempt the management authority of the board. Many such state statutes are modeled after The Model Business Act, which specifically authorizes any such agreements among the shareholders of a non-public company that "govern the exercise of corporate powers or the management of the business and affairs of the corporation or the relationship among the shareholders, the directors and the corporation, or any of them, and is not contrary to public policy." Model Business Corporation Act § 7.32(a)(8).

The shareholders agreement should be carefully drafted, specify how long it will remain in effect (absent such a term provision, applicable state statutes may terminate the agreement after a specified term, such as 10 years), and be conspicuously referenced in written legends on all stock certificates that are issued by the corporation.

In select situations, a shareholder or group of shareholders may desire to strongly emphasize or reinforce specific deal points. Usually this happens when minority shareholders have secured important rights under the shareholder agreement that are essential to their participation in the enterprise. Their concern is that, at some point in the future, the majority owners may try to use their power or business leverage to frustrate the purposes of the minority. To mitigate against this possibility, a protective provision may be included in the shareholders agreement to provide that any such actions taken by the majority owners will presumptively constitute a breach of their fiduciary duties to the minority owners and may constitute evidence of an undisclosed intention that, if disclosed, would have been a material fact relative to the minority owners' involvement in the enterprise. The real value of such a provision is that it may help prevent future disputes. Beyond emphasizing the importance of the minority rights, the provision will estop any majority owner from claiming in the future that he or she did not understand or appreciate the permanence of the minority rights. In the event of a full-blown legal battle, the provision may help bolster any corporate fiduciary or security law claims, but clients should be cautioned against expecting too much from such a provision.

### b. Non-Corporate Organizational Documents

Fewer organizational documents are required for an LLC or partnership entity. There is still a need for asset transfer documents, tax filings, executive employment agreements, and simple state filings for LLCs and certain types of partnerships. But for these entities, the counterpart core provisions of the other corporate documents are all embodied in a single comprehensive operating agreement. For planning purposes, this single operating agreement does it all. It incorporates the essential deal points between the co-owners of the business. The planning and drafting challenges of such operating agreements are discussed in the following chapter.

## 2. Owner Operational Deal Points

Usually there is a need to document during the organizational process key operational deal points that will govern the relationship of the shareholders of a closely held corporation. The identity of the client affects how the potential deal points among the shareholders are discussed and analyzed in a given situation. If the client is a majority shareholder or a group that has voting control (over 50 percent of the voting interests), the preferred choice may be to refrain from initiating any dialogue with the other owners. The clients will resolve key issues among themselves, knowing that they are in the driver's seat by virtue of their control. The burden is on the minority shareholders to raise any issues that may require special treatment in a shareholders agreement. If the minority shareholders are not represented or are under-represented, nothing may surface as all shareholders get caught up in the exciting prospects of the new venture. The lawyer who represents a minority shareholder has a more difficult job. Key issues must be identified, discussed, and prioritized. A plan must be developed for creating minority rights for those issues that are of greatest concern. Then the plan must be sold and eventually incorporated into the shareholders agreement.

The lawyer who is engaged to organize and represent the corporation, not a particular shareholder or group of shareholders, must be sensitive to the conflicts that many of the key planning issues might create between the shareholders. In too many cases, the organization is formed "the normal way," with little or no dialogue on the potentially tough issues. The far better approach is for the entity's lawyer to initiate a dialogue with all the shareholders in a meeting or series of meetings that address the most important issues. Lawyers representing specific shareholders should be invited to attend. Following each session, a simply worded memo should be circulated to all the parties, summarizing what was agreed upon and any open issues, and soliciting corrections or additions. When the meetings have been concluded and the memos have been finished, a shareholders agreement should be drawn that reflects the understandings incorporated in the memos. A draft should be circulated to all shareholders and their individual lawyers. The process requires a modest commitment of time and expense, but it will go a long way in identifying and resolving on the front-end any fundamental differences between the parties. The corporation and the relationships between the shareholders will be stronger as a result.

Following are brief descriptions of 20 operational deal point that often need to be discussed during the organizational process.

**a. The Scope of the Enterprise.** It is often desirable to limit in the shareholders agreement the scope of the business activities of the entity. Some shareholders may feel more comfortable about their investment in the venture if they do not have to worry about their money being diverted into activities that are outside the scope of what was originally discussed. Liability exposure may also be an issue, particularly where key players have multiple business interests. Limiting the scope of the business activities may help limit the business entity's liability exposure for unrelated actions of these players. And then there's the "Tag Along" problem. Often owners prefer a written activity limitation that removes any expectations that other owners may have relative to their other business activities. They like the idea of an express, unequivocal line in the sand that defines the limit of their relationship with their co-owners. Some shareholders may object to a written limitation on scope of the enterprise, arguing that it restricts flexibility, creates potential confusion for third parties, and fosters notions of "separateness" and "temporariness."

**b. Business Plan Changes.** The issue of business plan changes raises some of the same concerns as the scope of enterprise limitation. But here the issue is not whether the corporation can venture into different directions, but rather whether it can accelerate its plan for moving in its authorized direction. Turning up the volume usually triggers more risk and requires some combination of more capital or debt. Some shareholders may want the comfort of a written agreement that limits the capacity of their co-shareholders to overreact to early success by trashing the plan they all bought into up front in favor of a new model that promises greater pressure, more risk, and a potentially faster track to the gold.

**c. Debt.** Rare is the business that can grow and succeed without debt. The first lesson of Business 101 is the value of leveraging the borrowed dollar. In the business context, debt often raises two concerns among co-shareholders: (1) the amount of the debt relative to the size of the invested equity and the business operations; and (2) the need for personal guarantees from the shareholders. Most start-up operations require personal guarantees because the business operations are not mature enough to carry the debt. As the business grows, the guarantees may disappear unless a decision is made to accelerate the growth rate of the business. The big issues for the shareholders are: How much debt is going to be incurred during the start-up phase? What guarantees are the shareholders going to provide? What priority will be given to eliminating personal guarantees in the future? As the business grows and develops the ability to carry its own debt, what is an acceptable debt level? Some owners may want a written understanding on these key issues, particularly as they relate to personal guarantees. They may want to limit expectations of others relative to their willingness to provide guarantees beyond the levels agreed to, while being assured that their colleagues will step up to the plate and provide the level of guarantees that all have accepted.

**d. Additional Capital Contributions.** The issue of additional capital contributions from the shareholders often requires dialogue and a written understanding. Some shareholders, even those with deep pockets, may want to kill any expectations that they will help provide whatever is needed to keep the venture afloat or fund growth. Others may be concerned with dilution; they do not want their equity interests reduced as those with greater means continually pony up more money and claim a bigger share of the whole. Preemptive rights that give all owners the right to protect their percentage interests with additional contributions are usually inadequate. When this issue is a major concern, the owners need to talk through their concerns and, with the aid of counsel, reach an agreement that, to the fullest extent possible, addresses the objectives of the shareholders. One approach is to specify that each owner must contribute his or her *pro rata* share of the capital needed to accomplish the purpose of the entity. Some owners may be unwilling to agree to an unlimited equity contribution requirement. In this situation, the agreement may have to place a cap on future required capital contributions. If there is no mandatory requirement for additional capital contributions, the shareholders agreement may need to spell out how future capital needs will be satisfied. For example, it may permit but not require any one or more shareholders to make additional contributions and receive additional stock. Another approach is to authorize any shareholder to make a loan to the corporation if additional cash is required, and then to provide that the loan is to be paid back, together with interest, before any cash distributions are made to the shareholders. In some situations, the financial institution that finances the corporation's operations may limit or prohibit the corporation from borrowing additional funds from shareholders. If this is the case and additional capital is required, then the shareholders agreement may provide that any one or more of the owners may make additional capital contributions to the entity, which will have a priority right of repayment – no distributions will be made until these additional contributions have been fully repaid with a specified preferred return equivalent to an interest rate. Thus, the new money is treated like a loan for distribution purposes, but it is structured as an equity capital contribution that does not violate any restrictive covenant of the lender.

**e. New Shareholders.** The policy for admitting new shareholders is a critical issue in professional service and family organizations and many service businesses. It is a major event that, except in large firms, usually requires the consent of all the owners. Often it raises the same dilution concerns as additional capital contributions. Plus, there is the added factor of a new personality. Where the investors are truly passive and have no involvement in the operations, a new personality, even an unpleasant one, may be of little or no concern. But in most closely held businesses, the owners have input and have the capacity to be a positive or negative force. This reality, coupled with the fear that divisive factions may develop or be fed as more bodies are added, may warrant special provisions dealing with the admission of new shareholders.

**f. Shareholder Roles and Service Commitments.** The roles of the shareholders need to be clarified in many situations. For those shareholders who are employed and compensated by the venture, the key issues are the level of their service commitment and their right to be involved in other activities. Are they expected to devote all of their time and energies to the enterprise? Many organizations quickly hit a wall when the shareholders discover that a key shareholder spends only a fraction of his or her time looking after the affairs of the business. For those shareholders who are not employed by the business, the challenge is to clarify expectations. Some shareholders may expect that they will be entitled to serve on the board or have some other advisory role that provides an opportunity for input. Having put up their money, they want a spot in the inner circle. Some may expect that the sage advice and wisdom of a particular shareholder will be available, when, in fact, that investor, although willing to put up a few dollars, has no interest in providing any input or otherwise being tied to the business.

**g. Owner Employment Rights.**    Often there is a need to clarify the relationship between an owner's interest in the corporation and that owner's employment by the business.  In many organizations, the two are tied together through the shareholders agreement – no employment, no equity.  The issue usually surfaces in a few different ways.  A key shareholder may have received stock for putting the deal together or as compensation for management services rendered or to be rendered or, as is usually the case, for some combination of all of these.  Often that key shareholder wants assurance that his or her right to manage the business is protected and cannot be disturbed by the other shareholders, except under the most extreme circumstances.  The other shareholders may want clearly defined termination rights if the key shareholder doesn't do the job to their satisfaction.  And, to add injury to insult, the other shareholders may want the key shareholder to forfeit some or all of his or her stock in such an event or, at a minimum, to be obligated to sell any residual stock back to the corporation at a price determined pursuant to the shareholders agreement.

**h. Business Location.**    In select situations, the location of the business' operations or headquarters may be a concern.  There have been situations where shareholders have attempted to frustrate the rights of key shareholder/employees, by threatening to move the business to a location that, as a practical matter, makes it extremely inconvenient for the key employees.  Usually, such a threatened move can withstand a bad faith claim because it is supported by valid business justifications, such as cheaper labor prices, lower taxes, or reduced shipping costs.  The shareholder who has a vested interest in the business' headquarters staying in a particular city may want a contractual provision in the shareholders agreement that protects that interest.  Usually it can be secured with no objection on the front end.

**i. Outside Shareholder Activities.**    Beyond the issue of outside activities of shareholder/employees discussed previously, sometimes there is a need to consider limitations on the outside activities of other shareholders.  Often there is a desire to restrict owners from investing in competitors, major suppliers, or important customers of the business.  The fear is that such investments may create conflicts that could compromise future opportunities.  Some shareholders may strongly resist such limitations.  They may be unwilling to surrender their investment flexibility and options to a single investment, as they oppose any contractual corporate opportunity limitations.  Often their willingness to participate will be conditioned on an express provision to the contrary.

**j. Related Party Transactions.**  Transactions with related parties often are a source of contention in closely held businesses.  Examples include leasing facilities from a major shareholder, purchasing supplies or raw materials from a business controlled by a shareholder or a relative, licensing proprietary rights from a shareholder, purchasing capital assets from a shareholder, and employing relatives of a shareholder.   To avoid the conflicts and the uncomfortable embarrassments that often accompany these situations, the parties may include approval mechanisms in the shareholders agreement that assure that any such related party transactions are structured to include pricing terms, termination rights, and other provisions that serve the best interests of the corporation.

**k. Tax Elections.**   To avoid future conflicts, often it is advisable to document how certain tax matters are going to be handled.  Examples include the selection of a fiscal year, cost recovery deductions, and inventory valuation methods. There also is the issue of a potential future S election, which requires the consent of all owners, or the potential termination of an S election, which requires the consent of owners owning over half the outstanding stock.  In both situations, a different approval percentage may be desired and fixed by agreement.  For S election purposes, the preference may be a supermajority vote that gives no single shareholder a veto power.  For S termination purposes, something more than a simple majority may be warranted before the S election is discarded.  A shareholders agreement is an excellent tool for nailing down how key tax elections are going to be handled.

**l. Confidentiality Covenants.**  Employees, including shareholders who are employees, are often required to sign confidentiality agreements that are structured to protect the trade secrets and proprietary rights of the business. Sometimes it is desirable to extend these agreements to all shareholders of the corporation, particularly in those situations where the shareholders may have access to trade secrets or proprietary information critical to the success of the business.  Some investors may resist any such agreements or any mechanism that limits other investment options or exposes them to any future claims relating to the use of proprietary information.  When the issue is important and the potential shareholders won't budge, it may be necessary to start shopping for some different investors.

**m. Accounts Payable Management.**  There are different perceptions about paying bills.  Some see it as an opportunity to generate easy, low-cost financing by implementing a practice of delayed payment that pushes the envelope but keeps all vendors on board.  Others view it as an easy way to show strength, establish an admirable Dunn and Bradstreet rating, and build vendor loyalty and confidence (which may be badly needed in rough times) by not missing a due date. Plus, with the discounts many vendors offer for prompt payment, an on-time payment strategy may add to the bottom line.  This issue can become a source of contention between shareholders as the business begins to mature. Some may not want to be involved with a slow-pay enterprise that always looks strapped for cash, while others may want to maximize all financing options within definable limits.  Any up-front discussion between the shareholders may result in an understanding that avoids a future conflict when the business is in full swing and the issue is hot.

**n. Cash Distributions and Allocations.**   Are cash distributions to the shareholders a priority concern?  Some shareholders may want to know that the plan includes regular distributions to the shareholders as the business ramps up. Others may expect that all after-tax profits will be invested to finance growth and that no cash will flow for some time.  It is a fundamental part of the plan that should be clear to all shareholders.  The problem is that the issue is tied to other key factors, including the growth rate of the business and the use of debt.  Often the answer is to set guidelines regarding growth and debt that, once hit, will begin to trigger cash distributions to the owners. Typically, a provision is structured to ensure that cash is only distributed when all other cash needs of the business have been met, including ensuring appropriate reserves for working capital and other potential future needs. Also, loan agreements with the business' bank likely will impose restrictions on the timing of cash distributions that the agreement should recognize. An agreement regarding cash distributions is particularly important with an S corporation, where the earnings of the corporation are not taxed to the entity but instead are passed through and taxed to the shareholders. The shareholders of an S corporation often want some contractual assurance that cash distributions will be made to fund their pass-through tax liabilities. It is not possible to structure such cash distributions based on the size of the respective tax liabilities of the individual S corporation shareholders. Any such attempt would likely result in a claim that the S corporation has more than one class of stock and end up killing the S election. In an S corporation, cash distributions must be allocated among the shareholders according to their respective common stockholdings. So when there is a need to contractually commit an S corporation to make cash distributions to cover the shareholders' pass-through tax liabilities, often the best approach is to specify in the shareholders agreement that a designated percentage of the income allocated to shareholders (e.g., 40 percent) will be distributed in cash to the shareholders in accordance with their respective stockholdings. Such a flat percentage approach will likely result in some shareholders getting more than is needed for their tax bill, and others may get slightly less than is needed, based on their unique tax situation.

   **o. Shareholder Compensation Benefits.** In those situations where certain shareholders are employed by the corporation, there is a need to clarify the compensation rights of those shareholders and how such compensation rights will take priority over any dividends to the shareholders. The compensation rights may include a specified salary, period salary adjustments, cash bonuses based on the performance of the corporation, deferred compensation benefits, life insurance benefits, and compensation in the form of stock or stock rights. Typically, these compensation rights are spelled out in an executive employment agreement with a key shareholder/employee that is coordinated with the buy-out provisions of the shareholders agreement. A discussion of executive employment agreements is provided in Chapter 11.

   **p. Selection of Professionals.** Business entities need the assistance of outside professionals, including lawyers, accountants, appraisers, actuaries, investment firms, employee benefit firms and so forth. The method of selecting such professionals is often a potential source of conflict. Too often the organizer selects professionals who have a history with, and a loyalty to, that person. Those selected may not be the best qualified, nor the best suited to represent the interests of the corporation. Depending on the circumstances leading up to the lawyer's involvement in the start-up planning process, this may be an uncomfortable issue to deal with during the organizational effort. Nevertheless, it is often smart to do so. It makes it easy for all shareholders to vent any concerns, and actually may help build credibility for the lawyer. Often it leads to a procedure for selecting and monitoring the performance of all outside professionals that eliminates future concerns or conflicts among the owners.

**q. Indemnifications.**  Will those shareholders or employees who act on behalf of the entity be protected against any personal loss, damage or liability they incur as a result of such activity?  The answer is usually "yes."  An indemnification and hold harmless provision is included to protect against such liabilities and any associated legal fees.  But significant limitations are often included.  First, the agreement may provide that the indemnification may be recoverable only out of the assets of the entity and not from the owners of the entity.  The shareholders may not want any personal exposure for the acts of others.  If the primary assets of the business have been pledged to secure financing, the assets available for any such indemnity may be very limited.  Second, the indemnification may extend only to acts or omissions undertaken in good faith and with a belief that they were in the best interests of the corporation.  This places a proof burden on the employee or shareholder who is the target of the claim.  Third, the agreement may require that the targeted employee or shareholder tender the defense or resolution of the claim to the company so that the company can control expenses and dispose of the matter on its own terms.

**r. Dispute Resolution Procedures.**  An important issue that usually needs to be addressed by agreement is how disputes among shareholders are to be resolved.  No matter how carefully the up-front planning is handled, there is always the possibility that a dispute may erupt among the shareholders.  It's usually prudent to have all the shareholders agree to a method for quickly and inexpensively resolving any dispute that may surface.  Absent such a mechanism, the likely result is expensive, time-consuming, destructive litigation.  A common method of resolving any disputes is arbitration.  The agreement lays out the necessary procedures, including where the arbitration will be held and how the costs will be shared and allocated.  All agree that the decision of the arbiters will be binding on the parties.  The agreement also may require mandatory mediation prior to any litigation or arbitration proceeding.

**s. Life-After Rights.**  In many businesses, particularly in service and professional service organizations, it is advisable to spell out the "going forward" rights that each shareholder will have in the event there is a falling out and the group fractures.  Absent such an agreement, the shareholders may find themselves tangled up with shutdown issues that may make it difficult for some to immediately shift gears and preserve the continuity of their business activities.  Most professionals and service providers cannot afford a major disruption that stops their careers.  Key issues include the right to engage in the same business as the fractured entity, the right to pursue and service clients of the entity, the right to hire employees of the entity, the right to deal with vendors and financial institutions used by the entity, the right to make copies of client documents, files and other important documents, the right to use the same personal business email addresses and phone numbers, and the right to disclose the prior affiliation with the entity.  The shareholders often want the ability to immediately exercise these rights when things blow up, even while the affairs of the corporation are being resolved and settled.

**t. Sell-Out Options.**  Often the shareholders desire to clarify how a decision will be made for the corporation to sell out and cash in down the road. Potential future transactions could include a sale of substantially all the assets and goodwill of the business, a sale of all the stock or equity interests of the business, or a merger of the corporation into a larger company whose stock is publicly traded. The owners may want to require something more than a majority vote for such a "that's the ball game" transaction, and may want the assurance of knowing that all are required to play ball and go along if the requisite percentage approves the transaction.

### 3. SOLUTION TECHNIQUES

Resolving a planning issue that is of concern to the shareholders requires a solution. The range of potential solutions in any given situation is limited only by the imagination of the parties involved. Following is a brief description of solution techniques that are often used.

**a. Definitive Contractual Provision.** The shareholders agreement resolves the issue by spelling out the "deal" and what is expected of each party. Examples: All owners must sign confidentiality agreements; accounts payable will be paid in a timely manner to take advantage of early pay discounts; an S elections will be made; arbitration is mandated in the event of a dispute; each owner will be required to make additional contributions equal to 25 percent of his or her original contribution if such funding is needed; all owners will have specified life-after rights in the event of a falling out; and so forth. The parties reach an agreement that is incorporated into the shareholder or operating agreement.

**b. Supermajority Vote.** The parties agree that resolution of the issue will require a supermajority approval vote of the shareholders. Seventy or 80 percent will be required in order to accelerate the business plan, to incur additional debt beyond the approved limits, to trigger or revoke an S election, to approve a merger or sale of substantially all the assets, and so forth. The provision comforts both those who want something more than a simple majority and those who want the assurances that individuals cannot block certain actions, such as the making of an S election.

**c. Designated Board or Management Committee.** Often the solution is to delegate all future decisions regarding an issue or group of issues to a board of directors that has been carefully structured by agreement to protect the interests of all parties. Assume, for example, a hybrid entity where 40 percent of the equity interests are owned by employees and 60 percent are owned by investors. The parties agree to have a four-person board, comprising two employee-shareholders and two investors. Since any decision will require a vote of at least three members, all shareholders have the comfort of knowing that any affirmative decision on a particular issue will require the approval of at least one of their representatives.

**d. Specified Conditions.** Sometimes an issue can be resolved by specifying the conditions that must exist in order for the board of directors of the corporation to move forward on a specific issue. Often such conditions are combined with a supermajority back-up provision. For example, the agreement might specify that, absent a 70 percent approval by the shareholders, the board will not incur any additional bank financing beyond the approved limits if such financing would cause the company's debt-to-equity ratio to exceed 4-to-1.

**e. Individual Veto Right.** In select situations, an issue can be resolved by giving a particular owner an individual veto right. For example, a key employee who is also an shareholder may be concerned that the board may choose to change the business plan by reducing employee health insurance benefits. The other shareholders appreciate their colleague's concern, but suspect that any changes in the short-term are unlikely. To resolve the issue, all agree that any reductions in employee health insurance benefits over the next five years are subject to the approval of the specific shareholder.

**f. Opt-Out Rights.** Sometimes an shareholder issue can be resolved by giving shareholders the right to opt out of the effects of a given decision. For example, any concerns regarding debt expansion may be eliminated by granting individual shareholders the right to opt out of any personal guarantee requirement for the additional debt. One or more individual dissenters may protect their own pocketbooks without stopping the entity from moving forward. Of course, if too many owners exercise the opt-out privilege, the additional financing becomes unobtainable.

**g. Buy-Out Trigger.** A buy-out trigger under the buy/sell provisions may be justified in some extreme situations. For example, a shareholder may be adamantly opposed to any business plan acceleration or debt expansion changes without his or her consent. To resolve the concern, that shareholder is given an option to trigger a purchase of his or her interest under the buy-sell agreement if the others choose to move forward with such a change in the future. The concerned owner is satisfied with the exit option protection, and the others are comfortable with a provision that may create an opportunity for them to increase their equity positions and rid themselves of a difficult colleague once things are going strong.

**h. Cumulative Voting.** In select situations, a cumulative voting provision may be used to give minority owners the capacity to elect an individual to the board of directors or managing committee of the organization. The provision grants each shareholder votes equal to the number of shares he or she owns multiplied by the number of directors to be elected and the right to cast those votes among one or more directors. A few states mandate cumulative voting; most states allow it if it is authorized in the Articles of Incorporation. The following basic formula helps in determining the number of minority shares (one vote per share) needed to elect a designated number of directors with cumulative voting, where "A" equals the total needed shares, "B" equals the total shares to be voted by all owners, "C" equals the number of directors the minority would like to elect, and "D" equals the total number of directors to be elected:

$$A = [(B \times C) / (D + 1)] + 1$$

For example, if the minority shareholders want the capacity to elect one of four directors and there are 1,000 votes outstanding, the minority shareholders would need 201 shares [((1,000 x 1) divided by 4 + 1) + 1].  For planning purposes, cumulative voting often sounds better than it really is.  A single seat on the board may do little or nothing to enhance the minority's position on key issues.  Plus, if the board seat is vitally important, it may be obtained by a specific agreement among the shareholders, without the complexity and arithmetic challenges of cumulative voting.  But there are situations where the minority's counsel, hearkening back to his or her law school days, regards it as a big deal, and the majority concludes that it is a relatively harmless alternative to other solutions that may have more teeth.

**i. Preemptive Rights**.  A preemptive rights provision in the Articles of Incorporation is sometimes used to pacify the concerns of those shareholders who fear that future fundraising efforts may dilute their interests in the enterprise.  The provision gives each owner the right to acquire his or her proportionate share of any newly issued stock under specific conditions spelled out in the Articles of Incorporation or, in the absence of such conditions, according to the applicable state statute.  There are three primary concerns from a planning perspective.  First, although preemptive rights may seem harmless on their face, often they can stymie a company's flexibility to move quickly and decisively in resolving its capital needs.  The rights can trigger delays and uncertainties that can hurt the company and cause potential new investors to quickly lose interest.  Considerable thought should be given to the use (or better yet, the nonuse) of such rights.  Second, if preemptive rights are to be granted, care should be taken to structure the necessary exceptions in the Articles of Incorporation and not to automatically rely on the default provisions of the applicable state statute. Important exceptions may include, among others, shares issued to compensate key employees, shares issued for property other than cash, shares issued in time of financial crisis to secure important financing guarantees, and shares issued to satisfy option and conversion rights.  Finally, the timing requirements of the preemptive rights should be carefully structured.  The company may be stuck on hold as shareholders ponder their decision to exercise or waive their preemptive rights and consult with their financial advisors.  Short time requirements will turn up the heat and help preserve the interest of potential new investors.

**j. Different Equity Interests.**  Sometimes conflicting objectives of the owners can be resolved by issuing different types of equity interests.  Voting and nonvoting stock may be used to separate voting and control rights from growth and income interests in both C and S corporations.  Preferred stock is not permitted in an S corporation.  But in C corporations, preferred stock may be used to grant income, capital and liquidation preferences for specific shareholders. There is significant flexibility in structuring the terms and limitations of the preferences. The wise use of such different interests often can facilitate an agreement that addresses the competing objectives of different owners.

### PROBLEMS 4–A AND 4-B

**4-A**. Jason, Lucy, and Sam are organizing a new corporation ("Newco").  Newco will develop and exploit a new product that is designed to make it easy to produce low-cost vinyl fencing. All three will serve on the board of Newco, and Jason and Lucy will be officers, employed full-time by Newco.

Sam plans on investing $1.2 million in the new company ("Newco"), far more than Jason and Lucy. But, as things now stand, Sam will be only one of three directors. Sam wants some protection against Jason and Lucy (who control the board) taking the company in a direction that is not acceptable to him. Sam is concerned about any attempts to (1) change the basic business plan, (2) incur additional debt, (3) pay bonuses to officers, or (4) accelerate the growth targets. Sam feels strongly that he should have some additional control rights because of the size of his investment.

If you represent only Sam, how would you advise him? Be specific in addressing the four concerns that Sam has identified. If you represent only Jason, what suggestions would you have to accommodate Sam's concerns while preserving flexibility for Jason and Lucy?

**4–B.** Four individuals are organizing a C corporation to exploit and market a line of relatively small (up to 40 feet), high-quality Italian yachts in the United States. They believe the superb quality, competitive pricing and Italian mystique (the best boats in the world come from Italy) will allow them to "bury the competition." They have collectively agreed to fund the new venture with $2.5 million of equity capital.

Roger, a deep-pocketed yacht fanatic, has committed to put up $1 million for 40 percent of the stock. He "feels strongly" that the group should have an understanding as to how it will raise an additional $2.5 million of equity if "necessary to maximize the opportunity." He has made it clear that he can and will contribute whatever is needed, so long as his equity increases proportionately. He does not like the idea of using his wealth "to secure financing that just preserves the equity of the others."

Luke, a man of means but not in Roger's league, has committed to pay $625,000 for 25 percent of the stock. He is willing to "put up more to fund growth if things are going strong, but not to fund a black hole if things stall out."

Joyce, also a 25 percent player for $625,000, has a financial background. She is opposed to any more equity contributions because she feels the company can "easily" finance any growth with "low risk" bank financing secured by pre-sale contracts and deposits and guarantees from the owners.

Finally, there's David, a yacht marketing guru who has "powerful" contacts in the industry. David will be the only owner who will work for the company, serving as its CEO. David is putting up $250,000 for a 10 percent interest and will draw a comfortable salary. He has emphatically exclaimed, "I will not put up another dime, and my interest had better never drop below 10 percent."

You've been retained to represent the new venture. Describe your recommendations for structuring an equity and debt understanding between the parties that will address, at least in part, the concerns of each shareholder. Get creative.

# B. LIMITED LIABILITY TRAPS

*Keypoint*

Limited liability is often trumpeted as a supreme benefit of a corporation. If the corporation defaults on a contract or loan, the aggrieved creditor cannot go after the shareholders, directors and officers unless they personally guaranteed the obligation. If an employee, while on the job, injures another in an auto accident, the corporation may be held liable for the employee's actions, but the corporation's shareholders, directors and officers are not exposed personally. As sweet as the corporate shield may appear, it has its limits.

There are various ways that shareholders of a closely held corporation may have personal liability exposure, including the following:

1. Key creditors, such as banks, other lenders, and important vendors often require the personal guarantees of the shareholders as a condition to extending credit.

2. If a shareholder or any person acting on behalf of a corporation negligently injures another, that person cannot escape personal responsibility for his or her tort even though the corporation is also legally responsible.

3. State corporate statutes personally obligate a shareholder, in certain situations, to return any dividend or distribution received by the shareholder if the shareholder, at the time of the distribution, knew that the corporation could not pay its creditors or that the corporation's liabilities exceeded its assets.

4. If a shareholder, acting as a promoter before the corporation is organized, enters into contracts on behalf of a soon-to-be formed corporation and the corporation is never properly formed or fails to adopt or perform the contract, the shareholder/promoter may have personal liability for the contract. However, if the corporation was never officially formed and the creditor knew that the corporation was going to be the responsible party, courts have sometimes employed a *de facto* corporation doctrine to extend the protection of limited liability and prevent a windfall to the creditor.

5. Corporate directors and officers also face personal liability exposure. Directors may be exposed to shareholders if they violate their fiduciary duties of care and loyalty. Plus, there are various statutory liabilities: corporate state laws usually make directors personally liable if they approve payments to shareholders when the corporation cannot pay its debts or is insolvent; securities laws impose liability for insider trading or not properly disclosing facts; antitrust laws impose liability for price-fixing, market division schemes and other competitor-related activities that hurt the competitive process; tax laws impose personal liability for failing to properly handle employee withholdings; the list goes on.

6. Sometimes shareholders of a closely held corporation face a "piercing the corporate veil" or "alter ego" threat from creditors. The creditors seek to pierce the corporate veil to get to the personal assets of the shareholders, arguing that the corporation and shareholders are one and the same and that there would be an unjust or inequitable outcome if the shareholders escaped personal liability. As the following *Kinney Shoe* case illustrate, it is never an easy burden of proof

for the plaintiff-creditor, and there are a host of factors that often come into play. After reviewing the facts of Problem 4-C, read the case and apply the factors discussed in the case to answer the questions raised in the problem.

## MBCA § 6.22  Liability of Shareholders

(a)  A purchaser from a corporation of its own shares is not liable to the corporation or its creditors with respect to the shares except to pay the consideration for which the shares were authorized to be issued (section 6.21) or specified in the subscription agreement (section 6.20).

(b)  Unless otherwise provided in the articles of incorporation, a shareholder of a corporation is not personally liable for the acts or debts of the corporation except that he may become personally liable by reason of his own acts or conduct.

## PROBLEM 4-C

Last year Jerry found the yacht of his dreams, a posh 75-foot, three-year-old pilothouse named "Magic." Jerry was able to purchase Magic for the bargain price of $2 million through a newly-formed corporation. A recently-retired couple, the Morgans, had purchased Magic three years earlier for $3.5 million, with the hope of endless luxury cruising.

The Morgans soon discovered that they could not safely handle their new, expensive toy. It quickly became something to fear, not enjoy. Plus, the moorage and maintenance costs (about $75,000 a year) were intolerable. Magic was soon on the used yacht market, with no interested buyers in a chronically sick economy.

But finally Jerry had surfaced, agreeing to pay $250,000 as a down payment and to provide the Morgans with a 10-year, 6-percent promissory note for $1,750,000 ("Note"). The obligor on the Note was Cruise Luxury, Inc, ("Cruise"), a new corporation that would use Magic 42 weeks a year to provide cruise trips to paying customers. Jerry planned to enjoy Magic for the balance of the time. The Note was guaranteed by Cruises' sole shareholder, Franklin Associates, Inc. ("Franklin"), a corporation that had been in existence for 10 years. Jerry was the sole shareholder of Franklin.

The Morgans weren't excited about the deal, but they figured that they didn't have an alternative for getting clear of their expensive boat. The bulk of the down payment would simply pay broker commissions. But the deal promised to end the high moorage and maintenance costs and to provide the Morgans with interest and principle payments each month for the next 10 years.

The transaction was closed by the brokers and a yacht title company. Lawyer involvement was minimal. The Note was secured by a first lien on Magic and a guarantee from Franklin. When asked about Franklin, Jerry just said, "It's the company that I have conducted all my business through for years." Since Jerry projected substantial wealth, nothing more was said.

To fund the deal, Jerry contributed $250,000 to Franklin. Franklin loaned the $250,000 to Cruise and put a second lien on Magic (behind the Morgan's interest) to secure its loan. Cruise insured Magic for only $1 million and secured $1.2 million of liability insurance.

On Cruise's sixth trip with paying customers, the captain made a fatal error and caused Magic to strike a long underwater cable that attached a tug to a huge barge. Four customers died, six others were seriously injured, and Magic was destroyed.

Cruise's only assets were the insurance proceeds. The $1 million Magic insurance was paid to the Morgans and the liability coverage was available to satisfy customer claims. The Morgans ended up with a loss on the Note in excess of $700,000, and the customers' claims far exceeded the insurance limits.

The focus has quickly turned to Franklin and Jerry. Franklin conducts substantial business (as Jerry represented), but it has never had any significant assets, and its note from Cruise is now worthless. Franklin's income is withdrawn by Jerry as dividends and salaries. Jerry's net worth is around $14 million.

The Morgans and the customers know that their only hope for any recovery is to reach Jerry's personal assets. What are their chances? What additional facts would help in making this assessment? What additional steps could Jerry have taken to help protect against the risks of such attempts to reach his assets?

## KINNEY SHOE CORP. v. POLAN
939 F.2d 209 (4th Cir. 1991)

CHAPMAN, Senior Circuit Judge:

Plaintiff-appellant Kinney Shoe Corporation ("Kinney") brought this action in the United States District Court for the Southern District of West Virginia against Lincoln M. Polan ("Polan") seeking to recover money owed on a sublease between Kinney and Industrial Realty Company ("Industrial"). Polan is the sole shareholder of Industrial. The district court found that Polan was not personally liable on the lease between Kinney and Industrial. Kinney appeals asserting that the corporate veil should be pierced, and we agree.

The district court based its order on facts which were stipulated by the parties. In 1984 Polan formed two corporations, Industrial and Polan Industries, Inc., for the purpose of re-establishing an industrial manufacturing business. The certificate of incorporation for Polan Industries, Inc. was issued by the West Virginia Secretary of State in November 1984. The following month the certificate of incorporation for Industrial was issued. Polan was the owner of both corporations. Although certificates of incorporation were issued, no organizational meetings were held, and no officers were elected.

In November 1984 Polan and Kinney began negotiating the sublease of a building in which Kinney held a leasehold interest. The building was owned by the Cabell County Commission and financed by industrial revenue bonds issued in 1968 to induce Kinney to locate a manufacturing plant in Huntington, West Virginia. Under the terms of the lease, Kinney was legally obligated to make payments on the bonds on a semi-annual basis through January 1, 1993, at which time it had the right to purchase the property. Kinney had ceased using the building as a manufacturing plant in June 1983.

The term of the sublease from Kinney to Industrial commenced in December 1984, even though the written lease was not signed by the parties until April 5, 1985. On April 15, 1985, Industrial subleased part of the building to Polan Industries for fifty percent of the rental amount due Kinney. Polan signed both subleases on behalf of the respective companies.

Other than the sublease with Kinney, Industrial had no assets, no income and no bank account. Industrial issued no stock certificates because nothing was ever paid in to this corporation. Industrial's only income was from its sublease to Polan Industries, Inc. The first rental payment to Kinney was made out of Polan's personal funds, and no further payments were made by Polan or by Polan Industries, Inc. to either Industrial or to Kinney.

Kinney filed suit against Industrial for unpaid rent and obtained a judgment in the amount of $166,400.00 on June 19, 1987. A writ of possession was issued, but because Polan Industries, Inc. had filed for bankruptcy, Kinney did not gain possession for six months. Kinney leased the building until it was sold on September 1, 1988. Kinney then filed this action against Polan individually to collect the amount owed by Industrial to Kinney. Since the amount to which Kinney is entitled is undisputed, the only issue is whether Kinney can pierce the corporate veil and hold Polan personally liable.

The district court held that Kinney had assumed the risk of Industrial's undercapitalization and was not entitled to pierce the corporate veil. Kinney appeals, and we reverse.

We have long recognized that a corporation is an entity, separate and distinct from its officers and stockholders, and the individual stockholders are not responsible for the debts of the corporation. *See, e.g., DeWitt Truck Brokers, Inc. v. W. Ray Flemming Fruit Co.,* 540 F.2d 681, 683 (4th Cir.1976). This concept, however, is a fiction of the law and it is now well settled, as a general principle, that the fiction should be disregarded when it is urged with an intent not within its reason and purpose, and in such a way that its retention would produce injustices or inequitable consequences. *Laya v. Erin Homes, Inc.,* 352 S.E.2d 93, 97-98 (W.Va.1986).

Kinney seeks to pierce the corporate veil of Industrial so as to hold Polan personally liable on the sublease debt. The Supreme Court of Appeals of West Virginia has set forth a two prong test to be used in determining whether to pierce a corporate veil in a breach of contract case. This test raises two issues: first, is the unity of interest and ownership such that the separate personalities of the corporation and the individual shareholder no longer exist; and second, would an equitable result occur if the acts are treated as those of the corporation alone. *Laya,* 352 S.E.2d at 99. Numerous factors have been identified as relevant in making this determination.

(1) commingling of funds and other assets of the corporation with those of the individual shareholders;

(2) diversion of the corporation's funds or assets to noncorporate uses (to the personal uses of the corporation's shareholders);

(3) failure to maintain the corporate formalities necessary for the issuance of or subscription to the corporation's stock, such as formal approval of the stock issue by the board of directors;

(4) an individual shareholder representing to persons outside the corporation that he or she is personally liable for the debts or other obligations of the corporation;

(5) failure to maintain corporate minutes or adequate corporate records;

(6) identical equitable ownership in two entities;

(7) identity of the directors and officers of two entities who are responsible for supervision and management (a partnership or sole proprietorship and a corporation owned and managed by the same parties);

(8) failure to adequately capitalize a corporation for the reasonable risks of the corporate undertaking;

(9) absence of separately held corporate assets;

(10) use of a corporation as a mere shell or conduit to operate a single venture or some particular aspect of the business of an individual or another corporation;

(11) sole ownership of all the stock by one individual or members of a single family;

(12) use of the same office or business location by the corporation and its individual shareholder(s);

(13) employment of the same employees or attorney by the corporation and its shareholder(s);

(14) concealment or misrepresentation of the identity of the ownership, management or financial interests in the corporation, and concealment of personal business activities of the shareholders (sole shareholders do not reveal the association with a corporation, which makes loans to them without adequate security);

(15) disregard of legal formalities and failure to maintain proper arm's length relationships among related entities;

(16) use of a corporate entity as a conduit to procure labor, services or merchandise for another person or entity;

(17) diversion of corporate assets from the corporation by or to a stockholder or other person or entity to the detriment of creditors, or the manipulation of assets and liabilities between entities to concentrate the assets in one and the liabilities in another;

(18) contracting by the corporation with another person with the intent to avoid risk of nonperformance by use of the corporate entity; or the use of a

corporation as a subterfuge for illegal transactions;

(19) the formation and use of the corporation to assume the existing liabilities of another person or entity.
entity.

*Laya,* 352 S.E.2d at 98-99

The district court found that the two prong test of *Laya* had been satisfied. The court concluded that Polan's failure to carry out the corporate formalities with respect to Industrial, coupled with Industrial's gross undercapitalization, resulted in damage to Kinney. We agree.

It is undisputed that Industrial was not adequately capitalized. Actually, it had no paid in capital. Polan had put nothing into this corporation, and it did not observe any corporate formalities. In this case, Polan bought no stock, made no capital contribution, kept no minutes, and elected no officers for Industrial.

In addition, Polan attempted to protect his assets by placing them in Polan Industries, Inc. and interposing Industrial between Polan Industries, Inc. and Kinney so as to prevent Kinney from going against the corporation with assets. Polan gave no explanation or justification for the existence of Industrial as the intermediary between Polan Industries, Inc. and Kinney. Polan was obviously trying to limit his liability and the liability of Polan Industries, Inc. by setting up a paper curtain constructed of nothing more than Industrial's certificate of incorporation. These facts present the classic scenario for an action to pierce the corporate veil so as to reach the responsible party and produce an equitable result. Accordingly, we hold that the district court correctly found that the two prong test in *Laya* had been satisfied.

For the foregoing reasons, we hold that Polan is personally liable for the debt of Industrial, and the decision of the district court is reversed and this case is remanded with instructions to enter judgment for the plaintiff.

## C.  CORPORATE FORMATION TAX PLANNING

No new business venture wants to trigger a tax hit out of the box. In most situations, the challenge is to get assets into the new entity and equity interests into the hands of the owners with as little tax damage as possible. Fortunately, the Internal Revenue Code is structured to accommodate the tax-free formation of corporations and entities taxed as partnerships. The key is to closely adhere to some relatively simple rules and to avoid traps that can trigger unpleasant surprises.

Two general observations are helpful up front. First, when cash is the consideration for an equity interest, there is no threat of taxable income being recognized. The owner's basis in the equity interest is the amount of cash paid, and the business entity recognizes no taxable income.[9] Second, when property other than cash is the consideration for an equity interest, a taxable event triggering income or loss for the owner will result unless the transaction fits

---

9.  I.R.C. §§ 721, 1012, 1032.

within a specific statutory exception that provides otherwise.  So, for example, if Linda transfers to XYZ Inc. equipment that has a basis of $100,000 and a fair market value of $300,000 in return for 100 shares of XYZ Inc. common stock in a transaction that does not qualify for nonrecognition treatment, Linda will recognize $200,000 of taxable income, the tax basis in her newly-acquired stock will be $300,000, and her holding period for the stock will be measured from the date of the transaction.[10]  To avoid this distasteful outcome, Linda needs to fit within the 351 Rule.

### 1. CORPORATE FORMATIONS: EIGHT RULES AND RELATED TRAPS

**a. Rule 1: The 351 Rule.**  No gain or loss is recognized by a shareholder on the transfer of property to a corporation in exchange for stock of the corporation if:

- Property is transferred,

- The transfer is solely in exchange for stock, and

- The transferring parties are in "control" of the corporation immediately after the exchange.  "Control" means that the property transferors own at least 80 percent of the total combined voting power of all classes of stock entitled to vote and at least 80 percent of the total number of shares of all other classes of stock.[11]

**Example:** If Linda is the sole shareholder of XYZ Inc. in the above example, the 351 Rule would apply to prevent any recognition of income because *property* is transferred *solely* in exchange for stock and Linda *controls* the corporation immediately following the transaction.

**The Traps.**  Traps under the 351 Rule surface in a number of different ways, including the following:

**(1)  Stock for Services.**  One or more of the shareholders receives stock in exchange for services.  Although the term "property" for Section 351 purposes has been broadly defined to include cash, accounts receivable, capital assets, patents, licenses and even industrial know-how, it does not include services.[12]  So if one shareholder receives 30 percent of the corporation's stock in return for services rendered or to be rendered, no shareholder can qualify under the 351 Rule because the required control was not acquired with property.  Suppose the shareholder who receives stock in exchange for services also transfers some property in exchange for stock; that is, there is dual consideration.  The regulations state that a dual consideration transferor will not qualify as a property transferor if the property transferred is "of relatively small value" when compared to the value of the stock already owned or to be received for services.[13]  In Revenue Procedure 77-37 (here's the good news), the Service stated that this "relatively small value" standard can be avoided if the value of the property transferred equals 10 percent or more of the fair market value of the stock owned

---

10.  I.R.C. §§ 1001, 1012.
11.  I.R.C. § 351(a).
12.  I.R.C § 351(d)(1) specifically excludes services from the property definition.
13.  Reg. § 1.351-1(a)(1)(ii).

(or to be received for services) by the shareholder.[14]  So the planning point is straight-forward: Where necessary to qualify a transaction under the 351 Rule for the benefit of all the transferors, make certain that those receiving stock in exchange for services also transfer property that exceeds this 10 percent requirement.

**(2) Timing Differences.**  Shareholders may transfer property in exchange for stock at different times.  To fit within the 351 Rule, the participants who end up with control must have acted in concert under a single integrated plan.  If in the example above, Linda's transfer of equipment results in her owning 100 percent of the stock following her transfer, but six months later Jim contributes equipment in return for stock in a completely separate transaction and ends up with 50 percent of the stock, Linda's transfer would qualify under the 351 Rule because she owned more than 80 percent after her transfer, but Jim's would not.  The transfers need not occur at the same time to be part of a single plan.  What is required is that "the rights of the parties have been previously defined and the execution of the agreement proceeds with an expedition consistent with orderly procedure."[15]  So if at the time Linda transfers her equipment in return for stock it is contemplated that Jim will do the same six months out, the board resolutions approving Linda's transaction should make specific reference to Jim's future transfer and leave no doubt that it is part of a single, integrated plan to form the corporation.  This will help ensure that Jim's transaction falls within the 351 Rule.

**(3)  Immediate Subsequent Stock Transfers.**  Shareholders who receive stock in the exchange and constitute part of the "control" group dispose of their stock immediately following the exchange.  If the disposition is pursuant to a prearranged or legally binding plan, it will likely kill the "control immediately after" requirement to the detriment of all those who participate in the transaction.[16]  Absent a prearranged binding commitment to make such a transfer, there may still be a problem under the step transaction doctrine if the second transfer was expected and was dependent on the exchange transaction.[17]  Gifts and other donative transfers after the exchange generally do not present a problem.[18]  The planning precaution is to provide in the shareholders agreement that no post-exchange transfers will be permitted that may threaten application of the 351 Rule.  Most shareholder agreements include transfer restrictions that are broad enough to provide such protection.

**(4)  Accommodation Transfers.**  Existing shareholders choose to accommodate the admission of a new shareholder by contributing a nominal

---

14. Rev. Proc. 77-37, 1977-2 C.B. 568.

15. Reg. § 1.351-1(a)(1).

16. See, e.g., Intermountain Lumber Co. v. Commissioner, 65 T.C. 1025 (1976) and Rev. Rule 79-70, 1979-1 C.B. 144.  But see Rev. Rule 2003-51, 2003-1 C.B. 938 where a prearranged subsequent transfer did not preclude section 351 treatment when the subsequent transfer was tax-free and the overall result could have been directly accomplished on a tax-free basis.

17. See Rev. Ruling 78-330, 1978-2 C.B. 147; Rev. Rule 75-406, 1975-2 C.B. 125; and American Bantam Car Co. v. Commissioner, 11 T.C. 397 (1948), affirmed 177 F.2d 513 (3d Cir. 1949).

18. See D'Angelo Associates, Inc. v. Commissioner, 70 T.C. 121 (1978) and Stanton v. United States, 512 F.2d 13 (3d Cir. 1975).

amount of property in return for more stock in order to be included in the "control" group. If the existing shareholders do not participate, their stock ownership does not count in the "control" calculation, and the new shareholder has no hope of qualifying under the 351 Rule. If the existing shareholders participate, all their stock counts in the control calculation. This accommodation strategy will work only if the property transferred by the existing shareholders has a value equal to at least 10 percent of the total value of the stock already owned by the existing shareholders.[19]

**(5) Immediate Subsequent Property Disposition.** The corporation that receives property in the exchange immediately disposes of the property. If the disposition is consistent with the corporation's ordinary business practices (e.g., inventory dispositions), there should be no problem. However, if the disposition is part of a prearranged plan that looks as if the corporation is just being used as a conduit for disposing of unwanted assets, there is a risk that the Service may claim that the original transaction was a sham that did not fall within the scope of the 351 Rule.[20] The planning point is to avoid any such near-in-time asset dispositions that fall outside the scope of the corporation's ordinary business practices.

**(6) Nonvoting Stock Class.** Immediately after the exchange, the transferors in the control group own at least 80 percent of all the voting stock and over at least 80 percent of the value of all the stock, but do not own 80 percent or more of the shares of a particular class of nonvoting stock.[21] The exchange will not qualify under the 351 Rule. The planning point: Make certain that the transferors meet the two-pronged control test – at least 80 percent of each class of nonvoting stock and at least 80 percent of the voting power. Only direct ownership counts; options, conversion rights, and attribution won't get the job done. Treasury stock and authorized but unissued stock are not counted.

**(7) Loss Asset.** A shareholder intends to transfer a loss asset (tax basis exceeds value) to the corporation in return for stock and would like to recognize the loss on the transaction. The key is to structure the loss transaction to be after and completely unrelated to any 351 Rule transaction that may occur. Plus, the loss will not be allowed if the shareholder actually or constructively owns more than 50 percent of the corporation's outstanding stock.[22]

**(8) Nonqualified Preferred Stock.** Shareholders are issued "nonqualified preferred stock" in the transaction or such stock is outstanding at the time of the transaction. This is stock that is limited and preferred as to dividends, that does not significantly participate in equity growth, and that has one of the following characteristics: (1) the holder may require the corporation or a related party to redeem or purchase the stock; (2) the corporation or a related party is required to redeem or purchase the stock; (3) the corporation or a related party has a right to

---

19. Rev. Proc. 77-37, 1977-2 C.B. 568.
20. See Kluener v. Commisioner, T.C. Memo 1996-519, affirmed 154 F.3d 630 (6th Cir. 1998); Stewart v. Commissioner, 714 F.2d 977 (9th Cir. 1983); and Hallowell v. Commissioner, 56 T.C. 600 (1971).
21. I.R.C. § 368(c); Rev. Rule 59-259, 1959-2 C.B. 115.
22. I.R.C. §§ 267(a) & (b)(2).

redeem or purchase the stock, and it is more likely than not that the right will be exercised; or (4) the stock's dividend rate varies with reference to interest rates, commodity prices or other similar indices.[23]  Essentially, it is preferred stock that looks much like debt.  For purposes of the 351 Rule, nonqualified preferred stock has a split role.  Until the IRS says otherwise, for planning purposes it should be treated as stock for applying the "control" test.[34]  Thus, the control group transferors had better make certain that they end up with 80 percent or more of the nonqualified preferred stock.  But for applying the general nonrecognition provision of the 351 Rule, nonqualified preferred stock is not considered stock, but rather is treated as other property.  If it is the only consideration received by a transferor, the exchange will be completely outside the scope of the 351 Rule and will trigger taxable gain or loss.  If the nonqualified preferred stock is received along with other stock, it will constitute "boot" and will fall within the scope of Rule 2.[25]

**(9) Investment Company Transfer.**  The assets contributed by the shareholders qualify the corporation as an "investment company" within the meaning of Section 351(e).  When this happens, the 351 Rule is out and gain or loss is recognized on the transfers.[26]  For this trap to apply, two conditions must exist: (1) the transfer must result in a direct or indirect diversification of the shareholders' interests, and (2) more than 80 percent of the corporation's assets (excluding cash and non-convertible debt obligations) must consist of stock or securities – broadly defined since 1997 to include all stock and securities (not just the readily marketable); other corporate equity interests; evidences of indebtedness; options; forward and futures contracts; notional principal contracts and derivatives; foreign currencies; interests in real estate investment trusts, regulated investment companies, and publicly-traded partnerships; precious metal interests unrelated to an active trade or business; and more.[27]  Real estate and tangible business assets are not included in the definition.  The diversification requirement is met when two or more persons transfer non-identical investment assets to the corporation.[28]  So, for example, if A, B and C each transfer a different appreciated stock to the corporation and the corporation has no other assets, the diversification requirement would be met, the 351 Rule would not apply, and each party would recognize a taxable gain on the transfer.  If, however, A, B and C each contributed the same stock or identical interests in more than one stock, there would be no diversification impact and the 351 Rule would apply.  Transfers that are insignificant (i.e., less than one percent) are ignored in testing for diversification.[29]  Plus, diversification will not result from the transfer, and thus section 351 treatment will not be denied if each shareholder transfers a portfolio of stock and securities that is already diversified.[30]

---

23.  I.R.C. § 351(g).

24.  See Staff of Joint Committee on Taxation, General Explanation of Tax Legislation Enacted in 1997, 105th Cong., 1st Sess. 210 (1997) and I.R.C. § 351(g)(4).

25.  I.R.C. § 351(g)(1).

26.  I.R.C. § 351(e)(1).

27.  I.R.C. § 351(e)(1)(B); Reg. § 1.351-1(c)(1)(i).

28.  Reg. § 1.351-1(c)(5) & (7), Examples (1) & (2).

29.  Reg. § 1.351-1(c)(5); PLRs 200006008, 200002025.

30.  Reg. § 1.351-1(c)(6).  The regulations adopt a slightly modified version of the 25 percent and 50 percent tests of section 368(a)(2)(f) for determining whether the contributed portfolios are already "diversified."

**b. Rule 2: The Boot Rule.** If the 351 Rule would apply to an exchange except that the corporation transfers to the shareholder other property (boot) in addition to stock, the shareholder recognizes gain equal to the lesser of (i) the fair market value of the boot or (ii) the built-in gain on the property transferred by the shareholder to the corporation.[31] Plus, the corporation recognizes income equal to any built-in gain on the property transferred to the shareholder.[32]

**Example:** Linda transfers to XYZ Inc. equipment with a basis of $100,000 and a fair market value of $300,000 in exchange for 100 shares of XYZ Inc. common stock and $80,000 cash. Linda recognizes gain equal to the $80,000 of boot received. If Linda was paid $220,000 cash with the stock, her recognized gain would be limited to her $200,000 equipment built-in gain – the excess of the fair market value of the equipment she transferred over her basis in the property. If the boot paid to Linda was land that had a value of $220,000 and a basis of $150,000 in the hands of the corporation, Linda would still recognize $200,000 of income (the built-in gain on the equipment she transferred), and the corporation would recognize $70,000 of income (the built-in gain on the land).

**Traps:** The Boot Rule is subject to a few traps. First, losses are never recognized at either the shareholder or corporate levels – only gains.[33] Second, notes, bonds and other securities issued by the corporation along with its stock are considered boot. The shareholder may defer the boot gain on any such debt obligations by electing installment sales treatment under Section 453.[34] Third, as previously described, "nonqualified preferred stock" is treated as boot in a 351 transaction.

**c. Rule 3: Shareholder Basis Rule:** The basis of the stock acquired by a shareholder in a 351 exchange equals (i) the shareholder's basis in the property transferred to the corporation, plus (ii) any gain recognized by the shareholder under the Boot Rule, less (iii) the fair market value of any boot received.[35] The shareholder's basis in any boot received equals the fair market value of the boot.[36]

**Example:** If Linda in the above example received $80,000 cash boot, her basis in the 100 shares of XYZ Inc. stock received would be $100,000 ($100,000 equipment basis, plus $80,000 of boot gain recognized, less $80,000 boot received). If Linda received $220,000 of cash boot, her stock basis would be $80,000 ($100,000 equipment basis, plus $200,000 of boot gain recognized, less $220,000 boot received). If Linda received land worth $220,000 as boot, her basis in the stock would still be $80,000 (same calculation as in prior sentence) and her basis in the land would be $220,000, its fair market value.

**d. Rule 4: Shareholder Tacking Rule.** If the property transferred by a shareholder in a 351 transaction is a capital asset or a 1231 trade or business

---

31. I.R.C. § 351(b).
32. I.R.C. § 311(b).
33. I.R.C. §§ 311(a), 351(b)(2).
34. See I.R.C. § 453(f)(6) and Prop. Reg. § 1.453-1(f)(3)(ii).
35. I.R.C. § 358(a)(1).
36. I.R.C. § 358(a)(2).

asset, the shareholder's holding period of the asset is "tacked on" in determining the shareholder's holding period for the stock.[37]

**Example:** In the above example, the equipment transferred by Linda would qualify as a capital or a 1231 asset. If she had held such equipment for two years before the exchange, her holding period in the XYZ Inc. stock would be deemed to be two years when received.

**e. Rule 5: Corporate 1032 Rule.** A corporation recognizes no gain or loss on the receipt of money or property for its stock.[38]

**Example:** In the above example, XYZ Inc. would not recognize any gain or loss when it issues its stock to Linda in exchange for the equipment.

Note that the Corporate 1032 Rule applies even if the exchange does not qualify under section 351. As provided in the Boot Rule, if the corporation transfers other property (boot) in addition to its stock, it must recognize income on any built-in gain on such other property.

**f. Rule 6: Corporate Basis Rule:** A corporation's basis in any property acquired from a shareholder in a 351 exchange equals (i) the shareholder's basis in the property, plus (ii) any gain recognized by the shareholder under the Boot Rule.[39] But if built-in loss property is transferred by a shareholder, the corporation's adjusted basis in all property transferred by that shareholder may not exceed the fair market value of such property unless the corporation and the shareholder agree that the shareholder's basis in the stock shall not exceed the fair market value of the stock.[40]

**Examples:** If Linda in the above example received $80,000 of cash boot, XYZ Inc.'s basis in the equipment it received in the exchange would be $180,000 ($100,000 carryover equipment basis, plus the $80,000 boot gain recognized by Linda). If Linda received $220,000 of cash boot or $220,000 of land boot, XYZ Inc.'s basis in the equipment would be $300,000 (the $100,000 carryover equipment basis, plus the $200,000 boot gain recognized by Linda). Suppose in the example that Linda contributed equipment with a basis of $200,000 and a fair market value of $150,000 in exchange for 100 shares of XYZ Inc. stock. Since there is a built-in loss of $50,000, the corporation's basis in the property would be limited to its $150,000 fair market value. Alternatively, the corporation could have the full $200,000 carryover basis if Linda agreed to reduce her basis in the stock to $150,000, its fair market value.

**Traps.** Traps are triggered by the new basis limitation that kicks in when built-in loss property is transferred in a 351 exchange. The built-in loss determination is based on the aggregate basis and fair market values of all property contributed by a shareholder. Thus, the limitation may be avoided by pumping up the contributed built-in gain property to offset any built-in losses. Plus, great care should be taken before making the alternative election to reduce

---

37.  I.R.C. § 1223(1).
38.  I.R.C. § 1032.
39.  I.R.C. § 362(a).
40.  I.R.C. § 362(e).

the shareholder's outside stock basis, particularly if an S corporation is involved. For example, assume in the above scenario where Linda contributes property with a $50,000 built-in loss that the corporation is an S corporation and the alternative election is made to reduce her stock basis to $150,000, the fair market value of the stock.  If the S corporation sells the equipment for its fair market value of $150,000, a $50,000 loss is recognized and passed through to Linda, further reducing her stock basis to $100,000.  If Linda then sells her stock for its fair market value of $150,000, she recognizes a $50,000 gain that offsets the recognized loss.  The bottom line effect is that the tax benefit of her built-in loss on the equipment is lost completely.  Alternatively, if the election is not made and the corporation takes a reduced basis of $150,000 in the equipment, no loss is recognized on the sale of the equipment for $150,000 and there is no reduction in Linda's stock basis.  A sale of Linda's stock for its value of $150,000 would generate a loss of $50,000 because her stock basis would still be $200,000, her carryover basis in the equipment.  Under this approach, she would recognize a net tax benefit for her $50,000 built-in loss.

**g. Rule 7: Corporate Tacking Rule.**  In a 351 transaction, the shareholder's holding period in the property transferred to the corporation is "tacked on" in determining the corporation's holding period in the asset.[41]

**Example:**  If in the above example Linda held the equipment two years before the exchange, the two years would be tacked on in determining the corporation's holding period.

**h. Rule 8: Assumed Debt Rule.**  A shareholder debt assumed by a corporation in a 351 exchange is not considered boot for gain purposes, but does reduce the shareholder's stock basis.  But if the total of all debts assumed exceeds the basis of all property transferred to the corporation, the excess is treated as taxable boot.[42]

**Example:**  Linda transfers to XYZ Inc. equipment that has a basis of $100,000 and a fair market value of $300,000 and which is encumbered by an $80,000 debt.  In exchange, XYZ Inc. issues Linda 100 shares of its common stock and assumes the $80,000 debt obligation.  Linda recognizes no taxable income because the debt assumption is not treated as boot for gain purposes.  However, Linda's basis in the stock is only $20,000 (her $100,000 basis in the equipment less the debt assumed by XYZ Inc.).  If the debt assumed by XYZ Inc. was $120,000, Linda would recognize $20,000 of income (the excess of the debt over her basis in the equipment), and her basis in the stock would be zero (her $100,000 basis in the equipment, plus the $20,000 gain recognized, and less the $120,000 debt assumed).

**Traps:**  The Assumed Debt Rule has a number of potential traps, including the following:

**(1) Tax Avoidance Purpose.**  The debt assumed by the corporation will be treated as taxable boot if the shareholder's principal purpose was tax avoidance

41.  I.R.C. § 1223(2).
42.  I.R.C. §§ 357(a) & (c), 358(d).

and not a bona fide business purpose.[43]  This trap usually surfaces when a shareholder loads an asset with debt just prior to the transfer.  If the bad purpose exists for a single assumed debt, its taint will extend to all debt that is assumed in the exchange.[44]  The burden is on the shareholder to prove a bona fide business purpose by a clear preponderance of the evidence.[45]  For planning purposes, care should be taken to ensure that no assumed debts have recently been incurred and to document in written director's resolutions the business rationale for the corporation's assumption of the debts.

**(2) Lingering Shareholder Liability.**  If the shareholder remains liable for the debt, the corporation will still be deemed to have assumed the debt if, based on all facts and circumstances, the corporation is expected to satisfy the debt.[46]  The planning challenge is to leave no doubt as to the parties' expectation as to who is going to pay off the debt.  In the situation where the debt exceeds the basis of assets transferred and the shareholder does not want to recognize any taxable income, the preferred option may be to clarify that the shareholder, not the corporation, is expected to pay the debt.  The unique circumstances of each situation need to be evaluated.  The key is to decide on a course of action and then remove all ambiguities through the documentation.

**(3) Nonrecourse Debts.**  Nonrecourse debts are deemed to be assumed by the corporation if the assets transferred to the corporation are encumbered by the debts.  If the debts also are secured by assets not transferred to the corporation, the amount assumed by the corporation is reduced by the lesser of (i) the fair market value of such other assets or (ii) the portion of the debt agreed to be satisfied out of such other assets.[47]  The planning challenge is to specify the amount to be paid out of the other assets while assuring that the amount does not exceed the value of the outside assets.  This provides an opportunity to reduce the assumed amount to avoid a liability-in-excess-of-basis problem.

**(4) Future Accountable Debts.**  A debt assumed by a corporation in a 351 exchange is not considered boot and is not subject to the Assumed Debt Rule if payment of the debt would create a tax deduction for the corporation or be treated as a capital expenditure by the corporation.[48]  Examples include accounts payable of a cash basis shareholder and environmental liabilities that were never accounted for by the transferring shareholder.  The rationale is that such an item should not be considered an assumed debt because it was never taken into account by the shareholder before the transfer.

**(5) Basis Pumping.**  Where the assumed liabilities will exceed the basis of the transferred assets, one option to avoid the recognition of income is to contribute more cash or other assets and increase the basis of the transferred assets.  A few courts have even recognized the validity of a shareholder

---

**43.** I.R.C. § 357(b).
44. Reg. § 1.357-1(c).
45. I.R.C. § 357(b)(2).
46. See, e.g., Seggerman Farms, Inc. v. Commissioner, 308 F.3d 803 (7th Cir. 2002); Owen v. Commissioner, 881 F.2d 832 (9th Cir. 1989), cert. denied 493 U.S. 1070 (1990); Smith v. Commissioner, 84 T.C. 889 (1985), affirmed 805 F.2d 1073 (D.C. Cir. 1986).
47. I.R.C. § 357(d).
48. I.R.C. § 357(c); Rev. Rule 95-74, 1995-2 C.B. 36.

increasing the basis by transferring a personal note to the corporation and claiming that the basis of the note is its face amount.[49] This personal note technique pushes the outer-limits of basis pumping and may trigger a dispute with the Service.

## 2. FORMATION EQUITY FOR SERVICE

Often one or more owners are transferred an equity interest in a new enterprise in return for services that have been rendered or will be rendered in the future. As we saw above, such an interest may create a big 351 problem for all the contributing shareholders in a corporate context if it is too large. Chapter 11 of this book analyzes and discusses the planning factors and strategies that need to be considered whenever equity interests or rights are transferred to key employees. This discussion focuses on the narrower planning options for transferring equity interests to service owners during the formation process. Following is a brief description of five scenarios.

**a. The 83(a) Scenario.** XYZ Inc. is formed by Larry and Sue transferring $900,000 of cash and property to the corporation in return for 900 shares of common stock. Linda is transferred 100 shares of XYZ Inc. common stock in return for her promise to manage the company. Assuming the stock has a value of $1,000 a share, Linda recognizes $100,000 of income in the year she receives her stock under section 83(a). [50] XYZ Inc. is entitled to a $100,000 ordinary business expense deduction in year one when Linda recognizes the income.[51]

**b. The Deferral Scenario.** Linda does not want a tax hit on $100,000 of phantom income (income with no cash) in year one. Plus, Larry and Sue do not want Linda to keep her stock if her employment is terminated during the first four years. So the stock transferred to Linda is subject to a forfeiture restriction that kicks in if her employment comes to an end for any reason other than death or disability during the first four years. This restriction is a "substantial risk of forfeiture" that defers the recognition of any taxable income to Linda (and corresponding corporate deduction) so long as it is in effect.[52] That's the good news for Linda. The bad news is that she could lose her stock and, if she doesn't lose her stock, her phantom taxable income at the end of year four is based on the fair market value of the stock at that time. So if the share value has appreciated to $4,000 a share when the restriction lapses at the end of year four, Linda will have to recognize $400,000 of ordinary taxable income, and XYZ Inc. will get a corresponding ordinary business expense deduction. A restriction will constitute a "substantial risk of forfeiture" and trigger the deferral only if it "requires future performance of substantial services." [53] A forfeiture restriction based upon the commission of a felony or some other bad act won't do the job.[54]

---

49. Peracchi v. Commissioner, 143 F.3d 487 (9th Cir. 1998); Lessinger v. Commissioner, 872 F.2d 519 (2d Cir. 1989).

50. I.R.C. § 83(a).

51. I.R.C. § 83(h). Note, however, that if the service provided is capital in nature, the corporation will have to capitalize the expenditure. Reg. § 1.83-6(a)(4).

52. I.R.C. §§ 83(a) & (h). The restriction also must prevent the shareholder from transferring the stock free of the restriction. Reg. § 1.83-3(d).

53. I.R.C. § 83(c)(1).

54. Reg. § 1.83-3(c)(2).

**c.  The 83(b) Scenario.**  Linda decides that she would prefer to take her tax lumps in year one so that any future growth in the stock will only be taxed at capital gains rates when she sells the stock.  XYZ Inc., Larry and Sue decide that they still want the forfeiture restriction for the first four years just in case Linda takes a hike or doesn't measure up.  Linda may elect under section 83(b) to recognize the $100,000 income in year one even though there is a forfeiture restriction.  If Linda makes the election, the corporation gets a corresponding deduction.[55]  The election must be made within 30 days of the transfer.  There is a harsh risk under this scenario; if the forfeiture provision is triggered and Linda loses the stock, she gets no deduction in the year of the loss.[56]  She will have paid tax on $100,000 of phantom taxable income and received nothing of value.  Despite this ugly risk, many opt for the 83(b) election when the going-in stock value is low and the prospects for big appreciation in the early years look good.

**d.  The Year One Gross-Up Scenario.**  Linda is going to take the tax hit in year one either because there is no forfeiture restriction (Scenario One) or there is such a provision and she has made an 83(b) election (Scenario Three).  But she does not want to bear the burden of the tax hit.  She argues that it is unfair for her to have to pay taxes when she has received no cash while the corporation gets a windfall cash tax benefit for issuing stock.  She uses her leverage and the strength of the argument to secure a gross-up cash payment from the corporation.  Essentially, the corporation agrees to use the cash benefit from its deduction to pay Linda a cash bonus to cover her tax hit on the stock and the cash bonus.  With marginal corporate rates in the 34 to 35 percent range after the low-end brackets (brackets for the first $75,000 of earnings) and top individual marginal rates in the 33 percent to 35 percent range, such a gross-up cash bonus can often be made with no after-tax cash cost to the corporation.  The formula for calculating the gross-up cash bonus is as follows:

$$[\text{Stock Value}/(1 - \text{Executive Marginal Tax Rate})] - \text{Stock Value} = \text{Gross-Up Bonus}$$

Assuming Linda is in a 33 percent marginal tax bracket, the formula would produce a gross-up bonus of $49,254 [[$100,000/(1 - .33)] - $100,000].  If the corporation is subject to a 34 percent marginal rate, the cash tax savings to the corporation will be $50,746 (34 percent of $149,254), which more than covers the cash bonus to Linda.  As an alternative to such a gross-up bonus, the corporation could offer to use its tax cash savings to loan Linda the funds needed to cover her tax hit in the year of recognition, with the understanding that the loan amount plus accrued interest would be repaid when Linda sells or forfeits the stock.  Obviously, Linda would much prefer the bonus structure.  We will see opportunities to use this gross-up concept many times in following chapters.

**e.  Deferral Gross-Up Scenario.**  Linda is not going to recognize any taxable income until the end of year four when the forfeiture period ends (Scenario Two).  Her taxable income and the corresponding corporate deduction

---

55.  I.R.C. § 83(b).
56.  I.R.C. § 83(b).

will be measured by the value of the stock at that time. But under this scenario, Linda uses her leverage to negotiate the payment of a gross-up bonus at that time. If she is subject to a marginal tax rate of 33 percent and the stock value at that time is $400,000, the cash gross-up bonus to cover her tax hit would equal $197,015 under the formula. If the corporation's marginal tax rate is 34 percent, its cash tax savings at the end of year four will be $202,985 (34 percent of $597,015), which more than covers the cash bonus to Linda.

### 3. THE SHAREHOLDER DEBT CRAPSHOOT

In C corporation formations, shareholders often conclude that it is advantageous from a tax perspective to receive corporate debt in return for a significant portion of the money they contribute to the enterprise. Take Sam, Dick and Joy, golfers who each agree to contribute $500,000 to a start-up corporation that they believe will "quickly take off." One option is to receive only common stock for their contributions. They each end up owning one third of the equity, and all cash distributions to them will be taxed as double-taxed dividends.[57] Suppose instead that they each receive stock for $100,000 of their contributed capital and corporate notes for the additional $400,000. They still each own one third of the equity, with equal voting rights and value appreciation rights. But the tax impacts of cash distributions as the business "takes off" have changed dramatically if (and it's a big "if") the debt works.

First, the double tax hit is gone because the interest payments on the shareholder debt are deductible by the corporation.[58] Even though interest is taxed to the shareholders at ordinary rates instead of the favorable dividends rates, the net tax cost between the corporation and the shareholders will still be reduced in nearly all situations. If the corporation is subject to a 34 percent marginal rate (a likely result if it is profitable)[59] and the shareholders are subject to a 33 percent marginal rate, the tax benefit realized by the corporation from the interest deductions will exceed the tax cost to the shareholders. Second (and here's the really big deal), the principal balance of the debt ($400,000 for each shareholder) can be paid off tax free to the shareholder as a return of capital. This gives the corporation the capacity to repay 80 percent of the contributed capital free of any double tax hit. Any such payments to a shareholder in redemption of a portion of his or her stock would almost certainly be taxed as a dividend, particularly if the payments were pro rata among the shareholders.[60] Finally (and of less significance), the need to repay the shareholder debt may constitute a "reasonable business need" for accumulating income in the C corporation and, thereby, help avoid the accumulated earnings tax.[61]

Will it work? Maybe. Obviously, the IRS has an interest in trying to characterize the shareholder debt as equity for tax purposes. This re-characterization fight has been the subject of countless cases. What has emerged is a body of vague muss, characterized as a "jungle" by one court[62] and a "viper's

---

57. I.R.C. § 1(h)(11).
58. I.R.C. § 163(a).
59. The 34 percent rate kicks in once income exceed $75,000. I.R.C. § 11(b).
60. I.R.C. § 302(b).
61. Reg. § 1.537-2(b)(3).
62. See Commissioner v. Union Mutual Insurance Co. of Providence, 386 F.2d 974, 978 (1st Cir. 1967).

tangle" by the leading commentator.[63]  We do know that greed – pushing the concept too far – promises problems.  We also know that key factors in assessing the greed include the debt-to-equity ratio (the higher, the riskier), the real intent of the parties (as manifested by the terms of the documents and the capacity of the company to service and discharge the debt), proportionality among shareholders (the more proportionality, the more it is suspect), equity conversion rights (usually a killer), and subordination of the debt to other creditors (hurts, but not fatal).[64]

As the courts wrestled with the issue, Congress tried to offer some clarity by enacting Section 385 as part of the comprehensive Tax Reform Act of 1969, heralded as the 1969 Act's "most important" provision[65] because it empowered the Treasury to promulgate definitive regulations for determining whether and when a shareholder debt instrument would be treated as debt or equity. Temporary regulations came 11 years later, followed by permanent regulations, but then (over the cries of too many) all was withdrawn and the effort abandoned in 1983.[66]  Nothing has happened since, suggesting that even the Treasury, specifically empowered by Congress, couldn't create acceptable standards that bring certainty to the muss.

So the muss remains.  This does not mean that shareholder debt should not be used in C corporation planning; the advantages are powerful.  It means that care and prudence are required, along with the willingness of the client to live with a little uncertainty and risk.  For planning purposes, there are a few semi-bright lights that have emerged from case law and the aborted 385 regulation effort that help in structuring shareholder debt that doesn't cross over the line. First, any hybrid equity characteristics, such as equity conversion rights, contingent interest obligations, or interest obligations tied to profitability, will kill any debt as debt for tax purposes.[67]  They just can't exist.  Second, the debt-to-equity ratio is often the key factor in determining if the debt is "excessive." Under the old 385 regulations, the "excessive" tag was avoided if the outside debt-to-equity ratio (based on all liabilities of the corporation) did not exceed 10-to-1 and the inside debt-to-equity ratio (based only on the shareholder debt) did not exceed 3-to-1.[68]  Third, the intent of the parties to treat the debt as real debt requires that the debt instrument be a commercially "normal" debt instrument (unconditional promise to pay, sum certain, payment dates certain, reasonable interest rate, etc.) and that there is a reasonable basis (supported by reasonable projections, one would hope) for concluding that the corporation will have no problem timely making all payments due under the debt instrument.  Fourth, shareholder debt that is proportional among the shareholders is highly suspect, but not necessarily deadly.  It has a chance if it is issued for cash or property, bears a reasonable rate of interest, satisfies the old 385 regulation's debt-to-equity

---

63. Bittker & Eustice, Federal Income Taxation of Corporations and Shareholders ¶ 4.04 (4th ed. 1979).
64. See, e.g., Hariton, "Essay: Distinguishing Between Equity and Debt in the New Financial Environment," 49 Tax L. Rev. 499 (1994).
65. Bittker & Eustice, Federal Income Taxation of Corporations and Shareholders ¶ 4.05 (3rd ed. 1971).
66. T.D. 7920, 48 Fed. Reg. 31054 (July 6, 1983).  The temporary regulations were published in 45 Fed. Reg. 18957 (1980) and the final regulations in 45 Fed. Reg. 86438 (1980).
67. Prop. Reg. §§ 1.385-3(d), 1.385-0(c)(2).
68. Prop. Reg. §§ 1.385-6(f)(2).

safe harbors (10-to-1 and 3-to-1), and has all the appropriate "intent" trappings.[69] Fifth, subordination of shareholder debt to outside creditors should not be fatal if all other factors are solid, but it can become a big negative if the "intent" issue is equivocal or the debt-to-equity ratios are at or beyond the outer limits. Finally, no matter how safely the debt is structured, the client should be advised of the inherent uncertainties and the importance of treating the debt as real debt.

## PROBLEM 4-D

**4-D**. Lucy has operated a successful Italian import supply business as a sole proprietor for five years. She now plans to dramatically expand her business. To this end, she has lined up some new capital and developed the following plan:

1. She will form a C corporation that will have four shareholders: Lucy, Jim, Sue and Dave.

2. Lucy will contribute to the corporation accounts receivable that have a value of $100,000 and a basis of zero. She will be issued 100 shares of common stock in return.

3. Jim will contribute $100,000 cash in return for 100 shares.

4. Sue, a recognized expert in Italian goods, will sign a five-year agreement to manage the business. As a signing bonus, she will be issued 100 shares of stock.

5. Dave will contribute a warehouse to the corporation in return for 100 shares of stock. The warehouse has a value of $500,000, a mortgage balance of $400,000, and a tax basis of $250,000. The company will assume the mortgage.

6. Each of the four shareholders also will loan the company $450,000. The loan, plus interest at prime, will be paid off in monthly installments over a ten-year period. No payments will be due the first twelve months, then interest-only payments will be due for three years, and then the principal plus interest will be amortized over a six-year period. The projections show that the company should have no problem with this payment schedule if things go as planned.

Advise Lucy on the tax impacts of her plan. What changes would you suggest? Why? How would your advice change if Lucy plans to use an S corporation, not a C corporation?

---

69. Prop. Reg. §§ 1.385-6.

# CHAPTER 5

# CORE PARTNERSHIP AND LLC ISSUES

---

## A. THE CHALLENGE

A planning lawyer must know the basics of partnerships (there are four types) and limited liability companies. These entities are essential planning tools for many successful businesses and families. Although LLCs continue to grow in popularity, a partnership option still emerges as the preferred candidate in many choice-of-entity analyses. An extended choice-of-entity planning discussion is provided Chapter 3.

Section B of this chapter briefly examines the often intolerable risks of undocumented partnerships. It illustrates the downside disasters of no planning – when the passion to get the business going trumps efforts to properly set up the entity.

The discussion then turns to the statutory schemes for the various entity types. Since 1914, uniform acts have been developed as needed to help states enact comprehensive acts dealing with partnerships and LLCs. Although states typically modify select uniform act provisions during the legislative process, this ongoing uniform act effort has had a powerful impact in promoting consistency between the states. Section C of this chapter summarizes the latest uniform act provisions for LLCs and the various types of partnerships. The hope is that this summary discussion, coupled with Problems 5-A through 5-D, will help students understand the core legal underpinnings of the various entity types and the primary differences between them.

Section D of this chapter examines the tax challenges of forming a partnership or an LLC that is taxed as a partnership. It is the partnership/LLC counterpart to the corporation formation tax discussion in the previous chapter.

Section E of this chapter focuses on the all-important operating agreement between the partners or LLC members. With limited exceptions, this document can establish the entire deal between the parties and preempt all statutory default rules. The smart customization of this document is the primary planning challenge during the organizational process. From the planning lawyer's perspective, it requires an understanding of core legal principles, the ability to help parties identify and prioritize operational issues of concern, and careful attention to detail. The ignorant use of forms can be dangerous. That said, this section illustrates this planning challenge by discussing the purposes and options of key provisions of the LLC operating agreement form that is included in Chapter 18.

Details relating to family partnerships and LLCs are the subject of section B of Chapter 16, partly in recognition of the fact that most businesses in the U.S. are dominated by a single family.[1] As explained in that discussion, partnerships and LLCs often are used to accomplish niche objectives as part of an overall business and family plan to protect and transition wealth.

# B. UNDOCUMENTED PARTNERSHIP RISKS

## PROBLEM 5-A

Answer the questions raised in the following two scenarios based on your reading of the *Holmes* case and the statutory descriptive materials that follow.

### SCENARIO ONE:

There are three components to a golf club; the grip, the shaft, and the head. Tool Swing Inc. ("Tool"), owned by Pete Mack, is a specialty manufacturer of clubs. Many around Pete consider him "rich."

Duke, Pete's neighbor, is a struggling scientist. Pete describes Duke as "a materials nut who has never swung a golf club but who has developed the perfect plastic composite for a golf grip." Pete claims that Duke's grip produces a "feel" unlike anything on the market, weighs "virtually nothing," and has a natural "tackiness" that assures no slippage in rain or in the toughest competition.

Pete calls Duke's discovery the "Ghost Grip". With Duke's permission, Pete has tested the "Ghost Grip" with 30 top professionals. All of the professionals enthusiastically endorsed the grip on the spot and requested permission to use it on their clubs.

Pete provided Duke $62,000 to cover third-party expenses incurred in developing the Ghost Grip. Pete also paid an additional $24,000 to test the grip with industry experts and professionals. Duke has always provided Pete with an accounting for all sums spent and has regularly asked Pete about documenting the money advances. Pete would always respond by saying, "Let's not get tangled up in paperwork now. Once this thing is perfected, I will take it to the moon, and we will both make a killing."

Pete and Duke never signed any document or discussed the specifics of their relationship.

---

1. Some estimate that nearly 80 percent of U.S. businesses are family-dominated. See, generally, R. Duman, "Family Firms Are Different," Entrepreneurship Theory and Practice, 1992, pp. 13–21; and M. F. R. Kets de Vries, "The Dynamics of Family Controlled Firms: The Good News and the Bad News," Organizational Dynamics, 1993, pp. 59–71; W. G. Dyer, Cultural Change in Family Firms, Jossey–Bass, San Francisco, 1986; and P. L. Rosenblatt, M. R. Anderson and P. Johnson, The Family in Business, Jossey–Bass, San Francisco, 1985; Arthur Anderson/Mass Mutual, American Family Business Survey, 2002.

Last Monday, Duke visited Pete's home and delivered Pete a check for $92,000. The memo on the check read, "Loan repayment in full, plus interest at a rate of 12% per annum." Duke thanked Pete and explained that he had just sold all rights in the Ghost Grip to Nike for $7.8 million. Pete went berserk and mutilated the check in a rage.

Was a partnership created between Duke and Pete? What additional facts might help in making a determination? If a partnership was created, what are Pete's rights?

### SCENARIO TWO:

Jake and Luke teamed up to import and sell a line of special yachts produced in Italy. Jake's sole obligation was to provide the start-up capital of $125,000. He spent the balance of his time teaching law school. Their documentation consisted of a few emails that confirmed that they would equally share the profits.

Luke was the driving force behind the effort. He lined up a design and manufacturing firm in Italy, developed super-slick marketing materials, and started hustling customers for pre-orders. He ultimately collected $1.4 million in "advances" from nine customers located in seven different states. Luke regularly advised Jake that Jake's investment and the pre-order advances provided all the capital that was required to launch the business. He would exclaim, "Once the yachts start arriving, we will be gold."

Last month, Luke's wife and young daughter died in a tragic automobile accident. Devastated, Luke left the country and absconded with roughly $1.3 million, having spent only $225,000 on advances to the Italian company and marketing related expenses. The yacht venture instantly collapsed.

The nine customers soon learned of Luke's departure. They are claiming that Jake must repay them the amount of their advances, plus interest. If they are right, Jake will be forced into bankruptcy.

Is Jake personally liable to the nine customers? Would he be personally liable if Jake and Luke had formed a limited liability company? How about a limited partnership, with Luke as the general partner and Jake as the limited partner? How about a limited liability partnership?

### HOLMES v. LERNER
88 Cal.Rptr.2d 130 (Cal.App. 1999)

MARCHIANO, J.

This case involves an oral partnership agreement to start a cosmetics company known as "Urban Decay." Patricia Holmes prevailed on her claim that Sandra Kruger Lerner breached her partnership agreement and that David Soward interfered with the Holmes-Lerner contract, resulting in Holmes's ouster from the business. Lerner and Soward appeal from the judgment finding them liable to Holmes for compensatory and punitive damages of over $1 million. Holmes appeals from the portion of the judgment imposing joint and several liability for the award of compensatory damages, and the court's order granting a nonsuit on various causes of action against Soward.

Sandra Lerner is a successful entrepreneur and an experienced business person. By the time of trial in this matter, Lerner was extremely wealthy. Patricia Holmes met Lerner in late 1993, when Lerner visited Holmes's horse training facility to arrange for training and boarding of two horses that Lerner was importing from England.

On July 31, 1995, the two women returned from England and stayed at Lerner's West Hollywood condominium while they waited for the horses to clear quarantine. While sitting at the kitchen table, they discussed nail polish, and colors. Len Bosack, Lerner's husband, was in and out of the room during the conversations. For approximately an hour and a half, Lerner and Holmes worked with the colors in a nail kit to try to create a different shade of purple. Holmes then said that she wanted to call the purple color she had made "Plague." Holmes had been reading about 16th-century England, and how people with the plague developed purple sores, and she thought the color looked like the plague sores. Lerner and Holmes discussed the fact that the names they were creating had an urban theme, and tried to think of other names to fit the theme. Len Bosack walked into the kitchen at that point, heard the conversation about the urban theme, and said "What about decay?" The two women liked the idea, and decided that "Urban Decay" was a good name for their concept.

Lerner said to Holmes: "This seems like a good [thing], it's something that we both like, and isn't out there. Do you think we should start a company?" Holmes responded: "Yes, I think it's a great idea." Lerner told Holmes that they would have to do market research and determine how to have the polishes produced, and that there were many things they would have to do. Lerner said: "We will hire people to work for us. We will do everything we can to get the company going, and then we'll be creative, and other people will do the work, so we'll have time to continue riding the horses." Holmes agreed that they would do those things. They did not separate out which tasks each of them would do, but planned to do it all together.

Although neither of the two women had any experience in the cosmetics business, they began work on their idea immediately. In early August, they met with a graphic artist, Andrea Kelly, and discussed putting together a logo and future advertising work for Urban Decay.

Prior to the first scheduled August meeting, Holmes told Lerner she was concerned about financing the venture. Lerner told her not to worry about it because Lerner thought they could convince Soward that the nail polish business would be a good investment. She told Holmes that Soward took care of Lerner's investment money. Holmes and Lerner discussed their plans for the company, and agreed that they would attempt to build it up and then sell it. Lerner and Holmes discussed the need to visit chemical companies and hire people to handle the daily operations of the company. However, the creative aspect, ideas, inspiration, and impetus for the company came from Holmes and Lerner.

On January 11, 1996, Lerner and Holmes met at a coffee shop. Holmes explained that she wanted "something in writing" and an explanation of her interest and position in the company. Lerner responded that a start-up business is "like a freight train ... you can either run and catch up, and get on, and take a piece of this company and make it your own, or get out of the way." As a result of this conversation, Holmes decided to double her efforts on behalf of Urban Decay. Because she was most comfortable working at the warehouse, she focused on that aspect of the business. Holmes was reimbursed for mileage, but received no pay for her work.

During January and February, Urban Decay was launching its new nail polish product. Publicity included press releases, brochures, and newspaper interviews with Lerner. An early press release stated: "The idea for Urban Decay was born after Lerner and her horse trainer, Pat Holmes, were sitting around in the English countryside." Lerner approved the press release. In February of 1996, an article was printed in the San Francisco Examiner containing the following quotes from Lerner. "Since we couldn't find good nail polish, in cool colors there must be a business opportunity here. Pat had the original idea. Urban Decay was my spin." The Examiner reporter testified at trial that the quote attributed to Lerner was accurate. Lerner was also interviewed in April by CNN. In that interview she told the story of herself and Holmes looking for unusual colors, mixing their own colors at the kitchen table, and that "we came up with the colors, and it just sort of suggested the urban thing."

Lerner had always notified Holmes whenever there was a board meeting, and she sent Holmes an agenda for the February 20, 1996 meeting. Lerner also sent a memo stating that she thought they should have an "operations meeting" with the warehouse supervisor first. Lerner's memo continued: "and then have a regular board meeting, including [Zomnir], me, David, and Pat, and no one else." Holmes understood that the regular board meeting would be for the purpose of discussing general Urban Decay business. At the operations meeting, Holmes made a presentation regarding the warehouse operations. The financial report showed $205,000 in revenues and $431,000 in expenses. The "directors" thought this early sales figure was "terrific." Soward handed out an organizational chart, which showed Lerner, with the title "CEO" at the top; Soward, as "President" beneath her; and Zomnir, as "COO" beneath Soward. Holmes asked "Where am I?" Lerner responded by pointing to the top of the chart and telling Holmes that she was a director, and was at the top of the chart, above all the other names.

In March of 1996, Holmes received a document from Soward offering her a 1 percent ownership interest in Urban Decay. Soward explained that Urban Decay had been formed as a limited liability company, which was owned by its members. For the first time, Holmes realized that Lerner and Soward had produced an organizational document that did not include her, and she was now being asked to become a minor partner. When she studied the document, she discovered that it referred to an exhibit A, which was purported to show the distribution of ownership interests in Urban Decay. Soward had given Zomnir a copy of exhibit A when he offered her an ownership interest in Urban Decay. However, when Holmes asked Soward for a copy of exhibit A, he told her it did not exist. By this time, Holmes was planning to consult an attorney about the document.

Despite the deterioration of her friendship with Lerner, and her strained relationship with Soward, Holmes continued to attend the scheduled board meetings, hoping that her differences with Lerner could be resolved. She also continued to work at the warehouse on various administrative projects and on direct mail order sales. As late as the April board meeting, Holmes was still actively engaged in Urban Decay business. She made a presentation on a direct mail project she had been asked to undertake. As a result of Holmes's attendance at a sales presentation when she referred to herself as a cofounder of Urban Decay, Lerner instructed Zomnir to draft a dress code and an official history of Urban Decay. Lerner told Zomnir that it was a "real error in judgment" to allow Holmes to attend the sales presentation because she did not project the appropriate image. The official history, proposed in the memo, omitted any reference to Holmes. Finally, matters deteriorated to the point that Soward told Holmes not to attend the July board meeting because she was no longer welcome at Urban Decay.

On August 27, 1996, Holmes filed a complaint against Lerner and Soward, alleging 10 causes of action, including breach of an oral contract, intentional interference with contractual relations, fraud, breach of fiduciary duty, and constructive fraud. Holmes eventually dismissed some of her claims and the court dismissed others. At the trial, cosmetics industry expert Gabriella Zuckerman testified that Urban Decay was not just a fad. In her opinion, Urban Decay had discovered and capitalized on a trend that was just beginning. She reviewed projected sales figures of $19.9 million in 1997, going up to $52 million in 2003, and found them definitely obtainable. Arthur Clark, Holmes's expert at valuing start-up businesses, valued Urban Decay under different risk scenarios. In Clark's opinion, the value of Urban Decay to a potential buyer was between $4,672,000 and $6,270,000. Lerner's expert, who had never valued a cosmetics company, testified that Urban Decay had $2.7 million in sales in 1996. He estimated the value of Urban Decay as approximately $2 million, but concluded that it was not marketable.

Lerner and Soward claimed that Holmes was never a director, officer, or even an employee of Urban Decay. According to Lerner, she was just being nice to Holmes by letting her be present during Urban Decay business. Lerner denied Holmes had any role in creating the colors, names, or concepts for Urban Decay. When Holmes asked Lerner about her assets and liabilities in Urban Decay, Lerner thought she was asking for a job. She explained her statements to the press regarding Urban Decay being Holmes's idea as misquotes or the product of her stress.

The jury found in favor of Holmes on every cause of action. The jury assessed $480,000 in damages against Lerner, and $320,000 against Soward. Following presentation of evidence as to net worth, the jury awarded punitive damages of $500,000 against Lerner and $130,000 against Soward. In the judgment, the court declined to add the two amounts together, but stated that the verdict of $320,000 was against Lerner and Soward, jointly and severally, and that the additional $160,000 verdict was against Lerner individually. Lerner and Soward moved for a judgment notwithstanding the verdict, which was denied on

December 16, 1997.

Lerner and Soward argue that there was no partnership agreement as a matter of law, that the evidence was insufficient to support the fraud judgment against Lerner, that damages were incorrectly calculated, that the evidence does not support the judgment against Soward and that the judgment for punitive damages must be reversed. In the consolidated appeal, Holmes argues that the trial court erred in granting a nonsuit on various causes of action and in awarding a lesser amount of damages than was reflected in the jury verdict.

Holmes testified that she and Lerner did not discuss sharing profits of the business during the July 31, "kitchen table" conversation. Throughout the case, Lerner and Soward have contended that without an agreement to share profits, there can be no partnership.

The UPA provides for the situation in which the partners have not expressly stated an agreement regarding sharing of profits. Former section 15018 provided in relevant part: "The rights and duties of the partners in relation to the partnership shall be determined, subject to any agreement between them, by the following rules: (a) Each partner shall ... share equally in the profits and surplus remaining after all liabilities, including those to partners, are satisfied." This provision states, subject to an agreement between the parties, partners "shall" share equally in the profits. Lerner and Soward argue that using former section 15018 to supply a missing term regarding profit sharing ignores the provision of former section 15007, subdivision (2). That section, headed "rules for determining existence of partnership," provided that mere joint ownership of common property "does not of itself establish a partnership, whether such co-owners do or do not share any profits made by the use of the property." Lerner and Soward are mistaken. The definition in former section 15006 provides that the association with the intent to carry on a business for profit is the essential requirement for a partnership. Following that definition does not transform mere joint ownership into the essence of a partnership.

The trial court in this case refused to add additional elements to the statutory definition and properly instructed the jury in the language of former section 15006. We agree with the trial court's interpretation of the law. The actual sharing of profits (with exceptions which do not apply here) is prima facie evidence, which is to be considered, in light of any other evidence, when determining if a partnership exists. In this case, there were no profits to share at the time Holmes was expelled from the business, so the evidentiary provision of former section 15007, subdivision (4) is not applicable. According to former section 15006, parties who expressly agree to associate as co-owners with the intent to carry on a business for profit, have established a partnership. Once the elements of that definition are established, other provisions of the UPA and the conduct of the parties supply the details of the agreement. Certainly implicit in the Holmes-Lerner agreement to operate Urban Decay together was an understanding to share in profits and losses as any business owners would. The evidence supported the jury's implicit finding that Holmes birthed an idea which was incubated jointly by Lerner and Holmes, from which they intended to profit once it was fully matured in their company.

Lerner and Soward argue that the agreement between Lerner and Holmes was too indefinite to be enforced. The cases they rely on do not support the argument. For example, in *Weddington Productions, Inc.* v. *Flick* (1998) 60 Cal.App.4th 793 [71 Cal.Rptr.2d 265], the court reversed an order enforcing a settlement agreement imposed by a mediator against the will of one of the parties. The issue was the lack of a meeting of the minds as to settlement. The court described the degree of certainty that is necessary to enforce a contract. "The parties' outward manifestations must show that the parties all agreed upon the same thing in the same sense. If there is no evidence establishing a manifestation of assent to the 'same thing' by both parties, then there is no mutual consent to contract and no contract formation." 60 Cal.App.4th at p. 811.) "The terms of a contract are reasonably certain if they provide a basis for determining the existence of a breach and for giving an appropriate remedy." *Ibid.* The evidence produced at trial in this case supplied the requisite degree of certainty described in *Weddington*.

The agreement between Holmes and Lerner was to take Holmes's idea and reduce it to concrete form. They decided to do it together, to form a company, to hire employees, and to engage in the entire process together. The agreement here, as presented to the jury, was that Holmes and Lerner would start a cosmetics company based on the unusual colors developed by Holmes, identified by the urban theme and the exotic names. The agreement is evidenced by Lerner's statements: "We will do ... everything," "[i]t's going to be our baby, and we're going to work on it together." Their agreement is reflected in Lerner's words: "We will hire people to work for us." "We will do ... everything we can to get the company going, and then we'll be creative, and other people will do the work, so we'll have time to continue riding the horses." The additional terms were filled in as the two women immediately began work on the multitude of details necessary to bring their idea to fruition. The fact that Holmes worked for almost a year, without expectation of pay, is further confirmation of the agreement. Lerner and Soward never objected to her work, her participation in board meetings and decision making, or her exercise of authority over the retail warehouse operation. Holmes was not seeking specific enforcement of a single vague term of the agreement. She was frozen out of the business altogether, and her agreement with Lerner was completely renounced. The agreement that was made and the subsequent acts of the parties supply sufficient certainty to determine the existence of a breach and a remedy.

## NON-PARTNERSHIP ARRANGEMENTS

A "partnership" will be deemed to exist when there is association of two or more persons who carry on a business as co-owners for profit, whether or not they intend to form a partnership. Property co-ownership alone doesn't meet the definition. Thus, a joint tenancy, tenancy in common, tenancy by the entireties, joint property, or common property arrangement generally is not deemed a partnership even if the co-owners share profits made by the use of the property. Similarly, an arrangement to share gross returns, even when the sharing parties have a joint or common interest in the property that generates the returns, doesn't rise to the level of a partnership. Under the Revised Uniform Partnership Act, a person who receives a share of the profits from a business is presumed to be a partner, but not if the profits are received in payment:

- of a debt by installments or otherwise.

- for services as an independent contractor or of wages or other compensation to an employee.

- of rent.

- of an annuity or other retirement or health benefit to a beneficiary, representative, or designee of a deceased or retired partner.

- of interest or other charge on a loan, even if the amount of payment varies with the profits of the business.

- for the sale of the goodwill of a business or other property by installments or otherwise.

# C. STATUTORY NUTS AND BOLTS

## 1. PARTNERSHIPS

The partnership is the oldest form of business entity between multiple parties. Its history predates corporations and business trusts. And it is the historical foundation for all the "limiteds": limited partnership, limited liability partnership, limited liability limited partnership, and limited liability company. Partnership statutes have been around for over 2,000 years, being tracked to King Khammurabi of Babylon.[2]

A partnership is formed when there is "an association of two or more persons to carry on as co-owners a business for profit..., whether or not the persons intend to form a partnership."[3] Two distinct theories have been forever advanced to explain the nature of a partnership: an "entity" theory that focuses on a partnership being separate and apart from its owners, and an "aggregate" theory that views a partnership as an amalgamation of owner rights and interests and deemphasizes the separateness of the entity.

Focusing on the underpinnings and reach of these theories does little to advance one's understanding of partnership law because both theories are evidenced in state statutory schemes. The reason is that all states, except Louisiana, have based their partnership statutes on the Uniform Partnership Act ("UPA"), first published in 1914. The latest version, known as the Revised Uniform Partnership Act ("RUPA"), was released in 1997 and has been adopted by 37 states. While the RUPA favors the entity theory, evidence of the aggregate theory shows up throughout the RUPA in issues dealing with owners' liability for a partnership's debts, the impact of an owner's disassociation from a partnership, and more.

---

2. 1 Reed Rowley, Rowley on Partnership 2 (2d ed. 1960)
3. RUPA § 202(a).

Following Problem 5-B is a recap of the key provisions of the RUPA that have been adopted in most states.

## PROBLEM 5-B

Son developed a unique internet marketing strategy (the "Strategy") that could be worth millions. He asked Dad to "invest" $50,000 to "get the business going." Dad transferred the $50,000 to Son, and Son insisted that Dad sign a document that simply stated, "I will run the whole show, but we are now partners in the OuterNet Company partnership." As to this venture:

1. Does Dad have any property rights in Strategy?

2. How will the profits of the enterprise be allocated between Dad and Son?

3. Will Dad bear the first $50,000 of losses?

4. Does Dad have the power to bind the enterprise to contracts with third parties? Does Son?

5. What duties do Dad and Son owe each other?

6. What would be the capital accounts of Dad and Son if the partnership loses the $50,000 and then shuts down after six months because future marketing prospects look hopeless and the entity has no assets? At the time of the shut down, would Dad or Son have a financial obligation to the partnership?

7. Would Dad have any personal liability exposure if Son borrowed $150,000 in the name of OuterNet Company from a local bank, the bank had no knowledge of Dad's involvement, and Dad did not know of the loan?

### a. The Partnership Agreement

A core feature of state partnership statutes is that they exalt the agreement between the partners as the primary governing source for the entity. With limited exceptions (all important), the agreement will preempt state statutory provisions, which kick in only when the partnership agreement does not address a specific issue.[4] This puts a huge premium on the development of a smart partnership agreement during the planning process. Typically, a partnership agreement may not:[5]

• Vary the statutory rights of the partnership or a partner to file a statement with the secretary of state or other designated state agency to define or limit the rights of individuals to deal with partnership real estate or take other actions on behalf of the partnership.

• Unreasonably restrict a partner's right of access to books and records.

• Eliminate a partner's duty of loyalty, but, if not manifestly unreasonable, the partnership agreement may identify specific types or categories of activities

---

4. RUPA § 103(a).
5. RUPA § 103(b).

that do not violate the duty of loyalty, and the partnership agreement may provide that all of the partners or a number or percentage specified in the partnership agreement may authorize or ratify, after full disclosure of all material facts, a specific act or transaction that otherwise would violate the duty of loyalty.

- Unreasonably reduce a partner's duty of care.

- Eliminate a partner's obligation of good faith and fair dealing, but the partnership agreement may prescribe the standards by which the performance of the obligation is to be measured, if the standards are not manifestly unreasonable.

- Vary the power of a partner to dissociate as a partner, except the partnership agreement may require that a notice to dissociate be in writing.

- Vary the right of a court to expel a partner who (1) has engaged in wrongful conduct that adversely and materially affects the partnership's business, (2) has willfully and persistently committed a material breach of the partnership agreement or a duty owned to the partnership or other partners, or (3) has engaged in conduct that makes it not reasonably practicable to carry on the partnership's business.[6]

- Vary the requirement to wind up the partnership's business if (1) continuation of all or substantially all of the partnership's business is unlawful, (2) a partner seeks a judicial determination that the economic purpose of the partnership is unreasonably frustrated, a partner has engaged in conduct that makes it not reasonably practicable to carry on the partnership's business, or it is not reasonably practicable to carry on the partnership's business in accordance with the partnership agreement, or (3) a transferee of a partner's interest seeks a judicial determination that the partnership's term or undertaking has expired or that the partnership's term was at will.[7]

- Vary the manner in which the state's law is applicable to a limited liability partnership.

- Restrict rights of third parties.

### b. Property Rights

Property acquired by a partnership is property of the partnership, not property co-owned by the individual partners.[8] A partner does not have an interest in partnership property that can be transferred, either voluntarily or involuntarily.[9] Property is presumed to be partnership property if purchased with partnership assets, even if not acquired in the name of the partnership.[10] Property acquired in the name of a partner, without use of partnership funds and a reference that the partner is acting on behalf of the partnership, is presumed to be separate property of the partner.[11]

---

6. RUPA §§ 103(b)(7), 601(5).
7. RUPA §§ 103(b)(8), 801(4)(5)(6).
8. RUPA §§ 203, 501.
9. RUPA § 501.
10. RUPA § 204(c).
11. RUPA § 204(d).

### c. Agency Authority

Each partner is an agent of the partnership with authority to bind the partnership in the ordinary course of the partnership's business or business of the kind carried out by the partnership, unless the partner had no authority to act for the partnership and the third person with whom the partner dealt knew or had reason to know that the partner had no such authority.[12] A partnership may file a statement (good for five years) with the secretary of state (or, in the case of real estate, with the county recorder) that states the authority, or limitations on the authority, of specific partners to enter into transactions on behalf of the partnership. Such grant of authority is conclusive in favor of a third party who gives value in reliance of the statement.[13] A person named in any such statement may file a written denial of the person's authority or status as a partner.[14]

### d. Liabilities.

*Partner-Created Liabilities.* A partnership is liable for any actionable loss or injury caused by a partner while acting within the ordinary course of the partnership's business or within the partner's authority.[15] Similarly, a partnership is liable if a partner, while acting in the course of the partnership's business or within the scope of authority, misapplies money or property that the partner receives or causes the partnership to receive from a third party.[16]

*Entity Obligations.* Partners are jointly and severally liable for all obligations of the partnership unless otherwise agreed to by the claimant or provided by law. Exceptions apply for a newly admitted partner's responsibility for pre-admission obligations and (as described below) for the partners of a limited liability partnership.[17]

*Purported Partner Liabilities.* A person who, through word or action, purports to be a partner or consents to being represented by another as a partner is liable as a partner to any third party who relies on any such representation. If the purported partner representation is made in a public announcement, liability may attach even if the purported partner had no knowledge of the specific claimant. Personal liability under this purported liability rule is not triggered simply because a person is incorrectly named in a statement of partnership authority.[18]

### e. Rights Between Partners.
Unless the partnership provides otherwise, the following provisions apply to the partners:

*Capital Accounts.* Each partner's capital account is increased by the amount of money and the value of any property (net of liabilities) contributed to the partnership and the partner's share of any partnership profits. Each partner's capital account is decreased by the amount of money and the value of any

---

12. RUPA § 301.
13. RUPA § 303.
14. RUPA § 304.
15. RUPA § 305(a).
16. RUPA § 305(b).
17. RUPA § 306.
18. RUPA § 308.

property (net of liabilities) distributed to the partner and the partner's share of any partnership losses.[19]

***Profits and Losses***. Partnership profits and losses are allocated equally among the partners.[20]

***Partner Advances***. A partnership is obligated to indemnify a partner for payments made and liabilities incurred in the ordinary course of business or to preserve the partnership's business or property. Any such payment constitutes a loan to the partnership that accrues interest.[21]

***Excessive Contributions***. A partnership is obligated to reimburse a partner for any contribution to the partnership that exceeds the partner's contribution obligation. Any such excessive contribution constitutes a loan to the partnership that accrues interest.[22]

***Management Rights***. Each partner has an equal right to manage and conduct the partnership's business.[23]

***Use of Property.*** A partner may use or possess partnership property only on behalf of the partnership.[24]

***Partner Compensation***. A partner is not entitled to any compensation for services rendered to the partnership, except for reasonable compensation for services rendered in winding up the affairs of the partnership.[25]

***New Partners.*** A person may become a partner only with the consent of all existing partners.[26]

***Dispute Resolution***. A majority of the partners may resolve any dispute that involves a matter within the ordinary course of the partnership's business. A matter outside the ordinary course or any amendment to the partnership agreement requires the unanimous consent of the partners.[27]

***In-Kind Distributions.*** No partner has a right to receive, and may not be required to accept, a distribution in kind of partnership property.[28]

***Records Inspection Access.*** A partner and the partner's agents and attorneys has access to the books and records of the partnership, which the partnership is obligated to maintain and keep at the partnership's chief executive office. The same rights extend to former partners and the legal representatives of a deceased and disabled partner. The partnership may impose reasonable charges for the costs (both labor and materials) of document copies.[29]

***Duty of Loyalty.*** A partner's duty of loyalty to the partnership and other

---

19. RUPA § 401(a).
20. RUPA § 401(b).
21. RUPA § 401(c).
22. RUPA § 401(d).
23. RUPA § 401(f).
24. RUPA § 401(g).
25. RUPA § 401(h).
26. RUPA § 401(i).
27. RUPA § 401(j).
28. RUPA § 402.
29. RUPA § 403.

partners is limited to (1) accounting and holding as trustee any property, profit or benefit derived by the partner in the conduct or winding up of the partnership's business or from the use of partnership property, including the appropriation of partnership opportunity, (2) refraining from dealing with the partnership as, on behalf of, a person having an interest adverse to partnership, and (3) refraining from competing with the partnership.[30]  A partner does not violate this duty or any other duty merely because the partner's conduct furthers the partner's own interests, nor is a partner prohibited from loaning money to a partnership or transacting other business with a partnership.[31]

**Duty of Care.**  A partner's duty of care to the partnership and the other partners is limited to refraining from engaging in grossly negligent or reckless conduct, intentional misconduct, or a known violation of law.[32]

**Duty of Good Faith.**  A partner is required to discharge duties to the partnership and other partners and exercise any rights in a manner that reflects good faith and fair dealing.[33]

**Enforcement Actions.**  A partnership may maintain an action against a partner for violation of the partnership agreement or a violation of a duty owned to the partnership.  A partner may maintain an action against the partnership or other partners for legal and equitable relief to enforce rights under the partnership agreement or state law and to enforce other interests of the partner.[34]

**Partner's Transferable Interest.**  The only transferable interest of a partner is the partner's share of profits and losses and the right to receive distributions. This interest is personal property.[35]  A partner's transfer of such interest (1) is permissible, (2) does not itself cause a dissolution or winding up of the partnership, (3) does not entitle the transferee to participate in the management or conduct of the partnership's business, to require access to information about partnership transactions, or to inspect or copy partnership books and records, and (4) entitles the transferee only to distributions and net dissolution amounts that otherwise would have been paid to the transferor partner and to seek a judicial determination that it is equitable to wind up the partnership's business.[36]

**Partner's Third Party Debts.**  The creditor of a partner may seek a judicial charging order that constitutes a lien on the partner's transferable interest in the partnership. The court may appoint a receiver and enter other orders to enforce the charging order and may order a foreclosure of the interest.  The acquirer at any such foreclosure sale receives only the rights of a transferee. Statutes usually specifically provide that this is the "exclusive remedy" of a partner's judgment creditor who seeks to satisfy a claim out of the partner's interest in the partnership.[37]

---

30. RUPA § 404(b).
31. RUPA § 404(e),(f).
32. RUPA § 404(c).
33. RUPA § 404(d).
34. RUPA § 405.
35. RUPA § 502.
36. RUPA § 503.
37. RUPA § 504.

## f. Partner's Termination (Dissociation).

*At Will Termination.* A partner may dissociate from a partnership by notice expressing a will to withdraw as a partner. When the partnership is at will, such a withdrawal will trigger a dissolution and winding up of the partnership.[38] A partnership is at will when the partners have not agreed to remain partners until the expiration of a definite term or the completion of a particular undertaking.[39]

*Other Triggers.* Statutes typically provide that a partner's interest also may be terminated by the:

1) Occurrence of a dissociation event specified in the partnership agreement;

2) Expulsion of a partner pursuant to the partnership agreement;

3) Unanimous vote of the other partners if (a) it is unlawful to carry on business with the partner, (b) there has been a transfer of substantially all of a partner's interest in the partnership, (c) the partner is a corporation that has filed a certificate of dissolution or has had its charter revoked or its right to conduct business suspended, or (4) the partner is a partnership that has been dissolved;

4) A judicial determination of expulsion due to the partner's wrongful conduct, willful and persistent breach of the partnership agreement or duties owed, or conduct that makes it not reasonably practical to carry on the business with the partner;

5) Partner becoming a debtor in bankruptcy, executing an assignment for the benefit of creditors, or having a trustee, receiver or liquidator appointed to handle the partner's property;

6) Partner dying, having a guardian or conservator appointed to handle the partner's property, or being judicially determined to be incapable of performing the partner's duties under the partnership agreement;

7) Transfer of the partner's interest in the partnership by a trustee or a personal representative of an estate holding the partnership interest; and

8) Termination of any partner who is not an individual, partnership, corporation, trust, or estate.[40]

*Purchase of Interest.* Typically, a partner's dissociation does not force a dissolution and winding up of the partnership unless the dissociation is due to the death of a partner or one of the triggers described in items (5) through (8) above and over half of the partners approve a winding up of the partnership. Absent such circumstances, the interest of the departing partner is purchased for a price equal to the greater of the liquidation value of the partner's interest or the value based on a sale of the business as a going concern. State statutes usually specify the procedures for establishing the value.[41]

---

38. RUPA §§ 601(1), 801(1).
39. RUPA § 101(8).
40. RUPA § 601.
41. RUPA §§ 603, 701.

***Dissociated Partner's Liabilities.*** A dissociated partner remains liable: (1) to the partnership and other partners for any damages or losses resulting from a withdrawal that violated the partnership agreement or actions taken by the dissociated partner after the dissociation; and (2) to third parties for joint and several exposure obligations and liabilities arising prior to the dissociation. The dissociated partner's exposure on such a pre-dissociation obligation may be eliminated by agreement with the creditor and the other partners or by a material change in the terms of the obligation with the creditor having notice of the dissociation. Continued use of a dissociated partner's name in the partnership's name does not expose the dissociated partner to obligations of the partnership incurred after the dissociation.[42]

***Third Party Protection.*** The partnership may be liable to third parties who reasonably believed that a dissociated partner was still a partner for actions taken by the dissociated partner within two years of the dissociation, provided the partnership may cut off this exposure 90 days after filing a notice of dissociation with the secretary of state.[43]

### g. Dissolution and Winding Up

***Triggering Events.*** A partnership is dissolved, and its business must be wound up when (1) a partner gives notice to withdraw in an at will partnership; (2) a majority of partners approve winding up when a partner dies or dissociates for one of the reasons described in items (5) though (8) above; (3) the partners all agree to a winding up of the business; (4) the partnership's specified term or undertaking has expired or been completed; (5) a dissolution event specified in the partnership agreement occurs; (6) an event (not curable in 90 days) occurs that makes it unlawful to carry on substantially all of the partnership's business; (7) on application of a partner, a court determines that the economic purpose of the partnership is unreasonably frustrated, a partner has engaged in conduct that makes it not reasonably practicable to carry on the partnership's business, or it is not reasonably practicable to carry on the partnership's business in accordance with the partnership agreement, or (8) on application of the transferee of a partner's interest, a court determines that it would be equitable to windup the affairs of the partnership.[44]

***Winding Up.*** A partnership continues after dissolution only for purposes of winding up the business. At any time after dissolution, the partners may unanimously agree to terminate the winding up and resume the partnership's business activities.[45] Any partner who has not wrongfully dissociated from the partnership may participate in the winding up, subject to a court's power to order judicial supervision of the winding up. A person winding up a partnership may seek to preserve the business as a going concern for a reasonable time, prosecute and defend actions, settle and close the partnership's business, dispose of assets, pay liabilities, resolve disputes, bind the partnership for acts taken in connection

---

42. RUPA §§ 702, 703.
43. RUPA §§ 702(a), 704.
44. RUPA § 801.
45. RUPA § 802.

with the winding up, and make distributions to partners.[46]

*Statement of Dissolution.* Any partner who has not dissociated may file a statement of dissolution which is deemed to give any third party notice of the dissolution and limitation on the partners' authority 90 days after filing.[47]

*Account Settlement and Deficit Restoration Obligations.* Proceeds from the winding up must first be used to discharge obligations to creditors. Remaining proceeds are distributed to the partners in accordance with the respective positive balances in their capital accounts. Any partner who has a negative capital account balance must make a contribution to the partnership in an amount equal to the negative balance. If such partner fails to restore the negative balance, any amount needed by the partnership to pay partnership debts as a result of such failure must be paid by the other partners in proportion to their loss sharing percentages, and such other partners may seek to recover such additional contributions from the defaulting partner. Any partnership obligations that surface after the settlement of all partner accounts must be paid by the partners making additional contributions in proportion to their loss allocation percentages.[48]

### h. Choice of Law

State statutes typically provide that the laws of the jurisdiction where the partnership maintains its chief executive office will govern relationships among the partners and between the partners and the partnership.[49]

## 2. LIMITED LIABILITY PARTNERSHIPS

A limited liability partnership ("LLP") is a partnership that has filed a statement of qualification (sometimes called an "application") with the state's secretary of state and that does not have a similar statement in effect in another jurisdiction.[50] The terms and conditions on which a partnership becomes an LLP must be approved by a vote necessary to amend the partnership agreement, but if the partnership agreement contains provisions that expressly consider obligations to contribute to the partnership, it must be approved by the vote necessary to amend such provisions.[51]

### a. Qualification Statement.
The statement of qualification usually must state the name of the partnership, the location of a registered office, the address of its principal office; and a statement that the partnership elects to be an LLP.[52] Some states require that the qualification statement also include the number of partners and a brief statement of the business in which the partnership engages. Typically, a majority of the partners, or one or more authorized partners, must execute documents submitted to the secretary of state. The LLP's registration is effective immediately after the date the application is filed, or at such later date

---

46. RUPA § 803.
47. RUPA § 805.
48. RUPA § 806.
49. RUPA § 706(a).
50. RUPA § 101(5).
51. RUPA § 1001(b).
52. RUPA § 1001(c).

specified in the application.[53]

**b. Name.** The name of an LLP must end with the words "Registered Limited Liability Partnership," "limited liability partnership" or the abbreviation "R.L.L.P.," "RLLP," "L.L.P.," or "LLP."[54]

**c. Annual Report.** An LLP must file an annual report with the secretary of state and pay an annual fee. The annual report must update the contact information for the LLP's chief executive office and registered agent.[55] Some states also require updated information on the number of partners currently in the partnership and whether there are any material changes in the information contained in the partnership's qualification statement.

**d. Liability of Partners.** A partner of an LLP is not personally liable for an obligation of the partnership incurred while the partnership is an LLP, whether arising in contract, tort, or otherwise, by reason of being a partner. This limited liability exists even if the partnership agreement contained inconsistent provisions before making the election to become an LLP.[56] This is the big advantage of an LLP over a general partnership.

**e. Applicable Law.** State statutes typically provide that the law under which a foreign LLP is formed governs relations among the partners and between the partners and the partnership, and the liability of partners for obligations of the partnership.[57] States require a foreign LLP to file a statement of foreign qualification before transacting business in the state and typically provide that such a statement does not authorize a foreign LLP to engage in any business or exercise any power that a partnership in the state could not engage in or exercise as an LLP.[58] Absent the filing of such statement, a foreign LLP usually cannot maintain an action or proceeding in the state.[59]

**f. Professional Service Providers.** LLPs are often used by providers of professional services. Licensed partners of a professional provider LLP may be liable under state law for the partnership's debts if the partnership fails to maintain professional insurance coverage required by state law.

### 3. LIMITED PARTNERSHIPS

A limited partnership is an entity that has one or more general partners ("GP") and one or more limited partners ("LP") and is formed under a state's limited partnership act.[60] GPs have the authority to manage and conduct the business of the partnership and are personally liable for the debts and obligations of the partnership.[61] LPs typically are investors who have limited or minimal control over daily business decisions and operations of the partnership and have no personal liability for the obligations of the partnership beyond their capital

---

53. RUPA § 1001(e).
54. RUPA § 1002.
55. RUPA § 1003.
56. RUPA § 306(c).
57. RUPA § 1101(a).
58. RUPA §§ 1101(c), 1102.
59. RUPA § 1103(a).
60. ULPA §102(11) (2001).
61. ULPA §§ 402, 404 (2001).

contributions to the partnership.[62] If properly organized and managed, the limited partnership form of business organization allows persons to contribute capital to a business enterprise and share in its profits and losses without having liability exposure to the creditors of the business.

Limited partnerships did not exist at common law; they are creatures of state statutory law. The Uniform Limited Partnership Act ("ULPA"), with origins dating back to 1916 and most recently revised in 2001, has served as the basic framework for limited partnership statutes in 49 states. The 2001 version of the ULPA differs from prior versions in two significant respects. First, it no longer "links" its provisions to the Uniform Partnership Act. It is a "stand-alone" act that is considerably longer than the prior versions. Second, its revisions are targeted at those situations where a limited partnership is often the preferred entity form – sophisticated, manager-entrenched commercial deals whose participants commit for the long term and family limited partnerships used for estate planning purposes. The management powers of the GPs are increased; the management role and exit rights of LPs are decreased.

Although the 2001 version is not linked to the Revised Uniform Partnership Act, many state limited partnership acts remain linked to their versions of the Uniform Partnership Act. State adoption of the 2001 stand-alone version proceeds slowly.

## PROBLEM 5-C

Assume Son and Dad in Case Problem 5-B form a limited partnership in a state that has adopted the Uniform Limited Partnership Act (2001), with Son as the general partner and Dad as the limited partner.

1. Does Dad have any property rights in Strategy?

2. How will distributions be allocated to Son and Dad if there is no specific agreement between the parties?

3. Would there be limits on the amount of distributions to Son and Dad?

4. Does Dad have the power to bind the enterprise to contracts with third parties? Does Son?

5. What duties do Dad and Son owe each other?

6. Would Dad have any personal liability exposure if Son borrowed $150,000 in the name of OuterNet Company from a local bank, the bank had no knowledge of Dad's involvement, and Dad did not know of the loan?

### a. Entity Characteristics

A limited partnership is an entity distinct from its partners and may be organized for any lawful purpose and for a perpetual duration.[63] It has the power to do all things necessary and convenient to carry on its business, including the

---

62. ULPA §§ 302, 303 (2001).
63. ULPA § 104 (2001).

power to sue, be sued and defend in its own name.[64] The partnership agreement governs the operation of the entity, but, as in the case of a general partnership, there is a list of statutory provisions that cannot be changed by agreement. In most states, such list is substantively identical (or nearly so) to the list applicable to a general partnership,[65] as are the provisions relating to when a person will be deemed to have constructive notice of a fact regarding a limited partnership.[66] The name of the entity must contain the phrase "limited partnership," "L.P.," or "LP."[67]

### b. Formation

A limited partnership is formed by filing a certificate of limited partnership with the state's secretary of state. At a minimum, state statutes require the certificate to state: the name of the limited partnership; the street and address of the entity's initial designated office; and the name, street and mailing address of each general partner and the entity's initial registered agent for service of process.[68] A limited partnership is actually formed when the secretary of state files the certificate.[69] Limited partnerships typically are required to file annual reports with the state's secretary of state.

### c. Rights and Liabilities of GPs and LPs

*Agency and Management Authority.* An LP has no power to act for or bind the entity.[70] A GP is an agent of the limited partnership with full authority to manage and conduct the affairs of the limited partnership and bind the entity.[71] Each GP has equal management rights, and any matter relating to the entity's activities may be exclusively decided by the GP or, if there is more than one GP, by a majority of the GPs.[72] A GP has the same reimbursement rights for advances and excessive contributions as a partner of a general partnership.[73] Absent a provision in the partnership agreement, a GP is not entitled to any remuneration for services rendered to the partnership.[74]

*Liability for Entity Obligations.* GPs are jointly and severally liable for the obligations of a limited partnership.[75] LPs have no personal liability for the entity's obligation.[76]

*Fiduciary Obligations.* A GP has the same duties of loyalty, care, good faith and fair dealing as a partner of a general partnership.[77] An LP has no fiduciary duties to the limited partnership or the other partners, but does have a good faith and fair dealing requirement in exercising rights under the limited

---

64. ULPA § 105 (2001).
65. ULPA § 110 (2001).
66. ULPA § 103 (2001).
67. ULPA § 108(b) (2001).
68. ULPA § 201 (2001).
69. ULPA § 201(c) (2001).
70. ULPA § 302 (2001).
71. ULPA § 402 (2001).
72. ULPA § 406(a) (2001).
73. ULPA § 406(c),(d),(e) (2001).
74. ULPA § 406(f) (2001).
75. ULPA § 404 (2001).
76. ULPA § 303 (2001).
77. ULPA § 408 (2001).

partnership agreement.[78]

*Dual Capacity Partner.* A person may be both a GP and an LP and have the rights, duties and liabilities of each of those capacities.[79]

*Information and Inspection Rights.* An LP typically has an unlimited right to inspect and copy select core documents (specified by statute) during normal business hours, at an office designated by the entity, and on limited advance notice (normally 10 days). Other LP document requests relating to the activities or financial condition of the entity require a written request that must state a purpose reasonably related to the partnership, describe with particularity the information sought, and demonstrate that the information sought is related to the purpose. The GPs then decide whether to honor the request and may impose restrictions on the use of the information and charge the requesting LP any cost (labor and materials) incurred in connection with the request.[80] A GP has much broader information and inspection rights, being entitled to receive all information and documents reasonably required for the exercise of the GP's management rights and authority.[81]

*Contributions.* A partner's contribution may consist of tangible and intangible property, including promissory notes, services performed, and services to be performed. A partner's contribution obligation is not excused by death, disability, or other inability to perform and may be compromised only be the consent of all partners. Any creditor who extends credit in reliance on a contribution obligation of a partner, with no notice that the obligation has been compromised, may enforce the original obligation.[82]

*Distributions.* Absent a contrary provision in the limited partnership agreement (which usually exists), distributions by a limited partnership are allocated among partners on the basis of the relative value of their contributions to the entity.[83] This default rule is significantly different from the corresponding default rule for general partnerships. A partner has no right to a distribution before the dissolution and winding up of the entity, nor does a partner have the right to demand or receive a distribution in any form other than cash. A limited partnership may elect to make a distribution of an asset in kind so long as each partner receives a proportionate share of the asset based on the partner's share of distributions. A partner who is entitled to receive a distribution under the partnership agreement has the rights of a creditor, subject to offset rights of the partnership for any amounts owed by the partner to the partnership. A limited partnership is prohibited from making a distribution in violation of the partnership agreement.[84]

*Transferee Rights and Charging Orders.* A state's limited partnership statutory provisions dealing with the "personal property" nature of a partner's

---

78. ULPA § 305 (2001).
79. ULPA § 113 (2001).
80. ULPA § 304 (2001).
81. ULPA § 407 (2001).
82. ULPA §§ 501, 502 (2001).
83. ULPA § 503 (2001).
84. ULPA §§ 504 through 507 (2001).

interest, the rights to transfer a partnership interest, the rights of a transferee of a partnership interest, and the rights of a partner's creditors to obtain and foreclose on a charging order are usually substantially identical to the corresponding statutory provisions for general partnerships.[85] The personal representative of a deceased limited partner may exercise the rights of a transferee or the rights of an existing limited partner, as applicable.[86]

### d. Prohibited Distributions

*Statutory Limitations.* A limited partnership usually is prohibited from making a distribution if, after the distribution, (1) the entity is unable to pay its debts as they become due in the ordinary course of business or (2) the entity's total assets have a value that is less than the sum of the entity's total liabilities plus the amount of any superior preferable distributions that would be due to other partners if the entity was dissolved and wound up. In applying this limitation, the limited partnership may value its assets based on financial statements prepared in accordance with accounting principles that are reasonable in the circumstances or on a fair valuation of the assets. Any indebtedness issued by a limited partnership to partners as part of a distribution is not considered a liability for purposes of the limitation calculation if, and only if, any payments of principal or interest on such indebtedness are to be made only if they would be permissible distributions at the time made.[87]

*Related Partner Liabilities.* A GP who consents to a distribution that exceeds the statutory limitations on distributions is personally liable to the limited partnership for any excess distribution if it is established that the GP violated a duty of loyalty, care, good faith or fair dealing to the entity. Any partner or transferee who knowingly receives a distribution in excess of the statutory limits is personally liability to the entity for the amount of such excess.[88]

### e. Partner Termination (Dissociation)

*Limited Partners.* Limited partners generally have no power to dissociate from a limited partnership prior to the termination of the limited partnership unless they are granted specific termination rights in the limited partnership agreement.[89] State limited partnership statutes that specify the circumstances in which a limited partner's interest may be terminated usually are substantively identical to the corresponding provisions for terminating a partner's interest in a general partnership.[90] The dissociation of a limited partner's interest terminates the rights of the dissociated partner, but does not terminate the entity, the dissociated partner's duties of good faith and fair dealing, or any obligation that the dissociated partner owes to the partnership or the other partners.[91]

*General Partners.* A GP may choose to dissociate from a limited

---

85. ULPA §§ 701 through 703 (2001).
86. ULPA § 704 (2001).
87. ULPA § 508 (2001).
88. ULPA § 509 (2001).
89. ULPA § 601(a) (2001).
90. ULPA § 601(b) (2001).
91. ULPA § 602 (2001).

partnership at any time, rightfully or wrongfully, by expressed will.[92] State limited partnership statutes that specify the circumstances in which a GP's interest may be terminated usually are substantively identical to the corresponding provisions for terminating a partner's interest in a general partnership.[93] A GP's dissociation is wrongful only if it violates the partnership agreement or, unless the agreement provides otherwise, it occurs before the partnership terminates and the dissociation is due to a voluntary withdrawal, a judicial expulsion, a bankruptcy of the GP, or the GP ceasing to exist as an entity.[94] A GP who wrongfully dissociates is liable to the limited partnership for any damages caused by the dissociation. The dissociation of a GP's interest terminates all managing rights, ongoing duties of loyalty and care, and (with very limited exceptions) the dissociated GP's liability for partnership obligations incurred after the dissociation. A dissociated GP remains personally liable for partnership obligations incurred prior to the dissociation unless the dissociated partner's exposure for a pre-dissociation obligation is eliminated by agreement with the creditor and the other partners or by a material change in the terms of the obligation with the creditor having notice of the dissociation.[95]

### f. Dissolution and Winding Up

*Triggering Events.* Statutory provisions generally provide that a limited partnership must be dissolved and wound up on: (1) the occurrence of a dissolution event specified in the partnership agreement; (2) the consent of all the GPs and LPs who own a majority of the distribution rights; (3) the dissociation of a GP with at least one remaining GP, and LPs who own a majority of distribution rights consent to the dissolution; (4) the dissociation of a GP with no remaining GP, unless within 90 days a GP is admitted and LPs who own a majority of distribution rights consent to continue business activities; (5) 90 days after the dissociation of the last LP, unless a new LP is admitted during such period; (6) a declaration of dissolution by the state's secretary of state for failure to file an annual report or pay required fees; or (7) by order of a court based on a determination that it is not reasonably practicable to carry on the activities of the limited partnership in accordance with the partnership agreement.[96]

*Impacts.* The statutory impacts of winding up a limited partnership are very similar to those of a general partnership with the clarification that if the entity does not have a GP, LPs who own a majority of the distribution rights may appoint a person to wind up and dissolve the entity. A GP who causes a limited partnership to incur inappropriate obligations during a winding up is liable to the limited partnership for such obligations.[97]

### g. Litigation Rights

Some state statutes specifically authorize a partner of a limited partnership to bring a direct action against the partnership or other partners for legal or

---

92. ULPA § 604(a) (2001).
93. ULPA § 603 (2001).
94. ULPA § 604(b) (2001).
95. ULPA § 607 (2001).
96. ULPA §§ 801, 802 (2001).
97. ULPA §§ 803 through 805 (2001).

equitable relief to enforce the partner's rights under the partnership agreement or applicable law. The partner must plead and prove an actual or threatened injury to the partner, not the partnership. A right to an accounting upon a dissolution and winding up does not revive a claim barred by law.[98] Such statutes also usually permit a limited partner to maintain a derivative action on behalf of the limited partnership only if (1) the partner first makes a demand on GP's to bring the action or pleads with particularity why such a demand would be futile and (2) any recovery from the litigation is paid to the limited partnership. If such a derivative action is successful, the court may award a reimbursement of the plaintiff's attorney fees and costs from the recovery.[99]

### 4. LIMITED LIABILITY LIMITED PARTNERSHIPS

The limited liability limited partnership ("LLLP") is to a limited partnership what an LLP is to a general partnership. Its role is to eliminate the personal liability exposure that general partners have for the obligations of a limited partnership. It's a relatively new entity form that has been adopted in roughly half the states.

The LLLP statutory provisions are additions to each state's version of the Uniform Limited Partnership Act that mirror the LLP additions to the state's version of the Uniform Partnership Act. They include statutory requirements to elect LLLP status in the limited partnership's filed certificate[100] and use of a name that includes the phrase "limited liability limited partnership," "LLLP," or "L.L.L.P."[101]

With LLLP status, a general partner is not personally liable for an obligation of the limited partnership incurred while the partnership is an LLLP, whether arising in contract, tort, or otherwise. This limited liability exists even if the partnership agreement contained inconsistent provisions before making the election to become an LLLP.[102]

### 5. LIMITED LIABILITY COMPANIES

### PROBLEM 5-D

Assume Son and Dad in Case Problem 5-B form a limited liability company in a state that has adopted the Revised Uniform Limited Liability Company Act. How would you answer questions 1 through 6 of Case Problem 2-3 if the LLC is a member-managed LLC? How would your answers change if the LLC is a manager-managed LLC with Son as the manager?

### a. LLC Characteristics

The limited liability company ("LLC") has emerged as the most popular form of non-corporate entity. It offers limited liability protection for the LLC's members and the flexibility of having an entity that is managed by designated

---

98. ULPA § 1001 (2001).
99. ULPA §§ 1002 through 1004 (2001).
100. ULPA § 201(a)(4) (2001).
101. ULPA § 108(c) (2001).
102. ULPA § 404(c)(2001).

managers or by the members generally. The framework for state LLC laws is the Uniform Limited Liability Company Act, originally adopted in 1995 and most recently amended in 2006.

A limited liability company is an entity distinct from its members and may be organized for any lawful purpose and for a perpetual duration.[103] It has the power to do all things necessary and convenient to carry on its business, including the power to sue, be sued and defend in its own name.[104] The LLC operating agreement governs: the relations among the members as members and between the members and the limited liability company; the rights and duties of a person in the capacity of manager; the activities of the company and the conduct of those activities; and the means and conditions for amending the operating agreement.[105]

As in the case of a partnership or limited partnership, there is a list of statutory provisions that cannot be changed by agreement. In most states, such list is similar in many respects to the list applicable to partnerships.[106] The name of the entity must contain the phrase "limited liability company," "limited company," "L.L.C.," "LLC," "L.C.," or "LC." The word "limited" may be abbreviated as "Ltd," and "company" may be abbreviated as "Co."[107]

### b. Formation

A limited liability company is formed by one or more organizers filing a certificate of organization with the state's secretary of state. At a minimum, state statutes require the certificate to state: the name of the LLC; the street and address of the entity's initial designated office; the name, street and mailing address of the LLC's initial registered agent for service of process; and a statement that the LLC has no members if there are no members at time of filing.[108] If the LLC certificate states there are no members at time of filing, the certificate will lapse and be void if, within 90 days of filing, a follow-up filing is not made confirming that the LLC has at least one member.[109] An LLC is actually formed when the secretary of state files the certificate and the LLC has at least one member.[110] LLCs typically are required to file annual reports with the state's secretary of state.

### c. Operating Agreement Limiting Provisions

State statutes often provide that, if not manifestly unreasonable, an LLC's operating agreement may:[111]

    1. Restrict or eliminate a member's duty of loyalty.

---

103. RULLCA § 104
104. RULLCA § 105
105. RULLCA § 110(a).
106. RULLCA § 110(c).
107. RULLCA § 108(a).
108. RULLCA § 201(b).
109. RULLCA § 201(e)(1).
110. RULLCA § 201(d)(1).
111. RULLCA § 110.

2. Identify specific types or categories of activities that do not violate the duty of loyalty.

3. Alter the duty of care, except to authorize intentional misconduct or a known violation of law.

4. Alter any other fiduciary duty, including eliminating particular aspects of that duty.

5. Prescribe the standards by which to measure the performance of the obligations of good faith and fair dealing.

6. Specify the method by which a specific act or transaction that would otherwise violate the duty of loyalty may be authorized or ratified by one or more disinterested and independent persons after full disclosure of all material facts.

7. Eliminate or limit any fiduciary duty that would have pertained to a responsibility that a member has been relieved of under the LLC operating agreement.

8. Alter or eliminate any indemnification rights of a member or manager.

9. Eliminate or limit a member or manager's liability to the LLC and members for money damages, except for a breach of the duty of loyalty, a financial benefit received by a member or manager to which the member or manager is not entitled, a breach of a duty for unauthorized distributions, intentional infliction of harm on the company or a member, or an intentional violation of criminal law.

### d. Agency and Management Authority

A member is not an agent of an LLC by reason of being a member.[112] An LLC is deemed to be a member-managed LLC unless the operating agreement expressly provides that it will be "manager-managed" or includes words of similar import.[113]

*Member-Managed LLC.* In a member-managed LLC: the management and conduct of the company are vested in the members; each member has equal rights in the management and conduct of the company's activities; any difference arising among members as to a matter in the ordinary course of the activities of the LLC may be decided by a majority of the members; an act outside the ordinary course of the activities of the LLC may be undertaken only with the consent of all members; and the operating agreement may be amended only with the consent of all members.[114]

*Manager-Managed LLC.* In a manager-managed LLC: any matter relating to the activities of the company is decided exclusively by the managers unless a statute specifically provides otherwise; each manager has equal rights in the management and conduct of the activities of the LLC; and a difference arising among managers as to a matter in the ordinary course of the activities of the LLC

---

112. RULLCA § 301(a).
113. RULLCA § 407(a).
114. RULLCA § 407(b).

may be decided by a majority of the managers. Also, consent of all members is required to: sell or otherwise dispose of all, or substantially all, of the company's property; approve a merger, conversion, or domestication; undertake any other act outside the ordinary course of the company's activities; and amend the operating agreement.[115]

*Manager Selection and Removal.* A manager may be chosen at any time by the consent of a majority of the members and remains a manager until a successor has been chosen, unless the manager at an earlier time resigns, is removed, or dies, or, in the case of a manager that is not an individual, ceases to exist. A manager may be removed at any time by the consent of a majority of the members without notice or cause.[116] A person need not be a member to be a manager, but the dissociation of a member who is also a manager removes the person as a manager. If a person who is both a manager and a member ceases to be a manager, that cessation does not by itself dissociate the person as a member.[117] A person who wrongfully causes dissolution of the company loses the right to participate in management as a member and a manager.[118]

*Written Consent.* An action requiring the consent of members may be taken without a meeting by use of a written consent. A member may appoint a proxy or other agent to consent or otherwise act for the member.[119]

*Compensation.* A member is not entitled to remuneration for services performed for a member-managed LLC, except for reasonable compensation for services rendered in winding up the activities of the company.[120]

*Indemnification.* An LLC must reimburse for any payment made and indemnify for any debt, obligation, or other liability incurred by a member of a member-managed company or the manager of a manager-managed company in the course of the member's or manager's activities on behalf of the LLC unless the action involved a violation of a fiduciary duty or a prohibited distribution.[121]

*Insurance.* A limited liability company may purchase and maintain insurance on behalf of a member or manager of the LLC against liability asserted against or incurred by the member or manager.[122]

*Statement of Authority.* An LLC may file a statement (good for five years) with the secretary of state (or, in the case of real estate, with the county recorder) which states the authority, or limitations on the authority, of specific persons to enter into transactions on behalf of the LLC. Such grant of authority is conclusive in favor of a third party who gives value in reliance of the statement.[123] A person named in any such statement may file a written denial of the person's authority.[124]

---

115. RULLCA § 407(c).
116. RULLCA § 407(c)(5).
117. RULLCA § 407(c)(6).
118. RULLCA § 407(e).
119. RULLCA § 407(d).
120. RULLCA § 407(f).
121. RULLCA § 408(a).
122. RULLCA § 408(b).
123. RULLCA § 302.
124. RULLCA § 303.

### e.  LLC Member Rights and Duties

*Liability for Entity Obligations.* LLC members have no personal liability for the entity's obligation, whether arising in contract, tort or otherwise. The failure of an LLC to observe any particular formalities relating to the exercise of its powers or management of its activities is not a ground for imposing liability on the members or managers for the debts, obligations, or other liabilities of the LLC.[125]

*Fiduciary Obligations in Member-Managed LLC.* A member of a member-managed LLC owes to the LLC and other members a duty of loyalty to: account to the LLC and to hold as trustee for it any property, profit, or benefit derived by the member in the conduct or winding up of the company's activities; refrain from dealing with the LLC as or on behalf of a person having an interest adverse to the company (subject to a defense of fairness to the LLC); and refrain from competing with the LLC. All members may authorize or ratify, after full disclosure of all material facts, a specific act or transaction that otherwise would violate this duty of loyalty. Such member also has a contractual obligation of good faith and fair dealing and, subject to the business judgment rule, has a duty of care to act with the care that a person in a like position would reasonably exercise under similar circumstances and in a manner the member reasonably believes to be in the best interests of the LLC. In discharging this duty, a member may rely in good faith upon opinions, reports, statements, or other information provided by another person that the member reasonably believes is a competent and reliable source for the information.[126]

*Fiduciary Duties in Manager-Managed LLC.* In a manager-managed LLC, members do not have any fiduciary duties to the LLC by reason of being a member, but do have a contractual obligation of good faith and fair dealing. Managers have the fiduciary duties of loyalty and care described above, along with a contractual obligation of good faith and fair dealing. Any approval or ratification of an act that violates the duty of loyalty requires the approval of all members.[127]

*Information and Inspection Rights.* In a member-managed LLC, a member typically has unlimited document inspection rights relating to the LLC's activities and financial condition. In a manager-managed LLC, such rights are reserved to the managers, and members must submit an inspection request that states a purpose material to the member's interests in the LLC, describes with particularity the information sought, and demonstrates that the information sought is related to the purpose. The LLC may then decide whether to honor the request, impose restrictions on the use of the information, and charge the requesting member the costs (labor and materials) incurred in connection with the request.[128]

*Contributions.* An LLC member's contribution may consist of tangible and intangible property, including promissory notes, services performed, and services

---

125. RULLCA § 304.
126. RULLCA § 409(a)-(f).
127. RULLCA § 409(g).
128. RULLCA § 410.

to be performed. A member's contribution obligation is not excused by death, disability, or other inability to perform and may be compromised only by the consent of all members. Any creditor who extends credit in reliance on a contribution obligation of a member, with no notice that the obligation has been compromised, may enforce the original obligation.[129]

*Distributions.* Absent a contrary provision in the LLC operating agreement (which usually exists), distributions by an LLC prior to a dissolution and winding up must be in equal shares among the members. A member has no right to a distribution before the dissolution and winding up of the entity, nor does a member have the right to demand or receive a distribution in any form other than money. An LLC may elect to make a distribution of an asset in kind so long as each member receives a proportionate share of the asset based on the member's share of distributions. A member who is entitled to receive a distribution under the operating agreement has the rights of a creditor.[130]

*Transferee Rights and Charging Orders.* A state's LLC statutory provisions dealing with the "personal property" nature of a member's LLC interest, the rights to transfer an LLC interest, the rights of a transferee of an LLC interest, and the rights of an LLC member's creditors to obtain and foreclose on a charging order are usually substantially identical to the corresponding statutory provisions for partnerships. The personal representative of a deceased member may exercise the rights of a transferee or the rights of an existing member, as applicable.[131]

## f. Prohibited Distributions

*Statutory Limitations.* An LLC usually is prohibited from making a distribution if, after the distribution, (1) the entity in unable to pay its debts as they become due in the ordinary course of business or (2) the entity's total assets have a value that is less than the sum of the entity's total liabilities plus the amount of any superior preferable distributions that would be due to other partners if the entity was dissolved and wound up. In applying this limitation, the LLC may value its assets based on financial statements prepared in accordance with accounting principles that are reasonable in the circumstances or on a fair valuation of the assets. Any indebtedness issued by an LLC to members as part of a distribution is not considered a liability for purposes of the limitation calculation if, and only if, any payments of principal or interest on such indebtedness would be permissible distributions at the time made.[132]

*Related Member and Manager Liabilities.* A member of a member-managed LLC or a manager of a manager-managed LLC who consents to a distribution that exceeds the statutory limitations on distributions is personally liable to the LLC for any excess distribution if it is established that the member or manager violated a duty of loyalty, care, good faith or fair dealing to the entity. A person who knowingly receives a distribution in excess of the statutory

---

129. RULLCA §§ 402, 403.
130. RULLCA §§ 404. RULLCA § 406.
131. RULLCA §§ 501 through 504.
132. RULLCA § 405.

limits is personally liable to the entity for the amount of such excess.[133]

### g. Member Dissociation

***Dissociation Rights.*** A member may choose to dissociate from an LLC at any time, rightfully or wrongfully, by expressed will. State LLC statutes that specify the circumstances in which a member's interest may be terminated usually are very similar to the corresponding provisions for terminating a partner's interest in a general partnership. A member's dissociation is wrongful only if it violates the LLC agreement or, unless the agreement provides otherwise, it occurs before the LLC terminates and the dissociation is due to a voluntary withdrawal, a judicial expulsion, a bankruptcy of the member, or the member being dissolved or terminated. A member who wrongfully dissociates is liable to the LLC and to other members for any damages caused by the dissociation.[134]

***Dissociation Impacts.*** The dissociation of a member interest terminates all managing rights, and, if the LLC is member-managed, all ongoing duties of loyalty and care end with regard to matters arising after the dissociation.[135]

### h. Dissolution and Winding Up

***Triggering Events.*** Statutory provisions generally provide that an LLC must be dissolved and wound up on: (1) the occurrence of a dissolution event specified in the LLC operating agreement; (2) the consent of all the members; (3) the passage of 90 days during which the LLC has no members; and (4) the entry of a court order dissolving the LLC on grounds that the LLC's activities are illegal or cannot be carried on in a reasonably practicable manner in accordance with the partnership agreement or that the managers or members in control have acted illegally or fraudulently or in an oppressive manner that has directly harmed the member initiating the proceeding.[136]

***Winding Up.*** A dissolved LLC continues after dissolution only for the purpose of winding up. In winding up its activities, an LLC must discharge its debts and obligations, settle and close the LLC's activities, and marshal and distribute the assets of the LLC. It may deliver to the secretary of state a statement of dissolution, preserve the LLC's activities and property as a going concern for a reasonable time, prosecute and defend actions and proceedings, transfer the LLC's property, settle disputes by mediation or arbitration, file a statement of termination stating that the LLC is terminated, and take all other action necessary or appropriate to wind up the LLC. If a dissolved LLC has no members, the legal representative of the last person to have been a member may wind up the activities of the company.[137]

***Notices Barring Claims.*** A dissolved LLC may notify its known creditors of the dissolution, specifying the required information and mailing address for a claim, stating the deadline for receipt of the claim (not less than 120 days after

---

133. RULLCA § 406.
134. RULLCA §§ 601, 602.
135. RULLCA § 603.
136. RULLCA § 701.
137. RULLCA § 702.

receipt of the notice date), and indicating that a claim will be barred if not received by the deadline. A claim against an LLC is barred if the notice is given and the claim is not received by the specified deadline. A timely received claim will be barred if the LLC rejects the claim and the claimant does not commence an action within 90 days of being notified of the rejection and the 90 day deadline for commencing an action.[138] In addition, a dissolved LLC may publish notice of its dissolution and request persons having claims against the LLC to present the claims in accordance with the notice, stating that a claim against the LLC will be barred if an enforcement action is not taken within five years to enforce the claim. If the notice is published in accordance with the statutory requirements, an unenforced claim not previously barred will be barred after such five-year period.[139]

**Enforcement of Claims.** A claim that has not been barred may be enforced against a dissolved LLC to the extent of its undistributed assets and, if assets of the LLC have been distributed after dissolution, against a member or transferee, but a person's total liability for such claims may not exceed the total amount of assets distributed to the person after dissolution.[140]

**Final Distributions.** After discharging its obligations to creditors, a dissolved LLC must first distribute any surplus proportionately to persons owning a transferable interest based on the amount of their respective unreturned contributions and then distribute any remaining surplus in equal shares among members and dissociated members. All distributions must be paid in money.[141]

## i. Litigation Rights

State statutes usually authorize a member of an LLC to bring a direct action against the LLC or other members for legal or equitable relief to enforce the partner's rights under the operating agreement or applicable law. The member must plead and prove an actual or threatened injury to the member, not just the LLC.[142]

Such statutes also typically permit a member to maintain a derivative action on behalf of the LLC if (1) the member first makes a demand on the manager in a manager-managed LLC, or the other members in a member-managed LLC to bring the action or pleads with particularity why such a demand would be futile and (2) any recovery from the litigation is paid to the LLC. If such a derivative action is successful, the court may award a reimbursement of the plaintiff's attorney fees and costs from the recovery.[143]

Some statutes specifically authorize an LLC to appoint a special litigation committee made up of independent, disinterested persons (who may be members) to represent the interests of the LLC in a derivative proceeding.[144]

---

138. RULLCA § 703.
139. RULLCA § 704.
140. RULLCA § 704(d).
141. RULLCA § 708.
142. RULLCA § 901.
143. RULLCA §§ 902-904, 906.
144. RULLCA § 905.

## j. Mergers

State statutes generally authorize the merger of an LLC with another LLC, a partnership, a limited partnership, or a corporation, domestic or foreign.[145] Usually such merger statutes are patterned after the state's corporate statutes.

*Documents and Process.* A plan of merger must be approved by the members. The plan of merger usually sets forth the name of each party to the merger and the name of the surviving entity, the terms and conditions of the merger, the manner and basis of converting interests in each merging entity into the surviving entity or into cash or other property, and any required amendment's to the surviving entity's organizational documents.[146] Absent specific provisions in the governing LLC agreement, the plan must be approved by all members of the LLC.[147] Following approval of the plan of merger, the surviving entity files the articles of merger with the appropriate secretary of state offices. The articles of merger set forth, among other things: the plan of merger; the date the merge is effective; a statement that the merger was approved by each party to the merger as required by its governing statute; and any other information required by the governing statute of any party to the merger.[148]

*Effect of Merger.* Following the filing of the articles of merger, all entities that were parties to the merger, other than the surviving entity, cease to exist. Title to all property previously owned by each merged entity vests in the surviving entity, and the surviving entity is responsible for all liabilities of all other entities in the merger. If there is a legal proceeding pending against any party to the merger, it may either be continued as if the merger did not occur or the surviving entity may be substituted as the party in the proceeding. The governing instrument of the surviving entity (whether a certificate of formation, a certificate of limited partnership, or articles of incorporation) is deemed amended to the extent provided in the plan of merger.[149]

## D. FORMATION TAX PLANNING FOR PARTNERSHIP-TAXED ENTITIES

An entity taxed as a partnership can usually be formed with no threat of taxable income being recognized by the partnership or its partners. Compared to the formation tax rules for its corporate counterparts (discussed in the previous chapter), the partnership rules are identical in some respects, generally are more forgiving, and are a bit more complicated. Care is still required to avoid the planning traps.

### 1. THE 721 RULE AND RELATED TRAPS

A partner recognizes no gain or loss on the contribution of property to a partnership in exchange for an interest in the partnership.[150] Any future income,

---

145. RULLCA § 1002.
146. RULLCA § 1002(b).
147. RULLCA § 1002.
148. RULLCA § 1004.
149. RULLCA § 1005.
150. I.R.C. § 721(a).

gain, loss or deduction is allocated among the partners to reflect the built-in gain or loss.[151]

**Example:** Linda contributes equipment with a basis of $100,000 and a fair market value of $300,000 to XYZ partnership in exchange for a one-third interest in the partnership. She recognizes no income or loss on the exchange even though she is only a one-third partner. Linda's built-in gain at the time of the contribution is $200,000. Assume that for the next two years the partnership depreciates the equipment on a straight-line basis over 10 years. The book depreciation each year (based on the fair market value of the equipment at the time of Linda's contribution) is $30,000 (10 percent of $300,000), with one-third allocated to Linda and two-thirds to her partners. The tax depreciation each year (based on Linda's $100,000 carryover basis in the property) is $10,000, allocated all to Linda's partners because tax depreciation is first allocated to the noncontributing partners to the extent of their book depreciation so as to not give the contributing partner any deduction attributable to the built-in gain.[152]

Then assume at the end of year two the equipment is sold for $270,000, when the book basis is $240,000 ($300,000 less $60,000 of book depreciation) and the tax basis is $80,000 ($100,000 less $20,000 of tax depreciation). Linda's remaining built-in gain at the end of year two would be $160,000, the excess of the $240,000 book basis over the $80,000 tax basis. The $190,000 tax gain (the excess of $270,000 realized over the $80,000 tax basis) would first be allocated to Linda to the extent of her remaining $160,000 built-in gain, and the $30,000 excess gain then would be allocated one-third to Linda and two-thirds to her partners. Thus, Linda would end up recognizing $170,000 of total gain and her partners would end up recognizing a $20,000 gain on the sale – which is just the amount of depreciation allocated to Linda's partners during the first two years.

**Comparison:** The partnership 721 Rule is easier to satisfy up front than its 351 corporate counterpart. Since there is no control requirement, the 351 traps relating to the "control" and "immediately after" requirements, and the associated voting and nonvoting interest issues, are of no concern in the partnership context. However, things get more complicated in the partnership context if there is a built-in gain or loss on the contributed property because the taint stays with the contributing partner. In contrast, once property is in a corporation, its attachment to the contributing owner is gone.

**Traps:** Following are some of the traps with the 721 Rule.

**a. Service Partner.** As with the 351 Rule, the "property" requirement of Section 721 does not include services.[153] Thus, a partner who receives a partnership interest in return for services is not protected by the rule. The tax consequences to such a partner and the related planning options are discussed in

---

151. I.R.C. § 704(c)(1).
152. Reg. § 1.704-3(b).
153. Reg. § 1.721-1(b)(1).

the following section. The good news is that, unlike the 351 Rule, the presence of such a partner will not jeopardize application of the 721 Rule to others who contribute property for partnership interests.

**b. Ordinary Income Taint.** Any unrealized receivable contributed to a partnership by a partner will be considered an ordinary income asset. Similarly, any contributed property that was inventory in the hands of the partner will be considered inventory property of the partnership for gain or loss purposes if sold within a five-year period.[154]

**c. Capital Loss Taint.** If a partner contributes to a partnership property that was a capital asset in the hands of the partner and the partnership sells the property within a five-year period, any loss recognized by the partnership on the sale must be treated as a capital loss to the extent of any built-in loss (the excess of basis over fair market value) that existed at the time of the contribution.[155]

**d. Mixing Bowl Trap.** Partner A contributes property in exchange for a partnership interest, and the partnership then distributes the property to another partner within seven years of the contribution. Partner A must recognize any remaining built-in gain to the extent such gain would be recognized if the partnership had sold the property for its fair market value on the date of the distribution to the other partner.[156] The purpose of this exception is to prevent partners from using the generous tax-free rules relating to property transfers in and out of partnerships to structure transactions between themselves.

**e. Property Exchange Trap.** Partner A contributes property in exchange for a partnership interest, and the partnership distributes *other* property to Partner A within seven years. Partner A must recognize gain equal to the lesser of (i) the excess of the fair market value of the distributed property over Partner A's basis in his or her partnership interest before the distribution or (ii) the pre-contribution gain that Partner A would have been required to recognize under the previous Mixing Bowl Trap if the *contributed* property had been distributed to another partner within the seven-year time frame.[157] The purpose of this trap is to force income recognition where there is exchange of properties between a partner and a partnership within a seven-year period.

**f. Book Gain Less than Built-In Gain.** Suppose in the above example that the equipment contributed by Linda was sold for $210,000 at the end of year two when Linda's remaining built-in gain on the property was $160,000 (the excess of the $240,000 book basis over the $80,000 tax basis). In that situation, the $130,000 tax gain on the sale (the excess of the $210,000 realized over the $80,000 tax basis) would be less than the remaining $160,000 of built-in gain. What is allocated to Linda and her other partners in such a situation? Under the traditional approach, a ceiling rule kicks in to limit the gain allocated to Linda to

---

154. I.R.C. § 724(a) & (b).
155. I.R.C. § 724(c).
156. I.R.C. § 704(c)(1)(B).
157. I.R.C. § 737.

the actual gain of $130,000.[158]   Although very common, the problem with this approach is that Linda's partners never get any tax benefit for their two-thirds share of the $30,000 economic loss (the excess of the $240,000 book basis over the $210,000 amount realized on the sale).  To correct this situation, the parties may elect to use a curative allocation or a remedial approach that would allocate to Linda her full remaining $160,000 built-in gain, and then allocate a $30,000 loss to the partners according to their interests in the partnership.[159]  Linda would end up recognizing a net $150,000 gain ($160,000 less $10,000) and her partners would end up recognizing a $20,000 loss.  For planning purposes, there is a need for an understanding and agreement between the parties when built-in gain property is contributed for a partnership interest and the contributing party is credited for the fair market value of the contributed property.

     **g.   Investment Company.**   The 721 Rule does not apply to any gain realized on the transfer of property to a partnership that would be treated as an investment company if it were incorporated.[160]

### 2. RULE 2: PARTNERSHIP BOOT RULE

     If a partner transfers property to a partnership in exchange for a partnership interest and other property (boot), the portion of the transferred property allocable to the boot will be taxed as a sale or exchange.[161]

     **Example:** Linda transfers to XYZ partnership equipment with a basis of $100,000 and a fair market value of $300,000 in exchange for a one-third interest in the partnership and $75,000 cash.  One-fourth of the transferred equipment (75,000/300,000) will be treated as a sale for cash, producing a taxable gain of $50,000 ($75,000 less one-fourth of the $100,000 basis).  The remaining three-fourths of the contributed property will be treated as a tax-free contribution.

     **Traps:** Traps kick in when the transferring partner actually or constructively owns more than 50 percent of the capital interests or profits interests of the partnership.  In such event, the transferring partner may not recognize any loss on the exchange component of the transaction.[162]

     Plus, if the transferred asset is not a capital asset in the hands of the partnership (i.e., is accounts receivable or inventory), any gain recognized by the more-than-50 percent partner is treated as ordinary income.[163]   Also, if the transferred property is depreciable by the partnership, any gain recognized by such a partner will be taxed as ordinary income and installment sale treatment generally will not be available.[164]

### 3. RULE 3: PARTNER BASIS RULE

     The basis of the partnership interest acquired by a partner in exchange for

---

158.  Reg. § 1.704-3(b).
159.  Reg. § 1.704-3(c) & (d).
160.  I.R.C. § 721(b).
161.  I.R.C. § 707(a)(2)(B); Reg. § 1.707-3(f), Example 1.
162.  I.R.C. § 707(b)(1).
163.  I.R.C. § 707(b)(2).
164.  I.R.C. §§ 453(g), 707(b)(2), 1239(a).

property equals the partner's basis in the contributed property.[165]

**Example:** In the above example where Linda received a one-third partnership interest and $75,000 cash in exchange for the contributed equipment, her basis in her partnership interest would be $75,000, that portion of her $100,000 equipment basis (three-fourths) allocable to the partnership interest received.

### 4. RULE 4: PARTNER TACKING RULE

If the property transferred by a partner in a 721 transaction is a capital asset or a 1231 trade or business asset, the partner's holding period of the asset is "tacked on" in determining the partner's holding period for the partnership interest.[166]

**Example:** In the above example, the equipment transferred by Linda would qualify as a capital or a 1231 asset. If she had held such equipment for two years before the exchange, her holding period in her XYZ partnership interest would be deemed to be two years when received.

### 5. RULE 5: PARTNERSHIP NON-RECOGNITION RULE

A partnership recognizes no gain or loss on the receipt of money or property for an interest in the partnership.[167]

### 6. RULE 6: PARTNERSHIP BASIS RULE

A partnership's basis in property acquired from a partner in exchange for an interest in the partnership equals the partner's basis in the transferred property.[168]

**Example:** In the above example where Linda received a one-third partnership interest and $75,000 cash in exchange for her equipment, XYZ partnership's basis in the equipment would be $75,000, the portion of her $100,000 carryover equipment basis (three-fourths) allocable to the partnership interest received.

**Comparison:** Partnerships have no special built-in loss basis limitation comparable to the built-in loss limitations that apply in a corporate 351 transaction.

### 7. RULE 7: PARTNERSHIP TACKING RULE

In a 721 transaction, the partner's holding period in the property is "tacked on" in determining the partnership's holding period in the asset.[169]

**Example:** If in the above example Linda held the equipment two years before the exchange, the two years would be tacked on in determining the partnership's holding period.

---

165. I.R.C. § 722. The basis also is increased by any gain recognized under Section 721(b) if the partnership constitutes an investment company. Note, however, if a partner recognizes gain by virtue of a deemed distribution of cash in excess of basis, such gain itself does not increase the basis.

166. I.R.C. § 1223(1).

167. I.R.C. § 721.

168. I.R.C. § 723. The basis also is increased by any gain recognized under Section 721(b) if the partnership constitutes an investment company.

169. I.R.C. § 1223(2).

## 8. RULE 8: PARTNERSHIP ASSUMED DEBT RULE

A partner's debt assumed by a partnership in a 721 exchange is treated as a distribution of cash to the partner to the extent the partner's share of the debt is reduced.[170] If the reduction in the partner's share of the debt exceeds the partner's basis in his or her partnership interest, such excess deemed cash distribution is taxed as a gain from the sale or exchange of the partner's interest in the partnership.[171]

**Example:** Linda transfers to XYZ partnership equipment that has a basis of $100,000 and a fair market value of $300,000 and is encumbered by a $90,000 recourse debt. In exchange, Linda receives a one-third interest in the partnership, and the partnership assumes the $90,000 debt obligation. Linda is deemed to have received a $60,000 cash distribution, the two-thirds portion of the assumed debt that she is relieved of and that is allocated to the other partners. This deemed cash distribution reduces Linda's basis in her partnership interest from $100,000 (her carryover basis from the equipment contribution) to $40,000. The basis of the other partners is increased by $60,000, because the increase in their share of the partnership's debts is treated as a deemed contribution.[172] If the debt assumed by XYZ partnership equaled $180,000, Linda would be deemed to have received a $120,000 cash distribution for the two-thirds share of the debt allocated to the other partners. This deemed cash distribution would exceed her $100,000 basis in her partnership interest (the carryover basis from the equipment contribution) by $20,000, and that excess would be taxed as a gain from the sale of her partnership interest. Her basis in her partnership interest would be reduced to zero as a result of the deemed cash distribution. The basis of the other partners would be increased by $120,000, their deemed cash contributions to the partnership.

**Comparison:** On its face, the partnership debt assumption rule looks much like its corporate counterpart, but in fact they operate quite differently. The corporate rule is based on the total debt assumed by the corporation; the partnership rule considers only the portion of the assumed debt allocated to the other partners. Also, any liability in excess of basis gain recognized in a corporate context will increase the shareholder's stock basis and the corporation's basis in the contributed property. Not so in the partnership context; the gain is treated as sale of a partnership interest. Note, however, that Section 733 precludes a partner's basis from ever going below zero as a result of a distribution.[173]

**Traps:** The toughest traps under the 721 Rule relate to how liabilities are allocated to the various partners, the critical component to the operative effect of the rule.

**a. Recourse Liabilities.** The allocation of recourse liabilities is based on who will bear the ultimate loss if things go bad.[174] Often, it is possible to

---

170. I.R.C. § 752(b).
171. I.R.C. § 731(a)(1).
172. I.R.C. §§ 722, 752(a).
173. I.R.C. § 733.
174. Reg. § 1.752-2.

determine how the partners will share the burden just by eyeballing the situation. In the more difficult situation, the determination is made by assuming a hypothetical liquidation under the following conditions: all partnership liabilities become due and payable; all assets that secure debts are used to pay debts; all other partnership assets are deemed worthless; all guarantees, partnership agreement terms, and rights under state law and loan documents are considered; and all partners are assumed to have the means to satisfy their obligations. The recourse debt allocation is based on the amount that each partner, under these assumptions, would be required to pony up to pay off the debt.[175] For planning purposes, this provides an opportunity to use agreements between the partners to allocate recourse liabilities in a way that minimizes any adverse tax impacts, such as where the allocated recourse debt may otherwise trigger a deemed cash distribution in excess of basis.

**b.   Nonrecourse Liabilities.**   Nonrecourse liabilities (those secured by assets, but for which no partner has any personal liability) must first be allocated to the contributing partner to the extent the amount of the nonrecourse debt exceeds the contributing partner's basis in the contributed property.[176]  Thus, if Linda contributes property to the partnership with a basis of $100,000, a fair market value of $300,000, and subject to a nonrecourse debt of $180,000, the first $80,000 of the nonrecourse debt must be allocated to Linda. The partners have flexibility in allocating the remaining $100,000 of nonrecourse debt among themselves.  Options include allocating the remaining nonrecourse debt (i) in a way that is reasonably consistent with how any other significant income or gain item is allocated under the partnership agreement, (ii) according to how deductions related to nonrecourse liabilities are expected to be allocated over time, (iii) to the contributing partner (Linda, in this case) to the extent the total built-in gain ($200,000) exceeds the allocation of debt in excess of basis to the contributing partner ($80,000), or (iv) in accordance with the partners' shares of profits, considering all facts and circumstances.[177]  Thus, in Linda's situation, the entire $180,000 recourse debt could be allocated to her because it is less than the $200,000 of built-in gain.  Of course, the other partners would likely object to such an allocation because they might favor an allocation that would increase their basis in their partnership interests and provide an opportunity for them to share in any nonrecourse deductions.  The planning challenge is to agree on a basis for allocating any such nonrecourse debt among the partners that best accomplishes the objectives of all the partners.  In most situations, the parties will opt for an allocation that tracks how profits are to be allocated among the partners.

**c.   Future Accountable Debts.**   A debt assumed by a partnership in a 721 exchange is not subject to the Partnership Assumed Debt Rule if payment of the debt would create a tax deduction for the partnership or be treated as a capital expenditure by the partnership.[178]  One example is the accounts payable of a cash

---

175.  Generally Reg. § 1.752-2.
176.  Reg. § 1.752-3(a)(2).
177.  Reg. § 1.752-3(a)(3).
178.  Rev. Rule 88-77, 1988-2 C.B. 128.

basis partner. This is the same as the corporate counterpart limitation described above.

**d. Basis Pumping.** The ability to structure the allocation of the assumed debt among the partners usually eliminates the need for any additional basis pumping technique in a partnership context when the assumed liabilities will exceed the basis of the transferred assets.

### 9. FORMATION EQUITY FOR SERVICE

Often one or more owners are transferred an equity interest in a new enterprise in return for services that have been rendered or will be rendered in the future. Chapter 11 of this book analyzes and discusses the planning factors and strategies that need to be considered whenever equity interests or rights are transferred to key employees. This discussion focuses on the narrower planning options for transferring equity interests to service partners or LLC members during the formation process.

**a. Profits Interest Scenario.** XYZ partnership, owned equally by Larry and Sue, has equity capital interests valued at $1 million. Linda is transferred a 10 percent interest in all future profits of the business in return for her promise to manage the company. Linda does not recognize any taxable income on the receipt of the profits interest (and the partnership gets no corresponding deduction) unless Linda disposes of the profits interest within two years or the profits interest relates to a substantially certain and predictable income stream (i.e., income from high-quality debt securities or a high-quality net lease).[179]

This profits interest option creates a planning opportunity in partnerships that doesn't exist in a corporate context. The service owner can be given an equity interest that makes him or her a true partner, but there are no phantom income tax concerns and usually no need for forfeiture provisions because the interest relates only to the future.

**b. Capital Interest 83(a) Scenario.** XYZ partnership, owned equally by Larry and Sue, has capital valued at $1,000,000 that has a basis of $200,000. Linda is transferred a 10 percent interest in the capital of the partnership in return for her promise to manage the business. Linda recognizes $100,000 of income in year one under section 83(a),[180] and XYZ partnership is entitled to a $100,000 business expense deduction, which is passed through to Larry and Sue.[181]

**c. Deferral, 83(b) and Gross-Up Scenarios.** In the partnership context, section 83 works the same as it does it in the corporate context (see prior chapter) with respect to the ordinary income recognized by a service partner on the receipt of a capital interest and the corresponding deduction to the partnership. Substantial forfeiture provisions can be used to defer the recognition of income,

---

179. Rev. Proc. 93-27, 1993-2 C.B. 343. See also Prop. Regs. § 1.83(l)(2005).
180. I.R.C. 83(a).
181. I.R.C. 83(h). There is a question as to whether the transaction also may be treated as a taxable transfer of the appreciated property from the other partners to Linda, followed by a contribution of such property to the partnership by Linda. If so, Larry and Sue would be required to recognize an $80,000 gain on the transfer ($100,000 less $20,000 allocable basis). Reg. 1.83-6(b). Proposed Regs. 1.83-6(b) and 1.721-1(b) (2005), if and when finalized, would not require the recognition of such a gain.

and a risk-laden 83(b) election may be used to accelerate the income recognition in those situations where it is warranted. Similarly, the gross-up scenarios discussed in Chapter 4 in connection with corporate formation tax planning may also work in the partnership context.

## PROBLEM 5-E

Assume the same facts as Problem 4-D from the previous chapter, except that Lucy plans on forming an LLC for the business rather than a C corporation. Advise Lucy on the tax impacts of her plan. What changes would you suggest? Why?

Then suppose that Lucy desires that an LLC own the real estate contributed by David, but a C corporation be used to operate the business. The LLC will lease the real estate to the C corporation. How would you propose restructuring the transaction to accommodate such a structure and still provide each owner an equal interest in the LLC and the C corporation?

# E. DESIGNING THE OPERATING AGREEMENT

### 1. SCOPE AND LAWYER'S ROLE

The primary planning challenge during the organization of a partnership or LLC is to prepare a comprehensive operating agreement that incorporates all of the essential deal points between the co-owners of the business. Often the parties are tempted to short-circuit the front-end planning effort. They perpetuate the common (but false) perception that there is a "normal" or "accepted" way of documenting issues between co-owners. The result is that, in far too many cases, the operating agreement effort is limited to filling in blanks on a stock form, and the dialogue is limited to descriptive pronouncements from the lawyers. The operating agreement looks complete and official, but does little or nothing to reflect thoughtful, negotiated deal points that the owners have resolved with the assistance of skilled planning advisors.

In nearly all situations, the planning lawyer must take the lead in defining the scope of the front-end planning effort. This is done by identifying key planning issues, explaining the significance of the issues, and then helping the client carefully evaluate his or her objectives or priority concerns with respect to each issue. Usually customization of the operating agreement increases as the planning effort improves. More customization leads to more complexity and, most importantly, to a better mutual understanding of the key deal points between the owners of the business.

The identity of the client affects how the potential deal points are discussed and analyzed in any given partnership or LLC situation. If the client will own the controlling vote in the entity, the preferred choice may be to refrain from initiating any dialogue on many deal points with the other owners. The client knows that he or she has the power to dictate the outcome of any dispute by virtue of the voting control. Typically, the burden is on the minority owners to raise any operational issues that may require special treatment in the operating agreement. So the lawyer who represents the minority owners usually has the toughest job. Key issues must be identified, discussed, and prioritized. A plan must be developed for creating minority rights for those issues that are of greatest concern. Then the plan must be sold and eventually incorporated into the operating agreement.

The lawyer who is engaged to organize and represent the partnership or LLC, not a particular owner of group of owners, must be sensitive to the conflicts that many of the key planning issues might create between the owners. In this situation, usually the best approach is for the entity's lawyer to initiate a dialogue with all the owners in a meeting or series of meetings that addresses the most important issues, with input from lawyers representing specific owners. The process requires a modest commitment of time and expense, but it will go a long way in identifying and resolving on the front-end any fundamental differences between the parties.

Following is a brief description of certain key provisions of an operating agreement and related options for customizing these provisions. Specific references are to the LLC operating agreement in section B. of Chapter 18.

## PROBLEM 5-F

Refer to Problem 5-D in which Son and Dad form a manager-managed LLC. Son lines up a deep-pocket investor ("Investor") who is willing to invest $1 million in the LLC if, and only if, the LLC operating agreement contains the following provisions:

1. Investor is the manager of the LLC and has the exclusive right to determine how Strategy is exploited, when it is sold, and the terms of any sale.

2. Investor is relieved of all liabilities to the LLC for any actions or omissions taken in good faith, even those that are determined to be grossly negligent or intentionally reckless.

3. All fiduciary duties of the Investor are eliminated.

4. The Investor is allocated 90 percent of the losses that are expected during the first three years of operation. This is regarded as a tax benefit for Investor.

5. Investor accrues an annual fee of $100,000 for management services, to be paid when the LLC has sufficient cash flow to pay this accrued compensation.

6. Investor is allocated 50 percent of all profits realized in any year or on the sale of Strategy.

7. Available cash flows from operations or the sale of Strategy are used: first, to pay any accrued management fees due Investor; second, to repay Investor's $1 million investment; and third, to pay Investor 50 percent of the excess and the other members the remaining 50 percent.

What problems, if any, will the parties encounter in designing the LLC operating agreement to meet these deal-braking demands of Investor?

## 2. AUTHORITY AND MANAGEMENT PROVISIONS

*Purpose of the Company (Section 5).* In a partnership or LLC, the preferred choice often is to use this provision to specifically define and limit the scope of the business activities of the entity. Partners and LLC members often want the comfort of knowing that their investment will not be diverted into activities that are outside the scope of what was originally discussed. Liability exposure may also be an issue, particularly where the managers of the venture have multiple business interests. Limiting the scope of the business activities may help eliminate the business entity's liability exposure for unrelated actions of its managers. A written activity limitation also may dash any expectations other owners may have relative to their other business activities by drawing an express, unequivocal line in the sand. Some partners and LLC member may object to a written limitation on the scope of the enterprise, arguing that it restricts flexibility, creates potential confusion for third parties, and fosters notions of "separateness" and "temporariness" between the owners.

*Limits on Manager Authority. (Sections 11.1 and 11.6).* Often the manager of the partnership or LLC is given broad authority to administer the business affairs of the enterprise. The planning challenge is to define those situations where the manager must seek approval of the partners or LLC members before taking action and what level of approval is required. In some circumstances, majority approval may be adequate. In other situations, a unanimous or super-majority vote may be justified. It all turns on the nature and scope of the business and the expectations and goals of the partners or LLC members. These are the sections of the agreement that can be used to define and protect minority rights and often justify significant dialogue during the planning process. Provisions that often require special attention in these sections include: required cash distributions; the admission of new partners or LLC members; outside or competitive activities of partners or LLC members; related party transactions; material changes to the business plan; debt limitations; confidentially covenants of managers, partners or LLC members; tax elections; selection of professionals; and dispute resolutions procedures.

*Limited Liability of Manager (Section 11.3).* The key issue is whether the manager should be relieved of personal liability to the partnership or LLC for actions taken or omitted by the manager with a good faith belief that such actions or omissions were in the best interests of the entity. Resolution of the issue in the partnership or LLC operating agreement often turns on the level of culpability that partners or LLC members are willing to forgive. Ordinary negligence usually isn't enough to override a good faith exculpation provision, while willful misconduct and criminal acts often render provision moot and trigger liability. But what about grossly negligence or intentionally reckless conduct? These are tougher issues in the planning process. Managers often do not want any liability exposure absent a showing of bad faith, willful misconduct or criminal activity. They don't want to get tangled up in line drawing between ordinary and gross negligence. In contrast, many owners want protection against a manager's gross negligence or intentionally reckless activities.

*Resignation, Removal and Replacement of Manager (Section 15).* This provision raises a number of potential issues in the design of the operating agreement. If a manager resigns in violation of specified conditions in the operating agreement, does the manager have any liability exposure to the entity? Will the manager be subject to any non-competition restrictions? What ongoing confidentiality covenants, if any, will apply to the manager? What level of partner or LLC member vote (majority, super-majority, unanimous) is required to remove and replace a manager? Is there any requirement to show "cause"? Is the manager entitled to any severance benefit if removed for no cause? Does the resignation or removal of manager entitle the partnership or LLC to purchase the partnership or LLC interest of the member or give the manager a right to compel such a purchase?

*Indemnification (Section 11.4).* Will partners and managers who act on behalf of the partnership or LLC be protected against any personal loss, damage or liability they incur as a result of their activities on behalf of the entity? Usually an indemnification and hold harmless provision is included in the operating agreement to protect against such liabilities and any associated legal fees, but limitations often need to be worked out between the partners or LLC members. The agreement may provide that the indemnification rights are limited to assets of the entity and are not obligations of the partners or LLC members. The owners may not want any personal exposure, and the primary assets of the business may have been pledged to secure financing. The net result is that the indemnification provision, as a practical matter, may mean little or nothing if the business fails. The indemnification provision may be limited to acts or omissions undertaken in good faith and with a belief that they were in the best interests of the entity, subject to exceptions for specified levels of culpability (see prior paragraph). The operating agreement also may condition any indemnification right on a tender of the defense or resolution of the claim to the partnership or LLC so that the entity can control expenses and dispose of the matter on its own terms. These indemnification limitations often create concerns for managers. A solution to ease these concerns may be an errors and omissions insurance policy for the managers that facilitates the agreed limitations while providing an additional level of protection for the managers of the enterprise.

*Compensation of Managers (Section 11 Insertion).* Often there is a need to specify how those partners or members who manage the enterprise are to be compensated for their services on behalf the partnership or LLC. Absent such an agreement, the statutory default rule usually will deny any compensation for services that are not related to dissolving and winding up the entity.

*Time Devoted to Enterprise (Section 11.2).* For partners or LLC members who manage the enterprise, key issues often include their service commitments and their right to be involved in other activities. Are they expected to devote all of their time and energies to the enterprise? Failure to adequately clarify this issue can lead to an early showdown when the investment partners or LLC members discover that the manager spends only a fraction of his or her time looking after the affairs of the enterprise and is heavily involved in other ventures. The stock language in many forms gives the manager significant flexibility to define the service level and pursue other ventures. This language won't do the job in many situations.

### 3. OWNER RIGHTS PROVISIONS

*Owner Transfer Rights (Section 14).*   State statutes generally permit a partner or LLC member to transfer the economic (but not voting or management rights) rights of partnership or LLC interest to a third party transferee. Often, it is necessary and smart to prohibit any such voluntary or involuntary transfer unless specified conditions exist. These conditions usually include the death of a partner or LLC member or the approval by the managers or a designated percentage of the partners or LLC members. Absent such approval, partners are unable to transfer interests in the partnership or LLC. In many situations, the operating agreement also needs to specify the procedures and conditions that must be satisfied in order for a third party transferee to be admitted as an owner with all the rights and privileges of a partner or LLC member.

*Buy-Sell Rights (Section 14 Insert).*   In many business enterprises, the operating agreement between the partners or LLC members needs to spell out buy-sell rights that are triggered when a partner or LLC member dies, becomes disabled, just desires to cash out and move on, experiences a messy divorce or bankruptcy, or needs to be expelled. These buy-sell provisions and the associated planning may be used to accomplish various objectives, including to ensure that (1) ownership interests in the enterprise are never transferred or made available to third parties who are unacceptable to the owners, (2) there is a mechanism to fairly value and fund the equity interest of a departing owner, (3) control and ownership issues will be smoothly transitioned at appropriate times so as not to unduly interfere with and disrupt the operations of the business, (4) owners have a fair "market" for their shares at appropriate points of exit, (5) owners have the power to involuntarily terminate (expel) an owner who is no longer wanted, (6) the amount paid for the equity interest of a deceased owner determines the value of the deceased owner's equity interest for estate tax purposes, and (7) cash and funding challenges of owner departures are appropriately anticipated and covered. An extended discussion of this planning challenge is included in section C. of Chapter 13. The substance of that discussion, including certain of the common mistakes that are often made in the buy-sell planning process, is directly applicable to partnerships and LLCs.

*Major Transaction Approval Rights (Section 11.6).*   The operating agreement usually requires partner or LLC member approval of transactions that involve a merger of the partnership or LLC, a combination with another entity, or a sale of all or substantially all of the entity's assets. Majority approval works for many partnerships and LLCs. In some situations, the parties desire to require a super-majority vote, such as two-thirds. Often it helps to clarify if the manager's approval also is a condition to the transaction. And sometimes the often-used "substantially all" standard for determining whether an asset sale triggers owner approval rights is perceived as being too undefined or capable of manipulation. In such situations, the operating agreement lowers the threshold by specifying objective criteria (a designated percentage of assets or revenues, or both) for determining whether owner approval rights are required for a sale of assets.

*Inspection Rights. (Section 13.4)*   Some operating agreements provide partners and LLC members with broad document inspection rights, conditioned only on reasonable notice, inspection at the location where the documents are kept, and reimbursement of any reproduction costs. Often those who manage a limited partnership or a manager-managed LLC desire to limit the inspection rights of limited partners or LLC members who have no management rights. The rationale is that broad inspection rights for such investors will not benefit the entity in any way and may create opportunities for abuse that frustrate management efforts. When limited investor inspection rights are desired, the operating agreement often requires that the requesting partner or LLC member provide a written request that specifies the entity-related purpose for making the request, the particularized list of the documents requested, and how such documents relate to the stated purpose. The manager has the final say on whether the conditions of the request have been satisfied.

*Fiduciary Exculpatory Provisions. (Section 11.5 and Section 12 Insertion).*  Statutory provisions impose fiduciary duties of care, loyalty, good faith, and fair dealing on those partners or LLC members who have the right to participate in the management of the enterprise. As explained in section E. of this Chapter, the operating agreement usually may include provisions that substantially reduce any liability for fiduciary breaches that do not involve bad faith. The only limitation in many states is that the exculpatory provision may not be "manifestly unreasonable." This presents a planning opportunity for those enterprises that want to deemphasize restrictions that come with the duties of care and loyalty.

*Amendment Rights (Section 18).*   The power to amend the operating agreement is always an important consideration. In many situations, nothing short of unanimous consent will work. The agreement is viewed as a contract that protects minority rights.  In those circumstances where ownership and management interests are separated (limited partnerships and manager-managed LLCs), the operating agreement specifies what may be amended by the approval of partners or members who own a majority or designated super-majority of the entity's interests. Also, in such situations, often the manager is authorized to amend the agreement without partner or member approval to cure ambiguities or inconsistencies in the agreement.

*Owner Confidentiality Covenants. (Section 12 Insertion).* Sometimes it is necessary to extend confidentially covenants to partners and LLC members, particularly in those enterprises where the owners may have access to trade secrets or proprietary information critical to the success of the business. Some investors may resist any such agreements or any mechanism that limits other investment options or exposes them to any future claims relating to the use of proprietary information.

*Dissolutions Rights (Section 16).*  The operating agreement should specify the conditions for dissolving the partnership or LLC, which often track the applicable statutory provisions.  A primary consideration is the approval requirement of the partners or LLC members to force a dissolution and winding up. Many require unanimous approval, while others impose a super-majority requirement. In limited partnerships and manager-managed LLCs, a dissolution decision generally always requires the consent of those who manage the enterprise.

*Life After Rights (Section 12 Insertion).* In professional organizations and other partnerships and LLCs where revenues are generated from the personal services of the owners, often it is advisable to spell out the "going forward" rights that each owner will have in the event there is a falling out and the group fractures. Absent such an agreement, the owners may find themselves tangled up with dissolution and wind-up issues that may make it difficult to immediately shift gears and preserve the continuity of their business activities. Most professionals and service providers cannot afford a major disruption that stops their careers. Key issues include the right to engage in the same business as the fractured entity, to pursue and service clients of the entity, to hire employees of the entity, to deal with vendors and financial institutions used by the entity, to make copies of client documents, files and other important documents, to use the same personal business email addresses and phone numbers, and to disclose the prior affiliation with the entity.

### 4. CAPITAL AND ALLOCATION PROVISIONS

*Initial Capital Contributions (Sections 7.1 and 7.6).* The operating agreement should describe the initial contribution obligations of the partners or LLC members. Most importantly, the value that is going to be assigned to non-cash contributions for capital account purposes should be specified in the agreement or an Exhibit. Such contributions may include tangible property (such as land or equipment), intellectual property rights, the business plan for the enterprise, past services rendered on behalf of the enterprise, future services to be rendered, and more. The planning challenge is to clarify the expectations of the parties with respect to any non-cash assets and properly value those assets that are going to be positive additions to the capital account of the contributing partner or LLC member. The agreement should authorize the partnership or LLC to take any action to enforce the contribution obligations of partners or LLC members, to recover any associated costs and attorney fees, and to settle any such disputes with a designated approval (usually majority) of the other partners or LLC members.

*Future Contribution Obligations (Section 7.4).* The issue of additional capital contribution obligations of the partners or LLC members should be documented in the operating agreement. Some owners, even those with deep pockets, may want to eliminate any expectations that they will provide additional capital to keep the venture afloat or fund growth. Others may be concerned with dilution; they do not want their equity interests reduced as those with greater means continually pony up more money and claim a bigger share of the enterprise. When this issue is a major concern (as it often is in start-up ventures), the owners need to talk through their concerns and, with the aid of counsel, reach an agreement that, to the fullest extent possible, addresses the objectives of the owners. One approach is to specify that each partner or LLC member must contribute his or her *pro rata* share of the capital needed to accomplish the purpose of the entity. Some owners may be unwilling to agree to an unlimited equity contribution requirement. In this situation, the agreement may have to place a cap on future required capital contributions. If there is no mandatory requirement for additional capital contributions, the operating agreement should spell out how future capital needs will be satisfied. Often this is done by specifying that owners may make additional contributions, as needed, and receive additional equity interests, while giving all partners or LLC members the right to participate in any such contributions on a *pro rata* basis.

**Capital Account Maintenance (Section 7.5).** The operating agreement must provide that a capital account will be maintained for each partner or member. This account ultimately determines what a partner or LLC member yields when the entity's business is sold or distributed and its affairs are wound up. The agreement should specify that each owner's account will be increased for capital contributions and allocations of income and will be decreased for distributions and loss allocations. It should also clarify the capital account impacts of contributions and distributions of non-cash assets and the rights of the partnership or LLC to restate and revalue capital account balances when a new owner is admitted and other designated conditions are satisfied. As section 7.5 illustrates, often this is accomplished by incorporating by reference the provisions of specific Treasury regulations to the Internal Revenue Code.

**Allocations of Net Income and Net Loss (Section 8).** The operating agreement should specify how the annual net income or net loss of the enterprise is going to be allocated to the partners or LLC members and reflected in their respective capital accounts. A benefit of partnerships and LLCs that are taxed as partnerships is that they have tremendous flexibility in structuring such allocations, far beyond that of a corporation. For example, one partner or LLC member may be allocated 60 percent of all income and 30 percent of all losses. A partnership allocation will be respected for tax purposes only if it has "substantial economic effect,"[182] three words that make section 704(b) of the Internal Revenue Code and its regulations one of the most complex subjects in the world of tax. Generally speaking (and I do mean generally), an allocation that does not produce a deficit capital account for a partner or LLC member will be deemed to have "economic effect" if capital accounts are maintained for all partners and, upon liquidation of the partnership, liquidating distributions are made in accordance with positive capital account balances.[183] In order for an allocation that produces a deficit capital account balance to have "economic effect," the partner or LLC member also must be unconditionally obligated to restore the deficit (i.e., pay cash to cover the shortfall) upon liquidation of the partnership,[184] or the partnership must have sufficient nonrecourse debt to assure that the partner's share of any minimum gain recognized on the discharge of the debt will eliminate the deficit.[185] An "economic effect," if present, will not be deemed "substantial" if it produces an after-tax benefit for one or more partners with no diminished after-tax consequences to other partners.[186] The most

---

182. I.R.C. § 704(b).
183. Reg. §§ 1.704-1(b)(2)(ii) (b)(1), 1.704-(b)(2)(ii) (B)(2).
184. Reg. § 1.704-1(b)(2)(ii) (b)(3).
185. Reg. §§ 1.704-(2)(c), 1.704-(2)(f)(1), 1.704-(g)(1), 1.704-2(b)(1) & (e).
186. Reg. § 1.704-1(b)(2)(iii).

common examples of economic effects that are not deemed "substantial" are shifting allocations (allocations of different types of income and deductions among partners within a given year to reduce individual taxes without changing the partners' relative economic interests in the partnership) and transitory allocations (allocations in one year that are offset by allocations in later years).[187]

*Required Cash Distributions (Section 10).* The operating agreement should clarify how and when cash distributions are going to be made to the partners or LLC members. Some owners want to know that the plan includes regular distributions to the owners as the business ramps up and distributions that will cover the tax burden of partners or LLC members as the entity's income is allocated and taxed to them. Others may expect that all after-tax profits will be invested to finance growth or that cash distributions will be left to the discretion of the managers. This issue usually is tied to other key factors, including the growth rate of the business and the use of debt. Often the answer is to set guidelines regarding growth and debt that, once hit, will begin to trigger cash distributions to the owners.

*Cash Allocation Provisions.* A related and equally important planning consideration is how cash distributions are allocated among the partners or LLC members. The most common and basic structure is to provide that any cash distributed will be allocated among the owners according to their respective percentage interests in the entity and then to insure, through forced allocations, that the respective capital account balances of the partners or LLC members at time of liquidation reflect these percentage interests. There is flexibility in structuring the distribution provisions in the operating agreement. Consider the situation where one person puts up all the capital and one provides services to the venture. The operating agreement might provide that cash distributions first will be allocated to the owner who provided the capital until that owner receives the equity contributed together with a specified preferred return. The important point is that there is flexibility in structuring cash rights among the owners, and preferences may be created in favor of certain owners.

*Anti-Deficit Account Provisions (Section 8.3 through 8.8).* Often the partners and LLC members want the operating agreement structured so that there is no risk that the capital account of a partner or member will have a negative balance when the affairs of the partnership or LLC are wound up. Such a negative balance would trigger an unwelcome contribution obligation to eliminate the negative balance. To protect against such a negative balance, the operating agreement often includes a number of relatively complicated provisions that limit net loss allocations, designate how net gains from non-recourse debt obligations ("Minimum Gain Chargebacks") are to be handled, force gross income allocations ("Qualified Income Offsets") in certain circumstances, authorize curative allocations and modifications, and clarify the overriding intention that no partner have a deficit capital account balance at liquidation. These provisions, illustrated by sections 8.3 through 8.8 of the form agreement, are a multifaceted attack on the risk of a negative capital account.

---

187. Reg. § 1.704-1(b)(2)(iii) (b) & (c).

# CHAPTER 6

# CAPITAL SOURCING CHALLENGES

## A. CORPORATE CAPITAL STRUCTURE BASICS

The capital structure of a closely held business reflects how the business has secured funds to finance its assets and operations. A business basically has three funding sources: sell equity, borrow funds, and reinvest earnings. The capital structure reflects how these sources have been used to create rights and values for different stakeholders. The sources appear on the right side of the balance sheet, not the left side that lists the assets of the business.

### 1. COMMON STOCK

Common stock is the foundational stock of a corporation. Every corporation has common stock. Common stockholders are the last in line in a bankruptcy proceeding and usually the big winners when a corporation performs well or is sold at a handsome profit. Dividends are often paid to common stockholders, but only after obligations to debt holders and preferred stockholders have been satisfied. Common stockholders usually have the exclusive right to elect the board of directors, are the primary beneficiaries of fiduciary duties imposed on the board of directors, and must approve major transactions, including substantial mergers and any sale of substantially all of the corporation's assets. Different classes of common stock and non-voting common stock may be issued.

The common stockholders do not manage the corporation. Management issues are the responsibility of the board of directors, which is elected by the shareholders. However, as explained in Chapter 4, shareholders in a closely held corporation usually have the statutory right to contractually bind themselves to operational matters in a manner that preempts the authority of the board.

Authorized stock refers to the number of shares of stock that the articles of incorporation authorize the board of directors to issue. Issued stock is the actual stock that the board has issued and that is currently outstanding. The authorized stock of a corporation typically exceeds by many times the number of issued and outstanding shares. If a corporation needs additional authorized stock, it must amend its articles of incorporation, and such an amendment requires shareholder approval.

Par value is a concept that many decades ago was designed to protect creditors of a corporation by designating a legal par value for stock and insuring that a corporation did not sell "watered stock" – stock that was supported only by water because it was sold below the designated par value. The entire concept fell apart as everyone discovered the safety of using very low par stock, and then the corporate laws were amended to permit no-par stock. The Model Business Corporation Act completely rejects the concepts of "par" or "stated" values, although a corporation may designate such a value in its articles of incorporation. MBCA § 6.21. The official comments to section 6.21 state, "There is no minimum price at which specific shares must be issued and therefore there can be no 'watered stock' liability for issuing shares below an arbitrarily fixed price."

What is the meaning of the following phrase that often appears on a corporation's balance sheet: "Paid-in capital in excess of par value"? If a corporation's articles of incorporation designate a par or stated value, then the par or stated value of the shares outstanding is disclosed in the owner's equity section of the corporation's financial statements. The amounts in excess of the par value that have actually been paid for the outstanding stock (usually many times the size of the par value) are reflected in this line item in the owner's equity section. If the corporation has no par or stated value, there is no need for this separate line item and the entire consideration paid for the stock is reflected as "Common Stock."

What constitutes valid consideration for common stock? The Model Business Corporation Act and most states define the scope of valid consideration broadly, permitting any "tangible or intangible property or benefit to the corporation, including cash, promissory notes, services performed, contracts for services to be performed, or other securities of the corporation." MBCA § 6.21. Historically, a promise of future services and promissory notes were not authorized consideration for common stock. Residues of these limitations still exist in certain states that have not implemented the expansion provision of the Model Act. Delaware, for example, did not amend its corporate laws to permit stock to be issued for future services until 2004.

The board of directors sets the terms for issuing common stock? State statures typically provide that the board's determination "is conclusive insofar as the adequacy of consideration for the issuance of shares relates to whether the shares are validly issued, fully paid, and nonassessable." MBCA § 6.21(c).

## 2. NON-VOTING COMMON STOCK

Often in closely held corporations, particularly those dominated by a single family, there is a desire to spread the economic benefits of stock ownership to heirs or other individuals without disrupting the existing voting power. And non-voting stock can help avoid an estate tax trap that is triggered when a parent transfers stock in a controlled corporation and, through some means, "directly or indirectly" retains the right to vote the stock. When this condition exists, Section 2036(b) kicks in and the stock is brought back into the parent's estate for estate tax purposes. The safest way to avoid this trap is to transfer nonvoting stock, an option available to both C and S family corporations. Plus, in addition to avoiding 2036(b) threats, use of nonvoting stock may enhance gifting options by buttressing application of a lack of control valuation discount. See Chapter 10 for an expanded discussion of the use of non-voting stock in the context of developing a family transition plan.

## 3. PREFERRED STOCK

Preferred stock is any stock that has economic rights that are senior to the rights of common stock. The rights may be preferences in the event of liquidation, dividend preferences, call preferences, or any combination of these preferences.

Typically the preferential terms of preferred stock do not need to be spelled out in the articles of incorporation. The different classes of stock and the number of authorized shares in each class must be set forth in the articles of incorporation. Beyond this basic requirement, the articles of incorporation may give the board the right to establish the terms and preferences of any preferred stock at the time it is issued. See MBCA § 6.02. Such a "blank check" provision promotes flexibility, greatly simplifies the articles of incorporation, enhances the board's authority, and reduces the need for shareholder approval.

What is the difference between cumulative and non-cumulative preferred stock? Preferred stock dividends typically are due annually or quarterly. Cumulative preferred stock requires the payment of all dividends that have accrued, including any that have been missed, before any dividends can be paid on common stock. The preferred dividends "cumulate." With non-cumulative preferred, a dividend payment obligation lapses once if it is not paid and ceases to be an impediment to common stock dividends. Obviously, cumulative preferred stock is the preference of most investors.

What is the difference between participating and non-participating preferred stock? Participating preferred stock pays the owner the dividend and liquidation preferences of the stock, plus it permits the owner to share (participate) in dividend and liquidation distributions made on the common stock. Non-participating preferred stock does not offer this sharing right with the common stock.

What is callable preferred stock? It is preferred stock that, by its terms, can be purchased ("called") by the corporation at specified times or under specified conditions. Often, the corporation is required to pay a call premium to exercise this right.

What is convertible preferred stock? It is preferred stock that is convertible into common stock at a specified exchange ratio. This is an attractive option for many investment groups. The preferred stock provides liquidation and dividend preferences while the company's value is being built. The conversion feature ensures a large common stock return when the corporation is sold or goes public.

Preferred stockholders may have voting and control rights. It's a matter of negotiation, and often preferred investors drive a hard bargain, demanding seats on the boards and preferential voting rights. Corporate statutes typically provide preferred stockholders with the right to vote on any corporate structural change that would adversely impact their rights or preferences.

"Subordinated" preferred stock is preferred stock that has rights that take a back seat (are subordinated) to the rights of another class of preferred shareholders. Subordination is common when multiple financing rounds are necessary to fund the growth of a business and the risks and stakes change with each round.

Why might a company prefer to issue preferred stock rather than common stock? The issuance of more common stock always dilutes the financial interests of the existing common stockholders in the growth of the value of the business enterprise. For an investor who is looking for a fixed income yield, a non-convertible, cumulative, non-participating preferred stock may fit the bill without any serious dilution impacts to the existing common stockholders. Of course, if the preferred stock has a conversion feature, common stock dilution is likely if the business does well.

Why might a company prefer to issue preferred stock rather than debt? A preferred stock often resembles debt obligation because it offers a fixed periodic yield and may offer the potential of being called ("paid off") at some point down the road. The big difference, though, is that it is not a debt subject to debt legal payment obligations and default risks. The holder of a debt instrument usually has the right to accelerate payment of the entire obligation if interest payments are not made or other covenants in the instrument are not satisfied. Plus, all parties know that the debt must be paid off at a given time in accordance with its terms. In contrast, preferred stock usually is far more forgiving. If a dividend payment is missed, it may "cumulate" and move forward as an obstacle to common stock dividends, but it will not trigger the burdens of a default on a debt obligation. And with preferred stock, there may be the possibility, and perhaps even an expectation, that it will be retired through redemption at some future point, but usually there is no legal obligation comparable to that included in a debt instrument. The bottom line is that a preferred stock, as compared to a debt, is more flexible for the corporation and offers fewer guarantees to the investor. For that reason, the stated yield on a preferred stock often must be higher than a debt obligation in order to attract investors.

## 4. DIVIDEND CHALLENGES

There are three ways that a shareholder realizes a yield on an investment in the stock of a corporation. First, the shareholder can hold the stock until the corporations sells its business to a third party and liquidates. We discuss corporate sales in Chapter 9.

Second, the shareholder can sell the stock to a third party. An investment in a public corporation whose stock is actively traded can easily be sold at any time. The sale of stock in a closely held corporation presents a much tougher challenge. Usually there is no market for the stock, and the other shareholders do not want stock in the enterprise being shopped to third parties. This is why the buy-sell agreement between the owners of a closely held corporation (discussed in Chapter 8) is such a big deal. It spells out those situations where a shareholder's stock will be purchased by the corporation or the other shareholders and the terms and conditions of such a purchase. It also lays out the conditions that must be satisfied for a shareholder to sell stock to third parties.

Third, shareholders can receive dividends from the corporation which represent distributions of the company's earnings. Preferred stocks often specify periodic dividends that are to be paid before any dividends are paid to those who own the common stock of the corporation. Payment of dividends on common stock is usually at the discretion of the board of directors. The dividend policies of the board can trigger problems if dividends are too low or nonexistent, or if dividends are too large.

When dividends are too low or nonexistent, minority shareholders of a closely held corporation may complain that they are being treated unfairly by those in control. In many situations, the essence of the claim is that the minority shareholder is being oppressed and squeezed out, with no opportunity to realize any yield on the stock because it can't be sold and no dividends are being paid. Often the claim is accompanied by allegations that the controlling shareholder is able to generate income from the corporation through lucrative compensation payments. Such oppression claims and planning options to avoid them are discussed in Chapter 8.

Legal problems also can surface when the board authorizes the payment of dividends that are too large. The overriding fear is that the corporation will be stripped of all its assets through generous payments to its shareholders and will not be able to meet its obligations to creditors. There have been statutory legal limitations on the payment of dividends from the beginning.

The old approach adopted a relatively complicated concept of legal capital – a designated minimum amount of capital (usually the par or stated value of the stock times the number of shares outstanding) that a corporation was required to maintain in the enterprise. Any capital or earnings in excess of the minimum capital was considered "surplus" that could be used to pay dividends or repurchase the corporation's stock. This minimum capital approach has proved inadequate over time because corporations routinely designated insignificant par or stated values that had no relationship to the stock's value or the corporation's capacity to honor its obligations. The result was that a corporation could pay large dividends, meet its minimum legal capital obligation, and be left with insufficient assets to pay its creditors. But this minimum capital approach is still part of the statutory schemes of certain states.

The modern statutory approach to excessive dividends, adopted by the Model Business Corporation Act and many states, imposes a two-prong test: a "Solvency" test and a "Balance Sheet" test. These are basically the same statutory standards that usually apply to limited partnerships and LLCs, as discussed in Chapter 5. The Solvency test prohibits a corporation from paying dividends or repurchasing its own stock if the corporation is unable to pay its debts as they become due in the ordinary course of business. The Balance Sheet test prohibits a corporation from paying dividends or purchasing its own stock if the corporation's total assets are less than the sum of its total liabilities and any liquidation preferences that would be owed if the corporation dissolved at the time of distribution. State statutes often provide that, for purposes of the Balance

Sheet test, asset values can be based on the corporation's financial statements prepared in accordance with generally accepted accounting principles or a reasonable fair valuation of the assets. Following is the provision of the Model Act that has been adopted in most states.

### MBCA § 6.40(c), (d). Distributions to Shareholders

(c) No distribution may be made if, after giving it effect:

(1) the corporation would not be able to pay its debts as they become due in the usual course of business; or

(2) the corporation's total assets would be less than the sum of its total liabilities plus (unless the articles of incorporation permit otherwise) the amount that would be needed, if the corporation were to be dissolved at the time of the distribution, to satisfy the preferential rights upon dissolution of shareholders whose preferential rights are superior to those receiving the distribution.

(d) The board of directors may base a determination that a distribution is not prohibited under subsection (c) either on financial statements prepared on the basis of accounting practices and principles that are reasonable in the circumstances or on a fair valuation or other method that is reasonable in the circumstances.

Under the Model Act and many state statutes, these dividend limitations carry three significant consequences. First, board members can be held personally liable for consenting to the payment of any dividend that exceeds the statutory limitation.[1] Second, a corporation may not relieve a board member of such personal dividend liability exposure by a "good faith" exculpatory provision in the corporation's articles of incorporation or bylaws.[2] And third, any shareholder who receives such a dividend with knowledge that it exceeds the limitations may be required to repay the dividend to a director who has been held liable for the unlawful distribution.[3]

How does Delaware, the controlling law for many corporations, deal with the risks of excessive dividends? Delaware still has the old minimum capital/surplus scheme for controlling the payment of excessive dividends. Dividends and share repurchases may be made out of "surplus," defined to mean capital that exceeds the par or stated value of the shares and any addition amounts that the board elects to add to the minimum stated capital. The board has tremendous flexibility in structuring dividends and share repurchases that fit within the limitations of this statutory scheme.

### PROBLEMS 6-A AND 6-B

**6-A.** Doug, Linda and Laura, unrelated parties, plan to form a new

---

1. MBCA § 8.33.
2. MBCA § 2.02(b)(5).
3. MBCA § 8.33(b)(2).

corporation ("Newco") under the laws of a state that has adopted the Model Business Corporation Act. Newco will issue 200 shares of common stock to Doug for $200,000. Linda has no money, but she has agreed to give Newco a $200,000 promissory note for 200 shares of Newco common stock. The note will bear interest at an annual rate of 4 percent, and all interest and principal will be due and payable in 10 years. Linda's hope is that dividends from Newco will be sufficient to cover required payments on the note. Laura will be issued 200 shares of common stock as a "signing bonus" under an employment agreement that will require that she manage the company for five years for a base salary and a cash bonus plan set forth in the agreement. The parties anticipate that Doug (a deep pocket player) will probably need to "pony up" more cash within a year or so. Their tentative thinking is that Doug will be issued preferred stock for any additional capital, and the specific terms of the preferred stock will be worked out at the time of his contribution. Regarding the formation of the corporation, the parties have asked that you advise them on the following questions:

1. Is it legal to issue common stock to the parties for the consideration each party has agreed to provide?

2. Should the common stock have a par value? Is this required? What are the benefits of having a par value?

3. Can any preferred stock issued to Doug in the future have voting rights?

4. Should any preferred stock issued to Doug in the future be participating or cumulative preferred stock? Why?

5. Can the preferred stock that Doug may receive down the road be authorized now in the articles of incorporation even though the specific terms of the preferred will not be ascertained until later?

**6-B.** Two years ago, Doug, Linda and Laura, unrelated parties, formed a corporation ("Newco") under the laws of a state that has adopted the Model Business Corporation Act. Newco issued 200 shares of common stock to Doug for $200,000, 200 shares of common stock to Linda in return for a 10-year $200,000 promissory note ("Note'), and 200 shares of its common stock to Laura as a "signing bonus" under an employment agreement

Newco struggled through its first year in business. Doug was asked to put in more money, but refused when he saw how bad things were going. By the end of year two, prospects still looked bleak as the company continued to struggle with anemic sales. It was able to stay afloat by selling its accounts receivable at a discount for cash and stringing out the payment of all its suppliers and creditors.

Doug and Laura came up with a plan "to salvage what we can for ourselves." Newco would purchase from Linda her 200 common shares in return for a complete discharge of Linda's $200,000 promissory note held by Newco. Plus, Newco would either (1) pay a dividend of $50,000 to both Doug and Laura or (2) redeem 50 common shares from both Doug and Laura for $50,000.

You have been asked to advise the parties whether any element of their "salvage plan" is illegal. What additional facts (if any) would you like to have? How would your answer change if Newco was incorporated in Delaware?

## B. RAISING CAPITAL

### 1. FUNDING SOURCES FOR CLOSELY HELD BUSINESSES

### Capital Opportunities for
### Small Businesses

The University of North Carolina's Small Business
and Technology Development Center (2009)

#### Getting Started

As a company moves through its life cycle, the sources it uses for capital change. In the early formation phase, capital is generally raised through sources independent of the operations of the organization. Capital is acquired chiefly through the personal resources of the owner or his immediate relations, and investor-related debt. Any cash generated from operations is generally used for setup costs including purchases of inventory and equipment. This initial phase calls for the use of techniques that maximize- or "stretch"- current funds, such as seeking longer credit terms from suppliers, procuring advances from customers, subcontracting, and leasing equipment, among other methods.

As the company grows, it begins to generate capital through its operations, and as it establishes a track record of profitability, it will have more opportunities to obtain outside financing. Capital needed for expansion may be available from external sources, including a greater emphasis on debt financing through commercial lenders or equity financing through private investors and firms. As the company matures, operations generally provide cash. Mature companies are in a better position to be able to afford the costs of further expansion through combinations of debt and equity financing, such as private placements or initial public offerings (IPOs).

#### Start-Up (or "Seed") Stage

External sources of financing refer to those funds not generated by business operations. During the start-up phase, among the most important sources are personal assets accessible to the owner. The emphasis is on external sources since the business is not yet generating positive cash flow. In the search for early-stage capital, loan opportunities are usually limited by the need for collateral and personal guarantees, which serve as protection to the commercial lender. It is unlikely for most start-up companies to obtain equity investments, in part due to the high risk involved in this stage of investment. Factors such as a well-developed business plan, or prior experience in the new business's area, improve one's chances of acquiring start-up or early-stage funding.

##### Personal Assets

Obtaining financing for a start-up enterprise is difficult because there is no track record on which the business can be judged. Personal assets are thus the first source of capital that must be considered. A personal stake in the enterprise shows a commitment to the business and provides lenders with a potential source of collateral to secure a loan. Most banks require at least a 30 percent personal equity investment in a start-up business and 10 percent to 30 percent in a more established business. If an owner does not have access to sufficient personal resources to get through the lean times of the start-up phase, it may be wise to reevaluate the decision of going into business at this time.

Sources of financing using personal assets (in the pre-seed stage, this is oftentimes referred to as "bootstrapping" or "bootstrap" funding) include: Checking and savings accounts (good source, if available); Credit cards (disadvantage: a credit line can come with a high interest rate); Stocks, bonds and other investments (disadvantage: may face capital gains tax on the sale of investments that have appreciated over the years); Retirement funds such as a 401K (disadvantage: may face a penalty for early withdrawal).

### Family and Friends

Family and friends can provide direct investment funds, loans, or serve as guarantors on a bank loan if their credit history and resources are strong. Unlike commercial sources, this group is personally acquainted with the entrepreneur, and though they must still be objective in assessing the proposal, intangibles such as personal character are often given more weight by family and friends than by more traditional sources. If an outright loan is not possible, this group can still provide aid in procuring financing through credit enhancement. Credit enhancements are assets of recognized value that can be borrowed to support a loan or other debt obligation. This technique bolsters the asset base so that additional debt financing can be acquired. This can be accomplished through the pledge of personal assets such as a CD, stocks, or bonds as collateral.

### Home Equity Loans

A home equity loan (sometimes referred to as a "second mortgage", though it may in fact constitute a third or even fourth lien on the collateral property) can be a source of funding for a small business. The feasibility of this source will vary with the amount of equity that has been built up in the home. It can usually be obtained through a bank, a mortgage company, a finance company specializing in secondary funding, or a savings-and-loan (S&L) association. The monthly payment will be a function of the length of the loan and the interest rate. Additionally, there are usually points or fees and closing costs (and sometimes other factors, such as balloon payments) to be considered when assessing the costs of this mode of financing. The proceeds from the loan can either be used as a source of direct financing or as collateral to secure a credit line.

## Growth Phase - Internal Financing

### Cash Management Tools

Effective cash management of a business is one of the best ways to raise capital, and it also helps avoid paying interest on unnecessary external debt. Since short term cash flow needs are vital to company operations, available cash flow management techniques must be maximized. Small business banking services are traditionally oriented around deposits and loans, with most services tied to checking accounts. However, specialized services once used primarily by larger companies are now available to smaller businesses. The following services can be used as part of an effective cash management program:

### a. Lockbox

An integral part of a profitable business is a fast, efficient accounts receivable process. A lockbox is a post office box maintained by the bank to receive payments made to a business. The bank empties the lockbox frequently and immediately deposits checks into your account. The advantage is that funds become available much faster than if they are first sent to the place of business.

### b. Controlled Disbursement Account

This tool enables the business to make timely payments while maintaining the maximum earning power of funds. With a controlled disbursement account, the business receives daily notification of the checks that will clear the account that day. Only the amount needed to cover those checks is transferred to the checking account, ensuring that no idle cash remains in the account.

### c. Sweep Account

A sweep account is an automatic system to move excess money into an interest bearing account every night. After all debits and credits are posted to the checking account at the end of the day, funds in that account are automatically swept into a money market or savings account.

### Accounts Receivable Management

Effective short-term cash flow management is vital to a company's operations. Short-term financing needs are decreased when cash flow is maximized through matching accounts receivable with accounts payable. This is done by carefully negotiating and managing credit terms with customers and suppliers.

Periods where payables exceed receivables must be handled through short-term financing such as a line of credit. If the business itself delays sending bills, the result is a longer period before payment is received. The use of that cash to cover payables or for investment is lost over that period. The same is true when the collection cycle is lengthened as a result of a failure of customers to pay according to the credit terms. Consider using discounts to encourage timely customer payment.

### Inventory Control

The less excess inventory carried, the greater the availability of funds for interest bearing accounts or working capital purposes. Excess inventory lowers a company's profitability due to the money spent to produce or purchase the idle goods that take up warehouse space and increase insurance costs. The goal of avoiding excess inventory must be balanced with a company's ability to consolidate inventory purchases to take advantage of volume pricing. Implementing an inventory control system can help reduce excess inventory and its associated costs.

### Electronic Commerce

Each of the preceding strategies for effective internal financing may be enhanced through the use of electronic commerce. Electronic commerce, mostly in the form of Electronic Data Interchange (EDI), has been around since the 1950s but until recently was primarily used by large companies doing business with the federal government over expensive private networks. Technological advancement and the increased accessibility of both personal computers and the Internet have made electronic commerce an increasingly popular and more affordable tool for small businesses. For many individuals and small businesses, some aspects of electronic commerce are a part of daily life—for example, direct deposit of payroll, credit card validations, and automatic bill paying.

Electronic commerce allows the computer-to-computer exchange of routine business information between a company and its suppliers, its customers, banks, and other trading partners. One aspect of such an exchange that offers an important financing opportunity to small businesses is the ability, through either EDI or the Internet, to establish a partner-like relationship with their suppliers. Suppliers are then able to manage their customers' material logistics, including a customer's onhand inventory. The supplier's goods may be moved on consignment and/or the small business customer may not be expected to pay in full until the goods are used or, in the case of manufacturing components, until the final product has been sold. In this way, the supplier provides a portion of the working capital for the small business.

Procurement cards are another aspect of electronic commerce that offers significant cost-cutting potential to the small business. A procurement (or purchasing) card is a specialized corporate credit card that can be customized to limit dollar amounts and types of purchases that can be made by individual employees. Since banks replace the vendor in the task of customer billing and collection, for a small business the ability to handle procurement card transactions could mean both improved cash flow and significant cost savings.

### Barter

Bartering is the trading of one item for another. Commercial trade exchanges serve as the mechanism for the transfer. Through the use of computers, exchanges can match the needs and wants of its clients. Barter is a good way to keep a business moving when cash is scarce. It is especially useful for a small business because it allows the business to trade unused or excess inventory in exchange for goods and services for which the business would otherwise have to pay. The resulting benefit to a business is that it cuts costs and eases cash flow. Trades are normally made at full retail value with a 10 percent commission paid to the exchange. The goods or services received are also considered as income for tax purposes.

## External Financing

As the business begins to grow, external financing sources should become more available, and debt or equity may be used to satisfy financing needs. The mix of financing sources varies depending on the growth stage of the business.

During the start-up stage, entrepreneurs most often rely on "family and friends" and internal debt financing, but as the business becomes more established, it develops a credit history and outside debt financing becomes more available. High-growth companies- those growing very quickly- are attractive to equity financers. Equity financing providers may be companies, funds, or individuals, but they all seek to invest in private companies in which they can anticipate a substantial rate of return for their investment. Debt financing is more varied, both in the types of entities that provide such financing and in the types of financing available.

### Short-term Financing

Short-term financing is used to address needs of one year or less in duration and is intended to take care of a mismatch in cash flow generated from receivables and expended as payables. It is used to satisfy a business's working capital needs and to support investments in short-lived assets such as inventory and accounts receivable. A working capital deficit indicates that a company has more short-term obligations (i.e., payables) than short-term assets (i.e., cash, accounts receivable, inventory). The gap can be bridged through accessing short-term financing (e.g., a revolving credit line).

The most common situation that challenges a company's ability to repay its debt on a timely basis is using short-term borrowing for long-term needs. This includes financing expenditures for fixed assets or intangibles with short-term credit. Though most banks may be reluctant, refinancing short-term borrowings into long-term debt typically resolves this problem. Balance sheet management is a key factor in determining the right type of borrowing to utilize at the current stage of development.

### a. Trade Credit

Accounts payable -- also called 'trade credit'- is a form of money management that is especially crucial for small firms. A business may finance itself by asking its vendors and suppliers to accept a comfortable payment schedule instead of insisting on full payment at the time of delivery. A business will seek to pay off its debts over many months (without the penalty of interest charges) while collecting payments from its customers in full. This system keeps the maximum amount of cash under the business's control.

### b. Term Loan

Commercial lenders are a key source of loans. A single loan obtained from a commercial lender by a business firm is not much different from a loan obtained by an individual. Commercial term loans are direct business loans with a maturity of five or fewer years. A major advantage of the term loan is that it assures the borrower of the use of the funds for an extended period. The interest rate on term loans varies with the level of prevailing rates, the size of the loan, and the quality of the borrower, and it may be fixed for the life of the loan or it may vary. Repayment of principal and interest is made in a lump sum at maturity or in installments throughout the life of the loan. Most term loans are installment loans repayable on an amortized basis, which allows the loan to be repaid gradually over its life rather than have it due in total at maturity.

### c. Line of Credit

A line of credit is a formal or informal understanding between the bank and the borrower concerning the maximum loan balance the bank will allow the borrower. This source is useful for short-term financing of working capital, seasonal needs, and unplanned expenses. The amount of the credit line is often linked to a percentage of a firm's short-term assets. In most cases, the line of credit must be paid off in full every 12 months.

### d. Letter of Credit

A letter of credit is a financial instrument issued by a bank to provide a credit guarantee to an outside supplier. The purpose is to guarantee that, if all terms and conditions of the letter of credit are met, the seller will receive payment from the bank even if the buyer defaults on payment. The risk of the buyer defaulting on payments is, therefore, transferred from the supplier to the bank.

### Long-term Financing

Long-term financing extends beyond five years and is generally used for investment in long-lived assets. Long-term needs can be met by debt or equity financing or a combination of the two.

Debt obligates the business to repay its lenders the debt principal along with a specified rate of interest. The lender does not acquire an ownership interest in the organization, as would be common with equity financing. When a business becomes insolvent, creditors or debt holders are entitled to payment before equity shareholders. Interest payments on the debt by a corporation are tax deductible; dividend payments are not. The lender looks closely at the borrower's current position, because current assets are the main source of repayment.

Debt financing entails borrowing either at a fixed or a variable rate. A fixed rate offers certainty, but variable rates are usually lower than fixed rates at the time the loan is extended and may decrease further if interest rates fall. In general, if interest rates rise, so will the variable rate and higher monthly payments will result. Some of the variable rate loans may be capped so as to guarantee not being raised above a certain rate.

A business owner may choose equity financing by selling part of the business to individuals, firms, or the public. A corporation can issue shares of stock as a form of financing. Issues to consider regarding the use of equity financing include:

- Owner must relinquish percentage of ownership for equity capital

- Equity investors fall behind debt holders in the event of liquidation

- Costs of preparing and placing private offerings can be relatively high

- Dividends may be subject to double taxation

### Grants

Generally speaking, grants given to business start-ups are very rare. An exception may be for a high technology business or for businesses producing products that can be used by certain agencies or departments involved in our nation's defense. Also, non-profit businesses are sometimes eligible for grants. For the most part, these grants are very specialized. In addition, many Government grants are not available year-round. That is, you can't apply for most of them at any time you please -- in general, you can apply for them only when they are announced by a Government agency.

## Financial Institutions

### Commercial Banks

Commercial banks are usually one of the least expensive providers of loan capital. This source of financing will be most helpful for a business that has demonstrated it can operate profitably. Banks are most interested in financing firms that can show an ability to repay the loan. This usually means a company must have a strong positive cash flow or assets as collateral that can be easily liquidated. The evaluation will consist of a detailed analysis of the company's income statement, balance sheet, and cash flow statement. Factors such as the content of the business plan and experience of the management are also considered. If a business has no consistent operating history or cannot demonstrate that funds will be available to repay the loan, it may be difficult to procure financing using this method.

Payment terms are usually up to five years for loans from commercial banks. Most debt is secured, although some unsecured lines may be available. Personal guarantees are generally required resulting in exposure of the borrower's personal assets in the event of a business failure. Even if the business is formed as a corporation, the limited liability feature is superseded by a personal guarantee.

The interest rate on a loan is typically expressed as a percentage in excess of the prime rate. Prime is the rate the nation's largest banks charge their best customers. The prime rate itself will vary according to economic conditions; it is primarily dependent on the rate the banks themselves are charged by the Federal Reserve to borrow money. The percentage over prime that a customer is charged is based on the banker's perception of the risk taken by granting the loan.

Lending institutions have different policies towards risk. Some are inclined to follow relatively conservative lending practices; others engage in more creative banking practices. Banks borrow money elsewhere at a lower rate and lend it out at a higher rate; therefore, the commercial bank's primary concern is a borrower's ability to cover principal and interest repayments. Although bankers are interested in all financial aspects of a borrowing firm, hard assets provide their primary insurance if the business fails.

Commercial banks are among the largest sources of credit to small businesses.

### Savings Institutions

Savings and loans (S&Ls) and savings banks primarily focus on the area of home mortgage lending. Savings institutions have not traditionally been aggressive in pursuing non-real-estate commercial loans such as lines of credit and unsecured loans. Savings institutions may be more aggressive in the area of commercial real estate loans. These institutions can also provide indirect sources of business financing, such as home equity loans or second mortgages.

## Non-Bank Lenders

Finance companies offer a growing alternative for the financing needs of small businesses. The major differences between banks and finance companies are the criteria used to evaluate borrowers and the level of risk the institutions are willing to assume. Finance companies usually assume higher risk and therefore charge higher interest rates than commercial banks.

### Asset-Based Lenders

Over the past several decades, business lending by finance companies has increased at a faster rate than business lending by commercial banks. Increasingly, finance companies are providing asset-based lending services. Instead of focusing on a firm's historical operating record and cash flow, finance companies will lend money based on the value of the company's equipment, inventory, or accounts receivable. Asset-based lending is secured lending in which money is loaned using the borrower's assets as collateral. The lender's risk is mitigated by closely monitoring the quality and performance of the asset. Asset-based lending is especially useful when the company confronts issues such as high growth or seasonal variations in business. In these environments, traditional unsecured lending is unlikely to satisfy all financing needs, and asset-based lending becomes a viable alternative.

This method of lending is generally focused on providing secured working capital loans (with the amount that can be borrowed determined by established percentages of the advance against accounts receivable or inventory). By borrowing against its accounts receivable, a company can accelerate its cash collection cycle and improve its ability to purchase additional inventory to build sales. The resulting improvement in cash flow can be accomplished without giving up any ownership control.

In a traditional arrangement, the asset-based lender extends credit against 80 percent of eligible receivables (with the remaining 20 percent serving as a reserve). Eligibility is generally determined by the quality of the receivable. As the invoices are paid, the amounts received are applied against the borrower's loan.

Purchase order financing is another example of asset-based lending. This may be attractive to a company that has stretched its credit relations with vendors and has reached its lending capacity at the bank. The inability to finance raw materials to fill all orders would leave a company operating under capacity. The asset-based lender finances the purchase of the raw material, and the purchase orders are then assigned to the lender. After the orders are filled, payment is made to the lender, and the lender then deducts its costs and fees and remits the balance to the company.

The interest cost of this source of financing can be relatively expensive. Terms can be as low as prime plus three percent, but can also be as high as prime plus ten percent. Asset-based lenders usually require first liens on assets and almost always require personal guarantees. Lenders may also move quickly to liquidate collateral where necessary. The advantage of this type of financing is that it is available to companies with a strong asset base but with insufficient cash flow to qualify for a traditional loan.

### Factors

Finance companies assist businesses that are expanding and experiencing a cash shortage by purchasing the business's accounts receivables. In factoring, the receivable is purchased at a discounted rate and the finance company pays the business immediately. There are two types of accounts receivable sales: recourse and non-recourse factoring. In a recourse transaction, the business retains part of the risk of customer default and is ultimately responsible for any shortfall. In a non-recourse situation, the finance company takes on all the rights and obligations of the receivable, including the risk of default by the customer.

Finance companies charge a fee that is usually 2 to 6 percent of the receivable. The calculation of this fee depends on the following variables: volume, size, and number of invoices; customers' credit; location of the customers; and length of time of payment. Some companies charge an additional fee if the customer is late on payment, while others have one flat rate. Upon payment by the customer, the remaining value (10 to 30 percent), minus the fee, is sent to the business.

There are two methods of factoring, called traditional and spot. With traditional factoring, the finance company obtains the rights to an entire stream of receivables. This is best for companies with at least $1 million in annual sales. Spot factoring is the buying and selling of a single order or account. Businesses that only use factoring for a limited time or purpose, such as seasonal employers, often prefer the spot factoring method.

It is important to keep in mind that, unlike banking, there are no regulatory agencies overseeing the business practices of factoring companies. Most factors will provide prospective clients with a list of former and current clients as well as references from local lending institutions.

### Leasing Companies

A typical lease involves three parties: the seller of equipment (vendor), the one who will use the equipment (lessee), and the leasing company (lessor). The leasing company buys the equipment from the vendor and leases it for a specified period of time to the business owner. Leases are best used by businesses that cannot afford the initial capital cost to buy the equipment. Usually nearly 100 percent of the cost of the equipment can be financed, and no down payment is required.

There are two types of leasing arrangements: capital and operating. In a capital lease, the lessee (person taking possession of the property) assumes the obligation to purchase the equipment under the lease. This is generally regarded as a form of medium-term debt financing. Both the value of the asset and the related debt are recorded on the lessee's financial statements. Under an operating lease, the lessee pays a fixed monthly payment for a specified period of time, after which there exists no further obligation, and the lessor retains ownership of the equipment. Neither the asset nor the debt is recorded on the lessee's financials.

Usually the leasing company will require small business owners to personally guarantee the lease. Typically a leasing company requires that a business be in existence for two years and have a strong cash flow history. There are leasing companies that work with new businesses if the owner has strong personal resources and good personal credit. Terms range from short-term to long-term depending on the underlying asset.

## U.S. Small Business Administration (SBA)

The Small Business Administration was established in 1953 to protect the interests of the nation's small business community. The SBA accomplishes this, in part, by working with intermediaries, banks, and other lending institutions to promote both loans and venture capital financing for small businesses. SBA makes small business loans available through its disaster loan assistance and 504 Certified Development Company (CDC) programs, and venture capital through its Small Business Investment Company Program (SBIC). SBA 7(a) guaranty loans are made to small businesses through banks and non-bank lenders.

The 7(a) Loan Guaranty Program is the SBA's primary lending program. Section 7(a) of the Small Business Act authorizes the SBA to provide loan guaranties to small businesses that cannot obtain financing on reasonable terms through normal lending channels. The program operates through commercial lenders and some non-banker lenders who elect to participate in the 7(a) program.

7(a) loans are only available on a guaranty basis. They are provided by lenders who choose to structure their own loans by SBA's requirements and who apply and receive a guaranty from SBA on a portion of the loan. The SBA does not provide a guaranty for the entire loan amount. The lender and SBA share the risk that a borrower will not be able to repay the loan in full. The guaranty is for payment default. It does not cover imprudent decisions by the lender or misrepresentation by the borrower.

Under the guaranty concept, commercial lenders make and administer the loans. The business applies to a lender for financing, not the SBA. The lender decides if they will make the loan internally or if the application has some weaknesses which, in their opinion, will require an SBA guaranty if the loan is to be made. The guaranty that SBA provides is only available to the lender. It assures the lender that in the event the borrower does not repay their obligation and a payment default occurs, the SBA will reimburse the lender for its loss, up to the percentage of SBA's guaranty. Under this program, the borrower remains obligated for the full amount due.

The repayment ability from the business's cash flow is a primary consideration in the SBA loan decision process. Good character, management capability, collateral, and owner's equity contribution are also important considerations. All owners having 20 percent or more ownership in the company are required to personally guarantee SBA loans.

The vast majority of businesses are eligible for financial assistance from the SBA. However, applicant businesses must operate for profit, have reasonable owner equity to invest, and use alternative financial resources (including personal assets). Also, the business must be engaged in, or propose to do business in, the United States or its possessions.

SBA loan programs are generally intended to encourage longer-term small business financing, but actual loan maturities are based on the ability to repay, the purpose of the loan proceeds, and the useful life of the assets financed. The maximum term depends on the purpose of the loan.

Interest rates are negotiated between the borrower and the lender but are subject to SBA maximums, which are pegged to the prime rate as published in the Wall Street Journal. Interest rates may be fixed or variable, but fixed-rate loans must not exceed the prime rate plus a set percentage based on the total value of the loan as well as length of the loan.

The agency charges lenders a guaranty and a servicing fee for each loan approved. The guaranty fee can be passed on to the borrower once the lender has paid it. The fee amount is determined by the amount of the loan guaranty. In addition, all loans will be subject to a ongoing servicing fee, which is applied to the outstanding balance of SBA's guaranteed portion of the loan.

## Equity Capital Sources

You may have heard of something called the funding "food chain". This occurs when bigger fish are participating in each subsequent round of equity investment in a company. Ideally, deals are structured, milestones met, and value created in such a way that the bigger fish takes a nourishing bite in return for larger and larger amounts of capital as opposed to swallowing all the smaller fish.

For "food chain" funding to be successful for everyone, the entrepreneurs and investors should make sure that there is room for everyone to profit from a successful company. To accomplish this, the valuation of the company has to continue to be attractive at each stage, including late in the funding cycle. Thus, even later stage investors need to have an opportunity for an attractive return commensurate with the risk they are taking. Of course, the early investors want to be rewarded for their significant risk.

All investors typically have an interest in the management team having sufficient equity or an option pool that will provide incentives and reward them for their successful contributions. The idea is to grow the pie so that the shrinking pieces of ownership are actually worth a lot more when some form of exit is achieved. It is critical that each participant figures out how everyone can win.

Having said this, "food chain" funding rarely occurs in a linear fashion and should not be counted on as the sure way to grow. In fact, very few companies will actually fit this model through to its conclusion. For companies that don't fit the high growth and exit mode, other types of approaches may be appropriate to satisfy the investors and entrepreneurs. Nevertheless, the "food chain" idea provides a framework to consider when looking at funding strategies and options. Be prepared for funding efforts to take incredible amounts of physical and creative energy.

Here is how it can work. As a founder, an entrepreneur often starts with her own funds in combination with or followed by funding from family and friends. Or a company may be formed out of a university with some start-up help and, on occasion some funding help, prior to or concurrent with its emergence. Although the following terms may vary in meaning from person to person, here is one way to look at them. The term, pre-seed funding, is being used more frequently. These are funds invested to help develop the idea.

Next comes seed funding, which is often used to get the business plan together and develop the initial work on the technology, market/industry research or business model. These funds can come from within or outside the founder or founding team.

The first outside money may come from private equity investors, often called "angel" investors. They are sometimes called angels because they are not always as tough on valuation as other sources, sometimes to their own detriment, and they are often or should be looked upon to pass on added value from their industry knowledge, experience and contacts to the entrepreneur. As angels and entrepreneurs learn more about the funding process and become more sophisticated in structuring deals, the understanding will be greater and the expectations more realistic and clear. This should lead to the reduction of unwelcome surprises that are sure to come. To help navigate a successful future, entrepreneurs need to look as carefully at their investors as the investors look at them.

Angels invest in a variety of ways: as individuals; informally with others to invest as individuals; through formal networks as individuals; through funds with existing pools of capital accompanied by additional funds from their personal accounts; or some combination of any or all of these options. Sometimes they invest alongside seed or early stage venture capital funds.

Venture capital funds differ from angel funds in that they typically have a professional management team responsible for decisions and have attracted capital from institutions. Many of the seed and early stage venture funds include a number of angel investors who, it is hoped, will be available to assist with portfolio companies.

Entrepreneurs can ask for too little or too much money. To do so can affect (1) the likelihood of success in obtaining the capital sought and (2) the success of that stage in the company's life once the capital is in the bank. Entrepreneurs need to be careful to not deploy capital faster than the markets for their products and services are prepared to respond.

Raising capital from investors, selling your equity for their cash, is not unlike approaching customers for your products or services. It is important for entrepreneurs to understand the needs and issues facing these types of equity "customers" and to recognize that certain venture capital needs are unique to the fund or funds in question.

As companies show more than just great promise, in the form of concrete results in products, services and revenues, even if they are only license fees, the later stage VC funds play a valuable role in providing larger amounts of capital to drive forward a company (e.g. a technology platform with strong evidence of its potential or a business model that shows it has growing power).

Throughout the above process, competitive grants to advance the science can be won and partnerships for product development or marketing outcomes, etc. developed. And, occasionally, loans can be obtained from specialized sources to bridge science grants, etc.

Other resources include private equity funds, including mezzanine funds, which may provide bridge funding to support an initial public offering (IPO) or may provide debt funding with warrants for management buyouts or as an alternative to bank financing which may not be available. Venture banks (or venture arms of depositary banks) are another source for loans, possible equity features against certain assets, and may provide such capital alongside a venture funded round. Another important source of capital is the investment banking community which serves as a vehicle for obtaining funding from a wide range of sources through private placements or public offerings.

Having an understanding of and keeping a focus on exit strategy alternatives is one key to a company's ultimate success. On occasion, an exit is through an IPO. Far more likely, it is an acquisition by or merger with another -- hopefully well funded -- company.

In short, no matter what happens you can't depend on the "food chain". Companies rarely turn out the way they are initially envisioned. The world changes and so must companies. Every entrepreneur must be prepared to adapt and survive through thick and thin. Like an aircraft pilot, an entrepreneur must always be looking for ways to soar while searching for a safe landing site should he temporarily run out of fuel. Sometimes this means cutting salaries and other overhead before you are ready and hunkering down in order to take off another day. This, again, is another form of "funding".

## 2. GOING PUBLIC REALITIES

The advantages of being a public company are compelling. The owners have liquid stock that facilitates the rapid growth and diversification of their wealth. The company has a larger, stronger capital base to fuel growth, pursue new ventures, or expand through the acquisition of other companies. The compensation paid to the corporation's executives often increases dramatically though higher salaries, bigger bonuses and stock equity incentives. There is often a perception that the prestige and presence of the entire enterprise and those who work for it has been pushed up to a whole new level.

Balanced against these advantages are risks, pressures, hassles, and costs that must be carefully considered and planned for. The pressure to show strength of earnings and growth is relentless and never-ending.  It's all about the short-term, the here and now.  The investing public, primarily though their guardians, the brokerage community, will scrutinize results and ask the tough questions.  The challenges of public disclosure and confidentiality will demand serious time and attention to avoid litigation burdens that often accompany bad disclosures or breached confidences.  Accounting, audit, internal control, and regulatory reporting and compliance pressures will balloon at all levels.  Management will be directly accountable to an active board of directors, partially comprised of outside, independent members who will be the sole players on the all-important audit and compensation subcommittees. Sales and purchases of company stock by corporate executives will have to be publicly reported and carefully monitored to avoid securities law liability risks.

And then there are the costs – the costs to go public and the ongoing increased costs that come with being a public company.  The baseline upfront costs to go public include substantial legal fees for a host of items, including preparation of the registration statement and securities law compliance, accounting and audit fees, printing costs, and various others direct fees and costs that are incurred during the launch period, which typically runs six to nine months.  In a survey of 26 companies that went public during the 2009 to 2011 timeframe, Ernst & Young LLP[4] found that the companies, on average, engaged 11 third-party advisors in connection with the their IPO, including investment bankers, attorneys, auditors, printers, D&O insurance carriers, stock transfer agents, Sarbanes-Oxley consultants, compensation advisors, investor relations firms, tax advisors, road show consultants, compensation advisors to the board, and internal audit advisors.

On average, the surveyed companies spent $13 million in one-time advisory costs associated with executing the IPO.  Of course, the core offering costs will typically be much less in smaller offerings. But the bottom line is always the same – the up-front costs of an IPO, which are not predicated on a successful offering, are very expensive.  And beyond these direct getting-started costs are the indirect and opportunity costs of personnel and management time and the substantial commissions and expenses that must be paid to those who sell the stock in the offering.

As for the additional costs that come with being a public company, in the same survey Ernst & Young reported that the new public companies, on average, incurred additional ongoing costs (not related to the IPO) of approximately $2.5 million a year as a public company. Of this amount, $1.5 million was attributable to executive compensation and directors' benefits, and the remaining $1 million represented increased compliance costs.

What does the process of going public involve? The starting point is a determination that the company is a good candidate for an initial public offering.  This often requires discussions with consultants, underwriters, accountants and attorneys to assess the state of the market and the appeal of the company.  The focus is on the proven ability of the company to maintain consistent growth, the

---

4. Ernst & Young IPO Cost Survey, November 2011.  Ernst & Young is a global leader in assurance, tax, transaction and advisory services that employs 141,000 people worldwide.

experiences and track records of the management team, the type of product or service offered by the company (the "hotter" the better), how the company stacks up against its competition, and whether the audit requirements for a public offering have been or can be satisfied.

A key challenge is to get an underwriter committed to the offering. Often the creditability and experience of the management team is the primary factor in attracting a quality underwriter. And, of course, size matters. Most companies who are seriously exploring a public offering have annual sales of at least $100 million. It's often impossible to reasonably justify the increased costs and regulatory burdens of being a public company when the annual sales drop much below this threshold. In select situations, an underwriter may have an interest in smaller companies that have a cutting edge product and promise sustained, extreme annual growth (say, 25 percent) for the next five years.

The registration statement is always a major challenge in an initial public offering. It must be carefully drafted to include the history of the company, details related to the market for the product or services offered by the company, how the proceeds of the offering are going to be used, the risk factors that accompany an investment in the company, the backgrounds of the officers and directors, any transactions with related parties, the identifies of any major shareholders, and more. Of course, audited financial statements must be included in the registration statement. Once completed, the registration statement is submitted to the Securities and Exchange Commission for review.

The selling begins when the registration statement is approved and the offering is effective. Often the key to the sales effort is a high-quality "road show" that smartly and quickly lays out key facts and stimulates investor interest in the company. Institutional investors generally have no interest in visiting the companies they invest in. They want an informative presentation at the road show meetings that gives them what they need to make an investment decision. This is the ideal time (often the only time) for the company's senior management to communicate directly with potential investors. Usually the sales presentation is carefully scripted in various formats (everything from a full-blown presentation to a two-minute pitch) to accommodate different sales opportunities.

When the offering wraps up and the money has arrived, the governance, management, performance, disclosure, and compliance challenges of being a public company take center stage.

### 3. CROWDFUNDING

Crowdfunding is where a group of individuals collectively contribute funds to a start-up effort in response to solicitations that usually come via the Internet. There are two kinds of crowdfunding: non-equity and equity. Non-equity crowdfunding is where the individual does not receive any equity interest for his or her contribution to the cause. The contributor's motive may be completely charitable or with the hope of receiving a tangible item (not a security) promised by the company. Kickstarter.com is one of the leading non-equity crowdfunding sponsors. A company that has a creative idea but no money can use Kickstarter in hopes of raising modest amounts to "kick start" its business. The average yield from a success Kickstarter effort is about $5,000 – enough perhaps to make some noise about a creative idea, but not nearly enough to finance a real business.

Equity crowdfunding is a much different, and far more controversial, concept. It will soon be legal, but, as of this writing, nobody knows when or what it will mean. The JOBS ("Jumpstart Our Business Startups") Act of 2012 mandates that the SEC implement rules for a new crowdfunding securities registration exemption within 270 days of the April 5 passage date. The President heralded crowdfunding as a "game changer" for "small businesses and start-ups," stating "for the first time, ordinary Americans will be able to go online and invest in entrepreneurs that they believe in."[5]

The concept of equity crowdfunding scares many. Within a short time, private business ventures of all types will be using the Internet to sell unregistered securities to "ordinary Americans" who will have no capacity to evaluate what's being offered. All the targeted investors will see are ground floor opportunities to play like the big dogs. The maximum amount that a business can raise through this crowdfunding tool in a 12-month period is $1 million – not serious money in the world of business development. Those who have an annual income and a net worth of less than $100,000 may invest the greater of $2,000 or five percent of their income or net worth in a single deal. Those who exceed the $100,000 threshold many invest 10 percent of their income or net worth up to a maximum of $100,000.

Proponents of equity crowdfunding compare it positively to buying lottery tickets. Opponents claim that the securities laws should at least seek to promote something greater than dumb luck gambling.

Here's the feared scenario. A budding entrepreneur with a hot-sounding business idea will use the internet to raise, say, $450,000 from 150 investors (average investment of $3,000) who have an average income and net worth of $60,000. The 150 investors will need attending to and will soon become a nuisance. They will have questions and concerns. They will want reports and information, to be assured that everything is on track. Of course, there will be no market for the stock, but some will want out anyway because of a lost job, a sickness, or a desire for a new car. A few will file bankruptcy, and their stock will end up in the hands of a bankruptcy trustee. An investor will die, and the heirs will demand the lowdown.

Meanwhile, the $450,000 will be spent on salaries, fees and start-up expenses. Soon more money will be needed to keep the plan alive. But what savvy investor will want to partner-up with 150 needy neophytes who can't bring any more to the table? If such an investor does surface, a plan will be developed to flush out the original 150 investors at the lowest possible cost. The more likely outcome is that the entrepreneur, having consumed the money, will just move on to the next deal after advising the investing crowd that there's no more money, the plan is dead, and they may be entitled to a tax deduction for a worthless investment.

5. President Obama's address on April 5, 2012 at signing of JOBs Act bill.

Is this fraud? It might be. It might just be incompetence, stupidity or greed. Either way, the uninformed investors end up losing. Investing in unregistered securities of start-ups is a super high-risk game that always poses serious risks of fraud, abuse, and complete loss. That's why, to date, it's a game that has been off limits to general solicitation and advertising and has been limited to sophisticated investors and those with a certain level of wealth. Many believe that it's no place for unsophisticated investors of modest means.

This assessment is not unique. The President of the North American Securities Administration Association (NASAA) recently stated, "Congress has just released every huckster, scam artist, small business owner and salesman onto the internet." Ralph Nader claimed that it's a "return to the notorious boiler room practices" where any start-up "can sell stock to investors like the old Wild West days with little disclosure or regulation."

Will there be any serious oversight? In announcing the passage of the JOBS act, the President stated that the SEC would play an "important role" to ensure that "the websites where folks go to fund all these start-ups and small businesses will be subject to rigorous oversight." Opponents are quick to point out that this is the same SEC that failed to spot Enron, Worldcom, Madoff, the dot-com bust, the derivative showdown banking industry, the subprime mortgage lunacy, the financial meltdown, and a host of other huge messes. How about state securities regulators helping out with oversight and regulation? There is no hope there. The new law specifically provides that the federal exemption will cut off all state involvement.

As of this writing, the SEC has announced that it will not meet the 270-day deadline for the crowdfunding rules. It's unclear when we can expect the rules. When announced, the rules will clarify the opportunities and obstacles of equity crowdfunding. Although there are now many unknowns, it appears highly likely that, at some point in the not too distant future and for better or worse, many start-up companies will be using the Internet and social media to raise capital from large groups of small, uniformed investors.

# C. SECURITIES LAW CHALLENGES

### 1. REGISTRATION EXEMPTION BASICS

How much do I need? From whom can I get it? Many business owners mistakenly assume that these two basic questions sum up the capital challenges for a start-up or thriving business. But there's a third and, in many respects, a more fundamental question: How do I do it legally?

Since the immediate fallout of the great crash of 1929, our laws have recognized that there is a big difference between selling a security and selling a used car. The former is an intangible; it's not possible to get the lowdown by kicking the tires, looking under the hood, and taking a test spin. So over the past 80 years, a body of federal statutory securities laws has developed to provide special protections for those who entrust their investment dollars with others.[6]

---

6. The federal securities statutes include the Securities Act of 1933 (15 U.S.C. §§ 77a et seq.), the Securities

All states have followed suit with their own statutory schemes.[7] The purpose of these laws is to protect the public from some of the risks inherent in investing money in intangible assets. Various means are used to accomplish this overriding purpose, including mandated disclosure requirements, industry player regulation, government law enforcement, and expanded causes of action for private litigation. Most good business lawyers do not possess the know-how or the experience to navigate a client through the SEC and state regulatory mazes to take a client public; that rare effort is left to experts who play in those mazes every day. But a business lawyer should understand the basics of this all-important body of law, be sensitive to the flags that indicate that a client is near (or far over) an important line, and know how to discuss key issues with business clients. For most businesses, the three primary security law considerations are the registration requirements, the resale restrictions, and the anti-fraud prohibitions.

Sections 4 and 5 of the Securities Act of 1933 (the 1933 Act) establish the general requirement that any security offered for sale by an issuer, underwriter or dealer must be registered with the Securities and Exchange Commission (SEC).[8] As explained in the previous section, only a tiny fraction of businesses would ever consider going through the expense and hassle of such a registration process. For this reason, the important registration issues for most businesses in need of investors are the exceptions to the registration requirement. Is there an applicable exception that fits so that the money can be raised without enduring the burdens of registration?

There are two big statutory exceptions that become the ball game for most privately owned businesses that want outside investors. The first is found in Section 4(2) of the 1933 Act that exempts from registration any "transactions by an issuer not involving a public offering."[9] It is commonly referred to as the "private offering exemption."

The second is in Section 3(a)(11) of the 1933 Act that exempts from registration securities offered and sold only to residents of a single state by an issuer who is a resident of and doing business within the same state.[10] It is commonly referred to as the "intrastate offering exemption." Of course, the challenge is to know what it takes to qualify for one of these exemptions. To this end, the SEC has published rules that set forth specific standards for meeting the exemptions. Rules 504 through 506 of Regulation D describe three private offering exemptions; SEC Rule 147 deals with the intrastate offering exemption.[11]

---

Exchange Act of 1934 (15 U.C.C. §§ 78a et seq.), the Public Utility Company Act of 1935 (15 U.S.C. §§ 79 et seq.), the Trust Indenture Act of 1939 (15 U.S.C. §§ 77aaa et seq.), the Investment Company Act of 1940 (15 U.S.C. §§ 80a–1 et seq.), the Investment Advisors Act of 1940 (15 U.S.C. §§ 80b-1 et seq.), the Securities Investor Protection Act of 1970 (15 U.S.C. §§ 78aaa et seq.) and the Sarbanes-Oxley Act of 2002 (miscellaneous provisions of 15 U.S.C.).

7. Most states have patterned their statutes after the Uniform Securities Act.

8. 15 U.S.C. §§ 77d and 77e.

9. 15 U.S.C. §§ 77d(2).

10. 15 U.S.C. § 77c(a)(11)

11. 17 C.F.R. §§ 230.504 through 230.506. The definitions and other provisions of sections 230.501-230.503 should be read in conjunction with these three rules.

### Rule 504 Exemption

SEC Rule 504 allows a company to issue unregistered securities with a value of up to $1 million to an unlimited number of unsophisticated investors who purchase the securities for their own account and not for resale. The offering must be completed within a 12-month period, which starts when the first investment agreement is signed by an investor. The rule itself does not mandate any specific disclosures, but the issuer must satisfy the basic antifraud provisions of the securities laws (discussed below). The rule permits general solicitation, but often this is prohibited or limited by state securities laws. Securities issued under Rule 504 are freed of certain resale restrictions because they are not considered "restricted securities." The company must comply with the securities laws of each state in which a purchaser is a resident, and usually must file a notice with that state's commissioner of corporations or similar official. Any person who purchases a security under a Rule 504 offering should sign an investment agreement as proof of his or her investment intent and other required representations. A Form D must be filed with the SEC within 15 days after the first sale.

### Rule 505 Exemption

SEC Rule 505 allows a company, within a 12-month period, to issue up to $5,000,000 worth of unregistered securities to 35 unsophisticated investors plus any number of "accredited investors." Generally, an "accredited investor" is an individual with a net worth of at least a $1,000,000 (primary home excluded) or an annual income of over $200,000 ($300,000 for a married couple) for the last two years. The definition also includes: banks and investment companies; private development companies; corporations, partnerships and trusts with assets over $5 million; and company insiders (officers, directors, and promoters). There are a number of required disclosures if any securities are sold to non-accredited investors. Advertising and general solicitations are prohibited. The securities are "restricted securities" and may not be readily resold. The company must comply with the securities laws of each state in which a person who buys the security is a resident, and usually must file a notice with that state's commissioner of corporations or similar official. Any person who acquires a security in a Rule 505 offering should sign an appropriate investment agreement. The company must file a Form D with the SEC within 15 days after the first sale.

### Rule 506 Exemption

Rule 506 is the most popular registration exemption because there are no dollar limitations and (this is the big one) an exemption under 506 preempts all state securities law registration requirements. This can save a great deal of time, hassle or expense for the company that intends to raise money from investors in various states. Under Rule 506, there can be any number of accredited investors and up to 35 non-accredited investors if, and only if, each non-accredited investor (or an authorized representative) has knowledge and experience in financial and business matters and is capable of evaluating the risks of the investment. Historically, all advertising and general solicitations were prohibited under 506, but the JOBS Act of 2012 (discussed below) now permits general solicitation of accredited investors in a 506 offering if all the purchasers in the offering are accredited investors and reasonable steps are taken to ensure the accredited investor status of all investors.[12]  The company must file a form D with the SEC and with the corporation's commissioner in each state where stock is sold.  Any person who buys stock in a Rule 506 offering should sign an appropriate investment agreement confirming that he or she is buying the stock for investment purposes, that there are serious restrictions on the resale of the stock, and that no attempt will be made to resell the stock without the approval of the company.

### Rule 147 Exemption[13]

Rule 147 exempts from federal registration a company that sells securities in an "intrastate offering" to residents of only that state. To qualify as an "intrastate offering," the principal office of the company must be located in the state, at least 80 percent of the company's gross revenues must be derived from operations in the state, at least 80 percent of the company's assets must be located in the state, and at least 80 percent of the proceeds realized in the offering must be used in the state. The company must comply with the state's securities laws. Any person who acquires a security should sign an appropriate investment agreement containing proof of residence.

### Regulation A Offerings

Regulation A provides an exemption allowing for public offers and sales of up to $5 million of securities in a 12-month period. It is sometimes referred to as a mini-registration. Investment companies and any company subject to the periodic reporting requirements of the Securities Exchange Act are not eligible. Regulation A requires the company to file an offering statement with the Securities and Exchange Commission containing disclosures similar to those made in a registration statement, certain exhibits, and financial statements prepared in accordance with generally accepted accounting principles (audited statements are not required). When the offering statement has been reviewed and qualified by the SEC, it must be delivered to prospective investors prior to any securities being sold. The company is required to file reports with the SEC detailing the securities sold and the use of proceeds from those sales.  But once the offering is complete – and unlike all public companies – there are no ongoing reporting requirements.   Securities sold in a Regulation A offering are unrestricted and may be transferred in a secondary market transaction. Regulation A offerings are seldom used because of the $5 million limitation and the amount of work they require.

### JOBS Act of 2012

On April 5, 2012, President Obama signed the Jumpstart Our Business Startups (JOBS) Act with strong bi-partisan support. The Act is intended to

---

12. On July 10, 2013, the SEC issued its final changes to Rule 506 to permit issuers to use general solicitation and advertising to offer securities provided (1) the issuer takes reasonable steps to verify that the investors are accredited investors and (2) all purchasers of the securities fall within one of the categories of persons who are accredited investors under an existing rule (Rule 501 of Regulation D) or the issuer reasonably believes that the investors fall within one of the categories at the time of the sale of the securities.

13.  17 C.F.R. § 240.147.

increase American job creation and economic growth by improving access to the public capital markets for emerging growth companies. Key provisions of the Act include the following:

- The maximum number of shareholders of record that a private company can have before it must register with the SEC as a public company is increased from 500 to 2,000, so long as fewer than 500 are non-accredited investors.

- The prohibition on general solicitation and advertising in a private offering under Rule 506 of Regulation D must be removed by the SEC. In August 2012, the SEC released proposed changes to Rule 506 that would permit general solicitation and adverting if all the purchasers in the offering are accredited investors and reasonable steps are taken to ensure the accredited investor status of all investors.

- The SEC must adopt rules that permit "crowdfunding" activities so that entrepreneurs could raise up to $1 million from a large pool of small investors, subject to limitations based on investor income levels. (See related discussion of crowdfunding in the previous section of this chapter.)

- The SEC must raise the limit for offerings under Regulation A from $5 million to $50 million and exempting Regulation A offerings from state securities laws so long as the securities are offered or sold over a national securities exchange or are sold to a "qualified purchaser" (a term the SEC will need to define). The revised Regulation A will require a company to file audited financial statements annually with the SEC, and the SEC is directed to develop rules relating to periodic disclosure by Regulation A issuers.

- **A** category of issuer called an "emerging growth company" is created under the Act. This is a company that has under $1 billion in annual revenues. The regulatory burden on such companies is eased by permitting them to include only two years of audited financial statements and selected other information in their IPO registration statement, not requiring an auditor attestation of management's assessment of internal controls for financial reporting created under Sarbanes Oxley, and exempting them from certain other accounting requirements. Also, the Act eases offering-pending research disclosure rules, marketing communication conflict of interest rules, and pre-filing institutional investor communication limitations. Furthermore, an emerging growth company will be exempt from shareholder approval requirements of executive compensation

## Antifraud Challenges

Beyond the registration exemptions are the anti-fraud prohibitions. Section 10(b) of the Securities Exchange Act of 1934 (the 1934 Act) prohibits "the use of a manipulative and deceptive device" in connection with the purchase or sale of any security.[14] SEC Rule 10b-5, promulgated under Section 10(b), makes it unlawful for any person, directly or indirectly in connection with the purchase and sale of a security, "to make any untrue statement of a material fact or to omit

---

14. 15 U.S.C. § 78j.

to state a material fact necessary in order to make the statements made, in the light of the circumstances under which they were made, not misleading."[15]  This rule takes all dealings in securities to a higher level.  The seller has an affirmative duty to accurately state material facts and to not mislead; the buyer has a solid cause of action if the seller blows it.  Rule 10b-5 and its state counterparts keep our courts packed with countless disgruntled investors who believe they were unfairly deceived when things didn't go as planned.

In offerings that are exempt from registration, the tool that is used to protect against antifraud risks is the private placement memorandum ("PPM"), a carefully prepared document that provides the necessary disclosures.  Items typically included in a PPM include: The name, address, and telephone number of the issuer; a description and the price of the securities offered; the amount of the offering (minimum and maximum amounts, if any); the plan and cost of the distribution of the securities; an identification and description of the officers, directors, and advisers of the company; a description of company's business and products or services and the related technology; a discussion of the market for the issuer's products and services and related competition; a description of all risk factors, including those related to the company and those related to general market or economic conditions; a description of applicable resale restrictions and the related lack of liquidity impacts; and an explicit warning that the company could become insolvent or bankrupt and any investment in the company could be a total loss; recent financial statements of the company (audit not required); projections of future revenues, expenses, and profits or losses (optional); a description of how the proceeds realized from the offering will be used; a statement that neither the Securities and Exchange Commission nor any state securities commission has approved the securities or passed on the adequacy or accuracy of the disclosures in the PPM; a statement describing how the offering price was determined; a description of the company's present capital structure, prior offerings, and any outstanding stock plans or stock options; a description of the restrictions on the resale of the company's securities and the fact that no market now exists or may ever exist for the securities; a disclosure of any contracts or agreements with management; a disclosure of all significant contracts that the company has with third parties; copies of key documents related to the offering (legal opinions, Articles of Incorporation, etc.); and an offer for investors to meet with management, tour the company's facilities, and ask questions.

### Resale Restrictions

The Securities Act of 1933 does not provide an exemption for private resale of restricted securities acquired through a private placement.  In order to qualify for the private placement exemption, there can be no immediate distribution or resell by the initial purchasers of the securities.  For that reason, companies should take precautions to protect against resells, which typically include confirming the investment intent of each purchaser, printing restrictive legends on the share certificates, issuing stop transfer instructions to any transfer agents, and obtaining purchaser representations in writing from each purchaser

---

15.  17 C.F.R. § 240.10b-5.

confirming that he or she is buying the security for his or her own account and not for resale or with a view to distribution.

There are options for a purchaser of restricted securities who desires to resell. SEC Rule 144[16] provides a non-exclusive safe harbor from registration for resells of restricted securities. Among other things, it imposes holding period and "dribble out" requirements. SEC Rule 144A[17] provides a separate safe harbor for resells to qualified institutional buyers. Also, the courts and the SEC have acknowledged an additional resale exception, known as the "Section 4(1 1/2)" exemption.[18] The SEC has characterized it as "a hybrid exemption not specifically provided for in the 1933 Act but clearly within its intended purpose" and has stated that it will apply "so long as some of the established criteria for sales under both section 4(1) and section 4(2) of the [1933] Act are satisfied."[19] Under this exemption, an investor holding restricted securities may resell the securities to another accredited investor who purchases them for his or her own account and not for distribution if the subsequent purchaser signs an appropriate investment letter and if the certificate issued bears appropriate legends for restricted securities.

## 2. COMMON SECURITY LAW MISCONCEPTIONS

The root cause of most trouble under the securities laws is ignorance. The client just didn't understand and didn't stop to think or ask for advice before charging ahead. There are many misconceptions that can get in the way. A challenge for the business advisor is to spot and eradicate these misconceptions before they become a problem. It's an ongoing educational effort with many business owners. Following is a brief summary of some of the most common misconceptions.

**a. Big Guy Rules**. Some business owners mistakenly assume that the securities laws apply only to public companies whose stock is regularly traded. It's the old "Why would the SEC want to mess with little old me?" notion. This misconception is supported by the little they read in the press (it's all focused on big companies), and the fact that none of their business owner friends have ever had to deal with the SEC. Although many securities law issues are uniquely directed at public companies and SEC efforts are focused on the public markets, the securities laws extend to any private security transaction between a company and individual investors. Size is not a prerequisite for Rule 10b-5. For most privately owned businesses, the fear is not a call from the SEC; it's a letter from a hungry plaintiff's lawyer who, armed with 10b-5 and a set of ugly facts, is making demands on behalf of unhappy investors at the worst possible time.

**b. This Ain't a Security**. The misconception is that the securities laws

---

16. 17 C.F.R. § 230.144.

17. 17 C.F.R. § 230.144A.

18. See SEC 1933 Act Release No. 33-6188 (Feb. 1, 1980) and Ackerberg v. Johnson, 892 F.2d 1328 (8th Cir. 1989).

19. SEC 1933 Act Release No. 33-6188 (Feb. 1, 1980). On this exemption, see Olander and Jacks, The Section 4 (1 1/2) Exemption – Reading Between the Lines of the Securities Act of 1933, 15 Sec. Reg. L.J. 339 (1988) and Schneider, Section 4 (1 1/2) – Private Resales of Restricted or Controlled Securities, 49 Ohio St. L.J. 501 (1988).

apply only to stocks. The term "security" is broadly defined in the 1933 Act to include, among other things, any note, bond, evidence of indebtedness, certificate of interest or participation in any profit-sharing agreement, and investment contract.[20] The Supreme Court has held that a "security" exists whenever money is invested in a common enterprise with profits to come solely from the efforts of others.[21] Applying this broad definition, courts have found a "security" in investment contracts involving worm farms, boats, silver foxes, oyster beds, vending machines, parking meters, cemetery plots, exotic trees, vineyards, fig orchards, chinchillas, beavers and more.[22] A flag should surface whenever a client claims or suggests that money can be raised by offering something that is *not* a "security."

**c. The Safe, Dumb, Poor Crowd.** Some mistakenly believe that it is "safer" to target unsophisticated investors who don't know the law and lack the means or the will to fight back if things go wrong. Plus, this group is "easier" because they don't know enough to ask the tough questions – that is, they can be fooled. This is dangerous thinking for a number of reasons. First, the most important registration exemption requires that the investors be accredited investors[23] or be non-accredited investors who are sophisticated in financial affairs or have representatives who possess such sophistication.[24] Second, the company loses the opportunity to bring in savvy investors who may contribute their wisdom and experience in addition to their money. Third (and this is the crux), besides just being a bad thing to do, the whole purpose of the securities laws is to protect the naive and uninformed from those who peddle intangible investments that promise riches. The dumb, poor investors may lack the capacity to evaluate what is being promised; but after things go bad, it doesn't take much to find an aggressive lawyer who is willing to spec the case against a contingent fee because, given the undisputed limitations of the plaintiffs, it's a slam dunk. Smart business owners generally limit their offers to accredited investors who have experience in financial and investment matters and who can afford the loss of their investment. In rare instances, they might consider a non-accredited individual, but only if that individual is sophisticated in financial matters and is investing a sum that he or she can afford to lose.

**d. Only "Really Important" Stuff.** The misconception is that only the "really important" information has to be disclosed because Rule 10b-5 speaks in terms of "material facts." Often this misconception is aggravated by the notion that the important information is the bottom-line conclusions that support the business plan. So, they reason, there's no need to sweat details that may complicate the money raising effort. The determination of a "material" fact within the meaning of Rule 10b–5 "depends on the significance the reasonable

---

20. 15 U.S.C. § 77b(1).

21. S.E.C. v. W.J. Howey Co., 328 U.S. 293 (1946).

22. See 2 L. Loss & J. Seligman, Securities Regulation (3rd ed. 1989-93) pp. 948-956.

23. Individuals are considered accredited investors if they have a net worth that exceeds $1 million (primary residence excluded) or an annual income of over $200,000 ($300,000 if married) for the most recent two years preceding the securities purchase. 15 U.S.C. § 77b(15) and 17 C.F.R. § 230.501(a).

24. The all-important Rule 506 exemption requires that nonaccredited investors be sophisticated investors. 17 C.F.R. § 230.506.

investor would place on the withheld or misrepresented information."[25] The "material" standard will be met if the misrepresentation or omission "would have been viewed by a reasonable investor as having significantly altered the 'total mix' of information made available."[26] It's a very broad definition that presents a mixed question of fact and law in most cases; it is decided as a matter of law only when reasonable minds would not differ on the issue.[27] It's a mistake to assume that the materiality requirement eliminates the need to provide details. Plus, there is another hard reality that always supports the conclusion that more, not less, should be disclosed. If things go bad and a significant contributing factor to the failure was not disclosed up front, it may be impossible, looking back, to claim that that factor was not material and worthy of disclosure. The wisest and safest approach is to lay out all known risk factors and the related details.

**e. My Successes Say It All.** Many business owners focus only on past successes when talking track record. Failures or disappointments are forgotten or "amended" to look like successes. The misconception is that it is appropriate to paint the best possible track record, even when it involves a little fudging or selective editing. A key executive's track record is important to any investor. What one has done in the past often is the best indicator of what might happen in the future. If things go bad, an investor who first learns after the fact that this was not the key person's first failure may be shocked into action. The challenge is to accurately and fairly summarize the background and experiences, both good and bad, of the key players in a way that suggests that they now possess the skills and abilities to successfully manage the proposed venture.

**f. Good Advertising Is The Key.** Some mistakenly assume that fundraising is all about advertising. They start a makeshift advertising campaign, only to learn that they have killed some of their best shots at a registration exemption. Although the JOBS Act of 2012 has opened up general solicitation and advertising in select Rule 506 offerings and presumably the crowdfunding world, usually the word of an exempt offering must be spread through friends, relatives and business associates.

**g. Safety in Numbers.** The misconception is that it is safer to have a large number of small investors, rather than one or two big players. It's based on the false assumption that a small investor will be more inclined to swallow a loss and less inclined to fight back. It ignores some basic realities. First, the size of one's investment does not govern the capacity to stomach a loss; many large players are better equipped to understand and suck up a loss than most small investors who have had unrealistic expectations from the get-go and can't afford any loss. Second, it ignores the capacity of many voices to stir each other up and to share the expense and burden of hiring a gladiator to fight their cause. Third, it ignores the burden, often horrendous, of having to respond to multiple ongoing inquiries all along the way from nervous, uninformed investors who just want to hear that all will pay off "as promised" and that there are "no problems." Finally, it ignores the significant value of binding a few key players to the effort. Inviting

---

25. Basic Inc. v. Levinson, 485 U.S. 224, 240 (1988).
26. TSC Industries, Inc. v. Northway, Inc., 426 U.S. 438, 449 (1976).
27. Id. at 450.

them into the inner circle gives the business the benefit of their advice and counsel and often eliminates any securities law exposure because they see it all, hear it all, and are part of it all.

**h. Dodge the Downside.** Some wrongfully assume that there is no need to talk about the potential of failure when trying to raise money. They figure that everyone knows there is risk. So why talk about it? The truth is that, from a securities law perspective, it is essential to spell out the risk factors in writing for any prospective investor. Nothing is more material than those factors that may potentially cause the business to fail. Thought should be given to risk factors that are specific to the business (competition, market condition changes, supply access, technology changes, skilled labor needs, capital and liquidity challenges, etc.) and the potential impact that general risks (e.g., interest rate increases) may have on the business. Often this is one of the most difficult tasks for business owners to embrace. As the risk factor list is committed to black and white, they begin to fear that everyone will be "spooked away." It helps to remind them that seasoned players are used to seeing such lists, and that they have all made money in ventures that started out with risk factor lists that were just as ugly as the one being created.

**i. Projections Are Just Projections.** The misconception is that since future projections, by their very nature, are speculative, they create an opportunity to strengthen the money raising effort by painting the rosiest possible picture of how things might play out. It's little wonder that such projections have been the driving force behind many securities law claims. The use of projections should be handled carefully. They should not be viewed as an opportunity to oversell, but rather as a means of illustrating the business' potential under a defined set of reasonable assumptions. If overdone, they may create unrealistic false expectations that cause an otherwise good performance to disappoint or, worse yet, fuel a legal dispute when things turn sour. There are a few important precautions that can be taken. First, make certain that the projections are based on reasonable assumptions that are spelled out. The operative word here is "reasonable;" the assumptions should not reflect an ideal, unrealistic set of conditions. Second, the predictions should be accompanied by a cautionary statement that identifies the predictions as forward-looking statements, warns that conditions and risks could cause actual results to differ substantially from the projections, and lists specific risks and conditions that may have such an effect. The effort may allow the company, if necessary, to rely on the "bespeaks caution doctrine" that provides a defense against allegations of false and misleading forward-looking statements when such precautionary language has been used.[28]

**j. "Puffing" Works.** Some business owners believe that the key to "legal money raising" is "puffing" – making vague overstated generalizations that get potential investors excited. Often they have heard about cases where defendants escaped securities law liability because the court concluded that the alleged misrepresentations were nothing more than "obviously immaterial puffery."[29]

---

28. See, e.g., In re Worlds of Wonder Sec. Litig., 35 F.3d 1407 (9th Cir. 1994); Gasner v. Board of Supervisors, 103 F.3d 351 (4th Cir. 1996); and Nadoff v. Duane Reade, Inc., 107 Fed. Appx. 250 (2d Cir. 2004).

29. See, e.g., Grossman v. Novell, Inc., 120 F.3d 1112 (10th Cir. 1997); Raab v. General Physics Corp., 4

Statements like "our fundamentals are strong," "our product is revolutionary and could change the world," and "the stock is red hot" have been dismissed as immaterial puffing.[30] The problem is when it goes too far. What may appear as harmless puffing can trigger liability under the securities laws if the speaker had no reasonable basis for making the statement. The court will examine whether the speaker really believed that the statement was accurate and had a factual or historical basis for that belief.[31] There is some room for harmless puffing, but in no sense is it a free pass without limits.

**k. Let 'Em Be.** The misconception is that investors, once they've bought in, should be free to deal with their stock as they see fit. As described above, the private offering exemption requires that the investors not be used as a device to disseminate the stock to a broader audience and thereby convert what would otherwise be a private offering into a public offering. This important factor, coupled with the obvious antifraud challenges, gives the company a huge interest in what the investors do with their stock. For this reason, as described above, it is common practice to ascertain the investment intentions of purchasers up front, to place resale restrictive legends on share certificates, to issue stop transfer instructions to those who control the stock register, and to obtain written representations from all purchasers that they are acquiring the security for their own account and not for resale or with a view to distribute the stock.

**l. Cashing In Is the Easy Part.** This misconception surfaces when everybody just assumes that an acceptable exit strategy will present itself at the most opportune time. Often a business plan is developed with little or no thought given to the ultimate strategy that will be used to realize a return for the owners of the business. The organizers assume if things work out and the business becomes profitable, an opportunity will surface to cash in at the best time. No serious effort is made to research the practicality and possibility of specific exit scenarios. The details of operating the business and generating revenues have been thought through, but the broader picture is left to fuzzy notions of market options and base ignorance. This gets scary when an organizer with little knowledge starts speculating on return strategies with a potential investor who has even less knowledge. The organizer often has no specific knowledge regarding the appetite others may have for the business. The sad reality is that many business owner/managers are shocked and disappointed to discover that there is little or no market for their business. This disappointment can be magnified many times for the outside investor who draws no compensation and has assumed all along that a big payday was within reach. And then there are the baseless, overstated "going public" expectations. This sounds great to the naive investor, even though the organizer has no real clue as to what a public offering entails or requires. A primary challenge for many business owners is to develop a realistic expectation of the business' capacity to create returns for the owners. Seasoned entrepreneurs do this instinctively. Experience has taught them to

F.3d 286 (4th Cir. 1993); and Helwig v. Vencor, Inc. 210 F.3d 612 (6th Cir. 2000).

30. Rosenzweig v. Azurix Corp., 332 F.3d 854 (5th Cir. 2003); Vosgerichian v. Commodore Int'l, 832 F.Supp. 909 (E.D. Pa. 1993); Newman v. Rothschild, 651 F.Supp. 160 (S.D.N.Y. 1986).

31. See, e.g., Kline v. First Western Government Sec., 24 F.3d 480 (3d Cir. 1994), cert. denied 513 U.S. 1032 (1994) and In re Allaire Corp. Secs. Litig., 224 F.Supp.2d 319 (D. Mass. 2002).

always have their eye on the big picture and the entire life cycle of the business. Plus, they understand that conditions can change; what is solid and profitable today can be weak and vulnerable tomorrow. So timing is often the key when it comes to cashing in the marbles. Less experienced owners, particularly those who are wrapped up in their first effort, often fail to see, let alone focus on, the broader picture and never develop such realistic expectations for themselves and those who have entrusted them with their money. As a result, they end up in a situation where they can only disappoint.

## PROBLEM 6-C

For the past three years, Wayne has been the sole owner and CEO of a corporation that manufactures and distributes a relatively expensive high-tech baby monitoring device known as "Hear All." The business has grown steadily, and Wayne is convinced that it's time to "shoot for the stars." To make this happen, Wayne needs $1.5 million of equity capital and an expanded bank line of credit that will be "doable without personal guarantees" based on the past record of the business and the new equity. Wayne is willing to give up 40 percent of the equity to secure the needed capital.

Wayne's brother-in-law Sam, a CPA and big fan of Wayne's product, claims to have "lined up the dough." Seven individuals will each contribute $200,000, and Sam will contribute $100,000. All Wayne knows is that the investors reside in three states, four of the seven are "doctor clients of Sam," two are mothers who "married right and love the product," and the last one is a "23-year-old kid who wants to be a musician and just inherited a bundle."

What additional facts do you need to advise Wayne relative to any registration exemptions under the federal securities laws? On the basis of the facts you have, which exemption likely will work best for Wayne?

# CHAPTER 7

# ENTITY CONVERSIONS: UNRAVELING PRIOR CHOICES

---

## A. INTRODUCTION

Many mature businesses need to switch horses – convert from one entity form to another. The cause may be an ill-advised decision in the first instance or changed circumstances. Whatever the reason, the challenge always is the same: to effect the conversion at the lowest tax cost. Some conversions trigger no taxes; others are prohibitively expensive.

## B. CONVERTING FROM PARTNERSHIP STATUS TO C STATUS

There are three options for transitioning assets and liabilities from a partnership-taxed entity to a newly formed C corporation.[1] Option one is the most obvious – the partnership transfers the assets and liabilities directly to the C corporation in exchange for stock and then liquidates by distributing the stock to its owners. No gain or loss is recognized by the partnership or its partners.[2] The partnership's basis in the assets transfers over to the corporation.[3] Each partner's basis in the stock received equals that partner's adjusted basis in his or her partnership interest, which is reduced by any liabilities assumed by the corporation in the transaction.[4] The partnership is terminated for tax purposes.[5]

Under the second option, the partnership liquidates by distributing all of its assets and liabilities to its partners. The partners then contribute the assets and liabilities to the new corporation in return for stock. The partnership recognizes no gain or loss on the liquidation and is terminated for tax purposes.[6] A partner recognizes no gain or loss on the liquidation unless the partner receives money in

---

1. See generally Revenue Ruling 84-111, 1984-2 C.B. 88.
2. I.R.C. §§ 351.
3. I.R.C. § 362(a).
4. I.R.C. §§ 358(a), (d), 733, 752.
5. I.R.C. § 708(b)(1)(A).
6. I.R.C. §§ 731(b), 708(b)(1)(A).

excess of his or her basis in the partnership.[7] Similarly, the transfer of the assets and liabilities to the corporation usually qualifies as a tax-free exchange.[8] Each partner's basis in the assets distributed by the partnership equals that partner's basis in his or her partnership interest.[9] That basis in the assets then carries over to the corporation. It also determines the partner's basis in the stock the partner receives from the corporation.[10]

Option three is the situation where the partners contribute their partnership interests to the new C corporation in exchange for stock. The assets and liabilities of the partnership are then liquidated into the corporation. No gain or loss is recognized on the transfer of the partnership interests for stock.[11] Each partner's basis in the stock received equals the partner's basis in the transferred partnership interest.[12] Similarly, the partners' basis in their partnership interests carries over to the corporation and determines the corporation's basis in the assets received from the partnership.[13]

Do the three options produce any different results when the dust settles? Consider the case where the partners' outside basis in their partnership interests totals $500,000 and the partnership's basis in its assets totals $400,000. In options two and three, there is a direct transfer of property between the partners and the new corporation in return for stock. In option two, the partners transfer assets whose basis would have been bumped up to $500,000 on the liquidation of the partnership. The new corporation would end up with a $500,000 basis in the assets, and the partners would have a $500,000 basis in their stock. The result would be the same in option three because the partners would transfer their partnership interests for stock. The $500,000 basis in their partnership interests would carry over to their stock and would carry over to the assets received by the corporation on the subsequent liquidation of the partnership.

Option one would turn out differently. When the partnership contributes the assets to the corporation, the partnership's $400,000 basis in the assets would carry over and become the corporation's basis in the assets. When the stock is distributed to the partners in liquidation of the partnership, it would have a basis equal to the partners' $500,000 basis in their partnership interests. The corporation will end up with a lower basis in its assets under option one whenever the outside basis of the partnership interests exceeds the partnership's inside basis in the assets.

Also, option one is different than options two or three in another potentially important respect. Unlike options two or three, under option one the partners are not the original issuees of the stock. The stock first goes to the partnership and then to the partners. This will present a problem if the corporation desires to make an S election in its first year because the partnership, an ineligible S

---

7. I.R.C. § 731(a).
8. I.R.C. § 351.
9. I.R.C. § 732(b).
10. I.R.C. §§ 358(a), 362(a).
11. I.R.C. § 351.
12. I.R.C. § 358(a).
13. I.R.C. §§ 362(a).

corporation shareholder, will have owned stock for some period of time.[14] The S election will have to be deferred until year two. Plus, ordinary loss treatment under Section 1244 will not be available.[15]

There is a fourth option for getting from partnership status to C status. As described in Chapter 3, a partnership now has the option of just checking a box and being taxed as a corporation. There is no need to form a corporation or transfer assets and liabilities. The tax status of the entity changes, but the entity remains. This option certainly reduces the paperwork and may be particularly valuable in those situations where difficult or uncomfortable third party consents may be a prerequisite to transferring certain assets and contracts. Such consents often are required in connection with real property leases, borrowing and line of credit arrangements, joint ventures, licensing arrangements, executive employment contracts, and other similar agreements. The easy answer in select situations may be to check the box and just change the tax status.

The tax consequences of checking the box are spelled out in Reg. Section 301.7701-3(c)(1)(i). The election is treated the same as in option one described above. The partnership is deemed to have contributed all of its assets and liabilities to a new corporate entity in exchange for stock, and then immediately thereafter is deemed to have distributed the stock to its partners in liquidation of the partnership. The same result applies in those cases where, under state law, an unincorporated business is allowed to convert to corporate form without having to actually transfer assets and liabilities.[16]

Are there benefits to going through the process of actually incorporating as opposed to just checking the box? Usually there are. First, if the outside basis of the partners' interests exceeds the partnership's basis in its assets (a common scenario), options two and three described above, both of which require an actual entity change, will produce a tax benefit for the new entity. Second, in many situations, the structure, durability and state law benefits of a corporate entity will be desired. The concept of actually having stock, a board of directors, corporate titles, and other corporate trappings may be attractive. Many still feel that having a company name that ends in "Inc." or "Incorporated" helps foster perceptions of stability, permanence and strength – perceptions that can make things easier in the business world. Third, employee benefits available to shareholder/employees of a C corporation may not be available if the partnership entity is continued.[17]

## C. CONVERTING FROM S STATUS
## TO C STATUS

Comparatively, a conversion from S corporation status to C corporation status is a piece of cake. There is no need to transfer assets or liabilities or to

---

14. I.R.C. § 1362(b)(2).

15. I.R.C. § 1244(a). The regulations provide that 1244 ordinary loss treatment is not available to a shareholder who receives stock via the liquidation of a partnership. Reg. § 1.1244(a)-1(b).

16. Rev. Rul. 2004-59, 2004-1 C.B. 1050.

17. For example, section 79 group term life insurance benefits are available only to an "employee," defined in Reg. § 1.79-0 by incorporating the legal relationship standard of Reg. § 31.3401(c)-1. Similarly, "employee" status is required for other benefits, including benefits under I.R.C. §§ 105 (accident and health plans), 125 (cafeteria plans), 127 (educational assistance), and 129 (dependent care assistance).

create a new corporate entity. There is no deemed contribution of assets and liabilities, followed by a liquidating distribution of stock. All that is required is a revocation of the S election, approved by shareholders holding more than 50 percent of the corporation's outstanding shares, or the corporation doing some act that disqualifies it from the S election (e.g., issuing a second class of stock).[18] The corporation remains intact, with the same assets, liabilities, and tax attributes, only now taxed as a C corporation. When such a conversion is made, there are four planning considerations.

First, the shareholders may specify an effective date for the revocation of S status. Absent such a specification, the revocation is effective on the first day of the taxable year of the election if the election is made on or before the fifteenth day of the third month; otherwise, the election is effective on the first day of the following taxable year.[19] The planning opportunity is to pick an effective date that will facilitate easy accounting cut-offs while maximizing the benefits that motivated the decision to convert to C status. If the S termination is the result of a failure to qualify for S status, the S election terminates on the first day after the disqualifying event.[20]

Second, if the S election terminates on a specified date during the taxable year, the year is divided into two short years – an S short year and a C short year.[21] The shareholders then have an option. They may allocate income, losses, deductions and credits between the two short years based on the number of days in each short year.[22] Alternatively, they may allocate the items between the two short years based on the corporation's normal accounting practices.[23] Again, the primary considerations affecting this option will be the ease of accounting cut-offs and the motivating factors for converting to C status.

Third, if an S election is terminated, a corporation cannot return to S status for five years unless the Secretary of the Treasury consents to an earlier election.[24] For planning purposes, the shareholders should assume that S status, once terminated, is off the table for at least five years.

Finally, and perhaps most importantly in many cases, care should be taken to ensure that all S corporation earnings that have been taxed to the shareholders during the corporation's S tenure are distributed as tax-free distributions. If they are timely distributed, the only tax consequence is a reduction in the shareholders' stock basis. If delayed, the C corporation dividend rules of Section 301 kick in. In this regard, the Code offers a grace period that should be carefully respected. Section 1371(e)(1) provides that, absent an election to the contrary, any shareholder distribution by a former S corporation made during the post-termination period (basically until one year from the last day as an S

---

18. I.R.C. § 1362(d).

19. I.R.C. § 1362(d)(1).

20. I.R.C. § 1362(d)(2)(B).

21. I.R.C. § 1362(e)(1).

22. I.R.C. § 1362(e)(2). This option is not available if there is a sale of 50 percent or more of the corporation's stock during the year. I.R.C. § 1362(e)(6)(D).

23. The option is available only if all shareholders during the S short year and all shareholders on the first day of the C short year consent. I.R.C. § 1362(e)(3).

24. I.R.C. § 1362(g).

corporation) is treated as a tax-free reduction of stock basis to the extent of the corporation's accumulated adjustment account.[25]  So a former S corporation has one year to get the previously-taxed earnings out tax-free.

## D.  CONVERTING OUT OF C STATUS

Often a corporation decides to throw in the towel on its C status.  The driving incentive usually is a desire to escape the hassles of the double tax structure and the traps that exist to ensure that the structure exacts its pound of flesh.  As the business grows and the owners size up the tax costs of getting earnings out of the business or selling the business in the future, the benefits of a pass-through entity look increasingly more attractive.  The C corporation perks, such as the rate bracket savings and tax-free fringe benefits for shareholder/employees, no longer justify forgoing the benefits of a pass-through entity.

The strategic option for a corporation that wants to shed its C status usually is a no-brainer.  We saw above that it is relatively painless to convert from partnership status to C status.  Unfortunately, the reverse isn't true; it just doesn't work.  Any attempt to move from C status to partnership tax status, either via a partnership or a limited liability company (LLC), will trigger a tax liquidation of the C corporation, resulting in a corporate level tax (at regular corporate rates) on the excess of the value of the assets, including  goodwill,  over the tax basis of the assets.   Plus, the shareholders will be hit with a capital gains tax on the excess of the liquidation proceeds over their stock basis.  With the 1986 demise of the statutory offspring of the General Utilities Doctrine and other more palatable liquidation options (i.e., Section 333 one-month blow-outs), there is no escaping this double tax mess if a partnership-taxed entity is the chosen successor to the C corporation.  So the strategic decision is simple: move to S status.

Unfortunately, the decision is convert to S status usually is much easier than the execution of the decision itself.  A clean break from the burdens and hassles of C status is not possible.  From a planning perspective, it is important to evaluate and plan for the eligibility requirements of S status, the mechanics of making the conversion, and the tax traps that may be triggered at the time of the conversion or later.

### 1.  BECOMING ELIGIBLE FOR S STATUS

The conversion will work only if the corporation qualifies as a "small business corporation" both at the time the election is made and on the first day of the corporation's first S tax year.[26]  Qualifying as a "small business corporation" has nothing to do with the size of the corporation's operations, revenues or profits.  It is based upon the number of shareholders, the types of shareholders, and the presence of only one class of stock.

Seldom will the 100-shareholder count limitation be a problem.  Spouses count as one shareholder, as do family members (six generations deep) that elect

---

25.  I.R.C. §§ 1371(e), 1377(b)(1)(A).
26.  I.R.C. § 1361(b).

to be treated as one.[27]  In the extreme case where this limitation is a factor, the option is to start redeeming or purchasing the stock of shareholders until the body count hits 100.  The qualifying shareholder limitation can be more troubling. Only individuals, estates and certain trusts may be S corporation shareholders.[28] Partnerships, corporations, and nonresident aliens do not qualify.  So if the C corporation has an ineligible shareholder, that shareholder will need to disappear before the S election is made and the first S year begins.  Options include having the corporation redeem the stock owned by the ineligible shareholder or having one or more eligible shareholders purchase the stock.  In either event, the transaction should qualify for sale or exchange capital gains treatment.[29]  Where the stock is owned by a partnership or corporation, another option is for the ineligible shareholder (the partnership or corporation) to distribute the stock to those of its owners who are eligible S corporation shareholders.  For those ineligible shareholders who are partnerships, such distributions may be accomplished without triggering any taxes.  Neither the partnership nor the partner will recognize any income,[30] and the partner will take the partnership's basis in the stock,[31] with a corresponding reduction in the basis of the partner's interest in the partnership.[32]  This distribution option is more difficult for an S corporation-ineligible shareholder because any built-in gain on the distributed stock will be recognized by the entity and taxed through to its shareholders.[33] And any such distributions by an ineligible C corporation likely will trigger a brutal double tax hit – a corporate tax on the built-in gain and a personal tax (likely as a dividend) at the shareholder level.[34]  For planning purposes, the challenge is to evaluate the options against the facts of the particular case and then develop a wise exit strategy for the ineligible shareholders that is acceptable to all parties.

The single class of stock limitation can be the most difficult hurdle in many cases.  If the corporation has preferred stock or a second class of common stock, the best options are for the corporation to redeem the prohibited class of stock before the S election is made or to permit shares of the prohibited stock to be exchanged for common stock shares.  The redemption may trigger dividend treatment for the shareholder unless the shareholder's entire interest in the corporation is terminated.[35]  The exchange for common shares likely can be structured to qualify as a tax-free recapitalization under Section 368(a)(1)(E),

---

27.  I.R.C. § 1361(c)(1).

28.  I.R.C. §§ 1361(b)(2), 1361(c)(2).  For a brief description of the trusts that qualify as S corporation shareholders, see the description of S corporations in the section of Chapter 3 entitled "The Entity Candidates."

29.  Because the shareholder's entire interest in the corporation will be terminated, a redemption should have no problem qualifying for sale or exchange treatment under Section 302(b)(3) of the Code.  Similarly, any section 306 preferred stock should escape the ordinary income snare of section 306 by virtue of the complete termination.  I.R.C. § 306(b).

30.  I.R.C. § 731(a)-(b).

31.  I.R.C. § 732(a)(1).

32.  I.R.C. § 733.

33.  I.R.C. §§ 1371(a), 311(b).

34.  I.R.C. §§ 311(b), 302(b), 316, 301(c).  Because the shareholders who receive distributions of the S corporation stock likely will continue to hold stock in the distributing C corporation, dividend treatment under section 301 will be mandated unless the distribution is not essentially equivalent to a dividend within the meaning of Section 302(b)(1) or qualifies as a substantially disproportionate redemption within the meaning of Section 302(b)(2).

35.  I.R.C. §§ 302(1), 302(b)(1)-(3).

with neither the corporation nor the shareholder recognizing any income on the exchange.[36]

Shareholder debt also can trigger a second class of stock issue in select situations. The easy solution is to do whatever is necessary to fit the debt within the broad "straight debt" safe harbor protection of Section 1361(c)(5)(B). This requires only that the debt be a written unconditional promise to pay on demand or on a specified date a certain sum of money where (1) the interest rate and payment dates are not contingent on profits, the borrower's discretion, or similar factors; (2) the debt is not convertible into stock; and (3) the creditor is an eligible S corporation shareholder or a party in the business of loaning money.[37] These are not tough standards. The fact that the shareholder debt is subordinated to other debts of the corporation makes no difference. Note: qualifying the debt under this safe harbor only protects the S election from a second class of stock attack; it does not guarantee debt treatment for other tax purposes.

There are other, more extreme alternatives for dealing with questionable debt that may raise a second class of stock issue. One is to retire the debt by paying it off before the S election. This takes cash. Another is to exchange the debt for common stock of the corporation before the S election. If the debt qualifies as a "security," the exchange likely can be structured as a tax-free recapitalization.[38] If not, the exchange will likely be a taxable event, which may be of no consequence if the value of the stock issued for the debt approximates the debt holder's basis in the debt, a likely result in most cases. But both these options are far more complicated than just qualifying under the safe harbor.

The regulations to Section 1361 provide comfort on other key planning issues discussed in later chapters that might otherwise cause concern with respect to the second class of stock issue. Stock options issued to employees or independent contractors in connection with the performance of services (discussed in Chapter 11) do not constitute a second class of stock if they are not transferable and do not have a readily ascertainable fair market value at time of issue.[39] Similarly, stock options issued to a commercial lender or that are not "in the money" on their issue date do not constitute a second class of stock.[40] Restricted stock (discussed in Chapter 11) and split dollar insurance (discussed in Chapter 12) do not raise a second class of stock issue.[41] Agreements and restrictions in shareholder buy-sell agreements (discussed in Chapter 6) do not violate the one stock class requirement unless they set an extreme price (too high or too low) and their purpose is to avoid the one stock class requirement.[42] Executive deferred compensation agreements (discussed in Chapter 10) do not violate the one stock class requirement if they do not confer voting rights and are unfunded and unsecured obligations of the corporation.[43]

---

36. I.R.C. §§ 368(a)(1)(E), 361(a), 354.
37. I.R.C. § 1361(c)(5)(B).
38. I.R.C. §§ 368(a)(1)(E), 354(a). "Securities" generally include long-term debt obligations, not short-term notes.
39. Reg. § 1361-1(l )(4)(iii)(B)(2).
40. Reg. § 1361-1(l )(4)(iii)(C).
41. Reg. § 1361-1(l )(2)(iii)(B); PLR 200914019.
42. Reg. § 1361-1(l )(2)(iii)(A).
43. Reg. § 1361-1(l )(4)(i).

## 2. ELECTION MECHANICS

An S election requires the consent of all shareholders on Form 2553.[44] If the stock is held as community property or income from the stock is community property, both spouses must consent to the election. Similarly, if the stock is owned by tenants in common, joint tenants, or tenants by the entirety, each person owning an interest in the stock must sign the consent.[45] If the election is made during the first two and one-half months of a tax year with the expectation that the election will be effective as of the first of such year, any former shareholder who owned stock at any time during the year must consent to the election.[46]

In many situations, the corporation will have to change its taxable year as a result of the election. C corporations have unlimited flexibility in selecting a fiscal year to accommodate the needs of the business. An S corporation has fewer options. It may use a calendar year or prove a business purpose for using a fiscal year.[47] It will meet the business purpose burden of proof if it can show that 25 percent or more of its gross receipts were generated during the last two months of the fiscal year.[48] Absent meeting this 25 percent test, the corporation will have to show compelling reasons, based on all facts and circumstances, to justify a business purpose for a fiscal year.[49] If no business purpose is shown, the corporation may still elect to use a fiscal year that results in an income deferral of no more than three months at the shareholder level, but only if the corporation pays and maintains a tax deposit under Section 7519 that effectively eliminates any deferral benefit.[50] So the planning options for any corporation converting to S status are to adopt a calendar year, meet the 25 percent test for a natural fiscal year, or select a fiscal year under Section 444 and make a tax deposit under Section 7519.

## 3. THE TAX TRAPS

A conversion from C to S status is subject to four potential tax traps. Planners sometimes mistakenly assume that these traps are justifications for not making the conversion. The traps, although annoying and potentially costly, are not reasons themselves for not getting into or out of S status. They are hazards. If compelling reasons exist for making the conversion, the traps need to be managed and minimized – or rendered moot. As we will see, they all go away over time.

### a. The LIFO Inventory Trap

A C corporation that uses the last-in-first-out (LIFO) method of valuing its inventories must recognize as gross income its LIFO recapture amount when it

---

44. Reg. § 1362-6(a)(2).
45. Reg. § 1362-6(b)(2)(i).
46. Reg. § 1362-6(b)(3).
47. I.R.C. § 1378(b).
48. Rev. Proc. 74-33, 1974-1 C.B. 489, Rev. Proc. 2002-38, 2002-1 C.B. 1037.
49. Tax deferral for shareholders is not a sufficient business purpose. I.R.C. § 1378(b). Nor is the use of a fiscal year for regulatory or accounting purposes, to accommodate the hiring patterns of the business, administrative purposes (such as hiring or compensating staff), or the timing of price lists or model changes. H.R. Rep. No. 99-481, 99th Cong., 2d Session II-319 (1986).
50. I.R.C. §§ 444(a), 7519.

makes an S election.[51] To ease the burden, the tax hit on the recapture is spread out over four equal annual installments, the first of which is payable on the due date of the final C year return. A subsequent installment (without interest) is due in each of the next three years. The LIFO layers recognized as taxable income are added to the corporation's ending inventory balance at the end of the last C year.[52] Thus, this trap is a timing nuisance that, in select situations, may trigger an acceleration of taxes over a four-year period following the conversion. Of the four traps, it is the only one that triggers a tax by virtue of the election itself. In most situations, it presents the fewest concerns from a planning perspective.

### b. C Corporation E & P Trap

Earnings and profits accumulated within a C corporation are taxable as dividends when distributed by the corporation to its shareholders.[53] That is the crux of the C corporation double tax structure. There is no way that a C corporation can avoid this double tax exposure on earnings accumulated during its C life simply by converting to S status. That's the bad news. The good news is that, unless otherwise elected, all shareholder distributions after the S election will first be treated as tax-free distributions of passed-through S corporation earnings, as reflected in the S corporation's accumulated adjustment account.[54] So no taxable dividends attributable to the corporation's prior life as a C corporation will be triggered so long as the distributions after the S election do not exceed the income generated during the S existence. The trap doesn't add to any burden that would have existed with continued C existence.

For planning purposes, the challenge is to manage shareholder distributions to minimize the impact of the old C corporation earnings and profits that lurk, waiting to be taxed. Usually this will mean monitoring distributions to ensure that they do not exceed earnings generated during the corporation's S existence. But in some situations, the shareholders may conclude that they would like to accelerate the old C dividends and the ultimate demise of the corporation's earnings and profits. This could happen if, for example, in a given year the shareholders generate significant personal tax losses from other activities that can be used to offset dividend income. And many shareholders may keep a close eye on Congress' affection for Bush's favorable 15 percent dividend rate as the 2012 drop-dead date approaches, with the expectation of cashing in on the 15 percent bonanza before it jumps to ordinary income rates (perhaps up to 39.6 percent). For those S corporations that desire to accelerate the recognition of old C corporation dividends, the solution is found in Section 1368(e)(3), which allows an S corporation to elect to first treat all distributions as dividends made from prior C corporation earnings and profits.

### c. S Passive Investment Income Trap

The next two traps are big exceptions to the concept that S corporations themselves pay no taxes. If either of these traps is triggered, the tax bill goes to the corporation, not the shareholders.

---

51. I.R.C. § 1363(d).
52. I.R.C. § 1363(d)(2).
53. I.R.C. § 316(a).
54. I.R.C. § 1368(a)(1).

The passive investment income trap is designed to prevent S corporations from being used as vehicles that pass through income from passive investment assets. The word "passive" in this context should not be confused with the use of the exact same word in Section 469, which limits the use of losses generated from "passive" activities. Regrettably, the exact same word is given two very different meanings. In the context of this trap, the term "passive investment income" includes interest, dividends, royalties, and rents.[55] In the context of the 469 passive loss limitations, such income items are considered portfolio income, not passive income. This trap exists to prevent a C corporation from selling all its operating assets and then deferring the recognition of any income at the shareholder level by making an S election and passing through to the shareholders the passive income generated from the investment of the sales proceeds.

The trap kicks in when an S corporation has undistributed earnings and profits from its prior C existence and its net passive investment income exceeds 25 percent of its gross receipts. If these conditions are met, the highest corporate tax rate (presently 35 percent) is applied to the excess of the net passive income over 25 percent of total receipts.[56] The actual calculation of the tax is complicated by factoring in any expenses directly connected to the passive income.

There are three ways to mitigate or eliminate the impact of the tax. First, the S corporation can distribute all prior C corporation earnings and profits. Once these are out and taxed to the shareholders, the threat of this tax disappears.[57] Second, the corporation can avoid the 25 percent hurdle rate by increasing its active gross receipts or rearranging its investments to reduce its passive investment income. Finally, the corporation can escape the tax by zeroing out its taxable income for the year via shareholder compensation payments and other deductible expenses. The excess net passive investment income on which the tax is calculated cannot exceed the corporation's taxable income for the year.[58]

This trap creates a much bigger problem for the S corporation that regularly ignores its impact. If for three consecutive years an S corporation has undistributed accumulated earnings and profits from its prior C existence and its passive investment income exceeds 25 percent of its total receipts, its S election will be terminated as of the first day of the first taxable year following the three year term.[59] The result is usually a disaster. An S corporation with prior C earnings and profits should never ignore this trap. If the S election is lost, relief may be possible by timely showing that the circumstances resulting in the termination were inadvertent.[60]

---

55. I.R.C. §§ 1375(b)(3), 1362(d)(3)(C). The Small Business and Work Opportunity Tax Act of 2007 (P.L. 110-28) eliminated capital gain from the sale or exchange of stock or securities from the "passive investment income" definition.

56. I.R.C. § 1375(a).

57. I.R.C. § 1368(e)(3) gives an S corporation the right, with the consent of all affected shareholders, to accelerate the distribution of prior C earnings and profits as taxable dividends.

58. I.R.C. § 1375(b)(1)(B).

59. I.R.C. § 1362(d)(3).

60. I.R.C. § 1362(f).

### d. The BIG Tax Trap

A C corporation that sells an asset and distributes the sales proceeds to its shareholders creates a double tax – one at the corporate level on the gain recognized on the sale and one at the shareholder level on the proceeds distributed. The built-in gains ("BIG") tax trap of Section 1374 is designed to preserve some of this double tax pain for an S corporation with a C past. It does this by imposing a tax on the S corporation itself if an asset owned by the corporation at the time of its conversion to S status is sold within a ten-year recognition period following the election. The Small Business Jobs Act of 2010 eliminated the built-in gains tax for the 2011 tax year for any S corporation whose fifth S recognition year ended before its 2011 year started. The tax is imposed at the highest corporate tax rate (presently 35 percent) on the lesser of (i) the gain recognized on the sale or (ii) the asset's built-in gain at the time of the S conversion.[61] This corporate level tax is in addition to the tax that the shareholders bear as a result of the S corporation's gain being passed through and taxed to the shareholders. The only relief to this forced double tax is that the tax paid by the corporation is treated as a loss to the shareholders in the same year.[62]

A simple example helps illustrate the impact of the BIG tax trap. Assume S corporation X Inc. sells an asset for $100,000. Its basis in the asset is $30,000. It owned the asset three years ago when it converted from C to S status. At the time of the conversion, the asset had a value of $70,000 and a basis of $30,000. Thus, the built-in gain at time of conversion to S status was $40,000. X Inc. would have to recognize the $40,000 built-in gain as income at the time of sale and pay a BIG tax of $14,000 (35 percent of $40,000). Plus, the $70,000 gain recognized on the sale ($100,000 realized less $30,000 basis) would be passed through and taxed to the shareholders of X Inc. The shareholders would be entitled to reduce the $70,000 by the $14,000 BIG tax paid by the corporation. So in addition to the BIG tax of $14,000 at the corporate level, the shareholders would have to pay taxes on $56,000 of income.

All assets owned by the corporation at the time of conversion, including intangible assets such as goodwill, are subject to the BIG tax. Those assets that have a built-in loss at conversion pose no risk of a future BIG tax and, as described below, may help reduce the future tax burden of the built-in gain assets. The BIG tax taint of an asset owned at conversion carries over to any other asset acquired during the ten-year recognition period in a transaction that qualifies for carryover basis treatment (i.e., a 1031 like-kind exchange).[63] If a built-in gain asset is sold during the ten-year recognition period in an installment sale transaction that extends beyond the ten-year term, the BIG tax will be extended to any payments received after the recognition period.[64]

There are four technical limitations on the BIG tax trap that can be very helpful in select situations. First, the built-in gains recognized in any year may be reduced by any losses recognized in that same year on the sale of assets

---

61. I.R.C. §§ 1374(a), 1374(b)(1), 1374(d)(3), 1374(d)(7)(B)..
62. I.R.C. § 1366(f)(2).
63. I.R.C. § 1374(d)(6).
64. Reg. § 1.1374-4(h)(1).

owned at conversion, but only to the extent of such assets' built-in losses at time of conversion.[65] For example, if the sale of one pre-conversion asset triggers recognition of a $30,000 built-in gain and a sale of another pre-conversion asset produces a loss of $40,000, half of which was built-in at the time of conversion, the recognized built-in loss ($20,000) would reduce the $30,000 recognized built-in gain. Second, the cumulative built-in gains recognized after the S conversion may never exceed the "net unrealized built-in gain" (defined as the fair market value of all assets owned at conversion over the adjusted basis of such assets) at time of conversion.[66] Thus, for example, if an S corporation's total net unrealized built-in gain (which factors in both gains and losses) at conversion five years ago was $400,000 and the corporation has recognized built-in gains totaling $350,000 over the last five years, the maximum additional built-in gains that could be subject to future BIG taxes is $50,000. Third, the built-in gains recognized in any year cannot exceed the S corporation's taxable income for that year, computed as if it were a C corporation.[67] Any recognized built-in gain not taxed because of this taxable income limitation is carried over to future years.[68] Finally, any net operating loss carry-forwards and capital loss carry-forwards from prior C years may be used to reduce any built-in gains recognized after the conversion.[69]

The BIG tax trap can be managed and mitigated by effective planning in anticipation of the S conversion. Strategies to consider include the following:

• If the business is growing in value and the double tax burden of C status promises problems in the future, convert early. Get the ten-year clock ticking. The BIG tax trap only gets worse as values and assets continue to escalate before the conversion.

• Carefully document all assets owned at conversion. Assets acquired after the conversion are never subject to the BIG tax. The taxpayer has the burden of proving which assets were acquired after the conversion.

• Obtain appraisals for all significant assets owned at conversion, including the goodwill of the business. The focus should be on reliable, but conservative, valuations. Absent such appraisals, it may be difficult in future years to prove that the bulk of the appreciation realized on the sale of a valuable asset, such as goodwill, occurred after the S election.

• Before the conversion, consider selling assets that are likely to trigger a built-in gain shortly after the conversion. This produces a double tax benefit; the tax on the gain at the shareholder level is eliminated because there is no pass-through from a C corporation, and the total net unrealized built-in gain at time of conversion (an overriding limiting factor during the ten-year recognition period) is reduced. A perfect example is unrealized accounts receivable owned by a cash-basis C corporation before the conversion to S status. Factoring or selling these receivables before the conversion may be the wisest course of action.

---

65. I.R.C. § 1374(d)(2)-(4).
66. I.R.C. §§ 1374(c)(2), 1374(d)(1).
67. I.R.C. § 1374.
68. I.R.C. § 1374(d)(3)(A)(ii).
69. I.R.C. § 1374(b)(2).

- Defer the payment of built-in deduction items (accrued expenses and payables) until after the conversion. These items will reduce the total net unrealized gain at time of conversion (a good thing) and, when paid, will trigger built-in losses that may offset built-in gains. Also, care should be taken to ensure that all accrual items are booked before the conversion.

- Defer the disposition of any assets with built-in losses until after the conversion. This will reduce the total net unrealized gain at conversion and provide an opportunity for such losses to offset built-in gains recognized after the conversion. Loading the C corporation with built-in loss assets prior to conversion is prohibited by an anti-stuffing provision.[70]

- During the ten-year recognition period after the S conversion, plan the timing of asset dispositions to net recognized built-in losses against recognized built-in gains. The taxable income limitation may help with such timing by deferring the recognition of built-in gains in those years when the corporation's taxable income is zeroed out.

- To get beyond the ten-year recognition period, consider disposing of built-in gain assets in transactions that defer the recognition of gain, such as 1031 exchanges. Although the BIG tax taint carries over to any assets acquired in such a transaction, it is of no consequence once the ten-year window has expired.

## E. CONVERTING A PARTNERSHIP TO A LIMITED LIABILITY COMPANY

### Revenue Ruling 95-37
### 1995-1 C.B. 130

#### Issues

(1) Do the federal income tax consequences described in Revenue Ruling 84-52, 1984-1 C.B. 157, apply to the conversion of an interest in a domestic partnership into an interest in a domestic limited liability company (LLC) that is classified as a partnership for federal tax purposes?

(2) Does the taxable year of the converting domestic partnership close with respect to all the partners or with respect to any partner?

(3) Does the resulting domestic LLC need to obtain a new taxpayer identification number?

#### Law and Analysis

In Revenue Ruling 84-52, a general partnership formed under the Uniform Partnership Act of State M proposed to convert to a limited partnership under the Uniform Limited Partnership Act of State M. Revenue Ruling 84-52 generally holds that (1) under Section 721 of the Internal Revenue Code, the conversion will not cause the partners to recognize gain or loss under Sections 741 or 1001; (2) unless its business will not continue after the conversion, the partnership will not terminate under Section 708 because the conversion is not treated as a sale or

---

70. Reg. § 1.1374-9.

exchange for purposes of Section 708; (3) if the partners' shares of partnership liabilities do not change, there will be no change in the adjusted basis of any partner's interest in the partnership; (4) if the partners' shares of partnership liabilities change and cause a deemed contribution of money to the partnership by a partner under Section 752(a), then the adjusted basis of such a partner's interest will be increased under Section 722 by the amount of the deemed contribution; (5) if the partners' shares of partnership liabilities change and cause a deemed distribution of money by the partnership to a partner under Section 752(b), then the basis of such a partner's interest will be reduced under Section 733 (but not below zero) by the amount of the deemed distribution, and, gain will be recognized by the partner under Section 731 to the extent the deemed distribution exceeds the adjusted basis of the partner's interest in the partnership; and (6) under Section 1223(1), there will be no change in the holding period of any partner's total interest in the partnership.

The conversion of an interest in a domestic partnership into an interest in a domestic LLC that is classified as a partnership for federal tax purposes is treated as a partnership-to-partnership conversion that is subject to the principles of Revenue Ruling 84-52.

Section 706(c)(1) provides that, except in the case of a termination of a partnership and except as provided in Section 706(c)(2), the taxable year of a partnership does not close as the result of the death of a partner, the entry of a new partner, the liquidation of a partner's interest in the partnership, or the sale or exchange of a partner's interest in the partnership.

Section 706(c)(2)(A)(i) provides that the taxable year of a partnership closes with respect to a partner who sells or exchanges the partner's entire interest in a partnership. Section 706(c)(2)(A)(ii) provides that the taxable year of a partnership closes with respect to a partner whose interest is liquidated, except that the taxable year of a partnership with respect to a partner who dies does not close prior to the end of the partnership's taxable year.

In the present case, the conversion of an interest in a domestic partnership into an interest in a domestic LLC that is classified as a partnership for federal tax purposes does not cause a termination under Section 708. See Revenue Ruling 84-52. Moreover, because each partner in a converting domestic partnership continues to hold an interest in the resulting domestic LLC, the conversion is not a sale, exchange, or liquidation of the converting partner's entire partnership interest for purposes of Section 706(c)(2)(A). See Revenue Ruling 86-101, 1986-2 C.B. 94 (the taxable year of a partnership does not close with respect to a general partner when the partnership agreement provides that the general partner's interest converts to a limited partnership interest on the general partner's death because the decedent's successor continues to hold an interest in the partnership). Consequently, the conversion does not cause the taxable year of the domestic partnership to close with respect to all the partners or with respect to any partner.

Because the conversion of an interest in a domestic partnership into an interest in a domestic LLC that is classified as a partnership for federal tax purposes does not cause a termination under Section 708, the resulting domestic LLC does not need to obtain a new taxpayer identification number.

Holdings

(1) The federal income tax consequences described in Revenue Ruling 84-52 apply to the conversion of an interest in a domestic partnership into an interest in a domestic LLC that is classified as a partnership for federal tax purposes. The federal tax consequences are the same whether the resulting LLC is formed in the same state or in a different state than the converting domestic partnership.

(2) The taxable year of the converting domestic partnership does not close with respect to all the partners or with respect to any partner.

(3) The resulting domestic LLC does not need to obtain a new taxpayer identification number.

The holdings contained herein would apply in a similar manner if the conversion had been of an interest in a domestic LLC that is classified as a partnership for federal tax purposes into an interest in a domestic partnership. The holdings contained herein apply regardless of the manner in which the conversion is achieved under state law.

This revenue ruling does not address the federal tax consequences of a conversion of an organization that is classified as a corporation into an organization that is classified as a partnership for federal tax purposes. See, e.g., Sections 336 and 337.

## F. CONVERTING IN AND OUT OF ONE-OWNER STATUS

**Revenue Ruling 99-5**
**1999-1 C.B. 434**

Issue

What are the federal income tax consequences when a single member domestic limited liability company (LLC) that is disregarded for federal tax purposes as an entity separate from its owner under Section 301.7701-3 of the Procedure and Administration Regulations becomes an entity with more than one owner that is classified as a partnership for federal tax purposes?

Facts

In each of the following two situations, an LLC is formed and operates in a state which permits an LLC to have a single owner. Each LLC has a single owner, A, and is disregarded as an entity separate from its owner for federal tax purposes under Section 301.7701-3. In both situations, the LLC would not be treated as an investment company (within the meaning of Section 351) if it were incorporated. All of the assets held by each LLC are capital assets or property described in Section 1231. For the sake of simplicity, it is assumed that neither LLC is liable for any indebtedness, nor are the assets of the LLCs subject to any indebtedness.

Situation 1.  B, who is not related to A, purchases 50% of A's ownership interest in the LLC for $5,000.  A does not contribute any portion of the $5,000 to the LLC.  A and B continue to operate the business of the LLC as co-owners of the LLC.

Situation 2.  B, who is not related to A, contributes $10,000 to the LLC in exchange for a 50% ownership interest in the LLC.  The LLC uses all of the contributed cash in its business.  A and B continue to operate the business of the LLC as co-owners of the LLC.

After the sale, in both situations, no entity classification election is made under Section 301.7701-3(c) to treat the LLC as an association for federal tax purposes ...

## Holding(s)

Situation 1.  In this situation, the LLC, which, for federal tax purposes, is disregarded as an entity separate from its owner, is converted to a partnership when the new member, B, purchases an interest in the disregarded entity from the owner, A.  B's purchase of 50% of A's ownership interest in the LLC is treated as the purchase of a 50% interest in each of the LLC's assets, which are treated as held directly by A for federal tax purposes.  Immediately thereafter, A and B are treated as contributing their respective interests in those assets to a partnership in exchange for ownership interests in the partnership.

Under Section 1001, A recognizes gain or loss from the deemed sale of the 50% interest in each asset of the LLC to B.

Under Section 721(a), no gain or loss is recognized by A or B as a result of the conversion of the disregarded entity to a partnership.

Under Section 722, B's basis in the partnership interest is equal to $5,000, the amount paid by B to A for the assets which B is deemed to contribute to the newly-created partnership.  A's basis in the partnership interest is equal to A's basis in A's 50% share of the assets of the LLC.

Under Section 723, the basis of the property treated as contributed to the partnership by A and B is the adjusted basis of that property in A's and B's hands immediately after the deemed sale.

Under Section 1223(1), A's holding period for the partnership interest received includes A's holding period in the capital assets and property described in Section 1231 held by the LLC when it converted from an entity that was disregarded as an entity separate from A to a partnership.  B's holding period for the partnership interest begins on the day following the date of B's purchase of the LLC interest from A.  See Revenue Ruling 66-7, 1966-1 C.B. 188, which provides that the holding period of a purchased asset is computed by excluding the date on which the asset is acquired.  Under Section 1223(2), the partnership's holding period for the assets deemed transferred to it includes A's and B's holding periods for such assets.

Situation 2.  In this situation, the LLC is converted from an entity that is disregarded as an entity separate from its owner to a partnership when a new member, B, contributes cash to the LLC.  B's contribution is treated as a contribution to a partnership in exchange for an ownership interest in the partnership.  A is treated as contributing all of the assets of the LLC to the partnership in exchange for a partnership interest.

Under Section 721(a), no gain or loss is recognized by A or B as a result of the conversion of the disregarded entity to a partnership.

Under Section 722, B's basis in the partnership interest is equal to $10,000, the amount of cash contributed to the partnership.  A's basis in the partnership interest is equal to A's basis in the assets of the LLC which A was treated as contributing to the newly-created partnership.

Under Section 723, the basis of the property contributed to the partnership by A is the adjusted basis of that property in A's hands.  The basis of the property contributed to the partnership by B is $10,000, the amount of cash contributed to the partnership.

Under Section 1223(1), A's holding period for the partnership interest received includes A's holding period in the capital and Section 1231 assets deemed contributed when the disregarded entity converted to a partnership.  B's holding period for the partnership interest begins on the day following the date of B's contribution of money to the LLC.  Under Section 1223(2), the partnership's holding period for the assets transferred to it includes A's holding period.

### Revenue Ruling 99-6
### 1999-1 C.B. 432

#### Issue

What are the federal income tax consequences if one person purchases all of the ownership interests in a domestic limited liability company (LLC) that is classified as a partnership under Section 301.7701-3 of the Procedure and Administration Regulations, causing the LLC's status as a partnership to terminate under Section 708(b)(1)(A) of the Internal Revenue Code?

#### Facts

In each of the following situations, an LLC is formed and operates in a state which permits an LLC to have a single owner.  Each LLC is classified as a partnership under Section 301.7701-3.  Neither of the LLCs holds any unrealized receivables or substantially appreciated inventory for purposes of Section 751(b).  For the sake of simplicity, it is assumed that neither LLC is liable for any indebtedness, nor are the assets of the LLCs subject to any indebtedness.

Situation 1.  A and B are equal partners in AB, an LLC.  A sells A's entire interest in AB to B for $10,000.  After the sale, the business is continued by the LLC, which is owned solely by B.

Situation 2.  C and D are equal partners in CD, an LLC.  C and D sell their entire interests in CD to E, an unrelated person, in exchange for $10,000 each.  After the sale, the business is continued by the LLC, which is owned solely by E.

After the sale, in both situations, no entity classification election is made under Section 301.7701-3(c) to treat the LLC as an association for federal tax purposes ...

Analysis and Holdings

Situation 1. The AB partnership terminates under Section 708(b)(1)(A) when B purchases A's entire interest in AB. Accordingly, A must treat the transaction as the sale of a partnership interest. Reg. Section 1.741-1(b). A must report gain or loss, if any, resulting from the sale of A's partnership interest in accordance with Section 741.

Under the analysis of McCauslen and Revenue Ruling 67-65, for purposes of determining the tax treatment of B, the AB partnership is deemed to make a liquidating distribution of all of its assets to A and B, and following this distribution, B is treated as acquiring the assets deemed to have been distributed to A in liquidation of A's partnership interest.

B's basis in the assets attributable to A's one-half interest in the partnership is $10,000, the purchase price for A's partnership interest. Section 1012. Section 735(b) does not apply with respect to the assets B is deemed to have purchased from A. Therefore, B's holding period for these assets begins on the day immediately following the date of the sale. See Revenue Ruling 66-7, 1966-1 C.B. 188, which provides that the holding period of an asset is computed by excluding the date on which the asset is acquired.

Upon the termination of AB, B is considered to receive a distribution of those assets attributable to B's former interest in AB, B must recognize gain or loss, if any, on the deemed distribution of the assets to the extent required by Section 731(a). B's basis in the assets received in the deemed liquidation of B's partnership interest is determined under Section 732(b). Under Section 735(b), B's holding period for the assets attributable to B's one-half interest in AB includes the partnership's holding period for such assets (except for purposes of Section 735(a)(2)).

Situation 2. The CD partnership terminates under Section 708(b)(1)(A) when E purchases the entire interests of C and D in CD. C and D must report gain or loss, if any, resulting from the sale of their partnership interests in accordance with Section 741.

For purposes of classifying the acquisition by E, the CD partnership is deemed to make a liquidating distribution of its assets to C and D. Immediately following this distribution, E is deemed to acquire, by purchase, all of the former partnership's assets. Compare Revenue Ruling 84-111, 1984-2 C.B. 88 (Situation 3), which determines the tax consequences to a corporate transferee of all interests in a partnership in a manner consistent with McCauslen, and holds that the transferee's basis in the assets received equals the basis of the partnership interests, allocated among the assets in accordance with Section 732(c).

E's basis in the assets is $20,000 under Section 1012. E's holding period for the assets begins on the day immediately following the date of sale.

## PROBLEMS 7-A AND 7-B

**7-A.** Colson Inc. is a successful C corporation. It has eight shareholders, six of whom are individuals and two of whom are family limited partnerships. None of the shareholders are related. Only one of the shareholders works for the company. In recent years, the company has paid substantially all of its income to its shareholders as dividends and anticipates that it will continue to do so. The shareholders are frustrated with the double tax burden. Many of them would like to explore the possibility of converting to a pass-through entity, such as an S corporation or a limited liability company.

The company has issued both common and preferred stock to its shareholders. Three of the shareholders have made substantial loans to the company. The tax basis of the company's balance sheet assets is substantially less than the fair market value of the assets. Plus, as a result of the company's significant profitability, the unrealized goodwill and going concern value is huge.

Analyze the options of converting to an S corporation or a limited liability company. Among other things, consider the following factors:

1. Timing flexibility of the election.

2. Eligible shareholder requirements.

3. Necessary consents.

4. Income tax consequences of the conversion.

5. Capital restructuring requirements.

6. The need and importance of current appraisals.

7. Tax planning considerations.

**7-B.** Joel Larson has been the sole owner and president of Larson Electronics, L.L.C., a fast-growing electrical contractor. The company has been an LLC since its inception five years ago. Joel's basis in his equity in the business is $450,000. The company has balance sheet assets with a basis of $300,000 and a fair market value of $500,000. Based on input received from others, Joel estimates that the company's goodwill is worth at least $500,000. So Joel believes that, at a minimum, the company has a value of $1 million.

Joel has decided to offer ownership interests to his top two managers. He will give each of them a right to purchase 10 percent of the company's equity for $100,000, which Joel will personally finance over a 10-year period at a floating interest rate equal to prime. Following their admission as owners, the company will continue to operate as an LLC until the end of the current calendar year (nine months out). Joel has determined that, on the first day of the next year, he will convert to a C corporation format to take advantage of lower C rates on accumulated earnings and the tax benefits of shareholder/employee fringe benefits.

How will Joel's admission of the new owners affect the company's tax entity status? How would you advise that Joel make the conversion to C status?

# CHAPTER 8

## STRUCTURING THE BUY-SELL PROVISIONS

---

### A. BUY-SELL AGREEMENTS: A PRIMER

#### 1. INTRODUCTION

For owners of closely held businesses, the buy-sell agreement or shareholders agreement, as it is sometimes called, is one of the most critical components of the planning process. It is the document that defines the value of the owners' equity interests in the business – that spells out what they will yield when it comes time to cash out. Yet, in far too many cases this all-important document is given woefully inadequate attention. When the entrepreneurial bug bites a group of charged-up business owners, they usually are focused on making the business succeed, maximizing revenues, and minimizing expenses. They have little interest in discussing potential breakups, the risks of the three big "Ds" – death, disability and divorce – and all the other issues that should be addressed in a well-structured buy-sell agreement. A good advisor will help the owners look at the big picture and consider the entire life cycle of the business.

Business owners need to prepare early for the day when they will part company for whatever reason. At some point down the road, they are each going to want to or have to cash out their equity interest in the business. Somebody is going to leave the business, die, become disabled, or experience a messy divorce. Plus, the owners should acknowledge the simple reality that no matter how good they feel about one another going into the enterprise, tough business decisions may create friction along the way. Friction often leads to a buyout or, worse yet, a legal blowup.

Potential separation issues are best addressed in a calm, planning-oriented atmosphere, not at the point of crisis. Preferably, the job should be done at the outset of the business when all parties are making important decisions to devote capital and energy to the business enterprise. Encouraging clients to collectively think about the key issues up front often will bring to the surface diverse expectations that may surprise everyone. It usually helps to have these expectations out in the open before irrevocable commitments are made to the venture. Too often, the parties plunge ahead with little regard for the consequences of their inevitable separation down the road.

The buy-sell agreement planning process usually involves a series of meetings of all of the owners where questions are asked and opinions are expressed. Two factors permeate these discussions: "control" of the business enterprise and "the need for liquidity" at the right time. An understanding of the importance of these factors is critical to the process of designing a buy-sell agreement.

The control of a closely held organization is always a major consideration. The impact of a future change in ownership on the control of the business must be considered in structuring the agreement among the owners. Often parties misunderstand the significance of shareholder voting control. The shareholders of a corporation elect the board of directors and approve major corporate transactions, such as mergers, consolidations and sales of the business. The shareholders do not manage the business; the business is managed by the board. Therefore, the composition of the board becomes a vital issue. Absent specific provisions in the shareholders agreement or cumulative voting rights provisions, a minority shareholder usually will have no power to affect the election of board members.

The liquidity factor also is critical in structuring the provisions of the agreement. Most owners want to be assured that at the right time in the future there will be a buyer for their interest and funds will be available to cover the purchase price. They want the comfort of knowing that their business interest will be fairly valued. They do not want an untimely death to leave their family with the burden of having to negotiate price and payment terms with little knowledge and no leverage.

In a closely held corporation, these control, separation buyout, and liquidity issues are dealt with in a separate contract among the shareholders. In partnerships and limited liability companies, the issues are dealt with in the partnership agreement or the LLC operating agreement.

This section first summarizes the primary objectives that usually should be considered and prioritized in the planning process. This is followed by a brief case study that illustrates the key structural issues. The discussion concludes by examining eight of the biggest mistakes that are commonly made in structuring buy-sell agreements among private business owners.

## 2. BASIC OBJECTIVES OF THE PLANNING PROCESS

A carefully designed buy-sell agreement will accomplish many important objectives of the parties. Often, it is helpful to start the process by identifying and prioritizing the primary objectives. Following is a brief summary of seven of the key objectives that often are considered in the planning process:

**a. Control Who Gets In.** The objective is to ensure that ownership interests in the company are never transferred or made available to third parties who are unacceptable to the owners. This objective may not be a big deal in some golfer organizations, but it usually is a top priority in all other situations. Absent careful planning, an untimely death, disability, bankruptcy, or employment termination may trigger a condition that exposes an equity interest to an unwanted third party.

**b. Fairness.** The objective is to ensure that there is a mechanism to fairly value and fund the equity interest of a departing owner. The goal is to avoid the necessity of divisive negotiations at a point of crisis, where one party may be in a weak position with no leverage. The agreement should contain fair provisions that will apply evenly to all parties.

**c. Smooth Transition.** The objective is to ensure that control and ownership issues will be smoothly transitioned at appropriate times so as not to unduly interfere with and disrupt the operations of the business. Unless properly planned, business ownership changes can create anxieties for lenders, key suppliers, employees, and customers of any business. The ideal is to plan for a seamless transition that generates as little concern as possible for those who regularly deal with the business.

**d. Market.** The objective is to ensure that all owners have a fair "market" for their shares at appropriate points of exit. Absent a well-structured buy-sell agreement there may be no market, either inside or outside of the company. As a practical matter, the only viable exit opportunity for a departing owner may be an inside sale to the other owners pursuant to the terms of a carefully structured and funded buy-sell agreement.

**e. Expulsion Right.** The objective is to ensure that the owners have the power to involuntarily terminate (expel) an owner who is no longer wanted. This may not be a concern in some golfer organizations, but it is important in all toiler organizations, professional service organizations, and most hybrids.

**f. Estate Tax Exposure.** The objective is to ensure that the amount paid for the equity interest of a deceased owner determines the value of the deceased owner's equity interest for estate tax purposes. This can be an important consideration in many situations. Few can stomach the concept of having to pay estate taxes on a value that exceeds the amount actually received for the equity interest. But, as we will see, this objective is easier said than done.

**g. Cash.** The objective is to ensure that the cash and funding challenges of owner departures are appropriately anticipated and covered. Often this will require the smart use of life and disability insurance. But insurance won't cover all the exit triggers. To protect the business, usually there is a need to lay out payment terms in the agreement, including mechanisms for determining the duration of the payments, the interest rate, and any special relief provisions for the company.

### 3. CASE STUDY AND SELECT PLANNING ISSUES

ABC Inc. is a manufacturing corporation that has been in business for 17 years. The business was started by Jim and Sue Olson, husband and wife. Although Jim is the president of the corporation and the driving person behind its success, Sue has always been involved in the business and, during the early years, played an important role in keeping the books and providing general business advice. Sue considers herself to be part of the business and still works part-time in the business. They have one son, Sam, age 26, who is now working in the business and who is interested in the business.  Jim and Sue together own 60 percent of the stock of the business.

The business has two key employees, Roger and Joyce.  They both have worked in the business for over 12 years.  Approximately five years ago, they each acquired a 20 percent stock interest in the business.  So at the present time, Jim and Sue jointly own 60 percent of the stock of the business, and Roger and Joyce each own 20 percent.

Following is a review of some of the key planning issues that the owners of ABC Inc. need to consider in structuring a buy-sell shareholders agreement.

### a.  What buyout triggers should be structured into the shareholders agreement?

The buyout triggers are those events that trigger one party's right or obligation to buyout another party under the agreement.  The transaction also transfers voting shares and may result in a shift in voting control.  The most common triggers in any buy-sell agreement include:

- Death of an owner

- Disability of an owner

- Voluntary termination of an owner/employee

- Divorce of an owner

- Bankruptcy of an owner

- Desire of an owner to cash out and move on

- Expulsion of an owner

Each of these triggering events creates a unique set of problems and may require a different solution.

Take death as an example.  In the case of ABC Inc., it's likely that the agreement should be structured to provide that if one of the 20 percent stockholders, Roger or Joyce, dies, his or her stock should be purchased by the other shareholders or the company.  Certainly, Jim and Sue, the majority owners, would want the comfort of knowing that they could purchase the stock of Roger or Joyce if one of them died.  Roger and Joyce also would want the comfort of knowing that their stock will be cashed out at a fair price in the event of their untimely death.  But if Jim were to die, it's doubtful that his stock should be bought by the other shareholders or redeemed by the company.  Sue may want the stock, or perhaps Jim would want the stock to be left to his son, who is moving up in the business.  There's no requirement that all shareholders be treated the same under each of the various triggering events.

Disability presents unique problems.  Usually a disability trigger applies only to owners whose ownership interests in the business are tied to their employment in the business – a common condition in toiler and professional service organizations.  Often the trigger operates in favor of both the company and the disabled employee; that is, either party can trigger the buyout.  The parties initially must agree on a definition of disability and a process for determining whether a shareholder/employee is disabled. As in the case of death, there is no requirement that the disability provision apply to all of the shareholders.

One of the questions often asked is: Why is it advisable to have divorce and bankruptcy included as triggering events in the agreement? The purpose of these provisions is to protect the company and the other shareholders if a shareholder's stock becomes tangled up in a messy divorce or bankruptcy proceeding. The other owners or the company have the option to purchase that stock at a fair value to keep the company out of the mess. If the particular proceeding does not disrupt the company or pose any threat, there may be no reason for the company or other shareholders to exercise their rights under the agreement. But if an estranged spouse's attorney or a bankruptcy trustee attempts to cause problems or create uncertainty for the company by exercising control over a block of stock, the buyout rights can be effectively used to neutralize the actions of the attorney or trustee.

Expulsion usually is a difficult trigger for owners to discuss and resolve. Nobody likes to think about kicking out one of their own. But in many privately owned businesses, the owners are the principal employees in the business. If there are a number of business owners, usually there is a need to develop a mechanism to permit the group to throw out the bad apple. The trigger usually is structured to require a unanimous or super-high majority (75 percent) consent of the other owners. Careful discussion usually is required on this trigger.

### b. What are the trade-offs between using a redemption approach versus a cross-purchase approach in structuring the agreement?

When the business entity purchases the interest of the departing shareholder, it's called a redemption. When the other owners purchase the interest, it's called a cross-purchase. Typically, whether a redemption or cross-purchase approach is used, the fundamental control results are the same. The remaining shareholders end up with the same resulting percentage ownership interests under either approach. Plus, under either approach the departing shareholder, or his or her estate, is given cash or other property in exchange for the interest in the business. But beyond these common end results, there are important factors that may favor one approach over the other in any given situation.

An important tax factor is the impact on the outside tax basis of the stock owned by the other shareholders of a C corporation. A stock redemption by a C corporation will not increase the basis of the stock held by the remaining owners. By contrast, stock acquired in a cross-purchase transaction will have a basis equal to the purchase price. This will result in a higher basis in the stock owned by the other shareholders. They will realize a lower capital gain on any subsequent sale.

Let's assume, for example, that in the case of ABC Inc., Roger, one of the 20 percent shareholders, leaves the company. His 20 percent interest has a fair market value of $400,000 at the time of departure, and his tax basis in the stock is $100,000. If ABC Inc. redeems his stock on his departure for $400,000, Jim and

Sue, the original 60 percent owners, would own 75 percent of the outstanding stock of the company, and Joyce, the other owner, would now own 25 percent of the outstanding stock in the company. If Joyce's basis in her 20 percent interest was $100,000, her basis in her increased 25 percent interest is still $100,000. As for Jim and Sue, if their original 60 percent interest had a very low basis, say $30,000, the basis in their 75 percent interest would remain at $30,000. The stock redemption approach generates no step-up in basis for the other owners.

If the remaining shareholders acquired Roger's shares through a cross-purchase on a proportionate basis, Jim and Sue would acquire three-fourths of Roger's 20 percent interest, and Joyce would acquire the other one-fourth. Roger and Sue would still end up owning 75 percent, and Joyce would end up owning 25 percent. But the basis in their stock would have changed. Under a cross-purchase, Jim and Sue would have paid $300,000 for three-fourths of Roger's stock, resulting in a total basis in their shares of $300,000 plus $30,000, or $330,000. Joyce will now have a basis in her shares equal to her original investment of $100,000, plus the $100,000 that she would pay to Roger for one-fourth of his stock. So her total basis would have increased to $200,000. On a subsequent sale of the stock or liquidation of the company, Jim and Sue have an additional $300,000 that could be recovered tax-free and Joyce has an additional $100,000 that could be recovered tax-free.

This basis issue is not a factor for S corporations, partnerships, and limited liability companies. In these pass-through entities, the owners will receive a basis step-up whether a redemption or cross-purchase approach is used. If the transaction is structured as a redemption, the receipt of life insurance proceeds or entity income to fund the redemption will increase the outside basis of the equity interests held by the other owners.[1]

Does this basis difference always make the cross-purchase approach the best choice for C corporations? Not always. In cases where there are many shareholders, the cross-purchase approach may be too cumbersome, particularly where there are multiple life insurance policies that need to be reshuffled every time an owner dies or is bought out. Beyond the complexity of the reshuffling are serious transfer-for-value problems that can destroy the tax-free character of the death benefits and ultimately force a conversion to a redemption strategy.[2] Also, often the shareholders don't have sufficient capital to fund a cross-purchase buyout. The capital is in the company, and there's no effective tax method to get the cash out of the company and into the hands of the shareholders to fund the buyout of their departing partner. Another factor that may favor a redemption strategy in a C corporation is the deductibility of interest payments on any installment obligation paid to the departing owner or his or her heirs. Interest paid by a C corporation pursuant to a redemption is deductible as trade or business interest, whereas interest paid by the shareholders in a cross-purchase

---

1. I.R.C. § 1367 sets forth the basis adjustments for stock held by S corporation shareholders. The counterpart provision for entities taxed as partnerships is I.R.C. § 705.

2. I.R.C. § 101(a)(2) eliminates the tax free death benefit on life insurance policies that are transferred for valuable consideration. There are exceptions for transfers among partners, transfers to a partnership in which the insured is a partner, and transfers to a corporation in which the insured was an officer or officer. But there is no exception for transfers among co-shareholders of a corporation.

would be subject to the investment interest limitations.[3] So in many cases, as a practical matter, the redemption approach is preferred simply from a funding standpoint.

In some situations, there are other factors that make the redemption approach unattractive. If the C corporation is large enough to be subject to the alternative minimum tax (AMT) (annual gross receipts over $5 million during the first three years and over $7.5 million thereafter), receipt of life insurance proceeds may trigger an AMT for the corporation.[4] Plus, accumulation of funds to buy out a major shareholder may not qualify as a reasonable business need for purposes of the accumulated earnings tax.[5] State law restrictions may limit the corporation's ability to redeem its own stock if it lacks sufficient capital surplus or retained earnings to fund the redemption.[6] At a minimum, such state law restrictions may trigger additional costs (e.g. appraisal fees) to get the deal done. Finally, restrictive covenants in loan agreements often limit a corporation's capacity to redeem stock by making substantial payments to the owners of the business. All of these factors should be evaluated when considering the redemption approach.

Note that many of these factors do not come into play with a pass-through entity, such as an S corporation, a partnership or an LLC. As stated above, the outside basis differential is not an issue. Plus, getting money out of the entity and into the hands of the owners usually presents no difficult tax issues.[7] There are no AMT or accumulated earnings tax issues to worry about. The deductibility of the interest on any installment purchase will turn on other factors. It may qualify as trade or business deductible interest for those who are material participants in the venture; for all other owners, it will be passive or investment interest or both, depending on the investment assets held by the entity. State law and loan agreement restrictions may be just as applicable.

In some situations, the solution is to draft the agreement to provide flexibility. The agreement allows for a redemption or a cross-purchase and gives the company and the other shareholders the right to select the preferred approach when a trigger is pulled. This flexible approach sounds better than it really is because advance planning for the funding – whether through the use of life insurance, disability insurance, or internal funding – usually requires a decision on which approach will be used at the time the funding vehicle is put in place.

---

3.  I.R.C. § 163(d).

4.  I.R.C. §§ 55(b)(2), 55(e), 56(g).

5.  I.R.C. §§ 535(c)(1), 537; see, e.g., John B. Lambert & Associates v. United States, 212 Ct. Cl. 71 (1976); Lamark Shipping Agency, Inc. v. Commissioner, 42 T.C.M. 38 (1981).

6.  In any such redemption, the applicable state corporate law must be carefully analyzed to ascertain any restrictions. Appraisals are often necessary. The Model Business Corporation Act prohibits a "distribution" (broadly defined to include proceeds from a redemption) if "after giving it effect: (1) the corporation would not be able to pay its debts as they become due in the ordinary course of business, or (2) the corporation's total assets would be less than the sum of its total liabilities plus (unless the articles of incorporation permit otherwise) that amount that would be needed, if the corporation were to be dissolved at the time of the distribution, to satisfy the preferential rights upon the dissolution of shareholders whose preferential rights are superior to those receiving the distribution." MBCA §§ 1.04, 6.40(c). These two tests, referred to as the "equity insolvency test" and the "balance sheet test," have been widely incorporated into state corporate statutes.

7.  If an S corporation has accumulated earnings and profits from a prior C period, distributions that exceed its accumulated adjustment account may trigger taxable dividends. I.R.C. § 1368(c).

### c. What mandatory buyout obligations should be in the buy-sell agreement?

The business owners need to decide whether a triggering event requires a mandatory purchase or simply grants an option to purchase. And if it's optional, which party will have the option? For example, upon the death of a shareholder, the remaining shareholders typically want an option to purchase the shares of the deceased shareholder to preserve control. The deceased shareholder's heirs will want a put, which is an option to require the corporation or remaining shareholders to buy their stock, or a mandatory purchase obligation. It also is possible to give options to both the heirs and the remaining shareholders, permitting either side to trigger the purchase. Making the purchase either mandatory or at the option of the heirs of the deceased shareholder puts the remaining shareholders in the position of having to come up with the purchase price at death. Life insurance often is essential.

Similar issues arise if an owner simply wants to cash out. Most owners view this event as a voluntary event and have less concern for the cash and liquidity desires of the owner who wants to exit. The shareholders agreement may give the remaining owners the option to buy the interest of the departing owner, but impose no obligation. In other situations, the owners will recognize the need for owners to come and go, particularly in toiler organizations and professional groups. In these cases, there is often a provision for a payout upon voluntary withdrawal, but the payment terms are usually over an extended period of time to avoid creating an undue burden on the cash flow of those who remain.

### d. Is it advisable to tie business ownership to continued employment?

Many businesses restrict stock ownership to those who are employed by the business. For these businesses, termination of employment is an important triggering event. This is typically true for professional service corporations, as well as numerous other toiler and hybrid organizations and even many big fish organizations where the minority shareholders are employees. For these businesses, it's advisable to provide for a mandatory buyout upon the termination of employment of an owner. Funding is a challenge for the remaining owners. It is common for the departing owner to be paid in installments over a time frame that accommodates the cash needs of the business.

The question that is often asked is: "What happens if one of the owners wants out and none of the other owners wants to buy that person's stock?" Usually the agreement should be structured to give the parties significant time to negotiate a solution to the stalemate. If the stalemate continues for a designated time, often the owner who wants out is given the right to trigger a sale or liquidation of the business or to find an outside buyer for his or her stock.

### e. What types of special exceptions should be structured into the agreement for unique shareholders?

There is no requirement that all shareholders be treated equally in a shareholders agreement. Often the expectations and the needs of the shareholders will result in different rights, particularly in big fish organizations. ABC Inc. is an example. Upon the death of one of the majority owners, Jim or

Sue, the surviving spouse will not want the two minority shareholders to have the right or the obligation to purchase the stock of the deceased. Upon the death of the survivor of Jim and Sue, they likely will want the stock to pass to their son, Sam. A similar exception may give Jim and Sue the right to transfer stock to Sam at any time. They also may want the flexibility to transfer stock to a trust for the benefit of their grandchildren for estate planning purposes. It's doubtful Jim and Sue would tolerate the minority shareholders having similar rights.

### f. Is there a need to structure special voting restrictions into the agreement?

Sometimes. For example, one shareholder may be willing to purchase 25 percent of the stock on the condition that he or she is assured a seat on the board of directors. The shareholders agreement could provide that all of the shareholders must vote their stock to maintain that shareholder's board position. That same 25 percent shareholder may want to have veto power over certain major corporate events, such as the liquidation of the business or a sale of the business. The agreement could provide that no such act will occur without at least a 76 percent approval by the shareholders. By carefully designing a shareholder agreement, a minority shareholder can be given important voting rights at the time of his or her investment in the enterprise. In the case of ABC Inc., the two minority shareholders, Roger and Joyce, insisted on such a provision to protect themselves against a substantial change in the direction of the business by Sam, the owners' son, at the time he inherits his parents' 60 percent interest. They wanted to prevent Sam from unilaterally starting a new business, shutting down existing plants, or incurring debt beyond certain limits without a supermajority approval by the shareholders. In Chapter 4, there is a short discussion of 20 potential operating deal points that may require special treatment and the different solution techniques that may be considered.

### g. How do the parties select the most appropriate method for valuing equity ownership interest and the business?

Carefully. Often the most difficult element in a buy-sell agreement is the determination of how an ownership interest will be priced upon the occurrence of a triggering event. There are a number of options. One common (and usually bad) approach is to use book value. Its only virtue in most cases is simplicity. The problem with book value is that it does not reflect changes in the asset values or the goodwill and going concern value of the business. For these reasons, a modified book value approach is sometimes used. It adjusts the value of the balance sheet assets to reflect their current fair market value, but it too often fails to account for the going concern and goodwill value of an operating business.

The third common approach is to have a formula based on the recent average earnings of the business. This approach focuses on the earning capacity of the business and is used to reflect the going concern and goodwill value of the enterprise. Perhaps its biggest drawback is that it is based on historical earnings and may not reflect recent changes, good or bad, in the future prospects of the business.

A fourth approach is to agree on a mechanism for having the business appraised when a triggering event occurs. The comparative advantage of this approach is that it is designed to derive the current fair market value of the business. The problem is that appraisals can be expensive, and often businesses are so unique that even appraisers are incapable of accurately assessing their true value.

The fifth approach is to specify in the agreement that the price will be a fixed price, subject to adjustment by the shareholders at their annual meeting each year. Then each year the shareholders establish a new price that will govern any transaction for the following year. The appeal of the approach is that it requires the owners to focus on the valuation issue each year and to reach an agreement for a limited future time frame under calm circumstances that are not stressed by the demands of an immediate deal. A key to the approach is a specified backup valuation method if the shareholders neglect or are unable to resolve the valuation issue for a period of time. For example, the agreement might require that the price be re-examined each year at the annual meeting, but that if it has not been re-examined within two years of the date of an event that triggers the buy-sell agreement, the value will be determined by agreement among the interested parties. If the interested parties cannot reach an agreement on price within 30 days, then each party selects an appraiser and the two appraisers jointly determine the price. This gives the interested parties an opportunity to agree on a price before incurring the expense and the time delay of a formal appraisal, but also provides for a binding mechanism for ultimately determining the price.

A three-tiered approach of this type often is used in situations where the owners cannot agree on a formula for valuing the business. Some may view this as avoiding the issue rather than facing it. But often the job of agreeing on a value at a given point in time is much easier than the task of developing a formula that will work in the future, especially for a business that has not matured or that is growing rapidly.

### h. Should the same valuation method apply for all triggers?

Often the owners will want to establish a different price or price formula, depending upon the event that triggers the buyout. Providing a discount from the regular price for a departing owner/employee who does not give the remaining owners adequate advance notice of departure can be an effective means of ensuring a smooth transition in the case of key employees. Another possible use of a discounted fair market value is the situation where the departing owner/employee may become a competitor of the business. The departing owner moves across the street and wants his or her former colleagues to help fund a new competitive business venture. A heavy discount in this situation may be justified in many cases.

*[handwritten margin note: Good reasons to discount the departees stock]*

### i. Will the amount paid under the agreement to the heirs of a deceased owner govern for estate tax purposes?

Not necessarily. The buyout price paid under a buy-sell agreement on the death of an owner will not necessarily be the same value used to determine the federal estate tax liability of the deceased. It is possible that the IRS could determine that the actual fair market value of the interest for tax purposes is greater than the buyout price under the agreement. The owner's family would end up receiving cash that is substantially less than the value that is used to compute estate taxes. This could be disastrous for the owner's family, particularly in situations where the business is the largest asset in the estate. The situation also may jeopardize the marital deduction if the ownership interest passes to a qualified terminable interest property ("QTIP")[8] trust that is required to sell the stock for less than its fair market value for tax purposes. The fear is that the QTIP may not qualify for the marital deduction because someone other than the surviving spouse benefits from the QTIP trust by virtue of the right to buy the ownership interest for less than full consideration.[9]

A buy-sell agreement often can be structured to fix the value of the transferred business interest for estate tax purposes. The difficulty of accomplishing this desired result depends, in part, on whether the business is considered a family business for purposes of Section 2703.[10] If non-family parties own more than 50 percent of the equity interests, the requirements of Section 2703 will not be an issue.[11] In such a situation, the value determined pursuant to the agreement will govern for estate tax purposes if (1) the price for the interest is specified or readily ascertainable pursuant to the terms of the agreement and the price was reasonable when the agreement was entered into; (2) the decedent's estate was obligated to sell at death for the price established by the agreement; and (3) the deceased was restricted from selling or transferring the interest during life.[12] This third condition is not satisfied if the decedent had the right to transfer the interest by gift during life to a person who was not subject to the restrictions imposed by the agreement. At a minimum, this provision generally requires that the interest have been subject to a right of first refusal at a fixed or determinable price under the agreement during the decedent's life.

If family members control the company, then the price determined pursuant to the buy-sell agreement will govern for estate tax purposes only if the forgoing three conditions are satisfied, along with the requirements of Section 2703. Section 2703 requires that the agreement be a *bona fide* business arrangement, not be used as a device to transfer property for less than full value, and contain terms that are comparable to similar arrangements entered into by persons in arms-length arrangements.[13] The "arms-length" requirement is the most challenging and difficult in almost every situation. It requires a determination of what unrelated parties are doing in the same industry or similar types of businesses owned by unrelated parties.[14]

---

8. I.R.C. § 2056(b)(7).

9. See I.R.C. § 2056(b)(7)(B)(ii)(II), and Estate of Rinaldi v. U.S., 80 AFTR2d 97-5324 (Fed. Cl. 1997), 97-2 USTC ¶ 60,281 (Ct. Cl. 1997), and TAM 9147065.

10. Reg. § 25.2703-1(b)(3). Family members include the transferor's spouse, any ancestor of the transferor or the transferor's spouse, any spouse of any such ancestor, and any lineal descendant of the parents of the transferor or the transferor's spouse (but not spouses of such descendants). Reg. § 25.2703-1(b)(3); Reg. § 25.2701-2(b)(5). Broad entity attribution rules are used to determine ownership, with an interest being deemed a family interest if it is attributed to both a family and non-family member. Reg. § 25.2703-1(b)(3); Reg. § 25.2701-6(a)(2)-(4).

11. Reg. § 25.2703-1(b)(3).

12. Reg. § 20.2031-2(h).

13. I.R.C. § 2703(b).

14. Reg. § 25.2703-1(b)(4)(i). It is not necessary that the provisions parallel the terms of any particular

## 4. BIG MISTAKES TO AVOID

### a.  Mistake One:  Improper Use of the Showdown Clause

The first common mistake is the improper use of the showdown clause.  A showdown clause is a mechanism that is often used in a buy-sell agreement to deal with an owner who wants to cash out.  Here's how it works.  If an owner wants to withdraw from the company, that owner presents an offer to the other owners in the form of a purchase price and payment terms.  The other owners then have the choice to be either buyers or sellers, at the specified price and payment terms.  It's like a child splitting a candy bar with a friend.  One cuts it in half, and the other chooses which half he or she wants.  The showdown clause, in theory, forces the price and payment terms to be fair, since the one proposing them doesn't know if he or she is going to be a buyer or a seller.

The attraction of a showdown clause is its simplicity and apparent fairness.  Many advisers wrongly believe that it is the ultimate solution to all difficult buyout situations, and, therefore, they use it as a standard in structuring buy-sell agreements.  But in many types of businesses, the appearance of simplicity and fairness is deceiving.  Let's look at the big fish business, for example, one dominated by a large owner and one or more small owners.  The showdown clause usually gives the big fish a huge advantage.  Not only is the larger owner likely to have a bigger net worth and more capacity to pay, but he or she only faces the possibility of buying a small interest in the business.  By contrast, the smaller owner is not only likely to have a smaller net worth, but also has to pay a much larger price to buy out the interest of the larger owner.  In this type of business, the showdown clause may be nothing more than a way for the larger owner to squeeze out the little guy.  The apparent fairness of the showdown clause evaporates quickly.  Similarly, the showdown clause can be unfair in a toiler business where all of the owners have relatively equal interests, but one or more of them have a greater net worth.  Again the showdown clause may become a means for the richer owners to squeeze out those who do not have sufficient means to be buyers in a showdown situation.

The third type of business where a showdown clause may be inappropriate is the hybrid business where some of the owners work in the business and others do not.  If some of the owners depend upon the business for their jobs and others do not, a showdown clause may force the inside owners to become unwilling buyers simply to preserve their jobs.  The nature of their employment relationship with the company and the lack of other job opportunities may leave the insiders no choice any time the showdown clause is triggered by one of the outside owners.  For all practical purposes, the outside owners have a put.

The showdown clause works best in golfer organizations where all the players are passive owners.  None of them depends on the business for his or her employment.  To be fair, the provision should be limited to those businesses where each owner owns roughly the same percentage interest in the business, and each has the financial capacity to be a buyer when the clause is triggered.

---

agreement.  Reg. § 25.2703-1(b)(4)(ii).

### b. Mistake Two: Failure to Recognize the Unique Rights of the Majority Owner

The second big mistake is found in the big fish businesses dominated by a single controlling owner. The buy-sell agreement too often is structured on the assumption that all owners have to be treated the same. In fact, many provisions under a buy-sell agreement should apply differently to the majority owner than to the other owners. If the owners stop to think about it and ask all the appropriate "what if" questions, they will usually accept the unequal treatment.

One area where this unintended equal treatment shows up is in the control of the board of directors of a corporation. Too many majority shareholders assume that they control the operations of the corporation solely by virtue of the fact that they control the majority votes of the stock. As stated above, the shareholders of any corporation, whether public or private, do little more than elect the board of directors. The real control of the operation of the business rests with the board. Unless the majority shareholder also controls the board, that majority shareholder does not control the operation of the business. But why wouldn't the majority shareholder control the board? A shareholders agreement may provide a shareholder with an assured seat on the board.

Take, for example, ABC Inc. where Jim and Sue own 60 percent of the stock and Roger and Joyce each own 20 percent. If the shareholders agreement specifies a board of three members and ensures Jim, Roger and Joyce each a seat on the board, Roger and Joyce, the 20 percent owners, would control the board and the company. In this situation, it may still be appropriate to assure all shareholders a seat on the board. Their input usually is important in running the business. But it's their input that's needed, not their control. If the two minority shareholders are going to be assured a seat on the board, the board may be expanded to five directors, so that Jim, the majority owner, could elect Sue and Sam to the board and, thereby, preserve board control in the family. A buy-sell agreement that deals with the composition of the board needs to be structured to ensure that the control of the corporation by a majority shareholder is not inadvertently forfeited.

Other buy-sell provisions that often have unintended results for big fish organizations involve equal application of the buyout rights that arise in certain events, such as death, disability, or retirement. In the typical buy-sell agreement, when one of these triggering events occurs, the other owners have the right, and often the obligation, to purchase the stock of the departing owner. This is appropriate and works well in a toiler organization, for example, where all of the owners have substantially equal interests. But in a big fish enterprise, the majority owner may have never intended that he or she would be subject to the provisions. While it may be entirely appropriate to permit the majority owner to purchase the stock of a departing minority owner, it may not be consistent with the majority owner's intention that the same rights exist when he or she dies, retires or is disabled.

### c. Mistake Three: The Constructive Dividend Trap

A mistake occurs in the context of a C corporation when the agreement imposes a primary and unconditional cross-purchase obligation on the individual shareholders, and the parties want to preserve the flexibility of a redemption by the corporation. Often the mistake is aggravated by sloppily putting ownership of the life insurance in the corporation to facilitate the payment of premiums with corporate dollars. If there is a primary and unconditional obligation of the individual shareholders to purchase the stock of the deceased or departing shareholder, and that obligation is paid and discharged by the corporation, all payments by the corporation to redeem the stock of the deceased or departing owners will be taxed as constructive dividends to the remaining shareholders.[15]

The key to avoiding this trap and preserving flexibility is to structure any cross-purchase obligation of the individual shareholders as a secondary, backup obligation. This is done by first giving the corporation the right to purchase the stock, and then providing that the shareholders will purchase the stock if the corporation fails to do so. It may look like form over substance, but it can be the difference between a clean deal and a horrendous constructive dividend.[16]

### d. Mistake Four: Use of Inappropriate Payment Terms

A common mistake regarding payment terms is the failure to provide for security. At a minimum, the deferred payments should be secured by a pledge of the stock or the equity interest being purchased. When a stock pledge is used, the buy-sell agreement should specify its terms. For example, usually it should provide that, as long as the payments remain current, the voting rights and the right to receive dividends and other distributions with respect to the stock are retained by the purchasers. Those rights automatically shift to the departed owner if there is a default in the payment of the installment obligation.

Consideration also should be given to the need for other forms of security. For example, if the departing owner's stock is being redeemed by the company, should the other shareholders be required to personally guarantee the payment of the redemption price by the corporation? The question should be considered, particularly in cases where the redemption price is being paid over an extended period of time. Owners often agree that it is appropriate for those who stay behind and reap the benefits of the ongoing business to personally guarantee the payment of the deferred price. Also, consideration should be given to restrictions on the payment of compensation or dividends to the remaining owners so long as the deferred purchase price is outstanding. Often this is done by requiring that the business maintain certain debt-to-equity and quick-asset ratios as a condition to making distributions to the other owners.

### e. Mistake Five: Poor Structuring of Life Insurance Ownership

A fifth common mistake in structuring buy-sell agreements (and an expensive one) relates to the purchase of life insurance to fund a buyout obligation on the death of an owner. Most properly structured buy-sell agreements will permit the buyout of the deceased owner to be made by either the corporation or the remaining owners. The surviving owners can examine the

---

15. Rev. Rule 69-608, 1969–2 C.B. 42.
16. Compare Situations 1 and 2 with Situation 5 in Rev. Rule 69-608, 1969-2 C.B. 42.

circumstances existing at the death of one of the owners and determine then whether it's most appropriate to have the corporation buy the stock of the deceased owner or to have that stock purchased by the remaining owners. As stated above, various factors may affect the decision to structure the purchase as a redemption or a cross-purchase.

The mistake is made when life insurance is purchased to fund that obligation. Because of habit, simplicity, lack of thought, or a combination of all these, the life insurance often is purchased by the corporation. The corporation pays the premiums, and the corporation is named as the beneficiary. Upon the death of an owner, the corporation collects the life insurance proceeds. The mistake is that the decision relating to the ownership of the life insurance also, by necessity, decides the redemption-versus-cross-purchase issue. So even though the buy-sell agreement has been carefully structured to retain the flexibility to have either a redemption or a cross-purchase buyout, the purchase of the life insurance by the corporation forces the election of the redemption approach. The life insurance proceeds cannot be made available to the other owners to fund a cross purchase without significant adverse tax consequences.

There are two advantages of a cross-purchase that need to be carefully examined at the time the life insurance is acquired. The first advantage is that, with a cross-purchase, each of the shareholders receives a stepped-up basis in the acquired stock. No such step-up occurs with a redemption by a C corporation. The second advantage of having the owners directly own the policies is that the risk of triggering a corporate AMT on the receipt of the insurance is avoided.

Another life insurance structuring blunder sometimes is made in big fish businesses. A huge amount of life insurance is acquired to fund the buyout of the majority owner at his or her death. The premiums are funded by the corporation. At death, the majority owner's family ends up with a death benefit, subject to estate taxes, and no equity in the business. The minority shareholders end up with the entire business. For many majority shareholders, an infinitely better structure would eliminate all buyout rights of the minority shareholders. The life insurance on the majority owner would be held for the benefit of his or her family in a life insurance trust that would not be subject to estate taxes. The majority owner's family ends up with the life insurance death benefit, tax free, and the majority interest in the business. Most majority owners, when presented with the huge contrasts in these two scenarios, will enthusiastically opt for the latter.

#### f. Mistake Six: Misused Right of First Refusal

A common provision in many buy-sell agreements is a right of first refusal provision. It provides that no owner can sell his or her interest in the business to a third party without first offering that interest to the other owners at the same price and on the same payment terms. It is the traditional method of preserving the identity of the group. Each owner has the comfort of knowing that he or she will have the ability to prevent an unwanted owner from becoming part of the ownership group. In most cases, the provision just doesn't work.

The first problem with the right of first refusal provision is that it assumes there is a market for the stock when, in fact, there is no market for a minority equity interest. A minority owner usually finds it impossible to locate a third party who will make a reasonable, *bona fide* offer to trigger the right of first refusal provision. The result is that the right of first refusal provision becomes an absolute prohibition on sale. The problem with the provision is that it creates the expectation that each owner has the capacity to liquidate his or her interest when, in fact, there is no such capacity. It also may encourage individual owners to try to market their interests to uninformed third parties who know nothing about the business. It is usually not in the best interests of the company or the owners to have all details relevant to the business being freely shopped to strangers who are being invited to kick the tires. Apart from requiring huge amounts of executive time and expense to ensure full disclosure for security law purposes, the effort may be counterproductive to the strategic development of the company's business plan. Most private business owners, if they stop to think, will conclude that they do not want to do anything that encourages minority owners to shop the stock to third parties.

The second problem with a right of first refusal provision surfaces in the rare situation where the departing owner actually finds someone who wants to buy into the business. The prospective buyer is willing to pay a premium to get a foothold in the business. It may be a competitor, a potential competitor, a strategic supplier, a huge customer, an obnoxious relative of the departing owner, or some other party that the other owners do not want. This puts the remaining owners in a tough position. They either have to come up with a large sum to match the price and terms or end up with a co-owner they don't like or want or who may pose a real threat to the business.

A right of first refusal provision usually gives the task of finding the new owner to the wrong person. The departing owner doesn't care who the new owner is going to be; he or she just wants the best price and terms for the stock. Yet, the right of first refusal provision puts the onus on the departing owner to find a potential candidate in order to trigger the provision. Those who really care about any new owner are the remaining owners, who are going to have to embrace the new owner as a partner.

What's the alternative? It is to structure a mechanism that permits an owner to withdraw and get cashed out, without creating the problems described above that are often triggered with a right of first refusal. For example, the buy-sell agreement could provide that if an owner wants out, that owner must trigger Stage One by giving the others significant advance notice, say three months. Stage One is a reaction period for the other owners. They have a period of time to find a new owner or prepare for the purchase of the departing owner's stock. The pricing mechanism and payment terms are set forth in the agreement. If, at the end of the three-month period, the existing owners have not found an acceptable replacement owner or developed a plan to pay the required price, Stage Two kicks in. This is a time (say, 30 days) designated for negotiation between the owner who wants out and the other owners. All will have had time to ponder the realities of the situation and assess their options. Of course, the remaining owners can always buy the equity interest for the price and terms specified in the agreement. But if Stage Two is triggered, they will probably be looking for some concessions from the other side. If there is still no deal at the end of Stage Two, there is an additional period of time, say six months, for the existing owners to find a replacement owner. This is Stage Three. During all these stages, the departing owner remains an owner and is entitled to all the benefits of ownership. If at the end of the extended period a replacement owner has not been found and the remaining owners are still unwilling to purchase the interest of the departing owner on the stated terms or on mutually acceptable renegotiated terms, the departing owner has the option to force a sale of the business. This is Stage Four. If the option is exercised, any owner or group of owners may be the purchaser. Essentially, the company is put up for sale and anyone can be a bidder. If sold, the owner who wants to depart is cashed out at a price that reflects the value of the business.

As a practical matter, it is highly unlikely that the process will ever get to Stage Four. The remaining owners will have had plenty of time to find a replacement owner, secure financing to fund the buyout pursuant to the terms of the agreement, or renegotiate a more palatable deal with the departing owner. A staged exit procedure of this type, or any version thereof, can provide the remaining owners with the time and the opportunity to solve the problem of the departing owner, while at the same time providing the departing owner with a means of ultimately getting cashed out.

There are a number of variations of this approach. The important point is that the right of first refusal should not be the automatic solution to the problem of an owner who wants to depart. A better mechanism usually can be structured to provide a more realistic solution to the problem.

### g. Mistake Seven: Failure to Cover the Downside

Another common mistake in structuring buy-sell agreements is to neglect the downside – the disaster scenario. Most buy-sell agreements are entered into when all parties are anticipating a successful company. Most don't even want to think about the business failing. But it frequently happens. It helps to deal with the potential fallout up front.

The most common problem in a disaster scenario is that one or more of the owners end up getting stuck with a disproportionately large share of the liabilities because of personal guarantees or other commitments made in connection with the business. Most guarantees by multiple owners are joint and several. The lender can go after any one or more of the owners to collect the entire debt. The owners should agree up front as to how they will share the debt burdens of the business. Typically, the agreement should provide that if an owner is forced to fund a company debt, the portion of the payment that exceeds that owner's percentage interest in the business constitutes a loan to the other owners, in proportion to their respective percentage interests in the business. The agreement should set forth a mechanism for the repayment of the loan and perhaps collateral to secure the obligation.

### h. Mistake Eight: Ignore S Corporation Issues

A common mistake in buy-sell agreements relates to S corporations. The mistake is the failure to address in the buy-sell agreement specific S corporation issues. The first and most obvious issue is the failure to prohibit a shareholder from making any stock transfer that would result in the termination of the S election. There are a number of shareholder requirements that must be met in order for a corporation to be taxed as an S corporation. There are limits on the number of shareholders and the permissible types of shareholders. Corporations, partnerships, most trusts, and nonresident aliens may not be shareholders of an S corporation. The buy-sell agreement should prohibit any transfer of stock that would terminate the S election and should provide that any such attempted transfer is void.

An S corporation also has the option of making certain tax elections. These elections often require the consent of all shareholders. In order to prevent a single shareholder or a minority group of shareholders from vetoing an election that the majority wants to make, the buy-sell agreement may provide that all shareholders will consent to any tax election that is approved by a specified percentage of shareholders (e.g., 70 percent). An example would be an S corporation that has C corporation earnings and profits. An S corporation may elect to treat distributions as first coming from its C corporation earnings and profits rather than from its accumulated adjustment account.[17] An S corporation might desire to make this election to avoid the tax on excess net passive investment income or to take advantage of the current favorable rates on dividend income.[18] The election requires the unanimous consent of all shareholders because the distributions will be taxed to the shareholders. A buy-sell agreement can soften the impact of the unanimous consent requirement.

Other elections relate to the timing of income recognition within a given year. A corporation that loses its S election in the middle of a year may elect under Section 1362 to close its books on the date of the termination and calculate its income accordingly. This avoids the requirement that income during the year be allocated on a pro rata basis. Again, it requires the consent of all S corporation shareholders. A similar "closing the books" election is available under Section 1377(a)(2), requiring the consent of all shareholders when a shareholder terminates his or her interest in an S corporation during the year.

Another issue that usually should be addressed in an S corporation buy-sell agreement relates to the payment of dividends. It's an issue that is common to all pass-through entities, including partnerships and limited liability companies. The income of the entity is passed through and taxed to the owners, even if it is not distributed. The owners may end up with a tax bill and no cash. To ensure that the owners will be distributed enough cash to at least cover their tax liabilities, the buy-sell agreement may contain a provision that obligates the entity to distribute cash to fund the tax liabilities of the owners. In order to avoid any risk that such a provision creates a second class of stock (a condition that would kill the S election), the tax distribution to the shareholders should not be based on the specific tax liabilities of the different shareholders. Rather, it must be based on the shareholders' respective stockholdings in the company.

---

17. I.R.C. § 1368(e)(3).
18. I.R.C. § 1375.

## 5. JUDICIAL ENFORCEMENT

# CONCORD AUTO AUCTION, INC. v. RUSTIN
627 F.Supp. 1526 (D.Mass.,1986)

YOUNG, District Judge.

Close corporations, Concord Auto Auction, Inc. ("Concord") and E.L. Cox Associates, Inc. ("Associates") brought this action for the specific performance of a stock purchase and restriction agreement (the "Agreement"). Concord and Associates allege that Lawrence H. Rustin ("Rustin") as the administrator of E.L. Cox's estate ("Cox") failed to effect the repurchase of Cox's stock holdings as provided by the Agreement.

Rustin alleges in his defense that Concord and Associates are not entitled to specific performance because 1) they have breached the Agreement which they seek to enforce; 2) they have unclean hands because they failed to effect a review and revaluation of the shares; 3) the value of the stock increased so substantially that specific enforcement would be unfair and unjust to Cox's estate; and 4) specific performance is conditional upon an annual review of share value to be held no later than the third Tuesday of February, here February 21, 1984.

Rustin alleges that all parties intended an annual revaluation, that Betsy Cox Powell ("Powell") and Nancy Cox Thomas ("Thomas"), sisters of the decedent Cox, as the only other shareholders in both Concord and Associates, knew that a revaluation would result in a higher price and failed to effect the annual review required by the Agreement, that this failure breached the Agreement and was "undertaken with the intent and effect of depriving the estate of E. Leroy Cox from receiving fair value for its shares of Concord and Associates." Rustin further alleges that by failing to establish new prices, Powell in particular as well as Thomas breached their fiduciary duties to the estate of Cox in light of their direct pecuniary interest in the value of the shares. Finally, Rustin alleges that the actions of Powell, Thomas, Concord and Associates constitute a willful violation of Mass.Gen.Laws, ch. 93A, § 11.

Concord and Associates move for summary judgment, specific performance of the Agreement and dismissal of the counterclaims. Pursuant to Fed.R.Civ.P. 56, the Court will treat the motion for dismissal as a motion for summary judgment because the Court has gone beyond the pleadings to consider various affidavits and exhibits. For the reasons set forth below, the Court allows the motions for summary judgment.

Both Concord and Associates are Massachusetts Corporations. Concord operates a used car auction for car dealers, fleet operators, and manufacturers. Associates operates as an adjunct to Concord's auction business by guaranteeing checks and automobile titles. Both are close corporations with the same shareholders, all siblings: Cox (now his estate), Powell, and Thomas. At all times relevant to this action, each sibling owned one-third of the issued and outstanding stock in both Concord and Associates.

To protect "their best interests" and the best interests of the two corporations, the three shareholders entered into a stock purchase and restriction agreement on February1, 1983. The Agreement provides that all shares owned by a shareholder at the time of his or her death be acquired by the two corporations, respectively, through life insurance policies specifically established to fund this transaction. This procedure contemplates the "orderly transfer of the stock owned by each deceased Shareholder." At issue in the instant action are the prerequisites for and effect of the repurchase requirements as set forth in the Agreement.

This dispute arises because Rustin failed to tender Cox's shares as required by Paragraph 2, *Death of Shareholder.* Rustin admits this but alleges a condition precedent: that Powell, specifically, and Thomas failed to effect both the annual meeting and the annual review of the stock price set in the Agreement as required by Paragraph 6, *Purchase Price:* "Each price shall be reviewed at least annually no later than the annual meeting of the stockholders ... (commencing with the annual meetings for the year 1984) ...," here February 21, 1984. Rustin implies that, had the required meeting been held, revaluation would or should have occurred and that, after Cox's accidental death in a fire on March 14, 1984, Powell in particular as well as Thomas were obligated to revalue the stock prior to tendering the repurchase price.

There is no dispute that the By-Laws call for an annual meeting on the third Tuesday of February, here February 21, 1984. There is no dispute that none took place or that, when Cox died, the stocks of each corporation had not been formally revalued. No one disputes that Paragraph 6 of the Agreement provides for a price of $672.00 per share of Concord and a price of $744.00 per share for Associates. This totals $374,976 which is covered by insurance on Cox's life of $375,000. There is no substantial dispute that the stock is worth a great deal more, perhaps even twice as much. No one seriously disputes that Paragraph 6 further provides that:

> ... all parties may, as a result of such review, agree to a new price by a written instrument executed by all the parties and appended to an original of this instrument, and that any such new price shall thereupon become the basis for determining the purchase price for all purposes hereof unless subsequently superceded pursuant to the same procedure. The purchase price shall remain in full force and effect and until so changed.

Rustin asserts that the explicit requirement of a yearly price review "clashes" with the provision that the price shall remain in effect until changed. He argues a trial is required to determine the intent of the parties:

> The question then arises, presenting this Court with a material issue of fact not susceptible to determination on a motion for summary judgment: Did the parties intend, either to reset, or at least to monitor, yearly, the correspondence between the Paragraph 6 price and the current value of the companies? If so, who, if anyone, was principally responsible for effecting the yearly review required by the Agreement, and for insuring an informed review?

In answering these questions the Court first outlines its proper role in the interpretation of this contract.

A Court sitting in diversity will apply the substantive law of the forum state. *Erie R.R. Co. v. Tompkins,* 304 U.S. 64, (1938), here Massachusetts. In Massachusetts as elsewhere, absent ambiguity, contracts must be interpreted and enforced exactly as written. *Freelander v. G. & K. Realty Corp.,* 357 Mass. 512, 515, 516, 258 N.E.2d 786 (1970). Where the language is unambiguous, the interpretation of a contract is a question of law for the court. *Edwin R. Sage v. Foley,* 12 Mass.App. 20, 28, 421 N.E.2d 460 (1981). Further, contracts must be construed in accordance with their ordinary and usual sense.

Contrary to Rustin's assertion, the Court in applying these standards holds that there is no ambiguity and certainly no "clash" between the dual requirements of Paragraph 6 that there be an annual review of share price and that, absent such review, the existing price prevails. When, as here, the Court searches for the meaning of a document containing two unconditional provisions, one immediately following the other, the Court favors a reading that reconciles them. *Kates v. St. Paul Fire & Marine Ins. Co.,* 509 F.Supp. 477, 485 (D.Mass.1981). The Court rules that the Agreement covers precisely the situation before it: no revaluation occurred, therefore the price remains as set forth in the Agreement. This conclusion is reasonable, for the Agreement is not a casual memorialization but a formal contract carefully drafted by attorneys and signed by all parties.

Moreover, the Court interprets Paragraph 2 to provide, in unambiguous terms:

> "In the event of the death of any Shareholder subject to this agreement, his respective ... administrator ... *shall,* within sixty (60) days after the date of death ... give written notice thereof to each Company which notice *shall* specify a purchase date not later than sixty (60) days thereafter, *offering to each Company for purchase* as hereinafter provided, and *at the purchase price set forth in Paragraph 6,* all of the Shares owned on said date by said deceased Shareholder...." [Emphasis by the Court].

Rustin, therefore, was unambiguously obligated as administrator of Cox's estate to tender Cox's shares for repurchase by Concord and Associates. His failure to do so is inexcusable unless he raises cognizable defenses.

All of Rustin's defenses turn on two allegations: that his performance is excused because the surviving parties failed to review and to adjust upward the $374,976 purchase price. Rustin contends that the parties meant to review the price per share on an annual basis. No affidavit supports this assertion, nor does any exhibit. In fact, absent any evidence for this proposition, Rustin's assertion is no more than speculation and conjecture. While Rustin contends that the failure to review and revalue constitutes "unclean hands" and a breach of fiduciary duty which excuses his nonperformance, he places before the Court only argument not facts.

It simply does not follow that because a meeting was not held and the prices were not reviewed that a trial of the parties' intentions is required. The

Agreement is the best evidence of the parties' intent. Although the text of the Agreement provides that share price "shall" be reviewed "at least annually," the Agreement also states that "The purchase price shall remain in full force and effect unless and until so changed."

Even giving all intendments to Rustin, the "favorable inferences" generally afforded parties opposing summary judgment must be reasonable and based on facts, not conjecture. *Hahn v. Sargent,* 523 F.2d 461, 464 (1st Cir.1975). There must be sufficient evidence supporting the claimed factual dispute to require a trial to resolve the parties' different versions; the evidence manifesting the dispute must be substantial. Although, as the party opposing the motion, Rustin is entitled to inferences from the evidence in the records, he "is not entitled to build a case on the gossamer threads of whimsey, speculation and conjecture." *Manganaro v. Delaval Separator Co.,* 309 F.2d 389, 393 (1st Cir.1962). Thus, conclusory allegations unsupported by facts, do not create an issue which should be reserved for trial. Rustin presents no evidence that would tend to suggest that Cox intended to depart from or rescind the Agreement. He presents only bare allegations that a revaluation would have occurred had the annual meeting been held.

Even if competent evidence adduced at trial would support Rustin's allegations, his proposition would of necessity require judicial intervention, a course this Court does not favor. Rustin produces not a shred of evidence that the parties intended that a court should intercede to set the share price in the event the parties failed to do so themselves. Every first year law student learns that although the courts can lead an opera singer to the concert hall, they cannot make her sing. *Lumley v. Guy,* 118 Eng.Rep. 749 (1853). While this Court will specifically enforce a consensual bargain, memorialized in an unambiguous written document, it will not order the revision of the share price. Such intrusion into the private ordering of commercial affairs offends both good judgment and good jurisprudence. Moreover, the record before the Court indicates that the parties fully intended what their competent counsel drafted and they signed.

Moreover, the nucleus of Rustin's premise is that somehow Powell should have guaranteed the review and revision of the share prices. On the contrary, nothing in the record indicates that a reasonable trier of fact could find that Powell's duties and responsibilities included such omnipotence. More to the point, the By-Laws suggest that several individuals shared the responsibility for calling the required annual meeting: "In case the annual meeting for any year shall not be duly called or held, the Board of Directors or the President shall cuase (sic) a special meeting to be held...." Pursuant to the By-Laws, Cox himself had the power, right, and authority to call a meeting of the stockholders of both companies, in order to review the price per share—or for any other purpose for that matter.

Furthermore, nothing in the record indicates that somehow Powell, Thomas, Concord, or Associates was charged with the duty of raising the share price. In fact, this is discretionary and consensual: "all parties *may,* as a result of such review, *agree to* a new price by a written instrument *executed by all parties....*" Nowhere can the Court find any affirmative duty to guarantee either an annual meeting or a share price revision. To fault Powell for not doing by fiat what must be done by consensus credits Powell with powers she simply does not have. The mere fact that, as a shareholder of Concord and Associates, Powell benefits from the enforcement of the Agreement at the $374,976 purchase price does not, as matter of law, create an obligation on her part to effect a review or revision of the purchase price. One cannot breach a duty where no duty exists, and Rustin cannot manufacture by allegation a duty where neither the Agreement nor the By-Laws lends any support.

Of Rustin's defense that the value of the stock increased so substantially that specific enforcement would be unfair and unjust to Cox's estate, little need be said. This defense as well as Rustin's counterclaims rest on the allegation that Powell, in particular, and Thomas "knew" that a revaluation would result in a higher price and "failed to effect an annual review." Of Powell, Rustin argues that she had a "special responsibility" to effect a review of the purchase price because her siblings looked to her for financial expertise and to call a meeting. Nowhere is this "special responsibility" supported by the Agreement or the By-Laws. Rustin also implies that the sisters "knew" that failure to revalue would inure to their benefit. This presumes they knew that Cox would die in an accidental fire three weeks after the deadline for the annual meeting. To call this preposterous understates it, for nothing immunized the sisters from an equally unforeseeable accident. Rustin's argument withers in the light of objectivity to a heap of conclusory straws.

Agreements, such as those before the Court, "among shareholders of closely held corporations are common and the purpose of such contracts are clear." *Brigham v. M & J Corporation,* 352 Mass. 674, 678, 227 N.E.2d 915 (1967). Moreover, such agreements are valid, bind the stockholder and his administrator or executor, and may be specifically enforced. *Donahue v. Rodd Electrotype Company of New England, Inc.,* 367 Mass. 578, 598, 328 N.E.2d 505 (1975), as limited by *Wilkes v. Springside Nursing Home, Inc.,* 370 Mass. 842, 848–852, 353 N.E.2d 657 (1976); *Smith v. Atlantic Properties, Inc.,* 12 Mass.App. 201, 205–206, 422 N.E.2d 798 (1981).

The validity of such agreements will be upheld absent any fraud, overreaching, undue influence, duress, or mistake at the time the deceased entered into the agreement, these conditions rendering the agreement void. *New England Trust Co. v. Abbott,* 162 Mass. at 155, 38 N.E. 432; *see Renberg v. Zarrow,* 667 P.2d at 470. Thus "fairness" and "good faith" in a closely held corporation generally means that each stockholder must have an equal opportunity to sell his or her shares to the corporation for an identical price. *Donahue v. Rodd Electrotype Company of New England, Inc.,* 367 Mass. at 598, 328 N.E.2d 505. The effect of the Agreement is "blind": regardless of who dies first, his or her administrator is required to sell the shares held to the corporations by set procedure for a set price. These circumstances are "fair": "[T]he stipulated price provision wherein no one knows for certain at the time the price is set whether he is to be a buyer or a seller is inherently fair and provides mutuality of risk." *Renberg v. Zarrow,* 667 P.2d at 471.

Moreover, specific performance of an agreement to convey will not be refused merely because the price is inadequate or excessive. *New England Trust Co. v. Abbott,* 162 Mass. at 155, 38 N.E. 432; *see Lee v. Kirby,* 104 Mass. 420, 430 (1870); *Allen v. Biltmore Tissue Corp.,* 2 N.Y.2d 534, 543, 161 N.Y.S.2d 418, 141 N.E.2d 812 (1957) ("The validity of the restriction on transfer does not rest on any abstract notion of intrinsic fairness of price. To be invalid, more than mere disparity between option price and current value of the stock must be shown"); *Renberg v. Zarrow,* 667 P.2d at 470 ("In the absense of fraud, overreaching, or bad faith, an agreement between the stockholders that upon the death of any of them, the stock may be acquired by the corporation is binding. Even great disparity between the price specified in a buy-sell agreement and the actual value of the stock is not sufficient to invalidate the agreement.") The fact that surviving shareholders were allowed to purchase Cox' shares on stated terms and conditions which resulted in the purchase for less than actual value of the stock does not subject the agreement to attack as a breach of the relation of trust and confidence, there being no breach of fiduciary duty.

Rather than evidence of any impropriety, the Court rules that the purchase prices were carefully set, fair when established, evidenced by an Agreement binding all parties equally to the same terms without any indication that any one sibling would reap a windfall. The courts may not rewrite a shareholder's agreement under the guise of relieving one of the parties from the hardship of an improvident bargain. The Court cannot protect the parties from a bad bargain and it will not protect them from bad luck. Cox, the party whose estate is aggrieved, had while alive every opportunity to call the annual meeting and persuade his sisters to revalue their stock. Sad though the situation be, sadness is not the touchstone of contract interpretation.

In the absence any genuine issues of material fact, Concord and Associates are entitled to judgment as matter of law. The Agreement shall be specifically enforced.

SO ORDERED.

### HALEY v. TALCOTT
864 A.2d 86 (Del.Ch. 2004)

STRINE, Vice Chancellor.

Plaintiff Matthew James Haley has moved for summary judgment of his claim seeking dissolution of Matt and Greg Real Estate, LLC ("the LLC"). Haley and defendant Gregory L. Talcott are the only members of the LLC, each owning a 50% interest in the LLC. Haley brings this action in reliance upon § 18-802 of the Delaware Limited Liability Company Act which permits this court to "decree dissolution of a limited liability company whenever it is not reasonably practicable to carry on the business in conformity with a limited liability company agreement." The question before the court is whether dissolution of the LLC should be granted, as Haley requests, or whether, as Talcott contends, Haley is limited to the contractually-provided exit mechanism in the LLC Agreement.

Haley and Talcott have suffered, to put it mildly, a falling out. There is no rational doubt that they cannot continue to do business as 50% members of an LLC. But the path to separating their interests is complicated by a second company, Delaware Seafood, also known as the Redfin Seafood Grill ("Redfin Grill"), a restaurant that, at the risk of slightly oversimplifying, was owned by Talcott and, before the falling out, operated by Haley under an employment contract that gave him a 50% share in the profits. The LLC owns the land that the Redfin Grill occupies under an expired lease. The resolution of the current case and the ultimate fate of the LLC therefore critically affect the continued existence of a second business that one party owns and that the other bitterly contends, in other litigation pending before this court, wrongly terminated him.

The question before the court is essentially how the interests of the members of the LLC are to be separated. Haley asserts that summary judgment is appropriate because it is factually undisputed that it is not reasonably practicable for the LLC to carry on business in conformity with a limited liability company agreement (the "LLC Agreement") that calls for the LLC to be governed by its two members, when those members are in deadlock. Therefore, urges Haley, the LLC should be judicially dissolved immediately. Such an end will force the sale of the LLC's real property, which is likely worth, at current market value, far more than the mortgage that the LLC must pay off if it sells.

In response, Talcott stresses that the LLC Agreement provides an alternative exit mechanism that allows the LLC to continue to exist, and argues that Haley should therefore be relegated to this provision if he is unhappy with the stalemate. In other words, Talcott argues that it is reasonably practicable for the LLC to continue to carry on business in conformity with its LLC Agreement because the exit mechanism creates a fair alternative that permits Haley to get out, receiving the fair market value of his share of the property as determined in accordance with procedures in the LLC Agreement, while allowing the LLC to continue. Critically, the exit provision would allow Talcott to buy Haley out with no need for the LLC's asset (i.e., the land) to be sold on the open market. The LLC could continue to exist and own the land (with its favorable mortgage arrangement) and Talcott, as owner of both entities, could continue to offer the Redfin Grill its favorable rent.

But the problem with Talcott's argument is that the exit mechanism is not a reasonable alternative. A principle attraction of the LLC form of entity is the statutory freedom granted to members to shape, by contract, their own approach to common business "relationship" problems. If an equitable alternative to continued deadlock had been specified in the LLC Agreement, arguably judicial dissolution under § 18-802 might not be warranted. In this case, however, Talcott admits that the exit mechanism provides no method to relieve Haley of his obligation as a personal guarantor for the LLC's mortgage. Haley signed an agreement with the lender personally guaranteeing the entire mortgage of the LLC (as did Talcott) in order to secure the loan. Without relief from the guaranty, Haley would remain personally liable for the mortgage debt of the LLC, even after his exit. Because Haley would be left liable for the debt of an entity over which he had no further control, I find that the exit provision specified in the

LLC Agreement and urged by Talcott is not sufficient to provide an adequate remedy to Haley under these circumstances.

With no reasonable exit mechanism, I find that Haley is entitled to exercise the only practical deadlock-breaking remedy available to him, and one that is also alluded to in the LLC Agreement, the right to seek judicial dissolution. Haley argues, convincingly, that the analysis under § 18-802 for an evenly-split, two-owner LLC ordinarily should parallel the analysis under 8 *Del. C.* § 273, which enables this court to order the judicial dissolution of a joint venture corporation owned by deadlocked 50% owners. Because Haley has demonstrated an indisputable deadlock between the two 50% members of the LLC, and that deadlock precludes the LLC from functioning as provided for in the LLC Agreement, I also grant Haley's motion for summary judgment and order dissolution of Matt and Greg Real Estate, LLC.

Haley and Talcott each have a 50% interest in Matt & Greg Real Estate, LLC, a Delaware limited liability company they formed in 2003. In 2003, the parties formed Matt & Greg Real Estate, LLC to take advantage of the option to purchase the Property that was the subject of the Real Estate Agreement. The option price was $720,000 and the new LLC took out a mortgage from County Bank in Rehoboth Beach, Delaware, for that amount, exercised the option, and obtained the deed to the Property on or about May 23, 2003. Importantly, both Haley and Talcott, individually, signed personal guaranties for the entire amount of the mortgage in order to secure the loan. The Redfin Grill continued to operate at the site, paying the LLC $6,000 per month in rent, a payment sufficient to cover the LLC's monthly obligation under the mortgage. Thus by mid-2003, the parties appeared poised to reap the fruits of their labors; unfortunately, at that point their personal relationship began to deteriorate.

Haley, having managed the restaurant from the time it opened in May 2001, and having formalized his management position in the Employment Contract, apparently believed that the relationship would be reformulated to provide him a direct stock ownership interest in the Redfin Grill at some point. The reasons underlying that belief are not important here, but in late October they caused a rift to develop between the parties. On or about October 27, 2003, the conflict that had been brewing between the parties led to some kind of confrontation. As a result, Talcott sent a letter of understanding to Haley dated October 27, 2003, purporting to accept his resignation and forbidding him to enter the premises of the Redfin Grill.

Haley responded on November 3, 2003 with two separate letters from his counsel to Talcott. In the first, Haley asserts that he did not resign, and that he regarded Talcott's October 27, 2003 letter of understanding as terminating him without cause in breach of the Employment Contract. Haley goes on to express his intent to pursue legal remedies, an intent that he acted upon in the related case in this court.

The Redfin Grill's lease has expired and, as a consequence, the Redfin Grill continues to pay $6,000 per month to the LLC in a month-to-month arrangement. The $6,000 rent exceeds the LLC's required mortgage payment by $800 per month, so the situation remains stable. With only a 50% ownership interest, Haley cannot force the termination of the Redfin Grill's lease and evict the Redfin Grill as a tenant; neither can he force the sale of the Property, land that was appraised as of June 14, 2004 at $1.8 million. In short, absent intervention by this court, Haley is stuck, unless he chooses to avail himself of the exit mechanism provided in the LLC Agreement.

That exit mechanism, like judicial dissolution, would provide Haley with his share of the fair market value of the LLC, including the Property. Section 18 of the LLC Agreement provides that upon written notice of election to "quit" the company, the remaining member may elect, in writing, to purchase the departing member's interest for fair market value. If the remaining member elects to purchase the departing member's interest, the parties may agree on fair value, or have the fair value determined by three arbitrators, one chosen by each member and a third chosen by the first two arbitrators. The departing member pays the reasonable expenses of the three arbitrators. Once a fair price is determined, it may be paid in cash, or over a term if secured by: 1) a note signed by the company and personally by the remaining member; 2) a security agreement; and 3) a recorded UCC lien. Only if the remaining member fails to elect to purchase the departing member's interest is the company to be liquidated.

But despite this level of detail, the exit provision does not expressly provide a release from the personal guaranties that both Haley and Talcott signed to secure the mortgage on the Property. Nor does the exit provision state that any member dissatisfied with the status quo must break an impasse by exit rather than a suit for dissolution.

Haley argues that dissolution is required because the two 50% managers cannot agree how to best utilize the sole asset of the LLC, the Property, because no provision exists for breaking a tie in the voting interests, and because the LLC cannot take any actions, such as entering contracts, borrowing or lending money, or buying or selling property, absent a majority vote of its members. Because this circumstance resembles corporate deadlock, Haley urges that 8 *Del. C.* § 273 provides a relevant parallel for analysis.

In examining the record, I must draw every rational inference in Talcott's favor. Here, even if I find that there are no facts under which the LLC could carry on business in conformity with the LLC Agreement, the remedy of dissolution, by analogy to 8 *Del. C.* § 273, remains discretionary.

Here, the key facts about the parties' ability to work together are not rationally disputable. Therefore, my decision on the motion largely turns on two legal issues: 1) if the doctrine of corporate deadlock is an appropriate analogy for the analysis of a § 18-802 claim on these facts; and 2) if so, and if action to break the stalemate is necessary to permit the LLC to function, whether, because of the contract-law foundations of the Delaware LLC Act, Haley should be relegated to the contractual exit mechanism provided in the LLC Agreement.

Section 18-802 of the Delaware LLC Act is a relatively recent addition to our law, and, as a result, there have been few decisions interpreting it. Nevertheless, § 18-802 has the obvious purpose of providing an avenue of relief when an LLC cannot continue to function in accordance with its chartering agreement...

The relationship between Haley and Talcott indicates active involvement by both parties in creating a restaurant for their mutual benefit and profit, and the Employment Contract shows that Haley was to be the "Operations Director" of the Redfin Grill, a position that, according to the Side Letter Agreement, would only be terminated if the restaurant was sold. Haley was also entitled to a 50% share of the Redfin Grill's profits. In short, Haley and Talcott were in it together for as long as they owned the restaurant, equally sharing the profits as provided in the Employment Contract.

Most importantly, Haley never agreed to be a passive investor in the LLC who would be subject to Talcott's unilateral dominion. Instead, the LLC agreement provided that: "no member/managers may, *without the agreement of a majority vote of the managers' interest,* act on behalf of the company." Under these terms, as a 50% member/manager, no major action of the LLC could be taken without Haley's approval. Thus, Haley is entitled to a continuing say in the operation of the LLC.

Finally, the evidence clearly supports a finding of deadlock between the parties about the business strategy and future of the LLC. The very fact that dissolution has not occurred, combined with Talcott's opposition in this lawsuit, leads inevitably to the conclusion that Talcott opposes such a disposition of the assets. Neither is Talcott's opposition surprising given his economic interest in the continued success of the Redfin Grill, success that one must assume relies, in part, on a continuing favorable lease arrangement with the LLC.

For all these reasons, if the LLC were a corporation, there would be no question that Haley's request to dissolve the entity would be granted. But this case regards an LLC, not a corporation, and more importantly, an LLC with a detailed exit provision. That distinguishing factor must and is considered next.

The Delaware LLC Act is grounded on principles of freedom of contract. For that reason, the presence of a reasonable exit mechanism bears on the propriety of ordering dissolution under 6 *Del. C.* § 18-802. When the agreement itself provides a fair opportunity for the dissenting member who disfavors the inertial status quo to exit and receive the fair market value of her interest, it is at least arguable that the limited liability company may still proceed to operate practicably under its contractual charter because the charter itself provides an equitable way to break the impasse.

Here, that reasoning might be thought apt because Haley has already "voted" as an LLC member to sell the LLC's only asset, the Property, presumably because he knew he could not secure sole control of both the LLC and the Redfin Grill. Given that reality, so long as Haley can actually extract himself fairly, it arguably makes sense for this court to stay its hand in an LLC case and allow the contract itself to solve the problem.

Notably, this court's authority to order dissolution remains discretionary and may be influenced by the particular circumstances. Haley and Talcott created the LLC together and while the detailed exit provision provided in the formative

LLC Agreement allows either party to leave voluntarily, it provides no insight on who should retain the LLC if both parties would prefer to buy the other out, and neither party desires to leave. In and of itself, however, this lack of priority might not be found sufficient to require dissolution, because of a case-specific fact; namely, that Haley has proposed-as a member of the LLC-that the LLC's sole asset be sold. But I need not-and do not-determine how truly distinguishing that fact is, because forcing Haley to exercise the contractual exit mechanism would not permit the LLC to proceed in a practicable way that accords with the LLC Agreement, but would instead permit Talcott to penalize Haley without express contractual authorization.

Why? Because the parties agree that exit mechanism in the LLC Agreement would not relieve Haley of his obligation under the personal guaranty that he signed to secure the mortgage from County Bank. If Haley is forced to use the exit mechanism, Talcott and he both believe that Haley would still be left holding the bag on the guaranty. It is therefore not equitable to force Haley to use the exit mechanism in this circumstance. While the exit mechanism may be workable in a friendly departure when both parties cooperate to reach an adequate alternative agreement with the bank, the bank cannot be compelled to accept the removal of Haley as a personal guarantor. Thus, the exit mechanism fails as an adequate remedy for Haley because it does not equitably effect the separation of the parties. Rather, it would leave Haley with no upside potential, and no protection over the considerable downside risk that he would have to make good on any future default by the LLC (over whose operations he would have no control) to its mortgage lender. Thus here, unlike in *Surgical Services,* the parties do not, in fact, "have at their disposal a far less drastic means to resolve their personal disagreement."

For the reasons discussed above, I find that it is not reasonably practicable for the LLC to continue to carry on business in conformity with the LLC Agreement. The parties shall confer and, within four weeks, submit a plan for the dissolution of the LLC. The plan shall include a procedure to sell the Property owned by the LLC within a commercially reasonable time frame. Either party may, of course, bid on the Property.

IT IS SO ORDERED.

## 5. SUMMARY

An effective and workable buy-sell agreement requires considerable thought by the business owners and guidance from their legal advisor. The owners should be encouraged to spend sufficient time to think through and hash out the issues. A careful record should be kept of the decision points in the discussions so that the agreement can be periodically reviewed to see if the reasons for the various provisions remain or have changed. As time passes, circumstances will change that will necessitate revisions to the agreement.

## PROBLEMS 8-A THRU 8-C

**8-A.** Alton Inc. provides take-out laundry services to hospitals and healthcare providers in the Northwest. It is a C corporation with three shareholders, all of whom work full time for the business. The three owners have been "buddies and partners" since high school, but now they are all north of 40. The business has 80 employees and continual growth. The owners have decided that they need some kind of "buyout" agreement in case something happens to one of them. What "triggers" would you recommend be included in the shareholders buy-sell agreement? How would you suggest structuring each trigger?

**8-B.** Clint Wade owns 70 percent of the stock of Knock-Down Inc., a demolition and gravel supply company. The remaining 30 percent of the stock is owned in equal shares by three of the key managers of the business. The minority owners recently had their attorney draw up a "standard" buy-sell agreement to protect them in case one of them dies, retires, or wants out of the business. The agreement gives all the shareholders equal rights in the event of a triggering event. You represent Wade. How would you advise him?

**8-C.** Sports Limited owns a small chain of profitable sporting goods stores. The company has three shareholders: Sam, who owns 40 percent of the stock and does not work in the business; and Lewis and Jake, each of whom owns 30 percent of the stock and works in the business full-time. Sam is independently wealthy; his investment in the company represents a tiny portion of his wealth. Lewis and Jake have their company stock and their salaries and nothing else.

Sports Unlimited has a shareholder agreement that contains a standard right of first refusal provision and a showdown clause. The right of first refusal requires any shareholder who wants out to obtain a bid for his stock from a third party and then give the company or the remaining shareholders a first right to match the third-party offer. The showdown clause gives any shareholder the right to set a price for the stock and then force the other shareholders to elect to buy or sell at that price.

You represent Jake. Advise him on the wisdom of having these provisions in the agreement. What alternatives would you suggest?

## B. PROFESSIONAL SERVICE ORGANIZATIONS: TRANSITION PLANNING

### 1. INTRODUCTION

Professional service organizations are challenging clients. They differ from most other businesses in many ways. The owners are the key employees and the principal instruments of production. Often the business has few hard assets, but generates substantial incomes and supports a large overhead. The key players are usually well-educated, very independent, and have the flexibility to make a move if things aren't to their liking.

Most professional organizations are fragile. Their existence is tied to professional talent that can die, become disabled, or simply decide to walk out. A bruised ego can jeopardize the entire group. For the entity to survive, new blood must be recruited and trained; the talent needs to be replenished. Transitioning in and out of a professional organization is a challenge that has become more difficult. No longer are there one or two stock solutions that fit all groups. Most groups are unique and present specific issues that must be factored into the transition planning.

This section focuses on some of these transition planning issues by reviewing three case studies. Before getting into the case studies, the discussion reviews certain factors that have made the transition planning process more difficult. It then examines the three case studies to illustrate the scope of certain structural issues that need to be considered in different organizations. These case studies are referred to as the "Fragile Five," the "Mega-Sellout," and the "Too-High Buy-In."

## 2. WHY IT'S TOUGHER

Transition planning in professional organizations has become more difficult for a variety of reasons. There are a number of contributing factors; of course, not all apply to all types of professions.

One of the major factors is that the professional service corporation has been a popular target of Congress for a number of years. The 1980s were especially hard on professionals. TEFRA, the Tax Equity and Fiscal Responsibility Act of 1982, severely cut back retirement benefits and ushered in Section 269A of the Code – the provision that prevented a professional service corporation from claiming corporate tax benefits if all of its income came from a single entity. The 1986 Tax Reform Act further limited the benefits of the professional corporation. It reduced individual rates below corporate rates (for the first time in many decades); it further limited retirement planning options; it required that professional service corporations adopt a calendar year (or at least distribute earnings ratably over the calendar year); and it put an end to the General Utilities doctrine. The 1987 Act dealt another blow, wiping out the bracket advantage of accumulating corporate earnings in professional corporations. All of these changes, coupled with interest deduction limitations, complicated the process of phasing professionals in and out of organizations.

Factors in the marketplace also have aggravated the challenge for some groups. The income of many professionals has flattened, and if it hasn't yet flattened, there is a fear that it might. In some professions, market pressures have precluded or limited revenue increases, while overhead expenses have continued to build. It is more difficult for many professionals to enhance their bottom line by increasing the gap between revenues and expenses. Existing owners often feel that they can't afford to be as generous with a new partner, and the new partner is sensitive to the fact that his or her income may be under pressure from the start. All of this aggravates the situation.

Another factor is that the carrying value of accounts receivable in many professions has gone up. The accounts receivable asset usually is the major asset that drives the machine and pays the bills. An increase in the accounts receivable can inflate the buy-in purchase price of a new partner by many thousands of dollars. In many practices, more equity capital is required simply to carry the receivables. A number of factors may contribute to the receivables increase, including delayed payment from third-party payers.

A fourth factor that often aggravates the difficulty of the transition is the undertaking of a major real estate commitment by the group. Many groups have bought real estate to house their practices, or have entered into long-term, expensive lease arrangements. The arrangement represents a major commitment and must be addressed when a partner arrives or leaves. As the equity investment or the overhead burden increases, pressure on the new partner also increases, and the pressure to allow retiring partners to cash in their equity interests in the real estate compounds the problem.

A final factor is that, in many professions, there is strong competition for the best candidates. Often there is a real need to make the buy-in option look attractive to recruit the right candidate. If the buy-in price is too high or the cash flow requirements too burdensome, the candidate may look for another place to land.

Having focused on some of the troublesome factors in today's environment, let's turn to the three case studies. Although each of these cases involves a medical group, the principles and ideas discussed apply to any professional organization faced with a similar challenge. Also, each of the case studies involves a professional organization that operates as a professional service corporation, not as a partnership. However, most of the concepts and ideas would be directly applicable to any professional service entity that is taxed as a partnership.

### 3. CASE STUDY 1: THE FRAGILE FIVE

Physicians A and B have been practicing together for approximately seven years. They've been successful and have now decided to hook up with two other physicians, C and D. The four also have agreed to hire a fifth —Physician E. The five have come together. They are going to lease new space, upscale their image, and strengthen their base. They also are going to undertake some serious financial commitments.

Their concern is that their practice plan is tied to their ongoing involvement with one another. If one of them left the group, it would significantly increase the financial burdens of the other four. And if, by chance, two of them were to depart for any reason, the results could be disastrous. They've decided that there is no way that three of them could carry the capital and overhead structure that they are creating for five.

These anxieties are heightened by the fact that they've had limited experience with one another. Although they are very positive about their relationship, they know that it's fragile and untested. Their challenge is to structure an arrangement that will protect the individuals in the group. This situation is becoming more common as professionals link up with one another to strengthen their market position, consolidate their expertise, and spread their overhead. There are five items that the group may want to consider to address their anxieties.

**a. Secure Key Person Disaster Protection**. Death or disability can cause a major problem for a group such as this. Key person life and disability insurance is almost essential. This should not be confused with life insurance that is intended to cover buyout obligations or to provide needed cash to the disabled professional or to the family of the deceased professional. It's something additional; it's key person insurance that will be retained to protect the group – to cover overhead, finance the hiring of new physicians, or replace lost revenues.

**b. The Long-Term Exit Notice Provision**. The employment agreements and the related buy-sell agreement may impose a significant advance notice provision on any professional who elects to leave the group. In some cases, the provision may require as much as a year's advance notice. This will give the group and the remaining physicians time to adjust and make necessary changes. It eliminates the quick exit. Usually, it is advisable to provide that if a professional violates the provision and does not give the required notice, the professional is required to cover his or her share of the overhead for the remainder of the notice period. This is done by charging the physician's share of the receivables or the physician's equity interest in the venture with the amount of this overhead expenditure. This type of sanction usually ensures that the notice provision will be respected and followed.

**c. The "Lights-Out" Provision**. Often the lengthy advance notice provision is accompanied by a "lights-out" provision. Suppose the group has a one-year advance notice requirement. Dr. B gives notice. During the year, Dr. C gets nervous and also gives notice. Each of those two doctors has triggered a one-year exit plan. The lights-out scenario gives the other members of the group the opportunity to call everything off. If the others choose to do so, neither B nor C has the exit rights provided under the buy-sell agreement or their employment agreements. Instead, it is "lights-out" for the group and the entire entity goes into liquidation.

Although liquidation may sound severe, it can be a fair process for everyone involved. Everyone has to deal with the liabilities – the space, the employees and all other items. Usually, this results in everyone sharing the burden of making changes. Sometimes the changes amount to nothing more than dividing up the assets and the liabilities. In most situations, amounts must be paid to terminate the lease and fund severance payments to employees.

The lights-out scenario requires that everyone join in the effort and share the burden of shutting down the operation. If the remaining owners do not trigger the lights-out provision, each of the other professionals who gave notice is allowed to terminate his or her involvement at the end of the notice period in accordance with the terms of the employment and shareholder agreements.

**d. The Locked-in Equity Option**. Suppose the five physicians choose to buy a building or condominium space to house their practice. Over time they accumulate a substantial equity in this real estate. One of the professionals then chooses to leave the group. Do the others have to buy out the departing owner's equity in the real estate?

Often, it is advisable to include a special provision that does not require the others to buy out the equity at the time of departure. Instead, the group is given a period of time (sometimes as long as five years) before they have to trigger the purchase. In effect, the equity of the departing physician is locked in. That professional continues to receive any tax and cash flow benefits from ownership in the real estate. Also, if the real estate continues to appreciate during the deferral period, the departing professional shares in the appreciation. The benefit is that the remaining owners do not have to come up with cash or commence making payments at the time of the departure. They have a long period of time to trigger the acquisition of the interest. During the deferral period, they may recruit another professional who chooses to purchase the equity interest of the professional who has left the group.

  **e. The Early Transition Payment**. Some professional groups recognize at the outset that they would be hurt if one of them chose to leave early in the venture. They may feel differently after they have had a chance to stabilize and reap some of the benefits of their combined effort. What concerns them is the member who gets cold feet and chooses to jump ship early.

  A possible solution in this situation is to require a significant transition payment from any member who chooses to leave the group within a designated period of time. In effect, all the parties recognize up front that an early departure may trigger a significant financial burden for the others. So the financial burden is shifted to the one who chooses to leave. This provision may have two benefits. First, it will protect the others from having to assume the burden. Second, it will discourage anyone from leaving too soon. Sometimes this transition adjustment payment is coupled with a non-competition restriction.

  These are measures that the fragile five may want to consider. No doubt there are other options that could be considered. What is critical is that the parties focus on their mutual fears and plan to properly allocate the risks among themselves.

### 4. CASE STUDY 2: THE MEGA-SELLOUT

  Dr. Wright is a successful plastic surgeon. He is a solo practitioner. He nets about $1.4 million a year, and he's turning away business. He's 64 years old and wants to retire now. Dr. Wright has identified two surgeons who would like to take over his practice. They believe that they could transition his practice and, through their combined efforts, build the practice even more. Dr. Wright is ready to turn over the reins and disappear into the sunset. The big question: How is he going to get paid?

  This is the classic "mega-sellout" situation. The two new physicians have no significant resources at this time. They can't write Dr. Wright a check for the practice. Dr. Wright believes that his practice is worth many millions and wants to be paid approximately $500,000 a year for a long time. He figures that, based on existing volumes, this leaves over $900,000 of earnings for the other two. Plus, they have the upside potential.

  A traditional structure that is often used in these situations is a simple sellout. The two new physicians execute a note and give it to Dr. Wright, and he leaves as the big creditor. Principal and interest payments are made on a monthly basis. The two new doctors take over and work hard to make the payments and carve out a healthy income for themselves. There are some significant problems with this sellout approach, from the perspectives of both the buyers and the seller. The two new doctors have to undertake a substantial debt burden of $500,000 a year for a long time. They don't like the idea of being personally liable for millions of dollars. Such a huge debt may get in the way of other things they want to do, and there is no assurance that they will be able to make all the required payments.

There's also a tax problem for the new players. All payments of principal will have to be funded with after-tax dollars. That imposes a significant added burden on their cash flow. And there may be a serious question as to whether the interest payments that they make to Dr. Wright are deductible. If no portion of the $500,000 annual payment to Dr. Wright is deductible and the other owners are in a 35 percent marginal tax bracket, nearly $770,000 of earnings will be needed to fund an after-tax payment of $500,000.

The buyout scenario may also create concerns for Dr. Wright. He is relegated to the status of a creditor. If the new doctors run into trouble or don't make the payments, he's going to have to exercise his rights as a creditor to get back in control. This could be difficult in certain situations.

There's an alternative solution that may be more attractive in this mega-sellout case. In effect, there is no sellout. Instead, the professional service corporation makes an S election. Employment agreements are carefully structured with the two new physicians. They are given salaries based upon their maintenance of the existing productivity, and are given a substantial economic interest in any increased productivity. Dr. Wright remains the principal, and perhaps the sole, shareholder of the enterprise. He rides off into the sunset.

Normally, it makes little sense for a professional service corporation to make an S election. But this is one situation where the election makes sense. Dr. Wright will be able to continue to draw pre-tax earnings from the corporation while substantially reducing his services to the business. He will need to retain his professional license in order to continue to qualify as the shareholder. The payments that he receives for the rest of his life will come in the form of distributions with respect to his stock.

The obvious question is: When will the new shareholders become the real owners? This can happen at any time along the way. But in most cases, the preferred time will be at Dr. Wright's death. There are a couple of reasons for this. First, at his death there will be a step-up in the tax basis of his stock. So all amounts paid to his estate can be received income tax free. Second, the other two owners can fund the buyout by maintaining a policy on the life of Dr. Wright. Perhaps Dr. Wright can be convinced to use a portion of his annual $500,000 draw to fund the insurance policy that will ultimately be used to redeem his stock when he dies.

If the other two doctors want to acquire some stock along the way, they can do so. However, they may have little incentive to acquire any large blocks of stock prior to Dr. Wright's death. They will be receiving substantial incomes based, in large part, on their productivity and their ability to make the business grow. If they are concerned about control, special provisions can be inserted that allow them to serve on the board of directors after certain targets have been hit. It may even be possible to require, at some point in the future, that some or all of Dr. Wright's stock be converted to nonvoting common stock. The S election may be maintained even if there is nonvoting common stock.

Although Dr. Wright does not receive a promissory note in this situation, he may be better off as a practical matter. If the two doctors sputter and have a problem, he can easily step back in and take control. Remember, he's still the big owner and has the ultimate say in matters. He may actually be in a stronger control position under this scenario.

The big loser under this alternative is the government. No substantial after-tax payments are being made from one party to another. That can result in significant tax savings over a long period of time and allow the parties to create a win-win scenario among themselves. This S election phase-out scenario may be the answer in certain mega-sellout situations. Great care should be taken in analyzing the impact and timing of the election.

### 5. CASE STUDY 3: THE TOO-HIGH BUY-IN

Four doctors own equal shares of the stock of a professional service corporation known as Medical Services, Inc. The professional corporation has been structured to provide full equality for each of the owners – "full partnership," as they say. Among the owners, there is an equal sharing of patients, on-call duty, overhead, capital, and income.

The four doctors are also the sole partners of a partnership that owns the building in which they conduct their practice. The building partnership leases the land and the building to the professional corporation. The partnership has owned the building since early 1992, and the partners believe that the building has appreciated significantly over the years.

Dr. Roy has been an employee of the professional corporation for the past 18 months. During this time period, he has worked hard as an employee, has been paid a monthly salary, and has had an opportunity to review the operations and the practice. In turn, the other doctors have had an opportunity to review the work of Dr. Roy.

The doctors now agree that the time has come to admit Dr. Roy as a full owner, or "full partner," in the business. The parties, like numerous other professional corporations, are faced with the challenge of how best to accomplish the objective of getting Dr. Roy into the group. There are countless buy-in strategies that can be used. Nearly all of the strategies fall into one or two general modes – the "full cost" mode or the "sweat equity" mode.

When the "full cost" mode is used, the new partner is required to pay a designated sum for his or her share of the equity of the practice. Receivables, equipment, real estate and, if appropriate, goodwill are valued, and a price is set. In very rare cases, the new owner pays the price up front. In the usual situation, the price is financed by the other owners over a period of years. So the new partner makes monthly or quarterly payments of principal and interest to the existing professionals or the entity over a designated time frame.

In contrast, the "sweat equity" mode is usually less direct. When this approach is used in its purest form, the new partner never really has to pay a designated amount for the equity up front, nor is the owner required to finance the designated amount over a period of years. Instead, the new owner agrees to take less income, usually expressed as a percentage, over a number of years. So up front the parties really don't know how much the buy-in will ultimately cost the new owner, because no one really knows how much income the new owner will forego in the future. The approach tends to spread out the cash flow burden of the buy-in because the new partner knows that, even in lean times, the lion's share of his or her draw will not be used to cover a fixed buy-in cost.

Often, buy-in strategies represent a hybrid of both modes. For example, in some situations the parties treat all the assets except accounts receivable under the "full cost" mode, while the new partner phases in to a full share of the receivables by taking a reduced income share under the "sweat equity" mode.

In many groups, neither mode works very well. This is a tough situation and is becoming more common. The new partner simply feels that the buy-in price under either mode is too high. The existing partners believe that their equity in the practice is significant, and they don't want to give it away. This is the problem that Medical Services, Inc. is facing. First, let's look at the building partnership.

The building partnership was 100 percent leveraged in 1992. The current outstanding mortgage on the building is $1.5 million. The partnership's tax basis in the land and building is $980,000, which is less than the outstanding mortgage balance. Based on a recent appraisal, the four existing partners believe that the land and the building have a current value of approximately $3.2 million. They believe that their combined equity in the building partnership is roughly $1.7 million – the difference between the fair market value and the existing mortgage.

Their professional service corporation has no significant liabilities. Its assets consist of cash of $50,000, furniture and equipment of approximately $350,000, and accounts receivable of $1.2 million. So the total assets, including the receivables, have a value of approximately $1.6 million. The professional corporation is a cash-basis taxpayer, so no income taxes have yet been paid on the receivables that are on the books.

The existing owners believe that Dr. Roy will be a valuable addition to the group, and they want to accommodate him in every way possible. They want to make certain, however, that Dr. Roy pays for any equity interest that he receives as a partner in the venture. In contrast, Dr. Roy is concerned about the cost of his equity contribution. If Dr. Roy pays for a full one-fifth interest in the building at its presumed equity value of $1.7 million, the cost could be as high as $340,000 – that is, one-fifth of the present equity in the building. The existing partners believe that the asset value of the professional service corporation, excluding any goodwill but including the accounts receivable, is $1.6 million. This is the sum of the cash, the basis of the furniture and equipment, and the face value amount of the receivables. One-fifth of this amount is $320,000. Thus, the total cost of

Dr. Roy's one-fifth interest in both of these entities could be as high as $660,000.

On the basis of these numbers, the four doctors have offered to sell Dr. Roy a one-fifth interest in the professional service corporation for $320,000, and a full one-fifth interest in the building partnership for $340,000. They have agreed to finance this buy-in over an eight-year period. They have pointed out to Dr. Roy that he is not being charged for any goodwill or going concern value of the professional corporation. The partners have also correctly pointed out that their suggested approach – a "full cost" approach – has been used by many other groups.

From Dr. Roy's perspective, the offer is troublesome for a number of reasons. First, how can he be sure that the land and building really have a value of $3.2 million? Appraisals can be wrong. Moreover, the building is not being held by the partnership as an investment asset that will be sold at the most opportune time. The parties intend to practice in the building indefinitely. Dr. Roy is concerned that the existing appraised value of $3.2 million is inflated, and that this value could actually drop at some point down the road. Should he have to run the risk of such a loss based on one appraisal?

Second, Dr. Roy is troubled about the receivables, valued at $1.2 million. Over the past 18 months, he has helped build this receivables base. Should he now have to purchase what he has helped build? The other doctors are quick to point out that he has been paid well for his efforts during the past 18 months and that, as the owners, they're the ones who really own the receivables. Also, Dr. Roy is disturbed that the receivables really represent a pre-tax deferred earnings amount. As they are collected, taxes will need to be paid on them. He correctly points out that their value should at least be reduced by the taxes that will be paid as they are collected.

Third, the tax aspects of the proposed transaction are disturbing from Dr. Roy's perspective. All principal payments made by Dr. Roy for the cost of the partnership interest and the stock in the corporation (a total of $660,000) will be paid with after-tax dollars. This payment structure, which is popular among sellers, is a tax-inefficient way to transfer dollars between parties. The payer, Dr. Roy, gets no tax deduction for the payments, and the recipient must pay tax on all income received, capital gains or otherwise.

Finally, like so many professionals in similar situations, Dr. Roy simply feels that the total amount ($660,000) is unbearable. It will take a huge chunk out of his after-tax income for the next eight years. At this price, he is tempted to shop for another opportunity.

The parties recognize that they have a challenge that is faced by many professional organizations today. How can they attract and admit the needed newcomer as a full partner without giving away the shop – the equity of the existing partners? Here are some of the strategies that Dr. Roy and his new colleagues might consider to help in resolve their situation.

First, with respect to the building partnership equity valued at $1.7 million, the answer might be a "tiered equity" structure in the partnership. Although the existing partners believe their present equity is $1.7 million, Dr. Roy is reluctant to pony up cash based on this value. The compromise is to structure the partnership so the first $1.7 million of equity – the first tier – is reserved for the existing four partners if and when it is realized. Dr. Roy makes no capital contribution now, but is only entitled to one-fifth of the equity realized in excess of $1.7 million. Thus, he has no interest in the first $1.7 million of equity. The equity in excess of $1.7 million is now known as the "second tier." All partners, including Dr. Roy, share equally in current rents, expenses, and profits and losses. Only the equity of the partnership is tiered. Such a structure usually raises a host of questions, including the following:

**First question:** What happens if the land and building are refinanced down the road at a higher amount? Additional monies are borrowed against the asset. The cash generated from this refinancing is first used to pay off the first tier – the first $1.7 million. For example, if in two years the partners refinance the building for $2.5 million and pay off the existing mortgage of $1.5 million, the remaining $1 million would be distributed to the existing four partners and would reduce the first tier of the equity from $1.7 million to $700,000. This would be a permanent reduction.

**Second question:** What happens if the land and building are sold down the road at a price of less than $3.2 million? In this situation, there would not be enough funds to cover the first tier, assuming no refinancing. All available funds would be used to pay the existing partners. Dr. Roy would receive nothing. The rationale is that Dr. Roy has paid nothing for the existing equity.

**Third question:** What happens if the land and building are sold down the road for more than their present value, say for as much as $4 million? In this situation, the first available proceeds from the sale would be used to pay off the balance of the first tier. The remaining proceeds would be used to pay off the second tier partners, which would include Dr. Roy. He would be entitled to one-fifth of all amounts realized in the second tier, which would be everything left after the first tier had been paid off.

**Fourth question**: What happens if another new partner is admitted two years down the road? In this situation, the parties would create a third tier. For example, if the equity in the partnership grows from $1.7 million to $2 million and the entire first tier remains, the first tier would have a balance of $1.7 million, and the second tier would have a balance of $300,000. Dr. Roy would fully participate in the second tier, but the new doctor would not. The new doctor would participate only in the equity that is allocated to the third tier, which would then be divided six ways.

**Fifth Question**: Isn't this structure simply too complicated? Not really, because the tiered equity structure does not affect the month-to-month operations of the building partnership or the rent structure. It only comes into play when a new partner is admitted, when a partner leaves, or when the land and building are refinanced or sold. It is something that an accountant can easily account for and track. It does require that the partners focus on the value of the asset at the time a partner is admitted or leaves, but this is a task that would generally be required in any event.

**Sixth Question**: What effect does this tiered equity structure have on a partner who leaves the partnership? Normally, that partner's interest in each of the tiers is bought out by all of the remaining partners. For example, if one of the original four partners terminates his interest in the partnership, all of the existing partners would participate in the acquisition of that partner's interest in the first tier and any additional tiers that may have been created.

**Seventh Question**: Is such a tiered equity structure legal? That is, can the provisions of the partnership agreement be drawn so that the partners have equal interests in the profits, losses and expenses of the partnership, but have different equity levels in the partnership? The answer is "yes," so long as the provisions of the partnership agreement are carefully drafted in accordance with the regulations promulgated under Section 704(b) of the Internal Revenue Code by one who understands those regulations. It is beyond the scope of this discussion to explain the intricacies of the regulations. Suffice it to say, the job can be done.

The next issue for the group involves the professional service corporation, Medical Services, Inc. The parties have to face the issue of the receivables. Dr. Roy does not like the idea of buying corporate stock with after-tax dollars when the value of the stock is based principally upon the receivables owned by the practice. Here are some suggested strategies that the parties may want to consider in resolving this issue:

**Strategy No. 1**. First, in order to address Dr. Roy's concern that he is really being asked to buy an interest in receivables that he helped generate, it might be helpful to ascertain the total receivables balance at the time Dr. Roy was first hired. This is the "Date of Hire" receivables balance. Suppose in our situation, for example, that the Date of Hire receivables balance was $900,000. This would mean that the total receivables had increased $300,000 during the term of Dr. Roy's employment. By focusing on the Date of Hire receivables balance, Dr. Roy would not be required to purchase any interest in the growth that occurred during the term of his employment. In some situations, this adjustment helps immensely during the negotiation process. This is an important point that can be stressed in recruiting Dr. Roy and other new physicians.

**Strategy No. 2**. Steps can easily be taken to structure Dr. Roy's buy-in of the receivables with pre-tax dollars rather than after-tax dollars. This can help the situation significantly because it essentially reduces Dr. Roy's up-front buy-in costs by the tax savings, which may be as high as 35 percent. How is this pre-tax buy-in of the receivables structured? The concept is logical and capable of being clearly understood by all. The mechanics can be a bit complicated.

To accomplish this task, the professionals essentially realize that the accounts receivable in the practice represent deferred earnings that have been generated from their efforts in the practice. The employment agreement between each of the doctors and the professional corporation recognizes this fact, and is structured to provide that each doctor, upon leaving the professional corporation, will be paid his or her share of these receivables as compensation payments following the departure ("exit payments"). Dr. Roy, as a full owner, would receive the same benefit in his employment contract. As consideration for this right to receive the exit payments and in recognition of the fact that Dr. Roy has only recently joined the party, Dr. Roy would agree to a reduction in his regular compensation over the next few years in an aggregate amount equal to his share of the receivables base – either the Date of Hire receivables base or the Date of Admission receivables base, whichever the parties choose.

Let's illustrate this point. Assume the parties elect to use the Date of Hire base of receivables of $900,000. Dr. Roy would agree to reduce his regular compensation over the next four years in an amount equal to his one-fifth share of this $900,000, or $180,000. This pay reduction, in essence, is his form of buy-in. Over four years, this would amount to a $45,000 per year reduction in the pre-tax income that is paid to Dr. Roy by the corporation. All of this would be pre-tax, which has a real benefit for Dr. Roy. This pay reduction would generate more for the other owners, all taxable as compensation. Great care should be taken to ensure compliance with the requirements of the new Section 409A of the Code. See related discussion in Chapter 10.

This structure substantially reduces the stock price to Dr. Roy. By entering into a compensation contract with all five doctors, the corporation has created a deferred liability which at all times should equal its receivable balance. The effect, in our example, is that the receivable balance is removed from the equity of the corporation in computing the stock value. Thus, in our example, the net asset equity of the corporation is represented only by the cash, furniture and fixtures, a total of $400,000. Dr. Roy's one-fifth share of this amount would be $80,000. Thus, the price of Dr. Roy's stock, to be paid with after-tax dollars, would have been reduced to $80,000. Financed over five years with a stated interest factor, this would be a highly acceptable result in any situation.

**Strategy No. 3**. There is another alternative for dealing with the receivables. If the goal is to lighten Dr. Roy's load up front and still preserve the equity of the existing owners, a tiered structure could be established for the receivables. The concept is very similar to the tiered equity for the building, but the mechanics are substantially different. Let's illustrate.

Suppose still that the parties have agreed to focus only on the Date of Hire receivables balance of $900,000. To establish the first tier, each of the existing owners would have an employment contract that gives him or her a deferred compensation benefit equal to his or her full one-fourth share of the first $900,000 of receivables, plus a one-fifth share of any receivables in excess of $900,000. Dr. Roy's employment contract would be a bit different because it would give him only a deferred compensation benefit equal to one-fifth of the receivable balance in excess of $900,000. Dr. Roy up front would have no interest in the first $900,000 of receivables. He would take no pay reduction, nor would the receivable balance be factored into the value of the stock. All he would pay for his stock would be $80,000 based on his one-fifth share of the net asset value of the cash, furniture, and equipment. Out of the box, Dr. Roy would get the same full earnings as the other doctors; but if he decided to leave the organization, he would not participate in the first tier of the receivables – that $900,000. The result for Dr. Roy would be a substantially reduced buy-in cost up front. If he outlasts the existing owners and the organization perpetuates itself, he will help fund the exit compensation payments to the other partners over lengthy intervals down the road as each of them leaves. This may be a far less painful way of funding his share of the receivables as opposed to having him take a pay reduction over the next four years.

When this tiered equity approach is used with accounts receivable, it usually generates a number of questions. An obvious one is: Will Dr. Roy ever acquire an interest in the first tier of the receivables, the first $900,000 in our example? The answer is "yes," but the buy-in will not occur until one or more of the existing partners leaves the group. As an existing partner leaves, the remaining partners, including Dr. Roy, will buy out the partner's interest in the form of pre-tax compensation payments. Thus, Dr. Roy then will begin acquiring an interest in the first tier of the receivables. After all of the existing partners have retired and left, Dr. Roy will have a full interest in the first tier of the receivables. Presumably, other doctors will have been hired to assist in the buyout of the original four physicians.

Second question: What effect does this receivables tiered equity structure have on a retiring partner? The answer to this one is simple. It entitles the retiring partner to receive more at the time he or she leaves. More is paid at retirement because the partner retained his or her full interest in the first tier. This is one of the positive aspects of the tiered structure. Instead of receiving a few more dollars while practicing, the retiring owner receives greater payments at retirement when he or she may be in greater need of an income stream. This can be particularly helpful in those situations where a retiring physician wants to phase down, pay a smaller share of the overhead, and receive a reduced income. If that partner has a significantly enhanced equity interest in the receivables, the payout of that interest can be used to facilitate a phase-out. Thus, the tiered structure, in addition to accommodating the admission of new partners, may facilitate the exit of seasoned partners.

There's another question that may be raised in connection with this tiered structure. If the new partner doesn't have an interest in the first tier of the receivables, is he or she nevertheless entitled to receive a full share of the cash flow of the practice? The answer to this question is "yes." In our example, Dr. Roy would be entitled to receive the income on the same basis as the other doctors. The only difference is that at the time he leaves, he would not be entitled to receive a payment for the existing receivables of the business in the same amount as the other partners. His exit compensation benefit would be based only on his interest in the receivables.

What effect will these strategies in combination have on Dr. Roy's buy-in? Let's assume the parties elect to go with the tiered equity structure in the building partnership, use the Date of Hire receivables basis for the receivables, and use the current pay reduction strategy for funding Dr. Roy's buy-in. With this approach, we're assuming that the tiered equity structure is not used with the receivables, only with the building. In this set of circumstances, Dr. Roy would pay $80,000 after tax for his interest in the stock, roughly $180,000 in pre-tax reduced earnings over a period of years for his interest in the Date of Hire receivables, and nothing for his tiered equity interest in the building. All this could be paid over a term of years with an interest factor if the parties desire. This is a far cry from paying $660,000 with after-tax dollars. And the existing owners, while clearly accommodating Dr. Roy, have not given away the shop. In time, they will receive their equity interests when they exit the building partnership and the professional corporation.

As an alternative, let's suppose the parties elect the tiered equity structure for both the building partnership and the receivables. In this situation, Dr. Roy would have a total after-tax buy-in price of $80,000 for the stock. That's all he has to pay up front. He would be paid income on the same basis as the other doctors out of the box. For the privilege of having this substantially reduced buy-in up front, Dr. Roy would have no interest in the first $1.7 million of the building equity and no interest in the first $900,000 of the receivables in the corporation. These amounts would be reserved for the existing owners, who in time would receive priority payments represented by these amounts.

## PROBLEM 8-D

**8-D.** Linda is a doctor who has worked for a well-respected clinic for the last two years. The clinic is a professional service corporation, operated as a C corporation. She has now been offered an equal ownership interest in the C corporation and a limited liability company that owns the office real estate in which the clinic is operated. The buy-in price for the privilege of becoming an owner "blew her away." The C corporation buy-in is $300,000, of which $200,000 is attributable to untaxed account receivables. The LLC buy-in, set at $350,000, is based on a current appraisal. Although the existing three owners financed the construction of the entire facility with long-term debt four years ago, the current appraisal now shows that the equity in the facility (the excess of the fair market value over the mortgage debt) has appreciated to $1.4 million. Linda needs some help. What options would you suggest?

## C. FUNDING BUY-SELL AGREEMENTS

### 1. INTRODUCTION

Funding the obligations under a buy-sell agreement is always a challenge. The method used to come up with the cash to buy out the departing owner obviously can have significant tax and liquidity consequences. If the funding strategy is not carefully planned and implemented, the consequences can adversely affect the business.

This section identifies and reviews seven strategies for funding buy-sell agreements. In selecting the best combination of strategies, each potential strategy should be weighed and evaluated against the following four criteria:

(1) Does the strategy create needed liquidity for the departing owner or his or her family on an acceptable schedule?

(2) Does the strategy offer financial security to the departing owner – certainty that the cash will be paid when due?

(3) Does the strategy minimize the risk that the payments to the departing

owner or his or her family will jeopardize the financial stability of the company or the remaining owners?

(4) Does the strategy minimize the tax cost of generating and paying the required cash to the departing owner?

## 2. THE STRATEGIES

### a. Strategy One:  Earnings Accumulations

The first funding strategy is the least complicated.  The company "saves" for the future by accumulating earnings within the business.  Although this often appears to be a safe, conservative approach, it has its problems.  First, an event triggering a purchase under the buy-sell agreement may occur before enough cash has been accumulated.  Most businesses can't predict the death of their owners.  One of the owners might die within months of signing the agreement, creating a sizeable purchase obligation.

Second, most businesses need their cash to finance internal operations and capital expansion.  Few have the luxury of being able to accumulate large sums of cash to cover contingent events.   And those few businesses that have substantial cash flows are typically under pressure from owners to distribute the surplus cash.  So two of the four criteria in funding buy-sell agreements are not met with this approach.  The right of the departing owner to receive the payment is not secure, and the payment obligation may jeopardize the financial security of the purchaser.

The third significant disadvantage is that cash accumulations are after-tax dollars.  The tax burden is enhanced in a C corporation by the threat of the accumulated earnings tax.  This is a tax on excess earnings accumulated within the corporation.[19]  The purpose of the tax is to force C corporations to distribute excess earnings as dividends.  The tax is not imposed on earnings accumulations up to $250,000 ($150,000 for personal service corporations), and that number may be higher if the company can demonstrate that the reasonable business needs of the company require additional accumulations.  The accumulated earnings tax puts a cap on the amount of earnings that a C corporation can accumulate.

There is no conclusive legal authority that funding a shareholder buyout is a reasonable business need for purposes of the accumulated earnings tax.  Case authority suggests that accumulations to redeem stock of a dissenting minority stockholder usually will be deemed a reasonable business need.[20]  However, accumulations to redeem the stock of a friendly minority shareholder or a majority shareholder may be viewed as benefiting the shareholder rather than the corporation and, therefore, may be subject to the accumulated earnings tax.[21]

The accumulation of earnings strategy often is the last resort method for

---

19. See generally I.R.C. §§ 531-537.

20. See, e.g., Mountain State Steel Foundries, Inc. v. Commissioner, 284 F.2d 737 (4th Cir. 1960); Wilcox Manufacturing Co. v. Commissioner, 38 T.C.M. 378 (1979).

21. See, e.g., John B. Lambert & Associates v. United States, 212 Ct. Cl. 71 (1976); Lamark Shipping Agency, Inc. v. Commissioner, 42 T.C.M. 38 (1981).

funding buy-sell agreements. Typically, it is used when no other method is feasible or as a supplement to other methods.

### b. Strategy Two: Death Benefit Insurance

The second strategy is death benefit insurance. Perhaps the most effective means of funding a buyout is with insurance, both life insurance and, where appropriate, disability insurance. The primary advantage of the death benefit insurance strategy is that it enables the beneficiary of the policy – the company or the other owners – to make a large cash payment to the heirs of the deceased who was the insured under the policy. When the buyout trigger is an event other than death or disability, often the departing owner's need for liquidity is less critical. The death benefit insurance strategy needs to be coordinated with one or more other strategies that will fund the departing owner's buyout over time if the triggering event is something other than death.

When life insurance protection is considered in the context of a private business, it's important to identify for everyone the specific objective of the insurance. Usually there are three basic, competing objectives, any one or more of which may be the purpose for obtaining insurance in a particular case. One of those objectives is to provide a perk for an employee. The second objective is key person insurance, often necessary to protect the interests of the business in the event of the death of a key employee. The third objective is to provide liquidity for the buyout of a departing owner. The need for insurance to meet the other two objectives should not be the factor that drives the selection of the funding strategy of the buy-sell agreement. In some situations a company will unreasonably inflate the redemption price of stock if an owner dies in order to justify the purchase of large amounts of insurance for a shareholder. This confuses the objectives for purchasing the insurance. Keep the buy-sell objective separate from the key-person and employee-perk objectives. The amount of life insurance available to the corporation to fund a redemption obligation under a buy-sell agreement should be based upon the actual value of the stock, not the shareholder's need for cash. If the shareholder needs cash, there are other, more tax-efficient methods of providing that cash through life insurance or non-insurance vehicles.

From an income tax perspective, the premiums paid by a corporation on a policy that it owns to fund a buyout are not deductible. The flip side is that the proceeds received on the death of the owner are tax-free.[22]

The decision to use insurance to fund a buyout must be coordinated with the decision to structure the transaction as a redemption by the company or a cross-purchase by other shareholders. Insurance can be used as a funding mechanism with either structure, but the consequences vary substantially. In deciding whether to use a cross-purchase or a redemption approach where death benefit insurance is the funding mechanism, four factors should be considered: (1) the

---

22. The exception, of course, is if the entity is a C corporation that is large enough to be subject to the alternative minimum tax and the receipt of the life insurance proceeds triggers an AMT exposure. See I.R.C. §§ 55(a)(1)(B), 55(e), 56(g).

number of shareholders involved; (2) the transfer-for-value issue and the problems it might present; (3) who will pay and bear the economic burden of the premiums; and (4) potential AMT problems.

How does the number of shareholders impact the decision? If a cross-purchase arrangement is used among many shareholders of a corporation, each of the shareholders will be required to own a policy on each of the other shareholders. This can be cumbersome and complicated if there are more than a few shareholders. If there are 10 shareholders, for example, each of the 10 shareholders will have an insurance policy, or an interest in a policy, on the life of each of the other nine, resulting in a total of 90 separate policies or interests in policies. That may prove to be an intolerable administrative burden.

A problem related to the number of shareholders is the transfer-for-value rule. This rule provides that, unless an exception applies, any transfer of a life insurance policy for value will destroy the tax-free death benefit.[23] The proceeds of the policy, when paid, will be taxable to the recipient. Consider again the cross-purchase arrangement where there are 10 shareholders. Upon the death or departure of one of the shareholders, that shareholder will have to dispose of the policies that he or she owns on the others, either in the form of a sale or a cancellation of the policies. If a policy is sold to the other shareholders, the sale constitutes a transfer-for-value with the result that the proceeds, when received by those other shareholders, are fully taxable. This can be a disastrous outcome.

The only alternative for avoiding the transfer-for-value taint is to sell the policies to the corporation. There is a specific exception in the transfer-for-value rules for transfers of policies to the corporation of which the insured is a shareholder.[24] There is not a similar exception for transfers of life insurance policies between co-shareholders. If the policies are transferred to the corporation as ownership changes, the buyout structure gradually will phase out of a cross-purchase structure and into a redemption structure. This may not be the desired result.

No similar disadvantage applies to partnerships. A partner may sell to other partners a life insurance policy on the life of a partner without a transfer-for-value problem. The sale is exempt from the transfer-for-value rule, and thus the proceeds will not trigger an income tax even though the policy has been transferred among partners.[25] This partnership transfer-for-value exception may be helpful in transferring life insurance policies used in a corporate buy-sell structure if the shareholders also are partners in an unrelated partnership. The fact that they also are partners will permit them to transfer life insurance policies among themselves without running afoul of the transfer-for-value rule.

Some believe that a trust can be used in a cross-purchase situation with multiple shareholders to avoid the transfer-for-value rule. The concept is that a trust is set up to own the policies on each of the shareholders. When one

---

23. I.R.C. § 101(a)(2).
24. I.R.C. § 101(a)(2)(B).
25. I.R.C. § 101(a)(2)(B).

shareholder departs, the trust continues to own the policy; when a new shareholder comes in, that shareholder has the benefit of the insurance protection owned by the trust. Although there is no concrete legal authority, there is a risk that this trust approach will still create a transfer-for-value problem. The transfer-for-value rule applies to any transfer of a policy "by assignment or otherwise."[26] When a trust is used, the beneficiaries of the trust change as shareholders come and go. This may be viewed as an indirect transfer of the policy, subject to the transfer-for-value rule. Another potential tax problem of using a trust is that the insurance proceeds will probably be included in the insured's estate for federal estate tax purposes.[27]

The third factor that affects the cross-purchase insurance versus redemption insurance approach is whether there are large differences in the percentage interests of the various shareholders. An extreme example would be a corporation owned by two shareholders, one owning 90 percent and the other owning 10 percent of the outstanding stock. If a cross-purchase arrangement is funded with life insurance, the 10 percent shareholder would need enough insurance to fund the buyout of 90 percent of the stock. The 90 percent shareholder would only need enough insurance to buy out 10 percent of the stock. The 10 percent shareholder may struggle trying to fund the premiums on such a large insurance policy.

On the other hand, if the corporation acquires the insurance in anticipation of a corporate redemption, then the 90 percent stockholder will bear 90 percent of the financial burden of the premiums. This may solve the cash flow problem for the minority shareholder, but it may not represent what the parties really intend. In some situations, the parties will want to structure the arrangement so that the entire financial burden of the insurance is allocated pro rata according to the parties' respective stockholder interests. In other situations, the parties will want to structure the premium burdens so that the shareholder who benefits from a particular policy must bear the premium burden associated with that policy. One possible way of dealing with the discrepancy, depending upon the objectives of the parties, is to make adjustments through compensation payments to the owners. What is important is that the parties decide how they want the financial burden of the insurance premiums to be allocated among the respective shareholders, and then come up with a structure that accomplishes that objective.

The fourth factor to be considered in the cross-purchase versus redemption decision relates to C corporations with average gross receipts in excess of $7.5 million. Such companies must treat as alternative minimum taxable income (AMTI) as much as 75 percent of the excess of book income over taxable income.[28] When a C corporation subject to AMT receives life insurance proceeds on the death of a shareholder, the excess of those proceeds over the cash value of the policy constitutes book income but not taxable income, and 75 percent of that amount will be added to the corporation's AMTI. This AMT

---

26. Reg. § 101-1(b)(1).
27. This is the position taken by the Service in TAM 9349002.
28. I.R.C. § 56(g).

burden can substantially decrease the attractiveness of the redemption approach for all but the smallest C corporations when life insurance is the sole or major funding vehicle. This factor alone may require use of a cross-purchase structure in some situations. Smaller C corporations, S corporations and partnerships are not subject to AMT.

### c. Strategy Three: Cash Value Insurance

The one shortfall of death benefit insurance as a funding strategy is that it provides liquidity only on the death of a shareholder. In many cases, it may be prudent to use cash value insurance as the funding vehicle because it may provide cash via policy loans for other triggering events. In the case of C corporations, keep in mind that cash accumulations within the policy are subject to the same accumulated earnings tax consideration that applies to cash accumulations in any investment medium. Also, they will produce differences in book and tax income that may trigger AMT. However, the amount of income buildup within the policy in any year may be within the AMT exemption; if so, there may not be any AMT consequences until the insured shareholder dies. Also, remember that Section 264 limits the amount of interest that a corporation can deduct on amounts borrowed on a policy that insures a shareholder or executive. The limitation is the interest on loans up to $50,000.[29] This interest deduction limitation can be a serious impediment if there is any intention of borrowing from the policies in order to fund payments before death.

The cash value insurance option is an accumulated savings program. It carries with it all of the limitations of any accumulated savings program, the most significant of which is that the premiums must be funded with after-tax dollars. A benefit of accumulating dollars within the insurance contract is that the income buildup on the accumulation is tax-deferred.

### d. Strategy Four: Split-Dollar Insurance Funding

A life insurance arrangement that offers some unique solutions to the buy-sell funding challenge is the split-dollar arrangement. Split-dollar insurance is another situation where the three purposes of life insurance in a private business context can become confused. The primary advantage of a split-dollar arrangement is the perk that it provides to a shareholder/employee in the form of relatively inexpensive death benefit insurance. But a collateral benefit is that it can provide a means for a corporation to accumulate funds for the redemption of stock of a shareholder who departs for any reason, including death. Usually the benefits of using split-dollar insurance to fund a buyout are not compelling if the client's only objective is to fund the buyout. To justify the expense to the company, typically there also must be an objective to provide an insurance perk to the executive.

In its simplest form, the split-dollar agreement requires the company to pay the portion of the premium equal to the yearly increase in the cash surrender value of the policy. The employee pays the balance of the premium. When the

---

29. I.R.C. §§ 264(a)(4), 264(e)(1).

employee dies, the company receives a portion of the insurance proceeds equal to the total amount of premiums paid by the company or the policy's cash surrender value immediately before the employee's death. The balance of the proceeds is paid to the employee's designated beneficiary as a death benefit under the policy. The company ultimately gets its cash back. A common variation on the funding of a policy is for the company to pay the entire premium.

The tax impact to the employee during the life of the split-dollar contract depends on who actually owns the policy. If the employee/shareholder owns the policy with a collateral assignment back to the company of its rights in the policy, the premiums paid by the company will be taxed as a below-market loan to the employee/shareholder, with compensation being imputed to the employee and an interest payment being imputed from the employee to the corporation.[30] If the corporation owns the policy with an endorsement that reflects the employee/shareholder's rights, the employee/shareholder will be deemed to have been paid compensation each year in an amount equal to the excess of the value of the death benefit over the amount paid by the employee/shareholder.[31] The company gets a corresponding deduction.

Here's how a split-dollar arrangement might work in the context of a buy-sell agreement. Consider Ed, a one-third shareholder of a small corporation. An $800,000 whole life insurance policy is purchased on Ed's life by the corporation. The corporation pays all the premiums, and Ed is taxed on the value of the insurance benefit each year. Ed dies at the time the cash value of the policy is $200,000. Assume Ed's stock at that time is worth $1 million.

Ed's estate is the beneficiary of the $800,000 life insurance death benefit, reduced by the $200,000 cash value portion paid to the corporation. The corporation redeems Ed's stock upon his death, as required under the buy-sell agreement. The corporation pays the $200,000 it received under the policy to Ed's estate as a down payment.

The $800,000 balance of the redemption price owing to Ed is paid in the form of a 10-year installment note, including a reasonable rate of interest. Ed's estate ends up with a $600,000 insurance death benefit, thus meeting the liquidity needs of his family. His family also gets from the corporation a $200,000 down payment for his stock and a payment of $80,000 plus interest each year for the next 10 years. The corporation has met its redemption obligations without an immediate impact on its cash flow.

A disadvantage of using a split-dollar arrangement is that the death benefit portion of the insurance – the amount payable to Ed's family – does not reduce the purchase price of the stock. The proceeds belong to Ed's family, not the corporation. The existence of the death benefit could possibly be taken into account by the shareholders in fixing the redemption price, but it cannot be deemed to be a payment of that price. As noted earlier, this death benefit really has to be viewed primarily as a perk to Ed, and not as a solution to the buy-sell

---

30. Reg. § 1.7872-15(e)(4) & (5).
31. Reg. § 1.61-22(d)(1).

funding issue.

### e. Strategy Five:  Installment Purchase

On the opposite end of the spectrum from insurance funding is the installment purchase.  It's really not funding at all.  Under this method the corporation, the remaining owners, or a combination of both become debtors of the departing shareholder or his or her estate.  The advantage of this strategy is that it eliminates the problem of accumulating funds to acquire the ownership interest in advance, either by purchasing life insurance or by saving earnings.  The disadvantage is that it provides no immediate liquidity to the departing owner or his or her estate.  It is the most insecure strategy from the perspective of the departing owner.

Since cash liquidity may become a critical issue on the untimely death of a shareholder, it is often advisable to fund the death buyout with insurance and rely on the installment method to fund buyouts triggered by other events, such as termination, withdrawal, divorce, or bankruptcy.  This combination of funding methods can be effective in keeping the costs down and in providing liquidity at the time it is most needed.

The mechanics of an installment buyout are simple.  If the buyout is structured as a redemption the corporation purchases the stock of the departing shareholder in exchange for a promissory note or a combination of cash and a promissory note.  The note allows the corporation to pay the purchase price out of future earnings.  The installment buyout can also be used to fund a cross-purchase.  There, the remaining shareholders purchase the stock of the departed shareholder in exchange for promissory notes, or a combination of cash and notes.  An added complexity in a cross-purchase situation (and it can be huge) is that the remaining shareholders must devise a way to get money out of the corporation if corporate funds are needed to make the payments under the note.  This may create a double tax problem for the shareholders of a C corporation unless the needed funds can be bailed out as compensation.

The obvious disadvantage to the installment purchase is that it will drain future earnings of the company in the case of any significant buyout. To the extent that the obligation can be pre-funded through the use of a cash value insurance policy or some other mechanism, this future burden is reduced. Another method of dealing with a possible down cycle is to permit the company to defer payment of a specified number of installments under the note if specific deteriorating financial benchmarks are hit.

Usually, an installment purchase is secured by a pledge of the stock that is being purchased. Occasionally, the agreement will call for the personal guarantee of the other owners.  The security of the installment note should be considered. Otherwise, it will be an unsecured obligation of the business, its other owners, or both.  This may not adequately protect the interests of a departing owner or his or her family.  In some circumstances, the owners may want to avoid any personal obligation on the part of other shareholders.  They may agree that if the company itself cannot provide the cash flow to fund the buyout, the other individual owners should not have to suffer individually for the buyout.

There are a few important planning points to consider in advising business owners regarding an installment buyout. With an installment purchase, a portion of each payment is going to be interest. That's usually a large portion if the payments are spread over a significant period. Whether that interest is tax deductible by the payer may have a significant impact in structuring the arrangement. If it is deductible, it will significantly decrease the overall after-tax cost of the buyout. In the case of a C corporation redemption, the interest on the installment note should be deductible by the business entity as business interest. In the case of a cross-purchase, S corporation shareholders and partners who are material participants in the business should be able to deduct the interest as active trade or business interest. On the other hand, S corporation shareholders and partners who are not material participants, and all C corporation shareholders, will probably have to treat the interest as investment interest or include it in the calculation of passive income or losses. Hence, the interest may not produce a current deduction.

### f. Strategy Six:  ESOP Funding

The sixth funding option works only for a relatively narrow group of clients. But for the right client, it can be a very effective means of funding a buy-sell agreement and at the same time produce positive collateral benefits. It's the employee stock ownership plan, or ESOP.

An ESOP is a qualified retirement plan designed to invest in stock of the employer. The benefit of an ESOP in funding a buyout is that it permits the accumulation of funds by the corporation on a tax-deductible basis, as well as the deferral of tax on the earnings of the fund. Over time a substantial fund can be accumulated with pre-tax dollars to redeem or purchase the stock of a deceased or retiring shareholder. This accumulation occurs without risking the accumulated earnings tax.

If sufficient funds have not been accumulated by the time the purchase is made by the ESOP, the ESOP can borrow funds, possibly guaranteed by the company. The loan can be repaid with tax-deductible dollars in the form of future contributions by the company to the ESOP, which are then used to repay the loan. A major advantage of using an ESOP to fund the buyout is that the contributions used to fund the buyout or repay the loan are tax deductible to the company.

But there is more. The second tax consequence that needs to be considered in any kind of buyout is the tax impact to the seller. If the buyout is a result of the owner's death, the buyout generally does not create any income tax hit because the purchase price is typically equal or close to the fair market value basis step-up at the time of death. But in the case of a buyout before death, the seller will likely be hit with a capital gains tax. In the case of a buyout from an ESOP, even that tax consequence can be eliminated. Under Section 1042, the seller of the stock can defer, and can possibly even eliminate, the recognition of gain on the sale of the stock when it is purchased by an ESOP. To qualify for this treatment, the ESOP must own at least 30 percent of the stock after the sale, the stock acquired by the ESOP cannot be allocated within the ESOP to accounts of family members of the seller (except that up to five percent can be allocated to accounts for lineal descendants), and none of the stock acquired by the ESOP can be allocated to the account of any shareholder who holds 25 percent or more of the stock of the company. Also, to qualify for the deferral, the seller must invest the sales proceeds in the marketable stock of U.S.-based companies within the 15-month period beginning three months before the date of the sale. If this investment is made, the basis of the owner in the stock of the company becomes the basis of the marketable securities acquired with those proceeds. If the owner eventually sells the securities, the owner will then recognize the capital gains that would have been recognized on the sale of the stock to the ESOP. But if the owner dies before the replacement securities are sold, the owner will get a stepped-up basis and will never recognize the capital gain.

So, in effect, an ESOP can be used to totally eliminate the capital gains tax of a selling shareholder while at the same time providing that shareholder with liquidity and financial security that otherwise wouldn't be available if he or she continued to own stock in the company. It provides an extremely attractive alternative for an older shareholder phasing out of the business.

One disadvantage of an ESOP is that it can be costly to maintain and administer. One of the most costly elements of an ESOP is that under most circumstances the company's stock must be appraised once a year. Also, a group of shareholders can lose control of a company through the use of an ESOP, since the nondiscrimination rules of ESOPs require that other employees receive benefits under the ESOP. The dilution is usually mitigated somewhat by the fact that existing shareholders who are also employees may be the largest participants in the ESOP.

Another big potential problem is that voting control of the company can shift to the ESOP upon the death of a shareholder. The remaining shareholders may be the trustees and vote the stock in the ESOP, but they are required to vote the shares in the best interests of the ESOP participants. This can be a burden. The loss of unrestricted control can be a significant drawback to the use of an ESOP and always has to be considered in the design. Still, the ESOP is a vehicle worth considering if the circumstances are right to make it work.

### g. Strategy Seven:  The Supplemental Executive Retirement Plan

The seventh strategy for funding buy-sell agreements is not really a funding option; it is a technique to convert part of the purchase payments into tax-deductible payments. The normal stock redemption scenario in a C corporation creates a double tax. The corporation pays with after-tax dollars, and the selling shareholder pays a capital gains tax on the transfer, albeit at favorable rates. This strategy involves using a Supplemental Executive Retirement Plan or SERP. A SERP is a contract between a company and an owner-employee under which the company agrees to pay the owner-employee in the future a specified amount as a supplemental executive retirement benefit. This contract is a nonqualified retirement plan. It is not funded. It is an accrued liability on the books of the company that should be carefully structured to comply with the new Section 409A of the Code. For a discussion of SERPs and the related Section 409A challenges, see Chapter 11.

For purposes of a buy-sell arrangement, the accrued liability on the books reduces the fair market value of the stock of the company. So when the owner/employee departs, the company makes one payment in the form of a tax-deductible payment of the SERP benefit and another payment in the form of a non-tax deductible redemption of the stock. Alternatively, the stock could be purchased by the other owners through a cross-purchase arrangement, still using the reduced price based upon the accrued liability of the SERP.

The payments made under the SERP are tax deductible to the company, and are taxable as ordinary income to the departing owner. The departing owner forfeits the favorable capital gains rate on the SERP payments. But in most situations, the tax savings realized by the corporation will be greater than any additional income tax paid by the departing owner by virtue of receiving ordinary income rather than capital gains. The corporation can end up in a net positive position even if it increases the payments to compensate the departing owner for any lost capital gains benefits.

### PROBLEMS 8-E THRU 8-G

**8-E.**  David owns 75 percent of the stock of Smith Industries, which is operated as an S corporation. Walter owns the remaining 25 percent. David is the driving force behind the company. It is doubtful the company could survive without David. Walter is a purely passive investor.

Smith Industries has a standard cross-purchase buy-sell agreement that is triggered if one of the shareholders dies. The other shareholder is obligated to buy the stock of the deceased shareholder. The company is now valued at $12 million. Walter owns a $9 million policy on David's life, and David owns a $3 million policy on Walter's life. The company funds the premiums on the policies through bonuses to the shareholders.

You represent David. What is wrong with this situation? What changes would you recommend? How would you implement those changes?

**8-F.**  Mad Golf Inc., a successful C corporation, has three shareholders: Larry, Brice and Joe. All the shareholders are in their early fifties. The company has a redemption buy-sell agreement funded with corporate-owned life insurance. If a shareholder dies, the company will use the life insurance death benefit that it receives tax-free to redeem the stock of the deceased shareholder.

Joe recently attended a financial planning seminar and learned that their redemption structure was "all wrong" because the remaining shareholders receive no step-up in their stock basis for the amounts paid to the deceased shareholder. He claimed they were "wasting a huge income tax benefit" because it was likely that the surviving two would probably "sell the company and cash in if one of the partners kicked the bucket." Joe is adamant that the agreement be changed to a cross-purchase structure immediately. You have been retained by the company to deal with Joe's demands. How would you advise the shareholders?

**8-G.**  In the course of advising Mad Golf Inc. in 6–F above, the shareholders decided to cancel the life insurance. They think it is "way too expensive and not really needed." They are "sick and tired" of the escalating premiums. They have concluded that it is likely that they will sell the business in the next five to eight years so that they can all "retire and play golf until they drop." They figure that the odds of one of them dying in that time period is very low. If it does happen, the others will buy the stock of the deceased under an installment payment plan until the company is sold, at which time the family of the deceased shareholder will be paid off.

What do you think of the shareholders' plan? What changes, if any, would you suggest?

## D. MAJORITY OPPRESSION RISKS

Often the question is asked: What happens if a dispute breaks out and there is no buy-sell agreement? It can trigger a serious problem that tests the will of the combatants and may threaten the health or survival of the business. The minority shareholders may have no effective remedy other than a potential claim, often difficult to prove, that the controlling owners have been oppressive. Most states have corporate statutes patterned after the Model Business Corporation Act that empower a court to dissolve the corporation if a shareholder can prove that (a) the directors are deadlocked, and the deadlock cannot be broken by the shareholders and it is injuring the corporation or impairing the conduct of its business; (b) the shareholders are deadlocked and have not been able to elect directors for two years; (c) corporate assets are being wasted; or (d) those in control are acting "in a manner that is illegal, oppressive, or fraudulent."[32] As regards any oppression claim, the Official Comments to this section of the Model Act indicate that courts should be "cautious" so as "to limit such cases to genuine abuse rather than instances of acceptable tactics in a power struggle for control of a corporation."[33] A disgruntled minority shareholder, armed with such a statute, may claim that the majority is being oppressive and threaten an action to dissolve the entity.

But usually there is no basis for believing that a court will go beyond the confines of the applicable corporation code to protect unhappy minority shareholders. The hardnosed sentiment of some courts, when faced with a claim of minority shareholders who failed to protect themselves with a buy-sell agreement, was aptly described by the Delaware Supreme Court in *Nixon v. Blackwell*[34] as follows:

> We wish to address one further matter which was raised at oral argument before this Court: Whether there should be any special, judicially-created rules to "protect" minority stockholders of closely-held Delaware corporations.

---

32. Model Business Corporation Act § 14.30(a)(2). If a shareholder petitions to dissolve the corporation under the statute, the corporation or other shareholders may elect to purchase the shares of the petitioning shareholder at the fair value of such shares and, thereby, turn the proceeding into a valuation case. Model Business Corporation Act § 14.34.

33. Model Business Corporation Act Official Comment 2. B. to § 14.30.

34. 626 A.2d 1366 (Del. 1993).

The case at bar points up the basic dilemma of minority stockholders in receiving fair value for their stock as to which there is no market and no market valuation. It is not difficult to be sympathetic, in the abstract, to a stockholder who finds himself or herself in that position. A stockholder who bargains for stock in a closely-held corporation and who pays for those shares (unlike the plaintiffs in this case who acquired their stock through gift) can make a business judgment whether to buy into such a minority position, and if so on what terms. One could bargain for definitive provisions of self-ordering permitted to a Delaware corporation through the certificate of incorporation or by-laws by reason of the provisions in 8 Del.C. §§ 102, 109, and 141(a). Moreover, in addition to such mechanisms, a stockholder intending to buy into a minority position in a Delaware corporation may enter into definitive stockholder agreements, and such agreements may provide for elaborate earnings tests, buyout provisions, voting trusts, or other voting agreements. See, e.g., 8 Del.C. § 218.

The tools of good corporate practice are designed to give a purchasing minority stockholder the opportunity to bargain for protection before parting with consideration. It would do violence to normal corporate practice and our corporation law to fashion an ad hoc ruling which would result in a court-imposed stockholder buy-out for which the parties had not contracted.[35]

So the real planning challenge, in the words of the Delaware Supreme Court, is to use the "tools of good corporate practice" and "bargain for protection before parting with consideration."

Of course, with the right set of facts, a minority shareholder may prove actual oppression and trigger the statutory remedies. The following two cases illustrate the potential impact of a bona fide oppression claim against a majority shareholder and the various standards courts use in evaluating such claims.

## BONAVITA v. CORDO
692 A.2d 119 (Ch. Div. 1996)

LESEMANN, J.S.C.

Gerald Bonavita, the holder of one-half the stock of Corbo Jewelers, Inc., instituted this suit claiming that the corporation was deadlocked and that he was the victim of oppression by Alan Corbo, holder of the other 50% of the corporation's stock, who is also its president and chief executive officer. He sought relief under *N.J.S.A.* 14A:12-7 and also under this court's common-law power to remedy such oppression. Gerald Bonavita died before trial, and the suit has been continued by his executrix and widow, Julia Bonavita.

The oppression claim is based on Alan Corbo's rejection of plaintiff's attempt to have the corporation either pay dividends or buy out the Bonavita stock interests. With both demands rejected, plaintiff claims she is locked into a

---

35. 626 A.2d at pages 1379-80.

corporation which provides her with no benefit of any kind. At the same time, she says, Alan Corbo and his three sons are employed full time by the corporation, and his wife and daughter are employed part time. Thus, the Corbo half of the stock ownership receives substantial benefits-with fringe benefits, the total annual family compensation is between $300,000 and $400,000-while the Bonavita half receives nothing.

Defendants deny any obligation to buy the Bonavita stock. They also maintain that the refusal to pay dividends is merely an application of the "business judgment rule" and is amply justified by sound business reasons. There is no evidence that defendant's "no-dividend" policy is motivated by animus toward plaintiff, or by anything other than their view of what is best for the corporation. Thus, the case presents the question of the extent to which the business judgment rule will insulate a corporation's power structure from a claim of oppression when application of that rule has the effect of providing substantial benefits to some of the holders of the corporation's stock and no benefits to the others.

In the mid 1980's, as Gerald Bonavita aged and his health deteriorated, he told Alan Corbo that he wanted to retire and wanted to have the corporation (or Alan) purchase his stock. Some discussions ensued, but the parties did not reach agreement on a buy out. Gradually, Bonavita reduced the time he was spending on corporate business, until he completely retired in March 1991. Julia continued working for a short time thereafter, until she too ceased all work in January 1992.

Plaintiff's complaint was filed in December 1991. It alleges a deadlock within the meaning of *N.J.S.A.* 14A:12-7 and also alleges stockholder "oppression" within the meaning of that statute. Plaintiff sought interim relief, and the court, pursuant to Subsection (1) of *N.J.S.A.* 14A:12-7 appointed Thomas Herten, Esq., as a "provisional director" to function while the litigation proceeded.

In early 1994, Bonavita formally requested the corporation to pay a dividend of approximately $650,000 to each of the two shareholders-a total of $1,300,000. That sum represented a portion of the corporation's retained earnings on which income tax had already been paid-a point discussed further below. The request was denied, with Alan Corbo opposed to the request and the provisional director declining to join Bonavita in what he regarded as a matter of "business judgment." An attempt to have the court overrule that decision while the suit was pending was unsuccessful and thus no dividend was paid. Bonavita thereafter modified his request to propose a smaller dividend, but that, too, was denied, and Alan Corbo has remained, ever since, adamantly opposed to the payment of any substantial dividend.

Although plaintiff claims there is a corporate "deadlock," that charge is not sharply drawn, and it is not clear just what constitutes the alleged deadlock of which plaintiff complains. *N.J.S.A.* 14A:12-7 contains two deadlock provisions. Subsection (1)(a) provides that the court may take remedial action upon proof that:

[t]he shareholders of the corporation are so divided in voting power

that, for a period which includes the time when two consecutive annual meetings were or should have been held, they have failed to elect successors to directors whose terms have expired or would have expired upon the election and qualification of their successors.

As noted above, the Corbo certificate of incorporation requires three directors. A by-law provision of questionable validity provides for two directors and, in fact, the corporation has functioned for many years with just two directors.

Plaintiff seems to claim that three directors are required; that the by-law amendment providing for a two-member board is invalid; and that the failure to select a three-member board evidences deadlock. The claim is not persuasive. Gerald Bonavita had long acquiesced in a board composed of two directors and had voted to amend the by-laws to authorize such a board. An attempt to change that position now would raise substantial issues of waiver and estoppel.

Plaintiff claims that the rejection of her demand for payment of a dividend or a buy-out of the Bonavita stock constitutes such an inability to effect corporate action. However, rather than characterizing the refusal to accede to her demands as an inability "to effect action," it is more accurate to describe those decisions as what they really are: determinations by defendants to reject plaintiff's demands.

In short, this is not a case where a corporation is unable to act. It can act. And it did act. It acted by denying plaintiff's demands. And it is the result of that action-not an inability to act-which is the basis for plaintiff's claim that she has been left in a hopeless, "no-win" situation. Whether those actions, leading to those results, constitute shareholder oppression is the significant issue presented.

The essence of plaintiff's claim is that the corporation, as operated by defendant Alan Corbo, provides substantial benefits for Alan Corbo and his family but no benefits for Bonavita. That is certainly an accurate statement.

As noted, the six Corbo family members on the corporate payroll realize approximately $400,000 per year in salary and other benefits. And while there is no claim that the salaries are excessive, neither was there a showing that if the "inside" employment were terminated those family members could earn as much elsewhere. In addition, of course, a job in the family business probably provides considerably more security than one might find in other employment.

Such employment is, of course, a frequent and perfectly proper benefit of stockholders in a closed corporation. The difficulty here is that the benefit flows in one direction only: to the Corbos, and not to Bonavita, and there is no compensating, alternative benefit for the Bonavita interests.

Mrs. Bonavita testified that she and her husband had no children who could move into the jewelry stores' operation. She also said, as did her husband in his *de bene esse* deposition before trial, that Mr. Bonavita had hoped to receive some benefits from the corporation before he died, and she has a similar hope now for herself. Otherwise, as she put it, her husband's interest, which she now owns, will be locked forever within Corbo Jewelers, Inc., and will be of absolutely no benefit to her, as it was of no benefit to her husband.

Absent employment, and absent any thought of long-term growth (inapplicable to Julia Bonavita as it was to Gerald Bonavita because of age), the normal corporate benefit which one in the position of Mr. or Mrs. Bonavita might expect would be the payment of dividends. This corporation, however, pays no dividends.

Plaintiff argues that Alan Corbo's "no dividend" policy is particularly harsh in view of the extraordinary financial condition of the corporation. That argument has considerable merit. As of June 30, 1993, the corporate balance sheet showed retained earnings of more than $5,000,000 and, after adjustment for treasury stock held as a liability, showed total stockholders' equity of approximately $4,600,000. In addition, on June 30, 1993, the corporation had cash, or liquid assets easily convertible into cash, of approximately $1,100,000 and current liabilities of only $12,000.

Defendants' stated reason for the refusal to pay dividends is the corporation's need for cash. Alan Corbo testified that the business is seasonal and that the corporation's continued profitability requires it to have substantial cash available to buy quickly when "bargains" become available. The ability to do that, without the need to borrow money and pay interest, he maintained, is one reason for the corporation's success over the years. Alan Corbo also pointed to the anticipated need for substantial renovation expenses for two of the corporation's stores which were approaching the end of leaseholds. In each case, he said, the landlord would require such expenditures as a condition to lease renewal.

While the facts just described strongly indicate that the corporation can well afford to pay dividends, a contrary decision could hardly be called irrational. Indeed, from Alan Corbo's point of view, the "no dividend" policy undoubtedly makes good sense. Since the primary benefit that he receives from the corporation is continued employment for himself and his family, the maintenance of a $5,000,000 earned surplus, large cash balances, and the non-payment of dividends is certainly in his best interest.

If the Corbo's and Bonavita were in essentially the same position, and each was similarly affected by the decision against paying dividends, that policy could hardly be characterized as anything other than a permissible exercise of business judgment. It would, presumably, be unassailable under the principle that a court will not normally overturn the exercise of such judgment..

But that, of course, is not this case. The problem here is that the operation of the corporation benefits only one of its shareholders-Alan Corbo. It provides no benefit of any kind to Julia Bonavita. She receives, and she will receive, no salary. The long range future of the corporation will not benefit her. And the "no dividend" policy is not a short term measure adopted to meet some pressing financial necessity. It is what Alan Corbo sees as the norm, and a policy from which he does not intend to deviate.

What Julia Bonavita has, and what she will continue to have so long as Alan Corbo is able to make the kinds of decisions he has been making, is a block of stock which has absolutely no value. Alan Corbo has made and will continue to make decisions which are in his best interests (and those of his family) and which ignore the wishes, needs, and best interests of his co-shareholder.

Given the effect of those actions on plaintiff, and regardless of whether defendants' actions might otherwise be termed "wrongful" or "illegal," there is no question that defendants' conduct has destroyed any reasonable expectation that plaintiff may have enjoyed respecting her stock interests. As such, it is clear from the decision of our Supreme Court in *Brenner v. Berkowitz,* 134 *N.J.* 488, 634 *A.*2d 1019 (1993), from other New Jersey case law, from comments and analyses by leading text writers, and from decisions in other states, that defendants' actions do indeed constitute "oppression" within the meaning of *N.J.S.A.* 14A:12-7.

*N.J.S.A.* 14A:12-7 sets out four remedies which a court "may" order to remedy "oppression." A court may appoint a custodian, appoint a provisional director, order a sale of the corporation's stock as provided below, or enter a judgment dissolving the corporation…The statutory power to order a stock sale, is a power to order an unwilling party to *sell* stock. It does not authorize a mandatory *purchase* by someone otherwise unwilling to buy.

In *Brenner v. Berkowitz, supra,* however, the Court held that the statutory list of remedies was non-exclusive and that the statute "was not intended to supersede the inherent, common law power of the Chancery Division to achieve equity." One of those equitable remedies, it held, is the power to order an involuntary *purchase* of stock held by one of the corporation's shareholders. That power, however, should be exercised sparingly.

Dissolution, of course, is a "last resort" remedy and something which neither defendant nor plaintiff wants here. What plaintiff does want is an order directing the corporation, or Alan Corbo, to purchase the Bonavita stock. That remedy, as noted, is available, but should be imposed only if the court is satisfied that it represents "the only practical alternative" to dissolution and that some lesser remedy will not suffice.

Neither side in this case has focused on any such alternative remedy. The reason for that seems clear: there is no reasonable, practical lesser remedy which will solve the problem inherent in this relationship and provide plaintiff with the long-range relief to which she is entitled. In short, no other remedy will work.

Thus, the corporation could certainly be ordered to pay the dividend which plaintiff requests-or at least some smaller dividend. But if that were done, what about next year? Or the year after? Alan Corbo will continue to see such payments as antithetical to the best interests of the corporation. And as he defines the best interests of the corporation-consistent with his best interests and those of his family-his viewpoint would hardly be irrational. But it will continue to be inconsistent with the reasonable expectations of the Bonavita interests.

Similarly, the court could continue the appointment of the present provisional director or appoint someone else with a direction for that person to participate more actively in the business of the corporation. But given the ongoing divergence between the interests of the two shareholders, no such appointment could "solve" the existing problem.

In sum, there is no rational basis on which this corporation can continue to exist and operate with half its shares owned by the Corbo interests and half by the Bonavita interests. There must be a "divorce." One method of accomplishing that, raised and explored at trial but shown to be unworkable, would be a division of the corporation's stores between the two shareholders. The difficulty with such a division is that there is nothing that Mrs. Bonavita could do with three or four of the seven Corbo stores. She is not in a position to operate them. And Alan Corbo made emphatically clear that there is today no market for retail jewelry stores. She would not be able to sell them.

That brings us back, then, to plaintiff's request for a compulsory buy out of her stock. And since such a mandatory purchase by the corporation or Alan Corbo represents a less drastic measure than dissolution of the corporation, it is clear that the only feasible, rational remedy here is an order that the corporation (or perhaps Alan Corbo) be required to purchase the Bonavita stock interests.

Based on an analysis and evaluation of the extensive evidence submitted at trial as to the value of the Bonavita stock interests, the court has concluded that the price at which that sale should take place is $1,900,000.

What remains to be resolved, however, are the terms and conditions under which a sale at that price should take place....To investigate and consider all of these issues, and any others that must be resolved in order to effect the purchase of the Bonavita stock, this court will appoint a special fiscal agent. The agent will consult with the attorneys for the parties; make such independent investigation as may be deemed necessary or appropriate; and may consult with banks, other possible lending sources, accountants, and anyone else deemed helpful. The agent will then submit a proposal as to the terms and conditions on which the sale will take place. The parties will have an opportunity to be heard concerning the agent's report, and thereafter, the court will enter a final order fixing the terms and conditions of sale.

## KIRIAKIDES v. ATLAS FOOD SYSTEMS & SERVICES, INC.
541 S.E.2d 257 (S.C. 2001)

TOAL, Chief Justice:

This is a case in which respondents, minority shareholders in a closely held family corporation, claim the majority shareholders have acted in a manner which is fraudulent, oppressive and unfairly prejudicial. They seek a buyout of their shares under South Carolina's judicial dissolution statutes.

Respondents are 72–year–old John Kiriakides and his 74–year–old sister Louise Kiriakides. John and Louise are the minority shareholders in the family business, Atlas Food Systems & Services, Inc. (Atlas). Petitioners are their older brother, 88–year–old Alex Kiriakides, Jr., and the family business and its subsidiaries, Marica Enterprises, Ltd. (MEL), and Marica, Inc. (Marica).

Atlas is a food vending service which provides refreshments to factories and other businesses. Atlas was incorporated in 1956. Currently, Alex is the majority stockholder, owning 57.68%; John owns 37.7%, and Louise owns 3%.

Throughout Atlas' history, Alex has been in charge of the financial and corporate affairs of the family business; he has had overall control and is Chairman of the Board of Directors. John is also on the three member Board. In 1986, John became President of Atlas, after years of running client relations and field operations. Two of Alex' children are also employed by Atlas, his son Alex III, and his daughter Mary Ann. Alex III is (since John's departure as discussed below) President and is on the Board; Mary Ann is a CPA who performs accounting and financial functions; their brother Michael worked for Atlas in the past, but is no longer employed there.

For years, Atlas operated as a prototypical closely held family corporation. Troubles developed, however, in 1995, when a rift began between Alex and John. The relationship between the two became very strained. Several incidents served to heighten the tension.

In December 1995, the Board and shareholders of Atlas decided to convert Atlas from a subchapter C corporation to a subchapter S corporation. However, in March 1996, Alex, without bringing a vote, unilaterally determined the company would remain a C corporation. Later, in mid–1996, a dispute arose over Atlas' contract to purchase a piece of commercial property. Notwithstanding the contract, John, Alex III and William Freitag (Senior Vice President of Finance and Administration) decided not to go through with the sale. Alex however, without consulting or advising John, elected to go through with the sale. When John learned of Alex' decision, he became extremely upset and allegedly advised Alex III he was quitting his job as President. The next day, Alex III made plans with managers to continue operations in John's absence; John, however, went to the Atlas office in Greenville and visited Atlas offices in Columbia, Orangeburg and Charleston.

The following Monday, John went to work at Atlas doing "business as usual." He was told later that day (by Alex' son Michael) that management was planning John would no longer be President of Atlas. John circulated a memo indicating he intended to remain President; Alex III replied in a memo prepared with the aid of his father, refusing to allow John to continue as president of the company. The following day, Alex refused to allow John to stay on as president of Atlas, and designated Alex III as President. John was offered, but refused a position as a consultant.

In September 1996, Atlas offered to purchase John's interest in Atlas, MEL and K Enterprises, for one million dollars, plus the cancellation of $800,000 obligations owed by John. John refused this offer, believing it too low. John filed this suit in November 1996, seeking to obtain corporate records. The complaint was subsequently amended, naming Louise as a plaintiff, and adding claims for fraud under the judicial dissolution statute. The complaint sought an accounting, a buyout of John and Louise's shares, and damages for fraud. The trial was bifurcated on the issues of liability and damages.

After a five day hearing, the referee found Alex had engaged in fraud in numerous respects, and found Atlas had engaged in conduct which was fraudulent, oppressive and unfairly prejudicial toward John and Louise. The referee held a buyout was the appropriate remedy under S.C.Code Ann. § 33–14–

300(2)(ii) and § 33–14–310(d)(4). The referee found that, at the bifurcated damages hearing, it would be determined whether John and Louise had suffered any damages from the fraud in this regard. The Court of Appeals affirmed in result.

Atlas contends the Court of Appeals applied an improper standard of review to the referee's findings of fraud. We disagree.

An appellate court's scope of review in cases of fraud, where the proof must be by clear, cogent and convincing evidence, is limited to determining whether there is any evidence reasonably supporting the circuit court's findings. It is not for the appellate court to weigh the evidence to determine whether it is sufficient to meet the burden of proof. We find evidentiary support in the record for each of the referee's findings of fraud. Accordingly, the referee's findings of fraud are affirmed.

The referee found that, taken together, the majority's actions were "illegal, fraudulent, oppressive or unfairly prejudicial," justifying a buyout of John and Louise's interests under S.C.Code Ann. § 33–14–300(2)(ii) and § 33–14–310(d)(4).

The Court of Appeals affirmed the referee's holdings. In making this ruling, the Court of Appeals defined the statutory terms "oppressive" and "unfairly prejudicial" as follows:

1) A visible departure from the standards of fair dealing and a violation of fair play on which every shareholder who entrusts his money to a company is entitled to rely; or

2) A breach of the fiduciary duty of good faith and fair dealing; or

3) Whether the reasonable expectations of the minority shareholders have been frustrated by the actions of the majority; or

4) A lack of probity and fair dealing in the affairs of a company to the prejudice of some of its members; or

5) A deprivation by majority shareholders of participation in management by minority shareholders.

Atlas contends the Court of Appeals' definitions of oppressive, unfairly prejudicial conduct are beyond the scope of our judicial dissolution statute. We agree. In our view, the Court of Appeals' broad view of oppression is contrary to the legislative intent and is an unwarranted expansion of section 33–14–300.

South Carolina's judicial dissolution statute was amended in 1963 in recognition of the growing trend toward protecting minority shareholders from abuses by those in the majority. Section § 33–14–300(2)(ii) now permits a court to order dissolution if it is established by a shareholder that "the directors or those in control of the corporation have acted, are acting, or will act in a manner that is illegal, fraudulent, oppressive, or unfairly prejudicial either to the corporation or to any shareholder (whether in his capacity as a shareholder, director, or officer of the corporation)." The official comment to section 33–14–300 provides:

No attempt has been made to define oppression, fraud, or unfairly prejudicial conduct. These are elastic terms whose meaning varies with the circumstances presented in a particular case, and it is felt that existing case law provides sufficient guidelines for courts and litigants.

Given the Legislature's deliberate exclusion of a set definition of oppressive and unfairly prejudicial conduct, we find the Court of Appeals' enunciation of rigid tests is contrary to the legislative intent.

Under the Court of Appeals' holding, a finding of fraudulent/oppressive conduct may be based upon any one of its alternative definitions. We do not believe the Legislature intended such a result. In particular, we do not believe the Legislature intended a court to judicially order a corporate dissolution solely upon the basis that a party's "reasonable expectations" have been frustrated by majority shareholders. To examine the "reasonable expectations" of minority shareholders would require the courts of this state to microscopically examine the dealings of closely held family corporations, the intentions of majority and minority stockholders in forming the corporation and thereafter, the history of family dealings, and the like. We do not believe the Legislature, in enacting section 33–14–300, intended such judicial interference in the business philosophies and day to day operating practices of family businesses.

In adopting the "reasonable expectations" approach, the Court of Appeals cited the North Carolina case of Meiselman v. Meiselman, 309 N.C. 279, 307 S.E.2d 551 (1983). In Meiselman, a minority shareholder in a family-owned close corporation was "frozen out" of the family corporation in much the same fashion as John and Louise claim they have been frozen out of Atlas. The minority shareholder brought an action requesting a buyout of his interests under N.C.G.S. § 55–125.1(a)(4), which permits a North Carolina court to liquidate assets when it is "reasonably necessary for the protection of the rights or interests of the complaining shareholders." (Emphasis supplied).

In holding the minority shareholder was entitled to relief, the Meiselman court noted that the trial court had focused on the conduct of the majority shareholder, using standards of "oppression," "overreaching," "unfair advantage," and the like. The Court found this was error because the North Carolina statute in question required the trial court to focus on the plaintiff's "rights and interests," his "reasonable expectations" in the corporate defendants, and determine whether those rights or interests were in need of protection. The focus in Meiselman, based upon the language of the North Carolina statute, was upon the interests of the minority shareholder, as opposed to the conduct of the majority.

Unlike the North Carolina statute in Meiselman, section 33–14–300 does not place the focus upon the "rights or interests" of the complaining shareholder but, rather, specifically places the focus upon the actions of the majority, i.e., whether they "have acted, are acting, or will act in a manner that is illegal, fraudulent, oppressive, or unfairly prejudicial either to the corporation or to any shareholder." Given the language of our statute, a "reasonable expectations" approach is simply inconsistent with our statute.

We recognize that a number of leading authorities advocate a "reasonable expectations" approach to oppressive conduct. Although several jurisdictions have adopted "reasonable expectations" as a guide to the meaning of "oppression," it has been noted by one commentator that "no court has adopted the reasonable expectations test without the assistance of a statute." Ralph A. Peeples, *The Use and Misuse of the Business Judgment Rule in the Close Corporation,* 60 Notre Dame L.Rev. 456, 505 (1985). One criticism of the "reasonable expectations" approach is that it "ignores the expectations of the parties other than the dissatisfied shareholder." See Lerner v. Lerner Corp., 132 Md.App. 32, 750 A.2d 709, 722 (Md. 2000). Similarly, it has been suggested that the reasonable expectations approach is "based on false premises, invites fraud, and is an unnecessary invasion of the rights of the majority." J.C. Bruno, Reasonable Expectations:A Primer on An Oppressive Standard, 71 Mich. B.J. 434 (May 1992).

We find adoption of the "reasonable expectations" standard is inconsistent with section 33–14–300, which places an emphasis not upon the minority's expectations but, rather, on the actions of the majority. We decline to adopt such an expansive approach to oppressive conduct in the absence of a legislative mandate. We find, consistent with the Legislature's comment to section 33–18–400, that the terms "oppressive" and "unfairly prejudicial" are elastic terms whose meaning varies with the circumstances presented in a particular case. As noted by one commentator:

> While business corporation statutes may attempt to provide certainty and clarity in the law to enhance the attractiveness of doing business, the definition of oppression has been left to judicial construction on a case-by-case basis. Such an approach has been suggested by the Model Close Corporation Supplement which expressly indicates that no attempt has been made to statutorily define oppression, fraud or prejudicial conduct, leaving these "elastic terms" to judicial interpretation.... The judicial construction of the definition of oppressive conduct is well-suited to the diversified, fact-specific disputes among shareholders of closely-held corporations. However, the judicial development of a meaningful standard for defining oppressive conduct, apart from fraud or mismanagement, is a difficult task.

Sandra K. Miller, *Should the Definition of Oppressive Conduct by the Majority Shareholders Exclude a Consideration of Ethical Conduct And Business Purpose?* 97 Dick. L.Rev. 227, 229–230 (Winter 1993).

We find a case-by-case analysis, supplemented by various factors which may be indicative of oppressive behavior, to be the proper inquiry under S.C.Code § 33–14–300. Accordingly, the Court of Appeals' opinion is modified to the extent it adopted a "reasonable expectations" approach.

The question remains whether the conduct of Atlas toward John and Louise was "oppressive" and "unfairly prejudicial" under the factual circumstances presented. We find this case presents a classic example of a majority "freeze-out," and that the referee properly found Atlas had engaged in conduct which was fraudulent, oppressive and unfairly prejudicial. Accordingly, the referee properly ordered a buyout of their shares pursuant to S.C.Code Ann. § 33–14–310(d)(4).

The right of the majority to control the enterprise achieves a meaning and has an impact in close corporations that it has in no other major form of business organization under our law. Only in the close corporation does the power to manage carry with it the de facto power to allocate the benefits of ownership arbitrarily among the shareholders and to discriminate against a minority whose investment is imprisoned in the enterprise. The essential basis of this power in the close corporation is the inability of those so excluded from the benefits of proprietorship to withdraw their investment at will.

This unequal balance of power often leads to a "squeeze out" or "freeze out" of the minority by the majority shareholders. At its extreme, this harm manifests itself as the classic freeze out where the minority shareholder faces a trapped investment and an indefinite exclusion from participation in business returns. The position of the close corporation shareholder, therefore, is uniquely precarious.

Common freeze out techniques include the termination of a minority shareholder's employment, the refusal to declare dividends, the removal of a minority shareholder from a position of management, and the siphoning off of corporate earnings through high compensation to the majority shareholder. Often, these tactics are used in combination. In a public corporation, the minority shareholder can escape such abuses by selling his shares; there is no such market, however, for the stock of a close corporation. "The primary vulnerability of a minority shareholder is the specter of being 'locked in,' that is, having a perpetual investment in an entity without any expectation of ever receiving a return on that investment." Charles Murdock, *The Evolution of Effective Remedies for Minority Shareholders and Its Impact Upon Valuation of Minority Shares,* 65 Notre Dame L.Rev. 425, 477 (1990).

The present case presents a classic situation of minority "freeze out." The referee considered the following factors: 1) Alex' unilateral action to deprive Louise of the benefits of ownership in her shares in Atlas, and subsequent reduction in her distributions based upon the reduced number of shares, 2) Alex' conduct in depriving John and Louise of the 21% interest of Marica stock, 3) the fact that there is no prospect of John and Louise receiving any financial benefit from their ownership of Atlas shares, 4) the fact that Alex and his family continue to receive substantial benefit from their ownership in Atlas, 5) the fact that Atlas has substantial cash and liquid assets, very little debt and that, notwithstanding its ability to declare dividends, it has indicated it would not do so in the foreseeable future, 6) the fact that Alex, majority shareholder in total control of Atlas, is totally estranged from John and Louise, 7) Atlas' extremely low buyout offers to John and Louise, and 8) the fact that Atlas is not appropriate for a public stock offering at the present time.

These factors, when coupled with the referee's findings of fraud, present a textbook example of a "freeze out" situation. Short of a buyout of their shares, it is unlikely John and Louise will ever receive any benefit from their ownership interests in Atlas. We find the referee properly concluded the totality of the circumstances demonstrated that the majority had acted "oppressively" and "unfairly prejudicially" to John and Louise. Accordingly, we affirm the referee's finding that a buyout of John and Louise's shares is the appropriate remedy under the circumstances of this case.

Under South Carolina's judicial dissolution statute, the Court of Appeals erred in attempting to define oppressive and unfairly prejudicial conduct. Further, we reject the "reasonable expectations" approach adopted by the Court of Appeals. Under section 33–14–300, the proper focus is not on the reasonable expectations of the minority but, rather, on the conduct of the majority. Such an inquiry is to be performed on a case-by-case basis, with an inquiry of all the circumstances and an examination of the many factors hereinabove recited. We believe such an inquiry is in keeping with the Legislature's intention in enacting sections 33–14–300 and 33–14–310.

Under the factual circumstances presented here, we find the majority's conduct clearly constitutes oppressive and unfairly prejudicial conduct entitling John and Louise to a buyout of their shares.

## PROBLEM 8-H

**8-H.** Manu Inc. ("Manu") is a specialized manufacturing corporation that has been in business for 22 years. Walter and Jane Smith, husband and wife, founded the business and own 60 percent of Manu's outstanding common stock. They are Manu's only directors. Manu has always been profitable. Walter annually draws a salary and bonuses totaling $400,000 to $500,000.

Manu has had four executive employees, including Linda, for many years. Approximately five years ago, they were each granted, as additional compensation, 10 percent of Manu's outstanding common stock. Historically, they have each annually been paid a salary and bonus equal to $180,000 to $210,000. There has never been a shareholder buy-sell agreement between Manu and its stockholders.

Seven months ago, Walter and Linda had a major falling out over the termination of a junior employee. Linda wailed in protest until Walter finally exclaimed, "That's it, Linda. I've had it with you and your complaining. You are now finished. I can't put up with you any longer." Linda was instantly terminated and escorted out of the building. She was paid six months of severance pursuant to a simple employment agreement.

After cooling off for a month, Linda sent Walter an email requesting that either Manu or Walter buy her Manu stock. Walter's respond was curt: "Manu doesn't need your stock. I don't want your stock. No one else will want to buy your stock. There is no market for the stock, and there never will be. Manu has never paid a dividend and never will. As you well know, Manu pays its earnings to the team that makes it happen here. Because of your intolerable complaining, you are no longer part of that team. Thus, you should not expect any return on the Manu stock that you were given years ago."

Linda wants to know if she has any rights as a minority shareholder in this situation.  What additional facts would you like to have?  In a legal proceeding, how should the issues and allegations be framed on behalf of Linda? What standard of review should the court use?

# CHAPTER 9

# BUYING AND SELLING A BUSINESS

———

## A. STRUCTURING THE DEAL

### 1. THE NON-TAX AGENDA

Businesses are bought and sold every day. For most owners, it's a momentous event. They are using their power and means to grow through acquisition; or they are selling out, cashing in on a profitable adventure that may have lasted a lifetime. But whether they are buying or selling, and whether they are dealing with a business that's lasted three generations or three months, the structure of the transaction is a big deal. It sets the parameters for getting the deal done and allocates risks, liabilities, and administrative burdens. Most importantly, it directly impacts the net cost to the buyer and the net yield to the seller.

Many mistakenly assume that it's only about taxes. Tax consequences are always important and often drive the structure of the deal. But in some transactions, non-tax factors, deemed critically important by one or both of the parties, will trump all other considerations and dictate whether the transaction should be structured as a sale of assets or a sale of the entity itself. In many more situations, important non-tax objectives, while not controlling, must be evaluated and prioritized against the tax consequences of alternative structures. A useful starting point in any transaction is to identify key non-tax considerations that are impacted by structure and then assess their relative importance. Some of the most compelling non-tax factors that often surface include the following:

a. **Undisclosed Liability Exposure**. Often buyers fear exposure to undisclosed liabilities attributable to the operation of the business prior to the acquisition. Such liabilities may come in many different forms – product liability exposures; employee claims, including sexual harassment, discrimination or wrongful termination claims; environmental liabilities; unpaid taxes; contractual disputes and related expenses and exposures; regulatory violations; and many more. The buyer knows that if the entity is acquired, either through merger or stock purchase, it comes with all its skeletons. The acquisition agreement usually includes seller representations and warranties, indemnification provisions, and escrow holdback procedures, all designed to shift the ultimate risk of any material undisclosed liabilities back to the seller. But even with these, there is still the possibility – often the probability – that the buyer, as the new owner of the old entity, will get tangled up in a dispute over issues that pre-date the buyer's involvement. Many buyers want a structure that provides protections greater than those offered through a contract. For them, an asset acquisition, though not completely bullet-proof from all pre-acquisition liabilities, is a preferred structure because the old entity remains with the seller.

b. **Third-Party Disruptions**. The impact of the transaction on employees, customers, vendors, and other third parties often is an important consideration. Banks and key executives usually are knee-deep in the details, no matter the structure of the deal. But an acquisition that keeps the old entity intact and functioning, just with new owners, often can be accomplished with no knowledge of, let alone any involvement with, rank-and-file employees, customers and vendors. If the business and assets are transferred to a new entity, these other players soon discover that they too are being transferred. The result may be heightened insecurities, the need for additional assurances or, worse yet, new demands.

c. **Third-Party Consents**. An asset acquisition structure usually requires more third-party consents. Typically, such consents are required for leases, licenses, permits, and contracts that the new buyer needs to maintain in order to run the business. The consent process itself may result in added costs and delays. Also, and much worse, the need for the consent may provide a key third party with an exit opportunity that wouldn't exist otherwise. This opportunity may result in the loss of a valuable contract right or a forced unfavorable renegotiation. Although an entity acquisition, either through merger or stock purchase, often requires some third-party consents based on the breadth of transfer-of-control provisions in specific contracts, the burden is usually much tougher with an asset structure.

d. **Unwanted Assets.** Sometimes the buyer wants to cherry-pick specific assets that are necessary for the operation of the core business. The remaining assets are left for the seller to deal with. An entity acquisition structure can work in this situation if the seller can get the unwanted assets out of the entity before the deal is done. But, depending on the nature and value of the unwanted assets, often an asset structure is preferred because the old entity remains with the owner of the unwanted assets and, as a result, the seller has greater flexibility in dealing with any future transfers of the unwanted assets and the associated tax impacts.

e. **Sales and Use Taxes.** A sale of tangible assets often triggers a state sales tax or use tax, typically paid by the buyer. This is often an added expense of using an asset acquisition structure. In some transactions, it is a material cost that affects the structural decision.

f. **Insurance Rating.** Sometimes the selling entity has a favorable historical workmen's compensation insurance rating that will be lost if only assets, not the entity, are transferred. This can be a major factor in some situations. When it is, an entity acquisition structure becomes more appealing.

g. **Closing Complexities**. The closing of an entity deal is usually much

easier than an asset deal.  A stock certificate or ownership interest is transferred.
In an asset transaction, there is a need for transfer documents (e.g. assignments,
bills of sale, deeds, assumption agreements, etc.) covering the tangible assets,
licenses, leases, contract rights, intangibles, and other assets being transferred
and all the liabilities being assumed by the buyer.  It requires more effort, more
paperwork and more attention to detail.  Usually this factor is less important than
other considerations.  Often it is cited as an added reason or excuse by a party
who, for more compelling reasons, is advocating an entity structure.

   h.  **Securities Law Exposures**.  Some sellers are spooked by the anti-fraud
provisions of the securities laws.  They hate the idea of being legally obligated to
eliminate all misleading material facts related to a complex business operation
and its potential acquisition by a buyer who may see only the surface.  Often their
fear is grounded in a prior bad experience involving securities.  They feel safer
with an asset structure that does not involve the sale of stock.  Usually in any
transaction, either entity or asset, the buyer will expect and demand extensive
representations and warranties from the seller; and often it is standard practice to
include a catchall representation that is the verbatim equivalent of Rule 10b-5,
the securities law antifraud provision.[1]  A seller who is spooked enough by the
burdens of 10b-5 to let it influence the structure of the deal will often refuse to
make such a catchall representation.  This can complicate the negotiation.  If the
seller is adamant, the solution, in many situations, is to have the seller represent
that he or she has not "knowingly misrepresented any material facts" (usually the
specific "knowingly" limitation removes any objection) and to carefully design
other representations and warranties to give the buyer the comfort needed to
move forward.

## 2. CASE STUDY FACTS

   Michael Manufacturing (Seller) has been in business 30 years.  Its two equal
owners, Larry and Sue, both age 58, have decided that it's time to sell.  They both
have worked for the company their entire careers.  Each currently pulls about
$300,000 a year from the business.  They have concluded that a transition to
family members is out of the question.  And although the business has a seasoned
second level management team that would love to own what it has built, the
economics of an inside sale make no sense.  Larry and Sue would end up bearing
all the risk, against the hope that they would receive a fair yield over a very long
time.  These factors and a serious offer from a strategic deep-pocketed C
corporation buyer (Buyer) have convinced them that it is time to cash in and start
enjoying the good life.

   The value of Seller's equity is $12 million, the excess of the $17 million fair
market value of its assets over its liabilities of $5 million.  The book value of
Seller's equity is $5 million, the excess of the book value of its assets ($10
million) over its liabilities of $5 million.  Of the $7 million of asset value in
excess of book value, $1 million is attributable to tangible assets (equipment) and

---

1.  17 C.F.R. § 240.10b–5.

$6 million to goodwill and going concern value. The company's tangible assets – primarily cash, accounts receivable, inventories and equipment – have a book value and basis of $10 million and a fair market value of $11 million. For the last three years, the company's earnings, before interest, taxes, depreciation, amortization and any payments to Larry and Sue, have averaged $2.4 million on average sales of $30 million.

The following sections review the tax consequences to Seller, Buyer, Larry, and Sue under different transaction structure scenarios. The first section assumes that Seller is a C corporation, that Larry and Sue each have a $250,000 basis in their stock, that Larry and Sue are subject to a combined federal and state marginal income tax rate of 40 percent on ordinary income and 20 percent on long-term capital gains, and that Seller and Buyer, both C corporations, are subject to a combined federal and state marginal income tax rate of 40 percent (remember, C corporations get no capital gains tax rate break).

## 3. C CORPORATIONS – 11 SCENARIOS

### a. Asset Sale-Liquidation

Under this common scenario, Buyer pays Seller $12 million for all the assets of the business and assumes all the liabilities of the business. Seller pays its taxes and then distributes the net after-tax proceeds to Larry and Sue in a complete liquidation of Seller. Larry and Sue pay a long-term capital gains tax on the excess of the proceeds received over their stock basis. Seller disappears. The net result is a double tax – a corporate level tax and a shareholder level tax. [2]

Here's how the numbers shake out. Seller would recognize a taxable gain of $7 million, the excess of $17 million (the sum of the $12 million received and the $5 million of liabilities assumed by Buyer) over its assets' basis of $10 million. At a 40 percent combined federal and state tax rate, seller's tax hit would total $2.8 million. The net distributed to Larry and Sue would be $9.2 million, the excess of the $12 million paid by Buyer over the $2.8 million in taxes paid by Seller. Larry's and Sue's recognized long-term capital gains would total $8.7 million ($9.2 million less their $500,000 combined stock basis), and their tax hit at a combined federal and state rate of 20 percent would total $1.74 million. All said and done, they walk with $7.46 million after tax ($3.73 million each). The taxes on the deal total $4.54 million – $2.8 million at the corporate level and $1.74 million at the shareholder level. See Illustration A.

When faced with such consequences, Larry and Sue may ask: Can the $12 million paid by Buyer be allocated to reduce the overall tax bite? If it all goes to Seller, the answer is usually "No" because, as a C corporation, all of Seller's income is taxed at the same rate. The only exception is where Seller has an unused capital loss, a rare situation. In that case, care should be taken to create enough capital gain for Seller to use up any available capital loss. Also, there may be an opportunity to reduce overall taxes by having a portion of the consideration paid directly to Larry and Sue for their personal covenants not to

---

2. I.R.C. § 331.

compete with Buyer. Assume, for example, that $1 million of the price was paid for such personal covenants. This would be ordinary income to Larry and Sue, triggering a tax of $400,000. Seller's tax bite would drop by $400,000, and Larry and Sue's capital gains tax would drop by $120,000 (20 percent of $600,000). The net result would be a tax savings of $120,000.

### Illustration A: Asset Sale-Liquidation

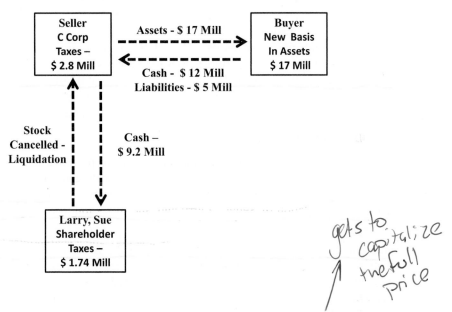

For tax purposes, the big winner under this scenario is Buyer, who gets to allocate the full purchase price to the acquired assets. This results in a basis step-up that will produce larger depreciation or amortization deductions in the future. Section 197 permits a buyer to amortize intangible assets ratably over a 15-year period.[3] Such assets include goodwill, going concern value, covenants not to compete, information bases, customer lists, know-how, licenses, franchises, trade names and more.[4] No longer does the Buyer need to sweat out a fight with the IRS over how much of the price constitutes goodwill or some other type of intangible that, prior to Section 197, produced no future tax benefit. Now there's a solid 15-year write-off period for intangibles.

So, asks Buyer, how much latitude is there in allocating the price to tangible assets that have a depreciation life of less than 15 years? After all, Seller has no interest in the allocations because it pays the same tax on all its income. Section 1060[5] spells out the rules for allocating the total consideration paid in an asset acquisition to the various assets. It mandates a priority residual approach that

---

3. I.R.C. § 197.
4. I.R.C. § 197(d)(1).
5. I.R.C. § 1060.

breaks assets into seven classes and then requires that the total consideration (which includes all liabilities assumed) be allocated to the assets (up to their fair market value) in each priority class.[6] In this case, Buyer would allocate the $17 million total consideration ($12 million paid plus $5 million of assumed liabilities) in the following priority: cash and cash equivalents (Class I priority); marketable securities, foreign currencies, certificates of deposits (Class II priority); accounts receivable, mortgages and credit card receivables (Class III priority); inventories and other dealer property (Class IV priority); all other tangible assets, including equipment (Class V priority); intangible assets other than goodwill and going concern value (Class VI priority); and, lastly, goodwill and going concern value (Class VII priority).[7] Seller and Buyer may, without changing the allocation priority, agree on the value of various assets in their agreement, and any such agreement will be binding on both parties for tax purposes unless the IRS determines that the value is not appropriate.[8] The IRS may use any appraisal method to challenge any allocation of value, especially in those situations (like this) where there are no conflicting interests between the parties to provide a basis for an arm's-length value negotiation.[9]

### b. Liquidation-Asset Sale

Under this scenario, the liquidation of Seller precedes the asset sale to Buyer. Seller distributes all of its assets to Larry and Sue in a complete liquidation, and Larry and Sue then sell the assets to Buyer. The bottom line tax results are identical to the first scenario, although the road traveled is different.

The liquidation of Seller triggers a gain for Seller equal to the excess of the fair market value of its assets ($17 million) over the assets' basis of $10 million.[10] The result is a $7 million gain that triggers a corporate tax of $2.8 million that Larry and Sue must pay because Seller no longer has any assets. Larry and Sue receive assets that have a value of $17 million, and their capital gain is determined by reducing this total asset value by the $5 million of corporate liabilities they assume, the $2.8 million in taxes they pay on behalf of Seller, and their combined stock basis of $500,000. The net result is a long-term capital gain of $8.7 million that, as in the first scenario, triggers a tax of $1.74 million.

Following the liquidation of Seller, Larry and Sue have a tax basis of $17 million in the assets they have just acquired by virtue of the taxes they've paid and the liabilities they've assumed. So the sale to Buyer for $12 million plus the assumption of the $5 million of liabilities produces no gain. The end result is taxes totaling $4.54 million, the same as in scenario one. Again, Larry and Sue each walk with $3.73 million after tax.

As an asset purchaser, the consequences for Buyer under this scenario also are the same as in scenario one. Intangibles qualify for 15-year amortization treatment under Section 197, and the whole Section 1060 priority regime will

---

6. I.R.C. § 1060(c); Reg. §§ 1.1060-1(a)(1), 1.1060-1(b)(1).

7. Reg. §§ 1.1060-1(c), 1.338-6.

8. I.R.C. § 1060(a); Staff of the Joint Committee on Taxation, General Explanation of the Tax Reform Act of 1986, 100th Cong., 1st Sess. 355-360 (1987).

9. Reg. § 1.1060-1(c).

10. I.R.C. § 336(a).

apply.  See Illustration B.

**Illustration B:  Liquidation-Asset Sale**

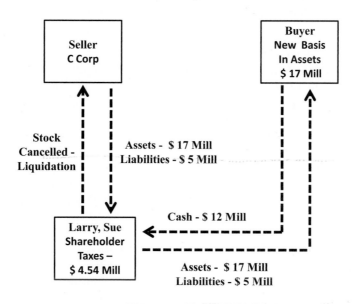

### c. Cash Merger

Under this scenario, Seller is merged into Buyer or a subsidiary of Buyer in a statutory merger, and Buyer distributes cash directly to Larry and Sue. The value of the structure is that the statutory merger will automatically transfer all of Seller's assets and liabilities to Buyer or its subsidiary, thereby eliminating the need to document the transfer of specific assets and the assumption of specific liabilities. For tax purposes, the IRS treats this scenario the same as an asset sale by Seller followed by a complete liquidation of Seller – scenario one.[11]

Since the surviving entity in the merger (Buyer or its subsidiary) is going to have a $2.8 million tax bill as a result of the merger, the cash paid to Larry and Sue in the merger will be $9.2 million ($12 million less $2.8 million).  Again, they incur a capital gains tax of $1.74 million, and they each end up netting $3.73 million.  Since Buyer is deemed an asset purchaser, its tax consequences are the same as under the first two scenarios.

### d.  Installment Asset Sale – Liquidation

This scenario is the same as scenario one, with an important twist.  A portion of the $12 million paid by Buyer is represented by an installment note that, with interest, will be paid off over many years.  Let's assume in this case that the note obligation is equal to $7 million.

The tax issue is whether the note obligation will permit Seller or Larry and

---

11.  Rev. Rule 69-6, 19690-1 C.B. 104.

Sue to defer the taxes they would otherwise have to pay. There is no hope for Seller; the distribution of the installment obligation on the liquidation of Seller triggers an immediate recognition of all gain that might otherwise have been deferred for Seller's benefit under the note.[12] So Seller still owes $2.8 million in taxes that it will pay out of the $5 million cash received from Buyer.

Although Seller gets no deferred tax benefits from the note obligation, Larry and Sue will get a deferral benefit if Seller adopts a plan of complete liquidation and then sells its assets and distributes the note and any other proceeds to its shareholders within 12 months following the adoption of the plan.[13] So Larry and Sue would end up receiving $2.2 million in cash ($5 million less the $2.8 million of taxes paid by Seller) and a $7 million note issued by Buyer, for a total of $9.2 million. Their total capital gain, after subtracting their combined basis, is $8.7 million. So their gross profit fraction is 94.5 percent (8.7/9.2). Of the $2.2 million cash they receive on the liquidation, $2.079 million (94.5 percent) will be taxable as a long-term capital gain. Then 94.5 percent of all future principal payments they receive under the note will be taxable as long-term capital gain.

### e. Asset Sale – No Liquidation

Under this scenario, Seller sells its assets to Buyer, but Seller is not liquidated. The proceeds from the sale ($12 million) are used to pay Seller's $2.8 million tax bill and the remainder ($9.2 million) are kept inside of Seller. There is no liquidation. This scenario raises two questions: Why would any shareholder want to do it? What are the tax consequences of leaving the money in Seller?

The answer to the "Why" question is found in Section 1014 of the Code. If Larry, for example, dies before Seller is liquidated, the basis in his Seller stock is stepped up to its fair market value at death.[14] So if the liquidation follows Larry's death, Larry's estate or heirs will not recognize any capital gain to the extent the proceeds do not exceed the stock's fair market value on Larry's death. The strategy makes little sense for a 58 year-old in good health. But for someone twenty years older or a shareholder dealing with serious health issues, the prospect of completely avoiding the tax at the shareholder level might be appealing, which raises the second question.

If the proceeds of the sale are maintained in Seller and invested to generate portfolio income (interests, dividends, rents, etc.), Seller will become a personal holding company subject to the personal holding company tax penalty. What this means, as a practical matter, is that Seller will need to distribute its earned portfolio income as dividend income to Larry and Sue to avoid the personal holding company penalty tax. Although this results in a double tax on the portfolio income, it may not be a serious problem if the double tax burden continues only for a short period. It might end up being a relatively small cost for eliminating a huge capital gain in the deceased shareholder's estate.

What about converting to S status after the sale in order to eliminate the

---

12. I.R.C. § 453B(a).
13. I.R.C. § 453(h).
14. I.R.C. § 1014(a).

double tax hit on the portfolio income as Seller holds the proceeds and waits for a shareholder to die? Won't work. Section 1375 imposes an entity level tax at the maximum corporate rate on any S corporation with C corporation earnings and profits (which Seller would have in spades by virtue of the sale) that has net investment income in excess of 25 percent of its total gross receipts. Plus, if the condition persists for three consecutive years, the S election is terminated.[15] The Code drafters saw this one coming.

### f. Straight Stock Sale

*Hot Option*

This scenario is the easiest and one of the most popular. Larry and Sue just sell their stock in Seller to Buyer. Buyer becomes the new sole shareholder of Seller. Since Seller is not a party to the transaction, it recognizes no income. The only income recognized is the capital gain at the shareholder level – the excess of the amount Larry and Sue receive from Buyer over the basis in their stock.

The trade-off for the single tax hit is that Buyer takes Seller with its historic basis in its assets. There is no basis step-up at the corporate level for the additional value paid by Buyer. In this case, the basis loss is $7 million (the excess of the $17 million fair market value over the $10 million basis). Had the transaction been structured under any of the prior scenarios, Buyer would have received additional future tax write-offs of $7 million. Since Buyer loses this tax benefit under this scenario, it is reasonable to expect that Buyer will not be willing to pay as much.

The big question then becomes: How large of a haircut in price will the Buyer require for this structure? If we assume that Buyer's combined federal and state marginal income tax rate will remain at 40 percent, the additional $7 million in basis would produce future tax savings of $2.8 million. But this number must be reduced by two factors to arrive at a fair estimate of the value of the lost tax benefits to Buyer. First, if the transaction were structured as an asset sale under any of the prior scenarios, Buyer would have to start new depreciation and amortization periods for all assets acquired. Many of these new write-off periods may be longer than the historic write-off periods that would be inherited under this scenario. Thus, while future write-offs will clearly be less under this scenario, this scenario may result in faster write-offs (and thus faster tax benefits) for some assets. Second, the difference in the future annual tax benefits of the write-offs under an asset scenario and this scenario, as adjusted, must be discounted by an interest factor to arrive at the present value of such benefits. Since much of the difference will be realized over a 15-year period, this present value discount often is huge. In theory, the present value of the lost tax benefits represents the additional tax cost of this scenario to the Buyer and would be the basis of any price reduction. If in this case these two reduction factors result in a present value of $1.5 million (from a starting point of $2.8 million), the price Buyer would pay for the stock of Seller would be reduced from $12 million to $10.5 million.

Note that even with such a $1.5 million price reduction, Larry and Sue net

---

15. I.R.C. § 1362(d)(3).

more on an after-tax basis under this scenario than under any of the previous asset sale scenarios. Their recognized long-term capital gain would be $10 million (the excess paid by Buyer over their $500,000 stock basis). Using the assumed combined capital gains rate of 20 percent, Larry and Sue's tax hit would equal $2 million, reducing their net yield to $8.5 million. They would each net $4.25 million, nearly a 14 percent increase over the $3.73 million realized under the prior asset scenarios.

Now, suppose the parties agree to a total stock price of $10.5 million, but Buyer only wants to purchase 80 percent of Larry and Sue's stock for $8.4 million (80 percent of $10.5 million). The remaining $2.1 million will come from Seller, who will pay this amount to Larry and Sue to redeem the balance of their Seller stock. Larry and Sue end up getting their $10.5 million, and Buyer ends up owning all of Seller's outstanding stock by using only $8.4 million of its cash. Of course, Seller is out $2.1 million.

### Illustration C: Bootstrap Stock Acquisition

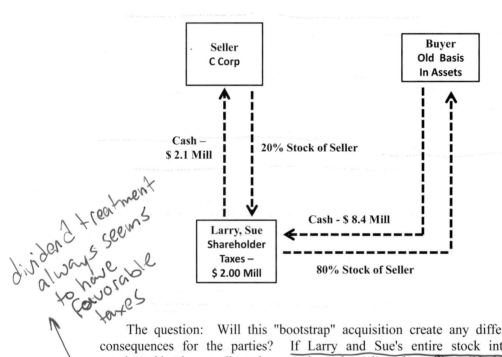

The question: Will this "bootstrap" acquisition create any different tax consequences for the parties? If Larry and Sue's entire stock interest is terminated by the coordinated transactions, the redemption will qualify for sale or exchange treatment (as opposed to dividend treatment), and they will end up in the same after-tax position.[16] The only significant difference is that Buyer's basis in its newly-acquired Seller stock will be $2.1 million less. See Illustration C.

There is one other potential twist under this bootstrap scenario. Suppose Seller's stock is owned by a C corporation ("LS"), not Larry and Sue. Could the transaction be structured so that the amount paid by Seller to LS would qualify as

---

16. Zenz v. Quinlivan, 213 F.2d 914 (6th Cir. 1954); Rev. Rule 75-447, 1975-2 C.B. 113.

a dividend that would trigger a dividend deduction under 243 (available only to corporate shareholders) and eliminate the tax on $2.1 million of the proceeds realized in the transaction? This technique will not work if the transactions are linked for tax avoidance purposes and not supported by independent business purposes.[17] The proceeds will not be treated as dividends subject to the 243 deduction.

### g. Statutory Merger          *Hot option*

In this scenario, Seller and Buyer merge under state law and Buyer issues to Seller's shareholders, Larry and Sue, its stock as part of the purchase price. The goal is to qualify the transaction as a tax-free A reorganization under Section 368(a)(1)(A).[18] Assume in this case that the consideration paid to Larry and Sue totals $10.5 million – $2.5 million in cash and $8 million in Buyer's common stock. If the transaction qualifies as an A reorganization, Seller recognizes no taxable income,[19] Buyer recognizes no taxable income,[20] and Larry and Sue recognize only $2.5 million of taxable income – the amount of cash that they receive.[21] Their total tax hit, at a combined federal and state rate of 20 percent, is $500,000, a far cry from the total tax bill under any of the previous scenarios.

There are a few trade-offs for this wonderful tax treatment. First, Larry and Sue's basis in the Buyer stock they receive would equal their basis in their old Seller stock ($500,000), increased by their recognized gain ($2.5 million) and decreased by the cash received ($2.5 million).[22] Thus, in this case, their basis remains at $500,000 ($250,000 each). If either of them sells their Buyer stock before death, a large capital gain will be triggered on the sale because of the low carryover basis. If they hold the Buyer stock until death, its basis will be stepped up to its fair market value at death.[23] Second, Seller's basis in the assets acquired by Buyer in the merger carries over to Buyer.[24] There is no step up in basis. And third, in select situations, the income recognized by the shareholders, Larry and Sue in this case, may be taxed as dividend income, but will never exceed their gain realized in the exchange.[25] So long as the dividend rate and the long-term capital gains rate remain the same, this possibility will be of no significance to individual shareholders.

So now the big question: What does it take to qualify as an A reorganization? Four requirements must be satisfied. First, there must be a statutory merger or consolidation under applicable state law.[26] With the merger in this case, all assets and liabilities of Seller are transferred to Buyer without the

---

17. See Waterman Steamship Corp. v. Commissioner, 430 F.2d 1185 (5th Cir. 1970). Also see TSN Liquidating Corp. v. United States, 624 F.2d 1328 (5th Cir. 1980) and Litton Industries v. Commissioner, 89 T.C. 1086 (1987) where technique worked under the specific facts of the case.
18. I.R.C. § 368(a)(1)(A).
19. I.R.C. § 361(a).
20. I.R.C. § 1032(a).
21. I.R.C. §§ 354(a)(1), 356(a)(1).
22. I.R.C. § 358(a)(1).
23. I.R.C. § 1014.
24. I.R.C. § 362(b).
25. I.R.C. § 356(a)(2).
26. I.R.C. § 368(a)(1)(A).

need for specific asset or liability transfer documents, and Seller is dissolved by operation of law.

Second, the continuity of interest doctrine must be satisfied. In this case, the doctrine requires that the stock issued by Buyer in the transaction equal a certain percentage of the total consideration paid by Buyer.[27] How large must that percentage be? Case law suggests that 40 percent will do the job,[28] and the IRS has said that 50 percent will qualify for a favorably ruling.[29] In this case, the percentage is in excess of 76 percent ($8 million as a percent of $10.5 million). Note that the percentage requirement focuses on the nature of the consideration paid by Buyer, not the shareholder's ownership percentage in the merged entity, which often is very small. Also, this requirement places no limitation on Larry or Sue's capacity to sell some of their Seller stock to a party unrelated to Seller or Buyer immediately before the merger, nor their capacity to sell any of their Buyer stock to a party unrelated to Buyer immediate after the merger (even if prearranged).[30]

Third, the continuity of business enterprise doctrine must be satisfied. This requires that the purchaser continues the business of the selling entity or uses a significant portion of the selling entity's assets for business purposes.[31] The requirement would not prevent Buyer from transferring Seller's business or assets to a subsidiary corporation or a partnership that is controlled by Buyer.[32]

Finally, there must be a business purpose for the merger. In a merger designed to strengthen two corporate entities, the business purpose requirement usually is not a problem.

### h. Stock Swap

This scenario is designed to qualify as a tax-free B reorganization under Section 368(a)(1)(B).[33] Here, Buyer would transfer its voting stock to Larry and Sue in exchange for all of their stock in Seller. The tax consequences for all the parties would be the same as in the previous merger scenario, except that Larry and Sue would not recognize any taxable income on the exchange because they would not receive any cash.

What does it take to qualify as a tax-free B reorganization? The big factor (and major difference from other reorganizations) is the "solely" requirement – the consideration paid by the purchaser must consist solely of the purchaser's voting stock.[34] Thus, Buyer could not use any other consideration, including nonvoting stock, without killing the tax-free treatment of the exchange. In addition to the "solely" requirement, the continuity of interest (a slam dunk with only voting stock), continuity of business enterprise, and business purpose

27. Reg. § 1.368-1(e)(1).
28. See, for example, John A. Nelson Co. v. Helvering, 296 U.S. 374 (1935), Miller v. Commissioner, 84 F.2d 415 (6th Cir. 1936), and Ginsburg and Levin, Mergers, Acquisitions and Buyouts ¶ 610 (2004 edition).
29. Rev. Proc. 77-37, 1977-2 C.B. 568.
30. Reg. § 1.368-1(e)(1).
31. Reg. § 1.368-1(d).
32. Reg. § 1.368-1(d)(4) & (5).
33. I.R.C. § 368(a)(1)(B).
34. I.R.C. § 368(a)(1)(B); Reg. § 1.368-2(c).

requirements must also be satisfied. The "solely requirement makes the B reorganization one of the least favored strategies.

### i. Stock for Assets

Under this scenario, Buyer would transfer its voting stock to Seller as consideration for Seller's assets and business. Seller would then liquidate by distributing the Buyer stock to Larry and Sue. The goal would be to qualify the transaction as a tax-free C reorganization. If successful, the tax consequences to all the parties would be the same as in the previous two reorganization scenarios. One is hard pressed to imagine why this scenario would ever be preferred over a statutory merger ("A") reorganization. The execution is far more difficult because specific assets and liabilities must be transferred; with a merger, this happens automatically by operation of law. Plus, as we will see, the qualification requirements are more demanding.

As for what it takes to qualify, the continuity of interest, continuity of business enterprise, and business purpose requirements must be satisfied. That's the easy part. There also is a "solely" voting stock requirement similar to the stock swap B reorganization, but it is not as strict.[35] It is not violated by the purchaser's assumption of liabilities.[36] Plus, consideration other than voting stock is permitted if (and this is a big "if") the value of the other consideration and the assumed liabilities do not exceed 20 percent of the total consideration paid. In this case, for example, Buyer's assumption of Seller's liabilities of $5 million would not violate the C reorganization "solely" requirement. But because those liabilities exceed 20 percent of the total consideration paid by Buyer ($15.5 million if Buyer issues $10.5 million of voting stock and assumes $5 million of liabilities), no other consideration can be paid. If the liabilities were less than 20 percent of the total, different consideration would be permitted up to the 20 percent mark. So, unlike the statutory merger, there is no capacity for Larry and Sue to get any cash out of the deal without killing the tax-free treatment for all parties.

There are a few additional C reorganization requirements that aren't a problem in this and many cases, but can be issues in select situations. C reorganization treatment requires that Buyer purchase "substantially all" of Seller's property, which, to be safe, means it must acquire at least 90 percent of the fair market value of Seller's net assets and 70 percent of the fair market value of its gross assets.[37] Finally, Seller must distribute all its assets (principally the Buyer's stock) to its shareholders pursuant to the reorganization plan.[38]

### j. Forward Triangular Merger

Under this very popular scenario, Buyer forms a wholly owned subsidiary ("Subsidiary"), Seller is merged into Subsidiary, and Buyer's stock is issued to

---

35. I.R.C. § 368(a)(1)(C).
36. I.R.C. § 368(a)(1)(C).
37. I.R.C. § 368(a)(1)(C); Rev. Proc. 77-37, 1977-2 C.B. 568, 569.
38. I.R.C. § 368(a)(2)(G). The statute authorizes the Treasury Secretary to waive this requirement in accordance with conditions prescribed by the Secretary. See Rev. Proc. 89-50, 1989-2 C.B. 631.

Seller's shareholders, Larry and Sue. Buyer ends up owning Seller's assets and business through its new subsidiary, Seller disappears, and Larry and Sue get Buyer stock. The tax consequences for all the parties are the same as under a statutory merger ("A") reorganization. The key is to qualify under Section 368(a)(2)(D), which specifically permits tax-free reorganization treatment for such a triangular merger.

In addition to the regular continuity of interest, continuity of business enterprise, and business purpose requirements, three other conditions must be satisfied. First, Subsidiary must acquire substantially all of Seller's property.[39] It's the same "substantially all" requirement applicable to C reorganizations. No problem here. Second, none of Subsidiary's stock can be used in the transaction. Again, no problem. Third, the transaction must be structured so that it would have qualified as a statutory merger ("A") reorganization if Seller had been merged into Buyer.[40] This third condition (and here's the good news) just requires that the continuity of interest requirement for an A reorganization must have been satisfied.[41] Thus, a substantial portion of the consideration paid by Buyer (50 to 60 percent) may be property other than its stock and the transaction will still qualify as a tax-free reorganization. Of course, Seller's shareholders, Larry and Sue, must still recognize income for the non-stock consideration (as in the case of an A reorganization), but otherwise the tax-free treatment applies.

### Illustration D: Forward Triangular Merger

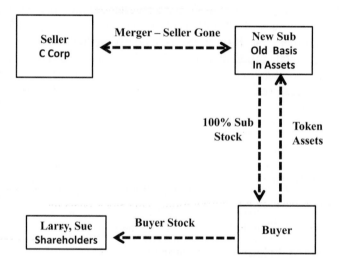

The value of this strategy is that it offers the flexibility and simplicity of a

---

39. I.R.C. § 368(a)(2)(D).
40. I.R.C. § 368(a)(2)(D).
41. Reg. § 1.368-2(b)(2).

statutory merger, enables the purchaser to acquire the assets in a new subsidiary, and permits the use of substantial non-stock consideration without threatening the tax-free character of the reorganization. See Illustration D.

### k. Reverse Triangular Merger

This scenario is a close cousin to the last. The difference is that Seller, not Subsidiary, is the surviving entity of the merger. As in the last scenario, Buyer forms Subsidiary, Subsidiary merges with Seller, and Buyer's stock is issued to Seller's shareholders, Larry and Sue. Here, Seller ends up as a wholly owned subsidiary of Buyer, and Subsidiary disappears. This reverse triangular merger[42] is attractive in those situations where Seller's continued existence is important for non-tax reasons (e.g., contractual rights, leases, licenses, franchises, etc.). The tax consequences to all parties are the same as under the prior scenario, but qualification is slightly tougher.

With one major exception, the qualification requirements for a reverse triangular merger generally are the same as a forward triangular merger. The exception relates to the amount of non-stock consideration that may be paid to the shareholders, Larry and Sue. For a reverse triangular merger to qualify as a tax-free reorganization, 80 percent of the Seller's stock must be acquired with voting stock of Buyer.[43] So the non-stock consideration cannot exceed 20 percent of the total consideration. As compared to a forward triangular merger, the reverse merger allows the selling entity to survive (which is important in many situations), but offers less flexibility with regard to the amount of non-stock consideration that can be used in the transaction.

### 4. S CORPORATION SCENARIOS

How do the structural scenarios change if Seller is an S corporation, not a C corporation? The impact of four primary factors must be assessed. First, if Seller has been an S corporation for a significant length of time, Larry and Sue's basis in their stock will be higher. Their basis in their S corporation stock is increased as the earnings of the S corporation are passed through and taxed to them but retained inside the company.[44] Seller's equity now has a book value of $5 million. Thus, depending on when Seller elected S status, Larry and Sue's basis in their stock may be as high as $5 million, a ten-fold increase over their $500,000 stock basis in a C corporation. This stock basis increase, a big benefit for S corporation shareholders, pays off at time of sale. Under all structural scenarios, the shareholder's stock basis affects the amount of gain recognized at the time of sale or, in the case of a reorganization, the amount that carries over to become the basis of the stock acquired in the reorganization.

Second, any corporate level gain triggered on the sale of assets or a liquidation of the S corporation will be passed through and taxed to the S corporation shareholders, Larry and Sue. The character of the gain is based on

*[handwritten margin note: Since the S corporation avoids the double tax hit]*

---

42. I.R.C. § 368(a)(2)(E).
43. I.R.C. §§ 368(a)(2)(E), 368(c).
44. I.R.C. § 1367.

the assets transferred by the S corporation.[45]    The real plus is that the shareholder's basis in their stock is increased by the amount of the gain.[46]   As a result, there is little or no shareholder-level tax triggered on the distribution to the shareholders.   Thus, the double tax hit is eliminated even in those situations where the transaction is structured to give the purchaser a basis step-up in the acquired assets.

For example, assume in this case that Buyer purchases all of Seller's assets (which have a value of $17 million), assumes the liabilities of $5 million, and pays $12 million cash (first scenario above).   As an S corporation, Seller recognizes a $7 million gain, $1 million of which is ordinary income (1245 recapture) and $6 million of which is capital gain.  This income is passed through and taxed to Larry and Sue, resulting in a tax of $1.6 million (40 percent of $1 million and 20 percent of $6 million).  Larry and Sue's basis in their stock also is increased $7 million.  If we assume that Seller has always been an S corporation and that Larry and Sue's basis in their stock before the sale equaled the book value of Seller's equity before the sale ($5 million), Larry and Sue would have a basis of $12 million in their stock when the $12 million of sales proceeds are distributed to them.  Thus, the $12 million distribution triggers no additional tax on its receipt.  Plus, as a purchaser of assets, Buyer gets a basis step-up.  The net after-tax yield to Larry and Sue is $10.4 million ($5.2 million each), a 36 percent increase over the $3.73 million they each would have netted after the double tax hit with a C corporation.

The practical effect of this difference is huge.  No longer is there a need to balance the purchaser's desire for a step up in basis against the burdens of a double tax hit, or to hassle with a negotiated price reduction to induce the purchaser to forego the basis step-up.  Even when the transaction (for whatever reason) is structured as a stock purchase with the purchaser buying the stock of the S corporation shareholders, the parties may jointly make an election under 338(h)(10) to have the transaction treated as an asset sale followed by a liquidation.  The purchaser ends up with a basis step-up, and no double tax is generated.

Third, if the S corporation has a C past, the potential impacts of the built-in gains (BIG) tax must be assessed.[47]   The BIG tax applies when an S corporation disposes of assets that it owned at the time of its conversion to S status within 10 years of the conversion.   It's an entity level tax imposed at the maximum corporate rate on the built-in gain at the time of conversion.  This tax is in addition to the tax that is realized and passed through to the S corporation's shareholders on the sale.  Its purpose is to preserve, at least in part and for a period of ten years, the double tax burdens of the corporation's C past.

Finally, an S corporation may be a party to any of the tax-free reorganization scenarios described above.  The challenge is to assess the impact of the reorganization on the corporation's continued S status if the corporation survives the reorganization.  If the stock of the S corporation ends up being

45. I.R.C. § 1366(b).
46. I.R.C. § 1367.
47. See generally I.R.C. § 1374.

owned by a C corporation after the reorganization (as might happen in a B reorganization or a reverse triangular merger), S status will be lost. If the S corporation is the purchaser in the reorganization, care should be taken to ensure that no S corporation eligibility requirements are violated (e.g., the 100 shareholder limitation, no corporate or partnership shareholders, etc.).

### 5. PARTNERSHIP-TAXED ENTITY SCENARIOS

How do the structural scenarios change if Seller is a partnership-taxed entity? If Buyer's stock is used in the deal, the tax-free reorganization options are out. They require corporate status of all parties. So any Buyer stock used in the transaction will be treated the same as any other consideration. As for the other structural options, the partnership's presence eliminates the burden of a double tax. The basis increase on the income passed through is the same as with an S corporation – both as income is accumulated during the life of the entity and when it is recognized at the time of sale.[48] Thus, the tax consequences are similar, but not identical, to those for an S corporation.

If Seller, as a partnership-taxed entity, sells all its assets to Buyer for $12 million and Buyer's assumption of all liabilities, a $7 million gain will be triggered and passed through to the partners, Larry and Sue. The character of the gain will be determined at the partnership level; thus, $1 million will be ordinary income (1245 recapture) and $6 million will be capital gain (goodwill and going concern value). Larry and Sue's basis in their partnership interests will be increased by the $7 million pass-through gain. Thus, assuming Larry and Sue had a combined basis in their partnership interests of $5 million before the transaction, there will be no second tax on the gain when the proceeds from the sale are distributed to Larry and Sue. Buyer will get a stepped-up basis in the assets under the 1060 regime and the ability to write off intangibles over 15 years under Section 197.

Although the consequences of this asset sale scenario look just like its S corporation counterpart, there are a few potential differences. First, if Larry or Sue had contributed to Seller any of the property sold by Seller and that contributed property had a built-in gain or built-in loss at the time of contribution (that is, a fair market value different from its transferred basis), any gain recognized on the sale of the contributed property would first be allocated to the contributing partner to account for such built-in gain or loss, and the balance would then be allocated to the two partners.[49] Thus, although the total gain recognized by Larry and Sue on such a sale would be the same as with an S corporation, the gain would be allocated differently among the owners. Second, unlike an S corporation with a prior C past, a partnership-taxed entity that sells its assets need not worry about any entity level tax comparable to the ten-year BIG tax under Section 1374. If the business had a prior C history, it would have taken its tax lumps at the time of its conversion from C to partnership status.

---

48. I.R.C. § 705(a).
49. I.R.C. § 704(c)(1); Reg. § 1.704-3(a)(3).

Suppose Larry and Sue liquidate Seller and receive all Seller's assets and liabilities and then sell all the assets to Buyer for $12 million and Buyer's assumption of the liabilities. The partnership would terminate on the liquidation, and its tax year would close.[50] Generally, Larry and Sue, as the partners of Seller, would not recognize any gain or loss on the liquidation of Seller.[51] Their basis in their partnership interests would carry over to the basis in the assets received in the liquidation.[52] Their subsequent sale of the assets would trigger a taxable gain equal to the excess of the amount they received over their basis in the assets ($7 million under these facts). The character of the gain would be based on the assets sold; thus, $1 million would be ordinary income and $6 million would be capital gain. But, again, the gain might be allocated differently between Larry and Sue if, within the seven years preceding the liquidation, one of them had contributed some of the property distributed in the liquidation.[53] Also, any attempt to allocate the ordinary income element of the gain disproportionately between the Larry and Sue (if, for example, one of them was in a lower personal tax bracket) by distributing more equipment (1245 recapture property) to one partner and more of the other assets to the other partner will fail.[54] As a purchaser of the assets, Buyer would get a new basis in the assets.

Suppose, as an alternative, Buyer purchased Larry and Sue's interests in the partnership for $12 million. Seller, the partnership, would terminate for tax purposes. Larry and Sue would recognize income equal to the excess (here $7 million) of the amount received over their basis in the partnership interests.[55] But, unlike a sale of corporate stock, the sale of a partnership interest may trigger ordinary income if the partnership holds ordinary income assets (e.g., unrealized receivables and inventory items).[56] Thus, the gain represented by such assets will affect the character of the gain recognized by a partner on the sale of a partnership interest. Here, $1 million of the gain recognized by Larry and Sue would be taxed as ordinary income. As for Buyer, the transaction would be treated as a purchase, as if Seller had made a liquidating distribution to Larry and Sue followed by Buyer's purchase of the former partnership assets – exactly as in the prior scenario.[57]

## PROBLEM 9-A

**9-A.** Circle Inc. (CI) is a calendar year C corporation that has two equal shareholders – Doug and Jane. Doug, age 81, owns 1,000 shares of CI's common stock, with a basis of $300,000. Jane, age 34, also owns 1,000 shares, but her basis is $7 million. Jane inherited the stock from her father. CI's balance sheet assets and liabilities are set forth below.

Olson Inc. (Olson) wants to buy CI, and Doug and Jane are ready to sell.

---

50. I.R.C. § 708(b).
51. I.R.C. § 731(a).
52. I.R.C. § 732(b).
53. I.R.C. § 704(c)(1)(B).
54. I.R.C. § 751(b); Reg. § 1.751-1.
55. I.R.C. § 741.
56. I.R.C. § 751(a); Reg. § 1.751-1(d).
57. Rev. Rule 99-6, 1999-1 C.B. 432.

Assume that CI is subject to a combined federal and state income tax rate of 40 percent, and Doug and Jane's combined federal and state ordinary marginal income tax rate is 40 percent and capital gain rate is 20 percent.

### CI's Assets and Liabilities

|                     | Book Value Basis | Fair Market Value |
|---------------------|------------------:|------------------:|
| Cash                | $ 1,500,000       | $ 1,500,000       |
| Inventory           | 2,500,000         | 3,000,000         |
| Accounts Receivable | 2,000,000         | 2,000,000         |
| Equipment           | 2,000,000         | 3,000,000         |
| Customer Lists      | -                 | 500,000           |
| Copyrights          | 200,000           | 500,000           |
| Goodwill            | -                 | 11,000,000        |
| Total Assets        | $ 8,200,000       | $ 21,500,000      |
| Accounts Payable    | $ 1,500,000       | $ 1,500,000       |

a. CI sells its assets to Olson for $20 million plus an assumption of all liabilities. CI pays its taxes and distributes all remaining proceeds to Doug and Jane. Calculate the tax impacts to CI, Doug, and Jane. What is Olson's basis in the assets? Any suggestions for Doug or Jane?

b. Olson buys CI's stock from Doug and Jane for $18 million. Is this a sensible price under the circumstances? Calculate the tax impacts to CI, Doug, and Jane. What is Olson's basis in its CI stock?

c. Olson buys 70 percent of CI's stock from Doug and Jane for $12.6 million. CI redeems the remaining 30 percent by paying $2.7 million cash to Doug (it will borrow an additional $1.2 million) and distributing the equipment to Jane. Calculate the tax impacts to CI, Doug, and Jane.

d. Olson forms a new subsidiary (S). CI is merged into S, and Doug and Jane are each issued 100,000 shares (value $90 per share) of Olson's common stock. What are the tax impacts to CI, Doug, Jane, Olson and S in such a reorganization? If Doug and Jane wanted some cash out of the deal, how much cash could they be paid without destroying the tax-free reorganization?

e. Same as **d.**, except S is merged into CI. What are the tax impacts to CI, Doug, Jane, Olson and S in such a reorganization? If Doug and Jane wanted some cash out of the deal, how much cash could they be paid without destroying the tax free character of the reorganization for everyone?

f. Same as **a.** except CI is and always has been an S corporation and Doug's basis in his stock is $3 million and Jane's basis is $8 million.

g. Same as **b.** except CI is and always has been an LLC taxed as a partnership, and Doug's basis in his partnership interest is $3 million and Jane's basis is $8 million.

# B. DOCUMENTING THE DEAL

## NEGOTIATING THE PURCHASE AGREEMENT
Richard A. Goldberg[58]

## 1. Introduction

   **a. Function of the acquisition agreement**. In addition to setting forth the principal financial terms of a transaction, the acquisition agreement also sets forth the legal rights and obligations of the parties with respect to the transaction. It provides the buyer with a detailed description of the business being acquired and affords the buyer remedies where the description proves to be materially inaccurate. The agreement indicates the actions which must be taken by the parties to properly consummate the transaction and requires the parties to take these actions. Finally, the acquisition agreement allocates the risks associated with the purchased business among the parties to the agreement. Special consideration may be applicable to the structuring of an acquisition and/or sale of divisions and subsidiaries. Certain legal issues are unique to these divestiture transactions, and may require particular attention, such as: fiduciary issues, financials; shared assets and liabilities; antitrust issues, taxes and employee matters.

   **b. Main components**. The objectives of the purchase agreement are accomplished through the operation of the representations and warranties, covenants, conditions and indemnification provisions.

   **(1) Representations and warranties**. The primary function of the representations and warranties is to provide the buyer with a "snapshot" of the acquired business at a particular point in time, typically on the date the agreement is signed and again on the date of the closing.

   **(2) Covenants**. The covenants govern the relationship of the parties over a certain time period. Certain covenants apply from the signing of the agreement until the closing date and provide assurance that the proper actions are taken to facilitate the closing of the transaction and preserve the business pending the closing. Other covenants survive the closing for a certain length of time, such as covenants requiring cooperation of the parties with respect to the post-closing transition of the business or sharing of facilities.

   **(3) Conditions**. Acquisition agreements contain conditions precedent that must be met in order for the party receiving the benefit of the condition to be legally obligated to consummate the transaction. If one party fails to satisfy a condition by the date of the closing, the other party has the right to terminate the agreement and walk away from the transaction.

   **(4) Indemnification**. The indemnification portion of the agreement requires the parties to pay damages in the event of a breach of their respective

---

58. Copyright © Practicing Law Institute and the author. Reprinted with permission. Mr. Goldberg is a partner in the law firm of Dechert LLP. His practice focuses on mergers and acquisitions, and he has counseled public and private companies, as well as investment banking firms. He has lectured and written extensively on legal topics, including mergers and acquisitions.

representations, warranties and covenants. Indemnification provisions also serve to allocate specific post-closing risks associated with the transferred business.

### c. Simultaneous versus delayed closing.

**(1) Purposes of a delayed closing**. In most instances, the parties would prefer to sign the agreement and close without any delay. However, it is often necessary to delay the closing to provide time to obtain third party and/or governmental consents which are required to consummate the transaction or to facilitate the financing of the transaction. For example, transactions exceeding a certain size require the approval of the Federal Trade Commission, and others necessitate filings with the Securities and Exchange Commission (SEC), e.g., where securities of the purchaser are issued as consideration for the transaction in a manner which constitutes a public offering. In addition, the seller and possibly the buyer may need to obtain shareholder consent to the transaction. In such an event, if the seller or the buyer, as the case may be, is a public reporting company, subject to the SEC's proxy rules, an SEC filing would also be required. The two-part signing and closing allows the parties to reach an agreement as early as possible and attend to these matters after the agreement is signed.

The Delaware Supreme Court held, in a 1996 decision, that in a two-step merger, the value added to the business being acquired following a change in majority control and during the transition period "accrues to the benefit of all shareholders and must be included in the appraisal process on the date of the merger." Accordingly, when a buyer is considering a two-step acquisition, the buyer should consider the possibility that dissenting shareholders who do not sell their shares in the first step of an acquisition may be entitled to their pro rata share of the value added to the business being acquired by the buyer during the transition period, thereby forcing the buyer to pay a higher price to such shareholders at the second step of the acquisition than the original price paid.

**(2) Effects on the agreement**. Acquisition agreements involving a simultaneous signing and closing are much simpler than those involving delayed closings. The reason for this is that the covenants which govern between the signing and the closing and the conditions to closing may be eliminated. For example, no shop provisions, options and break-up fees are only necessary in the event of a delayed closing (see section IIIC "Specific covenants; effects of termination: no shops, options and break-up fees" below). Other than the principal financial terms, only the representations and warranties, the related indemnification provisions and the post-closing covenants need to be included in the Agreement.

**(3) Disclosure**. During the period between the signing and the closing, the buyer is typically given full access to the seller's books, records and other pertinent data. Prior to the signing, the buyer's access will be less extensive because of the seller's reluctance to provide certain information in the absence of a signed agreement.

### 2. Representations and Warranties

**a. Seller's representations**. The seller's representations and warranties serve various purposes from the buyer's perspective. First, the buyer seeks assurance that the seller has the authority and power to enter into the transaction, and that once the buyer pays the consideration, it will own the business being acquired. Second, the representations serve as a means to acquire information from the seller regarding the nature and value of the business. Representations force the seller to carefully consider and disclose material that may not otherwise be discoverable by the buyer through due diligence. In addition, through the operation of the conditions to closing, the representations provide the buyer with the right to terminate the agreement in the event that any of the representations prove to be false at the time of the closing. The representations also provide the groundwork for indemnification after the closing.

**b. Buyer's representations**. The seller will also want to obtain representations to the effect that the transaction is properly authorized and is binding on the buyer. Aside from these, the form of payment will govern the extent of any other representations and warranties that the seller will require from the buyer. If the consideration is in the form of cash, the seller will usually not seek many other representations and warranties, provided that it is satisfied with the buyer's ability to pay. However, if the consideration includes securities of the buyer, the viability of the buyer's business and associated risks become material to the seller. Accordingly, in these situations, the seller will seek the same type of business disclosure that it is providing to the buyer.

**c. Specific seller representations**. The following is a brief discussion regarding specific types of representations typically made by the seller.

**(1) Financial statements**. The seller's financial statements are a significant source of information regarding the seller's business. A set of year end and stub period (if applicable) financial statements is usually attached as an exhibit to the acquisition agreement or otherwise delivered to the buyer. The seller represents that the financial statements are complete and correct, fairly represent the financial condition of the business (including the liabilities of the seller) for the periods indicated, and were prepared in accordance with generally accepted accounting principles (GAAP). Additional representations might also be sought that mirror Sarbanes-Oxley certification requirements. See section 13 below.

**(2) Assets and liabilities**. The seller will frequently also be asked to make representations about specific assets and liabilities included in the financial statements. This gives the buyer greater protection than the financial statement representation alone because a representation that the financial statements have been prepared in accordance with GAAP may not be breached for a minor variation from the balance sheet with respect to the value of certain assets which are of particular importance to the buyer. The following are examples of these types of representations:

**(i) Accounts receivable**. Negotiations frequently revolve around the seller's reluctance to state that the accounts receivable are collectible, which is in effect a guarantee of collection. Although the seller typically refuses to give such a guarantee, it will usually agree to represent that the accounts receivable arose in the ordinary course of business and represent the actual obligations of its customers. The seller also typically agrees to represent that, except for amounts reserved in allowance for doubtful accounts, there are no known claims or offsets against the receivables. If the collectability of the accounts receivable is an integral part of the value of the business being acquired, the parties sometimes agree that the buyer has the right to "put" or sell back to the seller the receivables that remain uncollected after a certain period of time. A buyer may be reluctant, however, to turn over the collection process to the seller who may not have the same customer sensitivities as the buyer.

**(ii) Inventory.** The objective of a representation regarding inventory is to flush out obsolete or unsalable inventory that has not been written off and to make sure that the inventory has been accounted for on a consistent basis.

**(iii) Plant and equipment**. The seller typically represents that the plant and equipment is in good operating condition and that no fundamental structural problems exist. The seller may also be asked to represent that the plant and equipment is sufficient to run the business. The seller will not want to make this representation so stringent as to turn it into a warranty that the equipment will not break down.

**(iv) Liabilities**. A representation stating that the financial statements have been prepared in accordance with GAAP will not cover liabilities which are not required to be included on a balance sheet (e.g. certain contingent liabilities and lease liabilities which are not capitalized) or which occur after the date of the financial statements. As a result, it is important to obtain a representation that there are no undisclosed liabilities except as set forth in the financial statements or on an attached schedule and except those that have been incurred in the ordinary course of business subsequent to the date of the balance sheet. The schedule typically excludes liabilities below an agreed upon dollar threshold.

**(v) Taxes.** A buyer will typically want a representation that all of the require tax returns have been properly prepared and filed and that all taxes shown to be due thereon have been paid, e.g., income taxes, excise taxes, customs taxes, sales taxes, etc. It is helpful for the representation to specify the years through which the seller's income tax returns have been audited and to indicate whether the seller has waived the statute of limitations with respect to any tax years. Of course, a tax representation is less significant in a sale of assets than a sale of stock.

**(3) Leases, contracts and other commitments**. The buyer needs to be familiar with all of the seller's material agreements in order to be forewarned about the obligations that the buyer will be undertaking. In addition, the buyer will review these documents to be sure that they are assignable. The buyer typically seeks a schedule of material agreements and a representation that the seller is not in default under any material agreement. The definition of a "material" contract will depend upon the size of the business being acquired and the cost to the seller of compiling the agreements.

**(4) Customers and suppliers**. Where material, the seller is asked to represent that customer and supplier relations are satisfactory.   Frequently, a schedule of the principal customers and suppliers is provided.

(5)  **Employee matters**.  This representation covers the seller's potential liability under employee benefit plans such as health plans, pension plans, retirement plans, etc. and their respective compliance with ERISA.   Typically, the representation also covers unions, if any, and labor relations, as well as a statement that there are no unfair labor practices or proceedings pending.

(6)  **Patents, trademarks, copyrights, trade names, etc**.  Where material, all patents, trademarks and licenses are listed on a schedule to the purchase agreement.   In addition, the seller may be asked to represent that to its knowledge, its intellectual property is not being infringed upon by any third party and that it is not infringing the intellectual property rights of a third party.

(7)  **Litigation and compliance with law**.  This representation typically covers threatened as well as pending claims.   Knowledge qualifications are usually permitted for threatened litigations but not for those that are pending.

(8)  **Absence of certain changes**.  This representation assures the buyer that there have been no material adverse changes in the business subsequent to the date of the most recent financial statements.   Frequently, the representation will also cover changes in the industry in which the seller operates.

(9)  **Insurance.**   This representation typically provides that the seller maintains adequate insurance with reputable insurance companies.   In addition, the buyer will often want to know whether the seller has been refused any insurance or has experienced any insurance cancellations, as these are often indications of operational problems or uninsurable risks.   A schedule of all the types and amounts of insurance maintained by the seller is sometimes included as part of the representation.   Care should be taken to identify insurance coverage that is maintained on a "claims made" basis, e.g., product liability or directors and officers liability insurance.   "Tail" coverage is often available for purchase by the buyer to avoid gaps in coverage which would otherwise arise under a "claims made" policy.   It is also useful to ascertain whether there is "entity" coverage as part of any directors and officers liability insurance policy.

(10)   **Environmental protection**.   Representations with respect to environmental protection are often one of the more significant representations in the acquisition agreement.   If lenders are involved, they are particularly concerned with these representations in view of the potential lender liability associated with environmental noncompliance.   Environmental representations typically encompass compliance with applicable environmental laws.   However, this is often an area of negotiation because environmental laws are so comprehensive that sellers are typically unwilling to represent that they are in compliance will all such laws.

(11)  **Data Backup and Redundancy**.  In an environment of heightened concern about data redundancy capabilities, a representation should be sought which provides assurances about protections against loss of critical data.

(12)   **Regulation FD**.  Regulation FD adopted by the Securities and

Exchange Commission (SEC) and effective as of October 23, 2000, generally applies whenever a senior official of a U.S. public company or another employee or agent who regularly communicates with the investment community discloses material nonpublic information to a security market professional or to a security holder where it was reasonably foreseeable that the security holder would trade based on the information. When the disclosure obligations of Regulation FD are triggered, the issuer is required to either simultaneously, for intentional disclosures or promptly, for non-intentional disclosures, make public disclosure of the same information. Thus, the buyer might ask the seller to represent that no disclosure violating Regulation FD has been made since the effective date of the Regulation.

**(13) Sarbanes-Oxley**. The Sarbanes-Oxley Act of 2002 (SOX) was enacted on July 30, 2002, with the aim of increasing corporate responsibility. Among other things, SOX imposes two separate certification requirements on the chief executive officer (CEO) and chief financial officer (CFO) of a public company. Section 302 of SOX requires that the CEO/CFO make specific representations in their respective certifications to each annual report on Form 10K and each quarterly report on 10Q. Section 906 creates a new CEO/CFO certification requirement in connection with all periodic reports that contain financial statements.

In 2003, the SEC adopted requirements relating to executive management internal control over financial reporting as required under the SOX mandate. The rules adopted pursuant to Section 404 of SOX require that the CEO/CFO include in their annual reports a report of management on the company's internal control over financial reporting. A company that is an "accelerated filer" as defined in Exchange Act Rule 12b-2, commencing with reports for its fiscal year ending on or after November 15, 2004, must comply with Rule 404 management report on internal control over financial reporting disclosure requirements in its annual report for that fiscal year. A company that is not an "accelerated filer" must comply with Rule 404 disclosure requirements commencing with reports for its first fiscal year ending on or after July 15, 2005. The CEO's/CFO's internal report must certify their responsibility for establishing and maintaining adequate control over financial reporting for the company; assess the effectiveness of the company's internal control over financial reporting as of the end of the company's most recent fiscal year; identify the framework used by management to evaluate the effectiveness of the company's internal control over financial reporting; and certify that the public accounting firm that audited the Company's financial statements included in the annual report has issued an attestation report on management's assessment of the company's internal control over financial reporting. Furthermore, the CEO/CFO must evaluate any change in the company's internal control over financial reporting that occurred during a fiscal quarter that has materially affected or is reasonably likely to materially affect, the company's internal control over financial reporting. In view of the requirements of SOX, the buyer might ask a public company seller to represent that it has complied with the requirements of SOX and to make further representations that mirror the contents of these certifications.

The effect of complying with Section 404 of SOX may add significant challenges to due diligence.  With a looming deadline for certification of internal controls, there may be pressure to integrate an acquired division or subsidiary rapidly so that the certification can be made.  Due diligence will be necessary to determine whether there are weaknesses in internal controls that will prevent certification in a timely manner.  Poor internal controls of a target company were once less significant during the due diligence process because it was viewed that the poor internal controls would be fixed post-acquisition.  Poor internal controls can now impact the acquirer to the extent that management and the auditor may conclude that the acquirer and the target, taken as a whole do not have effective internal control over financial reporting.  In addition, some seemingly small acquisitions can affect the acquirer's Section 404 compliance process if the operations of the new entity represent specific risks to the acquirer or cause a previously insignificant business location to become significant when combined with the acquired entity.  Acquisitions of private companies may cause additional difficulties in this area because private companies are less likely to have devoted much time to documenting their controls.  If an acquisition is closed before the end of a buyer's fiscal year end, the SEC recognizes that it is not always possible to conduct an assessment of an acquired business' internal control over financial reporting in the period between the consummation date and the date of management's assessment.  Management may exclude the acquired business from their assessment and explain why they have done so.  This is, in effect, a one year grace period for compliance for acquisitions made late in the year.  However, management may not make this exclusion for more than one year after the acquisition date or in more than one annual management report.  Although the acquirer may have an extended period of time to prepare its report under Section 404 covering the acquired entity, the first Section 302 certification under SOX after acquisition must include the operations of the acquired entity, and that certification must be made as of the end of the quarter in which the acquisition closes.  As also required by the SOX mandate, the SEC has implemented two additional disclosure requirements pursuant to Sections 406 and 407 of SOX.  Section 406 of SOX requires a company to disclose whether it has adopted a code of ethics that applies to the company's executive management including the CEO, CFO, Controller, or other persons performing similar functions.  Section 407 requires a company to disclose whether its audit committee includes at least one member who is a financial expert.  Rules 406 and 407 are effective for annual reports for fiscal years ending on or after July 15, 2003.  If a company does not adopt a code of ethics nor appoint an audit committee financial expert, the company must disclose these facts.  This disclosure should be reviewed as part of due diligence and might result in additional representations in the purchase agreement.

It is also worth noting that the requirements of SOX may affect public companies acquiring private companies that were not subject to the same SEC oversight prior to the acquisition.  Under the securities laws, if the acquisition is large enough, as defined by SEC regulations, a buyer that is a public company must disclose the historical audited financial statements of the seller on a Form 8-K and in some cases, in a proxy statement or registration statement related to the proposed acquisition. Depending upon the size and nature of the transaction, the buyer may have to include the target company's audited financial statements from the previous year or up to three years prior to the transaction. These requirements make it incumbent upon the buyer to ensure that the audited financial statements are available or can be made available prior to the due date of the SEC filing. In addition, though SOX does not impose new obligations on the officers of the buyer to certify the target company's historical financial reports, it does create new criminal penalties and increase already existing civil and criminal penalties under pre-existing securities laws. For example, Sections 13(a) and 18 of the Securities Exchange Act of 1934 (Exchange Act) impose personal liability (and criminal liability) on the CEO and CFO of a buyer for the contents of any Exchange Act filings and corporate officers signing such filings can be held liable for material misstatements or omissions under Section 10(b) of the Exchange Act. As SOX increases, considerably, the civil and criminal penalties for violations of these laws it is critical that the parties to a merger or purchase agreement conduct extensive due diligence throughout the process in order to carefully review the financial statements and information concerning the target.

**(14) Catch-all representations**. The buyer will sometimes ask the seller to make the general representation that there are no material misstatements or omissions in the representations. This type of representation can be a shortcut in cases where the principals desire to consummate the transaction quickly, without extensive due diligence or time spent on preparing schedules to the agreement.

**d. Schedules**. Schedules are typically the most illuminating portions of an acquisition agreement because they disclose all of the exceptions to the representations and warranties. For example, a representation will often provide that there are no defaults in material agreements except as set forth in the attached schedule. In evaluating a potential acquisition candidate, a review of schedules to previous acquisition agreements by such candidate (which may be publicly available if the candidate is publicly held) can provide a useful source for due diligence.

The information contained in the schedules can often be competitively sensitive. For example, the schedule may contain a list of the seller's largest customers and the volume of business done with these customers during a certain time period. If the buyer is a public company and the acquisition agreement is material to the buyer, the schedules must be filed with the SEC as exhibits to the purchase agreement. In these circumstances, the buyer may be willing to accept, in lieu of a schedule, a representation in the agreement that would have an exclusion for items "previously disclosed to the buyer." This may refer to items delivered during the due diligence process. If this approach is used, thought should be given as to whether these items are intended to be included within the integration clause of the agreement.

It should also be noted that under 8-K disclosure requirements, which became effective August 23, 2004, a merger or similar asset or stock purchase agreement must be disclosed on Form 8-K and filed as an exhibit within four business days of execution. Under prior 8-K rules, while some issuers filed merger agreements earlier, they were not required to be filed until the date of filing of the next quarterly report on Form 10Q or annual report on Form 10K after the execution of the merger agreement.

### e. Limitations on representations and warranties.

**(1) Materiality qualification**. The manner in which a representation is drafted plays an important role in the allocation of risk between the parties. It will determine whether the existence of certain previously undisclosed facts will permit the buyer to terminate the transaction or, after the closing, seek indemnification. One way to shift risk to the buyer is to qualify some or all of the representations with materiality exceptions, e.g., "except for those which do not have a material adverse effect upon the Company, its financial condition or the transaction contemplated hereby." Accordingly, the buyer bears the risk and costs with respect to any non-material items.

Different materiality standards may be used in the various sections of the acquisition agreement. For example, the seller may agree to disclose all litigation (without any materiality qualification) but limit the right to indemnification to situations in which exposure from the undisclosed litigation exceeds a certain dollar threshold. This option allows the buyer to flush out any potential problems with the seller's business through detailed disclosure schedules, but without triggering indemnification obligations for immaterial matters. Another alternative would be to require disclosure and indemnification for all litigation, but permit the buyer to terminate the agreement only in the event that the undisclosed litigation has a material adverse effect on the acquired business. The parties typically arrive at compromises on these issues depending on the particular facts related to the transaction.

**(2) Double materiality**. The buyer should bear in mind the pitfall of double materiality. This occurs when a representation is qualified by materiality and the corresponding indemnification provision is conditioned upon the breaches resulting in a certain threshold level of damages. The result is that the representation would not be breached, and any resulting loss would not be counted toward the minimum threshold level, unless there exists a material obligation or liability which is not disclosed. Due to the interplay of these provisions, the buyer may suffer substantial damages without triggering indemnification, leaving the buyer without adequate protection.

**(3) Knowledge qualification**. The seller can also limit the scope of its representations by having them qualified by a phrase such as "to the best of Seller's knowledge." This qualification limits the duty to disclose to only such information as is within the seller's knowledge. Often, the seller will argue that it can only make representations as to what it knows. However, the issue is not the veracity or trustworthiness of the seller. Instead, it is purely a question of who among the parties will bear the risk of unknown liabilities. By adding a knowledge qualifier, the risk is shifted from the seller to the buyer.

Frequently, the parties negotiate over what the appropriate meaning of "knowledge" should be. The seller will sometimes argue that it cannot be held responsible for the knowledge of all of its employees while the buyer will claim that, as between the seller and buyer, the seller should bear the risk of information known by its low level employees.  A frequent compromise is to define the individual(s) whose knowledge is subsumed within the meaning of the term.  Often, these individuals will be limited to the seller's officers (or just its executive officers) and its directors.  The definition of knowledge may also clarify whether it includes constructive knowledge.

**f.  Incorporation of SEC filings into representations and warranties**.  In situations where the party providing the representations and warranties is a public company, it may be sufficient to simply have a representation regarding the accuracy of the company's SEC filings coupled with limited additional representations concerning transaction specific matters, such as the authorization and execution of the agreement.  However, the buyer is likely to want more specific representations about specialized areas of concern such as environmental and ERISA compliance and customer relations.

### 3.  Covenants

**a.  General**.  Many of the covenants contained in the acquisition agreement require the parties to obtain the necessary approvals and consents from various governmental agencies and third parties, which are required for the consummation of the transaction.  The delayed closing provides the parties with sufficient time to perform these covenants.  Other covenants ensure that the seller's status quo is preserved during the hiatus between the signing and the closing.   Where the parties have a simultaneous signing and closing, the covenants will be limited to post-closing items such as payment of relevant taxes, filing of tax forms and the general covenant to take any further actions which may become necessary to consummate the transaction.

**b.  Covenants pending the closing**.

**(1)  Best efforts qualification**.  When a third-party consent is necessary to consummate the transaction, the buyer may seek an affirmative covenant that the seller will use its "best efforts" to obtain such consent.  "Best efforts" is an ambiguous phrase which parties are sometimes reluctant to use.  For example, a party may be concerned that such a covenant may require it to commence litigation, if necessary, in order to obtain such consent.   A compromise sometimes entails the phrase "reasonable efforts" instead of "best efforts."

**(2)  Stringency of certain covenants**.  The buyer will typically desire strict covenants aimed at preserving the seller's status quo by requiring the seller to seek the buyer's consent prior to taking certain actions.  However, the covenants should not be drafted so strictly as to materially interfere with the business of the seller pending the closing.

**(3)  Examples of specific covenants.**

**(i)  Affirmative:**

- To obtain all necessary consents;

- To carry on the business only in the ordinary course;

- To maintain plant, property and equipment;

- To comply with all applicable laws;

- To pay all taxes when due and avoid liens; and

- To maintain qualifications to do business in appropriate jurisdictions.

**(ii) Negative:**

- Not to introduce any method of accounting inconsistent with that used in prior periods;

- Not to enter into any transaction other than in the ordinary course of business, e.g., sales or purchases of a material amount of assets, bank borrowings;

- Not to amend the seller's charter and by-laws or principal agreements, except in the ordinary course;

- Not to grant any increase in the salary or other compensation of any employee, except in the ordinary course of business (absent previously anticipated increases or scheduled bonuses);

- Not to enter into any long-term contracts or commitments (specific dollar thresholds can be employed);

- Not to release any claims or waive any rights against third parties.

**c.  Covenants effective after the closing.**  Earn outs provide flexibility in determining a purchase price of the acquired business.  Earn outs allow the buyer to pay most of the agreed upon purchase price at the closing, and then make subsequent additional payments which are contingent upon how the business performs after the acquisition.  When using earn out provisions, it is important to clearly define the performance criteria that trigger the additional payments.  Performance criteria may include attaining specified revenue or earnings levels, or other defined targets such as completing the development of a new product line or receipt of awards relating to the acquired business' performance or products.  It is critical to clearly define the accounting terms to be used in earn out provisions (reference to generally accepted accounting rules is helpful).  In that regard, it would be advisable to have an accountant review the earn out provisions to lessen the potential for ambiguity in interpretation, e.g. review by one or more certified public accounting firms.  Further, the period of time over which the contingent payments may be earned, and the timing of computation and payment of the subsequent payments (whether annually or incrementally) must be clearly stated in the earn out provision.  Since disputes with respect to earn out provisions are common, a clause providing for an alternate dispute resolution method may be useful.

**d.  Specific covenants; effects of termination: no shops, options and break-up fees**.  In the event that the agreement has a delayed closing and the seller is publicly held, the seller's board of directors could be faced with an unsolicited offer between signing and closing which it could not ignore without violating its fiduciary duties.  To protect against this possibility, the buyer often requests certain covenants which minimize the actions the seller can take in respect of a third party, discourage third-party offers and compensate the buyer if a transaction is consummated with a third party. These protections generally prohibit the seller's board from soliciting or negotiating with alternate purchasers (subject to the seller board's fiduciary duties, as discussed below). The provisions may also grant the buyer certain rights in the event that the contemplated transaction is never consummated, such as reimbursement of the potential purchaser's expenses, a specified termination fee or an option to purchase certain assets or stock of the seller. These provisions are discussed below.

**(1) No shop provisions**. The agreement will generally contain a no shop provision prohibiting the seller from soliciting other offers. However, the seller will generally insist upon an exception that enables the seller to entertain unsolicited third party offers if the failure to do so would violate the fiduciary duties of the seller's board to its shareholders. This exemption is typically referred to as a "fiduciary out." The "fiduciary out" generally plays a more important role when the seller is a publicly held, as opposed to a closely held, company for two reasons. First, in a closely held company, it is likely that the shareholders have agreed to the transaction with the initial purchaser and may indeed all be parties to the acquisition agreement. Second, since there is no public market for the shares, it is less likely that a competing bid would emerge without cooperation of the shareholders.

**(2) Stock or asset options**. As a result of the "fiduciary out" typically included in the no shop provision, the potential buyer is at risk of the transaction not being consummated due to a competing bid. Accordingly, a purchaser will often ask for an option to purchase stock or assets of the seller upon the occurrence of a triggering event in order to deter, and give itself an advantage over, other potential purchasers. The triggering event is typically the termination of the acquisition agreement or the acquisition by another potential purchaser of a certain percentage of the seller's stock.

**(i) Stock options**. A stock option grants the initial purchaser the right to purchase authorized but unissued stock of the seller upon the occurrence of a triggering event. Such an option is advantageous to the initial purchaser in three respects. First, in the event the seller is considering a competing offer from another potential buyer, the initial purchaser can exercise its options and vote the shares in favor of its transaction with the seller and against the competing offer. Second, by increasing the number of shares outstanding, the issuance of the option would make the purchase by a competing bidder more costly. Finally, in the event a competing offer is commenced and the initial purchaser is outbid, the initial purchaser can realize a profit by exercising its options and tendering its shares for the higher bid.

**(ii) Asset options**. An asset option provides a buyer with the option to purchase a particular asset of the seller at an advantageous price upon the occurrence of a triggering event. Since the particular asset underlying the option is often a significant division or subsidiary of the seller (sometimes referred to as a "crown jewel"), the asset option can be successful in deterring potential purchasers who are mainly interested in, or unwilling to consummate the transaction if the seller were to lose, that asset.

**(3) Expense reimbursement or break-up fees.** Often, the acquisition agreement will contain a provision whereby the seller will be required to reimburse the initial purchaser for expenses incurred in connection with the transaction and/or pay a termination fee in the event that the acquisition agreement is terminated because of a specified reason, including the consummation, or recommendation to the seller's shareholders, of an alternative offer. These payments deter competing offers by making them more expensive and reimburse an unsuccessful potential purchaser for expenses incurred in connection with the failed acquisition.

**(4) Legality.** In the event of a change of control, the primary objective of the seller's board of directors must be "to secure the transaction offering the best value reasonably available for [its] stockholders." No shop provisions, options and termination fees are generally material features of a transaction to be considered by the board of directors in the exercise of their fiduciary duties to further that end.

      **(i) No shop provisions.** While no shop provisions are not per se illegal, they must not limit the fiduciary duties of the seller's board of directors or they will be unenforceable.

      **(ii) Options.** Asset and stock options have generally been upheld in Delaware courts if the granting of the option is necessary, and is used, to encourage either the initial offer or other competing offers on terms more favorable to the seller's shareholders. However, these options generally have been enjoined where they have been used to favor one buyer over another in the bidding process, and to exclude or limit competing offers, to the detriment of the seller's shareholders.

      **(iii) Break-up fees.** Break-up fees are generally upheld if they are reasonable in relation to the size of the whole transaction. In each case, the test would be whether the defensive measure used enhanced the bidding process in order to maximize the value to the seller's shareholders. In addition, Courts will take into account the overall effect that all of the protective measures have collectively on competing bids. Break-up fees average generally between 1 percent and 3.5 percent of the overall deal value, with smaller deals at the higher end of the range.

## 4. Conditions

      **a. General.** The parties' obligation to close the transaction is subject to certain conditions precedent which, absent a waiver, must be fulfilled before the party to whom the condition runs is obligated to close. Certain conditions are reciprocal, such as the requirement to obtain the necessary governmental or third party consents to the transaction. Other conditions encompass circumstances beyond the parties' control, such as the absence of an injunction against the transaction. In addition, there may be conditions that are specific to the seller, such as the absence of a material adverse change in the seller's business.

**b.  Material Adverse Effect/Change**.  The Delaware Court of Chancery, in a 2001 decision in the Tyson case, highlighted the importance of the careful drafting of a "material adverse effect" (MAE) or "material adverse change" (MAC) clause.    Basing its decision on New York law (because the merger agreement was governed by New York law), the Court determined that the seller had not suffered a MAE and ordered the buyer's specific performance of the merger agreement.   In its analysis of the MAE clause, the Court looked at the information available to the parties during and after closing.   The Court paid particular attention to the buyer's access to information during its due diligence review and to any additional material disclosed in the schedules to the merger agreement.   Despite a significant drop-off in earnings during the seller's first quarter, the Court found that, when examined in connection with the cyclical nature of the seller's business and its consistently fluctuating economic performance over time, the drop-off did not indicate a material change in the financial situation of the seller over a long period.   In addition, rather than judging the buyer's dealings under the standard of a reasonable purchaser, the Court subdivided the reasonableness standard into that of an acquirer looking at the long-term prospects of the business and a short-term speculator.   The Court reasoned that a short-term speculator may well consider a first-quarter drop-off in earnings as "material" while a long-term acquirer would need to look at the seller's earnings over a long period of time: "a MAC embraces a development that is consequential to a company's earning power over a commercially reasonable period, measured in years rather than months."   The Court's analysis leaves the interpretation of a MAC clause dependent on the nature of the buyer. For example, the MAC clause in a highly leveraged transaction (which is dependent on financing) is more likely to be judged on a short-term basis.

A well-drafted MAE clause should provide exceptions to a MAE to account for unavoidable circumstances such as changes to general industry conditions or natural disasters.  The parties in the case discussed above had not included such exceptions and though the Court determined that in that specific case it was not necessary, subsequent Delaware decisions have since held that if the parties desire that such exceptions apply they must be written into the agreement and will not be assumed by the court.  The tense of the MAE is also important.  The clause should be both immediate and prospective in nature.   For example, a clause that outlines events that "have" a MAE would be more narrowly construed and include only those consequences that occur simultaneously with the happening of the MAE and have an immediate effect on the seller's business, such as the destruction of the seller's primary manufacturing plant.  In contrast, a clause outlining events that are "reasonably likely to have" or "could" have a MAE involves a more sweeping definition and might include an event that is more difficult to measure, such as the loss of a major supplier or employee.

There is no definitive test for determining whether a MAE has occurred. The "materiality" of an event is normally a question of fact.  Case law provides no definitive standard for evaluating the concept of materiality.  The Tyson case, though very specific in its application, emphasizes the importance of the parties paying greater attention to the drafting of the MAE clause.  Proper language and the tailoring of the MAE clause to the nature of the business involved are critical.

**c. Standards of compliance with conditions**. Covenants may also include materiality qualifiers, requiring only that the condition be satisfied in all material respects. However, this will usually be inappropriate with respect to regulatory approvals.

**d. Effect of failure of certain conditions**. The failure to satisfy a condition will generally provide the non-breaching party with the option to terminate. However, the agreement may also permit the non-breaching party to seek damages for breach of the covenant not performed. Under certain circumstances (e.g. where a buyer ends a deal on MAC grounds) the non-terminating party may seek legal remedies against the terminating party for terminating the deal. Another potential consequence that a buyer terminating a deal must consider is that the target company's shareholders may commence an action against the buyer. Shareholders may seek to enforce the acquisition agreement, to recover damages based upon a theory of diminution in value of the target company's stock, or may make securities fraud claims alleging that the buyer failed to disclose that it was aware of material adverse information about the target at some point prior to its termination of the agreement or that buyer misrepresented its intention to close the transaction to the detriment of the target's shareholders. A review of case law in this area indicates that, absent exceptional circumstances, the Courts will generally deny shareholders' claims based on a lack of standing to sue or in the case of securities fraud claims, on the grounds that the buyer does not owe a duty to disclose information about the target to the target's shareholders. The Courts generally stress the importance of drafting a merger or acquisition agreement with precise language to make clear the intent of the parties. Most merger agreements contain explicit language providing that neither the agreement nor the transaction itself is intended to confer any rights or remedies on anyone who is not a "party" to the agreement. Current case law suggests that a court will deny shareholders the ability to sue the buyer directly where the agreement includes such language and, if other documents accompany the agreement, the agreement includes an integration clause, and nothing in the agreement suggests an intent to grant such rights to a third party. Despite the failure of the majority of such claims, their increasing frequency suggests that the buyer should be aware from the inception of a deal through post-closing of the risk of shareholder lawsuits not only in the drafting of the purchase agreement but in its internal statements and public disclosures, including e-mails, concerning the transaction.

**e. Legal opinions.** The scope of legal opinions is typically the subject of much negotiation.

**(1) Purpose**. The main purpose of a legal opinion is to force opposing counsel to perform the due diligence required to ensure that the transaction is handled properly. It is not a vehicle for making the opinion giver a guarantor of his client's representations.

**(2) Who can rely on the opinion**. The opinion giver will explicitly specify who is entitled to rely on the opinion. Typically, the opinion giver limits such reliance to only the opposing party. However, in certain instances the buyer's financing sources will also be entitled to rely on the opinion.

**(3) Opinion giver**. The opinion can be given by either inside or outside counsel. In most instances, the recipient of the opinion will prefer to receive an opinion from outside counsel as an independent party and a deeper pocket.

**(4) Contents of opinion**. The contents of a legal opinion are usually negotiated as part of the operative document. In most cases, the opinion will be limited to providing the opposing party with comfort that the objectives of the transaction have been accomplished. Typical portions of the opinion include the following:

**(i) Incorporation and good standing**. A basic component of most legal opinions is an opinion as to the due incorporation and valid existence of the opinion giver's corporate client. As a safeguard, the opinion giver should obtain and explicitly rely upon one or more certificates from state authorities attesting that the corporation is an existing corporation, in good standing and that all franchise tax returns have been filed to date.

**(ii) Qualification**. Opinion givers may be reluctant to opine that their corporate client and all of its subsidiaries are qualified to do business in every state in which such qualification is necessary, because businesses are often not in full compliance with these provisions. A frequent compromise is the use of a materiality qualification whereby the opinion giver states that his client is qualified in specific states and all other states wherein the failure to be qualified would have a material adverse effect on the seller.

**(iii) Enforceable in accordance with its terms**. Unless the only obligation under the agreement is a cash payment, many opinion givers are unwilling to give an unqualified opinion that such agreement is "enforceable in accordance with its terms" because of the uncertainty surrounding the meaning of the phrase. However, as a compromise, the opinion giver will make this opinion subject to creditors' rights and equitable principles. Care should be taken that the governing law clause of each of the operative agreements provides for the law of a state in which the opinion giver is qualified to opine.

**(iv) Consents**. The opinion giver will also be asked to give the opinion that no consents are required in order to consummate the transaction or that the required consents have been obtained.

**(5) Transaction specific matters**. It is typical for the opinion giver to opine that the transaction contemplated by the acquisition agreement will not result in any violation of law known to be applicable to their client or breach the certificate of incorporation or bylaws or any material agreement to which their client is a party.

**(6) Factual matters**. The party receiving the opinion will often ask the opinion giver to opine as to factual matters such as the existence of any breach of current agreements or the existence of any pending litigations. Most firms resist giving opinions involving such factual matters. For example, in order to opine as to the absence of breaches of existing agreements, the opinion giver would have to rely almost entirely on his client's representation that no breaches exist. Some firms will agree to provide such an opinion to the best of their knowledge. In such cases, they will typically limit the scope of the opinion to specified agreements and will exclude compliance with financial covenants. An opinion as to the absence of pending legal claims should specify, if true, that no search of court dockets was made. Otherwise, even if such opinion is qualified as being given to the best of the opinion giver's knowledge, an assumption can be drawn that a docket search was made.

(7) **Multiple jurisdictions**. In certain instances, opinions will be required as to matters that involve the laws of a number of different jurisdictions. Often, the principal counsel for the parties will not be an expert in the laws of each of these jurisdictions. This issue can be dealt with in various ways. The opinion giver can assume that the laws of each jurisdiction, other than the jurisdiction in which he is an expert, is identical to the laws of such counsel's jurisdiction or limit the scope of the opinion to the text of a particular statute, such as the corporate law of such state. In the alternative, the parties may retain local counsel in each jurisdiction for the purpose of giving an opinion. When making this decision, the parties weigh the sensitivity or importance of the issue requiring local counsel and the cost of retaining such counsel. Local counsel's opinion may be rendered directly to the opposing party or to the principal opinion giver, who in turn relies on such opinion in rendering its own opinion to the opposing party. Choosing the latter alternative ensures that the principal opinion giver is confident with the choice of local counsel.

## 5. Indemnification

**a. General.** The indemnification provisions are the principal mechanism in the purchase agreement for monetary risk shifting among the parties. The most common effect of the indemnification provisions is to provide the buyer with a remedy for any losses or expenses suffered in the event that the seller breaches the agreement or any of the representations or warranties. The indemnification may come in the form of a direct claim by the buyer against the seller for damages, or as a demand by the buyer to be indemnified from a third party claim regarding a matter for which the seller has assumed the risk.

(1) **Who should be the indemnitors?** One of the most hotly debated issues in an acquisition agreement, regardless of the form of the transaction, is whether the shareholders of the acquired company will be required to stand behind the seller's indemnification provisions. In the case of a sale of stock, if the shareholders do not agree to provide indemnification, there is no party available to provide the indemnity. If the seller is publicly held, its shareholders can provide indemnity in the form of a hold-back from the consideration paid by the buyer or some form of deferred or contingent consideration. Alternatively, if there are one or more principal shareholders of a publicly held company who are intimately familiar with the seller's business, they may be willing to provide indemnity, at least to a limited extent. The seller's shareholders often argue that the buyer has ample opportunity to perform a complete investigation of the seller's business through due diligence prior to the signing of the agreement. They also argue that they no longer wish to be subject to any potential liability relating to the business after the closing. That, in essence, is why they are selling the business. (The second argument is especially relevant to shareholders who

are individuals.) The buyer typically argues that the due diligence process never uncovers all liabilities and that they are unwilling to assume all of the risks in the transaction. If the seller is an individual and the buyer is relatively comfortable with the potential risks, the buyer may compromise by not seeking the shareholders' indemnity in return for a reduction in the purchase price. However, if the seller has a parent company, the buyer will typically insist on indemnification by the parent entity.

**(2) Scope of the indemnity**.

**(i) Substantive elements**. The general indemnification provision will ensure that the buyer is made whole for breaches of the seller's representations and warranties or covenants. Typical examples include misrepresentations as to the value of inventory and the absence of undisclosed liabilities of the seller. The parties may also agree that the seller will continue to be liable with respect to certain specific liabilities, which will be stated separately from the general indemnification provision. For example, the seller may agree to remain liable for liability under specified ongoing litigation.

**(ii) Fees and expenses.** The indemnified party will be entitled to indemnification for fees and expenses incurred in the process of enforcing its indemnification claims. Such fees and expenses include attorneys' fees, accountants' fees and fees of experts. Expenses that are not recoverable by the buyer include consequential damages (unless the indemnification provision explicitly allows such recovery).

**(iii) Third party claims.** The indemnification provisions will also cover post-closing claims by third parties against the buyer. Examples of these include products liability litigation based on products sold by the seller prior to the closing, claims for unpaid taxes and environmental liabilities. The agreement will typically enable the indemnifying party to control the defense of the claim and require the indemnified party to cooperate in the defense of the claim (with appropriate reimbursement). In addition, the indemnifying party will be prohibited from settling a claim without the indemnified party's consent, unless the latter is released in full.

**(3) Who may be indemnified?** The indemnification provision typically covers the buyer, the seller and their respective directors, officers, employees, shareholders, affiliates and funding sources or other assignees.

**(4) The amount of indemnification**. The amount of indemnification is usually left for negotiation at the time the breach is discovered or ultimately to the courts. However, the parties are also free to agree in advance on liquidated damages in order to define the amount of indemnification. This is useful where the determination of damages is ambiguous. However, if the amount agreed upon is too high and is in effect a penalty, courts may not enforce such a provision.

**b. Limitations on indemnification.**

**(1) The "basket."** The seller will want to include a provision setting a minimum loss requirement beneath which the buyer will not be entitled to indemnification. Minimum loss provisions may take the form of a threshold or a deductible.

**(i) Threshold.** If a threshold is built into the indemnity, the buyer will be entitled to indemnification only if the damages exceed a specified amount, e.g., if the damages exceed 5 percent of the purchase price. Once the damages exceed this amount, the buyer recovers from the first dollar of the loss.

**(ii) Deductible**. If a deductible is built into the indemnity, the buyer will only be indemnified for losses that exceed the agreed specified minimum amount. The buyer therefore bears the loss up to that minimum amount.

**(iii) Specific concerns.** If the representations and warranties include materiality exceptions, the inclusion of a basket in the indemnity section can result in having an overprotected seller. Buyers may seek to side-step the basket by suing directly under the representations and warranties. To avoid this, seller should include a provision that provides that the sole remedy for breach of representations is through a claim for indemnification.

**(2) Survival.** Sellers generally impose time limitations on the survival period of representations and warranties, and indemnification rights. This refers to the period during which a claim for indemnification must be asserted. The survival period should be long enough to allow discovery of inherent problems in the acquired business. A typical survival period is about two years, however, certain representations are typically held open for longer. At a minimum, the buyer should seek survival until the first audited financial statements following the closing are available. Representations concerning taxes, ERISA and environmental compliance often extend until the expiration of the applicable statute of limitations. Representations on issues that go to the essence of the transaction such as capitalization, corporate organization and authority to enter into the transaction are often perpetual. If the agreement simply provides for the survival of representations and warranties, and indemnification rights, without any time limitation, the survival will be equal to the appropriate statute of limitations within which to bring any actions under the acquisition agreement.

**(3) Caps on amount of indemnification**. Sellers may try to limit their liability by including a specified amount beyond which the buyer will not be entitled to indemnification. This may apply only with respect to the seller's shareholders and may be agreed to in the context of negotiating whether the selling shareholder will stand behind the indemnity.

**(4) Defense of actual knowledge of buyer before the closing**. Seller may seek to include a provision prohibiting the buyer from recovering for the breach of a representation if the buyer had actual knowledge of such breach on or before the closing of the misrepresentation. This provision can make it more difficult for the buyer to obtain indemnification by imposing a burden on it to prove that it was not aware of such breach prior to the closing. Often the buyer will insist that the agreement affirmatively state that the indemnification provision will apply regardless of any investigations conducted on behalf of the buyer.

**c.  Arbitration clauses**.  A clause requiring arbitration can facilitate a speedy and inexpensive resolution of indemnification claims.  Such clause should specify the method of selecting the arbitrator or arbitrators and the rules and jurisdiction for arbitrating.  However, arbitration does have certain disadvantages.  Often, the arbitrators are not lawyers and may have difficulty resolving complex legal issues.  In addition, the discovery process in arbitration is limited.  For the party who is likely to have to provide indemnification rather than receive it, litigation provides greater opportunities for delay which in turn benefit the payor.  Another typical complaint about arbitration is that arbitrators tend to push the parties to compromise and settle on a middle ground.

## PROBLEM 9-B

**9-B.**  Roger is preparing to purchase all of the stock of FlyNet Inc., a successful C corporation that is owned by five individuals.  He knows that there are others in the wings, ready to make an offer for the stock.  He needs to move fast, and he needs to be reasonable.

The term sheet for the deal sets the price of the stock at $18 million and lays out the other key terms.  It also references one of Roger's real concerns with the deal – a potential dispute over a patented product ("the Patent") owned by FlyNet and developed by Walter Larson.  The term sheet states that this concern "will be appropriately addressed to the mutual satisfaction of all parties in the definitive agreement between the parties."

FlyNet claims that Larson owns no financial interest in FlyNet, that it purchased the Patent from Larson for $250,000, and that it has documents to support these claims.  Roger's preliminary due diligence has confirmed that Larson has a reputation as a trouble maker and has stated to others on various occasions that FlyNet "did a number on me when FlyNet stole my patent."  Three weeks ago, in a drunken stupor, Larson called the CEO of FlyNet and ranted that he still owned the Patent because he was never given the 20,000 shares of FlyNet stock that he was promised.

Roger is concerned that a dispute with Larson could surface after the acquisition is closed and Larson discovers that each of the five stockholders of FlyNet walked with millions from the sale.  If FlyNet's ownership of the Patent was lost, Roger would still have an interest in purchasing the stock of FlyNet, but the price would be no more than $15 million.

Describe how Roger's concerns with respect to the Patent may be addressed in drafting each of the following elements of the definitive stock purchase agreement between the parties:  (1) the recitals;  (2) the covenants;  (3) the representations and warranties;  (4) the conditions;  (5) the indemnification provisions;  and (6) the legal opinions provided by FlyNet's counsel.  Which of these would be most effective from Roger's perspective?  Should certain of these options be used in combination?  What options will reduce an overkill risk that may incent the owners of FlyNet to reopen discussions with other interested buyers?

# CHAPTER 10

---

# FAMILY BUSINESS TRANSITION PLANNING

---

## A. HARD FACTS; HARD CHALLENGES

Mom and Dad have labored a lifetime building a profitable business that services a market niche and regularly delivers a paycheck to two hundred hard-working employees. On paper, most would consider them rich, but they fully appreciate that the bulk of their wealth is tied up in a business operation that could be derailed by changing market conditions, a breakthrough technology, a new tenacious competitor, sloppy management, or a host of other factors. They have witnessed the demise of other businesses that were all considered "rock solid" at some point in their existence. The time has come for Mom and Dad to slow down, turn over the reins, and enjoy their retirement. One child is immersed in the business, fully prepared and anxious to run the show, and two other children are off pursing other careers. The family wants a plan that will ensure the parents' financial security, treat all children fairly, protect the business, promote family harmony, and minimize all tax bites. It's a tall order.

Family business transition planning is big business. Oft quoted statistics say it all. Family dominated businesses comprise more than 80 percent of U.S. enterprises, employ more than 50 percent of the nation's workforce, and account for the bulk (some estimate as much as 64 percent) of America's gross domestic product.[1] According to a 2007 survey of family businesses with annual gross sales of at least $5 million, 60 percent of the majority shareholders in family businesses are 55 or older, and 30 percent are at least age 65.[2] And although more than 80 percent of the senior family owners claim that they want the business to stay in the family, less than 30 percent acknowledge having a transition plan.[3] The result is that most family businesses do remain in the

---

1. See generally R. Duman, "Family Firms Are Different," Entrepreneurship Theory and Practice, 1992, pp. 13–21; and M. F. R. Kets de Vries, "The Dynamics of Family Controlled Firms: The Good News and the Bad News," Organizational Dynamics, 1993, pp. 59–71; W. G. Dyer, Cultural Change in Family Firms, Jossey–Bass, San Francisco, 1986; and P. L. Rosenblatt, M. R. Anderson and P. Johnson, The Family in Business, Jossey–Bass, San Francisco, 1985; Arthur Anderson/Mass Mutual, American Family Business Survey, 2002.

2. Family to Family: Laird Norton Tyee Family Business Survey 2007, page 5.

3. Id. The survey also indicated that (1) only 56 percent of the respondents have a written strategic business

family, but at a dear cost. Best estimates are that less than 30 percent of family dominated businesses survive a second generation, and the survival rate is even uglier for those businesses that make it to generation three.[4]

Strategic transition planning takes time, energy, and a willingness to grapple with tough family, tax and financial issues. It cannot make a weak business strong or provide any guarantees of survival. But it can trigger an analytical process that prompts a frank assessment of available options, facilitates better long-term decision making, and saves taxes.

Although many successful family business owners enjoy a net worth that rivals or exceeds that of other well-heeled clients, the planning dynamics usually are much different when a family business takes center stage. For many clients, wealth transition planning focuses on a potpourri of investment and business assets, packaged in a medley of partnerships, trusts, limited liability companies (LLCs), and corporate entities. The challenge is to analyze, reposition where necessary, and ultimately transition the various marbles in the most tax efficient manner possible, consistent with the family objectives of the owners. With a family business, it's usually not about rearranging marbles; it's about trying to move a mountain. In the recent survey referenced above, a startling 93 percent of the senior business owners acknowledged that the business is their primary source of income and security.[5] With little or no diversification, everything gets tougher. Strategies that easily accommodate marble shifting often become more challenging, sometimes impossible, when applied to a sliver of the mountain. And, more often the not, the process is further complicated by strong emotional ties to the mountain and historical perceptions regarding essential bonds between the family and the mountain.

This chapter explores many aspects of the intergenerational transition challenges of family-dominated businesses. The chapter begins with the initial challenge in the planning process, the threshold "Keep vs. Sell" question: Should the business be sold or kept in the family? The focus then changes to not "whether", but "how". Section C discusses the challenge of developing a transition plan once the decision has been made to keep the business in the family. A simple case study is used to explain essential plan elements and related planning traps and to illustrate and contrast strategic options for moving the mountain. The facts of the case study are common to many successful family businesses: parents preparing to slow down; a successful business that represents the bulk of the parents' estate; children inside and outside the business; looming estate tax problems; and a compelling need to prepare for the future.

The plan design process for each family necessarily must be detail oriented, strategic, and forward focused. Care must be exercised to avoid planning traps and the temptation to tack on complicated strategies that offer little or nothing for the particular family. Each situation is unique and should be treated as such.

plan, (2) nearly 64 percent do not require that family members entering the business have any qualifications or business experience, and (3) 25 percent do not believe that the next generation is competent to move into leadership roles.

4. J. I. Ward, Keeping the Family Business Healthy, Jossey–Bass, San Francisco, 1987. This study suggests that the survival rate to generation three is less than 15 percent.

5. Family to Family: Laird Norton Tyee Family Business Survey 2007, page 5 (Executive Summary).

There is no slam-dunk solution; all strategies have limitations and disadvantages that mandate careful evaluation, and some pose risks or legal uncertainties that many just can't stomach. Above all, the specific objectives of the family must drive the planning process. The objectives, once identified, must be prioritized to facilitate an effective analysis of the trade-offs and compromises that inevitably surface in the planning process. The ultimate goal is to design a plan that effectively accomplishes the highest priority objectives over a period of time and at a level of complexity that works for the family.

## B. THE FAMILY BUSINESS: KEEP OR SELL?

### 1. THRESHOLD QUESTION

The owners of most successful family businesses sooner or later face a threshold question: Should the family business be sold or should it be transitioned to the next generation? Of course, the decision to transition the business triggers a major obstacle: estate taxes. The government extracts a large price for the privilege of moving the ownership of a successful business to the next generation. There are ways that this estate tax obstacle can be planned for, massaged, reduced, frozen, and ultimately funded. And there is the likelihood, perhaps virtual certainty, that Congress will change the tax in the future, and the potential long shot that it may choose to eliminate the tax in its entirety. For discussion purposes in this section, it is assumed that the estate tax obstacle can be handled through proper planning if the decision is made to transition the business to the next generation. The focus here is on the broader issue of whether transitioning the business to the next generation is the best course of action for the family.

Before focusing on the details, a few preliminary reminders are helpful. First, it's important to remember that, in many situations, the parents automatically will assume that the business is going to be kept in the family and transitioned to the next generation. The thought of selling the business to an outside party may have never seriously crossed the parents' mind. Some may even regard the issue as a taboo subject that is not to be discussed. The planner needs to be discerning in this situation and assess the risks of saying nothing. Often the planner does a client a disservice by ducking the issue at the first sign of any resistance. This is one area where a little artful devil's advocacy can shake loose the cobwebs, open minds, and get the thought process started by planting smart seeds.

Second, it's critically important to remember that priorities, objectives, biases, family dynamics, and business risk factors continually evolve and change over time. So too, the answer to the sell-keep decision may change over time. The patriarch who would never consider selling out at age fifty-five may have a very different attitude at age seventy, particularly if he has been subjected to many enlightening discussions over the years that have focused on a number of key factors that rightfully influence the analysis and the decision.

Third, the planner must be careful to never substitute his or her judgment for that of the clients'. Successful planners often spend hours with their clients over many years discussing this important issue. During these discussions, it's easy for the planner to formulate a personal opinion and to inadvertently become an advocate, rather than an adviser. The key is to remain an adviser at all times, encouraging the client to focus on the key factors and the business indicators and to honestly evaluate the situation. The adviser who is able to skillfully play such a role will grow closer to the client over time and will not end up in the uncomfortable position of having to defend an ultimate conclusion on the threshold issue. The adviser should always resist the temptation to become an advocate.

Fourth, simply going through the process of evaluating the sell-keep decision factors often has considerable value even though the parents refuse to seriously consider the sellout alternative. By focusing on the key factors and business indicators that affect the decision, the parents will become more tuned-in to steps that should be taken to prepare the business for transitioning to the next generation. They will better understand and be more sensitive to the non-tax problems and obstacles that will be triggered when the transition kicks in. This increased sensitivity will often enable them to plan more effectively in structuring the business to face the challenges that will inevitably surface.

Finally, the adviser who is able to meaningfully assist a family in dealing with this issue will gain a deeper understanding and knowledge of the family and the business and will have the opportunity to strengthen his or her ties to both generations. Plus, this challenge, more than many others, is best served by those who have had many similar experiences with other families. Every opportunity to help a family through this process adds to the adviser's experience bank and strengthens insights and perspectives that may enhance the adviser's future effectiveness.

## 2. KEY KEEP–SELL DECISION FACTORS

**a. Emotional Ties.** In many situations, no factor is more compelling than the parents' emotional ties to the business. They conceived the business and made it grow. They've sacrificed, and the sacrifice has paid off. The business has become a fundamental part of their identity. For many, the business is like another child that could never be disinherited. The challenge for the advisor is to help the parents acknowledge their emotional ties to the business to facilitate an honest assessment of the other issues that impact the threshold question. Usually this is easier said than done. Nevertheless, an attempt should be made if there's going to be any objectivity in addressing the primary issue.

There are a few suggestions that the advisor may want to consider in defusing the emotions. First, ask the parents whether their children have the same type of intense emotional attachment to the business. Often this may require that the parents do a little checking. In most situations, the parents will end up honestly acknowledging that the children do not have the same attachment. This acknowledgement may help facilitate a more objective discussion about the children and the prospects for the business. Second, try to plan the discussion to reduce the risk of emotional eruptions that will hinder thoughtful, objective analysis.  For example, usually it's helpful to have the discussions without the children present.  Parents are often willing to be more candid and objective if they do not feel the need to play to their children by reconfirming their emotional attachment to the business.  The effectiveness of the discussions can be quickly diluted if too many people are present.  It's usually helpful to keep non-family members who may fuel emotions away from the dialogue. Often an honest, bottom-line assessment of the issues between two or three people is the best way for diluting the emotions and objectively assessing the factors.

**b. The Risk World.**  The next factor that is often helpful to the discussion relates to the risks of operating the business and how those risks may change and evolve over time.  Any person who has operated a business over an extended period of time understands that the economic risks are higher today than in the past.  And all indications suggest that the risks are only going to intensify in the future.  This stark reality has prompted many parents to reevaluate their willingness to sell the business.  The increased risks have heightened their anxieties and frustrations, and they know that the risks will have the same effect on their children.

The risks come in many forms.  For many businesses, there's more risk in the marketplace.  New products are being introduced at a faster pace. Technology is changing.  Methods of operation are changing.  Consumer expectations are higher, and there are more competitors to deal with.  Often, the most serious increased risks are coming from offshore.  Many countries have paid a dear price for the privilege of embracing free enterprise and operating in a free trade environment.  Every day our markets are flooded with more competitive products that have been manufactured by a labor force that is paid a fraction of that paid to comparable groups of employees in the United States.

Business risks often are heightened by the costs and the risks of increased regulation and the expansion of the rights of the employees and customers of the business.  Businesses of all sizes are forced to comply with a variety of government regulations that take time, cost money, and hinder business operations.  The scope of the regulations is broad, including everything from massive health care changes to environmental issues, OSHA regulations, hiring laws, product liability risks, increased building access regulations for disabled persons, complex tax laws, drug testing, and more.  Beyond the state or federal agency that's been organized and staffed to monitor and enforce each set of regulations, the business is exposed to private claims that aggrieved third parties may choose to pursue with the aid of a tenacious lawyer.  Even the adoption of a qualified retirement plan for the employees of the business triggers a huge set of regulations that escalate the risks and costs of non-compliance.  The simple fact is that the business world is becoming more complicated, and there are more ways to fail than there were previously.  For many, this reality may affect the keep or sell decision process.

**c. The "Trapped Child" Syndrome.**  Many parents feel pressure to keep the business in the family because they have adult children who have become dependent on the business. It is the "trapped child" syndrome. At some point in time, one or more of the children decided to make the family business a career. They may have short-circuited their education by entering the business, or they may have foregone other opportunities. The parents are north of sixty-five, and the child who is in the business has a spouse, two children, a mortgage, and a fortieth birthday in his or her past. Since the child has made the business a career, the parents feel compelled to keep the business for the child. This syndrome can be extremely powerful in many situations.

The advisor may confront this syndrome at two different crossroads, and may be in a position to be an effective counselor at each crossroad. The first crossroad occurs when the owner of the business first considers the prospects of having a child join the business. Usually this happens after the child has completed his or her education and is looking for work. Since the child is familiar with the business and wants some security, the business provides a convenient career option. Often it ends up being an effective buffer against cutting short a college education or foregoing another opportunity that may pose more risks and create more discomfort. The parent in this situation usually is delighted with the prospect of working with his or her child. For many, it's perceived as the best possible scenario for the family.

An advisor who spots a family business at this crossroad can help by suggesting that the business owner evaluate whether an effective transition plan can be developed. The parent often needs to be reminded that the child may be paying a dear opportunity cost for joining the business and may quickly become dependent on the business. By having the child join the business, the parent may be creating a difficult situation down the road. If the parent chooses to sell the business and cash-in twenty years later, what is the child going to do? Usually, it's harder to make changes and get re-tooled as a forty-five year old than it is as a twenty-five year old. Does the parent really want the responsibility of having the child pay such an opportunity cost? Is it the best thing for the child in the long run? It's a hard reality that many business owners have to evaluate when they hit the crossroad that offers the opportunity of having a child join the business as a career option.

The second crossroad comes when the child has worked for the business for many years and has become dependent on the business. Absent this trapped child syndrome, the parents may conclude that the wisest course of action would be to sell the business, get rid of the risks and hassles, and enjoy their retirement. They may feel that there is no effective heir apparent to the management of the business, or that the risks of trying to carry the business through another generation are just too great. The most prudent course of action from a financial and risk perspective is to sellout. The major obstacle is the trapped child.

In this situation, there are a few factors that should be explored. First, the child may have a different perception of the trap or its severity. The forty-year-old child may be more resilient to change than his or her seventy-year-old parent ever imagined. The child may have witnessed many contemporaries change jobs and career paths in the current, fast-paced labor market that may be foreign to an elderly parent. In some cases, the child may actually welcome the idea of a second career and a release from the ties of the old family business, particularly if there is some back-up financial security. Second, the economic benefits of selling the business and cashing in may have substantial appeal to the middle-aged child. It may offer increased financial security and the opportunity to become involved in a new effort that may be more interesting than the family business. This is one situation where it may be particularly helpful to involve the child in the decision-making process at the right point in time. When the child sees the numbers and realizes that the burden of maintaining the business may be lifted off of his or her shoulders, the child may become a proponent of the sell alternative.

A related factor that often influences the discussion is the varying attitudes family members may have regarding retirement. Many seventy-year-old business entrepreneurs want to continue to work for the duration because their primary day-to-day satisfaction comes from working hard. Although they're willing to slow down a little, they have no interest in a full-time retirement of leisure. Many baby boomers and their offspring have a very different attitude about retirement. They are members of a lifestyle generation. Many boomers approaching fifty years of age envy their contemporaries who have the resources to retire early and pursue a variety of special interests for a long period of time. The patriarch business owner may be shocked to learn that his forty-seven-year old child is beginning to think about retirement and may actually welcome the idea of a business sell-out that would provide the financial basis for such a retirement. Such discussions inevitably lead to dialogue about different planning tools that will enable the inside child who is tied to the business to participate in the financial rewards of selling the business. There may be special buy-sell agreement provisions, stock options, stock equivalency programs, deferred compensation programs, bonus plans and other similar arrangements, all of which are discussed in other chapters. An honest discussion of these issues by the family members may uncover a number of surprising attitudes and perspectives and a basis for some creative planning to spread the financial benefits resulting from the sale of the business.

**d. Is There a Qualified Heir Apparent?** A business cannot be effectively transitioned to a second generation unless there is a qualified heir apparent to run the show. The key word is "qualified." Many parents mistakenly assume that their offspring are qualified to manage the business. They embrace the false notion, "If I can do it, my kid can sure do it." In many cases, it's a misconception that ultimately leads to business failure.

Too often the parents believe that the critical management factor is the day-to-day operation of the business. They mistakenly assume that the child's ability to understand and manage the day-to-day affairs of the business confirms that he or she can manage the entire business. To survive and succeed today, most businesses require a single leader who has the respect of the work-force, the ability to formulate a vision to carry the business forward, a thorough knowledge of the markets that impact the business, the ability to solicit and evaluate advice and make sound decisions, and the nerve and capacity to take and endure big risks. These qualities do not come easily. Many families are not able to develop an effective second-generation leader.

There is one option that almost never works. That is the concept of having the business run by a committee of children. Often the parents find themselves in a situation where two or more children are actively involved in the business. They don't want to designate an anointed leader because they're afraid the other children will feel offended or short-changed. Since the day their second child was born, they've embraced an unwavering concept of equality among the children. It's a rare situation where a business can survive and prosper under the management of a committee of siblings. The potential for internal problems that frustrate and stagnate effective management is enormous. The concept of management by committee makes little sense in most family businesses.

In some situations, the parents will designate a management group that consists of the inside children and a few non-family advisors, such as an accountant or an attorney. The thought is that the outsiders will provide objective advice and serve as a referee or a tiebreaker in disputes among the children. In most situations, it's highly unlikely that such a structure will provide any effective long-term management. The structure does not compare to the efficiency and effectiveness of developing a single heir apparent who possesses the tools, wisdom, and leadership skills to really carry the business forward. For most businesses, the notion of just preserving the status quo under a caretaker management structure doesn't work. The business is either moving forward and evolving under sound leadership or is in the process of withering and dying under poor leadership.

**e. Is There a Sellout Alternative?** Many family business owners do not want to focus on the keep-sell decision because they do not believe that there's a sellout option. No one has ever offered to buy the business so they doubt that a market for the business even exists. Moreover, they have no real clue as to what the business is worth. On this issue, there are a couple of ways that the advisor can be helpful. The advisor can encourage the business owner to investigate whether there is an effective sellout alternative. This may require discussions with business brokers and others who are involved in selling closely held businesses. Sometimes there is a strategic player that might have an interest in acquiring the company. The options can be assessed and evaluated without actually putting the business on the market. Often this process will give the business owner a better feel for what the business is actually worth. Some may be pleasantly surprised; others hopelessly disappointed. In either case, the knowledge will provide a basis for more effective planning in the future. If a determination is made that there is no effective sellout alternative, the process of evaluating the business as a transition candidate may have given the owner a better understanding of the risks, rewards and challenges of transitioning the business.

**f. Key Business Indicators.** There are a variety of business indicators that can be analyzed to determine whether the business is a good candidate for surviving another generation. Some businesses are better suited for a transition strategy than others. Obviously, if a review of the relevant business indicators suggests bleak prospects after the exit of the parents, a sellout may be the best alternative.

### 3. Key Business Indicators

**a. Strategically–Based vs. Relationship–Based.** The strength of some businesses is primarily attributable to key personal relationships that have been developed over many years. The relationships may be with suppliers, customers, key employees or all three. These relationships give the business its advantage and make it possible for the business to succeed. In contrast, there are other businesses that are strategically-based. They have identified and filled a market niche that is not dependent or tied to personal relationships. The business succeeds because it is strategically situated to competitively deliver goods or services in its identified market niche.

Obviously, a strategically-based business has a better chance of surviving through a second generation than a relationship-based business. Relationships are often difficult, if not impossible, to transfer. The child may develop a friendly interface with the crucial vendor, but that interface will never match the strength of the personal relationship that the father had with the vendor. The challenge becomes even more difficult when the vendor's successor takes charge. The reality is that, over time, the strength of personal relationships often breaks down and fizzles out as attempts are made to transition relationships. As this occurs, there is a substantial risk that the business activity between the parties will diminish unless both parties identify a strategic business advantage for maintaining the relationship.

Often it is assumed that a family business is strategically-based, when, in fact, the basis of its success is personal relationships that have been developed over many years. Similarly, there are some businesses that appear to be propped up by relationships, but that could be strategically strengthened with some careful analysis, restructuring and public relations. The advisor should encourage the parents to identify key personal relationships, assess the importance of those relationships to the overall success of the business, and evaluate the capacity of the business to enhance its strategic base.

**b. Is Institutionalization Possible?** A central challenge for many family-owned businesses is to begin the process of institutionalization. In this context, an institutionalized business is one that is bigger than any one individual. Its operations and growth do not primarily depend on the person that started it all. It has developed systems, personnel, management structures, and expertise to allow it to function like an institution. Usually, this condition is easily recognized by the employees of the company and outsiders who deal with the company on a regular basis. The contrast is the family business that is operationally dependent on one individual. That individual is the key to all that happens. Without the daily presence of that individual, the business lacks direction and suffers. The systems, support personnel, and expertise are not present. An institutionalized family business has a much better chance of being successfully transitioned than a business that is primarily dependent on its leader.

Many owners of family-owned businesses do not want to invest the time or capital required to build systems and personnel that will allow the business to effectively function on its own. In some cases, it takes a financial commitment that the owners are not willing to make. In others, it's an issue of control or ego. The owner enjoys the importance of his or her invaluable presence. The advisor can help by having the business owner fairly assess whether appropriate steps are being taken to institutionalize the business. Usually these steps are critical if the business is going to survive a second generation.

**c. Margin Tolerance.** The next business indicator relates to price and margin tolerance. The question is whether the business can survive and prosper if it is faced with some tough price competition. Ask this: What would be the impact if the business was forced to cut its gross margin by three or four percent to remain competitive? If the business owner responds by a roll of the eyes and a "No way" exclamation, this may suggest that the business will struggle trying to survive for another generation. In most businesses, price competition is intensifying. Others have found better ways of producing the same products or delivering comparable services at lower prices. New manufacturing techniques and operating systems are being developed to allow businesses to operate more efficiently. Businesses are "right sizing" to cut out the fat and to have the capacity to operate on lean, tough margins. New players are not tied to old systems and old investments.

Often a family business finds itself at an extreme competitive disadvantage as bigger and stronger players, sometimes from foreign lands, enter the market. It does not have the capital or the sales volume to justify the development of the economies of scale and operating systems that would allow it to remain tough on price. If this situation exists, the better alternative may be to consider selling while the company's market share is still intact. If the opportunity is missed, the owner may be forced to sacrifice or eliminate profitability by cutting margins to preserve the business. This has been the fate of many family-owned businesses that have been unable to survive a second generation.

**d. Asset Base.** The asset base of a business may be an indicator of whether the business can successfully survive another generation. Some businesses have a very unique, substantial asset base that cannot be readily duplicated. The assets have been developed over a long period of time. The key asset may be a unique, custom manufacturing capacity that gives the business a competitive advantage in the marketplace. In some cases, there may be valuable patents, trade names or other intellectual property rights that protect the position of the business. When such assets exist, the business has a better chance of surviving a transition. In contrast, the asset base of many businesses is not significant or unique in any respect. It can be readily duplicated by any new player entering the market.

**e. Low–Tech vs. High–Tech.** A low-tech business is one that does not rely heavily on new technology to sustain its market position. It does not have to keep coming up with new technology concepts to support the viability of its product mix. It offers a group of products that are readily recognized as non-technical. In contrast, a high-tech business is dependent on its ability to create new ideas and new products. Often the success of the high-tech business is tied directly to the talent of individuals that work in the business.

From a transition standpoint, a low-tech business usually is in a much stronger position than a high-tech business. A high-tech business today can quickly end up being a defunct no-tech business of tomorrow if it cannot keep pace by producing new products that play well in the marketplace. The competition in high-tech businesses continues to grow at a rapid pace as players from around the world enter the market. The low-tech/high-tech nature of a business is an important factor to consider in evaluating the transition capacity of the business.

**f. Barriers to Entry.** What are the barriers to getting into the business? Some businesses have very substantial barriers that make it difficult for a competitor to enter the market. The barriers may be tied to customer relations, brand strength, government regulations, production technologies, historical market positions, intellectual property rights, or financial commitments. If the barriers to entry are high, the chances of successfully transitioning the business go up. If the barriers to entry are low and others can easily access the same market, the prospects of the business succeeding a second generation are reduced.

**g. Capital Structure.** The capital structure of the business may influence the parents' attitude regarding the need to sell or transition the business. Often changes in the business' capital structure may cause the parents to look at a transition plan differently.

A common scenario is the family business that has done everything in its power to reduce or eliminate debt. The parents determined long ago that the business had a better chance of succeeding with little or no debt. As a result, the parents have taken steps over an extended period of time to reduce or eliminate all debt in the business and, in doing so, have committed substantially all their assets to the business. This situation significantly increases the stakes of the keep-sell decision. If the business is sold, the parents free up their capital, are able to diversify their holdings, and are in a much safer financial position. If the business is kept in the family, the lack of diversification increases the pressure for everyone.

In this situation, it is often advisable to consider restructuring the capital base of the business in order to enhance the strength and diversity of the parents' capital. This can be done by having the business take on an appropriate amount of debt that will be secured by the assets of the business and will be funded over an extended period of time through the business' operations. As the business increases its leverage to an acceptable debt-to-equity ratio, the parents are able to implement diversification strategies that allow them to pull funds out of the business. These funds may be used to develop investment portfolios, fund life insurance programs, and accomplish other financial planning objectives that are not tied to the business. The planning process usually gets easier as the parents diversify their financial base.

## C. ESSENTIAL PLAN ELEMENTS AND TRAPS

### 1. CASE STUDY: WILSON INCORPORATED

The Wilson family owns a business that is going to be transitioned to the next generation. The sellout option is off the table. Wilson Incorporated is a privately owned C corporation that has been in a specialized distribution business for 26 years. It has an established reputation with its customers and suppliers. Earl Wilson, age 65, is the founder and President the company and historically has been the principal force behind the company. Earl and his wife Betty, age 60, own as community property 90 percent of the outstanding common stock of the company. Betty serves on the board but spends no serious time in the business. Jeff Wilson, Earl and Betty's oldest child, owns the remaining 10 percent of the outstanding stock. Jeff is married and has been actively involved in the business for years. Technically, Jeff is considered the second-in-command behind Earl, but all close to the company recognize that Jeff now is the driving force in the company. In addition to his strong financial background, Jeff has a proven knack for sales and marketing, is skilled in dealing with people, and is adored by key employees and valued customers. Jeff is anxious to take over the reins and wants to aggressively grow and expand the business. If Jeff's involvement in the business was terminated for any reason, the loss to the business would be substantial.

The company's growth was dynamic in the earlier years, but recently the growth has been modest. Earl has been slowing down and has been reluctant to aggressively reinvest or borrow funds to expand the operation into new markets. This has been a frustration for Jeff, who wants to conquer new frontiers. The business has consistently generated sufficient profits and cash flow to pay generous salaries and to allow Earl and Betty to draw approximately $400,000 from the business each year in compensation payments.

Earl and Betty have two other children—Kathy and Paul. Both are grown and married, and neither has ever worked in the business. Paul is a dentist; Kathy used to work in commercial real estate before becoming a stay-at-home mom. Earl and Betty have four grandchildren and hopes of one or two more. All family members get along with each other. Earl is recognized as the family patriarch, although all acknowledge that the continued success and future of the business rests in Jeff's hands.

Earl estimates that the business is worth approximately $24 million. That's the price that he believes the business could be sold for today. Earl and Betty's total estate, inclusive of their share of the business, is valued at approximately $32 million. Their assets, all community property, include the building that houses the business. Earl and Betty own the building outside of the corporation and lease the building to the company. The building is presently valued at $4 million.

Earl and Betty have various personal hobbies and interests that they've neglected in the past in order to accommodate the demands of the business. They're anxious to move forward; they're looking forward to retirement. They would like to develop a plan that will accomplish the following objectives.

- Earl will phase out of the business over the next year and will continue to receive payments from the business that will enable Earl and Betty to ride off into the sunset and enjoy their retirement for the rest of their lives.

- Jeff will take over the control and management of the business. Earl wants some ongoing involvement as a hedge against the boredom of retirement and to ensure that the financial integrity of the business is protected for the sake of his retirement and Betty's welfare. Earl will be freed of all day-to-day responsibilities.

- Jeff will have the freedom to diversify and expand the business. Jeff would like the plan structured so that the value of all appreciation in the future will be reflected in his estate and will not continue to build Earl and Betty's estates or the estates of other family members, specifically Kathy and Paul, neither of whom play any role in the business.

- Earl and Betty want to make sure that, at their passing, each child receives an equal share of their estates. They are particularly concerned about Kathy and Paul, the two children who do not participate in the business. They appreciate that the business represents the bulk of their estate. They want Jeff to control and run the business, but they want to make certain that Kathy and Paul are treated fairly.

- Earl and Betty want to minimize estate taxes, consistent with their other objectives and their overriding desire to be financially secure and independent. They never want to be dependent on their children, and they always want to know that their estate is sufficient to finance their lifestyle for the duration. They are willing to pay some estate taxes for this peace of mind. As a hedge against future estate taxes, they would like to start transitioning assets to other family members. They generally understand that, as of right now, their unified credits[6] will shelter $10.5 million of their estate ($5.25 million each) from estate tax exposure and the excess will be taxed at 40 percent by the federal government. Given the value of their estate, the math is frightening.

- All family members want to minimize negative income tax consequences to the fullest extend possible.[7]

## 2. ESSENTIAL PLAN ELEMENTS: STARTING POINTS AND TRAPS

The design of a business transition plan requires that certain key elements be carefully considered on the front end to ensure that the financial interests of the parents are protected, estate taxes are minimized and deferred, family liquidity needs are satisfied, adverse income tax hits are eliminated, and sloppy planning

---

6. The estate tax unified credit under IRC § 2010 is $5.25 million for 2013 and, under the Taxpayer Relief Act of 2012, is adjusted for inflation each year.

7. The Wilson family's situation mirrors that of most successful family-owned businesses in America. According to the 2007 Laird Norton Tyee Family Business Survey, 60 percent of the responding family companies had a CEO over age 55, 71 percent had no succession plan, 97 percent had one or more additional family shareholders, 91 percent had at least one additional member employed by the company, and 74.5 percent had less than five shareholders. Family to Family: Laird Norton Tyee Family Business Survey 2007, pages 5, 7, 9, 12–15.

does not derail the effort. There are various planning traps that need to be avoided.

### a. Timing to Fit the Family

Timing is a critical element in the design of any transition plan. The temperament and anxieties of the parents can affect all timing decisions. Some are anxious to move at full stream; many need to take it slow, to walk before they run. A variety of other factors can influence important timing decisions, including the stability of the business, the parents' capacity to accept and adapt to change, the demands and expectations of the children, the strength of parents' financial base outside of the business, the age and health of the parents, and personal relationships between specific family members. Often the pace of implementing specific plan elements accelerates as circumstances change and the parents become more comfortable with the transition process and their new roles.

The planning process usually is helped by focusing on three timeframes: the period both parents are living, the period following the death of the first parent, and the period following the death of the surviving parent. So long as both Earl and Betty are living, top priorities must include their financial needs and security, their willingness to let go and walk away from the business, and their appetite for living with any fallout resulting from the transition of serious wealth and control to their children. From a tax perspective, all transfers during this timeframe are going to trigger either a transfer of the parents' existing stock basis (often very low)[8] or recognition of taxable income predicated on such basis.

The death of the first parent often creates more flexibility, particularly in a community property state. A double tax benefit is realized on the death of the first parent; the income tax basis in all community property is stepped-up to its fair market value,[9] and the marital deduction may be used to eliminate any estate taxes.[10] Any gifts to other family members during this timeframe now will transfer high-basis assets. Any sales will likely be income tax free. If the deceased parent had the strongest ties to the business (as is so often the case), officially surrendering total control may no longer be an issue. In our case, for example, Betty presumably would have no interest in being involved in the business following Earl's death. Plus, if the life insurance planning correctly eyeballed the parent most likely to die first (Earl in our case), the receipt of tax-free life insurance proceeds[11] may substantially reduce or completely eliminate the surviving parent's financial dependence on the business. For these reasons, often a transition plan is designed as a "targeted first death plan" to shift into high gear the wealth transition process on the death of the first parent.

Of course, the death of the surviving parent triggers the moment of truth for the two big consequences that have been the focus of the planning from the

---

8. For all gifts of property, the donee's tax basis in the transferred property equals the donor's carryover basis plus the amount of any gift taxes paid with respect to the gift, but in no event may the basis exceed the fair market value of the property at the time of the gift. I.R.C. § 1015(a)(d).

9. I.R.C. § 1014(a),(b)(6). For non-community property, the basis step-up is applicable only to property acquired from the decedent. IRC § 1014(a).

10. I.R.C. § 2056.

11. I.R.C. § 101(a)(1).

outset: (1) the ultimate transition of the business and the parents' other assets, and (2) the estate tax bill. As regards the first, the goal is to ensure that the parents' objectives for the family are satisfied without compromising the strength and survival prospects of the business. The objective for the second is to keep the bill as small as possible, while ensuring a mechanism for payment that won't unduly strain the business.

If substantial taxes are expected on the death of the surviving parent, it may be very important to structure the timing of various asset transitions to ensure that at least 35 percent of the surviving parent's adjusted taxable estate consists of the company's stock. Two valuable benefits may be triggered if this threshold is met. First, a corporate redemption of the stock held by the estate may qualify for exchange treatment under Section 303 to the extent the redemption proceeds do not exceed the estate's liability for death taxes (both federal and state) and funeral and administrative expenses.[12] The result is that the redemption proceeds are income tax free to the estate because of the basis step-up in the stock at death. The 35–percent threshold may be satisfied by aggregating stock owned the decedent's estate in two or more corporations if at least 20 percent of the outstanding stock value of each such corporation is included in the decedent's gross estate. Solely for purposes of satisfying the requisite 20 percent ownership for an included corporation, the interest of the decedent's surviving spouse in stock held as community property, joint tenants, tenants by the entirety, and tenants in common may be considered property included in the decedent's gross estate.[13] Absent this Section 303 benefit, and to the extent any redemption proceeds exceed the 303 limits, the redemption proceeds will likely constitute taxable dividends to the estate under section 302 because all stock owned by beneficiaries of the estate and their family members will be attributed to the estate. The family and estate ownership attribution rules of section 318 usually make it impossible for the transaction to qualify as a redemption that is not essentially equivalent to a dividend under 302(b)(1), that is a substantially disproportionate redemption under 302(b)(2), or that is a complete redemption of the estate's stock under Section 302(b)(3).[14] As a result, any redemption proceeds not protected by Section 303 are taxed as dividends under section 301.[15] When corporate funds are needed to fund the estate's tax burden, as is so often the case, this section 303 benefit becomes very important.

Second, if the 35–percent threshold is met, the estate may elect under Section 6166 to fund the federal estate tax burden over a period of up to 14 years at very favorable interest rates. The interest rate is 2 percent on the "2 percent portion," a number adjusted annually, and 45 percent of the normal underpayment rate for any amounts over the "2 percent portion."[16] For 2013, the "2 percent portion" is $1,430,000.[17] The favorable rates come with a cost; the interest is not deductible for estate or income tax purposes.[18]

---

12. I.R.C. § 303(a),(b)(2)(A).
13. I.R.C. § 303(b)(2)(B).
14. I.R.C. §§ 302(a), 302(b), and 318(a)(1), (a)(3)(A).
15. I.R.C. §§ 302(d), 301.
16. I.R.C. §§ 6601(j).
17. Rev. Proc. 2012–41.
18. I.R.C. §§ 163(k), 2053(c)(1)(D). In Estate of Roski v. Commissioner, 128 T.C. 113 (2007), the Tax

In those situations where either the Section 303 redemption benefit or the Section 6166 installment payment benefit is important, the timing of the parent's stock transition program prior to death and the value of parent's non-stock assets must be carefully monitored to ensure that the 35–percent threshold will be met at death.

### b. Valuation: Expert Disappearing Acts

An interest in a business must be valued for tax purposes before it can be transferred.  The standard is "fair market value"– the price a willing buyer would pay a willing seller with neither being under any compulsion to deal and both having reasonable knowledge of the relevant facts.[19]  In 1959, the Service issued Revenue Ruling 59–60,[20] which set forth guidelines to be used in valuing the stock of a closely held corporation.  The ruling did not use a mathematical formula; it discussed factors that should be considered in arriving at a fair market value.  It recognized that the size of the block of stock was a relevant valuation factor in a closely held corporation, specifically noting that a minority interest would be more difficult to sell.  Although the fair market value standard has been around forever and nearly a half century ago the Internal Revenue Service provided guidance on how it should be applied in valuing closely held business interests, serious valuation tax disputes regarding family business interests routinely erupt.

These disputes teach three important lessons.  First, secure the services of a professional appraiser. Valuing a closely held business interest requires judgment calls that must be made by a pro.  Second, get the best appraiser available.  If a dispute breaks out, the quality, reputation, and competence of the appraiser may be the ultimate deciding factor.  The Tax Court has consistently refused to accept an appraisal on its face; it has followed a practice of carefully examining the underlying details and assumptions and the quality of the appraiser's analysis.[21] A quality appraisal by a competent appraiser may shift the ultimate burden of proof to the government or result in a complete victory.  Section 7491 provides that, in any court proceeding, the burden of proof with respect to any factual issue relevant to ascertaining the liability of the taxpayer will shift to the government if the taxpayer introduces credible evidence with respect to the issue.[22]  In *Thompson v. Commissioner*,[23] the Second Circuit refused to hold for the taxpayer even though evidence had been submitted to shift the burden of proof under Section 7491 and the IRS had failed to submit a competent appraisal. The Court stated, "[Section 7491] does not require the Tax Court to adopt the taxpayer's valuation, however erroneous, whenever the Court rejects the

---

Court held that the Internal Revenue Service had abused its discretion by requiring that all estates who elect the installment option of section 6166 to provide a bond or security in the form of an extended tax lien. In Notice 2007–90, the Service announced that it had changed its policy and the requirement for security would be determined on a case-by-case basis.

19.  Regs. §§ 20.2031–1(b), 25.2512–1.

20.  1959–1 C.B. 237. Years later in Revenue Ruling 68–609, 1968–2 C.B. 327, the Service stated that the valuation principles of 59–60 also would apply to partnership interests.

21.  See, for example, Rabenhorst v. Commissioner, 71 TCM(CCH) 2271 (1996) and Estate of Kaufman v. Commissioner, 77 TCM (CCH) 1779 (1999).

22.  I.R.C. § 7491.

23.  499 F.3d 129 (2007), vacating T.C. Memo 2004–174.

Commissioner's proposed value; the burden of disproving the taxpayer's valuation can be satisfied by evidence in the record that impeaches, undermines, or indicates error in the taxpayer's valuation."[24]

A quality appraisal may also result in a complete victory. In a celebrated case decided in 1980,[25] the Tax Court refused to "split the difference" in a valuation dispute, opting instead to declare a winner based on a comparative assessment of the credibility of the experts on each side. The court stated:

> [E]ach of the parties should keep in mind that, in the final analysis, the Court may find the evidence of valuation by one of the parties sufficiently more convincing than that of the other party, so that the final result will produce a significant defeat for one or the other, rather than a middle-of-the-road compromise which we suspect each of the parties expects the Court to reach.[26]

With full knowledge of this winner-take-all approach, which has been followed in other key cases,[27] an IRS agent must carefully size up the company's appraiser in assessing the value of starting any fight. Of course, in some cases the court weighs the competing appraisals and makes its own determination.[28] In select instances, the Tax Court has rejected the appraisals submitted by both the Service and the taxpayer on the grounds that the appraisals were defective or unreliable.[29] When both appraisals are rejected, the Service prevails because the burden of proof ultimately is on the taxpayer. All the cases confirm the importance of having a quality appraisal from a reputable firm.

Finally, never get too aggressive on value; it can put into play a costly 20 percent penalty (computed on the tax understatement) if the value used by the client is 65 percent or less than the ultimate determined value.[30] The penalty jumps to 40 percent if the client's number falls to 40 percent or less.[31] A taxpayer may avoid the penalties by proving reasonable cause and good faith.[32] Reliance on a professional appraisal alone won't do the job.[33] The taxpayer must show that

---

24. 499 F.3d at 133.

25. Buffalo Tool & Die Manufacturing Co. v. Commissioner, 74 T.C. 441 (1980), acq. 1982–2 C.B. 1.

26. 74 T.C. at 452.

27. See, for example, Spruill Estate v. Commissioner, 88 T.C. 1197 (1987), Estate of Gallo v. Commissioner, 50 T.C. 470 (1985), Dailey v. Commissioner, 82 TCM 710 (2001), Estate of Strangi v. Commissioner, 115 T.C 478 (2000), Smith v. Commissioner, 78 TCM 745 (1999), Estate of Furman v. Commissioner, 75 TCM (CCH) 2206 (1998); and Kohler v. Commissioner, T.C. Memo 2006–152.

28. See, for example, Estate of Lauder v. Commissioner, TCM (CCH) 985 (1994) (court's value nearly average of values asserted by the respective parties); Estate of Fleming v. Commissioner, 74 TCM (CCH) 1049 (1997) (Court valued company at $875,000, with Service arguing for value of $1.1 million and taxpayer asserting value of $604,000); and Estate of Wright v. Commissioner, 73 TCM (CCH) 1863 (1997) (Court valued stock at $45 a share, with Service's appraisal at $50 a share and taxpayer's appraisal at $38 a share).

29. See, for example, Rabenhorst v. Commissioner, 71 TCM (CCH) 2271 (1996) and Estate of Kaufman v. Commissioner, 77 TCM (CCH) 1779 (1999).

30. I.R.C. § 6662(a),(g).

31. I.R.C. § 6662(h).

32. I.R.C. § 6662(c)(1). In Wandry v. Commissioner, T.C. Memo 2012-88, the Tax Court upheld the taxpayer's use of a defined value formula clause that was designed to eliminate any gift tax liability if valuation changes were imposed by the IRS. In Wandry, the taxpayer used a fixed dollar amount to define the gift of limited partnership units and provided that the number of gifted units, not the value of the gift, would be adjusted for any valuation changes imposed by the IRS. Many now regard Wandry as a landmark case that opened the door to the use of such valuation formula clauses.

33. Reg. § 1.6664–4(b)(1).

the appraiser was a competent professional who had sufficient expertise to justify reliance, that the taxpayer provided the appraiser with all necessary and accurate information, and that the taxpayer relied in good faith on the appraisal.[34]

In every situation involving a closely held business, valuation discounts become the name of the game and play an essential role in the plan design. In a very real sense, they are the ultimate disappearing act because big transfer taxes are saved as the values plummet. Usually, there is a dual focus in planning the valuation discounts. First, all stock transfers by the parents during life should be structured to qualify for the largest possible discounts. Discounts reduce the value of the stock transferred, which in turn reduces gift taxes or permits a greater leveraging of the gift tax annual exclusion[35] and unified credit.[36] In our case, for example, Earl and Betty will be able transition to Jeff, over time and gift tax free, a larger percentage of the company's stock if the value of the shares transferred is heavily discounted. Second, the stock transition program should be designed to ensure that any stock remaining in a parent's estate at death qualifies for the maximum discounts in order to minimize any estate tax burden attributable to the stock.

The two most significant discounts associated with an interest in a closely held business enterprise are the minority interest (lack of control) discount and the lack of marketability discount. The minority interest discount recognizes that a willing buyer will not pay as much for a minority interest; there is no control. The lack of marketability discount reflects the reality that a willing buyer will pay less for an interest in a closely held business if there is no ready market of future buyers for the interest. Usually both discounts are applied in valuing the transferred interest.[37] The size of the discounts is determined by appraisal. The average lack of marketability discount applied by the Tax Court over the last forty years is 24 percent. In *Janda v. Commissioner*,[38] the Tax Court noted:

> Mr. Schneider [IRS's expert appraiser] then listed various studies made on marketability discounts which are cited by Shannon Pratt in his book Valuing a Business: The Analysis and Appraisal of Closely–Held Companies (2d ed.1989). The studies, which deal with marketability discounts in the context of restricted, unregistered securities subsequently available in public equity markets, demonstrate mean discounts ranging from 23 percent to 45 percent. Mr. Schneider also cited several U.S. Tax Court cases that established marketability discounts ranging from 26 percent to 35 percent. Finally, Mr. Schneider stated in his report that he had consulted a study prepared by Melanie Earles and Edward Miliam which asserted that marketability discounts

---

34. Decleene v. Commissioner, 115 T.C. 457 (2000). See also Thompson v. Commissioner, 499 F.3d 129 (2007), vacating T.C. Memo 2004–174, where the court held that the penalty is mandatory absent proof from the taxpayer of good faith reliance.

35. The annual gift tax annual exclusion is presently $14,000. I.R.C. § 2503(b)(1). See related discussion in section D.I., infra.

36. The estate tax unified credit under IRC § 2010 is $5.25 million for 2013 and, under the Taxpayer Relief Act of 2012, is adjusted for inflation each year.

37. See, for example, Dailey v. Commissioner, 82 TCM 710 (2001); Janda v. Commissioner, 81 TCM 1100 (2001); Barnes v. Commissioner, 76 TCM 881 (1998); Litchfield v. Commissioner, T.C. Memo 2009-21.

38. 81 TCM 1100 (2001).

allowed by the Court over the past 36 years averaged 24 percent.

Often the two discounts total 35 to 40 percent.[39] These discounts can have a powerful impact in leveraging the use of annual gift tax exclusions and unified credits to transfer business interests to family members.

In this regard (and this is real good news), there is no family attribution in applying the discounts.[40] The fact that all the business interests stay in the family will not eliminate or reduce the discounts. Even the separate community property interests of spouses are not aggregated for valuation purposes.[41] In one case where a 100 percent business owner transferred his entire ownership to 11 different family members, the Service recognized that each gift would qualify for a minority interest and lack of marketability discount.[42] Absent such discounts, each family member would have received a business interest valued at more than nine percent of the total value (100/11 = something more than 9). Simple by breaking the ownership interest into minority pieces, the discounts reduced the value of each gift to less than six percent of the total.[43] For tax valuation purposes, the math can be exciting: 100/11 = something less than 6.

In the planning process, care must be taken to avoid the step transaction doctrine in structuring transactions to qualify for minority and lack of marketability discounts. If, for example, Earl and Betty transfer a minority stock interest in the corporation to Jeff and then have the corporation redeem the balance of their stock, the step transaction doctrine will kick in to deny any valuation discounts on the transfer to Jeff.[44] A linking of the two transactions kills the discounts because Jeff ends up owning a controlling interest in the company.

Care is required whenever voting control is transferred to a family member. The flipside of the discount game is that a control premium, often as much as 35 percent, must be considered when voting control is transferred.[45] The result is a higher valuation on the transferred interest and more taxes. The math can be just as weird, but in the wrong direction. In one case, the court sustained control premiums of 35 percent and 37.5 percent on two blocks of stock that aggregated 83 percent of the total stock.[46] The net result apparently was a value arguable higher than the total value of all outstanding stock. When voting control is

---

39. See, for example, Dailey v. Commissioner, 82 TCM 710 (2001); Janda v. Commissioner, 81 TCM 1100 (2001); Barnes v. Commissioner, 76 TCM 881 (1998).

40. Rev. Rule 93–12, 1993–1 CB 202; Mooneyham v. Commissioner, 61 TCM 2445 (1991); Ward v. Commissioner, 87 T.C. 78 (1986).

41. See Estate of Bright v. United States, 658 F.2d 999 (5th Cir. 1981).

42. TAM 9449001.

43. Courts have consistently held that, where a donor makes gifts of multiple shares of the same security to different donees at the same time, each gift is to be valued separately. See Bosca v. Commissioner, 76 TCM (CCH) 62 (1998); Mooneyham v. Commissioner, 61 TCM (CCH) 2445 (1991); Ward v. Commissioner, 87 T.C. 78 (1986). See also Rev. Rule 93–12, 1993–1 C.B. 202, revoking Rev. Rule 81–253, 1981 C.B. 187.

44. See TAM 200212006 where the Service stated "It is well established that where the steps of a donative transaction have no independent significance, the courts will collapse the individual steps in determining the substance of the transaction." See also Heyen v. United States, 945 F.2d 359, 363 (10th Cir.1991); Griffin v. United States, 42 F. Supp.2d 700 (W.D. Tex. 1998); and Estate of Bies v. Commissioner, T.C. Memo. 2000–338; and Senda v. Commissioner, 433 F.3d 1044 (8th Cir. 2006).

45. See Rev. Rul. 59–60, 1959–1 C.B. 237, section 4.02(e); Reg. 20.2031–2(f); Rev. Rul. 89–3, 1989–1 C.B. 278; Estate of Salibury v. Commissioner, 34 TCM 1441 (1975).

46. Lewis G. Hutchens Non–Marital Trust v. Commissioner, T.C. Memo. 1993-600.

ultimately transferred and a premium value kicks in for tax purposes, the planning challenge is to have the control premium attach to the smallest equity interest possible. Often this requires a strategic plan that is implemented over many years.

### c. The Entity Form: Nothing Easy

The form of entity usually has a significant impact in the plan design. Far and away, corporate entities are the preferred choice for family operating businesses. A 2002 survey of family businesses with average annual sales of $36 million confirmed that over 89 percent were corporations, split relatively equally between C and S status.[47] All entity forms present planning challenges; none of them are easy. For C corporations, it is the double tax structure that drives up the cost of redemption and dividend strategies, the locked-in stock basis that discourages lifetime gifting and puts a premium on the basis step-up at death, and the alternative minimum tax threat that complicates corporate funding of life insurance.[48] For S corporations, it is the eligibility requirements that preclude partnerships, corporations and most trusts[49] from owning stock and prevents the use of any preferred stock. For partnership-taxed entities, including limited liability companies, it is enhanced self- employment tax burdens,[50] the family partnership income tax rules, the "real partner" requirement for family transfers, potential gift tax annual exclusion problems if the operating agreement is too restrictive, and the threat of a wealth "recycling" claim that may trigger enhanced estate tax exposure under Section 2036.[51]

Often a desire for a different entity form quickly surfaces in the planning process. The most common scenario is the family that is fed up with the double tax burdens of its C corporation status and longs for the flexibility of a pass-through entity. For example, as discussed below, Wilson Incorporated may want to shed its C status in order to have more restructuring flexibility. Conversion from C status to partnership tax status, via a partnership or LLC, is usually out of the question; it will trigger a prohibitively expensive double tax on the liquidation of the C corporation.[52] If, for example, the corporation is subject to a 34 percent marginal tax rate and the shareholder pays a 20 percent capital gains rate, the combined tax burden on any distributed appreciation in the liquidation will be 47.2 percent.[53] Conversion to S status is the only viable option, but it's not free of hassles.

A conversion from C status to S status creates potential tax traps that need to be carefully evaluated and monitored.[54] First, if the company values its inventory

---

47.  Arthur Anderson/Mass Mutual, American Family Business Survey, 2002.

48.  For a discussion of the relative tax advantages and disadvantages of each entity form, see Chapter 3, supra.

49.  For a discussion of the S status eligibility requirements and trusts that may own the stock of an S corporation, see Chapter 3, supra.

50.  For a discussion of the self-employment tax challenges of partnership-taxed entities, see Chapter 3, supra.

51.  For a discussion of each of these issues in the context of family transition planning, see Chapter 16, infra.

52.  I.R.C. §§ 331, 336.

53.  [34 + (20 x (1–34))].

54.  For an expanded discussion of the conversion challenge, see Chapter 7.

using the last-in-first-out ("LIFO") method, conversion to S status will trigger a recapture of the LIFO recapture amount, to be funded over a four-year period.[55] The size of the recapture amount is a function of the historical increases in inventory costs and how fast the inventory turns.[56]

Second, accumulated earnings and profits from the company's prior C period will trigger a taxable dividend to the shareholders if shareholder distributions from the S corporation exceed earnings during the S period.[57] The taxable dividend exposure is limited to the amount of the corporation's earnings and profits from its C corporation existence and ends once the earnings and profits have been distributed. An S corporation, with the consent of all shareholders, may elect to accelerate such dividends by treating all distributions as earnings and profits distributions.[58] Such acceleration may facilitate the use of the favorable tax rates on dividends.

Third, a corporate level built-in gains tax will be triggered if assets owned by the corporation at time of conversion are sold within the 10–year period following the conversion.[59] The tax is imposed at the highest corporate tax rate (presently 35 percent) on the lesser of (i) the gain recognized on the sale or (ii) the asset's built-in gain at the time of the S conversion. This corporate level tax is in addition to the tax that the shareholder bears as a result of the S corporation's gain being passed through and taxed to the shareholder. The only relief to this forced double tax is that the tax paid by the corporation is treated as a loss to the shareholders in the same year. This trap requires a careful monitoring of any asset sales during the 10–year window.

Finally, if the net passive income received by the S corporation exceeds 25 percent of its receipts during a period that it has undistributed earnings and profits from its C existence, a corporate level tax will be triggered and the S status could be put in jeopardy if the condition persists.[60] For purposes of this provision, the term "passive investment income" includes interest, dividends, royalties, and rents, items that are considered portfolio income under the Section 469 passive loss limitations. If the 25 percent threshold is met, the highest corporate tax rate (presently 35 percent) is applied to the excess of the net passive income over 25 percent of the total receipts.[61] The actual calculation of the tax is complicated by factoring in any expenses directly connected to the passive income. Plus, an S corporation can lose its S status—a disaster—if the condition exists for three consecutive years.[62]

In many family situations, conversion from C to S status will help the transition planning process by opening up more restructuring options. The potential tax traps described above, all of which are triggered by the conversion,

---

55. I.R.C. § 1363(d).
56. I.R.C. § 1363(d)(3).
57. I.R.C. § 1368(c)(2).
58. I.R.C. § 1368(e)(3).
59. See generally I.R.C. § 1374.
60. See generally I.R.C. § 1375 and § 1362(d)(3).
61. The actual calculation of the tax is complicated by factoring in any expenses directly connected to the passive income.
62. If the S election is lost, relief may be possible by timely showing that the circumstances resulting in the termination were inadvertent. I.R.C. § 1362(f).

prompt some to take the conversion option off the table. Usually this is ill-advised. These traps should be viewed as serious nuisances that are capable of being monitored and can often be mitigated or eliminated entirely. Seldom will they justify rejecting a conversion that will provide needed planning flexibility in the given situation.

### d. Life Insurance: Structural Blunders

The stock transition plan must be coordinated with the parents' life insurance planning. In many family businesses, life insurance provides essential liquidity to pay the death taxes, to cover the cash needs of the family, and to free the business of cash burdens that otherwise might adversely affect operations or threaten its survival.[63] A central challenge in the planning process is to ensure that the life insurance proceeds are not taxed in the parents' estates. Usually, but not always, the best strategy to accomplish this essential tax objective is to park the ownership of the policy in an irrevocable trust that has no legal connection to the corporation.[64] However, in many situations, the cash flows pressures of funding the premiums and the interests of the other shareholders result in the policy having close ties to the business. In every such situation, the policy ownership and beneficiary decisions need to be carefully evaluated up front to eliminate tax problems and unintended consequences. This usually requires some basic "what if" analysis to avoid blunders that can undermine the entire effort. Following are key traps to avoid.

### (1) Constructive Premium Dividend Trap

To illustrate how this trap surfaces, assume in our case study that Earl and Betty, owners of 90 percent of the corporation's stock, enter into a cross-purchase buy-sell agreement with Jeff, the owner of the remaining 10 percent. To ensure funding of the cross purchase on the death of a shareholder, the parties agree that corporate resources will be used to fund life insurance policies on Earl and Jeff. Jeff, the minority shareholder, owns a $9 million policy on Earl's life to cover the 90 percent of the stock owned by Earl and Betty, and Earl and Betty own a $1 million policy on Jeff's life to cover the stock owned by the Jeff. Absent careful planning, it is likely that the payments made by the corporation to fund the premiums on these policies owned by the shareholders will be treated as distributions with respect to stock for tax purposes. In a C corporation, these payments will trigger constructive taxable dividends—an added tax burden.[65] In an S corporation, it is possible that the arrangement (which produces larger distributions for the benefit of the minority shareholder Jeff) could be considered a second class of stock that would kill the S election–a bombshell.[66] Cash pressures often require that corporate resources be used to fund premiums on

---

63. In a 2002 survey of successful family business owners (average annual sales of $36.5 million), nearly half (47.7%) of the responding owners listed life insurance as their primary source of funds to pay death taxes and life insurance trusts was listed as the most frequently used estate planning technique. Arthur Anderson/Mass Mutual, American Family Business Survey, 2002.

64. For an extended discussion of life insurance trusts, see Section D of Chapter 12, infra.

65. See, for example, Johnson v. Commissioner, 74 T.C. 1316 (1980), Ashby v. Commissioner, 50 T.C. 409 (1968), Hood v. Commissioner, 115 T.C. 172 (2000) and Rev. Rul. 69–608, 1969–2 C.B. 42.

66. See Reg. § 1.1361–1(l )(2)(i) and (vi) Example 6. If there is a binding agreement to use corporate funds to pay the premiums, the risk of a second class of stock finding is very high and the S status may be in jeopardy. See also Mintor v. Commissioner, T.C. Memo 2007–372.

policies that are going to be owned by other parties, including life insurance trusts. Whenever this common condition exists, great care must be exercised to structure compensation and other arrangements that account for such premium payments in the most tax efficient manner possible. It adds complexity, but the complexity is essential in this situation.

### (2) The Lopsided Cross Purchase Disaster

Assume the same cross-purchase scenario as described above, except the parties have eliminated the constructive dividend threat by implementing a compensation structure to account for the premium payments. Earl then dies, and Jeff uses the tax-free $9 million death benefit that he receives to acquire Earl and Betty's stock. Soon after Jeff's acquisition of the stock, he sells the company for its $15 million value. The income tax hit to Jeff on the sale is peanuts because of the high stock basis resulting from his purchase of the stock. Jeff walks from the sale with roughly $14.7 million after-tax.[67] In contrast, Earl and Betty's heirs, including Jeff, collectively net about $8 million from Earl and Betty's 90 percent stock interest after the estate tax hit on the $13.5 million purchase price is paid.[68] Jeff, having shed the business, nets a monstrous benefit from the company compared to his siblings, a result Earl and Betty may have never intended.

The simple lesson is to carefully factor in family dynamics before ever adopting a buy-sell or insurance structure commonly used by unrelated parties. In this situation, fundamental family objectives would likely have been immeasurably improved by having a life insurance trust own the policy on Earl's life. The trust could be structured to provide benefits for all the children and their descendants and to ensure that the policy would not trigger adverse income, estate, or generation skipping transfer tax consequences. Chapter 12 includes an expanded discussion of life insurance trusts.

### (3) The Majority Shareholder Trap

Assume in the prior example that, in order to facilitate corporate funding of the premiums on the policy that insures Earl's life, the corporation actually owns the policy. Thus, the corporation just pays premiums on an asset that it owns.[69] The corporation, as the policy owner, then names Jeff as the beneficiary. If Earl owns more than 50 percent of the corporation's outstanding voting stock on his death, the entire death benefit paid under the policy will be taxed in his estate because he will be deemed to have retained incidents of ownership in the policy by virtue of his majority stock position in the company.[70] Earl's estate tax bill will have mushroomed even though the death benefit is paid to Jeff.

This trap kicks in when the death benefit of a corporate-owned policy insuring the life of a majority stockholder is paid to a party other than the corporation. The trap can be avoided by naming the policy's corporate owner as the policy's sole beneficiary or by making sure that the insured does not own a

---

67. Jeff's only income tax cost on the sale would be the capital gains hit on the gain recognized on the 10 percent stock interest that he has historically owned.

68. The calculations assumes that the present 40 percent marginal estate rate is in effect.

69. For an expanded discussion of corporate-owned life insurance, see Section B. of Chapter 12, infra.

70. Reg. § 20.2042–1(c)(6).

majority of the corporation's outstanding voting stock. As regards the stock ownership threshold, the good news in a community property state is that, for purposes of this trap, an insured will not be deemed to own his or her spouse's community property interest in any stock.[71]

### (4) Corporate Ownership Traps

As previously stated, if the corporation is the named beneficiary on a corporate-owned policy that insures the life of the majority shareholder, the death benefit paid to the corporation on the death of the majority shareholder will not be included in the shareholder's estate.[72] But that's not the end of the story. The corporation's ownership of the policy may trigger other burdens. First, the family usually needs to get the insurance proceeds out of the corporation to satisfy the cash objectives of the family. This often creates unpleasant dividend income tax burdens when a C corporation is involved. The same burdens exist, but not to the same degree, for an S corporation that has undistributed earnings and profits from a prior C corporation existence.[73]

Second, the death benefit may trigger an alternative minimum tax (AMT) for the corporation because the amount by which the death benefit exceeds the corporation's basis in the policy will add to the corporations adjusted current earning AMT purposes.[74]

Finally, although the death benefit of an insurance policy owned by and payable to a corporation will not be included in the taxable estate of the shareholder, the value of the stock in the insured's taxable estate may be adversely affected by the corporation's receipt of the insurance proceeds. Depending on the existence of a buy-sell agreement, its compliance with the Section 2703 requirements,[75] and the underlying purpose of the corporation's ownership of the insurance, the valuation impact will vary, but in most cases the proceeds will not have a dollar-for-dollar impact.[76]

### (5) Transfer-for-Value Trap

Unraveling a corporate ownership life insurance structure can trigger a transfer-for-value trap that will destroy the income tax-free receipt of the death benefit. Assume, in our case, that the corporation is both the owner and the beneficiary of the policy insuring Earl's life and that the family later determines

---

71. See PLR 9746004 (August 8, 1997), where the majority voting stock requirement was not met when the decedent and his spouse each owned a 36 percent community property interest in the corporation's stock.

72. Reg. § 20.2042–1(c)(2) & (6).

73. The tax-free receipt of the life insurance proceeds by the S corporation does not increase the accumulated adjustment account of the S corporation. I.R.C. §§ 101(a)(1), 1368(e)(1)(A) and Reg. § 1.1386–2. 1368(a)(1). Any distributions by the S corporation in excess of its accumulated adjustment account (a likely result if life insurance proceeds are distributed) will trigger a taxable dividend to the shareholders to the extent the S corporation has any undistributed earnings and profits from its C corporation existence. I.R.C. § 1368(c)(2).

74. I.R.C. § 55(g). Not all C corporations are subject to an alternative minimum tax. There are blanket exceptions for a C corporation's first year of operation, any C corporation with average annual gross receipts of less than $5 million during its first three years, and any C corporation with average annual gross receipts of less than $7.5 million during any three-year period thereafter. I.R.C. § 55(e).

75. See related discussion in paragraph e. (1). of this Section, infra.

76. For a discussion of this issue and a leading case dealing with the valuation issue in the context of key person insurance is Estate of Huntsman, 66 T.C. 861 (1976), acq. 1977–1 C.B. 1, see Question 17 in Section B. 3. of Chapter 12, infra.

that the AMT impacts and the tax problems created by having the death benefit paid to the corporation are intolerable. To remedy the situation, the corporation transfers ownership of the policy to Jeff as additional compensation or as part of a dividend distribution. This shift in ownership will trigger the transfer-for-value rule under Section 101(a)(2), effectively destroying Jeff's capacity to receive the death benefit income tax free. It's a disaster. Exceptions to this harsh result exist for transfers to the insured, gratuitous transfers from the insured, transfers to (but not from) a corporation in which the insured is a shareholder or officer, and transfers among partners.[77] The lesson is to carefully set the best insurance structure up front. Changes can be costly and sometimes tax-prohibitive.

As stated above, often the smartest life insurance strategy is to use an irrevocable trust that has no legal ties to the corporation. The trust is both the owner and beneficiary of the policy. The identity and rights of the trust beneficiaries need to be carefully coordinated with the entire transition plan to protect the respective interests of the inside and outside children. This structure avoids corporate ownership traps and tax burdens, ensures that a structure commonly used by unrelated business parties does not become the default option for the family, and, if done right, protects the death benefit from estate tax exposure. The life insurance proceeds will not be included in the insured's taxable estate if the insured held no incidents of ownership in the policy at death or during the three-year period preceding death.[78] The premium funding burden might still exist; careful planning may be necessary to get funds out of the corporation and into the trust to cover the premiums on the policy. Often, this will require compensation payments or S corporation distributions to the parents, followed by annual gifts to the trust that are carefully structured to be sheltered from gift tax by the parents' annual exclusions or unified credits.[79]

### e. Multiple Family Owners: More Is Tougher

The planning takes on a new dimension as multiple family members and trusts begin acquiring stock in the company. The rights and interests of the various shareholders need to be clarified by agreement to keep expectations in line, protect the business, and mitigate the risk of ugly confrontations. Plus, care must be exercised to avoid certain tax traps that can surface as the parents implement their stock transition plan.

A buy-sell agreement between all the shareholders becomes essential once the transition process begins. The agreement should anticipate how and when the balance of the parents' stock in the company will be transitioned. Often special provisions tailored to the unique needs of the parents and not applicable to the stock held by the children will be required. The agreement must also address the stock held by the children to ensure that all stock stays in the family and that a

---

77. I.R.C. § 101(a)(2). For a related discussion of the transfer-for-value rule, see Questions 11 thru 13 of Section B.3. of Chapter 12, infra.

78. I.R.C. §§ 2035(a)(2), 2042.

79. The challenge in many plans is to build provisions into the trust that will enable the gifts that are made to fund the premium burden to qualify for the annual gift tax exclusion. In almost all situations, this is done by including special Crummey withdrawal rights in the trust that convert a trust beneficiary's future interest in the gifts to a present interest, which in turn qualifies the gifts for the annual gift tax exclusion. For a discussion of this funding challenge, see Questions 9 thru 18 of Section D. 3. of Chapter 12, infra.

child has a fair exit sellout option if the child dies or needs to cash-in because of bankruptcy, divorce, disability, sibling discord, or some other compelling circumstance. This family buy-sell agreement should be carefully crafted to meet the specific needs of those family members who own, or in the future may own, stock in the company.

### (1) Buy–Sell Valuation Trap

The buy-sell valuation trap surfaces when the stock owned by a deceased family member is sold pursuant to the terms of a buy-sell agreement, but the price paid under the agreement is less than the value of the sold stock for estate tax purposes. The decedent's estate ends up paying estate taxes on a value that was never realized.

The key to avoiding this trap is to structure the buy-sell agreement so that it fixes the value of the company's stock for federal estate tax purposes. The IRS perceives buy-sell agreements as potential tools to abuse the valuation process, particularly in family situations. For this reason, Section 2703 was added to the Code in 1990 to specify certain criteria that must be satisfied in order for a buy-sell agreement price to control for estate tax valuation purposes. Section 2703 imposes a three-part test:

1. The agreement must be a bona fide business arrangement;

2. The agreement must not be a device to transfer property to members of the decedent's family for less than full value and adequate consideration in money or money's worth; and

3. The terms of the agreement must be comparable to similar arrangements entered into by persons in an arms-length transaction.[80]

Each of the three requirements must be satisfied, along with the requirements imposed by regulations before the adoption of Section 2703. There are three pre–2703 requirements that must be satisfied: (1) The price must be specified or readily ascertainable pursuant to terms of the agreement and the value must have been reasonable when entered into; (2) The decedent's estate must be obligated to sell at death at the specified price; and (3) The decedent must have been restricted from selling or transferring the interest during life. This third condition is not satisfied if the decedent had a right to transfer the interest by gift during life to a person who was not subject to the same restrictions. As a minimum, this provision generally requires that the interest be subject to a right of first refusal at the fixed or determinable price under the agreement during the decedent's life.[81]

In most cases, the third requirement of section 2703 will prove to be the most difficult. The comparable arms-length determination is made at the time the agreement is entered into, not when the rights under the agreement are exercised.[82] This third requirement will be satisfied if the agreement is

---

80. I.R.C. § 2703(b).

81. Reg. § 20.2031–2(h).

82. Reg. § 25.2703–1(b)(4)(i). See Estate of Amlie v. Commissioner, T.C. Memo 2006–76, where the court held that evidence of price in other arms-length transactions may be used to sustain the burden of proof.

comparable to the general practice of unrelated parties under negotiated agreements in the same industry.[83]  An effort must be made to determine what others in the same industry are doing.  If multiple valuation methods are used in the industry, the requirement can be satisfied by showing that the valuation mechanism in the agreement is comparable to one of the commonly used methods.[84]  If there are no industry standards because of the unique nature of the business, standards for similar types of businesses may be used to establish the arms-length terms of the agreement.[85]

Because Section 2703 is targeted at abuses among family members, the regulations to Section 2703 provide an exception in those situations where over 50 percent of the equity ownership interests in the business are owned by non-family members.  In order for the exception to apply, the equity interests owned by the unrelated parties must be subject to the same restrictions and limitations as those applicable to the transferor.[86]  If this 50 percent test is met and three basic pre–2703 requirements are met,[87] the requirements of Section 2703 are deemed satisfied and the value determined pursuant to the agreement will govern for estate tax purposes.  This exception substantially reduces the proof burden.

### (2)  Preferred Stock Traps

In many situations, the parents desire to use preferred stock to facilitate the stock transition process to other family members.  Extreme caution is required whenever preferred equity interests are considered in the plan design.  The issuance of preferred stock will kill an S election, and the existence of preferred stock may make a future S election impossible if the holder of the stock is unwilling to surrender his or her preferred rights.[88]  Of far greater concern is Section 2701, the provision that assigns a zero value to a retained preferred interest that does not contain a "qualified payment" right when there is a transfer of a common equity interest to a family member.[89]

Assume, for example, that a C corporation has outstanding common stock valued at $3 million and non-cumulative preferred stock valued at $2 million, all owned by the parent.  If the parent sold the common stock to an unrelated party for $3 million, the parent would simply report capital gain income on the excess of the $3 million sales price over the parent's tax basis in the stock sold.  If, however, the parent sold the common stock to a child for $3 million, the parent would also be deemed to have made a $2 million taxable gift to the child. This extreme result is mandated by Section 2701, which requires that the preferred stock retained by the parent be valued at zero and the common stock sold to the

---

83. Reg. § 25.2703–1(b)(4)(i). It is not necessary that the provisions parallel the terms of any particular agreement. Reg. § 25.2703–1(b)(4)(ii).

84. Reg. § 25.2703–1(b)(4)(ii).

85. Reg. § 25.2703–1(b)(4)(ii).

86. Reg. § 25.2703–1(b)(3). Family members include the transferor's spouse, any ancestor of the transferor or the transferor's spouse, any spouse of any such ancestor, and any lineal descendant of the parents of the transferor or the transferor's spouse (but not spouses of such descendants). Reg. § 25.2703–1(b)(3); Reg. § 25.2701–2(b)(5). Broad entity attribution rules are used to determine ownership, with an interest being deemed a family interest if it is attributed to both a family and non-family member. Reg. § 25.2703–1(b)(3); Reg. § 25.2701–6(a)(2)-(4).

87. Reg. § 20.2031–2(h).

88. I.R.C. § 1361(b)(1)(D).

89. I.R.C. § 2701(a)(3)(A).

child be assigned a value of $5 million.  This taxable gift can be avoided only if the parties agree that qualified dividend payments henceforth will be made to the parent on a regular basis and actually make such payments.[90]  In that event, the retained preferred stock would be valued based on the size of the qualified payments, and the gift would be reduced accordingly.  But such qualified payments can be burdensome; they trigger double-taxed dividend income to the parent, drain cash from the corporation, and pump up the parent's taxable estate. The lesson is to keep a very close eye on Section 2701 whenever preferred equity interests are part of the mix.

### (3)  Voting Stock Trap

This trap is triggered when a parent transfers stock in a controlled corporation and, through some means, "directly or indirectly" retains the right to vote the stock. When this condition exists, Section 2036(b) kicks in and the stock is brought back into the parent's estate for estate tax purposes. The transfer will have done nothing to reduce the parent's future estate tax burden.  A corporation will be considered a "controlled corporation" if at any time after the transfer or within three years of death, the transferring parent owned, or is deemed to have owned under the broad family and entity attribution rules of Section 318,[91] at least 20 percent of the total combined voting power of all stock[92]—a condition that is easily satisfied by nearly every family corporation.  The "directly or indirectly" language extends the reach of the 2036(b) trap to many situations, including those where the parent votes transferred stock held in trust, where the parent is a general partner of a partnership that owns the transferred stock, and where the parent, through an express or implied agreement, retains the right to reacquire voting authority or has the right to influence or designate how the stock will be voted.[93]

The safest way to avoid this trap is to transfer nonvoting stock, an option available to both C and S family corporations.[94] Plus, in addition to avoiding 2036(b) threats, use of nonvoting stock will usually buttress the application of a lack of control valuation discount.  The need for nonvoting stock often requires a simple tax-free recapitalization to convert outstanding voting common stock to both voting and nonvoting stock.

The transition planning process should anticipate and avoid problems with the family buy-sell agreement and the preferred stock and voting stock traps.  As other family members begin acquiring stock, the process also should address the expectations of the new shareholders and their perceptions of their new wealth. They are no longer just family members; they are now owners.  Usually there is a need for education and dialogue on a broad range of basic issues, including limitations imposed by the buy-sell agreement, the rationale for using nonvoting stock, cash flow expectations, future transition plans, and more. The goal is to

---

90. I.R.C. § 2701(c)(3)(B)(ii).

91. I.R.C. § 318.

92. I.R.C. § 2036(b)(2).

93. See, for example, TAM 199938005 (transferor general partner of partnership) and Rev. Rul. 80–346, 1980–2 C.B. 271 (oral agreement with transferor).

94. Use of nonvoting stock does not trigger the trap. Rev. Rul. 81–15, 1981–1 C.B. 46; Pro. Reg. 20.2036–2(a).

keep all shareholders informed and to ensure that expectations are in line with reality.

### f. Marital Deduction Traps

Smart use of the marital deduction is essential in most plans. It's the tool that eliminates any estate tax bite on the death of the first spouse, deferring all taxes until the survivor's death. Although rationales are sometimes spouted for paying some taxes at the first death, they're always based on problematic assumptions and ignore the simple reality that most clients, particularly business owners, have no stomach for paying taxes any sooner than absolutely necessary. In most situations, the game plan is to transfer to a qualified terminable interest property ("QTIP") trust the smallest portion of the deceased spouse's estate necessary to eliminate all taxes in the estate. Although both a direct bequest to the surviving spouse and a bequest to a QTIP trust may qualify for the marital deduction and eliminate any estate tax liability on the death of the first spouse, the QTIP offers advantages that often make it the preferred option. With a QTIP, the first spouse to die can specify and limit the surviving spouse's access to the principal (not income) of the trust, can designate how the trust remainder will be distributed on the death of the surviving spouse, can help protect the trust estate against creditor claims of the trust beneficiaries, and can help preserve valuable discounts. To qualify for the marital deduction, the QTIP must mandate that, during the life of the surviving spouse, all QTIP income will be currently paid to the surviving spouse, and no person other than the surviving spouse may receive property distributions from the trust.[95] A closely held business interest that comprises the bulk of the estate can trigger problems with a QTIP.

### (1) The Minority Discount QTIP Trap

The minority discount QTIP trap surfaces when a controlling interest in the business is included in the estate of the first spouse to die, but only a minority interest in the business is used to fund the QTIP. The same specific shares in the estate are given a high value for gross estate valuation purposes and a lower discounted minority interest value for marital deduction purposes. This whipsawing nets a marital deduction that's too low, and the estate of the first spouse to die ends up with an unanticipated estate tax liability.[96] Plus if the underfunded marital deduction resulted in an overfunding of a credit shelter trust, a likely result in many cases, the surviving spouse may be deemed to have made a taxable gift to the credit shelter trust.[97] And there's more. If the surviving spouse has an income interest in the credit shelter trust, the property that constituted the constructive gift likely will be pulled back into the taxable estate of the surviving spouse at death under Section 2036.[98] The key to avoiding this mess is to make certain that, if the estate owns a controlling stock interest in the business, the QTIP is funded with other estate assets or with stock that represents a controlling interest.

The trap can also surface when a controlling stock interest is designated to

---

95.  I.R.C. § 2056(b)(7).
96.  See DiSanto v. Commissioner, T.C. Memo 1999–421, PLR 9050004, and PLR 9147065.
97.  See TAM 9116003.
98.  See I.R.C. § 2036(a) and TAM 9116003.

pass directly to the surviving spouse under the will or living trust of the first spouse to die, but the surviving spouse disclaims a portion of the bequest[99] and, as a result, ends up receiving a minority stock interest. In calculating the estate tax on the first death, the size of the marital deduction will be predicated on the discounted minority valuation of the stock, triggered by the surviving spouse's disclaimer.[100] Again, the same shares are given a higher valuation for gross estate inclusion purposes than for marital deduction purposes.

There's a flipside to this trap that may produce a positive result in the right situation. If the QTIP is funded with a controlling interest in the stock and the credit shelter trust is funded with a minority stock interest, the stock passing to the QTIP may qualify for a control premium for marital deduction valuation purposes. The end result is that fewer shares may need to pass to the QTIP to secure the needed marital deduction, leaving more shares for the credit shelter trust.[101]

### (2) The Buy–Sell QTIP Trap

The buy–sell QTIP trap may be triggered when the QTIP is funded with corporate stock that is subject to a buy-sell agreement. If the agreement gives other family members the right to buy the stock pursuant to a price established under the agreement and the requirements of section 2703 are not satisfied,[102] the price paid for the stock under the agreement will not be controlling for estate tax purposes. As a result, the value of the stock for estate tax purposes, as ultimately determined, may be greater than the price paid under the buy-sell agreement. In that event, the buyers of the stock may be deemed to have received an economic benefit from the QTIP during the life of the surviving spouse by virtue of their right to buy the stock for less than full consideration, and the entire QTIP marital deduction may be blown.[103]    The key to avoiding this trap is to ensure compliance with the 2703 requirements or to make certain that any stock passing to the QTIP is not subject to a buy-sell agreement.

### (3) The Non–QTIP Trap

Assume in our case study that, at Earl's death, his estate owns 45 percent of the stock and Betty owns 45 percent of the stock. The 45 percent owned by the estate would constitute a minority interest for estate tax purposes.[104] Assume that Earl's will or living trust mandates that a portion of his stock pass directly to Betty in order to secure a marital deduction to eliminate any estate tax liability. Betty would end up directly owning a controlling interest in the stock, which would be valued as such for estate tax purposes on her death. In contrast, assume that Earl had left the requisite marital deduction stock to a QTIP trust to secure

---

99. Such a disclaimer is effective for transfer tax purposes if (1) it is in writing and delivered within 9 months of the date the property interest is created, (2) the disclaiming party has not accepted the property interest or any related benefits, and (3) the property interest passes without any direction by the disclaiming party. IRC § 2518.

100. See DiSanto v. Commissioner, T.C. Memo 1999–421.

101. See Estate of Chenoweth v. Commissioner, 88 T.C. 1577 (1987).

102. See related discussion in paragraph e.1. of this section, supra.

103. See I.R.C. § 2056(b)(7)(B)(ii)(II), and Estate of Renaldi, 97–2 U.S.T.C. 60,281 (Ct. Cl. 1997), and TAM 9147065.

104. Estate of Bright v. United States, 658 F.2d 999 (5th Cir. 1981). See also Rev. Rule 93–12, 1993–1 CB 202; Mooneyham v. Commissioner, 61 TCM 2445 (1991); Ward v. Commissioner, 87 T.C. 78 (1986).

the marital deduction. The stock owned by the QTIP, although not directly owned by Betty, would be taxed in her estate. Both Betty and the QTIP would own minority stock interests that, if aggregated, would constitute a controlling interest. Even though both interests would be taxed in Betty's estate, they would be valued for estate tax purposes as two separate minority interests, not one controlling interest.[105] The lesson is that use of a QTIP in designing any marital deduction components of the plan may preserve valuable discounts that otherwise would be lost with direct inter-spousal transfers.

### (4) The Permission Sale QTIP Trap

This trap surfaces when the QTIP trust is funded with stock of the family corporation and the trustee of the QTIP is restricted from selling the stock without the consent of a third party. Suppose, for example, that Earl dies and a portion of his stock is used to fund a QTIP trust that is intended to qualify for the marital deduction, and the family buy-sell agreement prohibits any family member or trust from selling stock without the consent of Jeff, the CEO. Such a consent requirement would likely prevent the QTIP trust from qualifying for the marital deduction. A key QTIP requirement is that all income of the trust must be paid to the surviving spouse at least annually.[106] To protect this right of the surviving spouse, regulations provide that the QTIP trust must require the trustee to convert stock into income producing property on the request of the surviving spouse.[107] The Service has ruled that this requirement will not be satisfied if any stock sale is conditioned on the consent of another family member.[108] The key to avoiding the trap is to ensure that any stock consent requirements imposed by the family buy-sell agreement are not applicable to the trustee of any QTIP trust.

The QTIP trust is an essential element of most transition plans. It bridges the gap between the deaths of the parents, eliminates estate taxes on the death of the first parent, ensures that each parent can control the ultimate disposition of his or her property, provides management and creditor protection benefits, and preserves precious valuation discounts. Although it adds complexity on the death of the first spouse, in most cases the QTIP will be far superior to the alternative of leaving stock directly to the surviving spouse. The challenge is to customize each spouse's QTIP to meet the parents' objectives and to avoid the technical traps that compromise the all-important marital deduction.

### f. Compensation Transition Opportunities

In most situations, one or more children are key officers in the company at the time the transition plan is set in motion. Frequently the fear is that stock passing to these children will be deemed to be taxable compensation, not gifts that are income tax-free. In our case study, for example, this could be a concern as Jeff starts receiving more stock. In fact, it is usually preferable to actually structure the stock transfers as compensation income from the corporation.

---

105. Estate of Bonner v. U.S., 84 F.3d 196 (5th Cir. 1996); Estate of Mellinger v. Commissioner, 112 T.C. 26, (1999); AOD 1999–006.

106. I.R.C. § 2056(b)(7)(B)(ii)(I).

107. Reg. § 20.2056(b)–5(f)(4).

108. See PLR 9147065.

Although such transfers trigger taxable income to the child,[109] the corporation receives an offsetting tax deduction,[110] and, in nearly all cases, the corporation's income tax savings will equal or exceed the child's income tax cost.[111] The result is a zero net income tax burden, and a simple gross-up cash bonus can be used to transfer to the child the corporation's tax savings to cover the child's income tax hit.[112] So from a current income tax perspective, the compensation structure is usually no worse than a push with the gift option. But the compensation structure offers two big advantages that could never be realized with a gift. First, unlike a gift where the child takes the parent's carryover basis in the stock,[113] a compensation transfer results in the child receiving a basis in the stock equal to its fair market value at time of transfer.[114] Second, with the compensation structure, the parent has no gift tax concerns, and there are no gift tax opportunity costs. The transaction does not consume any of the parent's gift tax annual exclusion or unified credit benefits.

There are often opportunities to use the compensation process to dramatically accelerate the equity transition process. Suppose, for example, that in lieu of receiving more stock, or perhaps in addition to receiving more stock, Jeff is given a contractual right to compensation that is structured to provide the same economic benefits as stock. A deferred compensation contract is used to pay benefits based on Jeff's hypothetical ownership of a designated number of common stock shares. The written contract offers a medley of economic benefits based on the "phantom" stock, including dividend equivalency payments and payments based on the value of the phantom shares (determined at the time of the event) if the company is sold or merged or if Jeff dies, becomes disabled, or otherwise terminates his employment.[115] The arrangement offers a number of tax benefits. First, there is no threat that Jeff will end up having to report taxable income without having received a like amount of cash, a "phantom income" condition that is often triggered when stock is transferred to an employee as compensation.[116] Since all amounts paid to Jeff are compensation under a contract, Jeff will not have any taxable income until he actually receives payment. Second, there are no gift tax concerns for Earl and Betty even though the rights under the contract transfer substantial value to Jeff. Third, since all amounts paid to Jeff represent compensation, the company receives a full deduction at the time of payment.[117] In many ways, such a contractual arrangement is one of the most efficient strategies, from a tax perspective, for transferring equity value.

---

109. I.R.C. § 83(a). Recognition of taxable income is deferred so long as the stock is subject to a substantial risk of forfeiture unless the recipient makes an election under section 83(b) to accelerate the recognition of income.

110. I.R.C. § 83(h). Note, however, that if the service provided is capital in nature, the corporation will have to capitalize the expenditure. Reg. § 1.83–6(a)(4).

111. This common outcome is a result of the comparative marginal tax rates applicable to C corporations and individuals. A C corporation will be subject to a marginal rate of at least 34 percent once its annual income exceeds $75,000. I.R.C. § 11(b)(1)(C).

112. For a discussion of the "gross up" and how it is calculated, see Section C.2.d of Chapter 4, supra.

113. I.R.C. § 1015(a).

114. Reg. § 1.83–4(b), I.R.C. § 1012.

115. For a discussion of the planning opportunities and traps of such arrangements, see Sections D. 3. of Chapter 11.

116. See I.R.C. § 83(a).

117. I.R.C. § 162(a).

Are there any tax disadvantages to such an arrangement? Historically, the biggest disadvantage has been the absence of any capital gains break for the child. Because the child never receives real stock under the contract, there is no possibility of creating a capital gain at time of sale. To sweeten the deal for the child, an added bonus may be provided to produce a net after-tax yield to the child that is equal to the yield that would result if the phantom stock payment was taxed as a capital gain. Again, the company gets a full deduction for all amounts paid. Often this capital gains "make-up" bonus can be paid with the company still incurring a net after-tax cost that is less than would be incurred if it issued real stock and later had to purchase the real stock under a buy-sell agreement. For example, assume in our case that Jeff's marginal ordinary income tax rate is 33 percent and his capital gain rate is 15 percent. Jeff would net 85 cents on every dollar of capital gain recognized on the sale of real stock to the corporation under a buy-sell agreement. Under a phantom stock contract with a capital gain gross-up bonus, the corporation would have to pay Jeff $1.27 to net Jeff the same 85 cents after Jeff's 33 percent marginal ordinary income rate is applied. But if the corporation is subject to a marginal rate of 34 percent, the $1.27 payment would cost the company only 84 cents on a net after-tax basis, which is 16 percent less than the after-tax cost the company would need to expend to buy real stock from Jeff under a buy-sell agreement.

With any such deferred compensation plan, great care must be taken to ensure that it avoids the reaches of Section 409A, added by the American Jobs Creation Act of 2004.[118] Generally, this will require that (1) any compensation deferral elections of the employee be made before the close of the taxable year preceding the taxable year in which the related services are actually rendered, (2) the authorized events that may trigger payment of benefits under the contract (i.e. separation from service, specified time, change in control, unforeseen emergency) be specified in the contract (i.e. no elections are allowed as to timing of payments), (3) there be no acceleration or further deferral of benefits, (4) assets not be placed in a trust or other arrangement outside of the United States to pay benefits under the contract, and (5) assets not be restricted to the payment of benefits under the contract based on changes in the company's financial health.[119]

## D. CORPORATE TRANSITION STRATEGIES

The plan design usually includes a program for transferring stock to other family members while one or both of the parents are living. The strategic options include gifts of stock to other family members or trusts, sales of stock to the corporation, and sales of stock to other family members or trusts. No option is clearly superior to the others; each has disadvantages and limitations that need to be carefully evaluated. Often a combination approach is the best alternative. Plus, in some cases the need to actually transfer stock while the parents are living may be mitigated or eliminated entirely by business restructuring techniques that have the effect of transitioning future value without actually transferring stock.

---

118. I.R.C. § 409A.
119. Reg. §§ 1.409A–2(a)(b), 1.409A–3; I.R.C. § 409A(b)(1),(2).

## 1. GIFTING STRATEGIES

The gift strategy is clearly the simplest and easiest to comprehend. The parents seek to reduce their future estate tax exposure by gifting stock and other property to family members. The challenge is to structure the gifts to avoid or minimize gift tax on the transfers. In our case study, Earl and Betty could commence a program of gifting Wilson corporate stock to Jeff, the child involved in the business, and gifting other assets to other family members. For gift tax purposes, the value of any gifted stock may qualify for lack of marketability and minority interest discounts, which together may equal as much as 40 percent.[120]

Earl and Betty each have a gift tax annual exclusion which shelters from gift taxes any gifts of present property interests up to $14,000 (2013 amount) to a single donee in a single year.[121] All gifts of stock and other assets that fall within the scope of this $14,000 annual exclusion will be removed from Earl and Betty's estates for estate tax purposes.[122] Earl and Betty have 10 potential donees in their immediate family: three children, three spouses of children, and four grandchildren. At $28,000 per donee ($14,00 for each parent), Earl and Betty's annual gift tax exclusions would enable them to collectively transfer tax-free $280,000 of discounted value each year to immediate family members. If discounts are factored in at 40 percent, this simple strategy could shift nearly $467,000 value out of Earl and Betty's estates each year. Over a ten-year period, the total future value of property removed from Earl and Betty's taxable estates and transitioned tax-free with their annual gift tax exclusions could reasonably be expected to exceed $6 million.[123] Simple 2503(c) trusts could be used for all heirs under age 21 to avoid future interest problems that would otherwise compromise the availability of the annual exclusion. If grandchildren are the trust beneficiaries, care should be taken to meet the requirements of section 2642(c)(2) to insure an inclusion ratio of zero for generation skipping transfer (GST) tax purposes and no GST tax liability.[124]

In addition to their annual gift tax exclusions, Earl and Betty each have their lifetime gift tax unified credits and their GST exemptions.[125] Under the Taxpayer Relief Act of 2012 passed during the final days of 2012, the lifetime gift tax unified credit was increased in 2013 to tax-protect gifts of up to $5.25 million that are not otherwise sheltered by the annual exclusion. Under the same bill, the GST exemption for 2013 permits GST tax-free transfers of up $5.25 million during life or at death. If the company stock and other gifted assets are expected to grow in value (a reasonable assumption in many cases), early use of the gift tax unified credits and the GST exemptions will produce future estate tax benefits because all appreciation in the value of the gifted property' accruing subsequent to the date of the transfers will be excluded from the parents' taxable estates.

---

120. See, for example, Rakow v. Commissioner, 77 TCM 2066 (1999), Dailey v. Commissioner, 82 TCM 710 (2001), and Janda v. Commissioner, 81 TCM 1100 (2001).

121. I.R.C. §§ 2503(b).

122. I.R.C. §§ 2001, 2503(b).

123. This assumes that the annual gift tax exclusion continues to escalate in $1,000 increments as it has done in the past and that the value of the business grows at a rate of 6 percent per annum.

124. The grandchild must be the sole beneficiary of the trust during life, and the trust assets must be included in grandchild's estate if the grandchild dies before the trust terminates. I.R.C. § 2642(c)(2).

125. I.R.C. §§ 2505, 2631.

Gifts also have income tax consequences. As the common stock is transferred, any income rights attributable to that stock also are transferred. If, as in our case study, the corporation is a C corporation, any future dividends attributable to the gifted stock will be paid and taxed to the family members who own the stock. If the entity is an S corporation, the pass-through tax impacts attributable to the gifted stock will flow to the children and grandchildren who own the stock.

### a. Gift Taxes Now? A Hard Sell

Many parents have an interest in the gifting strategy so long as no gift taxes need to be paid. The strategy becomes much less appealing when the possibility of paying gift taxes is factored into the mix. In our case study, should Earl and Betty consider making taxable gift transfers—transfers that exceed the limits of their annual exclusions and their gift tax unified credits—in hopes of avoiding larger estate tax burdens down the road? There are two potential benefits to such transfers. First, all future appreciation on the gifted property will be excluded from the donor's taxable estate. Second, if the gift is made at least three years before death, the gift taxes paid by the transferring parent are not subject to any transfer taxes, resulting in a larger net transfer to the donee.[126] For example, if Betty dies with an additional $1 million included in her taxable estate that is subject to a 40 percent marginal estate tax rate, the net after-tax amount available to her heirs will equal $600,000. In contrast, if Betty had expended that same $1 million at least three years prior to her death by making a gift of $714,000 to a child and paying gift taxes at the rate of 40 percent on such gift ($286,000), the child would end up netting an additional $114,000 (the taxes otherwise imposed on the gift taxes), plus any appreciation on the property occurring subsequent to the gift. If the donor parent dies within three years of the gift, Section 2035(b) pulls the gift taxes paid by the parent back into the parent's taxable estate, and the tax benefit is lost.

Do these potential benefits justify writing a big gift tax check now in hopes of saving bigger estate taxes down the road? Most private business owners have little or no appetite for this potential opportunity. Their reluctance to seriously consider the possibility is bolstered by their understandable desire to defer any and all taxes as long as possible and wishful dialog they've heard regarding the potential demise of the federal estate tax. As a result, many families confine their gifts of stock to transfers that are fully tax-protected by the annual exclusion or the unified credit.

### b. Gifting Disadvantages

Although the gifting strategy may result in a reduction of future estate taxes and a shifting of income, it has its disadvantages and limitations. For many parents, the biggest disadvantage is the one-way nature of a gift; they receive nothing in return to help fund their retirement needs and provide a hedge against an uncertain future. In our case study, for example, the strategy does nothing to address Earl and Betty's primary goal of having a secure retirement income from the business for the balance of their lives. Their insecurities may be heightened as

---

126. Any gift taxes paid within three years of death are taxed in the decedent's estate. I.R.C. § 2035(b).

they see their stock being gifted away over time. The receipt of life insurance on the death of the first spouse may reduce or eliminate the insecurities of the survivor, but so long as they are both living and trying to adjust to their new, less-involved life style, their financial security will be priority one. To help secure their retirement income, the company may agree to pay Earl ongoing compensation benefits for consulting services or perhaps an agreement not to compete. There are disadvantages to this compensation approach. There is always the risk that the payments will not be recognized as deductible compensation for income tax purposes, but rather will be characterized as nondeductible dividends.[127] Plus, compensation payments will trigger ongoing payroll taxes.[128]

Another option for securing a steady income for Earl and Betty is to pay dividends on the stock that they retain. There are a number of disadvantages with the dividend alternative. First, it produces a double tax—one at the corporate level and one at the shareholder level. Conversion to S status may help eliminate the double tax hit moving forward, but, as explained above, the conversion itself is not tax-hassle free.[129] Second, since children will be receiving stock, corresponding pro rata dividend payments will need to be made to the children. This just aggravates the double tax problem and does nothing to accomplish the parents' objectives.

Another disadvantage of the gifting strategy relates to Jeff's plan for the future. Because a gifting strategy is usually implemented in incremental steps over a lengthy period of time to maximize use of the annual gift tax exclusion and to ensure that the parents have retained at all times sufficient stock for their future needs, the plan may frustrate or at least badly dilute Jeff's goal of garnering the fruits of his future efforts for himself. If Jeff is successful in expanding and growing the business, his success will be reflected pro rata in the value of all of the common stock, including the stock retained by Earl and Betty and any common stock gifted to Kathy and Paul and other family members.

Finally, there's an income tax disadvantage to the gifting strategy. The tax basis of any stock owned by a parent at death will be stepped up to the fair market value of the stock at death.[130] If Earl and Betty make gifts of stock, their low basis in the stock is carried over to their donees,[131] and the opportunity for the basis step-up at death is lost forever. This can be significant if a donee sells the stock down the road. In a community property state, this disadvantage is substantially eliminated for all gifts made after the death of the first spouse because all community property (even the surviving spouse's interest) receives a tax basis step-up on the death of the first spouse.[132]

---

127. Reg. §§ 1.162–7, 1.162–8.

128. The payroll tax burden is 15.3 percent of the annual threshold compensation amount ($113,700 for 2013) and 2.9 percent of any compensation paid in excess of the threshold. Starting in 2013, the rate jumps to 3.8 percent on a married couple's earnings in excess of $250,000 and an unmarried individual's earnings in excess of $200,000.

129. See related discussion in section C.2.c. supra.

130. I.R.C. § 1014(a).

131. I.R.C. § 1015(a).

132. I.R.C. § 1014(a),(b)(6).

These potential disadvantages need to be carefully evaluated in the design of any transition plan. The result in many situations is a gifting program that starts slowly, perhaps geared to the limits of the annual gift tax exclusion, then accelerates as the parents become increasingly more secure in their new "uninvolved" status, and then shifts into high gear following the death of the first spouse. In other cases, the fear of future estate taxes prompts the parents to aggressively embrace the gifting strategy and explore methods of enhancing their stock gifting options. Following is a description of enhanced stock gifting strategies that are often considered.

### c. The GRAT—A Square Peg?

The grantor retained annuity trust (GRAT) is a proven darling in the estate planning world. For large estates wrapped up in the challenge of juggling many valuable marbles, its allure often is irresistible. Its value in transitioning a family business, a mountain, is far more problematic. Often, when all factors are fairly considered, the GRAT ends up being the proverbial square peg that just doesn't fit the situation.

With a GRAT, the parent transfers property to a trust and retains an annuity, expressed as either a fixed dollar amount or a percentage of the fair market value of the property transferred, for a specified timeframe, expressed as a term of years, the life of the grantor, or the shorter of the two. The annuity must be paid at least annually, and its payment may not be contingent on the income of the trust.[133] That is, if necessary, annuity payments must be funded out of trust principal. The trust may not issue a "note, other debt instrument, option, or other similar arrangement" to pay the annuity.[134] No additional property may be contributed until the annuity term ends,[135] nor may payments be made to any person other than the grantor.

The contributed property is deemed to have two valuation components for gift tax purposes. The first component (Annuity Component) has a value based on the size of the designated annuity payment and the annuity tables under section 7520 (which are based on an interest rate equal to 120 percent of the applicable Federal midterm rate).[136] The value of the second component (Reminder Component) is the excess of the value of the property transferred to the trust less the value of the Annuity Component. At the time the trust is created, the parent is deemed to have made a gift equal to only the value of the Remainder Component. At the end of the annuity term, all remaining property in the trust is transferred to the designated beneficiaries, usually children, with no further gift tax consequences. Plus, the property is removed from the parent's estate for estate tax purposes.

A GRAT creates two key risks: a mortality risk and a yield risk. The mortality risk is that all tax objectives will be lost if the parent dies before the end of the designated annuity term. If the parent dies prematurely, the entire value of the property will be subject to estate taxes in the parent's estate under Section

---

133. Reg. § 25.2702–3.
134. Reg. § 25.2702–3(b)(1)(i).
135. Reg. § 25.2702–3(b)(5).
136. I.R.C. § 7520.

2036(a).[137] The entire effort will have produced nothing. The yield risk recognizes that the GRAT will not produce any net transfer tax benefit if the yield on the property held in the trust (including its growth in value) during the annuity term does not exceed the Section 7520 rate used to value the Annuity Component. If the property's yield can't beat the 7520 rate, the parent would be better off for transfer tax purposes if he or she, in lieu of the GRAT, had simply made a completed gift of property equal in value to the Remainder Component free of any mortality risk factor.[138] For the GRAT to pay off, the parent must beat both risks—live longer than the annuity term and have the trust property produce a yield superior to the 7520 rate.[139]

### (1) The Real Goal—Something for Nothing

Given the mortality and yield risks, often the GRAT is a tough sell if a substantial gift tax burden is triggered on its creation. Since the Remainder Component is a future interest, the gift tax annual exclusion is not available. The parent's unified credit is usually better spent on other transfers (e.g., life insurance dynasty trust insurance premiums) that are guaranteed to produce real transfer tax benefits; the opportunity cost of expending the credit on a risk-laden GRAT often just doesn't pencil out. And the thought of actually paying significant gift taxes on a transfer that might produce no estate tax benefits is rejected outright by many as absurd. So often the strategy of choice is to structure the annuity so that the Annuity Component nearly equals the value of the contributed property, and the Remainder Component has little or no value.

This "zero-out" strategy, made possible by the Tax Court's 2000 decision in *Walton v. Commissioner*,[140] is accomplished by structuring the annuity to be paid to the parent or the parent's estate for the designated term and setting the annuity payments high enough to create the desired Annuity Component value. When this strategy is used, the GRAT becomes a "Heads I win, tails I break even" scenario. If either the mortality or the yield risk becomes a problem, the parent, although back to square one, has lost nothing because no gift tax costs (either real

---

137. I.R.C. § 2036(a) is triggered because the parent will possess a retained income interest at death. Although technically I.R.C. § 2039 would also be triggered on death because the annuity payments likely will continue after the death of the parent, the Service recently issued Proposed Regulation § 20.2036–1(c) that mandates the application of 2036(a), not 2039, in such a situation. Proposed Regulation 119097–05, IRB 2007–28.

138. There are other differences that could favor a direct gift when the yield risk is a problem. A direct gift may qualify for the gift tax annual exclusion under I.R.C. § 2503(b); a future interest transfer to a trust has no hope of qualifying. Plus, any appreciation on property subject to a direct gift will be excluded from the donor's taxable estate; any property trust property will be taxed in the donor's estate under section 2036(a) at its full date of death value.

139. Arguments are sometimes advanced for the proposition that, in extreme situations, a GRAT may pay in the end even if it doesn't beat the yield risk. An example is the situation where a large block of marketable stock subject to a blockage discount is transferred to a GRAT and then sold off in pieces. See, for example, Blattmachr and Zeydel, Comparing GRATs and Installment Sales, Heckerling Institute on Estate Planning, Ch. 2 (2007). Such theories, although potentially applicable to marble shifters, are of no help with a transition plan for a closely held family corporation.

140. 115 T.C. 589 (2000). In Walton, Tax Court struck down old Example 5 in regulation 25.2702–3(e) in holding that an annuity payable for a term of years to a grantor or the grantor's estate is a qualified annuity for a specified term of years and can be valued as such, regardless of whether the grantor survives the term. The case opened the door to zero-out GRAT's because the fixed term can be used to value the Annuity Component. The result was a new Example 5 and 6, which are commonly referred to as the "Walton" Regulations. Reg. § 25.2702–3(e), Examples 5 & 6.

or opportunity) were incurred.

If, however, both risks are avoided and any property remains in the GRAT at the end of the annuity term, that property will pass to the designated remainder beneficiaries free of all transfer taxes. It offers a clear shot at "something for nothing." With this "zero-out" strategy, even the mortality risk can be mitigated by setting a short annuity term[141] and mandating big annuity payments that, in large part, will be funded from trust principal. The Service doesn't like this zero-out strategy; it will not issue a private letter ruling on the qualification of a GRAT if the Reminder Component has a value of less than 10 percent of the contributed property.[142] Many are not deterred by this position of the IRS and purse the zero out strategy on the theory that it is consistent with the regulations to Section 2702 and that any future changes to the regulations would likely be applied on a prospective basis only. Others build a formula into the GRAT that would automatically adjust the retained annuity if there was a subsequent determination as to the legally required value of the Remainder Component.

### (2) The GRAT and Closely Held Stock

Stock of a closely held corporation may be used to fund a GRAT. Even stock in an S corporation will work because a grantor trust is an eligible S corporation shareholder,[143] and the GRAT can qualify as a grantor trust by requiring that the annuity payments first be paid out of trust income.[144] But the issue isn't whether it can be done; it's whether it makes any sense to do it. There will be rare situations where the company's growth and cash flow prospects are so strong that the GRAT will be a smart vehicle to leverage the parents' unified credits or even the payment of gift taxes. But the cash and yield demands of the GRAT may prove troublesome for many mature family businesses that are struggling to maintain market share while sustaining a modest growth curve.

Any person who contemplates funding a GRAT with family stock should carefully focus on following four practical questions that, if ignored or understated, may result in the family spending a great deal of effort and money on a structure that backfires in the end.

First, how is the trust going to fund the annuity payments? Many businesses may conclude that double-taxed dividends from their C corporation or single-taxed income from their S corporation won't do the job unless the annuity term is very long (thus escalating the mortality risk beyond any reasonable period) or the parent incurs substantial gift tax costs (either real or opportunity) up front against the risks inherent in the GRAT. And if a decision is made to bail out corporate

---

141. The minimum term of a GRAT is a concern of some, based on an earlier position of the IRS that it would not rule on any GRAT that had a term of less than five years. The GRAT in the famous Walton case (see previous note) was two years; the Service did not challenge the 366 day term of a GRAT in Kerr v. Commissioner, 113 T.C. 449 (1999), aff'd 292 F.3d 490 (5th Cir. 2002); and the Service ruled favorably on a two year GRAT in PLR 9239015. In Rev. Proc. 2013-3, IRB 2013-1, the Service indicated that it would not rule on a grantor retained annuity trust if the value of the annuity payment in a year was more than 50 percent of the value of the property contributed to the trust. The Obama Administration's 2013 Budget Proposal recommended a minimum term of 10 years for a GRAT.

142. Rev. Proc. 2013–3, section 4, IRB 2013–1. See also Technical Advice Memorandum 2003–72, 2003–44 IRB 964.

143. I.R.C. § 1361(c)(2).

144. I.R.C. § 677(a).

earnings as fast as possible to help the GRAT, what impact will this bail out strategy have on other shareholders and the strength of the business? If large sums of cash are regularly withdrawn from the business, what will be the resulting negative impacts on the value of the business which, among other things, might magnify many times the yield risk factor of the GRAT?

Second, does the zero-out strategy (the play that gets so many so excited) make any sense in the situation? If the GRAT is structured to have a "zero-out" Remainder Component by funding large annuity payments out of principal, the trust will likely end up transferring stock back to the parent to fund the annuity. Huge cash payments from the company would often be impossible or certainly would make no sense if the expectation is that the company will grow in value and thereby produce transfer tax benefits through the GRAT. So often the only hope of zeroing out the Remainder Component is to transfer stock back to the Grantor to fund the huge annuity payments.

This stock recycling will necessitate costly annual stock valuations that will serve conflicting objectives. For GRAT purposes, it will be desirable if such valuations confirm high growth to beat the GRAT's yield risk, when in fact such high growth confirmations will likely create larger transfer tax problems on all other fronts, not the least of which is the future estate tax impacts on the very shares that are being transferred back to the parent in the form of annuity payments.

Third, will the need to beat the yield risk inherent in the GRAT be at cross purposes with other efforts the family takes to facilitate transition planning by holding down the stock value? Such efforts, for example, may include strategies to segregate new expansion growth opportunities and to adopt equity-based compensation structures for key children in the business.

Finally, what will the GRAT say to key inside children, such as Jeff, who are anxious to take over the reins and build the business? "We are going expend to real effort and money on a complicated trust structure that possibly may save some taxes and net you a few shares many years down the road if Dad can outlive the term of the annuity, if we can blow big money out of the corporation, and if we can still demonstrate that the value of the stock is escalating at a fast pace that may make other transfer strategies more difficult and may result in higher estate taxes when Dad dies." The inside child might start looking for a new job.

The forgoing questions should be carefully evaluated whenever a GRAT is being considered as an element of a family business transition plan. Often, though not always, the analysis will quickly demonstrate that the GRAT serves no critical objectives of the family. For many families, it will once again confirm the reality that stock of the family business often should not be treated the same as a portfolio of publicly traded securities.

### d. The Preferred Stock Freeze–A Very Rare Fit

Another enhanced gifting strategy is the preferred stock freeze. It requires that the family corporation be recapitalized with both preferred and common stock. All of the growth in value is reflected in the common stock that is gifted or sold to the children over time. The parents retain significant voting and income rights through the preferred stock that has a fixed value. The goal is to reduce future estate taxes by transferring the future growth in the business to the children through the common stock. Note that this preferred stock strategy will not work for an S corporation because of the single class of stock eligibility requirement.[145]

The recapitalization can be accomplished as a tax-free reorganization.[146] If common stock is exchanged for common and preferred stock, the shareholders will not recognize any gain,[147] and the corporation will be entitled to nonrecognition treatment.[148] Each shareholder's basis in his or her old common shares will carryover and be allocated to the new common and preferred shares based on their respective fair market values.[149]

This freeze strategy will work only if the valuation rules of Section 2701 of the Code are satisfied.[150] Under these rules, the value of the common stock transferred to the children for gift tax purposes is based on a subtraction method of valuation, which subtracts the value of the parent's retained preferred stock and other non-transferred family equity interests from the fair market value of all family-held interests in the corporation.[151] If the income rights of the preferred stock retained by the parents are not "qualified payment" rights, such preferred stock will be deemed to have a zero value under Section 2701.[152] In such an event, the transferred common stock's value for gift tax purposes will be based on the value of the parents' entire equity interest—a disastrous gift tax result.

Section 2701 applies to transfers among family members. Family members include the transferor's spouse, lineal descendants of the transferor or the transferor's spouse, and spouses of such descendants.[153] In order for the preferred stock to have a value under Section 2701 (and thus reduce the value of the gifted common stock), the preferred stock must mandate a "qualified payment," which is defined as a fixed rate cumulative dividend payable at least annually.[154] A fixed rate includes any rate that bears a fixed relationship to a specified market interest rate.[155]

---

145. I.R.C. § 1361(b)(1)(D).

146. I.R.C. § 368(a)(1)(E).

147. I.R.C. § 354.

148. I.R.C. § 1032.

149. I.R.C. § 358(a),(b). Reg. § 1.358–2(a)(2).

150. I.R.C. § 2701.

151. Reg. §§ 25.2701–1(a)(2). The subtraction method requires application of a four-step procedure. See Reg. §§ 25.2701–3(a)–(d).

152. I.R.C. § 2701(a)(3)(A).

153. I.R.C. § 2701(e)(1).

154. I.R.C. § 2701(c)(3).

155. I.R.C. § 2701(c)(3)(B); Reg. § 25.2701–2(b)(6)(ii). Election options are available to treat, in whole or in part, a qualified payment right as not qualified, in which event it will be valued at zero under Section 2701, or to treat a nonqualified payment right as a qualified payment, in which event it will be valued at its fair market value under Section 2701. I.R.C. § 2701(c)(3)(i),(ii); Reg. § 25.2701–2(c)(i),(ii). The determination to elect in or out of qualified payment status depends on the certainty of the fixed payments actually being made. If the interests are valued as qualified payments and the fixed payments are not made, additional transfer taxes are imposed on a compounded amount that is calculated by assuming that the unpaid amounts were invested on the payment due date at a yield equal to the discount rate used to value the qualified payments. I.R.C. § 2701(d); Reg. § 25.2701–4. Since gift or estate taxes on unpaid qualified payments can be painful under this compounding rule, some may choose to forgo the qualified payment status and avoid the tax risks of

The value of the preferred stock under section 2701 is based on the fair market value of the qualified payment.[156]  An appraisal will set the value by considering all relevant factors, including comparable rates paid on publicly traded preferred stock.  Thus, as a practical matter, the preferred stock must pay a market-rate dividend in order for its value for gift tax purposes to equal its face value.  If the preferred stock is valued under Section 2701 based on a "qualified payment" right, the value of the common stock transferred to the children for gift tax purposes may not be less than a special "minimum value."[157]  The special minimum value is the children's pro rata value of all common stock if all the outstanding common stock had a value equal to 10 percent of all equity interests in the corporation.[158]

The strategy triggers two tough challenges that preclude its use except in the rarest circumstances.  First, the cumulative dividend requirement on the preferred stock is an expensive burden from both a business and tax perspective.  Many closely held corporations simply can't afford the cash drain.  And all cash distributed will trigger a double tax hit–first at the corporate level when the income is earned and then at the shareholder level when the dividends are paid.  It is one of the most tax-expensive strategies for moving income.  Second, for many mature businesses, the fair market value of the preferred stock (set by appraisal) will have a value equal to its face value only if the fixed dividend rate on the preferred is set at a level that, as a practical matter, exceeds the projected annual growth rate of the business.  So the preferred dividends paid to the parents will continue to increase the value of the parents' taxable estate at least as fast as the status quo.  The result is that the strategy may start producing an immediate double income tax hit with little or no transfer tax savings.  For these reasons, the strategy, although useful in very unique fast-growth situations, does not fit most family businesses.

### e. The Three–Year GRIT: A Potential Add–On

The three-year grantor retained income trust (GRIT) strategy may be helpful in those situations where a parent has decided to pay gift taxes now in hopes of saving bigger estate taxes in the future.  If the parent makes a taxable gift and then dies within three years of the gift, all gift taxes paid by the parent will be subject to estate taxes in the parent's estate under Section 2035(b).  However, the gifted property itself is not brought back into the parent's estate and, therefore, does not receive a stepped-up tax basis under Section 1014.  If the parent lives for three years after the gift, the gift taxes are not pulled into the estate and the transfer avoids all transfer taxes.[159]

A three-year GRIT may be used to generate a basis step-up if the parent dies

---

nonpayment.  Similarly, against the risk of this compounding rule kicking in for nonpayment, an election may be made to treat a nonqualified payment right (i.e. noncumulative preferred stock dividend right) as a qualified payment right and value it as such under Section 2701 on the assumption that it always will be paid.

156.  I.R.C. § 2701(a)(3)(C). See Example 1 in Reg. § 25.2701–1(e). If the preferred stock that contains the qualified payment also contains a liquidation, put, call, or conversion right, the value of the preferred stock must be the lowest value based on all such rights. I.R.C. § 2701(a)(3)(B), Reg. § 25.2701–2(a)(3).

157.  Reg. § 25.2701–1(a)(2).

158.  I.R.C. § 2701(a)(4)(A).

159.  For an illustration of this transfer tax savings, see related discussion in paragraph 1.a. of this section, supra.

within three years and the gift taxes are subject to estate taxation. It works by transferring the gifted stock to a trust that requires that "all income" of the trust be paid to the parent for three years. At the end of the three-year term, the property passes to a designated donee, presumably a child. The annuity component of the trust will have a zero value because the annuity is not specified as a fixed dollar amount or a percent of the contributed property.[160] So the remainder interest for gift tax purposes will equal the full value of the property.[161] If the parent dies during the three-year term, the property and all gift taxes paid will be taxable in the parent's estate, the estate will receive a credit for the prior gift taxes, and the donee's basis in the property will be stepped-up to its fair market value at the parent's death.[162] If the parent outlives the three-year term, the GRIT will end, and the risk of the paid gift taxes being included in the estate will have ended.

The disadvantage of this strategy is that, if death occurs within three years of the gift, any appreciation in the value of the gifted property from the date of the gift to the date of death will generate an added estate tax burden. This disadvantage needs to be balanced against the value of the stepped-up basis to the donee. The 3–year GRIT may make sense in those rare situations where gift taxes are paid, the basis of the gifted property is very low in relation to its value, and meaningful appreciation during the three-year term is unlikely.

All gifting strategies, enhanced or not, require the parents to transfer something for nothing. Many parents want or need something in return. They need a strategy that will convert their stock into cash to fund their retirement while stopping or slowing down the growth in the value of their taxable estates. A sale of stock might do the job. If the company is going to stay in the family, the potential buyers include the corporation, the children, or a trust established for the children.

## 2. THE REDEMPTION STRATEGY — A COMPLETE GOODBYE

A corporate redemption can be used to transition stock in a family business. It works best in those situations where other family members already own a substantial percentage of the corporation's outstanding stock, the company's cash flow is strong, the prospects of future stock value growth are high, and the parents have fully surrendered the reins to the business or are prepared to do so. It is not a viable option for many.

In our case study, the corporation would contract to purchase all of Earl and Betty's stock in the corporation for a price equal to the fair market value of the stock. The corporation would pay the purchase price, plus interest, over a long period of time, as much as 15 years.[163] Immediately following the redemption,

---

160. I.R.C. § 2702(a)(b); Reg. §§ 25.2702–1 thru 3.
161. Reg. §§ 25.2702–1(b).
162. I.R.C. § 1014.
163. The IRS ruling guidelines indicate that the Service will ordinarily not issue a favorable ruling on a redemption if the note payment period exceeds 15 years. Rev. Proc. 2013–3, § 4.01(20), I.R.B. 2013–1. If the note term is too long, the risk is that the parents will be deemed to have retained an equity interest that (1) violates the "creditor only" requirement of I.R.C. § 3.02(c)(2)(A)(i), (2) precludes waiver of the family attribution rules of I.R.C. § 318(a)(1) and a complete termination of the parents' interest within the meaning of I.R.C. §§ 302(b)(3), and (3) results in the amounts distributed to the parents being taxed as dividends. I.R.C. §§

the only outstanding stock of the corporation would be the stock owned by Jeff. Although not a party to the redemption, Jeff ends up owning 100 percent of the outstanding stock of the corporation and is in complete control. The corporation has a large debt that is payable to its former shareholders, Earl and Betty. This debt will be retired with corporate earnings over an extended period of time. The interest and principal payments on the indebtedness will provide Earl and Betty with a steady stream of income during their retirement. If they die prior to a complete payout of the contract, the remaining amounts owing on the contract would become part of their estates and, together with their other assets, would be allocated to their children in equal shares.

In any redemption, the applicable state corporate law must be carefully analyzed to ascertain any restrictions and impacts on the corporation. Often appraisals are necessary. The Model Business Corporation Act prohibits a "distribution" (broadly defined to include proceeds from a redemption) if "after giving it effect: (1) the corporation would not be able to pay its debts as they become due in the ordinary course of business, or (2) the corporation's total assets would be less than the sum of its total liabilities plus (unless the articles of incorporation permit otherwise) the amount that would be needed, if the corporation were to be dissolved at the time of the distribution, to satisfy the preferential rights upon the dissolution of shareholders whose preferential rights are superior to those receiving the distribution."[164] These two tests, referred to as the "equity insolvency test" and the "balance sheet test," have been widely incorporated into state corporate statutes.

The primary tax challenge that always exists with a corporate redemption is determining the character of the payments made by the corporation to the departing shareholders: Will they be taxed as corporate dividends or as true principal and interest payments made in exchange for stock? If the payments are treated as dividends, they will be fully taxable to the extent of the corporation's earnings and profits, and there will be a tax hit at both the corporate and shareholder levels on the distributed income. And even though dividends are currently taxed at rates lower than ordinary income rates, in many situations the double tax hit will be unacceptable. And if the tax rate on dividends bounces back up to a level at or near ordinary income rates, the dividend scenario tax burden will be intolerable for most. If, on the other hand, the payments are treated as stock consideration payments, the parents will be allowed to recover their basis in the transferred stock tax-free, the interest element of each payment will be deductible by the corporation, and the gain element of each payment to the parents will be taxed as a long-term capital gain. In nearly all cases, the planning challenge is to structure the redemption to ensure that the payments qualify as consideration for stock, not dividends.

The answer to this challenge is found in Section 302(b) of the Code,[165]

---

302(b)(3), 302(c)(1),(2), 302(d), 318(a)(1). The Tax Court has been more forgiving. In Lisle v. Commissioner, 35 TCM 627 (1976) the court found that a valid 302(b)(3) complete termination had occurred even though the payment term was 20 years, the shareholder retained voting rights through a security agreement, and the stock was held in escrow to secure the corporation's payment obligation.

164. MBCA §§ 1.04, 6.40(c).

165. I.R.C. § 302(b). The family ownership attribution rules of section 318 usually make it impossible for

which specifies the conditions that must be met in order for the redemption to qualify for exchange treatment. In a family situation, the only hope is to qualify the redemption as a complete termination of the parent's interest under Section 302(b)(3). For the Wilson clan, this would essentially require that (1) Earl and Betty sell all of their stock to the company in the transaction; (2) Earl and Betty have no further interest in the business other than as creditors; (3) Earl and Betty not acquire any interest in the business (other than through inheritance) during the ten years following receipt of all payments made to them; (4) Earl and Betty not have engaged in stock transactions with family members during the last 10 years with a principal purpose of avoiding income taxes; and (5) Earl and Betty sign and file with the Secretary of the Treasury an appropriate agreement.[166] If all of these conditions are met (and often they are), then the family attribution rules are waived and the parents are able to treat the payments as consideration for their stock, not dividends.

Usually the most troubling condition is the requirement that, following the redemption, the parents have no interest in the corporation other than that of creditors.[167] In our case, neither Earl nor Betty could be an officer, director, employee, shareholder or consultant of the corporation following the redemption.[168] It must be a complete goodbye. This requirement is often viewed as an insurmountable hurdle by a parent who is departing and turning over the reins with the hope that payments will keep coming over a long period. One of Earl's prime objectives was to stay involved enough to hedge the boredom of retirement and to ensure that the business remains strong during the payout period. To qualify for tax exchange treatment under a redemption strategy, this objective would have to be abandoned.

The redemption approach offers a number of advantages that need to be carefully evaluated in each situation. It provides a long-term payment stream directly from the corporation to the parents. It effectively freezes the value of the business in the parents' estates, subject to the accumulation of interest income that is paid on the installment note. In our case, all future growth in the stock value would pass to Jeff, the sole shareholder. Finally, it makes it easy for the accumulated proceeds paid on the debt and the unpaid balance of the debt to be transferred to the children in equal shares at the appropriate time, thereby accomplishing the parents' objective of giving each child an equal share of their estates.

There also are some compelling disadvantages with the redemption approach that provide a strong incentive for many families to look for an alternative. First, the principal payments made to Betty and Earl on the indebtedness will need to be funded by the corporation with after-tax dollars. This may create an intolerable cash burden for the corporation in redeeming the

---

the a family transaction to qualify as a redemption that is not essentially equivalent to a dividend under 302(b)(1) or that is a substantially disproportionate redemption under 302(b)(2). The only hope is to qualify for a waiver of the family attribution rules and, thereby, qualify the redemption as a complete redemption of the parent's interest under section 302(b)(3). IRC §§ 302(a), 302(b), and 318(a)(1), (a)(3)(A).

166. These are the conditions imposed by section 302(c)(2) to secure a waiver of the family attribution rules and qualify the redemption as a complete termination under 302(b)(3). I.R.C. §§ 302(b)(3), 302(c)(2), 318(a).

167. I.R.C. § 302(c)(2)(A)(i).

168. See, for example, Lynch v. Commissioner, 801 F.2d 1176 (9th Cir. 1986).

stock. Second, even though large sums of after-tax dollars will be paid to the parents for their stock, Jeff, the sole shareholder of the corporation, gets no increase in the tax basis of his stock. Because the corporation is redeeming the stock and making the payments, there is no basis impact at the shareholder level. Third, as previously stated, Betty and Earl are precluded from having any further involvement in the management and affairs of the company if they want to meet the requirements of Section 302(b)(3) and qualify for exchange tax treatment. For many family patriarchs, this complete goodbye requirement alone will kill the strategy. Fourth, the amounts payable to Betty and Earl will terminate when the note is paid off. Given the size of the payout in our case, it is unlikely that this potential disadvantage will be significant. In situations where the payments are smaller, the parents may want and need a regular cash flow that will last as long as one of them is living. Fifth, if the parents die before the contract is paid in full, the children who inherit the unpaid contract will pay income taxes on their receipt of interest and principal payments under the contract. The contract payments are treated as income in respect of a decedent for income tax purposes.[169] There is no step-up in basis for the children; the income tax burden survives the parents' deaths. Sixth, the company takes on a tremendous debt burden in redeeming the stock. The company may not have the cash flow to foot such a huge bill and the associated tax burdens. At a minimum, the cash burden of the debt may adversely impact Jeff's capacity to move the company forward or to secure financing that may be necessary to expand the business and accomplish his objectives for the business.

These disadvantages cause many families to reject the redemption strategy in the plan design. They prefer a strategy that can be implemented on an incremental basis over time and that will allow the parents to have a continuing, but reduced, role in the business.

### 3. Cross–Purchase Strategies: Where's the Cash?

A cross-purchase is similar to a redemption, with one big twist: The purchasers of the parent's stock are the other shareholders, not the corporation. In our case, Earl and Betty would still be paid principal and income payments for a long term, but the payments would come from Jeff.

How does a cross-purchase strategy compare with the redemption approach? The cross-purchase offers two significant benefits over the redemption. First, the fear of Section 302 dividend treatment goes away because the parents are not receiving payments from the corporation. This means that the parents can stay involved in the business as much as, and for as long as, they want. Earl can remain on the board and keep his hands in the operation to the extent he chooses. Plus, there is no requirement that all the parent's stock be sold in a single transaction. Piecemeal sales work. Thus, the biggest impediment to the redemption strategy—the complete goodbye—is gone. Second, Jeff's tax basis in the purchased stock will equal the purchase price he pays for the stock.[170] Unlike the redemption scenario, the amounts paid to Earl and Betty in a cross-

---

169. I.R.C. § 691(a).
170. I.R.C. § 1012.

purchase produce a basis increase for the other shareholders.

Apart from these benefits, the cross-purchase approach has many of the same limitations and disadvantages as the redemption approach. Principal payments on the installment note must be funded with after-tax dollars. Jeff's credit capacity may be tapped. The payouts to the parents will not extend beyond the contract term. Any basis step-up on the parents' deaths is lost. Payments under the contract received by other family members following the deaths of the parents will be taxed as income in respect of a decedent.

Plus, the cross-purchase approach presents a whole new problem. Where is Jeff going to get the cash to cover the payments for the stock? This problem, alone, eliminates the cross-purchase option in many situations. If Jeff has an independent source of income or cash that he is willing to commit to the deal, this funding problem may be solved. Absent such an independent source, Jeff will be forced to turn to the corporation for the cash. The challenge then becomes getting enough corporate cash to Jeff on an ongoing basis to fund the current payments on the installment note. This can be a tough, often insurmountable, problem. The extra compensation payments to Jeff must be large enough to cover the current interest payments on the note, the after-tax principal payments on the note, and the additional income and payroll taxes that Jeff will be required to pay as a result of the increased compensation. Beyond the cash burden to the corporation, if the compensation payments to Jeff are unreasonably high, there may be a constructive dividend risk that could put the corporation's deduction in jeopardy.[171] An S election will help the tax situation, but there is still a cash drain on the company and the double tax risk of a constructive dividend is avoided only to the extent of earnings during the S corporation period.[172]

Corporate loans to Jeff might be an option, but corporate loans always present independent problems. First, the loans will need to be repaid at some point down the road with after-tax dollars. Figuring out how the repayments to the corporation will be funded may be more difficult than Jeff's current funding challenge with his parents' note. The loan approach may simply defer and magnify the problem. Second, the loans themselves need to be funded with after-tax corporate dollars. The corporation must pay current income taxes on the funds it loans. And third, there is always the risk that substantial shareholder loans may trigger an accumulated earnings tax.[173] That is, the corporation may be forced to unreasonably accumulate earnings in order to fund the loans. The bottom line is that the shareholder loan approach to solve the funding problem in a cross-purchase situation generally is not a satisfactory solution.

---

171. Reg. §§ 1.162–8, 1.301–1(j). See, for example, Elliotts, Inc. v. Commissioner, 716 F.2d 1241 (9th Cir. 1983), Charles McCandless Tile Service v. U.S., 191 Ct.Cl. 108, 422 F.2d 1336 (1970), and Exacto Spring Corp. v. Commissioner, 196 F.3d 833 (7th Cir. 1999).

172. Even with an S election, a taxable dividend exposure remains to the extent of the corporation's earnings and profits from its C corporation existence. I.R.C. § 1368(c)(2). The exposure ends once the earnings and profits have been distributed. An S corporation, with the consent of all the shareholders, may elect to accelerate such dividends by treating all distributions as earnings and profits distributions. I.R.C. § 1368(e)(3).

173. See generally I.R.C. §§ 531–537, Reg. § 1.537–2(c)(1) (loans to a shareholder for the shareholder's personal benefit may indicate that earnings are being unreasonably accumulated).

This funding challenge often requires a combination approach that integrates a cross-purchase with a gift or redemption strategy, or both. The parents may gift some stock and have the balance of their stock redeemed by the corporation or purchased by other family members. It is possible to structure a corporate redemption of a portion of the parents' stock and a cross-purchase of the balance of the parents' stock and still qualify the redemption for exchange treatment under Section 302(b).[174] The benefit of a combination approach is that the disadvantages of each strategy are watered down because only a portion of the stock is subject to the strategy. For example, only the gifted shares will do nothing to provide a retirement income to the parents; only the redeemed shares will need to be funded with corporate after-tax dollars that do not increase the other shareholders' stock basis; and only the shares subject to the cross-purchase obligation will create a funding challenge for the other shareholders.

There are circumstances where the cross-purchase funding challenge for the other shareholders is not a big deal. This may be the case, for example, if the entity is an S corporation with strong earnings, if other family members already own a substantial percentage of the outstanding stock or, as previously stated, if other family members have substantial investment assets unrelated to the company. When a cross-purchase is the strategy of choice in the plan design, two options for enhancing the strategy are often considered.[175] These are the intentionally defective grantor trust installment sale and the self-canceling installment note.

### a. The IDGT Sale—A Dream Deal?

With the intentionally defective grantor trust installment sale strategy, the parent establishes a trust that names one or more children as beneficiaries. However, the trust is structured so that the parent is deemed to be the owner of the trust property for income tax purposes, but not for estate and gift tax purposes. The trust is an income tax nullity, but triggers real gift and estate tax consequences. The strategy requires that one have some capacity to speak out of both sides of the mouth. The entire basis of the strategy is the incongruity between the income tax grantor trust rules[176] and the estate tax rules applicable to grantor-retained interests.[177] Although there is a broad overlap between these rules, there are a few instances where a trust may be crafted to fall within the income tax rules without triggering the estate tax inclusion rules. One such instance (commonly used to achieve the desired result) is where the parent retains a non-fiduciary power to reacquire trust property by substituting other property of equivalent value. With such a power, the parent may be deemed to be the owner of the trust for income tax purposes,[178] but not for estate and gift tax

---

174. See Zenz v. Quinlivan, 213 F.2d 914 (6th Cir. 1954) and Rev. Rule 75–447, 1975–2 C.B. 113.

175. The private annuity, a cross purchase strategy that has been popular in the past, is not discussed because recent regulations proposed by the Internal Revenue Service have effectively eliminated the tax deferral benefit of the annuity and, thereby, destroyed the private annuity as a viable transition option. See Prop. Reg. § 1.1001–1(j) that provides that any person who sells property in exchange for any annuity contract will be deemed to have received "property in an amount equal to the fair market value of the contract, whether or not the contract is the equivalent of cash."

176. I.R.C. §§ 671 thru 679.

177. I.R.C. §§ 2036.

178. I.R.C. § 675(4)(C); Reg. § 1.675–1(b)(4).

purposes.[179]

The parent then sells his or her corporate stock to the trust in return for an installment note that has a principal balance equal to the fair market value of the transferred stock. The principal balance of the note, together with interest at the applicable federal rate (a rate that generally is less than the Section 7520 rate applicable to annuities), is paid by the trust to the parent over the term of the note. The trust's income and any other assets owned by the trust are used to fund the amounts due the parent under the installment note. The strategy can be used with either C or S corporation stock because a grantor trust is an eligible S corporation shareholder.[180]

### (1) The Dream Scenario

Here's the dream tax scenario of this strategy. Because the trust is an income tax nullity, the parent does not recognize any taxable income on the sale of the stock to the trust. For income tax purposes, the transaction is treated as a sale by a person to himself or herself - a nonevent. Under the same rationale, the interest and principal payments on the installment note from the trust to the parent trigger no income tax consequences. Any income recognized by the trust on the stock or other trust assets is taxed to the parent as the owner of the trust. Ideally, the parent's sale to the trust triggers no gift tax consequences because the trust is deemed to have paid full value for the stock in the form of the installment note. Similarly, the parent's payment of income taxes on the trust income will not trigger a gift tax. When the parent dies, the stock is not included in the parent's estate under Section 2036(a) because the parent is deemed to have sold the stock for full consideration. Thus, all future growth in the value of the transferred stock is removed from the parent's estate. The one disadvantage is that the parent's tax basis in the stock (often very low) will probably transfer over to the trust and ultimately to the children. But even this negative might be eliminated if the parent, before death, uses the retained non-fiduciary asset substitution power to trade high-basis assets (i.e. cash) for the low-basis stock at equal values, thus ensuring that the reacquired low basis stock is included in the parent's estate at death and thereby receives a full basis step-up. The trust will still have accomplished its estate tax goal of removing the growth in the stock's value from the parent's estate because the substituted cash pulled from the estate will equal the higher stock value. And, once again, no income tax consequences will be triggered on the substitution because the parent will still be deemed the owner of the trust for income tax purposes.

### (2) Key Question: Will It Work?

There are some aspects of the strategy that seem relatively certain. First, a retained non-fiduciary power to reacquire trust assets by substituting other property of equivalent value should make the trust a grantor trust for income tax purposes.[181] Second, such a power, in and of itself, probably should not trigger estate tax inclusion. To remove any doubt regarding the estate inclusion issue

---

179. Estate of Jordahl v. Commissioner, 65 T.C. 92 (1975), acq. 1977–1 C.B. 1; PLR 9227013.
180. I.R.C. § 1361(c)(2)(A)(i).
181. I.R.C. § 675(4)(C); Reg. § 1.675–1(b)(4).

related to this power, some recommend giving this non-fiduciary power to a party other than the grantor.[182]  Third, no gain or loss will be recognized by the parent on the sale of appreciated property to a grantor trust in return for a promissory note that bears a rate of interest equal to the applicable federal rate.[183]  Fourth, the stock should not be included in the parent's estate if the parent dies after the note has been fully paid.[184]  Finally, the parent's payment of income taxes on the trust's income will not trigger a gift tax.[185]

Beyond these relative tax certainties, there are two fundamental questions that are troubling.  First, how will the promissory note be valued for gift tax purposes? Second, if the parent dies while the note is outstanding, will the parent be deemed to have retained a life estate in the stock, such that it will be taxed in the parent's estate at death?  If the answer to the first question is that the note will be valued in the same manner as a retained equity interest under Section 2701 (fair market value), a substantial gift tax will be triggered when the stock is transferred because the applicable federal rate likely will be far below the market rate needed to give the note a market value equal to the transferred stock.  The net effect would be that the strategy would be no more effective than a preferred stock freeze under Section 2701 because it would be subject to the same yield challenges.  The answer to the second question turns on the potential application of Section 2036(a), which requires that any property transferred by the decedent during life be taxed in the decedent's estate if the decedent owned an income interest in the property at death.[186]  If the answer to this second question is "Yes," the whole effort will produce no estate tax savings if the parent does not outlive the note.  The existing cases and rulings suggest that the answer to both questions will likely turn on whether the note will be considered real debt or rather be viewed as disguised equity.[187]  This will be a question of fact in each situation.  If the only source for payment of the interest and principal on the note is income generated on the stock owned by the trust, the equity risk goes way up, and the entire transaction is put in jeopardy.[188]  For this reason, many sensibly believe that when stock in a closely held corporation is the asset sold to the trust, the parent would be well advised to transfer other income-producing assets to the trust that have a value equal to at least one-ninth of the value of the stock.[189]  Even with such a transfer of additional assets, there still is no guarantee that the equity risk will be eliminated.  Also, the client should understand that an

---

182.  See PLR 9227013 and Estate of Jordahl v. Commissioner, 65 T.C. 92 (1975).

183.  Rev. Rule 85–13, 1985–1 C.B. 184.

184.  Since the parent will not be receiving any payments at death, there is no risk of estate tax inclusion under 2036(a).

185.  Rev. Rul. 2004–64, 2004–2 C.B. 7.

186.  I.R.C. § 2036(a).

187.  In Sharon Karmazin, Docket 2127–03, the Service took the position that both 2701 and 2702 were applicable because the note was not real debt, but the case was settled. See PLR 9515039 (real debt only if trustee/obligor has other assets); TAM 9251004 (2036 applied where closely held stock only source of note payment and plan was to have trust retain stock for family purposes); PLR 9639012 (no 2036 inclusion where note would be paid off in three years from earnings on S corporation stock); Estate of Rosen v. Commissioner, T.C. Memo 2006–15 (loans from partnership characterized as retained interests that trigger 2036 inclusion); and Dallas v. Commissioner, T.C. Memo 2006–212 (notes not challenged; trust funded with other asset that exceeded 10 percent of stock purchase price).

188.  See Keebler and Melcher, "Structuring IDGT Sales to Avoid Sections 2701, 2702, and 2036", Estate Planning Journal (October 2005).

189.  Id.

unfavorable answer to one or both of these critical questions would probably be the result if Congress or the Service decided to really attack this strategy (a justifiable fear given the blatant attempt to secure huge tax benefits by taking advantage of a technical incongruity in the Code).

If the parent dies before the note is paid off, there are a few tax questions that can only be answered with guesswork at this time. The trust will cease to be a grantor trust on the parent's death, but will continue to owe the parent's estate (or its beneficiaries) payments on the note. First, will such payments be treated as income in respect of a decedent under section 691, triggering income to the recipients as paid? The payments don't fit the technical definition of income in respect of a decedent,[190] but logically it's difficult to justify tax-free income treatment to the parent's heirs. Second, what will be the trust's basis in the stock on the parent's death? The options are the amount of the note at time of purchase (a purchase step-up), the fair market value of the stock at the parent's death (full basis step-up), or the parent's transferred basis in the stock.[191] The best guess is the carryover basis provision of section 1015 because of its technical "transfer in trust" language and the fact that the whole strategy is predicated on the theories that there is no sale for income tax purposes (which is inconsistent with a basis step-up under section 1012) and that the stock is not part of the grantor's estate (which makes a step-up under section 1014 a real stretch). But wait, who said anything about being consistent? Maybe talking out of three sides of the mouth to get a basis step-up will work. Finally, will the parent's death before the note is paid off trigger any taxable gain to the parent's estate because the trust has ceased to be a grantor trust? Most think not.[192]

Often an IDGT is compared to a GRAT. In some respects, they are close cousins; they both involve a transfer of property to a grantor trust, followed by the trust making payments to the grantor over a defined period of time. But in no sense are they twins. There are many key differences, some of which can be compelling for a family business. First, a GRAT is specifically authorized by the Code and Regulations; an IDGT is a quasi-freak creation of an incongruity in the Code that triggers uncertainties. Thus, a GRAT may be viewed as a "legally safer" option. Second, a GRAT creates a mortality risk; the grantor must outlive the GRAT term for the GRAT to produce any transfer tax savings. No such mortality risk is mandated by an IDGT; ideally only the unpaid portion of the installment note at the grantor's death will be taxed in the grantor's estate. Third, although both a GRAT and an IDGT impose a yield risk, the IDGT hurdle rate is presumably easier because the Applicable Federal Rate, required by the IDGT, is always lower than the Section 7520 rate required for the GRAT. Fourth, the GRAT produces less valuation discount leveraging benefits because such benefits will be lost for any stock that is transferred back to the grantor as required annuity payments. Fifth, the risk of an inadvertent gift or estate tax is higher with an IDGT because of existing uncertainties regarding the potential

---

190. Since the parent never treated the sale as a taxable event under the rationale of Revenue Ruling 85–13, 1885–1 C.B. 184, the post-death payments do not fit the technical definition of IRD under section 691.

191. The relevant code sections are 1012, 1014 , and 1015.

192. See Peebles, Death of an IRD Noteholder, Trusts & Estates 28 (August, 2005) and Blattmachr, Gans, Jacobson, Income tax Effects of Termination of Grantor Trust Status by Reason of Grantor's Death, 97 Journal of Taxation 149 (September, 2002).

application of codes Sections 2701, 2702, and 2036(a). Finally, although the IDGT will require the commitment of other assets to the trust to hedge the disguised equity characterization risk of the installment note, the period payment burden of an IDGT will often be far less than a GRAT because the presumed lack of a mortality risk will allow the payments on the note to be stretched out over a long term.[193] Often when the GRAT and the IDGT are laid side by side in the planning process, the IDGT will appear the most attractive in spite of its inherent legal uncertainties and the need for other assets. The presumed absence of a mortality risk, the lower yield hurdle rate, the greater discount-leveraging benefits, and the smaller periodic payment burden will carry the day. But even if the IDGT wins its beauty contest with the GRAT, it will not be a sensible candidate for many family transition plans.

### (3) Family Business Factors to Consider

The potential benefits of the IDGT cross-purchase strategy are compelling. A few key factors should be carefully considered before employing the strategy in a family business transition plan. First, is a cross-purchase of stock funded primarily with income from the corporation the best strategy for the family and the business, given the other transition strategies that are available? If so, using a grantor trust as the purchaser may be justified. The key is to not let the allure of the grantor trust strategy short circuit the analysis of other options that may in the end do a better job of accomplishing the family's objectives. Obviously, if a grantor trust purchase is used, it will be easier with S status because the double dividend income tax hit triggered in C corporation situations is avoided.

Second, does the client have the means and the gifting capacity to fund the trust with other income producing assets equal to at least one-ninth of the value of the stock sold to the trust? If not, the gift and estate tax risks of the whole effort may just be too great. The significance of fudging on this protective measure should not be understated. For many families, this requirement will be too burdensome.

Third, if the basis of the parent's stock is high (such as would occur on the first death of a spouse in a community property state),[194] the value of the strategy is reduced significantly. Compared to a straight cross-purchase with a child, the only real significant benefit of a grantor trust purchase in such a situation is the tax-free shift of value resulting from the parent's payment of income tax on corporate income that would otherwise be taxed to the child.[195] Even this potential benefit is watered down if the child's marginal income tax rate is lower than the parent's marginal rate, a likely condition in many situations. So the net benefits of the strategy may be substantially reduced in cross-purchase transactions targeted to occur after the death of the first parent.

Finally, the client's capacity to stomach tax uncertainty must be factored into the mix. The whole strategy is predicated on a technical incongruity that could easily be eliminated on a retroactive basis. A vulnerable element of the strategy

---

193. See generally Blattmachr and Zeydel, Comparing GRATs and Installment Sales, Heckerling Institute on Estate Planning, Ch. 2 (2007).

194. I.R.C. § 1014(b)(6).

195. Rev. Rul. 2004–64, 2004–2 C.B. 7.

is the basis of valuing the note for gift tax purposes. The argument would be that, since the transaction is considered a nullity for income tax purposes, the note should not be valued against the applicable federal rate standards used to assess income tax impacts in family loan situations, but rather as a retained interest by using market standards to compare the value of the transferred asset (the stock) against the true value of the retained asset (the note). If this were done, the strategy would trigger a significant gift tax hit (if the rate on the note equaled the applicable federal rate) or would require that the note rate be set at a high market rate that would significantly reduce (if not entirely eliminate) the transfer tax benefits of the entire effort (ala Section 2701). And in its 2013 budget proposal, the Obama Administration recommended a change to eliminate the estate tax benefits of an IDGT by requiring that the assets in the grantor trust be included in the grantor's gross taxable estate.

The strategy offers mystery, uncertainty, and a potential dream ending. Its allure will be irresistible to some, but for many families it will demand too much and promise too little.

### b. The SCIN: A Bet Against Life

The self-canceling installment note (SCIN) is a cross-purchase enhancement strategy that may produce an additional estate tax benefit if the parent dies before the note is paid off. The parent sells stock to a child or a grantor trust in return for a promissory note. The note, by its terms, provides that all amounts due under the note will be cancelled if the parent dies before the note is paid. The benefit to the obligor on the note (child or trust) is that the obligation ends on the parent's death. From the parent's perspective, no residual note balance will be included in the parent's taxable estate,[196] nor will any taxable income in respect of the decedent be paid to the parent's estate or heirs.

The key to the SCIN is valuing the self-canceling feature. The determination of this amount (the Premium) requires an actuarial calculation that is impacted by the parent's age, the length of the note term, and the size of the periodic payments.[197] The value of the Premium must reflect the economic reality of the given situation if, for example, the parent has a short life expectancy due to poor health.[198] If the note itself is not adjusted for the Premium, the parent will be deemed to have made a taxable gift equal to the amount of the Premium. This gift tax impact can be eliminated by increasing either the note's interest rate or principal balance, or both, so that the value of the Premium is reflected in the terms of the note. If the parent dies before the note is fully paid, the note is cancelled, but the basis in the stock is not reduced.[199] However, any unrealized gain in the note must be included in the first income tax return of the parent's estate as income recognized on the

---

196. Estate of Moss Estate v. Commissioner, 74 T.C. 1239 (1980), acq. 1981 C.B. 2; Rev. Rul. 86–72, 1986–1 C.B. 253; Estate of Frane v. Commissioner, 98 T.C. 341 (1992), affirmed in part and reversed in part, 998 F.2d 567 (8th Cir. 1993).

197. Presumable the Premium calculation could be based on Table H in the Alpha Volume of the IRS actuarial tables or Table 90CM of such tables.

198. See, for example, Estate of Musgrave v. United States, 33 Fed. Cl. 657 (Fed. Cl. 1995).

199. Estate of Frane v. Commissioner, 98 T.C. 341 (1992), affirmed in part and reversed in part, 998 F.2d 567 (8th Cir. 1993).

cancellation of an installment obligation under Section 453B(f).[200]

There are some potential disadvantages with a SCIN. If the parent outlives the note, the strategy will have produced no benefits but will have triggered added tax costs—the parent's taxable income and taxable estate will have been increased by the amount of the Premium or the parent will be deemed to have made a taxable gift equal to the Premium. Plus, if the note is adjusted to incorporate the Premium, the purchaser will have paid more and will have received no tangible economic benefit in return. Finally, in situations where multiple children are beneficiaries of the estate, a self-canceling note in favor of only one child may conflict with the parent's overriding objective to give each child an equal share of the estate.

The forgoing discussion of gifting, redemption and cross purchase strategies assumes a need for the parents to rid themselves of some or all of their stock during life. Often this is necessary and desirable to reduce future estate tax burdens, provide a secure retirement income stream to the parents, and give the children the necessary incentives to carry the business forward. But there are circumstances where the business can be restructured to facilitate these essential family objectives without the parents having to aggressively sell stock. Such a restructuring may allow the parents to phase-out without selling out.

### 4. BUSINESS RESTRUCTURING: A PHASE-OUT OPTION

Some simple business restructuring often can help immensely in the design of a family transition plan. Suppose, for example, that Wilson Incorporated is restructured to take advantage of two basic realities. First, the distribution of S corporation earnings presents no double tax issues.[201] Second, Jeff's desire to expand into new markets and to garner all of the benefits of expansion for himself can be accomplished by having him form and operate a new business that finances the expansion, takes the risks of expansion, and realizes all of the benefits. The restructuring may be implemented as follows:

- Wilson Incorporated would make an S election. The stockholders of the company would remain the same, at least for the time being. Earl and Betty would keep their stock for now. Earl would make plans to retire and ride off with Betty.

- The company would either employ Jeff as its CEO or it would contract with the new company to be formed by Jeff (described below) to provide top-level management for the company. The compensation structure would be designed to provide attractive bonus incentives to Jeff if the income of the company is improved under the new management. It may include deferred compensation tied to increases in the value of the company's stock.

- Jeff would form a new company. This new company would be structured to finance and manage the growth and expansion of the business. It would take

---

200. I.R.C. §§ 453B(f), 691(a)(5)(iii); Estate of Frane v. Commissioner, 98 T.C. 341 (1992), affirmed in part and reversed in part, 998 F.2d 567 (8th Cir. 1993).

201. I.R.C. § 1368(c)(1). If the distributions exceed the S corporation's accumulated adjustment account, a taxable dividend exposure remains to the extent of the corporation's earnings and profits from its C corporation existence. I.R.C. § 1368(c)(2). The exposure ends once the earnings and profits have been distributed.

the risks; it would reap the benefits. Appropriate provisions would be drawn to ensure that the new company does not adversely impact Wilson Incorporated's present operation, but that it has the latitude to enhance the existing markets and expand into new markets. Preferably, the new company would be a pass-through entity—an S corporation or an LLC. Jeff would select the entity form that works best for him.

• Earl and Betty would structure a gifting program to transfer to their children Wilson corporation stock and possibly other assets if and when they determine that they have sufficient assets and income to meet their future needs. These gifts, when made, would be structured to maximize use of their annual gift tax exclusions and the unused gift tax unified credits of Earl and Betty.

• Earl and Betty's wills or living trust would be structured to leave each child an equal share of their estates. Jeff would have a preferred claim to the Wilson stock, and Kathy and Paul would have a priority claim to the other assets in the estate. If it becomes necessary to pass some of the Wilson stock to Kathy and Paul in order to equalize the values, the will or living trust would include buy-sell provisions that give Jeff the right to buy the Wilson stock passing to Kathy and Paul under stated terms and conditions. Jeff's management rights would remain protected by the existing employment or management contracts.

This simple restructuring would offer a number of potential benefits. First, since Earl and Betty retain their stock, they would have an income for life. If that income grows beyond their needs, they would have the flexibility to begin transferring stock (and the related income) to their children and grandchildren as they choose. Since the cash distributions would be stock-related distributions, the unreasonable compensation risk would be eliminated, as would any payroll tax burdens. Second, by virtue of the S election, the income distributed to Earl and Betty each year would be pre-tax earnings, free of any threat of double taxation. So long as the corporation has sufficient current earnings, this income would be taxed only once. No longer would a party be forced to make payments with after-tax dollars to another family member. Third, Jeff's management and control rights would be protected by the employment and management agreements. Earl could play as much or as little of a role in the business as he chooses. The parties could sculpt their control and management agreement in any manner that they choose, free of any tax restrictions or limitations. Fourth, Jeff would be the primary beneficiary of the future growth in the business through the new business entity. The operating lines between the old company and the new company would need to be clearly defined. The goal would be to preserve the existing business operation for the old company and its shareholders (principally Earl and Betty) and to allow any new operations and opportunities to grow in the company that would be owned, financed, and operated by Jeff. Fifth, stock owned by Earl and Betty at their deaths would receive a full step-up in income tax basis.[202] Sixth, future increases in the value of Earl and Betty's estate could be limited and controlled by (i) the incentive employment and management contracts with Jeff, (ii) the new company owned, financed and operated by Jeff, and (iii) a controlled gifting program implemented by Earl and Betty. Finally,

---

202. I.R.C. § 1014(a).

hopefully the income stream for Earl and Betty would be insulated from some or all of the financing risks taken by Jeff to expand into new markets. These financing risks would be in the new company, not the old company

There are limitations and potential disadvantages with such a restructuring approach that need to be carefully evaluated and may require some creative solutions. First, Jeff may need the operating and asset base of Wilson Incorporated in order to finance the expansion efforts. Various factors may influence this issue, including historical success patterns, the likelihood of future success, Jeff's track record and expertise, and other assets owned by Jeff. If this condition exists, it may significantly complicate the situation. Workable alternatives are usually available, depending on the flexibility of the lenders and Earl and Betty's willingness to take some risk to help with the financing. But clearly this can be a troubling complication.

The second potential disadvantage is the possibility that the value of Earl and Betty's common stock in the old company continues to grow, with a corresponding increase in their estate tax exposure. There would be no automatic governor on the stock's future growth in value. Hopefully, this growth fear could be mitigated or entirely eliminated with a carefully implemented gifting program, the operation of Jeff's new company, and special incentives under the employment or management agreements.

A third potential disadvantage is that the employment or management contracts for Jeff would be subject to a special provision in Section 1366(e) of the Code that requires that a family member who renders services to an S corporation be paid reasonable compensation for those services.[203] Presumably, this requirement would not be a problem because the goal would be to adequately compensate Jeff and provide him with attractive economic incentives to preserve the existing operations for the security of Earl and Betty.

Fourth, conversion to S corporation status would likely create additional tax challenges that are usually regarded as serious nuisances, not reasons for rejecting the strategy. An immediate tax hit will be triggered if the company values its inventory under the LIFO method.[204] Additional taxes may be incurred in the future if shareholder distributions from the S corporation exceed earnings during the S period,[205] if assets owned by the S corporation at the time of conversion are sold within the 10–year period following the conversion,[206] or if the net passive income received by the S corporation exceeds 25 percent of its receipts during a period that it has accumulated earnings and profits from its C existence.[207] Usually these tax risks of conversion can be reduced to acceptable levels or eliminated entirely with careful monitoring and planning.

The plan design process should include an evaluation of business restructuring options that address specific family objectives. This may allow the parents to rethink or slow down their stock transitions or to target the transitions

---

203. I.R.C. § 1014(a).
204. I.R.C. § 1363(d).
205. I.R.C. § 1368(c)(2).
206. See generally I.R.C. § 1374.
207. See generally I.R.C. § 1375 and § 1362(d)(3).

to occur at key times, such as upon the first death of a parent. Although the tax challenges of a stock redemption require a complete disposition of the parents' stock, gifting and cross-purchase options may be implemented on a piecemeal basis to complement the business restructuring and to flexibly accommodate changed circumstances.

## 5. THE FAMILY PARTNERSHIP OR LLC—A COMPANION PLAY

Many family business owners want financial and estate plans that protect assets, preserve control, and save taxes. Perhaps no planning tool has historically been more effective in meeting these basic family objectives than the family partnership and the family limited liability company (LLC). These are flexible tools that can be crafted to accomplish specific, targeted objectives, including shifting income to other family members, maximizing wealth scattering gifting opportunities, protecting assets from creditors, and (the one that drives the IRS crazy) creating valuation discounts in the parents' estate by repackaging investment assets into discounted limited partnership interests. The wise use of a family partnership often can boost the performance of other planning tools, such as children and grandchildren trusts, dynasty trusts, and structured gifting programs.

If the family business is operated in corporate form, as most are, the family partnership or LLC usually will not be a vehicle for directly transitioning the stock of the corporation. A partnership or LLC may not own stock of an S corporation. And although stock of a closely held family C corporation could be contributed to a partnership or LLC, the benefits of doing so are highly questionable. There are three compelling tax problems. First, any earnings of the C corporation distributed as dividends to the shareholder, including the partnership, will be subject to both a corporate level tax hit and a shareholder dividend tax hit. This double tax burden eliminates the pass-through income benefits that partnership-taxed entities typically enjoy and will increase the expense and hassle of trying to use the partnership vehicle to shift income to other family members. Second, all losses generated by the C corporation will be trapped inside the corporation and will not pass through to its shareholders. Thus, the typical loss pass-through benefits of a partnership won't exist. Third, and of far greater concern, there is a high risk that Section 2036(a) would be applied to deny the parents the benefits of any valuation discounts that they might seek to claim as a result of the partnership structure. Section 2036(a) has been the most potent weapon used by the Service in racking up a series of victories against family partnerships in cases where the family has been unable to prove a legitimate and significant non-tax reason for the partnership.[208] If stock of a closely held family C corporation was transferred to a partnership in hopes of securing any valuation discount benefits on the death of a parent, a compelling argument could be made that the partnership served no legitimate and significant

---

208. Estate of Rosen v. Commissioner, T.C. Memo 2006–115; Estate of Rector v. Commissioner, T.C. Memo 2007–367; Estate of Erickson v. Commissioner, T.C. Memo 2007–107; Estate of Bigelow v. Commissioner, 503 F.3d 955 (9th Cir. 2007); Strangi v. Commissioner, 417 F.3d 468 (5th Cir. 2005); Estate of Hillgren v. Commissioner, T.C. Memo 2004–46; Kimbell v. United States, 371 F.3d 257 (5th Cir. 2004); Estate of Thompson v. Commissioner, 382 F.3d 367 (3d Cir. 2004); Estate of Bongard v. Commissioner, 124 T.C. No. 8 (2005).

non-tax purpose. The partnership would simply hold stock in a closely controlled family corporation, would never have engaged in any meaningful business activities, and would never have provided any additional limited liability or significant asset protection benefits. It may be considered nothing more than a "recycling" vehicle motivated primarily by tax considerations. This was the reasoning that the Service argued and the Tax Court adopted in *Estate of Bongard v. Commissioner,*[209] a 2005 case where Section 2036(a) was applied to tax in the decedent's estate interests in an LLC that had been transferred to a family limited partnership in a futile attempt to obtain valuation discounts.

The formidable obstacles of using a family partnership or LLC to transition stock in a family corporation do not preclude such partnership or LLC from being part of the transition plan in many cases. If the family business is operated in a partnership or LLC or as a sole proprietorship, use of a partnership or LLC as the primary transition vehicle is a given. But in the great bulk of cases, those where the family business is conducted in a C or S corporation, the family partnership or LLC will serve as a companion or supplemental transition strategy for valuable assets held outside the corporation that are ultimately targeted for those children who do not have career ties to the business.

For example, in our case study Earl and Betty could form a limited partnership and transfer the real property that houses the business to the partnership in return for limited partnership units. Kathy and Paul, the outside children, would transfer other assets to a newly formed S corporation that they would own and control. The S corporation, in turn, would transfer its newly acquired assets to the partnership in return for general partner units. The S corporation, owned by Kathy and Paul, would be the sole general partner and have complete management authority of the partnership, and Earl and Betty would start out as the sole limited partners of the partnership. With this tiered structure, all parties would have limited liability protection for the activities of the partnership. Earl and Betty, the retiring parents, would be relieved of the burden of having to manage the real estate and negotiate with Jeff on matters related to the company's use of the real estate. Kathy and Paul, the children targeted to ultimately own the real estate with their families, would directly manage and control all issues relating to the real estate.

This partnership structure may provide some valuable tax saving opportunities. Earl and Betty could maximize the use of their annual gift tax exclusions and unified credits by transferring limited partnership units each year to their children and trusts established for their grandchildren.[210] The limited partnership units would quality for substantial lack of marketability and minority interest discounts because they have no control rights. Lower values would permit more units to be gifted within the dollar limitations of the annual gift tax

---

209. 124 T.C. 95 (2005).

210. For grandchildren under age 21, simple 2503(c) trusts can be used to avoid future interest characterizations that would otherwise compromise the availability of the annual gift tax exclusion. I.R.C. § 2503(c). Plus, care should be taken to ensure that the each grandchild's trust is structured to avoid the generation skipping tax by having an inclusion ratio of zero. I.R.C. § 2642(c)(2). Generally, this will require that the grandchild be the sole beneficiary during his or her life, and that the trust assets be included in the grandchild's estate if the grandchild dies before the trust terminates.

exclusion. The gifts would not deplete Earl and Betty's more liquid investment assets, nor would they dilute the control rights vested in Kathy and Paul. As the gifts are made, the gifted units would be removed from Earl and Betty's taxable estates, and all distribution rights and income attributable to the gifted units would be shifted and taxed to other family members. Plus, any limited partnership units remaining in Earl and Betty's estates at death may also qualify for substantial lack of marketability and minority interest discounts because those units would have no control rights. The potential to generate these valuation discounts makes the family partnership an attractive candidate in many transition plans.

The powerful tax benefits of family partnerships and LLCs have made them a popular target of the IRS. The planning and tax challenges of family partnerships and LLCs are discussed in Chapter 16.

## E. THE INSIDE/OUTSIDE CHILDREN CONFLICT

### 1. THE CHALLENGE

Transitioning a family business is usually tougher when some children work in the business and others do not. This is a fairly common scenario. In our case study, Earl and Betty own a business that they worked their entire lifetimes to build. They have three children; Jeff is a key insider, and Kathy and Paul have careers outside the business. Like many parents in this situation, Earl and Betty view the business as an economic investment that has become part of the family culture. Since the business represents the bulk of their estate, they assume that each child will eventually inherit an interest in the business. The problems usually are centered in the three primary benefits of equity ownership—income rights, equity value growth, and control.

**a. Income.** In a corporation (either C or S), shareholders receive income cash distributions as dividends. In a partnership or limited liability company, the owner's cash income is received through distributions. Whatever the organization form, the amount available to the owners of the business is directly affected by the compensation and benefits paid to or for the benefit of the employees of the business. When only some of the children work in the business, there is always a potential income allocation conflict between the inside children, who have an interest in maximizing compensation and benefit payments, and the outside children, who know that their income rights will be negatively affected by any increase in compensation and benefit payments. It's the classic capital versus labor conflict. The inside children, who devote substantially all of their time and energy to making the business function properly, often see the profits coming primarily from their efforts. They may resent excessive profits going to the outside children who have never done anything to help the business. The outside children, who do not see up close what the inside children really do, often do not understand and appreciate the contributions made by the inside children. They view the business as something that Mom and Dad built to generate profits for everyone. They understand that compensation must be paid to the inside children, but a lifetime of sibling rivalries has removed any inhibitions toward questioning the amounts paid to the inside children.

Tax planning considerations often aggravate the conflict. If the company is a C corporation, the insiders may want higher single-taxed compensation payments and lower double-taxed dividends. Sometimes higher compensation payments are desired to permit larger contributions to the company's qualified retirement plan on behalf of the insiders. In a pass-through entity, such as an S corporation or an LLC, the pressure to reduce payroll tax burdens for both the insiders and the company may encourage higher dividends and owner distributions and lower compensation payments. But usually the overriding consideration is not taxes, but "how much?" While all profess fairness as the ultimate goal, the outsiders want insider compensation levels down, and the insiders want them up. Tax planning often takes a back seat.

**b. Stock Value**. Often the most significant income decision isn't whether to distribute income in the form of dividends or compensation, but whether to distribute it at all. The best choice in many situations is to retain the income in the business to help finance growth. This leads to the second benefit of stock ownership - equity value growth. Both the inside and outside shareholders hope and expect that the value of their equity interests will grow over time.

In many family businesses, the focus on the value growth potential ends up diluting the incentive of the inside children to make it happen. Often, there is insufficient cash to pay adequate compensation to the key management employees. So the principal economic incentive for those who are devoting all their time and energy to the business is not current income, but the prospects of building substantial value that will be realized in the future when the business is sold. The problem comes when the ownership is structured to provide the inside children with only a fraction of the upside growth potential of the business. The insiders watch their siblings pursue other careers and develop independent sources of wealth and still receive the benefits of any economic growth that the insiders are able to generate from the old family business. In addition to creating hard feelings, the structure often undermines the incentive of the insiders and the foundations of the company's success.

Most successful businesses require an immense commitment of management time and energy and a willingness to risk private capital. Owners often must personally guarantee bank financing essential to the operation and growth of the business. Mom and Dad just did it. What happens in the all-too-common scenario where the outside children, faced with the prospect of exposing their other assets and income resources to the risks of the business that employs their siblings, just say "no"? The inside children have a tough choice; they can step up to the plate by themselves or let the business suffer. The conflict often has significant detrimental affects, not only to the business itself, but also to the relationships between the inside and outside children.

**c. Control.** The third benefit of business ownership is control. Most business owners have some degree of control or voting rights with respect to the business itself. When inside and outside children possess the control, conflicts easily surface. For example, the inside children may want to arrange for a new source of financing, develop a new line of products, expand into new territories, or take some other action that requires the consent of the outside children. The outside children must cast a vote on an issue that they do not really understand because they are not involved on a day-to-day basis. As a result, the outsiders, like many in their situation, tend to be suspicious and risk averse. Growth is slowed; opportunities are lost. The insiders, who are critical to the success of the enterprise, become frustrated. Their need to secure the approval of an uninformed, uninvolved, hard-nosed, suspicious brother or sister makes everything harder and can quickly become an obstacle to sound management and profitable decision-making. Too often, deep-seated personal emotions, the foundations of which may be events that occurred decades earlier, take priority over sound business judgment.

These types of problems can lead to imprudent business decisions, costly tax consequences, and conflicts that can drive a permanent wedge into sibling relationships. The planning challenge is to anticipate the potential conflicts, based on an honest assessment of the specific facts, and then implement one or more strategies that may mitigate any adverse effects. Often the best strategies are those that eliminate the source of the conflict - joint ownership of the business. Each child gets a fair share of the parents' estate, but the insiders end up with sole ownership of the family business. When this is not possible, other strategies, often perceived as less attractive, may be used to mitigate adverse tax and control issues triggered by the joint ownership by inside and outside children.

## 2. THE PLANNING STRATEGIES

### a. The Insider Installment Sale

This strategy assumes that the parents, Earl and Betty in our case, are willing to exit the business while they are living. With this strategy, the parents sell their stock to the company, a grantor trust, or the insiders and take back a long-term note. If the company is the purchaser, the parents should have no further role in the business.[211] When the parents die, the note becomes part of their estate and passes to all their children, along with the other assets of their estate.

Although often used, this strategy has some significant disadvantages. The sale will trigger an income tax burden for the parents and any children who inherit the unpaid note obligation.[212] The lifetime sale eliminates any basis step-up potential at death unless the sale is structured to occur on the death of the first parent. Plus, the purchaser (either the insiders, a trust for the insiders, or the company) must fund the principal payments on the note with after-tax dollars, and the parents have a wasting asset (the promissory note) that may not sustain them, let alone provide anything for the outside children. For these reasons and

---

211. See explanation and related discussion in section D.2., supra.
212. Any remaining payments on the note that are paid to the children will be taxed to the children as income in respect of a decedent under I.R.C. § 691(a).

others, an insider installment sale during the life of the parents, although preferred in select situations, is often not the solution. Many parents prefer a strategy that will allow them to retain control, while ensuring that each child will ultimately receive a fair share of their estate.

### b. Other Asset Equalizing

The second strategy is simple and attractive if the numbers work. The solution is to leave the outside children assets other than the family business. The family business stock owned by the parents passes to the inside children, and other assets of equal value per child pass to the outside children. Any remaining assets after this equalizing allocation are distributed to all the children in equal shares. The result is that the inside children receive all of the interests in the business, plus possibly some other assets, and the outside children do not receive any stock in the family business, but end up with property having a value equal to that received by the inside children. In this situation, it is important to carefully coordinate the provisions of the parents' wills or living trust with the disposition of other assets that will pass outside such documents, such as the proceeds from life insurance policies and retirement plan benefits. These other assets must be considered in determining equality among the children and in properly structuring how the business interests are to be distributed to the inside children.

There is a common obstacle to the simple strategy. In many situations, the business constitutes the bulk of the parents' estate. There are not enough other assets to cover the outside children. In Earl and Betty's situation, the business, valued at $25 million, represents over 75 percent of their $32 million estate, and they have three children. The math doesn't work. In situations like this, often the preferred solution is to provide in the parents' wills that the estate of the parents will be divided among the children equally and that, in making the division, the inside children will first be allocated equity interests in the family business. To the extent that the value of total business equity interests owned by the estate exceeds the value of the equity shares allocated to the inside children, the inside children are given the option to purchase the additional business interests from the estate, before the final distributions are made to all children. This enables the inside children to acquire all of the equity business interests owned by the estate, while at the same time passing an equal date-of-death value to each child.

In creating the option, the two most critical elements are the price of the business interests to be acquired by the inside children and the terms of payment. The price may be set at the value finally determined for federal estate tax purposes. If there is no federal estate tax return required, or if the parents want a more specific basis for determining the purchase price, they may specify a valuation formula or an appraisal procedure, similar to what is often included in a buy-sell agreement among co-owners. The key is to make sure that there is either a value established or a method for determining the value so that there is little or no basis for a dispute over price. In rare cases, the parents may choose to name a non-child as the personal representative of the estate and allow that "independent" personal representative to determine the price, using whatever assistance he or she deems appropriate. In determining the method of payment for the option price, care should be taken to make sure that the required cash flow payments do not jeopardize the ongoing success of the business. For many businesses, the death of the owner may create a significant disruption in cash flow, apart from the need to make large cash payments to the outside children. One obvious solution is to provide for a long-term installment payout of the price, securing the payment obligation with the pledge of the stock being purchased. Since the inside children will be purchasing only a portion of the equity business interests owned by the estate, often the installment payment method will fit within the cash flow parameters of the business.

In some cases, it may be prudent to fund the buy-out price in whole or in part with life insurance on the parents. The inside child, Jeff in our case, owns the policies and uses the proceeds collected on the parents' deaths to buy the equity business interests from the estates. Often, the inside children do not have enough surplus cash flow to fund the premiums on the life insurance policies. So in many cases, the company bonuses the inside children sufficient amounts to cover the premiums and any tax hit on the bonuses. Some parents view this insider insurance funding bonus mechanism as a deviation from the overall objective to treat all children equally even though it ultimately provides the outside children with cash instead of an installment note from the insiders. If that's the case, the parents' wills or living trust may be structured to equalize such insurance bonuses among the children by requiring that, for allocation purposes only, all bonus insurance payments to the insiders must be added to the total estate value and be treated as payments already credited to the inside children.

The parents may prefer to have the company itself fund the insurance premiums, own the policy, collect the death benefit, and use the proceeds to redeem from the estate the business interests that exceed the equal shares of the estate allocable to the inside children. This approach has a few significant disadvantages. It eliminates the ability of the inside children to benefit from the stepped-up basis in the stock that would result if they purchased the stock directly. Plus, if the company is a sizable C corporation (annual gross receipts in excess of $7.5 million), the receipt of life insurance proceeds may trigger an alternative minimum tax.[213]

### c. Real Estate and Life Insurance Trade-Offs

A partial solution to the inside-outside child dilemma may exist when a portion of the value of the family business is real estate owned by the parents directly. Often the parents own business-related real estate outright or in a separate pass-through entity, such as a partnership or an LLC. The real estate is leased to the operating business, usually a corporation. In those situations where the value of the overall business, including the real estate, exceeds the value of the estate shares allocable to the inside children at the death of the parents, the preferred solution may be to leave the outside children the business real estate and the inside children the business. If the value of the real estate exceeds the equal shares allocable to the outside children, a portion of the real estate may also be allocated to the insiders, so that the overall shares passing through the estate are equal. If the value of the real estate is not sufficient to equalize the shares

---

213. I.R.C. §§ 55(e), 56(g).

(the more common scenario), this strategy may be combined with one of the other strategies to achieve an overall equal allocation.

When this real estate strategy is used, care must be taken to mitigate conflicts that may surface between the insiders who own the business and need use of the real estate and the outside children who own the real estate and want to maximize its earning potential. If the real estate is essential to the success of the business, leaving the real estate to the outside children creates a potential for conflict. The solution is to make sure that, at the appropriate time, the operating company enters into a lease that secures its rights to the use of the real estate. The lease should be long-term and provide the company with a series of renewal options. The lease payment obligation of the company should be adjusted periodically to reflect a fair market rent for a long-term single user tenant. This will help ensure that the outside children realize the benefits of the income and value elements of the real estate that is left to them. The lease, for example, may require that, unless the parties agree otherwise, independent appraisers will be used every five years to adjust the rent to reflect current market values and to set annual escalators in the rent for the next five years. The lease should spell out the rights and obligations typically included in commercial leases between unrelated parties, including the parties' respective obligations to maintain and repair the building and to pay real estate taxes and insurance premiums.

A similar trade-off opportunity may exist if one or both of the parents are insurable and there is no desire to hassle with the complexities of the other options. Life insurance may provide a solution. The parents acquire a life insurance policy through an irrevocable trust. It may be a second-to-die policy that pays off on the death of the surviving spouse. The beneficiaries of the life insurance trust are the outside children. The amount of the life insurance is based on the mix and value of the other assets in the parents' estate to ensure that there will be sufficient assets to fund the tax and liquidity needs of the estate and to provide each outside child with a benefit equal to the value of the family business interests that will pass to each inside child.

### d. King Solomon Solution[214]

In select situations, the best solution to the inside-outside children conflict may to do what King Solomon proposed - cut the baby into two pieces. One piece of the business goes to the inside children, who can manage and grow it. The other piece is sold for the benefit of the outside children. Of course, the solution has merit only in those situations where the business can be divided into profitable pieces, one of which can be sold. It is not a viable option for most businesses, but it may be attractive in situations where the business has separate divisions or facilities, only some of which are of interest to the inside children or are, because of their size, incapable of being purchased by the inside children. Also, it may be the answer in those situations where there are conflicts among different inside children who work in separate divisions of the family business. Instead of forcing the insiders to coexist in the same company, the company is divided so that each insider can be given his or her own company to manage.

---

214. The biblical King Solomon, when faced with two women each claiming to be the mother of a baby, proposed the ultimate solution–divide the baby in half. I. Kings Ch. 3, Verses 16–28.

In cases where a division makes sense, the tax challenge is to divide the company into pieces without triggering a taxable event. For partnership-taxed entities, there is seldom a problem. Corporate entities also can make it work if the division is structured as a spin-off, split-off, or split-up that qualifies as a tax free D reorganization.[215]

The foregoing strategies are geared at providing the outside children with a fair share of the parents' estate without them ever acquiring an interest in the business. Often it is inevitable that the outside children are going to end up owning an interest in the company on the death of the parents. There may be insufficient other assets and insufficient cash flow to implement a strategy that gives each child an equal share while keeping the outsiders out of the business. Or it may be one of those situations where the family business is an integral part of the family culture that binds everyone, and the parents and the children want all family members to own a part of the culture. Whatever the reason, the parents want a strategy that will enable each child to own an interest in the business and that will reduce or eliminate potential conflicts between the insiders and the outsiders. The following strategies are potential candidates in those situations.

### e. Preferred Stock Recapitalization

One option is for the parents to leave preferred stock to the outside children and common stock to the inside children. The value of the preferred stock often is capped so that all of the future growth in the business shifts to the owners of the common stock - the inside children. The preferred stockholders typically are given a priority right to receive their share values on liquidation before any amounts are paid to common stockholders (hence the name "preferred"). Generally, preferred stockholders are given a fixed, cumulative income right, although there are a wide variety of income rights that can be granted to preferred stockholders.

One advantage of using preferred stock for the outside children is that it reduces the potential conflict between the insiders and outsiders regarding income distributions being structured as compensation or dividend payments. If the insiders and outsiders both own common stock, the outsiders will have a vested interest in dividends, while the insiders will favor compensation payments. With preferred stock, the dividend rights of the preferred stockholders (the outside children) are fixed and are not dependent on the payment of dividends on the common stock. So the outsiders have no incentive to push for more common stock dividends and less compensation for the insiders. In fact, as owners of preferred stock, the outsiders may prefer the compensation characterization for all payments to the insiders because of the tax savings to the

---

215. I.R.C. § 368(a)(1)(D). If done right, the assets of a C corporation (referred to as the "distributing corporation") can be transferred to multiple C corporations (referred to as "controlled corporations"), and the stock of the controlled corporations can be distributed to the shareholders of the distributing corporation, all tax free. I.R.C. §§ 355(a), 361(a), 1032(a). Six requirements must be satisfied: (1) A control requirement governed by I.R.C. §§ 355(a)(1)(A) and 368(c); (2) A complete distribution requirement governed by I.R.C. § 355(a)(1)(D); (3) A five-year active trade or business requirement governed by I.R.C. § 355(a)(1)(C) and Reg. § 1.355–3; (4) A 50 percent continuity of interest requirement governed by Reg. § 1.355–2(c)(2); (5) A business purpose requirement governed by Reg. § 1.355–2(b)(2); and (6) A no dividend "device" requirement governed by I.R.C. § 355(a)(1)(B) and Reg. § 1.355–2(d). For a related discussion, see Section B. 6. of Chapter 13, infra.

company.   Although the outsiders' concern over the characterization of the
insider payments is gone, the amounts paid to the insiders, however
characterized, may still be a source of conflict to the extent there is any
uncertainty regarding the company's capacity to pay dividends on the preferred
stock, now or in the future.  Excessive compensation payments or common stock
distributions to insiders in early years may hinder the corporation's ability to fund
preferred stock dividend payments in later years.  A solution to this potential
conflict may be a shareholders agreement between the parties that conditions
additional payments to the insiders on the company maintaining minimum
liquidity ratios (e.g., current ratio or acid-test ratio) and debt-to-equity ratios.
Such ratio conditions, if fairly structured, may provide the outsiders with comfort
that the insider payments will not impair the company's ability to fund preferred
dividends and provide the insiders with the desired flexibility to increase their
incomes, free of outsider hassles, as they grow the business.

Preferred stock can either be voting or nonvoting.  If the objective is to keep
control in the hands of the insiders while the outsiders collect their preferred
dividends, nonvoting preferred may be the obvious choice.  But with nonvoting
preferred, the inside children have control over whether and when preferred
dividends get paid and, absent an agreement to the contrary, their own
compensation levels.  Of course, dividends on the insiders' common stock must
take a back seat to preferred dividends to the outsiders, but this likely will be an
irrelevant concern because of the insiders' capacity to set their own compensation
and bonus levels.

Often there is a need for creativity in this situation. As described above, one
option is ratio requirements, contractually protected through an agreement
between all the shareholders.  Another option is to make the preferred stock
nonvoting only so long as the dividends on the preferred stock are timely paid.  If
the dividends ever become delinquent, then the preferred stockholders acquire
voting rights that remain forever or until specified conditions are satisfied.  This
option gives the insiders a strong incentive to always keep the preferred
dividends current.  But if things get bad, the preferred stockholders have voting
rights and can involve themselves in the challenges of the business.

With this preferred stock strategy, there are three tax issues to consider.
First, the conversion of the parents' common stock to both common and preferred
stock should be structured to qualify as a tax-free recapitalization.[216]  Second,
after such a recapitalization, any gifts of common stock to the insiders by the
parents during life will be subject to the valuation rules of Section 2701.[217]
Generally, the value of the preferred (determined by appraisal) will be based on
its fixed dividend rate, and the value of the common will equal the total equity
value less the value of the preferred.  Third, and usually of greater significance,
dividends on the preferred stock will be subject to a double tax - one at the
corporate level and one at the preferred shareholder level.  The most common
solution to the double tax problem, the election of S corporation status, is not

---

216.  I.R.C. § 368(a)(1)(E).
217.  See generally I.R.C. § 2701 and related discussion in Section D.1.d. above.

available because S corporations cannot have preferred stock.[218] So although the preferred stock solution addresses some of the conflicts of passing business interests to both inside and outside children, it does so at a tax cost.

### f. Preferred Interests in a Limited Partnership or LLC

In select situations, a family limited partnership or family LLC may be used to transfer preferred units to the outside children and growth units to the inside children and avoid the double tax burdens of a C corporation. The preferred interest for the outside children is in the form of a preferred limited partnership or LLC interest rather than a preferred stock interest. The preferred partnership or LLC interest can be structured to have all of the elements of C corporation preferred stock: capped liquidation rights; preferred liquidation rights; and fixed, preferred income distribution rights. Also, the limited partnership or LLC agreement may be structured to give the preferred partnership interest holders voting rights in the event the preferred income distributions become delinquent, just as discussed in connection with preferred stockholders.

There are a few principal distinctions between the preferred interest approach using a family limited partnership or LLC and the preferred stock approach using a C corporation. The first difference is the elimination of the double tax problem. With the family partnership or LLC, the payment of preferred partnership distributions to the outside children does not result in double taxation because the partnership is not a tax-paying entity. A second distinction is a concern that usually can be neutralized with a little added complexity. When there is a family limited partnership, the general partners have personal liability exposure for the debts of the company. If the inside children are the general partners, they will have personal liability exposure. One solution to this liability problem is to have the inside children hold their general partner interests through an S corporation or an LLC. This introduces another entity into the equation, but the added expense and complexity usually are minimal. Another alternative is to use an LLC rather than a limited partnership. The LLC can be structured to eliminate personal liability exposure for all its members while spelling out the preferred and limited rights of the outside children. A potential negative of using an LLC is that the limited rights of the outside children are a function of negotiation and agreement. In a limited partnership, the status of being a "limited partner" usually does the job automatically.

There is a huge obstacle, often insurmountable, to this strategy of using a family partnership or LLC when the business has been operated as a corporation. That obstacle is the tax cost of converting from a corporation to a partnership-taxed entity. Such a conversion triggers a tax on all built-in gains for the corporation, followed by a tax at the shareholder level.[219] The impact of these taxes often makes it prohibitively expensive to even consider converting from a corporate form to a partnership or LLC form. For this reason, the strategy is limited to those situations where the business is already operated in a partnership or LLC or as a sole proprietorship.

---

218. I.R.C. § 1361(b)(1)(D).
219. I.R.C. §§ 331, 336.

### g. S Corporation Voting and Nonvoting Stock

An S corporation may issue voting and nonvoting common stock, but not preferred stock.[220] If the family business has been operated in an S corporation or has recently converted from C to S status, the transition plan may be structured to have the parents transfer nonvoting common stock to the outside children and voting common stock to the inside children. Often when nonvoting stock is used, the outside children are given limited control rights through a shareholders' agreement that kicks in under defined conditions. Usually income distributions are the biggest challenge with this S corporation strategy. The primary advantage, of course, is that dividends of S corporation earnings can be distributed to both the insiders and the outsiders free of any double tax concerns. But if the insiders have control, they will have the ability to pull out substantially all of the earnings of the corporation, or at least a disproportionately large amount, in the form of compensation payments. A solution is for the parents, either during life or through their estate plan, to impose contractual compensation limitations on the insiders. Usually this is done with mandated employment agreements. The insiders' compensation under the employment agreements can be based on a formula that provides strong incentives for the insiders to grow the business, while ensuring that the income interests of the outsiders are protected.

Two keys factors should be considered whenever equity interests are transferred to both the inside and outside children. First, future value growth may be a concern of the insiders. Depending on the nature and terms of the interest given to the outsiders, the outsiders may have a right to participate in equity growth generated by the business. This may dilute the insider's incentive to grow the business. The issue may be addressed, although usually not completely solved, by special compensation incentives for the insiders. The inside children may be granted stock appreciation or phantom stock deferred compensation rights that give them a larger stake in the future growth of the enterprise. Second, any strategy that passes ownership interests to multiple family members should include a properly structured buy-sell agreement to ensure that all interests are maintained within the family and that adequate exit options exist when a family members dies, becomes disabled, gets divorced, encounters credit problems, or wants out.

## PROBLEMS 10–A AND 10–B

**10-A**. Mark Crane is the second-generation owner of The Crane Company, a successful import and brand promotion company. Mark's father was the founder and visionary of the company. Mark, age 60, has been the CEO for the last twenty years. Mark's oldest son, Matthew, age 36, heads up the marketing division of the company. Matthew says that he intends to make the company his career. Mark and his wife Julie have two other adult children who have never worked for the company.

The company is an S corporation that for the last five years has generated average annual pre-tax earnings of $1.8 million (before any salary to Mark) on

---

220. Reg. § 1.1361–1(l )(1).

sales of about $28 million.  Mark typically withdraws about $1.4 million through a salary and owner distributions, pays about $600,000 in income taxes, and uses the remaining $800,000 to cover his semi-lavish lifestyle and fund his other investments.  Mark's assets outside the business have a value of approximately $6 million.

A large strategic competitor has offered Mark $16 million for the company. The competitor has two objectives: to obtain Crane's revenues and to substantially improve profitability by consolidating operations and "gutting most of Crane's support operations."  Most of Crane's employees, including Matthew, would be gone within six months. The only Crane employees who would have any real job security would be the account executives and account managers who have strong personal relationships with key accounts.

Mark is tempted by the offer.  The pressure of the company would be off his back.  He needs some counsel.  What additional facts would you need?  What specific questions would you ask Mark?  How would the answers to your questions influence your advice to Mark?

**10-B.**  Olson Consolidations Inc. is a successful shipping company owned by David and Kathy Olson, both age 62.  David is the chairman of the company. David's oldest son, Jason, age 39, is the president and CEO and has been the driving force behind of the company for the last five years. Jason joined the company at the age of 23 and took over the reins 11 years later.  The company's growth and admired position in the industry are due to Jason's efforts.

David and Kathy have four other children, two of whom work for the company.  Judy, age 35, heads up the company's customer service operation and, in Jason's opinion, does "an adequate job."  Luke, age 27, works in field operations because, according to Jason, "he can't find another job."  The other two children, Roger, age 32, and Julia, age 30, have never worked for the company.  Roger is a dentist, and Julia is a CPA.

The company has nearly 250 employees and sales of approximately $40 million a year.  Its pre-tax income is close to five percent, nearly $2 million a year.  It has always been a C corporation.  Its balance sheet shows total assets of $10 million (consisting primarily of account receivables and equipment), liabilities of $2.5 million, and equity of $7.5 million.  David believes the company is worth between $14 and $16 million, but he has no interest in selling the company.

Jason feels that he is at a crossroads in his life.  He is tired of building "Mom and Dad's Company."  He has made it clear to his parents that he will leave and start something on his own if they do not start the process of transitioning control and ownership of the business to him.  He is not demanding that he be given more than an equal share of his parents' estate at this time, but he is through building value for his brothers and sisters, none of whom understands the business or Jason's role.

David and Linda's other assets, apart from the business and life insurance, have a value or approximately $8 million, putting their total estate (exclusive of life insurance) in the $22 million to $24 million range.  These other assets include a $2 million debt-free building that is leased to the company. David and Linda have a $2 million survivorship life policy on their joint lives. The children are the named beneficiaries on the policy.

David and Linda are concerned about Jason. His loss would seriously hurt the company. David knows that there is no way that he could step back in and pick up the slack. And if Jason decided to stay in the same industry and compete, he could destroy the company very quickly. Nearly every employee and customer would be up for grabs, with the advantage to Jason. For these reasons, David has challenged Jason to come up with a plan that will be fair to all the children, ensure that David and Linda are protected for the rest of their lives, and give Jason what he wants.

Jason has requested your advice. What do you recommend? What additional facts would you like to have?

# CHAPTER 11

# EXECUTIVE COMPENSATION PLANNING

---

## A. THE EXECUTIVE EMPLOYMENT AGREEMENT

### 1. COMMON MYTHS

The use of carefully crafted employment agreements in large organizations is forever expanding down to deeper levels to hedge against the risk of expensive litigation and the loss or dilution of valued proprietary rights. Many closely held businesses still resist the need to get things in writing with those who can do the most damage. The owners cling to the old notion that a piece of paper can't make a bad employee good or a good one better. So why bother?

Usually the reluctance to come of age on this one is a result of inertia and ignorance. A program of using smart agreements with key employees takes real effort. Since many closely held businesses do not have a separate human resources person (much less a department), the burden of the effort falls on the chief executive officer or some other high-ranking officer who already has a more-than-full plate. Add to this a few common myths that question the whole value of the effort and it's easy to let this "priority" drop to the bottom of the stack. Following are a few of the myths that often get in the way.

**Myth 1: Advantage Employee.** The myth is that the document produces more for the employee, less for the company. Why else would only a privileged few in the company have their own agreement? The truth is that nearly all of the key provisions in an executive employment agreement primarily benefit the company in a big way. Such provisions include termination rights, confidentiality covenants, post-employment competition restrictions, intellectual property protections, work effort requirements, dispute resolution procedures, choice of law designations and more. Even the compensation provisions benefit the company by spelling out the limits and defining expectations.

**Myth 2: A Front-End Downer**. The myth is that it's counterproductive to get tangled up in legal minutiae during the courting phase with a new key executive. The focus should be on positive business challenges and synergies, not potential problems that may never surface between the company and its newest arrival. The myth ignores a basic truth – nearly all prospective employees long for the details of the whole deal. Showing that the key issues have been fairly thought through and incorporated into a document tailored for the new executive will not be viewed as a negative or an unjustified preoccupation with the dark side of business relationships. If done right, it will confirm that the company has its act together, values relationships based on detailed mutual understandings, and regards the prospective employee as a valuable part of the management team. It can actually be an "upper" that removes uncertainties and facilitates a more complete understanding of the objectives and priorities of both parties. And if an insurmountable conflict surfaces during the process, all will benefit from its early detection.

**Myth 3: It's Easier After the Honeymoon**. The myth is that the details of the employment relationship with a key employee are easier to hash out after the employee has been on board for a while. Everyone knows more; expectations are clearer. It's wrong. The problem is that the job won't get done. Once the employee is in the saddle, what interest will the employee have in dealing with post-employment noncompetition restrictions, broad employer termination rights, dispute resolution procedures and the like? In most situations, the company will be left with two lousy options to push the agenda along. It can get tough and demand its agreement, which may undermine morale, mutual respect, and all the other intangibles that strengthen individual business relationships; or it can offer something more, which can get expensive. Far and away the best time to work out the details and document the deal is just before the starting gun when both parties are anxious to find common ground and move forward.

**Myth 4: Money Vagueness Works**. The myth is that it's always smarter to not spell out the details of incentive compensation in an employment agreement. Far too often the matter is settled with a salary and some vague bonus discussions that create expectations of more money but do nothing to perpetuate individual performance objectives. The difference between real success and baseline mediocrity in many businesses is the ability and drive of the key employees who are charged with making it happen. The ability factor is tied directly to the executive's focus on specific targets of success. The drive factor is a function of how badly the executive wants to be better than good. Smart incentive compensation can keep the fire hot under both factors. Here are the key factors to consider.

- **Understandable.** The executive must be able to understand all specifics of the incentive. It can't be too complicated or tied to factors that are foreign to the executive.

- **Measurable.** The incentive should be objectively measurable. It should not be based totally on someone's discretion or will, although some subjectivity may be factored into the process. For example, the incentive for an accounts receivable manager may be a percentage of salary based on the percentage of accounts collected within 90 days (e.g., a 7 percent bonus for an 85 percent collection rate, a 10 percent bonus for a 90 percent collection rate, etc.). The plan also may give the company's CEO the discretion to increase any earned bonus by up to an additional 50 percent if the employee turnover rate in the accounts receivable department in a given year is less than 75 percent of the company's average. Such a bonus plan would be measurable and keep the manager focused on two critical success elements – collection percentages and employee turnover.

- **True Incentive.** The incentive must be large enough to matter. If the amount at stake is insignificant, the employee may pay lip service to the objectives without ever believing that there are serious concerns that warrant additional effort and commitment.

- **Calculation Factors.** The factors that affect the calculation of the bonus should be within the control of the executive. For the CEO and CFO, it may be the overall performance of the company. But there is usually a need for more specificity down the executive ladder. For the vice president of sales, it may be the volume from new customers. For a production VP, it may be the average employee cost for each unit produced. The key is to identify specific success factors that will result in the company becoming stronger as the executive makes more. It is the classic win-win.

- **Visible Time Monitors.** Techniques that enable the company and its executives to track and monitor progress on a regular basis, at least once a month, are vital. This need for regular monitoring may require some special periodic accounting reports or some custom adjustments to the company's computer information system, but the benefits usually easily justify any added up-front effort or expense.

## 2. KEY ELEMENTS OF THE AGREEMENT

### Ten Essential Considerations for Any Employment Agreement[1]
Theodora Lee, Lisa Chagala
Littler Mendelson, P.C.

As employment agreements become increasingly common, company counsel and human resources professionals must be alert to the specific terms of every employment contract. Failure to consider each and every term and how it will affect the employment relationship of each and every applicant and employee may have disastrous consequences. Thus, whether or not the agreement is a highly-tailored, long-negotiated agreement for an executive, or a standardized contract used for a rank-and-file employee, several key considerations apply. The following provides an overview of certain considerations; however, given the complexity of the subject matter, consultation with an experienced employment attorney is highly recommended.

### 1. Defining the Term of Employment

The determination of the employment term is essentially a question of management objective. Does management wish to have maximum flexibility to

---

1. Copyright © 2004 Practicing Law Institute and the authors. Reprinted here with the permission of the Practicing Law Institute and the authors. Ms. Lee is a partner in Littler, Mendelson, P.C.; Ms. Chagala is an associate in the firm.

terminate the employment relationship at any time without notice? Or, does management wish to create a contractual incentive to encourage an employee to remain in employment for a certain period of time? There are essentially three types of employment provisions that may be applied to achieve these management objectives. These provisions are commonly referred to as "at-will," "drop dead," and "evergreen" clauses.

In an at-will employment relationship, either party may terminate the employment relationship at any time. The primary advantage of an at-will employment relationship is flexibility. The main disadvantage of the at-will employment relationship is that there is no incentive, in the form of a "stick," for the employee to remain employed for any period of time. Some employers choose to combine an at-will provision with a notice period. This provides the employer – and the employee – a minimum time period to make alternative arrangements in light of the upcoming termination.

A "drop dead" clause is a provision that provides that the employment relationship will end upon a particular date. The advantage of this approach is that it provides a specific end to the employment relationship. The main disadvantage of this approach is that the employer will be bound to employing the individual through the specified date. This may be costly for the employer if, for example, technologies change or it is later discovered that the individual does not possess the necessary skills for the job. To address the chance that the employment relationship will continue beyond the specified date, employers may combine a "drop dead" provision with an at-will provision, providing that the employment relationship will continue for a specific period of time (until the "drop dead" date) and thereafter will be at-will.

An "evergreen" provision is a clause that states that the employment relationship will continue for a certain period of time and then automatically renew for successive periods unless either party gives notice of intent to terminate within a certain timeframe. This has the advantage of permitting the contract to continue indefinitely, such that the incentive to remain in the employment relationship continues indefinitely. However, the automatic renewal may become more of a hindrance than help. As years pass, the employer may forget to provide notice of termination within the required timeframe.

Regardless of what employment term the employer chooses, the duration of the contractual employment relationship should be defined within the contract. Even if employment is for a stated period, it should be clear that employment may be terminated for cause at any time, and cause should be defined.

If a "drop dead" or "evergreen" provision is used, the employer should include a provision that allows the employer to terminate the employment relationship "for cause" without penalty. Cause is normally defined within the contract and varies, including extreme levels of dishonesty and nonperformance on the part of the employee. The employer will, in most cases, want the contract to survive termination of the employment relationship, to ensure that contractual protections relating to intellectual property and arbitration, for example, are effective beyond the end of the term of the employment relationship.

## 2. Compensation

Traditionally, employment contracts set forth the terms of compensation for the individual, including the amount of base salary the individual is entitled to receive, when pay raises would occur, and what formula would apply to calculation of incentive compensation. Employers traditionally set forth each aspect of the total rewards structure, including base salary, future salary increases, incentive compensation arrangements such as bonus programs, commissions, and stock options, and benefits programs such as medical, retirement, and stock purchase programs.

## 3. Arbitration

An arbitration clause is a provision that secures an employee's consent to binding arbitration as a means of resolving disputes between the employee and the employer. Such clauses can be especially valuable in disputes over termination of employment, which often trigger large claims for damages. The value of arbitration clauses in the employment context have been debated among legal professionals and human resources professionals (and within the popular press) for years. Most employers have determined resolution of disputes through arbitration offer several advantages. Arbitration can be significantly less costly than resolving a dispute through the court. Disputes are often resolved much faster through arbitration than through the courts. Disputes resolved through arbitration are significantly more private than those resolved through the courts. Additionally, the outcome of the case may be more predictable with the use of an arbitrator than a jury. On the other hand, employers have also experienced several disadvantages in arbitration. Some employers experience an increased number of disputes, due to the reduced cost to an employee of bringing a claim. Judicial review (through appeal or otherwise) is extremely limited, leaving little wiggle room in the event of a disappointing arbitration result. Furthermore, arbitration may have negative employee relations consequences, as employees may believe (perhaps incorrectly) that arbitration erodes their substantive rights. These advantages and disadvantages must be weighed before deciding whether or not to implement a mandatory arbitration policy.

## 4. Protections of Intellectual Property

In today's increasingly competitive marketplace, employers must protect and preserve the key assets that are essential to competitive advantage. Often, these assets are in the form of intellectual property. Employers are willing to take great efforts to preserve confidential information and intellectual property from walking out the door (and to a competitor) with a terminated employee. Employment agreements are simply one factor within a program for protecting intellectual property. Normally, such program includes informing employees and others on an ongoing basis of confidentiality requirements and adopting company-wide policies for trade secret protection. Without a comprehensive, company-wide policy, it is not likely that any clause within any employment agreement will be effective.

One means of protecting valuable intellectual property is with a covenant not to compete. Such covenants restrict the activities of an employee after the employee stops working for the employer. Because non-compete covenants are post-employment restrictions on an employee's ability to earn a living, they are viewed in most states with disfavor and are narrowly construed. Generally, courts view covenants not to compete as enforceable only to the extent they are necessary to protect the employer's interest in its goodwill, confidential information, and customer relationships. Covenants not to compete must be narrowly tailored as to the time, geographic scope, and prohibited activity necessary to protect a legitimate employer interest. Defining what activity is prohibited is critical. Typically, the covenant will prevent persons from working for a competitor for a specific period of time in specific locations, may even name the competitors to which the clause applies, and specifies the particular work that is prohibited.

State law considerations cannot be ignored. States impose varying standards to determine whether or not covenants not to compete are enforceable, and some states altogether do not permit covenants not to compete. California is famous (or infamous) in this regard. An employer who uses a non-compete clause in California not only risks having the clause declared unenforceable, but also risks being found to have committed an unlawful business practice by including the clause in its agreements. For this reason, state law must be carefully analyzed before placing such a covenant into an employment agreement.

Non-disclosure covenants are clauses that preclude the employee from disclosing or making use of the employer's confidential information. Whether or not such provision is enforceable is a matter of state law. Generally, in order to be enforceable, such provision must be properly restricted as to time and territory and the employer must have a strong proprietary interest in protecting trade secrets. Again, analysis of state law is essential for ensuring that such a clause is enforceable and that the employer does not act unlawfully in requesting that the applicant or employee enter into such a covenant.

### 5. Work Effort

A provision regarding "work effort" generally states that the employee shall apply his or her best efforts at all times. The provision may also state that the employee must devote his or her entire work time and effort to the employer and will not engage in other gainful employment during the term of employment with the employer. This type of provision has certain advantages that are appealing to any employer. Restrictions on the employee's time avoids scheduling conflicts and prevents situations where transfer of intellectual property may occur.

However, important legal considerations exist for such provisions. Many jurisdictions prohibit certain restrictions on an individual's personal time. For these reasons, "work effort" provisions must be carefully drafted. A blanket prohibition on moonlighting may be replaced with a requirement that employees must avoid actual or potential conflicts of interest, or the appearance of conflicts of interest, as well as outside activities that would interfere with the employee's loyalty to the employer and ability to fulfill all job responsibilities.

## 6. Prior Commitments

A "prior commitments" clause is a clause that requires the employee (or applicant) to certify that he or she is not subject to any contractual commitments (such as employment agreement with former employers) that conflict with the obligations to the new employer. Such clause is important for two reasons. As a practical matter, an employer will want to know if it will only receive the benefit of part of the employee's knowledge.

## 7. Choice of Law Provision

A "choice of law" provision is a clause within an agreement that indicates what state law will apply in the event of a dispute. The choice of law provision is particularly important in the arena of the employment relationship. Many aspects of the employment relationship are governed by state law. Choice of law provisions are presumptively valid in most jurisdictions. However, a choice of law provision may be overcome if, for example, the jurisdiction does not have a reasonable relationship to the circumstances of the employment relationship. Choice of law provisions may also be overcome if they pose a hardship that effectively eliminates an individual's substantive rights. A provision that effectively precludes an individual from having his or her day in court (for example, requiring a disabled or financially-strapped individual to travel cross-country for litigation) will not likely be enforced. Furthermore, statutory protections (such as state wage and hour or anti-discrimination laws) may set forth specific provisions for extra-territorial reach and, thus, cannot be overcome with a contractual choice of law provision.

## 8. Integration and Amendment

An integration clause states that the terms of the contract constitute the complete and exclusive statement of the terms of the agreement, and that no other agreements, oral, written, or otherwise, which are not stated in the agreement will be valid. The integration clause is particularly important in the employment setting.

The provision for amendment of the agreement is similarly important. The provision for amendment specifies how the agreement may be amended. Such provision is important in the event that the employee claims that the agreement was modified after execution.

## 9. Liquidated Damages

A "liquidated damages" provision states an amount of money the employee will have to pay if he or she breaches the contract. Liquidated damages provisions will be enforceable only if the actual damages would be extremely difficult to ascertain. Additionally, the amount of the liquidated damages must be "reasonable." Determining whether to include a liquidated damages provision is not an exact science and is, thus, a matter of balance and judgment. With little or no potential for damages, the employee will have little incentive to comply with the terms of the agreement. For example, an employee considering termination before the end of the employment relationship will balance the cost of the breach of the employment agreement with the value he or she will receive by going to work for the new employer. Similarly, an employee considering improper use of an employer's confidential information will weigh the costs of violating the contract with the value he or she will receive from exploiting that confidential information.

### 10.  Execution and Document Retention Strategies

After all the effort in drafting the agreement, the final steps are most crucial: making sure the agreement is executed and retained. Retention and accessibility of the executed employment agreement is key. Steps must be taken to ensure that executed employment agreements make their way from supervisors' desks and file drawers to the company's formal document retention system.

### 3.  CONFIDENTIALITY AND NON-COMPETE PROTECTIONS

## Ten Traps to Avoid in Drafting Enforceable Confidentiality, Non-Compete, and Non-Solicitation Agreements
David J. Carr[2]

*"The mistakes may be easy to make, but they're also fairly easy to avoid."*

It exists as a realm of time and space, restrictions and caveats, prohibitions and exceptions, tricks and traps. The Twilight Zone? No. The Non-Compete Zone. Industrial espionage and violation of non-competes happen every day in the United States; often, they happen at the same time. What prevents your clients from being victimized? What prevents you from committing malpractice when you draft a non-compete agreement? Based on my years of practice in this area, I now provide you with my thoughts on how to avoid at least 10 (in reverse order) of the most common mistakes in this area of legal document drafting. Hopefully, this aids you in drafting the most bullet-proof, non-compete/non-solicitation/trade-secret-protecting documents possible, in this ever shifting area of practice.

**Mistake 10: "What Trade Secrets?"** In the recent case of *Rogerscasey, Inc. v. Nankoff,* 2002 U.S. Dist. LEXIS 7165 (S.D.N.Y. Apr. 22, 2002) *aff'd,* 50 Fed. Appx. 461 (2d Cir. 2002), two former employees of a pension fund investment consulting firm who started a competing firm were ordered by a court to not disparage their former employer, misappropriate its confidential information, or solicit its remaining employees. However, the employees were

---

2. Copyright © 2004 the American Law Institute and David J. Carr. Reprinted with the permission of Mr. Carr and the American Law Institute-American Bar Association Continuing Professional Education. David J. Carr is a Partner in the Labor and Employment Law section of Ice Miller. Mr. Carr is a veteran labor negotiator and has handled numerous labor arbitrations, union avoidance and other collective bargaining matters. He also has substantial experience representing employers in wrongful discharge lawsuits and employment discrimination investigations, including sexual harassment situations. This article is based on a paper the author prepared for the 2002 ABA Regional Institute Labor And Employment Law, The Basics: Trade Secrets, Covenants Not To Compete And Non-Solicitation Agreements, sponsored by the ABA's Section of Employment Law. This article is not intended as legal advice.

permitted to solicit their former employer's clients. Why? The judge found that the former employees' knowledge of clients' investment philosophies and strategies did not constitute a trade secret. Solution: Wrap your key customers and their information in:

- Trade secret status;

- Contractual proprietary status (fallback position); or

- Non-solicitation status.

You want to make as many claims as possible to protect your information. Perhaps you will not win on the non-compete claims, but you may get the same relief under your state's version of the Uniform Trade Secrets Act.

**Mistake 9: "Bigger Is Better."** Overbroad covenants often get thrown out, so restrictions must be reasonable. Covenants not to compete are enforceable in most states if there is a protectable interest and if the restraint is reasonable in light of legitimate interests sought to be protected. In many states, overbroad restrictions will cause the entire non-compete to be rendered unenforceable. *Licocci v. Cardinal Assocs., Inc.,* 445 N.E.2d 556, *vacated on other grounds* (Ind. 1983); *Donahue v. Permacel Tape Corp.,* 234 Ind. 398, 127 N.E.2d 235 (Ind. 1955); *Waterfield Mortgage Co. v. O'Connor,* 172 Ind. App. 673, 361 N.E.2d 924 (1977); *see also Seymour v. Buckley,* 628 So.2d 554, 558 (Ala. 1993) (applying Indiana law pursuant to license agreement's choice-of-law clause).

The employer must be able to show that the covenant is a "clear and specific restraint" not a "general restraint of trade," which is void as against public policy, and that it is "reasonable with respect to the covenantee, the covenantor, and the public interest." *Fumo v. Medical Group of Michigan City,* 590 N.E.2d 1103, 1109 (Ind. Ct. App. 1992) (*citing McCart v. H & R Block, Inc.,* 470 N.E.2d 756, 763 (Ind. Ct. App. 1984). "The ultimate determination as to whether a covenant not to compete is reasonable is a question of law for the court." *Smart Corp v. Grider,* 650 N.E.2d 80, 83 (Ind. Ct. App. 1995) (*citing Hahn v. Drees, Perugini & Co.,* 581 N.E.2d 457, 459 (Ind. Ct. App. 1991).

**Reasonableness Factors**.  Thus, to determine whether a covenant is reasonable, courts generally consider three factors:

- Whether restraint is reasonably necessary to protect the employer's business;

- The effect of the restraint on the employee; and

- The effect of enforcement upon public interest.

*Waterfield Mortgage Co.,* supra, *Donahue,* supra.

Courts have defined reasonableness as follows:

- "'Reasonableness is to be determined from the totality of the circumstances, i.e., the interrelationship of protectible interest, time, space, and proscribed activity.'" *Fumo,* supra, 590 N.E.2d at 1109 (*citing McCart,* supra, at 764, *quoting Frederick v. Professional Bldg. Maintenance Indus.,* 168 Ind. App.

647, 344 N.E.2d 299, 302 (Ind. Ct. App. 1976)). The length of time and geographic area restrictions should be no greater than is reasonably necessary to protect the employer's legitimate business interest;

- "A covenant not to compete is unreasonable when it is broader than necessary for the protection of a legitimate business interest in terms of the geographical area, time period, and activities restricted." *Smart Corp.,* supra, at 83 (*citing Fogle v. Shah*, 539 N.E.2d 500, 503 (Ind. Ct. App. 1989));

- "A covenant not to compete must be sufficiently specific in scope to coincide with only the legitimate interests of the employer and to allow the employee a clear understanding of what conduct is prohibited." *Id.* (*citing Field v. Alexander & Alexander of Ind., Inc.*, 503 N.E.2d 627, 635 (Ind. Ct. App. 1987)).

**Geographic Scope**. Absent special circumstances, such as an employee's knowledge of trade secrets or confidential information, the geographic restriction should be no broader than the employee's—not the employer's – geographic area of work. *See, e.g., Cap Gemini Am. v. Judd*, 597 N.E.2d 1272, 1288 (Ind. Ct. App. 1992) (noncompetition agreements purporting to restrict computer analysts – former employees of a company that provides computer software programming and analytical services for clients – from competing in the three-state area of Indiana, Ohio, and Kentucky, i.e., the area served by the branch in which they worked, were unreasonable because the area was broader than the geographic scope in which the employees, individually, actually worked); *Commercial Bankers Life Ins. Co. v. Smith*, 516 N.E.2d 110, 114-15 (Ind. Ct. App. 1987) (covenant restricting competition in state of Indiana was unreasonable where employee worked primarily in northern Indiana).

**Activity Restrictions**. With respect to activity restrictions as they relate geographic restrictions, note that: "the availability of the particular specialty practiced by the [employee] is a matter to be considered by the trial court in looking at the totality of the circumstances. Where a specialist offers services uniquely or sparsely available in a specified geographical area, an injunction may be unwarranted because the movant [former employer] is unable to meet the burden of showing that the public would not be disserved." *Fumo,* supra, at 1109. (declining to find, as a matter of law, that activity restriction on practice of gastroenterology was unreasonable and void as against public policy, given "intensely contested factual issue of whether the gastroenterology services (absent [former employee's] services) offered in the proscribed area are so deficient as to expose the public to unnecessary risks").

**"Unique Competitive Advantage."** The former employer must demonstrate "that the former employee has gained a unique competitive advantage or ability to harm the employer before such employer is entitled to the protection of a noncompetition covenant." *Hahn v. Drees, Perugini & Co.*, 580 N.E.2d 457, 459 (Ind. Ct. App. 2d Dist. 1991).

**Reasonable Duration**. The duration of the covenant must not be excessive. What is or is not excessive may vary with the nature of the former employee's job and the employer's protectable interest. But a duration of several years is not necessarily unreasonable. For example, Indiana courts have generally affirmed covenants for terms of one to three years after employment ends. *See, e.g., Licocci v. Cardinal Assocs.*, supra; *4408, Inc. v. Losure*, 373 N.E.2d 899 (Ind. Ct. App. 1978). However, Indiana courts have occasionally upheld covenants for terms of five years after employment ends. *See, e.g., Rollins v. American State Bank*, 487 N.E.2d 842, 843 (Ind. Ct. App. 1986); *Miller v. Frankfort Bottle Gas*, 202 N.E.2d 395 (Ind. Ct. App. 1964); *Welcome Wagon v. Haschert*, 127 N.E.2d 103 (Ind. Ct. App. 1955); *but see Captain & Co. v. Towne*, 404 N.E.2d 1159 (Ind. Ct. App. 1980) (two-year covenant not enforceable).

**Covered Employees.** In the absence of a geographical limitation, the covenant must list a specific limited class of persons with whom contact is prohibited. *Commercial Bankers Life Ins Co. of Am. v. Smith*, supra; *Field v. Alexander & Alexander of Ind.*, 503 N.E.2d 627 (Ind. Ct. App. 1987). *See also College Life Ins Co. of Am. v. Austin*, 466 N.E.2d 738 (Ind. Ct. App. 1984) (lack of durational and geographic limitations renders covenant void as against public policy); *Ebbeskotte v. Tyler*, 142 N.E.2d 905 (Ind. Ct. App. 1957) (a covenant indefinite as to time but very narrowly limited in geographic area is enforceable). In *JAK Productions, Inc. v. Wiza*, 986 E2d 1080 (7th Cir. 1993), the Seventh Circuit strongly reaffirmed the Indiana "blue pencil" rule for noncompete clauses in employment agreements, and highlighted the importance of defining the employer's protectable customers in the employment agreement. Here, the court allowed a customer restriction to be enforced by the employer, even where the restriction required court-imposed limitations to be enforceable.

**Mistake 8: "One Size Fits All, Right?"** A post-employment restrictive covenant also must be ancillary to the main purpose of an employment or compensation agreement. *Ohio Valley Communications v. Greenwell*, 555 N.E.2d 525 (Ind. Ct. App. 1990); *Woodward Ins. v. White*, 437 N.E.2d 59 (Ind. 1982) (covenant is valid when covenant and contract have significant nexus to employment situation such as to render covenant ancillary to employment situation and necessary to protect legitimate rights of the employer). So one size does not fit all. This maxim is also jurisdictional: You should never assume that a non-compete agreement enforceable in one state will be enforceable in all states, or that your choice of law provision will be respected in all states.

**Mistake 7: "We'll Let the Court Tell Us What's Enforceable."** Blue penciling is limited in many states. Some courts refuse to rewrite contracts after the fact; and some courts will only strike language, not add new language. *See, e.g., College Life Ins. Co. of Am v. Austin*, supra (absence of temporal and area terms made covenant overbroad and court declined to rewrite covenant so as to make it reasonable); *Donahue v. Permacel Tape Corp.*, supra (court declined to enforce three-year restriction that purported to restrict competition in United States and Canada). As the Indiana Court of Appeals put it in *Smart Corp. v. Grider,* supra, at 83-84 (Ind. Ct. App. 1995):

"If the covenant as written is not reasonable, the courts may not create a reasonable restriction under the guise of interpretation," because to do so would subject the parties to an agreement they have not made.  *Licocci v. Cardinal Associates, Inc.,* supra.  However, if the covenant is clearly separated into parts and some parts are reasonable and others are not, the contract may be held divisible and the reasonable restrictions enforced.  *Id.*  In such cases, unreasonable provisions are stricken and reasonable provisions may be enforced under the blue pencil process.  *Hahn [v. Drees, Perugini & Co.* (1991), Ind. App., 581 N.E.2d 457,] 462.  Blue penciling must be restricted to applying terms which already clearly exist in the contract and the court's redaction of a contract may not result in the addition of terms that were not originally part of the contract.  *Id.*  Simply put, if practicable, unreasonable restraints are rendered reasonable by scratching out any offensive clauses to give effect to the parties' intentions.  *Seach v. Richards, Dieterle & Co.* (1982), Ind. App., 439 N.E.2d 208, 215."  *See also Licocci v. Cardinal Assocs.,* supra, at 452 (if covenant is clearly separated into parts and some parts are reasonable and others are not, contract may be held divisible and reasonable restrictions may then be enforced); *Welcome Wagon v. Haschert,* supra (court upheld five-year limitation against former employee of advertising and sales promotion business as to city in which employee had performed services, but declined to enforce restriction as to any other city in which employer was doing, or planned to do, business).

**Courts Are Not Obligated to Blue Pencil.**  But the courts are not compelled to blue pencil.  *See Frederick v. Professional Bldg. Maintenance Indus.,* 168 Ind.App. 647, 344 N.E.2d 299, 302 (Ind. Ct. App. 1976) (if restrictive covenant is unreasonable, court may not enforce reasonable restriction under guise of interpretation).  For instance, where the geographic term is too severe, the court may decline to blue pencil, even if the terms of the covenant are separable.  *South Bend Consumers Club v. United Consumers Club,* 572 F.Supp. 209 (N.D. Ind. 1983) (a franchisee's covenant not to compete for two years within 25 miles of any of franchisor's outlets was unreasonable as a matter of Indiana law and court declined to blue pencil).

**Mistake 6: "We Don't Need No Stinkin' Consideration."**  We all know about the famed barleycorn (or was it a peppercorn?) at midsummer.  Many states require independent consideration for an employment contract.  Delay in signing the non-compete after employment commenced is dangerous, because the job is often sufficient consideration; continued employment may not be enough.  The consideration can be nominal: one day's extra notice on termination, a holiday – whatever.  But there has to be something.

In most states, a covenant not to compete signed at the inception of employment provides sufficient consideration for the covenant not to compete.  *Advanced Copy Prods. v. Cool,* 363 N.E.2d 1070 (Ind. Ct. App. 1977) (provision requiring 30 days' notice of termination is sufficient consideration to support covenant not to compete).  In *Ackerman v. Kimball Int'l Inc.,* 652 N.E.2d 507 (Ind. 1995) (employer's promise in employment agreement, made nine years after employment began, to continue to employ employee at-will, and ratification of non-superseding termination agreement, made in 1994, gave consideration for afterthought covenant in employment agreement; expressly adopting and incorporating by reference portion of court of appeals opinion on this issue, contained at *Ackerman v. Kimball Int'l Inc.*, 634 N.E.2d 778, 780-81 (Ind. Ct. App. 1994)); *see also Rollins v. American State Bank*, 487 N.E.2d 842 (Ind. Ct. App. 1986). In Indiana, the promise of continued employment is currently sufficient consideration for a covenant not to compete. *Leatherman v. Management Advisors*, 448 N.E.2d 1048 (Ind. 1983).

**Mistake 5: "Who Cares Whether It's Assignable?"** What was that in law school about non-assignability of personal service contracts? With respect to non-competes, they must be assignable and assigned in the purchase agreement. Failure to assign can be disastrous.

A number of courts follow the general rule that personal service contracts, including covenants not to compete, may *not* be assigned. *Norlund v. Faust*, 675 N.E.2d 1142 (Ind. Ct. App. 1997), *clarified on other points*, 678 N.E.2d 421 (Ind. App. 1997); *SDL Enters., Inc. v. DeReamer*, 683 N.E.2d 1347, 1349 (Ind. Ct. App. 1997). However, an exception to this general rule exists when:

• The original agreement specifically allows assignment by the employer (*Peters v. Davidson*, 359 N.E.2d 556, 562 (Ind. Ct. App. 1977)); or

• The employee consents to the assignment. *Norlund*, supra, at 1151; *SDL*, supra, at 1349-50.

Nonetheless, the wise counsel will always include a "savings clause" in the non-compete. *See Dicen v. New Sisco,* 806 N.E.2d 833 (Ind. App. 2004).

**Assignment Permitted In Original Agreement.** Many courts are able to apply the first exception by merely reading the original contract. If the original contract contains language which provides that the rights and obligations under the agreement are assignable and transferable, then the non-compete agreement may be assigned without consent from the employee. *Peters*, supra, at 558. It should be noted, however, that the actual facts in *Peters* were similar to those in *Norlund*, in that the employee continued to work without objection after the assignment. *Id.* Consequently, the court probably could have also based its holding on the "consent" exception discussed below, rather than merely relying on the language of the original contract.

**Employee Consent.** In Indiana, the second exception to the general rule forbidding assignment relies more heavily on the court's discretion. A non-compete agreement may be assigned absent any language in the agreement regarding assignability if the employee subsequently consents to the assignment. *Norlund*, supra, at 1151; *SDL*, supra, at 1349-50. The court in *Norlund* held that this "consent" may arise solely from the actions of the employee. *Norlund*, supra, at 1152. The court held that an employee has consented to an assignment if:

• The employee knew of the assignment; and

• The employee knowingly continues his employment with the assignee. In *Norlund*, the court found that an employee had consented to the assignment by continuing employment with the assignee after learning that the assignment took place. *Id.*

**Mistake 4: "It's Protectable if I Say It's Protectable, Dangnabit!"** An employer can't just pluck a "protectable interest" out of thin air. It has to exist independently of the non-compete. Customer goodwill and trade secrets are legitimate protectable interests. Putting janitors under a non-compete is futile and dangerous. Most courts will not enforce a covenant not to compete unless an employer can show a protectable interest. "It is evident where the underlying protectable interest appears minimal, courts are apt to closely scrutinize the terms of the restraint." *Slisz v. Munzenreider Corp.,* 411 N.E.2d 700, 705 (Ind. Ct. App. 1980). "In Indiana, a noncompetition covenant may be valid to prevent an employee from using his employment relationship for his own benefit or for the benefit of a competitor." *Cap Gemini Am. v. Judd,* 597 N.E.2d 1272, 1288 (Ind. Ct. App. 1st Dist. 1992) (*citing Commercial Bankers Life Ins. Co. v. Smith,* 515 N.E.2d 110, 112 (Ind. Ct. App. 1987)). In Illinois, existing customers are the employer's protectable interest; however, the employee also has a protectable interest in his or her pre-existing relationships. *See Lawrence & Allen, Inc. v. Cambridge Human Resource Group, Inc.,* 685 N.E.2d 434, 441 (Ill. Ct. App. 1997).

**Typical Protectable Interests.** Covenants have been enforced to protect an employer's confidential information, customer lists, goodwill, investment in special training or techniques, and actual solicitation of customers. *See, e.g, In re Uniservices,* 517 F.2d 492 (7th Cir. 1975) (former employer has no protectable interest in customer lists and information that can be obtained by lawful surveillance, but information on customer requirements, habits, and preferences may be confidential and, thus, a protectable interest); *McCart v. H & R Block, Inc.,* 470 N.E.2d 756 (Ind. Ct. App. 1984); *Captain & Co. v. Towne,* 404 N.E.2d 1159 (Ind. Ct. App. 1980); *Welcome Wagon v. Haschert,* supra. As stated in *Hahn,* supra, at 460:

> "[An employer is] entitled to protect the 'good will' of its business, which includes such things as 'names and addresses and requirements of customers and the advantage acquired through representative contact....' *Donahue [v. Permacel Tape Corp.,* 234 Ind. 398, 127 N.E.2d 235, 240, (1955)]. Included also in [the former employer's] protectable good will interest is the right, via a proper covenant not to compete, to restrict a former employee from enticing away the employer's old customers. *Id.* at 241; *see also Licocci [v. Cardinal Assocs.,* 445 N.E.2d 556, 563 (Ind. 1983).]"

Generally, an employer has no protectable interest in restricting contact with its past customers or clients. *Hahn,* supra, at 461. Although *Seach v. Richards, Dieterle & Co.,* 439 N.E.2d 208 (Ind. Ct. App. 1982), may be read to create a narrow exception to the general prohibition against restricting contact with a former employer's past clients, the *Seach* court itself expressed skepticism of the practice of restraining former employees from doing business with past customers of their employers. *Hahn,* supra, at 461. The *Seach* court stated:

> "Such a limitation [regarding when past clients with whom contact is prohibited may have been customers of the employer] *might* take the

form of proscribing contact with customers who have done business with the employer within one year prior to the employee's termination of employment. Any limitation would necessarily have to reflect the nature of the business involved in setting what is a reasonable time limit, and would also have to be formulated to protect and accommodate the valuable interests of the employer, such as customer lists and in-house knowledge." *Seach,* supra, at 214 n.4 (citation omitted); *Hahn, supra,* at 461 n.4. For purposes of this opinion, and generally, a "present" client is a client that did business with [the employer] during [the employee's] employment...."

*Hahn, supra,* at 460 n.3. *See also Smart Corp v. Grider*, supra, at 83 ("A former employer has a legitimate business interest in restricting its former employees from enticing away the employer's old customers"), citing *Hahn*, 581 N.E.2d at 460).

**No Protectable Interest In Employee's General Knowledge.** However, an employer has no protectable interest in the general knowledge, information, and skills gained by an employee in the course of his or her employment. *Brunner v. Hand Indus.*, 603 N.E.2d 157 (Ind. Ct. App. 1992) (metal polisher; clause in employment contract requiring employee to repay costs of training, on basis of sliding scale increasing from $2,200 for less than two months' work to $20,000 for 24-36 months' work, is unreasonable anticompetitive restraint rather than attempt to recoup legitimate training expenses; sliding scale could have made employees liable for amounts greater than all wages they had received from employer).

In *Brunner*, the defendant employee was a polisher of orthopedic products for plaintiff employer. As a condition of employment the employee was required to execute a noncompete agreement. The agreement stipulated that if he were to take employment with a competing business, he would have to reimburse the employer, ostensibly for the investment in his training, pursuant to a payment schedule based on length of service with the employer. The employee left the employer's service and the employer attempted to enforce the agreement. The court of appeals held that the agreement unreasonably restricted the protectable interests of the employee and was thus unenforceable. The court noted that the record did not disclose that the employee had taken customer lists, confidential information, or other trade secrets with him. In addition, although the agreement specified no definite duration of employment, the employer was attempting to impose a substantial burden on the employee for his acquisition of "general knowledge and skills." The final straw seemed to be the fact that, under the reimbursement scheme, it was possible for a departing employee to be liable for more than all of the wages he received during employment.

**Trade Secrets.** Courts will also enforce a covenant to protect a "trade secret" as that term is defined by the Uniform Trade Secrets Act, Ind. Code § 24-2-3-2 (2004). *Ackerman v. Kimball Int'l, Inc.*, supra. However, in 1995, the state supreme court in *Ackerman*, "wr[o]te to clarify that otherwise unenforceable covenants not to compete do not automatically become enforceable solely because an employee is in possession of trade secrets." *Id.* at 508. Information that is readily or easily available is not a trade secret under the Act. *College Life Ins. Co. of Am. v. Austin*, supra.

**Blacklisting/Tortious Interference Claims.** Many states will look very seriously at an employer's misuse of a non-compete provision in terms of potential counterclaims *against the employer!* In *Bridgestone/Firestone v. Lockhart*, 5 F.Supp.2d 667 (S.D. Ind. 1998), a federal district court not only refused to find for the employer on the employer's attempted enforcement of a non-compete, it found for the employee on the employee's claim against the employer for alleged "blacklisting" – using the non-compete as a means of interfering with the employee's future employment opportunities. In so doing, the court awarded the employee $50,000 in attorneys' fees, and seriously considered awarding punitive damages.

*Blacklisting can be a highly illegal*

Subsequent decisions have limited these "blacklisting" claims. *Burk v. Heritage Food Service Equipment*, 737 N.E.2d 803 (Ind. Ct. App. 2000). ("Blacklisting" may not be asserted by the employee if the employee voluntarily resigned from employment.) Nonetheless, tortious interference claims appear viable for many situations where an employer engages in overzealous pursuit of non-compete enforcement.

**Mistake 3: "I'm Not Paying an Ex-employee Not to Compete."** Courts show far more generosity to employers, and their non-compete provisions, when they are actually paying ex-employees not to compete. "In-term" covenants may be much broader in scope. Any issue of bad faith by the employer will hurt the enforcement of the covenant, and may create claims for breach of the duty of good faith and fair dealing. *See Weiser v. Godby Bros.,* 659 N.E.2d 237 (Ind. Ct. App. 1995). Consider adding language to your non-compete paying the employee some percentage of base salary to serve as a consultant for one year after the end of employment, with the additional caveat that no competing conduct will occur by the employee anywhere in the world during that period.

**Mistake 2: "Why Would I Want to Talk to an Employee Who Has Quit?"** There are a few good answers to this:

- To make sure they know their non-compete obligations;

- To make them commit to paper that they haven't taken anything; and

- To show you care about trade secrets.

**Mistake 1: "Warranties Are for Used Cars."** This notion is wrong on quite a few levels, but its potential for mischief with respect to non-competes is huge. Always ask questions, and be sure to get the employee's signature. You don't want to find something in the trunk of the employee's car after discovery has commenced. Key language:

*Employee hereby warrants and represents as follows:*

*a. That the execution of the Agreement and the discharge of Employee's obligations hereunder will not breach or conflict with any other contract, agreement, or understanding between Employee and any other party or parties.*

*b. Employee has ideas, information and know-how relating to the type of business conducted by SmartCo., and Employee's disclosure of such ideas, information and know-how to SmartCo. will not conflict with or violate the rights of any third party or parties.*

*I hereby affirm and attest that I have also returned, or will return by _____, all copies of any of the above listed items. I understand that while I have the right to use in any future employment any general knowledge of the trade/industry obtained as a result of my employment with SmartCo., I must at all times conform my conduct to the requirements of the applicable trade secrets law, and my SmartCo. non-compete obligations.*

*As required by the law of trade secrets, I will not misappropriate (e.g., use or disclose to any third party) any trade secret of SmartCo. I recognize that the penalties for a trade secret violation may include disgorgement of profits, payment of royalties, compensatory damages, punitive damages, and attorneys fees. I understand that I can ask SmartCo. to render an opinion as to whether SmartCo. considers certain knowledge to be a trade secret, if such a question should arise.*

**CONCLUSION.** Armed with these 10 tips, go forth and serve your clients well. However, beware that this area of law remains volatile, fluid, and oft-litigated. Admonish clients to review and update their agreements at least every two years.

## PROBLEM 11-A AND 11-B

**11-A.** Larry Smyth is the primary owner and CEO of a growing computer hardware distribution company. The company has 120 employees, which includes 10 managers. Larry feels that there is a compelling need to boost employee morale. He believes the problem is at the top. Seven of his 10 managers are "just logging time." Most employees are paid by the hour. The managers are all salaried. The company has sporadically paid bonuses in the past, but bonuses are not something any employee expects.

Larry has decided to adopt a cash bonus program for his 10 managers, in hopes that the plan will fire up the managers to get the place hopping. He has decided to divide 25 percent of the pre-tax income of the business among the 10 managers in equal shares each year. The bonuses will be paid within two weeks of the completion of the year-end financials.

Larry has asked you to draft a bonus plan document that can be reviewed and approved by the other two shareholders (both of whom serve on the Board) and the managers. He has also asked you to share your thoughts on his plan. What do you think of Larry's plan? Why might it be a waste of money? How might it backfire and create bigger morale problems? Is it oversimplified? What are the components of an effective cash bonus plan that Larry should consider? Is this something that a lawyer should even be concerned about? Why do you think Larry would ask your opinion?

**11-B.** Duke Longer, the CEO of Waldon Technologies, has just completed a negotiation to hire Jane Smith, a talented software designer. Jane will relocate from Boston to Seattle. Jane's salary will be high by Waldon's standards. Duke wants to ensure that Jane is "tied to the company for at least three years" but that the company "can get out of the deal after three years." Duke also wants to ensure that everything that Jane creates while working for the company will remain the exclusive property of the company.

Jane wants assurance that her high salary will be protected for the long-term. Her move from her hometown of Boston and her family is viewed as a sacrifice that is justified only by the promise of "big bucks" for the long-term. Plus, Jane routinely creates software on her off hours that has nothing to do with her job. She wants to make it clear that she will own all rights to such off-hour creations.

What middle-ground solutions should the attorneys for Waldon and Jane explore in putting together the employment agreement?

## B.  DEFERRED COMPENSATION: SERPs

### 1. THE RETIREMENT CHALLENGE

Many executives rank retirement planning as their number one financial concern. They want to know that they are going to "have enough" and are not going to outlive their financial resources. For many executives, the solution is a special supplemental executive retirement plan (SERP) provided by their employer. The company's regular qualified retirement plan is too watered down to do the job. An old-fashioned savings program is too tough, and social security, even if available, is hopelessly inadequate.

For decades companies have recognized the value of individually-tailored retirement arrangements for their key executives. These arrangements are routinely used to recruit and retain valuable executives. The substantial benefits that accrue under the plan over time create a powerful incentive for the executive to toe the line and not even consider flirting with the competition.

A key factor in many SERPs is life insurance. Often, it is the life insurance that breathes life into the SERP, hedges the financial risks for the company, and makes the whole effort "doable." The question is often asked: Why life insurance as opposed to some other investment? The answer lies in the three "tax-frees" of life insurance: the tax-free death benefit, the tax-free inside buildup within the policy, and the tax-free loan withdrawal privileges.

### 2.  A SERP EXAMPLE

Peter is 55 years of age. He is the chief executive officer of a growing manufacturing company and has served in that capacity for five years. The company is privately owned, and Peter has no hope of ever receiving any equity. The stockholders consider Peter indispensable to the ongoing success of the company and want to ensure that he remains in his position for at least another 10 years. They want to bind him to the business. Peter is concerned about his retirement needs and has voiced that concern to the owners.

A deal has been worked out to provide Peter a special supplemental retirement benefit that will commence on his retirement at age 65. The benefit, equal to 70 percent of Peter's highest average salary during any remaining three-year period of his employment with the company, will be paid monthly so long as Peter or his wife is living. Peter estimates that the annual benefit should be at least $250,000 if he continues to receive salary increases as he has in the past. Absent death or disability, Peter must remain with the company to age 65 in order to receive the benefit. If he dies or becomes disabled before age 65, the benefit will commence on the second month following his death or permanent disability.

The plan accomplishes the objectives of both parties. The company and its owners are assured of Peter's continued service and loyalty, and Peter's retirement concerns are put to rest. Following are brief reviews of the tax traps, structural options, collateral consequences, and funding alternatives that often need to be considered in the planning process for such a plan.

### 3. SERP TAX TRAPS

The plan for Peter is based on the premise that no income taxes will need to be paid on any SERP benefits accrued under the plan until the benefits are actually paid to Peter or his wife. As a deferred compensation plan, a SERP is subject to the tax traps that need to be carefully watched whenever income is deferred.

### a. The Constructive Receipt Trap

The first tax trap is the constructive receipt doctrine. Income is taxable in the year in which it is "received by the taxpayer."[3] If the constructive receipt doctrine applies to a SERP, the executive will be in the unfavorable position of having to pay taxes on money that he or she has not received. The mere deferral of the actual receipt of income will not guarantee deferral for tax purposes because the phrase "received by the taxpayer" encompasses "constructive receipt" as well as actual receipt of income.[4] Income is constructively received by a taxpayer when it is "credited to his account, set apart for him, or otherwise made available so that he may draw upon it at any time, or so that he could have drawn upon it during the taxable year if notice of intention to withdraw had been given."[5]

The constructive receipt trap can be an issue in those situations (unlike Peter's) where an executive elects to defer the receipt of compensation in order to fund a SERP benefit. The key is such situations is to ensure that the executive makes the election to defer the income before the services are rendered and the compensation is earned.[6] The constructive receipt doctrine may also become a problem if the executive at any point in time is given the unrestricted right to draw money out of the plan.[7]

---

3. I.R.C. § 451(a).
4. Reg. § 1.451-1(a).
5. Reg. § 1.451-2(a).
6. Rev. Proc. 71-19, 1971-1 C.B. 698, amplified Rev. Proc. 92-65, 1992 C.B. 428; I.R.C. 409A(a)(4)(B)(i).
7. Reg. § 1.451-2(a). See Martin v. Commissioner, 96 T.C. 814 (1991) for a discussion of the facts that

### b. The Economic Benefit Trap

The second trap is the economic benefit doctrine. Even if the employee is not deemed to have constructively received the income, the employee's opportunity to defer taxation may be derailed if he or she receives an economic benefit from the deferred amount that is the equivalent of cash.[8]

The doctrine usually surfaces when the employer's obligation to pay the deferred compensation is somehow "funded" and the employee acquires an interest in the funding vehicle. Examples include an escrow account for the executive, a trust vehicle to fund benefits for an executive,[9] an annuity contract naming the executive as an owner,[10] and a life insurance policy that guarantees the executive the cash value of the policy in the event of employment termination.[11]

In structuring any deferred compensation arrangement, the planner needs to keep both the constructive receipt doctrine and the economic benefit doctrine in mind. The economic benefit doctrine is clearly the more nebulous of the two and the one that often causes the greatest concern. A red flag should go up whenever an employee (1) receives a substantial economic or financial benefit from a non-qualified funding vehicle, particularly if the benefit is not forfeitable; (2) has the ability to assign his or her rights under that funding vehicle to an outside third party; or (3) has any other right or capacity to convert his or her rights under the funding vehicle to cash.

### c. The Section 83 Trap

The third trap is found in Section 83 of the Internal Revenue Code. It's similar to the economic benefit trap. Section 83 provides that, when property is transferred to an employee as compensation for services, the employee is taxed on the fair market value of the property at the time it is received if the property is transferable or is not subject to a substantial risk of forfeiture.[12] If the property is subject to a substantial risk of forfeiture, as is the case when the employee's rights to the property are contingent upon the employee remaining in the service of the employer, no tax will be incurred until that risk of forfeiture lapses or the property becomes transferable.

As regards a deferred compensation plan such as a SERP, the positive news is that the regulations under Section 83 provide that an unsecured and unfunded promise of an employer to pay deferred compensation does not constitute "property" for purposes of Section 83.[13] If the participant receives nothing more than the unsecured contractual promise of the company, there is no Section 83 problem. In all other cases where the participant is offered something extra, it is

impact such an application of the constructive receipt doctrine.

8. Rev. Rule 60-31, 1960-1 C.B. 174 (Example 4); Sproull v. Commissioner, 16 T.C. 244 (1951), affirmed per curiam 194 F.2d 541 (6th Cir. 1952); Rev. Rule 62-74, 1962-1 C.B. 68; Commissioner v. Smith, 324 U.S. 177 (1945).

9. Sproull v. Commissioner, 16 T.C. 244 (1951), affirmed per curiam 194 F.2d 541 (6th Cir. 1952); Jacuzzi v. Commissioner, 61 T.C. 262 (1973).

10. Brodie v. Commissioner, 1 T.C. 275 (1942).

11. See, for example, Frost v. Commissioner, 52 T.C. 89 (1969).

12. I.R.C. § 83(a).

13. Reg. § 1.83-3(e).

necessary to take a hard look to see whether Section 83 has been triggered.

Plus, as described below, section 409A has now breathed new life into Section 83 when an offshore funding vehicle or an employer financial health trigger is used in connection with a nonqualified deferred compensation arrangement.[14] If Section 83 applies and the deferred amounts are not subject to a substantial risk of forfeiture, the employee will be hit with a current tax.

### d. The Reasonable Compensation Trap

The fourth trap is the old "reasonable compensation" requirement of Section 162. This trap focuses on the tax treatment to the company, not the participant. The company wants to secure a deduction when the deferred compensation is paid to the employee. If the compensation is being paid to a shareholder/employee and is determined to be excessive within the meaning of Section 162, the company will lose its deduction.[15] The result is a double tax. Reasonableness is based on the facts and circumstances that exist at the time the contract is made, not those that exist when the contract is called into question.[16] For planning purposes, the challenge in any potentially troublesome situation is to carefully document the facts and circumstances that support a "reasonableness" determination at the time the plan is adopted by the company so that, if required, a sound case can be made at a later date.

### e. The 409A Traps

As deferred compensation tax traps go, the newest and toughest kid on the block is section 409A,[17] which was added by the America Jobs Creation Act of 2004. This section imposes specific statutory requirements that every nonqualified deferred compensation plan must meet. It does not replace the traps described above; it adds to them.[18] The 409A statutory requirements are not unduly burdensome in most normal situations; they are primarily designed to cause problems for those who play on the outer limits of the other traps. But they have real teeth. If a Section 409A requirement is violated, the participant is immediately taxed on all deferred amounts that are not subject to a substantial risk of forfeiture, plus he or she gets hit with an interest charge calculated at a rate one percent above the normal underpayment rate *and an extra 20 percent tax* on the deferred amount included in income.[19] Section 409A is not a "no harm, no foul" statute. It can hurt. Here are brief descriptions of some of the key Section 409A requirements:[20]

- Amounts deferred under the plan may not be distributed[21] before the participant's separation from service,[22] the participant's disability,[23] the

---

14. I.R.C. § 409A(b).

15. Reg. § 1.162-7(b)(1).

16. Reg. § 1.162-7(b)(3).

17. I.R.C. § 409A.

18. I.R.C. § 409A(c).

19. I.R.C. § 409A(a)(1).

20. Extensive regulations to Section 409A were finalized in 2007. Reg. § 1.409A.

21. I.R.C. § 409A(2).

22. For a "specified employee," the separation from service requirement is not met if a payment is made before the date which is six months after the separation of service. A "specified employee" is a key employee (as defined in section 416(i) without regard to paragraph (5)) of a corporation any stock of which is publicly

participant's death, the specified time or payment schedule in the plan, a change in the ownership or control of the corporate employer or a substantial portion of the assets of the corporate employer,[24] or the occurrence of an unforeseeable emergency.[25] What is not permitted is fuzzy payout language or schedules designed to give executives discretion over when they can get the deferred amounts.

- The plan may not permit the acceleration of the time or schedule for the payment of benefits, except as provided by regulations.[26]

- The plan may not give an employee an election to defer compensation earned during a taxable year after that year begins. The election must be made by the close of the preceding taxable year.[27] There are two exceptions. If it's the employee's first year in the plan, the election may be made within 30 days after the employee becomes eligible, but the election may relate only to services performed after the election.[28] Also, for performance-based bonuses that are based on services rendered over a period of at least 12 months, the deferral election may be made no later than 6 months before the end of the period.[29]

- The plan may not give an employee an election to further delay the payment of benefits under the plan unless the plan requires that (i) any such election not take effect until at least 12 months after it is made, (ii) the extended deferral period is not less than five years (except in the case of death, disability and unforeseeable emergency), and (iii) any additional delay in an election relating to a specified time or fixed payment schedule provision must be made at least 12 months before the first scheduled payment under such provision.[30]

*Keynote*

- Assets held outside the United States and set aside (directly or indirectly) to pay benefits under a deferred compensation plan will be considered property under Section 83, thus triggering a recognition of taxable income for the employees, plus the 409A interest charge and the 409A extra 20 percent tax.[31] Lesson: Do not earmark any assets that are held in offshore accounts as having anything to do with a deferred compensation plan.

- Employer assets that become restricted to the provisions of a deferred

---

traded. I.R.C. § 409A(a)(2)(B); Reg. § 1.409A-1(i)(1).

23. Disability generally requires a condition that can be expected to result in death or can be expected to last for at least 12 continuous months and that prevents any "substantial gainful activity" or that entitles the participant to receive income replacement benefits for not less than three months under an accident and health plan covering employees of the company. I.R.C. § 409A(a)(2)(C); Reg. § 1.409A-3(i)(4)(i).

24. See Reg. § 1.409A-3(i)(5).

25. An "unforeseeable emergency" means a severe financial hardship resulting from (i) an illness or accident of the employee, a spouse or a dependant, (ii) a loss of property due to casualty, or (iii) similar extraordinary and unforeseen circumstances beyond the control of the employee. I.R.C. § 409A(a)(2)(B)(ii); Reg. § 1.409A-3(i)(3)(i).

26. I.R.C. § 409A(a)(3). The Regulations provide that accelerated payments may be permitted to fulfill a domestic relations order, to pay income taxes due upon a vesting event under a plan subject to section 457(f), and to pay FICA taxes on compensation deferred under the plan. Reg. § 1.409A-3(i)(4).

27. I.R.C. § 409A(a)(4)(B)(i); Reg. § 1.409A-2(a)(3).

28. I.R.C. § 409A(a)(4)(B)(ii); Reg. § 1.409A-2(a)(7).

29. I.R.C. § 409A(a)(4)(B)(iii). Reg. § 1.409A-2(a)(8). At a minimum, the bonus must be contingent on performance criteria and may not be substantially certain at time of deferral. Reg. § 1.409A-1(e)(1).

30. I.R.C. § 409A(a)(4)(C); Reg. § 1.409A-2(b).

31. I.R.C. § 409A(b)(1),(3),(4).

compensation plan as a result of a change in the employer's financial health will be considered property under Section 83, thus triggering a recognition of taxable income for the employees, plus the 409A interest charge and the 409A extra 20 percent tax.[32] Lesson: Don't include in the plan any provision dealing with a change in the employer's financial health.

- If the company maintains a single-employer defined benefit plan that has not been adequately funded (i.e., is considered "at risk" within the meaning of Section 430(i)), any assets set aside for the payment of deferred compensation benefits to the company's chief executive officer, the company's four highest paid officers, or any individual subject to Section 16(a) of the Securities Exchange Act of 1934 will be treated as property taxable under Section 83.[33]

### 4. STRUCTURAL BASICS AND COLLATERAL CONSEQUENCES

A SERP is a private contract between the company and the executive. The primary components of the contract are: (1) the formula or basis for determining the amount of the SERP retirement payments; (2) the circumstances under which the SERP payments will be paid or not paid; and (3) the method of payment, such as a lump-sum cash-out, monthly installments, a life annuity, or some combination of these. The contract may contain other provisions based on the circumstances and the purpose of the SERP. The company gets no tax deduction until the amounts are actually paid to the executive, and the executive realizes no taxable income until the benefits are received.

**a. Plan Early.** The key to preserving the tax deductibility of the benefit payments under a SERP, particularly when the employee is also an owner of the business, is to establish the SERP many years prior to the date of retirement. If a SERP is established just prior to retirement, the IRS may challenge the company's deduction for the payments on the ground that they represent unreasonable compensation for a short period. If the employee is a stockholder, there is always the risk that the payments will be considered dividends or buy-out payments rather than true retirement benefits. In such a situation, the key is to make sure that the retirement benefit accrues over a sufficient number of years such that it is fair and reasonable compensation for services rendered during the years of accrual.

**b. Benefit Formula.** The company has flexibility in structuring the benefit accrual formula under the contract. The only limitation in structuring the arrangement is that it be reasonable. The formula may accrue a fixed sum each year, may be based on a defined monthly benefit at retirement, may be adjusted for inflation, may be based on accumulated years of service, or may consider any other factors that are reasonable. The retirement benefit accrual should be prospective, not retroactive. Typically a SERP does not involve deferral elections by the executive; it just specifies the benefits that will be paid by the company and the conditions of payment. From a tax standpoint, the safest approach is to structure the SERP so that the supplemental retirement benefit accrues after the date the agreement is executed. And, as previously noted, the amount of the

---

32. I.R.C. § 409A(b)(2),(3),(4).
33. I.R.C. § 409A(b)(3).

accrued benefit under the plan each year plus the amount of the current compensation must, in combination, constitute reasonable compensation for services rendered during the period.

**c. Elective Deferrals**. The SERP benefit can be structured as an elective benefit, similar to a 401(k) plan. With this approach, the employee is given the right each year to elect to defer an amount of compensation that will be paid out at retirement or termination of employment. Alternatively, the SERP can be structured as an add-on, employer-provided benefit that doesn't involve any employee election. If the elective approach is used, the key is to make sure that the deferral election is in writing and that the election to defer compensation for any given taxable year is made prior to the beginning of that year. If the election to defer compensation earned during a given year is made after the year begins, the employee will be taxed currently on the deferred amount and will be subject to the interest and extra 20 percent tax provision of Section 409A – a disaster.

**d. Method of Payout**. Another issue that must be addressed in the SERP agreement is the method of paying out the benefit. Typically the payout form is described in terms of a monthly payment for life or a term of years. Often the SERP provides for a lump-sum payment upon the death of the employee prior to retirement. The key is to ensure that the payout options are definitive enough to conform to the permissible payout options of Section 409A. Another important feature of many SERPs is a provision that gives the company the option to cash out any accrued benefits if the company is sold. This provision will help the company bail out proceeds received from the sale with tax-deductible dollars. Also, such a cash-out feature will benefit the purchaser who has no interest in picking up the SERP liability or perpetuating the SERP plan. A SERP can be structured to impose golden handcuffs on key employees. There are no restrictions on conditions or forfeiture limitations. The plan may provide that the benefits are reduced or eliminated if a key employee signs on with a competitor or voluntarily departs before retirement.

**e. Regulatory Requirements**. As with other nonqualified deferred compensation plans, SERPs are not subject to the same type of IRS and Department of Labor regulatory requirements that plague qualified retirement plans. A SERP needs to steer clear of any Section 409A foul-ups and the other tax traps. ERISA regulations are no big deal so long as the benefits are unfunded at all times and are made available only to a select group of highly compensated employees.

**f. Funding**. The SERP should be an unfunded obligation of the company in order to qualify for the ERISA exemption and avoid an early tax hit to the employee. This means that the company cannot set aside funds in a separate trust that is legally earmarked for the benefit of the SERP participants and is beyond the reach of the company's creditors. Although legal funding is taboo, the company can still prepare for the day when the SERP payments will commence. This is done by establishing an informal funding program. The company sets aside cash or other property to cover its future payment obligations to the executive. The key is that the assets set aside must continue to be owned by the company and be subject to the claims of the company's creditors.

**g. FICA and Social Security**. The SERP offers a potential FICA benefit. SERP benefits are considered earned for FICA purposes when the benefit is accrued and no longer subject to a substantial risk of forfeiture.[34] So, for example, if an executive accrues a $70,000 annual SERP benefit and is already receiving cash compensation in excess of the social security taxable wage base, the additional $70,000 of SERP accrual does not increase the amount of non-medical FICA taxes either for the executive or the corporation. And since the SERP benefit was potentially subject to non-medical FICA taxes when accrued, no non-medical FICA taxes are due when the SERP benefit is paid. The other social security issue is whether the SERP benefits, when paid, will reduce social security benefits. Fortunately, SERP benefits are counted as earned income when accrued, not when paid, for purposes of determining the benefit offset. So the receipt of the SERP benefit will not reduce social security benefits if the SERP recipient is otherwise eligible.

**h. Impact on Qualified Retirement Benefits**. Another aspect of a SERP that has to be kept in mind is its potential impact on qualified retirement plan benefits. If an executive's current income is less than it would be if a SERP benefit were not being accrued, this lower income level may reduce the amount that is being accrued for the executive under the company's qualified retirement plan. It depends on the benefit accrual formula of the qualified plan.

**i. Financial Statement Impact**. A factor to consider in designing a SERP is the effect it will have on the company's financial statements. Since the accrued SERP benefit is a liability of the company, it must show up on the books as a liability. Care will need to be taken to make sure that the SERP liability does not cause the company to violate any loan-to-net-worth ratios or other covenants in loan agreements that are tied to the company's book net worth. Loan agreements should be reviewed and possibly revised to avoid this result.

The foregoing are some of the basic factors to consider in structuring a SERP. Since the SERP offers a nonqualified benefit through a private contract between the employee and the company, there is considerable flexibility in structuring the terms to meet important objectives.

## 5. THE NO-FUND FUNDING OPTIONS

Let's return to the indispensable executive, Peter, in the above example. Peter understands that the supplemental retirement benefit he has worked out with the company is a special nonqualified benefit designed specifically for him. He further understands that the company's payment obligation is a general unsecured liability of the company. His payment rights are no better than those of a general, unsecured creditor of the company. Finally, Peter understands that if the company takes any steps to formally fund the benefit by legally earmarking a pot of money for him, the odds are that he will be taxed currently on the amount of the accrued benefit. Peter likes the idea of knowing that he will not have to pay any taxes under the program until he begins receiving benefits at age 65.

---

34. I.R.C. § 3121(v)(2)(A).

With all this understood, Peter would like to have the company take action to start informally funding the benefit. He realizes that the benefit could represent a significant liability of the company by the time he reaches age 65. He is concerned that, as he grows older, the owners may become nervous about the size of that liability and may try to renegotiate the liability or take some other action that could jeopardize his right to receive the promised benefit. Peter figures that the best way to head off any future problem is for the company to start preparing for the day when it will have to write his retirement checks.

### a. Company-Owned Insurance Funding

One option for funding the benefit is a high-cash-value life insurance contract owned by the company. The company would be both the owner and the beneficiary of the policy. Substantial premium payments would be made on the policy for the next 10 years. The earnings within the policy would accumulate on a tax-deferred basis. When Peter reaches age 65, there would be a substantial cash value in the policy that would offset, at least in part, the company's liability to Peter. The company could commence a program of borrowing from the policy the after-tax cost of the retirement payment that would be due Peter. The company's interest deduction on such borrowings would be limited.[35] When Peter dies, the company would receive a tax-free death benefit that would reimburse the company for all or a substantial portion of its payments to Peter under the program. Peter would have the comfort of knowing that the company has affirmatively taken steps to fund the program for his benefit. Although the policy would internally be tied to Peter's agreement, he would have no legal rights to the policy.

**Illustration A: Corporate Owned Insurance Funding**

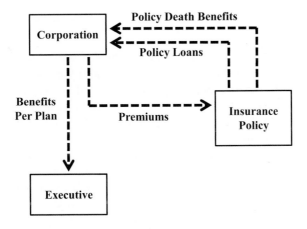

---

35. I.R.C. § 264(e)(1) limits interest deductions on indebtedness against policies insuring the lives of key employees to interest charges on $50,000 of such indebtedness.

## b. Rabbi Trust Option

A second option would be a "Rabbi" trust. The Rabbi trust is an irrevocable trust established by the company. The company would make periodic contributions to the trust that would be invested by the trustee. The trustee of the trust would be authorized to make investments and to use the assets of the trust for only two purposes. First, the assets could be used to pay Peter's benefit under his SERP. Second, the assets could be used to pay claims of the creditors of the company. Although the Rabbi trust would lock up funds for Peter's retirement benefit, it would not protect those funds from claims of the company's creditors. If the company were to experience serious financial problems, Peter's benefit might be lost.

**Illustration B: Rabbi Trust Option**

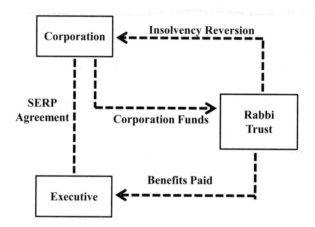

The value of the Rabbi trust is that it provides some protection to Peter while preserving the tax deferral. The trust precludes the company from using trust assets to finance other corporate priorities. For ruling purposes, the IRS has imposed a number of requirements in order for a Rabbi trust to qualify: (1) trust assets must be held for the sole purpose of paying benefits under the plan, except the assets may revert to the company if the company becomes bankrupt or insolvent; (2) the company's management must have an express duty to notify the trustee of the company's bankruptcy or insolvency; (3) if the trustee receives such a notice, the trustee must stop all payments from the trust and hold the assets until directed to make payments by appropriate court order; (4) state law must not grant Peter any priority rights to the amounts held in the trust; (5) the trust cannot be funded with securities of the company; and (5) the trust may not contain an insolvency trigger or any other provision that might frustrate the rights of other creditors of the company.[36] In addition, Section 409A prohibits use of a Rabbi trust that holds assets outside the United States or that springs into

Keynote

---

36. Rev. Proc. 92-64, 1992-2 C.B. 422.

existence or becomes subject to new restrictions upon a change in the company's financial health.[37]

The bottom line is that the Rabbi trust strategy may provide Peter with some protection in the event of a change in control, a change in management, or a change in the company's desire to pay the benefit.

### c. Rabbi-Owned Insurance Option

A third option is to combine the life insurance with the Rabbi trust. Here the trust is both the owner and the beneficiary of the policy that insures Peter's life. The trust makes all the premium payments with the amounts contributed to the trust by the company. The earnings in the policy accumulate on a tax-deferred basis. When Peter reaches age 65, there will be a substantial cash value in the policy that will be owned by the trust and used to fund Peter's benefits. The company could commence a program of borrowing from the policy to use such borrowings and other trust assets to make the retirement payments to Peter. When Peter dies, the trust would receive a tax-free death benefit that would cover all amounts due Peter's estate or spouse following his passing under the terms of the plan and potentially allow the company to recover a substantial portion of its payments to the trust. In this situation, Peter would have the added comfort of knowing that the company would not own and control the policy, so there would be no risk of the company choosing to use the policy to help fund some other corporate priority. The Rabbi trust would provide these added protections with respect to the policy.

### Illustration C: Rabbi Owned Insurance Option

### d. The Split-Dollar SERP

As Peter studies the insurance options for his SERP, he may decide that he would like to structure the insurance program to provide his family with an

---

37. I.R.C. § 409A(b)(1) & (2).

insured death benefit and to save substantial estate taxes. He proposes that the company fund the SERP with a split-dollar insurance program.

A split-dollar insurance contract is entered into between Peter and the company as part of the SERP agreement. The contract provides that the company is entitled to receive the cash value benefit under the policy, and Peter is entitled to receive the excess death benefit under the policy. The company is the owner of the policy, and Peter's rights under the split-dollar agreement are evidenced by an endorsement on the policy. If Peter's only right under the policy is a portion of the death benefit, the endorsement split dollar arrangement itself will not be considered a deferred compensation arrangement subject to Section 409A.[38] As the policy owner, the company has the right to borrow against the cash value to fund the after-tax cost of payments under the SERP. The contract is structured to have the company pay the entire premium. Peter must recognize as taxable income each year the value of the death benefit that he is provided, determined pursuant to a schedule published by the IRS. Peter transfers his rights in the policy to an irrevocable life insurance trust established for the benefit of his family. The value of the death benefit taxable to Peter each year is also deemed a gift from Peter to the trust.

### Illustration D: Split Dollar Insurance SERP

What has Peter accomplished with this structure? From Peter's perspective, the one negative is that he is going to have a current tax hit each year. Usually this tax hit is minimal, although it will grow each year. Also, the company gets a corresponding tax deduction, and it may choose to use the tax benefit from the deduction each year to fund Peter's tax hit with a grossed-up bonus. The trade-offs for the annual tax burden are a few significant benefits for Peter. First, the split-dollar agreement obligates the company to fund the insurance premium each year. Peter has more than a SERP agreement that he hopes the company will

---

38. See IRS notice 2007-34, which specifically discusses the impact of Section 409A on split-dollar arrangements.

informally fund with insurance each year; he has a contractual promise that the insurance will be funded.  Second, he has the assurance that, if he dies, the death benefit under the policy (to the extent it exceeds the cash value) will immediately be paid to his family.  This is because the family trust owns that death benefit.  Peter does not have to worry about the company collecting the death benefit and then deciding to pay his family out over time.  Finally, the structure permits the family to receive the death benefit free of income and estate taxes, assuming the trust's rights in the proceeds are established at least three years before Peter's death.  In contrast, if the company collects the death benefit and makes payments under the SERP contract, the payments are subject to estate taxes and to income taxes as income in respect of a decedent.[39]

How does the structure stack up for the company?  The structure contractually obligates the company to fund the insurance.  In return, the company is relieved of any liability under the SERP at the death of Peter, whether that death is pre-or post-retirement.  Perhaps the most negative impact is that, while the company does receive the cash surrender value under the policy at Peter's death, it does not receive all the life insurance proceeds.  If the portion of the proceeds payable to the trust established for Peter's family exceeds the amount the company would otherwise be required to pay at Peter's death under the plan, such excess would represent an added cost to the company and an added benefit to Peter's family.

The bottom line is that the split-dollar structure represents a stronger commitment by the company and will probably cost the company more in the long run.  The employee has a great death benefit, some tax benefits at death, and more assurance that the company will stick with the program.

### e. Bonus Insurance SERP

Assume the same facts, with one important twist.  Peter has determined that security for the payment of the benefit is far more important than the tax deferral.  He is willing to take a tax hit now for the security of knowing that his benefit is going to be paid, no matter what happens to the company.  Also, he has figured out that if he has to take a current tax hit, the company gets a current tax deduction.  He has convinced the owners of the company that the company should pass on to him the benefit of its early tax deduction by paying him a cash bonus to cover his current tax bill.  He figures that he will have the perfect plan if he can just figure out a way to legally earmark funds to cover his benefit. Peter wants something simple and easy – something that everyone can understand.

The answer for Peter may be a bonus insurance plan, which involves no trust at all and no tax deferral.  Here's how it works.

The company would adopt a bonus insurance plan for Peter.  Peter would be the owner of the policy.  Each year the company would bonus to Peter the amount necessary to fund the policy for Peter's retirement benefit, along with a gross-up bonus to cover any associated tax hit.  The after-tax amount paid as a

---

39.  I.R.C. § 691.

bonus to Peter each year would be structured to ensure that the value of the policy at Peter's retirement would be large enough to provide Peter his desired monthly benefits.

Peter would enter into an agreement with the company that would provide that, if Peter terminates his employment early, he would be obligated to repay to the company all or a portion of the amounts that the company had paid to Peter to fund the policy. This repayment obligation would arise by virtue of the employment contract, and the company would have no special right to enforce its rights against the insurance contract. If Peter terminates his employment and does not repay the amounts, the company would have a legal right to pursue Peter for all amounts due. When Peter retires, he could borrow against the cash value of the police to fund his monthly retirement benefits. At death, his family would be paid any residual death benefit under the policy.

**Illustration E: Bonus Insurance SERP**

This strategy may be an attractive candidate in those rare situations where the executive wants a secure asset, tax deferral is not an objective, the company wants some golden handcuff protections, and the company is willing to take the risk of recovering any forfeited amounts from Pete.

### f. The Guarantor Option

Another option that may be used to provide Peter with added protection that his promised benefits will be paid is to have the payment of the benefits guaranteed by a third party that has deep pockets. If the company goes under and is unable to pay the benefits, Peter can look to the third party for payment. An alternative is a surety bond that would guarantee the company's payment obligation to Peter. The IRS has ruled that if the company neither pays the premium on the bond nor reimburses Peter for the bond, the mere existence of the surety bond will not trigger tax on the deferred income, even though the employee has essentially acquired a guarantee of the payment.[40] If the company secures the bond and pays for the coverage, the likely result is that the employee will get hit with a current tax under the reaches of the economic benefit doctrine. Although some have felt that the surety bond may be the ultimate answer for the employee who has been promised a large supplemental retirement benefit, such surety bonds are not widely available and can be very expensive when they are available.

## PROBLEM 11-C

**11-C.** Jurden Windows Inc. hired Justin, a new sales vice president, two years ago. Justin is 51 years old. In the words of the company CEO, Justin has "taken the company to the moon." He has used his contacts in the industry to cherry-pick the best salespersons and to put together a sales effort that has everyone talking. That's the good news. The scary news is that everyone wants Justin and his sales team, whose loyalty is more to Justin than to the company. Bottom line: the company needs to lock Justin up.

The CEO of the company knows that Justin, a big spender, is concerned about his retirement down the road. The CEO doesn't know much about Justin's financial situation, but suspects that Justin doesn't save and invest much. Justin has inquired on a number of occasions if something can be done to enhance the company's retirement plan, which is a vanilla 401(k) plan that puts the funding onus on the employee.

The CEO would like to adopt a special retirement plan just for Justin. Ideally, it would be a plan that would bind Justin to the company for the duration. The CEO has many questions: Is such a plan for one person legal? What are the tax impacts? How would the benefits under the plan be funded? The CEO feels strongly that the plan must offer Justin more than just a "naked promise" down the road. There needs to be "some teeth" to show that the benefits will be paid. Plus, the CEO says it "can't create a bunch of tax problems for Justin before he starts collecting following his retirement from the company."

Advise the company.

# C. COMPENSATING WITH STOCK AND STOCK RIGHTS

Highly motivated executives often get to a point in their careers where something more than a salary and a bonus is required as an incentive. They want to own a portion of the business. They want to work *with* the business owner – not just *for* the business owner. Often the executive really doesn't understand or appreciate what an interest in the business represents. All the executive knows is that he or she wants to feel like an owner and be treated like an owner.

The lawyer may advise the employer who is faced with the challenge or the

---

40. PLR 84060022.

key executive who wants to be its beneficiary. Many employers view the challenge as a necessary evil and approach the task with suspicion, fear, and a natural propensity to drag out and procrastinate on the process. The employer usually recognizes the value of the key executive and wants to preserve loyalty and dedication. What the employer does not want to do is create a structure fraught with legal and tax complexities that unduly inflates the executive's expectations, diverts the executive's commitment or, worse yet, funds the executive's departure.

The advisor for the executive has a specific challenge – to clearly identify the real value of what is being offered or promised, and the associated pitfalls. This can be a formidable task, particularly sorting through the tax and legal tradeoffs. Complexity is the order of the day in dealing with stock options, restricted stock plans, phantom stock plans, stock right plans, and other types of ownership incentive programs.

## 1. BENEFITS AND BURDENS OF STOCK OWNERSHIP

For purposes of this discussion, let's assume that XYZ, Inc. is a closely held manufacturing corporation that is equally owned by two individuals, Larry and Sue. The company has 150 employees and is very profitable. Jim, age 42, has become a key ingredient in the company's success. Jim manages the day-to-day field operations of the company and is the primary contact with certain of the company's most important customers. Jim has reached a point where he feels that he should own part of the company.

What are the real benefits to Jim if he acquires stock of the company? Whenever stock is acquired by an executive, there are seven potential benefits. Depending on the circumstances, some of these benefits may be of great value, and others may be of no significance. Let's review the seven benefits in light of Jim's situation.

The first benefit is the privilege to vote the shares. If Jim is issued voting stock, he will have a vote that he didn't have before. Shareholders of a corporation have the power to elect the board of directors of the corporation and to vote on major transactions involving the corporation, such as mergers, liquidations, and sales of the corporation's assets. This new vote may be of no real value to Jim. As a minority stockholder, he can always be outvoted, and there's no assurance that he'll be given an opportunity to serve on the board of directors. Since it is the board of directors of the company that really controls its affairs, the opportunity to serve on the board may be far more important than the opportunity to vote a few shares.

The second benefit that Jim receives is the right to receive dividends. In a publicly held company that regularly pays a dividend, that right may have real economic value. Most closely held C corporations, however, such as XYZ, Inc., do not pay any significant dividends. Since dividends are subject to a double tax, the closely held corporation would rather bail out its earnings in the form of tax-deductible payments to its shareholders through salaries, bonuses, rental payments and other arrangements. For this reason, the dividend advantage in the closely held corporation often is not significant as a practical matter.

The third potential benefit of stock ownership is the right to participate in any sale or liquidation of the business. If Larry and Sue decide to dispose of XYZ, Inc. down the road and Jim owns a share of its stock, he will be in a position to participate in the rewards generated from the sale. This can produce a significant economic benefit if the company is sold at a handsome profit. But the prospects of any such sale may be nonexistent or, at best, remote. Maybe Larry and Sue have no interest in selling the business and want to preserve the business for their next generation. Maybe there is no market for the particular business. This is an important factor that needs to be analyzed in reviewing the potential benefits of any ownership program.

The fourth potential benefit is growth potential. By acquiring an interest in the stock of the company, Jim acquires an asset that has growth potential. As the earnings of the business increase, the value of his stock also should increase. The real question to ask is: How is Jim going to realize a profit on the value of that stock? There is no established market for XYZ, Inc. stock. Since XYZ, Inc. is a closely held corporation, there should be a buy-sell agreement between the shareholders of the company. That agreement will specify the terms and conditions for buying stock owned by a shareholder. In many closely held corporations, the terms of the shareholder buy-sell agreement are the most important factors in assessing the value of the stock incentive program that is offered to the executive. It is through that agreement that the minority shareholder executive will realize the value of the equity interest.

The fifth potential benefit is the capital gains tax break realized on the sale of a capital asset. One of the principal incentives for issuing an executive stock as compensation is the opportunity to generate capital gains that are taxed at favorable rates.

The last two benefits that executives usually long for in these types of programs are the "feel better" benefit and the "treat me more equal" benefit. These are purely subjective factors. Many executives are convinced that they will feel better and be more secure in their jobs if they own a part of the company. They also believe that the owners of the company will treat them more as equals, more like partners, if they own an interest in the business. Often these subjective factors are of greater importance to the executive than those factors related directly to the economic benefits of the program.

Frequently the question is asked: Are there any disadvantages to an executive receiving an equity ownership interest in the company that he or she works for? There are a few potential disadvantages that should be carefully reviewed in every situation.

First, there is the potential disadvantage of triggering the recognition of phantom taxable income – taxable income that is not accompanied by any cash. In many stock ownership programs, the executive ends up with a stock certificate and a tax bill, but no cash. More on this potential disadvantage later.

Second, in rare situations there is the possibility that the executive may take on some additional liability exposure by becoming an owner of the business. If there are uninsured risks in operating the business and the affairs of the corporation are neglected, there is a risk that the shareholders of the corporation may become personally exposed for certain debts and liabilities of the company. The executive may end up on the wrong side of a lawsuit in which a creditor of the corporation is trying to pierce the corporate veil to get directly to the corporate shareholders. Usually this risk can be mitigated or eliminated entirely by properly taking care of the corporate, legal and insurance affairs of the business. Suffice it to say, the executive who acquires stock in the corporation will want to be satisfied that the corporate legal affairs are in order.

There also are the potential disadvantages associated with the business losing money or possibly needing additional capital from its shareholders. If Jim is issued 10 percent of the stock of XYZ, Inc. and XYZ, Inc. then gets into financial trouble, Jim may have pressure put on him by Larry or Sue to help fund the operations of XYZ, Inc. by coughing up his share of the additional needed capital. Although Jim may have no legal obligation to make such a contribution, the pressure of being a co-owner with Larry and Sue may push him into having to fund his share of the shortfall.

Usually the biggest disadvantage is the opportunity cost in any situation where an executive takes an equity interest as part of his or her pay package. By taking stock in the company, Jim may lose the right to receive some alternative form of compensation that, in the end, may prove more valuable to him.

In each situation, the potential benefits and burdens of owning an interest in the company need to be carefully analyzed. In some situations, the executive may conclude that the benefits do not justify the burdens, the hassle, and the opportunity costs of alternative forms of compensation.

## 2. FACTORS IN ASSESSING AN OWNERSHIP PROGRAM

There are factors that should be analyzed in structuring or reviewing any equity ownership incentive program. Following are brief descriptions of eight key planning factors.

### a. The Real Cost Factor

Does the program require that the executive bear a real cost by making an investment to acquire his or her stock in the company? Most stock option programs are structured to require that the executive write a check and make an investment before the executive can acquire stock in the company. Employers often feel that such an investment on the part of the executive is essential to accomplish the real objectives of the plan. They argue that, absent such an investment, the executive can't really lose any money and may not fully appreciate the value of what's been given. In contrast, many executives do not want to make an investment or lack the resources to make a significant investment to acquire an interest in the company. Their argument is that their investment has been and will continue to be in the form of quality executive services to the company and their willingness to forgo other opportunities. This issue of whether the executive is going to be required to come "out of pocket" to acquire his or her interest is a threshold issue in structuring and analyzing any program.

### b.  The "Value Now" Factor

Will the program be structured so that the executive is given a stock interest that has a built-in economic value to the executive at the time it is given?  As we will see, many programs are structured to simply give the executive an economic interest in future appreciation that accrues in the company's stock.  The emphasis is on the future, not the present.  Many stock option programs, stock appreciation right programs, and phantom stock programs are designed to give the executive an economic interest in future appreciation.  There is no immediate economic value in the option or the right at the time it is given to the executive.  In contrast, other programs are structured to give the executive an interest in the company that has a demonstrable economic value at the time it is given.  Under such a program, the executive's net worth is increased at the time the executive is granted the option or the right.  Many employers are willing to part with a portion of the future value in their company, but are unwilling to simply grant the executive, free of charge, an interest in the value that has already been created.

### c.  The Golden Handcuffs Factor

Is the program going to be structured to ensure that the executive can enjoy the full economic benefits only if the executive satisfies certain specified employment criteria?  Many programs are structured to provide executives with significant economic benefits that depend entirely on the executive's willingness to remain loyal and dedicated to the company.  If the executive prematurely terminates his or her employment with the company, fails to measure up to designated performance criteria, or elects to go to work for a competitor, the executive  forfeits some or all of the economic benefits that accrued under the particular plan.

This factor can be extremely important from the executive's perspective.  The executive has been given something of value, but it is conditional and contingent.  It can be lost.  Often specified, custom-tailored conditions need to be negotiated with each executive in order to satisfy the interests of all parties.

### d.  The Cash-Out Factor

This factor focuses on the mechanism that will be used to allow the executive to convert his or her stock interest to cash at an appropriate point in the future.  This factor is not a consideration for the publicly held company whose stock is registered and regularly traded.  In contrast, this Cash-Out Factor is particularly important to the executive of the closely held business.  How is that executive going to realize a profit on the investment?  A carefully drafted shareholder buy-sell agreement that specifies a reasonable basis for valuing the stock at appropriate points in time is critically important.  It also is essential to develop a funding mechanism in many situations.  This often requires that the business purchase a life insurance policy on the life of the executive to ensure that the company will have the required funds to cash out the executive if there is an untimely death.  Cash-out provisions also have to be negotiated to deal with issues of employment severance, disability, retirement and expulsion.

### e. The Phantom Income Factor

Is the program going to create taxable income for the executive before the executive has any cash to pay the tax liability? Many programs are structured to confer an economic value for the executive at the time the particular option or right is granted. The result is that the executive may be taxed on the fair market value of that economic benefit at the time it is received, even though no cash has been paid to the executive. This can create an intolerable situation for the executive from a tax standpoint. To remedy the situation, employers often are forced to bonus additional cash sums to the executive to cover the tax liability. As we'll see, many programs attempt to deal with this Phantom Income Factor by eliminating the Value Now Factor – that is, by granting no present economic benefit – or by maximizing the Golden Handcuffs Factor, which presents a substantial risk of forfeiture to the executive. The trade-offs can be significant for any executive.

### f Employer's Tax Factor

The sixth factor focuses on the tax consequence for the employer. Does the program produce any tax advantages for the employer? The employer often find that the program has been structured to provide a tax deduction for options or rights granted to the executive, even though the employer has not expended any cash or liquid resources. Such a plan may reduce the tax liability of the employer and the overall costs of the plan. The executive, on the other hand, may be demanding that at least a portion of those tax savings should be reallocated to him or her to reduce the burden of any phantom taxable income.

### g. The Fall-Out Leverage Factor

This factor focuses on the relevant positions of the executive and the company if there is a major blow-up between them. Who has the most leverage? If there is a falling-out and the executive believes that he or she has been abused in the process, the executive may have substantially more leverage by exercising rights as a stockholder. For this reason alone, many employers prefer plans that grant stock equivalency rights or phantom stock rights, but never provide real stock. Carefully drafted transfer restrictions and buy-sell agreements can help mitigate the fear generated by this Fall-Out Leverage Factor when real stock is issued. Often it is difficult to get a handle on the significance of this factor in a given situation because the parties don't want to even acknowledge the prospect of a major blow-up.

### h. The Real Thing Factor

As we will see, incentive ownership programs can be structured without offering the executive any real equity interest in the company. Instead, the executive receives contractual payment rights structured to produce economic benefits that are the equivalent of stock ownership. Often these programs are unacceptable to the executive simply because they do not offer the "real thing." The executive isn't satisfied with anything less than stock, even though, from a tax and structuring standpoint, the executive may be better off receiving a carefully drafted stock substitute.

These eight factors are important considerations in analyzing any ownership incentive program. The following planning strategies focus on these factors. It is common to find that the company and the executive disagree on the importance of a particular factor or how it should be structured into the particular program.

### 3. SIX PLANNING STRATEGIES

#### a. Incentive Stock Options

The incentive stock option (ISO) is the strategy that presents the most technical requirements. It is available only to corporate entities, not entities taxed as partnerships.[41] The ISO gives the executive the right to buy stock from the company over a designated period of time on certain specified terms and conditions. It is designed to provide a tax benefit to the executive who receives the option.

With any stock option plan, there are three key points in time: the time the executive is given the option, the time the executive acquires stock through the exercise of the option and payment of the option price, and the time that the stock is sold by the executive and the sales price is realized in the form of cash. The appeal of an ISO is that the executive does not have to recognize any taxable income at the time of grant or the time of exercise, but rather only recognizes taxable income at the time of sale – when cash is available.[42] And any income recognized at the time of sale can qualify as capital gain income. There is one slight tax hitch. Although the executive does not have to recognize any phantom taxable income at the time of grant or at the time of exercise, if the fair market value of the stock at the time of exercise exceeds the option price (a circumstance that will exist in almost every case, for why else would the executive have exercised the option?), such excess fair market value at time of exercise will be treated as a tax preference item for purposes of the alternative minimum tax.[43]

What does it take for an option to qualify as an ISO so that the executive can enjoy the tax benefits of ISO treatment? There are a number of technical requirements, including the following:[44]

First, the plan under which the option is granted must be approved by the shareholders of the company within 12 months before or after the date the plan is adopted by the board of directors.

Second, each option must be granted within 10 years of the plan adoption. In other words, the plan is good for 10 years.

Third, the option period cannot be longer than 10 years, so the executive must make his or her election to exercise the option and acquire the stock within a 10-year time frame after it is granted.

Fourth, the option price cannot be less than the fair market value of the company's stock at the time the option is granted. Determining the fair market

---

41. I.R.C. § 422(b) requires that the recipient be an employee of a corporation.
42. I.R.C. § 421(a).
43. I.R.C. § 56(b)(3).
44. See, generally, I.R.C. § 422(a)-(d).

value of the stock of a closely held corporation can be a challenge. For this reason, there is a special provision that the ISO will qualify as long as a good faith effort is made to determine the fair market value of the stock.

Fifth, the option cannot be transferred, except in the case of the death of the executive.

Sixth, the executive who gets the ISO cannot own over 10 percent of the stock of the company.

Seventh, the total fair market value of all stock subject to ISOs which are first exercisable by the executive in any calendar year cannot exceed $100,000. The fair market value of the stock is determined at the time of grant.

Eighth, to claim the ISO benefits, the executive cannot sell the stock within two years of the date the option is granted, nor within one year from the date the stock is acquired through the exercise of the option. After exercising the option, the executive, Jim in our case, must hold the stock long enough to satisfy these periods in order to enjoy capital gains tax treatment.

Finally, the executive must have been an employee of the company or an affiliate of the company at all times from the date the option is granted until at least three months prior to the date upon which the option is exercised. In other words, if the executive leaves the employ of the company, the ISO must be exercised within three months of leaving in order to preserve the favorable ISO tax treatment.

The obvious question is this: Why wouldn't any executive and company (such as Jim and XYZ, Inc.) only want options that qualify as ISOs? After all, there is no taxable income until time of sale. The phantom income tax risks are eliminated. Also, the ISO can be structured with Golden Handcuffs features to protect the company. Usually this is done by providing that portions of the ISO can be exercised only after the executive has satisfied certain designated employment periods with the company. And once the option is exercised, the executive acquires the real thing – stock in the company.

Although certain advantages and structural opportunities exist, there are some major disadvantages to ISOs that are compelling in many situations. The result is that the ISO, although once very popular, has lost much of its appeal. First, from the executive's perspective, the ISO, by definition, flunks the Real Cost Factor and the Value Now factor tests. The executive must make a real investment before getting any stock, and the purchase price of the stock, by definition, must be equal to the fair market value of the stock at the time the option is granted. The option offers only a hope of future appreciation and no existing value. Jim may want some value now.

Second, the employer gets no deduction for the ISO. If the stock goes up in value and the employee, Jim in our case, recognizes a gain at time of sale, Jim will pay tax and the company will get no tax deduction. On a net tax basis, this is a costly, inefficient approach for moving value from the company to the executive. The executive is paying a tax bill with no offsetting tax benefit to the employer.

Finally, if the executive has an alternative minimum tax problem, the ISO may significantly aggravate that problem by creating an additional tax preference item at the time the option is exercised.

For these reasons, the ISO, although still a viable candidate and strategy, has lost much of its glitter. Many companies and their executives would be well advised to consider one of the less technical strategies.

### b. The Nonqualified Stock Option

The second strategy is the nonqualified stock option. A nonqualified stock option is an option that does not qualify as an incentive stock option; it flunks one of the technical requirements. The executive still is given the right to buy a designated number of shares of the company's stock on specific terms and conditions. However, there are no rules governing the option price, the option period, or any other items. The parties are completely free to sculpt their own deal.

Are nonqualified options taxed the same as ISOs? Not a chance. Generally, the executive will not have to recognize any taxable income at the time the option is granted unless the option can be transferred by the executive or the option itself is tradable and has a readily ascertainable fair market value. [45] Because such options are almost never transferable by the executive and usually never have readily ascertainable fair market values, the time of grant is not a problem – certainly not in a situation involving a closely held business such as XYZ, Inc.

The tax problem comes at the point of exercise. When Jim exercises the option by paying the price and receiving the stock, Jim is required to recognize taxable income equal to the excess of the fair market value of the stock over the option price. If, in our example, Jim is given an option to buy 100,000 shares of stock at a price of $1.00 per share (for a total of $100,000) and Jim exercises the option at a time when the shares have a fair market value of $3.00 per share (or $300,000), Jim would be required to recognize $200,000 of taxable ordinary income at the time of exercise. Yet Jim has no cash from the transaction at this point. Jim's tax basis in the stock would be $300,000. At the time that Jim sells the stock, he would only have to recognize income to the extent the sale price exceeds $300,000.

It's important to note that there is a tax benefit to the corporation at the time of exercise. When the exercise occurs, the corporation gets a tax deduction equal to the income that Jim is required to recognize.[46] In our example, the corporation would get a $200,000 deduction at time of exercise.

If the parties have determined that they want to use stock options, nonqualified options offer great flexibility in structuring their arrangement. The option requires some investment, so there is a Real Cost Factor. But the option price can be below the existing fair market value of the stock. If, in our example, the stock has a value of $2.00 per share at the time of grant and the option price

---

45. I.R.C. § 83(e)(3); Reg. §§ 1.83-7(b)(1) & (2).
46. I.R.C. § 83(h).

is $1.00 per share, Jim effectively would have been transferred $1.00 of real value for each share at the time the option is granted.  From Jim's perspective, this circumstance would satisfy the Value Now Factor because he has been given some of the existing equity in the company through the structure of the option price.  Many employers have used these types of options to set exercise prices that are substantially below the existing fair market value of the stock at time of grant.

If some Value Now is built into a nonqualified option, care must be taken to comply with the requirements of Section 409A.  Under Regulation § 1.409A-1(b)(5), a nonqualified stock option will be treated as a deferred compensation plan if the option price does not at least equal to the fair market value of the stock at time of option grant.  Thus, a nonqualified option that has a preferred Value Now option price will lose a great deal of flexibility as to the timing of its exercise.  To comply with Section 409A, the time of exercise would have to be specified at time of grant or be tied to a permissible payout event under Section 409A (separation for service, disability, death, change of control, or unforeseen emergency).

The executive would lose the capacity to pick the time to exercise the option.  In view of the penalties triggered by a violation of 409A, any company that issues nonqualified options that are not intended to comply with the exercise limitations of Section 409A should take extreme care to ensure that the option price is not less than the stock's fair market value at time of grant.  In recognition of the difficulty of valuing closely held business interests (and the high stakes for Section 409A non-compliance), the regulations to Section 409A permit the use of any reasonable valuation method, describe factors that will be used to determine the reasonableness of the valuation, impose consistency requirements, create a presumption of reasonableness for a one-year period, and create a special presumption for the good faith valuation of a start-up company's stock during the first 10 years of its active conduct of a trade or business. [47]

There is really no limit on the Golden Handcuffs feature that can be attached to the nonqualified option.  For example, XYZ, Inc. could grant to Jim an option to purchase 200,000 shares of the company's common stock at a specified price.  The option could be structured to provide that Jim would have the right to exercise the option with respect to one-tenth (1/10) of such shares (20,000) each year that Jim remains in the employ of XYZ, Inc.  The effect is that Jim would vest in his right to acquire the full 200,000 shares over a 10-year time frame.  If the company does well, Jim would have a strong incentive to remain loyal for a long period of time.

From Jim's perspective, the phantom taxable income created at the time of exercise is a real problem, but even this problem can often be resolved.  Remember, the corporation is getting an offsetting tax deduction. The transaction is often structured so that the corporation lends the amount of its tax benefit at the time of exercise to the executive.  This provides the executive with a source

47.  Reg. § 1.409A-1(b)(5).

of funding to cover his tax liability at the time of exercise. Interest would be paid or accrued on the loan. The loan would be paid off at the time the stock is sold.

As an alternative, the company could elect to simply bonus to the executive the amount of its tax saving from the exercise of the option. A calculation would have to be made to gross-up the bonus to take into account taxes also saved as a result of the bonus paid to Jim. This would provide Jim with a source of cash to cover his tax liability at the time of exercise.

The net effect from Jim's standpoint is that the nonqualified option gives him some real value now, provides a source of funding his phantom tax liability, and presents no alternative minimum tax problems.

Stock options are viable strategies. The nonqualified option provides more structural flexibility, but does raise a phantom income issue that needs to be addressed in the planning process. One major disadvantage of any stock option program is that the executive doesn't own the stock – the real thing – until he or she steps up and pays the option price. So the benefits of actual stock ownership usually are delayed. This may be a real negative from the standpoint of many executives.

### c. Bonus Stock

Bonus stock perhaps is the least technical and most straightforward strategy of all. Under this approach, XYZ, Inc. would adopt a stock bonus plan and transfer to Jim a specified number of its shares as compensation for services rendered. From Jim's standpoint, bonus stock offers some real pluses. There is no need to make a cash investment; there is no real cost. There is immediate value now; the existing value of the stock belongs to the executive, and the transfer of the stock is not deemed to be a deferred compensation plan subject to Section 409A.[48] A shareholder buy-sell agreement can be drafted to ensure that the Cash-Out Factor is satisfied. The executive owns the real thing now; there is no delayed enjoyment, as in the case of an option. Finally, the executive is entitled to vote the shares now and can immediately participate in all dividends and other rights.

But there are also disadvantages to bonus stock from the executive's perspective. Usually the executive is given fewer shares under a bonus stock plan than under some other type of plan, such as an option plan. It's only natural to expect that the company will be willing to transfer, free of charge, fewer shares under a bonus plan than it would be willing to sell for full value under an option program. The resulting disadvantage is that the executive has less opportunity to participate in the future appreciation of the company.

Bonus stock also presents a major phantom taxable income problem. The fair market value of the stock is taxed to Jim at the time the stock is transferred to him. As in the case of a nonqualified option, the company may find itself in the position of having to lend money to Jim to enable him to pay his phantom tax liability, or it may simply couple the stock bonus grant with a grossed-up cash

---

48. Reg. § 1.409A-1(b)(6).

bonus to cover the tax liability.

### d. Restricted Stock

Restricted stock is bonus stock with a twist. The twist is that the stock has strings attached – restrictions. If one of these restrictions is violated, the company yanks the string and retrieves all or a portion of the stock. Suppose, for example, that XYZ, Inc. is willing to transfer to Jim $100,000 worth of stock now. No investment is required on Jim's part. There is immediate value now. Jim gets the real thing now. And, presumably, there is a buy-sell agreement to ensure the Cash-Out Factor. Further, suppose that XYZ, Inc. wants to make certain that the stock will cement Jim's loyalty and dedication to the company. So it places a restriction on the stock. For example, the restriction may provide that, if Jim leaves the company at any time during the next 10 years, he will forfeit all of the stock. Alternatively, it may provide that Jim vests in his right to keep the stock at a rate of 10 percent each year. So if he leaves at the end of five years, for example, he will be paid for 50 percent of the stock under the buy-sell agreement, and he will forfeit the remaining 50 percent. Alternatively, the restriction may provide that all or a portion of the stock is forfeited if Jim fails to hit certain sales volumes, or otherwise fails to satisfy some other objective measure of performance.

There is a significant tax consequence to this forfeiture feature. As long as a substantial risk of forfeiture exists, the executive does not have to pay tax on the stock that's been transferred.[49] In our example, Jim could be transferred $100,000 worth of stock and pay no tax at the time of transfer. If, after 10 years, the forfeiture feature goes away, Jim would be taxed on the full value of the stock at that time. Often the forfeiture provisions are structured to lapse over a period of years so that only a portion of the tax liability is recognized in any year. On the other side, the company gets a tax deduction equal to the amount of taxable income that Jim is required to report in the same year that Jim reports the income.[50]

There is another tax planning option that should be considered whenever restricted stock is used. The executive may elect to be taxed on the stock at the time the stock is received, rather than at the time the forfeiture provision lapses.[51] Why would an executive ever want to elect to recognize taxable income at an earlier point in time? If the stock value at the time the stock is received is very low and there is a substantial prospect that it is going to appreciate rapidly in the future, the executive may prefer to recognize the taxable income at the time the stock is granted at the much lower value. If the election is made to recognize income at the time of grant, there is no need to recognize any future taxable income until the stock is actually sold. There is a disadvantage with this election. If the executive elects to recognize the income at the time the stock is granted

---

49. I.R.C. § 83(a)(1); Reg. § 1.83-3(c). The existence of the forfeiture feature and the related tax deferral does not make the arrangement a deferred compensation plan subject to the new section 409A requirements. Proposed Reg. § 1.409A-1(a)(6).

50. I.R.C. § 83(h).

51. See, generally, I.R.C. § 83(b).

and the stock is then forfeited, the executive gets no offsetting deduction at the time of the forfeiture. Thus, the executive may be in a position of having paid tax on something that never produced any value. It's a calculated risk. If the executive's choice is to make the election, the company gets a deduction at the same time the executive recognizes the income.

Restricted stock is a flexible tool that can be used in many situations. As many stock option programs have lost their appeal, the restricted stock alternative has become more popular.

### e. Stock Appreciation Right Strategy

The next strategy is different from the four previous strategies in one significant respect: the executive never gets the real thing. There is no stock. In lieu of receiving stock, the executive is given a contractual right to compensation that is structured to provide the same economic benefits as stock. Here is how it works.

Suppose XYZ, Inc. wants to give Jim the right to fully receive the value of all appreciation that accrues on 100,000 shares of its stock in the future. Jim doesn't want any stock options for a number of reasons. He doesn't want to have to pay a real cost, as is required by an option. The tax traps of options also are a problem for the parties. An ISO will produce no tax deduction for the company and may present an alternative tax problem for Jim. A nonqualified option, on the other hand, will produce phantom taxable income for Jim at time of exercise.

A stock appreciation right contract may be the answer. A contract is drawn that essentially states that the parties will pretend that Jim owns 100,000 shares of stock. He never really owns the stock. Usually the contract would establish a base price of the stock – say $1.00 per share – that would equal the current value of the stock. The contract would offer a number of economic benefits based on the pretend stock. It would provide that if a dividend is paid to the real shareholders of the company, then a corresponding amount of compensation would be paid to Jim on his 100,000 pretend shares. It would also provide that if the company is sold, merged, or goes public, Jim would receive the excess in the value of his pretend shares, at that time, over the base value of such phantom shares at the time the contract was awarded to him. For example, if the company is sold at a price of $3.00 per share down the road, Jim would be entitled to receive compensation income at a rate of $2.00 per share for the 100,000 pretend shares awarded to him under the contract. The contract would also provide that the stock appreciation rights would be valued at the time Jim dies, is disabled, or otherwise terminates his employment. The excess of the value of the rights at that time over the base value of $1.00 per share would be paid as additional compensation income to Jim. Golden Handcuffs features may be structured into the contract to provide Jim with incentives to remain loyal and dedicated to the company. Essentially, the contract is designed to provide Jim with the same economic benefits, in the form of compensation under the contract, that he would otherwise receive in the form of stockholder economic benefits if he actually owned the real stock.

What are the advantages to such a stock appreciation right arrangement?

There are a number of benefits. First, there is no threat of phantom income. Since all amounts paid to Jim are compensation under the contract, Jim will not have any taxable income until he actually receives payment. Second, there is no alternative minimum tax threat. Third, since all amounts paid to Jim represent compensation, the company receives a full deduction at the time of payment. This is a significant benefit to the company and may allow the company to pay Jim a larger benefit. In many ways, a stock appreciation right contractual arrangement is one of the most efficient strategies, from a tax perspective, for transferring upside stock value from the company to the executive.

Is there any tax disadvantage to such an arrangement? Historically, the biggest disadvantage to any such arrangement has been the absence of any capital gains or favorable dividend tax break for the executive. Because the executive never owns any stock, there is no possibility of creating a capital gain at time of sale or receiving dividends. To sweeten the deal for the executive, an added bonus may be provided to produce a net after-tax yield to the executive that is equal to the yield that would result if the pretend stock payment were taxed as a capital gain or dividend. Again, the company gets a full deduction for all amounts paid. Often, this capital gains or dividend bonus can be paid with the company still incurring a net after-tax cost that is less than what would be incurred if it purchased stock or paid a dividend under another strategy.

A stock appreciation right arrangement provides a number of flexible alternatives. There is no requirement that the executive make an investment in order to acquire rights to future appreciation in the stock. There is no risk of phantom income. The company gets a deduction. There is no alternative minimum tax risk. The Golden Handcuffs Factor and the Cash-Out Factor can both be accommodated in a variety of different ways through the contract. The company often prefers this type of arrangement because of the Fall-out Leverage Factor. If there is a major problem between the executive and the company down the road, the executive has a contractual right to payment, but does not own any stock in the company. Accordingly, the executive is not in a position to cause problems as a shareholder.

With a stock appreciation right plan, care must be taken to ensure that it avoids the reach of Section 409A or that it is structured to comply with the Section 409A requirements (i.e., no executive election rights as to timing or method of payout after the grant of the rights). There is no room for ambiguity. A stock appreciation right plan can avoid 409A treatment if there is no Value Now Factor (only appreciation following the grant is considered) and the plan includes no other deferred compensation element. [52]

The biggest disadvantage from the executive's perspective is that he or she never owns the real thing. The arrangement is a fancy employment contract. The subjective desires of being viewed and treated like an owner may never be realized. Often it's possible to overcome this fear by reemphasizing that the contract is being drawn to provide a real piece of the rock by offering economic

____

52. Reg. § 1.409A-(b)(5)(i)(C)(3).

benefits that, dollar for dollar, are structured to be the same as those that would be realized if stock were actually owned.

### f. Phantom Stock Plan

The next strategy is the phantom stock plan. This strategy is the same as the stock appreciation right strategy described previously, with one significant twist. The strategy is structured to give full effect to the Value Now Factor and falls squarely within the reach of Section 409A. A contract is drawn that gives the executive the right to be compensated on the basis of certain pretend shares, but there is no existing base value price. At the time the contract is entered into, the executive is promised payments down the road based on the current value of the phantom shares, together with all future appreciation on those shares. It's as if the executive actually owned the stock now. Hence, the name "phantom stock."

Jim, for example, could be provided a phantom stock benefit that gives him the right to 100,000 phantom shares that have an existing value of $2.00 per share. This would be an attractive contractual right from Jim's perspective. Moreover, as the value of the stock in the company increases, the value of Jim's phantom shares would similarly increase.

Since such a phantom stock plan is subject to Section 409A, Jim can have no timing or payout elections after the grant of the rights. To comply with Section 409A, the time and method of payout must be specified at time of grant or tied to a permissible payout event under Section 409A (separation from service, disability, death, change of control, or unforeseen emergency).

Assuming the requirements of Section 409A are satisfied, is Jim required to recognize this Value Now Factor ($200,000 in our example) at the time the contract is entered into? The answer is "no" so as long as Jim simply has the contractual right to receive a payment for this amount as compensation in the future.[53] Thus, unlike the bonus stock and the restricted stock strategies described previously, Jim can receive a Real Value Now factor and avoid any phantom taxable income. The key variable is that he has received a contractual right to future payments, rather than a property right represented in the form of stock.

Again, the biggest disadvantage from Jim's perspective is that he has not received real stock in the company. Also, because Jim never receives stock, there is no opportunity for capital gains treatment. These potential disadvantages may pale in significance compared to the economic benefits being offered under the program and the fact that there is no threat of phantom taxable income. Plus, as described above, the plan can be structured to pay Jim compensation for any lost capital gains benefits and put him in the exact economic position as if he had received real stock. When the plan is dolled up to include such benefits, it is sometimes referred to as a "stock equivalency plan" – a term that may sound more appealing than "phantom stock."

---

53. An unfunded and unsecured right to receive money or property does not constitute "property" under the provisions of Section 83. Reg. § 1.83-3(e).

## PROBLEM 11-D

Refer to Case Problem 11-C and Jurden Industries' challenge to lock in its star VP of sales, Justin. The CEO opened up discussions with Justin and, to everyone's surprise, Justin demanded a piece of the rock. He wants to participate in the equity growth of the company. He wants the rights of an owner. Specifically, Justin has requested (demanded?) the following:

1. He wants equity value now in recognition of the value he has already brought to the company. He doesn't want a deal that is based solely on the future appreciation of the company's stock.

2. He doesn't want to pay anything for his equity interest in the company. He figures that he has already paid through his efforts on behalf of the company.

3. He wants an official vote in the management affairs of the company. He isn't asking for control – just the right to be part of the inner circle.

4. He doesn't want to pay any income taxes on the equity interest that he receives until the stock is sold and cash is realized.

5. He wants the tax benefits of stock ownership – specifically preferred tax treatment on dividends and capital gains benefits at the time of sale.

Jurden's CEO is overwhelmed. He doesn't want to give Justin anything that is not tied to his future long-term performance on behalf of the company. The CEO asks: What happens if we give Justin stock and he stops performing or quits? How do we get the stock back? Do we have to buy it back? What happens to Justin's stock if there is a falling out down the road?

The CEO wants your advice. What do you recommend?

# CHAPTER 12

# BUSINESS LIFE INSURANCE PLANNING

---

## A. BUSINESS LIFE INSURANCE: A PRIMER

### 1. INTRODUCTION

Closely held businesses offer some of the greatest opportunities for life insurance planning. Careful planning can protect the business, its owners, and its key employees. Unfortunately, confusion and misinformation can get in the way of effective planning. Often the result is poor decisions or no decisions. Either way, the planning process is frustrated.

Often the core problem is the approach to the planning process. How does a business owner start to sort out the details? What bases need to be covered? Where are the traps? What is really being accomplished? An organized approach will promote understanding, enhance client confidence, remove the mystery, and facilitate sound decisions. This section presents a seven-question approach to business insurance planning. These basic questions will help focus the planning, promote understanding, and provide a primer for the client, particularly if they are reviewed periodically. They can help in structuring the initial business insurance program and in reevaluating the program from time to time.

### 2. THE SEVEN STARTER QUESTIONS

**Planning Question 1: What is the primary objective(s) of the business life insurance program?**

In the business context, there are three basic objectives for life insurance. These objectives can be, and often are, easily confused. The first objective is the "buy-out" objective: the insurance provides a fund that is used to acquire the stock of the deceased shareholder. In effect, the insurance is a funding vehicle for the buy-sell agreement.

The second objective is "business protection." The life insurance proceeds are retained by the company and used to protect the company from damage that the company may suffer as a result of the death of a shareholder or a key

451

employee. It's often called "key-person" insurance. The funds may be used by the company to hire a replacement executive, to stabilize financing for the company, or to compensate the company for lost customer or supplier relationships resulting from the death.

The third objective is "family protection." The life insurance is used to protect the family of the deceased shareholder or employee. It's paid to the family to cover taxes and to meet the cash needs of the family.

The three insurance objectives may become confused if the company purchases a substantial life insurance policy insuring the life of the owner but does not clearly focus on how the proceeds are to be allocated to the respective objectives. Often the policy is purchased and funded by the company, which is named as both owner and beneficiary. At death, a portion of the proceeds is used to buy the stock of the owner. The balance of the available proceeds is used to cover the other objectives – "business protection" and the "family protection." Problems set in when proceeds are insufficient to cover all the objectives, or when it is unclear how the funds are to be allocated to cover each.

The challenge is to design a life insurance program to eliminate any misunderstandings regarding the life insurance objectives, and to ensure that there are sufficient proceeds available to cover the various priorities. The following tips will help.

**Tip No. 1: Deal with Each Objective Separately**. The insurance program should be designed to deal with each objective separately. A designated amount of life insurance should be allocated to cover each objective. It is never advisable to have one large amount of life insurance and assume that at the time of death the parties will be able to agree on an allocation of the insurance.

**Tip No. 2: Use More Than One Policy**. Often the confusion or misunderstanding exists because there is one major insurance policy that is purchased and owned by the company with the expectation that it will cover all three objectives. In most cases, it will be better for all concerned if there is a specific policy for each objective. Also, the ownership of the policies often should be different. The policy that is targeted for "business protection" usually is owned by the company. In many businesses, particularly those with only a few owners, it will be preferable have the "buy-out" policy owned by the other shareholders, not the company. If the other shareholders own the policy, they will be in a position to acquire the stock of the deceased shareholder and to realize the tax and other advantages of a cross-purchase structure. Similarly, the "family protection" objective will often be enhanced if the policy designated for that purpose is not owned by the company, but rather is owned by the family of the insured or by a trust that has been established for them. This allows the "family protection" insurance to be coordinated with the overall estate planning of the insured shareholder.

**Tip No. 3: Watch the Tax Angles**. The business life insurance program should be structured to maximize the tax advantages of the insurance. As discussed in questions 5, 6 and 7 below, there are key tax issues to consider. In reviewing each objective, it is essential that these basic tax issues be separately evaluated.

**Tip No. 4: Use a Written Memorandum**. It's advisable to have a written agreement among the shareholders that succinctly describes the company-funded insurance program and the way that program is designed to accomplish all three of the objectives. The written statement should be simple, understandable, and designed to eliminate ambiguities. It always helps to put it in writing.

### Planning Question 2: Should the corporation own the insurance?

Designating the owner of the life insurance policy is a critical decision. In many planning contexts, the preferred choice will be to get the policy out of the corporation to avoid income tax problems, alternative minimum tax (AMT) issues, transfer-for-value problems and estate tax questions. Although non-corporate ownership often looks attractive, there is little doubt that many business owners will choose to park the policies inside the company. A solid understanding of the pressures of corporate ownership is important in the business planning process.

There are a variety of explanations for the common practice of having a corporation own life insurance policies. Any one or more of the explanations may apply in a given situation. Funding the premiums is usually the biggest challenge that must be addressed when a life insurance policy is purchased. Often it is easier to fund the premiums with corporate dollars. Other factors that contribute to corporate-owned life insurance are structural challenges of the buy-sell agreement and the fear of potential transfer-for-value problems. For a discussion of corporate ownership of life insurance, see section B of this chapter.

### Planning Question 3: How much insurance?

The planning process must determine how much life insurance is needed. The answer should not be a function of gut instinct; it should be the result of careful analysis. Businesses are different; there are no hard and fast rules.

A number of factors usually need to be considered. Obviously, if all three of the basic objectives discussed above are critical, more insurance will be needed than if only one of the objectives is viewed as a top priority. Twelve other key factors to consider include (1) the time frame for which the insurance will be needed, (2) the capital needs of the business, (3) the liquidity position of the company and its owners, (4) the role of the proposed insured within the business, (5) the capacity to fund premiums, (6) the willingness of the shareholders to allow stock to pass to future generations, (7) the size of the owners' estates, (8) the prospects that the company's stock will substantially increase or decrease in value over time, (9) prospects for changes in the capital or liquidity needs of the business, (10) the owners' attitudes and perceptions about life insurance, (11) the health of the owners and future insurability risks, and (12) any insurance requirements of lenders and investors. The key is to realize that all relevant factors need to be considered in addressing the all-important "how much" decision. There is no substitute for careful analysis.

In some situations, there is a natural temptation to overvalue the business and to purchase additional insurance to cover the overvaluation. This temptation is usually driven by a need to protect the family of a shareholder who might die. In other words, the owners confuse the "family protection" objective with the "business buy-out" objective and do this by overvaluing the business. If the business is overvalued to justify the acquisition of more business buyout life insurance, collateral problems may be created. For example, if one of the owners decides to leave the business, that owner may claim that the overvalued price that everyone accepted in the event of a death should also govern the buyout, even though there has been no death. By agreeing to a higher value to justify the purchase of a larger life insurance policy, the parties may set themselves up for a buyout dispute that is not triggered by death. Also, the overvaluation may create additional estate tax problems. Any amount paid to the family of a deceased shareholder for the stock owned by that shareholder is subject to federal estate taxes. However, as previously stated, if the family protection insurance has been properly structured, that insurance may completely avoid federal estate taxation. Generally, there is no advantage to overvaluing the stock of the business simply to justify the purchase of additional life insurance.

### Planning Question 4: Who really foots the premium tab?

Usually the answer to this question is "the company." If the company owns the policy, it's easy. If someone else is the policy owner, somehow corporate dollars need to be funneled to the owner of the policy to cover the premium payments. Mistakes are made when there is a failure to critically examine the real economic impact of having the company fund the premiums. Often the 80 percent owner may not like the idea of paying 80 percent of the premiums on a policy that will enable the 20 percent minority owner to fund a buyout of the majority owner upon death. The 80 percent owner may justifiably feel that the insurance primarily benefits the 20 percent owner and should be funded out of the 20 percent owner's share.

The key in each situation is to carefully examine who is really bearing the economic burdens of the premiums and then ask: Does this make sense? Often it is possible to shift the economic burdens through salary and bonus adjustments without rearranging underlying stock ownership.

### Planning Question 5: What is the income tax treatment of the premiums?

When the employee owns the policy and the corporation is paying the premiums on the policy, the employee receives a tangible economic benefit in the form of additional compensation. This is "bonus insurance." The corporation is entitled to a deduction, and the employee will have the amount of the premium included in his or her W-2 income. The corporation's tax deduction and the employee's taxable income usually go hand in hand.

What if the corporation is the sole owner of the policy, pays the premiums, and is the beneficiary? Such key person coverage provides no taxable benefit to the employee. The corporation cannot take a deduction for premium payments on a key person insurance policy that it owns. The Code expressly disallows any deduction for corporate-paid premiums if the corporation itself directly or indirectly benefits from the policy.[1]

The question is often raised: Are the rules always this black and white? Is there any way for the employee to receive the life insurance proceeds tax-free, for the business to pay and deduct the premiums, and for the employee to not recognize any taxable income on the business' payment of the premiums? Fortunately, this best-of-all-worlds result is available, within limits, with a group-term life insurance program under Section 79.

In addition to Section 79 group-term coverage, there are two other ways of offering an employee life insurance in a business context that mitigate the harsh income tax hit of the premium burden. The first exists with split-dollar life insurance arrangements; the second exists in those cases where life insurance is acquired in a qualified retirement plan.

### a. Group-Term Insurance → Tax advantaged

Group-term insurance offers the best combination: the employer gets a deduction for insurance premiums paid solely for the benefit of the employee, but the employee does not have to book any income for receiving the benefit of the insurance protection.[2] Because of its tax-favored status, group term life insurance is a popular option for many closely held businesses.

Section 79 has its limitations. It applies only to group term insurance; whole life and permanent policies do not qualify. Also, the favorable tax treatment exists only to the extent that the amount of the insurance coverage does not exceed $50,000 per employee. Finally, there is a complex set of nondiscrimination rules.[3]

If the group-term life insurance protection provided to any employee exceeds $50,000, that employee is required to include in his or her taxable income an amount representing the value of the excess protection. The amount taxable to the employee is determined under the "Table I" rates that are contained in the published regulations.[4] Table I lists the monthly costs per $1,000 of insurance protection at various ages, computed on the basis of five-year age brackets.

Key employees may not enjoy the tax-favored treatment under Section 79 if the plan is discriminatory.[5] Key employees include: (1) any officer of the employer, unless that person's compensation is less than an annual amount specified under Section 416(i)(1) (cost-of-living adjusted $130,000 from December 31, 2002); (2) any person who owns, directly or indirectly, five percent or more of the employer; and (3) any one-percent owner having an annual compensation exceeding the amount specified in Section 416(i)(1) (cost-of-living adjusted $150,000 from December 31, 2002).[6] The plan cannot discriminate in favor of key employees in terms of either eligibility or available

---

1. I.R.C. § 264(a)(1).
2. I.R.C. § 79(a).
3. I.R.C. § 79(a) & (d).
4. Reg. § 1.79-3(d).
5. I.R.C. § 79(d)(1)(A).
6. I.R.C. §§ 79(d)(6), 416(i)(1).

benefits. In applying the anti-discrimination rule, part-time employees, employees with a limited period of service, seasonal employees, and employees in a collective bargaining unit may be disregarded.[7]

To be considered nondiscriminatory as to eligibility, the plan must meet any one of the following four tests: (1) the plan benefits at least 70 percent of all employees of the employer; (2) at least 85 percent of all employees who are participants are not key employees; (3) the plan benefits employees in a classification found by the IRS not to discriminate in favor of key employees; or (4) the plan is part of a cafeteria plan that satisfies the requirements of Section 125.[8]

In addition to eligibility, the plan may not discriminate in the amount of benefits offered to key employees. However, a plan will not be deemed discriminatory as to benefits if the plan provides coverage that bears a uniform relationship to the total compensation of each eligible employee.[9] In other words, those who make more may be given greater insurance benefits.

### b. Split-Dollar Life Insurance

Split-dollar insurance is a popular strategy for providing life insurance to key employees as an executive perk. Often it's the answer for those companies that want a program that discriminates in favor of their key executives and provides their key executives with a significant permanent life insurance benefit that can be factored into their estate planning.

A split-dollar life insurance arrangement is a contract between an employer and an employee under which the benefits and burdens of a life insurance policy are split.[10] The classic split provides that the corporation will pay that part of each premium equal to the increase in cash value of the policy, and the insured employee will pay the balance of the premium. Alternatively, the corporation may also pay the employee's share of the premium. The major benefit of the arrangement is that the employee receives permanent life insurance protection with little or no cash outlay. There are no anti-discrimination rules, so the corporation can selectively offer the program to only certain employees.

The split-dollar agreement also provides for a split of the death benefit paid under the policy. When the key employee dies, the business typically is the beneficiary of that portion of the proceeds equal to the greater of the premiums it has paid or the cash surrender value of the policy. The balance of the proceeds (which is usually the lion's share) goes to the beneficiary designated by the key employee. Since the portion of the proceeds to be received by the employee gets smaller as the employer's benefit gets larger, many businesses elect to use dividends on the policy to buy one-year term insurance or paid-up additions so that there is a level death benefit paid to the beneficiaries designated by the key employee.

There are two methods of structuring a split-dollar arrangement. The first is

---

7. I.R.C. § 79(d)(2)(B).
8. I.R.C. § 79(d)(3)(A).
9. I.R.C. § 79(d)(5).
10. Reg. § 1.61-22(b)(1).

the endorsement method, where the corporation is the owner of the policy and there is an endorsement on the policy to reflect the interest of the employee. The second method is the collateral assignment method, where the employee owns the policy and "collaterally assigns" it to the corporation to secure the corporation's interest in the policy proceeds. The endorsement method gives the employer more control over the policy, including the ability to borrow from the cash surrender value.

What are the tax consequences of a split-dollar arrangement? If the endorsement method is used and the company owns the policy, the employee will be deemed to have received taxable compensation from the company for any portion of the premiums allocable to the employee's share of the policy that are paid by the company.[11] If the collateral assignment method is used and the employee owns the policy, any portion of the premium paid by the company, the non-owner, is treated as a below-market loan to the employee. The employee will be deemed to have received compensation income equal to the imputed interest on the loan and to have paid the interest to the company.[12] The death benefit ultimately received by the corporation and the employee's beneficiary will be tax-free under Section 101.[13]

### c. Life Insurance Within Qualified Retirement Plans

The income tax burden of funding a life insurance policy for a key employee also may be mitigated by acquiring the policy in a qualified retirement plan. The first question that always arises is: Why buy life insurance in a qualified plan? Many wrongfully assume that the payment to the beneficiary of life insurance proceeds passing through a qualified plan will be fully taxable. In fact, if a death benefit is paid to a beneficiary from a qualified retirement plan, the difference between the cash surrender value and the face amount is treated as tax-free under Section 101 to the same extent that such proceeds would have been tax-free if they were payable directly to the beneficiary.[14] The justification for this is that the cost of the insurance protection offered by the policy will have already been taxed to the employee on an ongoing basis as the premiums were funded with qualified plan dollars.[15] The portion of the proceeds equal to the cash surrender value are taxable as a long-term capital gain to the extent that they exceed the amounts previously taxed to, or paid by, the employee.[16]

The second most often asked question is: How much life insurance can be acquired within a qualified retirement plan? Existing regulations provide that life insurance is a permissible investment so long as it is merely "incidental" to the primary purpose of the qualified plan.[17] In determining whether the amount of life insurance provided by a qualified plan is incidental, coverage provided by

---

11. Reg. § 1.61-22(d)(1). If the endorsement method is used and the employee has legally binding rights in the policy beyond a share of the death benefit, it is likely that that the Section 409A requirements will be applicable to such rights. IRS Notice 2007-34. See Chapter 10 for a discussion the Section 409A requirements.

12. Reg. § 1.7872-15(e).

13. I.R.C. § 101(a)(1).

14. Reg. § 1.72-16(c).

15. I.R.C. § 72(m)(3)(B); Reg. § 1.72-16(b)(2).

16. Reg. § 1.72-16(c).

17. Reg. § 1.401-1(b)(1)(i) & (ii); Rev. Rule 54-51, 1954-1 C.B. 147.

insurance with an indeterminate premium, such as universal life insurance policies, will be incidental so long as the cost of providing the life insurance benefit does not exceed 25 percent of the contributions to the plan. The permissible percentage is increased to 50 percent in the case of coverage with a fixed premium, as with whole life policies. With regard to defined benefit plans, the insurance benefits will be considered incidental if the amount of the death benefit does not exceed 100 times the projected monthly life annuity that will be provided under the plan at the age of retirement.[18]

The cost of a portion of the life insurance protection provided through a qualified plan must be included in the employee's gross income in the year in which the premiums are funded with the pre-tax dollars contributed to the plan by the employer. The amount taxed to the employee is determined pursuant to IRS Table 2001, which approximates the cost of the mortality risk.[19]

### Planning Question 6: Are there any adverse estate tax impacts of business life insurance?

Potential adverse estate tax impacts always exist in structuring business life insurance programs. The regulations make it clear that the death benefit of an insurance policy owned by and payable to a corporation will not be included in the taxable estate of the insured shareholder, even if the shareholder is the sole shareholder of the corporation.[20] However, the value of the stock in the insured's taxable estate will be affected by the corporation's receipt of the insurance proceeds.[21] For a more thorough discussion of the estate tax impacts of corporate-owned insurance, see Section B of this chapter.

Assume that a controlling shareholder of a corporation establishes a life insurance trust and has a split-dollar contract structured between the life insurance trust and the corporation. The plan is structured to have the corporation fund most or all of the premiums, and to have the shareholder's share of the death benefit paid to a trust established for the benefit of the shareholder's family. The hope is that the death benefit will be excluded from the shareholder's taxable estate. This hope will fail if the corporation controls any incidents of ownership in the policy and the controlling shareholder owns more than 50 percent of the stock of the corporation.[22] If the corporation has any control over the policy, the control will be imputed to the controlling shareholder and the death benefit will be taxed in the shareholder's estate. So in a split-dollar situation such as this, it is critical that the collateral assignment be established in a manner that gives the corporation no control rights over the policy.

### Planning Question 7: Does the death benefit hit its ultimate destination income tax-free?

A major benefit of any life insurance policy is that the death benefit is not

---

18. See Rev. Rule 61-121, 1961-2 C.B. 65; Rev. Rule 68-453, 1968-2 C.B. 163; Rev. Rule 61-164, 1961-2 C.B. 99; Rev. Rule 66-143, 1966-1 C.B. 79.
19. Notice 2001-10, 2001-5 I.R.B. 459.
20. Reg. §§ 20.2042-1(c)(2), 20.2042-1(c)(6).
21. Reg. § 20.2031-2(f).
22. Reg. § 20.2042-1(c)(6).

*Keypoint*

subject to income taxes.[23] The importance of this result is a given in nearly all cases. The planning just assumes no income taxes on the death benefit. Unfortunately, sloppy planning can wipe out this essential income tax benefit. There are structural traps that may be triggered when the plan is designed to have the corporation own the insurance or to have policies transferred among shareholders when a death occurs. These are reviewed in the following section.

## B. CORPORATE-OWNED LIFE INSURANCE

### 1. INTRODUCTION

A common practice of many planners and insurance professionals has been to structure life insurance programs that end up with the company owning the policies. Tax laws create obstacles for any corporation that owns policies that insure the lives of its executives or shareholders. There are a variety of factors to consider in the planning process. This section reviews and analyzes many of the issues that affect corporate ownership of life insurance policies. It first examines why corporate ownership is used so often. The fact is that the obstacles have not deterred many from parking policies inside their corporations. The section then reviews, in a question and answer format, many of the issues that surface when life insurance policies are owned by a corporation.

### 2. WHY CORPORATE OWNERSHIP?

There are a variety of explanations for the common practice of having a corporation own life insurance contracts. Any one or more of the explanations may apply in a given situation.

Funding the premiums is usually the biggest challenge that has to be addressed when a life insurance policy is purchased. Except in extremely rare cases, life insurance premiums need to be funded with after-tax dollars. Historically, it has been easier in small companies to fund after-tax premiums with earnings accumulated in a regular C corporation because of the low corporate rates on the first $75,000 of corporate earnings each year. The tax rate for C corporations (other than professional service corporations) is 15 percent on the first $50,000 of accumulated earnings each year and 25 percent on the next $25,000.[24] The C corporation shareholder who is faced with a $40,000 annual insurance premium may find it easier to fund the premium with 15 percent tax dollars that are accumulated in the corporation, as opposed to dollars that are taxed at a higher rate in the shareholder's individual return. It's the old "bracket-racket."

The second major factor that contributes to corporate-owned life insurance is the structuring of buy-sell agreements. Often when these all-important agreements are designed, the end result is a number of life insurance policies being owned by the corporation. The alternative, of course, is to have cross-ownership of the policies among the individual shareholders. If there are many shareholders, the logistical problems of cross-ownership can be difficult.

---

23. I.R.C. § 101(a)(1).
24. I.R.C. § 11(b).

Assume, for example, that there are five shareholders, each of whom owns a policy or an interest in a policy on the other four shareholders. Simple arithmetic confirms that there would be 20 different ownership combinations, many of which would need to be juggled every time there is an entry or an exit. There are tools to help with this juggling, such as trusts and partnership arrangements, but these tools stack on more complexity. Many clients and advisors toss up their hands on this one and choose to avoid the hassles and the complexities by opting for corporate ownership.

Another major challenge with a cross-purchase structure is the premium burden. Where are the shareholders going to get the cash to fund the premiums? The obvious answer is the corporation. But how is the corporation going to move enough funds to the 20 percent shareholder to fund the policy on the life of the 80 percent shareholder? The answer may be bonuses. But a large bonus program may create income tax problems for the corporation and internal problems among the shareholders. How about dividends? Not a chance – a double tax burden and a pro rata distribution requirement.

Also, when the policies are individually owned in the cross-purchase format and there is a need to juggle the ownership, transfer-for-value problems may surface. If Shareholder A leaves the group and transfers to Shareholder B his interest in the policy insuring the life of Shareholder C, the transfer-for-value rule will kick in and Shareholder B will lose the tax-free death benefit on C's policy.[25] This problem is avoided with corporate ownership.

These problems of cross-ownership are not insurmountable. Often there are solutions that require some added complexity. But many clients just won't tolerate the added complexity. They want things simple and understood. For these clients, corporate ownership of the buy-sell insurance often is the answer.

In addition to buy-sell structuring, there are many other situations that dictate the use of corporate-owned life insurance. Key person insurance is probably the most obvious example. The purpose of the insurance is to provide the corporation with a cash infusion if there is an untimely death of a key person. The corporation funds the policy and is both the owner and the beneficiary of the policy.

Also, many companies have adopted nonqualified deferred compensation programs, including supplemental executive retirement programs, to augment benefits provided to their key executives under the company's qualified retirement plan. These nonqualified plans are usually structured to accomplish a number of objectives for both the employee/owners of the business and certain key executives who are not shareholders of the corporation.[26] Although the tax structuring usually requires that the liability of the corporation under these plans be an unfunded and unsecured obligation of the corporation, the company often chooses to implement an informal funding mechanism to assist the company in discharging its future obligations. This funding mechanism often involves

---

25. I.R.C.§ 101(b).
26. See generally the discussion in Section B of Chapter 11.

corporate-owned life insurance. The life insurance offers three significant tax benefits that help with a nonqualified plan: the ability to access funds prior to death through policy loans; the tax-deferred inside build-up within the policy; and the tax-free death benefit. These three characteristics of life insurance often make it the preferred choice in informally funding the future obligations of the company under such plans.

Perhaps the most prevailing reason for corporate-owned life insurance has nothing to do with taxes or technical structuring. Many business owners simply prefer to pay as many bills as possible with corporate funds. When it comes to any expenditure, they have a fixed mindset: corporate checkbook – good/ personal checkbook - bad. Corporate dollars are easy; personal dollars are off limits.

Whenever corporate ownership of life insurance is considered, a provision added by The Pension Protection Act of 2006 should be considered.[27] The provision subjects a portion of the proceeds paid on certain employer-owned life insurance policies to income taxation. If the provision is applicable to a policy, the excess of the death benefit received over the total premiums and other amounts paid for the policy will be taxable income. The section applies to an "employer-owned life insurance contract," which is generally defined to include any policy owned by and for the benefit of a business that insures the life of a person who was an employee of the business at the time the policy was issued.[28] There are huge exceptions that as a practical matter will render the provision irrelevant in most business and executive planning situations. The exceptions preserve tax-free treatment if the insured was an employee during the 12-month period before the insured's death; if the insured was a director or highly compensated employee of the business; if the proceeds were payable to the insured's estate, members of the insured's family or a trust established for their benefit; or if the proceeds were used to acquire an equity interest in the business from the insured's estate or members of the insured's family.[29] The one potential trap is that an exception will apply only if the notice and consent requirements of the new provision are met before the policy is issued. These requirements mandate that before the policy is issued the company must provide a written notice to the insured of the company's intention to own and be the beneficiary of the policy, and the insured must consent in writing to being the insured on a policy.[30]

### 3. THE CONSEQUENCES: QUESTIONS AND ANSWERS

**Question 1: Is corporate-owned life insurance for C corporations and S corporations treated similarly?**

The answer is "no." They are very different creatures when it comes to life insurance. S corporations do not pay corporate taxes and do not have to worry about the AMT. The interest deduction rules are different, along with just about everything else. Whenever an issue is presented regarding corporate-owned life

---

27. I.R.C. § 101(j).
28. I.R.C. § 101(j)(2)(3).
29. I.R.C. §§ 101(j)(2), 414(q), 105(h)(5).
30. I.R.C. §§ 101(j)(2), 101(j)(4).

insurance, the threshold question is whether the entity is an S corporation or a C corporation. It will usually make a huge difference in the analysis.

**Question 2: If life insurance proceeds are paid to a corporation, are the proceeds insulated from the claims of corporate creditors?**

Generally not. It makes no difference whether the corporation is a C corporation or an S corporation. Once the proceeds hit the corporate coffers, they become general assets of the corporation that may be reached by any corporate creditor. This is a disadvantage of corporate-owned life insurance. If the proceeds are paid to the shareholders, they will remain insulated from the claims of corporate creditors if the legal corporate veil that protects the personal assets of the shareholders is intact. If a corporation has substantial contingent liabilities that threaten its asset base, getting the insurance out of the corporation may be advisable.

**Question 3: If a C corporation receives a death benefit under a policy, can it distribute the proceeds to its shareholders and preserve the tax-free character of the proceeds?**

X, Y & Z Corporation is a C corporation with three equal shareholders, Jim, Larry and Sue. The corporation funds and owns a $500,000 life insurance policy on each of its shareholders. Jim dies, and the corporation collects $500,000. The issue is: can X, Y & Z Corporation distribute the $500,000 on a tax-free basis to Jim's estate and the other two shareholders?

The answer is "no." Although the proceeds are received tax-free by the corporation, the tax-free treatment stops there. A new tax burden is triggered if the corporation attempts at that point to distribute the proceeds to the shareholders by way of a dividend or some other distribution with respect to their stock. Note, however, that the shareholder who died, Jim in our case, will have received a step-up in his stock basis at death and, therefore, his estate may possibly avoid any income tax hit on a redemption of his stock.

Also, the income tax issue may not be a problem if the insurance is carried by the corporation to fund a deferred compensation payment to a shareholder/employee or a key executive or to fund some other liability that will generate a tax deduction for the corporation. Assume, for example, that the $500,000 policy on Jim's life is used to discharge a substantial deferred compensation liability that is payable to Jim's estate. In that situation, all payments that the corporation makes to Jim's estate following his death will trigger an income tax deduction for the corporation and an income tax hit to Jim's estate.

If the marginal corporate income tax rate approximates the estate's marginal income tax rate, the tax savings to the corporation will offset the tax hit to the estate. And if the corporation so chooses, it may transfer its tax savings to the estate through an additional gross-up bonus payment to cover the estate's income tax burden. In this situation, the life insurance proceeds would be received by the corporation tax-free and could then be transferred to discharge the deferred compensation obligation to Jim's estate without generating any additional net income tax between the parties.

**Question 4: If an S corporation receives a death benefit under a policy insuring the life of one of its shareholders, can it distribute the proceeds on a tax-free basis to its shareholders?**

It's the same situation as above, except X, Y & Z Corporation is an S corporation. Does the S status make it possible for the corporation to distribute the insurance proceeds to its shareholders tax-free? The answer is "maybe." If X, Y & Z Corporation has always been an S corporation or is an S corporation that has no accumulated earnings and profits from a C corporation past, then it's clearly possible for the corporation to transfer the death benefit to the shareholders tax-free. The reason is that when the corporation receives the death benefit, the basis in each of the shareholders' stock will be increased pro rata by the amount of the death benefit received by the corporation.[31] This permits the corporation to then distribute the death benefit to the shareholders tax-free because the distribution will be completely covered by the shareholders' basis in their S corporation stock.[32]

In contrast, if the S corporation has accumulated earnings from a prior period when it was a C corporation, the result may be different. The S corporation's accumulated adjustment account is not increased by the tax-free death benefit received under a life insurance policy.[33] Any distributions made by X, Y & Z Corporation, as an S corporation, in excess of its accumulated adjustment account will be deemed to come out of the accumulated earnings and profits from the C corporation period and will be taxed to the shareholders as a corporate dividend.[34] For this reason, it is important in dealing with an S corporation to determine whether it has accumulated earnings from a C corporation past. If so, additional care is required in structuring the corporate ownership of the life insurance.

**Question 5: Do payments made by a C corporation to fund corporate-owned life insurance constitute "reasonable business needs" for purposes of the accumulated earnings tax?**

All C corporations are potentially subject to an accumulated earnings tax. It's a penalty tax that is imposed on any C corporation that accumulates earnings beyond the greater of its reasonable business needs or $250,000 ($150,000 for personal service corporations).[35] Many closely held corporations accumulate substantial earnings and are understandably concerned about the reaches of this extra tax. The issue is whether earnings used to fund corporate-owned life insurance contracts constitute "reasonable business needs" and, therefore, avoid the reaches of this tax.

If the insurance is owned to provide the corporation protection from loss of a key person, there should be little difficulty establishing that the premiums are reasonable business needs. The IRS' Section 531 Audit Guidelines recognize that a corporation may accumulate a fund to compensate for the loss of a key

---

31. I.R.C. § 1367(a)(1).
32. I.R.C. § 1368(b).
33. I.R.C. § 1368(e)(1).
34. I.R.C. § 1368(e)(1).
35. See generally I.R.C. §§ 531-537.

person rather than to insure against the loss.[36] This would suggest that premiums paid to insure against the loss of a key person should constitute reasonable business needs.

If the insurance is owned by the corporation to fund the redemption of a shareholder's stock at death, the issue is more difficult. If the redemption is for the benefit of the corporation, the funding of the premiums should constitute reasonable business needs. However, if the redemption is deemed to be for the benefit of the stockholders, the funding of the premiums will not qualify under the Service's Audit Guidelines.[37] Generally, it is easier to establish a business purpose if the insurance is to redeem the stock of a minority shareholder. A valid business purpose would exist, for example, if the stock of the minority shareholder needed to be redeemed in order to prevent the minority shareholder's family from interfering with the management of the business.

The situation becomes much more difficult if the insurance is being funded to redeem a majority block of stock from the controlling shareholder. In fact, usually the burden of proof will be too great when the majority shareholder's estate will be the recipient of the funds. It is a facts and circumstances test in determining whether the redemption is primarily for the corporation or the shareholder. Obviously, when the majority shareholder's stock is being redeemed, the presumption is that the redemption is primarily for that shareholder's benefit. In all cases, great care should be taken to document the specific business purposes in the directors' resolutions approving the redemption. It is helpful to recite any detailed facts that support the directors' action.

**Question 6: If a C corporation borrows on its corporate-owned life insurance policies, is the interest paid on the indebtedness deductible?**

The answer is usually "yes" if the indebtedness is for the business, subject to a very important limitation that was added in 1986. This limitation provides that no interest deduction is allowed to a corporation for interest on indebtedness with respect to life insurance on the life of any officer, employee, or other person financially interested in the corporation's trade or business, to the extent that the aggregate amount of such indebtedness, per individual person, exceeds the sum of $50,000.[38] This interest deduction limitation is an outright prohibition; the deduction will never be allowed for the excess loans, even if the proceeds are used in connection with the corporation's trade or business. The business purpose of the loan is irrelevant.

**Question 7: If an S corporation pays interest on indebtedness borrowed on policies owned by the S corporation, is the interest deductible?**

The S corporation is not subject to a corporate tax, so the issue is not the deductibility of the interest by the S corporation. Interest in an S corporation is treated as a separately stated pass-through item to the shareholders. The question is whether the shareholders will be able to claim a deduction for the pass-through

36. IRS § 531 Audit Guidelines ¶ 637.4; See also W.L. Mead, Inc. v. Commissioner, T.C. Memo 1975-215, affirmed 551 F.2d 121 (6th Cir. 1977).
37. IRS § 531 Audit Guidelines ¶ 637.3(3).
38. I.R.C. § 264(a)(4) & (e)(1).

of the interest expense.

If the interest expense constitutes a trade or business expense of the corporation, an interest deduction may be available. If the expense does not constitute a trade or business expense, but rather a personal expense of the shareholder, the interest deduction is out. If the policy is owned by the corporation for a bona fide business purpose and the interest expense is incurred to assist in funding the premiums under the policy, there should be a legitimate basis for claiming that the interest expense constitutes a trade or business expense of the corporation. However, there is an additional issue that must be considered beyond the trade or business expense question. The S corporation constitutes a pass-through entity for each of its shareholders, and therefore each shareholder of an S corporation may be subject to the passive activity rule of Section 469. If the shareholder works for the company and is deemed to be a material participant in the activities of the S corporation, then it is likely that the shareholder will be able to claim the interest expense as an active trade or business expense. On the other hand, if the shareholder is not a material participant in the activities of the corporation, it is likely that the interest expense will be considered investment interest or an expense subject to the passive loss limitations.

The issue of interest expense pass-through deductions in an S corporation can be complicated. Whenever interest expense is incurred in connection with life insurance indebtedness owned by an S corporation, great care should be taken to analyze the character of the interest expense and how the indebtedness should be structured to maximize the income tax position of the shareholders.

**Question 8: What are the tax consequences of a corporation changing the named-insured under a corporate-owned policy that allows an exchange option?**

Often a corporation will acquire policies on a select group of executives. There is always the possibility that one or more of the executives will lose benefits under the plan as a result of an employment termination and that a new executive will surface for whom the corporation wants to provide benefits under the plan. To accommodate this situation, policies sometimes include special exchange privileges. Essentially, these exchange privileges allow the corporation to change the insured without incurring additional policy acquisition costs. This exchange feature is desired to facilitate the administration of the plan and the entry and exit of new participants in the plan.

The issue is whether the exchange privilege, when exercised, will trigger any adverse tax consequences. The Service has ruled that the tax-free exchange provisions of Section 1035 will not apply to a change in the insured under an exchange privilege.[39] As a result, if the corporation exercises the privilege, any gain in the policy at the time of the exchange will be taxed to the corporation.

**Question 9: What are the alternative minimum tax consequences to a C corporation that owns life insurance policies before the death benefit is paid?**

---

39. Rev. Rul. 90-109, 1990-2 C.B. 191.

At the outset, it is important to note that the corporate AMT does not apply to a corporation during its first year of operation, during its first three years of existence if its average annual gross receipts were less than $5 million, and during any other year if during the preceding three-year period its average annual gross receipts were less than $7.5 million.[40]  Bottom line: the AMT does not apply to small and many not-so-small companies.

If the AMT does apply, then the corporation's "Adjusted Current Earnings" (ACE) needs to be calculated.[41]  The ACE is designed to approximate the earnings and profits of the corporation, using federal income tax concepts, although it is not identical to the earnings and profits calculation. Seventy-five percent of the ACE adjustment affects the calculation of the corporation's AMT.[42]

To illustrate the ACE adjustment and the AMT consequences, assume that XYZ Corporation purchased a policy in year one on the life of its president. The corporation was the owner and the beneficiary of the policy. During year one, the corporation made premium payments totaling $15,000. At the end of year one, the cash value of the policy was $18,000. In this situation, the corporation would be deemed to have an ACE adjustment of $3,000 in the first year, the excess of the cash surrender value over the total premium paid. The corporation's alternative minimum taxable income (AMTI) would be increased by 75 percent of this amount, or $2,250. If the maximum AMT rate of 20 percent was applicable after all the other calculations, there would be an additional tax of $450 (20 percent of $2,250) attributable to the insurance ACE adjustment item.

In year two, the corporation made another $15,000 premium payment and, at the end of that year, the cash value in the policy was increased to $38,000. The ACE adjustment in year two would equal the excess of the current cash value ($38,000) over the sum of the cash value at the beginning of the year ($18,000) and the premium paid during the year ($15,000). The result would be an ACE adjustment of $5,000 in year two. Again, up to 75 percent of this amount could be subject to the AMT. If during any year the corporation received non-taxable distributions from the policy, they would also be added to the net cash value at the end of the year in calculating the ACE adjustment for the year.

The bottom line is that a corporation may increase its alternative minimum tax liability simply by owning life insurance policies. However, in most cases, the ACE adjustment and corresponding AMT impact will be insignificant during the holding period of a policy.

**Question 10: What is the alternative minimum tax impact when the death benefit is paid to a corporation?**

The serious AMT impact may surface in the year that the death benefit is paid. Assume in the case of XYZ Corporation that the president died at the beginning of year three and a $500,000 death benefit was paid to the corporation. The excess of the death benefit ($500,000) over the corporation's basis in the

---

40.  I.R.C. § 55(e).
41.  I.R.C. § 56(g)(4).
42.  I.R.C. § 56(g)(1).

policy would need to be computed. The corporation's basis for ACE purposes would include any amounts that had previously been included in its ACE. So in our example, the basis would be $38,000. The additional $462,000 would constitute the ACE adjustment for the current year. Up to 75 percent of this amount would be exposed to the corporate AMT.

In many situations, it is difficult, if not impossible, to predict whether or when a corporation is going to be exposed to an AMT. The corporation may already be paying enough regular taxes to avoid any serious risk of an AMT hit. However, if a closely held corporation bails out most of its earnings in the form of bonuses and compensation (as so many do), it may be apparent up front that a significant AMT may be triggered if a death occurs and the corporation receives a large tax-free death benefit. The AMT impact should be carefully evaluated for each corporate client large enough to be subject to its reach, particularly when the client owns significant life insurance policies.

### Question 11: If a corporation purchases a life insurance policy from a third party, should it be concerned about the transfer-for-value rule?

Suppose, for example, that ABC Corporation hires a new sales manager and, in order to protect itself, purchases a pre-existing policy that insures the life of the sales manager. The existing owner is anxious to sell the policy, and ABC Corporation would like to have the policy for its own protection. If, in this example, the new sales manager is an officer or shareholder of ABC Corporation, there is a clear exemption available under the transfer-for-value rule, and the rule will not be triggered.[43] If, however, the sales manager is not a shareholder or an officer, the rule will kick in. The result would be that the death benefit, when received, would constitute taxable income to ABC Corporation to the extent the death benefit exceeded the amount initially paid for the policy plus any premiums paid subsequent to the company's acquisition of the policy. The key to avoiding the trap in such a situation is to give the new sales manager a title in the company that confers officer status.

### Question 12: Can a C corporation convert from a stock redemption plan to a cross-purchase plan without violating the transfer-for-value rule?

Assume that a closely held corporation has a buy-sell agreement that provides for a corporate redemption in the event of a shareholder's departure or death. The agreement is funded with life insurance that is owned by the corporation. The shareholders of the corporation have determined that they would like to convert their buy-sell plan to a cross-purchase structure. They have a number of reasons for wanting to make this change. The conversion necessarily requires that the policies owned by the corporation be transferred to the shareholders. The question is whether such transfers will violate the transfer-for-value rule.

The simple answer is that the rule will be violated and the policies will be tainted for income tax purposes. Valuable consideration will be deemed to have passed between the parties due to the reciprocal nature of the transfers and the

---

43. I.R.C. § 101(a)(2)(B).

relationship of the corporation to the shareholders.[44]   No exception to the transfer-for-value rule will be applicable if the corporation transfers policies to co-shareholders of the insured. Note that this harsh result cannot be avoided by having the corporation first transfer each policy to the insured, followed by a subsequent transfer by the insured to his or her co-shareholders. The policy transfer to the insured will not trigger the transfer-for-value rule because any policy transferred to the insured is exempt under the rule.[45] However, there is no protection for any policy transferred from the insured to the co-shareholders.

There is one possibility for saving such a conversion from the rule. If the shareholders also are partners in a bona fide unrelated partnership, the exception to the transfer-for-value rule for transfers among partners or among a partnership and its partners may be applied to facilitate the conversion to the cross-purchase structure without violating the transfer-for-value rule.[46]

**Question 13: Can shareholders restructure the insurance to convert from a cross-purchase to a stock redemption structure without violating the transfer-for-value rule?**

This situation is the reverse of the prior scenario. For whatever reason, the shareholders determine that it is in their interest to convert from a cross-purchase structure to a stock redemption structure. In contrast to the prior scenario, such a conversion can easily be made without violating the transfer-for-value rule. Any transfer of a life insurance policy to a corporation in which the insured is an officer or shareholder qualifies under an exception to the rule.[47]

**Question 14: Will the proceeds received by the corporation on the death of a sole or controlling shareholder be included in the taxable estate of the shareholder?**

The regulations to the Code clearly indicate that the answer to this question is "no" to the extent the proceeds are payable to the corporation. None of the corporation's incidents of ownership in the insurance policy will be attributable to the insured, even if the insured is the only shareholder or the controlling shareholder of the corporation.[48] However, as discussed below, although the proceeds are not directly included in the estate of the insured, there may be an estate tax impact because they may increase the value of the stock that is included in the shareholder's estate.

**Question 15: Does the rule for estate tax exclusion apply if the life insurance policy is subject to a split-dollar contract between the corporation and an irrevocable life insurance trust established by the insured?**

Here is the situation.   Jim is the controlling shareholder of ABC Corporation. He establishes a life insurance trust and has a split-dollar contract structured between the life insurance trust and his corporation. The plan is structured to have the corporation fund the premiums and to have that portion of

---

44.  Reg. § 1.101(b)(4) & (5) (Example 1).
45.  I.R.C. § 101(a)(2)(B).
46.  I.R.C. § 101(a)(2)(B). See PLR 904504.
47.  I.R.C. § 101(a)(2)(B).
48.  Reg. § 20.2042-1(c)(2) & (6).

the death benefit that exceeds the policy's cash surrender value paid to the trust. The hope is that the portion of the death benefit paid to the trust will be excluded from Jim's taxable estate.

In this situation, Jim's plan to have the insurance excluded from his estate will fail if the corporation controls any incidents of ownership in the policy and Jim is the controlling shareholder (owns over 50 percent of the stock). If the corporation has any control over the policy, the control will be imputed to Jim, as the controlling shareholder, and the death benefit will be taxed in his estate.[49] This situation is very different than the scenario described above where the death benefit is paid to the corporation. In the split-dollar situation where a majority shareholder uses a family trust in hopes of keeping the death benefit out of his or her taxable estate, it is critical that the collateral assignment method of structuring the split-dollar agreement be used in a manner that gives the corporation no control rights over the policy.

**Question 16: What is the estate tax impact if the controlling shareholder of a corporation that owns a policy on the life of that shareholder arranges to have the death benefit paid to another corporation that the shareholder also controls?**

In TAM 8710004,[50] the National Office examined a situation where a decedent, who was the sole and controlling shareholder of a corporation that owned the policy, caused the proceeds of the policy to be paid to a second corporation controlled by the decedent. The National Office concluded that the policy's incidents of ownership were attributable to the decedent because the proceeds were not payable to the corporation that owned the policy, nor were they used for a valid business purpose of that corporation. As a result, the proceeds were taxed in the decedent's estate.

**Question 17: How will the corporation's receipt of life insurance proceeds on the death of a shareholder affect the value of the shareholder's stock for estate tax purposes?**

As stated above, the regulations make it clear that the death benefit of an insurance policy owned by and payable to a corporation will not be included in the taxable estate of the shareholder, even if the shareholder is the sole shareholder of the corporation. However, the value of the stock in the insured's taxable estate will be affected by the corporation's receipt of the insurance proceeds. A threshold issue is the purpose of the insurance. Is it key person insurance or buyout insurance? This question may affect the valuation issue. A leading case in dealing with the valuation issue in the context of key person insurance is *Huntsman Est. v. Commissioner*.[51]

In *Huntsman*, the IRS claimed that the proceeds of the insurance policies received by the corporation on the death of the decedent would have to be added in full in determining the value of the stock in the decedent's estate. In other words, the IRS claimed that the stock should first be valued without regard to the

---

49. Reg. § 20.2042-1(c)(6).

50. TAM 8710004, 1986 WL 372475 (IRS TAM).

51. 66 T.C. 861 (1976), acq. 1977-1 C.B. 1.

life insurance proceeds, and then the total amount of the insurance proceeds should be added dollar-for-dollar in arriving at the taxable value of the stock. The Tax Court rejected the IRS approach. It held that the insurance proceeds should be given "consideration" in the valuation process. Essentially, the court determined that, to the extent the valuation of the business was based on the net assets of the business, the insurance proceeds should be included in the asset value calculation. However, the court reasoned that to the extent the stock valuation was based on a price/earnings multiple, the insurance proceeds may strengthen the cash position of the company, which in turn may affect the multiple determination. But in such event there may not be a dollar-for-dollar increase.

The most interesting aspects of the *Huntsman* case are the final results that surfaced after all the calculations were in. In that case, the earnings multiple basis of valuation was weighted three times heavier than the net asset basis of valuation. In addition, the court discounted the value of the decedent's stock to reflect the loss of the decedent's value to the corporation. The bottom line was that for the first corporation in the case the ultimate value was increased approximately twenty-four cents for each dollar of insurance received. For the second corporation in the case the ultimate valuation was increased approximately thirty-three cents for each dollar of insurance received. The case demonstrates that the insurance will have an effect on the stock valuation, but in most cases not a dollar-for-dollar impact.

The other question that often surfaces with key person insurance is whether the insurance can be used to offset any discount to the stock value that is based on the loss of the key person. Two cases that dealt with this issue were favorable to the taxpayers. In each of these cases,[52] the court recognized that the receipt of the insurance would be included in the total asset value calculation for the corporation, and that this would have some impact on the ultimate value. However, the court also determined that the corporation's receipt of the insurance did not reduce the key person discount.

In *Huntsman*, a portion of the insurance proceeds received by the corporation was used to redeem some of its stock that was owned by the estate. The IRS tried to contend that the use of the insurance proceeds for the redemption had the effect of making the proceeds payable to the estate, rather than the corporation. The *Huntsman* court refused to consider this issue because it was untimely raised. The Service later abandoned this position.[53] Accordingly, it appears that insurance received by a corporation that will be used for redemption purposes will not be included in the estate, but will affect the value of the stock as previously discussed.

It may be possible within limits to improve the stock valuation issue in such a situation with an appropriate buy-sell agreement. As discussed in Chapter 8, in some cases a buy-sell agreement can be structured to establish a value that is binding on the Service for estate tax purposes.

---

52. Feldmar v. Commissioner, T.C. Memo 1988-429; Rodriguez v. Commissioner, T.C. Memo 1989-13.
53. Rev. Rule 82-85, 1982-1 C.B. 137.

**Question 18: Can stock transfers affect the application of the "three-year" rule[54] in determining the insured's estate tax liability?**

This issue was presented in Revenue Ruling 90-21.[55]  The Ruling presented two situations.  In the first, the insured owned 80 percent of the voting stock of the corporation, which had purchased a policy on the insured's life, payable to the insured's child.  Two years before the insured's death, the corporation transferred ownership of the policy to the child for less than adequate and full consideration.  The Service ruled that the insurance proceeds would be includable in the insured's estate because the corporation's transfer of the policy within three years of the insured's death was attributable to the insured, as the controlling shareholder.

The second situation was similar, except there was no transfer by the corporation.  The insured simply transferred to the child 40 percent of the stock of the corporation, thus reducing the insured's interest in the corporation to 40 percent.  The Service ruled that since the shareholder had given up a controlling interest in the stock, he had effectively transferred the incidents of ownership in the policy.

The lesson from this ruling is that any controlling shareholder should be extremely sensitive to any insurance policy transfers that the corporation makes and any transfers of stock that may result in a transfer of control over the policy.  Otherwise, the three-year rule of Sections 2035 and 2042 may be triggered.

## PROBLEMS 12–A AND 12–B

**12–A.**  Adoft Inc. is a C corporation with three shareholders: Jane, Lewis and Peter.  All three work full-time for the company, are in reasonably good health, and are between the ages of 40 and 45.  Two years ago a local "insurance tycoon" convinced them that the corporation should purchase a $1 million whole-life policy on each of their lives.  The corporation is the owner and beneficiary of the policies and pays all the premiums.

You recently met with the three shareholders to discuss their planning needs.  During the discussion, the topic of the insurance policies surfaced.  Jane said she was "delighted" with the policies because the company would really need an infusion of cash if one of the owners died prematurely.  Lewis said that he was comforted to know that there would be a source of cash to purchase the stock of any deceased owner, and he really was pleased by the fact that his stock was worth "a million big ones."  Peter said that he did not like insurance people and did not trust "money grubbing insurance companies."  He thinks the premiums are a waste of money.

After each had expressed his or her opinion, they asked for your thoughts.  Among other things, they asked that you explain any tax benefits or burdens associated with the company's ownership of the three policies.  How would you respond?

---

54.  I.R.C. §§ 2035(a) and 2042 require that the proceeds of any life insurance transferred by the insured within three years of the insured's death be included in the taxable estate of the insured.
55.  1990-1 C.B. 172.

**12–B.** After you advised the Adoft Inc. shareholders in 12–A above, the three shareholders began to rethink their situation. They all agree that each of their stock equity interests is worth about $750,000 and that it is unlikely that the equity value will grow much in the future. In other words, none of them could envision paying more than that amount if one of the shareholders left or died. They agree that if Lewis died prematurely, the company could use a cash infusion of about $500,000 because he would leave a "big hole" that would be difficult to fill and that would trigger some immediate setbacks. The situation would not be as tough if Jane or Peter died. All agreed that $200,000 would be sufficient if Jane or Peter died prematurely. The discussion then focused on the individual needs of the shareholders. Peter has a spouse and three minor children; he wants an additional million for family protection. Jane is single, has no children and says she doesn't need any life insurance. Lewis is divorced, has two teenage children, and says he would like to have an additional $300,000 of protection for the next eight years – "until the kids are through college." All agree that the company should pay all the premiums. How would you advise them regarding the restructuring of their life insurance program? What additional facts would you like to have?

## C. EXECUTIVE LIFE INSURANCE WRAP-UP

### 1. INTRODUCTION

Life insurance is a key ingredient of many executive compensation packages. It provides financial protection against an untimely death. It is often structured as an integral part of the executive's long-term estate plan and as a tool to encourage the executive to remain dedicated and loyal to the company for the long term. A major challenge for the lawyer who advises executives and companies is to identify and coherently explain insurance strategies that will accomplish the objectives of an executive in a given situation.

The prior chapter of this book discusses select life insurance planning strategies for key executives. Section B of Chapter 11 reviews deferred compensation strategies and how and why life insurance is often a component of a deferred compensation plan. Section C Chapter 11 focuses on different strategies for sharing equity with key executives. All equity sharing strategies that offer real stock must be coordinated with a buy-sell agreement that, as discussed in Chapter 8, is often funded with life insurance. Also, non-real stock strategies often include a life insurance policy that is designed to help fund the plan.

This section wraps up the discussion of executive life insurance planning strategies by reviewing three mini-case studies that illustrate the stock option backup, the group-term carve-out, and legacy insurance. The executive insurance strategies discussed in this chapter and the previous chapter do not include all potential life insurance strategies for key executives (it's difficult to comprehend the limits of such a list), but they do provide the student with a sampling of common strategies and a review of the relevant tax and non-tax considerations.

## 2. Case Study One: The Stock Option Backup

Julie has been appointed president and chief executive officer of a closely held company that is on the move. Although the company's growth trends have been good, Julie believes that the company, through its research and product development, is laying the foundation for some spectacular growth that could occur four to seven years down the road. If she is right, there will be another round of financing, followed by a major public offering. It could lead to big profits for everyone involved. She wants in on the action. She has worked for the company for many years and has been instrumental in its success.

Julie is paid a respectable salary, has the potential of earning a sizeable bonus each year, and receives various corporate perks. But from Julie's perspective, her biggest stake is in the stock options that she has been granted. Over the years, she has been granted options for nearly 120,000 shares and anticipates receiving more options in the future. Approximately 60 percent of Julie's stock options are incentive stock options. The big advantage of an incentive stock option to Julie is that she recognizes no taxable income when the option is granted, and she recognizes no taxable income when the option is exercised and the stock is acquired.[56] The tax is deferred until the shares are ultimately sold at a gain. If Julie plays her cards right, the gain recognized at the time of sale will be a capital gain.[57] All of Julie's incentive stock options have a ten-year term, which is the maximum term permitted under the Internal Revenue Code.[58] Although the incentive stock options trigger no regular taxes at the time of exercise, there may be an AMT impact upon exercise. The excess of the stock's value at exercise over the option price will increase her alternative minimum taxable income.[59] It's a tax trap for anyone who holds incentive stock options.

Julie's incentive stock options have some limitations mandated by the Code. The options are not transferable, except upon her death.[60] All options must be exercised within three months after she ceases to be employed by the company.[61] And in order for her to receive favorable ISO tax treatment, the stock acquired through the exercise of an option cannot be sold until two years after the option is granted and one year after the option is exercised.[62]

Julie also owns a substantial number of nonqualified stock options. These options also have a term of ten years. Julie knows that with these options she will have to recognize taxable income when the options are exercised. The amount of income recognized will equal the excess of the fair market value of the stock at the time of exercise over the price paid for the stock through the exercise of the option.[63] So, if a share has a fair market value of $100 at the date of

---

56. I.R.C. § 421(a).
57. To qualify for capital gain treatment, no disposition of the stock can be made within two years of the date of option grant or within one year of the date the stock is acquired. I.R.C. § 422(a).
58. I.R.C. § 422(b)(3).
59. I.R.C. § 56(b)(3).
60. I.R.C. § 422(b)(5).
61. I.R.C. § 422(a)(2).
62. I.R.C. § 422(a).
63. I.R.C. § 83(a).

exercise and the option price is $15, Julie will be required to recognize $85 of taxable income when she acquires that share. The nonqualified options, by their terms, are not transferable during Julie's lifetime and must be exercised within three months after Julie ceases to be employed by the company.

Both Julie's incentive stock options and nonqualified stock options carry stock appreciation rights (SAR). These rights provide that in lieu of exercising the option Julie may elect to receive cash equal to the excess of the fair market value of the stock over the option price. This right gives Julie the cash equivalent of exercising the option and immediately selling the stock.

Julie believes that her stock options promise her and her family a huge financial benefit if the company succeeds. But there are some aspects of the program that bother her. She presently is in no financial position to exercise the options and hold the stock. It would take substantial cash resources to cover the exercise price and pay the taxes that would result from the exercise of the options. Plus, she figures that it makes no sense to exercise the options any earlier than necessary. She also is concerned that the potential of the options may be lost if she dies prematurely. She has worked hard to earn the options, and she wants to make certain that her family will be in a position to realize the potential of the stock that may be acquired through the exercise of the options. If she were to die in the next few years, her family, as a practical matter, would have only two alternatives with respect to the options. First, they could exercise Julie's SAR rights and receive cash equal to the excess of the value of the stock at that time over the option price. All of the cash received would be taxable to the heirs. Second, the heirs could exercise the options within three months following Julie's death and then sell the acquired stock to cover the option price and all taxes due. In either case, the increase in the value of stock following Julie's death would be lost. The family would have no right to continue to hold the options (because that is not permitted under the terms of the options), nor would the family have sufficient cash resources to buy and hold the stock.

Julie is disturbed with this prospect. She would prefer a program that would provide her family with the resources to exercise her options and hold the stock for an extended period. The answer for Julie may be a stock option backup insurance program. Life insurance would be used to protect the potential of her options in the event that she dies prematurely. The stock option backup insurance program may be structured in a variety of ways. First, it could be structured as a straight bonus insurance program. Julie would be offered an insurance policy. As the owner of the policy, she would have the capacity to transfer the policy to an irrevocable life insurance trust for the benefit of her family. This would provide the opportunity to have the insurance excluded from her taxable estate after a three-year term. Each year the company would bonus Julie an amount sufficient to cover the cost of the premiums on the policy and the tax associated with the bonus. If Julie were to die prematurely, the funds in the trust could be used to cover the exercise price of the options and all taxes associated with the exercise of the options. The trust could then hold the stock as it grew in value.

Alternatively, the backup insurance program could be structured as a split-dollar arrangement. Julie's irrevocable life insurance trust would own the policy, but make a collateral assignment of the policy to the company. At Julie's death, the company would be entitled to recover from the death benefit the total amount of premiums it had paid on the policy. The balance of the death benefit would go to the trust, which would use the proceeds to exercise the options and cover any taxes associated with the exercise. If the company makes the entire premium payment under such a split-dollar arrangement, the company would be deemed to have made a below-market loan to Julie each year equal to the premium paid, and Julie would be taxed accordingly.[64] She would be deemed to have received compensation income equal to the imputed interest and would be deemed to have paid the interest to the company. The company would be deemed to have received the interest as income and would get a deduction for the deemed compensation paid.[65]

Julie, in turn, would be deemed to have made a gift of such amount to the trust. This gift to the trust would constitute a future interest that would not qualify for the $14,000 annual gift tax exclusion unless a *Crummey* procedure is followed for all such gifts to the trust.[66] The problem in this "employer pay all" situation is that there is no actual contribution of cash to the trust by Julie. So, it may be difficult to comply with a *Crummey* procedure that gives each trust beneficiary the option to withdraw from the trust his or her share of the contribution. The easy solution to this *Crummey* problem in an "employer pay all" split-dollar arrangement involving an irrevocable life insurance trust is to have the company actually pay Julie enough money each year to cover her share of the policy so she can contribute cash to the trust. Then there would be actual cash the beneficiaries could potentially reach through their *Crummey* withdrawal rights.

Another potential solution is to draft the *Crummey* power in the trust so broadly that the beneficiaries could exercise their *Crummey* withdrawal right each time the employee was deemed to have made a contribution to the trust, even though the contribution did not include any cash. In this situation, the trustee should be empowered to respond to any such *Crummey* demand by borrowing against the policy itself or by distributing any trust property, including the life insurance policy itself. This potential solution may be risky. A safer course of action is to have the employee actually make annual cash gifts to the trust.

One advantage of the split-dollar arrangement is that a permanent insurance policy would be acquired and funded over time. The split-dollar arrangement could continue to protect Julie's stock options until her retirement. If she remains with the company until retirement, the company could bonus to her at that time the entire policy. She could elect to maintain the policy as part of her permanent insurance program and possibly borrow against the cash value of the policy to facilitate the exercise of any options following her retirement from the company. Under this alternative, the split-dollar program becomes an integral part of her

---

64. Reg. § 1.7872-15(e).
65. Reg. § 1.7872-15(e).
66. See I.R.C. § 2503(b)(1).

customized retirement package and her stock option program.

To summarize, many executives hold stock options that have tremendous future value potential that could be eliminated by an untimely death. Often that potential can be protected with a backup insurance program.

### 3. CASE STUDY TWO: THE EXECUTIVE CARVE-OUT

Pete is a 62-year-old president of a successful company. He has been with the company for many years. The company offers a group-term insurance program that provides Pete a death benefit equal to twice his annual salary. Pete's annual salary is $300,000, so the total death benefit provided under the group-term program is $600,000.

This group-term program frustrates Pete. He does not believe it provides the key people in the company, including himself, with the protection they need. Since this term insurance ends at retirement, he cannot count on it as a real asset and incorporate it into his overall financial and estate plan. Also, the amount of taxable income that is imputed to him under the plan goes up each year, and the company is required to bonus to him a larger amount to cover the tax hit on this imputed income. He considers all this to be a waste because he doesn't anticipate dying before retirement at age 65. He believes this insurance is not going to produce any benefit for his family in the long run.

The company's board recognizes that this is a problem for Pete and other key executives. They would like to provide some type of permanent insurance benefit to their key people. They have explored the idea of continuing the group-term insurance beyond retirement. However, this poses two serious problems for the company. First, group-term coverage cannot be pre-funded for just select employees during their employment years, and it would be prohibitively expensive to cover all employees.[67] Second, the imputed income tax hit under any group-term program that extends beyond retirement would simply get worse for Pete as he grows older following his retirement.

The alternative for Pete and the other key executives may be a group-term carve-out program. Essentially, it's a permanent insurance program for a select group of employees that is carved out of the company's existing group-term insurance program. Under such a carve-out program, the company would fund a permanent insurance policy for Pete. The company would no longer pay the premium on Pete's $600,000 coverage under the group plan. The group-term benefit may be eliminated entirely, or may be reduced to $50,000, the maximum insurance amount that the company could fund under a group-term policy without triggering any imputed income to Pete.[68] In addition, the company would no longer need to bonus Pete any amounts to cover the tax hit on the income imputed to him under the group-term policy because the imputed income would be gone. The strategy would be to use the savings from the group-term policy and the related cost of the tax hit to Pete to help fund a permanent insurance benefit for him.

67. I.R.C. § 79(d)(4).
68. I.R.C. § 79(a)(1).

Pete's new insurance benefit may be structured in a variety of different ways. First, it may be structured as a simple bonus insurance program. The company would acquire a permanent insurance policy that Pete would own. Pete could protect the policy from estate taxes by transferring it to an irrevocable life insurance trust for his family. The company would make the premium payments and realize a deduction for the payments because they would be imputed and taxed to Pete as additional compensation income. The company could gross-up the amount of the payments to cover Pete's income tax exposure. Pete would have complete control over the policy and could incorporate it into his overall estate plan. The company could structure the funding so the policy would be fully funded by the time of Pete's retirement or, alternatively, the company could elect to pre-fund a portion of the policy prior to Pete's retirement and to fund the balance of the policy following Pete's retirement.

As an alternative, the company could elect to be the owner and the beneficiary of the policy. At Pete's death, the company would collect the insurance tax-free and pay the proceeds to Pete's designated heirs as a death benefit. As the owner of the policy, the company would not be entitled to any deduction as the premiums are made. Similarly, Pete would not have to recognize any income while the policy is funded. The benefits paid to Pete's heirs would be taxable,[69] and Pete would have no capacity to assign the policy to an irrevocable trust for estate planning purposes. Pete would have no equity interest in the policy and would have no capacity to exercise any rights over the policy. This alternative may be attractive for the company that is concerned about executive turnover and wants to make certain that its key executives acquire no interest in the policy until retirement. The plan could be structured so that the company would own the policy until Pete reaches a designated age, at which time the policy would be transferred to the executive as a bonus. The executive would be taxed on the value of the policy at time of transfer so the company may need to gross-up the bonus with cash to cover Pete's tax hit. Following the transfer, the company would continue to fund the policy through a cash bonus program.

A third alternative is a split-dollar arrangement. The company would fund the policy and be entitled to receive a portion of the death benefit equal to the premiums it pays. Pete would recognize taxable income each year, the amount of which would depend on whether the company or Pete (or a life insurance trust created by Pete) was the owner of the policy.[70] The company would only be entitled to receive a deduction equal to the amount of income recognized by Pete. Pete could assign the policy to an irrevocable life insurance trust for estate tax purposes.

Any company that considers adopting an executive group carve-out insurance program needs to consider a number of collateral issues that may affect the structure of the program. Following is a list of some of the planning questions that often surface in connection with such a group carve-out program:

---

69. I.R.C. § 691(a)(1).
70. See discussion accompanying footnotes 10 through 13, supra.

1. How is the underwriting going to be handled for the group of executives? The principal issue is whether there is going to be any preferred underwriting for the executive whose health is questionable.  As the group gets larger, the underwriting requirements may be simplified.  If a particular executive cannot satisfy the underwriting requirements, the best alternative for that executive may be for him or her to remain in the company's group-term plan until retirement and then for the company to structure some type of special uninsured death benefit plan for that executive following retirement.

2. Are insurance adjustments for salary increases automatically covered under the plan?  Under the present group insurance program, Pete is entitled to an insurance benefit equal to twice his annual salary.  He anticipates that his annual salary is going to increase substantially during the last three years of his employment with the company.  He believes other key executives are going to experience similar increases as they take on more responsibility.  Pete wants to be sure that any group carve-out program will continue to offer him a death benefit equal to at least twice his salary, which is rising.  The challenge is to structure a permanent carve-out insurance program with policies that will automatically reflect actual salary increases without a requirement for any new underwriting.  This can be a difficult challenge in some situations.  Some policies are limited to salary increases that do not exceed a designated percentage, such as ten percent.  Others are more flexible.  It's an important issue to consider in any group carve-out program for key executives.

3. How much flexibility is there in funding the policy prior to retirement? Suppose that one of Pete's key executives is 50 years old.  The company knows that, over the next 15 years, that executive's annual pay is going to increase at an annual rate of at least eight percent.  Therefore, the company is able to project the increasing death benefit that will be provided to that executive between now and age 65.  The company may prefer to structure the insurance program so that it makes a uniform annual payment to the insurance program over the next 15 years, based on the projected increases.  Essentially, the company would be pre-funding the death benefit obligation in the early years.  The challenge is to structure a policy that will allow pre-funding under this type of program.  It has significant appeal to many companies who would prefer to fund a level benefit and know that the policy will be fully funded when the executive reaches retirement age.

4. Is the program going to offer portability to the executive?  Group-term insurance programs usually offer the employee no portability advantages if the employee, for whatever reason, leaves the company.  Similarly, there may be little or no portability offered to the executive if the company is both owner and beneficiary of the carve-out policy and simply offers the executive a death benefit.  The portability feature may be significantly enhanced through a bonus insurance program or a split-dollar program.  This portability feature may be very attractive to the executive, but not so attractive to the company that wants to reduce the risk of turnover among its key people.

5. Who is going to cover the employee's tax burden?  Under a bonus insurance program or split-dollar program, the employee would recognize taxable

income each year as the policy is funded. Under a death benefit program where the company owns the policy, the employee's heirs would recognize a substantial tax hit when the benefit is paid. Is the employee going to be expected to absorb the tax costs under these arrangements, or is the company going to bonus the employee additional cash through a gross-up program to help the employee cover the tax burden? This is a critical structural issue.

6. How is the policy going to be structured and funded? The company needs to make a decision regarding the nature of the policy that is going to be used to fund the group carve-out program. Is the policy going to grow and endow by a designated age, such as age 95? How much cash value will be accumulated in the policy as of retirement? Is the policy going to be fully funded prior to retirement, or is the company going to continue the funding of the policy following retirement? How conservative or aggressive is the company going to be in projecting cash value increases under the policy? These are all important issues that the company needs to resolve in designing a permanent insurance policy for its key executives in a group carve-out plan.

There are a number of important issues that a company should consider in designing a carve-out plan for its key executives. If the issues are properly addressed and evaluated, it is often possible for the company to offer its key executives a permanent life insurance benefit at a reasonable increased cost to the company.

### 4. CASE STUDY THREE: LEGACY LIFE INSURANCE

Duke Lawson, age 59, made his millions three years ago when he sold his company. Following the sale, he played golf and was soon bored out of his mind. Two weeks ago (exactly two days after his non-compete expired), he started talking with Jake Moss, the majority owner of a C corporation that is a tough competitor of Duke's old company. Jake badly wants Duke to "come aboard for as much or as little as Duke wants." Duke likes the idea of getting "back involved" on a half-time basis. He misses the action. He'll be able to help grow Jake's company and will still have plenty of time for his golf. Duke's only problem is money; he has more than he or his family will ever need. He has no interest in accumulating more.

As Duke and Jake discussed the issue of pay, Jake struggled to find something that would excite and motivate Duke. What Jake discovered was that Duke's third great love in life (behind only his wife of 35 years and golf) was his religion. Duke has been a devout member of his church his entire life. Jake had his answer: a legacy life insurance program. Beyond a token salary, Jake's company would compensate Duke by funding a $1 million insurance policy on Duke's life for the benefit of Duke's church. Jake's company would be the owner and beneficiary of the policy and would enter into a simple agreement with Duke that would obligate the company to pay any death benefit received under the policy to Duke's church. As the owner of the policy, the company would not be entitled to deduct the premiums, and the proceeds would be received tax free, subject only to a potential corporate AMT.[71]  The company would be entitled to a charitable contribution deduction for the payment to Duke's church in an amount up to 10 percent of its taxable income, adjusted for select items.[72]  Any excess charitable contribution could be carried over five years.[73]  If Duke's role was limited to designating the charity to receive the payment, Duke would recognize no taxable income.[74]

Duke was motivated because his investment of time would produce a substantial tangible benefit for his church.  Jake was happy because Duke was motivated.  For those business owners who are no longer motivated by money, charitable planning often looks attractive.

*↳ Keypoint*

## PROBLEMS 12–C AND 12–D

**12–C.**     Bill Jones is the Operations Vice President of Fulton Communications Inc., a successful C corporation owned by six individuals.  Bill owns no stock in the company and has no hope of ever becoming a stockholder.  However, he has a powerful position in the company and serves on the board.  Bill is paid a substantial salary and has the opportunity to earn large bonuses each year through a generous executive incentive plan.  He also participates in the normal fringe benefit plans available to all employees, one of which is a Section 79 group term life insurance program.  Bill's term benefit under that program is $150,000.

Bill and a few other executives have become concerned about their life insurance benefits – or lack thereof.  They are meager term benefits that will terminate when they retire.  Bill would like to have $1.8 million of permanent coverage that he could count on until he dies.  He would prefer to have the insurance structured so that it would not be subject to estate taxes.  And he wants the company to fund the premiums as an executive perk.  The company's CEO has expressed interest in a new program and has asked Bill to come up with a specific proposal that would cover the company's top three executives.  Bill has requested your advice as the company's attorney.

**12–D.**     Dustin Wilson, the 56-year-old CEO of Wahshon Inc., has a substantial deferred compensation plan with his company.  The amount in the plan now exceeds $2.8 million, and he anticipates that the amount will exceed $4.1 million when he retires.  The company presently carries a $3.9 million insurance policy on Dustin's life to help fund the payment of its deferred compensation liability to him.

Recently, Dustin has become concerned about this life insurance policy.  He understands that if he dies and the company collects the death benefit and pays off his deferred compensation benefit, his heirs will have a double tax hit.  First, the amount paid under the deferred compensation plan will be income in respect of a decedent, taxable as ordinary income.  Second, the amount paid will be

---

71.  I.R.C. §§ 101(a), 56(g).
72.  I.R.C. § 170(b)(2); Reg. § 1.170A-11.  Adjustments are required for charitable deductions, the dividends received deduction, net operating loss and capital loss carrybacks and select other items.
73.  I.R.C. § 170(d)(2).
74.  See Knott v. Commissioner, 67 T.C. 681 (1977).

included in his estate for estate tax purposes. He considers this an intolerable result. He has asked for your advice. Is Dustin's analysis of the situation correct? What changes would you recommend?

# D. THE BUSINESS OWNER'S LIFE INSURANCE TRUST

## 1. INTRODUCTION

Business owners are often concerned with liquidity – the availability of cash. An untimely death can instantly create a liquidity crisis. For this reason, effective planning for most business owners requires the intelligent use of life insurance. Business owners typically focus on the cost/benefit ratio in structuring an insurance program. How much is the program going to cost? What is the real benefit that will be realized from the insurance? Does the cost justify the benefit? This cost/benefit analysis is substantially affected by tax considerations.

A primary tax threat is estate taxes. Are the proceeds going to be taxed in the owner's estate? If so, the policy may produce an after-tax benefit that is little more than half the face value. Put another way, the effective cost of each benefit dollar may be nearly twice the premium burden. In addition to this primary estate tax issue, there may be gift tax issues, income tax issues and generation-skipping transfer tax issues that have to be considered. Although these other tax issues are important, they are usually secondary to the primary issue of estate taxation.

The vehicle that is most commonly used to deal with the estate tax threat is the irrevocable insurance trust. It adds a layer of complexity that can produce a powerful tax benefit at death. But the complexity causes some to ignore it and others to use it ineffectively. This section focuses on the complexities of insurance trusts by addressing key questions that are often raised about these trusts in the planning process with business owners. A simple case study is used to help illustrate the significance of many of the questions and the related answers.

## 2. CASE STUDY: WALTER AND JANE BALLARD

Walter Ballard is 59 years of age. His wife, Jane, is 58. They have been married thirty-five years. Their estate is valued at approximately $33 million. Their principal assets consist of a closely held corporation (valued at approximately $24 million); a primary residence (valued at approximately $2.5 million); a secondary residence (valued at approximately $500,000); a retirement plan (valued at approximately $2 million); and a stock and bond portfolio (valued at approximately $4 million). They have no significant liabilities. They do not have a life insurance program.

The Ballards have two children – Walter, Jr., age 38, and Lucy, age 36. Their son is a civil engineer, and their daughter works part-time for their business. The Ballards have three minor grandchildren and another on the way.

The Ballards own all the stock of their closely held corporation. It is a light manufacturing business. They have 90 employees. Walter has been phasing out of the business for the past few years, although he continues to own all of the stock. There is no expectation that his children will become actively involved in the management of the business. Walter anticipates that he will eventually sell the business in stages to his second level management (which is quickly becoming the first level management), and, in return, will take back promissory notes that will be paid over a long period. He has no timetable for selling the business but hopes to defer the sale as long as possible.

The Ballards are seriously contemplating the acquisition of a $5 million life insurance policy. They want added liquidity in their estate for the benefit of their children and grandchildren. Walter is concerned about the impact his untimely death would have on the fate of the business. Plus, they are spooked by estate taxes, although they realize that Congress may change the estate tax in the future. They have not yet decided whether the policy should cover Walter's life only or be a survivorship policy that would pay only on the death of the surviving spouse. Although the premiums on the survivorship policy are substantially less, Walter likes the idea of Jane receiving a substantial cash boost if he dies first.

## 3. The Key Questions

### Question 1: Is it always advisable to protect life insurance from estate taxes?

No. In some cases it is unnecessary, and in other cases it is undesired. Of course, the challenge is to appropriately evaluate the circumstances and make sure the business owner understands the tradeoffs. In order to avoid estate taxation of the life insurance, it is necessary that all incidents of ownership in the policy be owned and controlled by someone other than the insured or the insured's spouse.[75] In the Ballards' situation, for example, their adult children or a trust established for the family could own the policy.

There is no question that separating the policy ownership from the parents creates an added complexity. Some couples just do not want this complexity, particularly if the primary purpose of the policy is to provide liquidity and support for the surviving spouse. If Walter's primary motive in acquiring a policy on his life is to provide liquidity for Jane's support following his death, neither he nor Jane may want the hassles of an irrevocable trust or the need to deal with their adult children. The estate tax burden can always be deferred until the death of the surviving spouse by making sure that the proceeds pass to Jane and qualify for the marital deduction. The only real issue then is estate taxation on the second death, and that may not be a big enough concern to justify the burdens of an irrevocable trust.

There also are situations where there is no need to protect the life insurance against estate tax. In many cases, the unified credits of both spouses, if properly maximized, may be large enough to cover any estate tax exposure. In some situations, the spouses may structure their estate plan so that the taxable portion

---

75. I.R.C. § 2042(2).

of the estate passes tax-free to charity on the death of the second spouse. Others may feel no need to lock their policy into an irrevocable trust because they are willing to bet that the federal estate tax will be watered-down or repealed altogether before their time comes.

There also is the situation where the client intends to use the life insurance policy as a tax-deferred retirement savings vehicle. In our case study, Walter may commence a program of rapidly building the cash value of the policy by aggressively funding the premiums. The income in the policy would accumulate on a tax-deferred basis. Down the road, Walter could borrow against the policy to supplement his retirement income. The policy would be used as a retirement savings program. In this situation, Walter would not want to transfer all of the incidents of ownership in the policy to his adult children or to an irrevocable family trust. Since he intends to personally benefit from the cash build-up within the policy, he would need to retain control of the policy. The tradeoff for the retirement savings benefit is that the policy would be exposed to estate taxation on the death of the surviving spouse.

**Question 2: Does it ever make sense to have the policy owned by a revocable living trust?**

If Walter and Jane establish a trust and reserve the right to alter, amend, revoke, or terminate it, they will accomplish nothing tax-wise. The assets of the trust, including the proceeds on any life insurance policy held by the trust, will be taxed in their gross estates. Nevertheless, Walter and Jane, like many couples, may establish a revocable living trust to avoid the hassles of probate, reduce the burden and expense of administration, and provide added privacy. But if they want to keep the life insurance proceeds out of their taxable estates, the revocable living trust won't do the job. They will need something more.

**Question 3: Can estate tax protection be obtained by having the adult children own the policy?**

Yes. If Walter's and Jane's two adult children own all of the incidents of ownership in their life insurance policies, the proceeds will not be taxed in their estates. Also, any amounts that Walter and Jane gift to their children to assist in making the premium payments should easily qualify for the gift tax annual exclusion without the necessity of going through the whole *Crummey* rigmarole discussed in Question 9 below. The obvious question: Why doesn't every couple have their children own the policy?

There are some disadvantages to this technique. If one spouse – Walter, in our situation – wants his surviving spouse to have access to the proceeds following his death, neither spouse may want to put control of the policy in the hands of the adult children. Jane may not like the idea of having her children control the funds that she is counting on for her support. A trust solves the problem by making her the primary beneficiary following Walter's death. For this reason, ownership by the adult children is usually limited to survivorship policies or policies in which neither spouse wants to claim any interest.

But even with a survivorship policy, ownership by the adult children may present problems. If the adult children do not get along or have spouses who routinely disagree, there may be problems with the control of the policy. If one of the children encounters serious financial difficulties, that child's interest in the policy may be exposed to his or her creditors. And if one of the children dies, that child's interest in the policy may become subject to a probate proceeding and may end up being passed to that child's heirs. A properly structured trust will avoid these potential problems. This is not to suggest that ownership by adult children should never be used. In some cases it is the easiest and, as a result, the preferred solution. But the client should understand the added protections that may be obtained by using a trust.

**Question 4: How much control over the policy do the parents lose with an irrevocable trust?**

All control! If Walter and Jane establish an irrevocable family trust to protect their life insurance from taxation, they must give up all incidents of ownership in the policy in order for the trust to accomplish its primary tax objective.[76] This means they must give up all control rights, including the rights to change the beneficiaries, assign the policy, surrender or cancel the policy, revoke any assignment of the policy, pledge the policy, borrow against the policy, change the time or manner in which proceeds will be received under the policy, or retain any veto right of any kind. The bottom line is that the new owner of the policy – the trustee of the trust or the adult children – must have all the control rights.

**Question 5: Can the parents serve as the trustees of their irrevocable family trust?**

Not a good idea. Suppose Walter and Jane want to use the trust, but do not want to give up control. Can they appoint themselves as trustees of the trust and still secure the estate tax benefits? In the leading revenue ruling on the issue,[77] the Service stated that an insured may serve as a trustee and not be deemed to own any incidents of ownership if all of the powers are held in a fiduciary capacity, if the insured did not transfer the policy to the trust or transfer any funds necessary to purchase or maintain the policy, and if the powers acquired by the insured as a fiduciary were not part of a pre-arranged plan involving participation by the insured. These standards are nearly impossible to meet. The most sensible course of action is to have someone other than the parents serve as the trustee and to include an express statement in the document prohibiting the insured and the insured's spouse from serving as a trustee of the trust.

**Question 6: Can the parents reserve the right to change or remove the trustee?**

Not if they want estate tax protection. If Walter has the power to remove or replace the trustee that he appointed at the outset, all of the powers held by that trustee may be imputed to Walter.[78] The result is that he will be deemed to own incidents of ownership in the policy, and the policy will be taxed in his gross

---

76. I.R.C. § 2042(2).
77. Revenue Ruling 84-179, 1984-2 C.B. 195.
78. TAM 8922003, Rev. Rule 79-353, 1979-2 C.B. 325.

estate. The bottom-line challenge is to make certain that the right trustee is selected at the outset.

**Question 7: What additional precautions should be taken if the insured's spouse is a beneficiary of the trust?**

Suppose Walter acquires a policy on his life, transfers the policy to a trust and names Jane the primary beneficiary of the trust for as long as she is alive. If there is a third-party trustee, are Walter and Jane home free tax-wise once the three-year rule has been satisfied? Maybe.

The issue in this situation is whether Jane ever owned any interest in the policy or the funds contributed to the trust to fund the policy premiums. If Jane owned an interest in the policy, she will be deemed to have retained that interest for life by virtue of the beneficiary designation; and, therefore, her portion of the policy will be taxed in her estate. This is a common problem in community property states where the spouses are deemed to own assets equally. It can also be a problem in a non-community property state where the spouse is an identified owner. The problem can usually be avoided by clearly documenting that the non-insured spouse has never owned an interest in the policy transferred to the trust and has no interest in any funds transferred to the trust. In a community property state, this will require documentation to clearly indicate that all assets transferred to the trust, including the policy, are the separate property of the insured. And, in many situations, it may be prudent to establish that the policy was held as the insured's separate property for a significant period before being transferred to the trust.

**Question 8. Can the trust agreement mandate that the life insurance proceeds be used to pay estate taxes?**

It can't be done without creating a serious tax problem. Section 2042 of the Code provides that life insurance will be included in the insured's estate if the proceeds are "receivable by the executor."[79] If the trustee is legally obligated to use the policy proceeds to pay estate taxes, the proceeds may be deemed to have been "received by the executor." The simple answer is to not mandate how the proceeds are to be used. The trustee may be given authority to loan funds to the estate to provide the estate with needed liquidity and to purchase assets from the estate at their fair market value. The key is to draft these sections to provide the trustee with broad discretion, but to not dictate specifically how the trustee is to handle the proceeds realized from the policy.

**Question 9: What are the tax consequences if the parents fund the premium payments by making cash contributions to the trust?**

Walter and Jane establish an irrevocable family trust that acquires a survivorship policy on their lives. The trust is in need of funds to cover the premium payments on the policy. Periodically, Walter and Jane give cash to the trust to cover the premium payments. Since the transfers constitute gifts, they do not trigger an income tax,[80] but do trigger a gift tax consequence.[81] And, in most

---

79. I.R.C. § 2042(1).
80. I.R.C. § 102(a).

family trusts, the trust provisions create future interests so that the gifts to the trust, standing alone, do not constitute present interest gifts that qualify for the $14,000 annual gift tax exclusion.[82]

Unless special measures are taken to have the transfers qualify for the $14,000 annual gift tax exclusion, the gifts will eat away at the parents' unified credits and may ultimately trigger a gift tax payment. The key of course is to build provisions into the trust that will allow the gifts to qualify for the annual exclusion. In almost all situations, this is done by including special *Crummey* withdrawal rights in the trust. If properly implemented, the *Crummey* provisions will convert a beneficiary's future interest to a present interest, which in turn will qualify the contributions for the $14,000 annual gift tax exclusion.

### Question 10: What is a *Crummey* Power?

Stated simply, it is a special provision in the trust that gives each beneficiary, for a limited period, the right to withdraw a portion of any contribution made to the trust. The mere existence of this right, even if it is not exercised and is allowed to lapse, will convert a future trust interest to a present trust interest so that the contribution will qualify for the annual gift tax exclusion. The power is referred to as a *Crummey* power because that is the name of the leading case that established the legal effectiveness of such a withdrawal right.[83]

Suppose, for example, that Walter and Jane's survivorship policy requires an annual premium of $22,000. If they contribute that amount to a trust and there is no *Crummey* withdrawal right, their unified credits will be reduced each year. If the trust includes a *Crummey* withdrawal right, each of their two children would have the right, for a limited period each year, to withdraw one-half of the contribution, or $11,000. Even though they are not expected to exercise the right and, in fact, do not exercise it, the contribution will be considered a gift of a present interest and will qualify for the $14,000 annual gift tax exclusion. As a result, there will be no impact on the parents' unified credits.

### Question 11: What should be included in the *Crummey* notice?

The IRS requires that each *Crummey* beneficiary be given prompt notice of his or her rights of withdrawal and a reasonable opportunity to exercise the power before it lapses.[84] The notice should explain the withdrawal right and also specify the amount of the contribution that is subject to the withdrawal right for the particular beneficiary.

### Question 12: How long does the *Crummey* election period need to be?

In various private letter rulings, the IRS has indicated that 30 days constitutes a reasonable time for the *Crummey* withdrawal period.[85] Any period less than 30 days is suspect and generally not recommended. If minors are involved, it may be prudent to lengthen the election period. There have been a

---

81. I.R.C. § 2501(a).
82. I.R.C. § 2503(b)(1).
83. Crummey v. Commissioner, 397 F.2d 82 (9th Cir. 1968).
84. Rev. Rule 81-7, 1981-1 C.B. 474.
85. See Private Letter Rulings 8813019, 8004172, 8024084 and Rev. Ruling 81-7, 1981-1 C.B. 474.

few rulings that have suggested that when there are minors the withdrawal period should be long enough to permit the appointment of a guardian under state law just in case that becomes necessary.[86]

### Question 13: How can a *Crummey* withdrawal right be given to a minor who is a beneficiary?

Suppose Walter and Jane name their grandchildren as primary beneficiaries of the insurance trust. Can a *Crummey* withdrawal right be given to a two-year-old?

The IRS has ruled that a *Crummey* withdrawal power can be given to a minor so long as there is no impediment under local law or the trust agreement to the appointment of a guardian who could exercise the minor's right to demand a withdrawal under the power.[87] The notice of the Crummey withdrawal right for the minor should be given to the minor's court-appointed guardian or, if there is no guardian, to the minor's parent as the natural guardian.

### Question 14: How is the *Crummey* power used in connection with a corporate-funded insurance program?

Group-term policies can present special challenges for a *Crummey* withdrawal provision if contributions are made on a periodic basis to pay insurance premiums. The IRS has taken the position that the trustee can satisfy the *Crummey* withdrawal right by making a single delivery of the future premium schedule to the beneficiaries.[88] If there is no published premium schedule, an alternative for a group term policy is to structure the *Crummey* withdrawal rights to extend over an entire year and to provide that the rights lapse annually at the end of the year and are not triggered by any specific addition to the trust itself. This technique may simplify the *Crummey* withdrawal procedure when periodic contributions are going to be made throughout the year to cover the premium payments.

### Question 15: What is the "5 and 5" rule?

This is a special rule that may apply whenever an individual is given a general power of appointment over property. If the individual who is given a general power of appointment[89] exercises the power or allows the power to lapse, he or she generally will be deemed to have made a transfer of the property for gift tax purposes.[90] The "5 and 5" rule is an important exception to this broad rule relating to general powers of appointment. The "5 and 5" rule provides that no taxable gift transfer will be deemed to have been made if the property subject to the general power of appointment does not exceed the greater of $5,000 or 5 percent of the total value of the assets out of which the general power of appointment could have been satisfied (usually 5 percent of the total assets in the trust).[91] It is a special rule that provides relief to one who is given a general

---

86. See, e.g., Private Letter Ruling 8825111.
87. Rev. Rul. 73-405, 1973-2 C.B. 321.
88. See Private Letter Ruling 8021058.
89. See I.R.C. § 2041(b)(1) for the definition of a general power of appointment.
90. I.R.C. § 2041(a)(2).
91. I.R.C. § 2041(b)(2).

power of appointment over property held in trust.

**Question 16: What impact does the "5 and 5" rule have on *Crummey* powers in an insurance trust?**

A *Crummey* power given to a trust beneficiary is considered a general power of appointment. If the amount subject to the Crummey power exceeds $5,000 or 5 percent of the total trust assets, the failure to exercise the Crummey withdrawal right (the lapse of the right as it's typically called) will be deemed a taxable transfer by the *Crummey* beneficiary. This transfer will be deemed to be a gift of a future interest and will trigger a gift tax use of the beneficiary's unified credit.

Let's look at a simple example. Suppose Walter establishes a trust and funds the trust with a policy that requires a $22,000 annual premium, or $11,000 for each of his two children. Assuming each of the children has a *Crummey* withdrawal right, the good news is that the entire transfer will qualify for the $14,000 annual exclusion. The bad news is that the "5 and 5" rule will protect only the greater of $5,000 or 5 percent of the trust property (in this case, the greater is $5,000) from a transfer tax by each child-donee who does not exercise the power. As a result, each child will be deemed to have made a taxable gift of $6,000, the excess amount over the maximum allowed under the "5 and 5" rule. Since that deemed transfer by each child-donee is a transfer of a future interest, each child's $6,000 taxable gift will either consume a portion of the child's unified credit amount (the likely result) or require the payment of a gift tax.

The point to remember is that the "5 and 5" rule has never been amended to match the increase in the gift tax annual exclusion of $14,000. Thus, in many family insurance trust situations, $5,000 is the real maximum amount that can be subject to one beneficiary's *Crummey* withdrawal right without creating a gift tax concern for the beneficiary.

**Question 17: Can the transfer capacities to an insurance trust be expanded by granting *Crummey* withdrawal powers to contingent grandchild beneficiaries?**

As stated above, if Walter's annual premium payment is $22,000 and the two children are the only beneficiaries of the trust, there is a problem under the "5 and 5" rule. Can this problem be eliminated by granting Walter's grandchildren *Crummey* withdrawal rights? Since he has three grandchildren, any transfer to the trust would be divided 5 ways. The amount that each beneficiary could withdraw under the *Crummey* power would be $4,400, which falls within the scope of the "5 and 5" rule.

The IRS has made its position clear that the *Crummey* technique will not work in the case of so-called "naked *Crummey* powers" – powers that are held by individuals who have no other interest in the trust.[92] So, as a general proposition, it's impossible to name friends or relatives in a trust instrument whose only interest is to exercise *Crummey* withdrawal rights. They must actually have a bona fide interest in the trust as beneficiaries. The question is whether the

---

92. TAM 8727003 (March 16, 1987); TAM 9045002 (July 27, 1990); Cristofani, Action on Decision, 1992-09 (March 23, 1992).

grandchildren, who have a contingent interest in the trust if one or more of their parents die, have a sufficient interest in the trust to justify the valid grant of *Crummey* powers to them. In TAM 9045002, the IRS ruled that a *Crummey* withdrawal power could not be given to a beneficiary who had only a remote contingent remainder interest in the trust. This IRS position was rejected by the Tax Court in *Cristofani Est. v. Commissioner*.[93]

In *Cristofani*, the trustor had two children and five grandchildren. He created an irrevocable trust that stated that his children were primary beneficiaries and his grandchildren were secondary beneficiaries. The trustor claimed seven annual gift tax exclusions on the grounds that each of the beneficiaries had a full *Crummey* withdrawal right. In focusing on the grandchildren's legal rights, the Tax Court determined that events could occur that would cause the children or the grandchildren, through their guardians, to exercise their withdrawal rights. The Tax Court specifically found that there was no agreement between the father, the trustees, and the beneficiaries that the grandchildren would not exercise their withdrawal rights. The court also determined that even though the grandchildren's interests were contingent, it was the intention of the settlor of the trust that each grandchild benefit from the trust in the event the grandchild's parent (the settlor's child) died. On the basis of these findings, the court determined that the *Crummey* powers could be appropriately granted to the grandchildren as contingent beneficiaries.

The bottom line is that uncertainty exists with respect to any insurance trust that grants *Crummey* withdrawal rights to contingent grandchildren as beneficiaries. Clearly the plan has a chance if it can fit squarely within the confines of the *Cristofani* case.

### Question 18: Are there any advantages to using multiple trusts to expand the Crummey withdrawal rights?

Suppose Walter establishes two separate trusts and puts a policy into each. He names his children as beneficiaries of each trust and contributes $10,000 to each trust. Does the use of the two trusts double the impact of the "5 and 5" exemption? The answer is "no" because the IRS will maintain that the "5 and 5" exemption must be applied on an aggregate basis. The result is that each beneficiary will be allowed only one "5 and 5" power each year to avoid a gift tax impact, even if the individual is a beneficiary of multiple trusts.[94]

### Question 19: What are the income tax consequences of an irrevocable insurance trust?

Usually the trust will be considered a grantor trust under the provisions of Section 677 of the Code because the income of the trust may be used to pay premiums on a life insurance policy that insures the life of the grantor or the grantor's spouse. Section 677 provides that the grantor is treated as the owner of any portion of a trust whose income, without approval or consent of any adverse party, may be applied to pay premiums on a policy of insurance on the life of the

---

93. 97 T.C. 74 (1991).
94. Rev. Rule 85-88, 1985-2 C.B. 201.

grantor or the grantor's spouse.[95] The same rule will apply even if the grantor did not transfer the policy to the trust.

The fact that the trust is treated as a grantor trust is not usually a significant concern. The income build-up within the life insurance policy will generally accumulate on a tax-deferred basis. Usually the trust has no other assets from which to generate any taxable income. If there is any additional income, it is usually nominal; the fact that it is taxed to the grantor will not be regarded as significant.

### Question 20: What are the Generation-Skipping Tax consequences of creating a life insurance trust?

Each transferor has a generation skipping tax (GST) exemption equal to the estate tax unified credit under Section 2010(c) of the Code.[96] This exemption is available to protect transfers to grandchildren and other descendants from the onerous GST. What does this mean from a practical standpoint for life insurance trusts? Here are four planning observations:

1. Even if the value of the parent's estate exceeds the GST exemption amount, remember that the GST is not even an issue until some portion of the estate passes to a "skip person," which is a grandchild or a more remote descendant.

2. Planners need not worry a great deal about the GST consequences where the life insurance trust is designed only to keep the proceeds out of the parents' estates. Since the ultimate beneficiaries of the trust are usually the children, there is not a major GST issue with this type of life insurance trust because the beneficiaries are all "non-skip" persons.

3. If grandchildren are given *Crummey* withdrawal powers, care must be taken to protect any amounts subject to the grandchildren's *Crummey* withdrawal rights from the GST.[97]

4. If the trust is set up as a "dynasty trust"[98] to pay benefits to multiple generations of beneficiaries, care should be taken to allocate the GST exemption to the contributions used to fund the premiums when the contributions are made. By doing so, the assets of the trust, including the death benefit, will be protected from the GST by virtue of such allocations.[99]

### Question 21: What are the primary administrative details that should be handled in setting up and maintaining a life insurance trust?

---

95. I.R.C. § 677(a).

96. I.R.C. § 2631(c).

97. A transfer to a trust, even a transfer that qualifies for the annual gift tax exclusion, must meet the requirements of I.R.C. 2642 to be assigned a zero inclusion ratio and be exempted from the generation skipping transfer tax. A typical life insurance trust will not satisfy the requirements of section 2642, which require lifetime income distributions to one individual and the trust's inclusion in that individual's estate. As a result, care must be taken to specifically allocate the GST exemption to all contributions to the life insurance trust, even those that are subject to a Crummey withdrawal right.

98. "Dynasty trust" is a term often used to describe a trust that is structured to provide benefits to members of multiple generations. Such trusts typically include provisions that allow them to last for the longest term permitted under the applicable state rule against perpetuities.

99. See HR Rep. No. 426, 99th Cong., 1st Sess. 1, 826 (1986), reprinted in 1986-3 C.B. (vol. 2) 1, 826.

The trust should obtain a federal employer identification number. This can be done by filing Form SS-4 with the IRS. The trustee should establish a bank account for the trust. All trust cash transactions should be handled through the bank account. Care should be taken to make sure that the trust is listed as both the owner and the beneficiary of all life insurance policies owned by the trust. Also, forms and procedures should be established to make certain that all of the *Crummey* withdrawal rights in the trust are carefully observed each time a contribution is made to the trust. The trustee should be instructed on the importance of these withdrawal rights and the need to observe the details.

If the contributions to the trust exceed the annual gift tax exclusion, the grantor will be required to file a gift tax return. In addition, if a *Crummey* power lapse triggers a taxable gift by the beneficiaries, they will be required to file gift tax returns.

The trustee must act as a fiduciary at all times in protecting and administering the life insurance policy and the other assets of the trust for the benefit of the trust beneficiaries.

### Question 22: What are the tax impacts of transferring an existing policy to an insurance trust?

Often an insured establishes an insurance trust after he or she has owned a policy for an extended period. The policy is contributed to the trust at the time the trust is established. There are three tax issues. First, if the transfer is structured as a gift, as is usually the case, there is no income tax consequence on the transfer to the trust.

Second, since the transfer constitutes a gift, there is a potential gift tax exposure. The amount of the gift is the replacement cost of the policy in the case of a fully paid-up policy, or the so-called "interpolated terminal reserve value" in the case of a policy where future premiums are due. The "interpolated terminal reserve value" is a fancy way of approximating the cash surrender value of the policy, plus any unearned premium as of the date of the gift, and less the amount of any policy loans.[100] This value will constitute a gift to the trust and will not qualify for the $14,000 annual gift tax exclusion unless the trust includes *Crummey* withdrawal powers that are applicable to the transfer of the policy to the trust. The third tax consequence is that the proceeds of the policy will be taxed in the insured's estate if the transfer is made within three years of the insured's death. Whenever an existing policy is to be transferred to a family trust, it is important to get the three-year clock ticking as soon as possible.

### Question 23: What are the consequences of the three-year rule?

Very simply, the three-year rule provides that the proceeds of a life insurance policy will be taxed in the estate of the insured if the insured has made any transfer of the policy to another party within three years of death.[101] So if Walter acquires a policy that insures his life, transfers that policy to a trust, and then dies within three years of that transfer, the policy will be taxed in his estate.

---

100. Reg. § 25.2512-6, Example (4).
101. I.R.C. §§ 2035(a) & 2042.

**Question 24: How difficult is it to avoid the three-year rule, and is it risky to try?**

Suppose Walter and Jane establish their insurance trust, appoint their adult children as trustees, and gift to the trust a sufficient amount of money to cover the initial premiums on a life insurance policy. Will the three-year rule be avoided if the trustees apply for a policy on Walter's life and directly acquire the policy? Neither Walter nor Jane will have owned any interest in the policy; and, therefore, they will not have made any policy transfer to the trust.

Historically, the cases have been all over the map on this issue, but careful taxpayers clearly have the upper hand at this time. A number of early cases adopted what is referred to as the "Beamed Transfer" theory, holding that the proceeds would be taxed in the estate of the insured in these circumstances. The argument was that the insured "constructively" transferred or "beamed" the policy to the trust by funding the premiums and establishing the trust. Under this line of cases, the proceeds were taxed in the insured's estate if death occurred within three years of the "beamed" transfer.

In *Kurihara Est. v. Commissioner*,[102] the Tax Court adopted an agency theory to require inclusion of the life insurance proceeds in the estate of the insured. In that case, Mr. Kurihara had transferred only a check to the life insurance trust, not the life insurance policy itself. But he specifically noted on the check that it was to cover the initial life insurance premium, and the trustee merely endorsed the check over to the insurance carrier. The court held that, in reality, Mr. Kurihara had transferred the insurance to the trust because the trustee was merely acting as his agent. As a result, the court held that the three-year rule was applicable.

More recent cases on the issue have clearly confirmed that there is a correct way to avoid the three-year rule where the policy has not yet been acquired. *In Leder Est. v. Commissioner*,[103] the policy was applied for and owned by the spouse of the insured, but the premiums were paid by the insured's corporation. In that case, the court held that the three-year rule did not apply because the insured never possessed any incidents of ownership in the policy. The same theory has worked for other taxpayers as well.[104]

These cases have given planners comfort in knowing that the three-year rule can be avoided if the insured transfers only cash to the trustee, and the trustee acts independently in acquiring a life insurance policy on the insured. Care should be taken to avoid any *Kurihara*-type agency argument. The trustee may be authorized but not required to acquire the life insurance, and the trustee should be given fairly broad investment powers. The key is to make certain that the insured never possesses any incidents of ownership in the policy.

The Service has now made it clear that it will throw in the towel on this issue if care is taken to avoid the three-year rule by following the standards

---

102. 82 T.C. 51 (1984)

103. 89 T.C. 235 (1987), affirmed 893 F.2d 237 (10th Cir. 1989).

104. Other leading taxpayer cases include the Estate of Headrick v. Commissioner, 93 T.C. 171 (1989) and Perry Est. v. Commissioner, 91-1 USTC ¶ 60,064, 927 F.2d 209 (5th Cir. 1991).

established in the *Leder, Headrick* and *Perry* cases.  In AOD 1991-012, the Service announced that, although it continues to believe that substance should prevail over form, it will no longer litigate this issue in light of the adverse opinions in these cases.  The bottom line is that the three-year rule can be avoided.

**Question 25: Are there any special precautions that should be taken in attempting to avoid the three-year rule?**

The following precautions will help in dealing with the issue:

1. The trust should be the applicant, owner and beneficiary of the policy.

2. Never require that the trustee pay premiums on the life insurance policy.

3. Never require that the insured make contributions sufficient to pay policy premiums.

4. Never make the amount of the contributions to the trust in the exact amount of the premiums.

5. Try to make the contribution to the trust well in advance of the time the premiums are due.  This will also help in dealing with the *Crummey* withdrawal powers.

6. Have an independent trustee.  Do not name the insured or the insured's spouse as trustee.

7. The trust document should grant the trustee broad investment discretion.

8.  Refrain from using the words "life insurance" in the name of the trust.

9.  Establish and document the trust before any insurance application is made.

**Question 26: Is it always advisable to attempt to avoid the three-year rule when a new policy is purchased?**

An attempt should be made to avoid the three-year rule whenever possible. In some cases, however, the insured may have already jumped the gun on the life insurance.  For example, in our case, Walter may have applied for the policy, taken a physical and written the first check.  He then decides that he wants to establish a life insurance trust and wants to avoid the three-year rule.

At this point, it is too late to avoid the reaches of the three-year rule.  Some planners make the mistake of trying to retroactively create the trust in an attempt to avoid the three-year rule.  This is a mistake that may compound the problem. Beyond the legal impropriety of attempting to avoid taxes in such a fashion, which itself can be serious, the client will be given a false hope that he or she has avoided the reaches of the rule, when in fact the transfer is squarely within its clutches.  The better course of action in this case is to face up to the fact that the gun-jumping has triggered the three-year rule, advise the client that the tax concern will disappear after three years, and then get the clock ticking.  This course of action properly keeps expectations in line with reality.

**Question 27: What is the estate tax impact if the parent-insured is named as a lifetime beneficiary of a trust established by his or her adult children?**

Suppose Walter and Jane's two adult children establish a trust. They contribute their own money. They designate themselves as trustees. They name their parents as income beneficiaries. They use a portion of the funds in the trust to acquire a policy insuring the lives of their parents. The parent's only connection to the trust is that they are named income beneficiaries of the trust. The issue is whether, under these limited, unique circumstances, the death benefit, when paid, will be taxed in the parents' estate.

In *Jordahl Est. v. Commissioner*,[105] the Tax Court was faced with a situation where the insured was entitled to receive the income from a trust that was in excess of any income needed to pay insurance premiums on life insurance policies on the insured's life that were owned by the trust. The Tax Court held that the insured did not possess any incidents of ownership by virtue of such income right. And the insured did not "retain" an interest in the trust because the insured had not established or funded the trust. Although logic and limited authority suggest that the insured may be a beneficiary without an adverse estate tax consequence in this limited situation, prudence would suggest that the insured be left out as a beneficiary if the estate tax considerations are paramount. The situation may become intolerably risky if there is any indirect pre-planning between the child and the parent.

## PROBLEMS 12–E AND 12–F

**12–E.** Jerry Bean is the sole owner of Bean Enterprises, Inc., a C corporation holding company that owns a number of small profitable businesses. Jerry has determined that he needs $3 million of permanent life insurance to help with estate taxes and potential family needs. Jerry has a wife, three married children, and five grandchildren. He has a revocable living trust, but has done no serious estate planning. He wants Bean Enterprises Inc. to pay all the premiums on the new policy. He adamantly refuses to use any of his own money for the policy premiums. What structuring options would you suggest? What additional facts would you like to have?

**12–F.** Whatever you advised Jerry in 12–E above, he worked with his insurance professional to purchase a $3 million policy that is owned by the company. The company funds all the premiums and is the designated beneficiary. Jerry figured that, because he was the sole owner of the company, his estate would always have complete access to the policy proceeds on a tax-free basis. Jerry now thinks his reasoning may have been flawed. Do you agree with Jerry? How would you recommend that Jerry proceed to correct the situation?

---

105. 65 T.C. 92 (1975).

# CHAPTER 13

# THE DIVERSIFICATION CHALLENGE

## A. THE CHALLENGE, THE PRESSURES

Owners of successful closely held businesses eventually face a basic decision regarding the profits generated by the business. Are the profits going to accumulate in the company or be distributed to the owners of the company? Although this is the type of decision that everyone would like to face, the answer can be difficult for many owners. The easy answer for many is to stockpile. Keep the profits in the company. Let them ride as the business expands and matures.

During the building period of most businesses, stockpiling usually is the only viable alternative. The earnings are needed to finance inventories, receivables, facilities, better technology, and new personnel. More debt isn't possible or prudent. As the business begins to mature, the retained profits are used to retire debt and the pressure to accumulate begins to fade and often disappears completely. But in many cases, this accumulation pattern has been set. The owners enjoy watching the net worth of the business expand every year with a corresponding increase in the value of their stock. Their success is measured and quantified by the accumulations. As time goes on, the balance sheet of the business becomes rock solid – lots of equity, little or no debt – while the balance sheets of the owners become lopsided – a large net worth and big taxable estate, the bulk of which is represented by a single business equity interest.

Some business owners recognize the value of distributing business profits to facilitate the diversification of their personal assets. They understood that concentrating wealth in the business can be risky, imprudent, and damaging in the long run. Their challenge is to figure out when and how to diversify their assets. Others don't see the need. They believe that the conservative, prudent approach is to accumulate while erasing all debt. And then there are those who acknowledge the value of diversification, but find it difficult to break out of the pattern of accumulating.

There are a host of pressures that, if properly considered, mandate the importance of diversifying once the business has matured. Often these pressures are not recognized or fully appreciated by the business owner. An understanding

495

of these basic pressures will allow the advisor to be more effective in dealing with those clients who do not see the need, or who lack the will, to start the process of leaning out their business and diversifying their personal holdings.

## 1. RISK MANAGEMENT PRESSURE

A program to distribute and diversify corporate profits may be used as an effective tool to manage and reduce risks for business owners. Many business owners are wedded to an internalized longing to have their business always exist and prosper. Their instinct is to do everything and anything that will reduce or mitigate any danger that could threaten the health or survival of the business. Experience has confirmed that this notion of eternal survival, although gratifying to ponder, is not something to bank on. Too many businesses, once perceived to be rock solid, have suffered or crumbled from the pressures of new technologies, international competition, and changing times.

Very few businesses are immune from the increased competitive pressures that exist today. The new world economy is offering more competition, price confusion, and product innovation than ever before. Most believe that this trend will expand significantly, if not exponentially, in the decades ahead. The increased need to be risk-tolerant provides a big pressure point for diversification. Many business owners no longer want to keep all their eggs in one basket. They see the value of a diversified financial portfolio that is not tied directly to the business. They want the comfort of knowing that if the business is wiped out by some unforeseen form of competition or new technology, their years of hard work will still have produced an independent economic base that will sustain them for the long haul.

Legal risks can also provide a big incentive for certain businesses to distribute and diversify profits. Some businesses, by their very nature, are exposed to potentially massive legal claims if something goes wrong. Many owners have read or heard about the damage that a tenacious plaintiff's lawyer can create with the right case at the wrong time. The sad fact is that many businesses have been damaged beyond repair by an ugly lawsuit that cripples the operation.

The answer for many owners is an investment portfolio that is beyond the operating risks of the business and the reaches of its creditors. The owners first understand, and then enthusiastically embrace, the comfort of knowing that an ever-expanding pool of assets is being protected. Often this protection is possible only if there is a program to distribute and diversify company assets.

As discussed in Chapter 16, an asset protection program may be structured to include a number of different components, including family limited partnerships and limited liability companies (LLCs), multiple business entities, a wide array of personal trusts, special gifting programs, and many other tools. But these tools will work only to the extent that assets exist separate and apart from the business. For the successful business owner, often such a block of assets can be created only through a program that facilitates the periodic distribution of business assets and profits.

## 2. Economic Leverage Pressure

The opportunity to create economic leverage in financing a successful business also may create pressure to distribute profits. This opportunity may manifest itself in a few different ways.

Simple arithmetic confirms that one who can generate an 11 percent return on money borrowed at seven percent will improve the yield on invested capital. Debt can be a valuable tool to increase a return on equity. It's Basic Business Leverage 101. The owner who persists in accumulating excess profits while eliminating all debt will usually experience a reduction in the return on each invested dollar.

Plus, the intelligent use of the right amount of debt inside the company usually makes sense from a tax standpoint. The interest on business indebtedness is tax deductible.[1] The use of business debt may allow the company to distribute earnings to the owners so that they can acquire assets and build alternative investment portfolios with little or no need for personal debt. This may avoid the tax complexities of the personal, passive, and investment interest limitations that often eliminate or postpone any tax benefit for the interest paid by individuals. Also, having cash to invest and being free of personal debt may make it easier for the business owner to implement estate planning strategies that do not work well with debt, such as residential grantor-retained interest trusts, charitable remainder trusts, family partnerships, dynasty trusts, and the like.

There also are those situations, far too common, where large accumulations inside the company are used to fund investments owned by the company that are unrelated to the company's business. The company's balance sheet improves as all the earnings, including the earnings from such investments, continue to balloon. Besides being exposed to the liabilities and risks of the business, such investments often generate a yield that is diluted by the two-tier tax system that applies to all C corporations. The earnings are initially taxed at the corporate level. At some point in time, a tax will be triggered at the shareholder level when the earnings are ultimately distributed. The after-tax performance of the investments would be improved if an effective program were implemented to distribute the earnings to the shareholders on a tax-wise basis and allow the appreciating investments to grow in a risk-protected vehicle that is not subject to a double tax regime.

## 3. Disposition Flexibility Pressure

The benefits of an earnings distribution plan that creates economic leverage may also be realized when the time comes to sell the business. Often the purchase price of a business is predicated on a price-earnings ratio, or some other measure that is not tied directly to the asset base of the business. The buyer assumes that the assets in the business are necessary for the business to function at its existing level of operations. The seller who has unreasonably accumulated earnings in the business and ballooned the asset base faces a double challenge at the time of sale. First, the seller must convince the buyer that certain assets in the

---

1. I.R.C. § 163(a).

company are not really necessary to sustain the operating level of the company. This discussion usually leads to further negotiations and adjustments. In the end, the seller often pays a price in the negotiating process for being able to exclude from the sale certain assets that, in the seller's mind, represent excess accumulations that do not need to be passed on to the buyer.

The second challenge faced by the seller is the huge tax cost of having the corporation rid itself of the excess assets at the time of sale. Often, the assets must be distributed by the company as a lump sum dividend or as additional consideration for the stock. In either event, a tax may be triggered at both the corporate and the shareholder level. It is an expensive way to distribute excess assets out of the company. Contrast this scenario with the owner who has intelligently distributed excess profits over a period of time and not unreasonably accumulated assets inside the corporation. There is no need to negotiate the release of excess assets, and the tax problems triggered on the disposition of excess assets are eliminated.

As unusual as it may seem, in some cases, the practice of leaning out the corporation and making intelligent use of debt may actually make it easier for the seller to get a better price for the business. In sizing up a business, many buyers focus on the potential return on their invested equity. They will pay more for a business that has yielded the prior owners 18 percent on their equity than one that has yielded 10 percent. As previously stated, the yield on equity is often tied directly to the size of the asset base and the intelligent use of debt. In most situations, the yield on the invested equity will go down if there are excess assets in the company and little or no debt. Of course, most semi-savvy buyers will be able to recognize and project the benefits of a reasonable debt-to-equity ratio and a leaner asset base in evaluating the potential return on their investment, even when the existing owners of the business apparently have not done so. But many buyers will not spot this opportunity, nor will they be impressed by a projection that shows the opportunity when the existing business owners haven't bothered to take advantage of the situation.

In many cases, a leaner asset base and the wise use of debt will allow a seller to show a stronger yield on equity, avoid unwanted and costly excess asset negotiations, eliminate double tax burdens, appear stronger, and negotiate a better deal.

### 4. TRANSITION PLANNING

Many closely held businesses are not destined to be sold; they are going to be transitioned to the next generation. The simple truth is that smaller mountains are easier to move. Of course, the big challenge is to make the transition at the lowest possible tax cost. A huge estate tax price tag may be triggered at the wrong time if the transition challenge is ignored. This tax burden alone can jeopardize the survival of the business. As discussed in Chapter 10, there are various transition strategies that can be used when the business is going to be transitioned to family members or second level management. Nearly all of them turn on the value of the business. The difficulty of the transition is often directly proportional to the value of the assets that need to be gifted or sold. For this reason, transition planning will usually be easier if business profits are regularly cleared out of the company and not allowed to accumulate. Many business owners reach a point where, for estate planning purposes, they want to maximize the pre-death transfers to family members without triggering any gift tax liability. They have their unified credits[2] their annual gift tax exclusions,[3] and their generation skipping tax exemptions[4] to do the job. The challenge is to maximize these tools – all of which have dollar limitations – to transfer the largest possible percentage of the business. In most cases, if the profits of the business have not been accumulated excessively and have been systematically distributed over time, these transfer tools will shelter a larger percentage of the equity ownership, resulting in lower taxes. Plus, a leaner business usually makes it much easier to resolve planning conflicts that often exist between the children who work in the business and those who do not.

Even when the transition is targeted at non-family members, such as a management team in the company, the challenge is easier when the equity of the business has not been excessively inflated. Buy-sell agreements and phase-out exit strategies work better. Plus, often the owner who is phasing out is able and willing to be more accommodating to the new owners, because he or she has already established a substantial net worth outside of the business through a program, implemented over many years, of regularly distributing and diversifying the profits of the business.

## 5. ESTATE PLANNING PRESSURES

A program to regularly distribute corporate profits can also help the owner take advantage of other estate tax saving strategies that are unrelated to the transfer of the business. If earnings are stockpiled in the company, the owner may not have sufficient independent resources to implement family partnerships, insurance trust programs, residential GRITS, charitable remainder trusts, dynasty trusts and other similar tools that require funding in order to work. Plus, as previously stated, lower values make it easier to leverage annual gift tax exclusions, unified credits, and generation skipping tax exemptions to transition larger equity percentages to other family members free of tax.

A well-structured estate tax plan will accomplish two primary objectives. First, it will hold down the value of the estate to reduce taxes. Second, it will ensure that sufficient liquidity is available at key points in time when cash is needed to provide for the needs of family members, pay estate taxes, and cover other obligations that require cash. Accumulating excess assets inside a closely held business makes it more difficult to accomplish these basic estate planning objectives.

## 6. INCOME TAX PRESSURES

There also are income tax pressures for adopting a program to systematically and regularly distribute profits from a mature privately owned business. The pressures come in the form of two traps. The first trap is the basic

---

2. See I.R.C. §§ 2010 and 2505.
3. See I.R.C. § 2503(b).
4. See I.R.C. § 2631.

double tax threat that all C corporations face. Most professional advisors and business owners fully appreciate that the prospect of paying a double tax is no fun. But that is the expected outcome whenever a C corporation indiscriminately accumulates earnings with no effective plan for distributing those earnings down the road. The corporation pays the tax on the earnings, and then the shareholders pay a second tax when the earnings are ultimately distributed. The bill goes even higher when a state income tax is involved. This provides a big incentive to structure a profit distribution program that avoids, to the fullest extent possible, the reaches of the double tax structure.

A second trap may also be triggered in certain situations. It is the accumulated earnings tax.[5] This tax is targeted at the corporation that wants to defer any tax on dividends at the shareholder level by having the corporation accumulate and retain its earnings. To discourage this practice of unreasonably accumulating earnings at the corporate level, the tax code imposes an extra tax at the corporate level. The accumulated earnings tax is now 20 percent of the excess accumulated earnings.[6] What are excess accumulated earnings? They are accumulated earnings that exceed the reasonable business needs of the business or $250,000, whichever is greater.[7] The $250,000 limit is a safe harbor for all businesses, except professional service corporations[8] who have a reduced safe harbor limit of $150,000.[9]

The accumulated earnings tax on excess accumulated earnings is designed to approximate what the individual shareholders would pay if the corporation distributed the earnings in the form of dividends. So it, too, is a form of double tax, although both taxes occur at the corporate level. What's worse is that the earnings are still stuck inside the corporation.

Many business owners, with the aid of their advisors, develop a program to avoid the accumulated earnings tax. They do this by documenting the "reasonable needs of the business" that justify the large accumulation of earnings. They often figure that, since they have avoided the accumulated earnings tax, they have done the right thing. In the process, they ignore the other pressures for keeping the business lean, and fail to realize that they are likely setting themselves up for a major double tax problem down the road. The ability to avoid the reach of the accumulated earnings tax by documenting reasonable business needs does not, in and of itself, justify the accumulation of earnings. The other pressures, in most cases, are more significant in the decision-making process.

## B. DIVERSIFICATION STRATEGIES

Partnership-taxed entities, including LLCs taxed as partnerships, have no serious tax obstacles to diversification. They just need to make the decision to do it. Property and cash distributions from the entity to its owners trigger no tax hit

---

5. See generally I.R.C. §§ 531-537.

6. I.R.C. § 531.

7. I.R.C. § 535(c).

8. This includes a corporation whose principal function is providing services in the fields of health, law, engineering, architecture, accounting, actuarial science, performing arts or consulting. I.R.C. § 535(c)(2)(B).

9. I.R.C. § 535(c)(2)(B).

unless the cash distributed to an owner exceeds the owner's outside basis,[10] an unlikely result in nearly all cases. Even if the entity borrows money to enhance its leverage and to have more available for the owners, there is usually no problem because the debt increase is treated as a cash contribution for outside basis purposes, thus increasing the outside basis of the owners.[11] And, when appreciated business assets are distributed by the entity, there is usually no tax triggered at either the entity or owner level. The entity's basis in the transferred asset is carried over to the owner, but may not exceed the owner's basis in his or her partnership interest.[12] So for partnership-taxed entities, the planning challenges are usually money and debt leverage, not taxes.

S corporations also have significant diversification flexibility, although nothing comparable to partnerships. S corporation income that has been passed through and taxed to the owners can be distributed free of any second tax hit.[13] So over time, a profitable S corporation can often distribute significant assets to its owners free of any double tax concerns. If the entity has no accumulated earnings from a prior C existence, either because it never was a C corporation or because it has already distributed all of its old C earnings and profits, owner distributions beyond the S corporation earnings will still not trigger a tax unless they exceed the owner's basis in his or her S corporation stock.[14] So, in effect, the S corporation shareholder, under such circumstances, can receive distributions equal to his or her share of all S corporation earnings and his or her investment in the enterprise before any tax is triggered as a result of a distribution. If the distributions exceed the stock basis, the excess is treated as proceeds from a sale or exchange, usually resulting in a long-term capital gain.[15] In those situations where there are accumulated earnings and profits attributable to a prior C existence, all distributions in excess of the S corporation earnings first will be taxed to the owners as C corporation dividends to the extent of the accumulated earnings and profits.[16] Any excess is then treated as a tax-free recovery of stock basis to the extent of the basis.[17] So even where there are prior C corporation earnings and profits, an S corporation can implement a diversification strategy to regularly distribute all of its S existence earnings to its shareholders free of any double tax concerns.

As compared to partnership-taxed entities, the S corporation falls short in two other important respects. First, any debt increase by the entity does not increase the owners' basis in their stock; the debt-basis adjustment is unique to partnership-taxed entities. Second, if the S corporation distributes appreciated property to its owners, a taxable gain equal to the appreciation is triggered at the corporate level that, of course, is passed through and taxed to the shareholders.[18] But even with these differences, an S corporation often can be just as tax-

---

10. I.R.C. § 731(a)(1).
11. I.R.C. § 752(a).
12. I.R.C. §§ 732(a), 733.
13. I.R.C. §§ 1368(b)(1), 1368(c)(1).
14. I.R.C. § 1368(b).
15. I.R.C. § 1368(b).
16. I.R.C. § 1368(c)(2).
17. I.R.C. § 1368(c)(3).
18. I.R.C. § 311(b)(1).

efficient as a partnership-taxed entity in implementing a diversification program based on regular distributions of current profits and the use of debt, not accumulated earnings, to finance growth.

A C corporation is a different animal. The inherent double tax structure makes nothing easy. Beyond the normal diversification issues of money and debt, there is a need to evaluate strategies that will eliminate or mitigate the double tax bite. Following is a summary of some of the key diversification strategies that are often considered for a C corporation.

### 1. DIVIDEND BLOW-OUT

One strategy, appealing to some, is to diversify by distributing earnings that are taxed at dividend rates that currently are much lower than ordinary income tax rates. The economic stimulus package of 2003 reduced the maximum tax rate on "qualifying corporate dividends" paid to non-corporate shareholders to 15 percent (5 percent for low-income shareholders otherwise subject to maximum marginal rates of 15 percent or less). These reduced rates applied to all dividends received from January 1, 2003 to December 31, 2012. The American Taxpayer Relief Act of 2012 (the "Fiscal Cliff" legislation signed into law during the final days of 2012)[19] increased this low dividend rate to 20 percent starting in 2013 for couples with taxable incomes in excess of $450,000 and individuals with taxable incomes in excess of $400,000. Plus, in 2013, the 3.8 percent Medicare tax kicked in on interest, dividends, capital gains, and other "net investment income" to the extent that this income, when added to the taxpayer's other modified adjusted gross income, exceeds $200,000 in the case of unmarried individuals, $250,000 in the case of married individuals filing jointly, and $125,000 in the case of married individuals filing separately. The net result is that a couple with an adjusted income of less than $250,000 or a single person with an adjusted gross income of less than $200,000 will continue to pay the pre-2013 dividend rates (a maximum of 15 percent).[20] Couples or individuals with higher incomes will pay a combined income and Medicare dividend rate of either 18.8 percent or 23.8 percent, depending on whether the new $450,000 or $400,000 thresholds are exceeded. For some successful enterprises, a simple diversification strategy may be to increase the leverage inside the company and then blow out dividends over a period of years. A 15 or 23.8 percent rate may hurt, but it's a far cry from a combined ordinary income and Medicare rate in the 44 percent range.

### 2. S STATUS CONVERSION

The need to diversify often prompts many C corporations to take a hard look at the S election. Once made, the S election will allow the company to start distributing all of its current earnings free of any double tax threat. The company will lose the benefit of low C rates on modest income accumulations (up to $75,000 each year)[21] and the ability to offer tax-preferred employee benefits to shareholder/employees,[22] but often these "losses" are not deemed significant to

---

19. Section 102 of the American Taxpayer Relief Act of 2012.
20. I.R.C. § 1411.
21. I.R.C. § 11(b).
22. Any shareholder/employee who owns more than two percent of the stock of an S corporation is treated as a partner, not an employee, for fringe benefit purposes. I.R.C. § 1372.

owners of a profitable C corporation in need of a diversification strategy. The benefit of the low corporate rates is quickly offset each year by the extra five percent "bubble" tax that kicks in at the $100,000 income mark (which has the effect of imposing a flat 34 percent rate on all corporate earnings from dollar one to $10 million).[23] The tax-preferred employee benefits offer no direct benefit to golfer owners and, when compared to the benefits of diversifying free of any double tax concerns, often are not viewed as a big deal by the key shareholder/employees.

The decision to enhance the diversification program by converting to S status is often much easier than the actual conversion itself. As discussed in Chapter 7, there are critical eligibility requirements, election mechanics, and tax traps that need to be factored into the planning. Only in the very rare case will these important nuisances justify a reversal of a decision to convert; they are usually hazards that just need to be navigated. The eligibility provisions require that the shareholder count be less than 100 (usually not a big deal),[24] that only individuals, estates, and certain types of trusts own stock (partnerships, corporations, nonresident aliens, and most trusts are out),[25] and that the corporation have only one class of stock (voting rights not considered).[26] Thus, to become eligible, sometimes it is necessary to say good-bye to certain shareholders or restructure the ownership of their shares, or to restructure the equity capital of the corporation to meet the one stock class requirement. The details of such restructuring options are discussed in Chapter 7.

The conversion tax traps (also discussed in Chapter 7) must be anticipated and may affect the "speed" of the diversification program. If there are accumulated C earnings and profits (a likely condition for a profitable C corporation), any post-conversion S corporation distributions in excess of S earnings will trigger a shareholder dividend tax to the extent of the accumulated C earnings and profits.[27] As a practical matter, this may put a governor on shareholder distributions to ensure they do not exceed the S earnings. Also, the existence of accumulated C earnings and profits may trigger the investment income trap of section 1375, a tax imposed on an S corporation at the highest corporate rate (presently 35 percent) on the amount by which its net passive income (interest, dividends, royalties, rents, etc.) exceeds 25 percent of its gross receipts.[28] This requires a monitoring to ensure that the 25 percent threshold is not exceeded. And then there is the built-in-gain (BIG) tax trap of section 1374, which imposes a tax on an S corporation that converts from C status and then sells assets owned at the time of conversion during the ten-year period following the conversion.[29] This entity level tax is in addition to any tax triggered at the S shareholder level on any recognized gain from the sale and is imposed at the maximum corporate rate (presently 35 percent) on the lesser of the built-in gain

---

23. I.R.C. § 11(b).
24. I.R.C. § 1361(b)(1)(A).
25. I.R.C. § 1361(b)(1)(B) & (C).
26. I.R.C. § 1361(b)(1)(D).
27. I.R.C. § 1368(c)(2).
28. See generally I.R.C. § 1375 and related discussion in Chapter 7.
29. See generally I.R.C. § 1374 and related discussion in Chapter 7.

at the time of conversion or the gain recognized on the sale.[30] A number of strategies for managing and mitigating this BIG tax are discussed in Chapter 5. For diversification purposes, it requires a careful evaluation of any sale of corporate assets that occurs within the ten-year window following the conversion.

### 3. S CONVERSION/DIVIDEND BLOW-OUT COMBO

This diversification strategy is just a combination of the last two discussed. An S conversion is made and then the company elects under section 1368(e)(3) to first treat all distributions as dividend distributions of C earnings and profits in order to ensure that such dividends are taxed at the favorable dividend rate of 15 percent.[31] This accelerates the diversification effort in two ways. First, distributions to clear out the C earnings and profits put more in the shareholders' pockets. Second, the S corporation, moving forward, is no longer shackled by the fear of taxable dividends or the passive income tax trap (which applies only if there are accumulated C earnings and profits). Thus, the S corporation, in addition to being able to distribute all of its current earnings free of any double tax concerns, could also make additional distributions that would not trigger any tax unless they exceed a shareholder's basis in his or her stock.

### 4. PIECEMEAL STOCK SALE

A simple shareholder diversification strategy is to sell some stock, thereby converting the non-liquid stock into cash or an interest-bearing debt obligation that is not tied directly to the success of the business. A stock sale to a party other than the corporation will generate only a single capital gains tax on the recognized gain. Installment sale treatment may be available to defer the gain if the proceeds are paid over time.[32] Popular buyer candidates may include key management personnel (who want a piece, or a bigger piece, of the rock), other existing shareholders (who may feel they are already sufficiently diversified and would like a larger stake in the enterprise), and new golfer shareholders (who are acceptable to the other shareholders and may view such an investment as an addition to their diversification program).

A piecemeal sale of stock to the corporation (a redemption) also will trigger only a single tax; but, in most cases, the tax will be based on all the proceeds being treated as a taxable dividend.[33] The piecemeal redemption may qualify for sale or exchange (not dividend) treatment if, after applying broad attribution rules,[34] it meets the "substantially disproportionate" standard of Section 302(b)(2) or the "not essentially equivalent to a dividend" standard of Section 302(b)(1), both very difficult in many situations.[35] So long as the maximum dividend rate equals the long-term capital gains rate, the only difference between dividend

---

30. I.R.C. §§ 1374(b)(1), 1374(c)(2).

31. If all the shareholders consent, an S corporation may elect to treat distributions as taxable dividends that reduce accumulated earning and profits from a prior C existence. I.R.C. § 1368(e)(3).

32. See generally I.R.C. § 453.

33. I.R.C. §§ 301, 302.

34. I.R.C. §§ 302(c), 318(a).

35. I.R.C. §§ 302(b)(1), 302(b)(2). Sale or exchange treatment also is available if there is a complete redemption of all the shareholder's stock, and, in making such determination, the family attribution rules of section 318(a) may not apply in many cases. I.R.C. §§ 302(b)(3), 302(c)(2), 318(a)(1).

treatment and exchange treatment is the tax-free recovery of the basis allocable to the sold shares, which may be no big deal if the shareholder (like many C corporation shareholders) has a very low stock basis. If and when the preferential dividend rate disappears, then, once again, there will likely be a significant rate differential between dividends and capital gains, and much more will be at stake in the dividend/exchange determination.

## 5. SECTION 1045 PIECEMEAL STOCK SALE

This diversification option is just a piecemeal stock sale with a twist. Section 1045 allows a noncorporate shareholder to elect to defer the taxable gain that would otherwise be recognized on the sale of small business stock held for more than six months by reinvesting the proceeds into new qualified small business stock within 60 days following the sale.[36] For the C corporation shareholder who feels he or she has too many eggs in one basket and wants to spread a few of those eggs into other business baskets, this option may allow the diversification with no tax hit at all. The key definition is "small business stock," which must be satisfied for both the stock being sold and the new stock being acquired.[37] The primary requirements of the definition are that the entity must be a C corporation; the stock must have been originally issued to the shareholder after the effective date of the Revenue Reconciliation Act of 1993 (re-sales won't work); the aggregate gross assets of the corporation cannot exceed $50 million; and the corporation must have always been engaged in the active conduct of a qualified trade or business.[38]

## 6. DIVIDE AND CONQUER

For diversification purposes, everything is usually easier when the business is operated through multiple corporations rather than one big C corporation. There's more flexibility and more options. One corporation can implement specific diversification strategies for the benefit of the owners, while other entities use different strategies or continue to accumulate earnings to finance growth. Take, for example, the situation where the owners plan to sell a part of the business to generate cash and diversify their holdings. If the portion to be sold is part of a large corporation, the only option is an asset sale that will trigger a taxable event at the entity level and a second taxable event when the proceeds from the sale are distributed to the owners. If, however, the portion to be sold is operated in a separate corporation, the stock of that corporation can be sold, generating a single capital gains tax at the shareholder level. Plus, beyond the capacity to develop different strategies for different entities, the use of multiple entities makes it easier to craft compromise solutions when owners have varying diversification needs and interests. And then there's the significant risk reduction benefit that always accompanies a structure segregating the operating and legal risks of one entity from the assets held in other entities. The simple truth: few little marbles work better than one big marble.

---

36. I.R.C. § 1045.

37. I.R.C. § 1045(b)(1), which incorporates by reference the "qualified small business stock" definition of Section 1202(c).

38. I.R.C. § 1202(c).

In many situations, the primary challenge is to bust up the big marble. Usually the best answer is a D reorganization.[39] If done right, the assets of a C corporation (referred to as the "distributing corporation") can be transferred to multiple C corporations (referred to as "controlled corporations"), and the stock of the controlled corporations can be distributed to the shareholders of the distributing corporation, all tax free. There are three different division structures, referred to as the "spin-off," the "split-off," and the "split-up." A spin-off division occurs when the distributing corporation contributes assets to a newly formed controlled corporation in return for the stock of the controlled corporation and then distributes that stock pro rata to its shareholders. A split-off division occurs when the distributing corporation contributes assets to a newly-formed controlled corporation in return for the stock of the controlled corporation and then distributes that stock to one or more of its shareholders in redemption of stock of the distributing corporation. A split-up division occurs when the distributing corporation contributes all of its assets to two or more controlled corporations in exchange for the stock of the controlled corporations and then distributes that stock to its shareholders in complete liquidation of their interests in the distributing corporation.

If the reorganization requirements are satisfied, the tax results of the division itself are wonderful, whether the transaction is structured as a spin-off, split-off, or split-up. The distributing corporation recognizes no gain or loss on the contribution of assets to the controlled corporation,[40] takes an exchange basis in the stock received from the controlled corporation,[41] tacks the holding period of the transferred assets onto the stock's holding period,[42] and loses a portion of its accumulated earnings and profits (based on the relative fair market values of the assets transferred and retained) to the controlled corporation.[43] Plus, the distributing corporation recognizes no gain on the distribution of the controlled corporation's stock to its shareholders, whether via straight distribution, redemption, or complete liquidation.[44] As for the controlled corporation, it recognizes no gain or loss on the issuance of its stock,[45] it takes its new assets with a carried-over basis[46] and a tacked holding period,[47] and it picks up a share of the distributing corporation's accumulated earnings and profits.[48] The shareholders of the distributing corporation make out just as well. They recognize no gain or loss on the receipt of the stock of the controlled corporation;[49] a portion of their basis in their stock of the distributing corporation is allocated to their newly acquired stock of the controlled corporation (based on relative fair market values);[50] and their holding period in their distributing corporation stock is tacked onto their controlled corporation stock holding

---

39. I.R.C. §§ 368(a)(1)(D), 355.
40. I.R.C. § 361(a).
41. I.R.C. § 358(a).
42. I.R.C. § 1223(1).
43. I.R.C. § 312(h); Reg. § 1.312-10(a),(c).
44. I.R.C. §§ 355(c), 361(c).
45. I.R.C. § 1032(a).
46. I.R.C. § 362(b).
47. I.R.C. § 1223(2).
48. I.R.C. § 312(h); Reg. § 1.312-10(a),(c).
49. I.R.C. § 355(a)(1).
50. I.R.C. § 358(b) & (c).

period.[51]  So the division is accomplished, and everyone gets off tax scot-free. Things can get a little messy and taxes can be triggered if the controlled corporation issues long-term notes, bonds or other similar debt securities[52] or the distributing corporation distributes property other than the stock of the controlled corporation (boot) to its shareholders,[53] but, even in such rare circumstances, the division can usually work from a tax standpoint.  However, if the D reorganization and Section 355 requirements are not satisfied, things get really messy because the key tax-free protections are lost.

So what does it take to qualify?  There are six primary requirements, all of which are important and some of which mandate careful advance planning and patience in order for a division to serve the diversification interests of the shareholders.

**a. Control.**  The distributing corporation must "control" the controlled corporation immediately before the distribution to its shareholders.  For this purpose, "control" has the same dual 80 percent definition that applies in corporate formations under Section 351.[54]  The distributing corporation must own 80 percent of all voting power and 80 percent of the shares of all other classes of stock.

**b. Complete Distribution.**  The distributing corporation must distribute to its shareholders all of its stock and securities in the controlled corporation or an amount sufficient to give the shareholders control (under the dual 80 percent definition) of the controlled corporation.[55]  If it retains any shares, it has the burden of establishing to the satisfaction of the Service that the retention was not pursuant to a plan that has tax avoidance as one of its principal purposes.[56]  The cleanest approach is to distribute it all.

**c. Five-Year Active Business.**  When the division is complete, the distributing corporation and all controlled corporations (or just the controlled corporations in a split-up) must be conducting an active trade or business that the distributing corporation conducted for at least five years before the division.[57] Passive investments that do not require significant management services won't work.[58]  There is no need to have more than one active business; a vertical division of a single business that the distributing corporation has conducted for five years will do the job.[59]  Geographical distinctions are not controlling; for example, a company can spin off a facility in a separate location that it has owned for less than five years and still qualify so long as the facility is part of a broader active business that it has been conducting for five years.[60]  Breaking off an active functional division (e.g., research and development) may also qualify in

---

51. I.R.C. § 1223(1).
52. I.R.C. §§ 355(a)(3)(A), 356(d)(2)(C).
53. I.R.C. §§ 356(b), 358.
54. I.R.C. §§ 355(a)(1)(A), 368(c).
55. I.R.C. §§ 355(a)(1)(D).
56. I.R.C. §§ 355(a)(1)(D)(ii); Rev. Proc. 96-30, 1996-1 C.B. 696.
57. I.R.C. §§ 355(a)(1)(C), (b); Reg. § 1.355-3.
58. Reg. § 1.355-3(b)(2)(iii) & (iv).
59. Reg. § 1.355-3(c), Examples (4) and (5).
60. Reg. § 1.355-3(c), Example (7); Lockwood's Estate v. Commissioner, 350 F.2d 712 (8th Cir. 1965).

select situations even when it generates no revenues from outside sources.[61] What won't qualify is an active business that the distributing corporation or its shareholders acquired in a taxable transaction within five years of the division.[62]

**d. Continuity of Interest.** The historic shareholders of the distributing corporation must own at least 50 percent of the equity interests in all the corporations that exist after the division.[63] There is no requirement that each shareholder own an interest in each company; the division can be used to realign the interests of different shareholders so long as the 50 percent historic requirement, in the aggregate, is satisfied.[64] Any person who acquired stock in the distributing corporation more than two years before the division will likely qualify as a historic shareholder.[65] A problem surfaces when a historic shareholder disposes of stock immediately following the division in a transaction that suggests or implies a pre-division intention (or worse yet, commitment) to sell.[66] As with the "No Device" requirement discussed below, this requirement mandates that the division be allowed to age for a while before any piecemeal sale efforts are initiated.

**e. Business Purpose.** There must be a "real and substantial non-federal tax" corporate business purpose for the division.[67] Sometimes this sounds easier than it is. An exclusively shareholder purpose, such as estate planning or the need for personal wealth diversification, won't suffice;[68] nor will a business purpose that can be satisfied without a shareholder distribution (e.g., segregating operations to reduce liability exposures).[69] Examples of business purposes that do work include increasing or improving credit facilities,[70] improving access to investment capital,[71] providing equity interests to key employees,[72] resolving or mitigating labor problems,[73] resolving shareholder disputes,[74] complying with regulatory decrees,[75] concentrating and focusing management resources,[76] and facilitating the parting of shareholders under circumstances that strengthen and benefit the business.[77] The fact that the division also serves the personal planning interests of the shareholders is not fatal so long as a real business purpose exists.[78] The planning challenge is to identify the key business purposes that will be served by the division and then to document those purposes and their significance in the board resolutions authorizing the division. Satisfaction of this

61. Reg. § 1.355-3(c), Examples (9) thru (11).
62. I.R.C. § 355(b)(2)(D).
63. Reg. § 1.355-2(c)(2), Example 2; Rev. Proc. 96-30, 1996-1 C.B. 696.
64. Reg. § 1.355-2(c)(2), with emphasis on Example 3.
65. Rev. Rule 74-5, 1974–1 C.B. 82.
66. See generally Shores, "Reexamining Continuity of Shareholder Interest In Corporate Divisions," 18 Va. Tax Rev. 473 (1999).
67. Reg. § 1.355-2(b)(2).
68. Reg. § 1.355-2(b)(2).
69. Reg. §§ 1.355-2(b)(3), 1.355-2(b)(5), Example (3).
70. Rev. Rule 77-22, 1977-1 C.B. 91.
71. Rev. Rule 85-122, 1985-2 C.B. 118.
72. Rev. Rule 88-34, 1988-1 C.B. 115.
73. Olson v. Commissioner, 48 T.C. 855 (1967).
74. Reg. §§ 1.355-2(b)(5).
75. Reg. §§ 1.355-2(b)(5).
76. Revenue Ruling 2003-74, 2003-2 C.B. 77.
77. Revenue Ruling 2003-52, 2003-1 C.B. 960.
78. Reg. § 1.355-2(b)(2).

requirement is not dependent on the corporation's successful accomplishment of its business purposes for the division.

**f. No Device.** The division may not be "used principally as a device for the distribution" of earnings and profits of the distributing corporation or any controlled corporation.[79] Although the requirement, on its face, suggests that a division cannot be used as a diversification strategy to mitigate the double tax burdens inherent in a C corporation, what it really mandates is forward planning, patience, and a focus on details. Of all the requirements, the "device" issue is the least defined – the vaguest. The determination is based on "all facts and circumstances."[80] The biggest smoking gun is a post-division sale that suggests or implies a pre-division intention or commitment to sell off part of the business.[81] This is so even though the statute specifically states that the "mere fact" of a subsequent shareholder sale will not be construed as "such a device."[82] As with the continuity of interest requirement, the division should be allowed to settle and age before any attention is given to potential sales of any of the pieces. Other factors can aggravate the device determination. Stuffing all excess liquid assets into one of the surviving corporations may appear incriminating.[83] Segregating a wholly dependent functional division into its own separate corporate entity may suggest a device in some situations.[84] And device concerns are heightened when the distributions to the shareholders of the distributing corporation are pro rata among the shareholders.[85]

## 7. NEW VENTURES

Many successful businesses have the opportunity to grow and expand. The common practice is to structure and finance the growth internally. The company just gets bigger. Some growth opportunities, by their very nature, can be structured separately from the existing business operations without losing any significant efficiency. This is possible in many situations, even when the growth opportunity is in the same line of business as the existing operations. When this situation exists, there is a valuable diversification option. The new opportunity can be owned and financed through a separate pass-through entity, such as an S corporation or an LLC. Often it can be financed with borrowed dollars, so that there is little or no equity value up front. The new pass-through entity allows cash generated from the new venture to be distributed free of any double tax concerns or the tax traps that accompany a conversion from C status to S status. Plus, the low going-in equity value often makes it possible to gift a large percentage of the ownership in the new venture to children, descendants, or trusts established for their benefit, at little or no transfer tax cost to the parents. If equity interests in the new pass-through entity are owned by other family members, cash flowing to the other family members from the new entity may be

---

79. I.R.C. § 355(a)(1)(B); Reg. § 1.355-2(d).
80. Reg. § 1.355-2(d)(1).
81. Reg. § 1.355-2(d)(2)(iii).
82. I.R.C. § 355(a)(1)(B) (Parenthetical).
83. Reg. § 1.355-2(d)(2)(iv).
84. Reg. § 1.355-2(d)(2)(iv)(C).
85. Reg. § 1.355-2(d)(2)(ii). In Rev. Proc. 2013-3, the IRS said that it will not rule on whether sections 355 and 361 will apply to a leveraged spin-off where a corporation distributes stock or securities in exchange for, or retirement of, any putative debt of the distributing corporation.

used to accomplish a number of targeted estate planning objectives, such as funding premiums on life insurance policies that insure the parents' lives and that will cover any estate tax burden triggered on the parents' death.

### 8. OWNER DEFERRED COMPENSATION

Effective use of compensation planning may be an attractive diversification option in toiler organizations where the owners work for the C corporation. Since reasonable compensation payments are deductible by the corporation, the double tax hit can be eliminated. Care needs to be taken to ensure that a case can be made for the reasonableness of the amounts paid.

Many toiler businesses enjoy periods of success where the cash flow of the business exceeds any amount that could be characterized as reasonable compensation for the current services rendered by the shareholder/employees who manage the business. Very few businesses start out that way. The typical scenario is that the business initially has low profit years, followed by a steady growth curve before the high profits are realized. In the early years, the owner/employees typically pay themselves no salaries or very low salaries. The cash just isn't available. In these cases, it may be prudent for each owner to be given a deferred compensation program under which the compensation level for the owner is initially set at a higher level than the company can afford to pay. The program provides that the unpaid compensation amounts are deferred until a future date.[86] Then when the good times arrive, the owners are not only paid appropriate current salaries, but are paid additional amounts that reflect the deferrals from the lean years. The unreasonable compensation risk is reduced because it is clear that the large amounts paid in the fat years are, in part, attributable to deferred amounts from the lean years.

This strategy cannot be implemented when the good years arrive. The deferred compensation must be accrued over the lean years. Many owners fail to focus on the problem until it has arrived, and then it is too late. A prudent course of action for any business starting out is to at least consider establishing some type of deferred compensation arrangement for those owner/employees who, by necessity, are being underpaid.

### 9. THE ESOP BAILOUT

An ESOP is a qualified retirement plan that is designed to invest in the stock of the employer.[87] The benefit of an ESOP is that it permits the accumulation of funds by the corporation on a tax-deductible basis, as well as the deferral of tax on the earnings of the fund. Over time, a substantial fund can be accumulated with pre-tax dollars that can be used to purchase the stock of a shareholder. It can provide an effective diversification tool to bail out substantial earnings to shareholders on a pre-tax basis. The accumulation occurs in the ESOP trust, not the corporation, so it does not enhance the risk of the accumulated earnings tax. If sufficient funds have not been accumulated in the ESOP by the time the stock of a particular shareholder needs to be acquired, the ESOP can borrow the needed

---

86. There are a number of tax issues that need to be carefully analyzed in structuring any non-qualified deferred compensation plan, including the requirements of the new Section 409A. See Chapter 11.
　　87. I.R.C. § 4975(e)(7).

funds, often with a loan provided through the company. The loan is then repaid with tax-deductible dollars that come from future contributions by the company to the ESOP.

An ESOP can be an effective tool to bail out accumulated earnings on a pre-tax basis to the shareholder who wants to diversify by selling some or all of his or her stock. Plus, if after the sale the ESOP owns at least 30 percent of the company's stock and the selling shareholder has held his or her stock for at least three years, there is an important additional tax benefit. The selling shareholder may elect to defer any capital gain on the stock sale by reinvesting the sale proceeds into the stock or securities of any one or more domestic operating corporations (including public companies) during the 15-month period commencing three months before the stock sale.[88] This provides an attractive deferral option to the shareholder of a closely held corporation who wants to reduce his or her illiquid holdings and reposition capital into a diversified portfolio of liquid investments. Plus, the portion of the gain attributable to any portion of the reinvestment portfolio that is held until death will permanently escape income taxation because of the basis step-up at death.[89] An ESOP works best in those situations where there is not a primary objective to pass the stock to family members or other substantial shareholders. The employees often end up with rights to a large block of stock through the ESOP.

An ESOP comes with burdens that must be evaluated. It can be costly to maintain and administer. One of the most costly elements is the need to have the company's stock formally appraised each year. Also, a group of shareholders can lose control of the company through the use of the ESOP because the anti-discrimination rules require that all participating employees receive the benefits of the ESOP. Another potential problem is that voting control of the company may shift to the ESOP upon the death of a major shareholder. The remaining shareholders may be the trustees who vote the stock in the ESOP, but they will be subject to a fiduciary duty to vote the shares in the best interest of the ESOP's participants. This can create a burden that is magnified by conflicting interests. The potential loss of unrestricted control must always be considered in the ESOP design. Then there is the burden of getting the employees involved in ownership, control and valuation issues of the company. Expectations may be unduly inflated, and management may find itself having to explain and justify its actions and decisions to a broad base of employees, many of whom are unsophisticated in financial matters. With such burdens, the ESOP is not for everyone. It is a vehicle worth considering only in select situations.

### 10. THE LIFE INSURANCE BAILOUT

Another diversification strategy for shareholder/employees of a C corporation is the life insurance bailout. With this strategy, the shareholder/employee does not receive cash from the corporation on a tax-favored basis, but rather corporate dollars are used to fund a life insurance program for the shareholder. Implementing the life insurance bailout presumes

---

88. I.R.C. § 1042.

89. The basis of appreciated property owned by a decedent is increased to its fair market value at the decedent's death. I.R.C. § 1014(a).

that the shareholder wants and needs life insurance protection and the liquidity it provides. The corporation's funding of the premiums is usually taxed as current compensation to the shareholder/employee, with a corresponding deduction to the corporation. The amount of the compensation hit depends on the structure of the program (bonus insurance, split-dollar, etc.). Alternative structures are discussed in Chapter 12. Often, the premium payment is augmented with a gross-up bonus to the shareholder/employee to cover any related taxes. During life, the shareholder/employee is saved the expense of having to fund a life insurance program. Of course, the big payoff comes at death when the proceeds show up (often in a family trust that is not subject to estate taxes) to cover family liquidity needs and assist in the funding of any tax exposures at death.

## 11. Family Employment

Another strategy for pulling earnings out of corporations is to employ children. If children render actual services to the corporation, the corporation may pay them reasonable compensation for their services. The compensation payments are deductible by the corporation and taxable to the children. To the extent the earnings do not exceed a child's standard deduction, the compensation is income tax free to the child. Of course, both the corporation and the children will still be obligated to pay employment taxes. Also, the "Kiddie Tax" is not an issue because it does not apply to earned income.[90] It makes no difference that the child is a minor. As long as the services are reasonable in relationship to the compensation paid, the compensation is deductible. The Tax Court has upheld the deduction of compensation payments to a child as young as seven years old.[91] The shareholder/parents can still claim the child as a dependent if they provide more than one-half the child's support.[92]

What about paying compensation to a spouse? Does it help? Obviously, if the spouse is rendering substantial services to the corporation, that fact can help overcome an unreasonable compensation problem and may provide a basis for bailing out additional earnings to the couple as compensation. Note, however, that the amounts paid to the spouse will trigger another round of payroll taxes. If all the compensation income can be paid to one of the spouses without creating a reasonable compensation problem, payroll taxes are usually saved.[93]

## 12. Shareholder Leased Property

Another popular diversification strategy is to have the shareholders acquire assets that the corporation needs and then lease those assets to the corporation. Real estate is the best example. The corporation's need for an office and warehouse is met by having the shareholders, or a pass-through entity owned by the shareholders, acquire the property. Owning real estate outside a C corporation offers important tax advantages. It eliminates a double tax on the

---

90. The "Kiddie Tax" refers to I.R.C. § 1(g) that taxes the unearned income of a minor under the age of 19 at the highest marginal rate of the minor's parents.

91. Eller v. Commissioner, 77 T.C. 934 (1981).

92. I.R.C. § 152(c)(1)(D).

93. The reason for this is that the social security portion of the payroll tax, presently 12.4 percent (equally split between the employee and the employer), stops for any employee whose income reaches a designated level ($113,700 for 2013).

appreciation when the property is sold. It provides estate planning flexibility for the shareholders. And it offers significant ongoing benefits to the owners relating to the withdrawal of earnings from the corporation on a tax-favored basis. There is one important caution: any net rental income received by the shareholders from the corporation may not constitute passive income that can be offset by other passive investment losses because of the relationship between the corporation and the shareholders.[94]

## PROBLEMS 13–A AND 13–B

**13–A.** Walton Industries Inc. is a successful, profitable family business. Walter Walton is the patriarch of the family and the founder, CEO and sole owner of the business. Walter and his wife, Betty, have four adult children, all of whom work in the business. The business has always been a C corporation. The business has always been profitable. The family members are paid generous salaries, and the net profits (ranging from $500,000 to $750,000) are retained in the business each year. Walter says that the balance sheet of the business shows total assets of $10.6 million, and the only liabilities are $300,000 of current accounts payable. Walter is very proud of the company's solid, growing debt-free equity base. Walter and Betty intend to transfer the business to the kids "at the appropriate time."

Advise Walter and Betty about the problems associated with their non-existent debt-to-equity ratio. What additional facts do you need to obtain? Based on the facts you obtain, what corrective action, if any, would you recommend?

**13–B.** David and Lou Smith are brothers and business partners. They have worked together their entire lives. They equally own the stock of Smith Industries Inc. (Smith), a C corporation that is a specialty furniture and door manufacturer. Smith has nearly 400 employees and facilities in four cities. David and Lou estimate that the company's value is approximately $24 million. The company's balance sheet shows assets with a book value of $14 million and debts totaling $3 million, for a net book equity of $11 million. The company's current pre-tax income is $3.2 million (before any payments to David and Lou) on sales of roughly $40 million. Although Smith has been in business nearly 30 years, its income and value started to really balloon only five years ago.

David and his wife Judy, both age 52, have three children, none of whom has ever worked for Smith. The "lion's share" of David's estate is "tied up" in Smith, and he's getting nervous about having "all his eggs in one basket." He enjoys running the two smallest facilities that the company has owned for three years (that account for about 35 percent of the sales and income), and he wants to "keep producing for 10 more years." Also, he appreciates Lou's passion for "growth, growth, growth." But David says he is anxious to start "seeing some of the money" and building some "serious wealth" outside and away from the risks of the business.

Lou's situation is different. He is a 56 year-old widower who loves to work

---

94. Reg. § 1.469-4(f), including example (2).

and never wants to "retire and wait to die."  Plus, his ultimate dream was realized when his only child Brandon joined the company eight years ago, quickly "learned the ropes and became a star," and "works with his old man to take it to the moon."  Lou has always conservatively spent and wisely invested his money. His personal estate, outside of Smith, is valued at approximately $10 million.  He just wants to keep building with his son.

David has asked for your advice and counsel.  What preliminary recommendations would you discuss with David?  What additional facts do you need?

# CHAPTER 14

# THE ENTERPRISE AND
# ITS COMPETITORS

## A. PERILS AND NAKED TRUTHS

Business is all about competition. Competition is what keeps markets thriving, prices down, output up, new innovation in high gear – at least in theory, and often in practice. To stay alive and healthy in an ever-faster-paced market whose geographical barriers are being shattered monthly by new technologies, most businesses need to develop a competitive strategy. They must determine how they are going to meet and beat new players, products, and technologies that threaten old ways, old prices, and old market shares. It requires knowledge; competitive intelligence itself is now big business. It requires forward planning and often bold actions designed to keep barriers up and outsiders out. And sometimes it requires, in the minds of those calling the shots, coordinated efforts with others, similarly threatened, who have forever been considered the "other guys," the competition.

Not all collaborations between competitors are bad. Some lead to increased efficiencies, more output, lower prices, and new innovation. But they are all potentially dangerous. The deal that promises every virtue of our competitive system may be a façade for (or soon lead to) an exercise of market power that controls output and discourages new products and innovation. The perils of getting mixed up in the wrong kind of coordinated effort, deemed smart and crafty on its face, can be severe. These perils can shake the business to its core, even threaten its survival. The fact that the line between good and bad often is fuzzy and can only be found by a court only magnifies the danger. The business owner who perceives such uncertainty as an opportunity or excuse for boldness lacks a fundamental understanding of how a plaintiffs' lawyer earns a living. The advisor's challenge is to help the business spot the danger flags and implement its competitive strategy clear of the danger zones.

The overriding goal of our antitrust laws is to preserve, protect and maintain public confidence in our free market system by deterring and eliminating economic oppression. The post-Civil War industrial revolution quickly taught all that unrestrained free market forces can produce combinations, driven by greed

515

*economics about efficiency*

and power, that will destroy the freedom of others.[1]  Therefore, for the past 116 years or so, the Congress, the Executive Branch, state legislators, academic commentators, and most importantly, our courts, have wrestled with the challenge of drawing the line between good and bad competition.  Although there have been many bumps and U-turns along the way, most now agree that the social objectives of antitrust are to promote the efficient allocation of goods and services; to prevent "deadweight loss," the loss that results when restricted output limits access to products and services; to stop "wealth transfer," the transfer of wealth from consumers to those who exercise market power to limit or restrict competitive conditions; and to promote "dynamic efficiency," the development of new products, innovations and technologies.  Of far less concern, although once deemed the essence of antitrust, are desires to decentralize power and to protect market entry for individual firms.  Now all have pretty much accepted the reality that big is not bad when it promotes efficiency and innovation and produces no serious signs of deadweight loss or wealth transfer.  It is against these fundamental objectives that each gray-area issue must ultimately be tested.

*Anti-price discrimination*

The antitrust statutes themselves clarify nothing.  Section 1 of the Sherman Act, the foundation for most antitrust disputes, just proscribes "any contract, combination and conspiracy in restraint of trade."[2]  Section 2, dealing with monopolies, offers nothing clearer.[3]  The Robinson-Patman Act's price discrimination prohibitions, although a bit more specific on their face, are just as difficult in their application.[4]  The Federal Trade Commission Act outlaws "unfair methods of competition" and "unfair and deceptive acts and practices."[5]  Justice Hughes characterized the antitrust statutes as a "charter of freedom," with a "generality and adaptability comparable to that found to be desirable in constitutional provisions."[6]  But, according to the beliefs of most, at least the Founding Fathers had "intentions" for what they put in the constitution.  No one really knows what Senator Sherman and his colleagues intended,[7] apart from the fact that they hated John D. Rockefeller and the deplorable tactics used by Rockefeller to build his powerful oil trust.[8]  So the courts, aided by the Department of Justice, the Federal Trade Commission (FTC), hordes of commentators, and masses of private litigants, have had free reign in exercising their charter of freedom to create a body of law that is anything but clear.

The need for some clarity has prompted the Department of Justice and the FTC to jointly develop and publish guidelines from time to time "to assist

---

1. See generally M. Josephson, The Robber Barons (Harcourt Brace Jovanovich, Inc., Copyright 1934, renewed 1962).
2. 15 U.S.C.A. § 1.
3. 15 U.S.C.A. § 2.
4. See, for example, J. Truett Payne Co. v. Chrysler Motors Corp., 451 U.S. 557 (1981) and Boise Cascade Corp. v. FTC, 837 F.2d 1127 (D.C. Cir. 1988).
5. 15 U.S.C.A. § 13.
6. Justice Hughes writing for the majority in Appalachian Coals Inc. v. United States, 288 U.S. 344, 359-60 (1933).
7. As Professor Bork wrote, "So far as I'm aware, Congress, in enacting these statutes, never faced the problem of what to do when values come into conflict in specific cases.  Legislators appear to have assumed, as it is most comfortable to assume, that all good things are always compatible."  Bork, The Role of the Courts in Applying Economics, 54 Antitrust L.J. 21, 24 (1985).
8. 21 Cong. Rec. 2,460 (1890).

businesses in assessing the likelihood of an antitrust challenge."[9]  One such set of guidelines, published in 2000, deals specifically with collaborations among competitors and lays out the analytical approach used by the Department of Justice and FTC in evaluating an agreement among competitors.  Excerpts from these guidelines are included in the following section of this chapter.  These excerpts are followed by five problems designed to test the student's ability to apply the guidelines to specific fact situations.

Business advisors often encounter clients who, yearning to secure what they have or to get more, are determined to push the envelope.  They have an opportunity; they want to "go for it."  They don't want to hear anything about dynamic efficiencies or dead-weight loss, and wealth transfer actually sounds pretty good.  When faced with this situation, the advisor might find some combination of the following 10 naked truths helpful.

**1.   Who's President Doesn't Matter.**   Some think a pro-business Republican president means no more antitrust.  After all, they say, compare Microsoft's fate under Clinton and Bush.  It's bad thinking.  The Department of Justice and FTC always are at work.[10]  Plus (and this is what many miss), the real threat often comes from a private party who has been hurt, not the government.  Or, perhaps more accurately stated, the real threat is the attorney of the private party who has allegedly been hurt.  The United States is the only country that allows private parties to seek redress for their injuries under the antitrust laws.  The simple truth:  There are 10 private lawsuits for every government action.  The ratio used to be 20-to-1; standing and other limitations have made it a little tougher for a plaintiff to latch onto antitrust.[11]  And these numbers do not include all those businesses (and there are many) that through calculated risk or ignorance stepped over the line, got caught, and quietly took their lumps.

**2. Forget the Odds.**  With antitrust, it's not about the odds of winning.  It's the stakes of losing.  Some risks with miniscule losing odds aren't worth messing with because of what's at stake.  Antitrust is one of those risks.  The antitrust statutes, although vague on many things, are very specific on one important detail: the plaintiff who wins is entitled to triple damages, plus attorney's fees.  This provides a powerful incentive for an injured party, aided by a hungry attorney, to explore all avenues for springboarding a contract or tort claim into an antitrust claim.  If successful, the potential yield just tripled.  An owner whose business has failed sometimes longs to salvage something by pinning blame on others.  When such an owner discovers a plausible antitrust claim from the "dirty pool" of others, the effort of recovering three times the business loss becomes a business venture unto itself.  Just the word "antitrust" gets some lawyers excited.

**3.  A Criminal?**  Add to any civil liability exposures the ugly reality, often overlooked, that antitrust violations are also criminal violations.  In 2004 Congress, with the support of the Bush Administration, increased criminal

---

9.  Antitrust Guidelines for Collaborations Among Competitors (April 2000), p.2.

10.  Many complained that the Bush Administration, to the surprise of everyone, was too aggressive in its antitrust efforts.  See, e.g., Stephen Moore, Bust the Antitrusters, NRO National Review (September 15, 2004).

11.  S. Salop & L. White, Private Antitrust Litigation: An Introduction and Framework in Private Antitrust Litigation, New Evidence, New Learning (L. White. ed. 1988), p.3.

penalties for individuals who violate the antitrust laws to $1 million and 10 years jail time (up from $250,000 and three years) and increased corporate penalties to $100 million (up from $10 million).[12]   Although criminal prosecutions are limited to the worst offenders (e.g. hard-core cartel offenders), the thought of getting involved in something that is a crime, not just a calculated business risk, may prompt some to think differently.

   **4.  Winning Is Losing.**  The fight itself can take an intolerable toll on a business, even when the business is declared the ultimate victor.  The high stakes provide powerful incentives for all parties to fight long and hard.  Often the mammoth out-of-pocket costs of the fight and the complete loss of huge amounts of otherwise productive time are too much for many closely held businesses. Usually the essence of the claims are factual allegations that demand intense scrutiny of the business, all of which adds to the expense, discomfort, disruptions, and opportunity costs of the effort.  As the dispute heats up, drags on and takes its toll, third-party observers, important to the business, may add to the mounting burdens.  Key employees may become insecure and jump ship. Important customers and vendors may start looking in other directions.  All of these costs and burdens are known to those who are throwing the darts.  Their challenge is to keep throwing and applying pressure because they know that, at some point, the business may conclude that winning is losing and cut its losses by settling.

   **5.  The Plagues: Price and Output.**  Agreements that make it easier to control market prices or outputs are the plague.  They are per se bad.  Arguments about market power (or lack thereof) and anticompetitive and pro-competitive effects won't help.  The challenge is to strip away all the proposed rationales and excuses for the deal and honestly answer one question: Does the company's proposed deal with its competitor make it easier to maintain or raise prices or control output of goods or services in the market?  If so, run.

   **6.  Signed Deal Not Required.**  A defective agreement among competitors can take many forms.  It need not be in writing or be an enforceable contract.  An informal understanding often is enough.[13]  Coordinated actions may be all that it takes.[14]  Circumstantial evidence becomes the ball game.  If the competitors' actions suggest some kind of agreement or understanding, the plaintiff's challenge is to present enough circumstantial evidence to get the case to the jury. Although some competitors, faced with a claim, have prevailed by refuting circumstantial evidence and proving the plausibility of their parallel conduct without any agreement or understanding,[15] the business owner who's tempted to play ball with his or her competitors by keeping prices up or output down would be foolish to bank on such an argument.

   **7.  Beyond Price and Output.**  An agreement between competitors that does not affect price and output might still be out of bounds.  For any such

---

12.  Antitrust Criminal Penalty Enhancement and Reform Act of 2004, Pub.L. 108-237.
13.  See, e.g., United States v. Paramount Pictures, 334 U.S. 131 (1948) and FTC v. Cement Institute, 333 U.S. 683 (1948).
14.  See, e.g., Interstate Circuit, Inc. v. United States, 306 U.S. 208 (1939).
15.  See, e.g., Matsushita Electric Industrial Co. v. Zenith Radio Corp., 475 U.S. 574 (1986).

agreement, a rule of reason is applied to determine the agreement's potential for anticompetitive harm. In the words of the Department of Justice and FTC, it's a "flexible inquiry and varies in focus and detail depending on the nature of the agreement and market circumstances."[16] Translation: No certainty; could go either way. Examples of competitor arrangements tested under the rule of reason include, among others, joint agreements for marketing, production, buying, research and development, and shared assets and facilities.

**8. Flying Solo Can Do It.** Antitrust risks are not limited to competitor collaborations. A company with dominant market power can get in trouble by itself. Being or becoming a monopoly is not illegal. But engaging in anticompetitive or exclusionary conduct to obtain or maintain monopoly power crosses over the line. Any company with substantial market power should realize that it will be held to a higher competitive standard than smaller players who are struggling for market share.

**9. Market Power Comes In Many Sizes.** Too often, market power is confused with company size. The sole newspaper in a small town may be a monopolist with market power.[17] Market power cannot be determined without first defining the limits of the relevant market, a tough challenge in many cases. Relevant markets come in many sizes.

**10. When Rule of Reason Rules.** In evaluating how any agreed restraint might fare under the rule of reason, it often helps to answer key questions. The purpose of these questions is to help assess the restraint's adverse impact on market output, efficiency, and innovation and to determine whether the agreement has any pro-competitive effects not available through less restrictive means. Ultimately, the end result is a balancing exercise between the pro-competitive and anticompetitive effects. Some of the important questions include the following:

- Does the restraint have the potential to strengthen the market?[18]

- Does the restraint have the capacity to impact market price-setting mechanisms?[19]

- Does the restraint promote or demand exclusivity?[20]

- Is the restraint imposed by a party possessing dominant market power?[21]

- Is the particular industry susceptible to collusion?[22]

- Does the restraint help get more output to market?[23]

---

16. Antitrust Guidelines for Collaborations Among Competitors (April 2000), p. 10.
17. Lorain Journal Co. v. United States, 342 U.S. 143 (1951).
18. See, e.g., California Dental Ass'n v. FTC, 526 U.S. 756 (1999).
19. See, e.g., FTC v. Indiana Federation of Dentists, 476 U.S. 447 (1986).
20. Compare, e.g., Broadcast Music, Inc. v. Columbia Broadcasting System, Inc., 441 U.S. 1 (1979) with NCAA v. Board of Regents of University of Oklahoma, 468 U.S. 85 (1984).
21. See, e.g., Eastman Kodak Co. v. Image Technical Services, Inc., 504 U.S. 451 (1992).
22. See, e.g., United States v. Container Corp. of America, 393 U.S. 333 (1969).
23. See, e.g., Broadcast Music, Inc. v. Columbia Broadcasting System, Inc., 441 U.S. 1 (1979) and Appalachian Coals v. United States, 288 U.S. 344 (1933).

- Does the restraint promote efficiency-enhancing infrastructures?[24]

- Is the restraint ancillary to a broader joint venture or business arrangement?[25]

- Does the restraint have the capacity to change the character of an established market?[26]

- Does the restraint affect access to a facility essential for all competitors?[27]

- Does the restraint force a blanket license, long-term lease or boycott that forecloses competition?[28]

- Does the restraint involve the legitimate exercise of intellectual property rights or the use of such rights as a phony pretext for foreclosing competition?[29]

## B. THE GUIDELINES

### ANTITRUST GUIDELINES FOR COLLABORATIONS AMONG COMPETITORS (EXCERPTS)

**Preamble**

In order to compete in modern markets, competitors sometimes need to collaborate. Competitive forces are driving firms toward complex collaborations to achieve goals such as expanding into foreign markets, funding expensive innovation efforts, and lowering production and other costs.

Such collaborations often arc not only benign but procompetitive. Indeed, in the last two decades, the federal antitrust agencies have brought relatively few civil cases against competitor collaborations. Nevertheless, a perception that antitrust laws are skeptical about agreements among actual or potential competitors may deter the development of procompetitive collaborations.[30]

To provide guidance to business people, the Federal Trade Commission ("FTC") and the U.S. Department of Justice ("DOJ") (collectively, "the Agencies") previously issued guidelines addressing several special circumstances in which antitrust issues related to competitor collaborations may arise. But none of these Guidelines represents a general statement of the Agencies' analytical approach to competitor collaborations. The increasing varieties and use of competitor collaborations have yielded requests for improved clarity regarding their treatment under the antitrust laws.

---

24. Med South FTC Advisory Opinion (February 19, 2002).

25. See, e.g., United States v. Addyston Pipe & Steel Co., 85 F. 271 (6th Cir. 1898).

26. See, e.g., Aspen Skiing Co. v. Aspen Highlands Skiing Corp., 472 U.S. 585 (1985).

27. Otter Tail Power Co. v. United States, 410 U.S. 366 (1973); United States v. Terminal R.R. Ass'n of St. Louis, 224 U.S. 383 (1912).

28. United States v. Griffith, 334 U.S. 100 (1948); Lorain Journal Co. v. United States, 342 U.S. 143 (1951); United States v. United Shoe Machine Corporation, 110 F.Supp. 295 (D. Mass. 1953), affirmed 347 U.S. 521 (1954).

29. See Eastman Kodak Co. v. Image Technical Services, Inc., 504 U.S. 451 (1992).

30. Congress has protected certain collaborations from full antitrust liability by passing the National Cooperative Research Act of 1984 (NCRA) and the National Cooperative Research and Production Act of 1993 (NCRPA) (codified together at 15 U.S.C. § § 4301-06).

The new *Antitrust Guidelines for Collaborations among Competitors ("Competitor Collaboration Guidelines")* are intended to explain how the Agencies analyze certain antitrust issues raised by collaborations among competitors. Competitor collaborations and the market circumstances in which they operate vary widely. No set of guidelines can provide specific answers to every antitrust question that might arise from a competitor collaboration. These Guidelines describe an analytical framework to assist businesses in assessing the likelihood of an antitrust challenge to a collaboration with one or more competitors. They should enable businesses to evaluate proposed transactions with greater understanding of possible antitrust implications, thus encouraging procompetitive collaborations, deterring collaborations likely to harm competition and consumers, and facilitating the Agencies' investigations of collaborations.

### Section 1: Purpose, Definitions, And Overview

#### 1.1 Purpose and Definitions

These Guidelines state the antitrust enforcement policy of the Agencies with respect to competitor collaborations. By stating their general policy, the Agencies hope to assist businesses in assessing whether the Agencies will challenge a competitor collaboration or any of the agreements of which it is comprised.[31] However, these Guidelines cannot remove judgment and discretion in antitrust law enforcement. The Agencies evaluate each case in light of its own facts and apply the analytical framework set forth in these Guidelines reasonably and flexibly.[32]

A "competitor collaboration" comprises a set of one or more agreements, other than merger agreements, between or among competitors to engage in economic activity, and the economic activity resulting therefrom.[33] "Competitors" encompasses both actual and potential competitors.[34] Competitor collaborations involve one or more business activities, such as research and development ("R & D"), production, marketing, distribution, sales or purchasing. Information sharing and various trade association activities also may take place through competitor collaborations.

These Guidelines use the terms "anticompetitive harm," "procompetitive benefit," and "overall competitive effect" in analyzing the competitive effects of

---

31. These Guidelines neither describe how the Agencies litigate cases nor assign burdens of proof or production.

32. The analytical framework set forth in these Guidelines is consistent with the analytical frameworks in the Health Care Statements and the Intellectual Property Guidelines, which remain in effect to address issues in their special contexts.

33. These Guidelines take into account neither the possible effects of competitor collaborations in foreclosing or limiting competition by rivals not participating in a collaboration nor the possible anticompetitive effects of standard setting in the context of competitor collaborations. Nevertheless, these effects may be of concern to the Agencies and may prompt enforcement actions.

34. Firms also may be in a buyer-seller or other relationship, but that does not eliminate the need to examine the competitor relationship, if present. A firm is treated as a potential competitor if there is evidence that entry by that firm is reasonably probable in the absence of the relevant agreement, or that competitively significant decisions by actual competitors are constrained by concerns that anticompetitive conduct likely would induce the firm to enter.

agreements among competitors. All of these terms include actual and likely competitive effects. The Guidelines use the term "anticompetitive harm" to refer to an agreement's adverse competitive consequences, without taking account of offsetting procompetitive benefits. Conversely, the term "procompetitive benefit" refers to an agreement's favorable competitive consequences, without taking account of its anticompetitive harm. The terms "overall competitive effect" or "competitive effect" are used in discussing the combination of an agreement's anticompetitive harm and procompetitive benefit...

### 1.3 Competitor Collaborations Distinguished from Mergers

The competitive effects from competitor collaborations may differ from those of mergers due to a number of factors. Most mergers completely end competition between the merging parties in the relevant market(s). By contrast, most competitor collaborations preserve some form of competition among the participants. This remaining competition may reduce competitive concerns, but also may raise questions about whether participants have agreed to anticompetitive restraints on the remaining competition.

Mergers are designed to be permanent, while competitor collaborations are more typically of limited duration. Thus, participants in a collaboration typically remain potential competitors, even if they are not actual competitors for certain purposes (e.g., R & D) during the collaboration. The potential for future competition between participants in a collaboration requires antitrust scrutiny different from that required for mergers.

Nonetheless, in some cases, competitor collaborations have competitive effects identical to those that would arise if the participants merged in whole or in part. The Agencies treat a competitor collaboration as a horizontal merger in a relevant market and analyze the collaboration pursuant to the Horizontal Merger Guidelines if appropriate, which ordinarily is when: (a) the participants are competitors in that relevant market; (b) the formation of the collaboration involves an efficiency-enhancing integration of economic activity in the relevant market; (c) the integration eliminates all competition among the participants in the relevant market; and (d) the collaboration does not terminate within a sufficiently limited period[35] by its own specific and express terms.[36] Effects of the collaboration on competition in other markets are analyzed as appropriate under these Guidelines or other applicable precedent...

### Section 2: General Principles For Evaluating Agreements Among Competitors

### 2.1 Potential Procompetitive Benefits

The Agencies recognize that consumers may benefit from competitor collaborations in a variety of ways. For example, a competitor collaboration may enable participants to offer goods or services that are cheaper, more valuable to

---

35. In general, the Agencies use ten years as a term indicating sufficient permanence to justify treatment of a competitor collaboration as analogous to a merger. The length of this term may vary, however, depending on industry-specific circumstances, such as technology life cycles.

36. This definition, however, does not determine obligations arising under the Hart-Scott-Rodino Antitrust Improvements Act of 1976, 15 U.S.C. § 18a.

consumers, or brought to market faster than would be possible absent the collaboration. A collaboration may allow its participants to better use existing assets, or may provide incentives for them to make output-enhancing investments that would not occur absent the collaboration. The potential efficiencies from competitor collaborations may be achieved through a variety of contractual arrangements including joint ventures, trade or professional associations, licensing arrangements, or strategic alliances.

Efficiency gains from competitor collaborations often stem from combinations of different capabilities or resources. For example, one participant may have special technical expertise that usefully complements another participant's manufacturing process, allowing the latter participant to lower its production cost or improve the quality of its product. In other instances, a collaboration may facilitate the attainment of scale or scope economies beyond the reach of any single participant. For example, two firms may be able to combine their research or marketing activities to lower their cost of bringing their products to market, or reduce the time needed to develop and begin commercial sales of new products. Consumers may benefit from these collaborations as the participants are able to lower prices, improve quality, or bring new products to market faster.

### 2.2 Potential Anticompetitive Harms

Competitor collaborations may harm competition and consumers by increasing the ability or incentive profitably to raise price above or reduce output, quality, service, or innovation below what likely would prevail in the absence of the relevant agreement. Such effects may arise through a variety of mechanisms. Among other things, agreements may limit independent decision making or combine the control of or financial interests in production, key assets, or decisions regarding price, output, or other competitively sensitive variables, or may otherwise reduce the participants' ability or incentive to compete independently.

Competitor collaborations also may facilitate explicit or tacit collusion through facilitating practices such as the exchange or disclosure of competitively sensitive information or through increased market concentration. Such collusion may involve the relevant market in which the collaboration operates or another market in which the participants in the collaboration are actual or potential competitors.

### 2.3 Analysis of the Overall Collaboration and the Agreements of Which It Consists

A competitor collaboration comprises a set of one or more agreements, other than merger agreements, between or among competitors to engage in economic activity, and the economic activity resulting therefrom. In general, the Agencies assess the competitive effects of the overall collaboration and any individual agreement or set of agreements within the collaboration that may harm competition. For purposes of these Guidelines, the phrase "relevant agreement" refers to whichever of these three – the overall collaboration, an individual agreement, or a set of agreements – the evaluating Agency is assessing. Two or more agreements are assessed together if their procompetitive benefits or anticompetitive harms are so intertwined that they cannot meaningfully be isolated and attributed to any individual agreement.

### 2.4 Competitive Effects Are Assessed as of the Time of Possible Harm to Competition

The competitive effects of a relevant agreement may change over time, depending on changes in circumstances such as internal reorganization, adoption of new agreements as part of the collaboration, addition or departure of participants, new market conditions, or changes in market share. The Agencies assess the competitive effects of a relevant agreement as of the time of possible harm to competition, whether at formation of the collaboration or at a later time, as appropriate. However, an assessment after a collaboration has been formed is sensitive to the reasonable expectations of participants whose significant sunk cost investments in reliance on the relevant agreement were made before it became anticompetitive.

### Section 3: Analytical Framework For Evaluating Agreements Among Competitors

#### 3.1 Introduction

Section 3 sets forth the analytical framework that the Agencies use to evaluate the competitive effects of a competitor collaboration and the agreements of which it consists. Certain types of agreements are so likely to be harmful to competition and to have no significant benefits that they do not warrant the time and expense required for particularized inquiry into their effects.[37] Once identified, such agreements are challenged as per se illegal.[38]

Agreements not challenged as per se illegal are analyzed under the rule of reason. Rule of reason analysis focuses on the state of competition with, as compared to without, the relevant agreement. Under the rule of reason, the central question is whether the relevant agreement likely harms competition by increasing the ability or incentive profitably to raise price above or reduce output, quality, service, or innovation below what likely would prevail in the absence of the relevant agreement. Given the great variety of competitor collaborations, rule of reason analysis entails a flexible inquiry and varies in focus and detail depending on the nature of the agreement and market circumstances. Rule of reason analysis focuses on only those factors, and undertakes only the degree of factual inquiry, necessary to assess accurately the overall competitive effect of the relevant agreement.[39]

#### 3.2 Agreements Challenged as Per Se Illegal

Agreements of a type that always or almost always tends to raise price or reduce output are per se illegal.[40] The Agencies challenge such agreements, once

---

37. See Continental TV, Inc. v. GTE Sylvania Inc., 433 U.S. 36, 50 n.16 (1977).
38. See Superior Court Trial Lawyers Ass'n, 493 U.S. at 432-3.
39. See California Dental Ass'n, 119 S. Ct. at 1617-18; Indiana Fed'n of Dentists, 476 U.S. at 459–61; NCAA, 468 U.S. at 104-13.
40. See Broadcast Music, Inc. v. Columbia Broadcasting Sys., 441 U.S. 1, 19-20 (1979).

identified, as per se illegal. Typically these are agreements not to compete on price or output. Types of agreements that have been held per se illegal include agreements among competitors to fix prices or output, rig bids, or share or divide markets by allocating customers, suppliers, territories or lines of commerce.[41] The courts conclusively presume such agreements, once identified, to be illegal, without inquiring into their claimed business purposes, anticompetitive harms, procompetitive benefits, or overall competitive effects. The Department of Justice prosecutes participants in hard-core cartel agreements criminally.

If, however, participants in an efficiency-enhancing integration of economic activity enter into an agreement that is reasonably related to the integration and reasonably necessary to achieve its procompetitive benefits, the Agencies analyze the agreement under the rule of reason, even if it is of a type that might otherwise be considered per se illegal.[42] In an efficiency-enhancing integration, participants collaborate to perform or cause to be performed (by a joint venture entity created by the collaboration or by one or more participants or by a third party acting on behalf of other participants) one or more business functions, such as production, distribution, marketing, purchasing or R & D, and thereby benefit, or potentially benefit, consumers by expanding output, reducing price, or enhancing quality, service, or innovation. Participants in an efficiency-enhancing integration typically combine, by contract or otherwise, significant capital, technology, or other complementary assets to achieve procompetitive benefits that the participants could not achieve separately. The mere coordination of decisions on price, output, customers, territories, and the like is not integration, and cost savings without integration are not a basis for avoiding per se condemnation. The integration must be of a type that plausibly would generate procompetitive benefits cognizable under the efficiencies analysis set forth in Section 3.36 below. Such procompetitive benefits may enhance the participants' ability or incentives to compete and thus may offset an agreement's anticompetitive tendencies.

An agreement may be "reasonably necessary" without being essential. However, if the participants could achieve an equivalent or comparable efficiency-enhancing integration through practical, significantly less restrictive means, then the Agencies conclude that the agreement is not reasonably necessary.[43] In making this assessment, except in unusual circumstances, the Agencies consider whether practical, significantly less restrictive means were reasonably available when the agreement was entered into, but do not search for a theoretically less restrictive alternative that was not practical given the business realities.

Before accepting a claim that an agreement is reasonably necessary to achieve procompetitive benefits from an integration of economic activity, the

---

41. See, e.g., Palmer v. BRG of Georgia, Inc., 498 U.S. 46 (1990) (market allocation); United States v. Trenton Potteries Co., 273 U.S. 392 (1927) (price fixing).

42. See Arizona v. Maricopa County Medical Soc'y, 457 U.S. 332, 339 n.7, 356-57 (1982) (finding no integration).

43. See id. at 352-53 (observing that even if a maximum fee schedule for physicians' services were desirable, it was not necessary that the schedule be established by physicians rather than by insurers); Broadcast Music, 441 U.S. at 20-21(setting of price "necessary" for the blanket license).

Agencies undertake a limited factual inquiry to evaluate the claim.[44] Such an inquiry may reveal that efficiencies from an agreement that are possible in theory are not plausible in the context of the particular collaboration. Some claims – such as those premised on the notion that competition itself is unreasonable – are insufficient as a matter of law,[45] and others may be implausible on their face. In any case, labeling an arrangement a "joint venture" will not protect what is merely a device to raise price or restrict output;[46] the nature of the conduct, not its designation, is determinative.

### 3.3 Agreements Analyzed under the Rule of Reason

Agreements not challenged as per se illegal are analyzed under the rule of reason to determine their overall competitive effect. Rule of reason analysis focuses on the state of competition with, as compared to without, the relevant agreement. The central question is whether the relevant agreement likely harms competition by increasing the ability or incentive profitably to raise price above or reduce output, quality, service, or innovation below what likely would prevail in the absence of the relevant agreement.[47]

Rule of reason analysis entails a flexible inquiry and varies in focus and detail depending on the nature of the agreement and market circumstances.[48] The Agencies focus on only those factors, and undertake only that factual inquiry, necessary to make a sound determination of the overall competitive effect of the relevant agreement. Ordinarily, however, no one factor is dispositive in the analysis.

Under the rule of reason, the Agencies' analysis begins with an examination of the nature of the relevant agreement, since the nature of the agreement determines the types of anticompetitive harms that may be of concern. As part of this examination, the Agencies ask about the business purpose of the agreement and examine whether the agreement, if already in operation, has caused anticompetitive harm.[49] If the nature of the agreement and the absence of market power,[50] together demonstrate the absence of anticompetitive harm, the Agencies do not challenge the agreement. Alternatively, where the likelihood of anticompetitive harm is evident from the nature of the agreement,[51] or

---

44. See Maricopa, 457 U.S. at 352-53, 356-57 (scrutinizing the defendant medical foundations for indicia of integration and evaluating the record evidence regarding less restrictive alternatives).

45. See Indiana Fed'n of Dentists, 476 U.S. at 463-64; NCAA, 486 U.S. at 116-17; Prof'l Eng'rs, 435 U.S. at 693-96. Other claims, such as absence of market power, are no defense to per se illegality. See Superior Court of Trial Lawyers Ass'n, 493 U.S. at 434-36; United States v. Socony-Vacuum Oil Co., 310 U.S. 150, 224-26 & n.59 (1940).

46. See Timken Roller Bearing Co. v. United States, 341 U.S. 593, 598 (1951).

47. In addition, concerns may arise where an agreement increases the ability or incentive of buyers to exercise monopsony power. See infra Section 3.31(a).

48. See California Dental Ass'n, 119 S. Ct. at 1612-13, 1617 ("What is required ... is an enquiry meet for the case, looking to the circumstances, details, and logic of a restraint."); NCAA, 468 U.S. 109 n.39 ("the rule of reason can sometimes be applied in the twinkling of an eye") (quoting Phillip E. Arccda, The "Rule of Reason" in Antitrust Analysis: General Issues 37-38 (Federal Judicial Center, June 1981)).

49. See Board of Trade of the City of Chicago v. United States, 246 U.S. 231, 238 (1918).

50. That market power is absent may be determined without defining a relevant market. For example, if no market power is likely under any plausible market definition, it does not matter which one is correct. Alternatively, easy entry may indicate an absence of market power.

51. See California Dental Ass'n, 119 S. Ct. at 1612-13, 1617 (an "obvious anticompetitive effect" would warrant quick condemnation); Indiana Fed'n of Dentists, 476 U.S. at 459; NCAA, 468 U.S. at 104, 106-10.

anticompetitive harm has resulted from an agreement already in operation,[52] then, absent overriding benefits that could offset the anticompetitive harm, the Agencies challenge such agreements without a detailed market analysis.[53]

If the initial examination of the nature of the agreement indicates possible competitive concerns, but the agreement is not one that would be challenged without a detailed market analysis, the Agencies analyze the agreement in greater depth. The Agencies typically define relevant markets and calculate market shares and concentration as an initial step in assessing whether the agreement may create or increase market power;[54] or facilitate its exercise and thus poses risks to competition.[55] The Agencies examine factors relevant to the extent to which the participants and the collaboration have the ability and incentive to compete independently, such as whether an agreement is exclusive or non-exclusive and its duration.[56] The Agencies also evaluate whether entry would be timely, likely, and sufficient to deter or counteract any anticompetitive harms. In addition, the Agencies assess any other market circumstances that may foster or impede anticompetitive harms.

If the examination of these factors indicates no potential for anticompetitive harm, the Agencies end the investigation without considering procompetitive benefits. If investigation indicates anticompetitive harm, the Agencies examine whether the relevant agreement is reasonably necessary to achieve procompetitive benefits that likely would offset anticompetitive harms.[57]

### 3.31 Nature of the Relevant Agreement: Business Purpose, Operation in the Marketplace and Possible Competitive Concerns

The nature of the agreement is relevant to whether it may cause anticompetitive harm. For example, by limiting independent decision making or combining control over or financial interests in production, key assets, or decisions on price, output, or other competitively sensitive variables, an agreement may create or increase market power or facilitate its exercise by the collaboration, its participants, or both. An agreement to limit independent decision making or to combine control or financial interests may reduce the

---

52. See Indiana Fed'n of Dentists, 476 U.S. at 460-61 ("Since the purpose of the inquiries into market definition and market power is to determine whether an arrangement has the potential for genuine adverse effects on competition, 'proof of actual detrimental effects, such as a reduction of output,' can obviate the need for an inquiry into market power, which is but a 'surrogate for detrimental effects.' ") (quoting 7 Phillip E. Areeda, Antitrust Law ¶ 1511, at 424 (1986)); NCAA, 468 U.S. at 104-08, 110 n.42.

53. See Indiana Fed'n of Dentists, 476 U.S. at 459-60 (condemning without "detailed market analysis" an agreement to limit competition by withholding x-rays from patients' insurers after finding no competitive justification).

54. Market power to a seller is the ability profitably to maintain prices above competitive levels for a significant period of time. Sellers also may exercise market power with respect to significant competitive dimensions other than price, such as quality, service, or innovation. Market power to a buyer is the ability profitably to depress the price paid for a product below the competitive level for a significant period of time and thereby depress output.

55. See Eastman Kodak Co. v. Image Technical Services, Inc., 504 U.S. 451, 464 (1992).

56. Compare NCAA, 468 U.S. at 113-15, 119-20 (noting that colleges were not permitted to televise their own games without restraint), with Broadcast Music, 441 U.S. at 23-24 (finding no legal or practical impediment to individual licenses).

57. See NCAA, 468 U.S. at 113-15 (rejecting efficiency claims when production was limited, not enhanced); Prof'l. Eng'rs, 435 U.S. at 696 (dictum) (distinguishing restraints that promote competition from those that eliminate competition); Chicago Bd. of Trade, 246 U.S. at 238 (same).

ability or incentive to compete independently. An agreement also may increase the likelihood of an exercise of market power by facilitating explicit or tacit collusion,[58] either through facilitating practices such as an exchange of competitively sensitive information or through increased market concentration.

In examining the nature of the relevant agreement, the Agencies take into account inferences about business purposes for the agreement that can be drawn from objective facts. The Agencies also consider evidence of the subjective intent of the participants to the extent that it sheds light on competitive effects.[59] The Agencies do not undertake a full analysis of procompetitive benefits pursuant to Section 3.36 below, however, unless an anticompetitive harm appears likely. The Agencies also examine whether an agreement already in operation has caused anticompetitive harm.[60] Anticompetitive harm may be observed, for example, if a competitor collaboration successfully mandates new, anticompetitive conduct or successfully eliminates procompetitive pre-collaboration conduct, such as withholding services that were desired by consumers when offered in a competitive market. If anticompetitive harm is found, examination of market power ordinarily is not required. In some cases, however, a determination of anticompetitive harm may be informed by consideration of market power.

The following sections illustrate competitive concerns that may arise from the nature of particular types of competitor collaborations. This list is not exhaustive. In addition, where these sections address agreements of a type that otherwise might be considered per se illegal, such as agreements on price, the discussion assumes that the agreements already have been determined to be subject to rule of reason analysis because they are reasonably related to, and reasonably necessary to achieve procompetitive benefits from, an efficiency-enhancing integration of economic activity. See supra Section 3.2.

### 3.31(a) Relevant Agreements that Limit Independent Decision Making or Combine Control or Financial Interests

The following is intended to illustrate but not exhaust the types of agreements that might harm competition by eliminating independent decision making or combining control or financial interests.

**Production Collaborations.** Competitor collaborations may involve agreements jointly to produce a product sold to others or used by the participants as an input. Such agreements are often procompetitive.[61] Participants may combine complementary technologies, know-how, or other assets to enable the collaboration to produce a good more efficiently or to produce a good that no one

---

58. As used in these Guidelines, "collusion" is not limited to conduct that involves an agreement under the antitrust laws.

59. Anticompetitive intent alone does not establish an antitrust violation, and procompetitive intent does not preclude a violation. See, e.g., Chicago Bd. of Trade, 246 U.S. at 238. But extrinsic evidence of intent may aid in evaluating market power, the likelihood of anticompetitive harm, and claimed procompetitive justifications where an agreement's effects are otherwise ambiguous.

60. See id.

61. The NCRPA accords rule of reason treatment to certain production collaborations. However, the statute permits per se challenges, in appropriate circumstances, to a variety of activities, including agreements to jointly market the goods or services produced or to limit the participants' independent sale of goods or services produced outside the collaboration. NCRPA, 15 U.S.C. §§ 4301-02.

participant alone could produce.  However, production collaborations may involve agreements on the level of output or the use of key assets, or on the price at which the product will be marketed by the collaboration, or on other competitively significant variables, such as quality, service, or promotional strategies, that can result in anticompetitive harm.  Such agreements can create or increase market power or facilitate its exercise by limiting independent decision making or by combining in the collaboration, or in certain participants, the control over some or all production or key assets or decisions about key competitive variables that otherwise would be controlled independently.[62]  Such agreements could reduce individual participants' control over assets necessary to compete and thereby reduce their ability to compete independently, combine financial interests in ways that undermine incentives to compete independently, or both.

**Marketing Collaborations**.  Competitor collaborations may involve agreements jointly to sell, distribute, or promote goods or services that are either jointly or individually produced.  Such agreements may be procompetitive, for example, where a combination of complementary assets enables products more quickly and efficiently to reach the marketplace.  However, marketing collaborations may involve agreements on price, output, or other competitively significant variables, or on the use of competitively significant assets, such as an extensive distribution network, that can result in anticompetitive harm.  Such agreements can create or increase market power or facilitate its exercise by limiting independent decision making; by combining in the collaboration, or in certain participants, control over competitively significant assets or decisions about competitively significant variables that otherwise would be controlled independently; or by combining financial interests in ways that undermine incentives to compete independently.  For example, joint promotion might reduce or eliminate comparative advertising, thus harming competition by restricting information to consumers on price and other competitively significant variables.

**Buying Collaborations**.  Competitor collaborations may involve agreements jointly to purchase necessary inputs.  Many such agreements do not raise antitrust concerns and indeed may be procompetitive.  Purchasing collaborations, for example, may enable participants to centralize ordering, to combine warehousing or distribution functions more efficiently, or to achieve other efficiencies.  However, such agreements can create or increase market power (which, in the case of buyers, is called "monopsony power") or facilitate its exercise by increasing the ability or incentive to drive the price of the purchased product, and thereby depress output, below what likely would prevail in the absence of the relevant agreement.  Buying collaborations also may facilitate collusion by standardizing participants' costs or by enhancing the ability to project or monitor a participant's output level through knowledge of its input purchases.

---

62. For example, where output resulting from a collaboration is transferred to participants for independent marketing, anticompetitive harm could result if that output is restricted or if the transfer takes place at a supracompetitive price.  Such conduct could raise participants' marginal costs through inflated per-unit charges on the transfer of the collaboration's output.  Anticompetitive harm could occur even if there is vigorous competition among collaboration participants in the output market, since all the participants would have paid the same inflated transfer price.

**Research & Development Collaborations**.   Competitor collabora-tions may involve agreements to engage in joint research and development ("R&D"). Most such agreements are procompetitive, and they typically are analyzed under the rule of reason.[63]   Through the combination of complementary assets, technology, or know-how, an R&D collaboration may enable participants more quickly or more efficiently to research and develop new or improved goods, services, or production processes.  Joint R&D agreements, however, can create or increase market power or facilitate its exercise by limiting independent decision making or by combining in the collaboration, or in certain participants, control over competitively significant assets or all or a portion of participants' individual competitive R&D efforts.  Although R&D collaborations also may facilitate tacit collusion on R&D efforts, achieving, monitoring, and punishing departures from collusion is sometimes difficult in the R&D context.

An exercise of market power may injure consumers by reducing innovation below the level that otherwise would prevail, leading to fewer or no products for consumers to choose from, lower quality products, or products that reach consumers more slowly than they otherwise would.  An exercise of market power also may injure consumers by reducing the number of independent competitors in the market for the goods, services, or production processes derived from the R&D collaboration, leading to higher prices or reduced output, quality, or service.  A central question is whether the agreement increases the ability or incentive anticompetitively to reduce R&D efforts pursued independently or through the collaboration, for example, by slowing the pace at which R&D efforts are pursued.  Other considerations being equal, R&D agreements are more likely to raise competitive concerns when the collaboration or its participants already possess a secure source of market power over an existing product and the new R&D efforts might cannibalize their supracompetitive earnings.  In addition, anticompetitive harm generally is more likely when R&D competition is confined to firms with specialized characteristics or assets, such as intellectual property, or when a regulatory approval process limits the ability of late-comers to catch up with competitors already engaged in the R&D.

### 3.31(b) Relevant Agreements that May Facilitate Collusion

Each of the types of competitor collaborations outlined above can facilitate collusion.  Competitor collaborations may provide an opportunity for participants to discuss and agree on anticompetitive terms, or otherwise to collude anticompetitively, as well as a greater ability to detect and punish deviations that would undermine the collusion.  Certain marketing, production, and buying collaborations, for example, may provide opportunities for their participants to collude on price, output, customers, territories, or other competitively sensitive variables.  R & D collaborations, however, may be less likely to facilitate collusion regarding R & D activities since R & D often is conducted in secret, and it thus may be difficult to monitor an agreement to coordinate R & D.  In addition, collaborations can increase concentration in a relevant market and thus increase the likelihood of collusion among all firms, including the collaboration

---

63. Aspects of the antitrust analysis of competitor collaborations involving R & D are governed by provisions of the NCRPA, 15 U.S.C. §§ 4301-02.

and its participants.

Agreements that facilitate collusion sometimes involve the exchange or disclosure of information. The Agencies recognize that the sharing of information among competitors may be procompetitive and is often reasonably necessary to achieve the procompetitive benefits of certain collaborations; for example, sharing certain technology, know-how, or other intellectual property may be essential to achieve the procompetitive benefits of an R & D collaboration. Nevertheless, in some cases, the sharing of information related to a market in which the collaboration operates or in which the participants are actual or potential competitors may increase the likelihood of collusion on matters such as price, output, or other competitively sensitive variables. The competitive concern depends on the nature of the information shared. Other things being equal, the sharing of information relating to price, output, costs, or strategic planning is more likely to raise competitive concern than the sharing of information relating to less competitively sensitive variables. Similarly, other things being equal, the sharing of information on current operating and future business plans is more likely to raise concerns than the sharing of historical information.

Finally, other things being equal, the sharing of individual company data is more likely to raise concern than the sharing of aggregated data that does not permit recipients to identify individual firm data.

### 3.32 Relevant Markets Affected by the Collaboration

The Agencies typically identify and assess competitive effects in all of the relevant product and geographic markets in which competition may be affected by a competitor collaboration, although in some cases it may be possible to assess competitive effects directly without defining a particular relevant market(s). Markets affected by a competitor collaboration include all markets in which the economic integration of the participants' operations occurs or in which the collaboration operates or will operate,[64] and may also include additional markets in which any participant is an actual or potential competitor.[65]

### 3.32(a) Goods Markets

In general, for goods[66] markets affected by a competitor collaboration, the Agencies approach relevant market definition as described in Section 1 of the Horizontal Merger Guidelines. To determine the relevant market, the Agencies generally consider the likely reaction of buyers to a price increase and typically ask, among other things, how buyers would respond to increases over prevailing price levels. However, when circumstances strongly suggest that the prevailing price exceeds what likely would have prevailed absent the relevant agreement, the Agencies use a price more reflective of the price that likely would have

---

64. For example, where a production joint venture buys inputs from an upstream market to incorporate in products to be sold in a downstream market, both upstream and downstream markets may be "markets affected by a competitor collaboration."

65. Participation in the collaboration may change the participants' behavior in this third category of markets, for example, by altering incentives and available information, or by providing an opportunity to form additional agreements among participants.

66. The term "goods" also includes services.

prevailed. Once a market has been defined, market shares are assigned both to firms currently in the relevant market and to firms that are able to make "uncommitted" supply responses. See Sections 1.31 and 1.32 of the Horizontal Merger Guidelines.

### 3.32(b) Technology Markets

When rights to intellectual property are marketed separately from the products in which they are used, the Agencies may define technology markets in assessing the competitive effects of a competitor collaboration that includes an agreement to license intellectual property. Technology markets consist of the intellectual property that is licensed and its close substitutes; that is, the technologies or goods that are close enough substitutes significantly to constrain the exercise of market power with respect to the intellectual property that is licensed. The Agencies approach the definition of a relevant technology market and the measurement of market share as described in Section 3.2.2 of the Intellectual Property Guidelines.

### 3.32(c) Research and Development: Innovation Markets

In many cases, an agreement's competitive effects on innovation are analyzed as a separate competitive effect in a relevant goods market. However, if a competitor collaboration may have competitive effects on innovation that cannot be adequately addressed through the analysis of goods or technology markets, the Agencies may define and analyze an innovation market as described in Section 3.2.3 of the Intellectual Property Guidelines. An innovation market consists of the research and development directed to particular new or improved goods or processes and the close substitutes for that research and development. The Agencies define an innovation market only when the capabilities to engage in the relevant research and development can be associated with specialized assets or characteristics of specific firms.

### 3.33 Market Shares and Market Concentration

Market share and market concentration affect the likelihood that the relevant agreement will create or increase market power or facilitate its exercise. The creation, increase, or facilitation of market power will likely increase the ability and incentive profitably to raise price above or reduce output, quality, service, or innovation below what likely would prevail in the absence of the relevant agreement.

Other things being equal, market share affects the extent to which participants or the collaboration must restrict their own output in order to achieve anticompetitive effects in a relevant market. The smaller the percentage of total supply that a firm controls, the more severely it must restrict its own output in order to produce a given price increase, and the less likely it is that an output restriction will be profitable. In assessing whether an agreement may cause anticompetitive harm, the Agencies typically calculate the market shares of the participants and of the collaboration.[67] The Agencies assign a range of market

---

67. When the competitive concern is that a limitation on independent decision making or a combination of control or financial interests may yield an anticompetitive reduction of research and development, the Agencies

shares to the collaboration. The high end of that range is the sum of the market shares of the collaboration and its participants. The low end is the share of the collaboration in isolation. In general, the Agencies approach the calculation of market share as set forth in Section 1.4 of the Horizontal Merger Guidelines.

Other things being equal, market concentration affects the difficulties and costs of achieving and enforcing collusion in a relevant market. Accordingly, in assessing whether an agreement may increase the likelihood of collusion, the Agencies calculate market concentration. In general, the Agencies approach the calculation of market concentration as set forth in Section 1.5 of the Horizontal Merger Guidelines, ascribing to the competitor collaboration the same range of market shares described above.

Market share and market concentration provide only a starting point for evaluating the competitive effect of the relevant agreement. The Agencies also examine other factors outlined in the Horizontal Merger Guidelines as set forth below:

The Agencies consider whether factors such as those discussed in Section 1.52 of the Horizontal Merger Guidelines indicate that market share and concentration data overstate or understate the likely competitive significance of participants and their collaboration.

In assessing whether anticompetitive harm may arise from an agreement that combines control over or financial interests in assets or otherwise limits independent decision making, the Agencies consider whether factors such as those discussed in Section 2.2 of the Horizontal Merger Guidelines suggest that anticompetitive harm is more or less likely.

In assessing whether anticompetitive harms may arise from an agreement that may increase the likelihood of collusion, the Agencies consider whether factors such as those discussed in Section 2.1 of the Horizontal Merger Guidelines suggest that anticompetitive harm is more or less likely.

In evaluating the significance of market share and market concentration data and interpreting the range of market shares ascribed to the collaboration, the Agencies also examine factors beyond those set forth in the Horizontal Merger Guidelines. The following section describes which factors are relevant and the issues that the Agencies examine in evaluating those factors.

### 3.34 Factors Relevant to the Ability and Incentive of the Participants and the Collaboration to Compete

Competitor collaborations sometimes do not end competition among the participants and the collaboration. Participants may continue to compete against each other and their collaboration, either through separate, independent business operations or through membership in other collaborations. Collaborations may be managed by decision makers independent of the individual participants. Control over key competitive variables may remain outside the collaboration, such as where participants independently market and set prices for the

---

typically frame their inquiries more generally, looking to the strength, scope, and number of competing R & D efforts and their close substitutes. See supra Sections 3.31(a) and 3.32(c).

collaboration's output.

Sometimes, however, competition among the participants and the collaboration may be restrained through explicit contractual terms or through financial or other provisions that reduce or eliminate the incentive to compete. The Agencies look to the competitive benefits and harms of the relevant agreement, not merely the formal terms of agreements among the participants.

Where the nature of the agreement and market share and market concentration data reveal a likelihood of anticompetitive harm, the Agencies more closely examine the extent to which the participants and the collaboration have the ability and incentive to compete independent of each other. The Agencies are likely to focus on six factors: (a) the extent to which the relevant agreement is non-exclusive in that participants are likely to continue to compete independently outside the collaboration in the market in which the collaboration operates; (b) the extent to which participants retain independent control of assets necessary to compete; (c) the nature and extent of participants' financial interests in the collaboration or in each other; (d) the control of the collaboration's competitively significant decision making; (e) the likelihood of anticompetitive information sharing; and (f) the duration of the collaboration.

Each of these factors is discussed in further detail below. Consideration of these factors may reduce or increase competitive concern. The analysis necessarily is flexible: the relevance and significance of each factor depends upon the facts and circumstances of each case, and any additional factors pertinent under the circumstances are considered. For example, when an agreement is examined subsequent to formation of the collaboration, the Agencies also examine factual evidence concerning participants' actual conduct.

### 3.34(a) Exclusivity

The Agencies consider whether, to what extent, and in what manner the relevant agreement permits participants to continue to compete against each other and their collaboration, either through separate, independent business operations or through membership in other collaborations. The Agencies inquire whether a collaboration is non-exclusive in fact as well as in name and consider any costs or other impediments to competing with the collaboration. In assessing exclusivity when an agreement already is in operation, the Agencies examine whether, to what extent, and in what manner participants actually have continued to compete against each other and the collaboration. In general, competitive concern likely is reduced to the extent that participants actually have continued to compete, either through separate, independent business operations or through membership in other collaborations, or are permitted to do so.

### 3.34(b) Control over Assets

The Agencies ask whether the relevant agreement requires participants to contribute to the collaboration significant assets that previously have enabled or likely would enable participants to be effective independent competitors in markets affected by the collaboration. If such resources must be contributed to the collaboration and are specialized in that they cannot readily be replaced, the participants may have lost all or some of their ability to compete against each other and their collaboration, even if they retain the contractual right to do so.[68] In general, the greater the contribution of specialized assets to the collaboration that is required, the less the participants may be relied upon to provide independent competition.

### 3.34(c) Financial Interests in the Collaboration or in Other Participants

The Agencies assess each participant's financial interest in the collaboration and its potential impact on the participant's incentive to compete independently with the collaboration. The potential impact may vary depending on the size and nature of the financial interest (e.g., whether the financial interest is debt or equity). In general, the greater the financial interest in the collaboration, the less likely is the participant to compete with the collaboration.[69] The Agencies also assess direct equity investments between or among the participants. Such investments may reduce the incentives of the participants to compete with each other. In either case, the analysis is sensitive to the level of financial interest in the collaboration or in another participant relative to the level of the participant's investment in its independent business operations in the markets affected by the collaboration.

### 3.34(d) Control of the Collaboration's Competitively Significant Decision Making

The Agencies consider the manner in which a collaboration is organized and governed in assessing the extent to which participants and their collaboration have the ability and incentive to compete independently. Thus, the Agencies consider the extent to which the collaboration's governance structure enables the collaboration to act as an independent decision maker. For example, the Agencies ask whether participants are allowed to appoint members of a board of directors for the collaboration, if incorporated, or otherwise to exercise significant control over the operations of the collaboration. In general, the collaboration is less likely to compete independently as participants gain greater control over the collaboration's price, output, and other competitively significant decisions.[70]

To the extent that the collaboration's decision making is subject to the participants' control, the Agencies consider whether that control could be exercised jointly. Joint control over the collaboration's price and output levels could create or increase market power and raise competitive concerns. Depending on the nature of the collaboration, competitive concern also may arise due to joint control over other competitively significant decisions, such as the level and scope of R & D efforts and investment. In contrast, to the extent that participants independently set the price and quantity[71] of their share of a

---

68. For example, if participants in a production collaboration must contribute most of their productive capacity to the collaboration, the collaboration may impair the ability of its participants to remain effective independent competitors regardless of the terms of the agreement.

69. Similarly, a collaboration's financial interest in a participant may diminish the collaboration's incentive to compete with that participant.

70. Control may diverge from financial interests. For example, a small equity investment may be coupled with a right to veto large capital expenditures and, thereby, to effectively limit output. The Agencies examine a collaboration's actual governance structure in assessing issues of control.

71. Even if prices to consumers are set independently, anticompetitive harms may still occur if participants

collaboration's output and independently control other competitively significant decisions, an agreement's likely anticompetitive harm is reduced.[72]

### 3.34(e) Likelihood of Anticompetitive Information Sharing

The Agencies evaluate the extent to which competitively sensitive information concerning markets affected by the collaboration likely would be disclosed. This likelihood depends on, among other things, the nature of the collaboration, its organization and governance, and safeguards implemented to prevent or minimize such disclosure. For example, participants might refrain from assigning marketing personnel to an R & D collaboration, or, in a marketing collaboration, participants might limit access to competitively sensitive information regarding their respective operations to only certain individuals or to an independent third party. Similarly, a buying collaboration might use an independent third party to handle negotiations in which its participants' input requirements or other competitively sensitive information could be revealed. In general, it is less likely that the collaboration will facilitate collusion on competitively sensitive variables if appropriate safeguards governing information sharing are in place.

### 3.34(f) Duration of the Collaboration

The Agencies consider the duration of the collaboration in assessing whether participants retain the ability and incentive to compete against each other and their collaboration. In general, the shorter the duration, the more likely participants are to compete against each other and their collaboration.

### 3.35 Entry

Easy entry may deter or prevent profitably maintaining price above, or output, quality, service or innovation below, what likely would prevail in the absence of the relevant agreement. Where the nature of the agreement and market share and concentration data suggest a likelihood of anticompetitive harm that is not sufficiently mitigated by any continuing competition identified through the analysis in Section 3.34, the Agencies inquire whether entry would be timely, likely, and sufficient in its magnitude, character and scope to deter or counteract the anticompetitive harm of concern. If so, the relevant agreement ordinarily requires no further analysis.

As a general matter, the Agencies assess timeliness, likelihood, and sufficiency of committed entry under principles set forth in Section 3 of the Horizontal Merger Guidelines.[73] However, unlike mergers, competitor collaborations often restrict only certain business activities, while preserving

---

jointly set the collaboration's level of output. For example, participants may effectively coordinate price increases by reducing the collaboration's level of output and collecting their profits through high transfer prices, i.e., through the amounts that participants contribute to the collaboration in exchange for each unit of the collaboration's output. Where a transfer price is determined by reference to an objective measure not under the control of the participants, (e.g., average price in a different unconcentrated geographic market), competitive concern may be less likely.

72. Anticompetitive harm also is less likely if individual participants may independently increase the overall output of the collaboration.

73. Committed entry is defined as new competition that requires expenditure of significant sunk costs of entry and exit. See Section 3.0 of the Horizontal Merger Guidelines.

competition among participants in other respects, and they may be designed to terminate after a limited duration. Consequently, the extent to which an agreement creates and enables identification of opportunities that would induce entry and the conditions under which ease of entry may deter or counteract anticompetitive harms may be more complex and less direct than for mergers and will vary somewhat according to the nature of the relevant agreement. For example, the likelihood of entry may be affected by what potential entrants believe about the probable duration of an anticompetitive agreement. Other things being equal, the shorter the anticipated duration of an anticompetitive agreement, the smaller the profit opportunities for potential entrants, and the lower the likelihood that it will induce committed entry. Examples of other differences are set forth below.

For certain collaborations, sufficiency of entry may be affected by the possibility that entrants will participate in the anticompetitive agreement. To the extent that such participation raises the amount of entry needed to deter or counteract anticompetitive harms, and assets required for entry are not adequately available for entrants to respond fully to their sales opportunities, or otherwise renders entry inadequate in magnitude, character or scope, sufficient entry may be more difficult to achieve.[74]

In the context of research and development collaborations, widespread availability of R&D capabilities and the large gains that may accrue to successful innovators often suggest a high likelihood that entry will deter or counteract anticompetitive reductions of R&D efforts. Nonetheless, such conditions do not always pertain, and the Agencies ask whether entry may deter or counteract anticompetitive R&D reductions, taking into account the likelihood, timeliness, and sufficiency of entry.

To be timely, entry must be sufficiently prompt to deter or counteract such harms. The Agencies evaluate the likelihood of entry based on the extent to which potential entrants have (1) core competencies (and the ability to acquire any necessary specialized assets) that give them the ability to enter into competing R&D and (2) incentives to enter into competing R&D. The sufficiency of entry depends on whether the character and scope of the entrants' R&D efforts are close enough to the reduced R&D efforts to be likely to achieve similar innovations in the same time frame or otherwise to render a collaborative reduction of R&D unprofitable.

### 3.36 Identifying Procompetitive Benefits of the Collaboration

---

74. Under the same principles applied to production and marketing collaborations, the exercise of monopsony power by a buying collaboration may be deterred or counteracted by the entry of new purchasers. To the extent that collaborators reduce their purchases, they may create an opportunity for new buyers to make purchases without forcing the price of the input above pre-relevant agreement levels. Committed purchasing entry, defined as new purchasing competition that requires expenditure of significant sunk costs of entry and exit – such as a new steel factory built in response to a reduction in the price of iron ore – is analyzed under principles analogous to those articulated in Section 3 of the Horizontal Merger Guidelines. Under that analysis, the Agencies assess whether a monopsonistic price reduction is likely to attract committed purchasing entry, profitable at pre-relevant agreement prices, that would not have occurred before the relevant agreement at those same prices. (Uncommitted new buyers are identified as participants in the relevant market if their demand responses to a price decrease are likely to occur within one year and without the expenditure of significant sunk costs of entry and exit. See id. at Sections 1.32 and 1.41.)

Competition usually spurs firms to achieve efficiencies internally. Nevertheless, as explained above, competitor collaborations have the potential to generate significant efficiencies that benefit consumers in a variety of ways. For example, a competitor collaboration may enable firms to offer goods or services that are cheaper, more valuable to consumers, or brought to market faster than would otherwise be possible. Efficiency gains from competitor collaborations often stem from combinations of different capabilities or resources. See supra Section 2.1. Indeed, the primary benefit of competitor collaborations to the economy is their potential to generate such efficiencies.

Efficiencies generated through a competitor collaboration can enhance the ability and incentive of the collaboration and its participants to compete, which may result in lower prices, improved quality, enhanced service, or new products. For example, through collaboration, competitors may be able to produce an input more efficiently than any one participant could individually; such collaboration-generated efficiencies may enhance competition by permitting two or more ineffective (e.g., high cost) participants to become more effective, lower cost competitors. Even when efficiencies generated through a competitor collaboration enhance the collaboration's or the participants' ability to compete, however, a competitor collaboration may have other effects that may lessen competition and ultimately may make the relevant agreement anticompetitive.

If the Agencies conclude that the relevant agreement has caused, or is likely to cause, anticompetitive harm, they consider whether the agreement is reasonably necessary to achieve "cognizable efficiencies." "Cognizable efficiencies" are efficiencies that have been verified by the Agencies, that do not arise from anticompetitive reductions in output or service, and that cannot be achieved through practical, significantly less restrictive means. See infra Sections 3.36(a) and 3.36(b). Cognizable efficiencies are assessed net of costs produced by the competitor collaboration or incurred in achieving those efficiencies.

### 3.36(a) Cognizable Efficiencies Must Be Verifiable and Potentially Procompetitive

Efficiencies are difficult to verify and quantify, in part because much of the information relating to efficiencies is uniquely in the possession of the collaboration's participants. The participants must substantiate efficiency claims so that the Agencies can verify by reasonable means the likelihood and magnitude of each asserted efficiency; how and when each would be achieved; any costs of doing so; how each would enhance the collaboration's or its participants' ability and incentive to compete; and why the relevant agreement is reasonably necessary to achieve the claimed efficiencies (see Section 3.36 (b)). Efficiency claims are not considered if they are vague or speculative or otherwise cannot be verified by reasonable means.

Moreover, cognizable efficiencies must be potentially procompetitive. Some asserted efficiencies, such as those premised on the notion that competition itself is unreasonable, are insufficient as a matter of law. Similarly, cost savings that arise from anticompetitive output or service reductions are not treated as cognizable efficiencies.

### 3.36(b) Reasonable Necessity and Less Restrictive Alternatives

The Agencies consider only those efficiencies for which the relevant agreement is reasonably necessary.   An agreement may be "reasonably necessary" without being essential.   However, if the participants could have achieved or could achieve similar efficiencies by practical, significantly less restrictive means, then the Agencies conclude that the relevant agreement is not reasonably necessary to their achievement.   In making this assessment, the Agencies consider only alternatives that are practical in the business situation faced by the participants; the Agencies do not search for a theoretically less restrictive alternative that is not realistic given business realities.

The reasonable necessity of an agreement may depend upon the market context and upon the duration of the agreement.   An agreement that may be justified by the needs of a new entrant, for example, may not be reasonably necessary to achieve cognizable efficiencies in different market circumstances. The reasonable necessity of an agreement also may depend on whether it deters individual participants from undertaking free riding or other opportunistic conduct that could reduce significantly the ability of the collaboration to achieve cognizable efficiencies.   Collaborations sometimes include agreements to discourage any one participant from appropriating an undue share of the fruits of the collaboration or to align participants' incentives to encourage cooperation in achieving the efficiency goals of the collaboration. The Agencies assess whether such agreements are reasonably necessary to deter opportunistic conduct that otherwise would likely prevent the achievement of cognizable efficiencies.

### 3.37 Overall Competitive Effect

If the relevant agreement is reasonably necessary to achieve cognizable efficiencies, the Agencies assess the likelihood and magnitude of cognizable efficiencies and anticompetitive harms to determine the agreement's overall actual or likely effect on competition in the relevant market.   To make the requisite determination, the Agencies consider whether cognizable efficiencies likely would be sufficient to offset the potential of the agreement to harm consumers in the relevant market, for example, by preventing price increases.[75]

The Agencies' comparison of cognizable efficiencies and anticompetitive harms is necessarily an approximate judgment.   In assessing the overall competitive effect of an agreement, the Agencies consider the magnitude and likelihood of both the anticompetitive harms and cognizable efficiencies from the relevant agreement.  The likelihood and magnitude of anticompetitive harms in a particular case may be insignificant compared to the expected cognizable efficiencies, or vice versa.   As the expected anticompetitive harm of the agreement increases, the Agencies require evidence establishing a greater level of

---

75. In most cases, the Agencies' enforcement decisions depend on their analysis of the overall effect of the relevant agreement over the short term.  The Agencies also will consider the effects of cognizable efficiencies with no short-term, direct effect on prices in the relevant market.  Delayed benefits from the efficiencies (due to delay in the achievement of, or the realization of consumer benefits from, the efficiencies) will be given less weight because they are less proximate and more difficult to predict.

expected cognizable efficiencies in order to avoid the conclusion that the agreement will have an anticompetitive effect overall. When the anticompetitive harm of the agreement is likely to be particularly large, extraordinarily great cognizable efficiencies would be necessary to prevent the agreement from having an anticompetitive effect overall.

### Section 4: Antitrust Safety Zones

### 4.1 Overview

Because competitor collaborations are often procompetitive, the Agencies believe that "safety zones" are useful in order to encourage such activity. The safety zones set out below are designed to provide participants in a competitor collaboration with a degree of certainty in those situations in which anticompetitive effects are so unlikely that the Agencies presume the arrangements to be lawful without inquiring into particular circumstances. They are not intended to discourage competitor collaborations that fall outside the safety zones.

The Agencies emphasize that competitor collaborations are not anticompetitive merely because they fall outside the safety zones. Indeed, many competitor collaborations falling outside the safety zones are procompetitive or competitively neutral. The Agencies analyze arrangements outside the safety zones based on the principles outlined in Section 3 above.

The following sections articulate two safety zones. Section 4.2 sets out a general safety zone applicable to any competitor collaboration.[76] Section 4.3 establishes a safety zone applicable to research and development collaborations whose competitive effects are analyzed within an innovation market. These safety zones are intended to supplement safety zone provisions in the Agencies' other guidelines and statements of enforcement policy.[77]

### 4.2 Safety Zone for Competitor Collaborations in General

Absent extraordinary circumstances, the Agencies do not challenge a competitor collaboration when the market shares of the collaboration and its participants collectively account for no more than twenty percent of each relevant market in which competition may be affected.[78] The safety zone, however, does not apply to agreements that are per se illegal, or that would be challenged without a detailed market analysis, or to competitor collaborations to which a

---

76. See Sections 1.1 and 1.3 above.

77. The Agencies have articulated antitrust safety zones in Health Care Statements 7 & 8 industry or to particular and the Intellectual Property Guidelines, as well as in the Horizontal Merger Guidelines. The antitrust safety zones in these other guidelines relate to particular facts in a specific types of transactions.

78. For purposes of the safety zone, the Agencies consider the combined market shares of the participants and the collaboration. For example, with a collaboration among two competitors where each participant individually holds a 6 percent market share in the relevant market and the collaboration separately holds a 3 percent market share in the relevant market, the combined market share in the relevant market for purposes of the safety zone would be 15 percent. This collaboration, therefore, would fall within the safety zone. However, if the collaboration involved three competitors, each with a 6 percent market share in the relevant market, the combined market share in the relevant market for purposes of the safety zone would be 21 percent, and the collaboration would fall outside the safety zone. Including market shares of the participants takes into account possible spillover effects on competition within the relevant market among the participants and their collaboration.

merger analysis is applied.**4.3 Safety Zone for Research and Development Competition Analyzed in Terms of Innovation Markets**

Absent extraordinary circumstances, the Agencies do not challenge a competitor collaboration on the basis of effects on competition in an innovation market where three or more independently controlled research efforts in addition to those of the collaboration possess the required specialized assets or characteristics and the incentive to engage in R&D that is a close substitute for the R&D activity of the collaboration. In determining whether independently controlled R&D efforts are close substitutes, the Agencies consider, among other things, the nature, scope, and magnitude of the R&D efforts; their access to financial support; their access to intellectual property, skilled personnel, or other specialized assets; their timing; and their ability, either acting alone or through others, to successfully commercialize innovations. The antitrust safety zone does not apply to agreements that are per se illegal, or that would be challenged without a detailed market analysis, or to competitor collaborations to which a merger analysis is applied.

## PROBLEMS 14–A THRU 14–E

**14–A.** Two competing software companies (S-1 and S-2) desire to form a joint venture partnership whose sole purpose will be to market and distribute the software products of their companies through a common sales and marketing force. S-1 and S-2 will have equal control rights over the joint venture, but each will generate profits based on how much of its product is sold through the joint venture. What antitrust risks might the joint venture pose? What additional facts would help?

**14–B.** Business A and Business B compete in the automobile carburetor market. Minor variations from year to year require annual retooling and redesigns of carburetors. In order to save money and promote efficiencies, Business A and Business B have an informal understanding. Business A will retool only in the even years, and Business B will retool only in the odd years. Is this understanding legal?

**14–C.** ABC Inc. and XYZ Inc. are both developing software that would allow an individual to use "flash" technology to easily create and publish on the Web multi-media presentations featuring voice, graphics and background music. The software could be offered as a desktop product that is loaded onto a specific computer or as a service that is hosted through a central server network. The advantages of the desktop version are that it is less expense and it will appeal to the individual user. The central server version would provide a business with a custom platform that could be used by many people from any location and would enable more than one person to participate in the creation of a presentation.

Luke Rogers, the president of the investment group funding ABC, ran into Linda Moore, general counsel of MNO, Inc., at a national conference in Las Vegas last week. MNO offers a competitive service that could be seriously threatened by the new products offered by ABC and XYZ. Linda said, "Just saw your boy Jason in the bar, downing vodka like water and bragging that you guys have locked up desktop with some deal with XYZ. That kind of talk gets us lawyers excited." Luke shook it off by responding, "Get real Linda. Just the vodka talking."

When Luke returned to his hotel room later that night and logged on, he discovered the following email from Jason Jones, President of ABC:

Luke,

> I had dinner with Jane Owen, President of XYZ last night. We go back a long way. She was glad to hear that we will be confining our efforts to desktop. And she made it clear that they plan only to offer a server-based product at this time. She said that, as a matter of professional courtesy, she would give us at least a year's notice before taking any steps to go to desktop, which would give us plenty of time to adapt. I, of course, would extend the same courtesy to her if our plans change. I trust this meets with your approval. – Jason

Does ABC have any legal exposure? What you would recommend moving forward?

**14–D.** Larry Carter recently completed his studies in orthodontics. He decided to establish his practice in town X. Larry was able to purchase equipment and take over a lease from a retiring dentist. Although the equipment picked up from the old dentist was usable, Larry planned on upgrading to state-of-the art stuff, including the new break-though "Soundless Drill" offered by Newwave Technologies.

During the first three months, Larry was able to generate minimal business from residents, but not a single referral from dentists. Larry knew that the lifeline of every orthodontist is dentist referrals and that he would "die on the vine" if he couldn't get some dentists on board. He scheduled a lunch with the old dentist whose assets he had purchased and two of the old guy's dentist buddies. The lunch was revealing.

Larry learned that the orthodontists in the town were members of the Orthodontists Study Group, a non-profit organization. This group meets regularly to study current professional topics of interest. In addition, the group has a "coverage program" that ensures that the members will "cover" for any member who becomes ill or disabled or who "develops an amount of business that exceeds a reasonable workload for a competent professional." The group also maintains a coordinated buying program to get the best deals from vendors and twice a year sponsors a gala affair to thank and honor all dentists in the community for their efforts. These gala affairs were described as "the biggest things any dentist and his or her spouse could hope to attend." The old dentist flatly told Larry, "If you're not part of that group, you're not going to get referrals from any dentists."

After three phone calls, Larry reached Bud Vary, the orthodontist who is the current manager of the group. Larry explained that he was a new orthodontist in town and inquired about membership in the group. Vary responded, "I thought we'd be hearing from you, what with all that advertising and price cutting. You can apply, but don't hold your breath."

Within the next seven days, Larry received bad news on two fronts. The group rejected his membership application, stating only that "membership is now full, but we anticipate one or more existing members may retire within the next ten years." Larry also heard from Newwave Technologies, the patent holder on the "Soundless Drill," stating that it was precluded from selling or licensing the drill to him pursuant to an exclusive arrangement with the Orthodontists Study Group. Approximately a year earlier all members of the group had acquired the first version of the drill in a joint purchase transaction that precluded Newwave Technologies ten years from selling or licensing its patented drill to any orthodontist in the same town who was not a member of the group.

Does Larry have any claims under federal antitrust laws? How would you advise the group moving forward?

**14–E.** Floatdock Inc. provides on-water yacht transport services. It has a fleet of eight large transport carriers, each of which can transport up to 20 yachts ranging in length from 30 to 120 feet. The appeal of Floatdock's service for the yacht owner is that the yacht is never taken out of the water. Floatdock provides transport services primarily to Europe and the Mediterranean, to the West Coast via the Panama Canal, and to ports far up the East Coast. It has recently extended its transport activities to short haul runs up the East Coast and in the Caribbean.

Yachtmove provides on-water yacht transport services with a single carrier that is larger, older, and less fuel-efficient than the carriers owned by Floatdock. Yachtmove had purchased the older carrier from Floatdock four years ago. Floatdock and Yachtmove always had the understanding that Yachtmove would use its older, less-efficient carrier to service the shorter, easier hauls on the East Coast and in the Caribbean, and Floatdock would handle the longer runs. To help coordinate their schedules with yacht brokers (who provide most the business) and independent customers, Floatdock, at its expense, has published "The On-Water Mover" each year to describe the services, schedules and prices of Floatdock and Yachtmove.

Six months ago, Floatdock resolved to "take over the short haul market." Yachtmove was advised that it would no longer be included in "The On-Water Mover." Plus, Yachtmove was shocked to discover that Floatdocks's short haul prices were less than Yachtmove's costs, and that Floatdock was offering huge volume discounts to yacht brokers who gave all their business to Floatdock. Yachtmove could try to compete, but would be at a huge disadvantage. Plus, if it did secure any volume, its big carrier usually would not be near capacity and losses would mount fast.

Does Yachtmover have any antitrust claims against Floatdock?

# Chapter 15

## THE ENTERPRISE EMPLOYEES

### A. THE COMPENSATION CHALLENGE

For most companies, a prerequisite to success is the ability to attract, retain and motivate quality employees. Effective employee motivation often is the key to achieving the company's goals and objectives. New technologies have increased productivity and enabled many companies to do more with fewer people; but, contrary to what some think, they have done nothing to reduce the importance of quality employees. Key challenges for most businesses today include improving employee skill levels, enhancing employee training, promoting employee stability, reducing employee turnover, and developing employees who care about the business.

Many factors can impact employee dissatisfaction and turnover rates. Some, such as the nature of the work or opportunities for career advancement, may be beyond the control of the owners of the business. But other critical factors, including the company's interest in the well-being of its employees, its vision for the future, and its willingness to embrace its employees as valued teammates, not expendable commodities, are completely within the control of management. There are many important steps that management can take in setting policy and operating day-to-day to bind and motivate employees.

The effectiveness of all efforts to build a productive, stable workforce is impacted by compensation and benefits, two important factors that every employee cares about. It's not about spending more (something most businesses cannot afford to do) or playing hardball when a demand surfaces. It is about spending smart and creating an environment of dialogue and understanding that eliminates the need for any hardball.

Every company needs to periodically analyze its compensation and benefit programs to make certain that they are competitive, are conducive to a productive work force, and are producing the best bang for the buck. For most companies, employee costs are the largest expense item on the income statement. As competitive pressures grow, often that expense item must produce greater results in order for the company to survive, let alone prosper. Too often compensation and benefit programs in closely held businesses are put together haphazardly. The owners offer what they have heard others are providing. Dollars are wasted on benefits that many don't care about. Opportunity costs are high. Smart options are never considered.

The advisor's challenge is to help business owners make wise decisions about compensation and benefit programs.  The advisor does not need to be an expert in the implementation, monitoring, and administration of employee benefit programs; there are many organizations that specialize in providing such services.  But the advisor needs to understand the options and how and when specific programs can be used to accomplish important objectives of the business.  Of equal and sometimes greater importance, the advisor often can help the business owner decide what *not* to do by clarifying and evaluating demands coming from inside the company and any confusing recommendations coming from service providers outside the company.

Of course, the nature of the business can have a profound impact on the owners' objectives regarding employee benefits.  In those toiler and professional service enterprises where the owners represent a significant portion of the total payroll, the objective may be to maximize owner benefits even at the expense of having to fund additional benefits for non-owner employees.  In all golfer and most big fish enterprises, the focus is not on benefits for the owners; the challenge is to maximize the value of each compensation dollar while creating a working environment that promotes and encourages loyalty, initiative, and hard work.

## B.  EMPLOYERS AND HEALTHCARE REFORM

This discussion starts with healthcare, a subject that all businesses must understand.  Unprecedented changes of mammoth proportions are just around the corner.  The focus here is on what American businesses are doing today and a few of the future business implications of the healthcare reform that is now the law of the land.

It is far beyond the scope of this effort to offer any specific insights into the comprehensive Patient Protection and Affordable Care Act (the "ACA") that was signed into law on March 23, 2010.  The ACA IS the hottest political issue of our time.  It has triggered the passage of countless "Repeal" votes in the Republican-led House, a landmark Supreme Court showdown, daily surveys of every variety, administrative setbacks and delays, a push at this moment for Congress to just "de-fund" the law, confusion galore, and the kind of fear and paralyzing uncertainty that often accompanies massive change.  It was a major factor in the 2010 and 2012 elections and promises to be the overriding factor in the 2014 mid-term battles for control of the House and the Senate.

### 1.  THE STATUS QUO

The leading source of health insurance in America is employer-sponsored plans.  Each year, researchers at the Kaiser Family Foundation, NORC at the University of Chicago, and Health Research & Educational Trust conduct a survey of current trends in employer-sponsored health coverage. The 2012 survey included 3,326 randomly selected public and private firms with three or more employees.  Following is a recap of certain of the key findings for 2012:

- **Scope.** Employers provided health benefits for about 149 million nonelderly people in America during 2012. Most American workers were offered health coverage at work, and the majority of workers who were offered coverage took it.

- **Coverage.** Among firms offering health benefits, 62 percent of workers were covered by health benefits through their own employer. When firms that did not offer health benefits are factored in, the percentage of workers covered by an employer plan dropped to 56 percent, a rate that has remained stable over time.

- **Eligibility.** Seventy-seven percent of workers in firms offering health benefits were eligible for the coverage offered by their employers. Employees in firms with a lower proportion of lower-wage workers (less than 35 percent of workers earn $24,000 or less annually) were more likely to be eligible for health benefits than employees in firms with a higher proportion of lower-wage workers (where 35 percent or more of workers earn $24,000 or less annually) (79 percent vs. 66 percent). Eligibility also varied by the age of the workforce. Those in firms with fewer younger workers (less than 35 percent of workers were age 26 or younger) were more likely to be eligible for health benefits than were workers in firms with many younger workers (35 percent or more of workers were age 26 or younger), at 79 percent versus 60 percent.

- **Electing Coverage**. In 2012, 81percent of eligible workers took up coverage when it was offered to them. Eligible employees in firms with a lower proportion of lower-wage workers were more likely to take up coverage (82 percent) than eligible employees in firms with a higher proportion of lower-wage workers (71 percent). Firms with a higher proportion of younger workers were less likely to take up coverage than those in firms with a smaller share of younger workers (71 percent vs. 81percent).

- **Waiting Period**. Seventy-four percent of covered workers faced a waiting period before coverage was available. Covered workers in small firms (3-199 workers) were more likely than those in large firms to have a waiting period (81 percent versus 71 percent). Workers in the West were more likely to face a wait for coverage (84 percent). The average waiting period among covered workers who faced a waiting period was 2.3 months. A third of covered workers faced a waiting period of three months or more, but only 8 percent had a waiting period of four months or more. Workers in small firms (3-199 workers) were more likely to have longer waiting periods than workers in larger firms.

- **Single vs. Family Distribution**. The distribution of covered workers electing single coverage, single plus one coverage, or family coverage was 46 percent, 17 percent, and 36 percent respectively in 2012. That distribution has remained stable over time.

- **Plan Shopping.** More than one-half (54 percent) of firms offering health benefits reported shopping for a new health plan or a new insurance carrier in the past year. Among firms that shopped, 18 percent changed insurance carriers and 27 percent reported changing the type of health plan provided to employees.

There were no significant differences between small firms (3 to 199 workers) and larger firms on these measures.

- **Section 125 Plans.** Forty-one percent of small firms (3 to 199 workers) and 91percent of larger firms had a plan under section 125 of the Internal Revenue Service Code to enable employees to use pre-tax dollars to pay for their share of health insurance premiums.

- **Flex Spending Accounts.** Seventeen percent of small firms (3 to 199 workers) and 76 percent of larger firms offered employees the option of contributing to a flexible spending account (or FSA). FSAs permit employees to make pre-tax contributions that may be used during the year to pay for eligible medical expenses.

- **On-Site Clinics.** Twenty-two percent of firms with 1,000 or more employees maintained an on-site health clinic at one or more of their major locations to treat employees for work-related or non-work-related conditions. Seventy-six percent of such firms with health clinics provided treatment for non-work-related medical conditions.

- **Average Cost.** The average insurance premium for single health coverage in 2012 was $468 per month ($5,615 per year). The average premium for family coverage was $1,312 per month ($15,745 per year).

- **Firm Size.** The average premium for family coverage for covered workers in small firms (3-199 workers) was $15,253, lower than the average premium for covered workers in large firms (200 or more workers) ($15,980). The average single premiums in small firms (3-199 workers) and larger firms were nearly the same.

- **Region.** The average single and family health premiums for covered workers were highest in the Northeast ($5,964 and $17,099) and lowest in the South ($5,445 and $14,988).

- **Age.** Covered workers in firms where 35 percent or more of the workers were age 26 or younger had lower average single and family premiums ($4,961 and $14,217) than covered workers in firms where a lower percentage of workers were age 26 or younger ($5,669 and $15,871). Covered workers in firms where 35 percent or more of the workers were age 50 or older had higher average single and family premiums ($5,860 and $16,392) than covered workers in firms where a lower percentage of workers were age 50 or older ($5,440 and $15,281).

- **Income Levels.** Covered workers in firms with a large percentage of lower-wage workers (at least 35 percent earn $24,000 per year or less) had lower average single and family premiums ($5,135 and $14,694) than covered workers in firms with a smaller percentage of lower-wage workers ($5,673 and $15,871). Covered workers in firms with a large percentage of higher-wage workers (at least 35percent earn $55,000 per year or more) had higher average single and family premiums ($5,789 and $16,427) than covered workers in firms with a smaller percentage of higher-wage workers ($5,448 and $15,087).

- **Large Variances**. Eighteen percent of covered workers were employed by firms that had a single premium at least 20 percent higher than the average single premium, while 19 percent of covered workers were in firms that had a single premium less than 80 percent of the average single premium. For family coverage, 19 percent of covered workers were employed in a firm that had a family premium at least 20 percent higher than the average family premium, while 20 percent of covered workers were in firms that had a family premium less than 80 percent of the average family premium.

## 2. THE FUTURE?

Looking ahead, business owners must assume that the ACA will be the controlling factor for employer-sponsored health plans as its provisions take effect over the next few years. Many businesses and politicians may hope for a major political reversal that would permanently unravel the ACA, but it would be foolish at this stage to count on such a change in the planning process. The best working assumption is that the ACA is here to stay, and its provisions will ultimately be implemented, some perhaps later than expected.

Given the uncertainties and confusion triggered by the ACA, the future relevance of any words written now is unclear. And the sheer breadth of the law precludes any comprehensive review of its terms and impact. So this discussion is limited to a brief description of five cornerstones of the law, a recap of a current survey of business owner reactions, and a series of related small business questions and answers recently issued by the Small Business Committee of the House of Representatives.

### a. Five Cornerstones

**(1) The Individual Mandate**. The individual mandate is a key element of the ACA. It requires individuals to purchase health insurance or pay a penalty tax. Those who are exempt from the penalty include the following:

- Individuals with religious beliefs that oppose acceptance of benefits from a health insurance policy

- Undocumented immigrants

- Incarcerated individuals

- A member of an Indian tribe

- Those whose family income is below the filing requirement threshold

- Those who have to pay more than eight percent of their income for health insurance coverage (net of employer contributions and tax credits)

- Those insured under an employer-sponsored plan, a personally-acquired Bronze level ACA plan, a grandfathered employer plan, a veteran's health plan, Medicare, Medicaid, the Children's Health Insurance Program, or TRICARE (for service members, retirees, and their families).

How much is the penalty?  In 2014, it's the greater of (1) $95 per adult and $47.50 per child (up to a maximum of $285 for a family) or (2) one percent of the family's income.  In 2015, it ratchets up to the greater of (1) $325 per adult and $162.50 per child (up to a maximum of $975 per family) or (2) two percent of the family's income.  After 2015, the penalty is the greater of (1) $695 per individual and $347.50 per child (up to a maximum of $2,085 per family) or (2) 2.5 percent of the family's income.  Bottom line:  It will very quickly get expensive for many.

Will the individual mandate really start in 2014?  Many strongly advocate delaying the individual mandate a year to coincide with the one-year delay in the employer mandate.  Pressure is building in Congress for such a delay.  Given the stakes of the 2014 mid-terms, the potential impact of this issue, and the perceived administrative chaos triggered by the ACA, such a delay wouldn't come as a surprise to many.

**(2) The Employer Mandate.**  The "employer mandate" is a requirement that all businesses with over 50 full time employees provide healthcare for their employees or face a tax penalty. The penalty is officially referred to as a "shared responsibility fee."  The shared responsibility fee kicks in for any business that has the equivalent of 50 or more employees who work 30 hours or more per week. The "equivalency" factor means that part-time workers are aggregated to determine if the 50-employee threshold has been met, as are workers who are split across multiple businesses controlled by the same owner.

How much is the penalty tax?  The penalty is $2,000 for each employee who works 30 hours or more and who is not provided with an acceptable employer-sponsored plan.  The penalty jumps to $3,000 for any employee who purchases insurance through an exchange with tax credits. The penalty does not apply to the employer's first 30 employees.  Hence, an employer with the equivalent of 49 full time employees would pay no penalty, but would face a penalty of $40,000 ($2,000 for employees 31 through 50) once the full time equivalent headcount jumps to 50.  The penalty does not apply to employees who work less than 30 hours, no matter how large the organization.  Small companies may have a strong incentive to stay below the 50 worker threshold and companies of all sizes may have a strong incentive to maximize their use of employees who work less than 30 hours per week.  Employers who have more than 50 employees may just choose to pay the penalty tax, avoid all the hassles of an employer-sponsored plan, and let their employees grapple with their responsibilities under the individual mandate.

What are the key elements of an acceptable plan that will avoid the employer mandate penalty?  The plan must provide benefits equal to the minimum benefits of a "Bronze" plan on a health insurance exchange, the employer must pay at least 60 percent of covered health care costs, and the employee's share of the cost many not exceed 9.5 percent of the family's income. If the plan costs an employee more than 9.5 percent of his or her income and the employee opts for a government subsidy on a health exchange, a $3,000 employer penalty will be triggered.

When does the employer mandate take effect? The law set the effective date as 2014. In July 2013, the Treasury Department announced a suspension of the mandate until 2015.

Are penalties paid under the employer mandate tax deductible? No. This potentially will be a major cost factor for those businesses that contemplate paying the penalty and not messing with a plan.

Is there any help for businesses with less than 50 employees? Small Businesses that have fewer than 25 fulltime employees who, on average, earn no more than $50,000 annually, may apply for tax credits of up to 35 percent (25percent for non-profits) of the cost of health insurance premiums for their employees. The employer must pay for at least 50 percent of the healthcare premiums. In 2014, the tax credit amount is increased to 50 percent (35 percent for non-profits) and the insurance must be purchased on the insurance exchange for at least two years.

**(3) The Exchanges.** The ACA requires the establishment in all states of health insurance exchanges that will serve as marketplaces where eligible individuals can compare and select among insurance plans offered by participating private issuers of health coverage. The Department of Health and Human Services' (HHS) Centers for Medicare & Medicaid Services (CMS) is responsible for overseeing the establishment of the exchanges. Enrollment in the exchanges is scheduled to begin on October 1, 2013, and the exchanges are to become operational and offer health coverage starting on January 1, 2014.

The exchanges are intended to provide an easy point of access for individuals to enroll into private health plans, apply for income-based financial subsidies established under the law and, as applicable, obtain an eligibility determination for other health coverage programs, such as Medicaid or the State Children's Health Insurance Program (CHIP).

The ACA directed each state to establish state-based exchanges by January 1, 2014. If a state elects not to establish and operate an exchange, the act requires the federal government to establish and operate an exchange in the state, referred to as a federally facilitated exchange. A federally facilitated exchange must carry out the same functions as exchanges established and operated by a state. Although the federal government bears responsibility for establishing and operating such exchanges, CMS has provided states the option to assist with certain operations as partnership exchanges.

The exchanges will offer qualified health plans (QHP) approved by the exchange and offered in the state by the participating issuers of coverage. The benefits, cost-sharing features, and premiums of each QHP must be presented in a manner that facilitates comparison shopping of plans by individuals. Once individuals wish to select a QHP, they will complete an application (via the exchange website, over the phone, in person, or by mailing a paper form) that collects the information necessary to determine their eligibility for enrollment in a QHP. On the basis of the application, the exchange will determine a person's eligibility for enrollment and eligibility for income-based financial subsidies.

In 2014, CMS will operate the exchange in 34 states, although it expects that states will assist in carrying out certain activities in almost half of those exchanges. As of May 2013, 17 states were conditionally approved by CMS to establish state-based exchanges. CMS will operate a federally facilitated exchange in the remaining 34 states, although it plans to allow 15 of the states to assist it in carrying out certain exchange functions.

The Congressional Budget Office has estimated that about 7 million individuals will enroll in exchanges by 2014, increasing to about 24 million by 2022.[1]

**(d) Taxes.** The ACA contains numerous tax changes designed to generate revenues to finance the cost of the federal government's expanded role in managing health care in America. Some of the changes establish new taxes, such as the taxes imposed under the individual and employer mandates described above, the expanded 3.8 percent Medicare tax on investment income (applicable to married couples earning over $250,000 and single taxpayers earning over $200,000) described in Chapter 3, a 2.3 percent tax on medical device manufactures, a 10 percent tax on indoor tanning services, a 40 percent excise tax on certain "Cadillac" insurance plans, and new taxes on brand name drugs and health insurers.

Other changes are designed to generate revenues by watering down tax benefits that have previously been available to assist with healthcare needs. Key examples include increasing the medical expense itemized deduction income threshold from 7.5 percent to 10 percent, reducing deductible contribution to flex spending accounts from $5,000 to $2,500, providing that over-the-counter medicines no longer are qualified expenses from a flex spending, health savings or Archer medical savings account, and increasing to 20 percent penalties for non-qualified medical expenses paid from a health savings account or a Acher medical savings account.

Of course, the big concern is the impact of these tax changes in covering the direct and indirect costs of the massive changes that will flow from the implementation of the ACA. Estimates and projections are all over the board. What is clear is that the magnitude of the change and related factors preclude projections accurate enough to provide any level of comfort. Only time will tell. Uncertainty and fear remain at heightened levels as we move closer to the key implementation dates.

**(e) Grandfather Rights.** Does the ACA provide grandfather rights for employer-sponsored plans that existed prior to its passage? Yes – kind of. Many of the new ACA standards for employer-sponsored plans will not apply to pre-existing plans that are not substantially changed. The interim final rules released by the Department of Health and Human Services on June 17, 2010, and amended on November 17, 2010, state that a firm desiring grandfather rights cannot significantly change cost sharing, benefits, employer contributions, or access to coverage, and must maintain consecutive enrollment in the plan.

---

1. Congressional Budget Office, Effects on Health Insurance and the Federal Budget for the Insurance Coverage Provisions in the Affordable Care Act—May 2013 Baseline (Washington, D.C.: May 14, 2013).

A grandfathered plan must still comply with many ACA provisions as they become effective.  For example, the plan must: (1) provide a uniform explanation of coverage, (2) report medical loss ratios and provide premium rebates if medical loss ratios are not met, (3) prohibit lifetime and annual limits on essential health benefits, (4) extend dependent coverage to age 26, (5) prohibit health plan rescissions, (6) prohibit waiting periods greater than 90 days, and (7) prohibit coverage exclusions for pre-existing health conditions.

Each company with a pre-existing plan will need to decide whether it wants to preserve its potential grandfather status, which severely limits future flexibility.  The Kaiser 2012 survey reference above found that 58 percent of companies offering health benefits reported that they had at least one health plan that was a grandfathered plan in 2012, down from 72 percent of offering firms with a grandfathered plan in 2011. A total of 48 percent of covered workers were enrolled in a grandfathered health plan in 2012, down from 56 percent in 2011. Workers in small companies (3 to 199 workers) were much more likely than workers in large companies to be in a plan that was not grandfathered under the ACA (55 percent vs. 19 percent).

Since September 23, 2010, the ACA has required all health plans to extend coverage to the children of covered workers up to age 26, whether or not the child is financially dependent.  Until 2014, grandfathered health plans are not required to extend coverage to a child of a covered worker if the child has access to employer-sponsored coverage either from a spouse or independently. The 2012 Kaiser survey found that 31 percent of firms that offer either family or single plus one coverage reported enrolling at least one adult child as a result of the new ACA requirement. Large firms (200 or more workers) were much more likely to have enrolled an adult child due to the ACA than smaller firms (90 percent vs. 29 percent).  The Kaiser survey stated that about 2.9 million adult children were enrolled in their parents' employer-sponsored health plan as a result of the ACA.

The ACA requires non-grandfathered health plans to provide coverage for certain preventive services without deductibles or other cost sharing. Grandfathered health plans have the option of conforming their coverage and cost sharing for preventive care without compromising their grandfathered status.  The 2012 Kaiser study found that 41 percent of covered workers are in a plan that reports it has changed its list of benefits to include services considered preventive under the ACA.

### b. Business Owner Perceptions

News media outlets feature on nearly a daily basis stories and ad hoc surveys that illustrate how Americans perceive the ACA.  Perceptions vary widely, constantly evolve, and are heavily influenced by specific events (such as the one-year delay in the employer mandate) and the words and actions of political leaders. Many believe that public perceptions will be a key factor in the successful implementation of massive changes to our entire healthcare system over the next few years.  As these words are being written, the Obama administration is gearing up to spend hundreds of millions of dollars on a public relations campaign to bolster the image of the ACA and the benefits its implementation will provide. And of course those who oppose the ACA are relentless in their efforts to publically emphasize what they term the "train wreck" that promises to hurt all Americans and particularly closely held businesses.

In early 2013, the ADP Research Institute surveyed human resource and employee benefits decision makers in a national sample of small companies in the United States. The key findings included the following:

• There is a lack of confidence among both employers and employees in their understanding of responsibilities required by the ACA and the impact on choices.

• Some employers have begun assessing risks and costs of compliance with the ACA, but many have not taken any substantial steps to develop a strategic plan. When the ACA's shared responsibility requirements take effect, penalties for noncompliance will apply only to certain organizations. Some small employers are looking ahead and crunching the numbers now to help avoid these penalties later, while others have yet to act. For example, 40 percent of respondents in the ADP Research Institute survey have run headcount estimates to determine whether their organization will be subject to penalties.

• Uncertainty abounds around public and private health insurance marketplaces, the "exchanges."

• Only 14 percent of small organizations feel "very confident" or "extremely confident" that their employees understand the impact that the ACA will have on their benefits and benefit choices.

• Only 28 percent of small organizations feel "very confident" or "extremely confident" that their employees will be able to effectively manage their healthcare when presented with a greater number of choices.

• Only 26 percent of employer respondents said they feel "very confident" or "extremely confident" that they themselves understand their responsibilities regarding compliance with the ACA.

• More than one-quarter of small employers said they have employed or are employing the following strategies:

1. Estimating the number of employees for whom the organization's current coverage may be deemed "unaffordable"

2. Estimating the number of employees eligible for Medicaid, or who are ineligible for Medicaid and have W-2 earnings that do not exceed 400% of the federal poverty level

3. Determining whether the organization has at least one current health plan that has a 60 percent actuarial value

• Half of small employers have not estimated the potential penalty amount their organization might have to pay under the mandate.

• Nearly 56 percent of employers said that their organization will feel at least a moderate impact from the establishment of federal and state health insurance marketplace exchanges in 2014, as required under the ACA. Fully one-third (33 percent) described the impact as "major" or "significant." There is still substantial uncertainty about whether to move employees to public and private exchange, offer them as an option, or not offer them at all. Nearly half of small employers indicate they have not investigated public exchanges and six out of ten have not investigated private exchanges.

• A U.S. Chamber of Commerce survey released in April 2013 showed that 77 percent of small-business executives believe that the ACA will make health coverage for their employees more expensive. (Source: *Bloomberg BNA's Daily Labor Report*)

• A 2012 U.S. government roundup of 27 published studies on the impact of the ACA on employers found that small employers are more likely than large employers to say that they are ready to drop health coverage for employees in response to the ACA's requirements.(Source: *Bloomberg BNA's Daily Labor Report*)

• According to an International Foundation of Employee Benefit Plans survey released in April 2013, smaller employers are more likely than larger employers to predict a big cost impact by the ACA, but they are less likely to have measured what that impact will be. (Source: *Bloomberg BNA's Daily Labor Report*)

• More than three-quarters of small-business executives in a U.S. Chamber of Commerce survey released in April 2013 said they expect "play or pay" penalties to negatively impact their businesses. To avoid these penalties, 32 percent said they expect to reduce hiring, 31 percent said they will cut back hours, and 27 percent said they expect to stop providing health insurance. (Source: *Bloomberg BNA*)

• Sixty-nine percent of employers said they will definitely continue to provide employer-sponsored healthcare even after health insurance marketplaces become effective in 2014, according to an International Foundation of Employee Benefit Plans survey released in April 2013. (Source: *Bloomberg BNA's Pension and Benefits Reporter*)

### c. Questions and Answers

**Frequently Asked Questions about the Health Care Law**
**House Committee on Small Business**
**May, 2013**

#### 1. Aren't small businesses exempt from the health care law?

Employers who have fewer than 50 full-time equivalent (FTE) employees are not subject to the employer mandate. However, all employers are required to do certain things, such as provide employees information about the exchanges and how to access them. Note: The regulation on how employers are supposed to notify employees about the exchanges has been indefinitely delayed.

The employer mandate covers firms that employed an average of at least 50 FTEs in the prior calendar year. According to the Department of the Treasury's proposed rule, businesses should look at the prior calendar year to determine if they meet the threshold of 50 FTEs for the following year, based on monthly averages. An employer calculates the number of full-time workers by counting each employee that worked an average of 30 hour per week that year. Second, employees who were part-time employees in the prior year are calculated by: 1) determining the number hours worked by all part-time employees who were not employed on average at least 30 hours per week; and 2) dividing the total hours by 120 to get an average FTE for a given month. This average FTE is added to the number of full-time employees to get the total number of FTEs.

If the number is 50 or higher, the employer is potentially subject to the employer mandate. If the number is under 50, he is not. Employers subject to the employer mandate (i.e., those with 50 or more FTEs) who do not offer coverage to full-time employees and whose employees access coverage on an exchange and receive a premium credit are subject to a penalty of $2,000 per full-time employee annually. Employers may exclude the first 30 full-time employees.

**2. Is it true that the first 30 full-time employees are exempted under the penalty (Ex: For a company of 100 full-time employees who did not offer health insurance, the penalty would be for 70 full-time workers, for a total of $140,000?**

Yes, that is correct.

**3. Can employers offer a high deductible plan? What is the highest deductible permitted?**

Yes, employers may offer a high deductible plan. The plan must be considered "adequate." Under the health care law, a plan is considered to provide adequate coverage if the plan's actuarial value (i.e., share of the total allowed costs that the plan is expected to cover) is at least 60%. According to a preliminary analysis done by the Actuarial Research Corporation for the Congressional Research Service, the majority of employer-sponsored plans would meet the actuarial value requirements in the health care law. Also, all high-deductible plans currently offered by employers today would meet the 60% actuarial value requirement.

**4. Is there a minimum plan offered under the law, and if so, what is it?**

An employer must offer full-time employees coverage that does not exceed 9.5% of their household income. If the employer does not, and a full-time employee uses a premium tax credit to access coverage on the exchange, the employer is subject to an annual penalty of $3,000 per full-time employee doing so. See further explanation of "affordability" in answer to number 5 below.

**5. How will an employer know if a plan is "affordable" for full-time employees?**

An employer probably won't know the employee's household income. The Internal Revenue Service (IRS) issued a notice stating that employers may use an employee's W-2 wages as an affordability test instead of their household income.

Employers may rely on this guidance at least through the end of 2014. A health plan's individual coverage would be considered affordable for an employee if their premium contribution for self-only coverage does not exceed 9.5% of their W-2 wages.

**6. Is it true that in year 1, companies are only required to offer employees coverage, and that coverage for dependents isn't required until Year 2?**

Employers with 50 or more FTEs who do provide health insurance coverage to avoid a potential penalty must offer coverage to employees and their dependents. According to the IRS' proposed regulation, the term "dependent" means the child of an employee who has not reached the age of 26, but does not include an employee's spouse.

**7. Will a "mini-med" plan satisfy the employer mandate? Are the HHS-issued waivers for these plans still effective?**

Mini-med plans are unlikely to satisfy the employer mandate in 2014. Current HHS waivers for these plans are effective through the end of 2013. By way of background, in September 2010, some companies requested a temporary waiver from the Medical Loss Ratio (MLR) requirements of the health care law for employees with minimum coverage (or "mini-med") insurance plans. Employers were concerned that higher costs of these plans meant they might not meet the new MLR requirement that 85% of premiums be spent on health benefits, so some received waivers. The majority of waivers were extended through 2013, but HHS has said that once the exchanges open and other coverage is available, waivers are unlikely to be extended.

**8. How will an employer determine if his full-time + part-time employees trigger the employer mandate?**

The employer mandate applies to businesses with an average of 50 or more full-time FTE employees during the preceding calendar year. To determine the number of FTEs, the IRS has proposed counting all employees who work an average of 30 hours per week as full-time employees. To determine average FTEs per month, an employer should add the number of hours part-time employees worked and divide by 120 (hours). Add both numbers together for the total number of FTEs.

If an employer offers coverage and the total number of FTEs is 50 or higher, the employer may be subject to a penalty if one of their full-time workers uses a premium credit to a premium tax credit to access coverage on the exchange. If the number of FTEs is below 50, the employer is not considered to be a large employer and is not potentially subject to a penalty.

**9. What is the penalty that an employer must pay if he is subject to the mandate and fails to offer insurance?**

If an employer is subject to the employer mandate (i.e., those with 50 or more FTEs), fails to offer coverage to their full-time employees and at least one full-time employee is eligible for a premium tax credit and purchases insurance on an exchange, the employer would be subject to an annual penalty of $2,000 per full-time employee, minus the first 30 full-time employees.

For example, an employer with 50 full-time employees who does not offer coverage and who has at least one employee who uses a premium tax credit to purchase coverage on the exchange would face an annual penalty of $40,000. [50 total full-time employees – 30 full-time employees excluded from the calculation = 20; 20 x $2,000 penalty = $40,000.] Note: Although the statute specifies the penalty calculation, or assessed, federal agencies have not yet issued regulatory guidance on how the penalty would be calculated or assessed.

**10. What are the minimum standards the policy offered to employees must meet? What are the penalties?**

Employers offering coverage in the individual and small group market must offer coverage that: 1) is affordable; 2) provides minimum value; and 3) (for small employers only) covers the essential health benefits package.

Minimum value is at least 60% actuarial value, according to the IRS/HHS minimum value calculator that will be available on HHS' website. Employers will be able to submit information about their coverage, such as deductibles and co-pays, into the calculator to determine whether the plan provides minimum value by covering at least 60% of the total allowed cost of benefits that are expected to be incurred under the plan. For essential health benefits, beginning in 2014, insurers must cover 10 broad categories of care, including emergency services, maternity care, hospital and doctors' services, mental health and substance abuse care and prescription drugs. Limits on annual out-of-pocket costs for consumers will apply to all policies. Those limits are: $6,250 for a single policyholder and $12,500 for a family based on this year's rate.

**11. If an employee is not offered insurance, or refuses it and purchases insurance on the exchange with a premium tax credit, what is the employer penalty? Does the penalty go to the IRS, and how is it assessed?**

The employer penalty for not offering insurance is $2,000 per full-time employee, minus the first 30. There will be no penalty if employers offer coverage to at least 95% of their full-time employees and their dependents up to age 26. If an employer offers insurance that does not meet the minimum value or affordability requirements, the penalty may be the lesser of $2,000 per full-time employee minus the first 30, or $3,000 per number of full-time employees receiving a tax credit. Penalties will be assessed by the IRS on tax returns.

**12. Under the individual mandate, if a person does not purchase insurance, or sufficient insurance, what is the dollar amount penalty? Will it be $95 the first year? Does it increase each year on a sliding scale?**

The individual mandate requires individuals to obtain minimum essential coverage for themselves (and their dependents) beginning in 2014 or pay a penalty. The penalty is the greater of:

• For 2014, $95 per uninsured person or 1% of household income over the filing threshold;

- For 2015, $325 per uninsured person or 2% of household income over the filing threshold; and

- For 2016 and beyond, $695 per uninsured person or 2.5% of household income over the filing threshold.

There is a family cap of 300% of the flat dollar amount listed above, and the overall penalty is capped at the national average premium of a bronze level plan purchases through an exchange. For individuals under 18 years of age, the applicable per person penalty is one-half of the amounts listed above.

Beginning in 2017, the penalties will be increased by the cost-of-living adjustment. Individuals under the age of 30 may purchase catastrophic plans to meet the individual mandate. Employers may not offer catastrophic plans to meet minimum essential coverage requirements. The requirement for individuals to obtain minimum essential coverage can be satisfied by participating in an employer-sponsored plan, purchasing individual policies, obtaining coverage under a state insurance exchange, or gaining coverage through Medicare, Medicaid or other governmental programs. There are several exceptions to the individual mandate; members of Indian tribes, illegal aliens, etc., are exempt.

**13. When will the employee premiums for policies under the employer mandate be available -- in 2014 or at some point in the future? Are they determined by the insurance companies, by statute or regulation?**

While the rate filings to each state are generally submitted by insurance carriers in the spring, the actual premium that a given employer group will pay for health insurance is subject to negotiation between each employer and each carrier. The announcement of the premium for an employer group is based on the plan year. Since not all plan years are the same (for example, some employer plan years do not follow the calendar year), when premiums are announced for a given employer will vary. For employers that already provide health insurance, premiums for 2014 will likely be made during the normal enrollment period.

Under the health care law, insurance carriers that sell insurance to small groups 1) must accept every applicant for health insurance, as long as the applicant agrees to the terms and conditions of the insurance offer; 2) must provide coverage for preexisting health conditions; 3) are prohibited from basing insurance premiums on health status; and 4) must abide by other insurance market reforms.

**14. Can premiums for employees vary based on factors such as their employees' age, weight, health status, whether they smoke, etc.?**

While the health status of an individual employee currently may not be used to increase premiums for just that employee, most states currently allow companies selling health insurance to small groups to use health status, age, gender and tobacco use to determine the premiums for the whole group.

In 2014, the health care law prohibits insurers from basing small group premiums on health status and gender. Insurers may vary premiums among small groups based on age and tobacco use, with some limitations, so long as such variation is not prohibited under state law.

Currently, employers are allowed to reward employees who participate in wellness activities, so long as these activities are non-discriminatory. The health care law increases the amount employers may reward participating employees, so long as the rewards meet the existing non-discrimination standards.

### 15. What about attempts to avoid the employer mandate?

The IRS, in its January 2, 2013 employer mandate proposed rule, noted that it anticipates the final rule will address practices that employers may contemplate to avoid the application of the mandate. For example, the proposed rule describes an arrangement where a company uses a temporary staffing agency to employ the company's employees for part of each week, which results in neither the company nor the staffing agency appearing to employ the employees on a full-time basis.

## C. EMPLOYEE BENEFITS

### 1. INTRODUCTION

This discussion briefly reviews, in a checklist type format, key benefit options and some of the related planning implications. It then presents a short case study (a true story) of how one closely held business did it right. There are a few important caveats. First, a checklist approach to employee benefits, if misused, can be dangerous; it can lead to a bloated budget that contains unnecessary, expensive bells and whistles. The checklist should not be viewed as a wish list for employees or a list of the benefits all good employers provide. It's simply a description of options and some of the key factors to consider. It should not be used as a tool to spend more.

Second, the focus here is on the rank-and-file employees of the business, not the key executives. As has been discussed in various prior chapters, most successful businesses need to provide special incentives and benefits for their key executive talent. Examples discussed in prior chapters include equity incentives, stock options, supplemental retirement programs, life insurance programs, and deferred compensation incentives, all embodied in employment agreements that protect the business and the executives. Although the key players in the company will have an interest in the type of company-wide benefits reviewed in this chapter, it usually takes exclusive custom-crafted perks to get them excited.

### 2. TIME–OFF BENEFITS

**a. Paid Vacations and Holidays**. Nearly every business offers paid vacations and holidays as a benefit to its employees. The primary challenge of this benefit is to set the parameters of the benefit and clearly communicate those parameters in writing to the employees. The written rules should indicate whether vacation benefits can be accrued and, if so, how employees can use or be paid for accrued vacation benefits. Some companies adopt a "use it or lose it" concept; if the vacation benefits are not used, they are lost. The owners of these companies typically do not want to hassle with the challenges of accrued benefits and often believe that the mental and physical health of the entire workforce will be stronger if each employee takes some time off each year. Other enterprises allow employees to accrue substantial benefits that are paid upon termination of employment.

Often an important consideration is the scheduling of vacation time. Some companies do not want employees using vacation time during a designated busy season or insist that vacation time be scheduled and coordinated with others to minimize any disruption to the business. For example, a department of 12 employees may allow only two members to be on vacation at the same time and may prohibit the manager and assistant manager of the department from taking vacations at the same time.

**b. Sick Leave**. Many companies have jumped on the bandwagon of offering paid sick leave benefits. The problem is that some of these programs backfire. The traditional sick leave program grants a unit of paid sick leave every month or pay period (e.g., one paid day for every two months). The employee is entitled to use the paid sick leave when the absence is due to an illness. The big problem with many paid sick leave programs is unscheduled absenteeism. Some studies suggest that companies with sick leave programs experience almost twice as much unscheduled absenteeism as companies without such programs. The employee reasons, "I'm going to get paid anyway, so why not take the day off?" or, "I need a mental health day" or, "They know I never get sick, so they must expect that I'll just take the days off." Unscheduled absenteeism often results in more overtime, less productivity, increased administrative hassles, and resentment by co-workers.

The challenge for many companies is to structure a paid sick leave program that discourages abuse. There are steps that a company can take to help cure the problem. Following is a brief description of four possibilities. They can be used separately or in combination with one another.

**(1) No Pay-First Day**. To preventive abuse, the program may be structured to provide no paid benefits for the first day of an illness. This discourages the one day discretionary absence. The technique has proven to be effective with many plans. Some companies that use this feature provide exceptions (and pay for the first day) if there is actual hospitalization, if the illness extends beyond a given period (such as five days) or if it is the first illness in a given year. The theory is that there is little potential for abuse in these situations.

**(2) A Well-Pay Bonus**. The sick leave policy may be amended to include a well-pay bonus. The employee is paid a bonus if no sick leave is claimed for a designated period, such as a quarter. The theory is that the increase in efficiency, productivity and employee morale will more than offset the cost of paying the bonus. Also, the well-pay bonus eliminates the need to accrue unused sick leave and pay it at some later point. Often the well-pay bonus is coupled with the "no pay-first day" provision to further eliminate any incentive for unscheduled absenteeism.

**(3) The Personal Time Bank**. Another technique to discourage unscheduled absenteeism is the "personal time bank." The company designates a number of days during the year that an employee may use for vacation time or paid sick leave. In some cases holiday time is added to the package. The employee knows up front that there are a designated number of paid days that can be used for all purposes. The employee may choose how to use his or her own time bank. The employee who experiences many illnesses may choose to take less vacation time. The healthy employee may have the luxury of additional vacation time. The program is administered in such a way that each employee schedules his or her own time, and that schedule is interrupted only by real illnesses. Such a plan eliminates the incentive for an employee to take additional unscheduled days off. It also allows the company to coordinate and schedule absences in order to minimize the impact on the operation of the business.

**(4) The Pooled Emergency Account**. A fourth technique to eliminate abuse is the "pooled emergency account." The company adopts a plan that allows employees to contribute their accrued sick leave to a pool that participating employees may draw upon in the event they suffer a major problem that requires extended time off. Each participating employee has the comfort of knowing that he or she will be paid if a prolonged absence from work is required as a result of a major personal or family emergency. This benefit discourages employees from abusing the paid sick leave policy by increasing peer pressure against such abuse.

**c. Family Leave.** The Family and Medical Leave Act ("FMLA"), administered by the United State Department of Labor's Employment Standards Administration, Wage and Hour Division, is applicable to all companies that have 50 or more employees in 20 or more workweeks during the current or preceding year.[2] Companies subject to FMLA must allow eligible employees to take up to 12 weeks of unpaid, job-protected leave in a 12–month period for specified family or medical reasons.[3] To be eligible, an employee must have worked for the company for 12 months, must have worked at least 1,250 hours during the previous 12-month period, and must work in a United States location where at least 50 of the company's employees are within 75 miles.[4] The specified reasons for the leave include (i) the birth and care of a newborn child, (ii) the adoption or foster care of a child, (iii) the care of an immediate family member (spouse, child or parent) with a serious health condition, and (iv) medical leave due to a serious health condition.[5]

FMLA raises a number of issues for many closely held enterprises. First, some companies with less than 50 employees may choose to voluntarily offer the same non-paid leave benefits as those required by FMLA. This may help to bind employees to the business and discourage employees from moving to larger companies. Often it makes sense to officially adopt and implement such a policy if, as a practical matter, the company would grant re-employment rights to any employee who is forced to take time off because of a family health emergency or the birth or adoption of a child.

---

2. 29 U.S.C. § 2611(4)
3. 29 U.S.C. § 2612(a).
4. 29 U.S.C. § 2611(2)
5. 29 U.S.C. § 2612(a)

Second, leave for a newborn, adopted, or foster child under FMLA may be taken at any time within 12 months of the birth or placement and may be spread over different blocks of time if approved by the company. This flexibility may benefit a company that must maximize its efforts during a busy season. Although the timing of the leave is the employee's decision, approving flexible options may make it easier for an employee to accommodate the needs of the company.

Third, companies subject to FMLA should be careful not to interfere with, restrain, or deny the exercise of any right by an employee or discharge or discriminate against any employee for exercising any right. It's unlawful to do so. This can become a problem, for example, if the owners promote and encourage an environment that discourages new fathers from exercising their family leave rights.

Fourth, group health insurance benefits must be made available to an employee who is on family leave.

Many business owners feel compelled to consider the big issue: Should their employees be compensated while on family leave? It's not required by federal law, but some estimate that American employers spend nearly $21 billion a year on direct costs related to family leave.

Various factors may impact the family leave compensation issue. Competition for quality employees may be a factor. In select situations, the owners may conclude that something needs to be offered to remain competitive. Cost is a huge factor, and care must be taken to avoid serious mistakes in assessing the cost. It's a mistake to assume that the incidents of family leave will remain the same if compensation is offered; many more employees who qualify for family leave will take time off if the checks keep coming. Some employees will consider it foolish not to do so. And it's a mistake to assume that the costs are limited to the direct compensation benefits. The indirect costs of overtime and lost efficiencies triggered by prolonged absences often exceed the direct costs. Plus, the costs and hassles of having to police a program that offers paid leave must be factored into the mix. If compensation is offered, many employees may be tempted to scream "serious family illness" to get three months off with pay. This may be particularly appealing to the employee who, fearing the loss of his or her job for substandard performance, may need some compensated time off and an opportunity to threaten unlawful family leave discrimination if the ax does fall. These added cost burdens often do not exist if the family leave triggers a loss in pay. And finally, opportunity costs need to be considered.

The question that needs to be asked: How might the additional direct, indirect, and administrative costs of a compensated family leave program be better used in other ways to provide stronger, more effective incentives for all employees? This opportunity cost factor often is decisive, particularly in those closely held businesses (and there are many) where all employees know that the company can afford to pay only so much for employee benefits and most of the hardest working, productive employees have no identifiable need for family leave and actually resent the fact that so many of the available dollars are allocated to "the few who choose" to take time off caring for infant children.

When all factors are considered, many closely held businesses conclude that the most they can offer is flexible vacation and sick leave policies that allow family leave participants to use accrued vacation and sick leave benefits to soften the income loss of the family leave.

### 3. TAX-PREFERRED EMPLOYEE BENEFITS

The law encourages companies to provide certain benefits to their employees by offering tax breaks. In most situations, the company is allowed to deduct the cost of providing the benefit while the employee is not required to recognize any income. In essence, the government subsidizes the benefit. In other cases, the same result is obtained by allowing the employee to exclude from his or her compensation the cost of the benefit that the employee chooses to fund. Following is a brief description of some of the most common tax-preferred employee benefits.

**a. Group Life Insurance**. Many companies choose to offer a group term life insurance benefit to their employees.[6] Often the amount of the life insurance benefit is based on the size of the employee's salary. Such a plan, if properly structured, will produce a cost benefit and a tax benefit. The cost benefit is attributable to the fact that the company may be able to acquire the insurance at lower rates because it is buying on a group basis, and it may be able to acquire insurance for individuals who might otherwise be uninsurable for health reasons. Also, if the insurance is structured as group term insurance, premiums on the first $50,000 of coverage for each employee are tax deductible to the company, but are not taxed to the covered employee.[7] If the insurance benefit for any employee exceeds $50,000, the company is still entitled to a deduction for the portion of the insurance that exceeds $50,000, but the employee is required to report taxable income for the excess coverage.[8]

The income tax benefit of a group-term life insurance plan will be available to key employees of the business only if the plan does not discriminate in favor of such employees. A key employee includes any officer whose annual compensation is over a specified amount (cost-of-living adjusted $130,000 from December 31, 2002), any person who owns more than five percent of the company, and any person who owns more than one percent of the company and receives annual compensation in excess of a specified amount (cost-of-living adjusted $150,000 from December 31, 2002) from the company.[9] Specific eligibility non-discrimination tests require that 70 percent of all employees be covered under the plan or that over 85 percent of all participating employees not be key employees.[10] The benefit discrimination rules are not violated if the amount of insurance provided to the employees bears a uniform relationship to the total compensation or regular or basic rate of pay of each employee.[11] Thus, higher-paid employees may be provided greater benefits so long as this uniform

---

6. See generally I.R.C. § 79

7. I.R.C. § 79(a)

8. See Reg. § 1.79–3(d) for the table of uniform premiums per five-year age brackets used to compute the value of the taxable benefit when an employee's term insurance benefits exceed $50,000.

9. I.R.C. §§ 79(d)(6)

10. I.R.C. § 79(d)

11. I.R.C. § 79(d)(5)

relationship standard is not violated in favor of key employees.

Some closely held businesses conclude that the cost savings and tax benefits of a group term life insurance program do not justify the overall costs of the program. They find that their rank-and-file employees do not really care about life insurance and would prefer having extra dollars added to an immediate cash incentive program. The key employees of the company, as discussed in Chapter 12, often want and need serious life insurance protection, but their needs go far beyond anything that can be offered in a company-wide plan that limits tax benefits to $50,000 of term life insurance. However, even when such factors exist and there is little or no enthusiasm for group term life insurance, the company may choose to maintain a modest program for a few important reasons. First, it may help in hiring; it's a basic benefit that can be cited as another example of how the company really cares about its employees. Its absence may look suspicious. Second, and often more compelling, is the company's fear that an untimely death of an employee may trigger an undue family hardship that will put pressure on the company to offer something. Many private business owners have concluded that the program paid for itself when the first untimely death triggered a life insurance check for $40,000 that the family proclaimed a "godsend." The company, having experienced the ultimate reward of term life insurance, thereafter deemed the program a necessity for the privilege of employing mortal human beings.

**b. Medical Insurance Benefits**. A company may deduct the cost of all premiums incurred to provide health insurance benefits to its employees. The premiums are not taxable to the employees, nor are any benefits paid by the insurance company as reimbursement for medical expenses for the employee, the employee's spouse, or the employee's descendants.[12] These tax benefits are not subject to any discrimination tests. But, as a practical matter, nearly every business must deal with the issue of health insurance coverage for its employees. Employees want access to company-wide group plans that offer benefits, premiums, and service provider discounts that are not available on an individual basis. As discussed above, the Affordable Care Act, its employer and individual mandates, and the new exchanges are going to require all employers to rethink their options for providing health insurance benefits to their employees. For most companies, no employee benefit challenge trumps in importance the need to offer its employees health insurance coverage.

**c. Medical Expense Reimbursement Plans**. A commonly overlooked benefit is an uninsured medical reimbursement plan. It is a written plan under which the company agrees to reimburse employees for uninsured medical and dental expenses up to a maximum dollar amount each year. The tax benefit of the plan is that the reimbursements are deductible by the company, but not taxable to the employee.[13] Thus, the plan permits medical expenses to be paid with pre-tax dollars. Some companies use a medical reimbursement plan to help employees pay deductibles and co-payment requirements under a group medical insurance programs, and to pay for services that are not covered, or only partially covered,

---

12. I.R.C. §§ 105(b), 106(a)
13. I.R.C. § 105(b).

by insurance plans (e.g., orthodontic services).

An uninsured medical reimbursement plan must not be discriminatory if it is to produce the desired tax results for "highly-compensated individuals," defined as the five highest paid officers, the highest paid 25 percent of all employees, and any shareholder who owns more than 10 percent of the company's stock.[14] As a practical matter, for most closely held businesses this means that the plan must cover all employees except seasonal and part-time employees, those with less than three years of service, and those under age 25.[15] Also, the annual cap on the company's maximum reimbursement to any one employee in a given year is very important. This cap cannot be expressed as a percentage of pay (no uniform relationship skewing in favor of the higher-paid employees, as with group-term life insurance). It must be the same dollar amount for all covered employees.[16]

**d. Dependent Expense Reimbursement Plans**. A company may offer a tax-preferred dependent care assistance benefit to its employees. Dependent care reimbursement plans work much like medical reimbursement plans in that the reimbursement is deductible by the company but not included in the income of the recipient.[17] The maximum annual reimbursement amount that may be excluded from an employee's income in a year is $5,000 ($2,500 for a married separate return filer).[18] The plan may not discriminate in favor of highly paid executives, and no more than 25 percent of the benefits under the plan may be paid to owners who own more than five percent of the company.[19] This type of plan may be appropriate for those companies that have a significant number of employees who pay day care expenses.

**e. Educational Assistance Programs.** A company also may offer its employees an educational assistance program that allows the company to deduct the cost of educational expenses paid on behalf of an employee.[20] An employee may receive up to $5,250 tax-free each year to assist with his or her education.[21] In order to qualify, the plan may not discriminate in favor of highly compensated employees, and no more than five percent of the amounts paid under the plan can be for the benefit of owners who own more than a five percent interest in the enterprise.[22] The plan may not offer the employee a choice to receive the educational assistance benefits or other remuneration included in gross income.[23] Thus, the plan cannot be part of a cafeteria plan. The plan need not be funded.[24]

**f. Cafeteria Plans**. Many closely held businesses struggle with employee fringe benefits. They find that their costs for fringe benefits are constantly increasing, often faster than the general rate of wage inflation. Yet, their employees are never satisfied and have little knowledge or appreciation for the

14. I.R.C. § 105(h)(5)
15. I.R.C. § 105(h)(3)(B)
16. I.R.C. § 105(h)(4)
17. I.R.C. § 129(a).
18. I.R.C. § 129(a)(2)(A).
19. I.R.C. § 129(d)(2) & (d)(4).
20. I.R.C. § 127(a)(1).
21. I.R.C. § 127(a)(2).
22. I.R.C. § 127(b)(2) & (3).
23. I.R.C. § 127(b)(4).
24. I.R.C. § 127(b)(5).

real cost of the benefits that are being provided. To satisfy the various antidiscrimination requirements, the company often ends up paying for benefits that certain employees don't really need or value.

The solution to this challenge for many companies is a cafeteria plan or a flex plan, as it is sometimes called. It is an arrangement that allows each employee to select from a menu of benefits only those benefits that the employee wants and needs. Those employees who have no need for any of the tax-free benefits can elect to receive cash. Section 125 of the Internal Revenue Code essentially provides for a waiver of the constructive receipt doctrine for flex plans that meet its provisions.[25] Without this provision, the ability of an employee to select cash always would trigger taxable income for the employee. If the plan qualifies under Section 125, the constructive receipt doctrine is out and the covered employees have flexibility to select from a menu of benefits that includes a cash option.[26]

A cafeteria plan offers a number of advantages. There are tax benefits; the employer deducts the cost of all amounts paid to or on behalf of the employees, and many of the benefits on the menu are tax-free to the employees. Plus, to the extent an employee selects tax-free benefits, both the company and the employee save employment taxes. Beyond the tax benefits, the company no longer pays for benefits that are not needed or desired, and employees quickly gain an understanding and appreciation of the costs and value of benefits because they are making the benefit purchase decisions. But perhaps the most significant advantage is that a cafeteria plan may be used to reduce the company's overall cost of fringe benefits. The plan can be structured so that the cost of the offered benefits are funded out of amounts presently paid employees, as each employee chooses. There are administrative burdens, but often the payroll tax savings to the company more than cover the administrative expenses of the plan.

There are important decisions to be made in the design of a cafeteria plan. The company must determine whether it is going to pay for certain benefits under the plan (e.g., health insurance) or simply give employees the opportunity to use their compensation to pay for benefits. The menu of benefits must then be selected. Typical benefits include group term life insurance, health insurance, mental and dental expense reimbursements, dependent care expenses, enhanced retirement plan contributions, and cash.[27] The plan must designate election procedures that limit the frequency of employee elections and that adopt a "use it or lose it" concept — dollars that an employee designates for a specific benefit (i.e., uninsured medical expense reimbursements or day care expenses) will be lost if they are not spent for that benefit. Elections may be changed for significant changes in family status, such as divorce, marriage, or the birth or death of a child.[28]

The tax-free benefits of a cafeteria plan are not available to highly compensated participants if the plan discriminates in favor of such participants as

---

25. I.R.C. § 125(a)
26. I.R.C. § 125(d)(1).
27. Reg. § 1.125–2T (Q–1).
28. Reg. § 1.125–4.

to eligibility or as to contributions and benefits.[29] Highly compensated participants include any officer, any more-than-five-percent shareholder, any highly compensated person based on a facts-and-circumstances determination, and any spouse or dependent of any such participant.[30] Plus, tax-free treatment is not available to key employees (as defined above for group term life insurance purposes) to the extent the nontaxable benefits provided to key employees under the plan exceed 25 percent of the nontaxable benefits provided to all employees under the plan.[31]

The bottom line is that a cafeteria plan cannot be used to provide extraordinary tax-free benefits to the owners or key executives of the business. Its value is not in what it offers top management but rather in how it may reduce the overall cost of benefits for all employees and, through flexibility, enhance the value of each benefit dollar spent.

### 4. EMPLOYEE RETIREMENT BENEFITS

Retirement planning for employees is a unique challenge, complicated by a host of issues and a hyper-technical body of law that has become a specialty unto itself. It's far beyond the scope of this work to discuss in any detail the different types of defined benefit and defined contribution plans and their comparative virtues and vices. But there are certain basic considerations and planning factors that an advisor should know and understand in order to help business owners through the objective identification and prioritization processes. As the objectives are formulated and basic trade-offs are understood, there usually is a need to involve a specialist who plays in this minefield every day.

In a perfect world, any business owner would like the comfort of knowing that all employees who stick it out for the long haul will retire from the company with a retirement package that will fund their lifestyles to the end. The appeal of this ideal magnifies as the business owner observers that most of his or her employees nearing 50, like their fellow American workers, have socked away little or nothing for retirement[32] and are banking on a Social Security benefit from an unsustainable government program that promises nothing more than a poverty level payment, if that.[33] It's a noble objective that regrettably is beyond the capacity of most companies. From experience, the business owner knows that turnover must be anticipated and that younger employees are focused on, and respond to, the here and now, not an exit date 30 or 40 years out.

Of course, all employees would love for someone to plan and fund their retirement three or four decades out; they just do not want to suffer any consequences now as a result. And that's the rub. Most closely held businesses cannot remain competitive by offering what must be offered to produce results now and aggressively fund a retirement program for their employees. It's just too expensive.

---

29. I.R.C. § 125(b).
30. I.R.C. § 125(e).
31. I.R.C. § 125(b)(2).
32. In a speech on February 28, 2002 at the 2002 National Summit on Retirement Savings, President Bush stated that the average 50–year old in America has less than $40,000 in personal financial wealth.
33. See Report of the President's Commission to Strengthen Social Security (December 2001).

The law aggravates the challenge because except for the company's key highly compensated executives it prohibits a company from cherry-picking a select group of employees (those most likely to last the duration) and providing a retirement program just for them.  As we saw in Chapter 11, a company may maintain a nonqualified deferred compensation plan, including a supplemental executive retirement plan, for a handpicked group of its highly compensated employees.  The law not only permits such discrimination, it mandates it.  But when it comes to rank-and-file employees, all those who do not qualify as highly compensated, discriminatory nonqualified arrangements are off the table.  The answer for the masses is a qualified retirement plan that mandates nondiscriminatory treatment and that, within varying limits, forces the company to offer the same retirement package to all — young and old, permanent and not-so-permanent.

There are some major positive trade-offs with a qualified plan.  It provides tax deferral benefits far superior to anything that a nonqualified deal for the company brass could ever provide.  The company gets an up-front deduction for all amounts contributed to the plan. Contributed amounts are deposited in a tax-exempt trust that grows on a tax-deferred basis.  No taxes are due until the accumulated amounts are paid to an employee during retirement, when the employee will presumably be subject to a low income tax bracket.  Plus, unlike a nonqualified plan that prohibits formal funding by the employer, a qualified plan for the rank and file must be formally funded along the way so that all contributed amounts are protected from the ongoing risks of the business.  And there's another plus: there are many different types of qualified retirement plans to accommodate the varying needs and objectives of different businesses. That's where the complexity begins.   As a business owner seeks to build an understanding that will lead to sound decision-making, the following basic eight considerations can help.

**a. A Tax Shelter for the Owners?** For many toiler and professional service organizations, the qualified retirement plan is viewed as a tax shelter opportunity for the owners.  The owners, as the company's highest paid employees, may be able to eliminate any current tax hit on a substantial portion of their incomes.  Plus, that income, year-in and year-out, will grow tax-free in a protected trust that they manage. For many, it is the ultimate savings tool, particularly considering the amounts that can be stashed away tax-free each year.

With a defined benefit plan, a toiler may make tax-deductible contributions to a plan that, based on actuarial calculations, will fund an annual retirement benefit up to 100 percent of his or her highest three years of compensation or $205,000 (the 2013 limit), whichever is lower.[34]   The size of the annual contributions to fund such a benefit will depend on the age of the owner when the funding starts (the older the age, the larger the contribution); but in nearly all cases, an aggressive defined benefit plan geared principally for the owners can be structured to produce huge tax-sheltered contributions every year.

Of course, the plan will qualify only if the company's other employees

---

34.  I.R.C. §§ 415(b)(1), 415(d).

participate in it. Many owners view the other employees' participation as a burden that must be balanced against the benefits the plan promises to produce for the owners, both long-and short-term. If the company has many non-owner employees who are expected to make the company their career, the cost of funding a lucrative defined retirement benefit for all employees might be prohibitive and force the owners to abandon their tax shelter dreams. However, for non-owner employees in many toiler and professional organizations, income levels are low, ages are young, and turnover rates are high. Very few will last long enough to accrue a substantial benefit under the plan. When this situation exists, often the planning exercise quickly becomes a "we-they" game. Steps are taken to minimize the costs attributable to the non-owner employees. The accrual of benefit and funding provisions are heavily weighted to age and income levels, all of which favor the owners. Promised benefits are integrated with social security to further reduce the plan benefits for lower-paid employees. And the company maximizes its vesting options (discussed below), provisions that cause an employee who leaves the company early to forfeit all or a portion of his or her benefits under the plan. The forfeited amounts are recycled to fund benefits for the plan's long-term participants, principally the owners.

**b. A "Do–It–Yourself" Opportunity?** At the opposite end of the spectrum are those business owners who will receive little or no direct benefits from any qualified retirement plan that the company may adopt. They may be golfers, a big fish, or key employees who know that, given the size and nature of the company's workforce, broader employee concerns trump any personal benefit they may get from the plan. In this situation, often the challenge is to offer all employees a tax-favored retirement plan at the lowest possible cost to the company. The answer for most is a 401k plan,[35] an option whose popularity now causes many employees to ask during the hiring process: "Do you offer 401k benefits?"

The distinguishing feature of a 401k plan is that, even though it is usually structured as a profit sharing plan, it contains a cash or deferred arrangement (typically called a "CODA" benefit). The CODA gives each participating employee the right to divert a portion of his or her regular pay into a retirement fund that will accumulate on a tax-deferred basis for the benefit of the employee.[36] The amount diverted to the fund each year is excluded from the employee's taxable income; thus, the employee has the opportunity to fund a retirement savings with pre-tax dollars. The popularity of the 401k has caused many to view it as a valuable benefit even though for many companies its adoption is an announcement to all employees, "The Company isn't going to fund it; You're on your own."

There are some important limitations with a 401k plan. First, there are limits on how much an employee can contribute each year. In 2013, the maximum employee contribution is $17,500.[37] Second, the contribution options for highly compensated employees (defined as a more-than-five-percent owner or an employee earning more than $115,000 (2013 limit)) often are dependent on

---

35. See generally I.R.C. § 401(k).
36. I.R.C. § 401(k)(2).
37. I.R.C. § 402(g)(1).

the amounts contributed by all eligible employees.[38] If the rank and file take their money home and elect to forgo the benefits of the plan, the company's key employees may be boxed out of any significant participation. Third, once an employee commits money to the plan, it may be very expensive to access that money before age 59 1/2.[39] Early withdrawals will trigger an immediate tax on the amounts withdrawn, plus a 10 percent penalty.[40] The prospect of being "worse off" if the money is needed down the road spooks many employees, particularly younger employees, away from the CODA option. A loan from a 401k plan is possible if the plan permits such loans, but it is not an easy solution. For example, the loan amount and all accrued interest must be repaid with after-tax dollars; a default is treated as an early withdrawal, triggering taxes and penalties; the loan must be repaid immediately in the event of a job change; and often fees are charged. Finally, to facilitate management of the plan, most companies limit the investment options that are available to employees who contribute to the plan. Although the investment menu often is broad enough to cover a wide risk-reward spectrum, the fund manager and fee options often are limited.

**c. Company Matching Money?** Often a company wants to sweeten the pot for those employees who contribute to the company's 401k plan. This is done by the company agreeing to match a portion or all of the contributions that an employee chooses to make. The company defines the terms of the match, which cannot discriminate in favor of highly compensated employees. A matching provision offers a number of benefits. Beyond encouraging participation, it is an effective pay raise for those employees who elect to participate in the plan. Plus, it can eliminate any participation problems for highly compensated employees if the match equals the employee's contribution for the first three percent of pay and then 50 percent of the excess employee's contribution up to 5 percent of pay.[41] A plan with such a match provision is deemed nondiscriminatory and may allow contributions from highly compensated employees without regard to the participation of other employees.

**d. Non–CODA Related Company Contributions?** Since the CODA 401k benefit usually is part of a profit sharing plan, the company has the capacity to make contributions to the plan unrelated to the contributions made by the participants. These company contributions are allocated to all plan participants, usually in proportion to their respective compensation levels. The maximum annual amount the company may contribute for any one employee is the lesser of 100 percent of the employee's compensation or a designated dollar amount ($51,000 in 2013).[42] But the total company deductions for such contributions to a profit sharing plan may not exceed 25 percent of the total compensation paid to the plan participants.[43]

The plan may be structured to give the company complete flexibility from

---

38. I.R.C. §§ 401(k)(3) & (5), 414(q).
39. I.R.C. § 401(k)(2).
40. I.R.C. § 72(t).
41. I.R.C. § 401(k)(12)(b).
42. I.R.C. § 415(c)(1).
43. I.R.C. § 404(a)(3)(A).

year to year; the board of directors each year may determine how much, if any, the company is going to contribute to the plan. Note however that if the plan requires the company to make such contributions each year equal to at least three percent of the participants' compensation, the plan is deemed nondiscriminatory for CODA purposes and the company's highly compensated employees may make CODA contributions without regard to the participation of other employees or any matching contributions of the company.[44]

**e. Who Handles the Money and Bears the Risk?** Getting money into a qualified retirement plan is only the start. Once in the trust, the money needs to be managed. This management challenge raises a number of issues. The manager of the money owes a fiduciary duty to all participating employees and will be held to a standard of care of an expert who is in the business of investing funds for others. This, plain and simple, means that a business owner should not undertake the responsibility and risk of making specific investment decisions. Pros need to be hired, and they cost money. Is the plan or the company going to pay their fees? Or should the plan be structured to offer employees a say in how their money is invested, such as through a family of mutual funds? This requires an ongoing communication and educational effort that costs money, sucks up productive time, and often creates a great deal of confusion.

*[margin note: has to → be managed by a pro investor]*

And then there is the issue of who bears the ultimate risk for the investment performance. In nearly all defined contribution plans, such as profit sharing and 401k plans, the employees reap the rewards of profitable investing and suffer the consequences of all investment setbacks. In defined benefit plans where the company promises a specific benefit at retirement, the ultimate risk of the investment performance is on the company. In these situations, the company will want to carefully control the investment performance of the funds.

**f. Reward Longevity?** Often a company does not want its contributions to the company's retirement plan to benefit employees who have short-term tenure with the company. They want the plan to provide an incentive for employees to remain with the company, not help fund the departure for those who move on. There is no capacity to impose any longevity limitations on amounts contributed by employees under a CODA arrangement; that money came from the employee and, along with any earnings it generates, cannot be forfeited.[45] But for any amounts contributed by the employer, including matching contributions, vesting provisions can be structured into the plan that provide for a full or partial forfeiture if the employee leaves too soon.

If the plan is a defined contribution plan, such as a profit sharing or 401k plan, the vesting schedule may (i) permit 100 percent vesting after three years of service, or (ii) permit 20 percent vesting after the first two years and then an additional 20 percent each year until 100 percent vesting occurs after six years.[46] All forfeited amounts are allocated to other plan participants. These vesting provisions, if properly used, can have a powerful concentration impact over time

---

44. I.R.C. § 401(k)(12)(c).

45. I.R.C. § 401(k)(2)(C).

46. I.R.C. § 411(a)(2)(B). This provision was amended by the Pension Protection Act of 2006 to require such vesting for all defined contribution plans.

*Keynote*

when a significant percentage of the company's employees have tenures of less than three years.

**g. Something Simpler?** Many closely held business owners long for simplicity. Administrative hassles and burdensome administrative costs scare them. They turn off when they start hearing about a custom-crafted qualified plan that requires up-front IRS approval, ongoing employee communications, careful monitoring, investment trust account management and administration and the related fiduciary liabilities, employee participation tracking just to find out how much key employees can contribute, vesting provisions that promise to confuse everyone and spawn a never-ending stream of questions, and much more. They like the tax deferral benefits and want to offer their employees something. They just want a simpler plan — one that will be easier and much less expensive to administer.

In this situation, the simplified employee pension (SEP) may be the answer. With a SEP, each participating employee establishes an individual retirement account (IRA) at any institution the employee chooses.[47] The company makes contributions directly to the IRAs of its employees. The company is saved all the hassles, expenses, and fiduciary liability concerns of administering and monitoring trust accounts, investment options, and all the other trappings of a qualified plan. Plus, SEPs are easy to set up; all it takes is filling in a few blanks on a government prototype form and then sending the form to the IRS. The maximum contribution limits to a SEP are the same as for any profit sharing plan — the company deduction is limited to 25 percent of total compensation, and the annual addition to any one employee's account is limited to a specified dollar amount ($51,000 in 2013).[48]

*no discrimination*

As with any profit sharing plan, the company has complete flexibility each year in deciding whether and how much to contribute, and the plan may not discriminate in favor of highly compensated employees. Contributions may be allocated to participants based on their compensation levels, subject to a maximum compensation factor for highly paid employees ($255,000 in 2011).[49] All employees who have attained age 21, have been with the company three of the past five years, and have earned at least $550 in a year must be allowed to participate.[50]

There are two significant disadvantages to a SEP. First, since all contributions go straight to IRAs set up by employees, no vesting provisions are allowed. All contributed amounts vest 100 percent. This disadvantage is mitigated by the three-year participation requirement. Second, a SEP may not contain a COLA feature similar to that offered by a 401k plan. Prior to 1997, a SEP could be structured as a cash or deferred arrangement. Not so now. With a SEP, the company, not the employees, must bear the cost. This factor alone forces many closely held businesses to forego the benefits of a SEP.

**h. A Simpler CODA?** Is there an option for a closely held business that

---

47. See generally I.R.C. §§ 404(h), 408(k).
48. I.R.C. §§ 404(h), 404(a)(3)(A), 415(c)(1).
49. I.R.C. § 408(k)(3).
50. I.R.C. § 408(k)(2).

wants to offer a tax deferred, "Do–It–Yourself" retirement opportunity to its employees, but does not want the administrative hassles and costs of a full-blown 401k plan? There is a solution if the company has no more than 100 employees who earn more than $5,000 a year and the company does not sponsor any other qualified retirement plan for its employees. Such a company may adopt a SIMPLE plan.[51]

A SIMPLE plan is similar to a SEP in that each participating employee opens and maintains his or her own individual retirement account into which all contributions are made. As with a SEP, the company is saved all the administrative hassles, expenses and fiduciary concerns of a retirement trust; and a SIMPLE plan can be easily set up in minutes. The big difference with a SIMPLE plan is that employees can be given an opportunity to contribute a portion of their pay to the plan, subject to a maximum dollar limitation ($12,000 in 2013).[52] But unlike a 401k plan that gives a company complete discretion in setting its own contribution levels, a SIMPLE plan requires the company to commit to certain contribution levels in order for the plan to qualify. The company must either (i) offer a matching contribution equal to the first three percent of the pay contributed by each employee or (ii) agree to make a contribution equal to at least two percent of compensation for each participating employee.[53] If the company elects the matching option, it may reduce the three percent amount to one percent in no more than two years in any five-year period.[54] And, of course, no vesting provisions are permitted.

Although a SIMPLE plan requires a fully vested contribution from the company, in many cases it will be the preferred option for the company that qualifies and wants to offer a CODA option to its employees. Often the savings in administrative costs and burdens will equal or exceed the company's obligations to the plan.

## 5. THE POWER OF CASH—A TRUE STORY

No employee benefit is more powerful than cash. Yet it is surprising that some closely held businesses never give much real strategic thought to the cash compensation they pay their employees. Of course, all business owners know that employee compensation is a huge expense that must be controlled. Salaries and hourly rates are carefully monitored against "the market." Cash bonuses, when paid, often are backward-focused, characterized as discretionary rewards for the company's past good fortunes. They do little or nothing to link what an employee does to what an employee gets. They become something to hope for, not work for; and sometimes the employees come to view them as an entitlement, part of the standard pay package that the company is expected to pay.

Some companies do it differently. They know that cash bonuses, if strategically forward-focused, can be the catalyst to a fully engaged work force that will work harder, think better, build stronger teams, and get results. The program can extend across the entire organization. It's not easy; it requires a

---

51. See generally I.R.C. § 408(p).
52. I.R.C. § 408(p)(2)(E).
53. I.R.C. § 408(p)(2).
54. I.R.C. § 408(p)(2)(C)(ii)(II).

strategic assessment of what the company can afford to create a win-win result for both the company and its employees under defined growth scenarios.  The rewards for the company are greater efficiencies, less turnover, reduced employee hassles, and a leaner, more productive workforce; all of which translate into a stronger bottom line.  If done right, the rewards for the employees go far beyond the extra money they are paid.  Complacency and an obsession to not give more than one gets disappear.  Employees at all levels develop an expanded purpose, a sense of belonging, as they discover that they really have a definable, measurable stake in the entire enterprise and that their peers, all similarly dependent on the efforts of all, expect the very best of everyone.

Following is a true story of one closely held company that did it right — and then did it wrong.  Only the names have been altered.  No doubt there are countless other successful companies that could tell similar tales.

Julian purchased Brand Inc ("Brand") in early 1993.  Brand provided promotional products and related services to a select clientele, all big public companies.  What attracted Julian to Brand were the marquee clients, the prospects of better mining those clients, and the potential of strategically adding more large clients over time.  Julian knew that the clients were under-serviced; Brand's sales (in the $13 million range) had been flat for three years, and its profits had disappeared.  Brand's present owners were worn out and ready to move on.  Julian bought the company for a little more than its book value, knowing that it would take some effort to turn things around.

Within 30 days, Julian knew that his biggest problem was the company's 80 rank-and-file employees, about three-fourths of whom were paid blue-collar hourly wages, and the seven managers who were charged with managing the employees.  The accepted management style was fear and intimidation.  Employee morale was non-existent.  Turnover was out of control. The managers were paid handsome salaries, and the company maintained expensive retirement and benefit programs that primarily benefited the prior owners and the managers, but did little for the rank and file.  The accepted perception throughout the company, forever fueled by the managers, was that the company needed many more employees just to remedy the substandard service of the present business.  All knew that if performance levels didn't improve, clients would start disappearing and everything could unravel.  The organization's goal was just to hang on; no thought was given to growing or taking on new clients.

Julian quickly concluded that the only real hope was to get more out of the existing rank-and-file employees.  They were the lifeblood of the company.  The answer was not more of the same; it was more *out of* the same.  Turnover in the ranks had to stop.  Tangible incentives were needed to start building morale.  A vision of a better, stronger future had to be developed.  Time was limited, so Julian promptly developed a plan that would be implemented at the beginning of the second quarter of 1993.

Julian's plan had many components.  The expensive retirement plan was replaced with a "Do–It–Yourself" 401k plan to which the company would not make any contributions until things radically changed.  The expensive benefit programs were replaced with a simple health insurance plan that met the basic needs of the rank and file. All production employees (silk screeners, sewers, embroiderers, etc.) were given specific incentive bonuses based on each department's increased piece productivity per employee. All account executives and managers were given bonus incentives based on the sales growth of their specific accounts. All other departments (warehouse, art, accounting, customer service, and administration) were given a designated bonus percentage of all sales growth, to be divided among each department's employees on a quarterly basis. Every employee had a financial interest in each dollar of growth and a financial incentive to make his or her department lean and efficient. Each manager was given a bonus incentive tailored to specific financial objectives of that manager's department. Julian carefully structured all bonuses to ensure that, if sales grew, the company would start making money. The whole plan was based on the premise that the existing workforce, if properly motivated, could do much more.

Julian presented his plan to a meeting of all employees in early April 1993, along with projections of wage and salary increases, bonus payments, and total employment increases if sales constantly grew to equal $25 million by the end of 1998. When this goal (a doubling of sales in five years) was announced, many employees including most managers laughed loudly. In immediate follow-up one-on-one meetings, five of the managers, as expected, expressed disgust with the cutbacks in their perks and told Julian his plan was a "pipe dream." They were terminated immediately and soon replaced with new blood that in Julian's words, "bought into the productivity-growth plan because it was their only hope for serious money." These dramatic, abrupt changes signaled to all employees Julian's commitment to the new plan.

Julian implemented the growth targets by announcing a minimum sales target for each quarter and then breaking the target into weekly goals. Bonuses would be paid at the end of each quarter based on all sales in excess of the target. Sales results were announced at the end of each week. After six weeks and many manager shake-ups, Julian knew something more was needed. The company had hit the weekly target in only two weeks, and it was difficult to keep employees focused on a potential bonus that might be paid at the end of the quarter. Plus, Julian knew that if no bonus was earned in the first quarter of the program (a likely result the way things were looking), the whole effort might fail. Brainstorming with the new management crew produced an idea for the remaining six weeks of the quarter. For each of those weeks that the company hit its sales target, the company would cater lunch for all employees on the following Wednesday as a celebration of the week's success.

The idea worked. Employees liked the weekly reward and soon realized, as one said, "If we eat together on Wednesdays, we get bonuses together at quarter end." Lunch was served in four of the last six weeks of the quarter. The average employee bonus for the first quarter was only $82. It wasn't much, but it was enough to show that the company would pay as promised and to illustrate the potential of the program.

The weekly lunch agenda became a permanent feature of the program. All employees quickly figured out that their bonuses would be larger if each department's productivity increased and new hires (who would share in the department's bonus percentage) were kept to a minimum. New ideas were regularly tested to improve productivity. Many worked. Cumulative sales results for the current week, measured against the weekly goal, were posted twice a day at different locations around the building to advise all employees of the week's progress. Customer service teams, the key interfaces with client purchasers, met on Thursday afternoons to brainstorm what they could do on Friday to maximize the week's sales effort and ensure that the weekly goal was hit. In the second half of 1993, lunch was served in 18 of the 26 weeks. All bonuses grew to meaningful amounts. Company sales increased to $15 million in 1993, and the company showed a pre-tax profit of $400,000. Most importantly, all had confidence in the growth capacity of the company and the rewards that it could produce for everyone. A healthy pride began to show.

In 1994, the weekly lunch target was hit 44 times. Quarterly bonuses became progressively more exciting. Sales grew to $19 million, generating a pre-tax profit of $1.5 million. During this year, Julian witnessed something he could not have imagined when he cooked up his bonus plan to save the company. The plan was causing employees at all levels to really learn the business of the company—how getting catalogs out on time, keeping product on the shelves, timely responding to all customer inquiries, getting all orders out daily, minimizing back orders, etc., all impacted the company's capacity to grow. No job was unimportant. What everyone did mattered. A team mentality developed throughout the company. Management was easier because fewer employees slacked off, and those who did soon discovered that their co-workers expected more.

Sales hit the original "laughable" $25 million mark by the end of 1995 (three years ahead of schedule). By 1997, the company was serving lunch 50 weeks a year. Sales totaled $38 million and produced a pre-tax profit of $3.4 million. The company had nearly 230 employees. Individual employee productivity was at an all-time high. The average base pay for employees had grown over 30 percent from the end of 1993, and large bonuses were paid every quarter.

At this time, a large public company ("Public"), a major player in a companion industry, offered to buy Brand. The price was nearly 10 times what Julian had paid for the company. All key employees were offered potentially lucrative stock options. Public offered capital and strategic resources that would enable Brand to provide better products and services and strengthen its already stellar reputation in its industry. For the first nine months following the purchase, all continued to work well; sales, income, and bonuses grew. Lunch was served every week. Then it happened — the consultants arrived.

Public's management explained that the outside expert consultants were being brought in to determine how Brand could grow even faster and continue to drop nearly nine points to the bottom line on a pre-tax basis. The consultants, all glorified accountants, found their answers in the numbers. Julian was advised that his management team, who had worked well together during the entire growth period, was too "thin" and lacked "proven expertise." The company could afford to build a solid "deep bench" management team if it stopped wasting money on its "bizarre" employment practices. Why spend $125,000 a year on employee lunches? Why pay large company-wide bonuses every quarter? Why were so many "blue collar employees" at pay levels that exceeded what they could be replaced for in the "market"?

The consultants had a heyday cutting out the "waste" and punching numbers that promised a much bigger and stronger company. Julian's objections soon became obstacles. He was terminated. One of his key mangers saw what was coming and quit. Six months later, the rest of his management team was summarily dismissed.

Public recruited a high-powered, high-priced management team to implement the plan developed by the consultants. Sales ballooned as Brand committed to many new programs that Julian's team would have never considered. As the consultants predicted, old employees began to leave in droves and were "efficiently replaced" with others who had "reasonable expectations." As the sales grew, the bottom line disappeared and then turned ugly. To counter the drop in service levels and productivity, the new management kept hiring. The employee ranks swelled, along with mountains of worthless inventories and customer complaints. Millions in red ink piled up and soon became an intolerable embarrassment. Public's board could not understand how Brand had "lost it so fast." Their question: How had Julian's management team managed to grow Brand at an annual rate of over 30 percent while dropping nearly nine percent pre-tax to the bottom line every year?

Without ever realizing that the answer lay in the will and hearts of those "blue collar" employees, Brand's high-priced, pedigreed management had only one response: "We have no clue." And, of course, the outside expert consultants were long gone. To cut its losses and rid itself of a mistake, Public dumped Brand as part of a broader reorganization for a price that was less than a third of what it had paid Julian.

Brand's experience, like that of many other companies, illustrates the value of a fully engaged, focused workforce. It can be the difference between real success and mediocre survival for a closely held business that must maximize every advantage to compete against bigger players. A smaller platform often makes it easier to design and implement programs that keep all employees engaged and provide a basis for tapping into the best the human spirit has to offer. It takes a catalyst. Smart cash often is the answer.

## PROBLEMS 15–A AND 15–B

**15–A.** Web–Master Inc. is a special Internet development firm owned equally by Louis, Joyce, and Bryan, all of whom work full-time for the company and are within a few years of age 50. Their company is a C corporation with 10 employees. The age range of their employees is 25 to 37; the compensation range is $38,000 to $75,000. The company has hit it big over the past three years. Presently, each owner is drawing salaries and bonuses slightly in excess of $400,000 a year. They anticipate their incomes will continue to grow and are hopeful their bonanza will run another ten years, at which time they'll "hang it up and enjoy the good life."

Their concern now is income taxes and employee benefits. They want a retirement program that will shelter a substantial portion of their incomes from current taxes. As for benefits, four of their employees have no need for health insurance; they are covered under their spouses' plans. Six of their employees incur substantial day care expenses. Their two oldest employees complain regularly about uninsured orthodontic bills for their children. The owners want "top-notch" benefits for their employees, but do not want to waste money or spend money that their employees do not appreciate.

What advice do you have for Louis, Joyce, and Bryan?

**15-B.** Luke Marsh is the majority owner and CEO of Valden Inc ("Valden"), a specialty light manufacturer that is operated as a C corporation. Valden has 73 employees, and its employee ranks grows, on a net basis, at the rate of two to three employees per year. More of its growth is continually being shifted to outside contractors. The average employee age is 31, and the turnover rate averages 13 percent a year.

Luke has become increasing concerned that Valden has never maintained a retirement plan for it employees. The costs and administrative hassles have always frightened him. Plus, given the young age of the employees and their appetite for current cash, he has never seen a need to offer something that would "cut-in" to current bonuses. Lately, though, more employees have been asking about a retirement plan. And during the hiring process, Luke is routinely asked if the company offers "401k" benefits. Luke believes his "no" answer has cost him a few good candidates. So Luke figures it's now time "to learn something about the retirement stuff."

Luke has asked for your advice. He wants an understanding of the options and issues before he starts talking to those that want to sell him a service. His objective is to offer the employees a retirement "tax break" that will keep the company's cost to a minimum. He is particularly concerned about administrative burdens that will "suck up valuable time and cause diversions that will hurt productivity." Please advise.

## D. PROTECTING EMPLOYEES' RIGHTS

Few businesses can survive without the loyal support of dedicated employees. But nearly all business owners appreciate (or certainly should appreciate) that the challenge goes beyond motivation and management. Laws have continually evolved to give employees more rights; and these rights pose risks for the uniformed business owner who is determined to run the show just as he or she did 20 years ago.

The challenge for the planning lawyer is to sensitize the owner to the importance of employee rights. Following is a brief review of some important planning pointers that a business owner should consider implementing in order to help protect the business and the rights of its employees. It discusses five employee risk areas and related planning ideas. It is not intended to be a comprehensive review of these areas.

## 1. PRESERVING RIGHTS OF TERMINATION

Once upon a time the law was clear. An employer could discharge an employee at any time for any reason without notice. This employment "at will" doctrine was the standard.

Uncertainty and new risks have now set in. While most employers believe they operate under the "at will" doctrine as regards their employees, the company takes a risk every time it terminates an employee. Wrongful discharge suits have popped up with increasing frequency throughout the country. Many employee victories have been publicized. New laws have been made in the courts and the legislatures, chipping away at the old "at will" standard. Each victory and law change has provided incentives to aggrieved, discharged employees and lawyers who are willing to fight their cases. Many companies have had to endure the pain of paying big legal fees to defend the termination, only to pay more when the employee prevails.

The operative word is "caution" when terminating an employee. It is beyond the scope of this discussion to outline all of the precautionary steps that might be taken, but here are nine ideas that will help.

**a. Clean Up the Paperwork**. Employment handbooks, application forms and other key documents should specifically state that the company has an "at will" termination policy. Any language that suggests that employment is "permanent" or that a discharge requires a showing of "good cause" should be deleted. It also is advisable to have each new employee specifically sign a statement acknowledging that the "at will" standard is used in the business. If the company uses a probationary employment period for new employees, great care should be taken to specifically document that completion of the probationary period of employment does not grant any special tenure rights.

**b. Watch the Sensitive Areas**. Specific federal statutes prohibit discrimination on the basis of race, creed, color, religion, sex, national origin, citizenship status, disability, and age. Many states have specific statutes that prohibit employment decisions based upon marital status, pregnancy, medical conditions or physical handicaps. If one of these sensitive conditions exists, great care must be taken. These are high-risk areas. A termination may not be possible absent a showing of strong cause.

**c. Spread the Word**. Managers and supervisors should be appropriately advised of the risks involved in terminating employees. Risks should be explained, along with the precautions to be taken. Do not assume that the word, once spread, will be understood by all. Repeat the effort often.

**d. Never Retaliate**. A termination decision should never be based on a desire to retaliate against an employee who has exercised a legitimate right, even if the exercise is contrary to the best interests of the company. The employee may have filed a safety or sexual harassment claim, filed a lawsuit against the company, reported an illegal act, or taken some other action that is distasteful to management. In many states, retaliation against such an employee will be viewed as a violation of public policy and provide a sound basis for a wrongful discharge suit.

**e. No Loose Talk**. Supervisors and managers should be cautioned against making verbal or written statements that might imply any right of permanent employment or a discharge standard of good cause. Many courts have recognized that an employee may acquire an implied contractual right to employment as a result of all the circumstances relating to the particular individual's employment. Irresponsible statements can aggravate the problem by creating a false sense of employment security.

**f. Do Not Overstate Procedures**. The company should have a process for periodically evaluating an employee's performance and providing feedback to the employee. The procedures should be structured so that they can be followed and easily implemented. If the company fails to comply with its own procedures, the employee may have a case. The key is to be realistic in drafting the procedures and tenacious in following them.

**g. Tell It Like It Is**. It is critical that managers and supervisors be candid in communicating job performance evaluations to employees. An over-sensitivity to the feelings of the employee may boomerang at a later date. If a problem is beginning to develop, be specific. Do not ignore or understate the problem. Many former employees have based their wrongful discharge case on the premise that they were never given any critical evaluations.

**h. Document The Story**. The basis for the termination should be documented in a written statement. If a fight breaks out, the company will not be able to advance grounds for the termination that were not presented to the employee at the critical time. The basis for the termination should be carefully thought out, documented and communicated in detail to the employee. There is no need to be brutal, but honesty and candor are the order of the day.

**i. Do it Right.** Firing a difficult employee is a challenge that all business owners face sooner or later. If the task is not handled properly, the hurt and frustration of the employee will be aggravated, and the risk of a wrongful discharge lawsuit increases. Following is a list of ten tips that often help in firing a difficult employee. They assume that the termination decision has been made.

**Tip 1: Time it Right.** Try never to fire an employee at the end of a week or the day before a holiday. If the termination takes place at the beginning of a week, the employee can immediately set about the task of finding a new job. There is less time for anger and frustration to build. Also, check personal files to make sure that the termination is not occurring on a birthday or some other personal date that may aggravate the situation for the employee. As for the time of day, make sure that the termination occurs at a time when there is not a large group of other employees to contend with.

**Tip 2: Detail the Evidence**. The evidence that supports the termination is important. It should be specific and documented. As the charges against the employee become more serious, the evidence should be stronger. If the reasons for the termination are vague and the facts are not specific, the employee may be suspicious and question the good faith of what is being said.

**Tip 3: Tighten the Script**. Carefully lay out what is going to be said to the employee in advance. Do not mince words or beat around the bush. Get to the heart of the matter quickly. The employee should be told that the termination is final, provided with the reasons for the termination, and advised of the benefits the employee can expect to receive. Direct, fair and compassionate communication is the key.

**Tip 4: Rehearse the Lines**. It's never easy to stick to the script. If the lines are not rehearsed, there is a high probability that the speaker will deviate from the script, talk too much and possibly say the wrong thing or communicate a false impression. It may be a sexist innuendo or some off-the-cuff comment that suggests an improper motive for the termination. Rehearse the lines.

**Tip 5: Select a Neutral Territory**. The termination discussion should take place in a neutral territory, such as a conference room. If it occurs in the manager's office, the manager may become entrapped in a protracted discussion that cannot be comfortably terminated. Having just dropped the bomb, it may be difficult to force the employee from the office. If a neutral territory is used, the manager can easily exit the room and give the employee a few moments alone to adjust and reflect on the discussion.

**Tip 6: Watch Out for Ambush Facts**. When a difficult employee needs to be terminated, a fact may exist that complicates the termination. For example, the employee may have participated in a union organizing activity, may have filed a grievance against the company, may be close to vesting in a retirement benefit, or may be on the verge of closing a big deal for the company that will generate a big commission for the employee. If one of these ambush facts exists at the termination, the employee may mistakenly assume that the real motive for the termination is retribution or greed. The key is to determine whether any such facts exist and do what is necessary to mitigate their impact on the termination.

**Tip 7: Know the Impact Answers**. A termination usually has a number of collateral impacts. Issues dealing with vacation time, accrued sick pay, severance pay, recommendation letters, health insurance benefits, and other items need to be addressed. The employee usually wants to know what he or she should do immediately following the termination discussion. The manager should anticipate these questions and provide all the answers without the employees having to ask. It gives the employee confidence that the termination is being handled properly and gives the manager an opportunity to show compassion and concern for the employee.

**Tip 8: Listen Smart**. In most situations, an employee, having been advised of the termination and the reason for it, will want to respond. The initial statements made by the employee may be critical, particularly if there is any dispute down the road. The listener must be patient and avoid the temptation to engage in a debate. Just listen smart.

**Tip 9: Document the Experience**. Take good notes and document the entire experience from beginning to end. Be specific. Memories fade quickly, and often there is a temptation to twist or embellish what was said. For this reason, sometimes it is advisable to have two individuals handle the termination discussion and document carefully all that was said.

**Tip 10: Embrace the Big "Cs"**. The two big "Cs" are "Consistency" and "Compassion." Consistency is word and action will reduce the risk of future problems. Being compassionate usually makes the experience easier for all the parties. But do not let compassion undermine the need to be direct and totally honest with the employee.

## 2. AVOIDING SEXUAL HARASSMENT PROBLEMS

Sexual harassment is a problem in the work place. More companies are facing charges and lawsuits by employees who allege that they've been sexually harassed while on the job. Although some statistics indicate that the actual incidence of sexual harassment may be dropping, the complaints are on the rise. This suggests that employees are more aware of their rights and are willing to assert those rights by filing claims.

The Equal Employment Opportunity Commission and the courts have established definitions for two forms of sexual harassment. The first form, often referred to as "quid pro quo" or "hard-core" harassment, occurs when an employment decision is based on an employee's willingness to engage in a particular activity. Every business owner knows that this type of harassment, beyond being just plain wrong, is fraught with liability.

The second form of harassment, known as "environmental harassment," is more subtle then the hard-core stuff but can be just as damaging. This second form exists when a company allows an unreasonable, intimidating or offensive working condition to exist, or where it tolerates conduct that unreasonably interferes with an employee's work performance. It comes in many forms: off-color jokes, racy calendars on the walls, inappropriate magazines in the lunchroom, ongoing lewd remarks, flirting with the staff — you name it.

A company can be liable for sexual harassment even though it has forbidden the particular activity and did not know it was taking place. Often the claim is brought by an ex-employee who wants to be reinstated or wants back pay. If the employee prevails, the company usually gets hit with an embarrassing order requiring that it clean up its act.

Following is a summary of an eight-step program that can be used by a company to reduce the risk of sexual harassment charges. It's not an exhaustive list, but it does provide a useful starting point for a company that has done no planning. And it may provide a useful cross-check for a company that already has an anti-harassment program in place.

**a. Develop The Word**. The company needs to develop a clear, written policy for preventing sexual harassment in the work place. This policy should broadly define sexual harassment and specifically condemn both forms of harassment. The policy should forbid specific conduct directed against employees, vendors, job applicants, sales representatives and others involved in the company. It also should spell out the steps that the company has taken to protect the work-place.

**b. Spread The Word.** All employees, especially supervisors, need to be instructed that both forms of sexual harassment are prohibited. The word needs to be spread more than once. Employees and supervisors need to be regularly reminded of the policy. It should also be prominently posted in conspicuous places and be part of the employee handbook or policy manual.

**c. Anti–Dating Policy**. Generally, it's not advisable to adopt a policy prohibiting employees from dating one another, but it may be appropriate in certain cases to have a policy that prohibits supervisors from dating those individuals who are directly subject to their supervision. The basis of many lawsuits is an allegation that the employee had to date his or her supervisor to protect a job. Union contracts and employee morale impacts should be considered before adopting any type of anti-dating policy. If it's known to the company that a particular supervisor is overzealous in pursuing those within his or her charge, there may need to be a policy just for that individual.

**d. Non–Threatening Grievance Procedure**. The company needs a procedure that encourages employees to report harassment. The procedure should ensure that an employee does not have to report the charges to the supervisor who may be the cause of the problem. There should be an independent person designated to review and act on the harassment charges. The grievance procedure should be absolutely non-threatening to the employee. Major disputes and lawsuits often can be avoided if the complaint surfaces early and the company has time to deal with the problem.

**e. Respond Quickly, Thoroughly and Consistently to Any Charge**. Speed and thoroughness are keys in responding to any charge. Getting truthful responses from others is much easier if the complainer or the alleged harasser has had no time to spread the word among the work-force. Allowing charges to linger for substantial periods can increase hard feelings and hurt the process. The investigation needs to be thorough. If the investigation is slipshod or viewed as just window-dressing, the whole process will fail, and negative emotions will build. Common sense needs to govern the scope of the examination, but the company should never underestimate the seriousness of a sexual harassment charge. The company must be consistent in responding to all charges. The consistency should extend to the scope of the investigation and any discipline and penalties that are meted out. The need for consistency requires that decisions regarding sexual harassment charges are handled by company officials who are thoroughly familiar with past cases and the company's policies. It's a mistake to have different employees handle every claim.

**f. Inspect the Work-Place**. Have someone who is acutely sensitive to sexual harassment issues periodically examine what's going on in the work-place. That person should check what's on the walls, what's being said in the lunchroom, and what's going on between the staff and various supervisors. It all boils down to sensitivity.

**g. Never Retaliate Against the Accuser.** A company should never take any type of retaliatory action against an employee who has filed a sexual harassment claim, even if the claim is frivolous. The law specifically provides that an employee cannot be discharged, disciplined or threatened with discharge or discipline for filing a sexual harassment claim. If the company, after conducting an investigation, determines that the claim is frivolous, the company should reinforce the reputation and authority of the accused, do nothing to retaliate against the employee who filed the claim, and specifically reaffirm the right of all employees to file these types of claims if they feel compelled to do so.

**h. Conduct Exit Interviews**. It's advisable to interview all employees who leave the company. Sexual harassment claims often are filed by employees after they have walked out the door. If during an exit interview the employee expresses no complaints or concerns regarding sexual harassment, that employee may be hard-pressed to complain at a later date. In addition, if an offensive or unreasonable environmental condition does exist, an employee who is walking out may be more apt to talk about the situation and voice a real complaint. It's a good way for the company to get useful information on what's really going on in the work place.

### 3. EMPLOYEE DRUG ABUSE

Employee drug abuse is a concern of many business owners and managers. They are worried not only about the impact drug abuse has on productivity and efficiency, but also on employee safety and general morale. An employee who is suffering from a drug addiction can cause significant problems for the company and its employees. In order to protect the business, an employer may take steps to test employees for drug abuse in order to prevent, detect or eliminate the problem. A private employer may adopt a drug-testing program as long as the program is set up and administered in accordance with applicable law.

The ability to conduct tests for employee drug use, as well as the ability to act on the results of those tests, is determined primarily by state law. Different standards apply in different states. As a result, any employer who desires to implement a drug testing policy needs to consult with a lawyer who is familiar with the laws relating to employee drug testing in the state in which those employees are located. Most state standards are directed at both pre-employment drug testing and drug testing for existing employees. There are a few states whose laws address only pre-employment drug testing. Generally, it is not feasible to test for alcohol abuse. Alcohol testing has limited value in the work place because alcohol can be detected only for a few hours after it is consumed. In contrast, the presence of illegal drugs can typically be detected for weeks after use.

In a typical state, there are a number of safeguards that will have to be built into the testing program to satisfy state law. The first is that the selection of the employee or applicant to be tested must be based on objective standards. In the case of pre-employment testing, it should be part of the regular procedures for pre-employment screening. For existing employees, the testing should involve everyone, or it should be conducted on a random basis that precludes the employer from pre-selecting the employees to be tested. The selection procedure should be independently witnessed and verified to ensure its objectivity. Usually it is a good idea (and sometimes it is required) to include management personnel in the testing.

The drug test is usually conducted by collecting a urine sample. Generally the collection should be unobserved, although some states require or permit an independent observation of the collection to eliminate any substitution risk. But usually the employee's right to privacy trumps any substitution concerns.

It's critical that the test be conducted by a reputable laboratory. The company desiring to implement a drug testing program should establish an arrangement with a reputable medical laboratory or other medical organization. Mistakes can be made. Using a reputable laboratory to conduct the tests can minimize the potential for mistakes. Typically the program should include a requirement that if the first, less-expensive drug test is positive, the same sample must be tested with a second, more expensive and more reliable technique. If both tests are positive, there is a very little possibility of a false reading.

Usually the information provided by the laboratory to the company must be limited to "positive" or "negative." No other information contained in the test results should be given, such as the type of drug detected. Similarly, the company personnel who have access to the test results should be kept to an absolute minimum. Only those who absolutely must know should know. Most state laws will encourage, if not require, that the employee or applicant be permitted to obtain the detailed test results. If the employee or applicant disagrees with the findings, he or she should be permitted to challenge the results, either by requiring that a different laboratory review the test procedures or by having a different testing method applied.

Some employers also will include a "second chance" policy as part of the drug testing procedure. When this policy is used, the first positive drug test may not result in any action by the company, at least in the case of current employees. Or the company may take some action short of employment termination. For example, the employee may be placed on probation. The employee is then given a follow-up drug test. If a positive result is obtained at the follow-up test, more drastic disciplinary action is taken. This type of "second chance" policy creates an appearance of fairness among all the employees, which is a critical part of any drug-testing program. With new applicants, often a company will have a policy permitting a job applicant rejected for a positive drug test to reapply after a stated period if he or she is able to successfully pass a second drug test.

Any company that announces a drug-testing program should anticipate a potential negative reaction from employees. However, where care is taken to present the program in a thoughtful manner, most employees will recognize and understand the necessity for the program. Usually, an employee meeting should be called to discuss the problems and risks associated with drug abuse. The procedure for conducting the drug-testing program should be described in detail, with special emphasis on the safeguards the employer has built into the procedure to protect each employee's privacy rights and to ensure accurate results. Generally, it is a good idea to make certain that employees at all levels, including management, are included in the program, even if the law does not require it. If a union is involved, the collective bargaining agreement will have to be taken into consideration, and the union may need to be consulted on the design and announcement of the program. Its support of the program will be important.

There is usually no legal requirement that a company cover the cost of a professional drug rehabilitation program for addicted employees. Each company needs to consider for itself the extent to which it wants to be involved in assisting with the rehabilitation, financially or otherwise. Many companies will keep an employee on the payroll after a first positive reading, so long as the employee enrolls in a drug rehabilitation program. Reinstatement of the employee may be contingent on the employee's successful completion of the program. Some employers are creative in dealing with rehabilitation. They permit the employee, at his or her option, to enroll in a drug rehabilitation program at the employee's own expense. Upon successful completion of the program, the employee resumes employment. If the employee then successfully passes another drug test after a specific period, such as one year, the company will reimburse the employee for the cost of the rehabilitation program. Also, some medical insurance programs will pay for all or a portion of the cost of the rehabilitation.

### 4. Probationary Employment Risks

Many companies use probationary employment periods. This is the period in which new employees are given an opportunity to prove themselves. It is usually a designated time frame, such as three or six months.

These probationary employment periods may create a problem when an employee who has successfully survived the probationary period is subsequently terminated. The employee may have reasoned that since the probationary period was successfully completed, he or she was home free. A sort of tenure had set in, and the employee should not have been given walking papers without the company first establishing just cause.

The central issue is whether the use of a probationary period changes the standard of termination. Many companies want to preserve the right to terminate their employees at will, without having to prove just cause for the termination. For this reason, care must be taken if some type of temporary employment period is going to be used during the early months.

There are many sound business reasons for using a temporary employment period for new employees. In some circumstances, it is a benefits issue: the company does not want new employees to receive sick leave, vacation time or other benefits until they put in a certain amount of time. Some companies want to designate a special period to train employees, or to carefully supervise their performance. Other companies want to have a period to test the employees. It boils down to a question of expectations and understanding. A primary reason employees challenge former employers is that they feel they've been treated unfairly. Therefore, if a probationary period is going to be used for new employees, steps need to be taken to keep expectations and understandings in line. The challenge for the company is to make certain that this initial employment period does not give the employee the impression that a different standard of termination will exist after the initial period.

Following are six steps that a business may take to protect itself if it is going to use a probationary period of employment.

**a. Use The Right Name**. The right term should be used for this different, initial employment status. Perhaps "probationary" is not the best adjective to use. The word "probationary" implies a test or a trial. It may give a false impression, particularly if the test is passed. It may be more appropriate to call the period a "start-up period" or a "phase-in period." If the initial emphasis is on training, it may be called a "training period" or a "supervised period." Or if the real purpose of having the period is to qualify for benefits, it may be called a "benefit qualification period." It may be appropriate to use the term "probation" if the company really wants to make it clear that the employee's status is tenuous and shaky during the initial period. The employee, in that situation, really is on probation.

**b. Sensitize Key Management**. The next step is to sensitize the key management personnel to the problem. Carefully instruct managers, particularly those responsible for hiring, on how to discuss this initial period of employment. It is important to remember that a misguided manager who is promising too much can bind the company to promises that were neither intended nor authorized. Employees often tend to put a great deal of stock in words spoken by executives and managers.

**c. Clean Up the Employee Policy Manual**. If the company has an employee policy manual, make certain that it carefully explains the purpose of the initial employment period. It also should specifically state that successful completion of the initial period does not guarantee subsequent employment or change the standard for employment termination. If the company has adopted an "employment at will" standard, the standard should be stated specifically in the policy manual. Any ambiguity or misstatement in the policy manual will arm any disgruntled employee with powerful ammunition.

**d. Up-front Written Notice**. Provide the employee with a specific written statement, describing the initial employment period and its purpose at the time the employee is hired. This will inform the employee of the situation up front. Also, it will create a valuable paper trail that one hopes will render moot any potential of a challenge down the road. The statement should be short and to the point. Avoid using legalese.

**e. Back End Statement**. At the end of the initial employment period, provide the employee with another statement, reminding the employee of the situation. The statement should state that the initial employment period has ended. It should summarize the positive consequences, but should not create any false expectations.

**f. Get the Word Out**. Clarify the situation for all those involved in the workplace. Many established and long-term employees may understandably assume, based on their experiences, that an employee is guaranteed employment or some form of tenure after completion of the probationary period. Through their discussions and conduct, these employees may give new employees the wrong impression and create false expectations. It's important to spread the word. It can be done in a very positive way without having to create undue alarm or concern. It will clarify the expectations of all employees and reaffirm the company's rights of termination.

## 5. FIXING THE HANDBOOK

A Sword or a Shield? An employee handbook is vital to communicate to employees the expectations of the company, the benefits of employment, and the company's policies regarding employment and other critical issues. There is no substitute. However, it's now clear that a poorly prepared employee handbook can be a trap for the company. If done wrong, the provisions of an employee handbook may be considered binding contractual commitments between the company and its employees.

The lesson is simple: take great care in preparing the handbook. If it's written properly, it can be a defensive tool that actually protects the company from liability down the road. It can be a shield rather than a sword.

Following is a brief description of six of the biggest mistakes often made in writing an employee handbook. Avoid them. Any company that already has a handbook should check it against these six items, and a company that is about to design one should have these items in mind.

**Mistake 1: No Disclaimer**. The handbook fails to contain an appropriate "no contract" disclaimer. This is a simple statement that the policy handbook is intended and designed to provide information and does not constitute a binding contractual commitment between the company and its employees. By including this statement, the company puts employees on notice that they may not claim that the handbook is the equivalent of a binding contract. This statement should appear in the front of the handbook. A helpful standard: draft the policy handbook as if it is a binding contractual commitment and then state throughout the document that that's exactly what it is not.

**Mistake 2: Fuzzy Employment Rights Language**. Many companies use fuzzy language in the employee handbook to describe an employee's rights to continued employment. A problem arises when the company wants to discharge an employee, and the employee claims that the handbook requires that the company show just cause for the termination. The handbook should never use the word "permanent" to describe employment, nor should it contain promises or assurances of continued employment that the company is not willing to live up to. Usually the best course of action is to specifically state that employment is "at the will" of the company, that it may be terminated by the company, and that no supervisor or other employee has the authority to alter this "at will" termination standard. As an added precaution, each employee may be asked to initial or sign this statement in the employee handbook.

**Mistake 3: Overstated Procedures**. In an effort to make the company look good, those responsible for drafting the handbook often include detailed procedures that are designed to protect the employees at the time they are reviewed or disciplined. The problem comes when the company is unwilling or unable to live up to the overstated promises of the handbook. An angry employee may file a lawsuit or a claim based on the company's failure to follow its own procedures. The company is in an embarrassing position, and the employee has a credible case. The lesson is for the company to avoid biting off more than it can chew in outlining its procedures. If anything, err on the side of understating the procedures in the handbook.

**Mistake 4: Too Narrow in Scope**. Often the employee handbook is too narrow in scope and ignores important issues and policies. Care should be taken up front to address comprehensively the important issues for the company. Some of the major policy issues to be considered include attendance, absenteeism, employee benefits, drug and substance abuse, sexual harassment, sick pay, smoking, termination, vacations, the work day and work week, performance evaluations, salary adjustments, overtime, leaves of absence, holidays, equal employment opportunities, educational assistance programs, and workmen's compensation benefits. The bottom line is that there is a broad range of issues to be covered.

**Mistake 5: The Copycat**. To save money and expedite the process, many companies borrow from other companies' handbooks. There's nothing wrong with examining what others are doing, but wholesale copying usually leads to problems. Careful consideration should be given to formulating policies that are tailor-made for the particular company and that fit the profile and philosophy of that company. It complicates the job, but always results in a better, safer product.

**Mistake 6: Too Much Salesmanship**. Often there is a tendency to puff up the company in the employee handbook. Statements are included describing how good, fair, and generous the company is going to be. This type of puffing or overstating does little to help the handbook and may come back to bite the company in the future. Eliminate unnecessary salesmanship.

## E. PROTECTING THE BUSINESS FROM ACTS OF ITS EMPLOYEES

How can a closely held business protect itself from liabilities that may be created by its employees? The issue of protecting a closely held business from acts of its employees is raised in a number of contexts. Nearly every business is dependent upon imperfect, fallible human resources. In order to carry out the business objectives and advance the profit-making plan, the company is required to hire employees and unleash them on behalf of the business. The law exacts a price for this privilege. Perhaps it's more accurate to say that it extracts a responsibility. In general, the company is responsible and liable for those acts of its employees that are carried out within the scope of their employment. This is a true vicarious liability. It is one of the broadest forms of vicarious, third-party liability in the law. The company may be fully liable, even though it had no direct involvement with, or knowledge of, the event creating the problem.

The scope of this vicarious liability should be a concern to every business owner. Too often the temptation simply is to toss up one's hands and conclude that, since the responsibility exists, there is nothing that can be done about it. This is a mistake. Steps can be taken to mitigate the exposure.

The company's vicarious liability can become a reality in a countless number of ways. In most instances, the liability pops up because an employee has committed one of four wrongs.  The first and perhaps most pervasive wrong occurs when the employee exceeds his or her authority in making a deal on behalf of the company, or goes beyond that authority in representing the interests of the company. The employee, justified or not, assumes too much authority and ends up making a deal, a commitment, a warranty, or a representation of some type that the company doesn't like.

The second wrong occurs when the employee, in the process of carrying out his or her duties, negligently or recklessly injures another party. It may be an injury to the other party's person, property, reputation, career or existing contractual rights.  Some third party ends up injured, and the company ends up holding the bag because an employee negligently or recklessly caused the injury while acting on behalf of the business.

The third wrong is where the employee ignores or violates a black letter law that has been established for the good of all.  For example, the employee refuses to hire someone on the basis of his or her sex, or fires someone on account of age.  The employee fixes prices with a competitor. The employee ignores basic environmental regulations.  The employee sexually harasses a co-worker. Whatever the event, when this condition exists, usually some combination of greed, bigotry and ignorance is at the root of the problem.

The fourth wrong is the worst and the rarest. It's intentional misconduct that, in some cases, may rise to the level of criminal conduct.  Fraud is probably the most common example.  But there are many others: bribery, extortion, embezzlement, malicious slander, insider trading, unlawful disposal of hazardous waste and a host of others.  These are the most ugly employee circumstances that business owners dread having to deal with. Fortunately, most business owners never experience this dark side.

There are specific steps that a business owner can take to reduce or mitigate the scope of the liability that may be created by employees.  These are reviewed below with no effort made to analyze the fine points of the law relating to masters and servants and principals and agents. or the limits of the vicarious liability *Respondeat Superior* doctrine.  The focus here is on third-party liability exposure, not actions or complaints that may come from employees. Not all of the steps reviewed will be applicable to every business.

## 1. TEN PROTECTION STEPS

### Step No. 1—Define the Scope

The whole concept of employer vicarious liability turns on the scope of the employee's authority or employment.  If an employee injures another outside the scope of employment — say by frolicking on off-hours — there generally is no employer liability.  But if the employee is within the scope of his or her duties, the liability will pass to the employer.  Therefore, it is advisable for a business owner to define the scope of the employment for each employee. If an executive is given authority to negotiate contracts on behalf of the business owner, clearly define the limits of that authority. If an employee is authorized to perform certain tasks on behalf of the business owner, define those tasks as specifically as possible. The vicarious liability of the employer extends only to the extent the employee is within the scope of his or her employment. Absent some definition of the scope, the business owner's exposure is increased.

The obvious question is: How is the scope defined? In most businesses, the best way to define the scope is through carefully prepared job descriptions. A business owner may conclude that Employee A should appropriately spend a portion of his or her time entertaining prospective customers, but is concerned about Employee B. Employee B likes the nightlife and particularly enjoys drinking and conversing with a broad range of buddies, all in the name and for the sake of business. The business owner may reasonably perceive that Employee B, while purporting to perpetuate the business through his actions, is really nothing more than a nocturnal accident waiting to happen. Thus, the business owner may determine that it is not within the scope of Employee B's employment to entertain perspective customers on off-hours. The owner does not want the responsibility for these activities of B. Employee B's job description is structured to specifically exclude any responsibilities for entertaining prospective customers outside of normal business hours.

In many businesses, it is impractical to fashion a specific job description for every employee. A description for classes of employees may be necessary. Certain prohibitions may be included in the employee manual. A reasonable effort should be made to craft a specific job description for each key executive employee whose primary responsibility is to interface with outsiders on behalf of the company. The description does not need to be elaborate, but it should make an effort to delineate the scope of the contractual authority of the executive and the scope of the executive's responsibilities and duties. In many cases, it will be included in a written employment agreement.

This task of defining the scope requires an effort up front, but this effort can mitigate the potential liability of the business owner in two important ways. First, if the scope of the employee's authority and activities is clearly defined at the outset, the possibility of the employee wandering beyond that scope and causing problems is reduced. The employee knows where he or she stands. The excuse "I didn't know" is gone. Second, if a problem is created because the employee did exceed the scope of his or her authority or responsibility, then the business owner, if required to defend against the liability claim, is in a much better position to establish that the employee was outside the scope of his or her responsibilities. The owner can point to a business record that was created before the incident to prove the limits of the employee's authority.

### Step No. 2—Mind the Memos and Emails

Whenever a business dispute ripens, lawyers go for the evidence. Often the best available evidence is file memoranda and emails that were prepared at the time the event took place. These documents can be killers or savers, depending entirely on how they are drafted. Key employees, particularly high-ranking executives, should be instructed on the appropriate preparation and retention of file memoranda and email documents.   Each memorandum should be prepared with a view that it may be scrutinized carefully in the future. Facts should be stated accurately and succinctly. Suspicions or innuendos should be deleted or at least clearly characterized as such. Inflammatory statements or rationales that are designed to make a competitive co-worker look bad if a problem arises down the road should be strongly discouraged.   Key employees should be specifically instructed against preparing documents that are designed only to protect themselves by pointing fingers at other people in the organization. If  a  written record needs to be prepared that may be damaging down the road, consider putting it in a confidential communication to a company lawyer.  This may keep the record out of the hands of an adverse party in a future dispute or lawsuit because of the attorney-client privilege.

All written records are not bad. Quite the contrary.  Executives should be instructed to carefully document the substance, time, and place of key statements made by others that may be helpful in a potential dispute down the road.  Often outside parties make admissions or statements that they later deny having made when the dispute surfaces.  A good executive will develop an ear for these types of statements, and will make a contemporaneous record of them in the form of a file memorandum.  This type of information can be invaluable when the dispute materializes.

### Step No. 3—Repudiate Fast

If an employee creates a problem by going beyond the scope of his or her authority, the business owner should act fast in determining whether steps are going to be taken to repudiate the actions of the employee.   The emphasis here is on speed.  Delay and equivocation may result in approval or ratification of the unauthorized act.  If, for example, a particular executive makes an offer that is outside the scope of his or her authority, fast action may enable the company to revoke the offer before it is accepted and ripens into a contract.  If the offer has already been accepted and presents a serious problem, the company immediately should consider the advisability of disclaiming the entire contract on the grounds that the executive did not have the authority to make the deal.  In many cases, the best course of action will be to honor the bad contract even though it is distasteful to do so.  But in some situations, the contract may be so bad that it is worth blowing the whistle and trying to find an exit.  The key is to move quickly before the other party has relied on it to its detriment.  Too many business owners assume that they can't do anything in this situation — that there is no out.  If it is clear that the employee exceeded his or her authority, moving quickly may create an opportunity to undo the damage.

In certain extreme instances, it may be necessary to fire the irresponsible employee to appropriately evidence the business owner's repudiation of the employee's actions.  This may be necessary in situations where the employee has been totally irresponsible, has been compromised by a conflict of interest, or has acted in bad faith.   Expulsion also may be required if the employee has demonstrated a pattern of unauthorized conduct that is likely to continue.  By acting swiftly and decisively, the business owner may cut off any exposure to future acts and may create a basis for disclaiming some responsibility for prior acts, on the grounds that the employee was clearly acting outside the scope of his or her authority.  If the owner ducks the situation and does nothing, the owner may get tagged for past acts and also future acts, on the ground that the future acts, although perhaps extreme, were being done with the knowledge and the consent of the owner.

### Step No. 4—Watch the Titles

In business, titles go a long way in defining the scope of a particular employee's authority.  Many business owners are careless with their titles.  Why not have a group of vice presidents?  They figure titles are cheap, so they can be generous with them.  The result is that many employees end up over-titled. This can present two problems from a liability perspective.

First, the over-titled employee may focus on the title and start acting like a bigger deal than he or she really is.  An employee who has an over-inflated image of his or her importance and role in the business can be dangerous.  The employee may embrace his or her concept of the authority and discretion of an executive vice president, even though the business owner had no intention of giving the employee the real authority and control that an executive vice president title would suggest.

Second, it is common practice in the business world to rely on the title of an individual in assessing the scope of that individual's authority.  By giving the title, the business owner may be presumed to have given the authority.  It may be difficult or practically impossible for the owner to disclaim the authority on the theory that company never intended to give the broad-based authority that the title suggested.

### Step No. 5—Customize the Insurance

A customized insurance program can be valuable in protecting the interests of a closely held business from the risks posed by its employees.  The key is to have an insurance program that covers specific risks of the business.  It is a mistake to assume that all risks can be insured against.  But many can. What is needed is a quality insurance person who understands the business, the nature of the risks involved, and the best available products in the marketplace.  Insurance policies can be deceiving. There is no effective substitute for an insurance professional who is thoroughly familiar with the exceptions and limitations of the policies.

### Step No. 6—Check the Pedigrees

Before hiring an employee, check out his or her background—carefully. Some employees are trouble wherever they go.  They can't play by the rules. They are always looking for shortcuts.  Over-reacting, overstating, and risk-taking are compulsions.  Sooner or later, they end up creating a problem for the business owner.  Often it is hard to get a handle on this factor.  Whenever possible, prior employers (listed or not as personal references) should be contacted.

These background checks can be critical in some situations, particularly where an employee is regularly exposed to members of the public.  Some employers have found themselves facing a charge of "negligent hiring" made by some injured third party. The charge is that the employer should have checked and determined that the particular employee posed an undue risk because of a social, mental or physical disorder. For example, there have been cases based on prior records for assault, sexual misconduct, theft and perjury. Obviously there are limits on how far any business owner can go in checking out a prospective employee. The lesson is to be sensitive to the company's needs, to watch for danger signs in the hiring process, and to do that amount of checking that is reasonable and practical under the circumstances.

### Step No. 7—Spread the Word

When the business owner delineates the authority and the scope of activities of the company's employees, the word needs to be spread — not only to the employees impacted, but also to those who are responsible for supervising and monitoring the activities of the employees. Hidden, undisclosed limitations will not be effective.

In certain instances, it may even be necessary to contact parties outside the business and inform them of limitations that have been placed on certain employees. It may be necessary to specifically warn prospective customers that employees and agents of the company have no authority to make any verbal representations or warranties outside of those that are specifically provided in writing by the company. In preliminary contract negotiations, it may be necessary to advise the other side that the company negotiators do not have the authority to bind the company to any specified set of terms and conditions, and that another layer of review and approval exists. In some situations, it will be necessary to advise third parties that all activities of employees outside the normal working hours are not the responsibility of the company. Spreading the word when necessary can be very helpful. It helps define the limits of the authority, reminds the employee of those limits, and puts third parties on notice.

### Step No. 8—Repeatedly Emphasize the Six "Big Nevers"

It is helpful to periodically emphasize to all employees the "Six Big Nevers." They are six things that generally should never be done.

1. Never talk or even joke about the possibility of hiring, firing or promoting on the basis of race, sex, age, national origin, disability or religion. A dumb comment, although intended to be innocent or fun-loving, may boomerang down the road to create a liability problem if some employee feels that he or she has been unlawfully discriminated against. Sensitivity is the name of the game on this issue.

2. Never discuss or attempt to resolve a conflict with the other side's lawyer. Many lawyers develop a knack for getting others to make admissions that will embarrass them when the dispute ripens. It is generally a good idea to advise all employees that when the other guy brings in a lawyer, you bring in yours.

3. Never encourage another party to breach a contract. This one recognizes that there is a difference between healthy competition in attempting to secure a contract and new business, and openly encouraging another party to breach an

existing contract with a third party. If A encourages B to breach a contract with C, C may have a direct liability claim against A for interfering with its contractual relationships. Many successful people have a hard time determining where selling ends and interference with contractual relationships begins. In some situations, the distinction is a bright light that is simply ignored. This can result in undue liability exposure.

Keep in mind that there is a difference between a party breaching a contract and a party simply allowing a contract to terminate or to lapse. There is nothing inappropriate about hustling business from a party who is about to rightfully terminate a contract or is a party to a contract that is ready to expire. It is a different matter when that party is being encouraged and enticed to actually breach an existing contractual relationship.

4. Never sign what you do not fully understand. This may sound axiomatic, but the truth is that many business executives sign agreements that they do not fully understand or that they have not carefully reviewed. Each employee should be instructed against the fear of appearing ignorant for not understanding the implication of a particular document. The lesson is to seek out appropriate counsel and advice on what the document actually says. When a dispute hits, the written word becomes all-important.

5. Never discuss with a competitor or a prospective competitor any matter involving prices, existing or potential market divisions, or existing or potential actions or plans to not do business with (boycott) a third party. The Sherman Act is always lurking. Lawyers love it. An aggrieved party can recover treble damages and attorney fees.

6. Never ignorantly look the other way. Many business owners have an employee who routinely breaks the rules, but who gets results. It is tempting sometimes to look the other way, take the risk of the liability exposure, and enjoy the benefits. What is important is not to be ignorant in assessing the magnitude of the risks. Look hard at the stakes before assessing the odds. There are some two-percent risks that should never be taken because the consequences of the risks are so utterly severe that they could mean an end to the business. Other 50-percent risks can be taken all day because the consequence of the risk materializing is not severe in light of the potential benefits to be obtained. What is required is an intelligent risk analysis. It requires a case-by-case review. No pat formula will work in all cases. Looking the other way can be dangerous, particularly if it is done ignorantly.

### Step No. 9—Education

Employees need to be educated. Do not assume that they know or appreciate basic laws or that they are sensitive to the risks that they may create for the business owner. Some areas of potential liability may require special education, such as price-fixing risks, hazardous waste disposal risks, employment discrimination, sexual harassment, and the like. Other areas of potential liability require one basic reminder: stay within your authority and be careful.

Some employees may need to be periodically reminded of their own personal liability if they wrongfully create a liability for the company. Many figure that since it's the company's problem, it can't be their problem also. This is faulty thinking. If an employee creates a problem, that employee will be in the middle of it all and, in many cases, will personally be on the hook. One important word of caution on this point: the business owner needs to be careful not to overdo it and spook employees into doing nothing, or make them so tentative and fearful that they become ineffective.

### Step No. 10—Reduce Turnover

In many respects, this last step is the most important. A stable, seasoned workforce is much safer than one that experiences high turnover rates. Plus, it's more efficient and productive. For many companies, a prerequisite to success is the ability to attract, retain and motivate quality employees.

Many factors can impact employee dissatisfaction and turnover rates. Some, such as the nature of the work or opportunities for career advancement, may be beyond the control of the owners of the business. But other critical factors, including the company's interest in the well-being of its employees, its vision for the future, and its willingness to embrace its employees as valued teammates, not expendable commodities, are completely within the control of management. There are many important steps that management can take in setting policy and operating day-to-day to bind and motivate employees.

Absent effective management, a workforce can quickly develop a destructive go-through-the-motions mindset that guarantees inefficiencies and waste and increases the potential of employee actions that create liability exposures for the company. Smart management can benefit everyone in an organization and reduce liability risks. The rewards for employees go far beyond any additional compensation they might net. The despair of complacency and an obsession to give only the minimum can soon disappear. Definable, measurable stakes in the effort can trigger an expanded purpose, a growing desire to excel and be careful, and an ongoing push to elevate the performance of the entire group.

Sound impossible? It happens every day in companies that, out of a desire to grow and protect their businesses, take positive actions to reward, incent, and cherish their employees by smartly tapping into the best the human spirit has to offer.

### 2. THREE MYTHS

There are three myths that often permeate a discussion about a company's liability for the acts of its employees. These myths can provide a false sense of security and divert attention from the real issues.

**Myth 1: If I make my employees independent contractors, I won't be liable for their actions.** Some business owners believe that if they make all of their employees independent contractors, they can escape liability for the employees' activities. While it is true that a business owner may have less responsibility for true independent contractors (such as outside accountants and lawyers), the answer is not to make all employees independent contractors. Titles alone won't do the job. If a person is designated as an independent contractor, but the business owner retains the right to control and supervise that person's conduct, the liability will be just as great as it would have been had the person been called an "employee."  There also are down sides to over-using the independent contractor title.  The business owner may develop a false sense of security and may end up foolishly granting the disguised employees additional rope with which to hang themselves and the company.  There also may be tax problems.  Independent contractors are required to pay their own income, self-employment and state business taxes.  If they fail to pay these taxes and it is established that, in reality, they were the equivalent of employees, the business owner may end up with a serious tax problem.

**Myth 2: If one of my employees does something wrong and I immediately fire that employee, I am off the hook.**  This is a gross over-generalization.  As discussed above, there may be extreme circumstances where an employee needs to be terminated in order to protect the business against future problems.  But there is no assurance that, by terminating the employee, the business owner will be able to absolve the business of responsibility for prior acts committed by that employee.  In addition, this myth can precipitate an over-reaction that results in an employee being needlessly terminated.  In many situations, the employer can reasonably take the position that the employee was outside the scope of his or her authority without firing the employee, particularly if the employee has no history of creating such problems.

**Myth 3:  If I didn't know about it, I'm not responsible for it.**  Some business owners mistakenly assume that if they can just demonstrate their own ignorance of the matter, they are home free.  It is natural for many to assume that they can't be liable for something that they did not know anything about.  It's a true myth.  As a general proposition, ignorance is no defense.

## PROBLEM 15–C

**15–C.** Web-Master Inc. ("WM") is a special Internet development firm that has 800 employees in six major cities and is posturing for some big growth.  WM's CEO has a problem with an account manager, Liz, who has always been regarded as a troublemaker that gets results with her accounts.  Liz has been with WM fourteen years.  She quickly moved up through the ranks and reached account manager status by the end of year five.  She has remained at that level for the past nine years, regularly complaining that she "has earned the right to be an account executive."

Liz has been vocal in her complaints, often suggesting that the company's management discriminates against women.  Two of the top six executives in the company are women, and three of the company's 11 account executives are women, all of whom started after Liz.  Liz has been "passed up" for a variety of reasons, none of which are related to her sex.  The reasons have been repeatedly explained to her in annual reviews.

Recently Liz has turned up the volume of her complaints by becoming a make-shift Internet blogger.  She maintains a website where she discusses many items, most of which are unrelated to WM.  But periodically, she "blows off steam" about WM's management.  She likes the company and the industry and cherishes the clients she serves, but she detests certain members of upper management, including the CEO and the two women who have attained executive status.   Her blog has become popular among many company employees from all six offices and many outside the company.   Beyond her complaints about her own situation and treatment of women in the company, she has recently stepped up her rhetoric to include speculations about the company's growth plans and alleged plans to cut out "older more expensive" employees, including herself.   Most of what she writes about has no basis in fact but it is starting to raise many questions around the company.   Liz regularly states on her blog site that the company cannot terminate employees for exercising their first amendment rights of free speech.   She encourages other employees to join in her complaints, but none do.

WM has an "at will" employment policy that all employees understand.   The CEO believes that the time has come to do something about Liz before she does any more damage.   How would you advise the CEO to proceed?

# CHAPTER 16

---

# ESTATE AND MULTI-ENTITY PLANNING

---

## A.  TROPHY-CHASERS AND WEALTH MANAGERS

A successful business client once explained, "It's not the hunt that excites; it's the spoils from the effort, the rewards of success."  For some clients, this simple statement says it all.  The prospect of acquiring "enough" personal wealth is why they put it all on the line every day to build a successful business.  These clients, the wealth managers, long for the time and freedom to enjoy their rewards with the comfort of knowing that all bases are covered.  On the other end of the spectrum are those who can't focus beyond the chase.  For them, the real thrill is in the hunt — the challenge of first making it happen and then proving, time and again, that they still "have it."  Why else would *so* many who have *so* much keep taking risks to conquer bigger prey?  For these clients, the rush is in the victory and scoping out the next target, not in figuring out how to enjoy the last kill.  Personal wealth accumulation is just a wonderful byproduct of their efforts, the ultimate trophy.  Their happiness is in chasing trophies.  Many business owners, perhaps most, fall somewhere between these extremes.   The rewards of wealth management are alluring, but they have a little trophy-chasing in their blood.

Where a client sits on this spectrum can have a powerful impact in the planning process.   Nearly all can embrace planning challenges that directly impact their business interests.   But big differences begin to surface when the planning extends beyond the business to matters of family and intergenerational wealth preservation.  Pure wealth managers are eager for the challenge — each component is viewed as another opportunity to get to the finish line faster.  Some compulsive trophy-chasers are impossible.  Their potential demise isn't a possibility worthy of serious discussion. Business challenges are viewed as comfortable, exciting opportunities; family challenges are uncomfortable, impossible burdens. When they do think beyond the next deal, they figure, "If I just keep raking it in, all will work out."  Sometimes they are right, even when big saving opportunities are lost all along the way.  And, of course, there are all those in the middle, some with wealth manager tendencies and others who naturally shy away from anything that isn't all business.

The high quality business advisor must be able to service all types.   There is no magic answer for the hardcore trophy-chaser, but there are steps that can be taken to make it easier for all clients to make the all-important planning leap to issues of family and intergenerational wealth preservation. Here are five suggestions:

**1. IGNORANCE IS THE CULPRIT.** The core problem in most cases is ignorance. Many owners understand complicated business issues, but really know nothing about the "estate planning malarkey" they have heard about in the past. And they figure there is no efficient, easy way to "get up to speed," let alone ponder the family dynamics that will impact tough decisions. This is one area where simple, user-friendly educational tools (such as those discussed in Chapter 17) can work wonders. The key is to create a plainspoken, non-reading learning opportunity that a client can experience at home in a private, non-threatening environment. Even modest replacements of base ignorance with simple understanding may ignite an interest that quickly shreds old barriers.

**2. DON'T LEAD WITH TAXES.** Taxes are important, but often it is counterproductive to make tax fears the centerpiece concern. All business owners accept taxes as a reality. If the primary pitch is the potential of less tax when the owner is gone, there may not be enough sizzle to trigger uncomfortable action now. Usually it helps to lead with business challenges and then family issues. Taxes should be an important, but distant, third priority.

**3. "CONTROL" OPTIONS.** Make it clear early and often that there are options for dealing with control issues. Wealth transfer talk often induces a fear that others will have unfettered control over assets that have always been in the sole dominion and control of the business owner. The owner hatches visions of adult children buying BMWs or the owner having to ask permission to chase the next trophy. Although some recent tax trends clearly favor less owner control in select situations, many options exist for ensuring that the owner's control fears are properly addressed.

**4. IT'S ALL BUSINESS.** It helps to make all the planning business-focused. The advisor usually accomplishes nothing by even acknowledging a distinction between business and estate planning — a distinction that gets very blurry and loses much of its significance when a closely held business is involved. It's all planning; and since the business activities are an integral part of everything, it's all about business. Many of the key planning challenges discussed in prior chapters, often characterized as business planning issues, have equally powerful impacts in resolving family and intergenerational challenges. These include, among others, choice of entity issues (Chapter 3), capital formation issues (Chapter 6), entity restructuring (Chapter 7), buy-sell agreements (Chapter 8), life insurance planning (Chapter 12), diversification planning (Chapter 13), business transition planning (Chapter 10), business acquisitions and dispositions (Chapter 9), and retirement planning (Chapter 15). Family partnerships and family LLCs, planning tools discussed in Part C. of this chapter, are business focused. The whole thrust of asset protection planning, discussed in Part D, is geared at protecting assets, particularly business assets. That planning often incorporates the trusts commonly used in planning an owner's estate. The point is that an integrated planning approach will promote understanding and keep everyone focused on the right target.

   **5. SIMPLE COMPLEXITY.** On its face, planning adds complexity. There are more entities, more pieces to deal with. The challenge is to keep the added complexity as simple and understandable as possible. Three steps can help. First, start with basic objectives. Examples: I want privacy when I die; I want to make sure my grandchildren have their college educations funded; I want to do something for my alma mater; I want my kids treated fairly; I want my business and my assets, to the extent possible, protected from unforeseen liabilities. Simplifying the objective identification process up front will allow the process to start. As it develops, specific, tougher family challenges can be tackled along the way. Second, in discussing each specific planning vehicle (e.g., family partnerships, dynasty trusts), focus first on the purpose and impacts of the vehicle, not the technical challenges of making it work. Once the client really understands what the vehicle does and how it might impact (or not) future business matters, any necessary technical dialogue can occur without losing sight of the big picture. Third, draw a picture of what the plan (integrated business and family) will look like and how it will work. For many business owners, this simple picture will be worth many more than a thousand words. It will become their ultimate planning cheat sheet. They will have a tool that instantly reminds them of the purpose and function of each piece. Many will quickly commit the picture to memory. Instead of being viewed as undue complexity, the multiple entities will be considered tools that are used to accomplish specific purposes. An example of such a simple picture is included in the following section.

   The purpose here is to illustrate the importance of multi-entity planning, not present a mini estate-planning presentation. The following section presents a short case study, a brief summary of how one successful couple used multiple entities to develop a plan to meet their various business and family objectives. This is followed in Part C. with a discussion of family partnerships and family LLCs, important business structures often used to bridge the gap between business opportunities and specific family objectives. Section D. discusses asset protection planning — strategies that can help protect business and personal assets from the risks of creditor claims.

## B.  MULTI-ENTITY PLANNING: AN EXAMPLE

   Duncan and Sandy Smith, both age 62, have built an estate valued at approximately $18 million. They have three children, all married and in their 30's. They have six grandchildren and hope to pick up one or two more. Duncan generates a substantial income in a consulting business ("Consulting") that he operates through a C corporation. He also is a one-third owner of a company ("Holding"), operated as an S corporation holding company that has a light manufacturing subsidiary and a distribution subsidiary. He plays an important role in the upper management and strategic decisions of Holding, but is not an employee. Sandy has always had an eye for quality real estate, principally raw land and small commercial properties. The couple owns two homes (in different states) and has significant stock and bond portfolios. The Smith's children and their spouses are all college-educated and gainfully employed; but none of them, as yet, has exhibited any of the entrepreneurial interests that have always driven Duncan and Sandy.

The Smiths have always been planners, but their serious planning started five years ago. They identified the following 10 objectives at that time, which still remain the focus of their planning:

1. Ensure that they always will have sufficient income and wealth for their personal needs, that they will never become a financial burden for their children, and that their privacy will be maintained with as little hassle as possible.

2. Ensure that their estate ultimately is shared equally by their children.

3. Establish a wealth accumulation program for each child that will provide a supplemental source of income and will be protected from the claims of creditors and the exposures of divorce.

4. Establish a wealth accumulation program for each grandchild that will help fund higher educational expenses and potentially provide some "getting started" support (i.e., a home down payment).

5. Provide their college alma maters with significant gifts that will fund in the future.

6. Defer any estate tax liabilities as long as possible — that is, until to the death of the survivor of Duncan or Sandy.

7. Minimize estate taxes by leveraging their annual gift tax exclusions, unified credits, generation skipping tax exemptions, and available transfer discounts, without compromising their other objectives.

8. Ensure that their estate always has adequate liquidity, including sufficient liquidity to cover all estate taxes.

9. Minimize income taxes.

10. Where possible, protect assets from exposure to unforeseen liabilities.

Duncan and Sandy have implemented a plan to accomplish these objectives. A simple diagram of the plan components is on the next page. Following is a brief description of each component (moving clockwise from the top of the diagram) and how it serves specific objectives.

The living trust is revocable. As such, it's a tax nullity. It holds title to Duncan and Sandy's assets. Its purpose is to eliminate the hassles and expense of probate (in their primary residence state and in any ancillary jurisdictions where they own real estate) and to protect the privacy of their affairs on death (with no probate, there is no public record of their holdings). The living trust provides for the establishment of an irrevocable qualified terminal interest property trust ("QTIP") on the death of the first spouse that will eliminate all estate taxes on the first death, provide the surviving spouse with a regular income stream and principal invasion rights as needed, protect the deceased spouse's remainder disposition preferences, and provide some creditor protection benefits. Duncan and Sandy also each have a will that pours over to the living trust any non-trust assets that they own at death.

# Duncan and Sandy Smith Plan

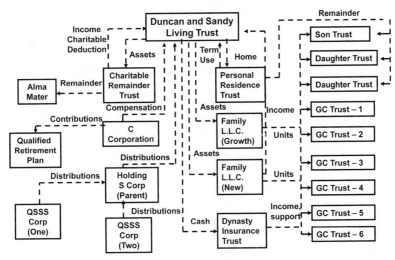

Duncan and Sandy have established a separate trust for each of their children. These children's trusts have been funded for many years. All contributions to the trusts come with *Crummey* withdrawal rights that allow maximum use of their annual gift tax exclusions. The trust balances are now large enough to eliminate any general power of appointment concerns on the lapse of *Crummey* rights (the "5 and 5" exception will cover the lapse). The trusts also provide protection from creditor claims and will help protect trust assets in a messy divorce proceeding.

A separate trust has been established for each grandchild. These trusts are used to fund annual gifts that quality for the annual gift tax exclusion. Until each child reaches age 21, the future interest gifts qualify for the exclusion without the need for *Crummey* withdrawal rights by virtue of the special exception in Section 2503(c). To comply with Section 2503(c), each grandchild is given the right for a limited period upon reaching age 21 to withdraw trust property. Property that is not withdrawn remains in the grandchild's trust for a longer term. All gift transfers after age 21 are subject to *Crummey* rights to qualify for the annual gift tax exclusion.

The qualified personal residence trust was set up to hold title to Duncan and Sandy's personal residence, a high quality property that has appreciated in value. The terms of the trust give Duncan and Sandy use of the residence for a specified term (there are 12 years remaining). At the end of the term, the residence passes to the children's trusts in equal shares. The trust permitted a substantial leveraging of a portion of Duncan and Sandy's gift tax unified credits. When the trust was established, the value of the remainder interest (then very small) was a taxable gift that consumed a portion of their unified credits. The benefit is that if Duncan and Sandy outlive the trust term (a probability), the home will pass to the children's trusts free of additional transfer taxes. The technique makes it possible to transfer a valuable residence by using a small portion of the couple's gift tax unified credits. Of course, at the end of the trust term, the residence passes to the children's trusts. If at that time Duncan and Sandy want to continue residing in the home, they will lease it from the trusts, which will create an additional opportunity to regularly transfer funds to the children free of any gift tax concerns.

The two family limited liability companies were established to facilitate the ownership of business and investment assets by the trusts established for the children and the grandchildren. Duncan and Sandy and two of their adult children are the managers. The entities own interests in real estate ventures. The "New" LLC invests in new ventures and was funded with cash contributions from Duncan and Sandy and the children and grandchildren's trusts, with the bulk of the cash coming from the trusts. The "Growth" LLC holds seasoned investments. Duncan and Sandy are the majority owners of the "Growth" LLC, but periodically gift membership interests to the children and grandchildren's trusts. See the following section of this chapter for an extended discussion on the use of family partnerships and family limited liability companies.

The dynasty life insurance trust is an irrevocable life insurance trust (see Section D of Chapter 12) structured to provide benefits for all Duncan and Sandy's descendants for as long as there are assets in the trust and the law will allow (in some states, in perpetuity). Hence, the name "Dynasty." The trust owns a $5 million second-to-die life insurance policy that will pay off on the death of the survivor of Duncan and Sandy. The premiums are funded by annual cash gifts to the trust from Duncan and Sandy that are tax-protected by their gift tax unified credits. Their generation skipping tax exemption also is allocated to all gifts to the trust. Their tax goal is to have the dynasty trust assets escape all future estate and generation skipping taxes. The proceeds of the life insurance policy may be used to help fund any estate taxes on the death of the surviving spouse by the trust purchasing assets that are included in the taxable estate (which will have received an income tax basis step-up at death).

The operations of Holding are conducted in the S corporation that owns two qualified subchapter S subsidiaries. The separate subsidiaries protect each company's operations from any liability exposures of the other's operation and facilitate the development and compensation of separate managements. All of the operations are consolidated for tax purposes. The S structure allows Duncan to regularly receive substantial distributions free of any double income tax concerns and payroll tax burdens.

Duncan's consulting business operates through the C corporation. The company funds a qualified defined benefit plan that primarily benefits Duncan, the sole shareholder and the highest paid employee. This enables Duncan to defer income taxes on a substantial portion of his consulting income. The C corporation structure also permits Duncan and the other employees to fund medical and insurance benefits with pre-tax dollars. Duncan "zeros out" the C corporation's taxable income each year with salary and bonus payments to himself.

The charitable remainder trust was set up principally to benefit Duncan and Sandy's alma maters, but it also provides some cash flow and tax benefits. Low basis unencumbered raw land was contributed to the trust. The time had come to sell the land. The trust sold the land but, as a charitable remainder trust, paid no income taxes on the sale. The total sales proceeds were invested to fund a monthly annuity that is payable to Duncan and Sandy for so long as either of them is living. Upon the death of the survivor, the trust property will pass to their two alma maters in equal shares. In addition to the lifetime annuity payments, Duncan and Sandy received a charitable contribution deduction for the value of the trust's remainder interests designated for the charities.

As depicted in the picture and briefly summarized above, the plan addresses all of Duncan and Sandy's objectives, at least in part. They receive income streams from the C corporation, the S corporation, the limited liability companies, the charitable remainder trust, and any assets owned by the living trust. The living trust provides probate and privacy protections. The children are treated equally, and the children's and grandchildren's trusts, funded via the family limited liability companies and the personal residence trust, meet Duncan and Sandy's objectives for their descendants. Their alma maters are taken care of through the charitable remainder trust. Estate taxes are deferred through the QTIP trust in the living trust and are reduced through the children's and grandchildren's trusts, the dynasty trust, the personal residence trust, and the charitable remainder trust, all of which are excluded from Duncan and Sandy's taxable estate. Liquidity is ensured through the life insurance in the dynasty trust, which will escape all future estate and generation skipping taxes. There are no double income tax concerns, payroll taxes are minimized, and taxable income can be shifted to children and grandchildren through the gifting of limited liability company units to the trusts. Duncan and Sandy have not surrendered any control of Consulting and Holding and have the opportunity to work with (and teach) two of their children in managing the limited liability companies. With the exception of the living trust, all the entities (the boxes) provide some level of protection against unforeseen liabilities (see Section D of this chapter).

## C. PLANNING WITH FAMILY PARTNERSHIPS AND FAMILY LLCS

### 1. INTRODUCTION

The powerful tax planning benefits of family partnerships and LLCs have made them a popular target of the IRS. The heat has been turned up over the past fifteen years as the Service has pulled out all the stops to shut down techniques that are designed to produce extreme tax savings. Some courts, including the Tax Court, have been willing accomplices on a few occasions. The thrust of the fighting has made everything harder. This is not to suggest that the family partnership or LLC is doomed as a planning tool or is only suited for those who have a cast iron stomach and the will to invite an encounter with the government. What it does confirm is the importance of careful attention to detail, reasonable expectations, and a willingness to not push the evolving limits.

Most investment assets offer three potential benefits: income, value growth, and control. Many mistakenly assume that these three components are tied together and must reside in the same individual. The assumption is that the person who controls the asset must necessarily be the one who receives the income generated by the asset and benefits from the appreciation of the asset. A family partnership or family LLC makes it possible to separate these benefits. Valuable economic benefits can be transferred to another and separated from the control element.

This discussion reviews some of the planning issues and opportunities associated with family partnerships and family LLCs. Although the primary focus is on the family partnership, the planning opportunities and issues are the same for any family LLC that is taxed as a partnership. The discussion first reviews five mini-case studies to illustrate how the family partnership can be applied in different situations to accomplish specific objectives. It then examines key questions that often are raised when a family partnership is being considered in a given situation.

## 2. FIVE MINI–CASE STUDIES

**a. The Shift.** Roger and Denise Moore have two children, ages 24 and 26. They also have strong incomes. Roger is a successful architect, and Denise owns and manages a profitable desktop publishing firm. Their combined taxable incomes exceed $450,000 a year. Their assets include a securities portfolio and real estate investments that produce a steady stream of interest, rental, and dividend income.

Roger and Denise's primary concern is income taxes. They pay big income taxes now and know that they will likely pay more as budgetary pressures promise higher rates for high-income taxpayers. Although they know that they are building an estate that will likely trigger an estate tax exposure on the death of the survivor, the estate tax threat is not their major concern at this time. The real issue now is income taxes.

In contrast to the parents' situation, each of their children is in a 15 percent tax bracket and will likely remain in that bracket for a long time. Simple arithmetic confirms that substantial income taxes could be saved if income could be shifted from the parents to the children. Plus, Roger and Denise would like to have a mechanism for transferring a steady income stream to each of their children. Since both children are over the age of 19, the Kiddie tax is not an issue.[1] The challenge is to figure out how to accomplish "The Shift."

After considering the alternatives, the Moores elect to use a family limited partnership to shift the income. A partnership is formed and funded with an income-producing securities portfolio and real estate investments. All of the general partner and limited partnership units initially are issued to Roger and Denise. Roger and Denise then embark on a program of gifting limited partnership units to each of their children. They initially make a gift of limited partnership units valued at $50,000 to each child. They use a portion of their

---

1. In 2007, the Kiddie tax age limit was raised to include children under age 19 and students under age 24. The tax requires that the unearned income of any such child be taxed at his or her parents' highest marginal rate. I.R.C. § 11(g).

combined unified credits to eliminate the gift tax impact of these initial transfers. They plan to gift to each child additional limited partnership units valued at $28,000 each year for the next five years. They will use their annual gift tax exclusions to shelter these gifts from gift taxes. They estimate that within five years, each child will have been given limited partnership units valued at approximately $180,000 for gift tax purposes. Appropriate minority interest and lack of marketability discounts will be used to maximize the value of the transfers to the children.

The income attributable to the gifted limited partnership units will be shifted and taxed to the children. This income will be used to help fund many of the children's financial needs down the road. The bottom line is that Roger and Denise have determined that a permanent shift of an income stream for the benefits of the children is a good idea. The family partnership accomplishes the shift.

**b. The Scatter**. Jim Bain is a 70-year-old, self-made real estate developer. He and his wife Lucy, age 66, have five children and 16 grandchildren. Jim's health is marginal; he has had some heart problems. Lucy's health is average. Jim and Lucy have a combined net worth of approximately $34 million. Most of their assets are illiquid real estate projects that Jim has developed over many years. Jim manages all of the assets. The couple's second son, Brandon, is the only child with any knowledge of the business. Brandon has worked with Jim for five years.

Jim and Lucy are concerned about their estate tax exposure. Although they have heard about estate taxes for many years, they've never really wanted to deal with the issue. Jim likes his real estate, and has never been able to get excited about the idea of transferring assets to his children and grandchildren. He has no intention of retiring and wants to keep developing. His desire to stay in the saddle is strengthened by the fact that Brandon is now involved in the business and wants to make real estate a career.

Jim and Lucy have determined that it's time to embark on a gifting program to save estate taxes. Income taxes have never been a serious issue; they have plenty of write-offs from their real estate projects. Their primary concern is estate taxes. They want to maximize the impact of the annual gift tax exclusion. They have figured that they have 24 potential donees each year. These include their five children, the spouses of their five children, and their 14 grandchildren. If Jim and Lucy embark on a program of scattering their wealth to these 24 donees each year by transferring to each donee (or an appropriate trust for minor donees)[2] $28,000 a year, their annual gift tax exclusions will shelter approximately $672,000 of transferred-wealth each year, **plus** all future appreciation on the property transferred. If the gifts are structured to maximize use of the minority interest and lack of marketability discounts, their estate reduction will be boosted by an additional $300,000 each year. Jim estimates, based on reasonable appreciation scenarios, that such a wealth-scattering program, if implemented over a 10-year period, could reduce their future estate

---

2. A trust may be used for any donees under age 21 and still qualify for the annual gift tax exclusion. I.R.C. § 2503(c).

value by at least $13 million. It would have all been done with their annual gift tax exclusions; their unified credits would still be available for other planning.

As Jim considered such a program, he had some initial reservations. First, he knew that he didn't have cash to make the gifts each year, and he felt that it would be extremely cumbersome to transfer interests in specific real estate investments to 24 different individuals each year. Transfers of undivided interests through deeds would be cumbersome, complicated, costly, and confusing. Second, he was concerned that he would lose control as these transfers were made. Finally, he was concerned that it would be complicated to transfer an interest in real estate to a minor grandchild who had no legal capacity to deal with property.

A family limited partnership eliminated these concerns, and made it possible for Jim and Lucy to embark on their family-scattering gifting program. Jim and Brandon each contributed real estate interests to a newly formed S corporation, which in turn contributed the interests to a new limited partnership in exchange for general partnership interests. Jim and Lucy contributed a substantial block of low-leveraged real estate investments to the limited partnership in exchange for limited partnership interests. Jim and Lucy then embarked on a program of transferring limited partnership units to each of the 24 donees (or trusts established for their benefit) each year. They structured the program so that, in even years, the gifts were made at the end of the year and, in odd years, the gifts were made at the beginning of the year. This technique eliminated the need for annual valuations; valuations every other year would do the job.

The S corporation general partner provided a means of transitioning control to Brandon or others without impacting the family partnership. The family limited partnership made it possible for Jim and Lucy to save substantial estate taxes by scattering their wealth to a broad range of descendants over an extended period of time.

**c. The Lock-Up**. George Judson is a surgeon. He has all the usual concerns. His malpractice rates have tripled over the last ten years. He knows that there is a risk that 10 or 20 years down the road he might be held responsible for a surgical procedure that he performed today. He also knows that a damage suit could potentially produce a judgment that far exceeds the limits of his malpractice policy. George and his wife Betty have worked hard to build an estate valued at approximately $9 million.

George and Betty would like to lock-up a portion of their assets that could not readily be confiscated by a judgment creditor in the future. In short, they want an asset protection strategy. They know that an asset protection strategy probably will not work if a claim has already been made. This type of planning should be done in calm waters. They figure that now is the time. George also understands that the strategy may not be completely fool-proof, and there may be some uncertainties. They figure that something is better than nothing. They know that some strategies are designed to make things difficult, unbearable and, hopefully in some cases, downright impossible for the judgment creditor who is going after the assets. Obstacles can be created. The hope is that most creditors, when they discover the obstacles and the potential legal implications, will conclude that the carrot isn't worth the fight.

George and Betty have decided to form a family limited partnership to help lock-up and protect certain commercial properties and investments that they own. Initially, they will own the limited partnership units and have a corporate entity be the general partner. Over time, they will transfer limited partnership units to other family members, including their children and perhaps grandchildren. Any such transfers will increase their protection from creditors. But for now, let's focus on the value of the limited partnership structure itself as an asset protection device, apart from any transfers that may be made to other family members.

The limited partnership, if properly structured and funded with assets, can itself become a major nuisance for a judgment creditor. If George has a large malpractice judgment entered against him, in many states a judgment creditor is limited to obtaining a charging order against the partnership. This charging order gives the creditor the right to receive income from the partnership when and if the income is distributed to George. The creditor gets no right to control or gain access to the assets that are owned by the limited partnership. The creditor has no right to become a general partner, nor can the creditor remove the general partner, vote in the partnership, or have any say in the management. All the creditor has is the right to receive the income and any other amounts that may be distributed to George. In some states, the creditor may petition to have the charging order "liquidated," which has the effect of transferring to the creditor all rights to the partnership interest.

The obvious question is: Can the creditor require that the partnership make distributions with respect to the partnership interest? Generally, the creditor has no such power. In this regard, if asset protection is a priority, it is usually advisable to include a clause in the partnership agreement that allows the general partners to retain cash in the partnership for the future business needs of the partnership. This type of clause may help if there is a need to retain cash in a partnership.

There is one additional aspect of the limited partnership device that makes it an even greater nuisance for the judgment creditor. It's a tax twist, and it can hurt. Based on Revenue Ruling 77–137,[3] many professionals believe that if a creditor secures a charging order against the partnership units and is entitled to receive all of the income distributed by the partnership, there is a high probability that the creditor will be taxed on its share of the partnership income as the owner of the units. If that income is retained in the partnership, the creditor may end up having to book phantom income for tax purposes. In effect, the charging order may become a poison pill for the creditor. If the creditor becomes a limited partner by having the charging order liquidated, there is little question that the income will be taxed to the creditor.

Once the limited partnership structure is in place, George and Betty can take other steps to strengthen their defense against a future judgment creditor. They can transfer units to their children, either outright or in trust. If the transfers are

---

3.  1977–1 C.B. 178.

timely made and properly structured, the transferred units will be completely beyond the reach of the creditors. If a creditor obtains a malpractice judgment against George, the creditor can only seek a charging order against partnership units owned by George, and cannot pursue the limited partnership units owned by the children. If George wants to add another layer of potential protection, he could consider the possibility of using a foreign trust to hold his limited partnership units or a trust established in a state with favorable asset protection laws. Although such a trust may provide another obstacle for the judgment creditor, it is far from bullet-proof, as discussed in the following section of this chapter.

**d.  The Freeze.** Sam and Joyce are both 65 years of age and looking forward to a long retirement. They have three children, and six grandchildren. Their estate is valued at approximately $25 million. A significant asset of their estate is an interest they hold in a bottling distribution partnership. They have owned this interest for about five years. This investment presently pays them an income of about $12,000 a month. They are looking forward to receiving this income for the rest of their lives.

They are concerned about estate taxes. They believe that their investment in the bottling distribution company will grow rapidly in value. It is postured to take off. Indeed, they anticipate that the value of the investment could increase eight to ten times over the next five to seven years. They are concerned that, as the value of the investment grows, their estate tax exposure will balloon. They want to take steps to reduce their estate tax exposure, without jeopardizing their current income stream.

The answer for Sam and Joyce may be a freeze family limited partnership. They would form a family limited partnership with an S corporation general partner, and then transfer their interest in the bottling distribution company to that partnership. That interest presently has a value of approximately $1.5 million. The partnership would issue two kinds of limited partnership units. The first would be limited partnership units ("Income Units") that allow the holders of the units to receive a fixed, guaranteed income from the partnership every year. This would be an ongoing, cumulative obligation of the partnership. The Income Units would be owned by Sam and Joyce, and would be structured to pay them a guaranteed income of 12,000 a month.

The remaining units would be growth limited partnership units ("Growth Units"). Unlike the Income Units, these units would not offer any guaranteed income rights. However, all appreciation in the value of the investment held by the partnership would be allocated to these units. Sam and Joyce would gift the Growth Units to their children.

This structure is called a "Freeze Limited Partnership" because it is designed to freeze the value of the investment in Sam and Joyce's estate, while at the same time preserving the income stream for them. All of the future growth in value is allocated to the children, who own the Growth Units. Congress attempted to forbid these types of estate freeze techniques in the Revenue Act of 1987 by adding former Section 2036(c) to the Code. Congress then reversed itself in 1990 by eliminating Section 2036(c) in the 1990 Revenue Reconciliation Act. It was replaced with Section 2701, which deals specifically with entity freezes. That section, among other things, requires that the interest retained by the transferor (Sam and Joyce in our case) must pay a fixed cumulative rate of return if that retained interest is to be given any value for gift tax purposes.[4] Plus, Section 2701 requires that the growth interest transferred to the children must have a value equal to at least 10 percent of the sum of all equity interests in the partnership owned by Sam and Joyce.[5] So in order for the freeze technique to work for Sam and Joyce in this situation, the partnership units that they retain must entitle them to receive a fixed, cumulative payment from the partnership. This is completely consistent with their desires to receive a steady retirement income from the partnership. Also, the professional who values the respective units must determine that the growth units transferred to the children have a value that meets the minimum 10 percent requirement.

The benefit of the family partnership freeze strategy is that it allows the parents to transfer future growth potential to the children, while at the same time retaining a fixed income yield for themselves. As is discussed in greater detail in Question 11 below, this strategy raises some important income and estate tax consequences that must be carefully evaluated and will only work in those limited situations where, as here, the expected appreciation in the partnership's assets is extraordinary.

**e. The Disappearing Act.** Rubin, age 75, is a widower with a $30 million estate that consists primarily of a large stock and bond portfolio, various real estate investments, investments in a handful of passive limited partnership ventures, and an expensive home. He has one son, Bruce, and three grandchildren. His health is marginal, but he knows of no life threatening condition. He is distressed over his estate tax exposure.

Rubin decides to "get aggressive." He forms a family limited partnership. A subchapter S corporation owned by his son, Bruce, is the sole general partner. Bruce separately funds the general partner, which owns one percent of the partnership. Rubin owns the remaining 99 percent of the partnership through limited partnership interests that are issued to him in exchange for all his assets except his home and $1.5 million of cash. Rubin estimates that the retained cash should cover his spending needs for the rest of his life. Bruce has complete control of the assets, and Rubin is relieved of all management burdens.

From a tax perspective, what Rubin hopes to accomplish with this technique is a substantial reduction in estate taxes at his death. As an owner of a limited partnership interest that provides no control and is subject to substantial marketability limitations, Rubin's estate would claim substantial lack of control and lack of marketability discounts in valuing the partnership interests. These discounts could total as much as 30 to 40 percent of the value of the underlying partnership assets attributable to the limited partnership units. Claiming these types of discounts to save big estate taxes when there has been a "circuitous recycling of value" often triggers a fight with the service. As discussed below,

---

4. I.R.C. § 2701(a)(3)(A) & (c)(3).
5. I.R.C. § 2701(a)(4)(A).

the limits for pushing this technique are being fought out in the courts.

## 3. BASIC PLANNING QUESTIONS

**Question No. 1: What is the difference between a general family partnership and a limited family partnership?**

The difference lies in who controls the assets and business of the partnership. A general partnership has only one class of partners: general partners. Each partner is allowed to participate in the management of the partnership and has personal liability for the debts and obligations of the partnership. The partnership exists by virtue of an agreement between the general partners.

A limited partnership is a very different creature. A certificate and limited partnership agreement is signed by the partners. The certificate is filed with the state. The agreement spells out the terms and conditions of the partnership. The agreement authorizes the issuance of general partnership units and limited partnership units. Those individuals who receive limited partnership units generally will have little or no say in the management or control in the partnership, but will also have no personal liability for the debts and obligations of the partnership. The general partners have the control and the liability of general partners. In most family situations, the limited partnership is the preferred form because it facilitates the separation of control and liability exposure.

**Question No. 2: How is a family partnership formed, operated and maintained?**

The partnership is formed through an agreement among the partners. The agreement should be in writing. As previously stated, if it is a limited partnership, a certificate must be filed with an official of the state in which the partnership is formed. Often the only parties to the initial agreement are the parents. As partnership units are transferred to other family members, those other family members, or trusts established for their benefit, become partners in the partnership.

The complexity of operating a family partnership is directly tied to the complexity of the assets held by the partnership. If the partnership holds real estate or other investment assets, the partnership's operations may be minimal. The assets should be titled in the name of the partnership; a separate partnership bank account should be maintained; and all partnership revenues and expenses should be transacted through that account. The partnership will be required to file a federal tax return each year on Form 1065, but will not be required to pay any taxes because the partnership will be treated as a complete pass-through entity. The individual partners will be provided Form K-1s that reflect their share of the partnership's annual income or loss. Many families operate their partnerships with a minimal amount of hassle and expense. However, the complexity and expense can rapidly escalate in those situations where the partnership owns operating businesses, employs family members, provides special allocation benefits to certain family members, or has other features that depart from a simple, straightforward investment partnership structure.

### Question No. 3: What types of provisions are typically included in the family partnership agreement?

The partnership agreement spells out the relationship between the partners. It should identify the partners and contain provisions that deal with all of the essential elements of the partnership. Above all, the agreement must carefully describe the non-tax reasons for the partnership, such as centralized management, enhanced investment opportunities and efficiencies, creditor protection benefits, asset pooling benefits, dispute mitigation benefits, business training benefits, continuity protections, institutionalized communication on family business matters, separate property status preservation (divorce protection), retention of business interests in the family, and the like. Care should be given to identifying and documenting the specific non-tax reasons for each situation. This "business reason" provision should not be stock boilerplate; it should be customized for each situation.

Beyond describing the non-tax reasons for the partnership, the agreement should include specific provisions dealing with the maintenance of capital accounts in the partnership; the requirement of partners to make additional contributions to the partnership; the scope of the business of the partnership; the basis upon which income and losses of the partnership will be allocated to the partners; the basis upon which cash will be distributed to the partners (which should be proportionate to partnership interests); procedures to be used in liquidating the partnership; the length of time that the partnership is going to exist (which should be coordinated with applicable state law to ensure that no limited partner has the unilateral right to withdraw); the management of the partnership, together with a succession structure (i.e., S corporation or trust as general partner) to ensure the partnership will continue and that no person has the unilateral right to dissolve the partnership; the fiduciary duties of the general partner; the handling of administrative affairs associated with the partnership; the basis upon which individual partners are to be compensated for services rendered to the partnership; reimbursement of partnership expenses; and buy-sell and transfer restrictions that apply to the partners.

The buy-sell and transfer provisions are extremely important. Most families want to structure their partnership to ensure that the partnership units will stay in the family. They also want to ensure that the control of the partnership will pass at the right time in an orderly fashion to family members who are designated to receive the general partnership units.

A family member will be deemed to be a partner for income tax purposes only if that individual is determined to be a "real partner", which requires that the transaction vest the family member with dominion and control over the partnership interest.[6] The IRS has established a number of guidelines for determining whether a particular family member is a "real partner."[7] All of the factors need to be weighed, and the test is not black and white. Usually there is

6. Reg. § 1.704–1(e)(1)(iii).
7. Reg. § 1.704–1(e)(2).

no serious problem, but care should be taken in structuring the agreement to ensure that each family member is deemed to be a "real partner". If the partnership agreement contains any one of a number of unusual features, this "real partner" requirement may become a problem and a red flag should surface. Following are brief descriptions of certain unusual provisions that should be avoided in drawing the partnership agreement:

(1) The partnership agreement should never state that there will be no cash distributions, or that a particular partner will not receive any cash distributions. Any family member who is precluded from participating in cash distributions may not be considered a real partner.[8] Generally, it is advisable to state in the partnership agreement that all cash in excess of the operating needs of the partnership will be distributed. If there is a need for the partnership to accumulate funds for a specific purpose, that need should be carefully documented from time to time.

(2) Generally, it is not advisable to preclude a general partner from participating in the management of the partnership. That individual may not be considered a "real partner."[9] The use of limited partnership units and general partnership units, in and of itself, will not create a problem.[10] For this reason, it is generally advisable to use the limited partnership format when there is a desire to preclude certain family members from participating in the management. It is not a good idea to use a general partnership structure, and then, by agreement, preclude certain general partners (the children) from participating in the operation of the partnership.

(3) A family partnership agreement should not contain severe buy-sell restrictions that prevent a partner from disposing of his or her interest in the partnership. Such provisions may preclude the partner from being considered a "real owner" for tax purposes.[11] The buy-sell provisions in the agreement may permit a partner to dispose of his or her interest in the partnership, but give other partners a first right to acquire such interest and other rights associated with the disposition of such interests. The key is to not be too strict in controlling the transfer of family partnership interests.

(4) It is never advisable to allow minors to directly own interests in the partnership. Minors usually do not have the legal capacity to protect themselves and may not be regarded as real partners for tax purposes.[12] A better alternative is to have the partnership interest of the minor held in a trust for the minor, held by a guardian, or held by a custodian under the applicable Uniform Transfer to Minors Act.

In structuring the family limited partnership agreement, the ideal situation is where the agreement is a collaborative effort among family members. In addition to promoting family understanding, harmony, and enthusiasm for the venture, it may help from a tax perspective by reducing any claims that a parent mandated

---

8. Reg. § 1.704–1(e)(2)(ii)(a).
9. Reg. § 1.704–1(e)(2)(ii)(d) & (ix).
10. Reg. § 1.704(e)(2)(ix).
11. Reg. § 1.704–1(e)(2)(ii)(c).
12. Reg. § 1.704–1(e)(2)(vii).

the terms as a "testamentary substitute."

### Question No. 4: What types of assets are best suited for a family partnership?

Clients often have flexibility in selecting assets to transfer to a family partnership. Following are a few key points to keep in mind in selecting the best assets in a given situation:

(1) Investments that generate income based on services rendered by a family member are never suitable candidates for a family partnership. As discussed below, the family partnership rule of Section 704(e) generally requires that capital, as distinguished from personal services or labor, must be a material income-producing factor in the partnership.[13] It would be futile, for example, for an individual to transfer all or a portion of his or her service income to a family partnership. In order for the partnership to shift the income, the income must be generated from capital, not personal services.

(2) The stock of an S corporation should not be transferred to a family partnership. A partnership is not a qualified shareholder of an S corporation.[14] Any such transfer to a partnership will destroy the S election for the corporation.

(3) Property that is expected to depreciate is not a good candidate for a family limited partnership. In most situations, transfer of partnership units to other family members will be sheltered from the gift tax through the use of the annual gift tax exclusion or through consumption of the parents' unified credits. If the property depreciates following the transfer, these gift transfer tax benefits will have been wasted, in whole or in part. Clearly, the preference is to transfer to the family partnership assets that are expected to appreciate in value.

(4) Usually, it is not advisable to transfer to a family partnership assets that are expected to generate income tax losses or write-offs for a period of time. In many situations, the parents will want to retain these assets in order to enjoy the write-offs.

(5) Great care should be taken in transferring to a partnership real estate and other assets that are subject to a mortgage or some other type of indebtedness. The transfer itself may trigger creditor's rights under a due on sale clause, or require some type of special consent from the lender.

### Question No. 5: Are there any limitations on the use of family partnerships to shift income to other family members?

Yes. Generally, when partnership units are transferred to another family member, the income allocated to those units flows to that other family member. But there is a potential trap whenever a family partnership is used to shift income among family members. The trap, found in Section 704(e) of the Code, can wipe out any income shifting advantage and require the parents to recognize all income of the partnership. Four requirements must be satisfied to avoid the trap.

The first is that capital, as distinguished from personal services, must be a

---

13. I.R.C. § 704(e)(1); Reg. § 1.704–1(e)(1)(iv).
14. I.R.C. § 1361(b)(1)(B).

material income-producing factor in the partnership. The capital can be in the form of tangible or intangible assets. Capital is not an income-producing factor when the partnership's income consists principally of fees, commissions, or other compensation for personal services. If the income is from investment assets or a business that requires substantial inventories or substantial investments in plant, machinery, or other equipment, this requirement usually will not be an issue.[15]

The second requirement is to make certain that the partnership is structured in such a way that each partner really owns his or her capital interest—has dominion and control over the interest. This is the "real partner" requirement previously discussed. A limited partnership structure itself will not cause a problem under this "real partner" requirement.[16] Make certain that none of the unusual provisions referenced in Question 3 are included in the partnership agreement.

The third requirement of the family partnership rule deals with whether the donors, usually the parents, are being adequately compensated for services that they render to the partnership. If, for example, a parent works for a business that is owned by the partnership, the parent must be adequately compensated for the services actually rendered by the parent.[17] If the parent is not fairly compensated, the trap kicks in to deny any allocation of the parent's service-related income to the children.

The fourth requirement is that the partnership agreement must not allocate to the donee partners (the children) an interest in the partnership's income that is greater than their respective interests in the partnership's capital.[18] This requirement prohibits the use of special allocations that have the effect of allocating disproportionately large income shares to the donee children. The partnership income allocated to any donee should be proportionate to the capital owned by the donee. Some advisors question whether this requirement precludes special allocations of deductions within a family partnerships agreement (e.g., depreciation deductions) that otherwise meet the requirements of 704(b) and that have the effect, directly or indirectly, of allocating a proportionately larger share of the partnership's income to the donee children. The safest and wisest approach is to assume that this requirement trumps any such special allocations.[19]

### Question No. 6: What are the creditor protection benefits of a family partnership?

These benefits were briefly illustrated in the "Lockup" case study. A family limited partnership, if properly structured and funded, can become a nuisance for judgment creditors. In most states, a judgment creditor is limited to obtaining a charging order against the partnership units and then petitioning to have the charging order "liquidated". The charging order gives the creditor the right to receive income from the partnership when and if the income is distributed. It does not give the creditor the right to control or gain access to the assets that are

---

15. Reg. § 1.704–1(e)(1)(iv).
16. Reg. § 1.704–1(e)(2)(ix).
17. I.R.C. § 704(e)(2).
18. I.R.C. § 704(e)(2).
19. See Reg. § 1.704–1(b)(1)(iii).

actually held by the partnership. The liquidation enables the creditor to become the owner of the limited partnership interest, but gives the creditor no access to the partnership property, no voting control or power, and no power to compel cash distributions. And the creditor may end up with some phantom taxable income. As the case study indicated, the nuisance factor of the limited partnership may be enhanced by transferring partnership units to other family members or to trusts established in select states or select foreign countries. A combination of steps can be taken to create a number of obstacles that may discourage any creditor.

### Question No. 7: Are valuation discount techniques available in valuing family partnership interests for transfer tax purposes?

Yes. In 1959, the Service issued Revenue Ruling 59–60,[20] which set forth guidelines to be used in valuing the stock of a closely held corporation. The ruling did not use a mathematical formula; it discussed factors that should be considered in arriving at a fair market value. It recognized that the size of the block of stock was a relevant valuation factor in a closely held corporation, specifically noting that a minority interest would be more difficult to sell. Years later in Revenue Ruling 68–609[21] the Service stated that the valuation principles of 59–60 also would apply to partnership interests.

The two most significant discounts associated with a minority interest in a closely held business enterprise are the minority interest (lack of control) discount and the lack of marketability discount. The minority interest discount recognizes that a willing buyer will not pay as much for a minority interest; there is no control. The lack of marketability discount reflects the reality that a willing buyer will pay less for an interest in a closely held business because there is no ready market of future buyers for the interest. Often, both discounts are applied in valuing the transferred interest[22] and total as much as 35 to 40 percent.[23] They can have a powerful impact in leveraging the use of annual gift tax exclusions and unified credits to transfer business interests to family members. In this regard (and this is real good news), there is no family attribution in applying the discounts.[24] The fact that all the business interests stay in the family will not eliminate or reduce the discounts.

A partner's rights in a partnership are governed by state law and the partnership agreement, both of which typically impose substantial transfer restrictions. However, as stated below, discounts for tax purposes should be based on state law restrictions, not restrictions in the agreement. Plus, care must be taken to ensure that the severity of the restrictions do not run afoul of the "real partner" requirement previously discussed. Usually, there is little difficulty striking a balance with reasonable transfer restrictions that work for the family

---

20. 1959–1 C.B. 237.

21. 1968–2 C.B. 327.

22. See, for example, Dailey v. Commissioner, 82 TCM 710 (2001); Janda v. Commissioner, 81 TCM 1100 (2001); Barnes v. Commissioner, 76 TCM 881 (1998).

23. Dailey v. Commissioner, 82 TCM 710 (2001); Janda v. Commissioner, 81 TCM 1100 (2001); Barnes v. Commissioner, 76 TCM 881 (1998).

24. Rev. Rule 93–12, 1993–1 CB 202; Mooneyham v. Commissioner, 61 TCM 2445 (1991); Ward v. Commissioner, 87 T.C. 78 (1986).

and stay clear of any "real partner" concerns.

In *Wandry v. Commissioner*, T.C. Memo 2012-88, the Tax Court upheld the taxpayer's use of a defined value formula clause in transferring limited partnership units to family members. The clause was designed to eliminate any gift tax liability if valuation changes were imposed by the IRS. In *Wandry*, the taxpayer used a fixed dollar amount to define the gift of limited partnership units and provided that the number of gifted units, not the value of the gift, would be adjusted for any valuation changes imposed by the IRS. Many now regard *Wandry* as a landmark case that opened the door to the use of such valuation formula clauses.

**Question No. 8: What rationale does the IRS use in challenging the tax benefits of a family partnership?**

Since the early 1990's, the IRS has used a variety of theories to attack the tax benefits of family limited partnerships. For simplistic purposes, the theories are lumped here into three categories.

The first category is the rejected theories. In the '90s, the Service issued a host of Technical Advice Memorandums that denied discounts on the theory that a family partnership was a sham transaction.[25] The theory was a loser in court, and the IRS threw in the towel on the theory when, after a string of losses, the tax court awarded attorneys fees to an estate that was forced to defend against the theory.[26] The Service also has unsuccessfully argued that Section 2703 (the Chapter 14 valuation provision for transfer restrictions) requires that partnership law restrictions should be disregarded in valuing transfers of property to limited partnerships and transfers of limited partnership interests.[27] Finally, the Service has futilely advanced a "gift on creation" argument, based on the theory that the excess of the value of the property contributed to a limited partnership over the discounted value of the partnership interest received in return constitutes a gift from the contributing partner to the other partners. This theory, like the other two, has gone nowhere in court.[28]

The second theory category is the traps. These have some substance, but can be easily avoided with some simple planning. They are traps for the uninformed. The first is the application of the valuation limitations of Section 2704(a) for lapsed voting or liquidation rights in the partnership agreement. The key is to ensure that no person has the unilateral right to dissolve the partnership, that the death of a general partner will not dissolve the partnership, and that distributions must be made in cash from the cash flow of the partnership (no in-kind distributions). The second is the application of the valuations limitations of section 2703 (the Chapter 14 valuation provision for transfer restrictions) to deny the valuation impact of restrictions in a partnership agreement to the extent that

---

25. Technical Advice Memoranda 9736004, 9735003, 9730004, 9725002.

26. Estate of Dailey v. Commissioner, T.C. Memo 2002–301. See also Estate of Thompson v. Commissioner, T.C. Memo 2002–246 and Knight v. Commissioner, 115 T.C. 506 (2000).

27. See Church v. United States, 85 A.F.T.R.2d 2000–804 (W.D. Texas 2000), affirmed 268 F.3d 1063 (5th Cir. 2001) and Estate of Strangi v. Commissioner, 115 T.C. 478 (2000), affirmed 293 F.3d 279 (5th Cir. 2002).

28. See Church v. United States, 85 A.F.T.R.2d 2000–804 (W.D. Texas 2000), affirmed 268 F.3d 1063 (5th Cir. 2001) and Estate of Strangi v. Commissioner, 115 T.C. 478 (2000), affirmed 293 F.3d 279 (5th Cir. 2002).

they exceed state law restrictions. To date, at least one district court has bought the theory.[29] What this means, as a practical matter, is that discount valuation appraisals should specifically identify discounts based solely on state law restrictions, which in most cases will do the job. Finally, if a partner makes an additional contribution to a family partnership and receives no additional partnership interests, the Service will argue (probably successfully) that the contribution is an indirect gift to the other partners.[30] The planning point is to ensure that additional partnership interests are issued to any partner who contributes property to the partnership.

The third category is the scary theories. These theories potentially have real teeth in select situations and, if sustained, can undermine the value of the entire effort. The first relates to the denial of the annual gift tax exclusion on the gift of family limited partnership interests. The second relates to the application of Section 2036(a) (the retained interest estate tax provision) to bring the value of the transferred partnership property back into the taxpayer's estate. These theories are discussed in the following questions.

### Question No. 9: Will the transfer of a family limited partnership interest qualify for the annual gift tax exclusion?

The gift tax annual exclusion is applicable only to transfers of a ***present*** interest.[31] The IRS has previously ruled that the transfer of a limited partnership interest would qualify as a gift of a present interest by virtue of the general partner's fiduciary duty to the limited partners and the limited partners right to sell or assign the interest.[32] In 1997, the Service denied the annual exclusion (and found no present interest) in a case where the partnership agreement gave the general partner unlimited discretion over distributions ("for any reason whatsoever") and effectively prohibited the limited partners from assigning their interests.[33]

This was followed in 2002 by *Hackl v. Commissioner*,[34] where the Tax Court and the Seventh Circuit held that no present interest was transferred on gifts to 41 donees where, among other things, the LLC would not produce any cash flow for many years and the donor, as the manager of the LLC, had control of all cash flow distributions, had the power to appoint his successor, had approval rights over any member's withdrawal, and had consent rights in his "absolute discretion" over any member interest sales. The court held that a transfer of an interest in a business entity did not automatically qualify as a present interest, stating that a present interest would exist only if the donee received "an unrestricted and noncontingent right to the immediate use, possession, or enjoyment" of the transferred property or income from the

---

29. Smith v. United States, 94 A.F.T.R.2d 2004–5627 (W.D. Pa. 2004).

30. Technical Advice Memorandum 200212006; Shepherd v. Commissioner, 115 T.C. 376 (2000), affirmed 283 F.3d 1258 (11th Cir. 2002).

31. I.R.C. § 2503(b).

32. Letter Ruling 9415007; Technical Advice Memorandum 9131006.

33. Technical Advice Memorandum 9751003.

34. 118 T.C. 279 (2002), affirmed 335 F.3d 664 (7th Cir. 2003). See also Price v. Commissioner, T.C. Memo 2010-2 where the Tax Court held that gifted limited partnership units did not represent present interests because they provided no immediate use, possession or enjoyment of the property.

property.[35] Unfortunately, neither the Tax Court nor the Seventh Circuit opinions clarify much for planning purposes. Surely, there is no requirement that the property be income-producing in order for the interest to qualify as a present interest if the donee has the power to sell the interest. And will the right to assign the interest suffice if the transferee has no right to become a substitute member or partner?

For planning purposes, what is clear is that, at a minimum, care should be exercised to spell out an objective standard for cash distributions, the general partner's fiduciary duty with respect to distributions, and the right of partners to transfer or assign their interests subject only to a right of first refusal. As an added precaution, some believe that a partner's transfer rights should include the absolute right of the purchaser to become a substitute partner or member. In those situations where no income will be generated for a period of time and there is no market for the interests (a common scenario), an added precaution would be to offer the donee a Crummey-type withdrawal right for a limited period of time after the gift to strengthen the present interest argument.[36] The entity would agree to buy back the interest for a limited period of time for its fair market value and would be authorized to borrow funds to finance any such purpose. All the normal Crummey procedures would be followed. It might make sense in select situations.

**Question No. 10: When will the donor of a family limited partnership interest be deemed to have retained a life interest in the partnership property?**

Section 2036(a) requires that a decedent's estate include any property transferred by the decedent during life if the decedent retains (1) the possession or enjoyment of the property or the income from the property or (2) the right (alone or in conjunction with others) to designate the persons who will enjoy the property. There is an exception that makes the provision inapplicable if the transfer is a bona fide sale for adequate and full consideration.[37] This provision is now the Service's most effective weapon against extreme family limited partnerships, and has provided the basis for a string of recent victories against "bad fact" family partnerships.[38] If it applies, the property transferred to the partnership is brought back into the decedent's estate for estate tax purposes. Any annual gift tax exclusions used in connection with gifts of limited partnership interests would have been wasted.

The starting point in the analysis is the exception. For it to apply so that 2036 is rendered moot, there must be a "bona fide sale" and "full consideration." In the context of a family limited partnership, the Tax Court and the circuit courts

---

35. 118 T.C. at 293.

36. N. Choate, Leimberg Estate Planning Newsletter (April 4, 2002).

37. I.R.C. § 2036(a).

38. Estate of Rosen v. Commissioner, T.C. Memo 2006–115, Rector Estate v. Commissioner, T.C. Memo 2007–367, Estate of Erickson v. Commissioner, T.C. Memo 2007–107, Estate of Bigelow v. Commissioner, 503 F.3d 955 (9th Cir. 2007); Strangi v. Commissioner, 417 F.3d 468 (5th Cir. 2005); Estate of Hillgren v. Commissioner, T.C. Memo 2004–46; Kimbell v. United States, 371 F.3d 257 (5th Cir. 2004); Estate of Thompson v. Commissioner, 382 F.3d 367 (3d Cir. 2004); Estate of Bongard v. Commissioner, 124 T.C. No. 8 (2005); Estate of Jorgenson, T.C. Memo 2009-66; Estate of Malkin, T.C. Memo 2009-212; Lockett Estate v. Commissioner, T.C. Memo 2012-123.

that have addressed the issue have held that the "bona fide sale" condition will exist if, as an objective matter, the transfer of property to the partnership serves a "substantial business or other non-tax purpose."[39] Subjective intentions of the parties won't suffice. Nor will non-tax purposes that are factually implausible or not supported by objective evidence. It's a factual issue that ultimately turns on whether the partnership has a bona business purpose or is just a vehicle to recycle the taxpayer's wealth in hopes of securing big tax discounts. Negative factors include the taxpayer's ongoing financial dependence on income from the partnership's property, the transfer of substantially all the decedent's assets to the partnership, the commingling of personal and business assets, the failure to observe partnership formalities, the failure of the partnership to conduct any business activities, the transfer of only passive investments to the partnership, and the lack of any business rationale to support a plausible hypothesis that the partnership's operations will produce an economic benefit at least as great as the claimed value loss triggered by the contributions to the partnership.[40]

If the "bona fide sale" condition is satisfied, the "full consideration" condition will usually be met if all formalities are respected and, in exchange for the property transfer to partnership, the taxpayer receives a proportional interest in the partnership.[41] Thus, as a practical matter, the presence of a legitimate non-tax business purpose is the key to both requirements. If both requirements are satisfied, the transfer of property to the partnership should not trigger the application of Section 2036.

If the exception does not apply, the issue becomes whether the taxpayer retained a "substantial economic benefit" from the property within the meaning of 2036(a)(1). This requires an express or implied agreement that the taxpayer will retain possession or enjoyment of the property transferred to the partnership.[42] It too is a factual issue that usually turns on whether the evidence supports the existence of an implied understanding or assurance that the partnership assets would remain available to meet the personal needs of the taxpayer. Negative facts, for example, include partnership distributions to pay personal expenses, the taxpayer's free use of partnership property (e.g., a residence), the taxpayer's inability to support himself or herself after transfers to the partnership, the commingling of personal and partnership assets, the failure to maintain partnership capital accounts or observe other formalities, the absence or waiver of fiduciary duties relating to partnership distributions, partnership decisions based on the personal needs of the taxpayer, the taxpayer's right to change a general power who is not subject to fiduciary duties, the taxpayer's

---

39. Strangi v. Commissioner, 417 F.3d 468 (5th Cir. 2005); Kimbell v. United States, 371 F.3d 257 (5th Cir. 2004); Estate of Bongard v. Commissioner, 124 T.C. No. 8 (2005). Estate of Rosen v. Commissioner, T.C. Memo 2006–115.

40. Strangi v. Commissioner, 417 F.3d 468 (5th Cir. 2005); Kimbell v. United States, 371 F.3d 257 (5th Cir. 2004); Estate of Bongard v. Commissioner, 124 T.C. No. 8 (2005); Estate of Thompson v. Commissioner, T.C. Memo 2002–246, affirmed 382 F.3d 367 (3rd Cir. 2004); Estate of Harper v. Commissioner, T.C. Memo 2000–202; Estate of Rosen v. Commissioner, T.C. Memo 2006–115, Rector Estate v. Commissioner, T.C. Memo 2007–367, Estate of Erickson v. Commissioner, T.C. Memo 2007–109.

41. Strangi v. Commissioner, 417 F.3d 468 (5th Cir. 2005); Kimbell v. United States, 371 F.3d 257 (5th Cir. 2004).

42. Reg. § 20.2036–1(a); United States v. Byrum, 408 U.S. 125 (1972); Estate of Bigelow v. Commissioner, 503 F.3d 955 (9th Cir. 2007); Estate of Rosen v. Commissioner, T.C. Memo 2006–115; Strangi v. Commissioner, 417 F.3d 468 (5th Cir. 2005).

power to liquidate the partnership, the taxpayer's power to control the income flow to the partnership, the use of partnership property to secure debts of the taxpayer, disproportionate distributions to the taxpayer, and payment of excessive management fees to the taxpayer.[43] The bottom line is that the taxpayer must be in a position to show that the partnership operates as a business in accordance with sound business practices and not as a personal tool of the taxpayer.

Even if the taxpayer is not deemed to have retained a substantial economic benefit, there may still be a problem under 2036 if the taxpayer is deemed to have retained the right to designate the persons who would enjoy the property within the meaning of Section 2036(a)(2). The application of this provision to family limited partnerships is unclear, at best. The few cases that have considered the issue involved extreme facts where the taxpayer had broad discretion to distribute income, free of any fiduciary restrains, or broad powers to replace general partners or liquidate the partnership.[44] Nevertheless, some of the dicta in these cases suggest that this provision could prove troublesome even in more vanilla scenarios where the taxpayer owns a substantial interest in the general partner. Some (including this author) do not believe that the provision should apply in such situations so long as there is an object standard for making distributions, the taxpayer is subject to normal general partner fiduciary duties, and the taxpayer possesses no special rights to liquidate the partnership or access partnership assets. Additional precautions may include vesting distribution decisions in a general partner who is not the taxpayer or having the taxpayer own no interest in the general partner.[45]

The uncertainty associated with Section 2036(a)(2) is particularly disturbing in those common scenarios where limited partnership interests are gifted. Such gifts will never fall within the "bona fide sale" exception, but generally should not present a retained economic benefit problem under Section 2036(a)(1) if there is no evidence suggesting that the taxpayer retained any right to enjoy the transferred partnership interest or the partnership assets attributable to the interest. Whether the right "to designate" prohibition can be extended to snare common, non-abusive uses of the family limited partnership is yet to be determined. The Supreme Court's interpretation of the provision's application to trusts in the famed case of *United States v. Byrum*,[46] coupled with the fact that the issue only has surfaced in factually difficult family partnership cases that have raised all the 2036 issues, suggest that the provision should not be applied in such a broad fashion.

---

43. Strangi v. Commissioner, 417 F.3d 468 (5th Cir. 2005); Estate of Hillgren v. Commissioner, T.C. Memo 2004–46; Kimbell v. United States, 371 F.3d 257 (5th Cir. 2004); Estate of Thompson v. Commissioner, 382 F.3d 367 (3rd Cir. 2004); Estate of Bigelow v. Commissioner, 503 F.3d 955 (9th Cir. 2007); Estate of Rosen v. Commissioner, T.C. Memo 2006–115; Estate of Bongard v. Commissioner, 124 T.C. No. 8 (2005).

44. Strangi v. Commissioner, T.C. Memo 2003–145, affirmed on other grounds 417 F.3d 468 (5th Cir. 2005); Kimbell v. United States, 244 F.Supp.2d 700 (N.D. Tex. 2003), reversed on other grounds 371 F.3d 257 (5th Cir. 2004).

45. See generally Gans & Blattmachr, Strangi: A Critical Analysis and Planning Suggestions, Tax Notes 1153 (Sept. 1, 2003) and Jensen, The Magic of Disappearing Wealth Revisited: Using Family Limited Partnerships to Reduce Estate and Gift Taxes, 1 Pitts. Tax Rev. 155 (2004).

46. 408 U.S. 125 (1972).

**Question  No.  11:  How  difficult  is  it  to  make  a  family  partnership  "freeze"  structure  work?**

The value of a family partnership freeze transaction was illustrated by the fourth mini-case study entitled "The Freeze." Great care should be exercised by anyone who is considering a family partnership freeze transaction. The 2701 limitations are an insurmountable barrier in most situations.  In order for the interest retained by the parents to have any value for gift tax purposes (and thus reduce the value of the interests transferred to the children), the parents must be entitled to receive a fixed, cumulative income interest that is the equivalent of a cumulative preferred stock interest.[47] In many cases, the required yield to be paid to the parents will exceed the anticipated increase of the value of the asset.  In such a situation, the freeze transaction will be of no value. For this reason, the freeze strategy is best used in those situations, such as the one described above, where there is a real expectation of huge future appreciation that will balloon an existing significant estate tax exposure.  It is important to realize that if the income interest of the parents is not properly structured, any transfer of an interest to the children may trigger an enormous gift tax. Great care needs to be taken in structuring the parents' income interest and valuing the interest transferred to the children.

The bottom line is that the demise of Section 2036(c) in 1990 opened the door for considering partnership freeze transactions once again, but the opening is very small.  There are still uncertainties, but the possibility of structuring an effective transaction in a given situation clearly exists. Great care must be taken to comply with the intricacies of the valuation rules of Section 2701.

**Question  No.  12:  How  does  the  partnership  structure  compare  to  a  C  corporation,  an  S  corporation,  and  a  limited  liability  company  in  accomplishing  specific  estate  planning  objectives?**

Corporate entities have disadvantages that often result in a family partnership or LLC being a preferred vehicle to use in accomplishing specific objectives.  The biggest drawback of the C corporation is that it is a tax paying entity, and there is an ongoing threat of double taxes. The income is taxed to the corporation, regardless of the identity of the shareholders. The only way to shift income to the children as shareholders in a C corporation is to pay dividends. That creates a double tax, and eliminates the advantage of trying to shift the income. Plus, the appreciation in the value of assets owned by the C corporation ultimately will be taxed twice if those assets are ever sold by the corporation or otherwise liquidated.  These problems have effectively eliminated the C corporation as an effective planning tool for many families.

The S corporation also has its limitations. Many trusts cannot be shareholders of an S corporation.[48] Also, S corporations cannot have different classes of stock that recognize different income and appreciation benefits. Finally, the S corporation does not provide the same creditor protection benefits of a partnership structure.

---

47.  I.R.C. § 2701(c)(3).
48.  See the related discussion in Chapter 3.

The limited liability company is a hybrid of the S corporation and the partnership. It has the advantages of both, and few of the disadvantages. The limited liability company, in nearly all situations, can offer planning benefits that equal and potentially exceed those of the family partnership structure. On the upside, it is clear that the limited liability company may eliminate any personal liability exposure for the managers. On the downside, it is unclear in some states whether the limited liability company can offer the same asset protection benefits of a limited partnership structure.

## D. ASSET PROTECTION PLANNING

### Excerpts From
### "Asset Protection: Trust Planning"[49]

Duncan E. Osborne, Mark E. Osborne
Osborne, Helman, Knebel & Deleery, L.L.P.

## I. Introduction

There is increasing demand from wealthy clients for asset protection planning advice. Many such individuals sense a risk of serious economic threats and liabilities no matter what professional, business, or personal activities they undertake. They genuinely believe that the plaintiff's bar can make a case and generate liability under even the most absurd and unlikely sets of facts, and they consider our legal system to be capricious, unpredictable, and unlikely to render a fair result. Running parallel with this cynicism toward the court system is a similar skepticism with respect to legislative and regulatory bodies. Because of laws like the Comprehensive Environmental Response, Compensation, and Liability Act ("CERCLA"),[50] the Sarbanes-Oxley Act of 2002,[51] and the Bankruptcy Abuse Prevention and Consumer Protection Act of 2005 (the "BAPCPA"), business men and women have become increasingly wary of the government's propensity to pass new legislation with potential liability consequences of dire and immediate impact.

Over the past decade, commentators have begun to raise the issue that a lawyer engaged in estate planning may have a duty to his clients to advise them about asset protection planning in addition to more traditional trust, estate, and tax planning advice. Whether or not such a duty exists, prudence suggests that estate planning attorneys be fully informed and able to address asset protection issues with their clients.[52]

---

49. Copyright (c) 2010 The American Law Institute and Duncan E. Osborne and Mark E. Osborne. The materials in this outline derive in part from Asset Protection: Domestic and International Law and Tactics, a four-volume treatise published by Clark Boardman Callaghan in 1995. Duncan E. Osborne and Elizabeth M. Schurig are co-authors and co-editors of the treatise. For information, call West Group Corporation at 1-800-221-9428.

50. 42 U.S.C. § 9601.

51. Sarbanes-Oxley Act of 2002, 15 U.S.C. §§ 7201 et seq. (2003).

52. See Peter Spero, Search and Rescue Missions, A.B.A. J., Oct. 1999 at 70; Samuel L. Braunstein and Carol F. Burger, Protecting the Wealth, A.B.A. J., Nov. 1999 at 58; Mario A. Mata, International Trusts and Related Wealth Preservation Strategies, in Texas Bar CLE: Advanced Estate Planning and Probate 2003, tab 26, available at http://www.texasbarcle.com; Ritchie W. Taylor, Note, Domestic Asset Protection Trusts: The "Estate Planning Tool of the Decade" or a Charlatan?, 13 BYU J. Pub. L. 163 (1998); Santo Bisignano, Jr. &

## II. Asset Protection Planning And Fraudulent Transfers

### A. The Client's Right to Asset Protection Planning

The debate between advocates of creditors' rights and advocates of asset protection is now, and long has been, a vigorous one. Articles on both sides of the debate from practicing lawyers are numerous and informative. Until recently, however, [53] most of the articles written by law professors on this topic were "Johnny-one-note" choruses of criticism of asset protection planning (almost polemical in some cases) punctuated with titles ringing of indictment, such as: "Putting a Stop to 'Asset Protection' Trusts," [54] "Domestic Asset Protection Trusts: Pallbearers to Liability?," [55] "Asset Protection Trusts: Trust Law's Race to the Bottom?," [56] and "Offshore Asset Protection Trusts: Testing the Limits of Judicial Tolerance in Estate Planning."[57]

While proclamations from the ivory tower have occasional value for the practitioner, it is far too easy for a legal purist peering down from high aloft to focus on a few instances of flagrant abuse by asset protection planners and their clients, such as the Anderson [58] and Lawrence [59] cases, stake out a position of moral outrage, and then universally condemn anyone who dares to engage in asset protection planning. Although perhaps satisfying to the author's sensibilities and finely-honed sense of moral rectitude after years in the academic community, such a reaction is simplistic, unhelpful, and unsupportable after even a cursory look at the law, the asset planning abuse protections already well established in the law (i.e., fraudulent transfer prohibitions and sanctions), and the equally well recognized legitimate nature and function of estate and asset planning activities (e.g., wills, trusts, homesteads, life insurance, annuities, retirement plans, family limited partnerships, tenancies by the entirety, and on and on and on...). [60]

Almost all estate planning lawyers, almost all of the time, represent honorable, law abiding clients, men and women who daily contribute to society by their productivity and with their generosity, who pay their bills and their

---

Toby M. Eisenberg, Asset Protection Without a Passport, in Texas Bar CLE: Advanced Estate Planning and Probate 2003, tab 25, available at http:// www.texasbarcle.com; Duncan E. Osborne & Jack E. Owen, Jr., Asset Protection Planning: The Estate Planner's Duty, Pers. Fin. Plan. Monthly, March 2003, at 11.

53. Robert T. Danforth, Rethinking the Law of Creditors' Rights in Trusts, 53 Hastings L. J. 287, 289 (2002)

54. Randall J. Gingiss, Putting a Stop to "Asset Protection" Trusts, 51 Baylor L. Rev. 987 (1999)

55. Henry J. Lisher, Jr., Domestic Asset Protection Trusts, Pall Bearers to Liability?, 35 Real Prop. Prob. & Tr. J. 479 (2000)

56. Stewart E. Sterk, Asset Protection Trusts: Trust Law's Race to the Bottom, 85 Cornell L. Rev. 1035 (2000)

57. David C. Lee, Offshore Asset Protection Trusts: Testing the Limits of Judicial Tolerance in Estate Planning, 15 Bankr. Dev. J. 451 (1999), see also Karen E. Boxx, Gray's Ghost — A Conversation About the Onshore Trust, 85 Iowa L. Rev. 1195 (2000)

58. Federal Trade Commission v. Affordable Media, L.L.C., 179 F.3d 1228 (9th Cir. 1999) (this case is usually referred to as "the Anderson case" in asset protection circles).

59. See Lawrence v. Goldberg, 573 F.3d 1265 (11th Cir. 2009); Lawrence v. United States Bankr. Court, 153 Fed. App'x 552 (11th Cir. 2005); In re Lawrence, 279 F.3d 1294 (11th Cir. 2002); In re Lawrence, 251 B.R. 630 (11th Cir. 2000); In re Lawrence, 244 B.R. 868 (Bankr. S.D. Fla. 2000); In re Lawrence, 238 B.R. 498 (Bankr. S.D. Fla. 1999); In re Lawrence, 227 B.R. 907 (Bankr. S.D. Fla. 1998); In re Lawrence, 217 B.R. 658 (Bankr. S.D. Fla. 1998); but see Petition for a Writ of Certiorari at 3, Lawrence v. Goldberg, 573 F.3d 1265 (2009). This civil contempt case has been litigated for the better part of ten years.

60. As early as 1890, the U.S. Supreme Court endorsed the notion of legitimate asset protection planning. Schreyer v. Scott, 134 U.S. 405 (1890)...

taxes, and who are not deadbeats, cheats, frauds, or criminals. These same good people, some of whom have acquired significant wealth by their own hard work or that of their forebears, are legitimately concerned about the excesses of an American litigation system which sometimes more resembles a lottery-like payoff game than it does a reliable forum for the settlement of genuine claims. These clients of integrity, the persons who make up the vast majority of the clients with whom ethical attorneys deal every day, are both willing and eager to plan and act within the time-honored and well established rules of estate planning and asset protection planning. Such clients have the right to conduct estate and asset protection planning, and, as some have argued, we attorneys have a duty to assist them in this endeavor. [61]

Let's be clear on this notion of duty. Even if some estate planning attorneys resist the idea, you can be assured the plaintiffs' bar will not. The next wave of creative malpractice actions could well be against estate planning attorneys who fail to advise clients about asset protection alternatives, filed by clients who have suffered financial reverses which could have been avoided with such planning. The estate planner's defense would be, of course, that "I do not do asset protection planning. I was engaged for estate planning purposes." And any semi-competent plaintiff's lawyer would have a field day with that response. Make no mistake about it; estate planning is about asset protection. Indeed, what are we estate planners about if not the preservation of wealth? Is the tax collector's grasp the only one we are charged to avoid by all legitimate means for our clients? The creditor's lawyer and the divorce lawyer can be every bit as much a predator as the tax collector. To ignore legitimate asset protection planning alternatives (including the asset protection trust) is to court disaster, for both your client and yourself... [62]

## B. Fraudulent Transfers

Asset protection planning is like tax planning, and all estate planning lawyers do tax planning. To do tax planning properly and legally, it must be done within the rules set forth in the tax code and tax regulations. In asset protection planning, the parallel rules are, in essence, the laws of fraudulent transfer.[63]

**1. General Principle.**[64]    The statutory law regarding fraudulent transfers derives from the Statute of Elizabeth enacted in the year 1570. Most notably, this

---

61. Howard D. Rosen & Gideon Rothschild, Asset Protection Planning, 810-2nd Tax Management Portfolios (2002); Peter Spero, Search and Rescue Missions, A.B.A. J. Oct. 1999, at 70; Dennis M. Sandoval, Judicial Foreclosures and Constitutional Challenges: What Every Estate Planning Attorney Needs to Know, Financial and Estate Planning, at ¶ 32,491 (2002).

62. See generally, Gunn v. Mahoney, 408 N.Y.S. 2d 896 (1978); In re Swift, 123 F.3d 792 (5th Cir. 1997).

63. The following series of articles by Neal L. Wolf is helpful in this regard: Understanding the Uniform Fraudulent Conveyance Act and Its Application in Creditor Attacks, J. Asset Prot., Sept./Oct. 1995, at 38; Fraudulent Conveyance Law as Contained in the U.S. Bankruptcy Code, J. Asset Prot., July/Aug. 1996; at 25; and The Right of 'Future Creditors' Successfully to Maintain Actions Under the Fraudulent Conveyance Statutes, J. Asset Prot., May/June 1997, at 52. If an individual makes a gratuitous transfer and later is subject to the fraudulent transfer rules of the United States Bankruptcy Code, the transfer may be invalidated, or set aside, if the transfer was made within two (2) years of the date that the bankruptcy petition was filed if either constructive or actual fraud is proved. 11 U.S.C. § 548 (Supp. 1990). As a practical matter, if the assets were transferred to a vehicle that is beyond the reach of the bankruptcy trustee (such as an offshore trust) and the judicial set aside is ineffective, the debtor is likely to be denied his discharge in bankruptcy...

64. Duncan E. Osborne, Advanced Practical Asset Protection Planning — Here, There or Everywhere? A Case Study, Address Before the Spring A.B.A. Meeting, (April 25, 2002) (transcript available from the author).

law declares "utterly void" conveyances, alienations, etc. designed to "delay, hinder, or defraud creditors."[65] The Statute of Elizabeth is the historical model for modern fraudulent transfer statutes. At its heart, the Statute of Elizabeth is a legal remedy.

The general principle upon which the remedy (i.e., fraudulent transfer law) rests is that if a court determines that an asset transfer is fraudulent, a creditor can set aside the transfer. The fraud can be actual or constructive, and the law protects both existing and future creditors.[66] While statutes provide the general legal framework, case law usually supplies guidance in the determination of whether a transfer was made sufficiently in advance of the ripening of a creditor obligation so as not to be deemed fraudulent, but rather be considered prudent and permitted planning.

**2. Types of Creditors.** At the risk of oversimplification, there are three categories of creditors one must consider when planning asset protection strategies.

**(a) Present Creditor.** A present creditor is one against whom a tort was committed, or with whom a debt was contracted, by the client prior to the asset transfer in question.[67] Credit card debt is an obvious example. Although intent to defraud always renders a transfer fraudulent, such intent need not be proved by a present creditor seeking to set aside a transfer. Rather, a transfer is fraudulent as to a present creditor if, regardless of the transferor's intent, the transfer renders the transferor insolvent.

**(b) Potential Subsequent Creditor.** A potential subsequent creditor is a creditor whom a client could reasonably expect to face, i.e., a reasonably foreseeable claimant. In this category, the obligation arises after the asset transfer, and so the law is, by definition, protecting a future creditor. However, the event giving rise to the obligation may occur before the asset transfer. For example, in the tort context, one person may injure another, then transfer assets, and subsequently become a debtor of the injured party through a court judgment. In these circumstances, the transferor's intent (whether actual or constructive) becomes critical. That is, a creditor whose claim arises after the transfer generally must show that the transferor intended to keep assets out of the creditor's reach. Because intent may be difficult to prove, "badges of fraud" have been identified and articulated as evidence of intent.

"Badges of fraud" are fact patterns that frequently accompany fraudulent transfers. Generally, no single badge of fraud is conclusive in and of itself, but more than one badge of fraud, considered together, may lead to an inference of fraud. Commonly recognized badges of fraud include the following: [68]

(i) The debtor retained possession or control of the transferred property after the transfer.

---

65. 13 Eliz. Ch.5 (1570).

66. See, e.g., United States v. Chapman, 756 F.2d 1237, 1240 (5th Cir. 1985)

67. Barry S. Engel, When is a Subsequent Creditor Not a Subsequent Creditor?, 3 J. Int'l Tr. & Corp. Plan. 105, 106(1994).

68. See Unif. Fraudulent Transfer Act § 4(b) & cmt. (1), 7A ULA 639, 653 (1984) for a comprehensive list of the most common badges of fraud cited by the courts.

(ii) The debtor transferred substantially all of his or her assets.

(iii) The transfer occurred shortly before or shortly after a substantial debt was incurred.

(iv) Before the transfer was made or obligation was incurred, the debtor was sued or threatened with suit.

**(c) Unknown Future Creditor.** An unknown future creditor is a creditor whom a client cannot reasonably foresee; for example, a party injured by the client in an auto accident at some future date, and for which accident the client is found liable. The courts have typically focused on protecting only those creditors whose claims are proximate in time to the asset transfer. Unknown future creditors removed in years and in events from the asset transfer have generally not been protected by the courts... [69]

## III. Domestic Strategies[70]

### A. Introduction: Multiple-Entity Planning

**1. Definition.** To help clients protect their wealth from potential creditor claims and possible future judgments, sophisticated attorneys engage in "multiple-entity" planning through the use of limited partnerships, corporations, various trust arrangements, foundations, retirement plans, life insurance and the like which, while perhaps originally conceived for the purpose of tax planning or wealth transfer, have the additional benefit of asset protection.

**2. Theory.** "Multiple-entity" planning dictates that wealth should be segregated and placed in isolated, sheltered legal compartments.

**3. Methods.** Opportunities for asset protection planning abound in domestic legal vehicles such as corporations, limited partnerships, limited liability companies, limited liability partnerships, trusts, retirement plans, life insurance, annuities, homesteads, spousal arrangements, inheritances, and foundations. Permutations and combinations of these entities and variations of the law between jurisdictions offer even more opportunities. For example, passive assets can be segregated from those with liability exposure (e.g., marketable securities can be segregated from an apartment complex); certain entities may be separated into multiple entities in order to achieve superior asset protection (e.g., two limited partnerships can be created to hold two pieces of real estate, each of which has an inherent risk or liability); limited partnerships can be deployed in conjunction with trusts; and corporations or limited partnerships can be formed in hospitable jurisdictions such as Delaware and Nevada.

**4. Laws Of The States.** The laws of the fifty United States vary markedly in what they offer by way of creditor protection.[71]   Recent attention has focused on

---

69. But see United States v. Townley, 77 A.F.T.R.2d (RIA) 2484 (9th Cir. 2006). In Townley, the defendants' repeated admission that they transferred property to avoid potential future creditors provided direct evidence of fraud on the IRS. The Townley case was contrary to most other cases dealing with unknown future creditors, but it may nonetheless be the law in Washington. See Gideon Rothschild and Daniel S. Rubin, Ninth Circuit Treads on an Established Right, Trusts. & Estates. (Nov. 1, 2006).

70. While effective utilization of federal bankruptcy law quite correctly can be considered a domestic asset protection "strategy," this outline focuses on preventive rather than remedial measures.

71. A state-by-state discussion of asset protection statutes can be found in Osborne & Schurig, supra note

Alaska and Delaware, and, to a lesser extent, Nevada, Utah, Rhode Island, Oklahoma, South Dakota, Missouri, Tennessee, Wyoming, and New Hampshire, which now have statutes that purport to protect self-settled discretionary trusts from creditor attack...[72]    The Bankruptcy Abuse Prevention and Consumer Protection Act of 2005 (the "BAPCPA") may have the effect of making it more difficult for debtors in bankruptcy to take advantage of a given state's protections simply by moving before filing for bankruptcy...[73]

**5. Marital Property Planning.** Planning for appropriate ownership of marital property can have important asset protection benefits. Of course, any marital property planning that has as its goal asset protection will have far-reaching implications to each spouse. It will alter the spouses' rights with respect to their property, including the spouses' rights to property in the event of divorce, and the division of property on death. Changing community property into separate property will allow only one-half of the property to receive a step up in basis at one spouse's death (whereby the basis of the property for capital gain purposes is deemed to be its value on the date of death, rather than the purchase price), whereas under current law, all of the community property will receive a step up in basis at one spouse's death. Due to these wide-ranging implications, it is preferable for each spouse to have separate legal counsel in marital property planning situations.

**a. Books and Records.** The most important step in any marital property planning is that the parties keep good books and records concerning the ownership of their property. The danger is that the different types of property unintentionally may become mixed together and lose any asset protection benefits that may be available. If only one spouse is to be liable for a specific debt, the spouses should take care in their representations to any potential lender that they do not lead the lender to believe that the other spouse's property may be available to satisfy the debt.

**b. Marital Property Agreements.** Spouses generally can change the nature of their marital property through premarital agreements or marital property agreements.[74]    These agreements can directly affect what property will be available to satisfy a creditor's claims by changing the ownership of the property. Sometimes the purpose behind these arrangements is to allocate all of the property to the spouse with the least creditor exposure. In other cases, the goal may be simply to divide the property equally, so that only half will be subject to the claims of the creditors of one spouse.

**c. Gifts Between Spouses.** Another way to accomplish the allocation of property to one spouse is for the spouses to make gifts to each other. A marital

---

49.

72. Some commentators have proposed that Colorado be included in this list of jurisdictions, citing Section 38-10-111 of the Colorado Revised Statutes. However, the judiciary has been inconsistent in its application of this statute to claims of creditors against self-settled trusts...

73. See Duncan E. Osborne, Joseph D. Martinec & Michael W. Johnson, Asset Protection Planning After the Bankruptcy Act, 68 Tex. Bar J. 1006 (2005).

74. For further reading, see Alexander A. Bove, Jr. & Melissa Langa, Using Spousal Agreements for Asset Protection — A New Tool for the Adviser, excerpted from Alexander A. Bove, Jr. & Melissa Langa, Use Spousals Agreements for Asset Protection, Tr. & Est. June, 2009.

property agreement specifying that the gift has taken place and addressing the future income from the gifted property may or may not be done in conjunction with such a gift. Any such gifts between persons contemplating marriage should be done after marriage, so that the marital deduction will be available and the gift will not be subject to gift tax.

Achieving asset protection by shifting the ownership of assets between spouses involves a determination as to which spouse is the most likely to be subject to creditors' claims, which is always a gamble with varying degrees of risk (depending mostly on the parties' professions). However, when that shifting is done by means of gifts, the spouse making the gift can create a trust for the benefit of the other spouse, thereby shielding the assets from the claims of both spouses' creditors.[75] The use of trusts also allows the gifting spouse to retain some control over the ultimate disposition and management of the assets.

**d. Tenancies by the Entirety.** In states where ownership of property as tenants by the entireties is possible it may provide significant asset protection benefits. This form of joint property ownership, available only between married persons, generally protects property from the claims of one spouse's creditors. When one spouse dies, the other takes the property free of the first spouse's debts. However, this protection is available only so long as the parties are married. Once the property is wholly owned by one spouse, the property may be reached by that spouse's creditors. Similarly, if the property is converted into some other form of joint ownership, each spouse's portion will be subject to his or her debts.

## B. Business Arrangements—Generally

**1. Liability Associated With Specific Activities.** Individuals are often engaged in activities that have inherent liability risk, such as the ownership of real property. By placing the activities that generate these risks into a limited liability vehicle, such as a corporation, a limited liability company, or a limited partnership, the client can insulate, to some degree, the rest of his wealth from liabilities associated with the activity. The choice of the specific entity will depend on an analysis of the complexity of administration of each business structure, the exposure of the activity and the entity to state taxes, and the client's estate planning goals with respect to the property. The shareholders of a corporation and the members of a limited liability company are not liable beyond their investments for claims arising out of the activities of the entity. Limited partners in a limited partnership have a status similar to that of shareholders in that regard. However, a limited partnership must have a general partner whose liability is not limited in this respect. Therefore, if this type of asset protection is desired, the general partner should not be an individual, but a limited liability company or corporation.

**2. Other Threats to Wealth.** Contribution of assets to family-owned

---

75. Of course, care should be given not to run afoul of the "reciprocal trust" doctrine. Reciprocal trusts are created when two settlers create identical or similar trusts for the benefit of the other, and each settlor is deemed to be the settlor of the trust created for his or her benefit. Although the doctrine is most often applied in the tax arena, it is also applicable in the context of asset protection. See Sec. Trust Co. v. Sharp, 77 A.2d 543 (Del. C. Chanc. 1950).

business entities may also provide some protection from an owner's general creditors. Creditors of an individual owner of an interest in a business entity generally have access only to that interest, not the assets of the entity. Any interest in a family-owned business entity will be subject to the claims of the creditors of the owner of that interest to some degree. However, ownership of such an interest may not be appealing to a creditor, which may be a factor influencing settlement of a case. There are two key reasons that such ownership may be unappealing. First, it may be a minority interest that gives the creditor little or no control over the manner in which the business is run. In addition, it may not be marketable, either due to transfer restrictions or simply because no buyers are willing to buy the interest. These are, of course, the same features that depress the value of interests in these entities for federal estate and gift tax purposes. The key feature of both of these "discounts" in value for interests in a business entity is ownership by multiple parties. In general, the more control an individual party has over the business entity, the more exposed the entity is to the claims of the individual's creditors.

**a. Corporations.** Corporations are probably the least effective of business entities in this regard. If a creditor seizes shares of a corporation, the creditor may exercise all of the rights of a shareholder. These rights may not be significant to the creditor if he or she has a small minority interest. If there are multiple owners of a corporation, some protection may still be available if the seizure triggers a buy-sell agreement that has been previously negotiated.

**b. Limited Liability Companies.** Limited liability companies, on the other hand, have significant asset protection features. These features vary on a state by state basis. Membership in a limited liability company is personal to the individual member. Only members or their designated managers have a voice in management of a limited liability company. A judgment creditor may petition a court for a charging order against the interest of a member in a limited liability company, so that the creditor has a right to receive distributions with respect to that member's interest and rights to certain information. The creditor has no right to become a member. The creditor may be subject to income taxes on the income attributable to a membership interest, even if it is not distributed.[76]

These rules are designed to protect the members of a limited liability company from the interference of an uninvited third party.[77] As such, the degree to which they will be respected if the limited liability company has only one member is still being determined by the courts. A limited liability company with only one member may not be afforded the same types of protection as a company having multiple members.[78]

---

76. See Rev. Rul. 77-137, 1977-1 C.B. 178 and Evans v. Commissioner, 447 F.2d 547 (7th Cir. 1971) (assignee treated as a partner for federal income tax purposes); but see Christopher M. Riser, Tax Consequences of Charging Orders: Is the "K.O. by the K-1" K.O.'d by the Code? 1 Asset Prot. J. No. 4 (Winter 2000).

77. In the bankruptcy context, an operating agreement that qualifies as an executory contract under 11 U.S.C. § 365 may afford significant protection from interference by the bankruptcy trustee. See Mark N. Berman, LLC Member Interests and Bankruptcy: Courts Begin to Sort Things Out, Bankr. L. Alert (Nixon Peabody, LLP), Fall 2003 at 1.

78. See Ehmann v. Fiesta Invs., LLC, 319 B.R. 200, 204 (Bankr. D. Ariz. 2005)...

**c. Limited Partnerships.** Limited partnerships also offer some asset protection features. Limited partners by their nature do not have rights in the day-to-day management of the partnership; this authority rests with the general partner. Typically, in a family-owned entity, there are also significant restrictions on the ability to transfer limited partnership interests. However, a creditor of a limited partner has even fewer rights than the limited partner himself.

Under most state statutes, a judgment creditor of a partner may petition a court for a charging order with respect to a limited partner's interest in the partnership, which gives the creditor the right to receive any distributions that would otherwise be made to the debtor/partner. Under some circumstances and in some states, the creditor may actually be able to obtain the underlying partnership interest, which also gives the creditor the status of an assignee. Assignees of a limited partner's interest have even fewer rights than limited partners have; they have only the rights to share in distributions to the extent the general partner chooses to make them. However, the assignee is subject to income taxes on the income earned by any pass-through entity, whether received or not. They cannot become limited partners without the approval of all of the other partners (or pursuant to any other procedure specified in the partnership agreement). Even if a creditor is able to sell the interest to a third party, he will likely have to discount the price substantially (if he can find a buyer in the first place) due to the lack of control and illiquidity that characterize interests in limited partnerships.

The general partner's role in a limited partnership is critical. If an individual is a general partner and his interest is alienated, it is generally treated as a withdrawal from the partnership. The general partner's interest may be converted to a limited partnership interest or may be purchased by the partnership or the other partners upon a vote by the limited partners. If any general partners remain, the partnership is continued if the agreement so provides. If no general partners remain, the limited partners may vote to continue the partnership and appoint a new general partner. The presence of more than one general partner is therefore important. If the general partner is a corporation or limited liability company, ownership by multiple parties is important so that the creditors of one party cannot gain control over the general partner and thereby the partnership.

**3. Respecting The Business Entity.** With each kind of business entity that might be used for asset protection purposes, protecting the integrity of the entity is important. The creditor's argument is basically "why should I be forced to respect the structure of the entity, if the owners have chosen not to?" In the corporate context, this theory has been used to impose liability on the shareholders for a corporation's debt, and is known as "piercing the corporate veil." The traditional concept of piercing the corporate veil is also being used by courts to ignore the business entity and allow the creditors of an individual owner to access assets owned by the business entity. This "reverse-veil piercing" theory is being used against corporations, limited partnerships, and limited liability companies. As illustrated by a leading case in this area, the courts' decisions are heavily influenced by the individual facts of each case, as well as the court's overall impression of the equities involved.[79]

As a practical matter, this issue is not as serious for limited liability companies and partnerships as for corporations, simply because there are fewer formalities to be observed. However, preserving the financial life of these entities separate and apart from that of their owners is critical to their success as asset protection vehicles. For this reason, owners should avoid such obvious pitfalls as paying personal expenses from business accounts, or having a business entity own a primary residence which a member or partner is allowed to use rent-free.

### C. Gifts, Trusts, and Disclaimers

Many U.S. asset protection opportunities exist in the traditional estate planning areas of gifts, trusts, and disclaimers. While state statutes differ in their treatment of disclaimers (in some states it can be a fraudulent transfer and in others it is not, even with an existing creditor), old-fashioned estate planning through gifts and trusts enables many patriarchs and matriarchs to insure the financial future of successive generations. Surprisingly, however, many states ignore or dilute the protection afforded by "spendthrift" clauses.[80] Therefore, a practitioner's knowledge in this area might lead to the conclusion that forum shopping within the fifty United States is appropriate even for life insurance trusts, Crummey trusts, and other commonplace estate planning trusts.

**1. Trusts: Asset Protection Checklist.** Leaving assets to a beneficiary in trust has been the traditional method of shielding the assets from the claims of the beneficiary's creditors, or saving the beneficiary from himself. Although the use of trusts is currently being pursued in many new contexts, the traditional spendthrift trust remains the most common asset protection planning device.

**a. "Spendthrift" Protection.** A spendthrift trust is one that contains a provision prohibiting the beneficiary from assigning his interest in the trust, and also prevents a beneficiary's creditors from reaching the beneficiary's interest. Spendthrift provisions are respected as being within the power of a donor to place conditions on any potential gifts. This principle does not extend to the individual himself - the large majority of American jurisdictions adhere to the traditional rule that a person cannot shield his own assets from the claims of his creditors...

**b. Interest of the Beneficiary.** If a creditor is able to reach assets held in a spendthrift trust, the creditor can reach only the beneficiary's interest in the trust. For this reason, defining and limiting that interest is very important.

**(i) Distribution Standard.** A creditor of a beneficiary will have more difficulty reaching a beneficiary's interest in a trust if distributions to that beneficiary are not fixed, but are subject to the discretion of the trustee. The broader the trustee's discretion, in general, the greater the protection. This protection is magnified if there are multiple beneficiaries among whom a trustee may "sprinkle" distributions. Finally, a beneficiary's interest in a trust may

---

79.  See C. F. Trust, Inc. v. First Flight Limited Partnership, 580 S.E. 2d 806 (Va. 2003)

80.  For an example of a judicial attack on spendthrift trusts, see Sligh v. First National Bank of Holmes County, 704 So. 2d 1020 (Miss. 1997).

change depending on his or her circumstances. For example, a trust providing for mandatory distributions might convert to a discretionary trust if the beneficiary becomes insolvent.

**(ii) Powers of Appointment.** Many trusts that are motivated by tax planning contain general powers of appointment which give a trust beneficiary the authority to vest trust assets in himself, his estate, his creditors, or the creditors of his estate. There is a split of authority as to whether or not a creditor may reach trust assets subject to a beneficiary's power of appointment. One line of authority is that a power of appointment is a property right, and a creditor should have all that the beneficiary may reach.[81] This view is certainly the case in bankruptcy proceedings. The more common rule under state law, however, is that a power of appointment is an inherently personal right, and exercise of that power may not be forced by a creditor…

**c. Duration of the Trust.** One limitation on spendthrift protection is that it only applies so long as trust assets remain in the trust. Once in the hands of the beneficiary, the assets are fair game to creditors. Placing the assets in trust for as long as possible therefore has asset protection advantages. Most states still subscribe to the traditional rule against perpetuities, which states that all interests in property must vest no later than twenty-one years after the death of the last survivor of "lives in being" on the creation of the interest. Translated in practical terms, the rule requires termination of a trust no later than twenty-one years after the death of the last survivor of a group of people who are living when the trust is executed. Several American jurisdictions have modified this rule or abolished it altogether.

**d. Selection of the Trustee.** Appointment of a trustee who is not a beneficiary of the trust is generally preferable for asset protection purposes. At common law, if the trustee was also the sole beneficiary of the trust, equitable and legal title to the trust assets were "merged," and the trust was disregarded. This rule has been eroded to a significant degree. For example, many state statutes provide that a spendthrift trust is by definition not subject to the merger doctrine. In addition, many courts have held that any interest, even a remote, contingent interest, held by any other beneficiary, will defeat the doctrine of merger. However, separation of these two roles continues to be the most effective course for asset protection. Recently, the authors of the Restatement (Third) of Trusts seem to have embraced a position that spendthrift provisions may be weakened or undermined when the beneficiary of a discretionary trust is also the trustee.[82] However, some states, including South Dakota and Texas, have responded to this position by enacting legislation that provides creditor protection to trustee-beneficiaries of discretionary trusts, and the Uniform Trust Code now provides that a creditor may not reach the assets of a spendthrift trust if the discretion of the trustee-beneficiary in making distributions to himself is limited to an ascertainable standard.[83] Although the view propounded in the Restatement

---

81. Restatement (Third) of Trusts, § 56, cmt. b.

82. Id. § 60, cmt. g; but see id. § 58, cmt. b; see also Harris & Klooster, Beneficiary-Controlled Trusts Can Lose Asset Protection, Trusts & Estates 37 (Dec. 2006).

83. See, e.g., Unif. Trust Code § 504(e) ("A creditor may not reach the interest of a beneficiary who is also a trustee or co-trustee, or otherwise compel a distribution, if the trustee's discretion to make distributions for the

(Third) of Trusts has not been widely accepted, if a beneficiary is also a trustee, a creditor can more easily make arguments that the trust should be disregarded due to a beneficiary's lack of observance of the trust terms, or easy availability of trust assets...

### 2. Asset Protection Implications of Commonly Used Estate Planning Trusts

**a. Credit Shelter Trusts/Bypass Trusts.** Probably the most commonly used type of trust in estate planning is a trust created at the death of one spouse for the benefit of the surviving spouse to utilize the deceased spouse's unified credit against estate and gift taxes... The very features that cause these trusts to escape estate tax at the surviving spouse's death make them effective asset protection vehicles. For maximum asset protection, an independent trustee should be appointed, and distributions should only be made in the trustee's discretion...

**b. Marital Deduction Trusts.** Many people today are reluctant to make gifts that require the payment of gift tax...[84] With exemptions from estate tax on the rise, it may very well be that the client's assets will not be subject to estate taxes at his death. Once a client has given away his full exemption from gift tax, if further gifts to a spouse are desired, a marital deduction trust should be considered. These types of trusts can be created at the death of one spouse, or during both spouses' lifetimes. Gifts to this type of trust generate no gift or estate tax when the trust is created. For this reason, the terms of these trusts are largely governed by the Internal Revenue Code. All income must be paid to the spouse/beneficiary. To the extent the spouse/beneficiary receives this income, spendthrift protection is lost, unless some other state exemption applies.[85] However, principal can be accumulated or distributed in the trustee's discretion. The trust assets are subject to estate tax at the spouse/beneficiary's death. However, the trust assets should not be subject to the claims of the spouse/beneficiary's creditors.

**d. Generation-Skipping Trusts.** Trusts that are designed to be preserved for several generations, or generation-skipping trusts, are generally designed to avoid estate tax at the passing of each generation... For maximum asset protection, a beneficiary should not be the sole trustee. Distributions to the beneficiary should be made in the trustee's discretion. Formalities of the trust must be observed. However, the spouse of the donor may be a permitted beneficiary of the trust if this type of safety net makes the donor more comfortable in making these gifts.

**e. Crummey Trusts.** Each person may give up to $14,000 per year to as many people as he wishes without gift tax.[86] Persons who wish to utilize these annual exclusions from gift tax by making gifts to minors often do so by making gifts to trusts. Crummey trusts give the beneficiary a power to withdraw the amount of any gift made to the trust, which lapses if unexercised after a short

---

trustee's own benefit is limited by an ascertainable standard.").

84. Id. § 2505.

85. For example, Delaware law might protect these payments if paid into a Delaware bank account. Del Code Ann. Tit. 12, §§ 3570(7) & 3572(1) (2007).

86. Id. § 2503.

period (often thirty days). This withdrawal power allows the gift to be eligible for the annual exclusion.

The property subject to the withdrawal power is vulnerable to creditors during the period the withdrawal power exists. Whether or not the lapse of a withdrawal power has adverse asset protection consequences is an open question in most states.[87] Although the asset protection exposure is generally limited with these types of trusts, it can become larger if "hanging" powers of withdrawal are used. These powers of withdrawal lapse only to the extent of the greater of $5,000 or 5% of trust assets per year, while the rest of the property continues to be subject to the power. This amount can grow quite large over a period of years, and it continues to be vulnerable as long as the power exists.

**f. Life Insurance Trusts.** Life insurance trusts are commonly structured as Crummey trusts. However, the investment of trust assets in life insurance may be a factor that increases the asset protection available for assets in these trusts.

**g. Charitable Remainder Trusts.** Charitable remainder trusts provide for the payment of a fixed amount (a percentage of the trust assets or a fixed dollar amount) to a beneficiary for a specified period of time, followed by a payment to charity at the trust's termination. These trusts allow the donor to obtain a charitable income tax deduction for the value of the charity's interest at the time the trust is created. The trust itself is not subject to income tax. Taxes are paid by the beneficiary as funds are received from the trust.

The fact that the payment is fixed reduces the asset protection available to a beneficiary, since a trustee generally has no discretion to accumulate the distribution rather than pay it to the beneficiary, unless some other state exemption would protect these payments.[88] In contrast, if a person creates a charitable remainder trust for his or her own benefit, some asset protection might be achieved. The settlor's interest in the trust would generally not be protected by a spendthrift clause. However, the settlor's only interest in the trust would be the right to the fixed payments; the corpus of the trust would be protected. In states that allow self-settled spendthrift trusts (see Part IV below), it may be possible to protect the settlor's undistributed interest in a spendthrift trust.

**h. GRATs, GRUTs, and QPRTs.** Grantor retained annuity trusts ("GRATs") and grantor retained unitrusts ("GRUTs") are creatures of the tax code. A settlor who establishes a GRAT or a GRUT retains the right to a payment of a certain amount (a fixed dollar amount or a percentage of the trust assets, respectively) for a specified period of time, after which the assets pass to another party. The value of the settlor's gift is the present value of the remainder interest on the day the trust is created. There is the potential for large value shifts if the trust "beats" the rate of return used to determine the value of the remainder interest when the trust is created. By definition, GRATs and GRUTs are self-

---

87. Some states have specifically addressed this issue through legislation. For example, Texas law provides a beneficiary will not be considered a settlor because of a lapse, waiver, or release of a beneficiary's right to withdraw trust property of the greater of (a) the greater of $5,000 or 5% of trust assets [IRC § 2041(b)(2) or § 2514(e)], or (b) the annual exclusion gift amount [IRC § 2503(b)]. Tex. Prop. Code § 112.035(e)(2).

88. For example, a state statute protecting annuity payments might apply to this type of payment.

settled trusts, and therefore, a spendthrift provision generally will not prevent a creditor from seizing the settlor's interests in them. The settlor's interest is the stream of payments that he retains when the trust is established. Like the charitable remainder trust, because the settlor's interest is fixed, the entire trust corpus cannot be reached by his or her creditors, and the settlor may actually achieve some asset protection that he would not have if he owned the assets outright. In states allowing self-settled spendthrift trusts (see Part IV below), additional protection for the settlor's interest may be achieved. The settlor's creditors can reach the payments he receives unless some other exemption applies.

In a qualified personal residence trust (a "QPRT") the settlor transfers his residence to a trust and retains the right to live there for a specified period of time. At the end of the term, the assets generally pass to the settlor's children. The value of the settlor's gift is the present value of the children's future right to the home on the day the trust is created. In this way, a 50 year old person could give away a $1,000,000 home at a gift tax value of $150,000. The settlor's retained right in a QPRT is merely the right to live in the residence during the term. An argument can be made that this type of right is personal and cannot be seized by a creditor. Consideration should be given as to whether contributing a residence to a QPRT affects the settlor's homestead exemption. In fact, the QPRT is often used in states where no (or limited) homestead protection is otherwise available to shelter homestead assets. It could also be used to provide some asset protection for a vacation home that would not be classified as a homestead.

**i. Self-Settled Trusts.** In many jurisdictions, an individual cannot shield his assets from the claims of his creditors by transferring assets to a self-settled spendthrift trust. However, in some jurisdictions (see Part IV below), self-settled trusts are permissible and may provide a level of protection from creditors provided certain conditions are met. The IRS has recognized that a transfer to a self-settled trust may be a completed gift for gift tax purposes under certain circumstances.[89]

## IV. Domestic Venues For Asset Protection Trusts[90]

### A. Introduction

Alaska, Delaware, Nevada, Utah, Rhode Island, Oklahoma, South Dakota, Missouri, Tennessee, Wyoming, and New Hampshire (the "Domestic Venues")[91] have enacted legislation with a view toward becoming viable venues for establishing asset protection trusts. Although all Domestic Venue statutes appear to offer substantial (or at least some) asset protection (especially against the claims of future creditors), none of these states can be as protective a site for establishing trusts as an offshore jurisdiction because they are bound by the

---

89. I.R.S. Priv. Ltr. Rul. 200944002 (July 15, 2009).

90. The following discussion is based, in part, on Leslie C. Giordani & Duncan E. Osborne, Will the Alaska Trusts Work?, 3 J. of Asset Prot. No. 1 (Sept/Oct 1997) and Leslie C. Giordani & Duncan E. Osborne, Stateside Asset Protection Trusts: Will They Work? in Estate and Personal Finance Planning (Edward F. Koren ed., 1997).

91. In addition to the existing Alaska, Delaware, Nevada, Utah, Rhode Island, Oklahoma, South Dakota, Missouri, Tennessee, Wyoming, and New Hampshire statutes, some commentators argue that Colorado statutes provide some basis for asset protection trusts against future creditors...

United States Constitution. By virtue of the "full faith and credit" mandate in the Constitution, the courts of one state must recognize judgments rendered under the laws of less debtor-friendly states.[92]   In addition (and as more fully discussed below), the enactment of laws enabling asset protection trusts may itself violate the Constitution's contract clause.[93]   Finally, due to the supremacy clause of the Constitution, no state statute can protect debtors from conflicting federal law (i.e., bankruptcy law).[94]   Even if state asset protection trust legislation passes constitutional muster, it does not necessarily defend an asset protection trust from some of the arguments available to a creditor through other existing state laws. The new statutes, existing statutory provisions, and common law provide various opportunities for a sympathetic court, whether in a Domestic Venue or elsewhere, to set aside or penetrate the trust structure in favor of creditors.[95]

## B. Overview of Domestic Venue Asset Protection Trust Legislation

### [Author's Note – Two Examples]

**1. THE ALASKA TRUST ACT.** Effective April 2, 1997, Alaska became the first state to offer a domestic alternative to offshore asset protection trusts with the passage of the Alaska Trust Act (the "Alaska Act").[96]   Alaska's legislature has subsequently strengthened the Alaska Act with new legislation, which, inter alia, tightened the statute of limitations for creditor claims, narrowed the definition of fraudulent transfers, and introduced elements that were previously unique to foreign trusts.[97]

To come under the protection of the Alaska Act, the trust instrument must: (i) state that the trust is irrevocable;[98]   (ii) state that Alaska law governs the validity, construction, and administration of the trust;[99]   (iii) contain a spendthrift clause;[100] and (iv) appoint a "qualified trustee."[101]   Only an Alaska resident, or a trust company or bank with trust powers headquartered in Alaska may serve as a qualified trustee.[102]   Notably, the settlor may serve as the trustee adviser or even a non-qualified co-trustee, provided the settlor does not have control over discretionary distributions.[103]   In addition, all qualified trustees must agree to be responsible for (i) maintaining trust records, (ii) preparing or arranging for the preparation of fiduciary income tax returns, and (iii) handling at least part of the administration, some of which must take place in Alaska.[104]   Finally, at least some of the trust assets must be deposited in Alaska,[105]   and the settlor must sign

---

92. U.S. Const., art. IV, § 1.
93. Id. art. I, § 10.
94. Id. art. VI, cl. 2.
95. In designing an asset protection structure, the lawyer must do more than simply read the Domestic Venue asset protection legislation. To probe for weaknesses, the lawyer must envision how the attack on the trust is likely to be played out. Also, note that the same thorough analysis is called for in reviewing asset protection features of foreign jurisdictions.
96. 1997 Alaska Sess. Laws 6.
97. 2003 Alaska Sess. Laws 138.
98. Alaska Stat. §§ 34.40.110(b)(2), 13.36.338 (2006).
99. Id. § 13.36.035.
100. Id. § 34.40.110(a).
101. Id. § 13.36.035(c).
102. Id. §§ 13.36.035(c), 13.36.390(3).
103. Id. § 34.40.110(f).
104. Id. § 13.36.035(c)(3)-(4).
105. Id. § 13.36.035(c)(1).

a solvency affidavit prior to any transfer.[106] If a trust satisfies these requirements, the trust assets are protected from creditors' claims, including a claim to enforce a judgment of a court in another jurisdiction...[107]

Alaska courts have exclusive jurisdiction over claims made against an Alaska asset protection trust.[108] Under the Alaska Act, claims that arose prior to the transfer in trust are extinguished by the later of four years after the date of the transfer or one year after the creditor discovers the transfer. To prevail on a claim against an Alaska asset protection trust that arose before the transfer in trust, the creditor must prove (by a preponderance of the evidence) that he or she asserted a specific claim before the transfer, or must file another suit against the settlor asserting a claim based on an act or omission of the settlor that occurred prior to the transfer. In addition, creditors' fraudulent transfer claims arising after the transfer in trust expire four years after the transfer.[109]

Importantly, claims may proceed against the trust if the settlor: (i) made the transfer with an intent to defraud creditors, (ii) was in default for 30 days or more in contravention of a child support judgment or order at the time of the transfer in trust, (iii) retained a right to mandatory distributions, or (iv) had a power to revoke or terminate the trust.[110] While an Alaska asset protection trust created before marriage is not subject to division in an Alaska divorce proceeding, a surviving spouse has the statutory right to elect against the settlor's will and might be able to pierce the trust and reach the trust assets.[111] Further, in such a case, the federal law providing for full faith and credit for child support orders might enable minor children to pierce an Alaska asset protection trust for support.[112] However, a creditor's access to trust assets is limited to the amount necessary to satisfy his or her claim and approved costs.[113]

In any event, the Alaska Act protects attorneys, trustees, and advisers from liability associated with the preparation or funding of Alaska asset protection trusts. [114] The Alaska Act also provides that certain assets of the trust, such as real property and tangible personal property, can be made available for the use of a beneficiary, without exposing such assets to a creditor as a "payment or delivery."[115] Such a "use" provision arguably permits the settlor to contribute a residence to an Alaska asset protection trust and continue to reside in that home. In addition, the Alaska legislature provided that a spendthrift trust restriction under Alaska law falls under the federal bankruptcy law exception for spendthrift trusts. [116] Further, a pre-existing non-Alaska trust may become an Alaska asset protection trust if it satisfies the requirements listed above. A trust that has its situs transferred to Alaska and has provisions that allow the trust to be perpetual

---

106. Id. §§ 34.40.110(j).
107. Id. § 34.40.110(b), (k).
108. Id. § 34.40.110(k).
109. Id. § 34.40.110(d).
110. Id. § 34.40.110(d).
111. Id. § 34.40.110(d).
112. 28 U.S.C. § 1738B(a), (h).
113. Alaska Stat. §§ 13.36.310(b), 34.40.110(c).
114. Id. § 34.40.110(e).
115. Id. § 34.40.110(a).
116. Id. ..

or are not expressly prohibited by the laws of Alaska is effective and enforceable.[117]

For all practical purposes, the Alaska Act eliminates the rule against perpetuities, although some interests must vest within 1,000 years.[118]

**2. THE DELAWARE TRUST ACT.** The Delaware Qualified Dispositions in Trust Act[119] (the "Delaware Act") attempts to achieve a result similar to the Alaska statute in a somewhat parallel manner.

To provide protection for assets transferred by a settlor to a Delaware asset protection trust, such trust must expressly name Delaware law as the governing law of the trust, be irrevocable, name a qualified trustee, and contain Delaware's statutory spendthrift language.[120] A qualified trustee includes an individual resident of Delaware other than the settlor, or a corporate trustee authorized by Delaware law to act as a trustee and whose activities may be supervised by the Bank Commissioner of Delaware, the Federal Deposit Insurance Corporation, the Comptroller of the Currency, or the Office of Thrift Supervision. However, the settlor may appoint trust advisers who have the power to remove and appoint trustees and advisers or who have authority over trust distributions, and the settlor may even serve as an investment adviser.[121] Further, the trust may also have nonqualified co-trustees other than the settlor.[122] The Delaware Act also provides that the qualified trustee must ensure that some of the trust property is located in Delaware or otherwise materially participate in the trust administration.[123]

The Delaware Act allows a settlor to be a discretionary beneficiary of the trust, and a settlor's retention of the following rights is protected under the act: (i) a right to income; (ii) a right to receive a percentage (not exceeding 5%) of the trust assets annually; (iii) a right to receive distributions from a charitable remainder annuity trust, a charitable remainder unitrust, or a GRUT; (iv) a right to use real property held in a QPRT; (v) a right to receive distributions of trust principal, if made in the qualified trustee's discretion or pursuant to an ascertainable standard; and (vi) a right to distributions of income or principal to pay income taxes on trust income. The Delaware Act also permits a settlor to retain the right to veto distributions of trust property and the right to remove and replace a trustee or trust adviser, as well as a special testamentary power of appointment over the trust corpus.[124]

Delaware courts have exclusive jurisdiction over claims against Delaware asset protection trusts.[125] The statute of limitations for claims existing on the date of the transfer is the later of (i) four years after the transfer, or (ii) one year after

117. Alaska Stat. § 13.36.043(b).
118. Id. § 34.27.051.
119. Del. Code Ann. tit. 12, § 3570 et seq. (2009).
120. Id. § 3570(7), (11).
121. Id. § 3570(8).
122. See id. §§ 3570(8)(f), 3570(11)(b), 3571 (2007).
123. See id. §§ 3570(8)(f), 3570(11)(b), 3571 (2007).
124. Id. § 3570(11)(b).
125. Id. § 3572(a) (2007).

the transfer was (or could reasonably have been) discovered by the creditor.[126] For claims arising after the date of the transfer, the statute of limitations is four years after the transfer.[127] In any action against a Delaware asset protection trust, the creditor has the burden of proving his or her claim by clear and convincing evidence.[128] As long as the settlor is not made a mandatory beneficiary, the assets in trust are free from the claims of the settlor's creditors, including claims based on a judgment of a court in another jurisdiction.[129] However, the protection from creditors does not extend to (i) claims for alimony or support of a spouse or former spouse who was married to the settlor on or before the date of the transfer, or children, (ii) a division of marital property, and (iii) existing tort claimants.[130] Furthermore, creditors' rights under the Delaware Fraudulent Transfer Act are expressly protected. [131] However, creditors are only allowed to reach trust assets to the extent of the debt and any costs the court allows.[132]

A trust created in another state may become a Delaware asset protection trust by transferring the trust to Delaware and meeting the requirements stated above.[133] Such a trust does not have to be governed by Delaware law.[134] If a trust is transferred to Delaware after June 30, 1997, the limitations period begins as of the date the trust was created, rather than as of the date of the transfer.[135]

In addition to the provisions noted above, the Delaware statute possesses some unique qualities. First, the statute permits a corporation or partnership (not solely individuals) to create an asset protection trust.[136] Second, the spendthrift clause contained in a Delaware asset protection trust is deemed to be a transfer restriction on the settlor's interest in the trust within the meaning of Section 541(c)(2) of the Bankruptcy Code.[137] Third, the Delaware Act provides that, in the event a non-Delaware state court declines to apply Delaware's law with respect to the validity, construction, or administration of a Delaware trust, the trustee's authority over the trust is immediately terminated and a successor trustee succeeds to the trusteeship. In the event the trust instrument fails to provide a successor trustee, the Court of Chancery appoints a successor.[138] Fourth, the statute provides that creditors may not bring claims against the trustee or trust adviser or any individual involved in the preparation or funding of such a trust.[139]

Finally, the Delaware rule against perpetuities is 110 years for real property and is nonexistent for personal property and with respect to certain types of trusts...[140]

---

126. Id. § 3572(b); id. tit. 6, § 1309 (1996).
127. Id. § 3572(b); id. tit. 6, § 1309 (1996).
128. Id. tit. 12, § 3572(b).
129. Id. §§ 3571, 3572.
130. Id. §§ 3570(9), 3573 (2005).
131. Id. § 3572(a); see id. tit. 6, §§ 1304, 1305 (1996).
132. Id. tit. 12, § 3574(a) (2007).
133. Id. §§ 3570(10).
134. Id. § 3570(11) (penultimate sentence of flush language at end).
135. Id. §§ 3572(c), 3575 (1998).
136. Id. §§ 3570(10), 3570(5), id. tit. 1, § 302(16) (1953).
137. Id. 3570(11)(c).
138. Id. § 3572(g).
139. Id. § 3572(d).
140. Id. tit. 25, § 503 (2008).

## C. Domestic Venue Asset Protection Legislation Vulnerabilities

## 1. Full Faith And Credit Problems

**a. Introduction.** In order for a judgment creditor of the settlor of an asset protection trust to enforce the judgment against trust assets, the creditor must involve a court that has jurisdiction over either the trust assets or a party in control of the trust assets (i.e., the trustee).[141] Accordingly, if trust assets are located outside of a Domestic Venue, or if another state's courts have jurisdiction over the trustee, the assets of a Domestic Venue trust could potentially be reached by a creditor who never even sets foot in the trust situs state's courts. More likely, however, the assets could be reached by a creditor who appears in the situs state court on a pro forma basis to have the court enforce a judgment rendered by the court of another state. As will be shown, this ability of creditors to sue effectively outside the trust situs state obviates some of the protection the drafters of the Domestic Venue statutes intended to provide.[142]

**b. Jurisdiction.** In order for a judgment creditor of the settlor to enforce a judgment against assets of a trust that the settlor has created and funded, the creditor must proceed in a court that has jurisdiction over some aspect of the trust. If the trust is a Domestic Venue trust, this does not necessarily mean a Domestic Venue court. Another state's court may have jurisdiction over the trustee, the settlor, or the trust assets.[143]

A leading case in the trust jurisdiction area is Hanson v. Denkla.[144] While this case is sometimes cited for the broad proposition that a judgment-rendering state court must have jurisdiction over the trustee for its judgment to receive full faith and credit in another state (e.g., a Domestic Venue state), a careful reading of the case fails to support this conclusion. In determining whether a Delaware court was required to give full faith and credit to a Florida judgment, the U.S. Supreme Court simply held that since Florida law made the trustee an indispensable party to a Florida lawsuit, and because the Florida court in this case had no personal jurisdiction over the trustee (or in rem jurisdiction over the trust assets), the Florida judgment was void (and therefore, quite logically, not entitled to full faith and credit treatment in Delaware or anywhere else). Hanson v. Denkla does not answer the question of whether jurisdiction over the trustee is an across-the-board requirement for a judgment creditor seeking full faith and credit treatment in another state. However, it may soon become required reading for judgment creditors' attorneys…

---

141. In many cases, an attack on an asset protection trust will be either the second phase of a lawsuit or a second suit entirely. The first action will have been the cause, cast in tort or contract, that gave rise to the liability. The second action will likely be against the trust in an effort to satisfy the judgment.

142. See, Jerry A. Schoenblum, Reaching for the Sky — or Pie in The Sky: Is U.S. Onshore Trust Reform An Illusion?, 3 Trusts E Àttivita Fiduciarie 340 (2003).

143. It can be argued that trustees are "necessary parties" to all suits involving trust assets, i.e., that they must be joined in such action for the court to validly adjudicate the dispute. However, since the revision of Federal Rule of Civil Procedure 19 in 1966, there has been a general trend by both state and federal courts away from characterizing any party not present as "necessary" or "indispensable." Instead, many states (and all federal courts) have moved to a more pragmatic analysis, mandating only that certain parties should be joined "if feasible." See, e.g., Fed.R. Civ. P. 19 (federal courts); C.C.P. § 389 (California); CPLR § 1001 (New York); Tex. R. Civ. P. 39 (Texas). This approach gives courts more latitude to adjudicate disputes without joining additional parties…

144. 357 U.S. 235 (1958).

A court could have jurisdiction over the trustee or settlor in a number of ways. First, individuals are always subject to the jurisdiction of courts within their domiciles.[145] Generally, this means that a non-Domestic Venue trustee or settlor is subject to the jurisdiction of his or her home state's courts. Jurisdiction may also exist under a long-arm statute if the trustee or settlor has sufficient contacts with the forum state.[146]

Corporations are subject to the jurisdiction of the courts in the state of their incorporation.[147] They are also subject to the jurisdiction of courts in any state in which they do business.[148] For large corporate trustees such as banks, including those based or with offices in a Domestic Venue, this could effectively give jurisdiction to the courts of many states.

A state's courts also will have jurisdiction over all property within the state's borders.[149] This includes real property, bank and brokerage accounts, and shares of stock issued by corporations incorporated in that state.[150] If a trust holds stock in many different corporations, its property may be subject to the jurisdiction of several states' courts. Furthermore, any non-Domestic Venue activities in which the trust participates will likely involve the maintenance of accounts outside that state, which would become targets of creditors seeking to pursue their claims outside of the Domestic Venue courts.

**c. Legal Theories.** The mere fact that a court outside of a Domestic Venue has jurisdiction to hear a creditor's post-judgment enforcement action does not guarantee a creditor victory. The judgment creditor must also advance an argument that convinces the court that it should enforce the underlying judgment on the merits against the assets of the judgment debtor's Domestic Venue asset protection trust. A judgment creditor's arguments typically will fall into one or more of the following categories, which might be pled individually or in the alternative: (i) the asset protection features of the Domestic Venue trust offend public policy in the state where the post-judgment action is brought and, therefore, the governing law of the trust (Domestic Venue law) should be ignored in favor of the law of such state;[151] (ii) the Domestic Venue trust is a "sham" trust or is the alter ego of the settlor and, because the settlor never really parted with dominion and control over the trust assets, the court should disregard the trust structure; or (iii) the settlor's transfer to the Domestic Venue trust was a fraudulent transfer and, therefore, should be set aside…[152]

**d. Enforcement.** Even if a court outside of the Domestic Venue renders a judgment in favor of the creditor pursuant to one of the three foregoing

---

145. See, e.g., Milliken v. Meyer, 311 U.S. 457 (1940)

146. See, e.g., Int'l Shoe Co. v. Washington, 326 U.S. 310 (1945).

147. Restatement (Second) of Conflict of Laws, § 41 (1971).

148. See, e.g. Int'l Shoe Co., 326 U.S. 310; Gulf Oil Corp. v. Gilbert, 330 U.S. 501 (1947).

149. See, e.g., Green v. Van Buskirk, 74 U.S. 139 (1868)

150. See id.

151. See, e.g., In re Brooks, 217 B.R. 98 (Bankr. E.D. Conn. 1998) (on grounds of public policy, court applied Connecticut law to determine the enforceability of spendthrift provisions of self-settled Jersey and Bermuda trusts; held, spendthrift provisions were unenforceable and trust assets therefore were property of the bankruptcy estate).

152. Cf. In re Esteem Settlement, 2003 JLR 188 (Royal Crt. Jersey). The creditor in this case employed other creative, if unsuccessful, theories to attack this trust.

arguments, the creditor's battle is not over. The creditor must also find a way to have this second judgment enforced against the assets of the Domestic Venue asset protection trust. If the court's jurisdiction is based on the situs of trust assets, the court should be able to force the turnover of those assets from the judgment debtor to the creditor by a court order (attachment, garnishment, etc.) that forces the party in possession of the assets to give them to the judgment creditor.

However, if the court has jurisdiction over the trustee or settlor but not over the assets, the situation will be different. The court might issue a turnover order against the trustee or the settlor or both.[153]   Failing that, the creditor would have to take the judgment to the jurisdiction where the trust assets are located to enforce the order obtained in the post-judgment proceeding. If that jurisdiction is any state of the U.S., including Domestic Venues, the judgment could be enforced pursuant to the application of the full faith and credit clause of the U.S. Constitution.

All state courts are bound by the Constitution and federal statutes to give full faith and credit to judgments rendered by the courts of sister states.[154]  As long as the rendering court had proper jurisdiction under its own law (as interpreted by the rendering court) and pursuant to the due process requirements of the Constitution, and the judgment was not procured by fraud, the sister state courts, including courts in Domestic Venues, must recognize it and give it the full effect that such judgment would have had if rendered by the sister state's court.[155]  This rule applies even if the rendering state's court based its judgment upon a misapprehension of Domestic Venue law and even if the judgment was based upon a cause of action that would be against law and public policy of the Domestic Venue.[156]

Of course, the trustee could be expected to vigorously defend such a proceeding on a number of fronts. [157]  In fact, some writers have argued that the full faith and credit clause should operate in favor of wealth protection as states must respect the legislative acts of their sister states.[158]  However, constitutional scholars point out that historically that has not been the case: "[Y]et virtually the entire effect of the clause and its implementing statute has occurred in the context of interstate enforcement of judicial decisions. The impact on the disregard of

---

153. Alternatively, the creditor would have the option of asking the court to issue a turnover order against the settlor with regard to future distributions. Presumably, the trustee would then cease making distributions to the settlor. The creditor would not benefit, but the settlor would lose the ability to enjoy the assets himself.

154. U.S. Const., art. IV, § 1; 28 U.S.C. § 1738.

155. See Scoles & Hay, Conflict of Laws 968-86 (1992).

156. See, e.g., Restatement (Second) of Judgments § 17 (1982); Fauntleroy v. Lum, 210 U.S. 230, 237 (1908). See also Douglas Laycock, Equal Citizens of Equal and Territorial States: The Constitutional Foundations of Choice of Law, 92 Colum. L. Rev. 249 (1992) (analyzing the constitutional principles on which choice-of-law rules must be based).

157. See, e.g., Nenno and Sparks, Delaware Dynasty Trusts and Asset Protection Trusts, Special Pamphlet to the 99-4 Supplement (1999) of Osborne & Schurig, supra note 36. An analysis of the possible defenses is beyond the scope of this discussion and is, in any event, too fact-specific for anything other than theoretical, treatise-length speculations.

158. Santo Bisignano, Jr. & Toby M. Eisenberg, Asset Protection Without a Passport, in Texas Bar CLE: Advanced Estate Planning and Probate 2003, tab 25, available at http://www.texasbarcle.com; Richard W. Nenno, Perpetual Dynasty Trusts, UPAIA Section 104 and Total Return Trust Statutes, and Domestic Asset Protection Trusts, in 4 Planning Techniques for Large Est. 1843 (ALI-ABA 2002).

other states' laws has been minimal..." [159]

### 2. Supremacy Clause Concerns.

**a. Federal Question/Diversity Jurisdiction.** Under the U.S. Constitution's Supremacy Clause, federal courts are not bound by state laws. [160] If a judgment creditor can obtain jurisdiction over a judgment debtor or the debtor's assets in a Domestic Venue asset protection trust by virtue of federal question jurisdiction [161] or diversity jurisdiction, [162] the creditor will have the opportunity to avoid the debtor-friendly provisions of the Domestic Venue asset protection laws, thereby stripping the judgment debtor of one of his most significant asset protection shields.

**b. Federal Bankruptcy Laws.** A judgment creditor facing a judgment debtor who has been rendered "insolvent" by virtue of a transfer to an asset protection trust may be able to force the debtor into involuntary bankruptcy. In that case, pursuant to a judgment against the settlor rendered by a United States Bankruptcy Court under Bankruptcy Code rules, it is again possible that the Constitution's supremacy clause will come into play. The Bankruptcy Code takes precedence over any conflicting state law as a result of the supremacy clause, and although the success of a creditor using this approach has heretofore been theoretical, the enactment of the BAPCPA in 2005 strengthened creditors' positions substantially...the BAPCPA made a number of revisions to the Bankruptcy Code that substantially increase the likelihood of successful creditor claims.

First, the BAPCPA enlarged the period for avoiding a fraudulent transfer under 11 U.S.C. § 548(a) and (b) from one year to two years... Second, the BAPCPA added subsection 548(e), which provides a ten-year clawback provision for transfers by the debtor to a "self-settled trust or similar device" if the transfer was made with the actual intent to hinder, delay, or defraud present or future creditors...

Moreover, the BAPCPA may have shifted the paradigm in asset protection planning because it significantly reduced a debtor's protections in bankruptcy. Whereas bankruptcy has sometimes been viewed by planners as a way to wash creditors away, the Bankruptcy Code is now outfitted with powerful tools for retrieving assets that were once believed to be free of creditors' claims. With these changes, a creditor who previously may have preferred to avoid bankruptcy court may now want to force the debtor into involuntary bankruptcy...

Of course, it is impossible to fully foresee or understand the practical effects that the BAPCPA will have on Domestic Venue trusts. However, it certainly seems to provide creditors with new weaponry in their attempts to assault Domestic Venue trusts.

---

159. Lea Brilmayer, Credit Due Judgments and Credit Due Laws: The Respective Roles of Due Process and Full Faith and Credit in the Interstate Context, 70 Iowa L. Rev. 95, 95 (1984).

160. U.S. Const., art. VI, sec. 2.

161. 28 U.S.C. § 1331.

162. Id. § 1332.

**3. Contract Clause Problems.** The Constitution prohibits states from enacting any law that impairs the "Obligation of Contracts."[163] This provision is known as the contract clause, and was specifically intended by the framers to prevent the states from passing extensive debtor relief laws.[164] In order to run afoul of the contract clause, the law in question must substantially impair the obligations of parties to existing contracts or make them unreasonably difficult to enforce.[165] Even when the law meets one of these criteria, it is not automatically void; instead, it is subjected to the "strict scrutiny" standard of review: that is, to be valid, it must be narrowly tailored to promote a compelling governmental interest.[166]

A creditor could argue that the Domestic Venue statutes violate the contract clause by eliminating the creditor's ability to seize assets to which he would otherwise have had access before the enactment of such statute. Even though the U.S. Supreme Court has in the past recognized a distinction between laws that regulate the substantive obligations of contracts and those that merely regulate the remedies for breach of those contracts, this distinction is no longer rigidly followed. Moreover, a creditor could argue that the new statutes do not just affect the remedies of the creditor, but that they also alter the substantive obligations of the settlor/debtor. Because the settlor can potentially continue to use the assets that have been "discretionarily" distributed, the settlor's enjoyment of the trust assets is not impaired, but the possibility of creditors reaching those assets is restricted. Because the debtor will not be harmed if he refuses to repay the debt, the debtor's obligation to do so becomes illusory. A creditor could argue that by changing their laws to allow the assets of discretionary self-settled trusts to be protected from creditor's claims, Domestic Venues have thwarted the repayment obligations of debtors who choose to set up such a trust.

## D. Aside from Constitutional Problems, the Status of Domestic Venues as Pro-Debtor Jurisdictions is Questionable

Although many of the barriers to the entry of the Domestic Venues into the asset protection arena exist because they are states of the United States and subject to American laws, problems also exist with the statutes as written, as well as with existing provisions of local laws. That is, even if Domestic Venues were

---

163. U.S. Const., art I, § 10.

164. Wright, The Growth of American Constitutional Law 64 (1967); Home Building & Loan Assoc. v. Blaisdell, 290 U.S. 398, 427-428 (1934) (Hughes, J. discussing historical background of the contract clause).

165. Wright, The Contract Clause of the Constitution (1938); Nowak & Rotunda, Constitutional Law, at 11.8 (1995).

166. The U.S. Supreme Court first used the contract clause to invalidate a state law on the basis of unreasonable interference with contracts in Fletcher v. Peck, 10 U.S. 87 (1810). The Court continued to use the clause for this purpose throughout the nineteenth century. See, e.g., Sturges v. Crowninshield, 17 U.S. 122 (1819); Ogden v. Saunders, 25 U.S. 213 (1827); Bronson v. Kinzie, 42 U.S. 311 (1843). However, the clause fell into obscurity during the Court's "substantive due process" era, because "substantive due process" gave the Court greater discretion in passing on the constitutionality of state legislation. Thereafter, the contract clause was considered of little or no importance until its revival in 1977 in United States Trust Co. v. New Jersey, 431 U.S. 1 (1977). The next year, it was used by the Court to invalidate a statute for unreasonable interference with private contracts in Allied Structural Steel v. Spannaus, 438 U.S. 234 (1978), and the Court has continued to use a contract clause analysis for this purpose. See, e.g., Exxon Corp. v. Eagerton, 462 U.S. 176 (1983); Energy Reserves Group, Inc. v. Kansas Power & Light Co., 459 U.S. 400 (1983); Keystone Bituminous Coal Assoc. v. DeBenedictis, 480 U.S. 470 (1987); General Motors Corp. v. Romein, 503 U.S. 181 (1992).

not prevented by the U.S. Constitution from becoming asset protection trust havens, the Domestic Venue statutes do not give the maximum possible protection to settlors. This is due to the failure of the legislation to control the effect of other aspects of Domestic Venue laws, such as their own creditor-friendly fraudulent transfer laws.

The new legislation of the Domestic Venues purports to give settlors a viable alternative to locating their asset protection trusts offshore. These laws are only partially successful. The statutes require significant work to close creditor-friendly loopholes, but the major problem faced by Domestic Venues is that each is one of the fifty states and is subject to the restrictions of the U.S. Constitution. Domestic Venues are unable to bring their laws in line with the more aggressive asset protection laws in some offshore jurisdictions, because to do so would violate constitutional mandates. Their statehood prevents them from being able to control fully a creditor's right to obtain and enforce judgments against trust assets. Therefore, a settlor who is contemplating choosing a Domestic Venue as the jurisdiction for an asset protection trust must realize that a stateside trust cannot protect assets as well as a trust in an offshore jurisdiction. Although there may be other reasons for locating an asset protection trust in a Domestic Venue,[167] those states cannot match offshore jurisdictions when it comes to the primary reason for creating such a trust: shelter from the claims of creditors.

## V. Offshore Trusts

### A. General Principles

There are two primary attractions of offshore trusts. First, like the domestic asset protection trusts discussed above, it is possible for a settlor to create a spendthrift trust and yet remain a beneficiary. Second, because it is jurisdictionally severed from the United States, an offshore trust is less likely than a domestic trust to be targeted as a source for satisfying a future judgment or claim. The difficulty in accessing the trust, both physically and legally, might influence a potential future claimant's decision to pursue an action, or, at a minimum, incline the claimant to settle in ways more favorable to the defendant.

### B. Methods of Attack

Typically, a creditor who is attempting to reach the assets of an offshore trust will first obtain a judgment against the debtor in a United States court. The judgment creditor will then attempt to satisfy this judgment with assets in the offshore trust. In order to reach such assets effectively, the judgment creditor may be forced to bring suit against the trustee in either the jurisdiction where the trustee is domiciled or in a jurisdiction where trust assets are located. In situations in which the creditor is alleging that a fraudulent transfer occurred or in certain other situations (e.g., in a bankruptcy context), the suit may also be brought in the jurisdiction of the settlor's domicile.

As with domestic asset protection trusts, the judgment creditor's arguments

---

167. One reason would be transfer tax planning. For a discussion of possible planning opportunities, see Douglas J. Blattmachr et al., A New Direction in Estate Planning: North to Alaska, Tr. & Est. (Sept. 1997).

generally will fall into one or more of the following categories, which might be pled individually or in the alternative: (1) the asset protection features of the offshore trust offend public policy in the jurisdiction where the post-judgment action is brought and, therefore, the governing law of the trust (i.e., the laws of the offshore jurisdiction) should be ignored in favor of the laws of the jurisdiction in which the action is brought; (2) the settlor's transfer to the offshore trust was a fraudulent transfer and, therefore, should be set aside; or, (3) the offshore trust is a "sham" trust or is the alter ego of the settlor and, because the settlor never really parted with dominion and control over the trust assets, the court should disregard the trust structure.

In planning and implementing an offshore trust for an American settlor/beneficiary, the asset protection lawyer should remember that any initial action against the settlor or the trust will usually be brought in the United States and will almost certainly involve one or more of the three legal theories cited above.

### C. Exporting the Assets Versus Importing the Law

There are two fundamental, and at times conflicting, methods of achieving asset protection through a foreign trust.

**1. Export The Assets.** The first method is to place the assets in a foreign jurisdiction with a foreign structure and a foreign trustee and to arrange the entire configuration to sever all jurisdictional ties with the U.S. federal and state judicial systems. This method requires a claimant seeking to satisfy a U.S. judgment to travel to the selected jurisdiction in an effort to enforce the claim, thereby entering a legal environment in which chances of success are bleak and costly. This method is known as "exporting the assets" to a foreign trust.

**2. Import The Law.** The second alternative is to select a foreign jurisdiction with a favorable (i.e., aggressive) body of trust and fraudulent transfer law enacted to be protective of the settlor and the beneficiaries and to implement the asset protection plan so that this favorable body of law is applicable to the trust entity even though the trust assets remain in the U.S.

Under this method, the settlor implements the foreign trust in conjunction with a U.S. family limited partnership or other domestic legal entity that holds some or all of the settlor's assets. The settlor conveys all or a portion of the domestic limited partnership interests or the domestic corporation's shares to the foreign trustee. Under this arrangement the hard assets remain in the domestic partnership or corporation and, therefore, are physically situated in the U.S. Of course, being situated in the U.S., the assets are theoretically susceptible to local in rem proceedings. The goal, however, is that the barricades of the aggressive foreign law applicable to the foreign trust will have been brought "onshore" to the U.S. in such a way as to defeat or severely discourage the claimant. Using this method, one "imports" the foreign law.

When one imports the foreign law, it may still be possible to export the assets at a later time. If the structure initially involves retaining the hard assets physically in the U.S., but a problem thereafter arises, the assets can then be moved offshore (for instance, by virtue of a liquidation right provided to the trustee/limited partner in the partnership agreement). The risks, of course, are that the assets will be frozen by a court order before they can be moved or that the timing of the asset move itself will be viewed as a fraudulent transfer. Some assets are difficult or impossible to move, such as real estate or a professional practice. Hypothecation of such assets and removal of the cash may provide some flexibility here. Nonetheless, in such a situation the timing of the asset removal is critical.

### D. Enforcement of Judgments

If the assets are physically offshore, a claimant or creditor pursuing the assets of a foreign trust typically will have to do so in, and under the law of, the jurisdiction in which the trust was created. Most offshore jurisdictions require that their own laws dictate the foreign claimant's rights. Some jurisdictions will not enforce foreign judgments or will only do so after the case is heard or retried under local law. In some countries, contingent fee arrangements are not permitted, and plaintiffs are required to make substantial down payments (e.g., ten to fifteen percent of the amount claimed) as a condition precedent to filing a lawsuit.

As additional protection, some foreign trust documents contain "anti-duress" provisions to shield assets from enforcement orders directed at a U.S. co-trustee or other party subject to U.S. jurisdiction. These provisions obligate the foreign trustee to ignore directions from any person who is acting under court compulsion...

### E. Transfer of Situs

For maximum flexibility, it may be advisable to plan mobility into the offshore arrangement. Structuring the transaction so that the trust or other entity can move from one jurisdiction to another provides further protection from claimants. The attorney should make sure that the law of the original jurisdiction permits this mobility, often called "redomiciliation," and should include appropriate facilitating language in the documents.

### F. Location of Trust Assets

It is usually possible to have trust assets in jurisdictions other than the trust situs. In protecting assets from creditors, this factor can be either a further advantage or a decided disadvantage, depending on the physical location of the assets and the additional jurisdiction laws to which the trust assets are subject. The primary benefit is the severance of the jurisdictional nexus (e.g., a lawsuit filed in the trust situs jurisdiction may be ineffective if the trust assets are not located there), but this benefit can be lost through incomplete or careless planning (e.g., a foreign trust with a custodial arrangement with a branch of a U.S. bank abroad may inadvertently expose trust assets to the jurisdiction of U.S. courts).

### G. Nest Egg vs. In Toto

What percentage of a client's assets should be offshore or in an offshore structure?

**1. In Toto.** Some attorneys argue that putting virtually all of a client's assets in a U.S. family limited partnership and putting 99% of the limited partnership interests into a foreign trust provides substantial protection, even if the underlying assets are located within the physical jurisdiction of U.S. courts. However, the possibility of judicial attachment of the ownership interest in the domestic entity held by the foreign trustee on the basis of in rem jurisdiction places the "in toto" approach at or near the "less creditor protective" end of the asset protection planning spectrum.

**2. Nest Egg.** At the other, "more creditor protective" end of the asset protection planning spectrum, representing perhaps the most conservative philosophy, is the "nest egg" approach. This strategy contemplates placing a limited percentage of assets in an offshore trust, severing all jurisdictional ties, and locating the cash, stocks, or other wealth physically offshore. Moreover, the arrangement should have well-documented purposes other than, or at least complementing, asset protection. The nest egg approach is less likely to give rise to fraudulent conveyance claims because the client, by definition, still passes a solvency test after settlement of the offshore trust.

Furthermore, there is not a well-developed body of conflicts of law cases, relatively speaking, in the area of offshore trusts. With respect to in toto-type arrangements in which all or a large portion of a client's wealth is ostensibly subject to the law of the foreign trust's situs, but the assets remain physically within the U.S., the possibility of an unfavorable conflicts of law ruling by a court (i.e., favoring the law of the jurisdiction in which the assets are physically located) poses a serious risk. That element of uncertainty must be considered in determining how much of a client's wealth should be subjected to the risk of an unfavorable outcome of a conflicts of law analysis.

### H. Control

Client control over assets is an overriding preoccupation in offshore planning. A core concept of offshore asset protection is that client control of assets is inversely related to achieving asset protection. Most clients resist surrendering control of their assets to a foreign trustee. That sacrifice must be made, however, to achieve the protection afforded under an exporting the assets approach. There are a number of specific methods of addressing the control issue (protectorships, letters of wishes, advisory committees, co-trusteeships, and the like), but the advising attorney must determine at what point the extent of retained client asset control renders the trust a sham and, therefore, indefensible in court.

The problem with all of the configurations designed to give the settlor some measure of control is that, no matter how elaborately structured or formally observed, there exists the possibility that the trust can be attacked as a sham either under U.S. law or applicable foreign law. The greatest danger exists when the settlor is aggressive about retaining control. If the arrangement is ultimately controlled by the settlor, and if the settlor has, in effect, complete beneficial enjoyment, a court could easily deem the entire structure a sham and order turnover of the assets.[168] With regard to those clients seeking a high degree of control, avoiding a sham arrangement presents a serious challenge.

## I. Beneficial Enjoyment

In addition to the desire to maintain control, the client generally wants to retain, either currently or prospectively, the right to beneficial enjoyment of trust assets. While the concept of shifting, expanding, and contracting beneficial enjoyment may be new to the U.S. trust practitioner, it is commonly used in foreign trust planning...

## VI. Practical Implementation...

**4. Possible Criminal Activity.** Attorneys engaged in foreign-based asset protection planning must be wary of the new client who wishes to move offshore in a hurry, lest the attorney become an unknowing participant in a money laundering operation, the fraudulent transfer of assets to avoid creditors, or a scheme to hide illegally obtained wealth.[169] The most common criminal activity associated with the creation of asset protection trusts is money laundering, which is a specific intent crime. In order to be convicted of this crime in the United States, an individual or entity must engage in a financial transaction knowing that the funds are derived from an unlawful activity and intending either to further the unlawful activity or to conceal the true nature of the funds.[170] If the attorney thoroughly investigates his new client and after such investigation has no reason to suspect criminal activity, then the attorney should be protected from criminal liability, even if the client is involved in criminal activity, unless the attorney deliberately ignores incriminating facts.[171] Because several U.S. courts have held attorneys liable for their role in attempts by clients to defraud others, if there is any question that a client might be involved in a criminal venture or in defrauding creditors, then the attorney should refuse (or cease) representation of the client.

**5. Competent Assistance.** The advice of co-counsel with expertise in creditors' rights and fraudulent transfers is strongly recommended...

**6. Costs.** Of particular concern to the client will be local fiduciary, legal, and accounting fees, formation costs, taxes (if any), etc. As a general rule, reputable professionals in foreign jurisdictions have reasonable charges.

---

168. See Hayton, When is a Trust not a Trust?, presented at the IBC Conference on Strategic Uses of International Trusts, London (Dec. 1993); United States. v. Grant, No. 00 -8986, 2005 WL 2671479 (S.D. Fla. Sept. 2, 2005). Because the beneficiary of a Bermuda trust had full discretion to remove and replace the trustee, the magistrate concluded that the beneficiary essentially controlled the corpus of the trust and recommended that the beneficiary be ordered to repatriate trust assets so that they would be subject to U.S. law.

169. See, e.g., Uniting and Strengthening of America by Providing Appropriate Tools Required to Intercept and Obstruct Terrorism Act of 2001 (USA Patriot Act), Pub. L. No. 107-56, 115 Stat. 272; see also Ethics Advisory Opinion 84-02, South Carolina Bar.. For general discussion of fraudulent transfers, attorney liability and ethics, and relevant criminal statutes, see Osborne & Schurig, supra note 36, ch. 2, 4 & 26.

170. 18 U.S.C. § 1956.

171. See, e.g., United States v. Ramsey, 785 F.2d 184, 189 (7th Cir. 1986), cert. denied, 476 U.S. 1186 (1986); see also In re Harwell, 414 B.R. 770, 787 (M.D. Fla. 2009) The Harwell court refused to determine whether Florida recognizes a cause of action for civil conspiracy. In that case, there was a preexisting judgment against the defendant attorney's client. The client completed interrogatories from the plaintiff and failed to disclose the client's receipt of settlement funds from another matter. In declining to address the issue of civil conspiracy, the court specifically noted that the attorney "played no part in answering the interrogatories."

Competition and professionalism seem to keep trustee, legal, and accounting fees at appropriate levels. It generally is advisable to consult with more than one attorney (or firm) and to inquire about that lawyer's charges as well as other costs and fees. Making it known that one will be conducting further inquiries before selecting professionals promotes competitive responses...

### F. Step Six: Review Case Law

The plan should be back-tested against recent case law. Several cases over the past decade have found in favor of the party seeking to penetrate the asset protection structure.[172] In response, the financial press has suggested that these decisions sound the death knell for offshore asset protection trusts.[173] A careful analysis of these cases reveals, however, that offshore planning is still alive and well, and the cases provide helpful guidance for practitioners seeking to better understand what can and cannot be done in the realm of asset protection.

The Anderson case[174] has received the most attention. The Andersons, a Nevada couple, operated a telemarketing venture that the Federal Trade Commission (the "FTC") successfully attacked as a fraudulent investment scheme. The Andersons had previously established a Cook Islands trust and transferred millions of dollars of telemarketing proceeds into it. The FTC argued that the Andersons were running a Ponzi scheme, and the trial court ordered the Andersons to repatriate the telemarketing proceeds in their offshore trust to repay defrauded investors. When the Andersons failed to do so, they were held in contempt of court and actually jailed for a period of time.[175]

In Brooks,[176] the debtor settled an asset protection trust in Jersey, a jurisdiction that honors self-settled spendthrift trusts. The bankruptcy court in Connecticut, however, found that Connecticut's long-standing public policy prohibiting its citizens from creating self-settled spendthrift trusts was an important enough public policy that Connecticut law (and not Jersey law) should apply; thus, the assets of the trust were held to be available to the trustee in bankruptcy. Portnoy, a New York bankruptcy case more complicated than Brooks, also held that the law of the settlor's domicile (in this case, New York)

---

172. In re Brooks, 217 B.R. 98 (Bankr. E.D. Conn. 1998); In re Portnoy, 201 B.R. 685 (Bankr. S.D. N.Y. 1996); In re Lawrence, 251 B.R. 630 (Bankr. S.D. Fl. 2000); Sec. & Exch. Comm'n v. Brennan, 230 F.3d 65 (2d Cir. 2000); Bank of America v. Weese, 277 B.R. 241 (Bankr. D. Md. 2002); Legendre v. Henkel, Case No. 01-06482-6J7 (Bankr. M.D. Fl. Orlando Div. 2002); FTC v. Affordable Media, Inc., 179 F.3d 1228 (9th Cir. 1999); Sec. & Exch. Comm'n v. Solow, No. 06-81041, 2010 WL 303959 (S.D. Fla. Jan. 15, 2010). See also Fed. Trade Comm'n v. Ameridebt, Inc., 373 F. Supp. 2d 558 (D. Md. 2005). The FTC aggressively pursued this case against Andres Pukke, accused of defrauding consumers with debt problems by structuring repayment plans which, not coincidentally, included huge fees to Pukke. Knowing full well he was under investigation by the FTC, Pukke nonetheless executed a deliberate plan to transfer (without consideration) nearly $24,000,000 of assets to relatives, friends, and asset protection trusts established in Delaware, Nevis, and the Cook Islands. The FTC obtained a freezing order, a preliminary injunction, an order to repatriate assets, and appointment of a receiver to marshal Pukke's assets. In May of 2007, Pukke was held in contempt and jailed for failing to turn over $35 million in assets, pursuant to a settlement with the FTC. Pukke spent about a month in jail and was released after he turned over $4.5 million, an amount agreed upon by the FTC and the court-appointed receiver.

173. William C. Symonds, Offshore Trusts: Not So Watertight, Businessweek, July 26, 1999; Lynn Asinof, Ruling in West May Chill Use of Offshore Trusts, Wall St. J., July 12, 1999 at A24.

174. FTC v. Affordable Media, LLC, 179 F.3d 1228 (9th Cir. 1999).

175. Civil contempt is imposed solely to force (or coerce) the contemnor to do a particular act--such as turn over assets. The contemnor must be released when he complies. Criminal contempt is punitive. The contemnor is sentenced and must serve the term, as in any criminal proceeding.

176. 217 B.R. 98 (Bankr. D. Conn. 1998).

should apply rather than the law governing the trust. The Portnoy court observed that "Jersey does not claim to have exclusive jurisdiction over its trusts."[177]

Most of the attention paid to the Anderson case focuses on the fact that the settlors were jailed for six months for civil contempt. Proponents of asset protection trusts are fully aware of this potential threat to settlors.[178] In the area of asset protection planning, concerns about imprisonment are often answered by the notion that "impossibility" is a defense to civil contempt. That is, an individual cannot be jailed for failing to perform an act (e.g., repatriate assets) that is impossible to perform. If a defendant is ordered to do an act, but he cannot comply, imprisonment for contempt is not permitted.[179]

The core question regarding the impossibility defense is, "What if the defendant created the impossibility by his or her own action?" In the world of asset protection trusts, the most convenient impossibility for a settlor is the inability to repatriate trust assets when so ordered by a court. This is usually accomplished by a "duress clause" in the trust which directs the trustee to refuse to make distributions to a beneficiary if the beneficiary is under a court order to repatriate trust assets. Conservative asset protection planners maintain that putting this clause into the trust instrument will be viewed as a form of lawyer trickery, enraging judges, and gaining immediate judicial sympathy for creditor claimants.[180] That seems to be the case...

However, these cases also provide very helpful and valuable lessons for the asset protection bar... The only solid asset protection trust structure is one in which the settlor cedes total control of the assets. The settlor should not serve as trustee, co-trustee, protector, co-protector, or retain a power to appoint a trustee or protector. All trustees and all protectors should be independent and not subordinate to the will or control of the settlor. In addition, no U.S. person or entity should fill those roles.

Likewise, the settlor should not attempt to maintain control through some other device. For example, neither the settlor, nor an LLC or corporation controlled by the settlor, should be the general partner in a limited partnership, the interests of which are in an offshore trust. A close reading of Anderson and Weese demonstrates that U.S. courts are both persuaded and moved by the issue of asset control. Settlors who want viable asset protection trust structures must be willing to forego control...

One significant failure of the Andersons' planning was that they put all of their wealth into the trust. Not only did that lend credence to the court's conclusion that the Andersons retained control, but it also supported the fraudulent transfer claim against them. In toto planning, by definition, brings a settlor to the very limits of solvency, and the Andersons' transfer of all their wealth offshore made them appear to be avoiding creditors.

---

177. In re Portnoy, 201 B.R. 685, 697 (Bankr. S.D.N.Y. 1996).
178. See David C. Lee, Offshore Asset Protection Trusts: Testing the Limits of Judicial Tolerance in Estate Planning, 15 Bankr. Dev. J. 451, 464 (1999).
179. Id. at 452. See United States v. Rylander, 460 U.S. 752 (1983)
180. Osborne & Schurig, supra note 36, § 26:06; Cf. Chadwick v. Janecka, Case No. 02-1173 (3rd Cir., 2002)...

All of these recent cases are instructive for asset protection planners in both offshore trust creation and implementation. Offshore trust creation should begin with a thorough due diligence review of the client's pending claims, threats, and creditors. Reserves should be set aside for these liabilities. Thereafter, only a limited percentage of a client's net wealth may be used to fund an offshore asset protection trust in an export-the-assets structure...

Finally, asset protection attorneys must be constantly attuned to (and avoid any involvement with) clients or potential clients who "push the envelope" on the issue of fraudulent transfers. Both at home and abroad, courts are taking an uncompromising position with regard to any such attorney involvement. In the Cook Islands litigation of the Weese case, the Cook Islands Court of Appeal upheld a lower court order of disclosure of otherwise attorney-client privileged documents. While paying the usual homage to the important role of attorney-client privilege in Western legal systems, the court determined that if a strong prima facie case of fraud by the client against a creditor can be established, then a court may require disclosure by the client of what would otherwise be privileged information. "We see an obvious need for disclosure of the advice the (client) received from their legal experts experienced in the intricacies of protective trusts in order to ascertain whether it is being advanced as mere window-dressing to conceal their alleged purpose of defrauding the (creditor)."[181]

Closer to home, the Third Circuit held that John DeLorean's attorneys (who allegedly actively participated in DeLorean's fraudulent scheme to hinder and delay a creditor's efforts to enforce a judgment against DeLorean) could themselves be liable to the creditor for fraud even though the attorneys made no misrepresentation to the creditor and even though the creditor did not detrimentally rely on any such misrepresentation (if it was made).[182] The harsh facts of this case may limit its impact on the larger world of asset protection planning—i.e., conspicuously bad acts by the attorneys, including making material misrepresentations to the court, fraudulent concealment of facts, and wrongful withholding of information, which occurred during the pendency of a claim and after judgment. However, creditor attorneys may try to launch similar civil conspiracy theories against asset protection attorneys in an effort to set aside asset protection plans which were in place well ahead of the creditor's claim and which (as intended) are making it hard for the creditor to collect on its claim...

## VII. Overview Of Selected Jurisdictions

### A. Introduction

Selection of a jurisdiction presents a challenge. Due to the logistical difficulties of having reliable contacts in every possible country and due to the burden of trying to follow the laws and the political and economic climates of many jurisdictions, it is very tempting to select one country and then do "cookie-cutter" structures for all clients. The attorney practicing in this arena should resist

---

181. Judgment of January 6, 2003, CA 8/02 [Cook Islands Court of Appeal held at Auckland, New Zealand], para. 14.

182. Inc., No. 3AN-97-7192-CIV, (Alaska Sup. 3rd Dist. 2002). Settlor's corporation suffered a judgment, and settlor attempted to drain the corporation of assets by a series of transfers to an offshore trust. Creditor sued everyone involved (including the attorneys who created this "plan") for civil conspiracy and fraud.

that inclination and become knowledgeable about the legal and nonlegal issues relevant to various jurisdictions. There are important differences among jurisdictions and the scene is not static. What works for one client may not be best for another; similarly, what works best this year may not work best next year. Trustees and lawyers in many jurisdictions are marketing their respective countries as being optimal for asset protection. Like marketing materials of any salesman, the information is helpful, but requires careful scrutiny...

### VIII. U.S. Tax Issues Applicable To Foreign Trusts

#### A. Introduction

When assisting a client in establishing an offshore trust, the practitioner must be aware of the tax implications of the plan. Although in most cases the trust is designed to be U.S. income tax-neutral during the settlor's lifetime (i.e., income of the trust will be taxable to the settlor under the grantor trust rules),[183] there are numerous ancillary tax issues raised by the international nature of the arrangement. In addition, Congress enacted much tougher enforcement rules relating to foreign trust information reporting in 1996...

### IX. Conclusion

The question most frequently asked of lawyers who specialize in asset protection trusts is "What jurisdiction do you prefer?" There is no single answer to this question. From the analysis of the Domestic Asset Protection Venues options presented above, and considering solely the issue of asset protection, foreign venues clearly offer U.S. citizens more secure solutions than domestic venues.

Among the foreign venues, ten jurisdictions have been summarized. Each is different, and each has its own strengths and weaknesses. From time to time, the authors have used these jurisdictions (as well as others) for asset protection trusts and related entities and structures. The list is neither comprehensive nor exclusive, but does perhaps represent the venues that at the present time are being selected, more often than not, by the authors and other practitioners.

However, the legal scene constantly shifts. Two or three years from now the list of ten might look different. Only by a careful and ongoing analysis of the client's objectives, the domestic legal environment, and the foreign options can a lawyer assure a client of the best in asset protection.

This is not to say that other venues will not work. As a practical matter, even poorly conceived and ineptly implemented offshore trusts have proven highly successful at asset protection. Penetrating an offshore trust and seizing assets held therein is a daunting prospect and an expensive, time-consuming, almost insurmountable task. Some creditors will simply walk away if informed that the debtor's assets are in an offshore trust or, in the alternative, will promptly settle their claims for a reasonable figure.[184]

---

183. I.R.C. §§ 671-679.
184. Cf. Engel, *Does Asset Protection Planning Really Work?*, 4 J. of Asset Prot. No. 1 (Sept/Oct 1998).

The multiple-entity theory of estate planning involves the creative use of a variety of different legal compartments. For many years, estate planners have employed homestead laws, marital property rights, trusts for family members, pension and profit sharing plans, limited partnerships, life insurance, and other arrangements to provide tax advantages for clients and leverage when dealing with client creditors and claimants. In the context of a multiple-entity plan, an offshore trust represents one more tool in the estate planner's tool box; not the solution for all asset protection worries, but an excellent tool if carefully integrated into a comprehensive estate plan.

Implicit in the notion of multiple-entity estate planning is that no single legal compartment is watertight. Each has its own vulnerability but, grouped together in complementary fashion, these various legal compartments (including offshore trusts) can constitute an estate planning vessel fully capable of navigating the hazardous rocks and shoals presented by the tax-man, the creditor, and the plaintiff's lawyer.

## PROBLEM 16-A

**16-A.** Derek Lawson, age 49, is in the syndication business. His job is to match money players with new ventures that promise high risk and high returns. He operates through a wholly owned C corporation that is a licensed NASD dealer. He has only six employees for whom the company offers a "do-it-yourself" 401k plan. His company gets paid an up-front fee on each venture, and he purchases a back-end interest in each venture. Many projects fail, but those that work pay off big. He zeros out the taxable income of his corporation each year with bonus payments.

Derek's present net worth, exclusive of various speculative back-end venture interests, is valued at $16 million and consists principally of two expensive homes, a yacht, five commercial properties, and a stock and bond portfolio. He has a solid income, more than his lavish spending habits require. He lives in a non-community property state, has been married 17 years (his wife, Joyce, works outside the home), and has three teenage children, ages 16, 15 and 13. His estate planning consists of a "will that is somewhere and leaves everything to Joyce and the kids." His life insurance consists of an $800,000 policy that is owned and funded by the company.

Derek now wants to "get things in order." He has a few major concerns. His biggest concern is protecting what he has accumulated. He has had a few "legal skirmishes" in the past when deals failed and upset investors "flexed their muscles." In each case, he was able to "get out with no damage." But, given the size of the deals he gets involved in (most very large), he fears that the wrong "blow up" could threaten all that he has accumulated. Beyond his asset protection fears, he wants "to have the right stuff for his family." He says that Joyce "has no capacity for money matters." If something happened to Derek, he would want his brother, a CPA, to "handle everything." He acknowledges that big expenses for his children are "just around the corner and will run for a long time." Income taxes are not a big concern, but he "doesn't want to pass up any easy opportunity." He claims that he "can't relate to estate taxes," particularly if nothing will be due so long as either he or Joyce is living.

Derek wants to understand the options. Consider how each of the following tools might impact his objectives and concerns:

- A revocable living trust
- A QTIP trust
- An expanded qualified retirement plan
- A life insurance trust
- A family partnership or LLC
- A minor's 2503(c) trust
- A trust in an asset-protection friendly state
- A trust in a foreign country
- A qualified personal residence trust

# CHAPTER 17

---

# THE LAWYER'S ROLE: BUILDING A PRACTICE

---

## A. PRACTICE TIPS IN SERVING CLOSELY HELD BUSINESSES

### 1. INTRODUCTION

Advising business owners sounds much easier than it really is. It is not something all lawyers should try. But for those who do choose to make it happen and learn how to do it right, it can be immensely rewarding. It can be done in a solo or very small firm practice, a medium size firm, or a very large firm.

The term "private business owner" goes far beyond small "ma and pa" businesses, although they are clearly included within the definition. The term includes any business that is not a publicly owned company. A drive through the business or commercial district of any town will pass by many successful, often very large, privately owned businesses. They are everywhere. Every one of these businesses and their owners need ongoing, high quality legal advice.

These businesses are the backbone of the American economy. They are the absolute best clients for the lawyer who wants a healthy, vibrant practice that offers real independence, real financial security, and the personal satisfaction of being able to provide constructive, positive, value-added services that really matter — that make a difference. The happiest, most financially secure, most energetic, most interesting, most fun-to-be-with people are those individuals who build private businesses. A few are really educated, Ph.D types, but many never graduated college and some never finished high school. Most of them are at a point and doing a thing that they would have never dreamed possible when they first entered the workforce. These people don't have to worry about a pink slip. But they have to think, and they have to be good. Many of them regularly experience the endless joy and wonder of self-discovery and improvement.

Most individuals look for a lawyer only in time of crisis—divorce, personal injury, death, bankruptcy, trouble with the law. But the massive client base of private business owners is different. They have important on-going planning and business needs, and they have budgets that reserve amounts every month for professional services. They need professionals who can help them with business and personal planning strategies that enable them to maximize their opportunities and minimize their risks. They need help in planning and executing important transactions. They need counsel and advice on how to minimize the dangers of dealing with employees, investors, financiers, competitors and customers. These ongoing needs, coupled with their ability to pay, are why this huge client base is the career answer for so many professionals.

The sad reality is that many private business owners are poorly served by the legal community. Many lawyers see the opportunity, rewards and benefits and try hard to plug into this client base. But they lack the necessary training and skills and do a miserably poor job of delivering value for their clients. They forever cycle in new clients with overstated expectations and false hopes as other clients routinely exit out the back, thoroughly frustrated. There are reasons why some are so bad. Some lawyers who try to play are nothing more than non-tech hip-shooters. They combine a little horse sense with some fancy forms and general legal knowledge picked up in law school as they attempt to bamboozle their clients. They have little or no core knowledge. When it comes to planning, out of sheer ignorance they use far too much "one size fits all." They have no real concept of different business types and structures, and they have little or no capacity to understand a business' unique challenges and objectives and how different strategies can be used to meet those objectives. Often what they end up doing for the client is worse than if they did nothing, and sometimes it takes serious effort just to untangle the mess.

This is why so many private business owners fear lawyers and often turn to other professionals for advice and counsel. They fear bad, sloppy advice that's presented in a way they'll never understand. They fear inefficient, poorly delivered services. And they fear undefined, open-ended fees that promise a bad value proposition. No businessperson wants to be on the wrong side of a bad deal.

There are many highly successful lawyers who learn how to overcome these fears by countering the bad experiences of many private business owners. They actually turn these fears to their advantage. These are lawyers who have the knowledge and the know-how to do it right. They end up with wonderfully successful, highly profitable practices that constantly put themselves in demand and enable them to pick and choose who they will serve and how fast they will grow. They have real independence and financial security.

## 2. CORE KNOWLEDGE PREREQUISITES

There are keys to this kind of real success. The first is core knowledge. The successful advisor to private business owners needs to have a base of core knowledge to build upon. There is no exception or short cut to knowledge. There are four core knowledge elements.

The first is basic accounting knowledge. The lawyer does not need to be an accountant or master the art of debits and credits, but he or she must be able to read and understand financial statements and know the purposes, functions and limitations of different financial statements. These are the scorecards. Accounting is the language of business. A lawyer who does not understand the language and cannot read the scorecards will not cut it as a successful advisor to business owners.

The second is core tax knowledge. The government is a financial partner of every private business owner. It wants a piece of the action every time a sale is made, an employee is paid, someone wants in, someone wants out, someone dies — you name it. Planning and advising with tax blindfolds promises disaster. What is required is a solid grounding in individual income taxes, corporate and partnership income taxes, and wealth transfer taxes.

The third core element is basic business law. An understanding of contracts and the Uniform Commercial Code is essential, as is knowledge of the different types of planning and business entities — corporations, partnerships, limited liability companies, and a broad menu of different trusts that can be used to accomplish a wide range of specific purposes. Basic knowledge of employee relations, employment law and the essential steps that a business can take to protect itself from its employees are important. Then there are the danger flags — those warnings that pop up when a client, by design or innocence, crosses over the wrong line. Three of the most sensitive areas are securities regulation, antitrust and employee relations. A good business advisor is sensitized to the danger flags in these arenas.

But core knowledge in all these areas by itself is not enough. The successful advisor learns how to make the leap from core knowledge to strategic planning. Some never get the necessary training on how to make this all-important leap. They are buried in the details of their knowledge with no capacity to analyze specific situations and develop smart, custom solutions that work.

### 3. SPOTTING WINNERS AND LOSERS

A successful business practice requires successful business clients. Unfortunately, many businesses fail. Of course, the ideal is the new client that is a proven winner. But the real world usually requires the lawyer to regularly work with unproven businesses that offer promise, but no guarantee of success. A competent business lawyer develops an ability to quickly spot those businesses that have a real chance at success and stays clear of those that are doomed to fail. No one bats 100 percent. The lawyer with a bad average often ends up wasting huge amounts of uncompensated time on unsolvable problems that are often compounded as desperate clients seek to do desperate things.

The obvious question: How does a lawyer size up a prospective unproven client's potential for success? The best way is to meet with the client before there is any engagement for the sole purpose of evaluating the potential fit. Tell the client that you want to know more about the business before you commit to help. Most clients will respect your candor and admire your will and ability to be selective. Get the client talking about his or her business plan and then listen very carefully. The ideal is the situation where the client provides solid affirmative answers to the following six basic questions without you ever having to ask them directly:

- Does the client have real industry expertise and experience?

- Does the client know and understand the target market and have the capacity to develop the necessary competitive intelligence along the way?

- Does the client have a written strategic business that addresses sales and marketing penetration, delivery issues (scalability, economies of scale, etc), and financing that is based on realistic benchmark numbers?

- Does the client have enough capital or have access to adequate sources of capital?

- Does the client have the requisite people skills to build a successful business?

- Does the client have a track record for playing by the rules?

Track record is particularly important. Smart business lawyers stay clear of potential clients who go from one business failure to another, who have a history of embracing greedy tax fantasies, who have little or no regard for the rules and limitations that govern their dealings with investors, competitors and employees, or who have a pattern of "good old fashion" cheating. It is always easier to *stay off* a bad team than to *get off* one. Always expect respect — no one is entitled to your service. Remember that your three most precious assets are your time, your wisdom, and your integrity.

### 4. TIPS TO BUILDING A SUCCESSFUL PRACTICE

Beyond acquiring the necessary core knowledge and making the essential leap to strategic planning, the successful lawyer knows how to build and manage a profitable, successful practice that services the needs of private business owners. It is a practice that causes private business owners to seek the lawyer's advice and counsel on an ongoing basis. It requires some of the same entrepreneurial spirit and know-how that drives the clients of the practice. The challenge is to develop systems and practices that (1) facilitate the cultivation of new clients and strengthen ties to existing clients, (2) ensure the timely and efficient delivery of high quality services that are understood and appreciated by all clients, and (3) generate fee revenues that equal or surpass the lawyer's expectations. With this client base, there are specific practice techniques that can be used to meet these challenges. Following is a brief description of fifteen of them.

#### Tip 1: Embrace Other Planning Professionals

Jump at any opportunity to work with other planning professionals — financial planners, insurance professionals, investment advisors and CPAs. These other professionals are invaluable allies. These professionals are indispensable to the planning process. They play on the front line every day, prospecting for new clients. Many of them are very good at what they do. The smart lawyer knows how to build relationships with these other pros, one person at a time; knows how to learn from these other professionals (there is much that can be learned from them); and, most importantly, knows how to support and help them do a better job with the planning needs of their clients. If done right, the rewards are huge because these front line pros become the smart lawyer's marketing force. They will deliver, educate, and "tee-up" business owners for the needed legal services. They often eliminate the need for the smart lawyer to waste large amounts of otherwise productive time prospecting on the front line for new clients.

How does a lawyer cultivate strong relationships with these other professionals? The starting point is to be able to honestly articulate why you are different — why you are better. You must constantly dispel the false myth that lawyers are fungible players who deliver the same fungible services. This does not mean that you should be a braggart or ever express the desired ultimate conclusion — that you are different, that you really are better. What it does require is your ability to confidently explain the values that drive your practice and the specific procedures and standards that you have incorporated to ensure that those values are honored. As you tell your story, your listener will get the message and come to the conclusion that you are different and do offer something better.

There are some basics in dealing with other professionals. First, you will be able to sell it only if you really believe it. Real pros spot phonies. Second, whenever another professional refers a client, that professional's biggest fear is that he or she will be embarrassed or let down by the referral. You can mitigate this fear by discussing your specific practice standards. Third, you will enhance your prospects of developing a permanent referral source by helping the other professional "play first chair" with the client, without compromising your quality or confidentiality standards. Fourth, in many situations, your growing relationship with the client will result in a loyalty shift from the referral source to you over time. Just let it happen. Never acknowledge it or allow it to impact your relationship with the other professional. Finally, avoid reciprocal deals where you are expected to provide return referrals. The odds of you disappointing are very high. When asked about this, emphasize your "back office" role in working with other professionals, your commitment to high quality service, and your deep regard for the referring professional's relationship with the client. A few opportunities may be lost for not promising what you can't deliver on, but the great bulk of high quality pros will be satisfied with your candor and the assurance that their client relationships will not be in jeopardy.

Once you have your pitch down, go out and sell it. Attend conferences, educational programs, and chamber meeting with other professionals and freely discuss what you do and how you do it. Always take a genuine, active interest in what others are saying about what they do. Line up one-on-one lunches or short office meetings to discuss your services and the services offered by the other professional. When you get a referral from another professional, send a short "thank you" by email. Then do a superb job. Your goal is to have that client thank the referring professional for the referral. All win when this happens. And you will soon discover that you have a permanent referral line from that professional.

**Tip 2: Become an Educator**

The best way for a lawyer to close credibility gaps and build strong relationships with front line pros and business clients, both new and old, is to liberally share his or her insights, ideas and wisdom for no charge. This requires that the lawyer learn how to communicate technical knowledge and strategies in ways that they can be understood by ordinary, non-legal folks. It is not easy, and many lawyers do not even want to make the attempt. But the lawyer who learns how to distill technical jargon into key issues, principals, and strategies that any reasonably intelligent person can understand ends up being a much better strategist and an infinitely better lawyer. Most business clients want to learn and understand anything that may improve or strengthen their business.

There are different ways to educate. One is to give live speeches to groups of front line pros or to audiences of potential clients that are routinely assembled by front line pros. As you demonstrate over time that you really know what you are talking about and that you can communicate in a way that educates and holds the interest of non-lawyers, you will receive many speaking opportunities, far more than you can handle. Beyond live speeches is the opportunity to develop simple educational tools that make it easy to share knowledge and ideas and leverage your expertise. The Internet provides a powerful opportunity to share knowledge as a quality educator. It is the most cost-effective communication tool that has ever existed.

These educational opportunities — live speeches and education tools— require an up-front investment of time and a little money, but the returns on the investment can be startling. As you provide the education and develop the right tools, you become the expert, and you'll be able to leverage your knowledge and wisdom in ways that make business owners want you to be on their teams. The lawyer who by design or default cloaks information in legalese to make it sound sophisticated or complicated, or who is unwilling to share information unless a fee paying client is sitting across the desk, just doesn't get it. That lawyer always will lose to the skilled educator who knows how to inform and interest others and is willing to share freely of his or her knowledge.

### Tip 3: Maintain A Smart Contact Program

Many lawyers mistakenly assume that contacts with an existing client should only be initiated by the client when the client needs service. The smart lawyer develops a program to constantly stay in touch with business owner clients. The program has three purposes: first, to continually strengthen ties with the client by reminding the client that he or she is part of your team; second, to provide an ongoing value-added educational service to the client; and third, to potentially generate more revenues by sparking a need for service that the client would not have otherwise recognized. Remember, successful private business owners often are highly-motivated, confident, ego-driven individuals. They like being reminded that they are important to you. It's likely that many of them regularly are being courted by your competition. Your challenge is to remind them that you value the relationship, that you are at the top of your game, and that you are ready and able to serve their needs.

Often an effective contact program has two components. The first component is a standard communication that goes to all business owner clients on a regular basis, either monthly or quarterly. It can be in a letter or newsletter format, sent by email or regular mail. It may recap tax and other developments that may impact private business owners, with a little personal commentary and opinion. The research effort is minimal. The entire effort, including the drafting, requires no more than a few hours of lawyer time each month or quarter. A staff member can finalize, format, and send the product.

The second and more important component is personal affirmative contact ("PAC"). A few times each year you affirmatively contact the client with a personal message. The message may refer to a news or sporting event of common interest, a comment on the client's financials (see Tip 7 below), or just a simple personal statement, such as, "I hope you are having another good year. Would very much like to have lunch and catch up." Each PAC is a custom reminder to the client that you care and that he or she is important to you.

An effective PAC program can be easily implemented with two simple procedures. First, a staff member is given the responsibility of identifying those clients who should be sent a PAC message each month (each client, for example, may be on the list every six months) and identifying suggested news items of interest. Second, the lawyer must pre-commit a specific hour or two each month to dictate or email PAC messages.

If these two simple procedures are used, PAC messages will flow from the office effortlessly each month. Absent these types of automatic procedures, the PAC chore may quickly be viewed as a desirable, but non-essential, nuisance that can be ignored for yet another month.

### Tip 4: Dial Down the Tech Talk

The law is technical, and many lawyers work hard to sound like lawyers. Planning lawyers often like to talk "Code," constantly referring to sections of the Internal Revenue Code to make a point. However effective this may be in conversing with other lawyers, it is a turn-off for most business owners. They want to understand. They want it in plain English. This creates a huge advantage for the lawyer who learns how to communicate like a businessperson. The lawyer who becomes an active educator, as suggested in Tip 2, will forever face this "Plain Talk" challenge. But apart from the speeches and the educational tools, there is a need to embrace the challenge in everyday dialogue with business clients.

Avoid "lawyer-like" transitions, such as "whereas", "therefore", "notwithstanding" and the like. Wherever possible, focus on objectives and potential solutions, rather than legal rules and exceptions. Often it is best to first summarize your bottom line conclusions and then provide the supporting details and rationale with logically organized points. The listener is spared the suspense and burden of waiting for the bottom line and can easily relate each point back to the conclusion.

When discussing a series of events or an interrelated set of different issues, try to just tell a story in simple words. Where appropriate, use drawings or diagrams to simplify the discussion. Often it is helpful to use short case studies. Many of the chapters in this book discuss a specific planning challenge or set of planning issues in plain-spoken terms. Use these as samples in developing your own capacity to communicate effectively with non-lawyer business owners.

### Tip 5: Assist with Risk Analysis

Peter Drucker once said, "Whenever you see a successful business, someone once made a courageous decision."[1] Truth is, someone probably made numerous courageous decisions. Business is about taking risks. The successful business owner needs to be a good risk-taker. Too many lawyers assume that their role is limited to spelling out the law and the legal issues. They do little or nothing to assist in effective risk analysis, which ends up being the tough, lonely job of the business owner. The lawyer who learns how to play an effective role in helping a client through a tough risk analysis may quickly become a valued advisor whose counsel is requested regularly.

Some business owners thrive on risk; they embrace it with a passion. It's a high. They cherish the thrill of letting it roll. To them, it's "no guts, no glory" all the way. So they have a tendency to just wing it, to go for it. Others loathe risk. They live with it, accept it as a reality, but detest it. Their natural tendency is to avoid and duck risk. But whether a client is a risk-lover or risk-hater is not all that important if the client has the discipline and know-how to deal with risk effectively. This is where trusted advisors can help most. Many business owners, even those who perceive themselves as risk-dreading wimps, can become excellent risk takers.

What separates the winners from the losers is the will and ability to tackle the risk — the ability to strip the risk to its bare essentials by synthesizing all relevant, credible information and then to properly analyze the stakes and the odds. It takes effort, energy, and some brain power. And because it takes some effort and is not easy, there are two mistakes that many poor risk takers routinely make.

The first is that they mistake risk taking for ignorance. They just do not expend the energy to gather useful, necessary information that is available with a little effort. This information, if known, would be critical to handicapping the risk and often would reduce or eliminate the risk. The cause usually is laziness, and the rationale is that nobody really knows what's going to happen in the future anyway. But with nearly every decision, usually there exist critical facts and important information that enable a good risk taker to smartly balance the odds, the stakes, and all the trade-offs. The person who never gets the information – or worst yet gets bad information from unreliable sources – is just betting on the state of his or her own ignorance. It becomes a game of dumb luck, not strategic, smart risk taking.

The second mistake that lousy risk takers often make is that they place too much emphasis on their perception of the odds. If the odds are favorable (that is, there is a good chance they are going to win), they go for it. They jump. If the odds are unfavorable, they walk. Smart risk takers do not start with the odds. They start by carefully and fairly assessing the stakes — the upside and the downside. Then before even looking at the odds, they ask these questions: Can I live with the downside if I lose this one? Will I still be a player? They understand that there are some risks with hugely favorable odds that they can never afford to take. The downside, no matter how small its chances, is just too catastrophic. On the flip side, they know there are other risks with unfavorable odds, often less

---

1. Encarta Book of Quotations (St. Martin's Acts 2000) p. 288.

than 50 percent, that they can afford to take all day. The reason is that the upside of being right is a huge deal while the downside of being wrong is no big deal, often peanuts.

The smart advisor helps the client through the process by pushing to ensure that all relevant information is on the table, that the stakes are properly evaluated, and that the odds then are appropriately assessed and evaluated.

### Tip 6: Brutal Honesty

There is no substitute for the truth, eEven when it hurts. No business owner wants to be finessed, even on the little things. Always tell the absolute truth. If you must cancel an appointment because something more important has surfaced, don't make up some phony excuse. Just tell it like it is. Your credibility with your client is supreme. It will be tested time and again. Make certain you pass every test.

### Tip 7: Be Genuinely Interested in the Business

Many business owners love their businesses. Often their whole lives, along with their dreams and aspirations, are wrapped up in the business. They spend nearly every waking hour trying to make the business stronger. Usually, they welcome the opportunity to talk about their business with an advisor who genuinely cares. Often they are honored and impressed when smart questions are asked about the business.

This kind of interest takes a little effort, but can pay huge "client loyalty" dividends. It's another way of showing that you care and that you understand the business of business. Before getting into the meat of any meeting or discussion, just ask the client how the business is doing. Listen for specifics. Then after the meeting, dictate a short memo to your file that summarizes what the client said. Before your next meeting, review the memo for details. In your next encounter, inquire as to those specifics that might be relevant or of interest. As you do this over time, you will develop a natural business dialogue with the business owner. This will help you be a better advisor and, most importantly, will continually reaffirm to your client the importance of you being a part of his or her team.

### Tip 8: Take an Interest in the Scorecards

The scorecards of every business are its financial statements. When you are retained to help on a specific matter, ask the business owner for permission to review the financial statements of the business. Explain that your review of the financials will give you a more solid understanding of the business. Most business owners will be impressed and honored by the request. Then review the financials. Learn from them. Discuss them with the client. Remember, these are your client's scorecard — the report card.

As your relationship with the client builds, you may be given the opportunity to automatically receive updated financials on a quarterly, semi-annual or annual basis. Take advantage of this opportunity to bind yourself to the client and learn more about the business. It often means that you have been accepted as a trusted advisor.

### Tip 9: Efficient, Timely Turnaround

Many lawyers talk a good game, but cannot get the product out the door on time. The business owner waits days for a promised document, perplexed as to why it takes so long and why the promised date of delivery has long since passed. Often little or no explanation is provided. When asked, the lawyer or an employee offers an excuse that suggests it is just "business as usual." The business owner's concern is heightened by the fact that he or she runs a far more complicated business that would never tolerate such delays and inefficiencies.

The smart lawyer avoids this syndrome like the plaque. Targeted turnaround dates are promised and hit. If something pops up that creates an unexpected delay, the client is advised immediately, provided a full explanation, and given a new turnaround date.

Two factors separate the good from the bad when it comes to turnaround. The first is office procedures designed to ensure that all promised deadlines are met. The lawyer must reserve blocks of time to prepare documents or give appropriate instructions for the preparation of documents that were discussed with clients on a given day. This should be followed by procedures that enable assistants or paralegals to prepare the draft documents and to timely return them to the lawyer for review and edit. A high quality, state-of-the-art form library that all key office personnel understand and know how to use can be invaluable. It is well worth a sizable investment of time and energy to create and update.

The second factor is a desire and commitment of all personnel to hit every promised deadline. It needs to be a matter of office pride. It's the old "ninety-nine percent right is one-hundred percent wrong" mentality. It often requires extra effort and diligence to ensure that no project is missed. It will set a standard of excellence that clients will see and appreciate. This commitment alone can distinguish an office from much of the competition.

### Tip 10: Make Certain All Your Employees Are Highly Engaged

In 2003, Towers Perrin, a global human resource professional service firm, published a comprehensive report and survey on employment in the United States entitled "Working Today: Understanding What Drives Employee Engagement".[2] A major purpose of the survey was to determine how many employees are really engaged in their jobs — which Towers Perrin defined as an employee's willingness and ability to contribute to a company's success by putting discretionary effort into his or her work in the form of extra time, brainpower and energy. Sadly, the report concluded that only 17 percent of America's workforce was highly engaged in their jobs.

A lawyer who wants to effectively service private business owner clients must ensure that his or her entire support staff is highly engaged. A smart business owner can determine in a matter of minutes if the non-lawyer employees of the firm are engaged and motivated. It is that obvious. The demeanor, reactions and speed of the staff say it all. The differences between a motivated, happy, engaged staff and a staff that is just logging another day are startling.

---

2. Tower Perrin, "Working Today" Understanding What Drives Employee Engagement (2003).

So the big question: How does a lawyer ensure that all of his or her coworkers are highly engaged? It's beyond the scope of this writing to discuss all the possibilities, but here are three practices to consider. First, ensure that every employee has a direct financial interest in the financial success of the practice. Nothing motivates like money. There are countless cash bonus programs that can be used to meet this objective. A smart bonus plan can help engage everyone. All know that more appointments, transactions and documents translate to more billings. All know that existing business clients are the best source for more work and higher billings. All appreciate the worn-out phrase, "It can take months to get a valued business client, and only seconds to lose one."

The second practice to engage employees is to include them in a monthly meeting that focuses on the firm's on-going commitment to high quality service. The meetings give all employees a forum to discuss problems and ideas for improvement. All are encouraged to participate and share ideas. The meetings eliminate the need for time-consuming ad hoc "complaint discussions."

The third practice is to hire upbeat, passionate people who enjoy being of service to others. Many just don't have it. They may be very talented and bright, but they act as though the world owns them a living, and they end up routinely bringing their personal problems, prejudices and petty hang-ups to the office. Quality driven employees understand the importance of parking their personal problems outside the door of a professional firm each day so they can contribute to a positive, upbeat professional environment that makes all clients want to return.

### Tip 11: Above All—A Fair Deal

All business owners want a fair deal when it comes to fees. They are willing to pay a fair price for high quality services, but they hate unpleasant surprises and uncertainties. Often this requires that the smart lawyer develop programs to generate revenues by eliminating the uncertainties of the billable hour game and the economic disincentives for a business owner to pick up the phone and ask a question. Smart business owners work hard to control their costs, and many have a natural aversion to routinely starting a meter that tracks at the rate of $350 an hour.

A threshold challenge for many business lawyers is to identify and maximize fixed fee opportunities — those situations where the lawyer can eliminate all uncertainties by offering a standard fixed fee up front for a particular job. A closely related practice is for the lawyer to quote a custom fixed fee in advance based on the parameters of the job worked out with the client. In both situations, the client is happy because the uncertainty is gone. The lawyer's focus also changes. The issue is no longer "how many hours can I bill on the job", but rather "how can I most efficiently deliver first-rate service on this job." As the efficiency improves, the yield on each expended hour goes up.

Beyond fixed fees is the opportunity to use monthly retainers that allow managers in the client's organization to call or email for business-related advice, knowing that the inquiry is covered by the retainer. Typically, the business owner and the lawyer will estimate how much legal time the retainer service will require for ad hoc calls for advice that do not require significant research. A monthly fee is set based on the estimate. The lawyer then monitors the actual performance, and the fee is periodically adjusted, prospective only. The lawyer takes the risk of any retroactive shortfall, but the risk is usually minimal and insignificant when compared to the value of strengthening the firm's ties to the business and the opportunity for non-retainer work.

Does this mean the billable hour game is gone? No, it just means that it is used less. Most business owners will greatly appreciate the lawyer's efforts to develop billing strategies that eliminate uncertainties. If done right, these efforts can generate increased revenues for the lawyer and provide firm wide incentives to promote efficiencies.

### Tip 12: Bring 'Em Together

Most private business owners enjoy socializing with and learning from other business owners, but often have limited opportunities to do so. The smart lawyer will help create such an opportunity once or twice a year by inviting his or her business owner clients to a special seminar that offers advice on a topic of interest and the opportunity for a little socializing and networking. Often other professionals who routinely refer clients to the firm are invited.

These informal, relatively inexpensive gatherings can accomplish a number of objectives. They provide another opportunity to showcase expertise and perhaps generate more work by sparking interest in a new idea. They reaffirm the lawyer's commitment to providing value-added information and experiences. They reinforce and strengthen the confidence of each business owner's decision to use the lawyer by allowing the owner to meet and hear from others who have made the same decision. They provide a simple venue for clients to discuss shared problems and challenges.

### Tip 13: Look Professional

Never underestimate the importance of looking professional. If you are going to be a business advisor, look like a business advisor. This doesn't mean that you must have an expensive high-rise office suite and lavish furnishings. It does help to have an office that is attractively decorated and comfortable. This usually requires some input from an interior designer. Usually how you spend the money is more important than how much you spend. Many attractive, comfortable client-oriented environments cost a fraction of that spend by others to make some kind of bold statement.

Dress is important. Keep the standards at medium-to-high business for everyone in the office. Ignore the casual Friday stuff. High dress standards help with clients and employees. Whether they admit it or not, most business owner clients prefer an environment that looks and acts professional. Employees who are required to "dress up" every day are continually reminded of the importance of their work in a professional office and the value of the clientele they are privileged to serve.

### Tip 14: Use Client's Name—Often

A simple but important technique to enhance the professionalism of the office is to greet each client by his or her name—often. It adds a powerful personal touch that makes the client feel welcome and important. It can be done effectively with just a little coordination. The receptionist needs to be briefed on who will be coming. When the receptionist announces a client's arrival, the client's name should be used. Each employee who interacts with the client should be encouraged to use the client's name.

### Tip 15: Ignore Talk of Your Business

You are the advisor. Your purpose is to strengthen the businesses of your clients. You accomplish nothing positive by lamenting about your business and the challenges you face. By way of comparison, you run a fairly simple business; you render professional services and send bills. Your business owner clients know this and will not be impressed with your complaints. Keep your problems to yourself. Always make your client's business the focus of your attention.

## B. BUSINESS ADVICE FROM A LAWYER?

### Recipe for An Overdue Change
### Why Corporate Lawyers Sometimes
### Need to Give Business Advice[3]

Business **lawyers** as **business advisers?** Could be. Read on. The recent series of corporate implosions should cause every business lawyer to wonder what counsel could have done to prevent these disasters. Many observers, in and outside of the profession, wonder the same thing. While it will take years for the courts and regulators to sort out exactly what happened in these corporate debacles, I suggest that a big part of the problem is the written and unwritten constraint taught to most aspiring business lawyers concerning the need to defer to their clients' business decisions. See, for example, the Model Rules of Professional Conduct, Sec. 1.2(a): "A lawyer shall abide by a client's decisions concerning the objectives of representation...." From law school through the associate and junior partner ranks, business transactional lawyers are taught the traditional paradigm that their job is to advise clients as to available options and legal implications and work diligently to implement the client's decision from among the options.

The product of the present approach has been noted in the pages of this magazine: "In this dramatic context, what has been the role of lawyers? Has our profession been battling misconduct, and taking heroic steps to protect companies and their investors? For the most part, our profession has not distinguished itself." Murphy, "Enron, ethics and lessons for lawyers," Bus. Law Today, January/February 2003 at 11. The author's thesis is that we must revisit this premise in order to make meaningful the current admonitions to public company counsel in Section 307 of the Sarbanes–Oxley Act (the act) and related regulations, to protest illegal acts of corporate management. SEC Release 2003–

---

3. Copyright © 2003 The American Bar Association and Martin B. Robins. Reprinted with permission. Mr. Robins is a sole practitioner, concentrating in corporate transactions. He holds a B.S. from the Wharton School at the University of Pennsylvania and a J.D. from Harvard Law School.

13 announcing the release of regulations under the act, Jan. 23, 2003, "SEC Adopts Lawyer Conduct Rule under Sarbanes–Oxley Act," at the SEC Web site, www.sec.gov (the "Implementing Release") summarizes the objective:

> The rules adopted today by the commission will require an attorney to report evidence of a material violation, determined according to an objective standard, 'up the ladder' within the issuer ... [ultimately to] the full board of directors;.... See also, Cramton, "Enron and the Corporate Lawyer: A Primer on Legal and Ethical Issues," 58 Bus. Lawyer 143, 179 (2002).

It is submitted that in the transactional context, a potential legal violation must in most cases be analyzed in the context of an economic transaction. Disclosure violations and fiduciary violations almost invariably involve a misrepresentation or diversion of economic consequences. Accordingly, counsel must be made responsible for understanding the economic basics of their client's business, industry and the financial marketplace as well as being responsible for a minimal critique as to whether a given major action is at least minimally viable in such context. Protest as to a legal violation will often require advice as to economic flaws in a proposed transaction or policy. This article suggests a new requirement to govern the manner in which a lawyer advises their client. Pending any change in formal requirements, lawyers engaged at an entity level are urged to take a broad view of their roles and speak up to their direct contacts whenever they see something that appears questionable, whether or not the matter is clearly legal in nature. Of course, they must in all events heed the language of the act to pursue "up the ladder" evidence of legal violations. Frequently, an objective perspective from counsel not directly involved in the matter will be sufficient to dissuade clients from disastrous paths that they have lost the ability to identify. Counsel choosing to act in this way should communicate their intention to their client, preferably at the inception of the representation in order to minimize any disruption from counsel's acting in a "nontraditional" way. The traditional approach may have worked well during the early and middle parts of the last century in the midst of a goods-based economy where it was frequently possible to easily distinguish business and legal issues. Today, however, things are different. With so many businesses based on intellectual capital, as opposed to plant and equipment, and so many businesses tied directly to the financial markets and the exotic strategies they now permit, it is often impossible to readily distinguish "legal" and "business" issues.

Yet, in the face of so much change, we still see lawyers seeking to limit their advice to legal matters when it is clear that such matters could not be meaningfully distinguished from business matters and that the client's fundamental approach to its business was seriously flawed and leading it toward disaster. A headline in the Wall Street Journal of May 10, 2002, is illustrative: "Lawyers for Enron Faulted its Deals, Didn't Force Issue." Perhaps the most graphic example of a lawyer standing by while the client careened toward business disaster is found in the case of Commercial Financial Services Inc. In this case, a partner in a large law firm that represented the now-defunct company in connection with numerous securitized financings is alleged to have been advised by the company's departing CEO (after five months on the job) that its business model was flawed in that it involved a scheme to provide investor returns by selling off assets, instead of from income generated by retained assets. However, the firm is alleged by its client to have said nothing to the client about the unsustainability of this approach but simply used carefully couched language pertaining to the CEO's departure in public disclosures pertaining to other financings. It was not until long after the CEO's departure that the problems came to light and litigation was brought against all concerned—including the law firm. The client's founder complained that "they were making so much stinking money on the deals that they didn't want it to end" and that "they didn't tell anyone not to do any more deals" and that "the advice we should have gotten is to slow down the operation and change the way we did business." Pacelle, "As Firm Implodes, Lawyer's Advice Is Point of Contention," Wall Street Journal, Oct. 29, 2002.

While the foregoing is necessarily anecdotal and considerations of lawyer-client privilege and client confidentiality make it impossible to say for sure what advice has been given in any particular situation, what is striking is the total absence of vigorous public pronouncements by lawyers involved in these situations as to their affirmative efforts to persuade their clients to stop doing things that in many cases must have appeared ex ante to be as perilous as they turned out to be ex post. Based on my own training and observations of numerous other transactional lawyers, I believe that in the majority of cases, well-meaning lawyers felt powerless to challenge their clients' "business decisions" despite the fact that it was clear that client management was either personally interested in the specific decision or policy or had become so close to the situation that they could no longer objectively analyze it—making a third-party critique that much more important. Our complex economy and financial markets and the critical "gatekeeper" role of lawyers vis a vis those markets demand that we banish this arcane distinction and require lawyers to use their objective perspective to advise their clients of significant reservations as to the prudence or propriety of the clients' business practices. Both client expectations and the public interest in these troubled times demand that those who are capable of heading off catastrophic losses be charged with the responsibility for making reasonable efforts to do so, as opposed to using their narrow specialty to rationalize looking the other way. When counsel sees their client headed for disaster, they should be required to speak up, whether or not the disaster is strictly "legal" in nature.

Are lawyers equipped to do so? From my observations, it appears that a business lawyer who has practiced at least 10 years or so will pick up enough of a feel for what makes economic sense and what doesn't, to make their comments meaningful at a high level. Senior-level lawyers by definition possess the talent and training to advise intelligently on all legal aspects of a given matter. Frequently, lawyers will have addressed a given situation enough times to develop a good idea of an intelligent business solution, in contrast to a client who may not have prior experience with the particular matter. It is suggested that if a lawyer does not develop or has not yet developed some feel for the business ramifications of major client actions, he or she should not be functioning in a senior capacity. The effort is not to constitute the business bar as some sort of super-board-of-directors or management committee sitting in judgment on day-to-day matters. The goal simply is to keep them alert for fundamental problems that imperil the future of the enterprise or its investors. That would include, among other things, major accounting irregularities that should be palpably evident without formal accounting training—such as drastic changes in accounting policy, financial statements that are not readily understandable and transactions producing material financial-statement benefit to the organization or its management without a discernible business purpose...

What is important is not the precise confines of counsel's obligations, but rather inducing counsel to take a broader view of their role. Make no mistake, these recommendations represent a substantial departure from the traditional—and at one time appropriate—role of the senior business lawyer as a technician and presenter of options. What is being urged here is to require counsel to educate themselves as to the broad confines of the client's business and industry and, most important, to sometimes confront the client on what some clients feel is the client's "turf."

However, it is clear that the traditional approach is simply not working; it is incomprehensible that senior level lawyers advising major companies will not see and have not seen the folly of the clients' approach in several of the widely publicized debacles. However, it appears that none of them has prevailed on their clients to change their ways. In addition to the compelling public policy issues discussed above, lawyers should also take into account that when the problem arises, there will be plenty of blame to go around. The client will not thank the lawyer for deference.

## C. COMMON ETHICAL CHALLENGES

### Ethical Issues In Advising Closely
### Held Businesses
Scott A. Schumacher[4]

### 1. INTRODUCTION

The ethical challenges faced by a business advisor can be varied and complex. Various sources must be considered, including state rules of professional conduct and ethics opinions, the American Bar Association's Model Rules of Professional Conduct, formal ethics opinions issued by the ABA, rules promulgated by the Department of Treasury in Circular 230 that govern practice before the Internal Revenue Service, and rules promulgated by the Securities and Exchange Commission pursuant to the Sarbanes–Oxley Act of 2002. Each of these bodies of law contains detailed rules and duties applicable to lawyers, many of which overlap and some of which conflict.

### 2. ETHICAL ISSUES AT FORMATION OF THE ENTITY

#### a. Identifying the Real Client

The threshold question a lawyer must always answer is: who is my client?

For most lawyers, the answer is obvious—it's the person sitting across the desk, asking all the questions. The answer is not so easy, however, when the lawyer is being retained to represent a closely held business. In this situation, the general rule for identifying the client is set forth in ABA Model Rule 1.13,[5] which provides simply that a "lawyer employed or retained by an organization represents the organization acting through its duly authorized constituents." With corporations, there usually is no confusion: It is well settled that a corporation is a separate legal entity, a separate legal "person." However, the law is much less settled with regard to partnerships, limited partnerships, limited liability partnerships, limited liability companies, and all of the other related hybrid entities.

Partnerships and LLCs are creatures of state law. Under § 101(b) of the Uniform Partnership Act of 1991, the term "partnership" means "an association of two or more persons to carry on as co-owners a business for profit." The predominate theory in cases that have examined this issue is that partnerships, LLCs, and similar structures are separate legal entities, rather than aggregates of their owners, and that the lawyer represents the entity and not the partners or owners.[6] However, other courts have found that the lawyer did in fact represent the owners as well as the entity.[7] Nearly every court to have addressed this issue has based its determination on the facts of the individual case. The Supreme Court muddied the water in *Carden v. Arkoma Associates*, 494 U.S. 185 (1990), where the Court held that, for purposes of diversity jurisdiction to permit a suit in federal court, the citizenship of an unincorporated association is to be determined by the citizenships of all its members. Thus, the Court in essence held that a partnership or other unincorporated entity should be treated, at least in some instances, as an aggregate of its individual members.[8]

---

4. Associate Professor of Law; Director, Graduate Program in Taxation, University of Washington School of Law.

5. Throughout this chapter, we will discuss only the ABA Model Rules, rather than any given state's rules of professional conduct. Since each state's rules vary slightly on many topics, it would be impossible in this context to address the numerous permutations amongst the rules. Moreover, given that ABA Model Rules are indeed the model rules for most state's rules, a discussion of the Model Rules should give a lawyer sufficient background to analyze the issue.

6. See, e.g., Quintel Corp., N.V. v. Citibank, N.A., 589 F.Supp. 1235 (S.D.N.Y. 1984) (lawyer representing the limited partnership and its general partners did not necessarily have a client-lawyer relationship with limited partners); Johnson v. Superior Court, 45 Cal.Rptr.2d 312 (Cal. Ct. App. 1995) (on facts presented, lawyer for limited partnership owed no duty to limited partners); In re Owens, 581 N.E.2d 633 (Ill. 1991) (lawyer who represented only the partnership did not violate prohibition on business dealings with clients by transactions with individual partners); Hopper v. Frank, 16 F.3d 92 (5th Cir. 1994).

7. See, e.g., Margulies v. Upchurch, 696 P.2d 1195 (Utah 1985) (holding that law firm's representation of a limited partnership in commercial litigation gave rise to and implied attorney-client relationship with respect to the individual partners, who according to the court reasonably believed that the law firm was acting for their individual interests as well as those of the partnership); Al–Yusr Townsend & Bottum Co. v. United Mid–East Co., Civ. A. No. 95–1168, 1995 WL 592548 (E.D. Pa. Oct. 4, 1995) (facts show that lawyer representing joint venture has attorney-client relationship with members of entity); Responsible Citizens v. Superior Court, 20 Cal.Rptr.2d 756 (Ct. App. 1993) (whether lawyer for partnership has lawyer-client relationship with individual partner depends on facts of case. Factors to be considered include type and size of partnership, nature and scope of lawyer's engagement by partnership, kind and extent of contracts between lawyer and individual partner, and lawyer's access to information relating to partner's interests); Arpadi v. First MSP Corp., 628 N.E.2d 1135 (Ohio 1994) (lawyers for limited partnership owed duty of care to limited partners).

8. See also Scott M. Rickard, Shoring Up The "Doctrinal Wall" Of Chapman v. Barney: In Support Of The Aggregate Approach To Limited Liability Company Citizenship For Purposes Of Federal Diversity Jurisdiction, 40 Willamette L. Rev. 739 (2004), stating that most courts that have considered the entity-vs.-aggregate issue in the context of an LLC has held that an LLC is an aggregate of its members for diversity of citizenship purposes.

The ABA has attempted to set forth a bright-line (or at least a brighter-line) rule on this issue of client identification in situations involving a partnership or a limited liability company. Model Rule 1.13(a) provides simply that a "lawyer employed or retained by an organization represents the organization acting through its duly authorized constituents." In ABA Formal Opinion 91–361 (1991), the ABA held that a partnership is an "organization" within the meaning of Rule 1.13, and that, generally, a lawyer who represents a partnership represents the entity rather than the individual partners. This rule would also be applicable to LLCs. Nevertheless, the ABA acknowledged that despite this general rule, an attorney-client relationship may nevertheless arise with the individual partners or owners, depending upon the facts of the case. Thus, while the ABA has clarified the issue as to whether an attorney represents the partnership as an entity (rather than an aggregate of individuals), the facts of any given case may well show that the attorney also represents one or more of the partners or owners.

How the tax laws treat partnerships, LLCs, and other related entities often is important in resolving the issue of client identity. Unfortunately, Congress has not been consistent on this issue.[9] The confusion and ethical dilemmas engendered by the tax code are perhaps most acute when a lawyer represents a partnership or LLC in an audit before the IRS or in litigation before the United States Tax Court. While the ABA has stated that a lawyer in a partnership case represents the entity, and not the individual partners, the unified audit and litigation procedures of the Code may provide otherwise. With the Tax Equity and Fiscal Responsibility Act of 1982 (TEFRA), Congress has chosen to have partnership tax cases handled by a partner but in the name of the partnership.

Congress promulgated the TEFRA partnership unified audit and litigation provisions of §§ 6221 through 6234 of the Internal Revenue Code intending to simplify and streamline the audit, litigation, and assessment procedures with respect to partnerships and their partners. These provisions centralized the tax treatment of partnership items and resulted in equal treatment for partners through the uniform adjustment of each partner's tax liability in a single, unified proceeding.[10] Congress enacted TEFRA so that "the tax treatment of items of partnership income, loss, deductions, and credits will be determined at the partnership level in a unified partnership proceeding rather than separate proceedings with the partners."[11] The TEFRA partnership rules also apply to LLCs being taxed as partnerships. The partnership is represented in the audit and litigation by the Tax Matters Partner (or "TMP"), who also represents his or her own interests in the dispute. For ethical purposes, does the lawyer representing the partnership and the TMP represent just the partnership's interest? Just the TMP's interest? Both? What if the interests of TMP and the partnership diverge? What if there is a dispute between the TMP (who may or may not have the best interests of the partnership in mind) and the other partners? The TEFRA

---

9. For an excellent discussion of the inconsistent approach to the taxation of partnerships under the code, see McKee, Nelson, and Whitmire, Federal Taxation of Partnerships and Partners, Warren Gorham & Lamont (2004), ¶ 102[3].

10. See, e.g., Chimblo v. Commissioner, 177 F.3d 119, 120–121 (2d Cir. 1999), aff'g. T.C. Memo 1997–535.

11. H. Conf. Rept. 97–760, at 600 (1982), 1982–2 C.B. 600, 662.

Partnership rules may give rise to unavoidable conflicts. It is essential that the lawyer communicate clearly with the partnership and the TMP from the beginning, to make sure that there are no misunderstandings about the nature of the representation, and also to learn as much as possible about the facts of the case in order to head off any potential conflict.

In *Goulding v. United States*,[12] the Seventh Circuit held that a lawyer who prepared partnership returns and schedules for a limited partnership was also liable for the preparer penalty of § 6694 for each of the limited partners' returns as well. The assessed liability against Mr. Goulding was more than $44,000. In so holding, the Court examined the structure of the Code and the nature of partnerships in general:

> *As the partnership is both entity and aggregate, the tax preparer's relationship to the partnership is necessarily dual—he is dealing with the partnership both as entity and as aggregate of partners.* Appellant was retained to analyze the partnership operation; however, the analysis of the partnership operation was a making of decisions and calculations for all the individual partners, to whom the tax liability or deductions would flow through the partnership. These decisions and calculations were directly reflected on the returns of the partners; *all the individual partners depended upon Mr. Goulding's analysis. Thus while appellant was retained by the partnership and compensated by the partnership, in reality his work was for all the partners.*[13]

According to the Court in *Goulding*, which analyzed and applied what it believed were the rules set out by Congress in the Code and by Treasury in its Regulations, a lawyer advising and representing a partnership "in reality" works for all of the partners, if under the facts of the case the partners depended upon the advice of the lawyer.

### b. Definitively Resolving the Question of Client Identity

The way in which nearly every ethical duty must be discharged will depend upon who the client is, that is, to whom the duties under the various ethical rules are owed. And yet, this most fundamental question often is unanswerable in the absolute when dealing with certain entities. While the inconsistent treatment of entities and owners is bad enough, what is especially troubling is that the determination of who the client is may in some cases be based on the subjective beliefs *of the clients*. ABA Formal Op. 91–361 provides that whether a relationship between a lawyer and one or more of the partners has been created almost always will depend on an analysis of the specific facts involved, including "whether there was evidence of reliance by the individual partner on the lawyer as his or her separate counsel, or of the *partner's expectation* of personal representation." Likewise in *Goulding*, the court held that while Goulding represented the partnership and made decisions on the tax treatment of certain partnership-level items, "these decisions and calculations were directly reflected on the returns of the partners; all the individual partners depended upon Mr.

---

12. 957 F.2d 1420 (7th Cir. 1992).
13. Goulding, 957 F.2d at 1427–1428 (footnotes omitted, emphasis supplied).

Goulding's analysis."

It is therefore imperative that a lawyer (1) determine as many facts as possible about the case and the parties (partnership and partners); (2) decide which of the parties he or she will represent; (3) clearly communicate to all parties involved (whether being represented or not) who the practitioner will be representing; and (4) to the extent possible, obtain consents or acknowledgements from all of the parties as to the extent and limitations of that representation.

In ABA Formal Opinion 91–361, the ABA stated:

> Lest the difficulties of representing both a partnership and one or more of its partners appear impossible to overcome, however, Rule 1.7(b)(2) and, to a lesser extent, Rule 1.13(d) suggest a procedure that may be helpful in many situations. If an attorney retained by a partnership explains at the outset of the representation, preferably in writing, his or her role as counsel to the organization and not to the individual partners, and if, when asked to represent an individual partner, the lawyer puts the question before the partnership or its governing body, explains the implications of the dual representation, and obtains the informed consent of both the partnership and the individual partners, the likelihood of perceived ethical impropriety on the part of the lawyer should be significantly reduced.

In his *Ethics Chat* Newsletter (Issue 2, Vol. 7, Spring 2003), Professor Walter W. Steele, Jr. sets out two clauses to be used in retainer agreements in order to avoid the common misunderstandings about whom the lawyer represents:

Suggested Clause for Initial Retainer Letter to Entity Organizers

> It will be necessary to discuss numerous issues with each of you as the process of forming [name of entity] takes place. I have already advised you that I have agreed to serve as the lawyer for the entity—I am not the lawyer for any of you in this transaction. As I told you during our initial conference, you have the right to engage another lawyer of your choosing to represent your personal interests in this matter. The fact that I discuss issues with you during the process of forming [name of entity] must not be interpreted by you as any indication that I am your lawyer or that I am guarding your own individual interest in this matter. Because I am not your lawyer, I have the right, and perhaps the obligation at times, to share any information you provide to me with the other entity organizers.

Suggested Clause for Affirmation by Organizers—Post Entity Formation

> We, the undersigned organizers of [name of entity] hereby ratify and confirm our agreement not to be represented personally as set forth in the retainer contract attached to this document, and we now confirm that at no point during the process of organizing [name of entity] did [lawyer] form an attorney-client relationship with any of us. Each of us

were free at any point during this process to retain a lawyer to guard and protect our own personal interests, and the fact that we chose not to do so is not any evidence that we relied on [lawyer] for that purpose.

### 3. REPRESENTING BOTH ENTITIES AND OWNERS

Even though the general rule is that a lawyer represents the entity and not the individual owners, the situation routinely arises in which the lawyer may be asked to represent one or more of the owners in addition to the entity itself. In addition, lawyers representing an entity will inevitably develop a relationship with one or more of the owners and, if the lawyer has been effective on behalf of the entity, an owner may wish to retain the services of the lawyer in an unrelated legal matter. Is it acceptable under the rules to represent an owner while also representing the entity? Rule 1.7 sets out the rules governing a lawyer representing more than one client:

Rule 1.7 Conflict of Interest

(a) Except as provided in paragraph (b), a lawyer shall not represent a client if the representation involves a concurrent conflict of interest. A concurrent conflict of interest exists if:

(1) the representation of one client will be directly adverse to another client; or

(2) there is a significant risk that the representation of one or more clients will be materially limited by the lawyer's responsibilities to another client, a former client or a third person or by a personal interest of the lawyer.

(b) Notwithstanding the existence of a concurrent conflict of interest under paragraph (a), a lawyer may represent a client if:

(1) the lawyer reasonably believes that the lawyer will be able to provide competent and diligent representation to each affected client;

(2) the representation is not prohibited by law;

(3) the representation does not involve the assertion of a claim by one client against another client represented by the lawyer in the same litigation or other proceeding before a tribunal; and

(4) each affected client gives informed consent, confirmed in writing.

Under Rule 1.7, a lawyer may represent parties with potential conflicts of interest, but only if the lawyer believes his or her representation will not be affected, and each client consents in writing. It is therefore essential that the lawyer do a full conflicts check at the outset, obtain as many facts as possible, and secure written consents from each of the clients.

As in the case of any potential conflict involving multiple representation, a lawyer may represent an entity and one or more of the owners. However, Rule 1.13(g) imposes the additional requirement that the consent on behalf of the entity that is required by Rule 1.7 must be given by an owner other than the owner who will be represented by the lawyer. Accordingly, if a lawyer will be representing both a corporate client and one of the shareholders or a partnership client and one of the partners, it is essential that the lawyer obtain written consents from both the entity and the other individual to be represented, with the consent on behalf of the entity from an owner other than the one to be represented. It may be advisable, if the number of owners is sufficiently small to make it practicable, to have each of the owners who will not be represented by the lawyer consent to the dual representation.

### 4. DUTIES OWED TO FORMER CLIENTS AND PARTNERS OF THE PARTNERSHIP CLIENT

Another common conflict of interest involves former clients. For example, a lawyer represents an entity with several owners and, during the course of this representation, the lawyer learns information about one of the owners. Later, that owner is an opposing party in another case. Can the lawyer represent his client against the former owner? This issue is governed by Rule 1.9.

Rule 1.9: Duties To Former Clients

(a) A lawyer who has formerly represented a client in a matter shall not thereafter represent another person in the same or a substantially related matter in which that person's interests are materially adverse to the interests of the former client unless the former client gives informed consent, confirmed in writing.

(b) A lawyer shall not knowingly represent a person in the same or a substantially related matter in which a firm with which the lawyer formerly was associated had previously represented a client

(1) whose interests are materially adverse to that person; and

(2) about whom the lawyer had acquired information protected by Rules 1.6 and 1.9(c) that is material to the matter; unless the former client gives informed consent, confirmed in writing.

(c) A lawyer who has formerly represented a client in a matter or whose present or former firm has formerly represented a client in a matter shall not thereafter:

(1) use information relating to the representation to the disadvantage of the former client except as these Rules would permit or require with respect to a client, or when the information has become generally known; or

(2) reveal information relating to the representation except as these Rules would permit or require with respect to a client.

This is yet another reason to make sure about the identity of "the client." If the lawyer is not careful, numerous owners could be considered to be clients, thereby increasing the list of "former clients." Thus, Formal Opinion 91–361 opines that "a lawyer undertaking to represent a partnership with respect to a particular matter does not thereby enter into a lawyer-client relationship with each member of the partnership, so as to be barred, for example, by Rule 1.7(a) from representing another client on a matter adverse to one of the partners but unrelated to the partnership affairs."

Nevertheless, Rule 1.9(c) prohibits a lawyer from revealing "information relating to the representation" except as otherwise permitted by the Rules (e.g., Rule 1.6). This prohibition is absolute and is not waivable. Given the breadth of the attorney-client privilege and the inclusion of partners as agents of the partnership for purposes of the privilege, a lawyer should be extremely careful about using facts learned from or statements made by an owner during the course of the lawyer's representation of the entity against the owner in a later proceeding against the owner.

## 5. LAWYER AS A DIRECTOR

It has long been accepted practice for corporations to ask their outside counsel to serve as a director of the client. The practice is common among closely-held businesses, as well as public companies. However, merely because it is common practice does not mean it is a good idea nor free of ethical dilemmas. Among the problems associated with a lawyer serving his or her client as a director are the possibilities that the attorney-client privilege will be jeopardized, the lawyer's independent professional judgment may be hindered, and the lawyer may be disqualified due to a conflict of interest.

Most of the issues surrounding the lawyer as director must be analyzed under Rule 1.7, which governs conflicts of interest. In short, Model Rule 1.7(a) provides that a lawyer may not represent a client if the representation of one client will be directly adverse to another client, or if there is a significant risk that the representation of one or more clients will be materially limited by the lawyer's responsibilities to another client or other third party. There is nothing in Model Rule 1.7 prohibiting a lawyer from representing a client of which he or she is also a director. Nevertheless, given the numerous ethical pitfalls, members of the profession sought guidance from the ABA on this question.

In Formal Opinion 98–410, the ABA addressed whether it would be appropriate for an attorney to act as a director for a corporate client. Formal Opinion 98–410 enumerated the steps attorneys must take to mitigate the problems inherent in this dual role.

At the beginning of the relationship, the lawyer should take steps to ensure that the corporation's management and the other board members understand the different responsibilities of outside legal counsel and director. For example, management and the board must understand the importance of, as well as the limitations of, the attorney-client privilege, and that in some instances matters discussed at board meetings will not receive the protection of the attorney-client privilege that would attach to conversations between the client and the lawyer *qua* lawyer. The client should also understand that conflicts of interest may arise that would require the lawyer to recuse himself or herself as a director or to withdraw from representing the corporation in a matter. The lawyer should also ensure that management and the other board members understand that, when acting as legal counsel, the lawyer represents only the corporate entity and not its individual officers and directors.[14]

The Formal Opinion goes on to advise that during the course of the dual relationship, the lawyer should exercise care to protect the corporation's confidential information and to confront and resolve conflicts of interest that may arise. The opinion noted that it is essential that the lawyer be particularly careful when the client's management or board of directors consults him for legal advice. If the purpose of the meeting or consultation is to obtain legal advice from the lawyer in his or her capacity as lawyer, the lawyer-director should make clear that the meeting is solely for the purpose of providing legal advice, and the lawyer should avoid giving business or financial advice, except insofar as it affects legal considerations such as the application of the business judgment rule. If during the course of the discussions the lawyer's presence and opinion is needed in his or her role as director, the lawyer should have another member of the firm present at the meeting to provide the legal advice. Vigilantly segregating the two roles of lawyer and director will provide the best support for a claim of privilege.

Formal Opinion 98–410 advises lawyers to "[m]aintain in practice the independent professional judgment required of a competent lawyer, recommending against a course of action that is illegal or likely to harm the corporation even when favored by management or other directors." It then advises the lawyer to "[p]erform diligently the duties of counsel once a decision is made by the board or management, even if, as a director, the lawyer disagrees with the decision, unless the representation would assist in fraudulent or criminal conduct, self-dealing or otherwise would violate the Model Rules."

Lawyers must also avoid conflicts of interest that may arise as a result of the insider status he or she enjoys on the board of directors. For example, a lawyer should recuse himself or herself as a director from board deliberations when the relationship of the corporation with the lawyer or the lawyer's firm is under consideration.

Likewise, Formal Opinion 98–410 points out that a lawyer should decline any representation as counsel when the lawyer's interest as a director conflicts with his responsibilities of competent and diligent representation. For example, a lawyer should not represent a client matter if the lawyer is concerned about potential personal liability as a director resulting from a course approved by the board. *Id.; see also* Model Rule 1.7(a)(2).

Finally, Formal Opinion 98–410 points out what may be an unavoidable conflict: A director, who also is the corporation's lawyer, may be under a duty to disclose information to third parties that, in his role as attorney for the corporation, he could not disclose without obtaining consent from the client. In this situation, the lawyer-director's knowledge as a director may prove inseparable from the lawyer's acts and knowledge as outside legal counsel. The lawyer may have to resign his or her role as director in order to protect client confidences.

---

14. See also Comment 35 to Model Rule 1.7.

### 6. Lawyer as an Officer of the Corporation

An officer, depending on the duties assigned, could be everything from a figurehead who performs ministerial functions to an officer involved in every aspect of the corporation's day-to-day operations. Depending upon the nature and extent of the duties performed by the lawyer, acting as an officer may violate the rules of professional conduct if the lawyer undertakes legal representation of the entity. While it may be appropriate for a lawyer to act as corporate secretary and receive all legal documents served on the corporation, in most situations it would not be appropriate for a lawyer to represent a corporate client while serving as its chief financial officer. The ethical issues applicable to the lawyer-director are equally applicable, if not more so, depending on the duties of the lawyer-officer. A lawyer should keep each of the potential problems in mind when considering service as an officer of a corporate client.

### 7. Ethical Issues in Investing With a Client

May an attorney properly invest in a business with a client, either as payment for services or as an independent investment? The general rule on conflicts of interests with respect to current clients is found in Model Rule 1.8, which provides:

Rule 1.8: Conflict Of Interest: Current Clients: Specific Rules

(a) A lawyer shall not enter into a business transaction with a client or knowingly acquire an ownership, possessory, security or other pecuniary interest adverse to a client unless:

(1) the transaction and terms on which the lawyer acquires the interest are fair and reasonable to the client and are fully disclosed and transmitted in writing in a manner that can be reasonably understood by the client;

(2) the client is advised in writing of the desirability of seeking and is given a reasonable opportunity to seek the advice of independent legal counsel on the transaction; and

(3) the client gives informed consent, in a writing signed by the client, to the essential terms of the transaction and the lawyer's role in the transaction, including whether the lawyer is representing the client in the transaction.

Thus, a lawyer may invest in a venture with a client or may take stock in the client's business in lieu of fees only if the terms of the deal are fair and reasonable, the client is fully informed in writing about the terms of the deal, the client consents in writing to these terms, and the client is advised to seek independent legal counsel on the deal and is given the opportunity to seek that advice. Comment 1 to Model Rule 1.8 explains the reasons for this rule: "A lawyer's legal skill and training, together with the relationship of trust and confidence between lawyer and client, create the possibility of overreaching when the lawyer participates in a business, property or financial transaction with a client." If the transaction with the client involves one in which the lawyer will actually be advising the client, the risks highlighted by Comment 1 are even greater, since the knowledge, trust, and confidence that creates the risk of overreaching are even greater under these circumstances.

The ABA weighed-in on this issue in Formal Opinion 2000–418. First, the ABA answered what should be an obvious question by holding, "In our opinion, a lawyer who acquires stock in her client corporation in lieu of or in addition to a cash fee for her services enters into a business transaction with a client, such that the requirements of Model Rule 1.8(a) must be satisfied." After reviewing the requirements of Model Rule 1.8, the formal opinion then outlined situations where, despite satisfying the literal requirements of Rule 1.8, the transaction, and the lawyer's role in representing the client, may raise other ethical issues not contemplated by Rule 1.8. The opinion notes an example where the lawyer might have a duty when rendering an opinion on behalf of the corporation in a venture capital transaction to ask the client's management to reveal adverse financial information even though the revelation might cause the venture capital investor to withdraw. Under those circumstances, an attorney must evaluate his or her ability to exercise independent professional judgment in light of the adverse impact the advice may have on his or her own economic interests.[15]

Formal Opinion 2000–418 notes that one way of reducing the risk that the stock-for-services fee arrangement will be deemed to be unreasonable is to establish a reasonable fee for the lawyer's services based on factors enumerated under Rule 1.5,[16] and then accept an amount of stock that, at the time of the transaction, equals the reasonable fee. The difficulty of course, especially with start-up companies, is to determine the value of stock of the company. The opinion nevertheless encourages the stock to be valued at the amount per share that cash investors have agreed to pay for similar stock.[17]

Joseph F. Troy has written a "Best Practices Checklist" for firms to follow when taking stock in clients, which is published in *Representing Start–Up Companies*, by Lee R. Petillon and Robert Joe Hull. Among the "Best Practices" Troy lists are:

- Impose firm control of all investments by lawyers in client's stock. Do not

---

15. See also Weiss v. Statewide Grievance Comm., 663 A.2d 22 (Conn. 1993) (lawyer who received an interest in his clients' hotel project instead of legal fees was disciplined for conflict of interest after he advised against the sale of the hotel proposed by some of the clients. Clients were unable to determine whether the lawyer's advice against the sale was motivated by his duty as legal counsel and his independent professional judgment or by his interest as an investor in the hotel.)

16. The factors listed in Model Rule 1.5(a) are: (1) the time and labor required, the novelty and difficulty of the questions involved, and the skill requisite to perform the legal service properly; (2) the likelihood, if apparent to the client, that the acceptance of the particular employment will preclude other employment by the lawyer; (3) the fee customarily charged in the locality for similar legal services; (4) the amount involved and the results obtained; (5) the time limitations imposed by the client or by the circumstances; (6) the nature and length of the professional relationship with the client; (7) the experience, reputation, and ability of the lawyer or lawyers performing the services; and (8) whether the fee is fixed or contingent.

17. Despite the ABA's Formal Opinion, the issue of attorneys taking stock in their clients as payment for services has engendered a great deal of commentary. See, e.g., Brandenburg & Coher, Going for the Gold: Equity Stakes in Corporate Clients, 14 Geo.J. Legal Ethics 1179 (2001); Kahrl & Jacono, "Rush to Riches:" The Rules of Ethics and Greed Control in the Dot.com World, 2 Minn.Intell.Prop.Rev. 51 (2001); McAlpine, Getting a Piece of the Action: Should Lawyers Be Allowed to Invest in Their Clients' Stock?, 47 UCLA L.Rev. 549 (1999); McQuiston, Ethical Issues in the Acceptance of Stock Options As Fee Payments for Legal Work, 6 Intell.Prop.L.Bull. 21 (2001); Miller, Lawyers As Venture Capitalists: An Economic Analysis of Law Firms That Invest in Their Clients, 13 Harv. J.L. & Tech. 435 (2000); Puri, Taking Stock of Taking Stock, 87 Cornell L.Rev. 99 (2001).

allow individual lawyers in the firm to make these investment decisions.

• Invest through a firm vehicle, and avoid direct investing by firm attorneys.

• Strictly limit the size of investments and the percentage of ownership. Troy lists a maximum of $25,000–50,000 or 1–2% of the company as typical or safe investment levels.

• Obtain a third-party valuation of the stock.

• Take all or the bulk of fees in cash.

• Do not take stock for future services without including vesting provisions and an express right of the client to terminate.

• Avoid flipping (immediate resale) of stock, and impose a voluntary lock-up.

• Impose strict insider trading rules.

• Require stock be held for investment and not with a view to resale. Do not permit trading of client stock.

• Disclose the stock ownership to third parties when appropriate.

• If you cannot fully and zealously represent your client on a matter because of your stock ownership, either do not invest or decline the representation.

• If your investment would compromise your independent professional judgment, either do not invest or decline the representation.

• Schedule a regular review of the conflicts and, when necessary, get a revised consent.

• Make a detailed and comprehensive disclosure of the conflicts; do not rely on boilerplate disclosures.

### 8. GENERAL DUTIES OWED TO OWNERS

The general rule is that a lawyer who is retained by a corporation, partnership, or LLC, represents the entity itself and not the individual owners. A lawyer may also represent an individual owner in the same matter or in an unrelated transaction, as long as he or she satisfies the requirements of Rule 1.7, dealing with conflicts of interest. The next question is what ethical duties are owed to the owners who are *not* clients? In one sense, the owners are merely third parties, and they are entitled, at a minimum, to the same treatment as other third parties. Model Rule 4.1 governs the treatment of third parties:

Rule 4.1: Truthfulness in Statements to Others.

In the course of representing a client a lawyer shall not knowingly:

(a) make a false statement of material fact or law to a third person; or

(b) fail to disclose a material fact to a third person when disclosure is necessary to avoid assisting a criminal or fraudulent act by a client, unless disclosure is prohibited by Rule 1.6.

Thus, Model Rule 4.1 requires at a minimum that a lawyer may not knowingly make a false statement of material fact or law to third persons, nor may the lawyer knowingly fail to disclose a material fact when disclosure is necessary to avoid assisting a criminal or fraudulent act by a client, unless disclosure is prohibited by Model Rule 1.6.[18]

In addition, since many owners will not have their own representation, the lawyer may be required to treat the owners as "unrepresented persons" and comply with Model Rule 4.3:

Rule 4.3: Dealing With Unrepresented Persons

In dealing on behalf of a client with a person who is not represented by counsel, a lawyer shall not state or imply that the lawyer is disinterested. When the lawyer knows or reasonably should know that the unrepresented person misunderstands the lawyer's role in the matter, the lawyer shall make reasonable efforts to correct the misunderstanding. The lawyer shall not give legal advice to an unrepresented person, other than the advice to secure counsel, if the lawyer knows or reasonably should know that the interests of such a person are or have a reasonable possibility of being in conflict with the interests of the client.

Ideally, the lawyer will have set out in the engagement letter that he or she represents the entity and not the individual owners. As a result, there should not be a misunderstanding as to the lawyer's role in the matter. However, Rule 4.3 imposes a continuing duty to correct any misunderstanding that a third party (i.e., partner/member/shareholder) may have.[19]

Moreover, Model Rule 1.13(f) reinforces the requirement that the lawyer representing an entity must ensure that the owners are reminded of where the lawyer's duty of loyalty lies:

Model Rule 1.13(f)

In dealing with an organization's directors, officers, employees, members, shareholders or other constituents, a lawyer shall explain the identity of the client when the lawyer knows or reasonably should know that the organization's interests are adverse to those of the constituents with whom the lawyer is dealing.

The Rules and comments make it plain that when dealing with owners, lawyers should ensure that there is no confusion as to who the lawyer represents.

---

18. See Model Rule 4.1(b).

19. See also Comment 2 to Rule 4.3: "So long as the lawyer has explained that the lawyer represents an adverse party and is not representing the person, the lawyer may inform the person of the terms on which the lawyer's client will enter into an agreement or settle a matter, prepare documents that require the person's signature and explain the lawyer's own view of the meaning of the document or the lawyer's view of the underlying legal obligations."

## 9. THE ATTORNEY-CLIENT PRIVILEGE AND REPRESENTING CLOSELY HELD BUSINESSES

One of the most common issues in representing a partnership, corporation, or other entity involves the application of the attorney-client privilege. During the course of representing an entity, a lawyer must routinely determine whether statements by officers, directors, partners, employees or other "constituents" are subject to the attorney-client privilege. Privilege issues also may impact what a lawyer may disclose to individual owners and what the lawyer may refuse to disclose to owners. Whether a lawyer may refuse to divulge a given statement under the attorney-client privilege will depend upon (1) the identity of the declarant (i.e., his or her role within the entity); (2) the identity of the person seeking to obtain the statement (i.e., whether the person is also an owner of the entity or and outsider); (3) the purpose for which the statements were made to the lawyer; and (4) whether the privilege has been waived.

The general rule in dealing with confidences is found in Model Rule 1.6, which provides that "a lawyer shall not reveal information relating to the representation of a client unless the client gives informed consent, the disclosure is impliedly authorized in order to carry out the representation or the disclosure is permitted by paragraph (b)." The exceptions of 1.6(b) include: (1) To prevent reasonably certain death or substantial bodily harm; (2) to prevent the client from committing a crime or fraud that is reasonably certain to result in substantial injury to the financial interests or property of another and in furtherance of which the client has used or is using the lawyer's services; (3) to prevent, mitigate or rectify substantial injury to the financial interests or property of another that is reasonably certain to result or has resulted from the client's commission of a crime or fraud in furtherance of which the client has used the lawyer's services; (4) to secure legal advice about the lawyer's compliance with these Rules; and (5) to establish a claim or defense on behalf of the lawyer in a controversy between the lawyer and the client. How is this rule applied in the context of an entity client?

The seminal case in this area is *Upjohn Co. v. United States*, 449 U.S. 383, 101 S.Ct. 677 (1981), in which the Supreme Court adopted a fairly broad application of the attorney-client privilege in the corporate context, holding that where communications were made by corporate employees to counsel for the corporation acting at the direction of corporate superiors in order to secure legal advice from counsel, and the employees were aware that they were being questioned so that the corporation could obtain advice, these communications were protected. Thus, the Court in *Upjohn* examined the purposes for which the attorney obtained the statements from the employees. Since each of the disputed statements was elicited pursuant to the attorney's representation, the statements were protected by the privilege. While this is certainly the general rule, the *Upjohn* test has not been uniformly adopted.[20] Accordingly, whether statements made by an employee or other constituent of an entity-client will be subject to the attorney-client privilege may depend upon the law of the jurisdiction involved.

---

20. See, e.g., Nalian Truck Lines, Inc. v. Nakano Warehouse & Transportation Corp., 6 Cal.App.4th 1256, 8 Cal.Rptr.2d 467 (Cal.App. 1992); Niesig v. Team I, 76 N.Y.2d 363, 559 N.Y.S.2d 493 (1990).

In addition, whether a lawyer can refuse to disclose statements obtained from an owner or other constituent will depend upon who is seeking disclosure. In Formal Opinion 91–361, which is the Formal Opinion declaring that the partnership is the client, the ABA stated that "information received by a lawyer in the course of representing the partnership is 'information relating to the representation' of the partnership, and normally may not be withheld from individual partners." The ABA went on to explain its opinion as follows:

> The mandate of Rule 1.6(a), not to reveal confidences of the client, would not prevent the disclosure to other partners of information gained about the client (the partnership) from any individual partner(s). Thus, information thought to have been given in confidence by an individual partner to the attorney for a partnership may have to be disclosed to other partners, particularly if the interests of the individual partner and the partnership, or vis-a-vis the other partners, become antagonistic.[21]

According to the ABA, since the partnership is the client, and not the individual partners, information received from the partners cannot be a "client confidence," at least with respect to the other partners. As a result, information received from a partner may not be withheld from other partners. Although the fiduciary duties owed by partners to their fellow partners are somewhat unique among business entities, the logic of Formal Opinion 91–361 would appear to apply equally to other entities types, and thus, in dealing with an entity and its owners, a lawyer may not normally refuse to disclose facts learned during the course or representing the entity. It is essential that the owners understand this and do not mistakenly make statements to an attorney, believing that the statement will be held in confidence. A lawyer should make this clear at the outset of the representation and remind owners of this during the course of the representation, if it appears that an owner may be mistaken as to the application of the attorney-client privilege. Moreover, as discussed more fully below, ethical rules may require an attorney to disclose certain facts and statements regarding the misconduct of an owner or employee learned during the course of representing the entity.

On the other hand, the Model Rules suggest that statements by an owner or employee of an entity may be subject to attorney-client privilege if the person seeking disclosure is an outsider.[22] Hence, the application of the privilege appears to depend upon who the declarant is, the declarant's role in the entity, the circumstances under which the lawyer sought and obtained the information and statements from the declarant, and who is seeking access to the statement or information. The lawyer must keep each of these factors in mind when dealing with owners and employees of the entity client in a situation that is or might soon become a sensitive or controversial matter. The problem, of course, is that statements are often obtained when neither the lawyer nor the client has any inkling that a controversy might soon erupt. The specific issue of an attorney's

---

21. Formal Opinion 91–361 (footnote omitted).

22. See Comment 2 to Rule 1.13, "When one of the constituents of an organizational client communicates with the organization's lawyer in that person's organizational capacity, the communication is protected by Rule 1.6 [attorney-client privilege]."

ethical duties when he or she learns of client misconduct is discussed in the following section.

### 10. THE ATTORNEY-CLIENT PRIVILEGE IN THE CONTEXT OF MISCONDUCT BY AN OWNER OR EMPLOYEE

Another common ethical issue concerns the situation where the lawyer learns that one or more of the owners, employees, or other constituents has done something that is either illegal or contrary to the best interests of the entity. As has been established, a lawyer represents the entity as a separate entity. Yet, entities can only act through individual owners and employees. Who speaks for the entity when there is a dispute and who should the lawyer listen to? Model Rule 1.13(a) provides that an organization acts through its "duly authorized constituents." However, particularly in the case of closely held businesses, it is not always clear who the duly authorized constituents are.

Comment 3 to Rule 1.13 emphasizes that the actions and decisions of the duly authorized constituent must generally be respected by lawyer: "When constituents of the organization make decisions for it, the decisions ordinarily must be accepted by the lawyer even if their utility or prudence is doubtful. Decisions concerning policy and operations, including ones entailing serious risk, are not as such in the lawyer's province."

One of the most difficult ethical issues a lawyer can face occurs when, for example, the general partner, who is the duly authorized constituent of the partnership, has taken some action that is either illegal or contrary to the interests of the partnership. Technically, the lawyer represents the partnership, not the general partner. However, in reality, the lawyer is retained by, paid by, and is answerable to a real person—the general partner. Lawyers must therefore resolve the inherent conflict in their duty to protect the "real" client (i.e., the partnership), not reveal confidences of a duly authorized constituent of the client, and still ensure that the best interests of the client and the other constituents are defended. Model Rule 1.13(b) sets out the basic rules on how the professional should act in these circumstances:

> Rule 1.13(b) If a lawyer for an organization knows that an officer, employee or other person associated with the organization is engaged in action, intends to act or refuses to act in a matter related to the representation that is a violation of a legal obligation to the organization, or a violation of law that reasonably might be imputed to the organization, and that is likely to result in substantial injury to the organization, then the lawyer shall proceed as is reasonably necessary in the best interest of the organization. Unless the lawyer reasonably believes that it is not necessary in the best interest of the organization to do so, the lawyer shall refer the matter to higher authority in the organization, including, if warranted by the circumstances to the highest authority that can act on behalf of the organization as determined by applicable law.

Thus, Rule 1.13(b) reemphasizes that the lawyer's primary duty is to act in the best interest of the organization. In addition, the lawyer must, if the circumstances warrant, report the misconduct to the "highest authority" within the organization. However, this does not answer the situation where the malevolent actor is the general partner who *is* the highest authority within the partnership.

Model Rule 1.13 was substantially revised in August of 2003. Under the prior version of the Rule, once the highest authority that can act on behalf of the organization was informed of the misconduct within the organization, it was proper for the lawyer to conclude that the organization as client has been notified and that the lawyer's professional obligation had therefore been fulfilled.[23] Significantly, however, no disclosure was permitted by the lawyer. The revised version of Rule 1.13 changes all that. Under the revised version of Rule 1.13(c), a lawyer may reveal information about the organization's (or constituent's) misconduct, even though revealing that information would not normally be permitted by Rule 1.6. Thus, if the lawyer knows that an owner or employee is engaged in action in a matter related to the representation that is a violation of a legal obligation to the entity, or that the action is a violation of law that reasonably may be imputed to the entity and that will likely result in substantial harm to the entity, then the lawyer shall proceed as is reasonably necessary in the best interest of the entity. The lawyer's action will be determined by the circumstances, but ordinarily this means referral to a higher decision-making person or group within the organization. The lawyer may, but is not required to, reveal facts relating to the representation, even if not expressly permitted by Rule 1.6, but only if and to the extent the lawyer reasonably believes necessary to prevent substantial injury to the organization.

The SEC's Standards Of Professional Conduct, § 205.3, contain a separate set of rules applicable to attorneys representing organizational clients before the SEC. Subsection (b) of 205.3 establishes an "up-the-ladder" reporting requirement similar to the provisions of Rule 1.13.[24]

### 11. THE ATTORNEY-CLIENT PRIVILEGE AND TAX ADVICE

A common area of the law about which business lawyers routinely give advice involves the client's tax liability. Business lawyers can give prospective tax advice as to how clients should structure certain deals, provide advice on reporting positions for tax returns that are to be filed, and represent clients in tax disputes with the IRS. A significant issue in these contexts is whether statements between a client and its lawyer are subject to the attorney-client privilege.

The attorney-client privilege is affected in the tax area by how "legal advice" is defined. If the advice is considered "accounting advice," the privilege does not apply. This can include preparation of tax returns.[25] The privilege does

---

23. See ABA Comm. on Professional Ethics, Formal Op. 93–375 (1993) (lawyer may not reveal client's lie to bank examiner but must "climb corporate ladder" or withdraw if client persists in fraudulent conduct). If the highest authority within the organization refused to take action against the misconduct, Rule 1.13(c) permits the lawyer to resign in accordance with Rule 1.16. See Ass'n of the Bar of the City of N.Y., Comm. on Professional Ethics, Op. 1994–10 (1994) (when general partner of limited partnership engages in activities that may harm entity, lawyer may be required to withdraw from representation of partnership, individual general partner, and individual limited partner if independent professional judgment likely to be affected by differing interests).

24. 17 C.F.R. § 205.3.

25. See, e.g., United States v. Lawless, 709 F.2d 485, 487 (7th Cir. 1983); United States v. Frederick, 182

not apply to return advice because there is no expectation that communications from the client would remain confidential, given that the communications were made for the purpose of reporting transactions on a tax return. Hence, to the extent the privilege may have attached to any of the communications, it was waived when the return was filed. However, if there is an expectation of confidentiality and that confidentiality is not later waived, an attorney's tax advice is privileged if client confidences would be revealed by disclosure of the attorney's advice.[26] The line between what is privileged and what is not has never been clear. As a result, a lawyer providing tax advice should assume that all communications may be discoverable by the IRS.

When a lawyer gives tax advice, the client's accountant often is involved in the conversations as well. In 1998, Congress enacted new § 7525 of the Internal Revenue Code that extends the attorney-client privilege to all authorized tax practitioners. Section 7525 extends the same common law protections of confidentiality that apply to communications between a taxpayer and an attorney to communications between a taxpayer and an accountant. However, the privilege may only be asserted in a non-criminal tax matter before the Service, and in non-criminal tax proceeding in Federal court brought by or against the United States.

Given the limited scope of the accountant-client privilege, an attorney should be careful in retaining the services of an accountant in certain tax matters. If the case involves a dispute with the IRS and has a potential for a criminal prosecution of the client, a lawyer must only employ the services of an accountant under certain conditions. While the client will most likely wish to use its current accountant, the lawyer should insist on retaining a different accountant because of the difficulty in segregating the non-privileged tax return advice from the later privileged communications.

Accountants retained under these circumstances are known as "Kovel" accountants, from the case *United States v. Kovel*, 296 F.2d 918 (2d Cir. 1961), where the court held that the attorney-client privilege extends to communications made by a client to an accountant *employed by the lawyer*, as part of the client receiving legal advice from the attorney. It is therefore essential that the *lawyer* retain the accountant directly and not have the client retain the accountant. In addition, all bills for services rendered by the accountant and all work-product produced by the accountant should go through the attorney before being distributed to the client.

### 12. CLIENT CONFIDENTIALITY AND DEALINGS WITH GOVERNMENT AGENCIES

Another set of ethical issues surface when a lawyer learns that his or her

---

F.3d 496, 500 (7th Cir. 1999)>; United States v. Ackert, 169 F.3d 136 (2nd Cir. 1999); Boca Investerings Partnership v. United States, 31 F.Supp.2d 9 (D.D.C. 1998); Saba Partnership v. Commissioner, 78 T.C.M. 684 (1999) (privilege does not cover factual content of communication between taxpayer and its in-house tax counsel regarding the transaction at issue), rev'd on other grounds, 273 F.3d 1135 (D.C. Cir. 2001).

26. See American Standard Inc. v. Pfizer Inc., 828 F.2d 734 (Fed. Cir. 1987) (opinion letter was not privileged because "it did not reveal, directly or indirectly, the substance of any confidential communication"); Mead Data Control v. United States Department of Air Force, 566 F.2d 242, 253 (D.C. Cir. 1977).

client has made false or misleading representations, or has engaged in "misleading silence," when dealing with a government agency. The lawyer's duties in these circumstances can be unclear and contradictory. Model Rule 3.3(a) provides one set of rules:

RULE 3.3: Candor Toward The Tribunal

(a) A lawyer shall not knowingly:

(1) make a false statement of fact or law to a tribunal or fail to correct a false statement of material fact or law previously made to the tribunal by the lawyer;

(2) fail to disclose to the tribunal legal authority in the controlling jurisdiction known to the lawyer to be directly adverse to the position of the client and not disclosed by opposing counsel; or

(3) offer evidence that the lawyer knows to be false. If a lawyer, the lawyer's client, or a witness called by the lawyer, has offered material evidence and the lawyer comes to know of its falsity, the lawyer shall take reasonable remedial measures, including, if necessary, disclosure to the tribunal. A lawyer may refuse to offer evidence, other than the testimony of a defendant in a criminal matter, that the lawyer reasonably believes is false.

Representing clients before the IRS illustrates the magnitude of the potential problems. In ABA Formal Opinion 314, the ABA states, "The Internal Revenue Service is neither a true tribunal, nor even a quasi-judicial institution." Formal Opinion 314 also provides that a lawyer appearing as an advocate before the IRS is under no duty to disclose weaknesses in the client's case if the case is "fairly arguable." And, to emphasize its position, the ABA stated that there is no duty to disclose weak facts. "Negotiation and settlement procedures of the tax system do not carry with them the guarantee that a correct tax result necessarily occurs ... just as it might happen with regard to other civil disputes."

Despite these rather broad statements, the ABA hastened to emphasize: "It by no means follows that a lawyer is relieved of all ethical responsibility when he practices before this agency. There are certain things which he clearly cannot do, and they are set forth explicitly in the canons of ethics." The ABA reinforced this notion in Formal Opinion 85–352, which states: "In all cases, however, with regard both to preparing returns and negotiating administrative settlements, the lawyer is under a duty not to mislead the IRS deliberately, either by misstatements or by silence or by permitting the client to mislead." But, as discussed above, Model Rule 1.6 prevents the disclosure of client confidences except to prevent the commission of a crime or fraud. But if the statements do not rise to the level of criminal or fraudulent behavior, may an attorney disclose client confidences? Arguably not without violating the affirmative prohibition against disclosure of Rule 1.6. At the same time, Circular 230, § 10.51 defines "incompetence and disreputable conduct" for which a practitioner may be censured, suspended or disbarred from practice before the Internal Revenue Service to include giving false or misleading information, or participating in any way in the giving of false or misleading information to the Department of the

Treasury.[27]

Thus, a professional may be caught between the duties imposed by the Model Rules, State Bar Rules (many of which do not follow the relatively liberal disclosure rules of Model Rule 1.6) and the duty not to mislead the IRS imposed by Circular 230. This already difficult situation is made even worse if the misleading statements can be seen to be continuing. For example, a client may have submitted a financial document to the IRS through its attorney, and the attorney later learns that the document contains misleading or incorrect factual information. Assume also that the IRS may rely on that false or misleading information in determining or resolving the client's tax liability. What do the rules require under these circumstances?

First and foremost, the attorney must recognize that he or she has been used to perpetrate what may be fraud or a crime. The attorney therefore may have exposure to both civil and criminal liability. Nevertheless, many states' ethics rules do not permit the attorney to reveal the client's confidences. The lawyer may be *required* to withdraw under Formal Opinion 314. ABA Formal Opinion 92–366 states that a lawyer should not only withdraw, but may have to disavow his or her prior work product and submissions, using what is known as a "noisy withdrawal." These various requirements (disclosure, nondisclosure, withdrawal, noisy withdrawal) put an attorney in a difficult ethical bind. In addition, regardless of what the attorney does under the ethical rules, there is a risk of being sued by his client or charged with conspiracy or disbarred from practice. As with other similar ethical quandaries, the best course of action is to solicit an opinion from the state bar association of which the attorney is a member.

## PROBLEM 17-A

**17-A.** Four years ago, you represented Jason, then age 28, in the implosion of a start-up venture. Four deep-pocket investors had funded a new company and selected Jason, boy wonder engineer, to be its president. Jason was given a "dream" employment contract that promised big riches if all played out as expected. Within six months, the investors were thoroughly dismayed with Jason's alleged incompetence, bizarre temper, and propensity to shade the truth. Jason was dismissed for cause and a brief legal battle ensued. You succeeded in quietly and quickly getting Jason out of the mess with a few bucks in his pocket.

Jason now has asked that you represent Lucy, Sam, and himself in organizing a new corporation ("Newco") that will develop and exploit a new product that is designed to make it easy to produce low-cost vinyl fencing. All three will serve on the board of Newco, and Jason and Lucy will be officers, employed full-time by Newco. Jason indicated that Newco may need your help in resolving a "frivolous" sexual harassment claim that likely will be triggered as a result of his efforts to recruit an office manager for the new venture.

Address the following:

---

27. See 31 C.F.R. § 10.51.

1. May you collectively represent Jason, Lucy and Sam in the organization of Newco? Should you?

2. May you represent just Newco?

3. What precautions should you take in connection with your representation of Newco or any of its owners?

4. Must you or should you advise Lucy and Sam of your prior experiences with Jason?

5. May you invest $100,000 in Newco for six percent of its stock? Jason promises that, if you make such an investment, you will be guaranteed a position on the board, will be elected secretary of the corporation, will be assured all of the corporation's legal work, and will realize a great return on your investment. If you can do this, should you do it?

# CHAPTER 18

# SELECT FORMS

---

## A.  THE FORM GAME:  BLESSING OR CURSE?

A good form library is a blessing for any planning lawyer. It's a necessity; no one has the time or the competence to start from scratch with every important document.  A quality form jumpstarts the drafting process and becomes a valuable aid in the planning process.  The competent lawyer knows his or her forms—what they say and, far more important, what they do *not* say. The limitations, shortcomings, and imperfections of each form (they all have them) are well understood.  A form never becomes a tool for short-circuiting or cheating the planning process.

Forms become curses when they are misused.  They make it possible for the lazy or ill-informed to create complete, official-looking documents without ever embracing the planning process.  Often the form's misuse is rationalized by perpetuating a dangerously false notion that there is a "standard" or "normal" way of doing things.  The perpetrator sometimes lacks a thorough knowledge of what the form really says and usually has no clue as to the form's flaws or shortcomings.  The foolishness of such a practice should be obvious to anyone who has read the foregoing pages.

Five sample forms are included in the following sections of this chapter. They were taken directly from the form file of one of the top Seattle-based firms.[1] As forms go, they are fine but nothing special. They are offered here not as examples of extraordinary quality, but rather as tools to assist each student's learning effort.  At the most basic level, it often helps to see how a document incorporates key provisions—a qualified income offset, a Crummey withdrawal procedure, a termination "for cause" provision, etc.  But the real educational value is in analyzing each form for its limitations and shortcomings.  This can be an individual or group effort. You will discover that these forms, like all their counterparts, contain limitations that a quality planning lawyer will easily spot and a phony often will miss. For example, you will see that neither the limited liability operating agreement nor the shareholders agreement addresses in any meaningful way many of the 20 co-owner operational deal points that were reviewed in Chapter 4.  You will discover that the shareholders agreement contains a stock right-of-first-refusal provision that, as we saw in Chapter 6,

---

[1]. The forms in this Chapter, included for educational purposes only, are from the form files of Foster Pepper PLLC, a Northwest-based firm with regional and national practices.

often is ill advised except in select golfer organizations. The hope is that your analysis of each form will enhance your understanding of the relevant planning challenges and promote a healthy respect for the value and limitations of all forms.

## B. FORM: LIMITED LIABILITY COMPANY OPERATING AGREEMENT

### OPERATING AGREEMENT OF

_____  _____

### A Washington Limited Liability Company

This Operating Agreement (the "Agreement") is made and entered into as of the ___ day of _____, 2011, by and between _____ ("_____") and _____ ("_____") (the "Members"). The parties agree to operate as a limited liability company under the laws of the state of Washington as follows.

The parties hereto agree as follows:

1. DEFINITIONS. The following terms used in the Agreement shall have the meanings specified below:

1.1 "Act" means the Washington Limited Liability Company Act, as amended from time to time.

1.2 "Adjusted Contribution Amount" with respect to each Member means the Capital Contributions pursuant to Sections 7.1 and 7.4, as reduced from time to time by distributions pursuant to Section 10.

1.3 "Agreement" means this Operating Agreement of the ABC, LLC as it may be amended from time to time.

1.4 "Assignee" means a person who has acquired a Member's Interest in whole or part and has not become a Substitute Member.

1.5 "Capital Account" means the account maintained for each Member in accordance with Section 7.5. In the case of a transfer of an interest, the transferee shall succeed to the Capital Account of the transferor or, in the case of a partial transfer, a proportionate share thereof.

1.6 "Capital Contribution" means the total amount of money and the fair market value of all property contributed to the Company by each Member pursuant to the terms of the Agreement. Capital Contribution shall also include any amounts paid directly by a Member to any creditor of the Company in respect of any guarantee or similar obligation undertaken by such Member in connection with the Company's operations. Any reference to the Capital Contribution of a Member shall include the Capital Contribution made by a predecessor holder of the interest of such Member.

1.7 "Cash Available for Distribution" means all cash receipts of the Company, excluding cash available upon liquidation of the Company, in excess of amounts reasonably required for payment of operating expenses, repayment of current liabilities, repayment of such amounts of Company indebtedness as the Manager shall determine necessary or advisable, and the establishment of and additions to such cash reserves as the Manager shall deem necessary or advisable, including, but not limited to reserves for capital expenditures, replacements, contingent or unforeseen liabilities or other obligations of the Company.

1.8 "Code" means the United States Internal Revenue Code of 1986, as amended. References to specific Code Sections or Treasury Regulations shall be deemed to refer to such Code Sections or Treasury Regulations as they may be amended from time to time or to any successor Code Sections or Treasury Regulations if the Code Section or Treasury Regulation referred to is repealed.

1.9 "Company" means the Washington limited liability company named ABC, LLC governed by the Agreement.

1.10 "Company Property" means all the real and personal property owned by the Company.

1.11 "Deemed Capital Account" means a Member's Capital Account, as calculated from time to time, adjusted by (i) adding thereto the sum of (A) the amount of such Member's Mandatory Obligation, if any, and (B) each Member's share of Minimum Gain (determined after any decreases therein for such year) and (ii) subtracting therefrom (A) allocations of losses and deductions which are reasonably expected to be made as of the end of the taxable year to the Members pursuant to Code Section 704(e)(2), Code Section 706(d) and Treasury Regulation Section 1.751–1(b)(2)(ii), and (B) distributions which at the end of the taxable year are reasonably expected to be made to the Member to the extent that said distributions exceed offsetting increases to the Member's Capital Account (including allocations of the Qualified Income Offset pursuant to Section 8.7 but excluding allocations of Minimum Gain Chargeback pursuant to Section 8.6) that are reasonably expected to occur during (or prior to) the taxable years in which such distributions are reasonably expected to be made.

1.12 "Interest" or "Company Interest" means the ownership interest of a Member in the Company at any particular time, including the right of such Member to any and all benefits to which such Member may be entitled as provided in the Agreement and in the Act, together with the obligations of such Member to comply with all the terms and provisions of the Agreement and the Act.

1.13 "Manager(s)" means those Member(s) and other persons who are appointed in accordance with this Agreement to exercise the authority of Manager under this Agreement and the Act. If at any time a Member who is a Manager ceases to be a Member for any reason, that Member shall simultaneously cease to be a Manager. The initial Manager of the Company shall be [_____].

1.14 "Mandatory Obligation" means the sum of (i) the amount of a Member's remaining contribution obligation (including the amount of any Capital Account deficit such Member is obligated to restore upon liquidation) provided that such contribution must be made in all events within ninety (90) days of liquidation of the Member's interest as determined under Treasury Regulation Section 1.704–1(b)(2)(ii)(g) and (ii) the additional amount, if any, such Member would be obligated to contribute as of year end to retire recourse indebtedness of the Company if the Company were to liquidate as of such date and dispose of all of its assets at book value.

1.15 "Member(s)" means those persons who execute a counterpart of this Agreement and those persons who are hereafter admitted as members under Section 14.4 below.

1.16 "Minimum Gain" means the amount determined by computing, with respect to each nonrecourse liability of the Company, the amount of gain, if any, that would be realized by the Company if it disposed of the Company Property subject to such nonrecourse liability in full satisfaction thereof in a taxable transaction, and then by aggregating the amounts so determined. Such gain shall be determined in accordance with Treasury Regulation Section 1.704–2(d). Each Member's share of Minimum Gain at the end of any taxable year of the Company shall be determined in accordance with Treasury Regulation Section 1.704–2(g)(1).

1.17 "Net Income" or "Net Loss" means taxable income or loss (including items requiring separate computation under Section 702 of the Code) of the Company as determined using the method of accounting chosen by the Manager and used by the Company for federal income tax purposes, adjusted in accordance with Treasury Regulation Section 1.704–1(b)(2)(iv)(g), for any property with differing tax and book values, to take into account depreciation, depletion, amortization and gain or loss as computed for book purposes.

1.18 "Percentage Interest" means the percentage interest of each Member as set forth on Appendix A.

1.19 "Substitute Member" means an Assignee who has been admitted to all of the rights of membership pursuant to Section 14.4 below.

2. FORMATION. The Members hereby agree to form and to operate the Company under the terms and conditions set forth herein. Except as otherwise provided herein, the rights and liabilities of the Members shall be governed by the Act.

2.1 Defects as to Formalities. A failure to observe any formalities or requirements of this Agreement, the articles of organization for the Company or the Act shall not be grounds for imposing personal liability on the Members or Manager for liabilities of the Company.

2.2 No Partnership Intended for Nontax Purposes. The Members have formed the Company under the Act, and expressly do not intend hereby to form a partnership under either the Washington Uniform Partnership Act or the Washington Uniform Limited Partnership Act or a corporation under the Washington Business Corporation Act. The Members do not intend to be partners one to another, or partners as to any third party. The Members hereto agree and acknowledge that the Company is to be treated as a partnership for federal income tax purposes.

2.3 Rights of Creditors and Third Parties. This Agreement is entered into among the Company and the Members for the exclusive benefit of the Company, its Members and their successors and assigns. The Agreement is expressly not intended for the benefit of any creditor of the Company or any other person. Except and only to the extent provided by applicable statute, no such creditor or third party shall have any rights under the Agreement or any agreement between the Company and any Member with respect to any Contribution or otherwise.

2.4 Title to Property. All Company Property shall be owned by the Company as an entity and no Member shall have any ownership interest in such Property in the Member's individual name or right, and each Member's interest in the Company shall be personal property for all purposes. Except as otherwise provided in this Agreement, the Company shall hold all Company Property in the name of the Company and not in the name or names of any Member or Members.

2.5 Payments of Individual Obligations. The Company's credit and assets shall be used solely for the benefit of the Company, and no asset of the Company shall be transferred or encumbered for or in payment of any individual obligation of any Member unless otherwise provided for herein.

3. NAME. The name of the Company shall be ABC, LLC. The Manager may from time to time change the name of the Company or adopt such trade or fictitious names as they may determine to be appropriate.

4. OFFICE; AGENT FOR SERVICE OF PROCESS. The principal office of the Company shall be _____. The Company may maintain such other offices at such other places as the Manager may determine to be appropriate. The agent for service of process for the Company shall be _____ at the above address.

5. PURPOSES OF THE COMPANY. The Company shall be in the business of providing _____ marketing products and services. In addition, the Company may engage in any other business and shall have such other purposes as may be necessary, incidental or convenient to carry on the Company's primary purpose or as determined by the Manager and Members from time to time in accordance with the terms of this Agreement.

6. TERM. The term of the Company shall commence on the date of the filing of the Articles of Organization for the Company in the office of the Washington Secretary of State, and shall continue until dissolved, wound up and terminated in accordance with the provisions of this Agreement and the Act.

7. PERCENTAGE INTERESTS AND CAPITAL CONTRIBUTIONS.

7.1 Initial Capital Contributions; Percentage Interests. The Members shall make the initial Capital Contributions to the Company in the amounts set forth on Appendix A for the Percentage Interests in the Company as shown on Appendix A.

7.2 No Interest on Capital. No Member shall be entitled to receive interest on such Member's Capital Contributions or such Member's Capital Account.

7.3 No Withdrawal of Capital. Except as otherwise provided in this

Agreement, no Member shall have the right to withdraw or demand a return of any or all of such Member's Capital Contribution. It is the intent of the Members that no distribution (or any part of any distribution) made to any Member pursuant to Section 10 hereof shall be deemed a return or withdrawal of Capital Contributions, even if such distribution represents (in full or in part) a distribution of revenue offset by depreciation or any other non-cash item accounted for as an expense, loss or deduction from, or offset to, the Company's income, and that no Member shall be obligated to pay any such amount to or for the account of the Company or any creditor of the Company. However, if any court of competent jurisdiction holds that, notwithstanding the provisions of this Agreement, any Member is obligated to make any such payment, such obligation shall be the obligation of such Member and not of any other Member, including the Manager.

7.4 Additional Capital. Except as otherwise provided for herein or mutually agreed upon by the Members, no Member shall be obligated to make an additional Capital Contribution to the Company.

7.5 Capital Accounts. The Company shall establish and maintain a Capital Account for each Member in accordance with Treasury Regulations issued under Code Section 704. The initial Capital Account balance for each Member shall be the amount of initial Capital Contributions made by each Member under Section 7.1. The Capital Account of each Member shall be increased to reflect (i) such Member's cash contributions, (ii) the fair market value of property contributed by such Member (net of liabilities securing such contributed property that the Company is considered to assume or take subject to under Code Section 752), (iii) such Member's share of Net Income (including all gain as calculated pursuant to Section 1001 of the Code) of the Company and (iv) such Member's share of income and gain exempt from tax. The Capital Account of each Member shall be reduced to reflect (a) the amount of money and the fair market value of property distributed to such Member (net of liabilities securing such distributed property that the Member is considered to assume or take subject to under Section 752), (b) such Member's share of non-capitalized expenditures not deductible by the Company in computing its taxable income as determined under Code Section 705(a)(2)(B), (c) such Member's share of Net Loss of the Company and (d) such Member's share of amounts paid or incurred to organize the Company or to promote the sale of Company Interests to the extent that an election under Code Section 709(b) has not properly been made for such amounts. The Manager shall determine the fair market value of all property which is distributed in kind, and the Capital Accounts of the Members shall be adjusted as though the property had been sold for its fair market value and the gain or loss attributable to such sale allocated among the Members in accordance with Section 8.1 or 8.2, as applicable. In the event of a contribution of property with a fair market value which is not equal to its adjusted basis (as determined for federal income tax purposes), a revaluation of the Members' Capital Accounts upon the admission of new members to the Company, or in other appropriate situations as permitted by Treasury Regulations issued under Code Section 704, the Company shall separately maintain "tax" Capital Accounts solely for purposes of taking into account the variation between the adjusted tax basis and book value of Company property in tax allocations to the Members consistent with the principles of Code Section 704(c) in accordance with the rules prescribed in Treasury Regulations promulgated under Code Section 704.

7.6 Default. In the event any Member shall fail to contribute any cash or property when due hereunder, such Member shall remain liable therefor to the Company, which may institute proceedings in any court of competent jurisdiction in connection with which such Member shall pay the costs of such collection, including reasonable attorneys' fees. Any compromise or settlement with a Member failing to contribute cash or property due hereunder may be approved by a majority by Percentage Interest of the other Members.

8. ALLOCATIONS.

8.1 Allocation of Net Loss from Operations. Except as otherwise provided in this Section 8 and in Section 16.3, the Company shall allocate Net Loss to the Members in proportion to each Member's Percentage Interest.

8.2 Allocation of Net Income from Operations. Except as otherwise provided in this Section 8 and Section 16.3, the Company shall allocate all Net Income as follows:

First, to the Members in proportion to the aggregate distributions of Cash Available for Distribution made to the Members in the current year and all prior years pursuant to Section 10 until such time as each Member has been allocated Net Income pursuant to this Section 8.3 in an amount equal to the excess of (i) the amount of Cash Available for Distribution distributed to such Member for the current year and all prior years pursuant to Section 10, over (ii) the amount of Net Income previously allocated to such Member pursuant to this Section 8.3; and

Thereafter, all remaining Net Income shall be allocated in proportion to each Member's Percentage Interest.

8.3 Limitation on Net Loss Allocations. Notwithstanding anything contained in this Section 8, no Member shall be allocated Net Loss to the extent such allocation would cause a negative balance in such Member's Deemed Capital Account as of the end of the taxable year to which such allocation relates.

8.4 Minimum Gain Chargeback. If there is a net decrease in Minimum Gain during a taxable year of the Company, then notwithstanding any other provision of this Section 8 or Section 16.3, each Member must be allocated items of income and gain for such year, and succeeding taxable years to the extent necessary (the "Minimum Gain Chargeback"), in proportion to, and to the extent of, an amount required under Treasury Regulation Section 1.704–2(f).

8.5 Qualified Income Offset. If at the end of any taxable year and after operation of Section 10, any Member shall have a negative balance in such Member's Deemed Capital Account, then notwithstanding anything contained in this Section 8, there shall be reallocated to each Member with a negative balance in such Member's Deemed Capital Account (determined after the allocation of income, gain or loss under this Section 8 for such year) each item of Company gross income (unreduced by any deductions) and gain in proportion to such negative balances until the Deemed Capital Account for each such Member is increased to zero.

8.6 Curative Allocations. The allocations set forth in Sections 8.3, 8.4 and 8.5 (the "Regulatory Allocations") are intended to comply with certain requirements of the Treasury Regulations issued pursuant to Code Section 704(b). It is the intent of the Members that, to the extent possible, all Regulatory Allocations shall be offset either with other Regulatory Allocations or with special allocations of other items of Company income, gain, loss, or deduction pursuant to this Section 8. Therefore, notwithstanding any other provision of this Section 8 (other than the Regulatory Allocations), the Manager shall make such offsetting special allocations of Company income, gain, loss, or deduction in whatever manner they determine appropriate so that, after such offsetting allocations are made, each Member's Capital Account balance is, to the extent possible, equal to the Capital Account balance such Member would have had if the Regulatory Allocations were not part of the Agreement and all Company items were allocated pursuant to other provisions of this Section 8.

8.7 Modification of Company Allocations. It is the intent of the Members that each Member's distributive share of income, gain, loss, deduction, or credit (or items thereof) shall be determined and allocated in accordance with this Section 8 to the fullest extent permitted by Section 704(b) of the Code. In order to preserve and protect the determinations and allocations provided for in this Section 8, the Manager shall be, and hereby is, authorized and directed to allocate income, gain, loss, deduction or credit (or items thereof) arising in any year differently from the manner otherwise provided for in this Section 8 if, and to the extent that, allocation of income, gain, loss, deduction or credit (or items thereof) in the manner provided for in this Section would cause the determination and allocation of each Member's distributive share of income, gain, loss, deduction or credit (or items thereof), not to be permitted by Section 704(b) of the Code and Treasury Regulations promulgated thereunder. Any allocation made pursuant to this Section 8.9 shall be made only after the Manager has secured an opinion of counsel that such modification is the minimum modification required to comply with Code Section 704(b) and shall be deemed to be a complete substitute for any allocation otherwise provided for in this Section and no amendment of this Agreement or approval of any Member shall be required. The Members shall be given notice of the modification within thirty (30) days of the effective date thereof, such notice to include the text of the modification and a statement of the circumstances requiring the modification to be made.

8.8 Deficit Capital Accounts at Liquidation. It is understood and agreed that one purpose of the provisions of this Section 8 is to insure that none of the Members has a deficit Capital Account balance after liquidation and to insure that all allocations under this Section 8 will be respected by the Internal Revenue Service. The Members and the Company neither intend nor expect that any Member will have a deficit Capital Account balance after liquidation and, notwithstanding anything to the contrary in this Agreement, the provisions of this Agreement shall be construed and interpreted to give effect to such intention. However, if following a liquidation of a Member's interest as determined under

Treasury Regulation Section 1.704–1(b)(2)(ii)(g), a Member has a deficit balance in such Member's Capital Account after the allocation of Net Income pursuant to this Section 8 and Section 16.3 and all other adjustments have been made to such Member's Capital Account for Company operations and liquidation, no Member shall have any obligation to restore such deficit balance, as provided in Section 8.9.

8.9 Deficit Restoration Obligation. No Member shall have an obligation to restore a deficit Capital Account balance upon liquidation of the Company or liquidation of its interest in the Company.

9. COMPANY EXPENSES. The Company shall pay, and the Manager shall be reimbursed for, all costs and expenses of the Company, which may include, but are not limited to:

9.1 All organizational expenses incurred in the formation of the Company and the selling of interests in the Company;

9.2 All costs of personnel employed by the Company;

9.3 All costs reasonably related to the conduct of the Company's day-to-day business affairs, including, but without limitation, the cost of supplies, utilities, taxes, licenses, fees and services contracted from third parties;

9.4 All costs of borrowed money, taxes and assessments on Company property, and other taxes applicable to the Company;

9.5 Legal, audit, accounting, brokerage and other fees;

9.6 Printing and other expenses and taxes incurred in connection with the issuance, distribution, transfer, registration and recording of documents evidencing ownership of an interest in the Company or in connection with the business of the Company;

9.7 Fees and expenses paid to service providers, including affiliates of the Manager;

9.8 The cost of insurance obtained in connection with the business of the Company;

9.9 Expenses of revising, amending, converting, modifying or terminating the Company;

9.10 Expenses in connection with distributions made by the Company to, and communications and bookkeeping and clerical work necessary in maintaining relations with, Members;

9.11 Expenses in connection with preparing and mailing reports required to be furnished to Members for investment, tax reporting or other purposes that the Manager deems appropriate; and

9.12 Costs incurred in connection with any litigation, including any examinations or audits by regulatory agencies.

10. DISTRIBUTIONS OF CASH AVAILABLE FOR DISTRIBUTION. At such times and in such amounts as the Manager in its discretion determines

appropriate, Cash Available for Distribution shall be distributed in the following order of priority:

10.1 First, among the Members in proportion to their Adjusted Contribution Amounts until such balances are reduced to zero; and

10.2 Thereafter, among the Members in proportion to their Percentage Interests.

11. POWERS, RIGHTS AND OBLIGATIONS OF MANAGER.

11.1 General Authority and Powers of Manager. Except as provided in Section , the Manager shall have the exclusive right and power to manage, operate and control the Company and to do all things and make all decisions necessary or appropriate to carry on the business and affairs of the Company. All decisions required to be made by the Manager or action to be taken by the Manager shall require the approval and action of only one Manager, acting alone, except as otherwise specifically provided in this Agreement. The authority of one Manager, acting alone, shall include, but shall not be limited to the following:

(a) To spend the capital and revenues of the Company;

(b) To manage, develop, and operate the business of the Company and the Company properties;

(c) To employ service providers to assist in the operation and management of the Company's business and for the operation and development of the property of the Company, as the Manager shall deem necessary in its sole discretion;

(d) To acquire, lease and sell personal and/or real property, hire and fire employees, and to do all other acts necessary, appropriate or helpful for the operation of the Company business;

(e) To execute, acknowledge and deliver any and all instruments to effectuate any of the foregoing powers and any other powers granted the Manager under the laws of the state of Washington or other provisions of this Agreement;

(f) To enter into and to execute agreements for employment or services, as well as any other agreements and all other instruments a Manager deems necessary or appropriate to operate the Company's business and to operate and dispose of Company properties or to effectively and properly perform its duties or exercise its powers hereunder;

(g) To borrow money on a secured or unsecured basis from individuals, banks and other lending institutions to meet Company obligations, provide Company working capital and for any other Company purpose, and to execute promissory notes, mortgages, deeds of trust and assignments of Company property, and such other security instruments as a lender of funds may require, to secure repayment of such borrowings;

(h) To enter into such agreements and contracts and to give such receipts, releases and discharges, with respect to the business of the

Company, as a Manager deems advisable or appropriate;

(i) To purchase, at the expense of the Company, such liability and other insurance as the Manager, in its sole discretion, deems advisable to protect the Company's assets and business; however, the Manager shall not be liable to the Company or the other Members for failure to purchase any insurance; and

(j) To sue and be sued, complain, defend, settle and/or compromise, with respect to any claim in favor of or against the Company, in the name and on behalf of the Company.

11.2 Time Devoted to Company; Other Ventures. The Manager shall devote so much of its time to the business of the Company as in its judgment the conduct of the Company's business reasonably requires. The Manager and the other Members may engage in business ventures and activities of any nature and description independently or with others, whether or not in competition with the business of the Company, and shall have no obligation to disclose business opportunities available to them, and neither the Company nor any of the other Members shall have any rights in and to such independent ventures and activities or the income or profits derived therefrom by reason of their acquisition of interests in the Company. This Section 11.2 is intended to modify any provisions or obligations of the Act to the contrary and each of the Members and the Company hereby waives and releases any claims they may have under the Act with respect to any such activities or ventures of the Manager or other Members.

11.3 Liability of Manager to Members and Company. In carrying out its duties and exercising the powers hereunder, the Manager shall exercise reasonable skill, care and business judgment. A Manager shall not be liable to the Company or the Members for any act or omission performed or omitted by it in good faith pursuant to the authority granted to it by this Agreement as a Manager or Tax Matters Partner (as defined in the Code) unless such act or omission constitutes gross negligence or willful misconduct by such Manager.

11.4 Indemnification. The Company shall indemnify and hold harmless the Manager from any loss or damage, including attorneys' fees actually and reasonably incurred by it, by reason of any act or omission performed or omitted by it on behalf of the Company or in furtherance of the Company's interests or as Tax Matters Partner; however, such indemnification or agreement to hold harmless shall be recoverable only out of the assets of the Company and not from the Members. The foregoing indemnity shall extend only to acts or omissions performed or omitted by a Manager in good faith and in the belief that the acts or omissions were in the Company's interest or not opposed to the best interests of the Company.

11.5 Fiduciary Responsibility. The Manager shall have a fiduciary responsibility for the safekeeping and use of all funds and assets of the Company, and all such funds and assets shall be used in accordance with the terms of this Agreement.

11.6 Restrictions on Authority of Manager.

(a) Except as provided in Section 11.6(b), the following Company decisions shall require the written consent of the Manager and Members holding a majority of the Percentage Interests in the Company:

(i) The dissolution and winding up of the Company;

(ii) The sale, exchange or other transfer of all or substantially all the assets of the Company other than in the ordinary course of business; or

(iii) A change in the nature of the business of the Company.

(b) Notwithstanding the provisions of Section 11.6(a), no consent or approval of the Members shall be required prior to a transfer of the Project or other Company property for no consideration other than full or partial satisfaction of Company indebtedness such as by deed in lieu of foreclosure or similar procedure.

(c) Notwithstanding the provisions of Section 11.6(a)(i), the dissolution and winding up or insolvency filing of the Company shall require the unanimous consent of all Members.

## 12. STATUS OF MEMBERS.

12.1 No Participation in Management. Except as specifically provided in Section 11.6 above, no Member shall take part in the conduct or control of the Company's business or the management of the Company, or have any right or authority to act for or on the behalf of, or otherwise bind, the Company (except a Member who may also be a Manager and then only in such Member's capacity as a Manager within the scope of such Member's authority hereunder).

12.2 Limitation of Liability. No Member shall have, solely by virtue of such Member's status as a Member in the Company, any personal liability whatever, whether to the Company, to any Members or to the creditors of the Company, for the debts or obligations of the Company or any of its losses beyond the amount committed by such Member to the capital of the Company, except as otherwise required by the Act.

12.3 Death or Incapacity of Non–Manager Member. The death, incompetence, withdrawal, expulsion, bankruptcy or dissolution of a Member, or the occurrence of any other event which terminates the continued membership of a Member in the Company, shall not cause a dissolution of the Company unless such Member is a Manager of the Company. Upon the occurrence of such event, the rights of such non-Manager Member to share in the Net Income and Net Loss of the Company, to receive distributions from the Company and to assign an interest in the Company pursuant to Section 14 shall, on the happening of such an event, devolve upon such Member's executor, administrator, guardian, conservator, or other legal representative or successor, as the case may be, subject to the terms and conditions of this Agreement, and the Company shall continue as a limited liability company. However, in any such event, such legal representative or successor, or any assignee of such legal representative or successor shall be admitted to the Company as a Member only in accordance with and pursuant to all of the terms and conditions of Section 14 hereof.

12.4 Death or Incapacity of a Manager Member. The death, incompetence, withdrawal, expulsion, bankruptcy or dissolution of a Member that is a Manager, or the occurrence of any other event which terminates the continued membership of such Member in the Company, shall cause a dissolution of the Company, unless the Company is continued in accordance with Section 16. If the Company is continued in accordance with Section 16, the rights of such Member to share in the Net Income and Net Loss of the Company, to receive distributions from the Company and to assign an interest in the Company pursuant to Section 14 hereof shall, on the happening of such an event, devolve upon such Member's executor, administrator, guardian, conservator, or other legal representative or successor, as the case may be, subject to the terms and conditions of this Agreement, and the Company shall continue as a limited liability company. However, in any such event such legal representative or successor, or any assignee of such legal representative or successor shall be admitted to the Company as a Member only in accordance with and pursuant to all of the terms and conditions of Section 14 hereof.

12.5 Recourse of Members. Each Member shall look solely to the assets of the Company for all distributions with respect to the Company and such Member's Capital Contribution thereto and share of Net Income and Net Loss thereof and shall have no recourse therefore, upon dissolution or otherwise, against any Manager or any other Member.

12.6 No Right to Property. No Member, regardless of the nature of such Member's contributions to the capital of the Company, shall have any right to demand or receive any distribution from the Company in any form other than cash, upon dissolution or otherwise.

13.  BOOKS  AND  RECORDS,  ACCOUNTING,  REPORTS  AND STATEMENTS AND TAX MATTERS.

13.1 Books and Records. The Manager shall, at the expense of the Company, keep and maintain, or cause to be kept and maintained, the books and records of the Company on the same method of accounting as utilized for federal income tax purposes, which shall be kept separate and apart from the books and records of the Manager.

13.2 Annual Accounting Period. All books and records of the Company shall be kept on the basis of an annual accounting period ending December 31 of each year, except for the final accounting period which shall end on the date of termination of the Company. All references herein to the "fiscal year of the Company" are to the annual accounting period described in the preceding sentence, whether the same shall consist of twelve months or less.

13.3 Manager's Reports to Members. The Manager shall send at Company expense to each Member the following:

(a) Within seventy-five (75) days after the end of each fiscal year of the Company, such information as shall be necessary for the preparation by such Member of such Member's federal income tax return which shall include a computation of the distributions to such Member and the allocation to such Member of profits or losses, as the case may be; and

(b) Within one hundred twenty (120) days after the end of each fiscal quarter of the Company, a quarterly report, which shall include:

(i) A balance sheet;

(ii) A statement of income and expenses;

(iii) A statement of changes in Members' capital; and

(iv) A statement of the balances in the Capital Accounts of the Members.

13.4 Right to Examine Records. Members shall be entitled, upon written request directed to the Company, to review the records of the Company at all reasonable times and at the location where such records are kept by the Company.

13.5 Tax Matters Partner. Should there be any controversy with the Internal Revenue Service or any other taxing authority involving the Company, the Manager may expend such funds as they deem necessary and advisable in the interest of the Company to resolve such controversy satisfactorily, including, without being limited thereto, attorneys' and accounting fees. _____ is hereby designated as the "Tax Matters Partner" as referred to in Section 6231(a)(7)(A) of the Code, and is specially authorized to exercise all of the rights and powers now or hereafter granted to the Tax Matters Partner under the Code. Any cost incurred in the audit by any governmental authority of the income tax returns of a Member (as opposed to the Company) shall not be a Company expense. The Manager agrees to consult with and keep the Members advised with respect to (i) any income tax audit of a Company income tax return, and (ii) any elections made by the Company for federal, state or local income tax purposes.

13.6 Tax Returns. The Manager shall, at Company expense, cause the Company to prepare and file a United States Partnership Return of Income and all other tax returns required to be filed by the Company for each fiscal year of the Company.

13.7 Tax Elections. The Manager shall be permitted in its discretion to determine whether the Company should make an election pursuant to Section 754 of the Code to adjust the basis of the assets of the Company. Each of the Members shall, upon request, supply any information necessary to properly give effect to any such election. In addition, the Manager, in its sole discretion, shall be authorized to cause the Company to make and revoke any other elections for federal income tax purposes as they deem appropriate, necessary, or advisable.

14. TRANSFERS OF COMPANY INTERESTS; WITHDRAWAL AND ADMISSION OF MEMBERS.

14.1 General Prohibition. No Member may voluntarily or involuntarily, directly or indirectly, sell, transfer, assign, pledge or otherwise dispose of, or mortgage, pledge, hypothecate or otherwise encumber, or permit or suffer any encumbrance of, all or any part of such Member's interest in the Company, except as provided in this Section 14. Any other purported sale, transfer, assignment, pledge or encumbrance shall be null and void and of no force or effect whatsoever.

14.2 Withdrawal of Member. A Member shall have no power to withdraw voluntarily from the Company, except that a Member may withdraw upon written approval of a majority of the non-withdrawing Members voting by Percentage Interests, which approval shall include the terms for redemption by the Company of the Interest of the such Member.

14.3 Transfers by Members.

(a) Subject to any restrictions on transferability required by law or contained elsewhere in this Agreement, a Member may transfer such Member's entire interest in the Company upon satisfaction of the following conditions:

(i) The transfer shall (A) be by bequest or by operation of the laws of intestate succession, or (B) be approved in writing by the Manager, which approval shall be withheld only if the proposed transfer does not comply with the requirements of this Section 14.

(ii) The transferor and transferee shall have executed and acknowledged such reasonable and customary instruments as the Manager may deem necessary or desirable to effect such transfer; and

(iii) The transfer does not violate any applicable law or governmental rule or regulation, including without limitation any federal or state securities laws.

(b) At the time of a transfer of any Member's interest, whether or not such transfer is made in accordance with this Section 14, all the rights possessed as a Member in connection with the transferred interest, which rights otherwise would be held either by the transferor or the transferee, shall terminate against the Company unless the transferee is admitted to the Company as a Substitute Member pursuant to the provisions of Section 14.4 hereof; provided, however, that if the transfer is made in accordance with this Section 14, such transferee shall be entitled to receive distributions to which his transferor would otherwise be entitled from and after the Effective Date. The Effective Date shall be the date that is the later of the following dates: (a) the effective date of such transfer as agreed to by the transferee and transferor and set forth in writing in the transfer documentation, or (b) the last day of the calendar month following the date that the Manager has received notice of the transfer and all conditions precedent to such transfer provided for in this Agreement have been satisfied including receipt by the Manager of all documents necessary to comply with the requirements of Section , provided that the Manager, in its sole discretion, may agree to an earlier effective date if an earlier date is requested by the transferor and transferee. The Company and the Manager shall be entitled to treat the transferor as the recognized owner of such interests until the Effective Date and shall incur no liability for distributions made in good faith to the transferor prior to the Effective Date.

(c) Notwithstanding any other provision of this Agreement, a Member may not transfer such Member's interest in any case if such a transfer, when aggregated with all other transfers within a twelve (12) month period, would cause the termination of the Company as a partnership for federal income tax purposes pursuant to Section 708 of the Code, unless such transfer has been previously approved by the Manager.

(d) A change in the custodian or trustee of a Member that is a IRA, Trust, or pension or profit sharing plan, will be reflected on Appendix A in connection with an amendment completed in the first quarter of each year following notification to the Company of such change by the Member and the new custodian or trustee. The IRA, trust or pension or profit sharing plan shall pay the costs incurred by the Company to amend the Company documents to reflect the change in custodian or trustee.

14.4 Admission of Transferees as Members.

(a) No transferee of a Member shall be admitted as a Member unless all of the following conditions have been satisfied:

(i) The transfer complies with Section 14.3;

(ii) The further written consent of the Manager, to such transferee being admitted as a Member is first obtained, which consent may be arbitrarily withheld;

(iii) The prospective transferee has executed an instrument, in form and substance satisfactory to the Manager, accepting and agreeing to be bound by all the terms and conditions of this Agreement, including the power of attorney set forth in Section 17 hereof, and has paid all expenses of the Company in effecting the transfer;

(iv) All requirements of the Act regarding the admission of a transferee Member have been complied with by the transferee, the transferring Member and the Company; and

(v) Such transfer is effected in compliance with all applicable state and federal securities laws.

(b) In the event of a transfer complying with all the requirements of Section 14.3 hereof and the transferee being admitted as a Member pursuant to this Section 14.4, the Manager, for itself and for each Member pursuant to the Power of Attorney granted by each Member, shall execute an amendment to this Agreement and file any necessary amendments to the articles of organization for the Company. Unless named in this Agreement, as amended from time to time, no person shall be considered a Member.

(c) In the event of a change in the custodian or trustee of a Member that is a IRA, trust, or pension or profit sharing plan that complies with Section hereof, the Manager, for itself and for each Member pursuant to the Power of Attorney granted by each Member, shall execute an amendment to this Agreement to reflect such change.

14.5 Assignment as Security Permitted. Notwithstanding any other provision of this Article 14, a Member may assign, as security for a loan or other indebtedness incurred by such Member, such Member's right to receive distributions from the Company, and the Manager, upon receipt of notification of any such assignment, shall acknowledge such assignment and shall agree to pay or distribute proceeds in accordance with instructions from such Member subject to such conditions, including indemnification, as the Manager may reasonably require; provided, however, that such lender shall acknowledge in writing to the Manager that such assignment of proceeds shall not entitle such lender to foreclose or otherwise acquire or sell the Company Interest and that the only right acquired by such lender shall be the right to receive distributions of cash and property, if any, made by the Company to the Members in accordance with this Agreement.

15. RESIGNATION AND ADMISSION OF MANAGER.

15.1 Resignation of Manager. A Manager shall be entitled to resign as a Manager 120 days after delivery of written notice to the Company and the Members of the Manager's intention to resign, or upon such earlier date as the Manager's resignation is accepted by Members holding a majority of the Percentage Interests in the Company. Resignation of a Manager, who is a Member, pursuant to this Section shall not affect its interest as a Member of the Company. Notwithstanding the foregoing, the transfer by a Manager, who is also a Member, of its Interest in the Company, shall constitute a resignation by such Member as a Manager, which resignation shall be effective as of the date of such transfer.

15.2 Death or Incompetency of Manager. A Manager who is a Member in the Company, shall cease to be a Manager upon the death, incompetence, bankruptcy or dissolution of such Manager, or any other event which terminates the continued membership of the Manager as a Member of the Company.

15.3 Removal of a Manager. A Manager may be removed as a Manager upon the written approval of Members holding a majority of the Percentage Interests of the Company. Removal of Manager who is a Member of the Company, pursuant to this Section shall not affect such Manager's interest as a Member of the Company.

15.4 Appointment of a New or Replacement Manager. A new or replacement Manager may be appointed with the written approval of Members holding a majority of the Percentage Interests of the Company.

16. DISSOLUTION, WINDING UP AND TERMINATION.

16.1 Events Causing Dissolution. The Company shall be dissolved and its affairs shall be wound up upon the happening of the first to occur of any of the following events:

(a) Expiration of the term of the Company stated in Section 6 hereof;

(b) Entry of a decree of administrative or judicial dissolution pursuant to the Act;

(c) The sale or other disposition of all or substantially all of the assets of the Company;

(d) The death, incompetence, withdrawal, expulsion, resignation, removal, bankruptcy or dissolution of a Manager, who is a Member, which is the last remaining Manager of the Company, unless (i) within 120 days of such occurrence, Members owning at least a majority of Percentage Interests in the Company, consent to the appointment of a new Manager(s) in accordance with Section 15.4, in which case the business of the Company shall be carried on by the newly appointed Manager(s), and (ii) the conditions of Section 14 are also satisfied;

(e) The death, incompetence, withdrawal, expulsion, bankruptcy, resignation, or dissolution of a Manager, who is a Member, or any other event that terminates the continued membership of such Manager unless at the time of the occurrence of any of such event there are at least two other Members, and within 120 days of such occurrence, remaining Members owning at least a majority of the Percentage Interests in the Company (or, if greater, remaining Members owning at least a "majority in interest" in the capital and profits of the Company as such term is used in Treas. Reg. Section 301.7701–2(b)(1)), consent to the continuation of the Company, in which case the business of the Company shall be carried on by the remaining Manager(s); or

(f) The unanimous vote of Members.

16.2 Winding Up. Upon dissolution of the Company for any reason, the Manager shall commence to wind up the affairs of the Company and to liquidate its assets. In the event the Company has terminated because the Company lacks a Manager, then the remaining members shall appoint a new Manager solely for the purpose of winding up the affairs of the Company. The Manager shall have the full right and unlimited discretion to determine the time, manner and terms of any sale or sales of Company property pursuant to such liquidation. Pending such sales, the Manager shall have the right to continue to operate or otherwise deal with the assets of the Company. A reasonable time shall be allowed for the orderly winding up of the business of the Company and the liquidation of its assets and the discharge of its liabilities to creditors so as to enable the Manager to minimize the normal losses attendant upon a liquidation, having due regard to the activity and condition of the relevant markets for the Company properties and general financial and economic conditions. Any Member may be a purchaser of any properties of the Company upon liquidation of the Company's assets, including, without limitation, any liquidation conducted pursuant to a judicial dissolution or otherwise under judicial supervision; provided, however, that the purchase price and terms of sale are fair and reasonable to the Company.

16.3 Allocation of Net Income and Net Loss Upon Termination or Sale. All Net Income and Net Loss upon dissolution of the Company or from sale, conversion, disposition or taking of all or substantially all of the Company's property, including, but not limited to the proceeds of any eminent domain proceeding or insurance award (respectively, "Gain on Sale" or "Loss on Sale") shall be allocated as follows:

(a) Loss on Sale shall be allocated among the Members as follows:

(i) First, proportionately to those Members having positive Capital Account balances until all positive Capital Accounts have been reduced to zero; and

(ii) Thereafter, among the Members in proportion to their Percentage Interests.

(b) Gain on Sale to the extent available shall be allocated among the Members as follows:

(i) First to those Members having negative Capital Account balances in proportion to such negative balances until they are increased to zero; and

(ii) Thereafter, any remaining Gain on Sale shall be allocated to the Members in proportion to their Percentage Interests.

16.4 Distributions. Prior to making distributions in dissolution to the Members, the Manager shall first pay or make provision for all debts and liabilities of the Company, including payment of any Manager Loans, and other loans to Members and their affiliates, and all expenses of liquidation. Subject to the right of the Manager to set up such cash reserves as it deems reasonably necessary for any contingent or unforeseen liabilities or obligations of the Company, the proceeds of liquidation and any other funds of the Company shall be distributed in the following order of priority:

(a) First, to Members in proportion to their Capital Account balances as adjusted by the allocations provided for in Section above; and

(b) Thereafter, the balance, if any, to the Members in proportion to their Percentage Interests.

It is intended and anticipated that the amount of cash distributable upon a termination or dissolution of the Company should equal the sum of the Members' Capital Accounts, after adjustment of such balances in accordance with Sections 16.3(a) and 16.3(b), and that therefore all cash will be distributable under this Section 16.4.

16.5 Certificate of Cancellation; Report; Termination. Upon the dissolution and commencement of winding up of the Company, the Manager shall execute and file articles of dissolution for the Company. Within a reasonable time following the completion of the liquidation of the Company's assets, the Manager shall prepare and furnish to each Member, at the expense of the Company, a statement which shall set forth the assets and liabilities of the Company as of the date of complete liquidation and the amount of each Member's distribution pursuant to Section 16.4 hereof. Upon completion of the liquidation and distribution of all Company funds, the Company shall terminate and the Manager shall have the authority to execute and file all documents required to effectuate the termination of the Company.

17. SPECIAL AND LIMITED POWER OF ATTORNEY.

17.1 The Manager, with full power of substitution, shall at all times during the existence of the Company have a special and limited power of attorney as the authority to act in the name and on the behalf of each Member to make, execute, swear to, verify, acknowledge and file the following documents and any other documents deemed by the Manager to be necessary for the business of the Company:

(a) This Agreement, any separate articles of organization, fictitious business name statements, as well as any amendments to the foregoing which, under the laws of any state, are required to be filed or which the Manager deems it advisable to file;

(b) Any other instrument or document which may be required to be filed by the Company under the laws of any state or by an governmental agency, or which the Manager deems it advisable to file; and

(c) Any instrument or document which may be required to effect the continuation of the Company, the admission of a Manager or Member, the transfer of an interest in the Company, the change in custodian or trustee of any IRA, trust or pension or profit sharing plan Member, or the dissolution and termination of the Company (provided such continuation, admission or dissolution and termination are in accordance with the terms of this Agreement), or to reflect any increases or reductions in amount of contributions of Members.

17.2 The special and limited power of attorney granted to the Manager hereby:

(a) Is a special and limited power of attorney coupled with an interest, is irrevocable, shall survive the dissolution or incompetency of the granting Member, and is limited to those matters herein set forth;

(b) May be exercised by the Manager (or by any authorized officer of the Manager, if not a natural person) for each Member by referencing the list of Members on Appendix A and executing any instrument with a single signature acting as attorney-in-fact for all of them;

(c) Shall survive a transfer by a Member of such Member's interest in the Company pursuant to Section 14 hereof for the sole purpose of enabling the Manager to execute, acknowledge and file any instrument or document necessary or appropriate to admit a transferee as a Member; and

(d) Notwithstanding the foregoing, in the event that a Manager ceases to be a Manager in the Company, the power of attorney granted by this Section 17 to such Manager shall terminate immediately, but any such termination shall not affect the validity of any documents executed prior to such termination, or any other actions previously taken pursuant to this power of attorney or in reliance upon its validity, all of which shall continue to be valid and binding upon the Members in accordance with their terms.

18. AMENDMENTS. Except as otherwise provided by law, this Agreement may be amended in any respect by a majority vote of the Members voting by Percentage Interests; provided, however, that:

18.1 This Agreement may not be amended so as to change any Member's rights to or interest in Net Income, Net Loss or distributions unless (i) such amendment is made in connection with an additional capital contribution to the Company or an additional guarantee of Company indebtedness, (ii) each Member is given the first opportunity maintain its Percentage Interest by participating in such contribution or guarantee in proportion to their existing Percentage Interest, and (iii) the amendment is approved by a sixty-six and two-thirds (66 2/3) of the

Members voting by Percentage Interests;

18.2 Without the consent of each Member to be adversely affected by the amendment, this Agreement may not be amended so as to increase the liability of or change the capital contributions required by a Member;

18.3 In the case of any provision hereof which requires the action, approval or consent of a specified Percentage Interest of Members, such provision may not be amended without the consent of the Members owning such specified Percentage Interest; and

18.4 In addition to any amendments otherwise authorized herein, amendments may be made to this Agreement from time to time by the Manager without the consent or approval of the Members, (i) to cure any ambiguity or to correct any typographical errors in this Agreement or (ii) to correct or supplement any provision herein which may be inconsistent with any other provision herein.

19. MISCELLANEOUS.

19.1 Notices. Any notice, offer, consent or other communication required or permitted to be given or made hereunder shall be in writing and shall be deemed to have been sufficiently given or made when delivered personally to the party (or an officer of the party) to whom the same is directed, or (except in the event of a mail strike) five days after being mailed by first class mail, postage prepaid, if to the Company or to a Manager, to the office described in Section 4 hereof, or if to a Member, to such Member's last known address or when received by facsimile if to the Company or Manager to the facsimile number for the office described in Section hereof, or if to a Member, to such Member's facsimile number. Any Member may change such Member's address for the purpose of this Section 19.1 by giving notice of such change to the Company, such change to become effective on the tenth day after such notice is given.

19.2 Entire Agreement. This Agreement constitutes the entire agreement among the parties and supersedes any prior agreement or understandings among them, oral or written, all of which are hereby cancelled. This Agreement may not be modified or amended other than pursuant to Section 18 hereof.

19.3 Captions; Pronouns. The paragraph and section titles or captions contained in this Agreement are inserted only as a matter of convenience of reference. Such titles and captions in no way define, limit, extend or describe the scope of this Agreement nor the intent of any provision hereof. All pronouns and any variation thereof shall be deemed to refer to the masculine, feminine or neuter, singular or plural, as the identity of the person or persons may require.

19.4 Counterparts. This Agreement may be executed in any number of counterparts and by different parties hereto in separate counterparts, each of which when so executed shall be deemed to be an original and all of which when taken together shall constitute one and the same agreement. Delivery of any executed counterpart of a signature page to this Agreement by facsimile shall be effective as delivery of an executed original counterpart of this Agreement.

19.5 Governing Law. This Agreement shall be governed by and construed in accordance with the internal laws of the state of Washington.

IN WITNESS WHEREOF the parties have executed this Agreement as of the date first hereinabove written.

MANAGER/MEMBER:_____

MANAGER/MEMBER:_____

SPOUSAL CONSENT

The undersigned acknowledges that she has read the foregoing Agreement, knows and understands its contents, and has had ample opportunity to consult with legal counsel of her own choosing. The undersigned is aware that by its provisions, her spouse agrees to hold their Percentage Interest in the Company subject to certain restrictions. The undersigned hereby approves of the provisions of this Agreement and consents to the imposition of certain restrictions on any interest he may have in the Percentage Interests, and agrees that she will not make any transfer of, or otherwise deal with, the Percentage Interests or with any interest she may have in the Percentage Interests except as expressly permitted by such Agreement.

DATED:_____

_____

DATED:_____

_____

## APPENDIX A

| Member | Cash Contribution | Percentage Interest | |
|---|---|---|---|
| | $ | _____ | % |
| | $ | _____ | % |
| TOTAL | $ | 100 | % |

## C.  FORM: CORPORATE SHAREHOLDERS AGREEMENT

### SHAREHOLDERS AGREEMENT of

_____

This Agreement dated as of _____, _____, is made by and among _____, a corporation (the "Company"), and the shareholders set forth on attached Exhibit A (the "Shareholders").

## RECITALS

This Agreement is intended to set forth the restrictions to which any transfer of any or all of the shares of the Company's capital stock now or hereafter outstanding ("Shares") will be subject. The Shareholders together own all the currently outstanding Shares as set forth in attached <u>Exhibit A</u>.

## AGREEMENT

### 1. RESTRICTIONS ON TRANSFER

1.1 Transfers by Shareholders. No Shareholder may transfer any Shares except as expressly permitted by this Agreement. For purposes of this Agreement, "transfer" is intended to be construed as broadly as the law allows and to include any change of legal or beneficial ownership with respect to the Shares or the creation of a security interest by any means. Any transfer made in connection with the foreclosure of a security interest will constitute a separate transfer.

1.2 New Stock Issues. The Company may not transfer Shares by new issue to anyone (including a Shareholder or an outside party) or permit anyone (including a Shareholder or an outside party) to subscribe to a new issue of Shares without the prior written consent of all Shareholders [or, if that consent cannot be obtained, without first offering to the Shareholders the right for a period of _____ days to subscribe to the proposed issue in proportion to the Shareholder's respective interest at the time of issue].

### 2. PERMITTED TRANSFERS

2.1 With Consent. A Shareholder may transfer Shares at any time with the written consent of [all] the other Shareholders [who hold at least _____ percent (_____) of the Shares of the Company at the time of the proposed transfer].

2.2 Without Consent. A Shareholder may transfer Shares to trusts created by the Shareholder for the Shareholder's benefit or for the benefit of family members of the Shareholder. For purposes of this Agreement, "family members" means lineal descendants of the Shareholder.

2.3 Binding on Transferees. No permitted transfer may be made unless the transferee (and, if applicable, the transferee's spouse) executes a document substantially in the form of attached Exhibit B evidencing the transferee's agreement to be bound by the provisions of this Agreement, as amended.

3. PERMITTED LIFETIME TRANSFERS. Any Shareholder desiring to transfer Shares in a bona fide voluntary transfer not permitted by Section 2 must first give written notice to the Company and the remaining Shareholders of the Shareholder's intention to do so. The notice ("Transfer Notice") must name the proposed transferee and the number of Shares to be transferred and, if the transfer constitutes a sale, must specify the terms of a bona fide offer, including the price per Share, and the terms of payment.

3.1 Company Option. The Company will have the option, exercisable within _____ days after receiving the Transfer Notice, to purchase the Shares. To exercise the option, the Company must give written notice to the offering

Shareholder. Subject to Section 3.4, the Company must pay the purchase price on the same terms and conditions set forth in the Transfer Notice.

3.2 Option of Remaining Shareholders. If the Company does not exercise its option as to all or any of the Shares set forth in the Transfer Notice, then the Company must so notify the remaining Shareholders.

(a) The remaining Shareholders will each have the option, exercisable within _____ days after receiving notice from the Company, to purchase any Shares not purchased by the Company. To exercise the option, a Shareholder must give written notice to the Company and to the offering Shareholder specifying the number of shares the Shareholder wishes to purchase.

(b) If the total number of Shares specified in the notices of election exceeds the number of offered Shares, each Shareholder will have priority, up to the number of Shares specified in the notice of election, to purchase the Shareholder's Proportionate Share of the available Shares. Proportionate Share means that proportion determined by dividing the number of the Company's Shares that the electing Shareholder holds by the total number of the Company's Shares held by all Shareholders electing to purchase as of the date the offer was made.

(c) The Shares not purchased on a priority basis will be allocated to those Shareholders that elect to purchase more than the number of Shares to which they have a priority right, up to the number of Shares specified in their respective notices of election to purchase, in the proportion that the number of Shares held by each of them bears to the number of Shares held by all of them as of the date the offer was made.

(d) Promptly after receiving the written notices of election of the remaining Shareholders, the Company must notify each Shareholder of the number of Shares as to which the Shareholder's election was effective and must provide to the offering Shareholder a notice summarizing these elections. Subject to Section 3.4, each Shareholder must pay the purchase price on the same terms and conditions set forth in the Transfer Notice.

3.3 Conditions of Transfer. If the Company and the Shareholders elect not to purchase all the Shares set forth in the Transfer Notice, then all those Shares may be transferred subject to the satisfaction of all the following conditions:

(a) Within thirty (30) days after receiving notice from the Company, the offering Shareholder must transfer the Shares to the transferee identified in the Transfer Notice at the price and on the same terms stated in the Transfer Notice; and

(b) The transferee (and, if applicable, the transferee's spouse) must execute a document substantially in the form of attached Exhibit B evidencing the transferee's agreement to be bound by the provisions of this Agreement, as amended.

(c) If all of the above-conditions are not satisfied, the offering Shareholder may not transfer the Shares under this Section 3 without giving a new written notice of intention to transfer and complying with this Section 3.

3.4 Right to Purchase Pursuant to Agreement. Notwithstanding any other provision to the contrary, the Company or the remaining Shareholders, or both, will be entitled to purchase all the Shares specified in the Transfer Notice at the price and on the terms set forth in this Agreement (and not at the price and on the terms set forth in the Transfer Notice), if any of the following occur:

(a) The price stated in the Transfer Notice is greater than the price set forth in this Agreement;

(b) The offering Shareholder has included in the Transfer Notice the terms of a gift, pledge, or other transfer not constituting a sale; or

(c) The terms of a bona fide offer in the Transfer Notice provide for the payment of nonmonetary consideration, in whole or in part, and the offering Shareholder and the Company or remaining Shareholders, or both (as applicable), are not able to agree on the equivalent cash value of that consideration.

(d) If appraisal is required to determine the value of the Shares under Section 8, the Transfer Notice will be deemed to be given on the date that the Company receives notice of the appraisal determination.

4. OBLIGATIONS OF TRANSFEREES. Unless this Agreement expressly provides otherwise, each transferee or subsequent transferee of Shares, or any interest in those Shares, will hold those Shares or interest subject to all the provisions of this Agreement and may make no further transfers except as provided in this Agreement.

5. PURCHASE ON DEATH

5.1 Mandatory Purchase on Death by Company or Shareholders

(a) Upon the death of a Shareholder, the Company must purchase all the decedent's Shares and all Shares that have been transferred to third parties under Section 2.2, and the decedent Shareholder's estate and any such third parties must sell those Shares, at the price and on the terms provided in this Agreement. Subject to Section 9.1, the purchase must be completed within a period commencing with the death of the Shareholder and ending sixty (60) days following the qualification of the Shareholder's personal representative.

(b) If the Company is not legally able to purchase all of the decedent's Shares and all Shares that have been transferred to third parties under Section 2.2 under applicable law, the remaining Shareholders must purchase all of the decedent's Shares and all Shares that have been transferred to third parties under Section 2.2 that the Company is legally unable to purchase at the price and on the terms provided in this Agreement.

(c) The obligation of the remaining Shareholders to purchase those Shares will be [joint and several] [several and not joint and will be prorated based on their respective shareholdings in the Company].

5.2 Insurance: Corporate Buyout. The Company [may] [must] apply for a policy of insurance on the life of each Shareholder to enable the Company to purchase the Shares of that Shareholder. Each Shareholder agrees to do everything necessary to cause a policy of life insurance to be issued pursuant to that application. The Company must be the owner of any policy or policies of life insurance acquired pursuant to the terms of this Agreement. Each policy, and any policies hereafter acquired for the same purpose, will be listed on attached Exhibit C.

6. DISABILITY

6.1 Optional Purchase on Disability. If any Shareholder who is then an employee of the Company becomes disabled, the Company and the remaining Shareholders will have the option, for the periods set forth below, to purchase all or any part of the Shares owned by the Shareholder and all or any part of the Shareholder's Shares that have been transferred to third parties under Section 2.2.

6.2 Exercise of Option

(a) To exercise its option, the Company must give written notice to the disabled Shareholder within _____ days after receiving notice of the determination of disability under Section 6.3.

(b) If the option is not exercised within that _____ -day period as to all Shares owned by the disabled Shareholder, the remaining Shareholders will have the option, for a period of _____ days commencing with the end of that _____ -day period, to purchase all or any part of the remaining Shares owned by the disabled Shareholder, at the price and on the terms provided in this Agreement. To exercise the option, a Shareholder must give to the disabled Shareholder written notice of election to purchase a specified number of the Shares.

(c) If the notices of election from the other Shareholders specify in the aggregate more Shares than are available for purchase by the other Shareholders, each Shareholder will have priority, up to the number of Shares specified in the notice of election, to purchase the Shareholder's Proportionate Share of the Shares. Proportionate Share means that proportion determined by dividing the number of the Company's Shares that the electing Shareholder holds by the total number of the Company's Shares held by all Shareholders electing to purchase as of the date the offer was made.

(d) The Shares not purchased on a priority basis will be allocated to those Shareholders electing to purchase more than the number of Shares to which they have a priority right, up to the number of Shares specified in their respective notices of election to purchase, in the proportion that the number of Shares held by each of them bears to the number of Shares held by all of them as of the date the offer was made.

(e) If this option is not exercised as to all the Shares owned by the disabled Shareholder, the disabled Shareholder will hold the remaining Shares [subject to] [free and clear of] the provisions of this Agreement.

(f) For purposes of this Agreement a Shareholder will be deemed to be "disabled" if one of the following conditions is satisfied:

(i) Under the terms of a bona fide disability income insurance policy that insures the Shareholder, the insurance company that underwrites the insurance policy determines that the Shareholder is totally disabled for purposes of the insurance policy.

(ii) A physician licensed to practice medicine in the state _____ of or _____, who has been selected by the Shareholder (or agent) and the board of directors of the Company, certifies that the Shareholder is partially or totally disabled so that the Shareholder will be unable to be employed gainfully on a full-time basis by the Company for a _____ -month period or more in the position that the Shareholder occupied before the disability. If the board of directors of the Company and the Shareholder (or agent) do not agree on the choice of a physician, these parties must each choose a physician who must in turn select a third physician. The third physician will have the authority to determine the Shareholder's disability. If the Shareholder refuses to choose a physician, the determination made by the physician selected by the Company will be conclusive. The Company must pay for the costs and expenses of the physician. As used in this Section 6.3(b), "agent" means, if applicable, the conservator of the Shareholder's estate or a person duly granted power-of-attorney to act on behalf of the Shareholder.

(iii) The Shareholder and the board of directors of the Company agree in writing that the Shareholder is partially or totally disabled so that the Shareholder will be unable to be employed gainfully on a full-time basis by the Company for a _____ -month period in the position that the Shareholder occupied before the disability.

7. TERMINATION OF EMPLOYMENT

7.1 Option to Purchase on Termination of Employment. If any Shareholder who is an employee of the Company [and who has not attained age _____ ] voluntarily terminates employment with the Company [or is discharged for cause], the Company and the remaining Shareholders will have the option to purchase all or any part of the Shares owned by the Shareholder and all Shares transferred to third parties pursuant to Section 2.2. The option will be exercisable first by the Company and thereafter by the remaining Shareholders, and the price, terms of purchase, and method of exercise of the option will be the same as are provided in Section 6.2. If this option is not exercised as to all of the Shares, the Shareholder and any third party to whom Shares were transferred under Section 2.2 will hold the Shares [subject to] [free and clear of] the provisions of this Agreement].

8. VALUATION

8.1 Agreed Price With Arbitration. The purchase price to be paid for each of the Shares subject to this Agreement will be equal to the agreed value of the Company divided by the total number of Shares outstanding as of the date the price is to be determined.

(a) The initial agreed value of the Company is $ _____ , and, at regular intervals hereafter, but no more often than quarterly and no less often than annually, the Shareholders to this Agreement will review the Company's financial condition. The Shareholders will at that time determine, by a vote of two-thirds of [the outstanding shares held by the Shareholders] [Shareholders (each Shareholder having one vote)], the Company's fair market value, which, if so voted, will be the Company's value until a different value is so determined or otherwise established under the provisions of this Agreement.

(b) If the parties are able to determine the value by that vote, they will evidence it by placing their written and executed agreement in the minute book of the Company. However, if the Shareholders have been unable to establish a value by that method within _____ years after the date on which the Shareholders last agreed on the value of the Company, the purchase price for each of the offering Shareholder's Shares will be determined by appraisal, in accordance with Section 8.2.

8.2 Appraisal. If required under Section 8.1(b), promptly after the occurrence of the event requiring the determination of the purchase price under this Agreement, the Company will appoint an appraiser to determine the fair market value of the Shares.

(a) If the Company and the offering Shareholder fail to agree on the identity of the appraiser, they will each appoint an appraiser to determine the fair market value of the Shares. If the appointed appraisers are not able to agree on the fair market value of the Shares, the appraisers will appoint a third appraiser, and the decision of a majority of the three appraisers will be binding on all interested parties.

(b) If a party fails to designate an appraiser within fifteen (15) days after receiving written notice from the other designating an appraiser and demanding appointment of the second appraiser, the first appraiser appointed may determine the fair market value of the Shares.

(c) The appraisal must be completed and communicated to the relevant parties not later than sixty (60) days after appointment of the first appraiser. [The appraisal fees must be paid by the Company.]

(d) Among other things, in making the appraisal, the appraiser must value real estate at fair market value; machinery and equipment at replacement cost or fair market value, whichever is lower; goods in process at cost, using the cost accounting procedures customarily employed by the Company in preparing its financial statements; receivables at their face amount, minus an allowance for uncollectible items that is reasonable in view of the past experience of the Company and a recent review of their collectibility; all liabilities at their face value; [bank orders]; good will based on probable future work; and must establish a reserve for contingent liabilities, if appropriate. The appraiser must also consider the value of other comparable companies, if known.

9. PAYMENT TERMS

9.1 Terms. Unless otherwise agreed, the purchase price for Shares purchased under this Agreement must be paid as follows:

(a) If the purchase price is $ _____ or less, the purchase price must be paid in full within ninety (90) days after the offering Shareholder receives notice of the mandatory or optional purchase of the offering Shareholder's Shares.

(b) Subject to Section 9.2, if the purchase price is greater than $ _____, a down payment of _____ percent (_____) of the purchase price must be paid within ninety (90) days after the offering Shareholder receives notice of the mandatory or optional purchase of the offering Shareholder's Shares.

(c) Subject to Section 9.2, the balance of the purchase price must be paid in _____ equal monthly installments, including interest at the prime rate announced from time to time in the Wall Street Journal, plus two percent. The installment payments must commence on the first day of the month next following the date on which the Company or the remaining Shareholders or both purchase the Shares, and like payments must be made on the first day of each month thereafter until the purchase price is paid in full. All or any part of the unpaid balance of the purchase price may be prepaid without penalty at any time. The purchase price for the Shares must be paid to the offering Shareholder or the offering Shareholder's estate, as the case may be.

9.2 Insurance. The purchase price for the Shares must be paid as follows if the Company has insurance under Section 5.2 on the life of a deceased Shareholder whose Shares are purchased in accordance with Section 5.1.

(a) If the purchase price for the Shares is less than or equal to the amount of the proceeds received by the Company or the remaining Shareholders or both from the insurance on the life of the deceased Shareholder, the purchase price for the Shares must be paid in cash on the date of the purchase of the Shares.

(b) If the purchase price for the Shares of the deceased Shareholder exceeds the amount of the insurance proceeds, an amount equal to the proceeds of the insurance on the life of the deceased Shareholder must be paid in cash on the date of the purchase of the Shares, and the balance of the purchase price must be paid in accordance with Section 9.1(b).

(c) The Company must file the necessary proofs of death and collect the proceeds of any policies of insurance described in Section 5.2 outstanding on the life of the deceased Shareholder. The decedent's personal representative must apply for and obtain any necessary court approval or confirmation of the sale of the decedent's shares under this Agreement.

9.3 Documentation

(a) The deferred portion of the purchase price for any Shares purchased under this Agreement must be evidenced by a promissory note executed by the Company or all the purchasing Shareholders or both (as applicable) substantially in the form of attached Exhibit D. Except to the extent otherwise provided under Section 5.1(c) (but in that event only with respect to purchases under Section 5.1), the obligations of the Company or the Shareholders or both (as applicable) under the note will be [joint and several] [several and not joint prorated based on the number of Shares that each purchaser is purchasing]. If the obligation is several and not joint, each purchaser must sign a separate promissory note substantially in the form of attached Exhibit D. If the obligation is joint and several, all purchasers must sign the same promissory note, substantially in the form of attached Exhibit D but appropriately modified to reflect the joint and several obligations of each.

(b) The note or notes must be secured by a pledge of all the Shares being purchased in the transaction to which the note or notes relate [and of all other shares owned by the purchasing Shareholders], as set forth in the promissory note attached in Exhibit D and must contain such other provisions as set forth therein.

9.4 Payment of Consideration; Procedures for Transfer. Upon the exercise of any option under this Agreement and in all other events, consideration for the Shares must be delivered as soon as practicable to the person entitled to it. The Company must have the certificates representing the purchased Shares properly endorsed and, on compliance with Section 11, must issue a new certificate in the name of each purchasing Shareholder.

## 10. ADMINISTRATIVE REQUIREMENTS

The Company agrees to apply for and use its best efforts to obtain all governmental and administrative approvals required in connection with the purchase and sale of Shares under this Agreement. The Shareholders agree to cooperate in obtaining the approvals and to execute any and all documents that may be required to be executed by them in connection with the approvals. The Company must pay all costs and filing fees in connection with obtaining the approvals.

## 11. SHARE CERTIFICATES

On execution of this Agreement, the Company must place the legend set forth in Section 12 on the certificates representing the Shareholder's Shares. None of the Shares may be transferred, encumbered, or in any way alienated except under the terms of this Agreement. Each Shareholder will have the right to vote that Shareholder's Shares and receive the dividends paid on them until the Shares are sold or transferred as provided in this Agreement.

## 12. LEGENDS ON SHARE CERTIFICATES

Each share certificate, when issued, must have conspicuously endorsed on its face the following legend:

> SALE, TRANSFER, PLEDGE, OR ANY OTHER DISPOSITION OF THE SHARES REPRESENTED BY THIS CERTIFICATE IS SUBJECT TO AND RESTRICTED BY THE TERMS OF A SHAREHOLDERS AGREEMENT DATED _____, _____, BETWEEN THE COMPANY AND ITS SHAREHOLDERS. A COPY OF THE SHAREHOLDERS AGREEMENT IS AVAILABLE AT THE OFFICE OF THE COMPANY. THE SHARES REPRESENTED BY THIS CERTIFICATE MAY BE SOLD, TRANSFERRED, PLEDGED, OR OTHERWISE DISPOSED OF ONLY UPON COMPLIANCE WITH THE SHAREHOLDERS AGREEMENT.

On the request of a Shareholder, the secretary of the Company must show a copy of this Agreement to any person making inquiry about it.

13. TERMINATION OF AGREEMENT. This Agreement will terminate upon the occurrence of any of the following:

(a) As to each Shareholder only, the transfer of all Shares held by that

Shareholder pursuant to the provisions of this Agreement;

(b) The written agreement of all parties who are then bound by the terms of this Agreement;

c) The dissolution [,or] bankruptcy, [or insolvency] of the Company; or

(d) At that time, if ever, that only one Shareholder or other transferee who is subject to the terms of this Agreement remains.

### 14. SHAREHOLDER WILLS

Each Shareholder agrees to include in his or her will a direction and authorization to the Shareholder's personal representative to comply with the provisions of this Agreement and to sell the Shareholder's Shares in accordance with this Agreement. However, the failure of any Shareholder to do so will not affect the validity or enforceability of this Agreement.

### 15. EQUITABLE RELIEF IN THE EVENT OF BREACH

The Shares of the Company subject to this Agreement are unique and cannot be readily purchased or sold because of the lack of a market. For these reasons, among others, the parties will be irreparably damaged if this Agreement is breached. Any party aggrieved by a breach of the provisions of this Agreement may bring an action at law or a suit in equity to obtain redress, including specific performance, injunctive relief, or any other available equitable remedy. Time and strict performance are of the essence of this Agreement. These remedies are cumulative and not exclusive and are in addition to any other remedy that the parties may have.

### 16. SUBCHAPTER S ELECTION AND STATUS

If all the Shareholders elect (or have elected) for the Company to be taxed as an "S Corporation" pursuant to Code Section 1362, then the Shareholders and the Company and will maintain that status until the Shares representing percent (_____ %) [NOTE TO DRAFTER: more than fifty percent (50%)] of the outstanding shares of Company are voted to terminate this election. Any provision of this Agreement is void that would prevent the Company from being able to make an effective election to be classified as an S Corporation once the decision has been made to elect S corporation status or that, once the Company becomes an S Corporation, would cause that status to be involuntarily terminated.

### 17. LEGAL LIMITATIONS

The obligation of the Company to purchase Shares under this Agreement is in all respects limited and by the ability of the Company to draw upon a legal source of funds from which to pay the purchase price. If the Company is legally unable to purchase and pay for any Shares that it is required to purchase under this Agreement, the Shareholders must promptly vote their respective Shares to take whatever steps may be appropriate or necessary to enable the Company to lawfully purchase and pay for all of the Shares.

### 18. MISCELLANEOUS PROVISIONS

18.1 Deletion and Addition of Parties. The secretary of the Company may add as a party to this Agreement any transferee of Shares or delete as a party any Shareholder who transfers all of the Shareholder's Shares. The secretary may take this action without the need for any further action by the board of directors of the Company or the consent of any party to this Agreement or of their respective heirs, personal representatives, successors, or assigns and regardless of whether or not a counterpart of this Agreement has been executed by that party. The Secretary may do so by amending the Shareholder list attached as Exhibit A.

18.2 Extension of Time for Closing. If in the opinion of legal counsel, additional time is needed in order to comply with applicable securities laws, the time of the closing of any sale or other transfer hereunder may be extended for a reasonable period not to exceed sixty (60) days.

18.3 Authorization. The Company is authorized to enter into this Agreement by virtue of a resolution duly adopted at a meeting of its Board of Directors dated effective _____ .

18.4 Employment Not Guaranteed. Nothing contained in this Agreement nor any action taken hereunder is intended to be construed as a contract of employment or to give a Shareholder any right to be retained in the employ of the Company in any capacity, or to be a director or officer of the Company, or to be retained by the Company as any type of independent contractor.

18.5 Notices. Any notice or other communication required or permitted to be given under this Agreement must be in writing and must be mailed by certified mail, return receipt requested, postage prepaid, addressed to the appropriate party or parties at the address(es) set forth in attached Exhibit A. Any notice or other communication will be deemed to be given at the expiration of the _____ day after the date of deposit in the United States Mail. The addresses to which notices or other communications are to be mailed may be changed from time to time by giving written notice to the other parties as provided in this Section.

18.6 Attorney Fees. If any suit or arbitration is filed by any party to enforce this Agreement or proceedings are commenced in bankruptcy or otherwise with respect to the subject matter of this Agreement, the prevailing party will be entitled to recover reasonable attorney fees incurred in preparation or in prosecution or defense of that suit or arbitration as fixed by the court or arbitrator, and if any appeal is taken from the decision of the court or arbitrator, reasonable attorney fees as fixed by the appellate court.

18.7 Amendments. This Agreement may be amended only by an instrument in writing executed [by all the parties] [by the Company and by Shareholders holding at least _____ (_____ %) of the Shares as of the date of the Amendment, except that, if another provision of this Agreement specifically requires the consent or vote of a lesser or greater percentage with respect to a particular action, that provision will control as to that action].

18.8 Headings. The headings used in this Agreement are solely for convenience of reference, are not part of this Agreement, and are not to be considered in construing or interpreting this Agreement.

18.9 Entire Agreement. This Agreement (including the exhibits) sets forth the entire understanding of the parties with respect to the subject matter of this Agreement and supersedes any and all prior understandings and agreements, whether written or oral, between the parties with respect to that subject matter.

18.10 Counterparts. This Agreement may be executed by the parties in separate counterparts, each of which when executed and delivered will be an original, but all of which together will constitute one and the same instrument. Signature pages may be detached from the counterparts and attached to a single copy of this Agreement to form an original document.

18.11 Severability. If any provision of this Agreement is held to be invalid or unenforceable in any respect for any reason, the validity and enforceability of that provision in any other respect and of the remaining provisions of this Agreement will not be in any way impaired.

18.12 Waiver. A provision of this Agreement may be waived only by a written instrument executed by the party waiving compliance. No waiver of any provision of this Agreement will constitute a waiver of any other provision, whether or not similar, nor will any waiver constitute a continuing waiver. Failure to enforce any provision of this Agreement will not operate as a waiver of that provision or any other provision.

18.13 Further Assurances. From time to time, each of the parties agrees to execute, acknowledge, and deliver any instruments or documents necessary to carry out the purposes of this Agreement.

18.14 Time Is of the Essence. Time is of the essence for each and every provision of this Agreement.

18.15 No Third–Party Beneficiaries. Except as may be expressly stated herein, nothing in this Agreement is intended to confer on any person, other than the parties to this Agreement, any right or remedy of any nature whatsoever.

18.16 Expenses. Each party agrees to bear its own expenses in connection with this Agreement and the transactions contemplated by this Agreement.

18.17 Exhibits. The exhibits referenced in this Agreement are a part of this Agreement as if fully set forth in this Agreement.

18.18 Governing Law. This Agreement will be governed by and construed in accordance with the laws of the state of _____.

18.19 Venue. This Agreement has been made entirely within the state of . If any suit or action is filed by any party to enforce this Agreement or otherwise with respect to the subject matter of this Agreement, venue will be in the federal or state courts in _____, _____.

18.20 Arbitration

(a) Any claim between the parties, under this Agreement or otherwise, must be determined by arbitration in _____, _____ commenced in accordance with applicable law. All statutes of limitations that would otherwise be applicable will apply to the arbitration proceeding. There will be one arbitrator agreed upon by the parties within ten (10) days before the arbitration or, if not, selected by the administrator of the American Arbitration Association ("AAA") office in _____, or failing that, the nearest AAA office. The arbitrator must be an attorney with at least fifteen (15) years' experience in commercial law and must reside in the _____ area. Whether a claim is covered by this agreement will be determined by the arbitrator. At the request of either party made not later than seventy-five (75) days after the arbitration demand, the parties agree to attempt to resolve the dispute by nonbinding mediation or evaluation or both (but without delaying the arbitration hearing date).

(b) The arbitration must be conducted in accordance with the AAA Commercial Arbitration Rules in effect on the date hereof, as modified by this Agreement. There will be no substantive motions or discovery except that the arbitrator may authorize such discovery as may be necessary to ensure a fair hearing, and discovery may not extend the time limits set forth in this Section. The arbitrator will not be bound by the rules of evidence or civil procedure.

(c) The arbitrator must hold a private hearing within one hundred twenty (120) days after the arbitration demand, conclude the hearing within three (3) days, and render a written decision within fourteen (14) calendar days after the hearing. These time limits are not jurisdictional. In making the decision and award, the arbitrator must apply applicable substantive law and must make a brief statement of the claims determined and the award made on each claim.

(d) Absent fraud, collusion, or willful misconduct by the arbitrator, the award will be final, and judgment may be entered in any court having jurisdiction thereof. The arbitrator may award injunctive relief or any other remedy available from a judge, including the joinder of parties or consolidation of this arbitration with any other involving common issues of law or fact or which may promote judicial economy, and may award attorney fees and costs to the prevailing party but will not have the power to award punitive or exemplary damages.

18.21   Legal Representation. Each of the undersigned recognizes and acknowledges that the law firm of _____ ("Counsel") has represented _____ with respect to this Agreement and no other party and that Counsel has advised each of the undersigned to obtain independent legal counsel.

|  | Shareholders | Spouses |
|---|---|---|
| Initials: | _____ |  |
|  | _____ |  |
|  | _____ |  |
| Company: | _____ |  |
|  | President |  |

DATED this ___ day of _____, _____.

COMPANY: _____

By: _____

Its: _____


SHAREHOLDERS:

_____

_____

SPOUSES:

    1. I acknowledge that I have read the foregoing Agreement and that I know its contents.

    2. I am aware that by its provisions my spouse agrees to sell all of my spouse's Shares of the Company (including, if applicable, my community interest in them) on the occurrence of certain events.

    3. I hereby consent to the sale, approve the provisions of the Agreement, and agree that those Shares and my interest in them are subject to the provisions of the Agreement and that I will take no action at any time to hinder operation of the Agreement on those Shares or any interest in them.

    4. In the event of a dissolution, divorce, annulment, or other termination of marriage of my spouse's and my marriage other than by reason of death, I hereby agree to release or transfer (or both) whatever interest I may have in the Company (including, but not limited to, any interest as a Shareholder or creditor, or interest in the Stock or debt of Company) to my spouse on the termination of our marriage.

    5. As part of any property settlement of our marital assets, my spouse must compensate me for my interest. In the event the parties cannot agree as to the value of my interest or upon terms of payment, the value of any Shares in which I have an interest will be determined and will be paid to me in accordance with the terms and conditions of the Agreement.

    6. If my interest in Company is in the nature of debt, the value of that debt will be deemed to be its outstanding principal balance plus any accrued and unpaid interest thereon and compensation therefore will be provided as agreed by the parties.

    7. I acknowledge that I have been advised to consult with independent legal counsel regarding this Agreement and this provision and, further, expressly acknowledge the provisions of Section [18.21] regarding legal counsel and conflicts of interest.

Name (Printed):_____

Signature: _____

Name (Printed): _____

Signature: _____

## EXHIBIT A

### LIST OF SHAREHOLDERS SUBJECT TO SHAREHOLDERS AGREEMENT

Dated _____

[Company name and address]

| Shareholder Name | Address | Number of Shares Held |
|---|---|---|
|  |  |  |
|  |  |  |
|  |  |  |
|  |  |  |
|  |  |  |

## EXHIBIT B

### LIFE INSURANCE SCHEDULE

| Name of Insured | Insurance Company | Policy Number | Type pf Policy | Initial Cash Benefit | Death Benefit |
|---|---|---|---|---|---|
|  |  |  |  |  |  |
|  |  |  |  |  |  |
|  |  |  |  |  |  |

## EXHIBIT C

### PROMISSORY NOTE

$_____

1. For good and valuable consideration, the undersigned promises to pay to the order of _____ ("Holder") the sum of _____ ($ _____), together with interest thereon, in monthly installments of not less than $ _____. The first installment is due on _____, _____, and a like installment is due on the same date of each successive month thereafter until _____, at which time the entire unpaid balance of this Note, any accrued but unpaid interest, and any other amounts payable under this Note, must be paid in full. The unpaid balance of this Note will bear interest at the rate of _____ percent (_____ %) per annum.

2. The undersigned may prepay a portion or all of the balance at any time without penalty.

3. With respect to any payment not made within ten (10) days after it is due and without waiving any other remedy the Holder may have under this Note or otherwise, the Holder may charge the undersigned a late payment charge of five percent (5%) of the unpaid amount.

4. If any payment required by this Note is not paid within fifteen (15) days

after receipt by the undersigned of notice of nonpayment from the Holder ("Event of Default"), at Holder's option, the unpaid balance will bear interest at a default rate of fifteen percent (15%) per annum from the date the payment was due until paid in full.

5. As security for the obligations of the undersigned evidenced by this Note, the undersigned hereby grants to Holder a security interest in _____ shares of the common stock of _____, (the "Shares") issued under certificate number _____ (the "Certificate"). The undersigned has delivered to the Holder the Certificate, together with a stock power endorsed in blank, to hold subject to the terms of this Agreement. Holder agrees to take reasonable care in the custody and the preservation of the Certificate. On payment in full of the principal and interest on the Note, Holder must deliver the Certificate to the undersigned, together with the stock power endorsed by the undersigned in blank.

6. The undersigned irrevocably appoints Holder as attorney-in-fact and grants Holder a proxy to do (but Holder shall not be obligated and shall incur no liability to the undersigned or any third party for failure to do so), after and during the continuance of an Event of Default, any act that the undersigned is obligated by this Note to do and to exercise such rights and powers as undersigned might exercise with respect to the Shares. With respect to voting the Shares, this Section 6 constitutes an irrevocable appointment of a proxy, coupled with an interest, which shall continue until the Note is paid in full.

7. Upon the occurrence of an Event of Default under this Note, the Holder may, in the Holder's sole discretion and with or without further notice to the undersigned and in addition to all rights and remedies at law or in equity or otherwise (a) declare the entire balance of the Note immediately due and payable, (b) register in Holder's name any or all of the Shares, (c) sell or otherwise dispose of the Shares, or (d) exercise Holder's proxy rights with respect to all or a portion of the Shares. In such event, the undersigned agrees to deliver promptly to Holder further evidence of the grant of such proxy in any form requested by Holder.

8. The undersigned hereby waives demand, notice of default, and notice of sale, and consents to public or private sale of the Shares upon the occurrence of an Event of Default, and the Holder will have the right to purchase at the sale.

9. If any action, suit, or other proceeding is instituted concerning or arising out of this Note, the prevailing party will be entitled to recover all costs and attorney fees reasonably incurred by such party in such action, suit, or other proceeding (including all bankruptcy courts), including any and all appeals or petitions therefrom.

_____
Signature

## D. FORM: EXECUTIVE EMPLOYMENT AGREEMENT

### [Employer]

### EXECUTIVE EMPLOYMENT AGREEMENT

### [Employee Name]

This Executive Employment Agreement (the "Agreement") is dated and made effective the _____ day of _____, 200 ___, the "Effective Date") by and between _____, a Washington _____ ("Employer") and ("Employee"). For purposes of Sections 12 through 17 hereof, the term "Employer" shall also be deemed to refer to subsidiaries and affiliates of Employer.

1. Employment. Employer employs Employee and Employee accepts employment on the terms and conditions in this agreement.

2. Duties. Employee is employed in the capacity of [inset title]. In this capacity Employee shall have responsibility for _____. Employee shall report directly to, and take direction from, [_____] (the "Manager") and to no other Employer employee. Subject to the provisions of this Agreement, Employee's precise duties may be changed, extended or curtailed, from time to time, at the Manager's direction, and Employee shall assume and perform the further reasonable responsibilities and duties that the Manager may assign from time to time.

3. Intensity of Effort; Other Business. Employee shall devote Employee's entire working time, attention and efforts to Employer's business and affairs, shall faithfully and diligently serve Employer's interests and shall not engage in any business or employment activity that is not on Employer's behalf (whether or not pursued for gain or profit) except for (a) activities approved in writing in advance by the Manager and (b) passive investments that do not involve Employee providing any advice or services to the businesses in which the investments are made.

4. Term. The term of this agreement starts on the Effective Date and expires on [insert date] (the "Initial Term"). This agreement shall automatically be renewed for successive one-year terms (each referred to as an "Extended Term") unless either party gives written notice of nonrenewal at least 90 days before the expiration of the term. Unless stated otherwise, the word "year" as used in this agreement refers to incremental periods of 365 days each (366 days in the case of a leap year), not calendar years. This agreement may terminate before the expiration of any term as provided below.

5. Compensation. Employee's compensation shall be as follows:

(a) Employee's salary initially shall be $[_____]per month ($[_____] per year on an annualized basis), which shall be computed and paid in equal installments consistent with Employer's normal payroll procedures. At the end of each calendar year, Employee's salary shall be reviewed by the Manager and adjusted as determined by the Manager in its sole discretion, provided that, absent cause or Employee's consent, it may not be adjusted downward and it

'ncreased annually by a percentage at least equal to the annual
 ~~ge~~ increase in the Consumer Price Index–All Urban Consumers (CPI–
~~U~~), U.S. Cities Average, All Items.

(b) [Employee may receive annual incentive compensation based on the following methodology: _____. This is simply a placemarker—we need to discuss how you want to structure incentive comp and probably put in place a separate bonus plan document.]

6. Benefit Plans. Employee shall be eligible for all benefit plans (including retirement or pension plans) that are provided generally to Employer's executive employees. At a minimum, during the term of this agreement Employer shall provide the following benefits to Employee:

(a) Term life insurance insuring Employee's life in an amount at least equal to times Employee's annualized salary, provided that Employer shall not be required to pay premiums in excess of $[_____]per year. Employee shall be the owner of the policy and shall designate the beneficiary of the policy. Employee shall be entitled to continue the policy, at Employee's own expense and subject to the terms and conditions of the policy, after Employee's employment by Employer ends. Employee shall reasonably cooperate with Employer in obtaining, at Employer's expense, any other life insurance policy insuring the life of Employee and naming Employer as beneficiary.

(b) Long-term disability insurance providing for a benefit of at least 60% of Employee's salary and an elimination period of no more than 180 days, provided that Employer shall not be required to pay premiums in excess of $[_____] per year.

(c) Medical insurance providing coverage for Employee and Employee's dependents.

7. Vacation and Sick Leave. Employee shall be entitled to [four] weeks of paid vacation and 10 days of paid sick leave per calendar year (prorated if this agreement begins and/or ends in the middle of a calendar year). Up to two weeks of vacation not used in any calendar year may be carried over into the next calendar year; otherwise unused vacation is forfeited at the end of the calendar year. Upon termination of employment for any reason Employee shall be paid for any available but unused vacation. Sick leave may be accumulated up to a maximum of 60 days. Unused sick leave is not paid upon termination of employment or expiration of this agreement.

8. Disability. If Employee is unable to perform the essential functions of the job because of Employee's own mental or physical illness or disability that continues for a continuous period of three weeks or more, the following shall apply:

(a) For the first 90 days of disability, Employee shall be provided paid disability leave, with full compensation and benefits.

(b) For the second 90 days of disability, Employee shall be on unpaid leave but with paid benefits continued to the extent allowed by the applicable benefit plan(s).

(c) After 180 days of continuous disability, Employer may terminate this agreement, provided that Employer shall grant additional unpaid leave to the extent required by law. During any additional unpaid leave, benefits will not be provided except as may be required by the applicable benefit plan(s) or COBRA.

(d) The foregoing notwithstanding, paid disability leave is limited to 90 days in any 24–month period. If this allowance has been exhausted, unpaid leave, with paid benefits continued to the extent allowed by the applicable benefit plan(s), shall be substituted for paid leave.

(e) Any available sick leave or disability benefits may be used to continue pay during any period of leave that otherwise would be unpaid.

9. Business Expenses. Employee is authorized to incur reasonable travel expenses to carry out Employer's business. Employer shall reimburse Employee for those expenses. Employee shall provide to Employer the itemized expense account information that Employer reasonably requests.

10. Termination. Employee's employment may be terminated before the expiration of this agreement as follows, in which event Employee's compensation and benefits shall terminate except as otherwise provided below:

(a) By Employer Without Cause. Employer may terminate Employee's employment at any time, with or without cause or advance notice. If Employer terminates Employee's employment when neither cause nor permanent disability exists, however, and provided that Employee releases Employer and its agents from any and all claims in a signed, written release satisfactory in form and substance to Employer, Employer shall pay to Employee termination payments equal to [_____] months of Employee's salary. If Employer gives Executive at least a full month's advance notice of termination, however, the termination payments shall be reduced by one month's salary for each full month of advance notice given; provided that this reduction shall not exceed three months' salary. These termination payments shall be paid out at Employee's normal salary rate on regular payroll days subject to normal payroll deductions. Employee shall not be required to mitigate the amount of these termination payments by seeking other employment or otherwise, and no income to Employee of any kind shall reduce the termination payments.

(b) By Employer for Cause. Employer may terminate Employee's employment for cause upon delivery of written notice to Employee indicating that such termination is for cause and the effective date of such termination.

For purposes of this agreement "cause" means and is limited to dishonesty, fraud, commission of a felony or of a crime involving moral turpitude, destruction or theft of Employer property, physical attack to a fellow employee, intoxication at work, use of narcotics or alcohol to an extent that materially impairs Employee's performance of his or her duties, willful malfeasance or gross negligence in the performance of Employee's duties, violation of law in the course of employment that has a material adverse impact on Employer or its employees, Employee's failure or refusal to perform Employee's duties, Employee's failure or refusal to follow reasonable instructions or directions, misconduct materially injurious to Employer, neglect of duty, poor job performance, or any material breach of Employee's duties or obligations to Employer that results in material harm to Employer, or a material breach of this Agreement or any other agreement between Employee and Employer.

For purposes of this agreement, "neglect of duty" means and is limited to the following circumstances: (i) Employee has, in one or more material respects, failed or refused to perform Employee's job duties in a reasonable and appropriate manner (including failure to follow reasonable directives), (ii) a representative of the Manager has counseled Employee in writing about the neglect of duty and given Employee a reasonable opportunity to improve (this written counseling and opportunity to improve shall satisfy the requirement of 30 days' written notice described above), and (iii) Employee's neglect of duty either has continued at a material level after a reasonable opportunity to improve or has reoccurred at a material level within one year after Employee was last counseled.

For purposes of this agreement, "poor job performance" means and is limited to the following circumstances: (i) Employee has, in one or more material respects, failed to perform Employee's job duties in a reasonable and appropriate manner, (ii) a representative of the Manager has counseled Employee in writing about the performance problems and given Employee a reasonable opportunity to improve (this written counseling and opportunity to improve shall satisfy the requirement of 30 days' written notice described above), and (iii) Employee's performance problems either have continued at a material level after a reasonable opportunity to improve or the same or similar performance problems have reoccurred at a material level within one year after Employee was last counseled.

(c) By Employee Without Good Reason. Employee may terminate Employee's employment at any time, with or without good reason, by giving [_____] days' advance written notice of termination.

(d) By Employee for Good Reason. Employee may terminate Employee's employment for good reason, in which event Employee shall be entitled to the same rights under this agreement as if Employer had terminated Employee's employment without cause. If Employee wishes to terminate employment for good reason Employee shall first give Employer 30 days' written notice of the circumstances constituting good reason and an opportunity to cure, unless the circumstances are not subject to being cured. Following the notice and opportunity to cure (if cure is not made), or immediately if notice and opportunity to cure are not required, Employee may terminate employment for good reason by giving written notice of termination. The notice may take effect immediately or at such later date as Employee may designate, provided that Employer may accelerate the termination date by giving five business days' written notice of the acceleration.

For purposes of this agreement, "good reason" means and is limited to the occurrence without cause and without Employee's consent of a material reduction in the character of Employee's duties, level of work responsibility or working conditions, a reduction in Employee's salary below the level initially established at the commencement of this agreement, Employer's failure to provide compensation or benefits owed to Employee, Employer requiring Employee to be based anywhere other than the greater Seattle/Bellevue area, except for reasonable travel on Employer's business, or any material breach by Employer of its duties or obligations to Employee that results in material harm to Employee.

(e) Death. Employee's employment shall terminate automatically upon Employee's death.

(f) Permanent Disability. Employer may terminate Employee's employment immediately if Employee becomes permanently disabled. For purposes of this agreement Employee will be considered "permanently disabled" if, for a continuous period of 180 days or more, Employee has been unable to perform the essential functions of the job (even with reasonable accommodation) because of one or more mental or physical illnesses and/or disabilities, provided that Employer shall grant additional unpaid leave to the extent required by law.

11. Additional Effects of Termination. Upon termination of Employee for any reason, Employee shall immediately resign all board of director seats, advisory board or observer seats held by Employee on account of investments by Employer or any of its Affiliates in the company to which such seat or board relates.

12. Indemnification. Employer shall defend and indemnify Employee from and against any and all claims that may be asserted against Employee by third parties (including derivative claims asserted by third parties on behalf of Employer) that are connected with Employee's employment by Employer, to the extent permitted by applicable law. The foregoing notwithstanding, Employer shall not be required to defend or indemnify Employee (a) in criminal proceedings, (b) in civil proceedings where Employee is the plaintiff or (c) to the extent it is finally adjudicated that Employee did not act in good faith and in the reasonable belief that Employee's actions were appropriate in the discharge of Employee's duties for Employer. Employer may fulfill its duty of defense by providing competent legal counsel of Employer's choosing. The foregoing rights are in addition to any other rights to which Employee may be entitled under any other agreement, policy, bylaw, insurance policy, ordinance, statute or other provision.

13. Confidentiality. Employee agrees that information not generally known to the public to which Employee has been or will be exposed as a result of Employee's employment by Employer is confidential information that belongs to Employer. This includes information developed by Employee, alone or with others, or entrusted to Employer by its customers or others. Employer's confidential information includes, without limitation, information relating to Employer's trade secrets, customer lists and contacts list, business modeling methods and related information, strategic investment plans, inventions, know-how, software (including source code and object code), procedures, accounting, marketing, sales, financial status or employees. Employee will hold Employer's confidential information in strict confidence and will not disclose or use it except as authorized by Employer and for Employer's benefit. If anyone tries to compel Employee to disclose any of Employer's confidential information, by subpoena or otherwise, Employee will immediately notify Employer so that Employer may

take any actions it deems necessary to protect its interests. Employee's agreement to protect Employer's confidential information apply both while Employee is employed by Employer and after Employee's employment by Employer ends, regardless of the reason it ends.

14. Limitations on Publicity. Except for actions in the course of employment for the benefit of Employer or as may be authorized by Employer in writing, Employee will not be involved in the preparation of any book, article, story, video or film about Employer, its business or activities, and Employee will not give interviews about those subjects.

15. Possession of Materials. Employee agrees that upon conclusion of employment or request by Employer, Employee shall turn over to Employer all documents, files, electronic media and other materials or work product in Employee's possession or control that were created pursuant to or derived from Employee's services for Employer.

16. Noncompetition. Employee agrees that Employer has many substantial, legitimate business interests that can be protected only by Employee agreeing not to compete with Employer under certain circumstances. These interests include, without limitation, Employer's contacts and relationships with its customers and entities in which Employer or its affiliates invest (each a "Portfolio Company"), Employer's reputation and goodwill in the industry, and Employer's rights in its confidential information. Employee therefore agrees that for 12 months after Employee's employment with Employer ends, regardless of the reason it ends, Employee shall not, directly or indirectly solicit, divert or attempt to divert on behalf of any other business competitive with Employer or any Portfolio Company, any customer, client or investment opportunity, or prospective customer, client or investment opportunity, of Employer or any such Portfolio Company as of the date of my termination or during the six month period preceding the date of Employee's termination.

17. Nonraiding of Employees. Employee recognizes that Employer's workforce and its relationship with its Portfolio Companies is a vital part of its business. Therefore, Employee agrees that for 12 months after Employee's employment with Employer ends, regardless of the reason it ends, Employee will not directly or indirectly solicit any employee to leave his or her employment with Employer or any Portfolio Company. This includes that Employee will not (a) disclose to any third party the names, backgrounds or qualifications of any Employer employees or otherwise identify them as potential candidates for employment; (b) personally or through any other person approach, recruit, interview or otherwise solicit employees of Employer to work for any other employer; or (c) participate in any pre-employment interviews with any person who was employed by Employer or a Portfolio Company while Employee was employed by Employer.

18. Intellectual Property Assignment. Employer owns all Inventions and Works Employee make, conceive, develop, discover, reduce to practice or fix in a tangible medium of expression, alone or with others, either (a) during Employee's employment by Employer (including past employment, and whether

or not during working hours), or (b) within one year after Employee's employment ends if the Invention or Work results from any work Employee performed for Employer or involves the use or assistance of Employer's facilities, materials, personnel or confidential information. Employer also owns all Inventions and Works of Employee that Employee bring to Employer that are used in the course of Employer's business or that are incorporated into any Inventions or Works that belong to Employer.

Employee will promptly disclose to Employer, will hold in trust for Employer's sole benefit, will assign to Employer and hereby do assign to Employer all Inventions and Works described in the prior paragraph, including all copyrights (including renewal rights), patent rights and trade secret rights, vested and contingent. Employee will waive and hereby does waive any moral rights Employee have or may have in the Inventions and Works described in the prior paragraph. Employee agree that all Works Employee produces within the scope of Employee's employment (which shall include all Works Employee produce related to Employer's business, whether or not done during regular working hours) shall be considered "works made for hire" so that Employer will be considered the author of the Works under the federal copyright laws. At Employer's direction and expense Employee will execute all documents and take all actions necessary or convenient for Employer to document, obtain, maintain or assign its rights to these Inventions and Works. Employer shall have full control over all applications for patents or other legal protection of these Inventions and Works.

"Inventions" means discoveries, developments, concepts, ideas, improvements to existing technology, processes, procedures, machines, products, compositions of matter, formulas, algorithms, computer programs and techniques, and all other matters ordinarily intended by the word "invention," whether or not patentable or copyrightable. "Inventions" also includes all records and expressions of those matters. "Works" means original works of authorship, including interim work product, modifications and derivative works, and all similar matters, whether or not copyrightable.

Employee understand that this agreement does not apply to any Invention or Work for which no equipment, supplies, facilities or trade secret information of Employer was used and which was developed entirely on Employee's own time, unless (a) the Invention or Work relates directly to Employer's business or actual or demonstrably anticipated research or development, or (b) the Invention or Work results from any work Employee performed for Employer.

19. Dispute Resolution. All disputes between Employee and Employer that otherwise would be resolved in court shall be resolved instead by the following alternate dispute resolution process (the "Process").

(a) Disputes Covered. This Process applies to all disputes between Employee and Employer, including those arising out of or related to this agreement or Employee's employment relationship with Employer. Disputes subject to this Process include but are not limited to pay disputes, contract disputes, disputes regarding equity or debt investments or interests held in

Employer, or its subsidiaries, affiliates or Portfolio Companies, wrongful termination disputes and discrimination, harassment or civil rights disputes. This Process applies to disputes Employee may have with Employer and also applies to disputes Employee may have with any of Employer's employees, agents or Portfolio Companies so long as the employee, agent or Portfolio Company with whom Employee has the dispute is also bound by or consents to this Process. This Process applies regardless of when the dispute arises and will remain in effect after Employee's employment with Employer ends, regardless of the reason it ends. This Process does not apply, however, to workers' compensation or unemployment compensation claims.

(b) Mediation. Before having an arbitration hearing, Employee and Employer agree to attempt to resolve all disputes by mediation using the Employment Mediation Rules of the American Arbitration Association. Mediation is a nonbinding process in which a neutral person helps the parties to try to reach an agreement to resolve their disputes. If the mediation is done after one party has started the arbitration process, the mediation shall not delay the arbitration hearing date. Temporary or interim relief may be sought without mediating first. Any failure to mediate shall not affect the validity of an arbitration award or the obligation to arbitrate.

(c) Arbitration. All disputes that are not resolved by agreement (in mediation or otherwise) shall be determined by binding arbitration. Arbitration is a process in which one or more neutral people decide the case after hearing evidence presented by both sides. The arbitration shall be governed by the Arbitration Procedures attached as Exhibit 1, which are a part of this Process. Employee and Employer agree that the disputes covered by this Process will not be decided in court by a judge or jury.

(d) Injunctive Relief. Either party may request a court to issue such temporary or interim relief (including temporary restraining orders and preliminary injunctions) as may be appropriate, either before or after mediation or arbitration is commenced. The temporary or interim relief shall remain in effect pending the outcome of mediation or arbitration. No such request shall be a waiver of the right to submit any dispute to mediation or arbitration.

(e) Attorneys' fees, Venue and Jurisdiction in Court. In any lawsuit arising out of or related to this agreement or Employee's employment at Employer, the prevailing party shall recover reasonable costs and attorneys' fees, including on appeal. Venue and jurisdiction of any such lawsuit shall exist exclusively in state and federal courts in King County, Washington, unless injunctive relief is sought by Employer and, in Employer's judgment, that relief might not be effective unless obtained in some other venue. These provisions do not give any party a right to proceed in court in violation of the agreement to arbitrate described above.

(f) Employment Status. This Dispute Resolution Process does not guarantee continued employment, require discharge only for cause or require any particular corrective action or discharge procedures.

20. Governing Law. This agreement shall be governed by the internal laws

of the state of Washington without giving effect to provisions thereof related to choice of laws or conflict of laws.

21. Saving Provision. If any part of this agreement is held to be unenforceable, it shall not affect any other part. If any part of this agreement is held to be unenforceable as written, it shall be enforced to the maximum extent allowed by applicable law. The indemnification, confidentiality, limitations on publicity, possession of materials, noncompetition, nonraiding and dispute resolution provisions of this agreement shall survive after Employee's employment by Employer ends, regardless of the reason it ends, and shall be enforceable regardless of any claim Employee may have against Employer.

22. Waiver. No waiver of any provision of this agreement shall be valid unless in writing, signed by the party against whom the waiver is sought to be enforced. The waiver of any breach of this agreement or failure to enforce any provision of this agreement shall not waive any later breach.

23. Assignment; Successors. Employer may assign its rights and delegate its duties under this agreement. Employee may not assign Employee's rights or delegate Employee's duties under this agreement.

24. Binding Effect. This agreement is binding upon the parties and their personal representatives, heirs, successors and permitted assigns.

25. Counterparts. This agreement may be executed in any number of counterparts, each of which shall be an original and all of which, taken together, shall constitute a single agreement.

26. Legal Representation. In connection with this agreement, the law firm of _____ has represented only Employer and has not represented Employee. Employee acknowledges that Employee has been advised to consult with independent legal counsel before signing this agreement and has had the opportunity to do so.

27. Complete Agreement. This agreement together with the attached Exhibit, is the final and complete expression of the parties' agreement relating to Employee's employment. This agreement may be amended only by a writing signed by both parties; it may not be amended orally or by course of dealing. The parties are not entering into this agreement relying on anything not set out in this agreement. This agreement shall control over any inconsistent policies or procedures of Employer, whether in effect now or adopted later, but Employer's policies and procedures that are consistent with this agreement, whether in effect now or adopted later, shall apply to Employee according to their terms.

DATED as of the date first written above.


EMPLOYEE:                          EMPLOYER

By: _____               By: _____

_____                   _____

## EXHIBIT 1

## ARBITRATION PROCEDURES

These arbitration procedures are a part of the Dispute Resolution Process (the "Process") set out in the agreement to which this Exhibit is attached.

**Commencement.** Arbitration shall be commenced by serving a written demand for arbitration on the other party, either personally or by both regular first class mail and certified mail, return receipt requested. The arbitration need not be filed with any arbitration administrator, but a party may file the arbitration with the American Arbitration Association ("AAA") if the party believes that administration by the AAA would be beneficial.

**Arbitrators.** There shall be a single neutral arbitrator, provided that if any party in good faith demands an award greater than $250,000, excluding interest, attorneys' fees, arbitration fees and costs, three neutral arbitrators shall hear the case and render the award while a single arbitrator shall hear and resolve all prehearing matters. The total award by a single arbitrator shall not exceed $250,000, excluding interest, attorneys' fees, arbitration fees and costs. If the parties cannot agree on the identity of the arbitrator(s) within 10 days of the arbitration demand, the arbitrator(s) shall be selected by the administrator of the AAA office nearest the arbitration site, in which case the arbitrator(s) shall be members of the AAA's Large, Complex Case Panel or shall have similar professional credentials. However selected, each arbitrator shall be a lawyer with at least 15 years' experience and shall reside in the metropolitan area in which the arbitration is to be conducted unless otherwise agreed.

**Representation by Counsel.** All parties shall have the right to representation by legal counsel at any stage of the proceedings.

**Location.** The arbitration shall be conducted in Seattle, Washington, unless the Employee is assigned to work in a state other than the State of Washington, in which case the arbitration shall be conducted in a city with a population of at least 100,000 that is closest to the location to which Employee reports to work, or at any other location to which Employee and Employer may agree.

**Rules.** The arbitration shall be conducted in accordance with the AAA Employment Dispute Resolution Rules to the extent not inconsistent with the other terms of this Dispute Resolution Process.

**Prehearing Matters.** There shall be no discovery or dispositive motion practice, except that the arbitrator shall authorize discovery that is appropriate to ensure a fair hearing. Discovery shall not extend the time limits set out below. The arbitrator may enter prehearing orders on any appropriate subject, including mediation, scheduling, discovery, witness disclosure, issues to be heard, preliminary injunctive relief, the joinder of parties (provided the party joined is bound by or consents to this Dispute Resolution Process) or consolidation of the arbitration with any other involving common issues of law or fact or which may promote economy. The arbitrator may impose reasonable sanctions on a party for failure to comply with the arbitrator's orders.

**Hearing.** The arbitrator(s) shall hold a private hearing within 120 days of the initial demand for arbitration and shall conclude the hearing within three days. These time limits are included to expedite the proceeding, but the arbitrator(s) may for good cause allow reasonable extensions or delays, and any extensions or delays shall not affect the validity of the award. The arbitrator(s) shall not be bound by the rules of evidence or of civil procedure, but rather may consider such writings and oral presentations as reasonable business people would use in the conduct of their day-to-day affairs and may require both of us to submit some or all of our evidence through written declarations or using any other manner of presentation that the arbitrator(s) decide is appropriate. Live testimony and cross-examination shall be allowed, but only to the extent necessary to ensure a fair hearing on material issues.

**Decision.** The arbitrator(s)' written decision shall be made within 14 calendar days after the hearing, but a failure to meet this deadline shall not affect the validity of the award. The decision shall contain a brief statement of the claim(s) determined and the award made on each claim. The decision and award need not be unanimous; rather, the decision and award of two arbitrators shall be final. Absent fraud, collusion or willful misconduct by an arbitrator, the award shall be final and binding and judgment may be entered in any court having jurisdiction.

**Law; Remedies.** In making the decision and award, the arbitrator(s) shall apply applicable substantive law. On issues of state law, the substantive law (not including choice of law rules) of the state in which Employee principally reports to work shall control. The arbitrator(s) may award injunctive relief or any other remedy that would have been available in court. If a court, applying applicable substantive law, would be authorized to award punitive or exemplary damages, the arbitrator(s) shall have the same power, but the arbitrator(s) otherwise shall not award punitive or exemplary damages. All statutes of limitations that would apply in court shall apply in the arbitration. Questions about whether a dispute must be arbitrated shall be determined by the arbitrator(s). The arbitrator(s) may award attorneys' fees, arbitration fees and costs to the prevailing party.

**Arbitration Law.** This Dispute Resolution Process is governed by the Federal Arbitration Act, 9 U.S.C. § 1 et seq. (the "FAA"). The provisions of the FAA (and to the extent not preempted by the FAA, the provisions of the law of the state in which Employee principally reports to work that generally apply to commercial arbitration agreements, such as provisions granting stays of court actions pending arbitration) are incorporated into this Dispute Resolution Process to the extent not inconsistent with the other terms of this Process.

## E. FORM: LIFE INSURANCE TRUST

THE _____ AGREEMENT

(Tax ID #_____)

THIS AGREEMENT is made effective _____ between _____ ("Grantor") and _____, her successors and assigns ("Trustee"). The Trust initially created by this Agreement is designated the _____ (the "Trust").

### 1. TRUST PROPERTY

In connection with the execution of this Agreement, Grantor is transferring certain property to the Trust and reserves the right to contribute additional property from time to time. In addition, the Trustee may accept contributions to the Trust made by other parties. With regard to contributions made by individuals other than Grantor, Trustee may, in Trustee's discretion, disregard the notice and withdrawal provisions and procedures set forth in Article 3 below. The Trustee agrees to administer all contributed property pursuant to the terms of this Agreement.

### 2. FAMILY

Grantor's immediate family now consists of Grantor's spouse, _____, and their children, _____ and _____. All references hereinafter to "Grantor's children" and the like shall include the children specifically named in this Article and any other children born to or adopted by Grantor after the date of this Agreement. Likewise, all references in this Agreement to "Grantor's descendants" or the like shall include only Grantor's children and their descendants.

### 3. ADMINISTRATION DURING GRANTOR'S LIFETIME

3.1 In General. The Trust is not expected to generate significant income during Grantor's lifetime. With this in mind, the Trustee shall have the authority to distribute among Grantor's spouse and Grantor's descendants so much of the income and principal of the Trust estate as the Trustee determines to be necessary or advisable to provide for their maintenance, education, support and health according to their accustomed standards of living, giving preference to Grantor's spouse's needs, considering other resources available to them and without being required to apportion benefits equally among them.

3.2 Withdrawal Rights. Each of Grantor's descendants shall have the right to withdraw portions of the Trust's assets on account of contributions made to the Trust, although, with respect to a given contribution, Grantor may confer withdrawal rights on select descendants, in which case the term descendants as used in this Article 3 shall refer only to those so selected. The amount withdrawable by a descendent on account of a given contribution shall be computed by dividing the contribution by the number of Grantor's descendants having withdrawal rights with respect to such contribution; provided, however, that the maximum amount withdrawable by a descendant on account of a given year's contributions shall be the amount allowed under IRC § 2503(b) as an annual exclusion to Grantor, presently $12,000.00. Although a descendant's withdrawal rights shall accumulate to the extent not exercised, the same shall lapse on each December 31 in the amount specified in IRC § 2514(e), presently the greater of $5,000.00 or 5% of the value of the Trust's assets minus the aggregate dollar amount of any rights waived by the descendant during the year; provided, however, that a withdrawal right on account of a given contribution shall not lapse prior to 30 days after notice thereof.

3.3 Withdrawal Procedure. The Trustee shall provide written notification of a given contribution to each descendant upon whom a withdrawal right has been conferred respecting such contribution. Withdrawal may be made only by written notification to the Trustee. A descendant may waive his or her withdrawal right as to a given contribution by written notification to the Trustee. Withdrawal rights may be satisfied by distributions of interests in insurance policies on Grantor's life or by issuance of promissory notes at prime rates with amortizations not to exceed five years, as well as by distributions of other trust assets. The withdrawal and waiver rights of a descendant who is under a legal disability may be exercised by such descendant's natural or legal guardian, other than Grantor. No amounts withdrawn may be used to satisfy Grantor's or such guardian's legal obligation to support the descendant or be made in any fashion that would have the effect of impairing or reducing an estate tax marital deduction otherwise applicable to all or a portion of the trust assets.

4. ADMINISTRATION FOLLOWING GRANTOR'S DEATH

4.1 During Spouse's Lifetime. If Grantor's spouse survives Grantor, then upon Grantor's death the trust assets shall be administered as follows:

(a) Assets Included in Grantor's Estate. Such of the trust assets as are included in Grantor's estate for federal estate tax purposes, if any, shall be administered for the exclusive benefit of Grantor's spouse. During Grantor's spouse's lifetime the Trustee shall pay to or for the benefit of Grantor's spouse all income from the assets at convenient intervals, preferably monthly, but at least annually. The Trustee shall pay to or for the benefit of Grantor's spouse such amounts from principal as are required for Grantor's spouse's maintenance, education, support and health according to Grantor's spouse's accustomed standard of living. Grantor's spouse may compel the Trustee to exchange any non-income-producing property for income-producing property by delivering a written direction to that effect. Any income remaining undistributed at Grantor's spouse's death shall be distributed to Grantor's spouse's estate. It is Grantor's intent that the assets administered under this section qualify for the estate tax marital deduction and that the Personal Representative of Grantor's estate or the Trustee make an election to treat some or all of the trust property as qualified terminal interest property, subject to the discretion of such fiduciaries.

(b) Assets Not Included in Grantor's Estate. Such of the assets of the trust as are not included in Grantor's estate for estate tax purposes, if any, shall be administered for the benefit of Grantor's spouse and Grantor's children in a trust share separate and apart from the share administered under the immediately preceding section. The income and principal of this share shall be paid to or applied for the benefit of Grantor's spouse and Grantor's children in the amounts determined by the Trustee for their maintenance, education, support and health according to their accustomed standards of living, giving preference to Grantor's spouse's needs, considering other resources available to them and without being required to apportion benefits equally among them.

4.2 Administration for Descendants.

(a) In General. If Grantor's spouse does not survive Grantor (or if Grantor's spouse survives Grantor, then upon Grantor's spouse's death), the trust assets shall be divided into equal shares, one share for each of Grantor's then surviving children and one share for all of the descendants of each then deceased child of Grantor which in turn shall be divided into separate shares by right of representation. The income and principal of each share shall be paid to or applied for the benefit of the beneficiary in the amounts determined by the Trustee for the beneficiary's maintenance, education, support and health according to the beneficiary's accustomed standard of living, considering other resources available to the beneficiary. One-third of the trust share shall be distributed to the beneficiary at age thirty, one-half of the balance then remaining at age thirty-five, and the balance at age forty.

(b) Upon Death of Descendant. If a beneficiary of a separate trust share dies before final distribution of the beneficiary's share, and the beneficiary is survived by one or more descendants, the share shall be divided among them by right of representation for administration under this Section, or, if such beneficiary has no surviving descendants, the share shall be added to the shares of Grantor's other descendants by right of representation for administration under this section.

4.3 Statement of Intent. It is intended that Grantor's family members enjoy the financial resources of the Trust without becoming dependent upon them. At the very least, it is intended that their respective standards of living be maintained. To this end, the Trustee is requested to be flexible and generous in assessing their situations and to use the trust assets to promote their personal growth and happiness without taking away their incentive to succeed on their own. For example, it is Grantor's intent that trust funds be made available, perhaps by loan, perhaps by distribution, to assist a responsible beneficiary in establishing himself or herself in a business or profession and in purchasing a home; subject, of course, to the Trustee's discretion. Grantor is mindful that, in order to avoid adverse tax consequences, the discretion of any trustee who is also a beneficiary must be limited by the standards expressed in the preceding sections, and this statement of intent shall not be considered to relax those standards as they apply to such trustee/beneficiaries.

4.4 Alternate Disposition. If all of Grantor's descendants fail to survive to the date of distribution hereunder, the trust assets then remaining shall pass as follows: in equal shares to _____, _____, and to _____ or, if deceased, their descendants by right of representation.

5. TRUSTEE SUCCESSION

5.1 In General. While serving as initial Trustee, _____ acting with

_____ shall have the power to designate a successor Trustee to serve when and if she becomes unable or unwilling to serve. If no such designation is made, and there is a Trustee vacancy, then BANK OF AMERICA, N.A. is designated to serve as Trustee. Notwithstanding the foregoing, upon the death of Grantor, _____ and BANK OF AMERICA, N.A. are designated to serve together as Co–Trustees. If, at such time, _____ is unable or unwilling to serve, BANK OF AMERICA, N.A., may serve alone as sole Trustee. After the death of Grantor, _____ shall have the lifetime power to designate for appointment without court proceedings a succession of alternate corporate or professional Trustees or Co–Trustees to serve from time to time in her discretion or when and if all of the foregoing designees are unable or unwilling to serve. Any such designation shall be written and acknowledged. If no successor Trustee has been designated and there is a Trustee vacancy, the majority of the adult beneficiaries may name a successor without court proceedings.

5.2 Trustees of Separate Shares. Notwithstanding the foregoing, each beneficiary of a separate trust share being administered under Section 4.2 above who has reached age twenty may serve as Co–Trustee of his or her trust share, and, upon reaching age thirty, may serve as sole Trustee of his or her trust share. At such time as the beneficiary is no longer able or willing to so serve the foregoing designees, in order of preference and successions, shall be reinstated as Trustee of the trust share for such beneficiary.

## 6. TRUSTEE POWERS AND COMPENSATION

6.1 In General. Except as otherwise limited herein, the Trustee shall have all of the power, authority and discretion conferred upon Trustees by Washington law. The Trustee shall not be bound by any requirement that may be imposed, under RCW 11.100.020 or otherwise, to diversify investments. The Trustee shall not be required to furnish annual statements of account under RCW 11.106.020; provided, however, that upon a beneficiary's reasonable request, the Trustee shall furnish such beneficiary with a current statement of assets and liabilities of the Trust together with a summary of current account activities of the Trust.

6.2 Extraordinary Powers.

(a) Extraordinary Action. The Trustee shall have sufficient authority to avail the Trust and its beneficiaries of such opportunities under existing and future laws as may require extraordinary action; S corporation shareholdership qualification and generation skipping transfer tax minimization being examples of such opportunities. To this end, the Trustee shall have the power to divide trusts into separate shares, to create new trusts for the purposes of holding specific property or for holding undivided interests in trust assets, to create limited, and, if necessary, general powers of appointment exercisable by specific beneficiaries, all to be consistent with, though not necessarily in literal compliance with, the dispositive scheme set forth in this instrument.

(b) Limited Power of Amendment/Power to Terminate Trust. In addition to the powers set forth above, the Trustee shall have the power, acting alone, to amend the Trust in any manner required for the sole purpose of ensuring that the Trust conforms with current and/or future laws affecting Trusts of this type. Any such amendment shall be deemed effective as of the date of creation of the trust or such other date as the Trustee shall select. Furthermore, the Trustee shall have the power to terminate the Trust, at any time, and to distribute the assets among Grantor's descendants by right of representation. The Trustee shall also have the power to amend the provisions of the QDOT as set forth herein solely to assure compliance with Internal Revenue Code Section 2056A and the regulations and rulings thereunder.

(c) Qualified Trustees. The only Trustees who shall have the extraordinary powers set forth in this Section 6.2 shall be those who are not beneficiaries of the Trust, and shall be referred to as qualified Trustees. If there are no qualified Trustees at the time that the exercise of such a power is called for, the Trustee may appoint a qualified Trustee to consider the situation then at hand and to proceed in the qualified Trustee's discretion with the powers as set forth herein.

6.3 Life Insurance—In General. The Trustee shall have the authority to accept, purchase and/or retain any type of life insurance policy on the life of Grantor or any beneficiary of the Trust. Such insurance may be obtained from one or more insurers. If the Trustee's investment decision respecting any policy is made in reliance upon the recommendation of an experienced insurance advisor, the Trustee shall incur no liability to anyone interested in the trust on account of such investment decision except as provided in RCW 11.98.070(27). The Trustee shall have all the incidents of ownership in any life insurance policies owned by the Trust and is authorized and employed to exercise, either before or after the death of Grantor, all the rights, options, elections or privileges exercisable in connection with such policies. Grantor shall have no rights or ownership interests of any kind in such policies.

6.4 Payment of Premiums. The Trustee may make payments of premiums or other charges on any trust owned policy out of annual cash contributions received by the Trust or from the principal and income of the Trust estate; however, the Trustee shall have no duty or responsibility for payment of premiums or other charges on account of any such policy. If sufficient funds are not available or provided to the Trustee to pay the premium or any other charge on any such policy, the Trustee shall have the authority, though not the duty, to allow any automatic premium loan feature of the policy to operate, or, if there is no such feature, to either borrow upon the cash values or reserves of such policy or of any other policy or policies held by the Trustee in order to pay the amounts due upon such policy, or to elect the automatic nonforfeiture feature of the policy, whichever procedure shall in the discretion of the Trustee be deemed to be in the best interests of the Trust estate.

6.5 Compensation. The Trustee shall be entitled to reasonable compensation payable not less frequently than annually together with current reimbursement for all reasonable expenditures. A determination of the Trustee's compensation shall take into account the Trustee's time commitment, the nature and magnitude of the Trustee's risks and responsibilities and the value of the assets being administered. The Trustee shall be entitled, though not directed, to obtain court approval of any compensation arrangement or payment upon notice to all interested parties as defined in RCW 11.9A.

## 7. TAXATION

The Trustee may pay any estate or inheritance taxes properly charged by law against the Trust estate by reason of Grantor's death.

## 8. GENERAL PROVISIONS

8.1 Protection from Creditors. No interest of any beneficiary in any trust or estate hereunder shall be subject to pledge, assignment, sale or transfer in any manner, nor shall any beneficiary have the power to anticipate, charge or encumber such interests in any manner, nor shall the interest of any beneficiary be liable for any claims against the beneficiary of any nature.

8.2 Mandatory—Trust Termination. Any trust or trust share created hereunder which has not terminated at an earlier date shall terminate at the expiration of the maximum term allowed under RCW 11.98.130. Except as otherwise provided above, the Trustees shall thereupon distribute the trust estate to the trust's beneficiaries then entitled to income in the same proportions as they were so entitled at the time of termination. If such proportionate income interests are not ascertainable, the trust estate shall be distributed as directed by court order under RCW 11.98.150.

8.3 Grantor Trust Status. Grantor acknowledges that on account of the Trust's ability to use income to pay premiums of insurance on Grantor's life, the Trust constitutes a Grantor Trust for federal income tax purposes. Grantor further acknowledges that Grantor shall not be entitled to reimbursement from the Trust for any income tax Grantor is required to pay on account of this provision.

## 9. DEFINITIONS AND CONSTRUCTION

9.1 Context. As the context may require, the gender of all words used herein shall include the masculine, the feminine and neuter, and the singular of all words shall include the plural and the plural the singular.

9.2 Contribution. The term "contribution" as used herein shall include direct transfers of property to the Trust and any indirect transfers to the Trust which constitute gifts by Grantor under the provisions of applicable federal tax laws.

9.3 Descendant. The term "descendant" when applied to a given person, shall include such person's children, grandchildren, great grandchildren etc. and shall include both descendants by blood and descendants by adoption.

9.4 Governing Law and References. This instrument shall be governed by Washington law and by applicable federal law. All references made to the statutes or legislative acts of any jurisdiction include any amendments and successor legislation.

9.5 Notice. For the purposes of this Agreement, notice shall be effective upon personal delivery to the recipient or by post to the recipient's last known address either by way of first class or certified mail.

9.6 Right of Representation. Where an estate or trust or any interest therein passes "by right of representation", the same shall be divided into as many equal shares as there are (i) surviving descendants in the generation nearest to the decedent which contains one or more surviving descendants, and (ii) deceased descendants in the same generation who left surviving descendants, if any. Each surviving descendant in the nearest generation shall be allocated one share. Shares in the latter category, if any, shall be divided among such deceased descendant's descendants, those more remote in degree taking together the share which their ancestor would have taken had he or she survived the decedent.

9.7 Survivorship. Any person who must survive or be living at the time of any event in order to take a beneficial interest of Grantor's estate or of a trust will be deemed to have survived or be living only if such person is still living forty-five days after the event giving rise to the vesting of the beneficial interest.

9.8 Support Obligations. No provision of this instrument shall be construed to permit Trust funds to be used to discharge Grantor's legal obligation to support any person.

9.9 Irrevocability. This instrument is irrevocable as is the Trust created hereby.

IN WITNESS WHEREOF, the parties have executed this Agreement effective the date first above written.

GRANTOR:                              TRUSTEE:

_____              _____

_____              _____

## F. FORM: ASSET PURCHASE AGREEMENT

### ASSET PURCHASE AGREEMENT

The parties to this Agreement are:

(i)_____, a_____("Seller");

(ii)_____,and_____(collectively Shareholders"); and

(iii)_____, a_____("Purchaser").

### RECITALS

A. Seller desires to sell to Purchaser and Purchaser desires to acquire upon the terms and conditions set forth in this Agreement substantially all of the property, assets and business of Seller.

B. Shareholders own all the issued and outstanding shares of stock of Seller.

In consideration of the mutual agreements set forth below, the parties agree:

1. SALE AND PURCHASE OF ASSETS. On the terms and subject to the conditions of this Agreement, at Closing Seller will sell, assign and convey to Purchaser and Purchaser will purchase from Seller, all of Seller's right, title and

interest in and to the "Assets," as defined below, free and clear of all liens, claims and encumbrances except as otherwise provided in this Agreement.

1.1 Description of Assets. The "Assets" are all of the assets and properties of Seller, except as specifically excluded below, existing as of Closing.

(a) Assets Included. The Assets include, without limitation, all of the following:

(i) Operating assets, furniture, fixtures, machinery, equipment, vehicles, computers (and related peripherals and software), including but not limited to the specific items listed in Exhibit 1.1.1(a) attached to this Agreement;

(ii) Inventories of raw materials, work in process, finished goods and supplies, all subject to the Closing audit described below;

(iii) Leasehold improvements at all leased premises occupied by Seller;

(iv) Accounts receivable;

(v) Trademarks, trade names (including the name _____ and any variation thereof), trade secrets, proprietary information, copyrights, patents, and other intellectual property rights of any and every nature, including but not limited to the specific items listed in Exhibit 1.1.1(e) attached to this Agreement;

(vi) Goodwill;

(vii) Business and accounting records, including product formulae, customer lists and supplier lists (including all such records and lists stored on computer disks and other similar media);

(viii) Telephone and fax numbers and post office boxes (effective as of Closing, Seller grants Purchaser the right to open all mail delivered to such post office boxes);

(ix) Credits and deposits with suppliers, utilities, taxing authorities and all other persons and entities including but not limited to the specific items listed in Exhibit 1.1.1(i) attached to this Agreement;

(x) Product warranties from Seller's suppliers;

(xi) The contracts and leases to which Seller is a party and which are listed in Exhibit 1.1.1(k) to this Agreement

(xii) Assignable permits, licenses and governmental approvals including but not limited to the specific items listed in Exhibit 1.1.1(*l* ) attached to this Agreement; and

(xiii) Stationery, forms, publications, office supplies, reference materials and other miscellaneous assets.

(b) Assets Excluded. Except as provided elsewhere herein, the Assets do not include the following:

(i) Corporate minute books, stock books and corporate seal;

(ii) Cash, bonds, savings certificates and other cash equivalents not included in the Assets;

(iii) Those specific items described in Exhibit 1.1.2 attached to this Agreement;

(iv) All Seller's rights under this Agreement and related documents; and

(v) All Seller's rights under any insurance policies in effect at or prior to Closing.

1.2 Liabilities and Obligations. Except for those liabilities, debts or obligations listed on Exhibit 1.2 to this Agreement, which Purchaser shall assume at Closing, Purchaser assumes no liabilities, debts or obligations of Seller of any nature whatsoever, whether absolute, accrued, contingent or otherwise, or whether due or to become due, including without limitation any liability for taxes or any liability under any lease, purchase agreement or other contract of Seller.

2. PURCHASE PRICE.

2.1 Amount and Payment. Subject to adjustment as provided below, the purchase price ("Purchase Price") for the Assets and for the covenant not to compete contained in section _____ of this Agreement (the "Covenant Not to Compete") is _____ _____ Dollars ($_____) payable as follows:

$_____ by cashier's check or wire transfer at Closing;

$_____ by assumption of those liabilities and in those amounts described in paragraph 1.2 above; and

The balance payable in accordance with the terms of a promissory note (the "Note") in the form of Exhibit 2.1 attached to this Agreement.

2.2 Security. As security for the Note, Purchaser will deliver to Seller at Closing a security agreement in the form of Exhibit 2.2 attached to this Agreement (the "Security Agreement"), granting to Seller a first-lien security interest in the Assets, together with appropriate financing statements and other documents necessary or appropriate to perfect the security interests granted in the Security Agreement.

2.3 Adjustment to Purchase Price. Immediately [prior to/following] Closing, an audit of the inventory and accounts receivable included in the Assets ("Closing Audit") shall be performed by _____, an independent certified public accountant ("Auditor"). The Closing Audit shall include a review of the relevant books and records and a physical inventory, using such procedures and to such extent as deemed necessary or appropriate by the Auditor to enable the Auditor to give an unqualified opinion to Purchaser. Inventory will be valued at the lower of actual cost or market value, reduced by a reasonable reserve for returned merchandise. Accounts receivable shall be valued by excluding those more than ____ days past due and shall be adjusted by a reasonable allowance for uncollectible accounts. The results of the Closing Audit shall be conclusive. Representatives of Purchaser and Seller may participate in the physical inventory. The cost of the Closing Audit shall be paid by _____, _____. In the event the Closing Audit indicates an adjusted book value for Seller's inventory and/or accounts receivable which is greater than or less than the amount of the Purchase Price allocated to inventory and/or accounts receivable below, then the Purchase Price shall be adjusted dollar-for-dollar for any such variance ("Purchase Price Adjustment"). The amount of the Purchase Price Adjustment shall be paid by, or credited to, Purchaser as follows: _____.

2.4 Allocation of Purchase Price. The Purchase Price, as adjusted, shall be allocated to the Assets as follows:

(a)  Inventory (subject to the Price Adjustment)          $_____

(b) Accounts receivable(subject to the Price Adjustment)    $_____

(c)  Fixed Assets                                          $_____

(d)  Intangible Assets and Goodwill                        $_____

(e)  Covenant Not to Compete                               $_____

The parties shall report consistently with the above schedule for all tax purposes.

2.5 Escrow. At Closing, Purchaser shall pay $_____ of the Purchase Price into escrow pursuant to the terms of the escrow agreement attached as Exhibit 2.5 to this Agreement (the "Escrow Agreement"). Purchaser and Seller shall sign and deliver the Escrow Agreement at Closing.

3. CLOSING. The Closing of the transactions contemplated by this Agreement (the "Closing") shall take place at the offices of _____ in Seattle, Washington, at __:_____ a.m., local time, on _____, 199__, or at such other date, time and place as Purchaser and Seller shall mutually agree in writing ("Closing Date"). Conveyance, transfer, assignment and delivery of the Assets shall be by bills of sale, certificates of transfer, endorsements, assignments and other instruments of transfer and conveyance in such form as Purchaser may request. Seller and Shareholders will from time to time after the Closing make such further conveyances, transfers, assignments and deliveries, and execute such further instruments and documents, as Purchaser deems reasonably necessary in order to effectuate and confirm the sale of Assets and other transactions contemplated by this Agreement.

3.1 Possession. Purchaser shall take possession of the Assets immediately following Closing.

3.2 Taxes and Fees.

(a) Any transfer, sales, use or other tax payable as a result of the sale of the Assets pursuant to this Agreement shall be paid by Purchaser and Purchaser shall timely remit such taxes to the applicable taxing authorities; provided, however, that Purchaser may withhold the amount of any such taxes from the Purchase Price and pay them itself.

(b) All real and personal property taxes attributable to any of the Assets and payable in the year in which Closing occurs shall be apportioned and prorated as of Closing. The proration of such taxes shall be made on the basis of the tax rate for the most recent tax year available applied to the latest assessed valuation of the Assets, and when the tax rate and assessed valuation are fixed for the tax year in which Closing occurs, Seller and Purchaser shall adjust such proration and, if necessary, to refund or pay such sums to the other party as necessary to effect such readjustment.

(c) Except as provided above, all Seller's taxes which are not yet due and payable and which relate to periods prior to Closing shall be paid by Seller no later than the date such payments are due.

3.3 Deliveries by Seller and Shareholders at Closing. At or before Closing, Seller and Shareholders shall deliver to Purchaser the following instruments, documents and agreements duly executed by the appropriate persons and entities:

(a) Warranty bills of sale, certificates of transfer, certificates of title, endorsements, assignments and other instruments of transfer and conveyance in such form as Purchaser may request;

(b) A certificate of Seller's president and each Shareholder certifying that all representations and warranties made by Seller and Shareholders in this Agreement are true and correct as of the Closing Date;

(c) An opinion of Seller's counsel in the form attached as Exhibit 3.3(d) to this Agreement;

(d) The Escrow Agreement;

(e) _____ ; and

(f) Such other documents, instruments and agreements as are necessary or appropriate to carry out the provisions of this Agreement.

3.4 Deliveries by Purchaser at Closing. At or before Closing, Purchaser shall deliver to Seller the following instruments, documents and agreements duly executed by the appropriate persons and entities:

(a) A cashier's check, wire transfer or other immediately available funds in the amount of $_____ ;

(b) An assumption of the liabilities and obligations that Purchaser is to assume pursuant to section 1.2 of this Agreement;

(c) The Note;

(d) The Security Agreement and associated financing statements and other documents of perfection described in section 2.2 of this Agreement;

(e) The Escrow Agreement;

(f) A certificate of Purchaser's president certifying that all representations and warranties made by Purchaser in this Agreement are true and correct as of the Closing Date;

(g) An opinion of Purchaser's counsel in the form attached as Exhibit 3.4(g) to this Agreement;

(h) _____ ; and

(i) Such other documents, instruments and agreements as are necessary or appropriate to carry out the provisions of this Agreement.

3.5 Covenant to Change Name. On or before the Closing Date, Seller shall change its name to a name wholly dissimilar to _____ and shall take such other and further actions as are necessary or appropriate to transfer that name to Purchaser.

3.6 Covenant Not to Compete.

(a) Seller and Shareholders agree that for the period of five (5) years following Closing, they will not, without the prior written consent of the Purchaser, directly or indirectly, whether as principal or as agent, officer, director, employee, salesman, consultant, independent contractor or otherwise, alone or in association with one another or with any other person, firm, corporation or other business organization:

(i) Enter into, participate in, engage in or own any interest in the business of any person, firm, corporation or other business organization which is engaged in or proposes to become engaged in any business which is in substantial competition with any part of the business now or hereafter engaged in by Purchaser in the state of Washington; or

(ii) Solicit any business of any type now or hereafter engaged in by Purchaser from any clients, customers, former customers or clients, or prospects of Purchaser; or

(iii) Solicit any employee, consultant or independent contractor of Purchaser to terminate his or her relationship with Purchaser.

(b) The period of time during which Seller and Shareholders are prohibited from engaging in certain activities pursuant to the terms of this section shall be extended by the length of time during which Seller or any Shareholder is in breach of the terms of this section.

(c) Seller and Shareholders acknowledge and agree that, in the event of any violation of this section 3.6, money damages will not provide Purchaser with a fully adequate remedy for such violation and Purchaser shall, therefore, be entitled to an injunction prohibiting any further violation. Seller, Shareholders and Purchaser agree that, any bond posted in connection with obtaining such an injunction shall not exceed ten thousand dollars ($10,000) in amount.

3.7 [If Accounts Receivable Not Purchased]. Accounts Receivable. After the Closing Date, Purchaser promptly will pay to Seller any amounts received by Purchaser on account of Seller's accounts receivable which Purchaser is not purchasing under this Agreement ("Accounts"). Seller and Shareholders agree to: (a) act in a business-like manner in the collection of Accounts; (b) consult with Purchaser regarding any collection problems; and (c) use reasonable efforts to retain for Purchaser the good will of all customers. In the absence of a designation by the customer of the invoices to which a payment is to be applied, payments shall be applied to the oldest invoices first.

4. REPRESENTATIONS AND WARRANTIES OF SELLER AND

SHAREHOLDERS. The "Disclosure Schedules" shall mean all of the disclosure schedules required by this Agreement, which are simultaneously delivered to Purchaser and initialed by all of the parties to this Agreement for identification. As of the date of this Agreement and as of Closing, Seller and Shareholders, jointly and severally, represent and warrant to the Purchaser:

4.1 Organization, Good Standing, Power. Seller (a) is a corporation duly organized, validly existing and in good standing under the laws of the state of _____; and (b) has the requisite power and authority to own, lease and operate its properties and to carry on its business as currently conducted.

4.2 Authorization. Shareholders and Seller have taken all necessary and proper corporate action, including approval by Shareholders' and Seller's boards of directors, to authorize and approve this Agreement, its consummation and the performance by Seller and Shareholders of all terms and conditions of this Agreement.

4.3 Property. Seller has good and marketable title to all of the Assets, free and clear of all liens, security interests, mortgages, conditional sale agreements, encumbrances or other charges whatsoever, except as set forth on the schedule of liabilities attached to this Agreement as Disclosure Schedule 4.3 and at Closing Purchaser will obtain good and marketable title to the Assets, free and clear of all liens, security interests, mortgages, conditional sale agreements, encumbrances or other charges whatsoever, except as set forth on Disclosure Schedule 4.3.

4.4 Leases. All leases under which Seller leases real or personal property are described in the schedule of leases attached to this Agreement as Disclosure Schedule 4.4. All such leases are valid and subsisting and no default exists under any of them and no event exists which, with the giving of notice or the passage of time, or both, will be a default. Except as otherwise noted on such schedule of leases, Seller does not occupy and is not dependent on the right to use any property of others.

4.5 Contracts. Except for this Agreement and the contracts and agreements set forth in the Schedule of Contracts attached to this Agreement as Disclosure Schedule 4.5, Seller is not a party to or subject to any agreements, contracts or other commitments (written or oral).

4.6 Taxes, Etc. Seller has filed all tax returns and paid all taxes or installments thereof, and all employment security premiums, workers compensation premiums and other governmental charges, required under applicable federal, state and other laws and regulations and will timely pay all such taxes and other items not yet due and payable which are owing with respect to any period before Closing.

4.7 Effect of Agreement. The execution, delivery and performance of this Agreement by Seller and Shareholders and the consummation of the transactions contemplated by it will not: (a) violate any provision of law, statute, rule or regulation to which Seller or Shareholders are subject; (b) violate any judgment, order, writ or decree of any court, arbitrator or governmental agency applicable to Seller or Shareholders; (c) have any effect on any of the permits, licenses, orders or approvals of Seller or Shareholders or the ability of Seller or

Shareholders to make use of such permits, licenses, orders or approvals; or (d) result in the breach of or conflict with any term, covenant, condition or provision of, or result in the modification or termination of, any charter, bylaw, commitment, contract or other agreement or instrument, to which Seller or any Shareholder is a party.

4.8 Financial Statements; Absence of Undisclosed Liabilities.

(a) The financial statements of Seller (the "Financial Statements") including but not limited to the unaudited balance sheet dated as of _____, ____ (the "Balance Sheet") as set forth on Disclosure Schedule 4.8 are correct and complete and fairly present the financial position of Seller as of the date thereof in accordance with generally accepted accounting principles consistently applied, and no event has occurred since the date of the Financial Statements which would render them misleading or inaccurate or incomplete in any material respect.

(b) Except to the extent reflected or reserved against or otherwise disclosed on the Financial Statements, as of the date of the Financial Statements, Seller had no liabilities, debts or obligations of any nature, whether absolute, accrued, contingent or otherwise, or whether due or to become due including, without limitation, liabilities for taxes. Subsequent to the date of the Financial Statements Seller has not incurred or become subject to any liabilities, debts or obligations other than in the ordinary course of business or otherwise disclosed in the Disclosure Schedules, and Seller has properly recorded in its books of account all items of income and expense and all other proper charges and accruals required to be made in accordance with generally accepted accounting principles and practice consistently applied. Since the date of the Financial Statements, no debts or liabilities of or to Seller have been forgiven, settled or compromised except for full consideration or except in the ordinary course of business, the aggregate amount of which has not had a material adverse effect of Seller's financial condition.

4.9 Litigation. Except as set forth on Disclosure Schedule 4.9, there is no claim, action, suit, proceeding, arbitration, investigation or inquiry pending before any federal, state, municipal, foreign or other court or any governmental, administrative or self-regulatory body or agency, or any private arbitration tribunal, or threatened against, relating to or affecting Seller or any of the assets, properties, employees or businesses of Seller, nor is there any basis for any such claim, action, suit, proceeding, arbitration, investigation or inquiry which may have a material adverse effect upon the assets, properties or business of Seller or the transactions contemplated by this Agreement.

4.10 Inventories. The inventories reflected on the Balance Sheet or thereafter acquired consist of items of a quality and quantity which are usable and salable at regular prices in the normal and ordinary course of business of Seller and the values at which such inventories are carried on the Balance Sheet are stated at the lesser of cost or market value. None of the Assets are held on consignment.

4.11 Purchase and Sale Obligations. All unfilled purchase and sales orders and all other commitments for purchases and sales made by Seller were made in the usual and ordinary course of its business in accordance with normal industry practice and Seller's normal practice.

4.12 Powers of Attorney. No person has any power of attorney to act on behalf of Seller in connection with any of Seller's properties or business affairs.

4.13 No Broker. Neither Seller nor Shareholders have taken any action which would give to any firm, corporation, agency or other person a right to a consultant's or finder's fee or any type of brokerage commission in connection with the transactions contemplated by this Agreement as a result of any agreement with, or action by, Seller or Shareholders.

4.14 Absence of Certain Changes or Events. Except as set forth in Disclosure Schedule 4.14, since the date of the Balance Sheet, Seller has not:

(a) Incurred any obligation or liability (of fixed or variable amount, absolute or contingent) except trade or business obligations incurred in the ordinary course of business;

(b) Suffered the occurrence of any events or gained the knowledge of the possibility of any events occurring (including, without limitation, events concerning customers, suppliers, equipment, employees, facilities, environmental issues or any other matter that is material to Seller's business) which, individually or in the aggregate, have had, or might reasonably be expected to have, an adverse effect on Seller's financial condition, results of operations, properties, business or prospects;

(c) Incurred damage to or destruction or other loss of any of its assets, in any material amount;

(d) Discharged or satisfied any lien or encumbrance or incurred or paid any obligation or liability (fixed or variable in amount, absolute or contingent), except (i) current obligations and liabilities included in the Balance Sheet and (ii) current obligations and liabilities incurred since the date of the Balance Sheet, in the ordinary course of business;

(e) Mortgaged, pledged or subjected to lien or any other encumbrance any of its assets or properties;

(f) Sold, transferred or leased any of its assets or properties, except for the sale of inventory in the ordinary course of business;

(g) Cancelled or compromised any debt or claim, except for adjustments made with respect to contracts for the sale of products or services in the ordinary course of business which in the aggregate are not material;

(h) Waived or released any rights of any material value;

(i) Transferred or granted any rights under any licenses, agreements, patents, inventions, trademarks, trade names, service marks, copyrights or other intellectual property rights;

(j) Made or entered into any contract or commitment to make any material expenditures;

(k) Declared or paid any distribution, whether in the nature of dividends or otherwise or purchased or redeemed any of its outstanding shares of capital stock; or

(*l* ) Made any commitments to any employees, sales representatives, dealers, sales agents, suppliers or customers, except in the ordinary course of business, consistent with part practices of Seller.

4.15 Trade Names and Trademarks. Seller has the right to use the following trade names and trademarks in its business: _____.

4.16 Environmental Matters.

(a) Except as set forth in Disclosure Schedule 4.16, Seller has obtained all permits, licenses and other authorizations which are required in connection with the conduct of its business under any and all laws, statutes, regulations, ordinances, zoning and land use requirements, directives, rules, and other governmental requirements, orders, decrees, judgments, injunctions, notices and demands relating to pollution or protection of the environment (collectively "Regulations"), including Regulations relating to emissions, discharges, releases or threatened releases of pollutants, contaminants, chemicals, or industrial, toxic or hazardous substances or wastes into the environment (including without limitation ambient air, surface water, groundwater, or land), or otherwise relating to the manufacture, processing, distribution, use, treatment, storage, disposal, transport, or handling of pollutants, contaminants, chemicals, or industrial, toxic or hazardous substances or wastes.

(b) Except as set forth in Disclosure Schedule 4.16, Seller is in full compliance in the conduct of its business with all terms and conditions of all required permits, licenses and authorizations, and is also in full compliance with all other limitations, restrictions, conditions, standards, prohibitions, requirements, obligations, schedules and timetables contained in any Regulations.

(c) Except as set forth in Disclosure Schedule 4.16, there are no (nor has Seller received any notice or claim of any) events, conditions, circumstances, activities, practices, incidents, actions or plans which may interfere with or prevent compliance or continued compliance with any Regulations, or which may give rise to any liability, or otherwise form the basis of any claim, action, demand, suit, proceeding, hearing, study or investigation, based on or related to the manufacture, processing, distribution, use, treatment, storage, disposal, transport, or handling, or the emission, discharge, release or threatened release into the environment, of any pollutant, contaminant, chemical, or industrial, toxic or hazardous substance or waste.

(d) Except as set forth in Disclosure Schedule 4.16, there is no civil, criminal or administrative action, suit, demand, claim, hearing, notice or demand letter, notice of violation, investigation, or proceeding pending or threatened against Seller in connection with the conduct of its business or any real property occupied by Seller relating in any way to any Regulation.

(e) Seller and Shareholders agree to cooperate with Purchaser in connection with Purchaser's application for the transfer, renewal or issuance of any permits, license, approvals or other authorizations or to satisfy any regulatory requirements involving Seller's business.

4.17 Insurance. Disclosure Schedule 4.17 contains a complete list of all insurance policies maintained by Seller. Seller shall keep all such insurance policies in full force and effect through the Closing Date.

4.18 Employment Agreements and Benefits. Disclosure Schedule 4.18 is a correct and complete list of every employment agreement, collective bargaining agreement, stock option, stock purchase, stock appreciation right, bonus, deferred compensation, excess benefits, profit sharing, thrift, savings, retirement, major medical, long-term disability, hospitalization, insurance or other plan, arrangement, commitment or practice of Seller providing employee or executive benefits or benefits to any person, including, but not limited to, plans administered by trade associations, area wide plans, plans resulting from collective bargaining and plans covering foreign employees. All reasonably anticipated obligations of Seller, whether arising by operation of law, by contract, by past custom or practice or otherwise, for salaries, vacation and holiday pay, bonuses and other forms of compensation which were payable to its officers, directors or other employees have been paid or adequate accruals therefor have been made in the Financial Statements.

4.19 Assets. Seller owns all the tangible assets used in the operation of its business or located on its premises except those listed in Disclosure Schedule 4.19 to this Agreement.

4.20 Compliance with Laws. Seller is not in violation of any law, ordinance or governmental or regulatory rule or regulation of any federal, state, local or foreign government to which Seller or its assets are subject. Seller has all governmental permits, licenses and authorizations necessary or appropriate for it to carry on its business as presently conducted.

4.21 Interests in Other Entities. Seller holds no shares, partnership interests or other investments or ownership interests in any other corporation, partnership, joint venture or other entity.

4.22 Corporate Matters.

(a) Shareholders own all the issued and outstanding capital stock of all classes in Seller and there are no other holders of shares in Seller.

(b) The following are all the directors of Seller: _____.

(c) The following are all the officers of Seller:

_____President

_____    _____

_____    _____

_____    _____

5.　REPRESENTATIONS　AND　WARRANTIES　OF　PURCHASER.

Purchaser represents and warrants to Seller and Shareholders:

5.1 Organization, Good Standing, Power. Purchaser (a) is a corporation duly organized, validly existing and in good standing under the laws of the state of _____; and (b) has all requisite corporate power and authority to execute, deliver and perform this Agreement and consummate the transactions contemplated by this Agreement.

5.2 Authorization. Purchaser has taken all necessary and proper corporate action, including approval by its board of directors to authorize and approve this Agreement, its consummation and the performance by Purchaser of all terms and conditions hereof and this Agreement constitutes the valid and binding obligation of the Purchaser fully enforceable in accordance with its terms.

5.3 Effect of Agreement, Consents, Etc. No consent, authorization or approval or exemption by, or filing with, any governmental or public body or authority is required in connection with the execution, delivery and performance by the Purchaser of this Agreement or the taking of any action hereby contemplated by this Agreement.

5.4 No Broker. There is no firm, corporation, agency or other person that is entitled to a consultant's or finder's fee or any type of brokerage commission in connection with the transactions contemplated by this Agreement as a result of any agreement with, or action by, Purchaser.

5.5 Effect of Agreement. The execution, delivery and performance of this Agreement by Purchaser and the consummation of the transactions contemplated by this Agreement will not: (a) violate any provision of law, statute, rule or regulation to which Purchaser is subject; (b) violate any judgment, order, writ or decree of any court, arbitrator or governmental agency applicable to Purchaser; (c) have any effect on any of the permits, licenses, orders or approvals of Purchaser or the ability of Purchaser to make use of such permits, licenses, orders or approvals; or (d) result in the breach of or conflict with any term, covenant, condition or provision of, or result in the modification or termination of, any charter, bylaw, commitment, contract or other agreement or instrument, to which Purchaser is a party.

6. INDEMNIFICATION.

6.1 Seller and Shareholders Indemnification. Shareholders and Seller will, jointly and severally, defend, indemnify and hold harmless Purchaser and any person claiming by or through either Purchaser or its respective successors and assigns (individually, an "Indemnified Party") from and against any and all costs, losses, claims, liabilities, fines, penalties, damages and expenses (including, without limitation, all legal expenses and reasonable fees and disbursements of attorneys and expert witnesses, with or without suit, on appeal and in bankruptcy or other insolvency proceedings) arising in connection with:

(a) Any breach of (i) any of the representations and warranties of Shareholders or Seller or (ii) any covenant or agreement made by Shareholders or Seller in this Agreement; and/or

(b) Any liability or obligation of Seller or Shareholders, whether known or unknown, absolute or contingent, except as specifically assumed by Purchaser under this Agreement.

6.2 Purchaser Indemnification. Purchaser will defend, indemnify and hold harmless Seller and Shareholders and any person or entity claiming by or through either Seller, Shareholders or their respective successors and assigns from and against any and all costs, losses, claims, liabilities, fines, penalties, damages and expenses (including without limitation, all legal expenses and fees and disbursements of attorneys and expert witnesses, with or without suit, on appeal and in bankruptcy or other insolvency proceedings) which arise in connection with:

(a) Any breach of (i) any of the representations and warranties of Purchaser or (ii) any covenant or agreement made by Purchaser in this Agreement; and/or

(b) Any liability or obligation relating to Purchaser's ownership or use of the Assets after Closing.

7. EMPLOYEES.

7.1 Immediately prior to Closing and effective no later than Closing, Seller will discharge and terminate the employment of each of its employees, contractors and others working in its business in compliance with any employment agreements or collective bargaining agreements then in effect and with applicable laws and regulations in a manner such as to ensure that those persons cannot and will not make any claim against Purchaser for reemployment, back pay, vacation or sick leave, vacation pay, expense reimbursements, benefits or any other obligations of Seller, whether arising under any such employment agreement, collective bargaining agreement or otherwise imposed by statute or common law, or otherwise. Upon such termination, Purchaser will have no obligation to any such persons (except as created by or at the direction of Purchaser) under any pension, profit-sharing, other benefit plans for Seller's employees or otherwise.

7.2 At its discretion, Purchaser may offer employment to any former employee of Seller on such terms and conditions as Purchaser shall determine.

7.3 The parties understand that Purchaser's ability to retain the good will of its employees through the transition from Seller to Purchaser is critical to Purchaser's future success. Seller agrees to coordinate its termination actions with the reasonable requirements of Purchaser and to consult with Purchaser on all matters affecting that process. Purchaser has the right to be present at, and to participate in, both the notification to Seller's employees that they are being terminated and the announcement of the sale to Purchaser.

7.4 Seller shall give all notices of the sale of the Assets required by any statute, regulation or contract, including but not limited to any notices required under the Worker Adjustment and Retraining Notification Act and any collective bargaining agreements.

8. CONDITIONS TO SELLER'S OBLIGATIONS. The obligations of Seller under this Agreement are subject to the fulfillment, at or prior to the Closing, of each of the following conditions, any or all of which may be waived in writing by

Seller, in its sole discretion.

8.1 Accuracy of Representations and Warranties. Each of the representations and warranties of the Purchaser contained in this Agreement shall be true in all material respects on and as of Closing with the same force and effect as though made on and as of Closing, except as affected by transactions contemplated by this Agreement.

8.2 Performance of Covenants. Purchaser shall have performed and complied in all material respects with all covenants, obligations and agreements to be performed or complied with by it on or before Closing pursuant to this Agreement.

8.3 Litigation. No claim, action, suit, proceeding, arbitration, investigation or hearing or notice of hearing shall be pending or threatened against or affecting Purchaser which might result, or has resulted, either in an action to enjoin or prevent or delay the consummation of the transactions contemplated by this Agreement or in such an injunction.

9. CONDITIONS TO PURCHASER'S OBLIGATIONS. The obligations of Purchaser under this Agreement are subject to the fulfillment, at or prior to Closing, of each of the following conditions, any or all of which may be waived in writing by Purchaser, in its sole discretion:

9.1 Accuracy of Representations and Warranties. Each of the representations and warranties of Seller and/or Shareholders contained in this Agreement shall be true in all material respects on and as of Closing with the same force and effect as though made on and as of Closing, except as affected by transactions contemplated by this Agreement.

9.2 Performance of Covenants. Seller and Shareholders shall have performed and complied in all material respects with all covenants, obligations and agreements to be performed or complied with by them on or before Closing pursuant to this Agreement.

9.3 Litigation. No claim, action, suit, proceeding, arbitration, investigation or hearing or notice of hearing shall be pending or threatened against or affecting Seller or Shareholders which: (a) might result, or has resulted, either in an action to enjoin or prevent or delay the consummation of the transactions contemplated by this Agreement or in an injunction; and (b) could have a material adverse effect on the Assets or the business of the Purchaser to be carried on following Closing and has not been disclosed in this Agreement.

9.4 Lease Negotiation. Purchaser shall have entered into an agreement, satisfactory to Purchaser in its sole discretion, regarding Purchaser's right to lease the premises at _____ currently occupied by Seller. If Purchaser has not entered into such an agreement by the date three (3) days prior to the Closing Date, Purchaser may terminate this Agreement by written notice to Seller, which notice shall be delivered by the date three (3) days prior to the Closing Date. If Purchaser has not terminated this Agreement pursuant to this Section, Purchaser shall be deemed to have waived this condition to Closing.

9.5 Due Diligence Investigation. Purchaser shall have completed, to its sole satisfaction, a due diligence investigation of Seller, the Assets and Seller's operations. If Purchaser is not satisfied with such investigation, Purchaser may terminate this Agreement by notice to Seller. If Purchaser has not terminated this Agreement pursuant to this Section by the date three (3) days prior to the Closing Date, Purchaser shall be deemed to have waived this condition to Closing.

9.6 Documents. Prior to Closing, Seller shall have delivered to Purchaser the following documents:

(a) Certified copies of Seller's articles of incorporation and bylaws;

(b) Certified copies of resolutions of Seller's board of directors and shareholders authorizing the execution, delivery and performance of this Agreement and the consummation of the transactions provided for in this Agreement;

(c) Certified copies of all documents evidencing any consents, permits or governmental approvals necessary or appropriate to the consummation of the transactions provided for in this Agreement; and

(d) An incumbency certificate of Seller's secretary certifying the names of the officer or officers of Seller authorized to sign this Agreement and the documents, instruments and agreements to be executed by Seller pursuant to this Agreement, together with a sample of the signature of each such officer.

10. TERMINATION. This Agreement may be terminated prior to Closing by either party:

10.1 No Closing. If the Closing has not taken place on or before _____ _____, _____; provided, however, that such termination shall not relieve any party from liability if such party, as of the termination date, is in breach of any of the provisions of this Agreement; and provided, further, that if the delay is caused by the act or omission of a particular party, such party shall not have the right to terminate this Agreement; or

10.2 Failure of Conditions. If on the Closing Date, any of the conditions set forth in Sections 8 or 9 have not been satisfied, or waived by the Purchaser or Seller, as applicable.

11. GENERAL.

11.1 Survival. The representations, warranties, covenants and agreements set forth in this Agreement shall survive Closing.

11.2 Expenses. Except as otherwise provided herein, whether or not the transactions contemplated by this Agreement are consummated, each party shall pay its own expenses and the fees and expenses of its counsel and accountants and other experts.

11.3 Assignment. Purchaser may assign its rights under this Agreement to a wholly-owned subsidiary, provided that such assignment shall not relieve Purchaser of its obligations under this Agreement.

11.4 Announcements. At Closing the parties will make a mutually agreeable joint press release announcing the consummation of the transactions contemplated in this Agreement. Other than the above press release, each party agrees that for the period commencing on the date of this Agreement and concluding forty-five (45) days after Closing, it shall not, except as otherwise required by applicable law or regulations, make or release any statement, announcement or publicity with respect to this Agreement or the transactions contemplated in this Agreement or permit any of its officers, directors or employees to do so unless the form and content of any such statement, announcement or publicity and the time of its release shall have been approved by the other party.

11.5 Waivers. No action taken pursuant to this Agreement, nor any investigation by or on behalf of any party, shall be deemed to constitute a waiver by the party taking such action of compliance with any representation, warranty, covenant or agreement contained in this Agreement. The waiver by any party of a breach of any provision of this Agreement shall not operate or be construed as a waiver of any subsequent breach.

11.6 Binding Effect; Benefits. This Agreement shall inure to the benefit of the parties and shall be binding upon the parties and their respective heirs, personal representatives, successors and permitted assigns.

11.7 Notices. All notices, requests, demands and other communications which are required or permitted under this Agreement shall be in writing and shall be deemed to have been given when delivered in person or three (3) days after deposit in the United States mail, certified postage prepaid, return receipt requested, addressed as follows:

        If to Seller or Shareholders, to:

           _____

           _____

           _____

           Attn: _____

        with a copy to:

           _____

           _____

           _____

           Attn: _____

        If to Purchaser, to:

           _____

           _____

           _____

           Attn: _____

with a copy to:

_____

Attn: _____

or to such other address as any party may designate by written notice to the other parties.

11.8 Further Assurances. Seller shall, from time to time, at the request of the Purchaser, and without further consideration, execute and deliver such other instruments and take such other actions as may be required to confer to the Purchaser and its assignees the benefits contemplated by this Agreement.

11.9 Entire Agreement. This Agreement (including its Exhibits and Disclosure Schedules) contains the complete and final expression of the entire agreement of the parties with respect to the subject matter of this Agreement and, except as otherwise expressly stated in this Agreement, supersedes and replaces any and all agreements, representations and understandings with respect to the subject matter of this Agreement. This Agreement may not be amended, modified, revoked, interpreted or waived orally, but only by means of a written document executed by the party against whom the amendment, modification or revocation is sought to be enforced. No party is entering into this Agreement in reliance on any oral or written promises, inducements, representations, understandings, interpretations or agreements other than those contained in this Agreement.

11.10 Headings. The section and other headings contained in this Agreement are for reference purposes only and shall not be deemed to be a part of this Agreement or to affect the meaning or interpretation of this Agreement.

11.11 Severability. The invalidity of all or any part of any section of this Agreement shall not render invalid the remainder of this Agreement or the remainder of such section, If any provision of this Agreement is so broad as to be unenforceable, such provision shall be interpreted to be only so broad as is enforceable.

11.12 Counterparts. This Agreement may be executed in any number of counterparts, each of which, when executed, shall be deemed to be an original and all of which together shall be deemed to be one and the same instrument.

11.13 Third Parties. Nothing in this Agreement, whether expressed or implied, is intended to confer any rights or remedies on any person other than the parties to this Agreement, nor is anything in this Agreement intended to relieve or discharge the obligation or liability of any third party, nor shall any provision give any third party any right of subrogation or action against any party to this Agreement.

11.14 Governing Law. This Agreement is made in and shall be governed and interpreted in accordance with the laws of the State of Washington without giving effect to their principles or provisions regarding choice of law or conflict of laws.

11.15 Jurisdiction and Venue. In the event of any litigation to enforce the provisions of this Agreement or recover damages for the breach of any provision of this Agreement, such litigation may be brought only in the Superior Court of Washington for _____ County or the United States District Court for the _____ District of Washington.

11.16 Gender and Number. Whenever appropriate to the meaning of this Agreement, use of the singular shall be deemed to refer to the plural and use of the plural to the singular, and pronouns of certain gender shall be deemed to comprehend either or both of the other genders.

11.17 Time of Essence. Time is of the essence of this Agreement.

DATED this _____ day of _____, ____.

SELLER: _____

By _____

Its _____

SHAREHOLDERS:

_____

_____

PURCHASER: _____

By _____

Its _____

## LIST OF EXHIBITS

1.1.1(a)   List of operating assets, furniture, fixtures, machinery, equipment, vehicles, computers, etc.

1.1.1(e)   List of trademarks, trade names, patents, copyrights and other intellectual property rights

1.1.1(i)   List of credits and deposits

1.1.1(k)   List of contracts and leases transferred to Purchaser

1.1.1(*l*)   List of permits, licenses and governmental approvals

1.1.2   List of Excluded Assets

1.2   List of assumed liabilities

2.1   Form of Note

2.2   Form of Security Agreement

2.5   Form of Escrow Agreement

### DISCLOSURE SCHEDULES

| | |
|---|---|
| 4.3 | Liens, encumbrances and charges |
| 4.4 | Real and personal property leases |
| 4.5 | Contracts, agreements and commitments |
| 4.8 | Financial Statements |
| 4.9 | Litigation |
| 4.14 | Certain changes or events |
| 4.16 | Environmental matters |
| 4.17 | Insurance policies |
| 4.18 | Employee benefits |
| 4.19 | Non-owned assets |

# G. FORM: ARTICLES OF INCORPORATION

## ARTICLES OF INCORPORATION

### OF

_____

_____ hereby executes these Articles of Incorporation for the purpose of forming a corporation under Title 23B of the Revised Code of Washington, the Washington Business Corporation Act.

#### ARTICLE 1

#### Name

The name of this corporation is:

_____

#### ARTICLE 2

#### Capital Stock

☐ This corporation has the authority to issue _____ shares, the par value of each of which is $_____.

☐ This corporation has the authority to issue _____ shares, and each share shall be without par value.

☐ The shares shall be classified as follows:

### ** Insert Text **

#### ARTICLE 3

#### Preemptive Rights

☐The shareholders of this corporation have no preemptive rights to acquire additional shares of this corporation.

☐The shareholders of this corporation shall have preemptive rights to acquire additional shares of this corporation.

## ARTICLE 4

### Cumulative Voting

☐The shareholders of this corporation shall not be entitled to cumulative voting at any election of directors.

☐Shareholders entitled to vote at any election of directors are entitled to cumulate votes by multiplying the number of votes they are entitled to cast by the number of directors for whom they are entitled to vote and to cast the product for a single candidate or distribute the product among two or more candidates.

## ARTICLE 5

### Action by Consent

Any action required or permitted to be taken at a shareholders' meeting may be taken without a meeting or a vote if either:

(i)    the action is taken by written consent of all shareholders entitled to vote on the action; or

(ii)   so long as the Corporation does not have any capital stock registered under the Securities Exchange Act of 1934, as amended, the action is taken by written consent of shareholders holding of record, or otherwise entitled to vote, in the aggregate not less than the minimum number of votes that would be necessary to authorize or take such action at a meeting at which all shares entitled to vote on the action were present and voted.

To the extent prior notice of any such action is required by law to be given to nonconsenting or nonvoting shareholders, such notice shall be made before the date on which the action becomes effective. The form of the notice shall be sufficient to apprise the nonconsenting or nonvoting shareholder of the nature of the action to be effected, in a manner approved by the board of directors of this Corporation or by the board committee or officers to whom the board of directors has delegated that responsibility.

## ARTICLE 6

### Approval by Majority Vote

Unless these Articles of Incorporation provide for a greater voting requirement for any voting group of shareholders, any action which would otherwise require the approval of two-thirds (2/3) of all the votes entitled to be cast, including without limitation the amendment of these Articles of Incorporation, the approval of a plan of merger or share exchange, the sale, lease, exchange or other disposition of all, or substantially all of the Corporation's property otherwise than in the usual and regular course of business, and the dissolution of the Corporation, shall be authorized if approved by each voting group entitled to vote thereon by a simple majority of all the votes entitled to be cast by that voting group.

## ARTICLE 7

### Limitation of Liability

A director of this Corporation shall not be personally liable to the Corporation or its shareholders for monetary damages for conduct as a director, except for liability of the director *(i)* for acts or omissions that involve intentional misconduct by the director or a knowing violation of law by the director, *(ii)* for conduct violating RCW 23B.08.310 of the Act, or *(iii)* for any transaction from which the director will personally receive a benefit in money, property or services to which the director is not legally entitled. If the Washington Business Corporation Act is amended in the future to authorize corporate action further eliminating or limiting the personal liability of directors, then the liability of a director of this Corporation shall be eliminated or limited to the full extent permitted by the Washington Business Corporation Act, as so amended, without any requirement of further action by the shareholders.

## ARTICLE 8

### Indemnification

The Corporation shall indemnify any individual made a party to a proceeding because that individual is or was a director of the Corporation and shall advance or reimburse the reasonable expenses incurred by such individual in advance of final disposition of the proceeding, without regard to the limitations in RCW 23B.08.510 through 23B.08.550 of the Act, or any other limitation which may hereafter be enacted to the extent such limitation may be disregarded if authorized by the Articles of Incorporation, to the full extent and under all circumstances permitted by applicable law.

Any repeal or modification of this Article by the shareholders of this Corporation shall not adversely affect any right of any individual who is or was a director of the Corporation which existed at the time of such repeal or modification.

## ARTICLE 9

### Directors

☐The initial board of directors shall consist of _____ (_____) directors. The names and addresses of the persons who are to serve as initial directors are:

_____

_____

_____

_____

_____

_____


_____

_____

_____

☐The initial board of directors shall consist of one director.  The name and address of the person who is to serve as the sole initial director is:

_____

_____

_____

Except with respect to the initial board of directors, the number of directors constituting the board of directors shall be determined in the manner specified in the bylaws.  In the absence of such a provision in the bylaws, the board shall consist of the number of directors constituting the initial board of directors.

### ARTICLE 10

### Registered Office and Registered Agent

The street address of the initial registered office of this corporation is:

☐          1780 Barnes Blvd. S.W.

Tumwater, WA  98512-0410


☐          1111 Third Avenue, Suite 3400

Seattle, WA  98101-3299

☐          _____

_____

_____

_____

and the name of its initial registered agent at that address is:

☐National Registered Agents, Inc.

☐FPS Corporate Services, Inc.

☐[Client]

## ARTICLE 11

### Incorporator

The name and address of the incorporator is:

☐    _____

1111 Third Avenue, Suite 3400

Seattle, WA  98101

☐    _____

_____

_____

Executed    this    _____    day    of    _____,

_____.

_____,

Incorporator

### CONSENT TO SERVE AS REGISTERED AGENT

National Registered Agents, Inc. ("NRAI"), hereby consents to serve as Registered       Agent       in       the       State       of       Washington       for _____ (the "Corporation"). NRAI understands that as agent for the Corporation, it will be its responsibility to receive service of process in the name of the Corporation; to forward all mail to the Corporation; and to immediately notify the office of the Secretary of State in the event of its resignation, or of any changes in the registered office address of the Corporation for which it is agent.

NATIONAL REGISTERED AGENTS, INC.

By:_____

Name: _____

Title: _____

NAME OF REGISTERED AGENT:  National Registered Agents, Inc.

ADDRESS OF REGISTERED AGENT:  1780 Barnes Blvd. S.W.

Tumwater, WA  98512-0410

## ARTICLE II

### TEXT INSERTS

[**INSERT:** Voting and Non-Voting Classes of Common Stock.]

The shares consist of _____ shares designated as "Class A Common Stock" and _____ shares designated as "Class B Common Stock". Each share of Class A Common Stock shall have unlimited voting rights. Class B Common Stock shall have no voting rights, and no separate vote of the holders of Class B Common Stock as a class shall be required for any purpose except as may be required by law. Other than with respect to voting rights, Class A Common Stock and Class B Common Stock shall have identical rights.

[**INSERT:** Special Class of Stock to Elect Designated Directors.]

The shares consist of _____ shares designated as "Class A Common Stock" and _____ shares designated as "Class B Common Stock". With respect to the election of directors, the holders of Class A Common Stock shall have the sole and exclusive right to elect _____ director(s), and the balance of the directors will be elected by the holders of Class B Common Stock. The holders of each class of stock shall have the sole and exclusive right to remove at any time the director(s) elected by such holders. The election and removal of the director(s) to be elected by the holders of any class of stock may be effected by unanimous written consent of all such holders, at a special meeting of such holders called for that purpose, or at an annual meeting of shareholders. Any vacancy with respect to a director elected by the holders of any class of stock shall be filled by a special election by the holders of that class, and not by a vote of the remaining directors. Other than with respect to rights relating to the election and removal of directors, Class A Common Stock and Class B Common Stock shall have identical rights.

The Board of Directors shall consist of not less than _____ directors.

[**INSERT:** Special Class of Stock to Elect Designated Directors. [All stock to elect balance of directors.]]

The shares consist of _____ shares designated as "Class A Common Stock" and _____ shares designated as "Class B Common Stock". With respect to the election of directors, the holders of Class B Common Stock shall have the sole and exclusive right to elect _____ director(s), and the balance of the directors will be elected by holders of all shares. The holders of Class B Common Stock shall have the sole and exclusive right to remove at any time the director(s) elected by such holders. The election and removal of the director(s) to be elected by the holders of Class B Common Stock may be effected by unanimous written consent of all such holders, at a special meeting of such holders called for that purpose, or at an annual meeting of shareholders. Any vacancy with respect to a director elected by the holders of Class B Common Stock shall be filled by a special election by the holders of Class B Common Stock, and not by a vote of the remaining directors. Other than with respect to rights relating to the election and removal of directors, Class A Common Stock and Class B Common Stock shall have identical rights.

The Board of Directors shall consist of not less than _____ directors.

[**INSERT:** "Blank Check" Stock Authorized.]

The shares consist of _____ shares designated as "Common Stock" and _____ shares designated as "Preferred Stock."

Except to the extent such rights are granted to Preferred Stock or one or more series thereof, Common Stock has unlimited voting rights and is entitled to receive the net assets of the corporation upon dissolution.

The preferences, limitations, and relative rights of Preferred Stock are undesignated. The Board of Directors may designate one or more series within Preferred Stock, and the designation and number of shares within each series, and shall determine the preferences, limitations, and relative rights of any shares of Preferred Stock, or of any series of Preferred Stock, before issuance of any shares of that class or series. [Preferred Stock, or any series thereof, may be designated as common or preferred, and may have rights that are identical to those of Common Stock.]

Shares of one class or series may be issued as a share dividend in respect to shares of another class or series.

## OPTIONAL PROVISIONS

[**INSERT:** Simple Majority Vote to Amend Articles, etc.]

### ARTICLE ____

Amendment of the articles of incorporation, approval of a plan of merger or share exchange, authorizing the sale, lease, exchange, or other disposition of all, or substantially all of the corporation's property, otherwise than in the usual and regular course of business, and authorizing dissolution of the corporation, shall be approved by each voting group entitled to vote thereon by a simple majority of all the votes entitled to be cast by that voting group.

### ARTICLE V

### TEXT INSERTS

To the maximum extent allowable bylaw, any action which may be authorized or approved by a vote of the shareholders at a meeting thereof at any time prior to the registration of any Corporation securities under the Securities Exchange Act of 1934, as amended, may be taken with the written consent of shareholders holding that number of shares as could authorize or approve the action at a meeting of all shareholders entitled to vote on such action. Except as otherwise provided by law, a notice describing the action taken and the effective date of such action shall be provided to each nonconsenting shareholder no later than ten (10) days prior to the effective date of any action approved pursuant to the preceding sentence

# H.  FORM: DIRECTORS' ORGANIZATIONAL CONSENT RESOLUTIONS

## CONSENT IN LIEU OF ORGANIZATIONAL MEETING OF [SOLE] DIRECTOR(S) OF

_____

The undersigned, being [all the] [the sole] director(s) of _____, a Washington corporation (the "Company"), pursuant to Section 23B.08.210 of the Washington Business Corporations Act (the "Act") hereby consent(s) to, and by this action approve(s) and adopt(s) the following resolutions:

### FORMATION

WHEREAS, the original Articles of Incorporation of the Company were filed in the office of the Secretary of State of Washington on _____; therefore it is

RESOLVED, that a certified copy of said Articles of Incorporation be inserted in the minute book of the Company; and

RESOLVED, that all the acts of the incorporator of the Company in forming and organizing the Company are hereby approved, ratified, and adopted as valid and binding acts of the Company.

### BYLAWS

RESOLVED, that the Bylaws, consisting of fifteen (15) pages inserted in the minute book following the Articles of Incorporation, are hereby adopted as the Bylaws of the Company.

### AGENT FOR SERVICE OF PROCESS

RESOLVED, that the appointment of _____ as the Company's registered agent for service of process in Washington is hereby ratified, approved and confirmed.

### FISCAL YEAR

RESOLVED, that the Company's fiscal year shall end on _____ each year.

### PAYMENT OF ORGANIZATIONAL EXPENSES

RESOLVED, that the officers of the Company or any of them be, and each hereby is, authorized and directed to pay the expenses of incorporation and organization of the Company.

## DIRECTORS

WHEREAS, the Bylaws of the Company allow for the number of directors to be set by the Articles of Incorporation or by resolution of the board of directors; therefore it is

RESOLVED, that the number of directors of the Company be fixed at _____ (_____) until such time as such number is amended by action of the Board of Directors or the shareholders of the Company.

## OFFICERS

RESOLVED, that the following persons be, and they hereby are, elected, effective immediately, as officers of the Company to serve until the next annual meeting of directors and until the election and qualification of their successors:

| Name | Title |
| --- | --- |
| _____ | President |
| _____ | Vice President |
| _____ | Secretary |
| _____ | Treasurer |

## FORM OF STOCK CERTIFICATE

RESOLVED, that the form of stock certificate attached hereto be, and the same hereby is, approved and adopted for use by the Company.

## ISSUANCE OF SHARES

WHEREAS, the Company is authorized to issue up to _____

(_____) shares of Common Stock, [no] [$_____] par value, and none yet have been sold or issued;

RESOLVED, that the board of directors hereby determines that $_____ per share is adequate consideration to be received by the Company for its Common Stock;

RESOLVED, that subject to compliance with the applicable state securities laws and the Securities Act of 1933, as amended ("1933 Act"), the Company shall issue shares of its Common Stock to the persons listed below at a price of $_____ per share, in cash, and for the number of shares set forth opposite their name:

| Name | Number of Shares |
| --- | --- |
| _____ | _____ |
| _____ | _____ |
| _____ | _____ |

RESOLVED, that upon receipt of the stated consideration and payment in full of any amounts payable pursuant to the terms thereof, such shares shall be duly and validly issued, fully paid and nonassessable.

RESOLVED, that the appropriate officers of the Company are hereby authorized and directed for and on behalf of the Company (i) to take all action necessary to comply with applicable state securities laws and the 1933 Act with respect to the above offer and issuance of shares, (ii) to thereafter issue shares on behalf of the Company pursuant to the above authorization, and (iii) to take such other action as they may deem appropriate to carry out the offer and issuance of shares and the intent of these resolutions.

## BANK ACCOUNT

RESOLVED, that the officers, or any of them, be, and each of them are hereby authorized to execute on behalf of the Company any and all forms of bank resolutions dealing with corporate banking matters, including the establishing and maintaining of corporate bank accounts, which in their judgment from time to time may be required for the proper fiscal management of the Company, including the designation thereon of such authorized signatures of corporate officers or other agents as may to them seem appropriate.  Such officers may execute such banking resolution or resolutions as if authorized to do so by a specific resolution of the board of directors adopted on the date this resolution was adopted by the board.  A copy of any such banking resolutions shall be placed in the corporate minute book.

## REGISTRATIONS AND LICENSES

RESOLVED, that the officers of the Company are hereby authorized and directed to cause the Company to be registered with federal and state taxing authorities, to obtain all necessary business licenses, and otherwise take all actions that are necessary or appropriate to enable the Company to commence business.

### * * * [S CORPORATION OPTION] * * *

## S CORPORATION ELECTION

RESOLVED, that for the first taxable year that is hereby designated to end on December 31, _____, the corporation shall make an election pursuant to Section 1362 of the Internal Revenue Code of 1986, as amended, to be treated as an "S corporation."  The shareholders shall execute such consents as are required thereby and the corporation shall timely file Internal Revenue Service Form 2553 and the required consents.

## OMNIBUS

RESOLVED, that any and all actions heretofore taken by the incorporator and/or officers of the Company resolutions are hereby ratified and confirmed as the acts and deeds of the Company; and

FURTHER RESOLVED, that the officers of the Company be, and each of them hereby is, authorized, directed and empowered to do all such other acts and things and to execute and deliver all such certificates or other documents and to take such other action as they deem necessary or desirable to carry out the purposes and intent, but within the limitations, of the above resolutions.

DATED this _____ day of _____, _____.


**DIRECTOR(S):**

_____

_____

_____

# INDEX

References are to pages.

## A

Access to capital, 6-7, 181–198
Acid test ratio, 31
Accounts receivable transition options, 263–270
Accredited investors, 199
Accumulated earnings tax,
    Generally, 62 - 63, 463–464
    Corporate-owned life insurance, 463–464
    Professional service organizations, 63
    Purpose, 62.
    Reasonable business needs, 63
    Tax rate, 63
Active trade or business requirement, 507–508
Affiliated group–definition, 59
Affirmative covenants, 323–324
Alaska asset protection trust laws, 638–640
American family business surveys,
    Generally, 14–22
    Advisors, 22
    Challenges, 15–16
    New horizons, 16–17
    Professionalism, 21
    Role of government, 16
    Succession planning, 17–18
    Women's roles, 20
Anticompetitive harms, 516, 523–527
Antitrust guidelines for collaborations
    among competitors,
        Generally, 523–541
    Agreements judged under Rule of
        Reason, 526–531
    Definitions, 521–523
    General Principals, 522–524
    Per se illegal agreements, 524–526
    Procompetitive benefit determinations,
        522, 537–539
    Purpose, 521–523
    Relevant market determinations, 531–537

Antitrust guidelines for collaborations among
    competitors (continued)
        Safety zones, 540–541
Antitrust safety zones, 540–541
Arbitration procedures: Form, 740–741
Articles of Incorporation, 93, 766–773
Asset protection planning,
        Generally, 624–656
    Alaska asset protection trust laws, 638–640
    Business arrangements, 630–633
    Bypass trusts, 635
    Charitable remainder trusts, 636–637
    Client's right to plan, 625–627
    Contract clause challenges, 646–647
    Corporations, 631
    Credit shelter trusts, 6635
    Criminal activity, 651– 655
    Crummey trusts, 636
    Delaware asset protection trust laws,
        640–642
    Domestic strategies, 628–647
    Exporting assets, 648
    Foreign trust U.S. tax issues, 655–656
    Fraudulent transfers, 625–628
    Full faith and credit challenges, 642–645
    Generation skipping trusts, 636
    Gifts, trusts and disclaimers, 633–638
    GRATs, GRUTs and QPRTs, 637
    Importing foreign law, 649
    Life insurance trusts, 636
    Limited liability companies, 631–632
    Limited partnerships, 632–633
    Marital Property Planning, 632– 633
    Nest egg vs. in toto, 650
    Offshore trusts, 647– 652
    Potential subsequent creditors, 627–628
    Respecting the business entity, 633
    Supremacy clause challenges, 645– 646
    Types of creditors, 627– 628
    Unknown future creditors, 628